CADOGANguides

W9-BNF-646

take the kids
England
JOSEPH FULLMAN

Contents

How to use this guide
England Touring Atlas
Snapshots of England

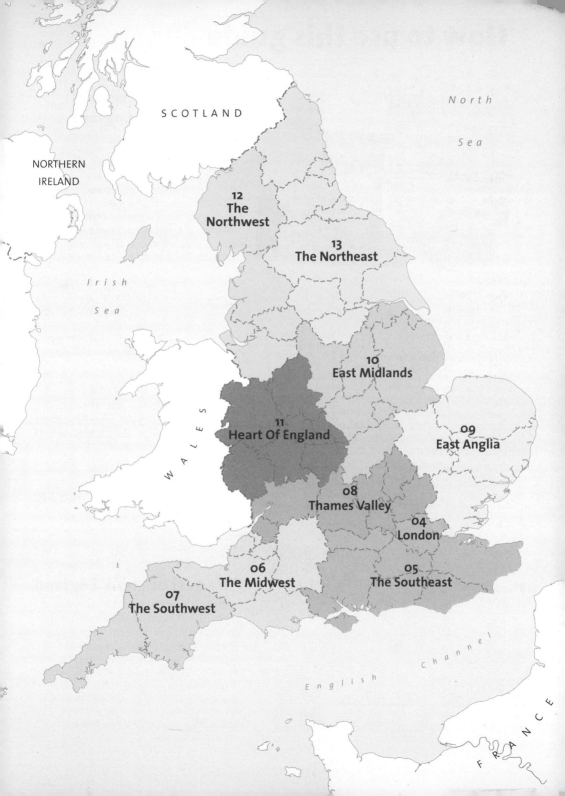

How to use this guide

Colour map atlas and Snapshots of England

This section kicks off with 15 pages of full-colour touring maps for easy-to-find orientation. These are followed by 11 pages of inspirational colour photographs that give you a flavour of each of the 9 regions and London at a glance. Browse through this album and get a taste of the types of things that characterize each collection of towns and counties. Every place or event is cross-referenced to the place where it is described in more detail later in the guide.

Practical advice and tips

The opening chapter provides advice on **Choosing Your Holiday**, with recommended activities for all ages, sources of information and specialist travel agents. The section on **Travel** covers getting to England and around by all practical means – from ferry crossings to bicycle hire. **Practical A–Z** provides information for residents and visitors alike on all essential matters, from discount passes to toilets.

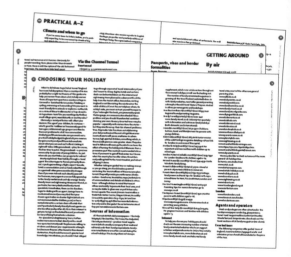

The best of 'mini' England

The body of the book, describing the best of what England has to offer kids, is organized geographically into 10 chapters covering London and the regions. It's jam-packed with ideas, but finding your way round is easy because every chapter is set out in the same way. Each opens with an orientation map of the region on which all necessary roads, cities, towns and attractions have been marked, and highlights boxes listing the best sights, activities and events.

Chapter contents

Top Towns are the ones you are bound to go to, to catch a train if nothing else, so we list them first and use them as a point of reference for other sights. For each town, we provide suggestions for 'Things to see and do' and give references to important places 'Around' that town. **Special Trips** (abbeys, castles, palaces, stately homes, historic houses or historical landmarks) comes next, followed by **Kids Out** (animal attractions, farms, sea life centres, beach towns and beaches, open air museums, parks and gardens, steam trains, theme parks, wide open spaces), **Sport and Activities** and **Kids In** (museums, cinemas, galleries). Our pick of places for **Eating Out** comes at the end of every chapter. For easy reference, entries appear in alphabetical order under these standard headings.

★ Top attractions are marked with a star.

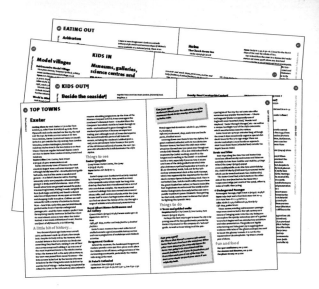

Boxed!

Quizzes and challenges, stories and anecdotes, jokes, special activities and foods… Entertaining information on things English, from crabbing to Pikelets, are boxed – so you can't miss 'em!

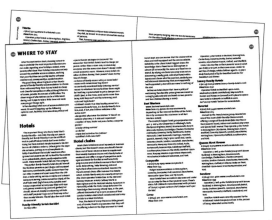

Where to stay

Our final chapter contains comprehensive reviews of over 100 recommended hotels and dozens of kids' camps, together with advice and contacts for all types of self-catering from boating to home exchange.

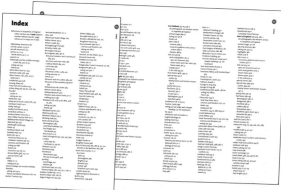

Reference

A comprehensive index allows you to find places quickly and easily, even if you don't know what area they are in.

About the series

take the kids guides are written specifically for parents, grandparents and carers. Each guide not only draws on what is of particular interest to kids, but also takes into account the realities of childcare – from tired legs to low boredom thresholds – enabling both grown-ups and their charges to have a great day out or a fabulous holiday.

Cadogan Guides
2nd Floor, 233 High Holborn
London WC1V 7DN
info@cadoganguides.co.uk
www.cadoganguides.com

The Globe Pequot Press
PO Box 480, Guilford,
Connecticut 06437–0480

Copyright © Joseph Fullman 2001, 2004, 2007

Maps © Cadogan Guides, drawn by
Maidenhead Cartographic Services Ltd

Art Director: Sarah Gardner
Managing Editor: Antonia Cunningham
Editor: Georgina Palffy
Assistant Editor: Nicola Jessop
Proofreading: Carla Masson
Indexing: Isobel McLean

Printed in Italy by Legoprint
A catalogue record for this book is available
from the British Library
ISBN 978-1-86011-353-6

The author and publishers have made every effort to ensure the accuracy of the information in this book at the time of going to press. However, they cannot accept any responsibility for any loss, injury or inconvenience resulting from the use of information contained in the guide.

Please help us to keep this guide up to date. We have done our best to ensure that information is correct at the time of printing, but places and facilities are constantly changing, and standards and prices fluctuate. We will be delighted to receive your comments concerning existing entries or omissions. Authors of the best letters will receive a copy of the Cadogan Guide of their choice.

All rights reserved. No part of this publication may be reproduced, stored in a retrieval system, or transmitted, in any form or by any means, electronic or mechanical, including photocopying and recording, or by any information storage and retrieval system except as may be expressly permitted by the UK 1988 Copyright Design & Patents Act and the USA 1976 Copyright Act or in writing from the publisher. Requests for permission should be addressed to Cadogan Guides, 2nd Floor, 233 High Holborn, London WC1V 7DN in the UK; or The Globe Pequot Press, PO Box 480, Guilford, Connecticut 06437–0480 in the USA.

take the kids
England touring atlas

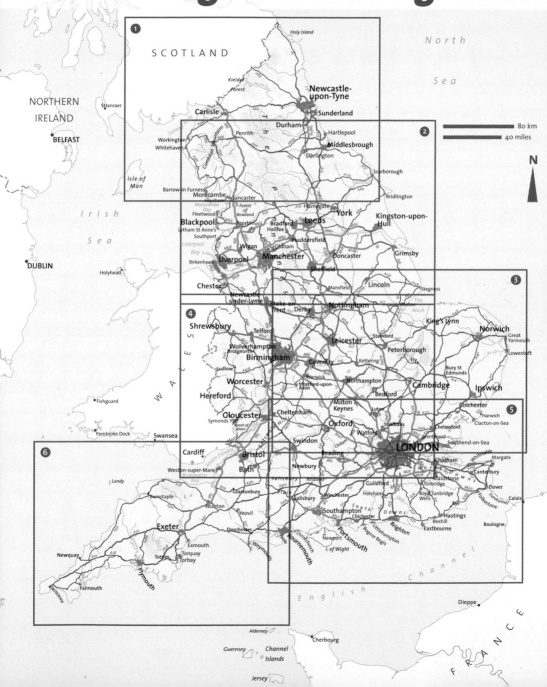

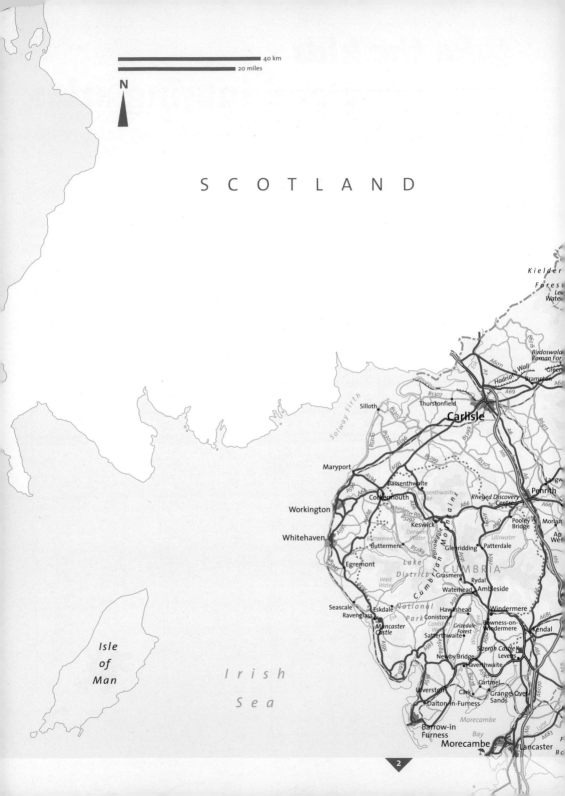

S C O T L A N D

40 km
20 miles

N

Kielder
Forest
Lev
Wate

Birdoswald
Roman For
Gree
Hadrian's Wall
Brampton

Silloth
Thurstonfield
Carlisle

Maryport
Bassenthwaite
Langw
Penrith
Cockermouth
Bassenthwaite
Lake
Rheged Discovery
Centre

Workington
Whinlatter Pass
Keswick
Derwent
Water
Pooley
Bridge
Morlan
Ullswater
Ap
Wes

Whitehaven
Buttermere
Buttermere
Glenridding
Patterdale

Egremont
Lake
District
Grasmere
Rydal
West
Water
Waterhead
Ambleside

Seascale
National
Hawkshead
Windermere

Ravenglass
Eskdale
Coniston
Bowness-on-
Windermere
Kendal
Muncaster
Castle
Grizedale
Forest
Satterthwaite
Szergh Castle
Levens

Newby Bridge
Haverthwaite
Ulverston
Cartmel
Grange Over
Sands
Dalton-in-Furness

Morecambe
Barrow-in
Furness
Bay
Morecambe
Lancaster

Isle
of
Man

I r i s h

S e a

C u m b r i a n   M o u n t a i n s

CUMBRIA

2

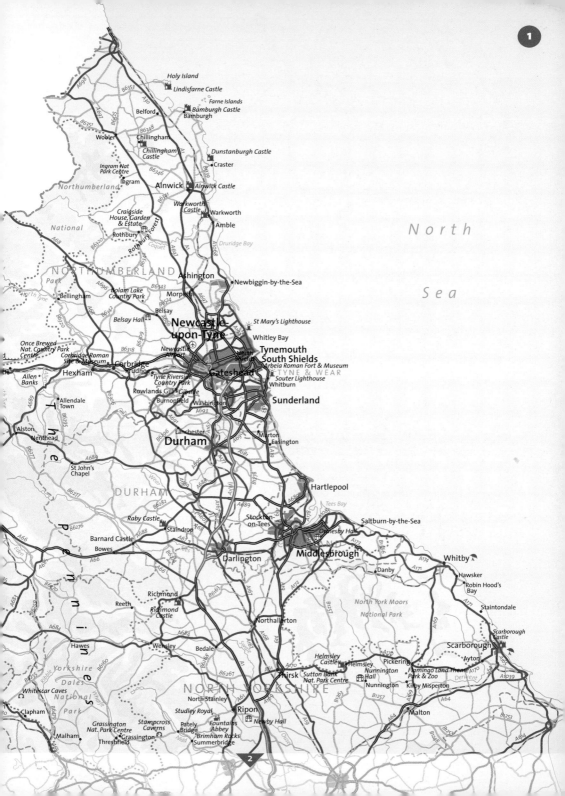

Holy Island
Lindisfarne Castle
Farne Islands
Belford
Bamburgh Castle
Bamburgh
Wooler
Chillingham
Chillingham
Castle
Dunstanburgh Castle
Craster
Ingram Nat
Park Centre
Ingram
Northumberland
Alnwick
Alnwick Castle
Warkworth
Castle
Warkworth
Craigside
House, Garden
& Estate
Rothbury
Amble
National
Bellingham
Druridge Bay
NORTHUMBERLAND
Ashington
Newbiggin-by-the-Sea
Bolam Lake
Country Park
Morpeth
Park
Belsay
North Tyne
Belsay Hall
Newcastle-
upon-Tyne
St Mary's Lighthouse
Whitley Bay
Once Brewed
Nat. Country Park
Centre
Newcastle
Airport
North
Shields
Tynemouth
South Shields
Corbridge Roman
Site & Museum
Corbridge
Prudhoe
Gateshead
Arbeia Roman Fort & Museum
TYNE & WEAR
Hexham
Allen
Banks
Tyne Riverside
Country Park
Gibside
Rowlands Gill
Souter Lighthouse
Whitburn
Allendale
Town
Burnopfield
Washington
Sunderland
Alston
Nenthead
Lanchester
Murton
Easington
Durham
St John's
Chapel
The Pennines
DURHAM
Hartlepool
Tees Bay
Raby Castle
Staindrop
Stockton-
on-Tees
Saltburn-by-the-Sea
Barnard Castle
Bowes
Ormesby Hall
Middlesbrough
Whitby
Darlington
Danby
Hawsker
Robin Hood's
Bay
Richmond
Richmond
Castle
North York Moors
National Park
Staintondale
Reeth
Northallerton
Scarborough
Castle
Hawes
Wensley
Bedale
Scarborough
Ayton
Yorkshire
Dales
Helmsley
Castle
Helmsley
Pickering
Flamingo Land Theme
Park & Zoo
Whitescar Caves
National
Park
Thirsk
Sutton Bank
Nat. Park Centre
Nunnington
Hall
Nunnington
Kirby Misperton
NORTH YORKSHIRE
Clapham
North Stainley
Studley Royal
Ripon
Newby Hall
Malton
Grassington
Nat. Park Centre
Grassington
Threshfield
Stampcross
Caverns
Pately
Bridge
Fountains
Abbey
Brimham Rocks
Summerbridge
Malham

North

Sea

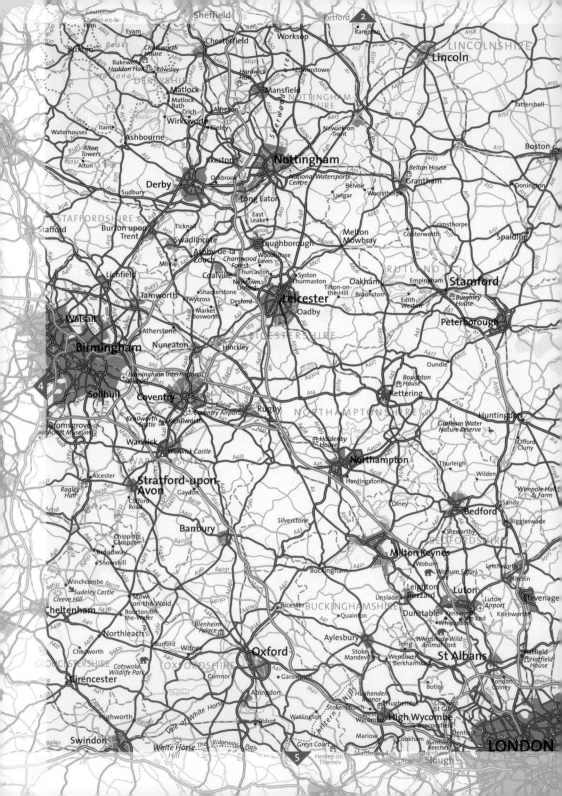

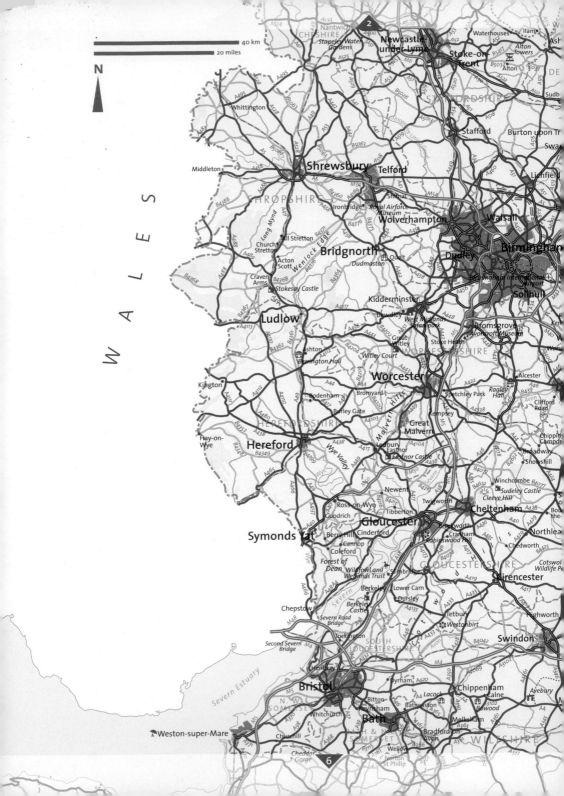

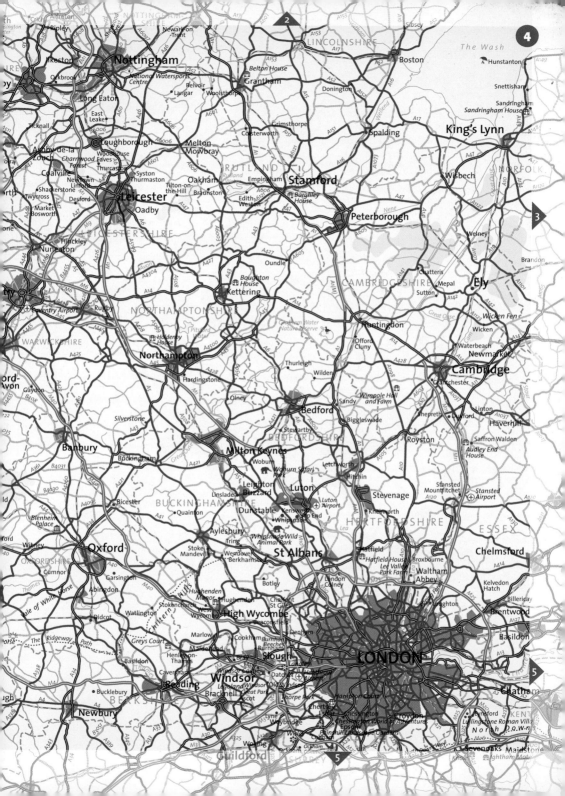

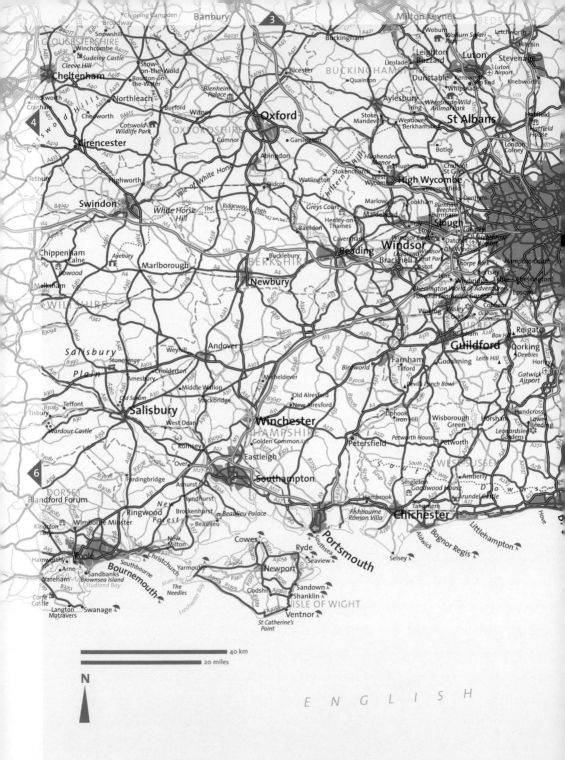

Castle Hedingham
Stour
Dedham
A120
Colchester
Stansted Mountfitchet
Stansted Airport
A120
Braintree
A12
Walton-on-the-Naze
Frinton-on-Sea
Brightlingsea
Clacton-on-Sea
ESSEX
Chelmsford
A414
A12
A414
oxbourne
e Valley Park Farm
Waltham Abbey
Kelvedon Hatch
Billericay
Loughton
Brentwood
A127
Basildon
A127
Thames
Southend-on-Sea
DON
Chatham
Herne Bay
Margate
Whitstable
North Foreland
Broadstairs
Ramsgate
Lynsford
Lullingstone Roman Villa
N o r t h
Sevenoaks
Ightham Mote
Knole
Maidstone
Leeds Castle
A2
M2
Canterbury
A257
Deal
D o w n s
KENT
Beltring
Childingstone
ver Castle
Penshurst
Penshurst Place
Tonbridge
Paddock Wood
Post Mill
Grinstead
Hadfield
Pooh Corner
Royal Tunbridge Wells
Lamberhurst
Scotney
Tenterden
Lympne
Hythe
Folkestone
Dover
Eurotunnel
Strait of Dover
Calais
Ashdown Forest
Bluebell Railway
Sheffield Park
Burwash
Etchingham
Bodiam Castle
Robertsbridge
Rye
Wilderness Wood
Bateman's
Heathfield
Uckfield
Horam
Battle
Battle Abbey
Halland
EAST SUSSEX
Hailsham
Hastings
Lewes
Polegate
Bexhill
Alfriston
Eastbourne
Langney Point
Eastdean
Beachy Head
Newhaven
Boulogne
FRANCE
C H A N N E L

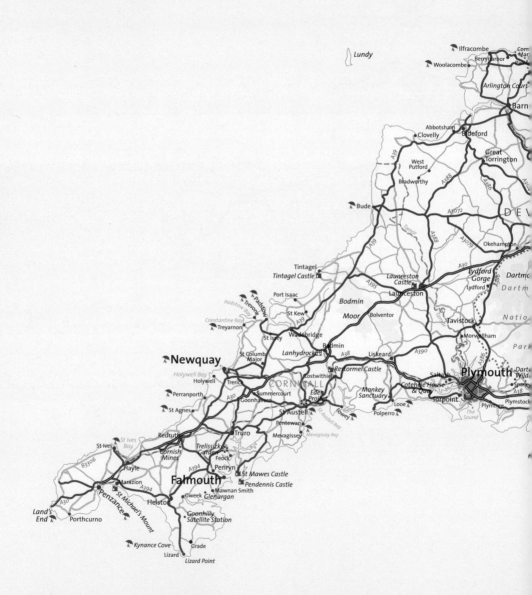

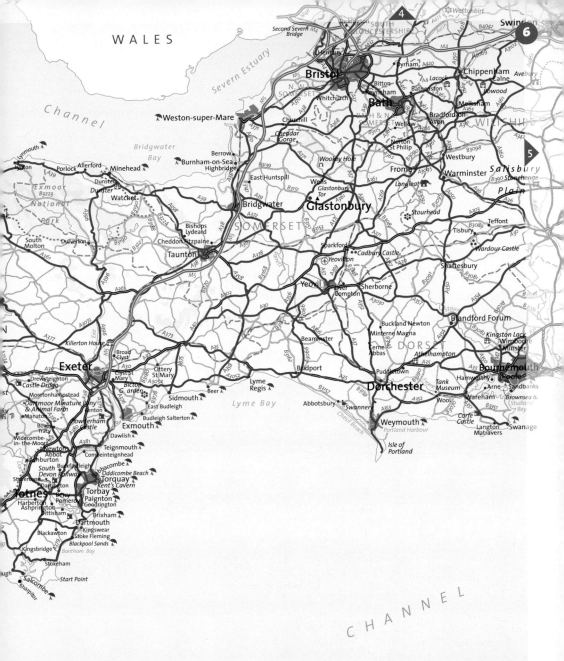

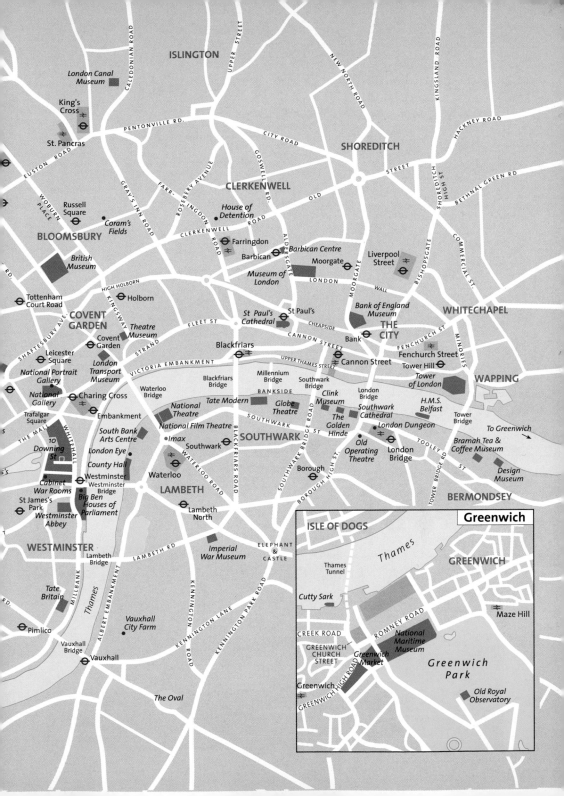

ISLINGTON

London Canal
Museum

King's
Cross

St. Pancras

PENTONVILLE RD.

CALEDONIAN ROAD

UPPER STREET

NEW NORTH ROAD

KINGSLAND ROAD

SHOREDITCH

HACKNEY ROAD

CITY ROAD

GOSWELL RD.

OLD

STREET

SHOREDITCH HIGH ST

BETHNAL GREEN RD

EUSTON ROAD

WOBURN PLACE

Russell
Square

Coram's
Fields

BLOOMSBURY

British
Museum

Tottenham
Court Road

GRAY'S INN ROAD

ROSEBERY AVENUE

FARRINGDON ROAD

CLERKENWELL

House of
Detention

CLERKENWELL ROAD

ALDERSGATE

Farringdon

Barbican

Museum of
London

Barbican Centre

Moorgate

LONDON

COMMERCIAL ST.

BISHOPSGATE

Liverpool
Street

WALL

MOORGATE

WHITECHAPEL

HIGH HOLBORN

Holborn

KINGSWAY

SHAFTESBURY AVE.

COVENT
GARDEN

Covent
Garden

Theatre
Museum

Leicester
Square

London
Transport
Museum

National Portrait
Gallery

National
Gallery

Charing Cross

Trafalgar
Square

THE MALL

Cabinet
War Rooms

St James's
Park

WHITEHALL

10
Downing
St.

Westminster
Abbey

WESTMINSTER

STRAND

FLEET ST

St Paul's
Cathedral

St Paul's

CHEAPSIDE

Bank of England
Museum

Bank

THE
CITY

CANNON STREET

UPPER THAMES STREET

Cannon
Street

FENCHURCH ST.

Fenchurch
Street

Tower Hill

Tower
of London

MINORIES

WAPPING

VICTORIA EMBANKMENT

Embankment

Waterloo
Bridge

Blackfriars
Bridge

Blackfriars

Millennium
Bridge

BANKSIDE

Tate Modern

National
Theatre

National Film Theatre

South Bank
Arts Centre

Imax

Southwark

Waterloo

County Hall

London Eye

Westminster
Bridge

Big Ben
Houses of
Parliament

Globe
Theatre

SOUTHWARK

Southwark
Bridge

Clink
Museum

The
Golden
Hinde

Old
Operating
Theatre

London
Bridge

Southwark
Cathedral

London
Bridge

London Dungeon

H.M.S.
Belfast

Tower
Bridge

To Greenwich

Bramah Tea &
Coffee Museum

Design
Museum

BERMONDSEY

TOOLEY ST.

TOWER BRIDGE RD.

BLACKFRIARS ROAD

SOUTHWARK BRIDGE RD

BOROUGH HIGH ST

SOUTHWARK STREET

Borough

Lambeth
North

WATERLOO ROAD

LAMBETH

Waterloo

LAMBETH RD.

Imperial
War Museum

ELEPHANT
& CASTLE

Lambeth
Bridge

Tate
Britain

Pimlico

MILLBANK

ALBERT EMBANKMENT

Thames

Vauxhall
City Farm

KENNINGTON LANE

KENNINGTON ROAD

KENNINGTON PARK ROAD

Vauxhall
Bridge

Vauxhall

The Oval

Greenwich

ISLE OF DOGS

Thames

GREENWICH

Thames
Tunnel

Cutty Sark

CREEK ROAD

GREENWICH
CHURCH
STREET

Greenwich
Market

Greenwich

GREENWICH HIGH ROAD

ROMNEY ROAD

National
Maritime
Museum

Maze Hill

Greenwich
Park

Old Royal
Observatory

Snapshots
of England
by region

London

The Southeast

The Midwest

The Southwest

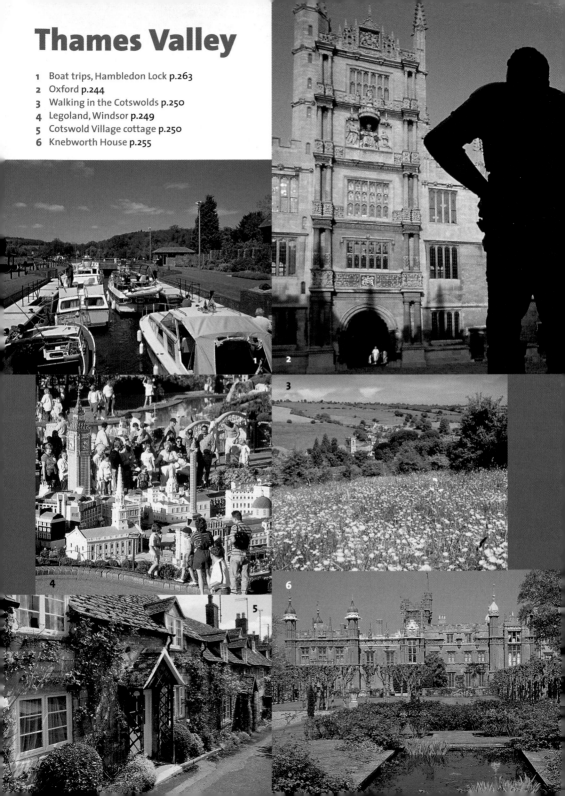

Thames Valley

East Anglia

East Midlands

Heart of England

The Northwest

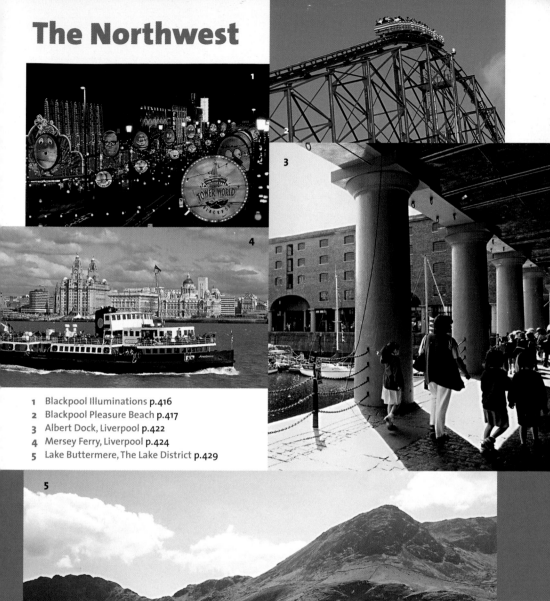

The Northeast

Introduction

01

INTRODUCTION

Attitudes in this country towards entertaining kids have changed greatly over the past few decades. Once, it was simply enough to find a safe area where kids could be left to create their own entertainment – a park, a beach, a square, etc. These days, however, we (and they) expect a little bit more. We (and they) expect to be actively entertained, to have our amusements laid on for us, hence the ever-increasing number of family attractions.

In many ways, England is now the antithesis of Mediterranean Europe, where children tend to be regarded as 'mini adults', welcomed everywhere their parents are, but with few attractions aimed directly at them. In England, children are more often viewed as a separate and distinct section of the population with needs and interests that must be specially catered for. In almost every aspect of life, there is now infinitely more on offer for children in England than there was just 25 years ago. In big restaurant chains, highchairs, children's menus and activity packs are now the norm rather than the exception. At pubs, children are no longer expected to sit outside with a glass of lemonade and a packet of crisps while dad quenches his thirst within, but are instead welcomed into special family rooms (where special family meals are served), or invited to play with a range of toys and games. At hotels, there are now greater numbers of family rooms available than ever before and, indeed, there are even a few establishments that choose to deal solely with families. The nation's high streets are lined with shops catering to younger tastes while, in the countryside, activity camps offer specialist training in mini sporting pursuits.

As the importance of the family market grows, so the nation's tourist attractions become ever more child friendly. For many, the watchword is now 'interactivity'. In the country's museums, dusty relics unimaginatively displayed in wooden cabinets have largely given way to lively, energetic exhibitions with hands-on areas and hi-tech graphics. Unfortunately, all the expensive interactive displays in the world don't count for much if they don't work, which is sometimes the case in our museums, but we're constantly improving services and the best are reflected in this book. Animal attractions, meanwhile, have cottoned on to the fact that kids don't just want to look at animals, they want to touch and hold them, too, which is why nearly all zoos and wildlife parks now offer children the chance to get up close and personal with the residents, more often than not in the form of a farm, where they can help milk the cows, bottle-feed the lambs and scatter corn for the chickens. Even the nation's stately homes now provide children's guides and organize special family events.

The turn of the millennium witnessed the opening of an unprecedented number of new attractions right across the country. Even if some of these fell by the wayside in the intervening years, a few, including the Eden Project in Cornwall, Tate Modern in London, and Leicester's National Space Science Centre have gone on to establish themselves as among the country's very top attractions.

In other words, there's never been a better time for a new edition of this book – a book designed to reveal the country from a family perspective, to show the best that England has to offer kids.

How this guide is organized

We've divided the country into 10 areas beginning with London, one of the world's great cities (at whatever age), and then taking in the Southeast, the Midwest, the Southwest, the Thames Valley, East Anglia, East Midlands, the Heart of England and the Northwest before finally finishing up in the Northeast. Each chapter begins with Top Towns, where we identify those urban centres that have the greatest number of child-orientated attractions and which, in our view, make the best base from which to explore the area as a whole. Special Trips – abbeys, castles, stately homes, historic ruins, etc. – is followed by Kids Out, which details the best animal attractions, theme parks, gardens, forests, resorts and beaches around. Sport and Activities provides details of the region's main sporting options while Kids In, the next section, lists those museums, galleries and science centres likely to be of interest to children, as well as the main theatres and cinemas. Each area chapter is completed by Eating Out, where you'll find detailed listings of family-friendly dining. There are also in-depth sections on accommodation, travel and practical matters. From Land's End to Hadrian's Wall, we've trawled the country on our mission to uncover the pick of 'mini' England – all the sights, rides, displays, attractions and exhibitions that make this one of the most fun-packed places on earth for younger visitors.

About the authors

Joseph Fullman

Joseph Fullman is a professional travel writer who has lived in London all his life and cherishes happy childhood memories of traipsing around the country with his determinedly enthusiastic mum and dad. He is the author of Cadogan's *take the kids London* and co-author of *take the kids Paris & Disneyland Resort Paris*, as well as guides to Britain's steam railways and London's markets.

Acknowledgements

Thanks to Mum and Dad, Sam and Beth, Steve and Lorin and everyone up and down the country (particularly in tourist offices) whose collective assistance has been invaluable. For the first edition I'd like again to thank everyone at Cadogan who rallied to the cause, especially Helen for all her hard work and cheerfulness editing my ever-late text, and for the second edition the updaters Rosie Whitehouse and Melanie Dakin whose sterling efforts immeasurably improved the book.

I would also like to thank Sarah Freeman for her expert advice on regional cooking, Matthew Tanner for his work on the London chapter and the following regional correspondents who have contributed valuable information from all corners of England and given local insight, tips and advice based on their personal experience with their children: Alex Bossman, Shona Cornthwaite, Denise Dawson, Kay Guttridge, Jenny Holdsworth, Helen Howells, Fiona Jack, Joanne Lipley, Judith Millidge, Janet Mills, Jan Mitchell, Eryl Rayner, Lesley and Chris Rayner, Louise Slarke, Suzanne Thompson, Heather Youd and Kate Young. But most of all I'd like to thank the wondrous Nicola who, after all, did most of the work.

Dennis Kelsall

The author of the Northeast chapter lives in Lancashire and is a member of the Outdoor Writers' Guild. He has written numerous books including *Walks with Children*, published by Questa, and a guide to the Pembrokeshire Coast Path, published by Cicerone.

Terry Marsh

The author of the Northwest chapter also lives in Lancashire and is a member of the Guild of Travel Writers. He is an intrepid traveller and writes regularly for travel guide publishers and also publishes his own books.

About the updaters

Nicola Mainwood

Nicola Mainwood regards her travels around the country on the hunt for the best family days out as simply a continuation of a trend started when she was little, as she moved in quick succession from Bedfordshire to Oxfordshire to Norfolk to Wales to London. To date, her writing career has seen her contribute to guides to Andalucia, Turkey and Costa Rica. She's also the co-author of Cadogan's *Belize*.

Acknowledgements

Many thanks to everyone who took the time to talk to me and answer my queries, either in person, on the phone or via email, especially Henry in Bristol, Anna in Manchester and Ray in London. Biggest thanks of all to my parents, Helen, Lauren and Joe.

About the series

take the kids guides are written specifically for parents, grandparents and carers. Each guide not only draws on what is of particular interest to kids, but also takes into account the realities of child-care – from tired legs to low boredom thresholds – enabling both grown-ups and their charges to have a great day out or a fabulous holiday.

Series consultant

Helen Truszkowski is series consultant of Cadogan's *take the kids* series, author of *take the kids Travelling* and co-author of *take the kids Paris & Disneyland® Resort Paris*. Helen is an established travel writer and photographer. Over the past decade her journeys have taken her around the globe, including six months working in South Africa. She contributes to a range of magazines worldwide and is a former travel editor of *Executive Woman* magazine. Helen's eight-year-old son, George, has accompanied her on her travels since he was a few weeks old.

Photo acknowledgements

Cover
(front) © Romilly Lockyer, © Adam van Bunnens/Alamy, © emmerichwebb (two photos) , Travel Pix, Richard T Nowitz, John & Eliza Forder; (back) © Ian Dagnall/Alamy

London
1, 2, 3, © Travel Pics/Peter Phipp; 4 © Natural History Museum; 5 © V&A Museum

The Southeast
1, 2, 3, 5 © Travel Pics/Neil Holmes; 4 © Chessington World of Adventure

The Midwest
1 © Longleat Safari Park; 2, 3, 4, 6 © Neil Holmes/Travel Pics; 5 © Wooky Hole Caves Ltd

The Southwest
1, 6 © Cornish Picture Library/Paul Watts; 4, 5 © Travel Pics/Neil Holmes; 3 © Newquay & Cornish Riviera; 2 © Vince Waterfall

Thames Valley
1, 6 © Travel Pics/Neil Holmes; 2 © Oxford City Council; 4 © Legoland; 3, 5 © Gloucester County Council

East Anglia
1, 2, 3, 5, 6, 7 © Travel Pics/Neil Holmes; 4 © Norfolk National Trust/J. Arnold

East Midlands
1, 2, 3, 4, 5, 6 © Travel Pics/Neil Holmes; 7 © National Space Science Centre

Heart of England
1, 3, 4, 5, 6 © Travel Pics/Neil Holmes; 4 © Alton Towers

The Northwest
1, 2, 3, 4, 5 © Travel Pics/Neil Holmes

The Northeast
1, 2, 3, 4, 5 © Travel Pics/Neil Holmes; 6 © By kind permission of the Dean and Chapter of York

Travel

CHOOSING YOUR HOLIDAY

What to do? Where to go? What to see? England has more holiday options than a country of its size probably has a right to. The aim of this guide is to help you narrow them down a bit, to help answer those all important questions: country cottage in Cornwall or furnished flat in London? Walking or cycling, swimming or horse-riding? Do you want to meet friendly farm animals or explore a castle, ride on a state-of-the-art rollercoaster or hop aboard a vintage steam train? Do you want big city thrills or small village quiet, seaside bustle or country calm?

Obviously, a variety of factors will affect your decision. The age of your children (*see* below), for instance – what's good for toddlers isn't necessarily good for teenagers, while mixed-age groups can often be the most problematic of all to accommodate. Similarly, you'll have to ensure you work out a practical holiday budget: England is not a bargain country and you'll have to be realistic about what you can and can't afford. Getting it right will take a little groundwork – plus, of course, the free time to put in the groundwork, a precious commodity for parents of young children. So, just where do you start? Who can you go to for advice?

Most people book their holiday through a travel agent. The advantages to this are primarily financial. A package involving a flight, airport transfer, hotel accommodation and car hire booked through an agent will often prove considerably cheaper than if you were to book each directly. Furthermore, many agents are now fully geared up to the family market and can help arrange family-friendly tours and sightseeing itineraries. The USA, in particular, has many dedicated family travel specialists. However, there can be disadvantages to dealing with an agent. Savings have to be made somehow and you may find that your chosen agent relies on charter flights (which are not recommended for children, p.10) or has a vested interest in a certain chain of hotels that is not particularly family friendly. Travel agents can also be rather pushy. After all, it's in their interest to get you to sign on the dotted line and you should be wary of being hurried into a decision.

For specialist and sightseeing tours, it often makes more sense to deal directly with a small tour operator. Not only will they be more willing to sit down and discuss your requirements at length but, because they are often based in the relevant destination, they should have much greater local knowledge. Nevertheless, you shouldn't feel obliged to go through any sort of travel intermediary if you don't want to. Cheap flights, hotels and car hire deals can be hunted down on the Internet and sightseeing tours planned in advance with a little help from the tourist office. Remember, visiting England is not like visiting the rainforest or the wilds of Africa. It's not the sort of place where, for safety's sake, you must entrust yourself to experts. If you've bought this book, you presumably speak the language so communication shouldn't be a problem and you should therefore feel confident devising your own itinerary. Escorted tours may be popular – especially with visitors from the USA – but they also throw up their fair share of problems. True, they may take the strain out of planning your daily routine, but the sort of rigid itineraries most adhere to will prove anathema to adventurous, high-spirited children; something which, in the end, will prove an even greater strain. They also tend to follow well-worn paths, which can have the effect of turning the holiday into little more than a procession past the country's most crowded attractions. If you want to get off the beaten track to see what the country has to offer when it's not furiously selling itself to the tourist market, you're better off going independently.

Whether taking a guided tour or making one up as you go along, you should make a point of contacting the tourist offices of the areas you plan to visit. They will provide you with reams of information – brochures, timetables, maps, leaflets, lists of accommodation and details of children's attractions – although do bear in mind that tourist offices exist solely to promote their local area, and so may be liable to gloss over any of its less salubrious aspects. The country's main tourist office is **Britain and London Visitor Centre**, 1 Lower Regent Street, Piccadilly Circus, London SW1; **open** Mon 9.30–6.30, Tues–Fri 9–6.30, Sat and Sun 10–4, (Jun–Sept longer hours Sat 9–5); **t** (020) 8846 9000, **www**.visitbritain.com.

Infants

Babies are surprisingly adaptable travel companions. They are mostly happy to go wherever you go, and love looking at new and interesting things (even if they can't tell the difference between Manchester and Margate). You rarely have to go out of your way to keep a baby occupied.

Comfortable in pushchairs or baby carriers, they are easily transported and will fall asleep just about anywhere. The biggest drawback to travelling with infants is the array of equipment and accessories they inevitably need, so holidays with an established base – self-catering in or near a town, for instance – are best. This will give you the freedom to do what you want, when you want and will provide you with easy access to supplies (and help in an emergency). There are details of self-catering options on p.529.

Toddlers

Toddlers are undoubtedly the most problematic age group to travel with. Notoriously difficult to keep restrained, prone to mystifying temper tantrums and capable of getting themselves lost in a flash, they can be exhausting to both themselves and their parents. The good news is that children of this age are invariably enthusiastic and insatiably curious. They take delight in the smallest things (or big things made small – model villages are always a big hit for some reason), but you will need both incredible patience and a holiday packed full of quick-fire, child-friendly diversions. Seaside holidays nearly always strike the right chord with toddlers. Not ready for castles or culture yet, they will find all the stimulation they need in a sandy beach, a bucket and spade, a stick of candyfloss and (if it's raining) a quick trip to the sealife centre. Furthermore, most resorts have plenty of family-friendly restaurants used to dealing with (occasionally) noisy, fidgety toddlers. Beach holidays are detailed in full in the area gazetteers. For a list of safe (and not so safe) beaches, log on to www.goodbeachguide.co.uk.

Primary-school age (5–11)

This is the easiest age; children still have the eagerness and interest of their younger years but are more independent and far less labour intensive. They can appreciate cultural visits and have the physical and mental ability to undertake somewhat more challenging excursions such as walking or cycling trips through the countryside. Visits to castles and historic sites will also be more appreciated at this age. Nonetheless, school-age children are quick to develop specific likes and dislikes and, unless you are prepared to take these into account early on, you could be heading for big trouble. For this reason, it's often an idea to base yourself in a large town or city (even if you plan to explore the

countryside) so as to have on hand a ready supply of distractions and attractions. Remember that a sizeable chunk of any city's population is made up of children, so it is guaranteed to contain a range of child-friendly museums, theatres, playgrounds, parks and shops, thereby making it easier for you to keep ahead of your children's limited attention spans. The country's most child-friendly towns are listed in the area gazetteers.

Teenagers

Teenagers can be a nightmare. Trapped between a child-like dependency and a burgeoning drive for adult independence, and with powerful new hormones coursing through their veins, they present a challenge. The primary focus for any teenager is spending time with other teenagers, so it is best if companions are a guaranteed part of the trip. Children's activity camps are excellent in this regard, allowing teenagers to interact with their peers in a safe environment away from their parents (pp.531–2).

Mixed-age groups

Finding a holiday that's suitable for children of varying ages can be the hardest trick of all to pull off. Family resorts (such as Centerparcs, Butlins and Pontins) may provide the answer. Young children will be well catered for with various dedicated amusements, while older teens are free to wander around in a safe, contained environment (p.531).

Sources of information

All the main British daily newspapers – from the upmarket *Daily Telegraph*, *Guardian*, *Independent* and *Times*, through the mid-market *Daily Mail* to the tabloid *Mirror* and *Sun* – produce travel pages or supplements (usually at weekends) as do their Sunday equivalents. Family-orientated features are often carried during school holidays. The *Sunday Observer*'s 'Escape' supplement, which runs a Kids section in summer, is worth checking out.

The number of family-orientated magazines is growing all the time. The best are listed below. As with family websites, most offer general parenting advice plus the odd travel feature.

BBC Parenting (monthly) **t** 0870 442 2092
Travel, food, fashion and features for parents with children ages 0–6.

Families (monthly) **t** (020) 8696 9680
www.familiesonline.co.uk
Series of regional magazines covering different areas of the country. Seven different titles in the Greater London area, others in the Home Counties, Edinburgh and Liverpool. Available in most local libraries.

The Green Parent (bi-monthly) **t** (01273) 401 012
www.thegreenparent.co.uk
Food, lifestyle, parenting and pregnancy articles for the environmentally conscious.

Junior (monthly) **t** (020) 7761 8900
www.juniormagazine.co.uk
Childcare, fashion, travel/lifestyle news for parents.

Mother & Baby (monthly) **t** (020) 7347 1869
www.motherandbabymagazine.com
For expectant and new mothers with children up to school age.

Practical Parenting (monthly) **t** (020) 7261 5058
www.ipcmedia.co.uk
Tips and articles for mums and mums-to-be.

Agents and operators

Deals and packages are often advertised in the Sunday and weekend editions of newspapers and in big, glossy international travel magazines like *Condé Nast Traveller* and *Wanderlust*. Also check out the travel sections of UK family magazines (*see* above).

Escorted tours

The following companies offer guided tours of England. Accommodation, luggage transfer and admission prices should all be included in the price of the tour. Do be aware that most will involve a hefty amount of coach travel. Make sure you check the proposed schedule thoroughly first and be prepared to ask a lot of questions. Does the schedule allow for plenty of relaxation time or will your holiday be spent constantly shuttling from one sight to another? What is their cancellation policy? Will they cancel the trip if not enough people sign up? If so, will you get a refund? How large is the group you will be travelling with? (Needless to say, the smaller the better.) Is every aspect of the tour covered in the original price?

British and Irish tours

Astral Travels UK Tours 72 New Bond Street, London W1S 9SS **t** 0700 078 1016 www.astraltravels.co.uk

Back-Roads Touring Company Ltd
14a New Broadway, London W5 2XA **t** (020) 8566 5312 www.backroadstouring.co.uk

Guidelines to Britain
89 Alleyn Park, London SE21 8AA **t** (020) 8299 3000 www.guidelinestobritain.com

Lionheart Tours/British Bobby Tours
15 Manor Avenue, London SE4 1PE **t** (020) 8691 0997 www.lionhearttours.com

London Country Tours
1 Hill Crescent, Worcester Park, Surrey KT4 8NB **t** (020) 8642 2193 www.londoncountrytours.co.uk

Internet
To help you choose your holiday, a number of British family-orientated websites can suggest activities and provide contacts.

Family travel sites
www.family-travel.co.uk
www.kidsintow.co.uk

General parenting sites
www.babycentre.co.uk
www.babyworld.co.uk
www.familiesonline.co.uk
www.familytravelguides.com
www.flyingwithkids.com
www.kidsinmind.co.uk
www.parentalk.co.uk
www.parents-news.co.uk
www.raisingkids.co.uk
www.ukparents.co.uk

General UK holiday sites
www.britannia.com
www.atuk.co.uk
www.beautiful-england.co.uk
www.britainexpress.com
www.britishholiday.com
www.britishresorts.co.uk
www.holidayuk.com
www.visitbritain.com

London
www.londontown.com
www.thisislondon.co.uk
www.timeout.com/london
www.visitlondon.com

US tours

About Family Travel 3555 South Pacific Highway 191, Medford, Oregon 97501 **t** (541) 535 5411 www.about-family-travel.com
Family-orientated guided coach tours of England and Scotland. London tours available.

British Holidays 462 Glenmont Avenue, Columbus, Ohio 43214 **t** (866) 202 6551 www.britholidays.com
Tailor-made tours.

Grandtravel 1920 N Street, NW, Suite 200 Washington DC **t** (800) 247 7651 www.grandtravl.com
Tours for grandparents and grandchildren.

Rascals in Paradise 500 Sansome Street, Suite 200, San Francisco, CA 94111 **t** (415) 921 7000 www.rascalsinparadise.com
Family-orientated coach tours throughout England.

Trafalgar Tours 801 East Katella Avenue, Anaheim, CA 90605 US **t** (866) 544 4434 www.ttuk.trafalgartours.com/USA
Probably the best-known name in the escorted tours business. Offers tours throughout the British Isles. Luxury and budget alternatives available.

Travcoa 2424 SE Bristol Street, Suite 310, Newport Beach, CA 92660 **t** (866) 591 0070 www.travcoa.com
Luxury coach tours.

Specialist holidays

Boating holidays
For information on boating holidays *see* p.531

Camping holidays
For information on camping holidays *see* pp.530–1

Cottage holidays
For information on self-catering holidays *see* pp.529–30

Cycling holidays
The following companies offer cycling holidays, providing you with pre-booked accommodation, detailed maps and luggage transfer between hotels while you cycle.

Compass Holidays Railway Station, Queens Road, Cheltenham, Gloucestershire **t** (01242) 250642 www.compass-holidays.com
Cycling tours through Cumbria, Cornwall, Cotswolds, Gloucestershire, Hampshire, Shakespeare Country, Bath and Wiltshire.

Country Lanes 9 Shaftesbury Street, Fordingbridge, Hampshire **t** 0845 370 0622 www.countrylanes.co.uk
Isle of Wight, Lake District, New Forest and Yorkshire Dales tours.

Wheely Wonderful Cycling Petchfield Farm, Elton, Ludlow, Shropshire **t** (01568) 770755 www.wheelywonderfulcycling.co.uk
Tours of Shropshire, Herefordshire and Wales (p.403).
For further information on cycling in England contact Sustrans, set up in the 1970s with the aim of lobbying the government for the creation of 6,500 miles of cycle paths, around half of which are now in place. They can provide maps of all current cycle paths, **t** 0845 113 0065, www.sustrans.org.uk. *See* also Sport and Activities in the area chapters.

Farms
For information on farming holidays *see* p.530

Hostelling
For information on youth hostels *see* p.529

Walking
Most walking holidays are aimed primarily at adults looking to cover large swathes of country-side each day. Some, however, are willing to accommodate older children (usually over 11).

Adventureline t (01209) 820847 www.adventureline.co.uk
Cornish and Cotswolds walks.

Sherpa Expeditions t (020) 8577 2717 www.sherpa-walking-holidays.co.uk
New tours throughout the country.
For further information on walking, *see* pp.16–17

Budget breaks

Youth hostels
t 0870 7708868 www.yha.org
Family holidays can be expensive, especially in high summer, but there are savings to be made. Youth hostels are worth considering (p.529). Many now have family rooms with bunk beds, central heating, carpets, en-suite facilities and offer organized activities (guided walks, steam train rides and nature reserve visits). Annual YHA membership for a family is £22.95 (for a single-parent family £15.95); prices for family rooms start from £40 per night for a family of four.

Luxury breaks

Luxury Family Hotels
t (01761) 240 121 www.luxuryfamilyhotels.co.uk
If money is no object, choose one of this group's four swish establishments (three in the Southwest, the other in East Anglia). There are games and outdoor activities for the kids (plus food and eating times to suit them), comfortable bedrooms and good restaurants for their parents (p.503).

GETTING THERE

By air

England is one of the world's most visited countries, welcoming thousands of flights every day. Competition between airlines on the major routes is fierce and, wherever you're flying from, you should be able to pick up some cheap deals. The New York–London route is a particularly rich hunting ground for bargains. Of course, if travelling with children, you may decide to forego any potential savings in return for a little extra comfort and some form of in-flight care and entertainment. Many larger airlines, including British Airways, Air Canada and Cathay Pacific, provide special on-board services for families, which can include designated flight attendants, play packs, seat-back computer games and children's TV channels. Charter flights may be cheap but can be particularly hellish for children, sitting in a cramped seat with nothing to do for eight hours or more.

Your first glimpse of England is likely to be at one of London's five airports. Transatlantic flights touch down at the two largest. Heathrow, **t** 0870 000 0123, 15 miles west of central London, is the world's busiest airport and has four terminals (a fifth will be complete by 2008). Gatwick, **t** 0870 000 2468, 25 miles to the south, has two terminals (*see* opposite for Connections to central London). London's other three airports, London City, **t** (020) 7646 0088, Stansted, **t** 0870 000 0303, and Luton, **t** (01582) 405100, mainly handle flights from Europe. Stansted is the furthest from central London – some 35 miles to the north.

Visitors travelling to the north of England should check out connections to the airports at Birmingham, Manchester and Newcastle, which have begun to welcome international flights.

An international air ticket for a child aged two or under should cost just 10 per cent of the adult fare (only one reduced fare allowed per adult), although some airlines do allow children to travel free so long as they don't take up a seat (or any baggage allowance). Between the ages of three and 11, your child will be charged between 50 per cent and 85 per cent of the full adult fare, but once over 12, your child is, in the eyes of the airline, officially an adult and no longer entitled to any type of discount.

Pushchairs are usually carried free on airlines and can often be taken up to the point of boarding. Carrycots, however, are not supposed to

Cheap flight websites
www.cheapflights.com
www.cheaptickets.com
www.expedia.com
www.farebase.net
www.lastminute.com
www.moments-notice.com
www.travelocity.com

be brought on board, although some airlines will allow the collapsible kind. It makes sense to pre-book a sky cot or bassinet, availability permitting.

Connections to central London

Both the city's main airports have good, frequent links with the centre of town. From **Heathrow**, you can catch the Heathrow Express train, **t** 0845 600 1515, to Paddington every 15 minutes between 5.10am and 11.30pm; adult single £13.50, 5–15s £6.70, under 5s free (the journey takes just 15 minutes). The Piccadilly Line tube runs into central London every 10 minutes or so between 5.10am and 11.45pm; adult single £4, child single £2 (roughly 50 minutes). Or you can take one of two airbuses (A1 and A2), which will deliver you to either Victoria or King's Cross stations; adult return £10, 3–15s £5, under 3s free (80 minutes).

From **Gatwick**, you can catch the Gatwick Express, **t** 0845 850 1530, to Victoria every 15 minutes between 5.50am and 12.50am (the last non-express train from Gatwick leaves at 1.35am); adult single £14, under 15s pay 50 per cent of an adult ticket, under 5s free (just over 30 minutes) or the cheaper (and slower) National Express Bus, which runs to Victoria between 5.15am and 10.15pm; adult single £6.60, child single £3.30 (the journey takes 80 minutes).

You also have the option of taking a taxi, which is obviously the most expensive but most convenient option of all. From Heathrow, the fare in a black cab should be in the region of £40. Expect to pay up to £90 from Gatwick.

From North America

The cheapest tickets offered by the major airlines are Apex and Super Apex, which must be booked 21 days before departure and involve a stay of at least seven nights. Also, check out the consolidators, companies that buy blocks of unsold tickets from major airlines in order to sell them at a discount. Because of the restrictions on flight

Major North American airlines
Air Canada
t (888) 247 2262 www.aircanada.com
American Airlines
t toll free 800 433 7300 www.aa.com
British Airways
t toll free 800 247 9297 www.britishairways.com
Continental Airlines
t toll free 800 231 0856 www.continental.com
Delta Airlines
t toll free 800 241 4141 www.delta.com
United Airlines
t toll free 800 538 2929 www.united.com
Virgin Atlantic Airways
t toll free 800 821 5438 www.virgin-atlantic.com

Consolidators in North America
Airline Consolidators
t (888) 465 5385 www.airlineconsolidators.com
Air Brokers Travel
t toll free 800 883 3273 www.airbrokers.com
Globester
t (650) 292 2331 www.globester.com
TFI Tours International
t toll free 800 745 8000 www.tfitours.com
Note: 'Toll free' numbers are only toll-free if called from within the USA or Canada.

Major airlines in Australia and New Zealand
Air New Zealand
Australia: t (13) 2476
New Zealand: t (0800) 737 000
www.airnewzealand.com
British Airways
Australia: t (1300) 765 177
New Zealand: t (09) 966 9777
www.britishairways.com
Cathay Pacific
Australia: t (13) 1747
New Zealand: t (09) 379 0861
www.cathaypacific.com
Qantas
Australia: t (13) 1313
New Zealand: t (09) 357 8900
www.qantas.com.au

times, high cancellations fees and the potential for stress-inducing delays, charter flights are not recommended when travelling with children.

By rail

Eurostar
t 08705 186 186 www.eurostar.com
20 trains a day from Paris and Brussels
Fares Standard class Apex return, adults from £59, children (4–11) from £50, under 4s **free**
Check-in time At least 30 minutes before departure. Two suitcases and a piece of hand luggage allowed per person
Wheelchair users need to inform Eurostar staff of their requirements when booking
It takes about two-and-a-half hours to reach London from Paris or Brussels aboard a super-sleek, super-speedy Eurostar train. Time spent under the sea whizzing through the Eurotunnel is just 25 minutes. At present, the trains arrive at Waterloo, although the new international rail terminus at King's Cross–St Pancras will open in 2007. For people travelling from places other than Brussels or Paris, there is still the option of the old-fashioned boat-train. The main ferry links land you at Harwich, Newcastle, Newhaven, Portsmouth and, by far the most popular choice, Dover (*see* below).

By car

There are two choices: the ferry or the Eurotunnel. The completion of the tunnel in the early 1990s transformed the cross-Channel travel industry. Despite their initial bravado, the ferry companies have taken a back seat ever since, forced through decreasing passenger numbers into a sustained period of retrenchment. The much-hyped advantages of ferry travel – duty-free shops, restaurants and bars, fabulously bad cabaret, etc. – which were intended to make it the route of choice for the discerning cross-channel traveller, have paled in comparison to a 25-minute seasickness-free and cabaret-less crossing. And now that duty-free shopping has finally been abolished, ferry companies are really beginning to feel the strain. A spate of mergers and route cancellations has been the result, with services to and from Belgium particularly hard hit.
For all its problems, ferry travel is still well worth considering. Prices are highly competitive with companies offering a range of deals in the hope of

drawing some custom away from the 'Chunnel' (under 4s usually travel free and there are discounts for under 14s). Most lines have excellent family facilities including restaurants, cafés, baby changing rooms, children's play areas and video rooms, and the trip provides a break from driving.

Calais–Dover is the fastest and most popular ferry crossing route. P&O Ferries, t 0870 980 333, www.poferries.com, operate 35 sailings a day in the high season; the journey takes one hour and 15 minutes. Check-in time 45 minutes before depature.

Via the Eurotunnel

Eurotunnel

t 0870 535 3535 www.eurotunnel.com
Four departures an hour between Folkestone and Calais during peak times
Fares Early booking discount tickets for a short stay start at £93 per car. The fare is for car space only regardless of the number of passengers. Day or overnight trips from £40
Check-in time 30 minutes before departure. No baggage weight limit
Disabled travellers should display badges on vehicles and inform Eurotunnel staff when checking in

Eurotunnel, the ferry companies' nemesis, transports cars on purpose-built carriers through the tunnel between Calais and Folkestone. The French Terminal is situated off junction 13 of the A16 motorway while the British equivalent can be reached via junction 11a on the M20. The journey time is 35 minutes platform-to-platform – most people choose to stay in their car, although you can get out to stretch your legs. It is advisable to reserve a space in advance, although you can just turn up and wait; you will be put on a standby list and given space on a first-come, first-served basis.

You may want to consider arriving in Britain carless and then renting once you get there. Most major airlines and many travel agents can arrange fly-drive packages for you on request. For rental companies in London, *see* **Getting Around**, p.13.

By bus

National Express

t 0870 580 8080 www.nationalexpress.com
Coach trips are invariably a balancing act, being both one of the cheapest and least comfortable ways of travelling long distances. National Express, which operates coach routes to all the major cities in Britain and Europe, does not charge for under 5s and charges only half fare for under 16s. Nonetheless, savings are tempered by the boredom of sitting down for hours on end.

Entry formalities

Passports and visas

Britain's 'shall we, shan't we' attitude towards Europe is amply demonstrated by its border policy. Although a member of the European Union (EU) – which technically gives all union citizens the right to move freely in and between member states – Britain has yet to institute a proper open border policy and thus it is still necessary for EU citizens to present their passports or identity cards upon entering the country.

Nationals from the US, Canada, Australia, New Zealand, South Africa, Japan, Mexico and Switzerland do not need a visa in order to visit the country for a holiday of up to three months but must present their passport upon arrival and should expect to answer a few routine questions relating to the nature of their visit: how long they expect to stay, how much money they're bringing into the country, etc.

Other nationals should check out their particular entry requirements with their respective embassies.

Customs

EU nationals over the age of 17 are no longer required to make a declaration to customs upon entry into another EU country and so can now import a limitless amount of goods for personal use. For non-EU nationals the limits are 200 cigarettes, one litre of spirits, two litres of wine, 60ml of perfume, two cameras, one movie camera and one television.

Retail Export Scheme

Visitors from non-EU countries can make savings on purchases made in England via the Retail Export Scheme. Simply pick up a form from participating shops, fill in the appropriate details and, upon leaving the country, you should be able to claim back the VAT paid on any goods you plan to take out of the country.

GETTING AROUND

By air

British Airways **t** 0870 850 9850
www.britishairways.com
British Midland **t** 0870 607 0555
www.flybmi.com
Easy Jet **t** 0890 5821 0905
www.easyjet.com
Eastern Airways **t** 0870 366 9100
www.easternairways.com
Ryanair **t** 0818 303 030
www.ryanair.com

England is a small country and once you've taken into account checking-in times, flying is not a great deal quicker (and in some cases, a good deal more expensive) than train travel. For the record, British Airways and British Midland operate domestic flights between London and the international airports at Manchester, Birmingham and Newcastle, while the newer budget airlines have brought destinations previously inaccessible without long car or train journeys within reach, such as the Cornish resort of Newquay, two hours from London.

By car

Despite severe under-investment – which has been exacerbated rather than improved by the privatization of the railways in the mid-1990s – Britain's public transport network is still relatively efficient. It is, however, by no means comprehensive and, if you plan to move around a lot during your holiday, especially in rural areas, then motoring is your only feasible option. Car hire prices are competitive (albeit still expensive; you'd be advised to arrange a package deal before you arrive) and England's roads are among the safest in Europe. Petrol is, unfortunately, pricey, certainly when compared with Europe – although, if you take into account European motorway tolls (which don't apply in England), the cost of driving more or less balances out.

England's motorways and A-roads are, in the main, well maintained and provide the fastest way of getting around. B-roads tend to be more circuitous, offering a slower but perhaps more pleasant driving experience, allowing you to see more of the scenery as you drive. Be aware that most major towns and cities do not lend themselves easily to motoring. Pedestrianized areas, incomprehensible one-way systems and draconian parking regulations are just some of the hazards awaiting you. London, in particular, is a city best explored on foot (especially since the introduction of a central pay zone) or using public transport. This is not to say that you shouldn't drive *to* a given city – many operate easy-to-use park-and-ride schemes – merely that you should, if at all possible, avoid driving *within* the city.

Motoring checklist

▶ If you belong to a motoring organization, you should check to see whether they have an arrangement with either of Britain's two main motoring organizations, the AA and the RAC, both of which operate a 24-hour emergency breakdown service. For instance, members of the USA's AAA are automatically covered when they drive in England.
**AA t 0870 600 0371
(international t (0161) 495 8945)
RAC t 0870 5722 722**
▶ Before starting to drive, you should first purchase a copy of the British Highway Code (available from post offices) in order to learn some of the peculiarities of the British way of motoring and to familiarize yourself with the road signs – which, unlike signs in America, are based on pictures rather than words.
▶ You will need to purchase a good road map, such as those produced by the RAC, the AA and Ordnance Survey, all of which are available at London's largest map shop, Stanfords, 12–14 Long Acre, Covent Garden, WC2, **t** (020) 7836 1321, **www.stanfords.co.uk**.
▶ Wearing front and back seatbelts is compulsory in Britain.
▶ Drive on the left. The thought of having to overcome this particular novelty is often a great worry to foreign drivers. It's actually a lot easier to get used to than you might think. Remember, if hiring a car, the steering wheel will be on the right hand side, which means you must change gears with your left hand. Unless specified, your rental car will have manual gears. Automatic drive cars are much less common in England than they are in the States and have to be requested specially.
▶ Drivers arriving from Continental Europe must remember to adjust the dip of their headlights for driving on the left.

Car rental firms

All rental companies require that the person driving be over 21 (more usually over 23) and that they have held their licence for over a year. Child seats should be available on request.

It goes without saying that you will need to bring a valid driving licence with you. If bringing your own car from the European Continent, you should also bring your vehicle registration and make sure that your car is insured (and that the insurance extends to driving in a foreign country).

You don't need to carry your driving papers with you when driving but, if stopped, you will usually be asked to present them at a police station within five days.

Car rental firms in the UK
Alamo t 0845 120 2071
Avis t 0870 608 6363
Hertz t (020) 7026 0077
Thrifty t (0149) 475 1500

Travelling times and distances from London

	Miles	By train	By coach
Bath	118	1hr 11min	2hr 10min
Birmingham	110	1hr 40min	2hr 20min
Brighton	51	51min	1hr 45min
Bristol	118	1hr 30min	2hr 30min
Cambridge	61	52min	1hr 50min
Canterbury	56	1hr 22min	1hr 45min
Chester	199	2hr 17min	5hr 10min
Dover	80	1hr 45min	2hr 30min
Durham	255	2hr 38min	5hr 05min
Exeter	174	1hr 59min	3hr 50min
Liverpool	193	2hr 45min	4hr 30min
Manchester	184	2hr 30min	4hr 15min
Newcastle	270	2hr 40min	5hr 20min
Norwich	115	1hr 35min	2hr 40min
Oxford	57	48min	1hr 40min
Penzance	283	5hr	8hr
Portsmouth	70	1hr 21min	2hr 05min
Salisbury	84	1hr 18min	2hr 40min
Southampton	80	1hr	1hr 35min
Stratford-upon-Avon	92	2hr 12min	2hr 45min
Windermere	259	3hr 16min	7hr 07min
York	188	1hr 42min	4hr 15min

Car rental firms in the US
Alamo t 800 462 5266
Avis t 800 331 1212
Hertz t 800 654 3001
Thrifty t 800 847 4389

By rail

If it's not a crisis currently afflicting Britain's railways, then it's something pretty similar. Delays, cancellations, baffling and occasionally contradictory ticketing arrangements, rising prices – these are just some of the problems the country's rail commuters face almost daily.

Many people cite the privatization of the railways in the mid 1990s as the root of the troubles. Certainly, the nationalized British Rail industry had its fair share of problems, but it was at least in total control of the system and, in some sense, accountable. Now, several different companies run the various routes, while tracks and signalling are under the control of a separate body entirely.

The benefits that privatization was supposed to bring – increased investment and a lowering of fares – have simply not been forthcoming and the railways remain severely underfunded, overcrowded at peak times and, on thankfully rare occasions, subject to accidents.

That said, Britain's railways do, in the main, provide a decent service. With over 2,500 UK stations offering access to most of the country's principal towns and some 18,000 daily departures, it's at least 90 per cent reliable – but that 10 per cent can cause a mountain of frustrations. All the major cities are linked by fast (up to 125mph) Intercity services which, despite the recent problems, still represent one of the most efficient ways of moving around the country. Sleeping carriages are available on long-distance journeys. For **National Rail Enquiries**, call t 08457 48 49 50 (from inside UK only) or t (020) 7278 5240 ; detailed information, including train times, is also available from the website, www.nationalrail.co.uk. For times and ticket bookings, check out the website www.thetrainline.com.

Train travel from London

London is the country's main transport hub with no fewer than eight mainline rail terminals serving all the major regions.

Charing Cross, The Strand WC2

For services to the Southeast – Canterbury, Chatham, Dover, Folkestone, Hastings, etc.

Euston, Euston Road NW1

For services to the Midlands and the Northwest – Birmingham, Chester, Manchester, the Lake District, Carlisle, etc.

King's Cross, Euston Road N1

For services to the east coast and the Northeast – Cambridge, Durham, Newark, York, etc.

Liverpool Street, Liverpool Street EC2

For the Skytrain to Stansted Airport and services to East Anglia – Cambridge, Colchester, Harwich, Ipswich, Norwich, etc.

Paddington, Praed Street W2

For the Heathrow Express to Heathrow Airport and services to the Southwest, Thames Valley and Heart of England – Bath, Cheltenham, Exeter, Gloucester, Stratford-upon-Avon, etc.

St Pancras, Euston Road N1

For services to the Midlands – Derby, Nottingham, Sheffield, etc.

Victoria, Terminus Place SW1

For the Gatwick Express to Gatwick Airport and services to the Southeast – Brighton, Canterbury, Eastbourne, Portsmouth, etc.

Waterloo, York Road SE1

For Eurostar services to Paris and Brussels via the Eurotunnel and services to the Southeast and the Midwest – Bournemouth, Portsmouth, Salisbury, Southampton, etc.

Safety note

There are two types of train currently in operation. Do be careful if you find yourself travelling on one of the older models with hinged, slamming doors. Not only is it possible to open the door whilst the train is moving but the windows open low enough for a determined child to be able to stick its head out. Therefore, always sit between your child and the door. The newer, more common style of train is much safer. The doors are automatic and can only be opened when the train is stopped in a station. Furthermore, the windows are quite high up and must be tilted backwards to open, thereby preventing any outside exploration. Beware that on some trains the emergency brake handles are situated conveniently at child height – a red rag to a bull if ever there was one.

Tickets and passes

The railways are expensive (British commuters pay the highest fares in Europe). Nonetheless, there are considerable savings to be made if you book in advance with **Apex** (seven days in advance) or **Super Apex** (14 days). Children aged 5–15 pay 50 per cent of the adult fare (although there are no discounts on Apex or Super Apex) while under 5s travel free so long as they don't take up a seat on a crowded train. For a long journey, it is advisable to book well in advance so that you can get both the lowest fare possible and reserve your seats.

There are two classes of railway travel: standard and first class. On Sundays, on some long distance services, you may be allowed to upgrade from standard to first class for as little as £10. It's well worth it, especially if you've got the family in tow, as you'll have more space and better seats.

You buy your ticket from the staff kiosk at the relevant station or, if booking an Intercity trip in advance, from a travel agent. Stations without a staff kiosk should have an automated ticket machine or, failing that, you should be able to buy your ticket from an inspector on the train. If caught trying to disembark without having paid your fare, you are liable for an on-the-spot fine of £10.

Family railcards are available from most major railway stations offering one-third off most fares for £20 (12-month pass) subject to restrictions.

Rail passes outside the UK

If coming from abroad and planning to do a lot of travelling by train, it's worth looking into the BritRail Consecutive Pass, which allows you unlimited travel on the rail network for a certain number of consecutive days, or the BritRail Flexipass, which allows you to pick a number of travel days out of a two-month period (*see above*). Buy any adult BritRail pass and one accompanying child (5–15) receives a free pass of the same type and duration. Passes must be bought before you enter the country and are available from BritRail Travel International in the US, **t** (866) 2748 7245, **www.britrail.com**.

BritRail Consecutive Pass

Adults	(prices in US dollars)	
Valid for	1st Class	2nd Class
4 days	$327	$218
8 days	$469	$311
15 days	$702	$469
22 days	$891	$592
1 month	$1954	$702
Children		
Valid for	1st Class	2nd Class
4 days	$164	$109
8 days	$235	$156
15 days	$351	$235
22 days	$446	$296
1 month	$527	$351

BritRail Flexipass

Adults		
Valid for	1st Class	2nd Class
4 days in 2 months	$409	$275
8 days in 2 months	$598	$399
15 days in 2 months	$901	$604
Children		
Valid for	1st Class	2nd Class
4 days in 2 months	$204.50	$137.50
8 days in 2 months	$299	$199.50
15 days in 2 months	$450.50	$302

National Express/Eurolines

Ensign Court, 4 Vicarage Road, Edgbaston,
Birmingham t 0870 580 8080
www.nationalexpress.co.uk

If you plan to take full advantage of the coach routes on offer then the Brit Xplorer Pass may be the most economical way to go about it. Xplorer Pass holders are entitled to unlimited travel for either 7, 14 or 28 consecutive days (£79/£139/£219) on all National Express services throughout England, Scotland and Wales. Family Coachcards are an additional way to save money entitling holders to free child travel. There are two available, the Family 1plus1 (one adult pays full fare with one child going free, £8 for 1 year) or 2plus2 (two adults pay full fare and two children travel free, £16 for 1 year).

Sightseeing buses

The City Sightseeing company offers sightseeing tours in open-top double decker buses with either live or recorded commentary in Bath, Cambridge, London, Oxford and Stratford all year round, as well as in 32 other British cities (including Brighton, Chester and Manchester) on a seasonal basis. Keep your ticket from one town and get a 10 per cent discount on City Sightseeing buses elsewhere. Details from t (01708) 866 000 or **www.**guidefriday.com.

Buses and coaches

Buses and coaches together make up England's most comprehensive public transport network. The term 'coach' is usually used to refer to long-distance services, while 'bus' is taken to mean city-specific ones.

National Express is the dominant player in the long-distance coach market, offering services to every major town in the country. Efficient and cheap, it has just one major drawback – the coaches are slow. Long journeys spent crawling from A to B whilst stopping off at every place of note in between are very much the norm. If travelling with a family, it's probably wise only to consider coach trips lasting no more than an hour or two. For details of local city and town buses, you should contact the relevant tourist authority.

Walking

Walking is one of the great British pastimes. Most major towns and cities have some kind of marked trail taking you past their attractions and many tourist offices offer guided walks. Indeed, in some of the more crowded and congested cities, such as London and Birmingham, walking is often the most efficient mode of transport, especially during the rush hour. For the best walking, however, you'll have to head away from the cities.

Although the English are mostly townies (according to the last census, around 83 per cent of the population live in urban areas), they also have a tremendous love of the countryside, which is why, every weekend, millions of them decamp there to put in a few hours of serious up-hill and down-dale strolling. Despite its small size, England has more than its fair share of walkable countryside. Areas like the Cotswolds, Dartmoor, the North Yorkshire Moors, the Peak District and the Lake District, which make up some of Europe's most stunning scenery, are criss-crossed by networks of trails.

The question of where you can and can't walk can be confusing. Much of the English countryside is in private hands. This is even true in the National Parks, areas of outstanding natural beauty that have supposedly been set aside for the whole country to enjoy. Thankfully, the population is protected by ancient laws governing 'rights of way' from being prosecuted for trespass. So long as you stick to the agreed path, which will be marked on any walking map – and sometimes on the ground by yellow (for footpaths) or blue (for bridlepaths) arrows – you have the legal right to cross private land (even farm land).

Some of the country's great long-distance walks are listed below, although if walking as a family, it's probably wise not to be too ambitious. A couple of miles is as much as the average small child is prepared to take, although teenagers may be willing to stretch their legs a little further. Whatever distance you decide upon, you'll need a good map. Ordnance Survey probably have the best selection. Their Pathfinder series is particularly good. Browse their list at **www**.ordsvy.gov.uk.

Every tourist office can provide details of local walks, but for a complete overview of Britain's walking options, contact the **Ramblers' Association** 2nd Floor, Camelford House, 87–90 Albert Embankment, London SE1, **t** (020) 7339 8500, **www**.ramblers.org.uk

Long-distance paths

Cotswold Way
One hundred miles across the great limestone escarpment from Chipping Camden to Bath (p.250).

Cumbria Way
Seventy miles of poet-inspiring Lake District countryside (p.429).

Hadrian's Wall
The remains of the great Roman wall can be followed for 70 miles from Newcastle-upon-Tyne to Bowness-on-Solway (p.473).

Offa's Dyke Path
These 177 miles follow the eight-century earthwork built by King Offa (p.380) to separate England from Wales.

The Pennine Way
The hardest walk of them all, it snakes along the mountains for 250 miles from the Peak District to Scotland (pp.344, 429).

The Ridgeway Path
85 miles from Overton Hill in Wiltshire to Ivinghoe Beacon in Bedfordshire taking in the Chilterns and Coombe Hill on the way (p.269).

South Downs Way
100 miles of rolling chalk downland between Eastbourne and Winchester (p.132).

Southwest Coastal Path
These 600 miles, from Minehead in Somerset, take in the coasts of Devon and Cornwall, before ending in Poole, Dorset. The Southwest chapter has details on many of the towns and villages lining the path (p.214).

The Thames Path
These 180 miles follow the Thames from its source to the sea (p.269).

Cycling

Though more cycle lanes are appearing each year, England's cities are still much less cycle-friendly than those in the Netherlands, Denmark and Germany. Indeed, those cycle lanes that do exist are often no more than token efforts – a green strip painted at the side of the road that may well peter out after 100 yards or so. Away from the cities, it's a different story. England's B-roads and country lanes are just begging to be cycled and provide a wonderfully scenic way of exploring the country. The British Tourist Authority's free booklet 'Cycling' will help you get started, while individual tourist offices can provide details of local routes and hire shops. Contact the **Cyclists' Touring Club**, **t** 0870 873 0060, **www**.ctc.org.uk.

Details of cycle routes and hire shops are provided throughout the guide. The average hire shop should be able to equip you with adult bikes, children's bikes, safety helmets, route maps, children's seats, tandems, tag-a-longs and child and dog trailers.

Cyclists' checklist

▶ Cycle helmets are, surprisingly, not compulsory in England but should nonetheless be worn and are available from all bike hire shops.

▶ Children can only be carried as 'passengers' on a bike with a properly fitted child seat.

▶ You will need a good D-lock. Though this can't guarantee that your bike won't be stolen by an organized gang armed with metal cutters, it will at least prevent petty opportunistic thievery.

▶ You will also need a good map. Ordnance Survey produce an excellent range of cycling guides. Browse their website list.

▶ Most airlines and ferry companies will carry bikes free of charge. Most bus companies won't carry them at all.

▶ For trains, there's no hard and fast rule. Most of the 25 rail companies will happily accept bikes outside peak hours. Intercity services tend to be a bit more reluctant and will often ask for a surcharge of around £3 for carrying a bike.

Practical A–Z

03

Climate and when to go

If you've never been to Britain before, you're probably expecting to be consumed by clouds of fog and drizzle the moment you step off the plane. Britain has a reputation for dismal weather and the state of the skies has long been the nation's favourite topic of conversation. Rainfall, however, is probably the greatest climatic hazard you'll have to face. Britain's weather could hardly be described as extreme. The summers are rarely too hot, the winters seldom too cold. You may get a brief heat-wave in July or the occasional week of snow cover in January (plus a small hurricane every 70 years or so) but these hardly warrant special precautions. It isn't even particularly foggy anymore – to tell the truth, it never was; the mist you see swirling down the streets in old films is smog, now largely eradi-cated thanks to stricter pollution laws. England is too small a country to have vast climatic contrasts.

The average temperature is 22°C (75°F) in July and August and 7°C (44°F) in December and January. Rainfall is at its heaviest in November (not, as the song says, April) with an average of 6.35cm (2.5in).

All in all, the best time to visit is probably late spring or late summer when you can look forward to mild temperatures, little rain, the odd sunny day and slightly less dense queues at the country's major tourist attractions.

Discount passes

When planning a family holiday, it's a good idea to think about buying a sightseeing pass. There are a variety of discount passes available giving you free or reduced entry to many of the country's attractions. Here is a selection of some of the best:

English Heritage membership

English Heritage Membership Department, PO Box 570, Swindon SN2 2UR **t** 0870 333 1181 **www.**english-heritage.org.uk
Prices Adults £38 each or £65 for 2, under 16s **free**

Gives you free entry for a year to all English Heritage properties including Audley End House, Dover Castle, Hadrian's Wall, Hastings Castle, Osborne House, Stonehenge and Tintagel Castle, as well as half-price admission to more than 100 historic sites in Scotland, Wales and the Isle of Man (free after your first year of membership). Members also receive a guide to English Heritage properties and quarterly editions of *Heritage Today*, the organization's magazine.

English Heritage Overseas Visitor Pass

US: BritRail Travel International, 2 Hudson Place, Suite 100, Hoboken, New Jersey, USA **t** (1-866) 2748 7245 **www.**britrail.com
Prices 7 days: adult £18/$34, 2 adults £34/$63, family £38/$71; 14 days: adult £22/$42, 2 adults £41/$77, family £46/$86

Gives you free entry to more than 120 historic properties throughout England. You will also receive a guide to English Heritage properties.

Great British Heritage Pass

UK: The Leisure Pass Group, PO Box 2337, London W1 **t** (020) 8846 9000
www.visitbritain.com/heritagepass
US: BritRail Travel International, 2 Hudson Place, Suite 100, Hoboken, New Jersey, USA **t** (1-866) 2748 7245 **www.**britrail.com
Prices 4 days: £28/$55; 7 days: £39/$77; 15 days: £52/$102; 30 days: £70/$137

Gives free entry to around 600 properties belonging to the National Trust, the National Trust for Scotland, English Heritage, CADW (Welsh Historic Monuments), the Treasure Houses of England, the Historic Houses Association, Historic Scotland and the Historic Royal Palaces Agency. Participating properties include Hampton Court Palace, Shakespeare's birthplace in Stratford-upon-Avon, Stonehenge, Warwick Castle and Windsor Castle. A gazetteer listing all the attractions along with opening times and maps showing their loca-tion is provided with each pass.

London Pass

British Visitor Centre, 1 Lower Regent Street, London SW1 **t** (020) 8846 9000
www.londonpass.com
Prices With/without travel: 1 day: adults £35/£30, children £20/£18; 2 days: adults £55/£42, children £33/£29; 3 days: adults £71/£52, children £40/£34; 6 days: adults £110/£72, children £68/£48

The pass entitles you to free entry to more than 50 of the capital's attractions, free public transport on buses, tubes and trains, commission-free currency exchange, free tours (Chelsea Football Stadium, Wimbledon All England Club and Royal Albert Hall) and special discount offers at galleries, restaurants and gift shops. You will also receive a free guidebook. Participating sites include HMS *Belfast*, the London Aquarium, St Paul's Cathedral, the Thames Barrier, Tower of London and Windsor Castle.

National Trust Membership

National Trust Membership Department
PO Box 39, Warrington, WA5 7WD t 0870 458 4000
www.nationaltrust.org.uk
Prices Adults £40.50 each or £68 for 2, young
person (13–25) £18.50, child £18.50, family (2+2
under 18s) £73, single-parent family £55
Free entry for a one-year period to all National Trust
and National Trust for Scotland properties plus
handbook, tri-annual *National Trust Magazine* and
regular newsletters.

Royal Oak Foundation

26 Broadway, Suite 950, New York t 800 913 6565
www.royal-oak.org
Prices Individual member $55 each or $80 for 2,
family (2+2, under 21s) $90
This is an American organization affiliated to the
National Trust. Members are entitled to free entry to
240 National Trust properties in England, Scotland,
Wales and Northern Ireland and receive an annual
National Trust Handbook plus the National Trust
Magazine.

Embassies and consulates

US Embassy, 24 Grosvenor Square, W1
t (020) 7499 9000 www.usembassy.org.uk (open
Mon–Fri 8.30–5.30; 24-hour helpline for US citizens)
Australian High Commission, Australia House,
The Strand, WC2 t (020) 7379 4334
www.australia.org.uk (open Mon–Fri 9–5)
Canadian High Commission, 38 Grosvenor St, W1
t (020) 7258 6600 www.canada.org.uk (open
Mon–Fri 8–11am; 24-hour telephone helpline)
Dutch Embassy, 38 Hyde Park Gate, SW7
t (020) 7590 3200 www.netherlands-embassy.org.uk
(open Mon–Fri 9–5)
French Consulate, 21 Cromwell Road, SW7
t (020) 7073 1200 www.ambafrance-uk.org
(open Mon and Fri 9–12 noon, Tues–Thurs 9–4)
German Embassy, 23 Belgrave Square, SW1
t (020) 7824 1300 www.london.diplo.de (open
Mon–Fri 9–11.30 pm)
High Commission of India, India House, Aldwych,
WC2 t (020) 7836 8484 www.hcilondon.net
(open Mon–Fri 9.30–5.30)
Irish Embassy, 17 Grosvenor Place, SW1
t (020) 7245 2171 (open Mon–Fri 9.30–5)
Japanese Embassy, 101–4 Piccadilly, W1
t (020) 7465 6500 www.uk.emb-japan.go.jp (open
Mon–Fri 9.30am–1pm and 2.30–4.30pm)

New Zealand High Commission, New Zealand
House, 80 Haymarket, SW1 t (020) 7930 8422
www.nzembassy.com (open Mon–Fri 9– 5)
South African High Commission, South Africa
House, Trafalgar Square, WC2
t (020) 7451 7299 www.southafricahouse.com
(open Mon–Fri 9.30–5)
Swedish Embassy, 11 Montagu Place, W1 t (020)
7917 6400 (open Mon–Fri 9–12.30noon)

Food

The importance of the family market to the
restaurant industry has become increasingly
apparent in recent years with many eateries now
offering specialized children's menus, highchairs
and activity packs. Some restaurants have even set
Sunday aside as a special Family Day when children's entertainment (puppet shows, face-painting
and magic demonstrations) is laid on.

England's huge multicultural population has bred
great culinary diversity. Chinese takeaways, French
bistros, Spanish tapas bars, American hamburger
joints and Japanese noodle bars are now common
sights on the nation's high streets. The country's
most popular restaurants, however, are its curry
houses. Every night the nation tucks into a mountain of poppadoms, samosas, biriyanis and baltis. In
the 50-odd years since the first Indian restaurant
opened in Britain, curry has become Britain's
unofficial national dish. Even if you're not into spicy
food, you should try curry at least once during your
holiday, especially if you're travelling near either of
the two great curry hot spots of Birmingham and
Bradford. There are four degrees of curry hotness:
korma (mild), *madras* (quite hot), *vindaloo* (very hot)
and *phall* (insanely hot).

Not all British culinary expertise is imported
though. Although as a nation Britain has never hit
great gastronomic heights, its traditional cuisine
has many devotees. Pubs are good sources of
sturdy olde English fare – shepherd's pie, toad-in-
the-hole, etc. – and many have become more child
friendly, offering family rooms, play areas and
children's menus. Try a full-fried 'English breakfast'
of sausages, bacon, eggs, tomato and mushrooms
served with toast and butter, beans and milky tea
to kickstart the day. It's available at hotels and
'caffs' or 'greasy spoons' (the British version of the
café) across the country. Sample regional dishes
such as Cornish pasties (p.236), Devonshire cream
teas (p.235), Whitstable oysters (p.124), Yorkshire

black pudding, pork pies from Melton Mowbray in Lincolnshire (p.369) and, for dessert, Bakewell puddings from Derbyshire (pp.345, 367).

Then there's fish and chips, the most quintessentially British meal of all. Battered fish – choose from cod, rock (dogfish), plaice and haddock – and big, chunky chips served in paper. For added authenticity, cover your meal in gallons of salt and vinegar.

The website www.speciality-foods.com is a comprehensive guide to high-quality British food and drink, and can be searched by region for local suppliers such as Produced in Kent, Tastes of Anglia, Scottish Enterprise, Taste of the Wear (to name but a few); there is an online marketplace where you can buy these delicacies direct.

If your children will not experiment with new culinary tastes and ideas, the nation's high streets are always lined with familiar fast-food names – McDonald's, KFC, Pizza Hut, Burger King, etc., whilst parents can enjoy a posh alternative to the more traditional type of takeaway foods by ordering a homecooked gourmet meal from t 0845 633699 www.cornucopia.co.uk.

Supermarkets

The rise of the supermarket has probably been the single most significant retail development of the last 25 years. Where previously most people would buy their food daily from small local shops, these days almost everyone makes a weekly trip to the supermarket. Many local high streets have suffered terribly as a result, with hundreds of grocers, butchers and bakers forced to close down. For most people, the attractions of supermarket shopping – convenience, choice, low prices, round-the-clock availability – have proved irresistible. Even the smallest supermarkets have a range of produce which little high street stores can never hope to match. If self-catering, you should certainly find out where your nearest supermarket is. Most have in-house bakeries and stock a wide range of fruit and veg, meat and fish, as well as aisles of ready-made meals. Supermarkets can also be tremendously helpful when it comes to feeding fussy kids as they always stock inexhaustible supplies of bland kiddies' favourites like hamburgers, fish fingers and alphabet spaghetti.

The main supermarkets are: Tesco, www.tesco.com; Asda, www.asda.co.uk; Sainsbury's, www.sainsburys.co.uk and Waitrose, www.ocado.com, and all of these offer online

shopping with direct home delivery. Organic foods can be ordered online from the supermarkets or from specialist companies such as www.abel-cole.co.uk or www.riverford.co.uk.

Markets

Not every old-fashioned shopping experience has been crushed under the wheels of big business. Village markets still thrive the length and breadth of the country where you can pick up good-quality fresh fruit and veg at a fraction of the price you would pay at a supermarket. Visit www.farmersmarkets.net for information on regional markets or ask about local market times at Tourist Information offices.

Insurance

It's vital that you take out travel insurance before your trip. This should cover, at a bare minimum, cancellation due to illness, travel delays, accidents, lost luggage, lost passports, lost or stolen belongings, personal liability, legal expenses, emergency flights and medical cover. You are not obliged to buy insurance from the travel company that sold you your holiday and it's well worth shopping around to see who offers the most extensive cover at the most competitive rates. Most insurance companies offer free insurance to children under the age of two as part of a parental policy. Also bear in mind annual insurance policies, which can be especially cost-effective for families with two or more older children. Keep the insurance company's 24-hour emergency number close to hand – if you have a mobile phone, store it in the memory.

The most important aspect of any travel insurance policy is its medical cover. You should look for cover of around £5 million. If a resident of the European Union, Iceland, Liechtenstein or Norway, you are entitled to free or reduced-cost medical treatment so long as you carry with you the appropriate validated form. In the EU, this is the European National Health Insurance Card (EHIC), which covers families with dependent children up to the age of 16 (or 19 if in full-time education). Despite this arrangement, you may initially have to pay for your medical treatment and then claim your expenses back at a later date so hang on to your receipts.

In the US and Canada, you may find that your existing insurance policies give sufficient medical cover – check them thoroughly before taking out a new one. Canadians, in particular, are usually

UK
Association of British Insurers t (020) 7600 3333
www.abi.org.uk
The Financial Ombudsman service t 0845 080 1800
www.financial-ombudsman.org.uk
The government-appointed regulator of the
insurance and financial industries.
Columbus Travel Insurance t 0870 033 998811
www.columbusdirect.com
Endsleigh Insurance t 0800 028 3571
www.endsleigh.co.uk
Insure and Go t 0870 901 3674
www.insureandgo.com
Medicover t 0870 735 3600 **www.**medi-cover.co.uk
World Wide Insure t 0870 112 8100
www.worldinsure.com

North America
Access America, US and Canada **t** 800 729 6021,
www.accessamerica.com
Carefree Travel Insurance, US and Canada
t 800 727 4874 **www.**carefreetravel.com
MEDEX Assistance Corporation, US **t** 800 732 5309
www.medexassit.com
Travel Assistance International, US and Canada
t 800 821 2828 **www.**travelassistance.com

covered by their provincial health plans. Few
American or Canadian insurance companies will
issue on-the-spot payments following a reported
theft or loss. You will usually have to wait several
weeks and engage in a hefty amount of correspon-
dence before any money is forthcoming. *See* box
above for a list of useful telephone numbers.

Medical matters

Visitors from the European Union, Iceland,
Liechtenstein and Norway can claim free or
reduced-cost medical treatment under the
auspices of Britain's National Health Service, so
long as they carry with them the appropriate
validated form (in the EU, this is the EHIC card). The
only things you will be expected to pay for are
medical prescriptions (currently £5.95 a pop, these
are dispensed at chemists, *see* opposite) and visits
to the optician or dentist – although these are free
to children, senior citizens and the unemployed.

There is now a free NHS helpline, healthcare
guide and website providing extensive health
advice free of charge – NHS Direct, **t** (0845) 4647,

www.nhsdirect.nhs.uk. Visitors from other
countries should take out an appropriate level of
medical insurance.

In an emergency
If you or a member of your family requires urgent
medical treatment, call an ambulance on 999 or 112.

Health advice
Most high streets have a dispensing chemist
where you must go to buy any medicine prescribed
to you by a doctor. In Britain, only a limited range of
drugs can be dispensed without a doctor's
prescription. Chemists will also often stock a selection of basic medical and cosmetic products such
as cough mixture, plasters (band-aids), bandages,
nappies and hairspray. Major branches of Boots the
chemist offer travel health clinics. Your local police
station can provide a list of late-opening chemists.
See useful telephone numbers and addresses below.
Action for Sick Children t 0800 0744519
www.actionforsickchildren.org
Provides advice to help parents get the best possible
healthcare for their children.
Dental Emergency Care Service t (020) 7937 3951
Eye Care Information Bureau t (020) 7928 9435
The Health Education Authority Hotline
t 0800 555777 (freephone advisory number)
Medical Advisory Service for Travellers Abroad
t 0891 224100
NHS Direct
t 0845 4647 **www.**nhsdirect.nhs.uk
St John Ambulance Supplies t (020) 7278 7888
www.nstjohnsupplies.co.uk
Provides baby and toddler first-aid guides.

Money and banks

The currency in Britain is the pound sterling
(written £) divided into 100 pence (written p). There
are eight coin denominations: 1p, 2p, 5p, 10p, 20p,
50p, £1 and £2 (all issued by the Royal Mint) and

Carrying money around with you
Use a money belt around your waist under a
tucked-in shirt or T-shirt. Pickpocketing is common
in the big cities, especially in busy shopping areas
like London's Oxford Street, but it's a skilful pick-
pocket who can undress you without you noticing.
Always keep wallets in your trouser pockets and
hold purses and bags close to your body with the
flap towards you and the strap over your shoulder.

four note denominations: £5, £10, £20 and £50; the last is the most easily forged and a number of shops and restaurants refuse to accept £50 notes in any circumstances. All notes are printed by the Bank of England (apart from the forgeries, that is).

Most shops and restaurants accept the big name credit and debit cards: Visa, Delta, Mastercard, Switch, Diners Club, American Express and Barclaycard.

The biggest high street banks are Barclays, NatWest, HSBC and Lloyds TSB. Most have automatic 24-hour cash dispensers (commonly known as a 'hole in the wall' rather than ATM machines) and will often dispense money on foreign bank cards, but you will usually have to pay a hefty commission for the privilege – your bank's international banking department should be able to advise you on this. All banks are open from 9.30am to 3.30pm (many until around 5pm) and some even open on Saturday mornings. The easiest and safest way to carry large sums of money is by using travellers' cheques. These can be changed for a small commission at any bank or bureau de change.

National holidays

Britain's national holidays always fall on a Monday – Christmas, Boxing Day, New Year's Day and Good Friday excepted – so people can enjoy a 'long weekend'; this stops the nation from being cheated out of a holiday that would otherwise fall on a Saturday or Sunday. Shops and services tend to operate according to their Sunday template and banks are always closed (Britain's national holidays are known as Bank Holidays). The full holiday list:

New Year's Day (1 Jan)
Good Friday
Easter Monday
May Day (first Monday in May)
Spring Bank Holiday (last Monday in May)
Summer Bank Holiday (last Monday in August)
Christmas Day (25 Dec)
Boxing Day (26 Dec)

One-parent families

There are various organizations offering advice and support for single parents travelling with kids:
National Council for One-parent Families
t (020) 7428 5400 Helpline: t 0800 018 5026
www.oneparentfamilies.org.uk
The Holiday Care Service t 08451 249971
www.holidaycare.org.uk

Help and travel advice for disabled travellers, their carers and families.
Holidays for One-parent families
t 0845 230 1975 **www.opfh.org.uk**
Holiday options and discounts on foreign and UK holidays for single parents.
Holiday Endeavour for Lone Parents
t (01302) 728791 **www.helphols.co.uk**
Low-cost and assisted holidays for single parents in the UK and overseas.
Single Parent Travel Club
t 0870 2416210 **www.sptc.org.uk** or write to SPTC, 6 Bentfield Road, Stansted, Mountfitchet, Essex CM24 8HW
Advice and social events across the UK.
Single Parents UK t 0117 951 4231
www.singleparents.org.uk
Online community with holiday ideas and support.
Gingerbread t (020) 7403 8500
www.gingerbread.org.uk
Advice on a variety of subjects, including holidays, for lone parents and their children.
Cruse t 0870 167 1677
www.crusebereavementcare.org.uk
Help for bereaved families and lone travellers.
YHA t 0870 7708868 **www.yha.org.uk**
Offer a single-parent membership for £15.95 and a series of events and activities for kids and families including sports weekends and talks.

Opening hours

The traditional opening times for shops and offices are 9am–5.30pm, with shops open the same hours on Saturdays, but these days, especially in cities and large towns, many shops observe a more Continental-style day (10am–7pm), and have one nominated day, usually Wednesday or Thursday, when they stay open until 8 or 9pm. Sunday opening, most commonly between 12 noon and 5pm, has also become the norm in towns in recent years, while some of the capital's corner shops and supermarkets stay open 24 hours a day. Opening hours are a little more restricted in rural areas where shops often have one nominated day (usually Wednesday) when they close early, usually around 1pm. Britain's strict licensing laws in pubs and restaurants have been loosened but in the vast majority of pubs and restaurants no alcohol is served outside 11am–11pm (12pm–10.30pm on Sundays). Motorway service stations stay open 24 hours.

Post offices

t 08457 740 740 **www.royalmail.com**
t 08457 223 344 **www.postoffice.co.uk**

You can buy stamps, send parcels and pay bills in post offices (Mon–Fri 9am–5.50pm and Sat 9–12 noon), but there's no need to go to one just to send a postcard (which is just as well as the number of rural post offices is being reduced year on year). Most newsagents sell stamps – it costs 28p to send a letter or postcard first class to anywhere in the UK or Europe; to America 47p – and red post boxes are common. There are usually four collections a day Mon–Sat, the last at 6pm, and one at 12 noon on Sunday. International express delivery services for letters and parcels are also available at post offices; the alternatives are Federal Express, **t** 08456 070809, **www.federalexpress.com/gb/** and DHL, **t** 08701 100 300, **www.dhl.co.uk.**

Safety

In the event of an emergency you can call the Police/Fire Brigade/Ambulance on 999 or 112.

You are at no greater risk on England's streets than in any other western country. England has its fair share of lawlessness but muggings and armed crime are still relatively uncommon. Few British policemen carry guns. As a tourist, the crimes you are most likely to fall victim to are pickpocketry and petty thievery. Big city shopping districts – such as London's Oxford Street – are often targeted by organized gangs of pickpockets but, so long as you remain vigilant and take sensible precautions with your valuables, you'll have a trouble-free holiday.

Special needs

Several specialist tour operators in Britain cater for the needs of physically disabled travellers – the Association of Independent Tour Operators, **t** (020) 8744 9280, **www.aito.co.uk**, can provide a list as can RADAR (Royal Association for Disability and Rehabilitation, *see* opposite), which also publishes its own guides to holidays and travel. *See* below for a list of organizations that will provide information and advice:

UK

Artsline, 54 Charlton Street, London NW1
t (020) 7388 2227 **www.artsline.org.uk**
Free information on access to arts venues.
Council for Disabled Children t (020) 7843 6000
www.ncb.org.uk/cdc/

Information on travel, health and further resources.
Disability Now, 6 Market Road, London N7
t (020) 7619 7323 **www.disabilitynow.org.uk**
Monthly newspaper and website with travel advice and holiday ideas written by the disabled.
Greater London Action on Disability, 1 London Bridge, London SE1 **t** (020) 7022 1890 **www.glad.org.uk**
Publishes a free London Disability Guide.
Holiday Care, The Hawkins Suite, Enham Place, Andover **t** 0845 124 9971 **www.holidaycare.org.uk**
Information on the best places for families with disabilities to visit in the UK and overseas.
RADAR (Royal Association for Disability and Rehabilitation), Unit 12, City Forum, 250 City Road, London EC1V **t** (020) 7250 3222 **www.radar.org.uk**
Produces excellent guide books and information packs for disabled travellers. The website now features an online UK accommodation search engine for disabled visitors at **www.radarsearch.org.**
Royal National Institute for the Blind, 105 Judd Street, London, WC1H **t** 0845 766 9999
www.rnib.org.uk
Advises blind people on travel matters.

USA

American Foundation for the Blind, Suite 300, 11 Penn Plaza, New York, NY **t** 800 232 5463
www.afb.org
Federation of the Handicapped, Basement, 40 Foley Square **t** (212) 233 4593
Mobility International, PO Box 10767, Eugene, Oregon **t** (541) 343 1284 **www.miusa.org**
SATH (Society for Accessible Travel & Hospitality), 347 Fifth Avenue, Suite 610, New York, NY **t** (212) 447 7284 **www.sath.org**

Australia

ACROD (Australian Council for the Rehabilitation of the Disabled), PO Box 60, Curtin, Act 2605
t (02) 6283 3200 **www.acrod.org.au**

Telephones

Although British Telecom lost its monopoly for supplying the nation with telephones in 1984 when it was privatized, it's still the most popular phone company in the UK. The majority of public phone booths are BT-owned, although there are now several other companies, including Mercury and AT&T, operating networks of payphones.

Most modern payphones accept coins (any denomination from 10p up, minimum call price

30p) and phone cards (available in denominations of £1, £2, £5, £10 and £20 from any newsagent or post office) although some are either/or. Some booths let you pay by swiping a credit card.

Britain's domestic phones employ an unusually wide type of phone jack and, if you need to plug in a phone brought from abroad or a modem, you may have to buy an adaptor. International calls are cheapest in the evening after 6pm and on weekends. Phone cards and direct-access phone numbers offering cut-rate international calls are widely available. Check the national press or websites such as www.niftylist.co.uk for details.

The phone numbers of local businesses and shops are listed in a directory known as the Yellow Pages, available for a small charge by calling t 0800 671 444 (t 0870 2408942 from outside the UK) and at www.yell.com or www.scoot.co.uk.

The internet can be accessed from most hotels, and from internet cafés.

Useful numbers

Emergency (Police, Fire Brigade, Ambulance)
999 or **112**
Operator **100**
Directory enquiries **118 500** (BT service, other enquiry numbers available)
International operator **155**
International directory enquiries **118 505** (BT service, other enquiry numbers available)

International dialling codes

United States and Canada **00 1**
Ireland **00 353**   France **00 33**
Italy **00 39**   Germany **00 49**
Australia **00 61**   New Zealand **00 64**
Britain (from overseas) **00 44**

Time

London is the official home of time. The prime meridian, the line of 0° longitude, runs through the quiet southeast London borough of Greenwich and, since 1884, Greenwich Mean Time (GMT) has been the standard against which all other times are set. GMT is usually one hour ahead of western Europe. In summer the country switches to British Summer Time (BST), one hour ahead of GMT. Britain is five hours ahead of New York, eight hours ahead of San Francisco and 10 hours behind Tokyo and Sydney. In everyday conversation, most people will use the 12-hour clock – 9am, 3pm, etc. – but

printed event times and transport timetables are often given using the 24-hour clock.

Tipping

The usual rate in restaurants, taxis, hairdressers etc. is 10–15 per cent. You are not obliged to tip, especially if the service was unsatisfactory. You would not normally tip a bartender in a pub. Restaurants may add a service charge of 10–15 per cent. Tipping staff, such as porters, is discretionary.

Toilets

Public loos are most commonly found in train and bus stations (where you may have to pay a small fee of around 20–30p), motorway service stations, department stores and most fast food outlets (notably McDonald's and Burger King). Pubs and restaurants will often only let you use their facilities (even in an emergency) if you're going to buy something. Street toilets are now an increasingly rare sight. Free-standing automatic toilets ('super loos') allow you 15 minutes' use of the facilities (for 20p), after which the door will swoosh open revealing you to the street so be prepared.

Tourist information

Britain and London Visitor Centre, 1 Lower Regent Street, Piccadilly Circus, SW1 (open Mon 9.30–6.30, Tues–Fri 9–6.30, Sat and Sun 10–4, June–Sep 9–5 on Sat) **t (020) 8846 9000 www.visitbritain.com**

Almost every town in the country has its own tourist office which will happily give you information on the local area. Many arrange overnight accommodation as part of their book-a-bed-ahead (BABA) scheme. Opening hours are Mon–Fri 9–5 for smaller offices, with big city branches often staying open over the weekend. Some UK cities now have tourist information online with a web address featuring the word 'visit'. For example, www.visitbath.co.uk, www.visitbristol.co.uk, www.visitliverpool.com or www.visitlondon.com.

London

04

London

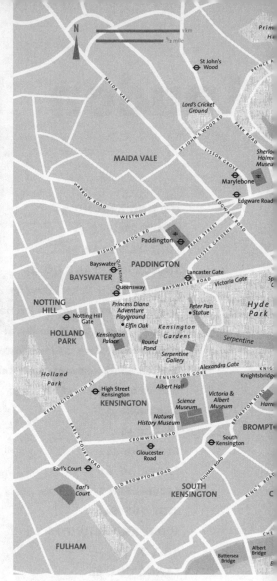

There's more for kids to do in London than you probably think. You may know that the Science Museum is one of the best interactive museums in the country, but do you also know that it organizes 'sleepovers' for children wanting to explore and experiment in the dead of night? And were you aware that kids can spend the night pretending to be pirates aboard the *Golden Hinde*, a replica 16th-century sailing ship? And did you realize that kids can stroke the snakes at London Zoo? Or that at the IMAX 3D cinema in Waterloo they can expore the cosmos or the ocean depths? Well, you do now.

And to cap it all, most of London's major museums and galleries are free. In fact there is quite a lot on offer that is free in the capital (p.84). Free foyer concerts are often given at the National Theatre (p.52), Royal Festival Hall (p.52) and the Barbican (p.56) at lunch time or in the early evening. Except for St Paul's and Westminster Abbey, entry to all churches is free. There are plenty of free events (pp.34–6), or how about a guided walk (pp.68–9), an afternoon in a park (pp.65–7) or a few hours at a city farm (p.64)?

London itineraries

There's nothing more tiring than trying to do too much, or more dreary than doing too much of just one thing. Variety is the key, whether this is your first time in the city or your fiftieth. Here is a selection of child-size itineraries, taking in most of the major sightseeing areas in London.

Bankside

Morning: Tate Modern (p.55)
Lunch: Museum Café or Fish!, Cathedral Street, SE1
t (020) 7407 3803
Afternoon: Millennium Bridge (p.54) to St Paul's (p.57), or Shakespeare's Globe Theatre (p.54)

Buckingham Palace

Morning: Buckingham Palace (p.44)
Lunch: Pizza Express, 154 Victoria Street, SW1
t (020) 7828 1477
Afternoon: St James's Park (p.67)

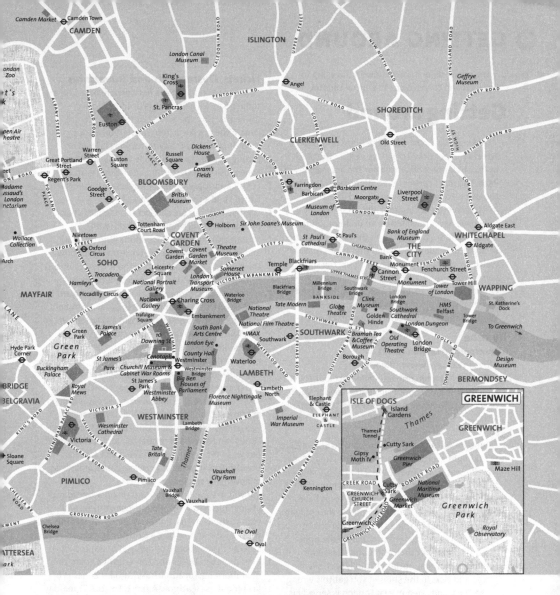

Regent's Park

Morning: London Zoo (p.37)
Lunch: Picnic in Regent's Park (p.67) or Giraffe (p.80)
Afternoon: Madame Tussaud's (pp.37–8)

South Bank

Morning: London Aquarium (p.50)
Lunch: Gourmet Pizza Company, Gabriel's Wharf
(p.82) or National Theatre Terrace Café
t (020) 7452 3555
Afternoon: British Airways London Eye (p.50) or
BFI IMAX 3D Cinema (p.73)

South Kensington

Morning: Natural History Museum (pp.47–8)
Lunch: Picnic in Hyde Park (pp.66–7) or
Pizza on the Park (p.82)
Afternoon: Boating on the Serpentine in Hyde
Park (pp.66–7) or shopping in Harrods (pp.49, 61)

West End

Morning: National Gallery (pp.41–2)
Lunch: Rainforest Café (for younger children, p.83)
or New World (for older children, p.81)
Afternoon: Trocadero (p.43)

See pp.10–18 for information on travelling to England and connections to Central London.

Getting around

Making your way around the maze of London's streets can be tricky. They have neither the block-by-block clarity of New York nor the accessibility of Paris. The most convenient option, if you are new to the city, is to take the underground (the 'tube'). This in itself can be exciting for children, especially if they have never travelled on an underground system before. When you, and they, are a little more at home in London, you'll find that buses make a welcome change, allowing you to see the sights as you travel around, albeit at a more leisurely pace. Other forms of transport, such as London's famous black cabs, can also be fun, although expensive. Why not see London from the river (p.32, pp.64–5)?

By tube

Transport for London Travel
t (020) 7222 1234 **www**.tfl.gov.uk

There are 12 interconnecting lines (colour-coded) which criss-cross London. In central London you're never more than five minutes from a tube station, although the system becomes more sparse the further from the centre you get.

Tube trains run from 5.30am (7am on Sundays) to 12 midnight every day apart from Christmas. Avoid travelling at peak times (Mon–Fri 7.30–9.30am and 5–7.30pm) if you can. This is especially important if you are using a pushchair. Few tube stops have lifts, which means taking the stairs or the escalator. Pushchairs must be folded up and held on the escalator. It is the custom to stand on the right-hand side and walk on the left and stressed Londoners may get uptight (usually with silent stares and kicks in the shins) if you get this wrong.

The Docklands area in east London is served by the DLR (Docklands Light Railway), an overground monorail which links up with ⊖ Bank and ⊖ Tower Gateway. For information, contact DLR customer services, **t** (020) 7363 9700, **www**.tfl.gov.uk/dlr. Trains run until 12.30am Mon–Sat, 11.30pm Sun.

By bus

Bus travel can make a very pleasant alternative to subterranean travel once the thrill of riding the escalators has worn off. Looking out of the window from the top deck of a slow-moving double decker is a great way of getting to know the city.

Tickets, Oystercards and Travelcards

Fares on London's **tube** network are based on a zonal system. The capital is divided into six concentric rings or 'zones'. Zone 1 is the centre, Zone 6 the outskirts. Your fare is worked out according to how many zones you travel in or through. For instance, a single tube fare within Zone 1 (using an Oystercard, see below) is adult £1.50, child 70p, whereas a single fare between Zones 1 and 2 rises to adult £2, child £1.

Single **bus** trips are cheaper than single tube or train journeys. All single bus tickets (with Oystercard) now cost £1 for adults (80p off peak) and 50p for 16–17-year-olds, while under-16s now travel free. Tickets cost £1.50 without the Oystercard.

Transport for London has recently introduced a pay-as-you-go discount card, called an **Oystercard**. It is well worth picking one of these up (at any tube station), as tickets bought without an Oystercard can cost twice as much as the discounted Oystercard tickets. For example, a Zone 1 adult single tube ticket purchased without an Oystercard costs £3, compared to £1.50 with one. It works like a pre-pay phonecard: you charge it up, then travel to your heart's content. The cost of all single trips taken in one day is capped at 50p less than the cost of a One-day Travelcard (*see* below). For example a One-day Travelcard for Zones 1 and 2 (most of central London) costs £4.90, but you will be charged no more than £4.40 for travel with an Oystercard in those zones, regardless of how many single trips you make.

If you're travelling after 9.30am on a weekday or at anytime on a weekend (off-peak times), and plan to use National Rail services within London as well as tube and/or bus, a One-day **Travelcard** is still the best option. It allows you unlimited journeys on tubes, buses and trains until 4.30am the next morning. An adult Travelcard for Zones 1–6 (as far out as Heathrow Airport) £6.30. A Three-day Travelcard is also available.

Children under 5 travel free at all times. Children's fares apply for 5–15-year-olds travelling at peak times on tubes and trains. Children under 11 travel free on tubes and trains at off-peak times (Mon–Fri after 9.30am, weekends and Bank Holidays) with a ticket-holding adult; 12–15-year-olds pay £1 (up to four children per adult).

You must buy your ticket before you travel, from tube and train station windows, machines or at some newsagents. Children aged 12–15 may need photo ID as proof of age.

Attempts are being made to speed up the bus service, which for years has been hampered by clogged-up, seemingly random bus lanes. The Congestion Charge (*see* right) has slightly reduced the volume of traffic during the week and most buses in central London now operate a 'pay before you board' policy to reduce stopping time. To take a ride on a conductor-less bus, you now have to purchase your ticket in advance from one of the new ticket machines located by the bus stop (or from a newsagent) rather than from the driver.

There are two types of bus stop: white, at which buses must stop, and red, which are request stops. To hail a bus at a red stop, stick your arm out. To alight at a request stop, ring the bell.

Night buses

Standard buses stop operating around midnight, at which point N-prefixed night buses take over until 5am the following morning. There are far fewer night bus routes – you can pick up a night route map from any Underground station and most newsagents. One-day Travelcards are valid on night buses until 4.30am.

By train

National Rail Enquiries t 08457 48 49 50

For nipping around central London, stick to the tube. For longer journeys out into the suburbs, however, you may wish to switch to the train. London's rail network links up with the tube at various points and, unlike the tube, there are certain services (particularly the airport routes) that run all night. All train and tube stations have a map, known as a Journey Planner, showing London's combined tube and train network. If you buy a One- or Three-day Travelcard (*see* opposite), you can chop and change your mode of transport throughout the day, using as many trains, tubes and buses as you like.

By taxi

London is justifiably proud of its black cabs. Though undeniably expensive, they make up one of the most efficient and reliable taxi services in the world. Cabbies must train for two years and pass a strict test before qualifying for their taxi licences. During this time they must learn every street and major building in the capital, as well as 468 separate routes – a mean feat of learning known simply as 'The Knowledge'.

London cabs are easily recognizable. Most are black although, in this consumer age, some now sport the coloured livery of advertisers. All have orange 'For Hire' signs on their roofs which light up when the cab is available. Carseats are fitted as standard in all TX1 black cabs. The seats are built into the central arm rest in the rear of the cab and can accommodate children between 22 and 36kg. You may hail a cab on the street (by sticking out your arm) or, if staying at a hotel, you can ask the doorman to do it for you. There are taxi ranks outside all major railway stations and also some tube stations. Alternatively, call Dial-A-Cab, **t** (020) 7253 5000. To track down that mislaid umbrella or teddy bear, call Black Cab Lost Property on **t** (020) 7486 2496. Black cabs are licensed to carry four people at a time (sometimes five), with space next to the driver for luggage. Most black cabs can accommodate wheelchairs (and pushchairs). Fares increase after 8pm when a higher tariff applies.

Minicabs are cheaper, but less reliable and largely unregulated. A driving licence is pretty much all that's required to qualify as a minicab driver. Hiring a minicab can therefore be rather a risky business; never ever pick one up on the street. There are some reputable firms, however, including:
Greater London Hire t (020) 8883 5000
www.glh.co.uk
Lady Cabs t (020) 7254 3501

A specialist service run by women (all the drivers are female) for women.

By car

If you're coming to London to see the sights, you're better off using public transport. Otherwise you'll have to cope with a heady cocktail of unfathomable one-way systems, draconian parking regulations and now also the Congestion Charge in central London – introduced in 2003 to deter drivers and raise revenue to improve public transport (a partial success). All drivers entering central London between 7am and 6.30pm Monday to Friday must pay a flat fee of £8. The Congestion Charge zone stretches from King's Cross in the north to Elephant and Castle in the south, and from Kensington in the west to Tower Bridge in the east. Entry points are clearly marked by a big red 'C' painted on the road. The system is enforced by a network of CCTV cameras that monitor number plates. Drivers have until midnight of the day of travel to pay the charge, when a £100 penalty is issued. Payment can be made online at **www.cclondon.com**, by phone, **t** 0845 900 1234, or at shops displaying the red 'C' symbol.

PRACTICAL A–Z

Beware the parking restrictions. Going over the allotted time at a parking meter can have dire consequences. Your car may end up with a fine, a wheel clamp or be towed away. To find out which pound to go to to reclaim your car call **t** (020) 7747 4747 – the main ones are at Marble Arch, Earl's Court and Camden. The fine is a staggering £200.

If you are still tempted to use your car in central London, you must be rich or crazy. Using a car for trips outside London, however, does make sense. These are some of the best-known car rental firms:

Avis t 0870 010 0287 **www**.avis.co.uk
easycar t 0906 333 3333 **www**.easycar.com
Hertz t 0870 844 8844 **www**.hertz.co.uk
Thrifty t (01494) 751 600 **www**.thrifty.co.uk

By bike

London is not very cycle-friendly – certainly not when compared with places like Copenhagen or Amsterdam. Extreme congestion, rising pollution and a limited number of cycle lanes are just some of the hazards. People still do it, however. Here are some rental companies that provide bikes and helmets for families. Hire rates are approximately adult £3 per hour, child £2 per hour.

On Your Bike 52–4 Tooley Street **t** (020) 7378 6669 **www**.onyourbike.net ⊖ London Bridge
Dial-a-Bike t (020) 7828 4040

Delivers rental bikes to major hotels in London.

Capital Sport Ltd t (01296) 631 671
www.capital-sport.co.uk

Offers guided tours along the Thames.

By riverboat

Thames Boat Service Guide t (020) 7941 4500
www.tfl.gov.uk/river

Daily riverboat services operate between most central London piers. The following companies also offer sightseeing boat trips

Bateaux London–Catamaran Cruisers
t (020) 7925 2215 **www**.bateauxlondon.com
City Cruises t (020) 7740 0400
www.citycruises.com
For further information *see* pp.64–5

On foot

London comes in two different sizes: Greater London, which is huge (28 miles north to south and 35 miles east to west) and Central London, where most of the capital's tourist attractions are located, which isn't very big at all. Touring on foot is the best way to get to know the smaller version.
For organized walks *see* pp.68–9

For information on climate, embassies, insurance and other national issues *see* pp.19–26.

Disabled travellers

Wheelchair access to London's public places – its theatres, cinemas, sports grounds, etc. – is relatively good. The London Tourist Board's website provides access details for all London's principal attractions, **www**.visitlondon.com/city_guide/disabled/index.html, or call **t** (020) 7932 2000. It also provides a list of wheelchair-accessible accommodation, as well as hotels that accept guide dogs.

Unfortunately, public transport is a nightmare for disabled travellers, although 'low-floor' wheelchair accessible buses have been introduced on 35 routes. Leaflets detailing routes and mobility buses are available from Transport for London, whose guide, 'Access to the Underground', has information on what little lift access there is to the city's tube stations. It's available free from stations or by post from Transport for London Access and Mobility Unit, Windsor House, 42–50 Victoria Street, SW1, **t** (020) 7222 1234. All black taxis are wheelchair accessible.

More transport information can be found in the 'Access in London' guide, produced by the Access Project, 39 Bradley Gardens, London W13 8HE, **www**.accessproject-phsp.org (donation of £10 requested). Wheelchair users and blind people are entitled to a 30–50 per cent discount on rail fares and can apply for a Disabled Person's Railcard (£14 a year) at major rail stations, **www**.disabledpersons-railcard.co.uk. A booklet providing advice on rail travel for disabled passengers can be downloaded from **www**.nationalrail.co.uk/info/disabled.htm.
Artsline 54 Charlton Street, NW1 **t** (020) 7388 2227
www.artsline.org.uk

Free information on access to arts venues in the capital on its websites, **www**.artslineonline.com and **www**.theatreaccess.co.uk.

The London Pass

t 0870 242 9988, **www**.londonpass.com

The London Pass allows free entrance to more than 50 attractions, among them London Zoo, the Tower of London and Shakespeare's Globe Theatre, and discounts for theatres, shops and restaurants, including a free Hamley's bear when you spend more than £20 at the toy shop. One-, two-, three- or six-day passes are offered, from £15 per day. Combined transport passes are also an option. *See* also p.20.

Infant matters

Babysitters

Large hotels usually offer a babysitting service, and smaller hotels may be able to arrange one. Listed below are some reputable childcare agencies.

Childminders 6 Nottingham St, W1
t (020) 7935 2049/3000 **www**.babysitter.co.uk
Hopes and Dreams 339–41 City Road, EC1
t (020) 833 9388 **www**.hopesanddreams.co.uk
Babysitting from 3 months–5 years, and 'hotel' for 2–11-year-olds.
Pippa Pop-Ins 430 Fulham Rd, SW6
t (020) 7385 2458
Award-winning 'hotel' for 2–12-year-olds; crèche, nursery school and babysitting services.
Universal Aunts t (020) 7738 8937
www.universalaunts.co.uk
Babysitters, entertainers, people to meet children off trains, and even guides to show them London.

Breastfeeding

Attitudes to public breastfeeding are as relaxed as your own. London's principal airports and train stations, and some of its department stores, have dedicated mother-and-baby rooms.

Nappies

You can pick up disposable nappies at any supermarket. Some stock 70% biodegradable Nature Boy & Girl nappies from Sweden. For washable nappies and eco-friendly disposables try the following:
Green Baby Leroy House, 436 Essex Rd, N13
t 0870 241 766 **www**.greenbabyco.com
For a nappy laundry service in your area try:
The National Association of Nappy Services (NANS) t 0121 693 4949 **www**.changeanappy.co.uk

Lost property

If you lose anything while out and about in London, the chances are it's gone for good. However, it's still worth trying:
London Transport Lost Property Office (incorporating the Black Cab Lost Property Office) 200 Baker Street, NW1 **t** (020) 7486 2496
Open Weekday mornings

Maps

Your first purchase upon arrival should be a copy of the London A–Z Street Atlas, an indexed book map of the city, which you can pick up at any newsagent. It's available in a range of formats from a big, colour, hardback version to a black-and-white pocket edition (£22.50 and £4.75 respectively), **www**.a-zmaps.co.uk. For a more varied selection try Stanfords, 12–14 Long Acre, Covent Garden, WC2, **t** (020) 7836 1321, **www**.stanfords.co.uk.

Train, tube and bus maps are available free from tube and train stations. The hybrid Journey Planner shows both tube and train links.

Medical matters

For urgent medical treatment, call an ambulance by dialling **t** 999 or 112, or drive to a hospital with an Accident and Emergency (A&E) Department.
Central Middlesex Hospital Acton Lane, Park Royal, NW10 **t** (020) 8453 2257 ⊖/ ⇄ Harlesden
Charing Cross Hospital Fulham Palace Road, W6 **t** (020) 8846 7490 ⊖ Hammersmith
Chelsea & Westminster Hospital 369 Fulham Road, SW10 **t** (020) 8746 8000 ⊖ Fulham Broadway
Ealing Hospital Uxbridge Road, Middlesex, UB1 **t** (020) 8967 5613 **www**.ealinghospital.org.uk ⊖ Ealing Broadway
Guy's Hospital St Thomas Street, SE1 **t** (020) 7955 5000 **www**.guysandstthomas.nhs.uk ⊖ London Bridge (*dedicated A&E for children*)
Royal London Hospital Whitechapel Road, E1 **t** (020) 7377 7000 **www**.bartsandthelondon.org ⊖ Whitechapel (*Dedicated A&E for children*)
St Mary's Hospital Praed Street, W2 **t** (020) 7886 6666 **www**.st-marys.org.uk ⊖ Paddington
University College London Hospital Gower Street, WC1 **t** (020) 7387 9300 **www**.uclh.org ⊖ Euston Square, Warren Street, Goodge Street
Whittington Hospital Highgate Hill, N19 **t** (020) 7272 3070 **www**.whittington.nhs.uk ⊖ Archway

For minor ailments, consider one of nine new NHS walk-in centres in the capital, open on a drop-in basis from 7am to 10pm. The most central is:
Soho Centre for Health and Care 29–30 Soho Square, W1 **t** (020) 7534 6500
⊖ Tottenham Court Road, Leicester Square
For more information, contact NHS Direct, **t** 0845 4647 or **www**.nhs.co.uk, which also provides a useful free medical helpline staffed by nurses.

In a dental emergency, contact the following organization to find a dentist:
Dental Emergency Care Service t (020) 7955 2186 **www**.bda-findadentist.org.uk

Chemists

Most high streets have a chemist, where you can buy prescription and over-the-counter medicines.

Boots, **www**.boots.com, is the biggest chain. Your local police station can provide a list of late-opening chemists. Otherwise try the following:
Bliss Chemist 5 Marble Arch, W1 **t** (020) 7723 6116
Open Daily until 12 midnight
Zafash Chemist 233–5 Old Brompton Road, SW5
t (020) 7373 2798
Open 24 hours a day, 365 days a year

Post offices

t 0345 740 740.**www**.royalmail.com
Many minor post offices have closed recently, but you'll still find main post offices at:
24–8 William IV Street, Trafalgar Square, WC2
t (020) 7930 9580
105 Abbey Street, SE1 **t** (020) 7237 8629
43–44 Albemarle Street, W1 **t** (020) 7493 5620
81–89 Farringdon Road, EC1 **t** (020) 7242 7262
54–6 Great Portland Street, W1 **t** (020) 7636 2205
24–27 Thayer Street, W1 **t** (020) 7935 0239

Toilets

Most mainline stations have public toilets (20p per visit!) as do London's principal department stores and some fast-food outlets. Public toilets are few and far between apart from the odd free-standing automatic toilet known as a 'super loo' (20–30p for 15 minutes). If in Covent Garden, check out the award-winning ambient loos in St Paul's Churchyard.

Tourist information

www.visitlondon.com **t** (020) 8846 9000
www.kidslovelondon.com.
Britain and London Visitor Centre
1 Regent Street, Piccadilly Circus, SW1
Open Mon–Fri 9–6.30, Sat–Sun 10–4
Heathrow Terminals 1,2,3 Underground concourse
Open Daily 8am–6pm
Waterloo International Terminal
Open Daily 8.30am–10.30pm
Accommodation booking service:
t (020) 7234 5800
Greenwich Tourist Information Centre
Pepys House, 2 Cutty Sark Gardens, SE10
t 0870 608 2000 **Open** Daily 10–5
Liverpool Street Station
Liverpool Street Underground station, EC2
Open Mon–Fri 8am–6pm, Sat–Sun 8.45am–5.30pm
Victoria Station
Station Forecourt, SW1
Open Mon–Sat 8am–7pm, Sun 8am–6pm

LONDON'S YEAR

From festivals and parades to major sporting events and exhibitions, hardly a week goes by without something big happening in the capital. For top sporting events such as the London Marathon or Wimbledon, *see* pp.69–72.
Unless otherwise stated, all events are free.

Daily events
Ceremony of the Keys
Tower of London, EC3 **t** 0870 756 6070
www.hrp.org.uk
⊖ Tower Hill **Bus** 15, 25, 42, 78, 100, D1
Time Daily at 9.53pm. Ceremony lasts 20 minutes.
The nightly locking of the Tower of London is one of the oldest military ceremonies in the world. For free tickets apply at least two months in advance (remember to include a SAE) to The Ceremony of the Keys, HM Tower of London, London EC3N 4AB.

Changing of the Guard
Buckingham Palace, SW1 **t** (020) 7930 4832
Infoline **t** (020) 7766 7300 **www**.royal.gov.uk
⊖ St James's Park, Green Park, Victoria
Bus 7, 11, 139, 211, C1, C10
Time Apr–June daily at 11.27am sharp; rest of year alternate days at the same time. Ceremony lasts around 45 minutes.
For further information *see* p.44

Annual events
January
London Parade
New Year's Day
Parliament Square to Piccadilly by way of Whitehall and Trafalgar Square
t (020) 8566 8586 **www**.londonparade.co.uk
⊖ Westminster, Embankment, Green Park, Piccadilly Circus
Ten thousand performers and more than a million spectators make this one of the the biggest New Year's Day parties in Europe.

Chinese New Year Festival
Late January or early February
Gerrard Street, Lisle Street & Newport Place, WC1
www.chinatown-online.co.uk
⊖ Leicester Square
Bus 6, 7, 8, 10, 12, 13, 14, 15, 19, 23, 25, 38, 53, 55, 73, 88, 94, 98, 139, 159, 176, X53
Chinatown celebrates with firecrackers, paper lanterns and dancing papier-mâché dragons.

February

Accession Day Gun Salute
Accession Day, 6 February, 12 noon
Hyde Park; ⊖ Hyde Park Corner, Knightsbridge,
South Kensington, Lancaster Gate, Queensway
Bus 2, 9, 10, 12, 14, 16, 19, 22, 36, 52, 70, 73, 74, 82, 94, 137
The first gun salute of London's year. The Royal
Horse Artillery gallop into Hyde Park and unleash a
noisy 41-gun salute. The practice is repeated several
times: on the Queen's birthday (21 April),
Coronation Day (2 June), Prince Philip's birthday (10
June) and the State Opening of Parliament in
November. If any of these dates fall on a Sunday,
the salute is fired on the following Monday.

Spitalfields Pancake Race Day
Shrove Tuesday
Spitalfields Market, E1 **t** (020) 7372 0441
⊖ Liverpool Street
Bus 5, 8, 26, 35, 43, 47, 48, 67, 78, 149, 242, 344
Competing teams race around Spitalfields
Market tossing pancakes as they go. A similar
event takes place in Soho, **t** (020) 7289 0907.

Easter

Oxford–Cambridge Boat Race
www.theboatrace.org
Saturday before Easter
Thames between Putney Bridge and Mortlake
For start ⊖ Putney Bridge; for finish ⇌ Mortlake
Bus For start 14, 22, 39, 74 85, 93, 220, 265, 414, 430;
for end 209, 485, R69
The two teams have been battling it out over the
4 1/2-mile Thames course for more than a century
now. Best views from Putney and Chiswick bridges.

Easter Parade
Easter Sunday
Battersea Park, SW11; ⇌ Battersea Park ⊖ Sloane
Square; **Bus** 44, 137, 319, 344, 345; **Open** Dawn–dusk
Easter Sunday carnival with a fairground, parade
and special children's village featuring a bouncy
castle, playground, clowns and puppet shows.

April

London Marathon
t (020) 7902 0184 www.london-marathon.co.uk
⇌ (*start*) Blackheath ⊖ (*finish*) Westminster
Takes place on a Sunday late in April between
Blackheath and Westminster Bridge via the Isle of
Dogs, Victoria Embankment and St James's Park.

May

May Fayre and Punch & Judy Festival
Nearest Sunday to 9 May
St Paul's Church, Covent Garden **t** (020) 7375 0441
⊖ Covent Garden, Leicester Square
Bus 9, 11, 13, 15, 23, 77a, 91, 176
An annual celebration of marital puppet
disharmony in the grounds of the actors' church.

June

Trooping the Colour
Second Saturday in June, starts at 10.45am
Buckingham Palace to Horse Guards Parade
t Booking line (020) 7766 7300/1 www.royal.gov.uk
⊖ Charing Cross, St James's Park
Buses 7, 11, 139, 211, C1, C10
The ceremony, which marks the official birthday
of the Queen, takes place at Horse Guards Parade
and is preceded by a Royal Air Force jet display.
Tickets for this top piece of British pageantry are
awarded by ballot. You must apply by the end of
February in writing to the Brigade Major (Trooping
the Colour), Household Division, Horse Guards
Parade, SW1, enclosing a SAE (max two tickets per
application). You can see a lot for free *en route*.

July

Coin Street Festival
Mid-July–mid-September
The South Bank at the Oxo Tower Wharf, Gabriel's
Wharf and the Bernie Spain Gardens
t (020) 7401 2255 www.coinstreetfestival.org
⊖ Waterloo, Westminster, Blackfriars
Bus 4, 68, 76, 77, 149, 168, 171, 176, 188, 211, P11, 501,
505, 507, 521, D1, P11
Three-month free arts festival on London's South
Bank organized by the Coin Street Community
Builders. Children's fancy dress parade a highlight.

Greenwich & Docklands Festival
Ten days in mid-July
Various venues in Greenwich
t (020) 8305 1818 www.festival.org
⊖ North Greenwich **DLR** Island Gardens
⇌ Greenwich
Bus 177, 180, 188, 199, 286, 386
This popular arts festival combines concerts and
theatre as well as children's events, and starts with
a bang with an opening night firework display.

Kenwood House Lakeside Concerts

July–August
Hampstead Lane, NW3 **t** 0870 333 1181
www.english-heritage.org
⊖ Archway **Bus** 210
Adm £18–26, under-5s **free**
    Families flock to this series of popular classical concerts and firework displays in the grounds of this grand old house. Bring a picnic!

August

Notting Hill Carnival

August Bank Holiday Sunday and Monday
Notting Hill and surrounding streets
t (020) 8964 0544
www.rbkc.gov.uk/nottinghill
⊖ Westbourne Park, Ladbroke Grove
    The largest carnival in the world after Rio. Steel bands, floats, costumed dancers, fancy dress, jugglers, face-painting, exotic food. There is a children's parade on the Sunday.

September

BBC Family Prom in the Park

Early September, Sun after 'Last Night of the Proms'
Hyde Park
t 0870 899 8001 **www.bbc.co.uk/proms**
⊖ Hyde Park Corner
Bus 2, 8, 9, 10, 12, 14, 16, 19, 22, 36, 39, 73, 74, 82, 94
Adm Adult £14, child £9, under-3s **free**
    The BBC Philharmonic club together with the latest pop sensations for easy classical listening.

Covent Garden Festival of Street Theatre

Early September
Covent Garden
t (020) 7836 9136 **www.coventgarden.org.uk**
⊖ Covent Garden, Leicester Square
Bus 9, 11, 13, 15, 23, 77A, 91, 176
    Fire-eaters, escapologists, stilt-walkers, unicyclists and comedians perform in Covent Garden's Piazza.

Thames Festival

Mid-September
Thames between Waterloo and Blackfriars Bridge
t (020) 7928 8998 **www.thamesfestival.org**
⊖ Embankment, Charing Cross, Southwark, Waterloo
Bus 1, 4, 26, 45, 63, 68, 76, 77, 149, 168, 171, 171a, 172, 176, 188, 501, 505, 507, D1, P11, X68, RV1
The Thames really comes to life with a range of events along the banks, from firework displays to lantern processions.

October

Costermongers' Pearly Kings and Queens Harvest Festival

First Sunday in October, starts at 3pm
St Martin-in-the-Fields, Trafalgar Square, WC2
t (020) 7766 1100
⊖ Charing Cross, Leicester Square
Bus 9, 24, 109
    London's East-end community of Pearly Kings and Queens descends on St Martin-in-the-Fields.

November

Bonfire Night

5 November
In parks and recreation grounds across London, *see* **www.visitlondon.com** for more details.
    Parks all over London hold firework displays on this date to celebrate the capture and execution of Catholic Guy Fawkes and his failure to blow up James I and the Houses of Parliament.

Lord Mayor's Show

Second Saturday in November, starts at 11am
Mansion House to the Old Bailey
t (020) 7606 3030 **www.lordmayorsshow.org**
⊖ Mansion House, Blackfriars
    The ceremonial parade to mark the beginning of the Lord Mayor of London's year in office starts at Mansion House and ends at the Old Bailey.

The Christmas Lights

Mid-November
Oxford Street, Regent Street and Bond Street
    The elaborate street illuminations are turned on in mid-November by a celebrity.

December

Carol Service

December–early January
Trafalgar Square, WC1
⊖ Charing Cross, Leicester Square
Bus 9, 24, 109
    Carol singing takes place around the huge Trafalgar Square Christmas tree every evening from Advent to Twelfth Night (6 January).

New Year's Eve in Trafalgar Square

    The traditional venue for London's end-of-year bash, Trafalgar Square is within chiming distance of Big Ben's 12 bongs at midnight. The celebrations can get rowdy and boisterous and are not really recommended for young children.

THINGS TO SEE AND DO

Regent's Park to Baker Street

Canal trips

Why not take a boat trip along Regent's Canal to London Zoo from Camden or Little Venice (p.65)?

Cinemas and theatres

For details of Regent's Park Open Air Theatre *see* p.65. For more on the Puppet Theatre Barge on Regent's Canal *see* pp.79–80

London Canal Museum

12–13 New Wharf Road, N1 **t** (020) 7713 0836
www.canalmuseum.org.uk
⊖ King's Cross **Bus** 10, 17, 30, 45, 46, 63, 73, 91, 205, 214, 259, 390, 476, A2 **Free** mooring for canal boats
Open Tues–Sun and Bank Hols 10–4.30 (last entry 3.45) **Adm** Adult £3, child £2, under-8s **free**

Back in the 19th century, 'canal kids' put in 18-hour days leading barge horses along tow paths, opening locks and cleaning boats. This evocative museum tells the story of all those who made a living ferrying cargo along London's industrial canals, in an era when childhood was far less sacrosanct.

★London Zoo

Regent's Park, NW1 **t** (020) 7722 3333
www.zsl.org/london-zoo
⊖ Camden Town or Baker Street, then **bus** 274, C2
Open Mar–Oct daily 10–5.30 daily, Nov–Apr 10–4
Adm Adult £13, child (under 15) £9.75, under-3s **free**, family £41

London Zoo is home to thousands of animals and is still a mainstay of school trips and family outings. Whatever you may think about the rights and wrongs of big city zoos, there's no doubt that London's famous menagerie does its best to justify its existence in the modern world. These days, its watchwords are conservation and education. All the animals are here for a reason, whether, as in the case of the Arabian Oryx, it's because they're now extinct in the wild or, as with the Sumatran tiger, because they soon could be. The zoo runs a very successful captive breeding programme and has played an important part in reintroducing many endangered species back into the wild.

The zoo's latest crowd-pleaser has been to remove the barriers (some of them literally): at the zoo's popular 'Meet the Monkeys' exhibition, visitors are invited into a 1,500 sq m (16,000 sq ft) squirrel monkey enclosure to watch the hyperactive mammals scamper, jump and chatter close up.

Every day the zoo organizes demonstrations and talks. Turn up at feeding time and you can watch pelicans and penguins gobbling their way through buckets of fish or a snake slowly swallowing a rat – whole. Spectacular animal shows are held in three special demonstration areas: you can see lemurs and parrots leaping, climbing and flying during Animals in Action in the Amphitheatre, Aerobatic Skills on the Display Lawn (birds of prey) and cute groups of social animals (meerkats, otters) at the Happy Families area; look out for pygmy marmoset – at 11–15cm (4–6in) tall the smallest monkey.

At the Children's Zoo there's a Touch Paddock, where kids can stroke and pet the resident sheep, goats and wallabies and help feed the pigs. They can even have their faces painted to look like a lizard, a butterfly or (the most popular) a tiger. Don't miss the real tiger enclosure in the main zoo, where you can peer through a round window at these fearsome beasts, just a few inches away.

Be sure not to miss the Web of Life Building, an imaginative exhibition which aims to demonstrate how animals and organisms combine to form ecosystems. You can see examples of habitats from around the world and discover how the resident animals have adapted to their surroundings – how butterflies camouflage themselves against tree bark, or how robber crabs set up home in the shells of other sea creatures .

Kids are specially catered for at the Activity Den where they can take part in crafts like badge-making.

The zoo has a central relaxation area with a café, gift shop, fountain and a small children's carousel. There are also several playgrounds dotted about with slides and climbing frames.

Madame Tussaud's and the London Auditorium

Marylebone Road, NW1 **t** 0870 400 3000
www.madame-tussauds.co.uk
⊖ Baker Street **Bus** 13, 18, 27, 30, 74, 82, 113, 159, 274
Open Daily 9–5.30
Adm Prices vary according to the time of day from adults £14, children £9 (after 5pm) to adults £22.99, children £18.99 (9–5), under-5s **free**
No pushchairs allowed (baby carriers provided)

This collection of waxen doppelgangers is now London's third most popular tourist attraction. It's world-famous, with queues that regularly stretch right round the block. Whatever its unfathomable attractions may be, your kids understand them and will undoubtedly have a whale of a time, running around pointing at all the famous faces and demanding to have their picture taken with Posh and Becks, Tom Cruise, J-Lo or the Queen.

There are several new interactive exhibits aimed squarely at children. They can play air guitar alongside The Darkness's Justin Hawkins, sing like a 'diva' with Beyonce and Britney or climb a wall to take their picture with Spiderman. The highlight is the Spirit of London Ride, where you are carried in a mock-up 'Time Taxi' through London history from Elizabethan times to the present day, although your kids' favourite section will inevitably be the Chamber of Horrors, with its collection of grisly exhibits (for some reason yet to be explained, all children are fixated with blood, gore and mayhem).

The adjacent London Auditorium (formerly the London Planetarium), set beneath a distinctive green dome, has been revamped and incorporated into the main Madame Tussaud's site. Its new show, 'Journey to Infinity' is its most hi-tech yet – a virtual reality ride through the cosmos past black holes and whirling supernovas to watch the 'universe explode', based on information provided by the Hubble space telescope.

Parks and Gardens

Don't miss Regent's Park (p.67) and all it offers and, in summer, the Open Air Theatre (p.65) which often puts on child-friendly productions.

Sherlock Holmes Museum

221b Baker Street, NW1 **t** (020) 7935 8866
www.sherlock-holmes.co.uk
Baker Street **Bus** 13, 18, 27, 30, 74, 82, 113, 159, 274
Open Daily 9.30–6 **Adm** Adult £6, child £4

It all depends whether your children know who Sherlock Holmes is. The older ones (10 and over) may well and if, by chance, they are actually fans of Conan Doyle's classic detective, they will be completely bowled over by this little museum. It is a fictional address, of course; number 221 is actually the Abbey Building Society, where a secretary is employed purely to tackle the thousands of letters sent to the great detective each year.

On entering the museum you are met by a 19th-century 'Bobby' and shown round the house by a Victorian maid. The rooms have been faithfully recreated (or should that be created) according to the descriptions in the book. Afterwards you can have a cream tea at Mrs Hudson's Old English

Madame Tussaud

Madame Marie Tussaud was born in France in 1761. When just six years old she was taken by her uncle to Paris, where he instructed her in the art of modelling anatomical figures. By her early twenties, Marie had become so accomplished that she was hired to give art lessons to Louis XVI's children at Versailles; something which, in any other era, would have set her up for life. Unfortunately for her, in 1789 France underwent the Revolution – the monarchy was abolished, the King was executed and Marie, suspected of having Royalist sympathies, was thrown into jail and only released on condition that she attend public executions and sculpt the death masks of the Revolution's more celebrated victims.

In 1802, following a failed marriage, she emigrated to England, taking her two children and 35 of her models with her. To make ends meet, she was forced to tour her waxwork gallery of heroes, rogues, victims and confidence tricksters around the country until, in 1835, a permanent home was found for them in London's Baker Street. By 1850, the year Madame died, 'Tussaud's' was sufficiently well known for the Duke of Wellington to have become a regular visitor. He was especially taken with the Chamber of Horrors and left instructions that he should be informed whenever a new figure was added to its gruesome ranks.

By 1884 the exhibition (now managed by Madame's sons) had grown to over 400 models, forcing it to move to new premises in Marylebone Road, where it has stayed ever since. Madame's last work, a rather eerie self-portrait, is still on display in the Grand Hall.

Restaurant next door (Mrs Hudson was Holmes's housekeeper in the books). Opposite the museum is a memorabilia shop.

Shopping

Older children will love Camden's bustling street markets (p.61).

Sport and activities

For all cricket enthusiasts, a visit to world famous Lord's, north of Regent's Park, is a must.
For further information *see* p.69

British Museum to Lincoln's Inn Fields

British Museum

Great Russell Street, WC1 **t** (020) 7636 1555
Infoline **t** (020) 7323 8000
www.thebritishmuseum.ac.uk
⊖ Tottenham Court Road, Russell Square, Holborn
Bus 7, 8, 10, 19, 22b, 24, 25, 29, 38, 55, 68, 73, 91, 98, 134, 188, 242
Open Galleries: Sat–Wed 10–5.30, Thurs–Fri 10–8.30; Great Court: Sun–Wed 9–6, Thurs–Sat 9–11 **Adm Free** (a £2 donation is recommended); charges apply for some temporary exhibitions

The British Museum has never looked so good. Its central courtyard (known as the Great Court), which had been closed to the public for nearly 150 years, reopened for the millennium following a spectacular architectural transformation. The circular Reading Room at its centre, which used to house the British Library, now holds a public reference library and exhibition galleries. The huge domed interior looks like a vast cathedral of books, while the surrounding two acres of courtyard have been landscaped and rebuilt to contain an ethnographic gallery, a new Clore Education Centre, a lecture theatre, a cinema and a young visitors centre offering a range of activities for children. The most stunning feature, however, is the new 6,000 sq m (64,600 sq ft) glass roof that arches over the court-yard, the largest covered public square in Europe.

There's so much to look at that you couldn't hope to do it all in one, or even two, trips. From the Great Court, you can choose from a number of routes into the main galleries: head west for Egyptian Sculpture, east for the impossibly huge King's Library and north for the new Wellcome Wing of Ethnography. Inside the courtyard, two massive staircases lead up to the restaurant from where a bridge takes you into the museum's upper galleries.

Whatever route you choose, however, you won't go far wrong if you take your children to the ever-popular Ancient Egyptian Galleries (rooms 62–6) on the first floor. Here, they'll immediately be captivated by the huge gold sarcophagi, the brightly coloured frescoes and, of course, the mummies. These 2,000-year-old dead bodies hold a strange fascination for kids. The Egyptians, it seems, had a bit of a thing about mummification. As well as mummified Pharaohs, you'll find mummified cats, fish and even cattle.

Elsewhere, look out for the enormous (11-m high) early 19th-century totem pole that stands by the North Stairs; Lindow Man, the perfectly preserved, leathery remains of a 2,000-year-old Briton (room 35); and the great fat, smiling, ceramic Buddhas in the Oriental Gallery (room 33).

The museum's other famous exhibits include the controversial Elgin Marbles (room 8), the frieze reliefs from the Parthenon in Athens which, depending on whom you believe, were either rescued or stolen by Lord Elgin, British Ambassador to the Ottoman Empire, in 1802; the Rosetta Stone (room 25), an ancient tablet with the same decree inscribed upon it in three languages, which allowed Egyptian hieroglyphics to be deciphered for the first time; and the Sutton Hoo Treasure (room 41), a jewel-encrusted collection of Saxon swords, helmets, bowls and buckles.

How to make a mummy

The ancient Egyptians believed that every human was made up of a *ka* (spirit) and a *ba* (body). When a person died, they could only enter the afterlife if their body had not decayed – hence the fascination with preservation through mummification.

The key to a successful mummification is to dry out the body as quickly and as thoroughly as possible. Embalmers used natron, a chemical that occurs naturally in Egypt, to suck the mois-ture out of the body. The eyes and most of the internal organs, including the brain, kidneys and liver, were taken out. The brain was removed through a nostril and thrown away (the Egyptians didn't consider the grey matter useful in the afterlife). All the other organs were stored safely inside jars and buried with the body ready for the post-life journey. The skull and body cavi-ties were filled with a mixture of natron and plaster, and the eyes replaced with stones in order to stop them becoming sunken.

Once the body was dry, it was wrapped in bandages. Sometimes more than 300 yards of bandages were used, with charms written on pieces of papyrus slipped between the folds. The mummy would then be put into its sarcophagus and entombed, but not before its mouth had been opened to make sure it could breathe and talk in the afterlife – although, without a brain, conversation was presumably limited.

The museum produces a number of themed family tours, known as 'Compass Tours', on subjects such as 'Animal Mummies', 'Anglo-Saxon England' and 'Sutton Hoo Treasure', which are available from the information desks in the Great Court and Reading Room (or can be downloaded from the museum website). You can also pick up a 'family audiotour', featuring the voice of Stephen Fry. The museum organizes free events including 'Family Eye-opener Tours' for ages six and over on the first weekend of each month, and free drawing activities in the school holidays.

The British Museum is vast, so there's always the danger it can turn into a huge blurry mass for many children, especially the younger ones. Head back to the courtyard for some quiet contemplation when the kids start to suffer from overload.

Cinemas and theatre

The West End and Covent Garden are good areas for behind-the-scenes theatre tours (pp.79–80), not to mention live performances.

Dickens' House

48 Doughty Street WC1 **t** (020) 7405 2127
www.dickensmuseum.com
⊖ Chancery Lane, Russell Square **Bus** 17, 19, 38, 45, 55
Open Mon–Sat 10–5, Sun 11–5, closed Bank Hols
Adm Adults £5, children (5–15) £3, family £14, under-5s **free**

Charles Dickens wrote a fair bit within the walls of this house, now a museum to his literary life, although he only spent two years here. It was here that the great writer finished *The Pickwick Papers*, and went on to write *Oliver Twist*, *Nicholas Nickleby*, *The Old Curiosity Shop* and *Barnaby Rudge*. Special family events are organized throughout the year, from storytelling to writing with a quill pen.

London's Transport Museum

Covent Garden, WC2 **t** (020) 7379 6344
www.ltmuseum.co.uk
⊖ Covent Garden/Leicester Square **Bus** 6, 9, 11, 13, 15, 23, 77A, 91, 176
Open 10–6 daily, except Fri when it opens at 11am
Adm Adults £5.95, children **free**
Please note: the museum is being revamped; due to reopen summer 2007

This is a great, child-friendly museum, which neatly combines education (tracing the history of transport in London from 1829 to the present day) with activity – there are buttons to push, levers to pull and exhibits to clamber over. Housed in a huge iron and glass structure (a flower market from the 1870s to 1974), the museum possesses a wonderful, colourful collection of horse-drawn and motorized trams, buses and trolley cars. A new gallery is being added to display.some of the marvellous collection of London Transport posters.

The revamped museum promises more hands-on activities for children in an updated learning centre, with plenty of chances to take the wheel on a tube or bus simulator, an expanded play area for the under-5s and a 120-seat theatre, as well as a new café and shop.

Shopping

Covent Garden

Covent Garden is London's oldest square and for much of its 300-year existence was home to the capital's great fruit 'n' veg and flower markets. In 1974 the markets were relocated and the square underwent a facelift. Today, these cobbled streets and shopping arcades are a far cry from the clamour of street hawkers and stench of rotten vegetables of days gone by. Specializing in unusual toy and gift shops, the Piazza is perhaps London's closest (if rather phoney) approximation to European street life and café culture. Sit and have coffee and ice cream while the kids are entertained by exuberant street performers strutting their stuff.

Oxford Street and around

This is the main shopping area in London, so you will be spoilt for choice. Hamleys, Niketown and The Disney Store are all here, as well as the reliable John Lewis and glitzy Selfridges department stores.

Sir John Soane's Museum

12–14 Lincoln's Inn Fields, WC2 **t** (020) 405 2107
www.soane.org
⊖ Holborn
Open Tues–Sat 10–5; first Tues of each month until 9pm (candlelit) **Adm Free**

Once the home of Sir John Soane, the celebrated 18th-century architect and collector *extraordinaire*, this is a real treasure trove. You'll find Egyptian relics, toys, models of buildings, artworks (including Hogarth's cartoons of the 'Rake's Progress' from wealthy young ne'er-do-well to the madhouse), statues and jewellery.

On Saturdays, the museum runs free architecture workshops for children aged 7–13, and in school holidays it organizes art workshops for the same age group. Book in advance.

Somerset House

The Strand, WC2 **t** (020) 7845 4600
www.somerset-house.org.uk
⊖ Temple, Charing Cross, Embankment, Covent
Garden **Bus** 6, 9, 11, 13, 15, 23, 77a, 91, 176
Open Daily 10–6
Adm Entry to Somerset House, the Courtyard and
River Terrace **free**; Courtauld Gallery: adults £5,
children **free**; Gilbert Collection: adults £5, children
free; joint ticket: adults £9; Hermitage Rooms:
adult £6, child £4

Somerset House reopened to the public in 2000
and now houses the Courtauld Gallery, a large
collection of Impressionist and Post-Impressionist
paintings (including Van Gogh's *Bandaged Ear*); the
Hermitage Rooms, where Russian imperial treasures
are displayed; and the Gilbert Collection of gold
and silver decorative arts. Use the family-friendly
'Royal Trail Guide' to find your way around the
dazzling treasures. At weekend workshops kids can
take part in activities such as 'making a silver
goblet' or 'animal safaris'.

One of London's great riverside palaces, the
Renaissance-style building you see today is in fact
an 18th-century construction erected on the site of
the original Tudor palace. Its River Terrace, with
wonderful river views, and the glorious courtyard,
set with dozens of water jets, are great places to
have a picnic or start a river walk. An ice rink is set
up in the courtyard for a few weeks each winter.

Sport and activities

For a heated outdoor pool in the heart of London,
visit Oasis Sports Centre, Endell Street, WC2 (p.72).

Theatre Museum

Russell Street, WC2 **t** (020) 7943 4700
www.theatremuseum.org
⊖ Covent Garden/Leicester Square
Bus 6, 9, 11, 13, 15, 23, 77A, 91, 176
Open Tues–Sat 10–6 **Adm Free**

The museum is actually dedicated to all aspects
of the performing arts, not just theatre; there are
displays on ballet, circus, opera, pop music and
magic (you can see the wheelbarrow that the
legendary tightrope walker Charles Blondin wheeled
across the Niagara Falls in 1859). The museum is big
on interaction, with free daily workshops and
demonstrations where kids can learn how to
operate puppets or try on costumes. Theatrical
make-up demonstrations, thespian guided tours
and backstage visits to nearby Theatre Royal and

Drury Lane Theatre are also on offer. A free theatre
workshop club for kids aged 8–12 runs on Saturday
mornings (£5 per child; booking essential), while
younger siblings can enjoy storytellings.

Walks

For details of the Jubilee Walkway and Original
London Walks (guided tours) *see* pp.68–9.

The Wallace Collection

Hertford House, Manchester Square, W1
t (020) 7935 0687 www.wallacecollection.org
⊖ Bond Street, Marble Arch
Bus 2, 10, 12, 13, 30, 74, 82, 94, 113, 137, 274
Open Mon–Sat 10–5, Sun 12 noon–5
Adm Free (charge for some children's activities)

Looking at one of the country's most important
collections of French 18th-century paintings,
furniture and porcelain is not every child's idea of a
great day out. However, the conservators have
made a real effort to involve children in the gallery,
offering trails and quizzes and running a full
programme of school holiday activities. So, while
parents examine the Sèvres porcelain, Poussins
and Fragonards, kids may be able to try on a suit of
princely armour or make jewel-encrusted daggers
and flying carpets, tiles and textiles inspired by the
collection. Book in advance for activities.

Trafalgar Square and Piccadilly

Cinemas and theatres

This is the heart of West End cinema and
theatreland (pp.79–80). Flanked by four giant
cinemas, Leicester Square is *the* place in London to
catch a film (p.73).

★National Gallery

Trafalgar Square, WC2 **t** (020) 7747 2885
www.nationalgallery.org.uk
⊖ Charing Cross, Leicester Square, Embankment
Bus 3, 6, 9, 11, 12, 13, 15, 23, 24, 29, 53, 88, 91, 109, 139,
159, 176, 184, 196
Open 10–6 daily, Wed 10–9
Adm Free (charges for some temporary exhibitions)

The National Gallery has more than 2,300 canvases
covering the last eight centuries of European art,
divided into four colour-coded wings (pick up a map
for details). All the great artists are here: Cézanne,
Constable, Leonardo da Vinci, Picasso, Turner, Van
Gogh. The sheer size and scope of the gallery can

make the prospect of a visit seem daunting for adults, let alone children.

To get the best out of the gallery, it's often a good idea to pick perhaps a dozen or so pictures in advance and then plan your tour accordingly. That way you can turn the experience into a sort of treasure hunt. Fortunately, the wonderful resources of the National allow you to plan your trip in exactly this fashion. Your first port of call should be the Micro Gallery in the Sainsbury Wing, where you can explore the gallery's entire collection on touch-screen computer terminals. For very young children, however, it's probably best just to let them wander and point – you'll be surprised at what catches their eye.

The Gallery produces special audio guides and paper trails for children and organizes a range of family events including free weekly gallery talks for 4–11 year-olds, storytellings for under-5s on the Gallery's 'magic carpet', holiday workshops and artist-led drawing events (see website). Most events are free; turn up early to get a place.

There's a decent self-service café, or you can eat your own picnic in the Education Centre's sandwich rooms. The Gallery shop is excellent and well worth a visit for good introductory art books and the print-on-demand poster service: you can have any painting in the collection reproduced while you wait for between £10 (A4) and £25 (A2).

The pictures

There are certain pictures here with special appeal to children. The colour and vibrancy of many of the Renaissance canvases (Sainsbury and West Wings) often touch a nerve with kids, and the subjects – St George slaying the Dragon, John the Baptist's head on a silver platter, St Sebastian shot full of arrows – are usually gory enough to impress. Paintings that employ overt forms of visual trickery also often grab children's attention. Here are four paintings they may enjoy.

Hans Holbein
The Ambassadors

This is a bright and colourful picture of two very grand 16th-century courtiers. Everything seems quite normal apart from a strange stretched shape at the bottom of the picture. Get your kids to go as close to the wall on the right hand side of the picture as possible and then look back at the picture. By changing the point of view in this fashion, the stretched shape should now have transformed itself into the picture of a skull.

Can you spot?

Hidden among the fruit and flowers of Jan van Os's picture are the following creatures and objects. How many can you find? There are two butterflies, three flies, a snail, a dormouse, a dragonfly and a bird's nest.

Jan van Eyck
Arnolfini Wedding Portrait

This 15th-century Dutch picture of a couple holding hands seems quite unremarkable on first glance. But if you look closely at the mirror hanging on the wall behind the couple, you should be able to see the reflection of the back of the couple stretching out their hands towards a visitor. The visitor is Van Eyck himself, come to paint the couple's portrait. The words 'Van Eyck fuit hic, 1434' appear on the wall above the mirror. Roughly translated they mean 'Van Eyck made this, 1434'.

Samuel van Hoogstraten
Peepshow (North Wing)

Created in the 17th century, this isn't a conventional painting at all, but a wooden box mounted on a plinth. In the side of the box is a peephole. If you look through the hole, you'll see what looks like a miniature house filled with what appears to be 3D furniture. It is, in fact, a 2D painting which cleverly uses perspective to make you think you are seeing things that aren't really there.

Jan van Os
Fruit, Flowers in a Terracotta Vase

This picture, from the late 18th century, is so realistic that it almost looks like a photograph. The trick is in the composition rather than the representation. Although the fruit and flowers in the picture appear quite fresh, in fact they couldn't possibly have all appeared together at the same time as they all ripen at different times of the year. The painting was therefore painted over the course of a year, each new fruit and flower being added as it came into season.

National Portrait Gallery

St Martin's Place, WC2 **t** (020) 7306 0055
www.npg.org.uk
⊖ Charing Cross, Leicester Square, Embankment
Bus 3, 6, 9, 11, 12, 13, 15, 23, 24, 29, 53, 88, 91, 109, 139, 159, 176, 184, 196
Open Mon–Wed, Sat–Sun 10–6, Thurs–Fri 10–9
Adm Free (charges for some temporary exhibitions)

The National Portrait Gallery is the nation's picture album. More than 2,000 portraits of the greatest figures from the last 700 years of British history are on display here. The collection is arranged chronologically, so it's best to start at the top (there's a lift) with the Tudors (look out for the clever picture of Edward VI by William Scrots which requires you to look at it from an acute angle in order to see the perspective) before making your way slowly down through the centuries via the Balcony Gallery (part of the new Ondaatje Wing) to the 20th-century works on the ground floor. On the way children will find themselves putting faces to names they had previously only read about in text-books or heard in history lessons: kings, queens, soldiers, statesmen, scientists, politicians, artists and sculptors, they're all here. The Gallery has also introduced themed Rucksack Tours for 4–12-year-olds; each tour contains eight different activities relating to the displays – puzzles, quizzes, drawing tasks and so on – in a rucksack. They're free for the duration, but may run out.

Because the Gallery's pictures have been chosen on the basis of identity rather than ability, the quality and style of the works varies enormously. Most of the older paintings have been painted in a traditional, formal style, while the more modern works have been rendered using a mish mash of different techniques. Kids will enjoy spotting the famous faces nonetheless: look out for Princess Diana, David Beckham and Kate Winslet.

Once you've finished, catch the lift back up to the top-floor café, which has wonderful views.

Shopping

One of London's best-known sports stores, Lillywhites, is on Piccadilly Circus (p.62), and Hamleys toy shop (p.62) is just up Regent's Street.

Trafalgar Square

Charing Cross, Leicester Square, Embankment
Bus 3, 6, 9, 11, 12, 13, 15, 23, 24, 29, 53, 88, 91, 109, 139, 159, 176, 184, 196

Things have changed in Trafalgar Square. The north side has been pedestrianized and prettified and most of the pigeons have been sent away. The grand new staircase at the square's northern end provides a great place to sit and admire the views, which are dominated by the 185-feet-high granite pillar of Nelson's Column. Kids will instinctively roll their heads back in an attempt to catch a glimpse of the one-eyed, one-armed British hero perched on its summit. Lord Horatio Nelson (for it is he) was Britain's greatest naval commander. The square and column were built in the early 19th century to

Can you spot?
Trafalgar Square is home to the world's smallest police station. See if you can find it. Hidden in a lamp post, in the southeast corner of the square, it has room for just one police officer.

commemorate his victory over the Franco-Spanish fleet at the Battle of Trafalgar back in 1805. Nelson was fatally wounded at the battle and was brought home in a barrel of brandy for a hero's funeral.

Keeping guard at the foot of the column are four magnificent iron lions, sculpted by Edward Landseer and unveiled in 1870, 25 years after the construction of the column. A photo of your kids sitting between a pair of giant protective forepaws is one of the classic snapshots of London. Or you could pose them in front of one of the square's great gushing, gurgling fountains, which spring into life every day at 10am. The stairs also provide a fittingly grand approach to the National Gallery (pp.41–2) and National Portrait Gallery (pp.42–3).

Trocadero

Piccadilly Circus, WC1 **t** 0906 888 1100 (60p/min) **www**.troc.co.uk
Piccadilly Circus, Leicester Square
Bus 3, 12, 14, 19, 22, 38
Open Sun–Thurs 10am–12 midnight, Fri–Sat 10am–1am **Adm Free**

Originally a plush hotel, the Trocadero is now a large, noisy arcade-cum-electronic entertainment centre with souvenir shops, fast-food restaurants, a seven-screen cinema and its biggest draw, Funland – six floors of the latest computer games.

Funland

t (020) 7439 1914 **www**.funland.co.uk
Open Sun–Thurs 10am–12 midnight, Fri–Sat 10am–1am **Adm Free** (charge for games and rides)

This is essentially a giant amusement arcade with six floors of flashing, beeping video games to explore – shoot-'em-ups, fighting games, flight simulators and racing games – interspersed with 3D simulator rides, as well as more traditional attractions such as pool tables, putting, 10-pin bowling, dodgems, etc. Don't be fooled by the free entry signs. Each video game costs at least £1 and each of the large 3D rides £2–£3 (there are small savings to be made by buying combined tickets).

Walks

For details of the Jubilee Walkway, which passes through this area, see pp.68–9.

Buckingham Palace to Westminster

Boat trips

Westminster Pier is an excellent starting point for a boat trip. You can also catch a boat from Tate Britain to Tate Modern, via the South Bank.
For further information see p.65

Buckingham Palace

**St James's Park, SW1. Ticket office in Green Park at Canada Gate t Booking line (020) 7766 7300/1
www.royal.gov.uk**
⊕ St James's Park, Green Park, Victoria
Bus 7, 11, 139, 211, C1, C10
Open Palace: Aug–Sept daily 9.30–5.30 (last entry 4.15); Queen's Gallery: daily 10–5.30 (closed 25–6 Dec)
Adm Palace: adults £12.95, children (under 17) £6.50, under-5s free; Queen's Gallery: adults £7.50, children £4, under-5s free, family £19

It's all change at the palace. Previously the very private London residence of the Royal Family, the famous 19th-century palace has, since 1993, been opening its doors to the public for two months each summer. Or at least some of its doors; in fact the official guided tour takes in just 18 of a possible 600 rooms. These include the Grand Hall, the Throne Room, the State Dining Room, the Music Room, the Royal Picture Gallery and the Silk Tapestry Room. All are splendid in a formal, rather haughty sort of way, although the Throne Room is a bit of a disappointment as it doesn't even contain a throne, just two pink and yellow chairs marked EIIR (Elizabeth Regina) and P (Philip). To be honest, the palace will probably prove a little dull for most children (and adults). For art fans the Queen's Gallery on Buckingham Palace Road offers rotating displays from the royal collection (Old Masters).

Remember, if the Union Flag is raised the Queen is at home; if it's lowered, she's out.

If it's just a little pomp and circumstance you're after, you would be better off watching the Changing of the Guard from the railings outside.

Changing of the Guard

⊕ St James's Park, Green Park, Victoria
Bus 1, 16, 24, 52, 73
Time Apr–Jun daily at 11.27am sharp; rest of year alternate days at the same time. Ceremony lasts around 45 minutes.
Adm Free

This daily costume drama has become a veritable symbol of Britishness, attracting hundreds of tourists every day, and yet, it has to be said, it can get a bit dull. It'll probably capture your interest briefly – the rows of bearskinned, red-coated soldiers, the barked orders, the military band, the complex, regulated marching patterns – but, after half an hour, you could be forgiven for wishing that they'd get to the point (which, in case you're wondering, is to replace the 40 men guarding Buckingham Palace with another contingent from Wellington Barracks). Nonetheless, it's extremely popular, and the views from outside Buckingham Palace can quickly become obscured. Even perched on your shoulders, kids may have trouble seeing. Your best bet for a glimpse of the marching soldiers is to take up one of the alternative vantage points at St James's or Birdcage Walk.

Alternatively, watch the Horse Guards march up to Buckingham Palace at 11am (in summer). London's own toy soldiers sit astride their horses in full dress uniform of red tunic, breastplate and sword. The stillness of the soldiers – both horse and man are trained not to twitch and to look straight ahead – fascinates children.

Guards' Museum

**Wellington Barracks, Birdcage Walk, SW1
t (020) 7414 3271**
⊕ St James's Park Bus 3, 11, 12, 24, 159
Open Daily 10–4
Adm Adult £2, under-16s free

The museum traces the history of British troops from Cromwell's New Model Army and Charles II's five regiments (who still make up the infantry) to the present day, with plenty of battle memorabilia on display and an excellent toy soldier shop.

The Royal Mews

**Buckingham Palace Road, SW1 t (020) 7766 7302
www.royal.gov.uk**
⊕ St James's Park, Green Park, Victoria
Bus 1, 16, 24, 52, 73
Open Mar–Jul and Oct 11–4 (last entry 3.15), Aug–Sept 10–5 (last entry 4.15)
Adm Adults £5.50, children (under 18) £3, family £14

These are the stables where the horses that work for the Royal Family are kept. As you would expect, the stalls are magnificent, with tiled walls and gleaming horse brasses. You can touch and pet the horses and admire the gold coach used for coronations – it's so heavy, it takes eight horses to pull it!

GETTING AROUND | PRACTICAL A–Z | LONDON'S YEAR | **THINGS TO SEE AND DO** | SHOPPING | SPECIAL TRIPS | KIDS OUT | KIDS IN | EATING OUT

Can you spot?
The statues in Parliament Square of three of Britain's most famous Prime Ministers: Palmerston, Disraeli and Winston Churchill. How is Churchill's statue different to the others? It is, how shall we put it, cleaner than the other statues. This is because it's heated from the inside to stop pigeon droppings from sticking.

Cenotaph

Near the junction of Downing Street and Whitehall stands the Cenotaph, the nation's chief memorial to the dead of the two World Wars. An official ceremony of remembrance takes place here each year on the Sunday nearest Armistice Day, 11 November, when wreaths of poppies are laid at the memorial.

Churchill Museum & Cabinet War Rooms

King Charles Street, SW1 **t** (020) 7766 0120
www.cwr.iwm.org.uk
↔ Westminster, St James's Park
Bus 3, 11, 12, 24, 53, 77a, 88, 109, 159, 184, 211
Open 9.30–6 daily (last entry 5)
Adm Adults £10, children **free**

A great place to take children with some knowledge of the Second World War. It contains both the Cabinet War Rooms – 21 cramped, low-ceilinged chambers 5m (17ft) underground that were, for the last years of the conflict, the nerve centre of the British war effort – and (opened in 2005) the country's first museum dedicated to the great wartime leader. The museum is divided into five sections covering Churchill's entire life, with exhibits ranging from his baby rattle and school reports to the periscope he used while on active service in the trenches of the First World War, as well as Second World War documents. There are also audiovisual and interactive displays giving a wealth of detail about the life story and legacy of the man recently voted the 'Greatest Briton' ever.

The war rooms themselves were, for a few years, the most important place in the country, for it was here that Churchill and his ministers made decisions that changed the course of history. To visit these rooms today is to take a step back into the past; they have remained untouched since the final days of the war in 1945. They are wonderfully evocative, their very smallness (Churchill's office was a converted broom cupboard) giving some sense of the desperate pressure of the times. Each individual detail, so ordinary in itself, becomes, in this context, charged with significance. You can even see Churchill's bedroom from where he made his legendary radio broadcasts. Make use of the free audio guides to hear Churchill's rousing speeches, children's memories of war, sound effects, recordings of conversations and period music.

Downing Street

You can catch a glimpse of No.10, the house where the Prime Minister lives, through a pair of black iron gates at the end of the road. Unfortunately, you are no longer allowed to go and have a close-up look. Britain's official centre of power is certainly not as grand as the White House in Washington or the Elysée Palace in Paris. But then, the man who built it, George Downing, never meant it to be more than a simple residential house. When Robert Walpole moved here in the mid-18th century (once the preceding tenant, a Mr Chicken, had moved out) he had no idea that all the Prime Ministers would follow in his footsteps, and to this day no one really knows why they have.

Houses of Parliament

Parliament Square, SW1. Ticket office is opposite the St Stephen's entrance
t (020) 7219 4272 **www.parliament.uk**
www.explore.parliament.uk
↔ Westminster
Bus 3, 11, 12, 24, 53, 77a, 88, 109, 159, 184, 211, X53
Open In the summer recess (Jun–Sept) daily guided tours are available. To watch a debate from the House of Commons Visitors' Gallery, you must queue from 2.30pm onwards Mon–Wed, from 11.30am Thurs and from 9.30am Fri. For details of PM's Question Time (Wed 12 noon) and guided tours of the palace when the house is sitting, open to UK residents only, write to your local MP.
Adm Summer tours: adults £7, children £5, family £22, under-5s **free**; debates: **free**

Its official name is the Palace of Westminster, but politicians refer to it simply as 'the House'. Whatever you call it, it is one of the unmistakable sights of London. Most of the huge building dates from the 1830s, the original medieval structure having burned down in a fire in 1834, although parts of the interior, including Westminster Hall, were built at the end of the 11th century.

This is where the British government goes about its daily business, and where the ruling party of the day debates policy with the opposition. Despite its importance, however, it was, until recently, very difficult for members of the public to take a look inside the neo-Gothic palace. Happily, guided tours are now available from July to September to all visitors. The tour includes the House of Commons chamber where the country's most important debates take place. It's surprisingly small, the chamber's plush leather benches having room for just 437 MPs (forcing many of the current 659 MPs to stand during popular debates). From here it's on to the 'Noes Lobby', where MPs vote on legislation.

Other places of interest include the Royal Gallery and Queen's Robing Room, where the Monarch prepares for the State Opening of Parliament; the House of Lords Chamber and the very Grand Westminster Hall, the oldest part of the palace. Though now only used for ceremonial occasions, it was once the setting for important state trials. Both Charles I and the Gunpowder plotters were tried (and found guilty) here.

Children wanting to find out more about parliament can visit www.explore.parliament.uk.

Big Ben

Big Ben, the great clock tower, completed in 1859, was named after a Mr Benjamin Hill, the portly commissioner of works at the time. Big Ben is actually the name of the bell rather than the tower – its distinctive sound is due to a crack that appeared during its installation. Tours of the clock tower are occasionally available to UK residents (no children under 11) via written application to your local MP.

Parks and gardens

For details of St James's Park see p.67. Green Park (p.66) and Hyde Park (pp.66–7) are also nearby.

Tate Britain

Millbank, SW1
t (020) 7887 8000 www.tate.org.uk/britain
⊖ Pimlico, Vauxhall ⇌ Vauxhall
Bus 2, 3, 36, 77A, 88, 159, 185, 507, C10
Open Daily 10–5.50
Adm Free (charge for some temporary exhibitions)

Originally intended as a showcase for British art when it opened in 1897, the Tate had ceased to fulfil its role until, in 2000, Tate Modern opened on Bankside, taking the European art collection with it. The old Tate was reborn as Tate Britain, a gallery once again devoted solely to British art.

As with its younger sibling, Tate Britain now organizes its collection according to themes as well as chronology. So within the major sections, British Art 1500–1900 and British Art 1900– 2005,

Can you spot?
The big beige office building with green windows opposite Tate Britain, on the other side of the river. This is the HQ of MI6, Britain's secret service. Until recently, the British government denied that this service existed, which meant that, officially, the building also didn't exist – and neither did the people who worked in it. You might just as well say James Bond doesn't exist.

you'll find sections named 'Inventing Britain', 'Making British History', 'Art and Victorian Society', 'The Cult of Youth' and 'Ways of Seeing Revisited', as well as no less than seven rooms dedicated to the works of Joseph Mallord William Turner.

Families are very well catered for at Tate Britain, whose curators have long understood that children can quickly grow bored staring at paintings, and so provide plenty of activities to keep them amused (most of which are free). In addition to 'Saturday Soundings', special artist-led family workshops, the gallery can provide 'Paths through Pictures' family trails (for ages 5 and over, from the information desk) and children's audioguides (8–12-year-olds) bringing pictures to life through stories, quizzes, riddles and sound effects.

The ever-popular art trolley is wheeled out on Sundays, Bank Holidays, and Thursdays during the school holidays between 12 noon and 5pm. Designed for adults and children to work on together, all you have to do is turn up to choose from a range of games and activities related to the many artworks on display.

Tate Britain is linked to Tate Modern by a ferry service (see p.65).

Walks

For details of the Jubilee Walkway, which passes through this area, see pp.68–9.

Westminster Abbey

Broad Sanctuary, SW1
t (020) 7222 5152 www.westminster-abbey.org
⊖ Westminster, St James's Park
Bus 3, 11, 12, 24, 53, 88, 109, 159, X53, 211
Open Mon–Fri 9.30–4.45 (last entry 3.45), Wed until 8pm (last entry 7), Sat 9–2.45 (last entry 1.45)
Adm Adults £7.50, children £5, under-11s free, family £15

The Abbey could be described, if you were feeling a little disrespectful, as a great indoor graveyard filled with the remains, relics and reminders of the last thousand years of British history. You enter through Statesmen's Aisle, which features memorials to three of the country's most famous past Prime Ministers: Gladstone, Disraeli and Palmerston. The Abbey houses the tombs of Elizabeth I and Mary, Queen of Scots, whom she beheaded, and the centrepiece of the Abbey – the shrine of St Edward. You'll also come across what is thought to be the last resting place of the two young princes, Edward V and his brother Richard, who were supposedly murdered by their uncle (later Richard III) in the Tower of London in 1483 (*see* p.57). The confused layout just makes it more interesting for kids who happily wend their way through, under and around the assorted statues, stones, memorials and shrines. See if they can find Poets' Corner where Geoffrey Chaucer was buried in 1400, and Shakespeare, Shelley and Keats, are memorialized.

The Abbey is a very beautiful place with great vaulted ceilings and richly coloured stained glass windows, but the best thing about it is that it manages to engage the macabre interest of children while, at the same time, offering a more serene, reflective air which adults will appreciate.

There's a café and a souvenir shop in the cloisters. Audio guides are available for £2 at the entrance.

Chelsea, South Kensington and Knightsbridge

Saatchi Gallery
Duke of York's HQ, Sloane Square SW1
t (020) 7823 2363 **www.saatchi-gallery.co.uk**
Open Mon–Thurs and Sun 10–8, Fri and Sat 10–10
Adm Adults £8.75, child £6.85, family £26

Following several years at County Hall, the city's leading independent modern art gallery recently upped sticks to the Duke of York's HQ building in Chelsea. Contact and admission price details were unavailable at the time of going to press. Check the website for up-to-date information.

Charles Saatchi was a prime mover in the 'Brit Art' movement of the early 1990s when he bought up works by young artists (many just out of art school) for huge sums. His acquisitions soon became talking points with countless 'is it art?' debates in the press. Such was the furore that a few pieces, including Damien Hirst's shark pickled in formaldehyde and Tracey Emin's unmade bed, took on the status of national icons. Though not to everyone's taste, the gallery's constantly rotating

> ### Can you spot?
> The Elfin Oak. Close to the Round Pond is Ivor Innes's sculpture – an ornate tree stump inlaid with scores of tiny woodland creatures. The famous Peter Pan statue is also near here (p.66).

display does provide a good introduction to British conceptual art. sBe aware that many of the pieces explore sexual themes and therefore may not be suitable for young children.

Kensington Palace
The State Apartments, Kensington Gardens, W8
t 0870 751 7050 **www.hrp.org.uk**
⊖ High Street Kensington, Notting Hill Gate, Queensway
Bus 9, 10, 12, 52, 73, 94
Open Mar–Oct daily 10–6, Nov–Feb 10–5
Adm Adults £10.80, children £8.20, family £32

On the western edge of Kensington Gardens, this rather reserved-looking palace is where Princess Diana, the 'People's Princess', lived following her divorce from Prince Charles. The gardens outside were covered in 1.5 million bunches of flowers in the week following her untimely death in 1997. There are guided tours between 10am and 3.30pm, when you can walk through the plush historic apartments and see clothes from the royal wardrobe, including some of Diana's outfits. The palace's very fancy Orangery restaurant offers a children's menu. Nearby are Kensington Gardens and the new Princess Diana Adventure Playground (p.66).

★Natural History Museum
Cromwell Road, SW7
t (020) 7942 5000 **www.nhm.ac.uk**
⊖ South Kensington
Bus 9, 10, 14, 49, 52, 70, 74, 345, 360, 414, C1
Open Mon–Sat 10–5.50, Sun 11–5.50
Adm Free

One of the must-see sights for both children and adults, the Natural History Museum is a fabulous place. Huge monsters, replica volcanoes, earthquake simulators, creepy crawlies, precious stones, big things, small things, shiny things – there's so much to look at. This is the sort of museum where kids rush off pointing at everything.

It's been revamped in recent years. All the old favourites are still here – the great fossil monsters, the impossibly huge blue whale suspended from the museum ceiling – but these have been augmented with new exhibits and more up-to-date technologies.

Whatever entrance you choose, there's an almost immediate 'Wow!' awaiting you. Walk through the main door and you'll be confronted by the great swooping head of a fossil *diplodocus* looming down above you. Nip around the side and you'll find yourself walking through a guard of honour made up of bizarre futuristic statues before riding up an escalator into a huge clunking, clanking metal globe. The two entrances mark the beginnings of the museum's two themed areas, the Life and Earth Galleries.

Pride of place in the Life Galleries goes to those perennial children's favourites, dinosaurs. There is an illuminated walkway to take you past the various superstar fossils (*T-Rex* and the horned-faced *Triceratops* among them). Videos, interactive displays and an intriguing display on how these long-extinct beasts have become staples of pop culture – from *The Flintstones* to *Jurassic Park* – all add to the experience. The *pièce de résistance*, however, is the new two-thirds size, animatronic *Tyrannosaurus Rex* – it growls, it slavers, it snaps its jaws, it even smells.

The Earth Galleries play to their strengths. Detailed, in-depth geology has been ditched in favour of spectacular volcano and earthquake exhibitions: videos of exploding craters, models of lava flows, plastercasts of the Pompeii victims petrified in mute agony and, best of all, an earthquake simulator – where you can feel a tremor.

The latest addition to this great cathedral of nature is the Darwin Centre. Built at a cost of £30m and covering some 10,000 sq m (108,000 sq ft), it provides a showcase for the museum's vast collection of preserved animal species (of which there are around 22 million, although the centre only has space for 450,000), some even collected by the great naturalist himself during his trip to the Galapagos islands. Free behind-the-scenes tours to see undisplayed specimens and laboratory facilities are given daily (kids 10 and over only). The new Clore Education Centre gives 7–14-year-olds a chance to examine their own specimen with microscopes, magnifiers and measures.

Discovery Guides, for ages 3–18, and Explorer backpacks, for under-7s, are available at the main entrances, and the museum organizes family workshops at weekends and in school holidays. They are free, and can be booked on the day in Gallery 10. For more details go to www.nhm.ac.uk/kids-only/.

★Science Museum

Exhibition Road, London SW7
t 0870 870 4868 www.sciencemuseum.org.uk
⊖ South Kensington
Bus 9, 10, 14, 49, 52, 70, 74, 345, 360, 414, C1
Open Daily 10–6 **Adm Free** IMAX: adults £7.50, children £6

The Science Museum, perhaps more than any other museum, understands that children like to be involved with the exhibits; they like to touch, to feel, to press and push as well as just see. Nowhere is this better demonstrated than in the four-storey Wellcome Wing, which offers state-of-the-art exhibits and lots of hands-on fun. There are three permanent exhibitions: 'Who am I?', which looks at how science helps us to understand what it means to be human (you can morph your features on a computer to make yourself look older or younger, or switch gender); 'Digitopolis', which explores today's digital landscape (digitally manipulate your voice to sound like Darth Vader or Mickey Mouse), and 'In Future', which predicts how technology will develop over the next 20 years – play the 'In Future' interactive game and decide for yourself which technologies you think will be most relevant in the decades to come. There is also an IMAX film theatre showing science films on a four-storey-high screen and a simulator ride, 'Virtual Voyages', which takes you on a ride across the solar system to intercept a comet hurtling towards Earth.

Impressive though this wing is, you'll want to save some time for some of the museum's other exhibits, several of which are specifically designed for children. These include the Launch Pad in the basement where there are various games and pieces of equipment through which kids can learn a few basic scientific principles – they can create a giant bubble, touch a plasma ball and see electricity following their fingers, build a rubber bridge or perhaps try and tiptoe past the vibration detector. Staff are on hand to guide the youngsters through the apparatus.

In the basement there are two further child-centric galleries – the Garden, for 3–6-year-olds, which gives children the chance to experiment with water using pumps, dams and buckets, and Things, aimed at 7–11-year-olds, with a wide range of interactive video displays. Try not to miss the Secret Life of the Home, which takes a humorous look at domestic gizmos from vacuum cleaners and washing machines to fridges and heaters.

Short of time?

There's far too much in the museum to be covered in a single day and you may prefer to plan your tour around a few headline exhibits. Here are some suggestions:

▶ A 1903 Burnley mill engine. This is the showpiece of the Power Gallery on the ground floor, dedicated to the great machinery of the Industrial Revolution.

▶ The Black Arrow. Britain's first and only satellite launch rocket. The enormous craft is attached to the ceiling of the Space Gallery.

▶ The Apollo 10 Command Module. In 1969 it flew three astronauts into space as a rehearsal for the moon landing mission later in the year. Note the scorch marks on the craft, which were caused when it re-entered the earth's atmosphere at great speed.

▶ Foucault's Pendulum. A giant pendulum suspended from the ceiling of the ground floor, designed to demonstrate the rotation of the Earth.

▶ One of the last working mechanical telephone exchanges in Britain. It can be found in the Telecommunications Gallery on the first floor.

▶ Charles Babbage's Difference Machine. This collection of cogs, gears and levers was the world's first ever computer. It is in Computing Then and Now on the second floor.

▶ On Air. Here, on the third floor, kids can learn how a radio station works.

▶ A model of a 16th-century medical teaching theatre and a life-size recreation of a modern operating theatre, in which waxwork doctors perform open-heart surgery. Both are in Glimpses of Medical History on the fourth floor.

Of course, there are plenty of other galleries which, while not specifically designed for children, will nonetheless appeal. The Flight Gallery, for instance, will bring out the latent pilot in both parents and children. Here, in the 'Flight Lab', you can pedal a propeller to see how helicopters work, sit in the cockpit of a single-seater aircraft, watch as a water-powered rocket is fired across the gallery, or take a ride in a state-of-the-art flight simulator which replicates the cockpit of a Harrier jump jet.

Before leaving, make sure you check out the museum shop which is filled with 'science' toys and games – junior astronomy kits, holograms, binoculars, models, kaleidoscopes and the like.

Themed children's trail guides are available both here and at reception for £1.

Science Nights

Kids will like the museum so much that they'll probably wish they could spend the night. Well, guess what? The museum runs Science Nights every month when children aged between 8 and 11 (plus an accompanying parent) can come and camp overnight. They are treated to midnight tours of the museum, workshops and bedtime stories. The sleepovers, which are only available to groups of 5–9 children, are very popular and need to be booked well in advance. They cost £30 per child.

★Shopping

Knightsbridge is home to two of London's most famous department stores – Harrods and Harvey Nichols (p.61). There are also some very chic children's shops on nearby Walton Street. Not far away – a short bus trip if little feet are tired – are the King's Road and High Street Kensington, also good for shopping. A little further off is Notting Hill and Portobello Road, now one of London's most upmarket shopping areas.

Victoria & Albert Museum

Cromwell Road, SW7 **t** (020) 7942 2000
www.vam.ac.uk
⊖ South Kensington
Bus 9, 10, 14, 49, 52, 70, 74, 345, 360, 414, C1
Open Daily 10–5.45, Wed and last Fri of month until 10pm **Adm Free**

Dedicated to the decorative arts, the Victoria & Albert Museum (the V&A) has a huge collection of treasures from all over the world: silverware from European royal palaces, ceramics from eastern temples, sculptures by African tribes and vast hoards of jewellery, furniture, textiles, tapestries and paintings. The Dress Gallery usually appeals to clothes-conscious teenage girls. It traces fashion from the 17th century to the present day, from ruffs and crinolines to mini skirts and trainers.

For something to gasp at, head to the Cast Court where you'll find plastercasts of some of the world's greatest (and biggest) statues and monuments – Michelangelo's *David* and the enormous Trajan's Column (in two huge pieces) among them.

The British Galleries 1500–1900 are a welcome addition, with play areas where kids can try on Victorian clothes or attempt to rebuild the Crystal Palace using perspex blocks, as well as touch-screen information, reconstructed room sets and computers. There's not much to push or pull in the other galleries, though the museum organizes plenty of kids' activities. These are usually themed according to the gallery – origami in the Japanese Gallery, paper clothes-making in the Dress Gallery and jewellery-making in the Silver Gallery. Free themed family trails are available from the information desk daily, and activity backpacks full of jigsaws, stories, puzzles and construction games can be picked up from the Grand Entrance on Saturday afternoons (1–4.30pm). Designed for ages 5–12, there are seven themed packs to choose from, including 'Murder Mystery' and 'Magic Glasses'. On Sundays and in the school holidays a roving activity cart tours the museum's seven miles of corridors, while on the first Sunday of each month the museum organizes drop-in events for 5–12-year-olds, based around the current temporary exhibitions and usually involving some artistic activity such as drawing or photography.

For generations rather fusty and dusty, the V&A is in the throes of a continuous upgrade, ranging from 21st-century gallery redesigns to new cafés.

Waterloo and the South Bank

Boat trips

Waterloo Pier is an excellent place to catch a boat up or down river (pp.64–5)

★British Airways London Eye

Next to County Hall, South Bank, SE1
t 0870 500 0600 www.ba-londoneye.com
Open Feb–Apr and Oct–Dec daily 9.30am–9pm; May and Sept Mon–Thurs 9.30–8, Fri–Sun 9.30–9; Jun Mon–Thurs 9.30–9, Fri–Sun 9.30–10; Jul and Aug daily 9.30–10
Adm Adults £12.50, children (5–16) £6.50, under-5s **free**. Purchase tickets in advance; online discounts

One of the few Millennium projects to have stood the test of time, this 138m (453ft) rotating observation wheel perched on the south bank of the River Thames has provided both tourists and Londoners with a whole new way of looking at the capital. Night rides are particularly spectacular, especially when the Christmas lights go on, although the best sightseeing opportunities are afforded during the day.

Officially the fourth-highest structure in the capital, each of the Eye's 32 enclosed glass-sided capsules (they hold up to 25 people each) takes around 40 minutes to complete its circuit. Don't worry though, it moves so slowly and smoothly there's little chance of travel sickness and there's a central seating area in each capsule.

Cinemas and theatres

Britain's largest cinema screen, IMAX 3D Cinema, can be found near Waterloo Station (p.73). You will also find the South Bank Arts Centre, one of the world's greatest art complexes (p.52).

County Hall

⊖ Waterloo, Westminster ⇌ Waterloo
Bus 11, 12, 24, 53, 76, 77, 159, 211, 341, 381, X53

After sitting empty for several years, County Hall, the beautiful Edwardian building that used to house the now defunct Greater London Council (GLC), has once again found a purpose (or two).

There's the London Aquarium in the basement, Namco Station, a sort of giant video game arcade, The Saatchi Gallery, displaying the latest 'Brit Art', and Dali Universe, a museum dedicated to the great, Spanish surrealist artist, as well as several restaurants and hotels.

Dali Universe

County Hall, Riverside Building, Belvedere Road, SE1
t (020) 7620 2720 www.daliuniverse.com
Open Daily 10–5.30
Adm Adults £8.50, children (8–16) £5.50, under-8s £3.50, under-4s £1, family £23

This museum is filled with bizarre sculptures and paintings of the Spanish surrealist. In particular, look out for the sofa designed to resemble an enormous pair of red lips (modelled on the lips of Hollywood actress Mae West) and the lobster telephone. An audio guide and activity sheets for children are available.

London Aquarium

County Hall, Riverside Building, Westminster Bridge Road, SE1
t (020) 7967 8000 www.londonaquarium.co.uk
Open Daily 10–6
Adm Adults £9.75, children £6.25, under-3s **free**, family £29

The London Aquarium has become established as one of the capital's top animal attractions. Its vast tanks are home to thousands of sea creatures, from water-spitting archer fish and gruesome-looking eels to multi-coloured corals and translucent floating jellyfish. It's arranged according to habitat and region, with displays on freshwater rivers, coral reefs, tidal mangrove swamps and rainforests, as well as the Indian, Pacific and Atlantic Oceans. The prime attractions, of course, are the sharks, which swim around the Pacific tank (they are fed on Tuesday, Thursdays and Saturdays at 2.30pm).

More serene pleasures can be found at the touch pool where visitors can stroke the resident rays. Children, who usually need little encouragement to get their hands wet and touch things, love this. Do make sure, however, that they treat the rays gently, remembering the untimely death of Steve Irwin.

Dotted in among the tanks are a number of interactive terminals where more can be learned about the aquarium's inhabitants. There are touch-screen quizzes and short-play videos in which cartoon sea creatures explain themselves and their environment to children.

More information can be gleaned at the free daily talks given by the aquarium's keepers at the Coral Reef and Pacific Tank (where the sharks live).

Namco Station

County Hall, Riverside Building, Westminster Bridge Road, SE1 t (020) 7967 1067
www.namcoexperience.com
Open 10am–12 midnight, daily
Adm Free (although each game costs £1–£2)

This arcade-ridden labyrinth is packed with hundreds of video games and simulators as well as a full-size car-racing game, bowls, dodgems and pool.

Florence Nightingale Museum

2 Lambeth Palace Road, SE1 t (020) 7620 0374
www.florence-nightingale.co.uk
Θ/ ⇌ Waterloo
Bus 12, 53, 76, 77, 148, 159, 211, 431, 381, 507
Open Mon–Fri 10–5, Sat–Sun 10.30–4.30 (last entry one hour before closing)
Adm Adult £5.80, child and concs £4.20, family £13

A wonderful place to bring aspiring medics. The museum tells the story of Florence Nightingale, the founder of modern nursing, using reconstructions, such as a ward scene from the Crimean War where 'the lady with the lamp' tends to the wounded. The museum is very much geared towards kids, so there are lots of audiovisual displays, including a short film on Florence's healthcare achievements. Free family events the second weekend of each month.

★Imperial War Museum

Lambeth Road, SE1 t (020) 7416 5000
Infoline t 0900 1600 140
www.london.iwm.org.uk
Θ Lambeth North, Elephant & Castle
Bus 1, 3, 12, 45, 53, 55, 63, 68, 100, 159, 168, 171, 172, 176, 188, 344, C10
Open 10–6, daily **Adm Free**

Upon catching sight of the 38cm (15in) naval guns by the entrance, you could be forgiven for thinking that this is a place that glorifies war and treats it as some gung-ho 'Boys Own' adventure. Quite the opposite – the museum is largely dedicated to exploring and demonstrating the human experience of war; the lives of the ordinary men and women charged with settling the arguments of nations on the battlefield. There are some impressive items of hardware to look at in the large central hall, including tanks, planes, one-man submarines and even a 9m (30ft) Polaris missile, but the museum never loses sight of the very real cost of conflict. For every piece of dazzling equipment, there's a more sobering exhibit – the Trench Experience, for instance, is an affecting recreation of the life of a foot soldier on the Western Front in the First World War, while the Blitz Experience lets you see what conditions were like for Londoners during the Second World War, huddled in shelters under the streets as Hitler's bombs rained down.

The exhibition on the Holocaust is perhaps the most moving of all, but is not recommended for children under 14. It charts the rise of Hitler and the Nazi party through to the horror of the Final Solution.

Until 2008, the museum will be hosting 'The Children's War', an exhibit that aims to explore the experience of the Second World War, as recalled by the children who lived through it. So the displays deal with matters that most affected children – evacuation (the mass evacuation of children at the start of the war was Britain's largest migration of people), rationing (kids were allowed 57g (2oz) of sweets a week – the equivalent of one small 'party-sized' chocolate bar) and school. There's also a replica wartime house to explore. See also p.50.

There's a good proportion of interactive exhibits – you can clamber around the cockpits of some of the fighter planes, take the controls of a fighter plane simulator or watch archive footage on touch-screen TV terminals. Children's trails are available at reception and there are workshops in the school holidays, including very popular 'In Their

Evacuation

When Britain declared war on Germany on 3 September 1939, Londoners began preparing for the worst. It would surely only be a matter of time, they reasoned, before the German air force began bombing raids on the city (it actually took over a year) and it was therefore crucial that the capital's children (up to age 15) were quickly evacuated to safer parts of the country. Soon London's stations were bidding farewell to train after train packed to bursting with children heading out to new lives in the countryside, each carrying with them just their bare essentials packed in a bag or case, a gas mask and a label with their name on it. Of course, finding places for all the children to stay (not to mention the blind and disabled people, teachers and helpers who were also evacuated) proved to be no easy task. The sheer numbers involved meant that there was no way of guaranteeing which child went where, with the result that many middle-class kids found themselves in labourers' cottages while slum children were billeted in stately homes – no bad thing: in this way, the evacuation process helped to foster a level of social integration that would have been impossible outside wartime. For some it proved to be a frightening and unhappy experience, although others, with fresh food to eat and space to run around in, saw it more as a holiday.

The Blitz

The deliberate and systematic bombing of London by the German airforce, or 'Luftwaffe', began on the afternoon of Sunday 7 September 1940. Squadron after squadron hit the East End where the warehouses at Surrey Docks, filled with rubber, paint and rum, were soon ablaze. That night the Luftwaffe struck again and by the dawn of 8 September, 448 Londoners had lost their lives. The 'Blitz', as it came to be known, had begun and continued unabated for the next 76 days, during which time vast swathes of the capital were flattened and thousands of lives lost. There were, however, some miraculous escapes along the way. Buckingham Palace was hit but escaped relatively undamaged, while St Paul's Cathedral, despite the destruction around it, survived the bombing virtually intact and became a symbol of London's defiance. Night after night, Londoners took cover in steel shelters or on the platforms of the Underground stations as the German planes attempted to crush their morale in preparation for a land invasion. Much to the Nazis' chagrin, however, the bombing, if anything, served to stiffen British resolve to resist the enemy at all costs. Even so, London paid a heavy price for its brave resistance. Over the next four years 20,000 people were killed in the air raids and a further 25,000 were wounded.

Shoes' days when kids (under supervision) are invited to handle artefacts from the collection in order to try and work out the stories behind them.

Afterwards, it may be a relief to take a walk to the Tibetan Peace Garden just outside, which was opened by His Holiness The Dalai Lama in 1999.

South Bank Arts Centre

The South Bank, SE1 t (020) 7921 0600
www.southbankcentre.org.uk
⊖ Waterloo, Embankment ≋ Waterloo
Bus 1, 4, 26, 68, 76, 77, 168, 171, 172, 176, 188, 211, 341, 381, 501, 507, 521, RV1, X68

One of the world's great art complexes, the South Bank comprises, at present, the Royal Festival Hall, the Queen Elizabeth Hall, the National Film Theatre, the Hayward Gallery and the Royal National Theatre. Together, they put on a range of events suitable for families throughout the year including dance classes, concerts by youth orchestras, ballet performances, theatre shows

and poetry sessions. There are often outdoor events by the riverbank in summer too.

Hayward Gallery

t (020) 7690 4242 www.hayward.org.uk
Open Daily 10–6, Wed and Thurs until 8pm
Adm Varies, depending on the exhibition

The Hayward has no permanent exhibition, but puts on a series of temporary shows throughout the year, with children's art trails and activities attached wherever possible. It often organizes art and photographic workshops for children in the holidays as well (usually for over-12s). Regular activities are held for younger children on Sunday afternoons. The shop has a good range of art and activity books for children

Walks

The South Bank is the place for a family walk along the Thames. You can walk the Millennium Mile (p.69) all the way to Tate Modern (p.55).

Southwark

Boat trips

You can catch a boat from outside Tate Modern (Bankside) up river to Tate Britain (Millbank) (p.65).

Bramah Tea & Coffee Museum

40 Southwark Street, SE1 **t** (020) 7403 5650
www.bramahmuseum.co.uk
⊖/ ≋ London Bridge **Bus** 15, 25, 42, 78, 100, 381, RV1
Open Daily 10–6
Adm Adult £4, children, £3, family (2+4) £10

Relocated from Butler's Wharf, this charming little museum details the history of the country's two favourite (non-alcoholic) beverages. Children will like the extraordinary collection of more than 1,000 teapots and coffee-makers, which come in all shapes and sizes – dragons, monsters, lions, pillar-boxes and even policemen. Head for the café to sample one of the museum's own blends.

Clink Museum

1 Clink Street, SE1 **t** (020) 7403 6515 www.clink.co.uk
⊖/ ≋ London Bridge **Bus** 17, 95, 149, 184
Open Daily 10–6
Adm Adult £4, child £3, family £10

The museum attempts to recreate the scenes of the medieval Clink Prison, which stood on this spot in the Middle Ages. Although the prison building was demolished in 1780, the name 'the Clink' has survived to this day as a nickname for all prisons. It's divided into a number of cells, each inhabited by some rather unhappy-looking mannequins undergoing some form of medieval torture – the Stocks, the Fure and the Cage among them.

Design Museum

28 Shad Thames, Butler's Wharf, SE1
t (020) 7940 8790 www.designmuseum.org
⊖ London Bridge, Tower Hill
Bus 15, 42, 47, 78, 100, 188, P11
Open Daily 10–6
Adm Adults £6, children £4, under-12s **free**, family £16

The museum's purpose is to explain why various ordinary, everyday objects – such as telephones, vacuum cleaners, toothbrushes and cars – look the way they do, examining them from both a func-tional and an aesthetic perspective. You can sit in some of the outlandish chairs of yesteryear. There's a good shop selling books, gadgets and design classics and an attractive (but expensive) café, Blueprint. 'Design Action Packs' and a 'Spot the

Building' game to identify famous surrounding landmarks (St Paul's, the Gherkin) are available free. Design workshops for 6–12-year-olds are held on Saturday and Sunday afternoons, where kids can turn their hands to anything from hat- and mask-making to animation.

The *Golden Hinde*

St Mary Overie Dock, Cathedral Street, SE1
t 0870 011 8700 www.goldenhinde.co.uk
⊖/ ≋ London Bridge **Bus** 17, 95, 149, 184
Open Call in advance
Adm Adults £3.50, children £2.50, family £10; guided tours: adults £4.50, children £3.50, family £15; Overnight Living History Experiences: £39.95 per person; Workshops: £12 for first child, £10 per additional child

This full-size replica of the 16th-century ship on which Sir Francis Drake became the first Englishman to circumnavigate the globe sits in dry dock, just back from the riverfront. There are five levels to explore including Drake's cabin and a 14-cannon gun deck. As the children roam the ship, the crew, dressed in Tudor costume, will entertain them with tales of adventure and treachery on the high seas. The vessel is fully functioning and has sailed the Atlantic several times since it was built in 1973, clocking up more than 10,000 miles (16,000km) at sea. It's available for children's parties, and school groups or families are invited to attend the ship's Overnight Living History Experiences, which run from 5pm until 10am the next day. During this time the whole family is expected to assume the roles of a crew of Tudor sailors: performing shipboard tasks, eating Tudor food and sleeping in the cabins on the lower decks. 'Drama', 'Pirate' and 'Tudor' workshops are also available.

HMS *Belfast*

Morgan's Lane, off Tooley Street, SE1 **t** (020) 7940 6300 www.hmsbelfast.iwm.org.uk
⊖/ ≋ London Bridge
Bus 21, 35, 40, 43, 47, 48, 133, 381
Open Mar–Oct daily 10–6 daily, Nov–Feb 10–5
Adm Adult £8, under-16s **free**

This huge, heavily armed, heavily armoured cruiser was used during the D-Day landings, the invasion of Normandy in 1944 that finally turned the progress of the Second World War in the Allies' favour. These days it's a kind of floating nautical museum, moored permanently between London

Bridge and Tower Bridge. Children love running around the ship's clunking metal decks, looking down the barrels of the huge naval guns, manoeuvring the lighter anti-aircraft guns and exploring the seven floors of narrow corridors.

London Dungeon

Tooley Street, SE1 t (020) 7403 7221
www.thedungeons.com
⊖/ ≋ London Bridge **Bus** 10, 44, 48, 70, 133
Open Nov–Mar 10.30–5, Apr–mid-Jul and Sept–Oct 10–5.30, mid-Jul–Aug 10–7.30
Adm Adults £12.95, children (under 14) £9.95, under-5s **free**

In the dark, candlelit 'dungeon' (actually a series of railway arches next to London Bridge Station), you'll find a series of gruesome waxwork tableaux depicting some of the more grisly episodes from British history: a human sacrifice by druids at Stonehenge; Boadicea stabbing a Roman soldier to death; Anne Boleyn having her head chopped off; blotchy, bloated victims of the Black Death in 1666 and the manacled maniacs of Newgate Prison. The highlight, however, is a recreation of the life and times of London's most notorious serial killer, Jack the Ripper.

The Millennium Bridge

Designed by Norman Foster, Anthony Caro and the engineering firm Arup, this elegant walkway linking Tate Modern with St Paul's had a shaky start: as the first people walked across the bridge, it started to wobble so alarmingly it was closed. It's now stable, and provides great views up and down the Thames, not to mention easy access to the City.

Old Operating Theatre

9a St Thomas Street, SE1 t (020) 7955 4791
www.thegarret.org.uk
⊖/ ≋ London Bridge
Bus 17, 21, 22a, 35, 40, 43, 47, 48, 133, 343, 344, RV1
Open Daily 10–5
Adm Adults £4.25, children £2.60, under-8s **free**, family (2+2) £11

The country's only surviving example of an early 19th-century operating theatre is thick with atmosphere and a very real sense of horror. You can see the gruesome medical equipment used for amputations (the most common form of surgery), the operating table (actually a wooden board that held screaming patients upright) and various pickled bits of unlucky patients in jars.

★Shakespeare's Globe Theatre

Bear Gardens, Bankside, New Globe Walk, Southwark, SE1 t (020) 7902 1400
www.shakespeares-globe.org.uk
⊖/ ≋ London Bridge
Bus 11, 15, 17, 23, 26, 45, 63, 76, 100, 344, 381, RV1
Open Daily 10–5; call for tour and performance times
Adm Museum: adults £8, children £5.50, under-5s **free**, family (2+3) £24; 'Child's Play' Workshops £10

The Globe is a perfect modern recreation of the Elizabethan theatre where Shakespeare premièred many of his most famous plays, including *Othello*, *Macbeth* and *Romeo and Juliet*. The original theatre burnt down in 1613 during a performance of *Henry VIII*, when an ember from a stage cannon set fire to the thatched roof.

You can take a guided tour of the new Globe (completed in the mid-1990s), visit the multimedia museum which explains the history of the Globe (old and new) or watch a performance of a Shakespeare play almost as his contemporaries would have done: seated on wooden benches or standing in the open in front of the stage. This can add to the atmosphere at performances, but can also serve to obscure children's views.

Children aged 8–11 can take part in Saturday afternoon 'Child's Play' workshops at the Globe's Education Centre (booking essential), which involve drama, storytelling and art.

Shakespearean theatre

Welcome to the bad side of town... In the 16th century, when the first Globe theatre was built, this was the area of town frequented by the city's reprobates and ne'er do wells – where people came to indulge in bawdy, rowdy entertainments such as drinking and gambling, bear and bull baiting, cock and dog fighting (any sort of mayhem with animals seems to have been particularly popular) and, of course, going to the theatre. While, today, we often regard theatre-going as something rather refined and elegant, in Shakespeare's day it was a much more rough and ready form of entertainment. The audiences at Shakespeare's plays were a particularly rowdy lot. Mostly drunk, they were determined to enjoy the show, and would cheer for the goodies, hiss for the baddies and pitch rotten food at the stage (and each other) if they were unhappy with the performance. Booing, catcalls and merriment are still very much part of the fun.

Tate Modern

Bankside, SE1 **t** (020) 7887 8000 **www.tate.org.uk**
⊖/ ≷ London Bridge, Blackfriars
Bus Bus 11, 15, 17, 23, 26, 45, 63, 76, 100, 344, 381, RV1
Open Sun–Thurs 10–6, Fri and Sat 10–10
Adm Free

Tate Modern was one of the unqualified success stories of the Millennium year and has been packing them in ever since the day it opened. Housed in the former Bankside power station, the collection is arranged around a vast turbine hall that serves as both entrance and exhibition space. Make sure you come in by the main entrance at the side for the full 'wow!' effect.

Inside, the museum has a mighty 9,290 sq m (100,000 sq ft) of display space dedicated to modern international works from the 19th century to the present day. That's a lot of art, but don't be put off. There are actually only four (very large) galleries to explore and there are lightweight collapsible stools for you to carry round and have a break whenever you need it. The galleries are arranged thematically rather than chronologically, with umbrella topics ('History/Memory/Society' and 'Nude/Action/Body') used to trace links and resonances between artists. Much of the work on show, such as Marcel Duchamp's *Fountain* (actually a urinal) and Carl Andre's *Equivalent VIII* (a pile of bricks), are the kind of works of art that the British public love to hate, although there are also many famous works by more 'traditional' artists such as Bacon, Dali, Freud, Hockney, Matisse, Picasso, Pollock, Rothko, Spencer and Warhol.

Tate Modern provides plenty of resources to help families understand and involve themselves in the collection. Free activity sheets, which encourage kids to draw their own impressions of the collection, and Family and Explorer Trails, which offer themed routes for ages 3 and over, are available. You can also hire a special children's audiotour (aimed at 8–12-year-olds), narrated by the celebrated children's author Michael Rosen from the audiotour desk on level 1 (£2). The gallery also organizes a programme of art-related activities for children including 'Start', a drop-in event on Sundays (11–5) in school holidays aimed at providing a basic introduction to art for under-5s, and Tate Tales, which offers storytelling and word games for ages 5 and over. Teenagers may be interested in the gallery's 'Raw Canvas' summer school courses for budding young artists aged 15–23.

Before leaving, head to the top floor, where the café offers wonderful views of the river, St Paul's and Millennium Bridge. At the shop on the ground floor you can pick up Tate memorabilia and art books.

Tate Modern is linked to Tate Britain by a ferry service from the pier outside (p.65).

Tower Bridge Exhibition

London Bridge, Fenchurch Street **t** (020) 7403 3761
www.towerbridge.org.uk
⊖ Tower Hill, London Bridge
Bus 15, 25 (Sat/Sun), 42, 78, 100, RV1
Open Daily 9.30–6 (last entry 5)
Adm Adults £5.50, children £3, under-5s **free**, family (2+2) £14

With its fairytale turrets and huge decks, which raise to let tall ships pass through, this is easily London's most recognizable and popular bridge. At the Tower Bridge Exhibition you can see the steam-powered machinery that was used to raise the decks in Victorian times (these days the bridge relies on hydraulics and electricity) and climb the 200 steps (or take the lift) to the covered walkway that runs along the top of the bridge some 46m (150ft) above the Thames. From here you can enjoy spectacular views up and down the river. Look out, in particular, for the new Greater London Authority building next to the bridge, which looks a bit like an enormous glass paperweight. The bridge is still raised at least once a day; you can find out exactly when by calling **t** (020) 7940 3984.

Family activities are put on throughout the year.

Walks

Try the walk along the river to the South Bank or take a Globe Walkshop (pp.68–9)

Did you know?
▶ That each bridge deck weighs an astonishing 1,000 tonnes? That's as much as 200 elephants.
▶ That the 'proper' name for one of Tower Bridge's decks is a 'bascule'.
▶ That in 1952 a double decker bus had to jump a three foot gap between the opening bridge decks when the traffic lights didn't turn red?
▶ That the bridge took eight years to build? It was completed in 1894.
▶ That the bridge was deliberately designed to look 'ancient', so as not to look out of place next to the very old Tower of London?

The City

Bank of England Museum

Threadneedle Street, EC2, entrance on
Bartholomew Lane t (020) 7601 5545
www.bankofengland.co.uk
✆ Bank, Cannon Street **Bus** 9, 11, 22
Open Mon–Fri 10–5 **Adm Free**

See how financial transactions have developed
from paper IOUs to whizzing numbers on a
computer screen. The curators have obviously
thought long and hard about how to make a rather
dry subject interesting for children. So there are
waxwork bankers, lots of interactive video screens
and, the highlight, a large Perspex pyramid filled
with gold bars. Activity sheets for kids (5–8, 9–12
and 13–16-year-olds) available from the front desk.

Boat trips

You can catch a boat from Tower Pier down to
Greenwich or up to Waterloo or Westminster
(pp.64–5).

Cinemas and theatres

One of London's major arts centres, the Barbican
has a family film club (p.73) and also puts on free
foyer concerts as well as special children's events
and performances in the school holidays (p.78).

Geffrye Museum

Kingsland Road, E2 t (020) 7739 9893
www.geffrye-museum.org.uk
✆ Old Street (south exit 8) ≋ Dalston Kingsland
Bus 67, 149, 242, 243
Open Tues–Sat 10–5, Sun 12 noon–5 **Adm Free**

Housed in a row of 18th-century almshouses, this
museum is dedicated to the evolution of Britain's
living rooms. It contains dozens of reconstructed
interiors from Tudor times to the present day. The
museum holds imaginative workshops for kids on
such diverse topics as wig-making, enamelling and
block printing. Occasional storytelling sessions.

The Monument

Monument Street, EC3 t (020) 7626 2717
✆ Monument **Bus** 15, 22a, 35, 40, 48
Open 9.30–5, daily **Adm** Adults £2, children £1,
under-5s **free**

If the Monument were to fall over, its top
(provided it fell in the right direction) would land
on the very spot in Pudding Lane where the Fire of
London broke out in the early hours of 2 September
1666. It was designed by Sir Christopher Wren as a

The Great Fire

Just as London was recovering from the horrors
of the Bubonic Plague, which ravaged the population in 1665, killing an estimated 100,000 people, a
new terror struck in the early hours of the morning
of 2 September 1666, when a fire broke out at
Farynor's bakery in Pudding Lane. At first no one
took it seriously: 'A woman could put it out,'
sneered one observer and went back to bed. He
was grossly mistaken. The warm, breezy night
fanned the flames which raced along, easily
consuming the timber-framed buildings of old
London. By morning London Bridge and 300 houses
were ablaze. People thronged the streets, desper-
ately trying to douse the fire with tiny water
pumps, designed for small domestic fires. Teams of
Londoners heroically destroyed buildings in the
path of the fire to starve it of fuel. Yet the flames
blazed on. Terrified, some ran naked from their
beds and plunged into the Thames. Hundreds
huddled on barges on the Thames. A few climbed
up inside church spires, only to be burned alive in
their ill-chosen sanctuaries. Four days later, when
the fire finally blew itself out, 13,200 houses,
44 livery halls and 87 churches, including old St
Paul's, had gone up in smoke. Two-thirds of London
had become a filthy, smouldering wasteland, its
citizens roaming the charred streets in search of
old homes and lost loved ones. Amazingly, though
the physical destruction was on a terrible scale,
only 18 people perished in the fire. And what
followed was a determination to build a cleaner,
safer London to replace the old plague-ridden city.

memorial for the victims of the Fire. At 62m (202ft)
high it was, on completion in 1677, the tallest free-
standing column in the world. You can climb the
311 steps to the top to get a close-up look at the
great bronze urn that sits on the monument's
summit spouting shiny metallic flames.

Museum of London

London Wall, EC2 t 0870 444 3851
www.museumoflondon.org.uk
✆ Barbican, Bank, St Paul's **Bus** 8, 22b, 56
Open Tues–Sat 10–6, Sun 12 noon–6 **Adm Free**

From prehistoric camps to concrete tower blocks,
the museum tells the story of life in the nation's
capital. It may not have the range of one of the
great Kensington collections, but this is still a
lovely little museum with a charm and style all of

its own. It has created some wonderful scale models that vividly illustrate the stages of London's history: a mammoth hunt, a Viking ship, Shakespeare's Rose Theatre and London during the Great Fire, each rendered in perfect miniature. There are also a number of restored and reconstructed interiors: a Roman kitchen, a Stuart dining room, a cell from the infamous Newgate Prison and a 1920s shop interior. Also on show, for 364 days of the year, is the ornate Lord Mayor's state coach.

The museum is constantly expanding as new building sites are excavated, uncovering hoards of Roman antiquities (from jewellery to kitchenware). It tries hard to make history come alive for its younger visitors, with artefact handling sessions at weekends, and school-holiday workshops, demonstrations and performances for children on subjects from metalwork to preparing Roman food.

St Paul's Cathedral

St Paul's Churchyard, EC4 **t** (020) 7236 4128
www.stpauls.co.uk
⊖ St Paul's, Mansion House
Bus 4, 8, 11, 15, 17, 23, 25, 26, 56, 76, 172, 242, 501, 521
Open Mon–Sat 8.30–4.30, Sun for religious services only **Adm** Adults £8, children £3.50, family (2+2) £19 (**free** for religious services)

St Paul's Cathedral, with its great dome dominating the city skyline, is undoubtedly one of London's most recognizable landmarks. Unfortunately much of the building may still be obscured behind scaffolding for renovations (due for completion in 2008, the 300th anniversary of its construction). It's still well worth a visit. It's a great place for kids to come and burn off some excess energy. The 521-step climb, though hard on the thighs, is worth it. The panoramic views from the top of the dome, 111m (365ft) up, are stupendous. You can see more or less the whole of London stretched out before you like a great 3D tapestry.

Designed by Sir Christopher Wren and built in the late 17th century after the original, wooden cathedral burnt down in the Great Fire in 1666, St Paul's is arguably London's most beautiful church. Feast your eyes on the fantastically decorated interior, particularly the massive domed ceiling. About halfway up the inside of the dome is the Whispering Gallery. You can put its name to the test by doing the following: stand on one side of the Gallery while a friend goes over to the other. Now, providing it's quiet enough, you should be

> **Q:** The Lord Mayor's gold coach resides in the museum for 364 days of the year. Where is it on the remaining day?
> **A:** Parading through the streets of London as part of the Lord Mayor's Show (p.36)

able to whisper something to the wall on your side and have your friend hear it quite clearly on the other, 33m (107ft) away.

In the crypt (the largest in Europe), you'll find the tombs of many of Britain's greatest military leaders – Admiral Nelson (his coffin is made out of the main mast of the flagship of the French fleet that was defeated at the Battle of Trafalgar in 1805) and the Duke of Wellington (who beat Napoleon at the Battle of Waterloo in 1815) among them – as well as one of Wren's original models of the cathedral (he made three in the design process). There's also a shop, restaurant, and a great, child-friendly café.

Sport and activities

For ice-skating fans, check out Broadgate Arena right by Liverpool Street Station (p.70).

Tower of London

Tower Hill, EC3 **t** 0870 756 6060 **www.hrp.org.uk**
⊖ Tower Hill **Bus** 15, 25, 42, 78, 100, D1
Open Mar–Oct Mon–Sat 9–6, Sun 10–6; Nov–Feb Tues–Sat 9–5, Sun–Mon 10–5
Adm Adult £13.50, child £9, family (2+3) £37.50
Limited pushchair access

Murders, executions, assassinations, conspiracies and betrayals – the Tower of London has seen them all. So that kids get the most out of their visit here, it's important that they know a little of the history. An old building is not particularly interesting in itself, but if children are told that this is the building in which two princes were murdered and bricked up behind a wall, perhaps by their wicked uncle so that he would become king instead of them, it suddenly becomes much more exciting. The famous Yeoman Warders or 'Beefeaters' come in very handy in this regard, as they are generally more than willing to regale children with tales of intrigue and murder.

At around 900 years old, the Tower is one of London's oldest major landmarks, and also one of the best-preserved medieval castles in the world. The White Tower, at its heart, was built by William the Conqueror soon after his invasion of England in 1066 in order to shore up his position and provide a stronghold against future rebellions. It was to prove a great success; its massive 4.5m (15ft) walls have never been breached. The Tower has not always served a purely defensive role, however. In the 16th and 17th centuries it proved just as good at keeping people in as it had been at keeping them out. You can visit the spot on Tower Green where the teenage Lady Jane Grey, Walter Raleigh and Anne Boleyn all met their grisly ends – and grisly, in this instance, really means grisly. The sword blow that killed Anne Boleyn, Henry VIII's second wife, was delivered with such speed that her lips supposedly continued to recite a prayer after her head had been removed.

The Tower's fantastic security record led to it being entrusted with the safekeeping of the nation's most precious treasure – the Crown Jewels. You can see them at the Jewel House, where you are carried past the priceless crowns, sceptres and orbs on a moving walkway. Look out for the Cullinans I and II, the largest top-quality cut diamonds in the world.

Elsewhere in the Tower you'll find Edward I's medieval palace, where guides dressed in period costume will demonstrate crafts such as calligraphy and quill-making; the Armouries, where there's a display of miniature suits of armour made for royal children (presumably the medieval equivalent of a modern millionaire giving their child a miniature Ferrari), and the White Tower where there's a display of grisly torture instruments. It was here that Guy Fawkes confessed to having tried to blow up James I (only after his legs and arms were almost pulled off on the rack). Do also look out for the Tower's most famous residents, the shiny black ravens which live in the Tower Gardens (although be sure to keep your distance as they can get a bit grumpy). According to legend, if the ravens ever leave the Tower, it, and the country, will topple.

The Tower is one of the most popular sites in London; if you're visiting in summer, you'll have to queue (get there early to beat the rush). Family trail booklets are available at the main gate and, during the school holidays, the Tower organizes a whole range of free family activities (having your children locked up is not an option).

Walks

As the oldest part of London, the City is an excellent place to take a guided walking tour (pp.68–9).

Greenwich

Boat trips

Arriving at Greenwich by boat is a great option if you have the time.
For further information *see* pp.64–5

The *Cutty Sark*

King William Walk, SE10 **t** (020) 8858 3445
www.cuttysark.org.uk
≥ Greenwich, **DLR** Greenwich, Cutty Sark
Bus 53, 54, 177, 180, 188, 199, 286, 380, 386
Open Daily 10–5 (last entry 4.30)
Adm Adults and children £4.25, family £10.50, under-5s **free**

In her time, the *Cutty Sark* was the world's fastest sailing ship, able to sail the round-Africa journey from Shanghai to London in a record 107 days. Sadly, the advent of steam-powered boats in the late 1800s, coupled with the opening of the Suez Canal, made her redundant. Such was her fame, however, that she was never dismantled, and is now the only surviving tea clipper in the world. You can explore her decks and cabins and learn all about her illustrious history through a display of pictures and models.

Gypsy Moth IV

King William Walk, SE10 **t** (020) 8858 2698
Open Easter–Oct Mon–Sat 10–6, Sun 12 noon–6 (last entry 5.30) **Adm** Adults 50p, children 30p

Next to the *Cutty Sark* stands the tiny, 16m (54ft) yacht in which Sir Francis Chichester sailed single-handedly around the world in 1966–7. In honour of his achievement, he was knighted with the same sword with which Elizabeth I had knighted Sir Francis Drake (the first Englishman to circumnavigate the globe) some 300 years earlier.

National Maritime Museum

Romney Road, Greenwich, SE10 **t** (020) 8858 4422
Infoline **t** (020) 8312 6565 **www.nmm.ac.uk**
≥ Greenwich, **DLR** Greenwich, Cutty Sark
Bus 53, 54, 177, 180, 188, 199, 207, 286, 380, 386,
Open Sept–Jun daily 10–5 (last entry 4.30), Jul–Aug 10–6 (last entry 5.30) **Adm** Free

The National Maritime Museum is a favourite family museum, and has always been good at sparking off controversy. After years of criticism that its exhibitions were too 'triumphalist', the creation of a more questioning 'Trade and Empire Gallery' led to the curators being accused of portraying the British Empire in an unremittingly hostile light. Certainly, the exhibition tries to show the spread of the Empire not just from view of the conquering British, but also from the vantage point of the conquered, who saw things differently.

Besides this controversial exhibition, there are galleries dedicated to 'Explorers', 'Passengers' and 'Hidden Treasures', all filled with great nautical exhibits to explore and study, including reconstructed engine rooms, boat decks and cabin interiors. There's also a special 'All Hands' children's area on the third floor, where kids can experience 'pulling flags', 'firing cannons', sending morse code messages and learning how to steer a Viking long-boat. For a little touch of gore, pop into the Nelson Gallery where you can see the bloodstained uniform worn by the famous Admiral during his final battle at Trafalgar in 1805 (see p.43 for more on this famous nautical encounter). The museum runs regulars 'Shipmates' sessions at the week-ends, in which children aged 7 and over can learn more about the lives and skills of sailors through a series of interactive workshops. Their younger siblings, meanwhile, can enjoy 'Crowsnest' storytelling sessions. Special events for families, themed around the museum's temporary exhibitions, are also put on in summer. Activity trails are available from the front desk.

Parks and gardens

As you head up to the Observatory, take time to stop and enjoy Greenwich Park (p.66).

Royal Naval College

King William Walk, SE10 **t** (020) 8269 4747
www.greenwichfoundation.org.uk
≋ Greenwich, **DLR** Greenwich, Cutty Sark
Bus 53, 54, 177, 180, 188, 199, 286, 380, 386
Open Daily 10–5 **Adm Free**

With its grand classical façades overlooking the river, the Royal Naval College provides an elegant first sight of Greenwich to anyone arriving from the riverside. The building is the work of three of Britain's most famous architects: Sir Christopher Wren, Nicholas Hamilton and Sir John Vanbrugh, and was originally used as a hospital for disabled sailors before being turned into a college in 1873. The chapel and Painted Hall are open to the public. Their fabulously painted interiors were designed by James Thornhill, who also decorated the dome of St Paul's (p.57). In between the Royal Naval College's façades stands the Queen's House, an earlier Italianate palace designed by Inigo Jones.

The search for longitude

Until the late 18th century nobody knew how to measure longitude – the distance east or west around the earth. People could work out latitude (the distance north or south) using the position of the pole star, but no such system existed for longitude. In 1754, the government put up a reward of £20,000 for anyone who could come up with a solution. The reward was finally claimed, in 1772, by a clockmaker called John Harrison. He constructed a clock which could measure time accurately at sea, and so permit navigators to calculate a ship's east-west position to within 30 miles (48km).

Royal Observatory

Greenwich Park, SE10 **t** (020) 8858 4422
Infoline **t** (020) 8312 6565 **www.**rog.nmm.ac.uk
≋ Greenwich, **DLR** Greenwich, Cutty Sark
Bus 53, 54, 177, 180, 188, 199, 202, 286, 380, 386
Open Daily 10–5 (last entry 4.30)
Adm Free to Observatory; Planetarium shows: adults £4, children £2

Just behind the Royal Naval College, the Royal Observatory stands on the Greenwich Meridian, the official dividing line between east and west, declared to be 0° degrees longitude. The line is marked out so you can stand with one foot in the western hemisphere and the other in the east. In 1884 the observatory was given the task of setting the time for the whole world, and Greenwich Mean Time (GMT) is still the standard against which all other times are measured. Every day at exactly 1pm, a red timeball on the Observatory roof drops to allow passing ships to set their clocks accurately.

The observatory, built in the late 17th century by Sir Christopher Wren, today houses the country's largest refracting telescope; a compelling attraction for anyone interested in the cosmos. You can visit the apartments of the Astronomers Royal and find out how astronomy has developed, attend a 'space show' in the dome or try some astronomical experiments at the children's 'science station'. The observatory organizes free 'drop-in' science events for children between 2 and 4pm every Saturday, as well as longer summer workshops where they can learn more about astronomy and make their own basic astronomical equipment.

Shopping

For details of Greenwich's excellent weekend markets, see p.61.

SHOPPING

London is one of the world's great shopping centres, with an outlet for every kind of taste. Children are particuarly well catered for, although it is beyond the scope of this guide to provide a comprehensive list. Below is a selection of the best of children's shopping in the capital, with the emphasis on one-off stores rather than chains.

Arts, crafts & hobbies

The Bead Shop
21a Tower Street WC2, **t** (020) 7240 0931
www.beadworks.co.uk
⊖ Covent Garden
Bus 6, 9, 11, 13, 15, 23, 77A, 91, 176
Open Mon 1–6, Tues–Fri 10.30–6.30, Sat 11.30–5
 Stocked with coloured baubles and beads, the Bead Shop, near Covent Garden, provides the essentials for kids to make their own jewellery.

Comet Miniatures
44–48 Lavender Hill, SW11 **t** (020) 7228 3702
www.comet-miniatures.co.uk
⇝ Clapham Junction **Bus** 77, 77A, 345
Open Mon–Sat 9.30–5.30
 A haven of hobbydom, Comet sells all manner of collectibles from rare Japanese toys to film figures, as well as thousands of aircraft kits.

Kite Store
48 Neal Street, WC2
t (020) 7836 1666 ⊖ Covent Garden
Bus 6, 9, 11, 13, 15, 23, 77A, 91, 176
Open Mon–Wed, Fri– Sat 10–6, Thurs 10–7
 Every size, shape and colour of kite imaginable, plus aerobatic toys including boomerangs, yo-yos and water-powered rockets.

St Martins Accessories
95 St Martin's Lane, WC2
t (020) 7836 9742 **www.stmartinsmodelcars.co.uk**
⊖ Covent Garden **Bus** 6, 9, 11, 13, 15, 23, 77A, 91, 176
Open Mon–Fri 9.30–6, Sat 11–5
 Everything the model car enthusiast could want: racks of sporting classics – Ferraris, Porsches, Aston Martins and more – in perfect miniature detail.

Stanley Gibbons
399 The Strand, WC2
t (020) 7836 8444 **www.stanleygibbons.com**
⊖ Charing Cross **Bus** 6, 9, 11, 13, 15, 23, 77A, 91, 17
Open Mon–Fri 9–5.30, Sat 9.30–5.30
 A mecca for stamp collectors. Why not start a collection with a £1 mixed bag of stamps?

Books & comics

The dominant bookselling chains (Waterstone's, Borders and Books Etc.) all have good children's sections. For a change of tempo, try anarchic Foyle's in Charing Cross Road, where tracking down a book is an adventure. The flagship Waterstone's on Piccadilly is Europe's largest bookshop, with cafés and juice bars as well as a bewildering range of books on several storeys. Dedicated children's book-shops and comic stores in central London include:

Children's Book Centre
237 Kensington High Street, W8 **t** (020) 7937 7497
www.childrensbookcentre.co.uk
⊖ High Street Kensington **Bus** 9, 10, 27, 28, 33, 49
Open Mon, Wed, Fri–Sat 9.30–6.30, Tues 9.30–6, Thurs 9.30–7, Sun 12 noon–6

Comic Showcase
63 Charing Cross Road, WC2 **t** (020) 7434 4349
⊖ Covent Garden **Bus** 6, 9, 11, 13, 15, 23, 77A, 91, 176
Open Mon–Wed 10–6, Thurs–Sat 10–7

Forbidden Planet
179 Shaftesbury Avenue, WC2 **t** (020) 7420 3666
⊖ Tottenham Court Road, Covent Garden
Bus 14, 19, 24, 29, 38, 176
Open Mon–Fri 10–7 (Thurs until 8), Sat 12–6
 A must for sci-fi fans.

Gosh! Comics
39 Great Russell Street, WC1 **t** (020) 7636 1011
⊖ Tottenham Court Road **Bus** 7
Open 10–6, Thurs–Fri 10–7
Open Mon–Sat 9–5.30, Sun 11–5
 Catch up on the exploits of your favourite super-heroes. Also sells cartoon strip compilations.

Clothes & shoes

Chainstores such as Marks & Spencers, H&M, Mothercare, Next, Gap and Clarks (for shoes) are the sensible places to shop for children's clothes. Here is a selection of (expensive) one-offs.

Buckle My Shoe
Selfridges, 400 Oxford Street **t** 0870 837 7377
www.bucklemyshoe.co.uk
⊖ Oxford Circus **Bus** 6, 7, 10, 12, 13, 15, 23, 73 94, 98, 113, 135, 137, 139, 159, 189
Open Mon–Sat 10–8, Sun 12 noon–6
 Snazzy, modern footwear for snazzy modern kids with the emphasis on soft leather and classic Italian designs. Also a small clothing range.

Catimini

52a South Molton Street, W1
t (020) 7629 8099 www.catimini.com
⊖ Bond Street **Bus** 6, 7, 10, 12, 13, 15, 23, 73 94, 98, 113, 135, 137, 139, 159, 189
Open Mon–Sat 10–6, Thurs 10–7
Bright printed romper suits, dresses and coordinating accessories. Top children's wear name.

Gymboree

198 Regent Street, W1 **t** (020) 7494 1110
www.gymboree.com
⊖ Oxford Circus **Bus** 3, 6, 12, 13, 15, 23, 53, 88, 94, 139, 159, X53
Open Mon–Sat 10–7, Thurs 10–8pm, Sun 11.30–5.30
Funky attire from swimsuits to winter coats.

Humla Children's Shop

Open Mon–Sat 10.30–6.30
⊖ Bond Street **Bus** 6, 7, 10, 12, 13, 15, 23, 73 94, 98, 113, 135, 137, 139, 159, 189
23 St Christopher's Place, W1 **t** (020) 7224 1773
Earthy Scandinavian designs (especially good for knitwear), traditional wooden toys and mobiles.

Joanna's Tent

289b King's Road, SW3 **t** (020) 7352 1151
⊖ Sloane Square **Bus** 11, 19, 22, 211, 319
Open Mon–Sat 10–6, Sun 1–5
Top-of-the-range designer kids' clothes.

Paul Smith for Children

40–44 Floral Street, WC2
t (020) 7379 7133 www.paulsmith.co.uk
⊖ Covent Garden **Bus** 6, 9, 11, 13, 15, 23, 77A, 91, 176
Open Mon–Wed, Fri 10.30–6.30, Thurs 10.30–7, Sat 10–6.30, Sun 1–5
Innovative designer clothes using fabulous prints for parents who really want to go to town.

Department stores

John Lewis (278–306 Oxford Street, W1) is England's most trusted and reliable department store, if a little short on glamour. Selfridges (400 Oxford St, W1) has gone upmarket, in the trail of Harrods (87–135 Brompton Road, SW1) and Harvey Nichols (109–125 Knightsbridge). All have good children's clothes departments, toilets and cafés. Liberty (214–20 Regent St, W1) is quaint and self-consciously old-fashioned. Fortnum and Mason (181 Piccadilly, W1) is posh and worth a visit for the food hall. There's one department store in London, however, devoted solely to children:

Daisy & Tom

181–3 King's Road **t** (020) 7352 5000
www.daisyandtom.com
⊖ Sloane Square **Bus** 11, 19, 22, 211, 319
Open Mon–Wed, Fri 9.30–6, Thurs–Sat 9.30–7, Sun 11–5
Daisy & Tom is a Harrods for the under-15s. It provides everything a child could want – books, toys, games, a play area, a carousel, an automated puppet show – as well as catering to the more mundane concerns of parents with its extensive range of clothes, baby equipment and pushchairs. It's even got a hairdressing salon where kids can pick up a First Haircut certificate.

Markets

For antique toys try Portobello (Notting Hill) or Camden Passage (Islington). For bric-a-brac and the odd find, Brick Lane on Sunday mornings is worth a visit (be sure to turn up early for bargains) and good on atmosphere. For trendy clothes, music and handmade jewellery, Camden is worth a mosey, while Greenwich at weekends has a good range of market fodder, from CDs and clothes to antique furniture, bric-a-brac and toys.

Brick Lane

Brick Lane, E1 and surrounds
⊖ Aldgate East, Shoreditch, Bethnal Green, Liverpool Street ⇌ Liverpool Street
Open Sun 6am–1pm

Camden Lock

Camden Lock Place, off Chalk Farm Road, NW1
t (020) 7284 2084 www.camdenlock.net
⊖ Camden Town, Chalk Farm ⇌ Camden Road
Bus 24, 27, 29, 31, 134, 135, 168, 214, 253, 274, C2
Open Sat–Sun 10–6

Camden Passage

Camden Passage, off Islington High Street, N1
⊖ Angel **Bus** 4, 19, 30, 38, 43, X43, 56, 73, 171a, 214
Open Wed 7–2, Sat 8–4

Greenwich

Stockwell Street, SE10 and surrounds
⇌ Greenwich **Bus** 53, X53, 177, 180, 188, 199, 286, 386
Open Sat–Sun 9–5

Portobello

Portobello Road, W11 and surrounds
⊖ Notting Hill Gate, Ladbroke Grove, Westbourne Park **Bus** 7, 23, 27, 28, 31, 52, 70, 302
Open Sat–Sun 5.30–3ish

Specialist shops

Anything Left Handed
57 Brewer Street, W1
t (020) 7437 3910 www.anythingleft-handed.co.uk
θ Piccadilly Circus
Bus 3, 6, 12, 13, 14, 15, 23, 38, 53, 88, 94, 139
Open Mon–Fri 10–6, Sat 10–5
Shop for left-handers selling everything from scissors to boomerangs.

Chappel of Bond Street
50 New Bond Street t (020) 7491 2777
www.chappellofbondstreet.co.uk
θ Bond Street Bus 6, 7, 10, 12, 13, 15, 23, 73 94, 98, 113, 135, 137, 139, 159, 189
Open Mon–Fri 9.30–6, Sat 9.30–5
This famous music shop is a great place to pick up that first recorder or quarter-size violin. The ground floor is full of pianos, keyboards and guitars while the basement has sheet music and songbooks.

Sports shops

JJB Sports
The Plaza, 120 Oxford Street, W1 t (020) 7636 0696
www.jjb.co.uk
θ Oxford Circus
Bus 6, 7, 10, 12, 13, 15, 23, 73 94, 98, 113, 135, 137, 139, 159, 189
Open Mon–Sat 10–7, Thurs 10–8, Sun 12 noon–6
Very busy and chaotic sportswear shop with good range of reduced-price clothing and footwear.

Lillywhites
24–36 Regent's Street, W1 t 0870 333 9602
www.lillywhites.com
θ Piccadilly Circus
Bus 3, 6, 12, 13, 15, 23, 53, 88, 94, 139, 159, X53
Open Mon–Sat 10–7, Thurs 10–8, Sun 12–6
Well-established sports equipment store catering for everyone from footballers and cricketers to abseilers, skateboarders and canoeists.

Soccerscene
56–7 Carnaby Street, W1 t (020) 7439 0778
www.soccerscene.co.uk
θ Oxford Circus Bus 6, 7, 10, 12, 13, 15, 23, 73 94, 98, 113, 135, 137, 139, 159, 189
Open Mon–Sat 9.30–7
Easily the best football shop in London. You can pick up the kit of almost any team in the world here, as well as any number of balls and boots.

Toys & games

Benjamin Pollock's Toy Shop
44 Covent Garden Market, WC2 t (020) 7379 7880
www.pollocks-coventgarden.co.uk
θ Covent Garden, Leicester Square
Bus 6, 9, 11, 13, 15, 23, 77A, 91, 176
Open Mon–Sat 10.30–6, Sun 12 noon–5pm
Pick up one of the theatre kits based on Pollock's original designs and bring Cinderella to life.

The Disney Store
360–66 Oxford Street, W1 t (020) 7491 9136
θ Oxford Circus
www.disneystore.co.uk
Open Mon–Sat 10–8, Sun 12 noon–6
The store is full of lovable characters as familiar as friends, as well as a vast array of cartoon-related merchandise. The video screen belting out classics never fails to attract children.

Early Learning Centre
36 King's Road, SW3, t (020) 7581 5764
θ Sloane Square
174 Kensington High Street, W8, t (020) 7937 6238
θ High Street Kensington
www.elc.co.uk
Branches open Mon–Sat 9–6, Wed 9–7, Sun 11–5
The toys, aimed mainly at the preschool age group, are uniformly excellent. The shop has special play areas where kids can try out the toys.

★Hamleys
188–196 Regent Street, W1 t (020) 7734 3161
www.hamleys.com
θ Oxford Circus
Bus 3, 6, 12, 13, 15, 23, 53, 88, 94, 139, 159, X53
Open Mon–Fri 10–8, Sat 9.30–8, Sun 12 noon–6
London's premier toy store, Hamleys has six floors of the latest must-have playthings.

Peter Rabbit & Friends
42 The Market, Covent Garden, WC2
t (020) 7497 1777 www.peterrabbit.com
θ Covent Garden
Bus 6, 9, 11, 13, 15, 23, 77A, 91, 176
Open Mon–Sat 10–8, Sun 10–6

Traditional Toys
53 Godfrey Street, SW3 t (020) 7352 1718
θ South Kensington
Bus 11, 19, 22, 49, 211, 319, 345
The name says it all.

This section offers some ideas of day trips from London that should take no more than an hour or two to reach. Be aware that you may have to take a bus or a short taxi ride from the nearest station.

For train information call National Rail Enquiries **t** 0845 748 4950.

Top towns

Brighton
Train from Victoria **Journey** 1 hour

There's a pier with a funfair and games, eight miles of pebbled seafront with good play facilities, unique Royal Pavilion and good shops (pp.88–91).

Cambridge
Train from Kings Cross **Journey** 1 hour 20 minutes

This famous university town has its own Botanic Gardens, the River Cam and good museums, notably the Fitzwilliam, as well as the colleges (pp.284–8).

Oxford
Train from Paddington **Journey** 1 hour

Soak up the atmosphere and appreciate the beauty, culture and history of this university town, which is also very child friendly (pp.244–6).

Windsor
Train from Paddington **Journey** 30 minutes

Dominated by its castle (the Queen's official residence), Windsor is also home to the famous public school Eton and theme park Legoland (pp.248–50).

Animal attractions

Bockett's Farm Park
Fetcham, Surrey **Car** only **Journey** 40 mins approx

More than just a working farm: pig races, animal petting, mini tractors and play facilities (pp.117–8).

Whipsnade Wild Animal Park
Dunstable, Buckinghamshire **Train** Kings Cross to Luton then bus (10 miles) **Journey** 1 hour

Its 2,428 hectares (6,000 acres) are home to 2,500 animals who roam wild. See elephants, rhinos, tigers (p.258).

Beside the Seaside

Eastbourne
Train from Victoria **Journey** 1 hour 30 minutes

A sand and shingle beach, indoor and outdoor playground and a huge leisure complex (pp.120–1).

Southend-on-Sea
Train from Liverpool Street Station **Journey** 1 hour

Tons of kids' entertainment, a sandy beach, watersports and the world's longest pier (pp.314–5).

Castles, palaces and historic houses

Bodiam Castle
East Sussex **Train** Victoria to Robertsbridge (5 miles) **Journey** 1 hour 40 minutes

A proper fairytale castle, with turrets, battlements, a portcullis and even a moat (p.111).

Hampton Court Palace
East Molesey, Surrey **Train** Waterloo to Hampton Court **Journey** 30 minutes

See Henry VIII's state apartments, a Real tennis court, huge Tudor kitches and a maze (p.114).

Knebworth House
Knebworth, Hertfordshire **Train** Kings Cross to Stevenage (2 miles) **Journey** 35 minutes

The grounds are the real draw, with the Fort Knebworth Adventure Playground (pp.255–6).

Open air museums

Weald and Downland Open Air Museum
Singleton, West Sussex **Train** Victoria to Chichester, then bus (7 miles) **Journey** 1 hour 40 minutes

More than 40 historic rural buildings (p.96).

Parks and Gardens

Richmond Park
Surrey ⊖ /≷ Richmond **Journey** 20 minutes

See the deer, rent a bike or go for a walk (p.67).

Steam trains

Bluebell Railway
Sheffield Park Station, near Uckfield, East Sussex **Train** Victoria to East Grinstead, then bus **Journey** 50 minutes

Take a 10-mile trip on a proper, puffing train (p.126).

Theme parks

Chessington World of Adventure
Chessington, Surrey **Train** Waterloo to Chessington South **Journey** 30 minutes

Rides for all ages, as well as a zoo (p.128).

Legoland
Windsor, Berkshire **Train** Paddington to Windsor and Eton (2 miles) **Journey** 30 minutes

A theme park and activitiy centre combined, this is one of the country's top family attractions (p.249).

KIDS OUT

There's no shortage of outdoor activities for kids in London, from river trips to petting animals at a city farm. Listed below are a few ideas and contacts.

Animal attractions

If you can't get out to the countryside, bring it to the city, and if you can't make it to the African savannah, bring that and its inhabitants too.

Battersea Park Children's Zoo

Albert Bridge Road, SW11 **t** (020) 7924 5826
www.batterseaparkzoo.co.uk
⊖ Sloane Square ⇌ Battersea Park, Queenstown Road **Bus** 19, 44, 49, 137, 319, 344, 345
Open Daily 10–5
Adm Adult £4.95, child £3.75, family £15.50

This small zoo's fate is constantly in the balance, but for now it's still with us, so get down there while you've got the chance. You'll find a small Reptile House as well as meerkats, flamingoes, emus and wallabies. Children can stroke and pet the long-suffering goats and sheep to their heart's content.

Coram's Fields

93 Guilford Street, WC1 **t** (020) 7837 6138
⊖ Russell Square **Bus** 17, 45, 46, 168
Open Summer daily 9–8, winter 9–dusk
Adm Free

Adults can only visit this park, aviary and farm (home to goats, sheep, pigs, geese, chickens, rabbits and guinea pigs) if accompanied by a child. Built on the site of a 1740 foundling hospital, the 'fields' have been set aside for children since its demolition in the 1920s. There's also a supervised playground, helter-skelter, paddling pool and sandpit, and year-round kids' events from dance competitions to circus performances. Vegetarian café.

London Aquarium

County Hall, Riverside Building, Westminster Bridge Road, SE1 **t** (020) 7967 8000
www.londonaquarium.co.uk
Open Daily 10–6
Adm Adults £9.75, children £6.25, under-3s **free**, family £29

One of the capitals' newest attractions, this hi-tech aquarium has sharks and stingrays.
For further information see p.50

London Zoo

Regent's Park, NW1 **t** (020) 7722 3333
www.zsl.org/london-zoo
⊖ Camden Town or Baker Street, then **bus** 274, C2
Open Mar–Oct daily 10–5.30 daily, Nov–Apr 10–4
Adm Adult £13, child (under 15) £9.75, under-3s **free**, family £41

The *ni plus ultra* of London's animal attractions, home to thousands of animals.

Vauxhall City Farm

Tyers Street, SE11 **t** (020) 7582 4204
⊖ Vauxhall **Bus** 2, 36, 77a, 88, 185
Open Tues–Thurs and Sat–Sun 10–5
Adm Free

Near the MI6 building, the farm is home to all the usual suspects, including pigs, rabbits, sheep, ducks and hens. Donkey-rides in summer.

Boat trips

The following companies offer sightseeing boat trips along the Thames. For more details, visit the London River Services website **www.tfl.gov.uk/river** or call **t** (020) 7941 4500. Travelcard holders are entitled to a discount on most scheduled services.

Catamaran Cruisers

t (020) 7987 1185
www.catamarancruisers.co.uk
Fares Hopper Pass: adults £9, children £4.50 (unlimited hop on hop off use of service for a day) Circular Cruise: adult return £9, child return £4.50, family £22.50 (non-stop 50 minute cruise from Westminster Pier)

River cruises on one of six purpose-built vessels with fun, informative commentary. Unrivalled views of some of London's best-loved sights. London Eye and Tower Passes also available, offering combined boat trip and entry to attractions.

City Cruises

t (020) 7740 0400 **www.citycruises.com**
Fares Westminster–Tower Pier: adults single £5.60, return £6.80; children single £2.80, return £3.40, under-5s **free**; Westminster–Greenwich: adults single £6.80, return £8.60; children single £3.40, return £4.30, under-5s **free**; Rail & River Rover: adult £9, child £4.50, family £22, under-5s **free**

Runs between Westminster Pier, Waterloo Pier, Tower Pier and Greenwich. The huge boats, which seat up to 500, are easily recognized by their bright red livery. The 'Rail and River Rover Ticket' allows unlimited travel for a day on boats and DLR.

Tate to Tate

t 0870 781 5049 www.thamesclippers.com
Fares Adult £4.50, child £2.25, family £10; tickets valid all day for maximum three return journeys

Damien Hirst-liveried boats run every 40 minutes between Bankside Pier (Tate Modern) and Millbank Pier (Tate Britain) and back, stopping off at Waterloo Pier (South Bank).

Thames River Services

t (020) 7930 4097
Fares Westminster–Thames Barrier: adult single £7.50, return £9; child single £3.25, return £4.50

Take a cruise way downriver beyond known land-marks to the impressive Thames Barrier.

Westminster Passenger Service

t (020) 7930 2062
www.wpsa.co.uk **Fares** Westminster–Kew (return): adults £16.50, children £8.25, family £41.25; Westminster–Richmond (return): adults £18, children £9, family £45; Westminster–Hampton Court (return): adults £19.50, children £9.75, family £48.75

Upriver to Kew Gardens, Richmond and Hampton Court, with salacious commentary.

Canal trips

Several companies make a leisurely journey along Regent's Canal between Little Venice and Camden Town, via London Zoo.

Jason's Traditional Canal Boat Trips

60 Blomfield Road, Little Venice **t** (020) 7286 3428
www.jasons.co.uk
⊖ Warwick Avenue **Bus** 6, 46
Open Dec–Sept daily at 10.30, 12.30 and 2.30; Bank Hols also 4.30; Oct–Nov daily at 12.30 and 2.30
Fares Adults single £6, return £7; children single £4.50, return £5.50, under-4s **free**; family single £20, return £22

London Waterbus Company

50 Camden Lock Place **t** (020) 7482 2660
www.londonwaterbus.com
⊖ Camden Town, Chalk Farm **Bus** 6, 46
Open Apr–Oct daily 10–5, Nov–Mar Sat–Sun only
Fares Adults single £5.50, return £7; children single £3.70, return £4.70, under-4s **free**; combined canal trip and zoo visit: from Little Venice adults £14.50, children £11.20, from Camden Lock adults £14, children £11, under-4s **free**

Trips aboard traditional, painted narrow boats, stopping off at London Zoo (p.37).

Outdoor music and theatre

BBC Family Prom in the Park

Hyde Park **t** 0870 899 8001 www.bbc.co.uk/proms
⊖ Hyde Park Corner
Bus 2, 8, 9, 10, 12, 14, 16, 19, 22, 36, 39, 73, 74, 82, 94
Adm Adults £14, children £9, under-3s **free**

The BBC Philharmonic club together with the latest pop sensations once a year in early September to bring an evening of easy listening classical music.

Kenwood House Lakeside Concerts

Kenwood House, Hampstead Lane, NW3
t 0870 333 1181 www.english-heritage.org
⊖ Archway **Bus** 210
Adm £18–£26, under-5s **free**

Families flock to this series of popular classical concerts and firework displays in the grounds of this grand old house. Bring a picnic!

Regent's Park Open Air Theatre

Regent's Park, NW1 **t** 0870 060 1811
www.openairtheatre.org
Adm Daytime performances £9.50–£26; evening tickets £6, family shows £9

This respected theatre company usually puts on a child-friendly show in summer as well as a selection from Shakespeare and a quality musical. *A Midsummer Night's Dream* often features.

Parks and gardens

All London parks are free.

Battersea Park

Prince of Wales Drive, SW11 **t** (020) 8871 7530
www.batterseapark.org
⊖ Sloane Square ⇌ Battersea Park, Queenstown Road **Bus** 19, 44, 137, 319, 344, 345
Open Daily dawn–dusk

One of London's best parks for children, Battersea is undergoing a major revamp, the first phase of which has installed a new running track and floodlit tennis courts. There's a small zoo (p.64), a breezy boating lake, a Victorian Pump House and, best of all, London's largest adventure playground – if it can be clambered over, you'll find it here. There's a branch of the London Recumbents, **t** (020) 7498 6543, where you can hire bikes. The park organizes lots of summer events for children, including a teddy bears' picnic.

Green Park

Piccadilly W1 & The Mall, SW1 t (020) 7930 1793
www.royalparks.gov.uk/parks/green_park/
⊖ Green Park Bus 2, 8, 9, 14, 16, 19, 22, 38, 52, 73, 82
Open Daily dawn–dusk

The name says it all – this is a green park, with lots of lush grass and trees, but little else: no pond, no playground, not even statues. Nonetheless, it's a lovely serene place. Every spring, for a few weeks, it becomes a yellow and green park when hordes of daffodils pop up.

Greenwich Park

Charlton Way, SE3 t (020) 8858 2608
www.royalparks.gov.uk/parks/greenwich_park/
Open Daily dawn–dusk

Everything in Greenwich Park has been touched by the brush of elegance, from the flower gardens and stately avenues to the ornate Ranger's House and landscaped heights offering stunning views over the Thames. Created as a hunting ground by Henry VI in 1433 – it still has a small deer enclosure on its south side – it was landscaped in the 17th century by the great French gardener André Le Nôtre. The park also has a boating lake, well-equipped playground and picnic tables, and in summer circus acts, storytellings and a carousel (£2 a ride).

Hampstead Heath

Hampstead, NW3 t (020) 7482 7073
⊖ Belsize Park, Hampstead ⇌ Hampstead Heath, Gospel Oak Bus 24, 46, 168, 214, C2, C11
Open Night and day

One of the few places in London that actually feels a little bit wild. Once the stomping ground of the poets Keats and Shelley and the highwayman Dick Turpin, these 324 hectares (800 acres) provide a wonderful setting for a family walk. Kids will enjoy the playground by Gospel Oak Station, complete with swings, slides and climbing frame, as well as the funfairs that regularly set up here in summer. It's ideal for kite-flying. There are some good views of the city, particularly from Parliament Hill (site of the lido, p.72), and the park is home to Kenwood House and its summer firework concerts (pp.36, 65).

Highgate Wood

Muswell Hill Road, N6 t (020) 8444 6129
www.highgatewoods.co.uk
⊖ Highgate Bus 144, W7
Open Daily 7.30am until dusk

There's a playground , a sports ground, an excellent vegetarian restaurant, Oshobasho (p.83), and a small patch of ancient woodland inhabited by a staggering array of flora and fauna – more than 70 species of birds, 12 species of butterfly, 180 species of bats, 80 species of spiders, foxes, squirrels, beetles, slugs and worms. Pick up a nature trail from the woodland centre.

Holland Park

Kensington High Street, W8 t (020) 7471 9813
www.rbkc.gov.uk
⊖ Holland Park, High Street Kensington
Bus 9, 10, 27, 28, 49
Open Daily dawn–dusk

Just off hustling bustling Kensington High Street, this is a lovely manicured park with an eco centre, t (020) 7471 9809, orangery, Japanese Water Garden, free-roaming peacocks and pheasants, and a groovy, multi-level adventure playground. Child-friendly Sticky Fingers restaurant is just around the corner at 1a Phillimore Gardens.

Hyde Park/Kensington Gardens

t (020) 7298 2100
www.royalparks.gov.uk/parks/hyde_park/
⊖ Hyde Park Corner, Knightsbridge, South Kensington, Lancaster Gate, Queensway, Marble Arch
Bus 2, 8, 9, 10, 12, 14, 16, 19, 22, 36, 39, 73, 74, 82, 94
Open 5am–12 midnight

Hyde Park provides a welcome oasis of calm in the hectic city. In fact, only the eastern side is officially called Hyde Park; the western side is known as Kensington Gardens, but there is no official border and it's really just one big park. In the middle is the Serpentine – as the name suggests, a great, snake-shaped lake – populated by swans, ducks, geese and other wildfowl. You can hire rowing boats – a great way to spend a lazy summer afternoon (adults 30mins £3, one hour £4; children 30mins £1, one hour £2; rowing lessons £5; no under-5s). Alternatively, if the kids would rather play on the grass, help yourself to one of the many green and white striped deckchairs that dot the park – an attendant will eventually find you and charge you £1. You can also swim in the Serpentine Lido (adults £3.50, children 80p, family £8), paddle in the children's pool (May–September) and clamber aboard the pirate ship in the Princess Diana Adventure Playground, located in the northwestern corner near the famous Elfin Oak and Peter Pan statue, erected secretly by author J.M. Barrie in the middle of the night. On the south side of the park, by Rotten Row, there's a small enclosed play area with slides and swings. Hyde Park Stables, on the north side, is one of the few places in London you can go riding (p.70).

Speaker's Corner

Some of London's more passionate (some would say barmy) citizens have, since 1872, been allowed to let off steam every Sunday at Speaker's Corner, which is located at the northeastern corner of the park. People can say whatever they want (about whomever they want) here and, standing on a makeshift platform (traditionally a soapbox), attempt to rally passing pedestrians to their cause – providing they can make themselves heard above the din from the traffic on Park Lane.

Regent's Park

t (020) 7486 7905
www.royalparks.gov.uk/parks/regents_park
⊖ Baker Street, Great Portland Street, Regent's Park, Camden Town then bus 274 **Bus** 2, 13, 18, 27, 30, 74, 82, 113, 135, 139, 159, 189, 274, C2
Open Daily 5am–dusk

One of London's great parks, Regent's Park has masses going on. There's the boating lake, home to a mass of wildfowl including ducks, moorhens and black swans, where you can hire a rowing boat. There are four playgrounds (open daily from 10.30), complete with children's toilets, sand pits, swings and play equipment. There are tennis courts, cricket and football pitches. In the centre are the neatly manicured Queen Mary's Gardens, best visited in summer when you'll find bed upon bed of wonderful, colourful roses. The gardens also house London Zoo (p.37), the Open Air Theatre (p.65), an ornamental lake, a sunken garden and a fountain depicting a man blowing water out of a conch shell. The park authorities also organize late-night 'Owl Prowls' (t (020) 7298 2000).

Richmond Park

Richmond, Surrey t (020) 8948 3209
www.royalparks.gov.uk/parks/richmond_park/
⊖/≳ Richmond **Bus** 72, 74, 85, 371
Open Daily dawn–dusk

This great swathe of west London parkland has long been closely associated with the monarchy. In the 15th century Henry VII had a viewing mound created in the park, allowing him to look out over his kingdom – the mound still stands today and the views remain magnificent, stretching from Windsor Castle in the west to St Paul's Cathedral in the east. Two centuries later, both Charles I and Charles II used the park as a hunting ground. Today, although the hunting has stopped, the park is still home to the Queen's own herds of red and fallow deer, which roam the park pretty much as the fancy takes them. A huge variety of other species of wildlife, among them foxes, weasels and badgers, have also made the park their home. There are two public golf courses, some great walking trails and you can hire bikes from Richmond Park Cycle Hire, t 07050 209 249. The very good Pembroke Lodge Cafeteria, perched high on Richmond Hill, offers a children's menu, t (020) 8940 8207.

St James's Park

The Mall, SW1 t (020) 7930 1793
www.royalparks.gov.uk/parks/st_james_park/
⊖ St James's Park
Bus 3, 11, 12, 24, 53, 77A, 88, 109, 159, 211, X53
Open Daily dawn–dusk

A must for all bird-lovers. In the 17th century the park held several aviaries (hence Birdcage Walk) and today is home to London's finest wildfowl ponds, a great stretch of water where you can find more than 20 species of bird including ducks, geese and even pelicans (fed between 2 and 3pm each day, but have recently been spotted swallowing pigeons whole). There's also a playground with a sandpit and a smart teashop. If your kids have seen the film *One Hundred and One Dalmatians* (the live action version), they may recognize certain parts of the park – it was the scene of the bicycle chase where poor old Pongo gets thrown into the lake. Brass, concert and military bands play on the bandstand on Saturday, Sunday and Bank Holiday afternoons in summer.

Wide open spaces

Kew Gardens

Kew, Richmond, Surrey, TW9
Infoline t (020) 8332 5655 www.kew.org.uk
≳ Kew Bridge, Kew Gardens ⊖ Kew Gardens
Bus 65, 391, 267, R68 (Sun only)
Open 9.30–dusk
Adm Adult £10, under-16s **free**

The Royal Botanic Gardens, to give Kew its proper name, is spread over a 121ha (300-acre) site on the south bank of the Thames. It has grown, over the course of 200 years, into the largest and most comprehensive collection of living plants in the world, with more than one in eight of all flowering plants. There are three enormous conservatories: the Palm House, full of tropical exotica; the late-Victorian Temperate House; and the 1980s Princess of Wales Conservatory, home to the giant Amazonian water-lily and Titan Arum, the largest and, possibly, the smelliest, flower in the world. There is also a 10-storey, 50m (164ft) high, 18th-century pagoda and a new botanical play zone for kids, Climbers and Creepers. There's a good restaurant, but where better for a picnic?

WWT Wetlands Centre

Queen Elizabeth Walk, SW13 t (020) 8409 4400
www.wwt.org.uk
≥ Barnes then **bus** 33, 72, 209, 283
⊖ Hammersmith then **bus** 283
Open Winter 9.30–5, summer 9.30–6 (last entry 1hr before closing); feeding times 12 noon and 3.30pm
Adm Adults £6.75, children (4–16) £4, family £17.50, under-4s **free**

This innovative site is split into 14 simulated habitats, including arctic tundra and tropical swamp, each inhabited by wildfowl. Picture boards help to identify what's what. There are numerous huts and hides from which you can see the wildlife and a visitors' centre where you can pick up children's trails and hire binoculars (£5). It also has a spacious café (kids' menu). Upstairs, in the observatory, there's an interactive area for kids. Weekend and holiday wildlife activities are organized.

Sightseeing tours

Various companies offer sightseeing tours of London, but the Big Bus Company – recognizable by its distinctive maroon and cream livery – is the pick of the bunch. It operates three routes: the West End and Bloomsbury; Knightsbridge and Mayfair; and Victoria to the Tower of London. Main departure points are Marble Arch, Green Park, Baker Street and Victoria, although you can board at any stop along the route.

The Big Bus Company

48 Buckingham Palace Road, SW1 t (020) 7233 9533
www.bigbus.co.uk
Fares Adult £20, child £8
Ticket allows 24 hours unlimited travel on Big Bus Company buses

London Duck Tours

County Hall, Belvedere Road, SE1 t (020) 7928 3132
www.londonducktours.co.uk
Open Feb– Dec 10–dusk daily
Adm Adults £16.50, children £11, family £49

A novel approach to sightseeing – London Duck Tours have adapted a number of Second World War amphibious vehicles into bright yellow sightseeing 'ducks' capable of tackling London by road and river. Each duck begins its 80-minute tour on land at County Hall, crosses Westminster Bridge and makes its way to Lacks Dock in Vauxhall, taking in key sights on the way, before 'splashdown' into the Thames for a half-hour sightseeing cruise down the river. It's a fun way of navigating through London and the plunge into the river is truly exciting. It may be advisable to wear waterproofs.

Walks

Blue Plaque Tours

www.english-heritage.org.uk
Have you noticed that some London houses have blue plaques on their walls? These show that a famous person has lived there. It can be fun to use the plaques as the basis for a walk around the city.

Globe Walkshop

Bear Gardens, Bankside, New Globe Walk, Southwark, SE1 t (020) 7902 1433
www.shakespeares-globe.org.uk
⊖/ ≥ London Bridge
Bus 11, 15, 17, 23, 26, 45, 63, 76, 100, 344, 381, RV1
Times Sat 10am–12 noon
Adm Adult £7

Find out more about the decadent history of Southwark on a Globe Walkshop – a guided tour taking in the prisons, inns and theatres that used to make up the bulk of the area's buildings (p.54).

Jubilee Walkway

This 10-mile walk is split into seven sections, which run from Leicester Square through Westminster across the river to the South Bank and then back through The City to Covent Garden, each topped and tailed by a tube stop, so you can walk as much or as little as you like. The route is marked by discs set in the pavement (there are 400 in total) – fun for kids to spot. The walk was created in 1977 to commemorate the Queen's Silver Jubilee, hence the name and was revamped for the Golden Jubilee in 2002.

Millennium Mile

www.southbanklondon.com/walk_this_way/

The Thameside path between Westminster Bridge and Tower Bridge has been spruced up since the millennium and rechristened the Millennium Mile. What was once one of the city's more tatty districts is now vibrant – and one of the best places to come to for a family walk. The route is dotted with some of the capital's best attractions, among them the London Aquarium, London Eye, South Bank Centre, Tate Modern, Shakespeare's Globe Theatre, HMS *Belfast* and Tower Bridge.

The Original London Walks

PO Box 1708 London NW6 4LW **t** (020) 7624 3978 **www.**walks.com

There are several companies offering walking tours of London, but this one (London's oldest) is easily the pick of the bunch and certainly the most child friendly (under-15s **free** if accompanied by an adult; adults £5.50). As well as organizing tours around several specific areas of London, including the City, Greenwich, Westminster and Hyde Park, London Walks offer various themed treks including 'Shakespeare's London', 'Ghosts of the West End', 'Jack the Ripper Haunts', all led by knowledgeable, entertaining guides.

The Thames Path

Thames Barrier Visitor Centre **t** (020) 8305 4188 **www.**thames-path.co.uk

For a more *ad hoc* walking experience, you might like to try a portion of the Thames Path, a designated nature trail along the banks of the Thames. You might have a job finishing the route, however, as it stretches the entire length of the river, all 180 miles of it.

Pub Signs

As you walk around the city, look out for the painted signs hanging up outside pubs, particularly old pubs. The names displayed are often very distinctive, not to say occasionally rather peculiar – Lamb and Flag, Hoop and Grapes, Black Friar, Old Cheshire Cheese, Bleeding Heart Tavern, Red Lion, White Swan, Coach and Horses, etc. They were chosen specially because of the ease with which they could be illustrated on the pub sign.

Remember, back in the 17th and 18th centuries, a large proportion of London's population couldn't read or write and would have had to rely on such images to make sure they found the right pub.

Cricket

London's two premier grounds are Lord's and the Oval. The county championship season runs from April to September, with four-day matches taking place between Thursday and Monday, and one-dayers on Sunday. Both grounds also host one-day international matches and five-day international Test Matches. Tickets cost £7–£25. Both run courses for children aged 8 and over, and are enthusiastic supporters of 'Kwik Cricket' for younger children.

Marylebone Cricket Club (MCC) and Middlesex County Cricket Club

Lord's Cricket Ground, St John's Wood Road, NW8 **t** (020) 7266 3825 **www.**lords.org
St John's Wood **Bus** 3, 82, 113, 139, 189

Surrey County Cricket Club

The Oval, Kennington, SW8 **t** (020) 7582 6660 **www.**surreycricket.com
Oval, Vauxhall **Bus** 36, 185

Football

London is home to more than a dozen professional football clubs. The biggest – Arsenal, Chelsea and Tottenham – play in the Premier League. Most grounds have family enclosures and the facilities are usually excellent. Book tickets as early as possible. Tickets cost £15–£60 (children half price).

Arsenal Football Club

Arsenal Stadium, Avenell Road, Highbury, N5 **t** (020) 7704 4040 **www.**arsenal.com
Arsenal **Bus** 4, 19, 29, 43, 153, 236, 253, 271
Tickets £26–£50

There is a six-year waiting list to become one of the club's 21,000 season ticket holders.

Chelsea Football Club

Stamford Bridge, Fulham Road, SW10 **t** 0870 300 1212 **www.**chelseafc.co.uk
Fulham Broadway **Bus** 14, 211
Tickets £29–£49

Tottenham Hotspur Football Club

White Hart Lane, Bill Nicholson Way, 748 High Road, Tottenham, N17 **t** 0870 420 5000 **www.**spurs.co.uk
Tottenham Hale, Seven Sisters
Bus 149, 259, 279, W3
Tickets £25–£50

Go-karting

London's indoor circuits offer training and racing for mini racing drivers aged 8–16. Helmets and overalls are provided. Approx £30 per hour session.

Docklands F1 City
Gate 119, Connaught Bridge, Royal Victoria Dock E16 t (020) 7476 5678 www.f1city.co.uk, DLR Royal Albert

Streatham Playscape Kart Raceway
390 Streatham High Road, SW16 t (020) 8677 8677 www.playscape.co.uk
⇌ Streatham Bus 57, 109, 118, 133, 201, 250, 255

Horse-riding

London has dozens of stables and horse-riding schools, some offering lessons to 2–3-year-olds.

Hyde Park Riding Stables
63 Bathurst Mews, W2 t (020) 7723 2813 www.hydeparkstables.com; ⊖ Lancaster Gate Bus 7, 15, 23, 27, 36; Adm £50 per lesson Age 5 and over

Ross Nye's Riding Stables
8 Bathurst Mews, W2 t (020) 7262 3791
⊖ Paddington Bus 7, 15, 23, 27, 36
Adm £40 per hour Age 7 and over

Wimbledon Village Stables
24a High Street, Wimbledon, SW19; t (020) 8946 8579 www.wvstables.com; ⊖ /⇌ Wimbledon Bus 93, 200; Adm From £35 per hour weekdays, £40 weekends; Age 3 and over

Ice-skating

London has several ice-skating rinks, many with popular disco nights. Most will not let under 3s on the ice. Boots can usually be hired. The average price, including skate hire, is adults £5–£7, children £3–£5.

Alexandra Palace Ice Rink
Alexandra Palace Way, N22 t (020) 8365 4386 www.alexandrapalace.com
⇌ Alexandra Palace Bus 184, W3

Broadgate Ice Rink
Eldon Street, EC2 t (020) 7505 4068 www.broadgateice.co.uk ⊖ /⇌ Liverpool Street Bus 133, 141, 172, 214, 271; Open Nov–Mar
One of London's few outdoor rinks.

Leisurebox
Queensway, W2 t (020) 7229 0172
⊖ Bayswater, Queensway Bus 70

Natural History Museum Ice Rink
Cromwell Road, London SW7, t (020) 7942 5000; www.nhm.ac.uk; Open Nov–Jan, Mon–Fri 10am–10pm, sat and sun 9am–10pm
Adm weekday (10–4pm) adults £10.50, child £7.50; weekday (5.15–10pm) and weekends adult £12, children £7.50; family tickets £30 (anytime)
Every Christmas the museum sets up a 1000 square metre adult rink, as well as a smaller junior rink. Lessons also available.

Somerset House
The Strand, WC2 t 0870 166 0423 www.somerset-house.org.uk; ⊖ Temple, Charing Cross, Embankment, Covent Garden Bus 6, 9, 11, 13, 15, 23, 77a, 91, 176; Adm adult £10 (10–5.30), £12–15 (evenings), children £7; family ticket £29 (1 adult and 3 children or 2 adults and two children)
An open-air ice rink is set up in the courtyard over Christmas and New Year. It is advisable to book as day tickets are restricted.

Tower of London Ice Rink
t 0870 602 1100; http://hrp.org.uk/tower; Open late Nov–mid Jan 10am–10pm, Adm adult £10, children £7.50, family (1+3 or 2+2) £30. (1hr sessions)

Play gyms & gymnastics

British Amateur Gymnastics Association
t 0845 1297 129 www.baga.co.uk

Crêchendo
7 locations across London
t (020) 8772 8120 www.crechendo.com
Classes using toys and soft climbing equipment, for kids from 4 months to 4 years (four age groups). Kids must be accompanied by an adult.

Tumbletots, Gymbabes & Gymbobs
Various venues across London
t (0121) 585 7003 www.tumbletots.com
Kids from crawling to school-age can climb, jump and hang on specially designed equipment to improve balance, co-ordination and physical ability.

Rowing

The famous Oxford–Cambridge Boat Race takes place on the Saturday before Easter between Putney Bridge and Mortlake. The best views (and atmosphere) are from Putney or Chiswick bridges.

Rugby

Rugby Football Union **t** (020) 8892 2000
www.rfu.com
All of London's professional clubs coach kids through the year. Professional club matches are usually played on Saturday afternoons.

Harlequins

Stoop Memorial Ground, Langhorn Drive, Twickenham, Middlesex; **t** (020) 8410 6000; **www.quins.co.uk**; ≥ Twickenham **Bus** 281; **Tickets** £12–£25

London Irish RFC

Madejski Stadium, Junction 11, M4, Reading, RG2 **t** (01932) 783 034 **www.london-irish.com**
≥ Reading; **Tickets** adult £10–£25, child £5

London Wasps

Twyford Avenue Sports Ground, Twyford Avenue, Acton, W3 **t** (020) 8993 8298 **www.wasps.co.uk**
⊖ Ealing Common; **Tickets** adult £25, under-16s £10

London Welsh

Old Deer Park, Kew Road, Richmond, Surrey TW9 **t** (020) 8940 2368 **www.london-welsh.co.uk**
⊖ Richmond **Bus** 65; **Tickets** £4–£11, under-16s **free**

Saracens RFC

Vicarage Road Stadium, Watford **t** 01923 475 222 **www.saracens.com**; ≥ Watford High Street **Bus** 298, 299, 307; **Tickets** £10–£30, under-16s £7–£10

Running

London Marathon

t (020) 7902 0184 **www.london-marathon.co.uk**
≥ (*start*) Blackheath ⊖ (*finish*) Westminster
Every April, more than 30,000 people run the 26-mile 385-yard (42km 166m) course from Blackheath to Westminster Bridge via the Isle of Dogs, Victoria Embankment and St James's Park.

Skateboarding

Ally Pally Skatepark

Alexandra Palace, Muswell Hill, N22
⊖ Wood Green ≥ Alexandra Palace **Bus** 184, W3
Open 24 hours a day **Adm Free**
Between the ice rink and children's playground.

Meanwhile

Meanwhile Gardens, Great Western Road, W9
⊖ Westbourne Park
Open Daily dawn–dusk **Adm Free**
London's first skate park, built back in 1976.

Stockwell Bowl Skatepark

Behind Brixton Academy, Stockwell Road, SW9
⊖ Brixton; **Open** 24 hours a day; **Adm Free**
South London's most popular skate park is of the 1970s generation of good, concrete outdoor parks, recently resurfaced with smooth pink concrete.

Sports centres

There are nigh on 200 sports centres in London. Many have swimming pools and most have special facilities for young children.

Britannia Leisure Centre

40 Hyde Road, Islington, N1 **t** (020) 7729 4485
www.britannia.leisureconnection.co.uk
⊖ Old Street **Bus** 67, 76, 141, 149, 242, 243, 243A, 271
Football, tennis, gym, basketball, swimming (including lessons), snorkelling and water polo.

Crystal Palace

National Sports Centre, Ledrington Road, Upper Norwood, SE19 **t** (020) 8778 0131
≥ Crystal Palace **Bus** 2, 3, 63, 122, 137a, 157, 202, 227, 249, 342, 358, 361, 450
Internationally renowned sports centre with an athletics stadium, an Olympic-sized pool and high diving board and excellent facilities for badminton, basketball, gymnastics, hockey and martial arts.

Oasis Sports Centre

32 Endell Street, WC2 **t** (020) 7831 1804
⊖ Holborn, Covent Garden **Bus** 1, 14, 19, 24, 29, 38, 176
Facilities for badminton, football, martial arts, swimming, table tennis and trampolining, as well as London's only heated outdoor pool.

Queen Mother's Sports Centre

223 Vauxhall Bridge Road, SW1 **t** (020) 7630 5522
⊖ /≥ Victoria, ⊖ Pimlico **Bus** 2, 36, 185
Badminton, football, martial arts, netball, rounders, swimming.

Swimming

Most indoor pools run mother-and-toddler sessions. Expect to pay around £3–£5 for adults, £2–£3 for children.

Indoor pools

Britannia Leisure Centre

40 Hyde Road, N1 **t** (020) 7729 4485
www.britannia.leisureconnection.co.uk
⊖ Old Street **Bus** 67, 76, 141, 149, 242, 243, 243A, 271

Open Mon–Fri 9–9, Sat and Sun 9–6

Water slides, wave machine and pool inflatables.

Crystal Palace Pool

National Sports Centre, Ledrington Road,
Norwood, SE19 **t** (020) 8778 0131

≋ Crystal Palace **Bus** 2, 3, 63, 122, 137a, 157, 202, 227, 249, 342, 358, 361, 450

Open Mon–Fri 9am–9pm, Sat–Sun 9–6

Huge pool complex with an Olympic-size (50m) pool, a 25m training pool, a 20m diving pool (with high diving boards) and an 18m teaching pool.

Fulham Pools

Normand Park, Lillie Road, SW6 **t** (020) 7471 0450

⊖ West Brompton **Bus** 74, 190

Open Mon–Thurs 6.30am–10.30pm,
Fri 6.30am–9.30pm, Sat–Sun 8–9

Water slide, water toys, wave machine and a swimming club for kids.

Latchmere Leisure Centre

Burns Road, SW11 **t** (020) 7207 8004
www.kinetika.org

⊖ Clapham Junction, Battersea Park

Bus 44, 49, 319, 344, 345

Open Mon–Thurs 7am–9.30pm, Fri and Sat 7am–7pm, Sun 7–6

Child-friendly indoor pool which includes a seashore slope, wave machine and toddler's pool.

Outdoor pools

Evian Lido

Brockwell Park, Dulwich Road, SE24
t (020) 7274 3088 www.thelido.co.uk

⊖ Brixton ≋ Herne Hill **Bus** 3, 37, 196

Open May–Sept Mon–Fri 7am–7pm, Sat–Sun 12 noon–6

Finchley Lido

Great North Leisure Park, High Road, N12
t (020) 8343 9830

⊖ Finchley Central **Bus** 263

Open May–Sept daily 10–7

Oasis Sports Centre

Endell Street, WC2 **t** (020) 7931 1804

⊖ Covent Garden **Bus** 1, 14, 19, 24, 29, 38, 176

Open Mon–Fri 7.30am–8pm, Sat–Sun 9.30–5

Heated outdoor pool in the heart of London. Also has a toddlers' paddling pool.

Parliament Hill Lido

Parliament Hill (off Gordon House Road),
Hampstead Heath, NW5 **t** (020) 7485 3873

≋ Gospel Oak **Bus** 214, C2, C11

Open May–Sept 7–6, Oct–Feb 7–10.30

Tennis

Wimbledon, the game's most prestigious tournament, is held in the last week of June and the first week of July. Demand for tickets is huge, to put it mildly. Getting tickets for Wimbledon is not impossible, but it is very difficult – and even if you do get lucky, they're not cheap. In order to buy tickets for Centre Court or No.1 Court, where all the big-name matches take place, you have to enter a ballot the previous September for tickets that cost £32–£79. Alternatively, turn up on the day and queue for a ground pass (about £15) which gives you access to all the outer courts, where star players are thinner on the ground. If you just want to see some grass court tennis and spot a few famous players, you'd be better off going to the men's tournament at Queen's a couple of week's before Wimbledon. The atmosphere is more relaxed and tickets easier to come by (and cheaper, at £10–£15). If your family fancies a game, many public parks have a couple of concrete courts and there are a few indoor clubs.

Wimbledon (All England Lawn Tennis and Croquet Club)

Church Road, Wimbledon, SW19 **t** (020) 8946 2244
www.wimbledon.org

⊖ Southfields, Wimbledon ≋ Wimbledon

Bus 39, 93 or shuttle bus from Southfields or Wimbledon stations

Queen's Club

Palliser Road, W14 **t** (020) 7385 3421
www.queensclub.co.uk

⊖ Barons Court **Bus** 28, 74, 190, 211, 220, 295, 391

Regent's Park Tennis Centre

York Bridge Road, NW1 **t** (020) 7486 4216
www.rptc.co.uk

⊖ Regent's Park **Bus** 274

Westway Indoor Tennis Centre

1 Crowthorne Road, W10 **t** (020) 8969 0992
www.westway.totaltennis.net

⊖ Latimer Road **Bus** 295

KIDS IN

Art activities

All of the major art galleries provide trails and activities for kids, in particular Tate Britain (p.46) and Tate Modern (p.55), the National Gallery (pp.41–2) and National Portrait Gallery (pp.42–3)

Art 4 Fun/Colour Me Mine

172 West End Lane, NW6 **t** (020) 7794 0800
www.art4fun.com
✈ West Hampstead
444 Chiswick High Road, W4, **t** (020) 8994 4100
www.chiswick.colourmemine.com
✈ Chiswick Park
212 Fortis Green Road, N10, **t** (020) 8444 4333
www.muswellhill.colourmemine.com
✈ East Finchley **Bus** 102, 234
Adm From £4, items from £2.50
Open Daily, call for times
Suitable for all ages

A magical place where children and parents can paint their own cups, plates (dishwasher safe), T-shirts or picture frames. Also great for original parties: ceramics, clay T-shirt printing and painting, tie-dye and face painting. Take away a souvenir ceramic hand- or foot-print of your little angel!

Ceramics Café

Branches at Hammersmith, Kew Green and West Ealing
t (020) 8741 4140 **www.ceramicscafe.com**
✈ Ravenscourt Park **Bus** 9, 10, 27, 94
Open Tues–Sat 10–6, Sun 11–6
Adm £2 studio fee, £3–£12 for materials

Personalize plates, mugs and other tableware. Party packages available.

London Brass Rubbing Centre

St Martin-in-the-Fields, Trafalgar Square, WC2
t (020) 7930 9306 **www.stmartin-in-the-fields.org**
✈ Charing Cross, Leicester Square, Embankment
Bus 3, 6, 9, 13, 15, 23, 24, 29, 53, 88, 91, 109, 139, 159, 176, 184, 196
Open Mon–Wed 10–7, Thurs–Sat 10–10, Sun 12–7
Adm Rubbings cost anything from £2.90 to £15, depending on the size of the brass

In the crypt, you'll find more than 100 brasses, including knights, dragons, griffins and elephants.

Cinemas

The biggest and best can be found in Leicester Square, London's cinematic heart, where star-studded premières take place and all the major blockbusters have their first runs. For a full, up-to-date list of what's on where and when, check the weekly listings magazine *Time Out* or the *Evening Standard*'s free 'Metro Life' supplement (Thursday).

IMAX 3D Cinema

1 Charlie Chaplin Walk, SE1 **t** 0870 787 2525
www.bfi.org.uk/imax
✈ Waterloo, Westminster
Bus 11, 12, 53, 76, 77, 109, 211, 507, D1, P11
Open Mon–Fri 12.30–8, Sat–Sun 10.45–8.45
Adm Adults £7.90 (£5.50 for each extra adult), children (5–15) £4.95 (£3.95 for each extra child), under-3s **free**

Britain's largest cinema screen is housed in a seven-storey glass cylinder in the middle of a roundabout. The screen itself is the height of five double-decker buses, the sound system transmits 11,000 watts and the films are recorded and projected using the most up-to-date 3D format available – it's an all-encompassing experience. You can usually see some kind of space or wildlife spectacular.

Leicester Square

Empire
t 0870 010 2030 **www.uci-cinemas.co.uk**
Odeon Leicester Square and **Odeon West End**
t 0870 505 0007 **www.odeon.co.uk**
Vue West End
t 08712 240 240 **www.myvue.com**

Both the Odeon and Vue Cinemas run special offers for kids – at all but Leicester Square branches.

Cinema clubs

There are several smaller picture houses that run kids' Saturday morning film clubs, usually a mix of Disney cartoons and family favourites.

Barbican Centre

Silk Street, EC2 **t** 0845 120 7528
www.barbican.org.uk/familyfilmclub
✈ Barbican, Moorgate **Bus** 8, 22B, 56
Times Sat 10.30am **Ages** 5–11
Adm Annual membership £7.50, films £4.50 non-members, £3 members

Kids can enjoy a family classic and take part in some film-related activities from the 'Movie Cart' in the foyer at the Family Film Club. Workshops on animation, make-up, set design, etc. are held on the last Saturday of the month (booking essential).

GETTING AROUND | PRACTICAL A–Z | LONDON'S YEAR | THINGS TO SEE AND DO | SHOPPING | SPECIAL TRIPS | KIDS OUT | KIDS IN | EATING OUT

Clapham Picture House

76 Venn Street, SW4 **t** 0870 755 0061
www.picturehouses.co.uk/site/cinemas/Clapham/kids-club.htm
⊖ Clapham Common **Bus** 88, 137, 155, 345, 355
Times Sat 11.15am (film starts at 11.45am) **Ages** 3–10
Adm Members £2, non-members £3, accompanying adults £3 (all children must be accompanied by an adult); annual membership £4

At the weekly pre-screening workshops, kids can design their own space ship, make a cartoon picture book or mould plasticine.

Electric Cinema

191 Portobello Road, W11 **t** (020) 7908 9696
www.electriccinema.co.uk/kids.php
⊖ Notting Hill Gate
Times Sat, films at 11am and 1pm **Ages** 4–12
Adm £3.50 members, £4.50 non-members, accompanying adults

Games and activities inspired by the screenings. Parents and Babies Club on Thursdays, when parents can take babies to a movie where snuffling, singing and crying babies are the norm.

Movie Magic at the NFT

National Film Theatre 2, BFI, South Bank, SE1
t (020) 7928 3232 **www.bfi.org.uk/moviemagic**
⊖ /≋ Waterloo **Bus** 1, 4, 26, 68, 76, 168, 171, 176, 188, 341, 501, 505, 521, X68
Times Sat afternoon, call for times **Ages** 6–12
Adm Children £1, accompanying adult £4.50

The NFT shows a range of classic family films, and organizes movie workshops on the first Saturday of the month, where kids can learn about the techniques of film-craft. Supervised by experts, they can try creating animation, making props and costumes or writing their own short film script.

Phoenix Cinema

52 High Road, East Finchley, N2 **t** (020) 8444 6789
www.phoenixcinema.co.uk/families/
⊖ East Finchley **Bus** 102, 143, 263
Times Every other Sat 11am (film starts 12 noon)
Adm Under-12s £5.50, under-8s £4.50, film only £3; 'Bringing up Baby' screenings £4 **Ages** 6–11

Screenings combined with hands-on activities such as painting and model-making aim to introduce children to the wonders of world cinema. Also 'Bringing up Baby' screenings on Tuesday mornings for parents with babies.

Ritzy Cinema

Brixton Oval, Coldharbour Lane, SW2
t (020) 7733 2229 **www.ritzycinema.co.uk**
⊖ Brixton **Bus** 35, 37, 118, 196, 250, P4, P5
Times Sat 10.30am **Ages** Under 12
Adm Child £1, accompanying adult £3

Special kids' events for over and under 7s; free tea, coffee and newspapers for parents.

Museums and Galleries

See 'Things to see and do', pp.37–60, for full details of Central London galleries and museums listed below.

Bank of England Museum

Threadneedle Street, EC2
t (020) 7601 5545 **www.bankofengland.co.uk**
⊖ Bank, Cannon Street (p.56)

Bramah Tea & Coffee Museum

40 Southwark Street, SE1
t (020) 7403 5650 **www.bramahmuseum.co.uk**
⊖/≋ London Bridge (p.53)

British Museum

Great Russell Street, WC1
t (020) 7636 1555 **www.thebritishmuseum.ac.uk**
⊖ Tottenham Court Road, Russell Square, Holborn (pp.39–40)

Churchill Museum and Cabinet War Rooms

King Charles Street, SW1
t (020) 7766 0120 **www.cwr.iwm.org.uk**
⊖ Westminster, St James's Park (p.45)

Clink Museum

1 Clink Street, SE1
t (020) 7403 6515 **www.clink.co.uk**
⊖/≋ London Bridge (p.53)

Design Museum

28 Shad Thames, Butler's Wharf, SE1
t (020) 7940 8790 **www.designmuseum.org**
⊖ London Bridge, Tower Hill (p.53)

Dickens' House

48 Doughty Street, WC1
t (020) 7405 2127 **www.dickensmuseum.com**
⊖ Chancery Lane, Russell Square (p.40)

Florence Nightingale Museum

St Thomas Hospital, 2 Lambeth Palace Road, SE1
t (020) 7620 0374 **www.florence-nightingale.co.uk**
⊖/≋ Waterloo (p.51)

Geffrye Museum
136 Kingsland Road, E2
t (020) 7739 9893 www.geffrye-museum.org.uk
Θ Old Street (p.56)

Hayward Gallery
Belvedere Road, South Bank Centre, SE1
t (020) 7690 4242 www.hayward.org.uk
Θ Waterloo, Embankment ≋ Waterloo (p.52)

HMS *Belfast*
Morgan's Lane, off Tooley Street, SE1
t (020) 7940 6300 www.hmsbelfast.iwm.org.uk
Θ/ ≋ London Bridge (p.53)

Imperial War Museum
Lambeth Road, SE1
t (020) 7416 5320 www.london.iwm.org.uk
Θ Lambeth North, Elephant & Castle (p.52)

London Canal Museum
12–13 New Wharf Road, N1
t (020) 7713 0836 www.canalmuseum.org.uk
Θ King's Cross (p.37)

London Dungeon
Tooley Street, SE1
t (020) 7403 7221 www.thedungeons.com
Θ/ ≋ London Bridge (p.54)

London's Transport Museum
Covent Garden, WC2
t (020) 7565 7299 www.ltmuseum.co.uk
Θ Covent Garden/Leicester Square (p.40)

Madame Tussaud's & London Auditorium
Marylebone Road, NW1
t (020) 7935 6861 www.madame-tussauds.co.uk
Θ Baker Street (pp.37–8)

Museum of London
London Wall, EC2
t 0870 444 3851 www.museumoflondon.org.uk
Θ Barbican, Bank, St Paul's (pp.56–7)

National Gallery
Trafalgar Square, WC2
t (020) 7747 2885 www.nationalgallery.org.uk
Θ Charing Cross, Leicester Square, Embankment (pp.41–2)

National Maritime Museum
Romney Road, Greenwich, SE10
t (020) 8312 6565 www.nmm.ac.uk
≋ Greenwich, DLR Greenwich, Cutty Sark (pp.58–9)

National Portrait Gallery
St Martin's Place, WC2
t (020) 7306 0055 www.npg.org.uk
Θ Charing Cross, Leicester Square, Embankment (pp.42–3)

Natural History Museum
Cromwell Road, SW7
t (020) 7942 5000 www.nhm.ac.uk
Θ South Kensington (pp.47–8)

Old Operating Theatre
9a St Thomas Street, SE1
t (020) 7955 4791 www.thegarret.org.uk
Θ/ ≋ London Bridge (p.54)

Saatchi Gallery
County Hall, Riverside Building, Belvedere Road, SE1
t (020) 7823 2363 www.saatchi-gallery.co.uk
Θ Waterloo, Embankment ≋ Waterloo (p.51)

Science Museum
Exhibition Road, London SW7
t 0870 870 4868 www.sciencemuseum.org.uk
Θ South Kensington (pp.48–9)

Shakespeare's Globe Theatre
Bear Gardens, Bankside, New Globe Walk, Southwark, SE1
t (020) 7902 1400
www.shakespeares-globe.org.uk
Θ/ ≋ London Bridge(p.54)

Sherlock Holmes Museum
221b Baker Street, NW1
t (020) 7935 8866 www.sherlock-holmes.co.uk
Θ Baker Street (p.38)

Sir John Soane's Museum
12–14 Lincoln's Inn Fields, WC2
t (020) 7405 2107 www.soane.org
Θ Holborn (p.40)

Somerset House
Strand, WC2
t (020) 7845 4600 www.somerset-house.org.uk
Θ Temple, Charing Cross, Embankment, Covent Garden (p.41)

Tate Britain
Millbank, SW1
t (020) 7887 8000 www.tate.org.uk/britain
Θ Pimlico, Vauxhall ≋ Vauxhall (p.46)

Tate Modern
Bankside, SE1
t (020) 7887 8000 www.tate.org.uk
⊖/⇌ London Bridge, Blackfriars (p.55)

Theatre Museum
Russell Street, WC1
t (020) 7943 4700 www.theatremuseum.org
⊖ Covent Garden/Leicester Square (p.41)

Tower of London
Tower Hill, EC3
t 0870 756 6060 www.hrp.org.uk
⊖ Tower Hill (p.57)

Victoria & Albert Museum
Cromwell Road, SW7
t (020) 7942 2000 www.vam.ac.uk
⊖ South Kensington (p.49)

The Wallace Collection
Hertford House, Manchester Square, W1
t (020) 7563 9500 www.wallacecollection.org
⊖ Bond Street, Marble Arch (p.41)

Outside Central London
The suburbs are home to some great local museums and galleries.

Bethnal Green Museum of Childhood
Cambridge Heath Road, E2
t (020) 8983 5200 Infoline t (020) 8980 2415
www.museumofchildhood.org.uk
⊖ Bethnal Green Bus 8, 106, 253, 309, D6
Open Mon–Thurs, Sat–Sun 10–6
Adm Free (donations welcome)
A wonderful collection of historic childhood artefacts, including clothes, toys, nursery furniture and baby equipment. Pride of place goes to the two Dolls' House Streets (three centuries' worth of miniature homes) and a display of dolls – from 17th-century porcelain beauties to plastic modern Barbies. Kids can dress up and play 'What Will I Be?' and the museum organizes lots of events for kids, such as art workshops where children can make their own finger puppets.

Dulwich Picture Gallery
Gallery Road, Dulwich Village, SE21
t (020) 8693 5254
www.dulwichpicturegallery.org.uk
⇌ North Dulwich Bus P4, P15
Open Tues–Fri 10–5, Sat, Sun and Bank Hols 11–5
Adm Adults £4, children free; Fridays free for all

Recently refurbished, this is one of the finest galleries outside central London (it was also one of the first). The collection includes Rembrandt's *Girl at a Window* and Gainsborough's *Linley Sisters*, as well as works by Rubens, Poussin, Canaletto and Raphael. The adjacent park is a great spot for picnics. Free, drop-in art workshops are held in the summer holidays, as well as Saturday morning and after-school art clubs.

Firepower Museum
Royal Arsenal, SE18 t (020) 8855 7755
www.firepower.org.uk
⇌ Woolwich Arsenal Bus 96, 161, 180, 472
Open Daily 10–5
Adm Adults £5, children (5–16) £2.50, family £12
Housed in a former arsenal, this is a more whizz-bang version of the Imperial War Museum, with an impressive range of military hardware but less emphasis on the human cost of weapons. It's noisy, with battlefield re-enactments and hands-on computerized simulators to trace the development of military firepower from sling-shot to computer-guided missiles. Kids wil enjoy the Command Post on the first floor, with a paintball range and climbing wall. Would-be cadets can stock up on combat gear, toys and ammo' in the shop.

Horniman Museum
100 London Road, SE23 t (020) 8699 1872
www.horniman.ac.uk
⇌ Forest Hill Bus 63, 122, 176, 185, 312, P4, P13
Open Mon–Sat 10.30–5.30, Sun 2–5.30
Adm Free (charge for temporary exhibitions)
Founded in the early 19th century by the tea magnate Frederick Horniman, the museum defies classification. It has a vast ethnographic collection, including South American tribal masks, African head dresses and Egyptian mummies; a fantastic array of animal exhibits – look out for the Goliath beetle, the largest insect in the world; and one of the country's most important collections of musical instruments, plus an interactive music display where, using touch-screen computers and headphones, kids can find out about (and listen to) some of the world's more obscure instruments. Perhaps it could simply be classed as South London's premier treasure trove.
Revamped in recent years, with a whole new layer of interactivity, the museum is now better than ever – but it's still the sheer clutter and variety that enthralls. At the new 'Hands-on Base',

kids have a chance to touch and examine more than 4,000 miscellaneous items, while the museum hosts family workshop events such as making an Ancient Egyptian mummy case. The gardens are equally wonderful.

Kew Bridge Steam Museum

Green Dragon Lane, Brentford, Middlesex, TW8 **t** (020) 8568 4757 **www.kbsm.org**
≥ Kew Bridge Station ⊖ Gunnersbury, Kew Gardens **Bus** 237, 267, 391 (Sun only)
Open Daily 11–5
Adm Mon–Fri adults £3.60, children £2, family (2+3) £10; Sat–Sun adults £5.20, children £3, family £15; **free** for all after 4pm

Kew Bridge Steam Museum offers a down-to-earth contrast to all those flower beds and neatly sculpted lawns across the river at Kew Gardens. It focuses on the development of London's water supply and sewage system from Roman times to the present day, with a collection of Victorian water-pumping machinery, including the two largest beam engines in the world (sometimes powered up at weekends). Kids love the replica London sewage system, rats and all, the Water of Life exhibition has plenty of levers and buttons to push and pull, and there's a full programme of family events in summer.

National Army Museum and Royal Hospital

Royal Hospital Road, Chelsea, SW3 **t** (020) 7730 0717
www.national-army-museum.ac.uk
⊖ Sloane Square **Bus** 11, 19, 22, 137, 239
Open Daily 10–5.30 **Adm Free**

Tells the story of British army life from the 16th century to the present day. Kids will like the recreation of the Battle of Waterloo using 75,000 toy soliders. The museum is next to Christopher Wren's Royal Hospital, founded by Charles II in the 17th century as a home for army veterans and still home to 400 red-coated Chelsea pensioners today.

Ragged School Museum

46–50 Copperfield Road, E3 **t** (020) 8980 6405
www.raggedschoolmuseum.org.uk
⊖ Mile End **Bus** 25, 277, 309, D6, D7
Open Wed–Thurs 10–5, first Sun of month 2–5
Adm Free

Dr Barnardo, a young missionary, ran this 'Ragged School' to provide free education for the poorest children of London's East End in Victorian Times.

Kids can walk through the classrooms, sit at the old desks and write on the slates. The museum also organizes activities, including parlour games and old-fashioned sweet-making sessions.

Royal Air Force Museum

Grahame Park Way, NW9 **t** (020) 8205 2266
www.rafmuseum.org.uk
⊖ Colindale ≥ Mill Hill Broadway **Bus** 204, 303
Open Daily 10–6 **Adm Free**

On the site of the former Hendon Aerodrome, the museum is made up of two huge hangars stuffed full of aeronautical hardware – from bi-planes and Battle of Britain Spitfires to the awesome vertical take-off Harrier jump jet. The highlight is undoubtedly the flight simulator in which you get to take the controls of a Tornado – be warned, it's intense.

Music
Listening to music

For details of forthcoming pop (rock, folk, jazz etc.) concerts, consult the weekly listings magazine *Time Out* or the *Evening Standard*'s free 'Metro Life' supplement (Thursday). Many will take obviously take place at night, in venues not licensed for children, but there are sometimes mellower Sunday music sessions, and in summer outdoor concerts in the parks. Classical music, on the other hand, adheres to a calendar (albeit a fluid one); you might like to keep an eye out for the following.

Kenwood House Lakeside Concerts

Hampstead Lane, NW3 **t** 0870 333 1181
www.english-heritage.org.uk
⊖ Archway, Golders Green then bus 210 **Bus** 210
Open July–Aug **Adm** £18–£26, under-5s **free**
For further information *see* pp.36, 65

London Coliseum

St Martin's Lane, WC2 **t** (020) 7632 8300
www.eno.org
⊖ Leicester Square, Charing Cross
Bus 14, 19, 24, 29, 38, 176
Open/Adm Call for dates, times and prices

Operatic workshops and short performances for ages 7 and over. Children and accompanying adults can take part in plot summaries and improvisation sessions, and listen to a sung excerpt from the opera in question.

London Symphony Orchestra Family Discovery Concerts

Barbican, Silk Street, EC2 **t** (020) 7638 8891
www.barbican.org.uk
⊖ Barbican **Bus** 4, 56
Open One or two a season; call in advance
Adm Adults £5, children (under 16) £3

A popular annual event designed to get children aged 7–12 interested in classical music. The programmes mainly comprise short pieces and there is lots of audience participation. Orchestra musicians mingle with the crowds during the interval and will give any child who brings along an instrument an impromptu music lesson.

Royal Festival Hall

South Bank Arts Centre, SE1 **t** (020) 7336 0777
www.rfh.org.uk
⊖ Waterloo, Embankment ⇌ Waterloo
Open/Adm Call for dates, times and prices

The resident London Philharmonic Orchestra programmes various child-friendly concerts during the year, such as the 'Little Red Riding Hood Songbook'.

Royal Opera House

Bow Street, WC2 **t** (020) 7304 4000
www.royaloperahouse.org
⊖ Covent Garden/Leicester Square
Bus 6, 9, 11, 13, 15, 23, 77A, 91, 176
Open Tours: Mon–Sat 10.30am, 12.30 and 2.30pm
Adm School matinées £6

As well as the free classical concerts now staged in its foyer, there is an education programme comprising six 'school matinées' a year, with opera and ballet performances for schools and colleges. Information packs are available online for teachers.

Wigmore Hall

36 Wigmore Street **t** (020) 7935 2141
www.wigmore-hall.org.uk
⊖ Bond Street
Bus 6, 7, 10, 12, 13, 15, 23, 73, 94, 98, 113, 135, 137, 139, 159, 189
Open Call for dates and times **Adm** £5

Organizes Chamber Tots sound workshops for under-5s, hands-on music-making sessions for over-5s (which culminate in a concert) and school holiday music groups for over-11s.

Making Music

Whether it's pop, classical or 'world' music, your kids will always have much more fun making a racket than listening to one.

Guildhall School of Music

Silk Street, Barbican, EC2 **t** (020) 7638 1770
www.gsmd.ac.uk
⊖ Barbican **Bus** 4, 56

This prestigious school runs weekly music courses for all abilities during term time. Children can learn an instrument or have vocal coaching and, if they reach a sufficient standard, join one of two youth orchestras.

Horniman Music Room Workshops

100 London Road, SE23 **t** (020) 8699 1872
www.horniman.ac.uk
⇌ Forest Hill **Bus** 63, 122, 176, 185, 312, P4, P13
Open Call for workshop dates and times **Adm Free**

The Horniman Museum houses one of Britain's largest and most important collections of musical instruments. Children can explore their sounds at one of the museum's regular workshops (pp.76–7).

The Music House for Children

Bush Hall, 310 Uxbridge Road, London, W12
t (020 8932 2652)
www.musichouseforchildren.co.uk
⊖ Shepherd's Bush
Bus 207, 260, 283, 607

The Music House for Children, run from Bush Hall, has an extensive music and arts education programme. It provides group tuition throughout the week involving music, dance and drama.

National Festival of Music for Youth

Royal Festival Hall, South Bank, SE1
t (020) 8878 9624 www.mfy.org.uk
⊖/ ⇌ Waterloo **Bus** 1, 4, 26, 68, 76, 168, 171, 176, 188, 341, 501, 505, 521, X68

In July, a vast collection of school orchestras and youth bands comprising some 12,000 musicians gather at the Royal Festival Hall for a huge musical jamboree (the biggest of its kind in the world), during which music workshops and classes for both adults and children are held. In November, the festival's best musicians also play three concerts at the Royal Albert Hall.

Theatre

On any given night, there will be more than 60 productions showing in the West End. Obviously not all are suitable for children, but many theatres specialize in all-singing, all-dancing shows targeted at a family audience. For details check newspapers and weekly listings magazines such as *Time Out*.

Performances are typically at 7.30pm Monday to Saturday with additional matinée performances on Wednesday and Saturday.

Behind the scenes

The following theatres offer backstage tours where you can explore dressing rooms, wardrobes and costume departments, and find out about the elaborate machinery used to get the scenery on and off the stage.

London Palladium

Argyll Street, W1 **t** (020) 7494 5091
⊖ Oxford Circus **Bus** 3, 6, 7, 8, 10, 12, 13, 15, 23, 25, 53, 55, 73, 88, 94, 98, 139, 159, 176, X53
Tours Mon, Tues, Thurs and Fri at 12.30 and 4.30pm; Wed and Sat at 12.30pm
Adm £4

National Theatre

South Bank, SE1 **t** (020) 7452 3400
www.nationaltheatre.org.uk
⊖ /≋ Waterloo **Bus** 1, 4, 26, 68, 76, 168, 171, 176, 188, 341, 501, 505, 521, X68
Tours Mon–Sat three times a day; lasts 1hr 15mins
Adm Backstage tours: £5, family £13

Children's theatre

London is home to several theatre companies that put on their own child-friendly performances, and offer training and advice to aspiring young thespians. Here are some of the best.

Battersea Arts Centre

Old Town Hall, Lavender Hill, SW11 **t** (020) 7223 2223
www.bac.org.uk
≋ Clapham Junction **Bus** 77, 77A, 345
Open Mon 10–6, Tues–Sun 10–9
Adm Drama workshops £4.50; children's theatre: adults £5.75, children £4.50; membership: children £10.75, family £16.50

Organizes theatre workshops for 3–16-year-olds and stages a children's drama performance every Saturday at 2.30pm. Be aware that they're hugely popular and places are limited.

Half Moon Young People's Theatre

43 White Horse Road, E1 **t** (020) 7709 8900
www.halfmoon.org.uk
⊖ Stepney Green ≋ Limehouse
Bus 5, 15, 15b, 25, 40, 106, 253
Open 10–6 (performance times vary)
Adm Performance: adults £5, children £3.50

This serious-minded theatre group runs weekday and Saturday theatre workshops on themes ranging from street dance to mask-making. It stages a programme of kids' theatre on Saturdays at 11.30am and 2pm.

Little Angel Theatre

14 Dagmar Passage, Cross Street, N1
t (020) 7226 1787 www.littleangeltheatre.com
⊖ Angel, Highbury & Islington
Bus 4, 19, 30, 38, 43, 56, 73, 341
Open Performances: Sat at 11am and 3pm
Adm Adults £7.50, children £5; puppet course £65

A wonderful puppet theatre which holds regular weekend performances and also runs 10-week puppet courses on Saturday mornings at which kids can make and learn how to use puppets, before performing on the Angel stage. Children must be aged 3 or over.

London Bubble

t (020) 7237 4434
www.londonbubble.org.uk
Open/Adm Call for dates, times and prices

This popular roving theatre company moves its mobile show tents around the parks of London in summer. The plays are aimed at 11-year-olds and under. It also holds workshops for ages 3–6.

Polka Theatre

240 The Broadway, SW19 **t** (020) 8543 4888
www.polkatheatre.com
⊖ /≋ Wimbledon ⊖ South Wimbledon
Bus 57, 93, 155
Open Tues–Fri 9.30–4.30, Sat 10–5
Adm Performances: £5–£10; workshops £55

The capital's only purpose-built children's theatre. Four shows a day in school holidays, two in term-time. It also runs drama and puppetry workshops and after-school clubs for all ages. The shows are usually of a very high standard and a mixture of classics and new work.

Puppet Theatre Barge

Bloomfield Road, Little Venice, W9
t (020) 7249 6876 www.puppetbarge.com

Bus 6, 18, 46
Open Call for times
Adm Adult £7, child £6.50
The Moving Stage Marionettes Company, which operates the barge, puts on puppet shows all year, although it moves from its mooring on Regent's Canal in summer, plying the Thames instead.

Regent's Park Open Air Theatre

Regent's Park, NW1 **t** 0870 060 1811
www.openairtheatre.org
Adm Daytime performances: £9.50–£26; evening tickets: £6; family shows: £9
⊖ Baker Street
Bus 2, 13, 18, 27, 30, 74, 82, 113, 139, 189, 205, 274
For further information see p.65

Shakespeare's Globe Theatre

Bear Gardens, Bankside, New Globe Walk, Southwark, SE1 **t** (020) 7902 1400
www.shakespeares-globe.org.uk
⊖/ ⇌ London Bridge
Bus 11, 15, 17, 23, 26, 45, 63, 76, 100, 344, 381, RV1
Open Daily 10–5; call workshop times
Adm 'Child's Play' Workshops £10
On select Saturdays, children aged 8–11 can take part in 'Child's Play' drama sessions at the Globe. For further information see p.54

Tricycle Theatre

269 Kilburn High Road, NW6 **t** (020) 7328 1000
www.tricycle.co.uk
⊖ Kilburn **Bus** 16, 31, 32, 98, 189, 206, 316, 328
Open Performances Sat at 11.30am and 2pm
Adm Performances: £5; workshops £20
The theatre holds about 300 workshops a year for all ages, offering nine-week courses in acting, singing, dancing, music, mime, puppetry and circus skills. Its own family theatre performances are both highly innovative and hugely popular, taking place every Saturday of the academic year (Sept–Jun) at 11.30am and 2pm.

Unicorn Theatre

147 Tooley Street, Southwark, SE1 **t** (020) 7645 0500, box office **t** 08700 534 534
www.unicorntheatre.com
⊖ London Bridge, Tower Hill **DLR** Tower Gateway
⇌ London Bridge **Bus** 47, RV1, 381
The Unicorn continues to stage award-winning productions for children at its new Southwark home. Family Days (£24) offer workshops, refreshments and a chance to meet the cast too.

EATING OUT

Cheap Eats

Café in the Crypt

St Martin-in-the-Fields, WC2 **t** (020) 7839 4342
⊖ Charing Cross
Open Mon–Sat 10–8, Sun 12 noon–8
Dungeonesque subterranean café which appeals to kids. Hot dishes, vegetarian meals and snacks. Half-price half portions and highchairs available.

Chelsea Kitchen

98 King's Road, SW3 **t** (020) 7589 1330
⊖ Sloane Square
Open Mon–Sat 8am–11.30pm, Sun 9am–11.30pm
Wide range of sandwiches, salads and pasta.

Ed's Easy Diner

12 Moor Street W1 **t** (020) 7439 1955
⊖ Tottenham Court Road
Open Sun–Thurs 11.30am–12 midnight, Fri–Sat 11.30am–1am
Fabulous burgers at this mock 1950s 'rock 'n' roll' diner. Kids' menu £4.45. Highchairs available.

Giraffe

6–8 Blandford Street, W1 **t** (020) 7935 2333
and branches everywhere www.giraffe.net
⊖ Baker Street; **Open** 8am–11.30pm daily
Bright décor, piped world music and children's menu of simple dishes and fruity shakes (£4.95), plus games and puzzles. Highchairs available.

Goddard's Pie House

45 Greenwich Church Street, SE10
t (020) 8293 9313, www.pieshop.co.uk
⇌ Greenwich, **DLR** Greenwich, Cutty Sark
Open Mon–Fri 10–6.30, Sat–Sun 10–7.30
Traditional London food served up by the fifth generation of Goddard's: minced beef, steak and kidney, eel or cheese and onion pie with mash, followed by blackberry and apple pie with ice cream.

Manze's

87 Tower Bridge Road, SE1 **t** (020) 2407 2985
www.manze.co.uk, ⊖ London Bridge, Tower Hill
Open Mon 11–2, Tues–Thurs 10.30–2, Fri 10–2.15, Sat 10–2.45
The oldest pie and mash shop in London (opened in 1862). Traditional food – minced beef pies, jellied eels and dollops of mash topped with liquor (parsley sauce) – has people queuing round the block. It's very cheap too: where else can you feed a family of 4 for under £15?

African

Calabash
Africa Centre, 8 King Street, WC2 **t** (020) 7836 1936
🚇 Covent Garden
Open Mon–Fri 12.30–3 and 6–11
   Couscous, groundnut stew and Yassa (grilled chicken in a lemon sauce). Cheap kids' portions.

American

Bodeans
17 Poland Street, W1 **t** (020) 7287 7575
www.bodeansbbq.com 🚇 Oxford Circus
Open Mon–Fri 12 noon–11, Sat–Sun 12 noon–10.30
   American-style smokehouse with kids TV lounge at weekends, when children eat free (otherwise £5).

Maxwell's
8/9 James Street, WC2 **t** (020) 7836 0303
🚇 Covent Garden, Embankment, Leicester Square
Open 11am–12 midnight daily
   Chicken nuggets, fish 'stix', burgers and hot dogs, topped off by deep-fried ice cream, on the daytime kids' menu. Good views of street entertainers.

British

Rock and Sole Plaice
47 Endell Street, WC2 **t** (020) 7836 3785
🚇 Covent Garden
Open Daily 11.30–10.30
   The oldest fish and chip shop in the capital (it opened in 1871). Large portions of battered fish and chunky chips. Outside seating and highchairs.

Seashell
49–51 Lisson Grove, NW1 **t** (020) 7224 9000
🚇 Marylebone
Open Mon–Fri 12 noon–2.30 and 5–10.30, Sat 12 noon–10.30
   Two floors serving crisp fish and crunchy chips; a long-time favourite of Londoners.

Greek

Daphne
83 Bayham Street, NW1 **t** (020) 7267 7322
🚇 Camden Town
Open Mon–Sat 12 noon–2.30 and 6–11.30
   Warm, welcoming and very popular Greek restaurant with a lovely sunny roof terrace. Children's portions and highchairs available.

Indian

Veeraswamy
99–101 Regent Street, W1 **t** (020) 7734 1401
www.veeraswamy.com 🚇 Piccadilly Circus
Open Mon–Sat 12 noon–2.30 and 5.30–11.30, Sun 12.30–3
   Child-friendly Indian restaurant (it claims to be the UK's oldest). Sunday is the designated family day, when a kids' menu of lightly spiced Indian dishes is on offer for £8 and there are crayons, colouring books and goodie bags. High chairs.

Italian

La Lanterna
6–8 Mill Street, SE1 **t** (020) 7252 2420
www.millstreetcafe.co.uk 🚇 Tower Hill
Open 12 noon–11pm
   Small, homely, traditional Italian restaurant serving good, reasonably priced fare. Half portions and highchairs available. Music in the evenings.

Monza
6 Yeoman's Row, SW3 **t** (020) 7591 0210
🚇 South Kensington, Knightsbridge
Open Tues–Sun 12 noon–2.30 and 7–11.30, Mon 7–11.30
   Small, quaint, family-orientated Italian restaurant offering a range of pizza, pasta and risotto dishes.

Oriental

Benihana
37–43 Sackville Street, W1 **t** (020) 7494 2525 and branches **www.benihana.co.uk**
🚇 Piccadilly Circus, Green Park
Open Mon–Tues 6pm–11pm, Wed–Fri 12 noon–3 and 6–11, Sat–Sun 12 noon–11
   Fun Japanese noodle chain. Several dishes are designed for children's tastes. Highchairs available.

New World
1 Gerrard Place, W1 **t** (020) 7734 0396
🚇 Leicester Square
Open Daily 11am–late
   On Sundays it's packed with families tucking into bowls of *dim sum*, the popular Chinese pick and mix meal, with an assortment of dishes wheeled around on trolleys. Chinese dumplings are the restaurant's speciality). Try the special child-size mini *dim sum*.

Royal Dragon

30 Gerrard Street, W1 t (020) 7734 1388
⊖ Leicester Square
Open Daily 11am–late

Excellent dim sum and a family-friendly atmosphere, particularly on Sundays.

Yo! Sushi

52 Poland Street, W1 t (020) 7287 0443
and branches www.yosushi.co.uk
⊖ Oxford Circus, Tottenham Court Road County
Open 12 noon–12 midnight daily

Pick sushi dishes from an enormous conveyor belt whilst your drinks are prepared by a special drinks-mixing robot. During the week under-12s eat for free. Highchairs.

Pizzas

Gourmet Pizza Company

Gabriel's Wharf, 56 Upper Ground, SE1
and branches t (020) 7928 3188 ⊖ Waterloo
Open 12 noon–10.30

Small, rather upmarket chain serving reliably excellent pizzas. Highchairs available.

Pizza on the Park

11 Knightsbridge, SW3 t (020) 7255 5273
www.pizzaonthepark.co.uk
⊖ Hyde Park Corner, Knightsbridge
Open Mon–Fri 8.15am–12 midnight, Sat–Sun 9.30am–12 midnight

A longstanding favourite for park- and museum-goers, this cheery pizzeria hands out colouring books, crayons and balloons at weekends, when live jazz is played. Children's portions and highchairs.

Pizza Organic

20 Old Brompton Road, SW7
t (020) 7589 9613, ⊖ South Kensington
www.pizzapiazza.co.uk
Open Daily 11.30am–12 midnight

Organic kids' menu designed by Jamie Oliver at this environmentally friendly pizzeria.

Posh Nosh

Locanda Locatelli

38 Seymour Street, W1 t (020) 7935 9088
www.locandalocatelli.com ⊖ Marble Arch
Open 12 noon–3 & 7–11 daily

Giorgio Locatelli is determined to bring the Italian tradition of good family eating to London with his upmarket, family-friendly restaurant.

Tea-Time Treats

Fortnum & Mason Fountain Room

181 Piccadilly, W1 t (020) 7734 8040
www.fortnumandmason.co.uk ⊖ Piccadilly Circus
Open Mon–Sat 7.30am–11pm

A wonderfully elegant tea room set in the basement of the Queen's grocers. Children's menu on offer, but the highlight here is definitely the wide and delicious range of ice creams, sorbets, sundaes and sodas. It's a haven of old-fashioned style and charm. When you've finished, pop outside to watch the famous Fortnum & Mason clock.

Gloriette Patisserie

128 Brompton Road, SW3 t (020) 7589 4750
⊖ Knightsbridge
Open Mon–Sat 7am–7pm, Sun 9–6

Tempting cakes, from creamy chocolate gateaux to glazed fruit tarts and a wide variety of snacks.

Patisserie Valerie

215 Brompton Road, Knightsbridge, SW3
and branches t (020) 7823 9971 ⊖ Knightsbridge
Open Mon–Fri 7.30–7, Sat 8–7, Sun 9–6

Established in the 1920s by Belgian-born baker Madame Valerie, this patisserie-cum-café chain has a pleasant Continental ambience and a wonderful array of sticky treats.

Ritz Hotel

150 Piccadilly, W1 t (020) 7493 8181
www.theritzhotel.co.uk ⊖ Green Park
Tea Daily 1.30pm, 3.30pm and 5.30pm

Afternoon tea at the Ritz is rather steep at £34 a head, but the setting and the sight of the cakes, sandwiches and scones piled high on silver platters make it an experience few children are likely to forget. Book well in advance (at least three months for a weekend) and dress smartly (no jeans).

Treat Eats

The Blue Kangaroo

555 Kings Road, SW6 t (020) 7371 7672
www.thebluekangaroo.co.uk ⊖ Fulham Broadway
Open Daily 9.30–8.30

Arguably London's best family restaurant, the Blue Kangaroo is a sort of combined dining room and play zone. The wipe-clean kids' menu (£4.95) is organic, offering free-range chicken nuggets and additive-free burgers, while downstairs is a great collection of soft play equipment –

nets, tunnels, slides, ball pools, and so on – where kids can run amok while their parents enjoy a more relaxing meal, but still keep a keen eye on their charges on the live video link.

Hard Rock Café
150 Old Park Lane, W1 **t** (020) 7629 0382
www.hardrock.com ⊖ Hyde Park Corner
Open Mon–Thurs 11.30am–12 midnight, Fri–Sat 11.30am–1am, Sun 11.30am–11.30pm

Younger kids can enjoy the colour-in menu (£4.25) and the collection of toys. Older siblings will love the videos and rock stars' jackets. Go downstairs to the Vault for a tour of curious bits and bobs left behind on the road to eternal stardom. Bo Diddley's home-made guitar, John Lennon's military jacket and Buddy Holly's trademark specs are among the highlights.

Planet Hollywood
13 Coventry Street, W1 **t** (020) 7734 6220
www.planethollywoodlondon.com
⊖ Leicester Square, Piccadilly Circus
Open Sun–Thurs 12 noon–11, Fri–Sat 12 noon–12 midnight

Kids like the garish posters and cabinets full of movie memorabilia. The food is expensive (the kids' menu costs £7.95).

★Rainforest Café
20 Shaftesbury Avenue W1 **t** (020) 7434 3111
www.therainforestcafe.co.uk
⊖ Leicester Square, Piccadilly Circus
Open Sun–Thurs 12 noon–11, Fri–Sat 12 noon– 12 midnight

The tables and chairs sit among the trees and foliage of an artificial rainforest. Inhabiting the dense undergrowth are various mechanical animals, including chimps, monkeys, alligators, birds and snakes, who come to life every 15 minutes after an artificial thunderstorm. The grill-style kids' menu costs a rather hefty £10.25.

Smollensky's
105 The Strand, WC2 **t** (020) 7497 2101
and branches **www.**smollenskys.co.uk
⊖ Embankment, Charing Cross
Open Mon–Wed 12 noon–12 midnight, Thurs–Sat 12 noon–12.30am, Sun 12 noon–5.30 and 6.30–11

Kids can have their faces painted, watch a Punch and Judy show, take part in magic tricks and eat something from the American-style kids' menu (£4.95). Book in advance.

Sticky Fingers
1a Phillimore Gardens, W8 **t** (020) 7938 5338
www.stickyfingers.co.uk
⊖ High Street Kensington, Holland Park
Open 12 noon–12 midnight daily

Rolling Stones' bass guitarist and restaurant owner Bill Wyman's collection of rock and roll memorabilia may be lost on kids, but they will enjoy the burgers and fries (children's menu £7.25) and the magic shows, activities and face painting that are laid on on Sunday afternoons. Highchairs.

TGI Friday's
6 Bedford Street, WC2 **t** (020) 7379 0585
and branches **www.**tgifridays.co.uk
⊖ Covent Garden, Leicester Square
Open Mon–Sat 12 noon–11.30, Sun 12 noon–11

An ever-popular choice, this lively Tex-Mex diner is a bargain for families, offering children's menus for £3.25 and £3.45, comprising the usual hamburger, hotdog and chicken finger combinations plus a dessert and a drink, as well as free organic baby food for children aged 4–15 months. Highchairs, booster seats and colouring books available.

Vegetarian

Food For Thought
31 Neal Street, WC2 **t** (020) 7836 0239
⊖ Covent Garden
Open Mon–Sat 12 noon–8.30, Sun 12 noon–5

Cheap and friendly, serving quiches, salads, soups, etc. It can get a little crowded, so turn up for an early lunch to be sure of a seat.

Manna
4 Erskine Road, NW1 **t** (020) 7722 8028
www.manna-veg.com ⊖ Chalk Farm
Open Mon–Sat 6pm–11pm, Sun 12.30–3 and 6–11

Spacious, popular and highly regarded veggie restaurant. No smoking throughout.

Oshobasho
Highgate Wood, Muswell Hill, N10
t (020) 8444 1505, ⊖ Highgate
Open Daily 8.30–7.30; park gates close at 8.30pm

Extremely popular vegetarian restaurant in the idyllic setting of Highgate Wood. Familes flock to its large outdoor seating area at the weekends. There's also a children's play area (see p.66).

LONDON FOR FREE

London is one of the most expensive cities in the world. Even so, it is possible to have a fun day out without breaking the bank.

Churches

Admission to all the churches in London is free – except for St Paul's Cathedral and Westminster Abbey. Free concerts and carol services take place several times a year – notably at Christmas.

City farms

Coram's Fields and Vauxhall City Farm allow families to pet and stroke their animals free of charge (p.64).

Entertainment

Free foyer concerts are often given at the National Theatre (p.52), Royal Festival Hall (p.52) and Barbican (p.56) in the early evening. Covent Garden plays host to some of the country's top buskers and street performers every day, and there's a Festival of Street Theatre every September (p.36).

Events & festivals

Ceremonial events such as the Changing of the Guard outside Buckingham Palace (p.44) and the Ceremony of the Keys at the Tower of London (p.34) take place daily, and can be watched free of charge. There are also various free annual events (pp.34–6).

Museums & galleries

Some of the capital's most prestigious collections, including the Natural History Museum, Science Museum, Museum of London, National Maritime Museum and the Imperial War Museum, have recently taken the decision to waive their entrance fees. Many more never charged in the first place.

Bank of England Museum (p.56)
Bethnal Green Museum of Childhood (p.76)
British Museum (pp.39–40)
Geffrye Museum (p.56)
Horniman Museum (pp.76–7)
Houses of Parliament (pp.45–6)
Imperial War Museum (p.52)
Kenwood House (pp.36, 65)
Museum of London (pp.56–7)
National Gallery (pp.41–2)
National Army Museum (p.77)
National Maritime Museum (pp.58–9)
National Portrait Gallery (pp.42–3)
Natural History Museum (pp.47–8)
Ragged School Museum (p.77)
Royal Air Force Museum (p.77)
Royal Observatory (p.59)
Royal Naval College (p.59)
Science Museum (pp.48–9)
Sir John Soane's Museum (p.40)
Tate Britain (p.46)
Tate Modern (p.55)
Theatre Museum (p.41)
Victoria & Albert Museum (p.49)
The Wallace Collection (p.41)

Museums free for children

Churchill Museum and Cabinet War Rooms (p.45)
Courtauld Gallery (p.41)
Dulwich Picture Gallery (p.76)
Gilbert Collection (p.41)
Guards' Museum (p.44)
HMS *Belfast* (p.53)
Kew Gardens (pp.67–8)
London's Transport Museum (p.40)

Parks & views

From elegantly manicured royal gardens to great swathes of ancient woodland, London's parks are all free (pp.65–7). Wherever you're staying in London there will be a park, usually with a children's playground, not too far away.
For stunning views try Hampstead Heath (p.66), The Mall (p.66), the Oxo Tower along the Millennium Mile (p.69), the Millennium Bridge (p.54) or Westminster Bridge (p.69).

The Southeast
Hampshire · Kent · Surrey
East and West Sussex

05

The Southeast

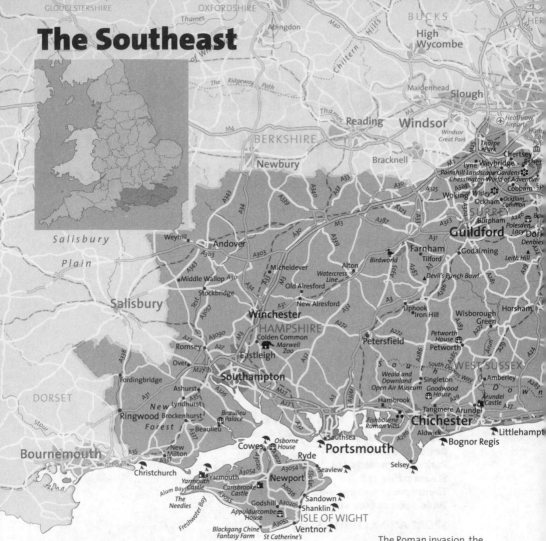

The Roman invasion, the coming of St Augustine to convert the population to Christianity, the Battle of Hastings, the evacuation of Dunkirk by the small ships – the Southeast has borne witness to some of the most significant events in English history. Just 21 miles from mainland Europe at its closest point, the region has, over the centuries, provided many people (both invaders and tourists alike) with their first glimpse of the country.

Littered with castles and fringed by lively day-trip-worthy resorts, it's a quintessentially English sort of place with lots of grand landscaped gardens to visit, plenty of steam trains to ride and, in the shape of the New Forest and South Downs,

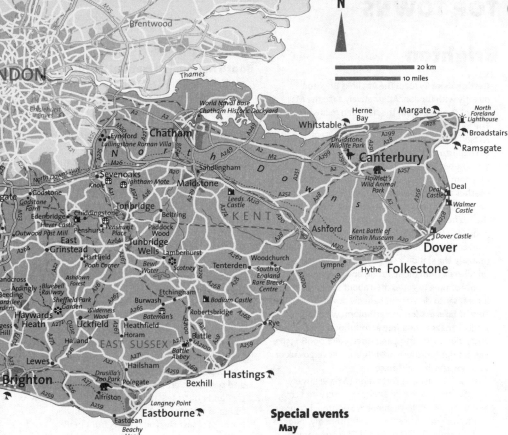

hundreds of square miles of idyllic countryside to explore. There are also boat trips to enjoy, particularly at the great naval town of Portsmouth, from where you can catch a ferry to the Isle of Wight, one of the country's most popular holiday destinations for families.

Day-trip itinerary

Morning: Battle Abbey – take a tour of the battle-field where King Harold was slain by William's conquering army (pp.110–1).

Lunch: At the nearby Copper Kettle – be sure to check out the scale model of the town just outside (p.141).

Afternoon: Train to Hastings (10 minutes) to play on the beach, explore the Smugglers' Adventure (p.122) and ride along the West Hill Railway up the cliff face (p.122).

Special events

May
Brighton Festival **t** (01273) 260819/709709
www.brighton-festival.org.uk

June
Biggin Hill: International Air Fair **t** (01959) 572277
www.airdisplaysint.co.uk

July
Cowes Week **t** (01983) 295744
www.cowesweek.co.uk
Chichester Festival **t** (01243) 780192
www.chifest.org.uk

August
Rye Medieval Festival **t** (01797) 226696
www.rye.org.uk

September
Leeds Castle Hot Air Balloon and Vintage Car weekend **t** (01622) 880 008
www.leeds-castle.com

November
London–Brighton Car Rally
t (01327) 856 024 www.lbvcr.com

Brighton

Getting there By road: The A23 links Brighton directly with London. Alternatively, take the M23 part of the way, rejoin the A23, then follow the signs. The journey should take a little over an hour. By rail: A regular train service runs from London Victoria (30 departures a day) and the journey takes around 50 minutes. Trains also run from London Bridge, Clapham Junction and King's Cross. National Express coaches and Southdown bus services arrive at Pool Valley bus station on Old Steine, not very far from the seafront. If your kids are aged five or over, it's a good idea to travel to Brighton by train. The seafront is an easy 10-minute downhill walk from the station (making the station a slightly harder 15-minute uphill walk from the seafront) and gives your kids plenty of time to get excited about seeing the sea. It comes into view about halfway down.

Tourist information 10 Bartholomew Square **t** 0906 7112255. For a free accommodation brochure and guide to Brighton and Hove, call **t** 0906 14597, **email** brighton-tourism@brighton-hove.gov.uk or visit **www.visitbrighton.com**

Britain's seaside resorts tend to have largely similar characteristics. They are cheery and cosy and somewhat old-fashioned. Brighton, however, is different. It's brash, loud, determinedly modern and remains so all year round. The great thing about Brighton is that it manages to be fashionable, with its clubs and designer stores, and yet extremely family orientated with lots of child-friendly attractions. There's the pier, with its funfair, arcades and giant teddy bears; the Marina, with its arcades and bowling alleys; and, last but not least, the beach itself. Brighton boasts a mighty eight miles of seafront made up of pebbles rather than sand, so bring your sturdiest pair of sandals. There are good play facilities along the beachfront, which are accessed via decking walkways, including an invitingly sandy volleyball pitch, a basketball court and, further up near the ruined West Pier, a children's play area *par excellence*. Here you'll find a large play pool, brightly coloured lookout posts complete with turrets and binoculars, a sand and water table and lots of space for families to have a picnic.

Things to see and do

Booth Museum of Natural History
194 Dyke Road **t** (01273) 292777
www.booth.virtualmuseum.info
Open Mon–Wed and Fri–Sat 10–5, Sun 2–5
Adm Free
Gift shop, mother and baby room, guided tours, wheelchair access

Based on the collection of Victorian naturalist and Brighton resident Edward Thomas Booth, this museum holds a fascinating display of insects, butterflies, fossils and animal skeletons. Kids can get up close to all manner of specimens in the new hands-on Discovery Lab, and special events are organized during the school holidays.

Brighton Marina
Brighton **t** (01273) 818504 **www.brightonmarina.co.uk**
Open Daily 10–6

East of the town centre, the Marina is still well worth a visit. It's a nice place to eat, shop and even stay at the stylish Alias Hotel Seattle, **t** (01273) 679799, **www.aliashotels.com**. There's also a leisure centre and a large entertainment complex with a cinema, an arcade, 10-pin bowling and pool. Boat cruises around the harbour, to the pier and out to sea are also offered. The best way to reach the Marina is on the Volk's Railway, Britain's oldest electric railway, built in 1883.

Please note: The journey, which starts at the Palace Pier, takes in views of the local nudist beach, which should give you something to talk about.

Brighton Museum
Royal Pavilion Gardens **t** (01273) 290900
www.brighton.virtualmuseum.info
Open Tues 10–7, Wed–Sat 10–5, Sun 2–5 and Bank Hols **Adm Free**
Gift shop, café, wheelchair access, monthly events for toddlers, families and ages eight and up

The museum reopened a few years ago following a £10-million redevelopment, which has relocated the entrance to the Pavilion Gardens and made the building much more accessible to visitors. The interior is spacious and light with a small gift shop and a café serving boiled eggs and soldiers among other comfort foods. The finishing touches, added in autumn 2003, are the archaeology galleries and the local studies centre, which complement the displays of art, photography and interior design. Families will mostly enjoy the masks and the costume galleries, where children can gawp at the PVC-clad Goths, gasp at the vast girth of George IV's pants or try an Edwardian costume on for size. Downstairs there's an artroom, where kids can experience different colours in the spectrum through reading, drawing and colouring, making structures, as well as writing down their impressions of the artworks they have seen.

Brighton Palace Pier

Off Madeira Drive **t** (01273) 609361
www.brightonpier.co.uk
Open Mon–Fri 10am–8pm, Sat–Sun 10am–10pm
Adm Free; individual charges for rides
Three bars, various fast food outlets, wheelchair access, disabled toilets

After the beach, this should probably be your first port of call. Vaguely reminiscent of an ocean liner on stilts, this beautiful snow-white pier stretches a mighty 525m (1,722ft) out to sea and is lined with snack bars, stalls and child-friendly attractions. About halfway down, you'll find an amusement arcade full of all the latest video games, a few fairground-style stalls plus a couple of old-fashioned and rather neglected one-arm bandits. Next door stands a 250-seat fish and chip restaurant while, beyond this, right at the end of the pier, is a fun fair, with several gentle carousel-type rides, a small go-kart track, a helter-skelter, a log flume, a 'Crazy Mouse' rollercoaster and for those that don't scare easily, the new 'Super Booster', which lifts you 38m (125ft) over the sea before dropping at a speed of 60mph. There's free family entertainment in summer ranging from comedy and magicians to live shows featuring favourite kids' TV characters and a host of tribute bands.

Brighton Toy and Model Museum

52/55 Trafalgar Street (under the railway station)
t (01273) 749494
www.brightontoymuseum.co.uk
Open Tues–Fri 10–5, Sat 11–5 (last admission 4)
Adm Adults £3.50, children (4–14) £2.50, family (2+2) £10
Gift shop, wheelchair access

Located in the arches of the Brighton Railway Station is this superb collection of more than 10,000 exhibits, made up of dolls' houses, puppets, toy theatres, tin cars and rare model trains (including a model railway featuring the

Sussex countryside). The attached shop has a nice range of souvenirs, vintage toys and games.

Bus tours

Devil's Dyke tour information t (01273) 886200 (Brighton and Hove Buses) **www.**buses.co.uk
Stops North Street, Palace Pier, Brighton Station
Tour times 16 times daily between 10–8 Jul–early Sept, weekends and Bank Hols only late Apr, May, Jun and late Sept. No service in winter.
Fares Adult SuperSaver ticket (available from newsagents) £2.60, children £1.75

The South Downs, which start a few miles inland from Brighton, make up some of England's most beautiful countryside. The no.77 open-top sightseeing bus makes 16 trips a day in high summer from the Palace Pier to the Devil's Dyke (p.132), one of the most famous local beauty spots. Its elevated position has long proved popular with both hang-gliders and kite-flyers. If you fancy joining in with the kite-flying, you can pick up a suitable stunter in Brighton at Air Born Kites, 42 Gardner Street, **t** (01273) 676740, **www.**airbornkites.co.uk.

Cinemas and theatres *See pp.136, 140*

Foredown Tower

Foredown Road, Portslade **t** (01273) 292092
www.foredown.virtualmuseum.info
Open Mar–Oct weekends and Bank hols 10–5, mid-Jul–late Aug Thurs–Sun 10–5 **Adm** Adults £2.50, children £1.50, family £6.50
Café, mother and baby room, wheelchair access, on-site parking

Just outside the town, this beautifully restored Edwardian water tower holds the only operational camera obscura in the Southeast and provides wonderful 'secret' views of the local countryside and the channel from its viewing gallery. There is also a weather station and interactive displays. Children can enjoy a programme of events looking at astronomy and the natural landscape of the South Downs. The tower is a good starting point for walks and information on family group trails.

Hove Museum and Art Gallery

19 New Church Road **t** (01273) 290200
www.hove.virtualmuseum.info
Open Tues–Sat 10–5, Sun 2–5 **Adm Free**
Café, gift shop, wheelchair access

Following refurbishment, the museum now has a lift to access the upper galleries for

Can you spot?
The silver dragon which holds up the one-tonne chandelier in the Banqueting Room at Preston Manor. Note its bright red forked tongue and the fire shooting out from its nostrils.

wheelchair users and families with pushchairs. The gallery space has also been transformed to enhance the museum's collection of local history, paintings, toys and early cinema. Children will enjoy the optical toys and the 'Wizard's Attic' with its workshop for broken playthings, working train sets and doll displays. There are monthly events for all ages and in the school holidays children can join in a range of activities including film-making, puppetry and costume design.

Preston Manor

Preston Park, Preston Road **t** (01273) 292770
www.prestonmanor.virtualmuseum.info
Open Apr–Oct Tues–Sat and Bank Hols 10–5, Sun 2–5 **Adm** Adults £4, children (under 16) £2.50, family (2+4) £10.30, (1+2) £6.30
Café, picnic areas, shop, guided tours (at extra cost, book in advance), on-site parking

Inside this beautifully maintained Edwardian museum house, kids can learn about life 'below stairs' during the early part of the century. For £35 visitors can hire a guide (well worth it for a large group or an educational birthday party). 'Edwardian experience days', where children get to role play as domestic servants, are available for school groups throughout the year.

★Royal Pavilion

North Street **t** (01273) 290900
www.royalpavilion.org.uk
Open Oct–Mar 10–5.15, Apr–Sept 9.30–5.45
Adm Adults £7.50, children (under 16) £5, family £19 (2+4), £11.50 (1+2)
Queen Adelaide Tearoom, gift shop, children's quiz sheets, mother and baby room, guided tours (at extra cost), free audio guides, disabled facilities

The Pavilion is Britain's most over-the-top Royal Palace. Designed by John Nash in the 1810s on the orders of the Prince Regent, it's described as being 'in the Indian style with a Chinese interior' – a bit of a mishmash. Forget notions of taste and style, just come and enjoy the excess: crystal chandeliers, lashings of gilt, hand-knotted carpets and bizarre *trompe l'oeil* décor. Kids usually respond well to its fairytale exuberance.

Sea Life Centre

Marine Parade **t** (01273) 604234 **www**.sealife.co.uk
Open Daily 10–6 (till 5 in winter; last entry 1hr before closing time)
Adm Adults £9.95, under 14s £7.50, under 3s **free** (ticket valid for unlimited visits all day)
Shop, restaurant, mother and baby room, disabled facilities

It's the world's oldest aquarium and is crying out for refurbishment, but it's still a good option to while away an afternoon. The centrepiece is the transparent tunnel running through the middle of a huge tank, where you can pretend to be walking along the ocean floor while various exotic sea creatures, from sharks to seahorses, swim and glide overhead. Elsewhere, you'll find floor-to-ceiling tanks, where freshwater and tropical fish swim through model wrecks and caves (many have bubble windows giving you the sensation of being in the tank with them). There is also a touch pool full of friendly rays and lots of interactive displays designed to keep kids informed as they gawp. Children are well catered for, with themed areas including 'Adventures at 20,000 leagues', where they can hear about the adventures of Jules Verne's *Nautilus* while perched on the edge of a mock-up submarine, a Victorian marine display, complete with waxworks in period costume, and a soft play area for under 5s. Feeding of most fish takes place twice a day (for sharks it is once every two days). In truth, the presentation is a bit uninspired in places, but this is more likely to bother parents than children, who'll simply be thrilled at the chance to see a shark close up and personal.
Tip: The aquarium tends to be cold and damp.

Shopping

Just back from the seafront are the Lanes, the heart of 'designer' Brighton, a maze of narrow alleyways and pedestrianized streets, full of antique shops, jewellers, designer clothes stores and restaurants. Look out for The **Toy and Model Museum**'s shop in Trafalgar Street, **t** (01273) 749494, next to the station, where kids can pick up souvenirs and gaze at all the vintage model toys, cars and trains. For something a little more mainstream, head to the Churchill Square Shopping Centre **t** (01273) 327428, where you'll find Mothercare for baby items, the Early Learning Centre for toys and games and Girl Heaven and The Bear Factory just for fun.

Did you know?
That Brighton is over 1,000 years old and the Lanes are its oldest part. The town is even mentioned in the Domesday Book, the catalogue of the country which William the Conqueror had compiled shortly after becoming king – although back then Brighton was known as Brithelmstone, much more of a mouthful.

Sport and activities *See pp.133–6*

Vintage Penny Arcade
On the beach, 50 yards west of the Palace Pier
Open Easter–Oct weekends and school hols 12 noon–late
Adm Free (depending how many pennies you buy)

A collection of original Edwardian penny slot machines (strength testers, fortune-tellers, 'what the butler saw' gizmos, etc.) that will probably prove as popular as the more modern whizz-bang stuff on offer at the pier. Buy a collection of old pennies at the entrance to feed into the machines.

Around Brighton

The South Downs (p.132)
Arundel Castle, 16 miles west (p.110)

Canterbury

Getting there By road: Canterbury is linked to London via the A2/M2 and to Ashford via the A28. The city centre is largely pedestrianized, but there's a good park and ride system in operation. By rail: There are two train stations, Canterbury East (northwest of the town centre), which receives services from London Victoria, and Canterbury West (south), which receives services from London Charing Cross and Waterloo; both are 10 minutes on foot from the city centre. By bus/coach: National Express services arrive daily from London, the bus station is on St George's Lane
Tourist information 12–13 Sun Street, Buttermarket
t (01227) 378100 www.canterbury.co.uk

This was where the seeds of English Christianity were first sown when, way back in AD 597, the Pope sent his emissary Augustine to Canterbury to convert the population to Christianity. During the Middle Ages, it was the country's most important pilgrimage centre and, even today, it's England's second most visited city after London. If possible,

try to avoid coming in high summer when its narrow streets are thronged with people. Also be aware that, though well worth visiting, the city's attractions are principally religious and/or historical, and may prove a little dry for very young children. This is true of the city's prime site, the imposing Christ Church Cathedral, the ecclesiastical and theological headquarters of the English Church, which, along with the remains of the abbey founded by St Augustine and St Martin's, the oldest parish church still in constant use, has been designated a World Heritage Site by UNESCO – the three are linked by a marked walk. Nonetheless, there's plenty here for families to do. Many of the city's museums and exhibitions (including the Canterbury Tales, Canterbury Museum and Roman Museum) are presented in a lively, hands-on way, and there are riverside gardens (notably the West Gate Gardens with its summer floral displays) and boat trips along the River Stour to enjoy.

The city centre, which is pedestrianized and filled with picturesque medieval buildings (particularly on Palace Street, Burgate and St Peter's Street) is fun to explore, with lots of good shops although, thanks to hefty wartime bombing, it does have its uglier parts as well. Canterbury is a short drive or bike ride away from the resort of Whitstable on the Kent coast (p.124).

Things to see and do

★Canterbury Cathedral
Cathedral House, The Precincts **t** (01227) 762862
Open Summer: daily 9–6.30, Sundays 9–2.30 and 4.30–5.30; winter: daily 9–5, Sundays 10–2 and 4.30–5.30. Restricted access 9–12.30 on Sundays during religious services
Adm Adults £6, children £4.50, under 5s **free**, family £14.50 (single-parent family £12), guided tours £4 per adult and £2 per child (family £8)
Shop, Welcome Information Centre, audiovisual presentations on the 'Story of the Cathedral' (groups only, £1 per person); advance notice of wheelchair visits needed

The multi-pinnacled Canterbury Cathedral is grand, imposing, highly evocative and looks particularly magical at night when spotlights pick out the detail in the exterior carving. Most of what you see was constructed in the 15th century although parts, including the crypt and some of the stained glass (among the very oldest in

Thomas à Becket

'Who will rid me of this turbulent priest?' These fateful words, spoken by Henry II in 1170, sealed the fate of Thomas à Becket, the then Archbishop of Canterbury. During his reign, Henry was in almost constant disagreement with the Pope in Rome – who, at that time, was still the head of the English Church – over religious policy. Henry didn't like the idea of a foreign leader having so much influence over his church and so appointed his close friend and advisor, Thomas à Becket, as Archbishop of Canterbury (the English Church's top job) thinking that Thomas would let him run the church the way he wanted. Unfortunately for Henry, Thomas proved much more devout and loyal to Rome than he had expected. Previously known for his fondness for fine living, upon assuming the archbishopric, Thomas immediately renounced his old hedonistic ways (and his friendship with Henry) and devoted himself to upkeeping church (the Pope's) law. Over the succeeding years, Henry and Thomas had numerous arguments and run-ins resulting, at one stage, with Thomas being banished from the country. Though they did manage to patch things up, and Thomas did return from exile, it proved to be a short-lived peace. The two men soon fell out again, this time so seriously that Henry was prompted to make his fateful

request. Upon hearing his words, four knights rushed to Canterbury, found Thomas preparing for evensong in the cathedral and slew him where he stood. When he learnt of the news, Henry was mortified. He claimed that he had only been speaking out loud, not issuing orders. Racked with guilt, he decided to pay penance by walking barefoot from Hambledon to the cathedral at Canterbury, where he allowed himself to be flogged as punishment for his sins.

Thomas, meanwhile, achieved even greater fame in death than he had in life. He was declared a saint and his tomb in Canterbury Cathedral became the country's most popular and important site of pilgrimage. Indeed, catering for the needs of pilgrims became the principal activity of most of the town's inns and taverns. In the *Canterbury Tales* (*see* opposite), Chaucer describes how the streets of medieval Canterbury were lined with tradesmen trying to sell souvenirs to visitors – not much changes.

Unfortunately for Thomas, in the 16th century, Henry VIII, like Henry II before him, began to argue with the Pope. This particular argument proved terminal. Henry removed the English Church from the Pope's control, abolished the country's monasteries and had all the saints' shrines, including Thomas's at Canterbury, destroyed.

Britain), date back to the 12th century. Look out for the Martyrdom in the northwest transept, the spot where Thomas à Becket was murdered in 1170 at the wish, if not the order, of Henry II (*see* above). Becket's shrine attracted thousands of pilgrims in the Middle Ages following his elevation to the sainthood, but was destroyed in the 16th century in the wake of the English Church's breach with Rome and replaced by the Trinity Chapel – you can still see the deep grooves worn into the steps by countless pairs of devotional knees. See if you can also find the stained glass images of Becket's murder and the saint performing miracles.

During the Second World War, Canterbury was targeted for bombing by Germany as part of its Baedeker Campaign – an attempt to break Britain's will by destroying its most precious religious and cultural landmarks (picked out of a Baedeker guide, hence the name). Miraculously, however, the cathedral and its beautiful stained glass managed to survive the war unscathed.

Pick up an audio guide or a children's 'Explorer' guide at the entrance, which will point out all the places of interest and fill you in on all the background stories and legends that, for children, will really help bring the place alive.

Canterbury Guild of Guides

Arnett House, Hawks Lane **t** (01227) 459779
Tours Apr–Oct daily at 2pm (Jul–Aug also 11.30am)
Prices Adults £4.15, children under 12s £3, over 12s £3.75, family (2+3) £12.50

Historic Walks that leave from the Canterbury Visitor Information Centre.

Museum of Canterbury and Rupert Bear Museum

Stour Street **t** (01227) 475202
www.canterbury-museums.co.uk
Open Mon–Sat 10.30–5 and summer Sun 1.30–5
Adm Adults £3.30, under 18s £2.20, under 5s **free**, family (2+3) £8.70
Guided tours, disabled access

Who is Chaucer?

Geoffrey Chaucer (b.1340–d. c.1400) is, after Shakespeare, probably the most famous writer of English that ever lived.

What did he write?

Many things including poems and treatises. His most famous work is *The Canterbury Tales*, a verse-story about a group of 30 pilgrims – including a knight, a monk, a cleric, a miller and a merchant – who gather at the Tabard Inn in Southwark on their way to Thomas à Becket's shrine in Canterbury to engage in a storytelling contest. The result is one of the funniest and bawdiest collections of stories in the English language.

I've seen his writing, it doesn't look much like English to me.

Not at first. English was pronounced and spelt very differently in Chaucer's day. It is, however, still recognizably the same tongue. Try reading the following passage (from *The Tale of Sir Thopas*) out loud. The spelling may look a bit odd but you can still get the sense of the words from the sound.

Listeth, lordes, in good entent
And I wol telle verrayment
Of mirthe and of solas;
Al of a night was fair and gent
In bataille and in tourneyment
His name was sir Topias
Y-born he was in fer contree,
In Flaundres, al biyonde the see,
At Popering, in the place;
His fader was a man ful free,
And lord he was of that contree,

As it was goddes grace.
How did he become a writer?

Seemingly by accident. His main job was as a government official. Born into a wealthy family of wine merchants, he became a page in the royal court in his mid twenties and was sent on numerous diplomatic missions to France and Italy. He also served for a while in the army and was captured by the French at the siege of Reims and only released after a ransom had been paid for him by Edward III. Back in England, he was given the job of controller of customs of the Port of London before later becoming MP for Kent.

When did he find time to write?

Intermittently. It seems that he first turned his hand to writing as a way of keeping in the good graces of his employers (one of his earliest works was a poem written to the memory of the Duchess of Lancaster in whose household he was employed), and later as a means of supplementing his income. He lived in turbulent times and was sacked from his positions with the royal court at least twice during his lifetime – although he always returned to favour and indeed died a relatively wealthy man in 1400. He was buried in Westminster Cathedral.

Why were his stories so popular?

First and foremost, because they're very good, filled with strong characters, lots of action (and plenty of rudeness). But, it did also help that they were among the very first published by William Caxton following his introduction of the printing process to England in the late 15th century.

Housed in a former Poor Priests' Hospital, the museum provides a good overview of the major events from the city's 2,000-year history - the coming of the Romans, the murder of Thomas à Becket, the burning of 40 heretics at the stake during the reign of Mary I, the bombing of the city during the Second World War, with plenty of hands-on activities for children (including looking at medieval poo under a microscope). The adjoining Rupert Bear Museum features the adventures of Rupert, the lovable soft toy with the bright checked trousers (created by local artist Mary Tourtel), where children can dress up, draw and play games. There are smaller displays of other children's TV favourites including Bagpuss, The Clangers and, for those of us old enough to remember, Pogles Wood. On the second Thursday of every month (10–11.30, £2 per child) there are also storytellings for 2–5-year-olds. It's much better presented than most local museums, with state-of-the-art video, computer and even hologram displays and well worth an hour or two of your time in Canterbury.

Canterbury Historic River Tours

Weavers Garden, St Peter's Street **t** (07790) 534744
www.canterburyrivertours.co.uk
Open Apr–Sept daily 7–5
Adm Adults £6, children £4, family (2+2) £17.50

Sightseeing trips (30–40 minutes) along the River Stour. Punts can also be hired from near the West Gate, **t** (07816) 760869, **www.crnc.co.uk**.

Canterbury Roman Museum
Butchery Lane, Longmarket **t** (01227) 785575
Open Mon–Sat 10–5 (last admission 4), Jun–Oct
also Sun 1.30–5 **Adm** Adults £3, under 18s £1.85,
under 5s **free**, family (2+3) £7.60
Gift shop, guided tours, disabled access
   Come and see what's left of *Durovernum Contiacorum*, the Roman town that preceded modern Canterbury, in this spirited underground museum. There are reconstructions of Roman house interiors and market stalls to explore, interactive computer displays and a special 'hands-on' area, where children can handle genuine Roman artefacts. You can also see the floor mosaics from a Roman villa that once stood on this site.

★Canterbury Tales
St Margaret's Street **t** (01227) 479227
www.canterburytales.org.uk
Open Daily 9.30–5.30 (winter 10–4.30) **Adm** Adults £7.25, under 16s £5.25, under 5s **free**.
Gift shop, café, guided tours, disabled access
   An exuberant, albeit slightly cheesy, retelling of Chaucer's literary masterpiece using jerky animatronic models enlivened by sound, lighting and smell effects. You can listen to the tales retold through a headset as you wander around. It's particularly good for kids and there are extra family events during the school holidays.

Cinemas and theatres *See pp.136, 140*

Downland Cycle Hire
Canterbury West Station **t** (01227) 479643
www.downlandcycles.co.uk
Open Tues–Sat 10–5.30 **Adm** £12/1-day hire + £25 returnable deposit
   Hires out bikes for tours along the famous 'Crab & Winkle' route between Canterbury and Whitstable.

Sport and activities *See pp.133–6*

St Augustine's Abbey
Longport **t** (01227) 767345
www.english-heritage.org.uk
Open Apr–Oct daily 10–6, Oct–Mar Wed–Sun 10–4
Adm Adults £3.70, children £1.90, under 5s **free**
Gift shop, picnic areas, free audio guide tours
   There's not a great deal to see at the place where English Christianity first took root. The main body of the Abbey was destroyed long ago, on the orders of Henry VIII following the Reformation. Nonetheless, it's an atmospheric place and worth a half-hour detour in the

company of an audio guide. Though founded in the 6th century, most of what remains dates from the 11th century. Various family-friendly events take place here in summer.

West Gate Museum
St Peter's Street **t** (01227) 789576
www.canterbury-museums.co.uk
Open Mon–Sat 11–12.30 and 1.30–3.30 **Adm** Adults £1.20, children 70p, under 5s **free**, family (2+3) £2.80
   The medieval city of Canterbury was enclosed behind a thick stone wall lined with a number of gatehouses where soldiers would have been stationed to look out for potential invaders. The West Gate is the last remaining such gatehouse. You can tour the battlements, from where there are good views over the city and look through the murder holes; unwelcome visitors would have been deterred from entry with a quick dousing of boiling oil poured through these holes. Kids can try on replica suits of armour and do brass rubbings (10p–£2.50 per item), and there's a family quiz.

Around Canterbury
Druidstone Wildlife Park, 5 miles west (p.116)
Howlett's Wild Animal Park, 5 miles southeast (p.117)
Whitstable, 8 miles north (p.124)

Chichester

Getting there By road: Chichester is 60 miles southwest of London, 31 miles west of Brighton and 14 miles east of Portsmouth on the A27 and A259; from London take the A3 then the A286. By rail: The station is on South Street and there is a regular service from London Victoria. By bus/coach: National Express Coastline buses run from Brighton and Portsmouth, National Express services leave daily from London; the bus station is next door to the train station
Tourist information 29a South Street **t** (01243) 775888 **www.chichester.gov.uk**
   Chichester is a quiet, attractive market town with lots of handsome architecture and a reserved, slightly stuffy atmosphere. Founded by the Romans in the 1st century AD, the roads still follow the Roman grid layout although most of the architecture is Georgian, the principal exceptions being the grand Norman cathedral and the

16th-century market cross which marks the centre of town – you can't miss it, it looks a bit like an enormous stone crown. Radiating out from this are the town's four main streets (North, South, East and West Street), which are pleasant, pedestrianized and lined with shops, tearooms and the sort of pubs which have large, curved glass windows jutting out into the street. In July, thousands of tourists flock here for the Chichester Festivities, a two-week celebration of theatre, dance and music (the choice of works on offer is famously traditional with nothing too racy or experimental allowed), which usually kicks off with a carnival and firework display.

Although the town boasts few out-and-out tourist sites (of most interest to children will be the Mechanical Music and Doll Museum on Church Road and the Chichester Canal, where you can hire canoes and rowboats and take narrow-boat trips), Chichester is within easy reach of a number of excellent attractions: the South Downs are just to the north (p.132), as is Goodwood Racetrack and the Weald and Downland Open Air Museum (p.130). Due south is Chichester Harbour, a popular sailing marina, where you can hire boats and take sightseeing trips along the coast. Three miles east of Chichester is the Tangmere Military Aviation Museum, while two miles west is Fishbourne Roman Palace, the largest Roman building in the country.

Things to see and do

Centurion Way Railway Path

A cycle and pedestrian path running around the west side of Chichester decorated with sculptures by local school children. Bicycle hire from **City Cycles**, 44 Bognor Road **t** (01243) 539992.

Chichester Canal Society

Canal Basin, Canal Wharf **t** (01243) 771363
Open/Adm Call for times and prices
Hires out rowboats and canoes, and organizes narrowboat canal trips and guided towpath walks.

Chichester Harbour Conservancy

The Harbour Office, Itchenor **t** (01243) 512301
www.conservancy.co.uk
Open/Adm Call for times and prices
Organizes guided walks (stream walks, bird walks, wild flower walks, cream tea walks, etc.) and activities (pond-dipping, butterfly collecting, etc.) around Chichester Harbour.

Chichester Harbour Water Tours

12 The Parade, East Wittering **t** (01243) 670504
www.chichesterharbourwatertours.co.uk
Open Mar–Oct **Fares** Adults £6.50, children £3
Tours (90 minutes) of the harbour from Itchenor.

Cinemas and theatres See pp.136, 140

Fishbourne Roman Palace

Salthill Road, Fishbourne near Chichester
t (01243) 785859 www.sussexpast.co.uk
Open Mar–Jul and Sept–Oct daily 10–5; Aug daily 10–6; Nov–Dec daily 10–4; Jan Sat–Sun 10–4
Adm Adults £6.50, under 15s £3.40, under 5s **free**, family £16.60
Café, gift and book shop, parking, disabled access
Although little of the actual building remains, there are four beautifully preserved mosaics, including a very famous one depicting Cupid riding a dolphin, and there's an exciting audio-visual presentation to give you some idea of what the complex must have looked like in Roman times. In school holidays, kids can try their hand at Roman activities including pottery and, of course, mosaic-making. Try some Roman recipes at home by visiting the website.

Goodwood Racetrack

Goodwood **t** (01243) 755055 (Goodwood House: **t** (01243) 755040) www.goodwood.co.uk
Getting there A few miles north of Chichester off the A286
Open Call in advance **Adm** Call in advance
Café, shop, disabled access
On its event days, you can watch sports cars whizzing around a track and helicopters and planes landing and taking off.

Mechanical Music and Doll Museum

Church Road **t** (01243) 372646
Open Jun–Sept Wed 1–4
Adm Adults £2.50, children £1.25
Gift shop, guided tours, disabled access, on-site parking
Collection of barrel organs, polyphons and Victorian wax and china dolls.

Sport and activities See pp.133–6

Tangmere Military Aviation Museum

Tangmere, near Chichester **t** (01243) 775223
www.tangmere-museum.org.uk
Open Mar–Oct daily 10–5.30, Feb–Nov 10–4.30 (last entry 1hr before closing)
Adm Adults £5, children £1.50, family (2+2) £11.50

One of the country's most important military aviation museums, with 20th-century exhibits. For further information *see* p.139

★Weald and Downland Open Air Museum

Singleton, near Chichester **t** (01243) 811348
www.wealddown.co.uk
Getting there About 7 miles north of Chichester off the A286
Open Mar–Oct daily 10.30–6; Nov, Dec and early Feb daily 10.30–4; Jan–mid-Feb Sat–Sun 10.30–4
Adm Adults £7.95, children £4.25, under 5s **free**, family £21.95

More than 40 assembled historic rural buildings recovered from all over southeast England.
For further information *see* p.130

Around Chichester

Arundel Castle, 8 miles east (p.110)
Bognor Regis, 5 miles southeast (p.120)
South Downs, 5 miles north (p.132)

Dover

Getting there By road: From London take the M20 then the A20. By rail: Dover Priory train station is half a mile northwest of the town centre and welcomes daily services from London (Victoria and Charing Cross) and Canterbury. By bus/coach: National Express coaches run from London to the Eastern Docks every hour. For ferry information, *see* pp.11–12
Tourist information, Old Town Gaol, Biggin Street **t** (01304) 205108 **www**.whitecliffscountry.org.uk

When people think of Dover, they think of ferries. This, after all, is the country's principal cross-Channel port and indeed, the world's busiest passenger harbour; a place for passing through, not hanging around in. A cursory look around the town centre would seem to confirm this view. Full of modern, purpose-built buildings, Dover town is quite horribly unattractive and yet, bizarrely, is still well worth an hour or two of your time. Beautiful it may never be, but Dover does have its attractions, most notably the wonderfully preserved 12th-century castle, which sits on a hill perched high above the town, from where there are towering views of the English Channel. In the town itself, do also check out the Roman Painted House, the remains of a small villa built some 1,800 years ago – its frescoed walls and elaborate underfloor heating system still intact – and Dover Museum and Bronze Age Boat in Market Square. Of course, no visit to Dover would be complete without a look at the famous white cliffs, which, over the centuries, have become a symbol of the nation itself. The visitor centre can provide details of all the best walks – on a clear day, you can see all the way to France. When Dover's charms start to pall, pay a visit to nearby Deal, which also boasts a castle (albeit a somewhat smaller one) and a fascinating Time Ball Tower. Deal is far prettier than Dover, with a small harbour and an indoor tropical lagoon, 'Tides', with water slides, waves and a Jacuzzi, **t** (01304) 373 399 **www**.vistaleisure.com

Things to see and do

Cinemas and theatres *See* pp.136, 140

★Dover Castle

Dover **t** (01304) 211067
www.english-heritage.org.uk
Open Apr–Jul and Sept daily 10–6; Aug 9.30–6.30; Oct 10–5; Nov–Jan Mon and Thurs–Sun 10–4; Feb–Mar 10–4 **Adm** Adults £9.50, children £4.80, family (2+3) £23.80
Gift and book shop, café, mother and baby facilities, disabled access, on-site parking

The castle is child friendly with lots of interactive exhibits, a children's activity centre and an audiovisual presentation on what life would have been like during a 13th-century siege and on preparations for a visit by Henry VIII. A range of family events is put on throughout the year including archery tournaments, battle re-enactments and storytellings by costumed characters. Within its walls are the remains of a *pharos* or lighthouse erected by the Romans in AD 50 (making it Britain's oldest standing building), while beneath the castle, is a network of subterranean passageways known as the 'Secret Wartime Tunnels' dug during the Napoleonic wars and extended in the Second World War. Spooky guided tours are offered every 20 minutes when you are also shown a short film on Operation Dynamo – the evacuation of Dunkirk. The views from the castle's battlements are dazzling.

Dover Museum and Bronze Age Boat

Market Square **t** (01304) 201066
www.dovermuseum.co.uk
Open Mon–Sat 10–5.30 **Adm** Adults £2, children £1.25
The centrepiece of the museum is the Bronze Age Boat Gallery with its interactive puzzles, models and, of course, the boat itself. While digging roadworks along Bench Street in 1992, workmen discovered an unusually large piece of wood. Archaeologists and conservationists were called in and slowly uncovered a boat consisting of two flat-bottom planks, four side planks and two end planks, all carved from three very large, old oak trees. The timbers were treated by the Mary Rose Trust in Portsmouth and returned freeze-dried to Dover for display. The museum holds special family days at least once a month.

Dover Transport Museum

Willingdon Road, White Cliffs Business Park
t (01304) 822409
www.dovertransportmuseum.homestead.com
Open Apr–Oct Wed–Fri 1.30–5, Sun and Bank Hols 10.30–5; Oct–Apr Sun only. **Adm** Adults £2.50, children £1, family £6
Tearoom open Sun
This newly relocated museum covers everything you need to know about getting from A to B. From bicycles to buses, model rail and tramways to maritime memorabilia, there's plenty for kids to see and do. The site also houses model towns, bygone shops and a 1930s garage.

Gateway to the White Cliffs and South Foreland Lighthouse

St Margaret's at Cliffe **t** (01304) 202756
www.nationaltrust.org.uk
Open Jan–Oct 11–5.30
Adm Adults £3.60, children £1.80, family £9
Coffee shop
The new visitor centre can provide details of clifftop walks, guided walks and treasure trails. Children will enjoy the interactive displays which tell them all about how the cliffs were formed. The South Foreland Lighthouse, where Guglielmo Marconi made the world's first ship-to-shore transmission in 1898, is a 30-minute walk away.

Roman Painted House

New Street **t** (01304) 203279
Open Apr–Sept Tues–Sat 10–5, Sunday 2–5
Adm Adults £2, children 80p
Gift shop, disabled access, on-site parking, guides

Housed within a modern building, you'll find this official Roman hotel (*Mansio*), with extensive and intact wall paintings, elaborate underfloor heating (hypocaust) and displays of Roman Dover.

Sport and activities *See pp.133–6*

Around Dover

Deal Castle, 8 miles northeast (p.111)
Kent Battle of Britain Museum, 7 miles west (p.138)
Walmer Castle, 5 miles northeast (p.113)

Portsmouth

Getting there By road: Portsmouth is 75 miles southwest of London, 14 miles west of Chichester, 19 miles southeast of Southampton on the south Hampshire coast at the end of the M275, just south of the M27. By rail: Trains arrive at Portsmouth Harbour Station daily from London (Victoria and Waterloo) and Brighton. By bus/coach: National Express services run from London (Victoria and Heathrow) and Brighton
Tourist information The Hard **t** (023) 9282 6722
www.visitportsmouth.co.uk
The tourist information centre organizes guided walks (£2 per person, accompanied children **free**)
If you and the kids are thinking of coming to Portsmouth, it would help if you're interested in ships. The city is the headquarters of the British Navy and its huge, seven-square-mile harbour is full of them. Spend a day here and you'll see almost every type of naval craft imaginable, from Tudor warships and 19th-century gunboats to Second World War submarines and modern aircraft carriers. The city's main draw is Flagship Portsmouth, which runs Portsmouth's four main naval attractions in and around the historic dockyard. These are: HMS *Victory*, Admiral Nelson's flagship at the Battle of Trafalgar (you can see the spot where he was fatally wounded by French sniper fire); HMS *Warrior*, the most fearsome fighting vessel of the 19th century; the *Mary Rose*, Henry VIII's Tudor flagship (sunk by the French in 1545, it was only rediscovered in 1965) and the Royal Naval Museum. These, along with the atmospheric Submarine Museum in Gosport and the Royal Marines Museum and D-Day Museum in Southsea, provide the most comprehensive overview of naval history you could ever wish for. Of course, if the

sight of all these ships makes you yearn for a life on the ocean waves, you could always put your sea legs to the test on a sightseeing tour of the harbour or a trip out to Spitbank Fort, a brick-and-iron fortress one mile out to sea with a network of spooky passageways. You could even pay a visit to the Isle of Wight, two miles off the coast (pp.103–10).

Portsmouth and its environs have recently undergone a multi-million-pound facelift, the results of which are the Gunwharf Quays leisure complex (with restaurants, a 14-screen cinema, a bowling alley and outlet/designer shops) and the Gosport Millennium Promenade, a six-mile-long walkway which runs from the Submarine Museum across the Forton Lake Bridge to Explosion! – Museum of Naval Firepower, taking in the newly opened 170m (558ft) Spinnaker Tower, the Halsar Marina and a giant 'Time Space' sundial (measuring a whopping 40m/131ft wide with a 17m/56ft-tall mast) en route.

Things to see and do

Blue Reef Aquarium

Clarence Esplanade, Southsea **t** (023) 9287 5222
www.bluereefaquarium.co.uk
Open Mar–Oct daily 10–6, Nov–Feb daily 10–5
Adm Adults £7.50, under 16s £4.99, under 3s **free**, family (2+3) £26.99, (2+2) £22.99
Café, gift shop, adapted toilets, baby facilities

Overlooking the Solent, this is a great place to introduce kids to the marine world – sharks, rays, jellyfish and colourful tropical varieties including the popular clownfish of *Finding Nemo* fame. Fish-eye viewing capsules and open-top tanks allow children to get up close to crustaceans, seahorses and local marine life, while the walk-through ocean tank brings the inhabitants of the coral reef into spectacular view. There's an otter enclosure, too. The aquarium has daily talks and activities and special trails and events in the school holidays.

Cinemas and theatres *See* pp.136, 140

D-Day Museum

Clarence Esplanade, Southsea **t** (023) 9282 7261
www.ddaymuseum.co.uk
Open Apr–Sept daily 10–5.30, Oct–Mar 10–5
Adm Adults £6, children £3.60, family £15.60, under 5s **free**
Gift shops, café, adapted toilets, baby changing facilities, on-site parking

On 6 June 1944, in the dead of night, thousands of Allied soldiers were landed on the Normandy coast

in the largest seaborne invasion ever staged. This would be the turning point of the war, the moment when the Allied forces were finally able to drive back the Nazis. This remarkable achievement is retold through audiovisual displays and you can even climb aboard one of the actual landing craft. The centrepiece of the display is the extraordinary 83m/272ft-long Overlord Tapestry ('Overlord' was the invasion's code name), based on the famous Bayeux Tapestry in France, a sort of enormous comic strip detailing every stage of the great invasion.

Explosion! – Museum of Naval Firepower

Priddy's Hard, Priory Road **t** (023) 9250 5600
www.explosion.org.uk
Open Apr–Oct daily 10–5.30; Nov–Mar Thurs, Sat and Sun 10–4.30 **Adm** Adults £5.50, children £3.50, family (2+4) £15, (1+3) £12.50
Shop, disabled access

This highly interactive and informative museum traces the history and development of naval armaments – in other words, things that go bang! on ships – from cannons to cruise missiles. There's touch-screens, gun-deck simulations, torpedos, mines and audiovisual displays that navigate you through the cavernous gunpowder magazine. Monthly family events and school holiday craft activities for children aged four and upwards.

★Flagship Portsmouth

Historic Dockyard, Portsmouth Harbour
t (023) 9283 9766 www.flagship.org.uk
Open Apr–Oct 10–5.30; Nov–Mar 10–5 **Adm** Ticket to all attractions: adults £16, children £13, family (2+3) £46; individual attractions: adults £10, children £8, family £30, under 5s **free**
Gift shops, restaurant, café, adapted toilets, baby changing facilities, on-site parking

Please note: Your Flagship Portsmouth ticket also allows you entry to the Dockyard Apprentice Exhibition, where you can try your hand at a range of shipbuilding skills; Action Stations ('see the Navy, be the Navy' is the catchphrase), where you learn naval training techniques from interactive games and simulator rides; and a 45-minute harbour cruise, t (023) 9272 2562, for a close-up look at the modern warships and aircraft carriers.

The *Mary Rose*

In 1982, when the *Mary Rose* was raised from the Solent silt in one of the greatest recovery operations in archaeological history, the ship turned out to be a genuine Tudor time capsule laden with hundreds of unique artefacts. She was built in 1509 on the orders of Henry VIII and led the King's fleet in his wars against the French before sinking in the Solent during a skirmish in 1545, where she lay for over 400 years until rediscovered in 1965. It would be a while yet, however, before she saw the light of day. Between 1978 and 1982, divers recovered some 19,000 objects from around the wreck, which are now on display in the building. Today, the great ship's hull sits in a specially constructed gallery, where the environment is carefully controlled to prevent her from decaying and can be observed from a viewing gallery. Audio guides are available and children can have hands-on fun with a replica Tudor longbow, listen to Tudor music, hoist the yard on the mast and don replica Tudor armour.

Royal Navy Museum

Housed in an 18th-century dockside building, this museum tells the story of the Royal Navy from its beginnings to the Falklands War. As you would expect, it holds a good deal of Nelson memorabilia, including his uniform, the furniture from his cabin on HMS *Victory*, his watch and a miniature of Emma Hamilton. In a new exhibition 'Horatio Nelson – the Hero and the Man', you can stand next to a waxwork model of the great man (shorter than you'd think) and watch an audio-visual presentation on his life. Elsewhere, there's lots of interactivity for the kids, especially in the 'Sailing Navy' gallery, which aims to show what life was like aboard a 19th-century warship – children can hold a musket, climb inside a leaguer barrel and even take the wheel of a virtual 74-gun ship – and the new 'Action Stations' exhibition on modern warships. Do also look out for the delightful exhibition tracing the evolution of the sailor's uniform – from frogging and riband to bell-bottom trousers.

HMS *Victory*

It was aboard this ship that Vice Admiral Nelson commanded the British naval victory at Trafalgar in 1805 over the combined Franco-Spanish fleet. Fatally wounded in the battle, it was also where he spent his final hours before being brought home to a hero's funeral, preserved in a barrel of brandy.

The ship, commissioned in 1759, was the most awesome fighting machine of its day. It carried 100 cannons and was manned by 821 officers and crew including 153 Royal Marines 'to provide accurate musket fire in battle'. It has been beautifully restored to look exactly as it would have done on that fateful day in 1805, with its huge cannon lined up along the gun deck. There are excellent guided tours and a multimedia walk-through experience, which really brings this star-attraction back to life.

HMS *Warrior*

With her masts and rigging, gangways and stairways, cannon and armour, this huge 19th-century warship provides the perfect setting for an afternoon of serious exploring. When she was built in 1861, HMS *Warrior* was the fastest, most heavily armed, most heavily armoured warship in the world. She was the first to be fitted with an iron hull and the first to carry 50kg (110lb) guns. Overnight, she made all other warships obsolete and was described by Napoleon III, the Emperor of France, whose naval threat she had been designed to curb, as 'a black snake amongst rabbits'. Just 15 years later, however, and without ever having been used in battle, she, too, was obsolete, surpassed by faster, nastier craft. For much of the 20th century she languished in a state of disrepair before being restored to her former splendour in the early 1980s and returned to Portsmouth in 1987.

Portsmouth Harbour Cruise

Gosport Ferry Company, departs from Gosport t (023) 9252 4551
Open Daily, call for cruise times
Fares Adults £5, children £4

A one-hour trip around the harbour to view HMS *Warrior*, HMS *Victory* and the ships in both the Naval and Commercial docks, with live commentary. Tours of Spitbank Fort, with its Victorian gun emplacements, are also available.

Royal Marines Museum

Eastney Esplanade, Southsea t (023) 9281 9385
www.royalmarinesmuseum.co.uk
Open Jun–Aug 10–5; Sept–May 10–4.30
Adm Adults £4.75, under 16s **free**
Gift shop, café, adapted toilets, on-site parking, disabled access

This is a very lively museum with plenty of interactive exhibits and lots of opportunities for kids to pretend to be soldiers. Check out the Jungle Room, where you can experience the conditions of a tropical campaign and see the types of hazard that the Marines have to deal with (like snakes, scorpions and blowpipe darts), the multimedia cinema, where you can watch footage of derring-do campaigns, and the junior assault course outside.

Southsea Castle

Clarence Esplanade **t** (023) 9282 7261
www.southseacastle.co.uk
Open Apr–Sept daily 10–5.30; Oct daily 10–5
Adm Adults £3, children £1.80, family £7.80
Gift shops, adapted toilets

Built as a coastal defence in 1544 on the orders of Henry VIII, Southsea Castle proved such a success that it was in use by the military until 1960. In its 'Amazing Time Tunnel' exhibition, a costumed guide will lead you through a series of gruesome waxwork tableaux depicting the most dramatic scenes from the castle's long history – prisoners being whipped in a damp Victorian cell is always a particular favourite. During the summer, various events (such as battle re-enactments and bird of prey days) are staged; at other times, children are happy just to climb about on the cannons outside.

Spinnaker Tower

Gunwharf Quays **t** (023) 9285 7520
www.spinnakertower.co.uk
Open Daily 10–10 **Adm** Adults £5.95, children £4.80, family £19
Café, gift shop
Please note: *No pushchairs allowed.*

One of the more recent, more prominent, additions to the Portsmouth skyline, the 30,000-tonne (30,480-ton), 170m/558ft-tall Spinnaker Tower takes both its name and design from a type of large, three-cornered sail, as modelled by many a yacht in Portsmouth Harbour. The tower offers three viewing areas. These are, in ascending order, View Deck 1, which boasts the largest glass floor in Britain and, on a clear day, views of up to 23 miles; View Deck 2, where the current Portsmouth cityscape can be compared to its historical forebear via a 'time telescope' and, the highest of all, the Crow's Nest, which is entirely open to the elements and only recommended to those with a good head for heights. The decks can be reached either by a slow-moving external panoramic lift (£2 per person) or via a more speedy (and free) internal lift.

Sport and activities *See* pp.133–6

Submarine Museum

Haslar Jetty Road, Gosport **t** (023) 9252 9217
www.rnsubmus.co.uk
Getting there The museum is reached by passenger ferry from the Harbour train station and a 10-minute walk along the Millennium Promenade

Open Apr–Oct 10–5.30; Nov–Mar 10–4.30
Adm Adults £6.50, children £5, family (2+4) £15
Gift shops, café, waterfront picnic area, adapted toilets, guided tours, on-site parking

This museum recreates the life of the undersea soldier through exhibits and audiovisuals. The highlight is a guided tour through the narrow, clunking decks of HMS *Alliance*, a Second World War submarine, to see its periscope, torpedo launchers and cramped sleeping quarters. A purpose-built visitor centre has been added to the site to house *Holland I*, Britain's first submarine. Children will be amazed at how small it looks and they'll enjoy peering inside the vessel. Talks, science workshops and museum trails are held in the school holidays.

Around Portsmouth

Chichester, 14 miles east (pp.94–6)
Isle of Wight, 2 miles off the coast (pp.103–10)

Rye

Getting there By road: Rye is 62 miles southeast of London off the A259 and A268. By rail: Trains run daily from London (Charing Cross), Ashford, Hastings and Dover. By bus/coach: Services link Rye with Hastings, Dover and Brighton
Tourist office The Heritage Centre, Strand Quay **t** (01797) 226696 **www.**visitrye.com

It has been called the most beautiful village in England and it certainly conforms to many people's expectations of an idealized English town, full of narrow, cobbled streets, half-timbered buildings and quaint tearooms. In truth, there's something rather theme park-like about Rye. Wonderfully preserved it may be, but look closely and you'll see a subtle commercialization at work. This is not a town cut off from the modern world but rather a sort of Ye Olde outdoor museum, a vision of an ideal England preserved in aspic for the bustling summer tourist trade. Nonetheless, it's a very pleasant place, especially if you manage to avoid the August crowds and, despite the overwhelming picturesqueness, surprisingly child friendly. Kids will certainly like the **Rye Town Model Sound and Light Show**, an audiovisual introduction to Rye using a large-scale model of the town. The **museum** is also well worth a visit. Housed in the

Ypres Tower, the town's small castle, it contains a fascinating display on smuggling. Rye Audio Walking Tours are available for hire from the Heritage Centre, including one on 'Ghost Walks' (adults £2.50, children £1, family £6, deposit required), either by the day or overnight. Every July the town hosts a medieval weekend when costumed characters (Lords and Ladies, Knights and jesters, etc.) parade through the streets, and on Bonfire Night there's a torchlight procession.

Should you tire of the town's attractions, Camber Sands, Hastings, Battle and the rest of Sussex's 1066 country are all close (a cycle path leads from Rye to Camber Sands), as is Romney Marsh in Kent. At New Romney, just north of Rye, you can go for a ride on the Romney, Hythe and Dymchurch steam railway and visit the Romney Toy and Model Museum with its toys, dolls and one of the largest model railways in the country.

If you had visited Rye in the Middle Ages, you could have gone for a swim. Unfortunately, the sea retreated several hundred years ago and Rye is now a coastal town without a coast. The sea's disappearance is the main reason for Rye's historically unchanged appearance. As soon as the sea retreated, Rye became frozen in time. There was no need to adapt to a way of life that no longer existed. If circumstances had been different, Rye would probably look something like Dover now, but then progress isn't always a good thing.

Things to see and do

Cinemas and theatres *See pp.136, 140*

Rye Castle Museum
Rye Castle, East Street **t** (01797) 226728
www.ryemuseum.co.uk
Open Easter–Oct Mon, Thurs and Fri 10.30–5.30, Sat–Sun 10.30–5; Nov–Easter Sat–Sun 10.30–3.30
Adm Tower and museum: adults £2.90, children £1.50, under 7s **free**, family £5.90
Gift shop, guided tours

Rye Town Model Sound and Light Show
Rye Heritage Centre, The Strand Quay
t (01797) 226696
Open Mar–Oct daily 9–5.30, Nov–Feb 10–4
Adm Adults £2.50, children £1, family £5

Sport and activities *See pp.133–6*

Around Rye
Battle Abbey, 11 miles southwest (pp.110–1)
Bodiam Castle, 9 miles northwest (p.111)
Kent and East Sussex Steam Railway, 10 miles northwest (p.127)
Romney, Hythe and Dymchurch Railway, 10 miles northeast (p.127)
South of England Rare Breeds Centre, 9 miles north (p.119)

Winchester

Getting there By road: Winchester is 70 miles southwest of London, 12 miles north of Southampton off the M3, A34, A31 and A3090. By rail: There are regular services from London (Waterloo), Portsmouth and Southampton. By bus/coach: National Express coaches arrive daily from London
Tourist information The Guildhall, High Street **t** (01962) 840500 **www.visitwinchester.co.uk**
Guided walks, which are a good way to bring the town's attractions alive for kids, leave from outside the tourist information centre most weekdays

Surrounded by water meadows and filled with medieval buildings, this beautiful cathedral city is timeless and serene. Even in summer, when the hustle and bustle of the tourist season is at its height, it remains tranquil. The special qualities of this location were first recognized more than 2,000 years ago, when an Iron Age fort was built here. The Romans replaced this with a thriving market town, which remained popular even after the collapse of the Roman Empire – both Alfred the Great and King Canute made it their capital. The town reached its zenith in the 11th century when it witnessed the coronation of William I and the creation of the *Domesday Book* (William's catalogue of the country) and rivalled London in importance. It's been on the wane ever since and, since the Civil War, has receded into middle-ranking provinciality – a blessing, as it has managed to escape the modern architectural ravages that have blighted its former rival.

Modern Winchester is an easy city to find your way around with most of its attractions – the cathedral, the Great Hall and the City Museum – located within a few minutes' walk of the largely pedestrianized High Street. Despite its legendary propensity for rain, Winchester is a city best appreciated out of doors. You could take a trip to St Giles Hill on the eastern edge of the city past the trout-filled River Ichen, where there's lots of green space for picknicking and wonderful views of the city, follow the picturesque Water Meadow Walk from Winchester College to St Cross Hospital, or perhaps pay a visit to the 18th-century working watermill near the city bridge. Alternatively, head out of town altogether to Alresford (six miles away), where you can board a steam train for a ride through leafy local countryside (it's known as the Watercress Line because the route wends its way through watercress beds, p.127) or to Marwell Zoological Park, a leading centre of wildlife conservation (p.117).

Things to see and do

Look out for The Toy Cupboard, an excellent old-fashioned toy shop on the adjacent St George's Street at no.65, **t** (01962) 849988, www.thetoycupboard.co.uk.

Cinemas and theatres *See pp.136, 140*

Great Hall
Castle Avenue **t** (01962) 846476
Open Mar–Oct 10–5, Nov–Feb 10–4 **Adm Free**
Gift shop, guided tours, disabled access

Just off the High Street, the Great Hall is all that remains of the 13th-century castle that was once the country's seat of government (and where the first-ever English parliament met in 1246). Its main claim to fame now is a vast 5.5m (18ft) circular table hanging on a wall. Painted in a variety of gaudy colours and divided into 24 place settings, it's claimed by some to be the legendary round table of King Arthur (it's actually a medieval fake).

INTECH
Hampshire Technology Trust Ltd, Romsey Road **t** (01962) 863791
Open Daily 10–4 **Adm** Adults £6.50, children £4, family £18.90
Gift shop, cafe, disabled access, on-site parking

Perhaps the city's best attraction for children, INTECH is a small, interactive science museum, where kids can build a bridge, operate a crane, turn themselves into a battery and see the effects of a hurricane on a house.

Sport and activities *See pp.133–6*

Alfred 'the Great'
The statue of King Alfred (the one who burnt the cakes) is on Broadway near the Guildhall. Alfred, the only English king ever to be called 'the Great', ruled the kingdom of Wessex in southern England from 871 until 899 during which time he fought and won numerous battles against the Vikings and instigated a widespread revival of learning. His most famous moment supposedly came during one of his least successful campaigns when, hiding out in the Somerset marshes disguised as a commoner, he was asked by a peasant woman to watch her cakes for her while she milked her cows. But Alfred had other things on his mind and let the cakes burn, prompting a severe scolding from the woman. It obviously did him some good, however, for just a few days later a rejuvenated Alfred led his troops to victory in battle.

Westgate Museum
High Street **t** (01962) 848269
Open Apr–Oct Mon–Sat 10–5, Sun 12 noon–5; Feb–Mar Tues–Sat 10–4, Sun 12 noon–4
Adm Free
Shop

One of the city's two remaining medieval gateways, the Westgate contains a small history museum. Items on display include weapons, armour and torture instruments – look out for the gruesome 18th-century gibbeting irons in which executed criminals were displayed as a warning to the general public. Children can take do brass rubbings and dress up in replica armour.

★Winchester Cathedral
The Close **t** (01962) 857200
www.winchester-cathedral.org.uk
Times Cathedral: daily, 8.30–6 (Sun closes 5.30); Library and Triforium Gallery: Apr–Oct Mon 1.30–4, Tues–Sat 11–1 and 1.30–4, Nov, Dec and Mar Wed and Sat 11–3.30, Jan–Feb Sat 11–3.30
Adm Cathedral only: Adults £4, children **free**; Library and Triforium Gallery: Adults £1, children 50p.
Restaurant, shop, guided tours, disabled access

This vast cathedral, begun during the reign of William I in 1079, although much altered since is, at over 168m (550ft) long, the longest medieval building in Europe. Within are the tombs of several kings, including Canute (the one who tried to send back the tide) and William II (the one who was shot by 'accident' by one of this

Can you spot?

The statue of a diver by the lady chapel. This was erected in the early 1900s to commemorate William Walker, a local diver who repaired the cathedral's foundations when serious flooding threatened to wash them away. The city has long had its problems with rainfall and flooding. Most people blame St Swithin, who was Bishop of Winchester in the 9th century. According to the legend, Swithin requested that, when he died, his body should be buried in the open air. Unfortunately, the townspeople forgot and had his remains interred within the cathedral whereupon a storm of such enormous dimensions erupted over Winchester that it continued to rain unabated for the next 40 days. Today, it is said that if it rains on 15 July (St Swithin's day), it will again continue raining for the next 40 days.

own men whilst out hunting in the New Forest), as well as memorials to St Swithin and to the writer Jane Austen, who died in the city in 1817. Look out for the 12th-century illuminated Bible in the cathedral library. Tours of the cathedral are available (Mon–Sat 10–3 on the hour), as are tours of the tower (one per day, over 12s only) although if it's been raining, the creepy crypt (particularly prone to flooding) may be out of bounds. Pictorial guides for children, as well as observation trails on subjects such as 'Dragons', 'Things' and 'Woodworm', are available.

Winchester City Mill

Bridge Street **t** (01962) 870057
www.nationaltrust.org.uk
Open late Mar–early Apr Mon–Sun 11–5; mid-Apr–June Wed–Sun 11–5; Jul–Dec daily 11–5
Adm Adults £3.20, children £1.60, family £8
Gift shop, guided tours
   Working watermill with an interactive exhibition, audiovisual display and children's quizzes.

Winchester City Museum

The Square **t** (01962) 848269
Open Apr–Oct Mon–Sat 10–5, Sun 12–5; Nov–Mar Tues–Sat 10–5, Sun 12–4 **Adm Free**
Gift shop, disabled access
   The history of the city plus reconstructed Victorian shops to wander through. Children's quizzes.

Around Winchester

Marwell Zoological Park, 4 miles south (p.117)
Watercress Line, 6 miles east (p.127)

ISLE OF WIGHT

A roughly diamond-shaped piece of land two miles off the coast of southern England, the Isle of Wight has long been one of the country's favourite family getaways. Its appeal is perhaps best characterized as a sort of detached Englishness. It is often said that the Isle of Wight languishes some 20 years behind the mainland so don't go expecting the latest whizz-bang thrills. This is a walking, horse-riding, cycling, sea bathing, pottering about sort of place – somewhere to relax and enjoy the summer sunshine. The south side of the island, in particular, has an almost balmy climate. It is also one of the country's prime fossil-hunting regions, with soft clay cliffs revealing dozens of preserved dinosaur skeletons each year – thus giving rise to the isle's nickname, 'Jurassic Island'.

Cowes

Getting there By road/boat: Cowes lies on the northern tip of the island, the closest town to mainland England, 4 miles north of Newport (via the A3020) and 6 miles northwest of Ryde (via the A3054 and A3021). Red Funnel operates a car ferry service (under an hour) between Southampton and East Cowes, **t** 0870 444 8898, www.redfunnel.co.uk
By train/boat: Trains run from London (Waterloo) to Southampton Central Station, from where passengers can make their way to the Town Quay Terminal for the Red Jet passenger service, which will whisk them up Southampton Water and across the Solent to West Cowes in a little over 20 minutes (*see* Red Funnel)
Tourist information The Arcade, Fountain Quay **t** (01983) 813818 www.islandbreaks.co.uk www.iwight.com
   Known for its boat-building industry and posh yachting regatta (held in August), Cowes is a lively, upmarket sailing town with interesting shops lining its narrow high street (including boatyards and chandlers) and good walking along the nearby cliffs. Osborne House, Queen Victoria's favourite home (and, following the success of the film *Mrs Brown*, English Heritage's most visited property) is in East Cowes across the River Medina (reached via a chain ferry).

Can you spot?

The brass cannon by the harbour used to start yacht races.

Things to see and do

Cowes Library and Maritime Museum

Beckford Road **t** (01983) 823433
Open Mon, Tues and Fri 9.30–5.30, Wed 11–7, Sat
9.30–4.30 **Adm Free**
Disabled access
 Maritime history of the island, plus model boats.

★Osborne House

York Avenue, East Cowes **t** (01983) 200022
www.english-heritage.org.uk
Getting there Just east of East Cowes off the A3021
Open Apr–Sept daily 10–5; Oct 10–4; call for spring
and winter times; pre-booking essential
Adm Adults £9.50, children £4.80, family (2+3)
£22.40
*Café, tearoom, souvenir shop, guided tours,
wheelchair access to ground floor and gardens only*

If ordinary people resemble their dogs, then
perhaps it could be said that monarchs resemble
their palaces. This certainly seemed true in the
19th century when the flamboyant, iconoclastic
George IV ordered the construction of the
Brighton Pavilion while the staid, conservative
Queen Victoria (who quickly rejected her prede-
cessor's effort) made her personality manifest in
the form of Osborne House. Built during the
1840s according to plans drawn up by Victoria's
husband, Albert, Osborne was intended to be a
'quiet, modest retreat' – a simple country house
where the royal family could holiday together.
The vast Italianate palace that resulted does not
conform to many people's ideas of 'modest' or
'simple', but in royal terms, it is rather restrained;
certainly when compared with grand chocolate
box palaces like Windsor and Buckingham.
Osborne was very much Victoria's house.
Responsible for much of the interior décor, she
referred to it as a 'place of one's own, quiet and
refined' and would eventually see out her final
days here in 1901. Her son Edward VII's decision,
soon after her death, to bequeath the house to
the nation had the effect of turning it into a sort
of unofficial memorial to the country's longest
reigning monarch and its apartments have been
carefully restored to look as they would have
done during Victoria's day. Though ornate and, as
you would expect, beautifully furnished, the
rooms have a distinctly sombre quality to them.
Following Albert's death in 1861, the Queen

Can you spot?
In the Swiss Cottage, look out for the rather odd
collection of marble arms modelled on the royal
children – Queen Victoria had them commissioned
as souvenirs.

remained in mourning for the rest of her life and
Osborne's rooms are littered with reminders of
her grief – you can see Albert's personal bathroom preserved just as he left it, a specially
commissioned portrait of the Prince Consort
which sat by the Queen's bed and a starkly
melancholic study of the Queen herself, 'The
Queen called Sorrow' by Landseer. In parts, the
house feels a little mausoleum-like, although it
does have its more light-hearted areas including
a billiard room where the Queen used to
challenge her ladies-in-waiting to games and
a room filled with furniture made from antlers.

The most charming part of the whole estate,
however, and the area that will most appeal to
children, is the Swiss Cottage, built in the
gardens in the 1850s for the nine royal children
to play in – there's a toy fort, a miniature kitchen
and a collection of miniature gardens, which the
children were encouraged to tend. The cottage
can be reached from the house aboard a grand
horse-drawn carriage – check out the views of the
Solent. There's a free activity sheet for children.

Newport

Getting there By road: Newport lies just north of
the island's centre, 4 miles south of Cowes, 6 miles
southwest of Ryde and 8 miles northwest of
Ventnor on the A3020
Tourist office The Guildhall, High Street
t (01983) 813818. Designed by John Nash (the man
responsible for the Brighton Pavilion) in the early
19th century, the Guildhall is also home to a
Museum of Island History with touch-screen
computers, hands-on displays and quizzes and
games for children.

The island's capital lies more or less at the
centre of the island. It's perhaps less visually
arresting than some of the Isle's lesser towns
although it does have some fine historic architecture including several Georgian and Victorian
houses, not to mention the remains of a 3rd-
century Roman villa. The island's second most
popular historic landmark (after Osborne House),
Carisbrooke Castle, lies just two miles southwest
of the town.

Things to see and do

Carisbrooke Castle Museum

Newport **t** (01983) 523112
www.carisbrookecastlemuseum.org.uk
Getting there Just southwest of Newport off the B3328
Open Apr–Sept 10–5, Oct–Mar 10–4
Adm Adults £5.50, children £2.80
Café, disabled access, guided tours, on-site parking

Occupying a strategically important location on a high ridge right at the centre of the island, Carisbrooke has long been the island's seat of power (it was the official seat of the governor right up until 1994). There's been a castle here since Saxon times, although most of what you see is Norman, albeit with a few later adornments, notably the grand Elizabethan gatehouse which forms the main entrance. Visitors hoping to see Carisbrooke's scars of battle may be a little disappointed. The castle has been involved in few conflicts. Indeed, its main contribution to the Civil War was to act as a prison for Charles I between 1647 and 1648 before the king's execution in London in 1649. Find out about the monarch's incarceration and his attempts to escape (on at least two separate occasions) at the interactive exhibition in the old Coach House while at the Donkey Centre you can meet the castle's more recent four-legged residents who, since the 17th century, have been used to power the treadmill that draws the castle's water from a deep underground well (in the Middle Ages, the labour was supplied by unlucky prisoners). Daily demonstrations of donkey-powered water drawing are given and there's a free children's activity sheet. The castle organizes various special events during the summer including medieval entertainments (find out about armour and archery) and Civil War Living History days when you can meet soldiers in a Civil War encampment.

Classic Boat Museum

The Quay **t** (01983) 533493
www.classicboatmuseum.org
Open Apr–Oct daily 10.30–4.30, Nov–Mar Tues and Sat 10.30–3.30.
Adm Adults £3, children £1, family £6 under 6s **free**
Café, shop, disabled access

Collection of modern and antique boats plus displays of maritime memorabilia.

Robin Hill Country Park

Downend, Newport **t** (01983) 527352
www.robin-hill.com
Getting there 2 miles east of Newport off the A3056
Open Open Apr–Oct daily 10–5
Adm Adults and children £7.50, under 4s **free** (toboggan run £1 extra); Saver Ticket: (x4) £27. All tickets are valid for a return visit within 7 days.
Café, shop, picnic areas, mother and baby facilities, disabled access

Run by the same people as Blackgang Chine, Robin Hill offers the same combination of gentle, almost dated-looking entertainments and pleasant countryside setting. Its most notable attractions are its 366m (1200ft) toboggan run, a motion platform cinema and a Roman galley-themed swing boat, 'Colossus', but families will also enjoy the nature walks, assault course and falconry displays.

Roman Villa

Cypress Road **t** (01983) 529720
Open Easter–Oct Mon–Sat 10–4.30; Jul–Aug also Sun 12 noon–4 **Adm** Adults £2.20, children £1.75, family £7
Shop, disabled access

You can see reconstructed rooms plus the original well-preserved baths of this 3rd-century villa.

Ryde

Getting there By road/boat: Ryde, in the island's northeast corner (6 miles southeast of Cowes off the A3054), provides the main link with the mainland. Car and passenger ferries run from Portsmouth to Fishbourne (just east of Ryde) every half hour in summer (every hour in winter). The journey takes just over half an hour. A passenger-only ferry also operates from Portsmouth to Ryde Pier (the craft dock at the tip every 15 minutes) **t** (0870) 582 7744 www.wightlink.co.uk for both. Hovercraft travel in good weather (and now the only operating Hovercraft service in Britain) from Southsea, just south of Portsmouth, to Ryde **t** (01983) 811000 www.hovertravel.co.uk
By train/boat: Trains link London (Victoria and Waterloo) with Portsmouth. Passengers are deposited directly onto The Hard (where the ferry

terminals are situated). Train arrivals are arranged to coincide with ferry departures. The Isle of Wight's own mainline railway runs from Ryde down the east coast of the island to Shanklin via Sandown and connects with the Isle of Wight Steam Railway at Smallbrook Junction
Tourist information 81–3 Union Street
t (01983) 813818

The island's largest and liveliest town, Ryde is a typically seasidey affair with six miles of sandy beaches, a pier (at half a mile, it's the second longest in the country), family-orientated attractions lining its esplanade including an ice rink, a swimming pool (with retractable roof) and a bowling alley with a children's play area, plus numerous arcades and fish restaurants. The promenade stretches from the Esplanade past Appley Gardens and Appley Tower, a Victorian folly, to Puckpool Park, where you'll find tennis courts, a crazy golf course and a children's playground. It's only a short ride from Ryde aboard the island's mainline railway to Smallbrook Junction, where you can connect with the Isle of Wight Steam Railway.

Things to see and do
Brickfields Horse Country
Newnham Lane, Binstead, Ryde **t** (01983) 566801
www.brickfields.net
Getting there Southwest of the town off the A3054
Open Daily 10–5
Adm Adults £4.95, children £3.75
Café, picnic areas, shop, mother and baby facilities, guided tours, disabled access, on-site parking

Lots of good horsey stuff. You can take wagon rides, go for tours of the stables, see the blacksmith at work in his forge, meet Sylvie the Shetland pony and watch the lively twice-daily horse parades (12 noon and 3.30pm), at which mounted Cowboys and Indians will show off their riding prowess and engage in mock pistol versus tomahawk battles. There are also occasional 'Shetland Grand Nationals' and pig races are held three times daily in high season.

Butterfly and Fountain World
Staplers Road, Wootton **t** (01983) 883430
www.butterfly-world-iow.co.uk
Getting there 4 miles west of Ryde on the coastal A3054 road
Open Apr–Oct 10–5.30
Adm Adults £5.25, children £3.25, under 4s **free**

Café, picnic areas, shop, guided tours, disabled access, on-site parking

A two-hectare (five-acre) garden centre with water gardens, 'jumping' fountains and a tropical butterfly house.

Isle of Wight Steam Railway
The Railway Station, Havenstreet **t** (01983) 882204
www.iwsteamrailway.co.uk
Open Apr–Oct Thurs and Sun; Jun–Sept daily
Adm Station: £1 (**free** after 4pm); train rides (unlimited travel all day): from £8.50, children £5.50 family ticket from £22
Café, gift shop, picnic area, children's play area, limited wheelchair access (call in advance), on-site parking

The geographic isolation of the Isle of Wight's railway means that a great proportion of its Victorian and Edwardian rolling stock has survived. At Havenstreet Station, the nerve centre of the railway, you can see a collection of Island Railway artefacts and watch locomotives being shunted and worked upon. From here, you can take a two-mile journey to Wootton Station, a traditional country terminus with an old wooden booking office and signal box, before travelling back along the line's entire five-mile length to Smallbrook Junction, where you can connect with the island's mainline railway and rejoin the modern world (or, at least, the 1930s, which is when most of the mainline rolling stock dates from). The Railway plays host to various events throughout the year including brake van rides, barbeque evenings, a Summer Extravaganza and Santa Specials.

Seaview Wildlife Encounter
Seaview **t** (01983) 612261
Getting there Just east of Ryde off the B3330
Open Easter–Sept 10–5 (last admission 4), Oct 10–4 (last admission 3)
Adm Adults £7.25, children £5.25, family £23, under 3s **free**
Shop, licensed café, disabled access, on-site parking

Formerly 'Flamingo Park', this wildlife centre is now home to a wide selection of animals including wallabies, beavers, meerkats, pelicans and parrots as well the original occupants – pink flamingos. There's an interactive discovery zone and events are held around the park throughout the day to keep youngsters entertained (they can even feed the penguins). Activity packs available.

Sandown and Shanklin

Getting there Sandown and Shanklin are 2 miles apart on the island's east coast off the A3055. Shanklin marks the southernmost station of the island's mainline railway which links it to Ryde
Tourist information Sandown: 8 High Street **t** (01983) 813818; Shanklin: 67 High Street **t** (01983) 813818

Sandown is a popular Victorian resort with a pleasure pier lined with entertainments, several fine gardens – including Los Altos and Sandham Gardens – a boating lake, a zoo, a fossil museum and a bustling market. The beach is wide and sandy and stretches for two miles along the coast to neighbouring Shanklin, which offers a similar array of seaside attractions including a crazy-golf course, arcades and a funfair as well as a natural gorge to explore, Shanklin Chine.

Things to see and do

Dinosaur Isle

Culver Parade, Sandown **t** (01983) 404344
www.dinosaurisle.com
Open Nov–Mar daily 10–4, Apr–Sept 10–6, Oct 10–5
Adm Adults £4.75, children £2.75, under 3s **free**, family (2+2) £13
Shop, café, disabled access and facilities

A purpose-built attraction with a large Dinosaur Gallery featuring skeletal and life-sized fleshed dinosaur reconstructions, fossils, atmospheric lighting, animatronics, sounds and smells.

Isle of Wight Zoo

Yaverlands, Seafront, Sandown **t** (01983) 403883
www.isleofwightzoo.com
Open Feb–Mar daily 10–4, Apr–Sept 10–6, Oct 10–4, Nov Sat–Sun (weather permitting) 10–4
Adm Adults £5.95, children £4.95, under 5s **free**, family tickets from £19.25
Café, shop, guided tours, mother and baby facilities, disabled access, on-site parking

Although it can count monkeys, birds, snakes and giant spiders among its residents, most people come here for the big cats, who live in a dedicated extension, the Tiger Sanctuary. As the name suggests, tigers are the star attraction. They have long been zoo owner Jack Corney's obsession; his captive breeding programme has resulted in the birth of dozens of cubs, including more than 30 born to the world's most productive captive tigers, Tamyra and Shere Khan.

Ventnor

Getting there By road: Ventnor lies in the island's southeast corner, 3 miles south of Shanklin on the A3055

The Victorian spa town of Ventnor, built on a series of terraces below St Boniface Down (which, at 240m (787ft), is the island's highest point), is linked by a collection of steep, windy roads. Famed for its sunny climate and with beautiful botanic gardens, it's one of the island's most well-to-do resorts. Look out for the elegant flower-lined cascade which leads down to the esplanade, where you'll find a narrow sand and shingle beach, as well as arcades and winter gardens. The pretty village of Bonchurch, with its working blacksmith's forge, lies just east of the town while the Isle of Wight Rare Breeds and Waterfowl Park is just west.

Things to see and do

Appuldurcombe House

Appuldurcombe Road, Wroxall, Ventnor
t (01983) 852484 **www**.appuldurcombe.co.uk
Getting there 3 miles northwest of Ventnor off the B3327
Open Apr–Jun and Sept–Oct daily 10–4, Jul–Aug 10–5; Falconry Centre: daily flying displays at 11am, 1pm and 3pm
Adm Adults £3, children £2, under 5s **free**, family (2+3) £9; combined ticket with Falconry Centre: adults £6.50, children £4.50, family £19
Café, picnic areas, shop, disabled access, parking

Once one of the grandest buildings on the island, this 18th-century house has been slowly decaying since it was vacated in the early 20th century. Appuldurcombe looks grand from afar; only when you get close can you see the ravages of time. Visit the ghost-like rooms and 4.5 hectares (11 acres) of ornamental gardens (designed by Capability Brown), but the real draw is the Falconry Centre.

★Blackgang Chine Fantasy Park

Blackgang, Ventnor **t** (01983) 730330
www.blackgangchine.com
Getting there Blackgang is on the south coast, 5 miles west of Ventnor off the A3055
Open Mar–Oct 10–5 (summer hols until 10pm)
Adm Adults and children £8.50, family £31 (tickets are valid for a return visit within 7 days)
Café, restaurant, shop, mother and baby facilities, disabled access

The attractions at this 16-hectare (40-acre) fun park are of the water-garden, pirate-ship, hedge-maze variety, with plenty to amuse younger children including a teacup ride and Sleeping Beauty's Castle. Lightweight it may be, but it has charm with its replica Wild West town, haunted mansion and fairytale castle. Explore the steep wooded slopes of the Chine itself, where you'll find themed areas populated by model goblins, trolls, dinosaurs and nursery rhyme characters.

Ventnor Botanic Gardens

Undercliff Drive **t** (01983) 855397
www.botanic.co.uk
Open Gardens and visitor centre: daily 10–6; temperate house: 10–5 **Adm Free**
Café, picnic areas, shop, guided tours, disabled access, on-site parking (at extra cost)

These nine hectares (22 acres) of landscaped gardens are the town's biggest draw, filled with subtropical blooms that flourish in south-facing climate. Visit the 100-year-old palm trees, the medicinal herb garden and the temperate house.

Yarmouth

Getting there Yarmouth is in the island's northwest corner on the A3054 and is linked to the mainland resort of Lymington via a car ferry **t** 0870 582 7744 **www**.wightlink.co.uk
Tourist information The Quay (01983) 813818

With a picturesque harbour filled with bobbing boats, this medieval port at the mouth of the River Yar makes a pleasant base for exploring the sights of the island's northwest tip – The Needles and Alum Bay. Its own sights are less well known but still worth a look. There's the castle, which was the last to be built as part of Henry VIII's programme to improve coastal defences – though small, it's well preserved, with views of the Solent – and, one mile west of the town, there's Fort Victoria Country Park – 20 hectares (50 acres) of wood-land around a 19th-century fort leading down to a shingle beach. Here you'll find a plane-tarium, an aquarium and an underwater archaeology centre plus a large model railway.

Things to see and do

Alum Bay and The Needles

Getting there The Needles can be found right at the western tip of the island. Alum Bay is slightly east off the B3322. A ferry service links the nearby resort of Yarmouth (about 4 miles east) with Lymington in the New Forest **t** 0870 582 7744

Alum Bay, with its layers of multicoloured sand, is particularly photogenic. Its appearance is caused by the slow crumbling of the different rock strata that make up the cliff face and is seen to its best effect in wet weather when the shore becomes a riot of pinks, oranges and ochres. You can fill a souvenir glass tube with coloured layers of sand at the nearby Needles Park, a gentle seaside amusement park (crazy golf, carousels, glass-blowing, etc.) and take a ride on the chairlift down to the beach, looking out on the way for The Needles, the row of chalky white pinnacles (with adjoining lighthouse) that have become the emblem of the island itself. There are even better views from The Needles Old Battery along the coast, a 19th-century sea fortress built 80m (262ft) above sea level. Walk through the 65m (213ft) tunnel for impressive views. Boat trips around The Needles are on offer nearby.

Amazon World

Watery Lane, Newchurch **t** (01983) 867122
www.amazonworld.co.uk
Getting there 2 miles west of Sandown on the A3056 Newport Road
Open Daily 10–5.30 **Adm** Adults £6.75, children £5.25, under 3s **free**, family £23
Café, shop, picnic areas, disabled access, on-site parking

An array of rainforest creatures (from toucans to tarantulas) living in an authentic jungle setting (albeit indoors). Though fun (there are 'meet the animals' sessions), it's all presented from an environmental perspective, with displays on ecological damage to the rainforest. Adventure playground (with toddlers' area), petting zone (where children can stroke rabbits and goats) and two daily displays of falconry.

Chessell Pottery Barns

Calbourne **t** (01983) 531248
www.chessellpotterybarns.co.uk
Getting there 5 miles west of Newport off the B3401
Open Daily 10–5 **Adm Free,** pottery from £4.95 + £2.50 studio fee for paints, etc.
Coffee shop, shop, disabled access, on-site parking

Families can watch the potters at work and decorate pieces to take home. There is an adjoining coffee shop (cream teas served).

Dinosaur Farm Museum

Military Road, near Brighstone **t** (01983) 740844
www.dinosaurfarm.co.uk
Open Apr–Jun and Sept–Oct Tues, Thurs, Sat and
Sun 10–5, Jul–Aug daily 10–5
Adm Adults £3.30, children £2.50, family £10
  Watch experts cleaning and repairing fossils or
go for a guided dinosaur hunt in nearby
Brighstone Bay. There's also a play area with
'educational' toys.

Fort Victoria Country Park

Sconce Point, Westhill Lane, Norton **t** (01983) 760860
www.fortvictoria.co.uk
Open Easter–Oct 10–6 **Adm** Park: **Free**; Aquarium:
Adult £2.50, children £1.50, family £7; Model
Railway: Adult £4, children £3, family £12;
Planetarium: Adult £1.50, children 50p; Underwater
Exhibition: Adult £2, children £1.10, family £6.
Café, picnic areas, shop, disabled access, on-site parking
  In addition to its coastal walks and areas of
woodland, this country park also boasts an
aquarium with tanks filled with local sealife and a
tropical fish display, a planetarium with an exhibi-
tion on the work of 17th-century scientist Robert
Hooke, a miniature railway and an underwater
exhibition on the Isle of Wight's sunken treasures.

Isle of Wight Shipwreck Centre and Maritime Museum

Sherborne Street, Bembridge **t** (01983) 872223/
873125
Getting there On the island's eastern tip, 5 miles
northeast of Sandown off the B3395
Open Mar–Oct 10–5 **Adm** Free
Shop, disabled access, on-site parking
  Maritime history of the island with six galleries
devoted to salvage from local wrecks and model
ships. The village of Bembridge is quiet with lots
of good walking options in the nearby cliffs.

Isle of Wight Waxworks

High Street, Brading, Sandown **t** (01983) 407286
www.thebradingexperience.co.uk
Getting there Brading is 3 miles north of Sandown
on the A3055. It's also a station on the island's
mainline railway between Ryde and Shanklin
Open Easter–Oct daily 10–5.30; Nov–Easter 10.30–5
Adm Adults £6.75, children £4.75, under 5s **free**,
family (2+2) £21, (2+3) £25
Café, shop, mother and baby facilities, on-site parking

Dinosaur hunting

  The Isle of Wight is one of the best places in the
entire country to go fossil-hunting. The southern
cliffs of Brighstone and Brook Bays are particularly
rich in dinosaur deposits. Not only are the rocks
here of the right age to contain fossils (65–200
million years old) but they are also mainly made
up of soft, easily eroded clay and numerous new
fossils are exposed by storms and high spring tides
each year. Around 20 different species of dinosaur
have been found here including *iguanodons* (a five
metre-high herbivore), *polycanthuses* (an
armoured dinosaur), *brachiosauruses* (one of the
largest dinosaurs that ever lived) and the recently
discovered *egyptyrannus lengi*, a fearsome meat-
eater, a bit like a miniature T-Rex. Its name
translates as 'Lengi's early tyrant' in honour of
Gavin Lengi, the local fossil collector who uncovered it. Fossil hunts along the coast are organized
by the Dinosaur Farm Museum (*see* left).

The history of the island presented as a series
of garish waxwork scenes ('The Chamber of
Horrors') plus a collection of stuffed animals and
birds. A new 'World of Wheels' exhibition has
recently been added, offering a display of steam
engines and veteran cars, as has a mock pier with
old bicycles (penny farthings, boneshakers, etc.)
and antique amusements.

Lilliput Doll and Toy Museum

High Street, Brading **t** (01983) 407231
www.lilliputshop.com
Getting there Brading is 3 miles north of Sandown
on the A3055. It's also a station on the island's
mainline railway, which links the town with Ryde
and Shanklin
Open Daily 10–5 **Adm** Adults £1.95, children £1,
under 5s **free**
Shop, guided tours, disabled access
  More than 2,000 toys and dolls from the last
two millennia.

Natural History Centre

High Street, Godshill **t** (01983) 840333
www.shellmuseum.co.uk
Open Mid-Feb–Dec 10–6 **Adm** Call for prices
  Displays of shells, minerals, precious stones,
fossils and (incongruously) replicas of the crown
jewels, housed in a 17th-century squire's cottage.

SPECIAL TRIPS

The Needles Old Battery

West High Down, Totland Bay **t** (01983) 754772
www.nationaltrust.org.uk
Open Apr–Oct Sun–Thurs 10.30–5 (Jul–Aug daily, although it is liable to close in bad weather)
Adm Adults £3.90, children £1.95, family £8.90
Café, guided tour

Needles Park

Alum Bay, Totland Bay **t** 0870 458 0022
www.theneedles.co.uk
Open Apr–Nov 10–5 (later in summer)
Adm Free; £1–£2 per attraction; chairlift: adults £4, children £3
Café, fast food, picnic areas, shop, mother and baby facilities, disabled access, on-site parking (£3 per car)

Children and parents can watch their favourite traditional sweets being made and taste the sticky results at the Sweet Manufactory, or view glass being shaped into paperweights, vases and bottles at the Glassmakers. Younger children (aged 4 and up) will enjoy the Junior Driver track, a miniature road complete with signs and working traffic lights, which can be traversed in child-friendly electric cars, at the end of which they'll be awarded a special Needles driving licence. On Thursday nights throughout August the park closes its doors every night for an impressive fireworks display.

Roman Villa

Brading **t** (01983) 406223
www.bradingromanvilla.org.uk
Open Mar–Oct daily 9.30–6, Nov–Feb 10–4
Adm Adults £3.95, children £1.95, family (2+3) £10
Café, shop, disabled access

The best-preserved Roman remains on the island, the villa has several mosaics including an image of Medusa, an interesting collection of Roman pottery and coins and a reconstruction of a Roman garden.

Yarmouth Castle

Quay Street **t** (01983) 760678
www.english-heritage.org.uk
Open Apr–Oct Mon–Thurs and Sun 10–4
Adm Adults £2.80, children £1.40
Disabled access, on-site parking

Commissioned by Henry VIII to defend the coast and completed in 1547, a coastal defences exhibition is now on display in the castle.

Abbeys and castles

★Arundel Castle

Arundel **t** (01903) 882173 **www**.castleexplorer.org
Getting there 4 miles north of Littlehampton, 8 miles east of Chichester off the A27 and A284
Open Apr–Oct Sun–Fri 12 noon–5
Adm Adults £12, children £7.50, under 5s **free**, family (2+5) £32
Café, gift shop, on-site parking, disabled access, picnic sites

Arundel was first acquired by the Duke of Norfolk some 700 years ago and has remained in the family ever since. Unlike many other stately home-style castles, which are often more stately home than castle, this has all the requisite features befitting a fairytale fortress. Parents and kids can tick them off together: moat (check), drawbridge (check), portcullis (check), battlements (check), suits of armour (check). Although there are many roped-off areas and plenty of 'do not touch' signs, this is still a pretty accessible place, although it's probably best toured in the company of a young person's guide (available at the museum shop), which will point out all the most interesting features, as well as providing activities (such as pictures to colour in) and interesting facts. In particular, look out for Mary Queen of Scots' prayer book and the keep – it's 120 steps to the top from where there are fantastic views out over the coast towards the Isle of Wight (pp.103–10). Do also check out the Arundel Toy and Military Museum in the town, a fascinating collection of old toys, games, dolls and teddy bears housed in a Georgian cottage.

★Battle Abbey

High Street, Battle **t** (01424) 773792
www.english-heritage.org.uk
Getting there About 6 miles northwest of Hastings on the A2100 and A271 (a 10-minute train ride away)
Open Apr–Sept daily 10–6, Oct–Mar daily 10–4
Adm Adults £5.50, children £2.50, family (2+3) £13.80
Gift shop, disabled access, picnic sites, free audio tour

The Battle of Hastings, the most famous battle in British history, actually took place here, a few miles inland from the seaside resort. William I had an abbey erected as a means of atoning for the blood shed during the fighting, although most of the buildings you see date from the later medieval and Tudor periods. Visitors to the site are taken on a virtual journey through the bloody conflict, beginning with an exhibition on the background history, a video on the battle, as well as a look at the changes the Norman invasion brought to the country – in the years after 1066, around half the land in England became the property of just 30 or so individuals, none of whom spoke English. Afterwards, you get to take an audio tour of the battlefield itself (you can hear the story of the battle retold from various viewpoints – a Saxon soldier's, a Norman knight's, etc.) and stand on the spot where Harold fell after being shot in the eye by a Norman arrow. Activity sheets and quizzes are provided and there's also a themed play area for very young children. Battle re-enactments take place every weekend in summer.

Housed in a barn near the abbey is Buckley's Yesterday's World (see right), which holds a collection of recreated shop and house interiors from the 1850s to 1950s, as well as a children's village, penny arcade, miniature golf course and toddlers' activity area.

★Bodiam Castle
Bodiam, Robertsbridge **t** (01580) 830436
www.nationaltrust.org.uk
Getting there 10 miles north of Hastings off the B2244. In summer there are river cruises to Bodiam from Newenden. The Kent and East Sussex Steam Railway also makes trips from Bodiam to the nearby town of Tenterden
Open Mid-Feb–Oct daily 10.30–6, Nov–mid-Feb Sat–Sun 10.30–4 **Adm** Adults £4.60, children £2.30, under 5s **free**, family £11.50
Café-restaurant, gift shop, picnic areas, mother and baby facilities, some disabled access, on-site parking

When children try to draw a castle, they nearly always come up with something that looks like Bodiam: a proper storybook castle with round turrets on each corner, crinkly battlements, arrow-slit windows, a portcullis and a deep surrounding moat. It has been uninhabited since the Civil War and much of the interior is open to the elements which means that, unlike many other castles where you have to stop your children bumping into precious relics and mementos, here kids can run about to their heart's content. And they do – they climb the

narrow spiral staircases, peer through the high windows at imaginary invaders and hunt for ducks and carp in the moat. If you can get them to sit still for long enough, they'll probably enjoy the 15-minute audiovisual presentation showing what life was like in a medieval castle (pretty grim in truth). After that, however, it's probably best just to let them off the leash to explore. See if they can find the castle's medieval toilets which emptied straight into the moat (those poor ducks). The inside of the castle, most of which is covered in grass, makes a perfect spot for a picnic and there are numerous family events organized throughout the year, including treasure hunts, donkey rides and open-air theatre performances. In summer there are boat trips from Bodiam up and down the river to Newenden and back (it's a 90-minute round-trip) and you can also take a ride aboard the East Sussex Steam Railway, which runs between here and the nearby town of Tenterden.

Buckley's Yesterday's World
80–90 Battle High Street, Battle **t** (01424) 775378
www.yesterdaysworld.co.uk
Open Daily 9.30–5.30 **Adm** Adults £5.95, children £3.95, under 4s **free**, family £16.99
Café, gift shop, mother and baby room

Deal Castle
Victoria Road, Deal **t** (01304) 372762
www.english-heritage.org.uk
Getting there Deal is on the east Kent coast, 7 miles north of Dover on the A258
Open Apr–Sept 10–6 **Adm** Adults £3.90, children £2, under 5s **free**
Gift shop, some disabled access, audio tour

A few miles north of Dover, Deal supposedly marks the spot where Julius Caesar and his Roman troops first set foot on British soil. Some 1,600 years later Henry VIII ordered the construction of this peculiarly shaped castle (from above it resembles a Tudor Rose) in order to prevent anyone else on the continent from getting a similar idea. With its towering views of the coast and long, dark passageways to explore, Deal Castle provides an excellent afternoon's entertainment. Call in advance for details of any family events that might be coming up, which include battle re-enactments, puppet-making workshops, Tudor printing workshops and special child-friendly guided tours.

A brief history of the Battle of Hastings

Who was it between?

Harold, King of England and William, Duke of Normandy (and their respective armies). Although we tend to think of the Normans as French, they could equally well be described as Viking. William and his army were the descendants of Viking raiders who had seized part of northern France in the 10th century. The name Norman is a corruption of 'Norse Man'.

When?

1066 – the most famous date in English history.

Why?

The battle was an argument over who should be king of England. William said that Edward the Confessor, who had been king before Harold, had promised the crown to him. Harold disagreed and, upon Edward's death, seized the crown for himself.

What happened?

William invaded in October 1066 with several thousand troops and set up camp in Hastings. Harold and his army were meanwhile in the north of England fighting invaders from Scandinavia. Hearing of William's arrival, Harold was forced to march his army back down south, where they arrived exhausted three days later. They took up position on the high ground of Battle and waited for William to make his move. William's forces made several unsuccessful attempts to gain control of the high ground but were repelled by Harold's troops. William then pretended to retreat, whereupon Harold's army charged down the hill, only for William's troops to turn round and engulf the English in a hail of arrows. Harold was shot in the eye and, as he tried to pull the arrow out, was cut to pieces by Norman soldiers. Upon hearing that their king was dead, the English army's morale collapsed and William marched on London and was proclaimed the new king of England.

Hever Castle

Hever, near Edenbridge **t** (01732) 865224
www.hever-castle.co.uk
Getting there 8 miles west of Tonbridge off the B2027
Open Mar–Nov daily 11–6 **Adm** Adults £9.80, children £5.30, under 5s **free**, family (2+2) £24.90
Restaurants, gift shop, guided tours, mother and baby facilities, disabled access, on-site parking

It may look similar, with its turrets, battlements and moat, but Hever is very much the antithesis of the rough-and-ready Bodiam; its interior sumptuously decorated with antiques, fine tapestries and suits of armour – although many of the more interesting areas are (frustratingly) roped off. There are, however, a few nooks and crannies worth exploring, as well as costumed waxworks of Henry VIII and his six wives (this was where Anne Boleyn, his second wife, lived as a child), a display of dolls' houses and the castle's picnic-perfect grounds contain a yew maze, an adventure playground, a lake and an Italian garden with a lakeside theatre, where a renowned season of plays, musicals and opera performances takes place each summer. There's also a water maze (from April to October) lined with water jets that spray visitors every time they take a wrong turning.

★Leeds Castle

Maidstone **t** (01622) 765400 **www**.leeds-castle.com
Getting there 40 miles southeast of London near Maidstone off the M20 and B2163. There are direct services from London Victoria to Bearsted, the nearest train station, from where there's a regular shuttle bus to the castle. Eurostar services from the Continent and slow trains from London Bridge stop at Ashford International, 20 minutes away
Open Castle: Apr–Sept 10.30–5, Oct–Mar 10.30–3; park and gardens: Apr–Sept 10–5, Oct–Mar 10–3
Adm Adults £13.50, children £8, under 4s **free**
Gift shops, restaurant, guided tours, some wheelchair access, baby changing facilities

Leeds Castle, Henry VIII's favourite castle, looks dramatic, romantic and mysterious set on two islands in the middle of a lake in 200 hectares (500 acres) of beautifully sculpted Kent countryside. He spent a fortune on it during his lifetime as seen in his fabulously opulent Banqueting Hall with its ebony wood floors and carved oak ceiling. Architecturally, it's a bit of a hotch potch – the cellar dates from the 11th century, the original gatehouse from the 12th (it contains a rare collection of dog collars, some over 400 years old), the Maiden's Tower is Tudor, whilst the main residential quarters were built in the last century – but it all hangs together perfectly and is an undeniably beautiful place. Unfortunately, beauty doesn't always cut it with children. The trouble with Leeds, as far as kids are concerned, is that it's a bit starchy and formal inside. The interior is stuffed full of precious paintings and furniture but the rarefied 'don't touch' atmosphere means that kids can't really interact with the space as much as they would like. A suit of armour quickly loses its appeal if you're not allowed to take it apart and get inside. It's a different story, however, in the castle grounds. With a maze, an underground grotto, an aviary and lots of wide grassy spaces to run around on, the grounds provide a wonderful opportunity for kids to let off steam. What's more, family entertainments are put on in the grounds throughout the year. These include Easter celebrations with face-painting, Punch and Judy shows, circus workshops, Half-Term Fun (when a range of impromptu mazes are constructed in the castle grounds) and the famous Balloon Festival in September, when the sky around the castle become filled with dozens of weird and wonderfully shaped hot air balloons.

Walmer Castle

Kingsdown Road, Walmer, Deal **t** (01304) 364288 **www**.english-heritage.org.uk
Getting there Deal is on the east Kent coast, 7 miles north of Dover on the A258
Open Apr–Sept daily 10–6 (Sat 4pm), Oct and Mar Wed–Sun 10–4
Adm Adults £6.20, children £3.10, under 5s **free**, family £15.50
Café, gift and plant shop, disabled access, audio tour, on-site parking

Built at the same time as nearby Deal Castle, Walmer has likewise been designed to look like a Tudor Rose (when viewed from above) and can offer equally splendid views of the Kent coastline, although it's perhaps slightly less child friendly. Unlike many other castles, Walmer is still used by the Royal Family, albeit only for ceremonial occasions. It is the official seat of the Lord Warden of the Cinque Ports, the military official who, in centuries past, was charged with overseeing Kent's coastal defenses. In the mid 19th century, this role was fulfilled by the Duke of Wellington, Napoleon's conqueror, and the castle contains an exhibition on his life and times featuring a pair of his famous waterproof boots. These days, however, it's a purely honorary title. Her Majesty the Queen Mother held the title during her lifetime and was a frequent visitor to the castle. A

special garden was built in the grounds in honour of her 95th birthday, which serves as a memorial to her today. Garden tours, Easter egg hunts and fairytale re-enactments are just some of the family events put on at the castle throughout the season.

Palaces and historic houses
★Beaulieu

Beaulieu **t** (01590) 612345 **www.**beaulieu.co.uk
Getting there In the New Forest, about 6 miles south of Southampton on the B3054, B3055 and B3056 (J2 from the M27). The nearest train station is Brockenhurst, 6 miles west
Open May–Sept daily 10–6; Oct–Apr 10–5
Adm Adults £16, youth (13–17) £9, children £8, under 5s **free**, family £44
Restaurant, gift shops, guided tours, some disabled access, adapted toilets

There are two distinct sides to Beaulieu: a quiet serene side as represented by the 16th-century Beaulieu Palace and its beautiful lakeside park, and the noisier, more exuberant side of its world-famous Motor Museum with its thousands of clanking, clunking, whirring exhibits. At this temple to all things mechanical, there are exquisitely preserved cars from throughout the history of the motoring age, from late 19th-century prototypes to ultra-modern speed machines. Priceless luxury cars (including a 1909 Rolls Royce Silver Ghost and a 1962 E-Type Jaguar) sit alongside archetypal people-carriers (Volkswagen Beetles, Minis and the original people's car, the Ford Model T). Yesteryear's record-breakers – their once unbelievable feats now long since surpassed – are also here, including the 1927 Sunbeam 1000hp, the first car to break the 200mph barrier, and Donald Campbell's 1964 Bluebird, the first vehicle to travel above 400mph. Elsewhere, you'll find a historic garage and an interactive gallery where children can unravel the mysteries of the internal combustion engine before sampling the museum's radio-controlled cars, mini bikes and hi-tech arcade simulators. A jaunty little monorail travels round the palace grounds at regular intervals. The museum's showpiece is its 'Wheels' ride in which a motorized car trundles you past seven tableaux designed to tell the story of motoring in the 20th century.

★Hampton Court Palace

East Molesey **t** (0870) 7527777 www.hrp.org.uk
Getting there Just southwest of London near
Kingston-upon-Thames, off the A3 and A309 (J12
from the M25). Trains run regularly from London
(Waterloo) to Hampton Court station or, alternately,
take a cruise up the Thames with the Westminster
Passenger Service from Westminster Pier
Open Nov–Feb daily 10–4.30, Mar–Oct daily 10–6
Adm Adults £12.30, children £8, under 5s **free**,
family ticket £36.40
*Café, restaurant, souvenir shops (in particular the
Tudor Kitchen shop which sells a range of Tudor
cooking implements and medieval herbs), children's
room with construction toys, guided tours, disabled
facilities, on-site parking*

Hampton Court provides a fabulous day out for
children of all ages. This grand old building is full
of 500 years' worth of historical treasures
including Henry VIII's sumptuous state apartments, a 'Real tennis' court and a Renaissance
picture gallery with works by Brueghel and
Mantegna. Your children's favourite area will
probably be the huge Tudor kitchens, where a
banquet complete with spit-roast is prepared
daily by cooks in Tudor dress. It's like stepping
into a time-warp – see the sights, hear the
sounds and inhale the smells of the past. The
highly recommended guided tours given by
costumed characters will enthrall your children
with tales of marriage and murder (this was
where Henry VIII lived, remember). Children's
trails are available and workshops and storytelling sessions are organized during the school
holidays. In winter, visitors can enjoy festive
events and an ice rink in the grounds.

Henry VIII's wives

Everybody knows that Henry VIII had six wives
Can you name them and, more importantly, do you
know what fate befell them?
Catherine of Aragon April 1506–April 1533 *Divorced*
Anne Boleyn January 1533–May 1536 *Beheaded*
Jane Seymour May 1536–October 1537 *Died*
Anne of Cleves January 1540–July 1540 *Divorced*
Catherine Howard July 1540–February 1541 *Beheaded*
Catherine Parr July 1543–January 1547 *Survived*
It's easy to remember. You just need to keep
repeating to yourself: 'divorced, beheaded,
died...divorced, beheaded, survived'.

Did you know...

That in Henry VIII's time, Hampton Court
contained an enormous multiple lavatory? It
could seat 28 people at a time and was known as
'The Great House of Easement'.

The building itself was begun in the 1520s by
Cardinal Wolsey, chief advisor to Henry VIII, who
offered the monarch the palace as a gift. Henry
refused, only to seize it anyway when Wolsey later
failed to secure Henry a divorce from his first wife,
Catherine of Aragon. During his reign Henry spent
a staggering £62,000 on Hampton Court (around
£18 million today), turning it into the most
modern, sophisticated palace in England. Only
part of the structure we see today, however, dates
from this time. Sir Christopher Wren undertook a
further £131,000 (an estimated £9.5 million today)
worth of rebuilding work in the late 17th century
and planted the landscaped gardens (p.125).

Lullingstone Roman Villa

Near Eynsford **t** (01322) 863467
www.english-heritage.org.uk
Getting there 7 miles north of Sevenoaks, just
outside Eynsford off the A225 (J3 from M25)
Open Apr–Sept daily 10–6, Oct–Nov daily 10–4,
Dec–Jan Wed–Sun 10–4, Feb–Mar daily 10–4
Adm Adults £3.90, children £2, under 5s **free**
*Shop, refreshments, on-site parking, **free** audio guide*

One of the largest Roman villas in Britain,
Lullingstone lay buried and forgotten after the
collapse of the Roman Empire in the 5th century
until it was rediscovered 1,400 years later in
the mid 20th century. Not much remains – the
site mainly consists of a series of small walls –
but there are some well-preserved mosaics and
wall paintings. The audio guide will help you to
fill in the gaps and there's a children's activity
sheet available. It's best to come on one of the
numerous English Heritage-organized event
days when children get the chance to meet a
Roman soldier, eat Roman food or try their
hand at making Roman jewellery or mosaics.

Penshurst Place

Penshurst, Tonbridge **t** (01892) 870307
www.penshurstplace.com
Getting there 6 miles northwest of Tunbridge
Wells off the B2176 and B2188

Open Apr–Nov daily 10.30–6, Mar Sat–Sun 10.30–6
Adm Adults £7.50, children £5, family £21
Restaurant, some disabled access, on-site parking

This medieval manor house is surrounded by a wonderful array of formal and informal gardens, where you'll find lots of wide grassy spaces, flowerbeds, orchards and ponds, and an excellent adventure playground with a sandpit, slides and some commando-style climbing equipment. There's a nature trail through the adjoining woods and, in summer, the gardens hosts falconry displays, craft demonstrations and theatrical performances. The house itself is rather dry and dusty but contains a delightful toy room filled with dolls and teddy bears collected from ancient nurseries.

Polesden Lacy

Great Bookham, Dorking **t** (01372) 458203/452048
www.nationaltrust.org.uk
Getting there 2 miles north of Dorking off the A246
Open Garden: daily Mar–Oct 11–5, Nov–Feb 11–4; house: Apr–Oct Wed–Sun 11–5
Adm Adults £9, children £4.50, family £22.50; Gardens only adults £6, children £3, family £15
Refreshments, guided tours, some disabled access, on-site parking

This beautiful Regency house was once one of the most fashionable addresses around, the venue of the most lavish society parties. Although the chatter, dancing and merriment have long since faded (leaving behind a rather workaday museum-house), it's still worth visiting for its fabulous gardens, picknicking lawns, woods, hedges and flowers for admiring (if you're an adult) or for playing hide-and-seek in (if you're a child). For anyone wanting something a little more structured, there are four marked walks through the gardens and woods, ranging in length from one to three miles, and croquet sets can be hired during the summer. Various family events take place here during the year including Easter egg hunts, country fairs and classical concerts (with firework finales). The famous London–Brighton car run also makes a designated stop here mid route. There's an activity book and quiz for families wishing to tour the house.

Animal attractions

Ashdown Forest Llama Farm

Wych Cross, Forest Row **t** (01825) 712040
www.llamapark.co.uk
Getting there On the A22, near Wych Cross, just south of the junction with the A275
Open Daily 10–5 (or dusk if earlier) **Adm** Adults £4.75, children £4
Tearoom, picnic area, gift and alpaca knitwear shop, museum

Friendly farm where you can meet sheep, goats (angora and cashmere), llamas and alpacas and visit a World of Wool Museum in an 18th-century barn.

Bentley Wildfowl and Motor Museum

Harveys Lane, Halland, Lewes **t** (01825) 840573
www.bentley.org.uk
Getting there 7 miles north of Lewes and signposted from the A22, A26 and B2192
Open Apr–Oct daily 10.30–5.30 **Adm** Adults £6.50, children £4.50, under 3s **free**, family (2+3) £21
Café, gift shop, guided tours, disabled access, on-site parking

It's a slightly odd combination of attractions but definitely well worth a visit. Start at the museum, which is full of bright, gleaming sports cars from throughout the history of motoring – Ferraris, Aston Martins, etc. Kids will be attracted to all the shiny metal but may find the lack of interaction frustrating. Visitors are not even allowed to touch these speed machines (much less climb inside, which is what they really want to do). The grounds offer much more scope for kids to get their hands dirty, with woodland trails and a miniature steam train offering rides in summer. The main attraction, however, is the birds. Pick up an identification chart and a bag of seed at the entrance and see what you can find. There are well over 1,000 birds living on the park's collection of ponds and enclosures with three marked routes taking you past all the assorted ducks, geese and swans, who will rush up to meet you as soon as they hear the first faint rustle of seed.

★Birdworld

Holt Pound, Farnham **t** (01420) 22140
Infoline: **t** (01420) 22838 **www.**birdworld.co.uk
Getting there 3 miles southwest of Farnham off the A325
Open Mar–Oct daily 10–6, Nov–Jan Sat–Sun 10–4.30

Adm Adults £10.95, children £8.95, under 4s **free**, family £35.95

Restaurant, gift shop, mother and baby facilities, disabled access, on-site parking

You wil meet many feathered friends at this imaginatively presented 11-hectare (28-acre) animal centre near Farnham. All birdlife is here – green, squawking parrots, beautiful pink flamingoes and white, haughty-looking pelicans with their huge fish-hungry bills. You'll see ostriches up close, chicks in the incubation centre and penguins, oyster catchers and an aviary full of free-flying exotic birds. There's lots to see, which can be quite hard on little legs, but there's plenty of opportunity for sitting down. Take a seat at the Heron Centre, where talks are given on the park's inhabitants at 1pm and 3pm every afternoon (usually accompanied by a demonstration of flying or feeding by one of the park's tamer residents), or take a 10-minute tour of the park on the free road train, which runs daily from the beginning of June. The park contains a good café and picnic area, a small farm, a children's playground and a marine creature display.

Druidstone Wildlife Park

Honey Hill, Blean, Canterbury **t** (01227) 765168
www.druidstone.net
Getting there Blean is 5 miles northwest of Canterbury off the A290
Open Mar–Nov daily 10–5.30
Adm Adults £5.10, children £3.80, family £15
Café, gift shop, mother and baby facilities, disabled access, on-site parking

Lots of small, friendly animals to meet, including wallabies, deer, owls and monkeys, as well as a woodland walk, an adventure playground and an under-5s play area.

★Drusilla's Zoo Park

Alfriston **t** (01323) 874100 **www.drusillas.co.uk**
Getting there 7 miles northeast of Eastbourne off the A27
Open Apr–Sept 10–5, Oct–Mar 10–4
Adm Adults £11.50, children £10.50, under 3s **free**, family £21–£56.25
'Explorers' restaurant, gift shop, mother and baby facilities, disabled access, on-site parking

There are no tigers, elephants or giraffes here, no animals your kids will simply stand and point at because of their sheer size or fearsomeness. At Drusilla's the watchword is small. As one of the country's most child-orientated zoos, it understands that the best way to get kids to appreciate animals is by providing them with as much access as possible to the animals' own world – which isn't really a feasible option with a tiger. Here, animals are displayed in new and different ways and from imaginative viewpoints. Children can watch meerkats running and frolicking from inside a plastic dome within the meerkat enclosure; they can walk through a bat house as the bats fly over and around their heads, and look at penguins cavorting underwater from a special viewing area. The zoo encourages participation and organizes lots of activities and games to help kids understand the zoo's inhabitants better – they can hang upside down like a monkey or a bat on a climbing frame, try to run as fast as a llama on a treadmill or get up close and personal with an owl, snake or monkey at an animal encounter session. There are art competitions, talks by the keepers and themed weekends (Reptile Weekend, Primate Weekend, etc.) – everything, in fact, for a perfect day at the zoo. And, should the animals lose their appeal, you could climb aboard a miniature train or head to the play area, where you'll find swings, slides, a tractor and even an old fire engine, as well as a soft play area for toddlers.

The Hawk Conservancy Trust

Sarson Lane, Weyhill, Andover **t** (01264) 773850
www.hawk-conservancy.org
Getting there On the A303 4 miles west of Andover
Open Mid-Feb–Oct 10.30-5.30 (last entry 4)
Adm Adults £8.75, children £5.50, under 3s free, family £27.50
Café, gift shop, parent and baby room, picnic areas

The hawk conservancy gives children and adults the chance to meet and learn about hawks, kites, falcons, owls, eagles, vultures and other birds of prey. Flying demonstrations take place at 12 noon, 2 and 3.30pm. After the 2pm display adults can have a turn flying a Harris' Hawk, while after the 12 noon and 3.30pm demonstrations, children can hold one of the British birds of prey. The grounds cover six hectares (15 acres) of woodland, which contain trails (children's nature sheets available from the gift shop), ponds, adventure and toddlers' play areas, and an education centre with interactive displays and quizzes. At weekends and in school holidays there are ferret races, duck races and tractor rides.

Howlett's Wild Animal Park

Bekesbourne Lane, Bekesbourne, Canterbury
t (01227) 721286 **www.howletts.net**
Getting there 5 miles southeast of Canterbury and signposted from the A2
Open Daily 10–6 (or dusk) **Adm** Adults £13.95, children £10.95, under 4s **free**, family (2+2) £42, family (2+3) £49
Café, restaurant, gift shop, disabled access, adapted toilets, on-site parking

Howlett's and Port Lympne (*see* right) were founded by the late conservationist John Aspinall as wild animal conservation parks. Howlett's is home to the largest family group of gorillas outside the African jungle and the largest breeding population of elephants in Europe. Both parks have successfully reintroduced captive bred animals back into the wild. Animal sessions and kids' activities all year.

Marwell Zoological Park

Colden Common **t** (01962) 777407
www.marwell.org.uk
Getting there 8 miles south of Winchester off the B2177 (J12 from the M3)
Open Daily 10–6 (winter until 4)
Adm Adults £13.50, children £10, family £45
Restaurant, café, gift shop, mother and baby room, adapted toilets

As one of the country's leading conservation zoos (its logo features the endangered Oryx), Marwell's enclosures are designed to imitate the animals' natural environments as closely as possible. In particular, look out for the leopards' enclosure, where poles and platforms are used to replicate the African tree tops – leopards spend much of their time in trees and often drag their kills up into the branches to prevent them being stolen by other predators. All the headline beasts are here, from lions, tigers and even black panthers to zebras, giraffes and rhinos. Animal encounter sessions are organized in summer.

New Forest Otter, Owl and Conservation Park

Longdown, Ashurst, Southampton
t (023) 8029 2408 **www.ottersandowls.co.uk**
Getting there About 5 miles southwest of Southampton off the A35
Open Daily 10–5.30 (winter until dusk)
Adm Adults £6.95, under 14s £4.95, under 4s **free**, family (2+2) £20.50
Café, gift shop, disabled access, on-site parking

Port Lympne

Aldington Road, Lympne, Hythe **t** (01303) 264647
www.totallywild.net
Getting there Lympne is about 5 miles inland from Hythe on the Kent coast off the A261 and B0267
Open Daily 10–6 (or dusk) **Adm** Adults £13.95, children £10.95, under 4s **free**, family (2+2) £42, family (2+3) £49
Café, restaurant, gift shop, disabled access, adapted toilets, on-site parking

One of two wild animal parks founded by the late conservationist (and controversialist) John Aspinall (*see* left), Port Lympne is home to the largest captive group of black rhinos in the world. The animals are kept in large, natural-looking enclosures, and there are regular talks, meet the animals sessions and children's activities throughout the year.

Seven Sisters Sheep Centre

The Fridays, East Dean, Eastbourne **t** (01323) 423302
www.sheepcentre.co.uk
Getting there West of Beachy Head off the A259
Open May–Sept Mon–Fri 2–5 Sat–Sun 11–5
Adm Adults £4, children £3, family (2+2) £13
Café, gift shop, guided tours, disabled access, on-site parking

As well as meeting the woolly favourites (over 45 breeds), you can watch demonstrations of sheep-shearing, wool-spinning, milking and cheese-making. In spring and early summer, there are baby lambs to cuddle and feed and tractor rides are offered around the centre. The Seven Sisters Country Park, which lies on the South Downs Way (p.132), is a few miles to the west.

Farms

★Bockett's Farm Park

Young Street, Fetcham **t** (01372) 363764
www.bockettsfarm.co.uk
Getting there Fetcham is 2 miles south of Leatherhead, 2 miles north of Polesden Lacy off the A24 and A246
Open Daily 10–6 (winter till 5.30)
Adm Adults £5.95, children (3–17) £5.40, under 2s £4.25
Café, picnic area, mother and baby facilities, disabled access, on-site parking

It may be a proper working farm, but Bockett's has clearly thought long and hard about how best to present its animals to younger visitors. You'll find lots of enclosures surrounded by small fences offering easy viewing for little people. Most of the animals (which include pigs, goats, cows, a donkey and a big, shaggy Shire horse) live in a large open barn, although there is a separate area for small animals, where kids can get a little more hands-on with the ever-so-strokable rabbits and guinea pigs, or help feed the free-roaming chickens. Outside, there's a small enclosure of tame red deer and a very good playground with the rural equivalent of climbing equipment: hay bales, tyres and even an old tractor (by far the most popular choice), as well as a few more traditional items – swings, slides and a wooden fort. Tractor and pony rides are offered on the weekend in summer.

Burpham Court Farm

Clay Lane, Jacob's Well, Guildford **t** (01483) 576089
www.burphamcourtfarm.co.uk
Getting there Just north of Guildford off the A3
Open Daily 10–6 **Adm** Adults £4.75, children £3.95, under 2s **free**
Café, on-site parking
Burpham is much less polished and touristy than many of its competitors, but no less enjoyable for that. Unlike other show farms, where the animals are often corralled into one small child-size area, here they are spread out in the fields and you must follow a trail through the farm to find them. So, pick up some seed at the entrance for feeding the sheep and chickens and get searching. The route starts with a pleasant amble alongside the banks of the River Wey wending your way past overgrown plants and clambering over stiles (not suitable for pushchairs). In summer, you should be able to see ducks and butterflies and, if you're lucky, perhaps the odd dragonfly or two (which will probably delight and terrify your children in equal measure). After that, you come to the open paddocks separated by wide grassy paths, where you'll find woolly sheep (who'll rush up to be fed) and long-horned cows (who won't), as well as goats, pigs, ponies and even llamas. In spring, children can help bottle-feed the lambs and goat kids. One of the great things about Burpham is that at the end of the day (between 4 and 6pm, depending on the season), you can help the farmer put the animals away for the night (which gives kids a great sense of importance) and collect any hens' eggs that may have been laid during the afternoon. Tea is served in the farmhouse or you can picnic outside.

Finkley Down Farm Park

Andover **t** (01264) 324141 Infoline **t** (01264) 352195
www.finkleydownfarm.co.uk
Getting there Just northeast of Andover off the A303 and A342
Open Mar–Oct daily 10–6 **Adm** Adults £5.75, children £4.75, under 2s **free**, family (2+2) £20
Refreshments, mother and baby facilities, disabled access, gift shop, on-site parking
Good, solid working farm with animals and poultry to pet and feed, a pets' corner, an adventure playground and trampolines. Activities for children are organized throughout the day.

Fishers Farm Park

Newpound Lane, Wisborough Green, near Billingshurst **t** (01403) 700063
www.fishersfarmpark.co.uk
Getting there 7 miles south east of Horsham off the A272
Open Daily 10–5 **Adm** Low/mid/high season Adults £7.75/£9.75/£10.75, children £7.25/£9.25/£10.25, under 3s £4/£6/£7
Café, picnic area, gift shop, mother and baby facilities, on-site parking
Your day begins at the barns by the entrance, where you can meet the farm's resident cows, pigs, goats and sheep and, in early summer, kids and lambs – children may even be allowed to get into the lamb enclosure for a cuddle. Then, after a brief inspection of the games in the play barn, it's off to the farm's open-air section, where you can enjoy tractor, combine harvester and pony rides, go for a spin on a 1950s carousel, take the wheel of a go-kart, climb over the equipment at the adventure playground and visit the cows and sheep in their paddocks.

★Godstone Farm

Tilburstow Hill Road, Godstone **t** (01883) 742546
www.godstonefarm.co.uk
Getting there Godstone is just south of the M25 (J6) on the A25
Open Mar–Oct daily 10–6, Nov–Feb 10–5
Adm Children (2–16) £5.80, accompanying adult **free**
Café, gift shop, mother and baby facilities, disabled access, on-site parking
England has many children's farms. In recent years, they have become almost as ubiquitous as playgrounds and, in truth, it is sometimes hard to tell them apart with their standard collections of animals and run-of-the-mill playgrounds.

Occasionally, however, you come across a park that surprises you with the range and quality of its attractions. Godstone is one such farm. It is made up of four sections: a 16-hectare (40-acre) working farm with enclosures holding goats, sheep, cows and pigs, which kids are encouraged to pet; a large expanse of fields and woods; an outdoor play area with elaborate climbing frames, tunnels, sandpits and even a mini dry-slope toboggan run (not suitable for toddlers); and a large indoor play barn full of toy vehicles galore (perfect for winter visits). There is an incubation shed too, where you can help feed the chicks, ducklings and piglets and, in summer, sheepdog trials are held. All in all, an excellent day's fun. It can get very crowded in summer.

Horton Park

Horton Lane, Epsom **t** (01372) 743984
www.hortonpark.co.uk
Getting there 65 miles east of Guildford off the A246
Open Mar–Oct daily 10–6, Nov–Feb 10–5
Adm Children (2–16) £5.80, accompanying adult **free**
Refreshments

Just south of London, Horton Park is very popular with the capital's schoolchildren. Its pens are home to goats, cows and sheep among others, and there are special standing platforms so kids can get a good look at what's going on. They can even get in with the rabbits and guinea pigs for a quick stroke if they wish and, if you come in spring or early summer, you should be able to help bottle-feed the lambs and goat kids. Once you've finished bonding, take a wander through the rest of the complex – you'll come across numerous free-roaming ducks and chickens – or, if you want to take the weight off your feet, try a tractor tour (offered in summer only). Any remaining energy can be used up at the adventure playground and children's activity centre, which is filled with an assortment of climbing equipment.

Longdown Dairy Farm

Ashurst, near Southampton **t** (023) 8029 3326
www.longdownfarm.co.uk
Getting there 5 miles southwest of Southampton off the A35 in the New Forest
Open Feb–Oct daily 10–5 , Nov–Dec Sat–Sun 10–5
Adm Adults £6, children £5, under 2s **free**, family £22
Refreshments, gift shop

Much less developed and commercial than many of its competitors, Longdown nonetheless offers a wide range of farm animals to look at and feed including pigs, sheep, goats and cows. There may even be the chance to watch the daily milking session from a viewing gallery and, if you come in spring, you may be able to see a calf being born. There's also a new indoor play area featuring trampolines and a ball pool.

South of England Rare Breeds Centre

Woodchurch, Ashford **t** (01233) 861493
www.rarebreeds.org.uk
Getting there 9 miles north of Rye, 6 miles south of Ashford on the B2067 between Hamstreet and Tenterden (J10 from the M20)
Open Summer daily 10.30–5.30, winter Tues–Sun 10.30–4.30
Adm Adults £6.60, children £6.60, under 3s **free**
Café, picnic areas, shop, disabled access, on-site parking

Extremely well laid out, this 36-hectare (90-acre) working farm has a large collection of rare animals for children to meet with lots of unusual-looking breeds on display (cows with long twirly horns, shaggy goats, giant rabbits, etc.), a children's barn, where 'meet the animals' sessions are organized, and a reconstructed Georgian farmstead. There's also a paddling pool, a sandpit, an adventure playground and lots of special events – including 'piggy picnics', car rallies and 'pudding days' – are laid on in summer.

Do make sure you pay a visit to the farm's most famous residents, a pair of pigs (nicknamed the 'Tamworth 2' by the press) who escaped from an abbatoir in 1998.

Tulley's Farm

Turners Hill **t** (01342) 718472
www.tulleysfarm.com
Getting there Off the B2026
Open Daily 10–6 (last entry 5)
Adm Adult £7, children £6, under 3s **free**, family £5.50
Café, shop, on-site parking

This farm has a little bit of everything. There's an animal patch with goats, bunnies and pigs, pick-your-own berries (seasonal) and an adventure park with a giant pirate-themed maze, pedal go-karts and giant games. Special events are held during Easter, Halloween and Christmas.

Sea-life centres

Blue Reef Aquarium

Clarence Esplanade, Southsea **t** (023) 9287 5222
www.bluereefaquarium.co.uk
Open Mar–Oct daily 10–6, Nov–Feb 10–5
Adm Adults £7.50, under 16s £4.99, under 3s **free**,
family (2+3) £26.99, (2+2) £22.99
   Marvel at marine life through viewing capsules.
For further information *see* p.98

Sea Life Centre

Marine Parade, Brighton **t** (01273) 604234
www.sealife.co.uk
Getting there Brighton is on the south Sussex
coast and is linked to London by the A23
Open Daily 10–6 (10–5 in winter) last admission 1hr
before closing time
Adm Adults £9.95, under 14s £7.50, under 3s **free**,
(ticket valid all day)
   Pretend to be walking along the ocean floor.
For further information *see* p.90

Beside the seaside

Brighton *See* pp.88–91

Bognor Regis

Getting there Bognor is on the south coast 5 miles
east of Chichester and 6 miles west of
Littlehampton on the A259. There are regular train
services from London (Victoria) and Brighton
Tourist information Belmont Street **t** (01243) 823140
   The Regis suffix was awarded by George V, a
frequent and appreciative visitor in the early
part of the 20th century. Indeed, such was his
fondness for the place that, on his deathbed,
his aides suggested he might like to pay it one
final visit. His last words were reputedly
'Bugger Bognor'.
   In truth, there is nothing particularly regal
about it these days (it is the site of a Butlins
Holiday Camp, after all, the epitome of simple
knees-up entertainment), although the town is
pleasant enough and, what's more, officially the
sunniest place in England. According to the Met
Office, it enjoyed more sun on average per day
in the 1990s than anywhere else including such
traditional hotspots as the Isle of Wight and

the English Riviera. And, if that isn't reason
enough to come, there's always the beach, one
of the cleanest and best maintained on the
south coast. Wide, sandy and over eight miles
long, it's lined along its entire length with ice
cream kiosks, snack bars and pubs. Donkey rides
are offered in summer and a dog ban operates
between May and September.

Butlins

Gloucester Road **t** (01243) 822445
www.butlins.com
Open Apr–Oct 10–8 **Adm** Adults £15, children £7.50,
family £39
Fast food outlets, cafés, picnic site
   Circus acts, splash pools, rollercoasters,
puppet shows, jugglers, singers, costumed
characters, go-kart tracks, indoor and outdoor
adventure playgrounds, Butlins has them all. It's
loud, it's garish, it's unashamedly tacky and it's
exactly what your kids want.

Eastbourne

Getting there Eastbourne is on the south coast
21 miles east of Brighton, 18 miles west of Hastings
on the A259, just south of the A27. There are regular
train services from London (Victoria) and Brighton
Tourist information 3 Cornfield Road, Eastbourne
t (01323) 411400 www.eastbourne.org
   Part owned by the Duke of Devonshire,
Eastbourne has a cultured, almost dignified air
to it. Indeed for a popular British seaside resort,
there's a distinct lack of the normal tourist tat.
There are no souvenir shops or candyfloss sellers
along the seafront, just elegant Victorian homes
and a few hotels and restaurants. Nothing is
allowed to disturb the town's relaxed and (some
might say) slightly stuffy atmosphere. Perhaps
unsurprisingly, this haven of south coast
tranquillity has become a popular retirement
home with all the benefits (peace and quiet) and
problems (too much peace and quiet) that this
implies. Nonetheless, the authorities haven't
managed to stamp out all the fun yet. Despite its
polished veneer, Eastbourne actually has a good
deal to offer in terms of family entertainment.
There's the pier, one of the best and most visited
in the country; a 'Treasure Island' adventure playground; an adventure fun park, 'Fort Fun', and, of
course, the beach, a long stretch of sand and
shingle with numerous rock pools, patrolled by
lifeguards in summer. The seafront is framed by

two old towers: the Redoubt Fortress, where classical concerts and firework displays are held in summer, and the Wish Tower, which holds a collection of puppets.

Every summer (in early June), Eastbourne plays host to a prestigious women's tennis tournament, which attracts many top players hoping to get in some grass-court practice before Wimbledon at the end of the month.

There is no need to restrict your holidaying to the town itself. Eastbourne makes a good base for exploring the South Downs Way, which starts a couple of miles west at Beachy Head and continues all the way to the Sussex-Hampshire border. The head itself is well worth visiting for its spectacular 175m/575ft-high cliff overlooking a crashing sea and interactive countryside centre. The Seven Sisters Sheep Centre is four miles west (p.117), Drusilla's Zoo Park seven miles northeast (p.116), the Wilmington Long Man four miles northwest (p.132), while the Herstmonceux Science Centre, one of the best science museums in the country (p.138), and the Knockhatch Adventure Park (p.129) are nine miles north in Hailsham.

Beachy Head Countryside Centre

Beachy Head Road **t** (01323) 737273
Open Summer daily 10–4, winter Sat–Sun 10–3.30
Adm Free
Disabled access
  Hands-on exhibits, play areas and guided walks along the clifftops.

Fort Fun

Royal Parade **t** (01323) 642833 **www.fortfun.co.uk**
Open Rocky's Adventure Land: daily 10–6, Fort Fun: Jun–Oct daily 10–6, Feb–May Sat–Sun 10–6
Adm Individual charges for rides
Café-restaurant, some disabled access
  Rollercoaster, slides, go-karts, miniature railway and 'the largest indoor soft play area in Sussex'.

How We Lived Then Museum of Shops and Social History

20 Cornfield Terrace **t** (01323) 737143
Open Daily 10–5
Adm Adults £4, children £3, under 5s **free**
Gift shop
  You can wander through four floors of authentic shop and house interiors including a grocer's, a chemist's, a wartime living room, a seafarer's inn and, for the kids, a toy shop.

The Pier

t (01323) 410466 **www.eastbournepier.com**
Open 7am–2am **Adm Free** (also **free** deckchairs)
Restaurants, cafés, fast food, souvenirs, disabled access
  Lined with arcades and restaurants; speedboat rides are offered from the tip.

Treasure Island

Royal Parade **t** (01323) 411077
www.treasure-island.info
Open Daily 10–5
Adm Children (2–12) £4, accompanying adult £1.50
Picnic area, fast food outlets
  Well-equipped adventure playground.

Wish Tower Puppet Museum

King Edward's Parade **t** (01323) 417776
Open Easter–Jun and Sept–Oct Sat–Sun 11–5, Jul–Aug daily 11–5 **Adm** Adults £1.80, children £1.25, under 2s **free**, family £5
Picnic site, toilets
  Explores the history of puppetry.

Hastings

Getting there Hastings is on the south coast 18 miles northeast of Eastbourne on the A259. There are frequent train services from London (Victoria and Charing Cross), Gatwick, Brighton, Eastbourne, Portsmouth and Rye. National Express coaches arrive from London; South Coast buses from Brighton and Dover
Tourist information Queen's Square **t** 0845 274 1001 **www.visithastings.com**
  Hastings is where William conquered in 1066, when his Normans beat the English army and poor old Harold was shot through the eye with an arrow. Despite its name, the Battle of Hastings actually took place at Battle, seven miles inland (and so should really have been called the Battle of Battle). Still, the Hastings tourist industry has always made the most of the connection and the town does boast a castle, erected on the orders of William himself, where you can see the 1066 Story, an audiovisual presentation on the battle in a mock-up siege tent. Hastings has had its problems in recent years and parts of it are rather run-down; however, the old town is still very pleasant with its rickety old 15th-century timber-framed buildings and 13th-century church of St Clements, and there are two rather

Can you spot?

The Stade, a traditional working fishing beach in East Hastings, just below the old town, where fishermen still haul their boats on to the beach. It's a fascinating place. Look out, in particular, for the net shops, three-storey wood and tar sheds, where fishermen hang their nets out to dry. In the mid 19th century, the town council attempted to get the fishermen to move off the beach by increasing ground rents – these constructions were the fishermen's response.

jaunty Victorian funicular railways (the West Hill Railway, which ascends Hastings cliff face, is the most fun). Down by the seafront, there's a very good Sea Life Centre (Underwater World) with a walkthrough sea bed tunnel and, jutting out from the wide sandy beach, a pier lined with arcade games and candyfloss sellers. Perhaps the most fun attraction the town has to offer is the Smugglers' Adventure, a labyrinth of deep caves and passageways used by 18th-century duty-dodgers and now inhabited by life-size waxworks arranged in a variety of nefarious tableaux (with the obligatory spooky lighting and sound effects).

Smuggler's Adventure

St Clement's Caves, West Hill t (01424) 422964
www.discoverhastings.co.uk
Open Easter–Sept daily 10–5.30, Oct–Easter daily 11–4.30 **Adm** Adults £6.40, children £4.40, under 4s free, family (2+2) £18.75
Gift shop

★1066 Story in Hastings Castle

Castle Hill Road, West Hill t (01424) 781111
www.discoverhastings.co.uk
Open Easter–Sept daily 10–5, Oct–Easter daily 11–3
Adm Adults £3.40, children £2.25, family £10
Gift shop, disabled access

Underwater World

Rock-A-Nore Road t (01424) 718776
www.underwaterworld-hastings.co.uk
Open Easter–Sept daily 10–5.30, Oct–Easter 11–4
Adm Adults £6.40, children £4.40, family £18.75
Café, gift shop, mother and baby room, disabled access

Littlehampton

Getting there Littlehampton is on the south coast, 6 miles east of Bognor, 14 miles west of Brighton off the A259
Tourist information 63–5 Surrey Street
t (01903) 721866

Come to Littlehampton to experience the archetypal British seaside weekend – making sandcastles, collecting seashells and hunting for crabs in pools. Littlehampton's charms are as familiar and timeless as the sea itself. Its seafront is lined with fish and chip restaurants, seaside rock emporiums and shops selling plastic buckets, spades, beach balls and other such seaside essentials, and there's a small road train offering trips up and down the front. Low tide exposes a vast expanse of sand and the gentle slope of the beach means that the sea remains shallow many metres from the shore making it perfect for paddling. The River Arun meets the sea at the western end of the beach and sightseeing boat trips are offered up the river to Arundel, where you can visit the famous castle (p.110), as well as around the harbour and along the coast. Beyond the river is an extensive area of unspoilt sand dunes. The only downside of a trip to Littlehampton will be the crowds, which, in summer, can be pretty intense – although nothing compared with the hordes that descend on Brighton during the season. Look out for Harbour Park on the seafront, a small, very seasidey children's fun park with a soft play area, a ball pond, an assault course, an ice rink, a log flume and that evergreen seaside favourite, a crazy-golf course.

Harbour Park

Seafront t (01903) 721200 www.harbourpark.com
Open Summer daily 10–8, winter 10–6
Adm Individual charges for rides
Fast food outlets

Margate

Getting there Margate is on the Isle of Thanet at the northeastern tip of Kent, 14 miles northeast of Canterbury, 4 miles northwest of Broadstairs. Train services run regularly from London (Victoria), Chatham, Canterbury West and Dover
Tourist office 12–13 The Parade t (01843) 583333

It's not St Tropez. Neither, for that matter, is it Yalta, the swanky Black Sea resort with which it is twinned. Margate is a mess of arcades, budget cafés, cheap B&Bs and lurid seaside entertainments. The last word in tacky, or refreshingly unpretentious, depending on how you look at things. London's holidaymakers have been giving it the thumbs up for over two centuries now and, for many, Margate represents the very essence of the traditional British seaside experience; the sort of place where you can still occasionally spot sunburnt heads sporting knotted hankies. Kids – often the most enthusiastic consumers of tack – will have a whale of a time. There are four main attractions: the beach, which is sandy and small; the Shell Grotto, an underground shell 'temple' discovered by children in 1835 and made up of no less than 185 sq m (1,991 sq ft) of passageways decorated with intricate shell mosaics (nobody knows who built it or why); the Margate Caves, a network of spooky caverns; and Dreamland, a very Margate sort of theme park, full of mildly scary rides including a rollercoaster built in 1863 (perhaps scary for all the wrong reasons).

Dreamland Park

Marine Terrace **t** (01843) 299244
www.dreamlandfunpark.com
Open Easter–Oct Sat–Sun 11–6 (Aug daily)
Adm Individual charges for rides
Cafés, fast food, mother and baby room, some disabled access, adapted toilets, on-site parking

The Shell Grotto

Grotto Hill **t** (01843) 220008
www.shellgrotto.co.uk
Open Easter–Nov daily 10–5, winter Sat–Sun only
Adm Adults £2.50, children £1.50, family £7
Gift shop, café

Ramsgate and Broadstairs

Getting there Ramsgate and Broadstairs lie about 4 miles apart from one another on the Isle of Thanet at the northeastern tip of Kent and can be reached via the A253 and the A256
Tourist information Ramsgate: Albert Court, York Street **t** (01843) 583333; Broadstairs: 2 Victoria Parade **t** 0870 2646111

Ramsgate and Broadstairs are Margate's slightly posher, slightly swankier siblings. Broadstairs is easily the most refined of the three despite (according to legend) having been founded on the proceeds of smuggling. A pleasant clifftop resort overlooking a calm bay, it boasts five sandy beaches. The main one, Viking Bay, has a tidal pool, a children's play area and a Punch and Judy theatre, and is cleaned daily during the season – there are lifeguards and a dog ban in operation from May to September. Ramsgate, by contrast, can offer just two beaches (both sandy and with lifeguards and a dog ban in summer), a harbour and a Maritime Museum with shipwreck and naval exhibitions.

Just north of Broadstairs stands the North Foreland Lighthouse, which marks the entrance to the River Thames. When converted to automatic operation in 1988, this was the last manned lighthouse in the UK. Tours are now offered in summer.

Smuggling

In the 13th century, Edward I became the first English monarch to introduce duty tax on exported and imported goods with the result that his subjects soon became the country's first smugglers. Throughout the Middle Ages duty-dodging thrived right along England's coast, helped in no small part by the tolerant attitude of the general population, who welcomed the cheap goods (typically small, easily portable luxury items such as tea, tobacco, silks, spices and spirits) that this illicit trade provided. Measures introduced to curb smuggling in the 17th century had little effect. Customs officials were usually severely underpaid and thus easy to bribe. Nonetheless, smugglers would often go to extreme lengths to keep their activities hidden from the authorities. Rather than secreting their goods in cliff-face caves in the traditional manner, by the 18th century some smugglers had entire coastal villages at their disposal with each house linked to the other via a network of secret passageways. The best smugglers even had getaway vehicles. Small galleys, powered by oarsmen rather than sails, were their vessels of choice as they were not only highly manoeuverable but very fast (especially over short distances) and could easily outrun the lumbering craft of the customs officials.

Though the age of mass smuggling came to an end in the late 19th century when Britain began to adopt free-trade policies, it's a problem that has never fully died out. So long as the duty paid on alcohol and cigarettes on the Continent remains lower than it is in England, there will always be people willing to take the risk.

Ramsgate Maritime Museum

Pier Yard, Royal Harbour
t (01843) 231213 **www.ekmt.fogonline.co.uk**
Open Easter–Sept Tues–Sun 10–5, Oct–Easter
Thurs–Sun 11–4.30 **Adm** Call for admission charges

North Foreland Lighthouse

Two miles north of Broadstairs on the B252
t (01843) 861869 **www.trinityhouse.co.uk**
Open/Adm Call for times and prices

Whitstable

Getting there Whitstable is 7 miles northwest of
Canterbury on the north Kent coast off the A299
Tourist office 7 Oxford Street **t** (01227) 275482
www.visitwhitstable.co.uk

Whitstable offers a calmer, more sedate
alternative to traditional seaside resorts. It has
few arcades, ice cream kiosks or fish and chip
restaurants, just lots of charm. And, despite the
rather grown-up attractions of its narrow
streets, quaint fishermen's cottages and old-
fashioned tearooms, there's still plenty for kids
to do. There's the beach, of course, a great
pebbly expanse surrounded by grassy slopes
leading onto a working harbour, where you can
experience all the hustle and bustle of the sea
harvest – watch the boats unloading their
mountains of shellfish, including the famous
Whitstable oysters, which have been the town's
principal export since Roman times. In
Whitstable Museum, there's an Oyster and
Fishery Exhibition, which traces the history of
the town's reliance on the sacred bi-valve.

Whitstable Museum and Gallery

Oxford Street **t** (01227) 276998
Open Mon–Sat 10–4 (Jul–Aug also Sun 1–4)
Adm Free

The museum has exhibits exploring the
seafaring traditions of Whitstable with special
features on the oyster industry and on diving.

Parks and gardens

Claremont Landscape Garden

Portsmouth Road, Esher **t** (01372) 467806
www.nationaltrust.org.uk
Getting there Just south of Esher on the A307
Open Apr–Oct daily 10–6, Nov–Mar Tues–Sun 10–5
(or dusk) **Adm** Adults £4, children £2, under 5s **free**,
family £10
*Café, shop, guided tours, disabled access,
on-site parking*

One of the country's oldest landscaped gardens,
Claremont's 50 neatly arranged acres contain a
lake, a grotto, a turf amphitheatre and dozens of
dazzling flower beds. There's a children's trail and
family events, such as Easter egg hunts, treasure
trails and fêtes, are held here annually.

Groombridge Place Gardens and Enchanted Forest

Groombridge, Tunbridge Wells **t** (01892) 863996
www.groombridge.co.uk
Getting there Follow A264 from Tunbridge Wells
to East Grinstead and follow signs to
Groombridge village.
Open Mid-Mar–Oct 10–5
Adm Adults £8.70, children £7.20, under 3s **free**,
family £29.50
Restaurant, shop, disabled access

The setting for many a TV show and movie,
including the latest film adaptation of Jane
Austen's 'Pride and Prejudice', Groombridge
boasts beautiful 17th-century formal walled
gardens with neatly manicured lawns, tinkling
streams and plenty of quiet spots to sit and
contemplate. Children, however, who usually have
little interest in either quiet or contemplation will
be much more interested by the adjoining
enchanted forest – with its fantasy gardens,
mythical 'Groms' village (with child-sized houses
and baby giant rabbits), and adventue playground
– the Dinosaur Valley (with its plesiosaur nests)
and the giant chess board in the knot garden.
Other attractions include a vineyard (the wine
from which can be bought in the gift shop), the
photos and memorabilia of the Conan Doyle
Museum (who used the gardens as a setting for
one of his Sherlock Holmes mysteries) and canal
cruises (£1 per person).

★Hampton Court Gardens

East Molesey **t** 0870 9504499 **www.**hrp.org.uk
Getting there Hampton Court is just southwest
of London near Kingston-upon-Thames, off
the A3 and A309 (J12 from the M25). Trains run
regularly from London (Waterloo) to Hampton
Court station, or you can take a cruise up the
Thames with the Westminster Passenger Service
from Westminster Pier
Open Summer daily 10–7, winter 10–5.30
Adm Palace and gardens: Adults £12.30, children £8,
under 5s **free**, family £36.40; gardens only: Adults
£3.50, children £2.50, under 5s **free**
*Café, restaurant, souvenir shops (in particular
the Tudor Kitchen shop, which sells a range of
Tudor cooking implements and medieval herbs),
guided tours, wheelchair access, adapted toilets,
on-site parking*

These beautiful gardens have always been as
big a draw as the palace itself, attracting around
1.3 million visitors a year. They contain many
wonders: a 1,000-year-old oak tree, the oldest
and longest vine in the world planted in 1768 (in
the 1920s and '30s, the grapes were harvested in
baskets made by soldiers blinded in the First
World War); 100,000 rose bushes; 250,000 flowering bulbs and the most famous maze in the
world. It was planted in 1690 for William III and
lures in around 300,000 people a year (and lets
roughly the same number out again, give or take
a few). It takes about 20 minutes to reach the
centre and at least 40 minutes to negotiate the
way back through the third of an acre of yew-
lined paths. Once you have made your escape,
head to nearby Bushy Park, a picturesque picnic
spot with herds of deer and ornamental ponds.
For further information on Hampton Court Palace
see p.114

Leonardslee Gardens

Lower Beeding, Horsham **t** (01403) 891212
www.leonardslee.com
Getting there 8 miles west of Haywards Heath,
just off the A281
Open Apr–Oct daily 9.30–6
Adm Adults £6 (£9 in May), children £4, under 5s
free
Refreshments, gift shop, on-site parking

Set in a 97-hectare (240-acre) valley on the
edge of the ancient forest of St Leonard's, these
grand, sweeping gardens – full of azaleas,
camelias, rhododendrons, magnolias and
conifers – contain no fewer than seven lakes, as
well as a rock garden, a Japanese garden and
wallaby and deer enclosures. There's also a
collection of vintage cars and a miniature 1:12
scale scene of life in the 1900s.

Painshill Landscape Gardens

Portsmouth Road, Cobham **t** (01932) 868113
www.painshill.co.uk
Getting there Just west of Cobham off the A3
Open Mar–Oct daily 10.30–6, Nov–Feb 10.30–4
Adm Adults £6.60, children £3.85, under 5s **free**,
family (2+4) £22
*Café, gift shop, mother and baby room, guided
tours, disabled facilities, on-site parking*

These 18th-century landscaped gardens are
packed full of interesting follies – a Gothic
temple, a Chinese bridge, a ruined abbey, a
Turkish tent, a fairy grotto waterwheel – all of
which can be examined and explored to your
kids' hearts' content. There's also a Gothic tower
which you can climb (99 steps) for views out
over the surrounding countryside, a six-hectare
(14-acre) lake and lots of grassy banks for sitting
on (or rolling down, depending on your fancy)
while you decide where to go next. To help you
get your bearings, pick up a map at the entrance
(30p each). Activities, including water games,
dressing up and nature trails, are laid on for children in the gardens throughout the year. A trip
to the park can easily be combined with a trip to
the nearby Cobham Bus Museum, a private
collection of vintage buses, some of which can
be ridden on the museum's special open days.

Scotney Castle Gardens

Lamberhurst, Tunbridge Wells **t** (01892) 891081
www.nationaltrust.org.uk
Getting there 6 miles southeast of Tunbridge
Wells, just outside the town of Lamberhurst off
the A21
Open Apr–Oct Wed–Sun and Bank Hols 11–6
Adm Adults £5.20, children £2.60, under 5s **free**,
family £13
Café, gift shop, some disabled access, on-site parking

Surrounding the ruins of a 14th-century castle
(check out the tiny child-sized rooms), these
beautiful gardens are wonderful for exploring
with their thick, lush flowerbeds, overhanging
trees, mossy slopes, grassy lawns and ponds.

Sheffield Park Garden

Sheffield Park, Uckfield **t** (01825) 790231
www.nationaltrust.org.uk
Getting there Between East Grinstead and Lewes,
just northwest of Uckfield off the A275
Open Mar–Oct Tues–Sun 10.30–6 (or dusk if
earlier), Nov–Dec Tues–Sun 10.30–4, Jan–Feb
Sat–Sun 10.30–4
Adm Adults £6.20, children £3.10, under 5s **free**,
family £15.50
*Café, picnic areas, shop, guided tours, disabled
access, on-site parking*

Huge 49-hectare (120-acre) Capability Brown-
landscaped park filled with flowers in summer
– azaleas, rhododendrons, etc. – and with five
lakes lined by cascades and waterfalls. Family
events, such as Teddy Bear picnics and nature
walks (to look for bats, fungi, birds, etc.), are
organized in summer. The Bluebell, probably the
country's most famous 'proper' steam railway,
departs for trips through the local countryside
from Sheffield Park Station.

RHS Garden Wisley

Wisley, Woking **t** 0845 2609000 **www.**rhs.org.uk
Getting there Wisley is just south of the M25 (J10),
5 miles northeast of Guildford. The nearest train
station is West Byfleet, 3 miles away
Open Mar–Oct Mon–Fri 10–6, Sat–Sun 9–6,
Nov–Feb Mon–Fri 10–4.30, Sat–Sun 9–4.30
(Sun members only)
Adm Adults £7.50, children £2, under 6s **free**
*Restaurant, café, plant centre, book and gift shop,
disabled facilities, on-site parking*

Set up by the Royal Horticultural Association
(RHS) in 1904, Wisley has become one of the
country's best loved gardens. The 98-hectare
(240-acre) site boasts a traditional country
garden, a farm, an orchard, delightful woodland,
a Garden of the Senses and a Temperate Glass
House containing a waterfall and pool. It's definitely at its best on a hot summer's day when
the magnificent flowers are in full bloom. Every
August there's a flower show and a Family
Fortnight with children's activities and entertainers. Garden trails are offered for
7–12-year-olds.

Steam trains

★Bluebell Railway

Sheffield Park station, near Uckfield **t** (01825)
720800 talking timetable: **t** (01825) 720825
www.bluebell-railway.co.uk
Getting there Sheffield Park station is 8 miles
south of East Grinstead on the A275, 2 miles north
of the A272 junction. You can book direct to the
Bluebell Railway from London Victoria and
intermediate stations on South Central's East
Grinstead line. There is also a special bus service
from East Grinstead station
Operating times Easter–Sept and school hols daily
10.30–5; winter Sat–Sun 10.30–5
Fares Adults £9.50, children £4.70, family £27
*Restaurant, real ale bar, gift shop, wheelchair access,
adapted toilets*

Kids love the experience of old-style railway
travel aboard a proper puffing train, à la
Thomas the Tank Engine. The Bluebell wends its
way through fields and meadows between
Sheffield Park and Kingscote in Sussex. A
10-mile round trip aboard one of the stylishly
restored 1930s carriages takes about 90
minutes. Every last detail has been meticu-
lously restored from the elegant fittings in the
sumptuous Pullman dining cars to the period
advertisements on the station walls. At
Sheffield Park, there's a collection of railway
memorabilia and in spring the trains trip
through fields of bluebells (hence the name).

Great Cockcrow Railway

Hardwick Lane, Lyme, Chertsey **t** (01932) 255500
(Mon–Fri), **t** (01932) 565474 (Sun; no phone Sat)
www.cockcrow.co.uk
Getting there The railway is located 1.5 miles
northwest of Chertsey on the A320
Operating times May–Oct Sun 2–5.30, Aug also
Wed 12–4
Fares Adults £3, children £2.50, family £8.50

Rides on jaunty miniature steam trains over a
two-mile length of track passing through
tunnels and over viaducts.

Hollycombe Steam Collection

Iron Hill, Liphook **t** (01428) 724900
www.hollycombe.co.uk
Getting there South of Liphook off the A3 and B2131

Open Apr–Oct Sun and Bank Hols 12–5; Aug daily 12 noon–5 **Adm** Adults £9, children £7.50, under 2s **free**, family £30
Café, disabled access

Experience all the fun of an old-fashioned fairground. While an antique barrel organ chortles away excitedly in the background, you can go for a spin on a painted carousel, check out the views from atop the big wheel or take a ride on a swingboat. The rides may be steam-powered (the constant sound of pumping pistons combined with the noise of the organ make this a very noisy day out) and rather old-fashioned, but they are still a lot of fun. The big wheel, in particular, is quite hairy although there are gentler entertainments (such as a helter-skelter) and a chain swing for younger kids.

Once you've had your fill of fairground attractions, you might like to take a ride aboard a narrow-gauge steam train through a mile and a half of leafy countryside, or climb aboard the steam tractor for a quick trip down to the centre's small farm to bond with the resident animals. If you feel like a break from the constant whirring and hissing, you could always just go for a wander through the grounds – perfect for picnics – with their flower gardens and patches of woodland.

Kent and East Sussex Steam Railway

Tenterden Town Station, Tenterden **t** 0870 6006074 **www.kesr.org.uk**
Getting there 7 miles northeast of Bodiam off the A28
Operating times Mar Sun, Apr–Oct Sat–Sun and Bank Hols, Jun and Sept also Tues–Thurs, Jul and Aug daily, Dec Santa Specials
Fares Adults £10.50, children £5.50; platform tickets £1
Refreshments, wheelchair access, adapted toilets, on-site parking

The first full-size light railway in the world when it opened in 1900, the Kent and East Sussex Railway has been carefully restored in recent years by a team of dedicated volunteers. Its puffing engines and beautiful 'blood and custard' carriages (the nickname for the red and yellow colour scheme) transport passengers on a scenic journey through seven miles of Kentish countryside from Tenterden, where there is a small museum of railway memorabilia and an

adventure playground, to Bodiam, site of the famous castle (p.111), passing streams, lily ponds and acres of hop farmland on the way.

Romney, Hythe and Dymchurch Railway

New Romney Station, Littlestone Road, New Romney **t** (01797) 362353 **www.rhdr.org.uk**
Getting there The railway stretches along the Kent coast from Dungeness to Hythe. There are six stations of which New Romney (10 miles northeast of Rye off the A259 and B2071) is the main one
Open Easter–Sept daily, Oct–Easter Sat–Sun only
Adm All-day ticket: Adults £10.90, children £5.45 (includes entry to Toy and Model Museum)
Cafés, souvenir shops, wheelchair access on trains (but call in advance), adapted toilets

A true historical oddity, this miniature railway was built in the 1920s for the racing driver Captain Howey, who hoped to operate it as a full mainline railway carrying freight, as well as passengers. British industry, however, didn't share his vision and the railway was forced to rely on holidaymakers for its main source of income. It fell into disrepair during the Second World War, but was restored and reopened in 1946 (at a ceremony attended by Laurel and Hardy) and can today claim the honour of being the world's longest 15-inch gauge railway. It runs for 13.5 miles across Romney Marsh close to the coast from Hythe to Dungeness passing through New Romney Station, where there's a large collection of toys and models (including one of the largest model train layouts in the country) on the way.

Watercress Line

Station Road, Alresford, near Winchester **t** (01962) 733810 **www.watercressline.co.uk**
Operating times Feb–Oct Sat–Sun and Bank Hols, May–Sept also Tues–Thurs; eight trains a day
Fares Adults £10, children £5, family £25
Café, gift shop, mother and baby room

The name derives from the watercress beds which still grow in Alresford, the railway's headquarters and a picturesque Georgian town. From here, it's a 10-mile trip to Alton passing through Ropley, where there's a locomotive yard and picnic area, and Medstead and Marks, the highest station in southern England, on the way.

Theme parks and open-air museums

Amberley Industrial Museum

Amberley, near Arundel **t** (01798) 831370
www.amberleymuseum.co.uk
Getting there Amberley is 4 miles north of
Arundel, 8 miles north of Littlehampton, 12 miles
northeast of Chichester off the B2139
Open Mar–Oct Wed–Sun 10–5.30, school hols daily
Adm Adults £8.20, children £5, under 5s **free**,
family £23
Café, gift shop, disabled access, on-site parking

Dedicated to the industrial history of southeast England, this museum is busy, bustling and
child friendly. A former chalk quarry, the 15-
hectare (36-acre) site is now home to more than
20 recreated workshops, where you can see
skilled craftsmen demonstrating traditional
rural crafts like pottery, printing and boat-
building. It's a fascinating experience; kids will
be drawn like magnets to the noise and dirt – all
the banging, bending, sanding and hammering
– and will, on occasion, even be invited to join in.
If the noise gets a bit much, take time out to
enjoy the beautiful South Downs setting aboard
the open-top 1920s bus which tours the site, or
take a ride through the woods on a workman's
steam train (you can choose to ride in a covered
carriage or an open trailer depending on the
weather) to the small railway museum where
kids can clamber over an assortment of ancient
steam engines. There's a small interactive electricity museum and nature trails. Vintage car
rallies, fire engine days and craft workshops for
children, plus numerous other special events, are
put on during the year, usually on weekends.

★Chessington World of Adventure

Chessington **t** 0870 444 7777 **www.chessington.co.uk**
Getting there Chessington is 2 miles north of
Epsom, just off the A243, 2 miles from the A3 and
M25 (J9 from the north, J10 from the south). There
are regular train services to Chessington South
Station from London (Clapham Junction)
Open Apr–Oct daily 10–5, peak days 10–6 **Adm**
Adults £29, children £19, one child (under 12) per
paying adult is admitted **free** and all children
under 1m tall enter **free**

*Fast-food outlets, baby changing facilities, on-site
parking, some disabled access, safety restrictions
apply on some rides (call for detailed leaflet), a
limited number of wheelchairs available on request*
Note: Height restriction 1.2–1.4m for most rides

Chessington has rides for all ages from top of
the range rollercoasters to gentle carousels and
roundabouts. The park's most intense rides are
the 'Rattlesnake', a somewhat rough and jerky
wild-west themed rollercoaster, 'Rameses
Revenge', which looks a bit like a great big bread
tin and flips its passengers over several times
before squirting them in the face with jets of
water and the suspended coaster 'Vampire',
which swoops and loops over the park's
rooftops. Younger children are well catered for
at Toytown, the Dragon River log flume, the
recently renovated Professor Burp's Bubble
Works and Beanoland, where you can enjoy a
range of rides themed on Beano characters
(such as Billy Whizz's Waveslinger and the Bash
Street Bus) and watch comic characters
behaving badly. In amongst all the hi-tech
gadgetry, there is also a zoo. You can take a look
at the resident Sumatran tigers, Persian and
Clouded leopards and Asian lions, gorillas and
meerkats aboard the Safari Skyrail. There are
daily displays by sea lions, penguins and hawks
and, at the 'Creepy Cave', you can all grimace at
spiders, insects and other crawling horrors, or
soar with the birds in the walk-through aviary.

Hop Farm Country Park

Beltring, Paddock Wood **t** (01622) 872068
www.thehopfarm.co.uk
Getting there 7 miles east of Tonbridge on the A228
Open Daily 10–5
Adm Adults £7.50, children £6.50, family (2+2) £27
*Café, picnic areas, shop, disabled access,
on-site parking*

Pleasant, family-friendly country park laid out
around the largest complex of Victorian oast
houses in the world. There are exhibitions on hop
farming and old-fashioned farming life, nature
trails (including a treasure trail which children
follow using mini metal detectors), a 'Time
Tunnel' Museum, farm, Shire Horse Centre, adventure play area, indoor play centre and pottery
workshop. Numerous family events in summer.

Knockhatch Adventure Park

Hempstead Lane, Hailsham **t** (01323) 442051
www.knockhatch.com
Getting there 9 miles north of Eastbourne off the A22
Open Apr–Sept Sat–Sun and school hols 10–5.30
Adm Adults £7.25, children £6.25, under 3s **free**,
family £25
*Café, gift shop, mother and baby room, disabled
access, adapted toilets, on-site parking*

Knockhatch has a 186-sq-m (2,000-sq-ft)
indoor play area, an adventure playground, freefall slides, go-karts, a laser shooting-range, a dry
ski and snowboard slope, a boating lake, a bird of
prey centre and a children's farm.

Museum of Kent Life

Lock Lane, Sandling, Maidstone **t** (01622) 763936
www.museum-kentlife.co.uk
Getting there 2 miles north of Maidstone off the
A229 (J6 from the M20)
Open Daily 10–5 **Adm** Adults £7, children £5, under
4s **free**, family (2+2) £20
*Tearooms, beer garden, picnic sites, gift shop, some
disabled access, on-site parking*

In centuries past, workers used to come to Kent
every autumn to pick hops, a small, bitter fruit
used to make beer. Everything was done by hand
and the fields would be full of people picking as
fast as they could – they were paid according to
the number of hops they picked after a back-
breaking day's work. Find out all about it here –
you can see the tiny hop-pickers' huts, where 10
people or more stayed in one room during the
harvest, the conical oast houses, where the hops
were laid out to dry over a hot kiln, and explore
reconstructed farm buildings, including an
18th-century thatched barn and a granary, with a
gruesome exhibition on rats, the biggest enemy
of the harvest. There's a traditional farm, a duck
pond, a craft village, where pottery, blacksmithery and stained glass-making are
demonstrated, a playground and mini tractors
plus acres of delightful countryside.

Paulton's Park

Ower, Romsey **t** (023) 8081 4455
www.paultonspark.co.uk
Getting there Ower is at the northern end of the
New Forest, west of Southampton, near the
junction of the A31 and A36 (J2 from the M27).
A bus service runs from Southampton
Open Daily 10–6.30

Adm Adults £15.50, children £14.50, family £56
*Café, fast food, mother and baby facilities, some
disabled access, on-site parking*

Like a mini Chessington with the same mix of
rides and animals but on a gentler, kiddy-size
scale. The 57-hectare(140-acre) park contains
woodland and gardens (home to tropical birds
including flamingoes) plus its rollercoasters, log
flumes, bumper boats, go-karts, radio-controlled
cars and animated dinosaurs. It's a little bit
lightweight and perhaps best suited for very
young children (there's a Tiny Tots Town and a
small petting zoo) but it's a cheerful, welcoming
place and more family friendly than many of its
larger, more overtly commercial competitors.

Rural Life Centre

Old Kiln Museum, Reeds Road, Tilford, Farnham
t (01252) 795571 **www**.rural-life.org.uk
Getting there 5 miles southeast of Farnham off
the A287
Open Apr–Sept Wed–Sun and Bank Hols 11–6,
Oct–Mar Wed only 11–4 **Adm** Adults £5.50, children
£3.50, under 5s **free**, family £16
*Café, gift shop, guided tours, mother and baby
facilities, disabled access, picnic area, on-site parking*

A collection of traditional farm implements
and machinery illustrating more than 150 years
of rural life. Wander through the buildings in a
recreated 19th-century farming village, which
include a wheelwright's shop, a smithy, a school
room and a village hall. There's also a children's
playground, a miniature railway and acres of
grounds.

★Thorpe Park

Staines Road, Chertsey **t** 0870 444 4466
www.thorpepark.com
Getting there On the A320 between Chertsey and
Staines (J11 or 13 from the M25). There's a regular
train service from London (Waterloo) to Staines
and Chertsey, from where you can catch a bus
Open Mar–Oct, times vary but it usually opens
some time between 9.30 and 10 and closes
between 5 and 7.30
Adm Adults £28.50, children £20, children under 1m
free, family £78
*Fast-food outlets, gift shop, baby changing facilities,
first aid centre, some wheelchair access, adapted
toilets, on-site parking*

Thorpe Park's showpiece ride is the bizarrely
titled 'X:/No Way Out', which, although not the

first rollercoaster to operate in pitch darkness, is the first to force its passengers to travel at speeds of around 65mph in the dark...backwards. Thorpe's impressive range of water rides and slides make it the perfect option for a hot day but do pack waterproofs, swimwear and a spare T-shirt for good measure. The most fun to be had is on Tidal Wave, where you plunge 26m (85ft) into a wall of water. Daredevil kids like to wait on the bridge after their ride to get another soaking as the next boatload of bold adventurers hit the briney. Serious white-knucklers can also enjoy Nemesis Inferno's volcanic rumblings through 750m (2,460ft) of suspended track, or head in all directions at once on Quantuum. Then there's the might of Colossus to sample, the world's first 10-looping roller coaster and the new Stealth ride (the fastest and tallest launch coaster in Europe). These concessions to modern super-thrill-seeking trends aside, most of the attractions have clearly been designed to cater for families. Children are particularly well provided for with various themed areas, such as Mrs Hippo's Jungle Safari and Mr Monkey's Banana Ride, as well as Model World, which features miniature versions of the Eiffel Tower, the Pyramids and Stonehenge. They can also take a boat ride to Thorpe Farm to bond with the resident goats, sheep and rabbits.

★Weald and Downland Open-Air Museum

Singleton, near Chichester **t** (01243) 811348 **www**.wealddown.co.uk
Getting there 7 miles north of Chichester off the A286
Open Mar–Oct daily 10.30–6; Nov, Dec and early Feb daily 10.30–4; Jan–mid-Feb Sat–Sun 10.30–4
Adm Adults £7.95, children £4.25, under 5s **free**, family £21.95
Gift shop

The 20-hectare (50-acre) site contains more than 40 historic rural buildings recovered from all over southeast England and reassembled here by a team of volunteers. There are shepherds' huts, cottages, a blacksmith's forge, a 17th-century watermill, a Tudor farmstead, a charcoal burners' camp and even an old Victorian village school. You can sit at a school desk, lie down on one of the tiny beds or work out how the archaic toilet system might have worked. There are also demonstrations of rural crafts such as woodturning, spinning and candle-making. Children can try bricklaying, roof-pegging, willow-hurdle-making or grinding flour at the watermill.

Wide open spaces

Ashdown Forest

Getting there Just to the southeast of East Grinstead off the A22
Tourist information East Grinstead Tourism Initiative, The Library, West Street, East Grinstead **t** (01342) 410121 **www**.ashdownforest.com

Visit this great swathe of West Sussex forest and heathland armed with a picnic and a few *Winnie-the-Pooh* books. It inspired AA Milne's tales of the famously forgetful bear, Christopher Robin and friends. Visit the 'Hundred-Aker' Wood, where the Pooh stories were set, and have a game of Poohsticks off the real Poohsticks bridge near Hartfield village, which contains 'Pooh Corner', a 17th-century house with the world's largest collection of 'Pooh-phernalia'. Otherwise, Ashdown is serious walkers' territory with lots of nature trails and sandy tracks.

Pooh Corner

High Street, Hartfield **t** (01892) 770456 **www**.poohcorner.co.uk

Chislehurst Caves

Old Hill, Chislehurst **t** (020) 8467 3264 **www**.chislehurstcaves.co.uk
Getting there Off the A222 on the B264 near Chislehurst railway station
Open Wed–Sun daily 10–4 **Adm** Adults £5, children £3
Café, gift shop, on-site parking

Experienced guides take you on 45-minute tours down into this winding 4,000-year-old network of stony tunnels and passageways stretching deep beneath the Old Hill.

★The New Forest

Getting there The National Forest occupies a vast swathe of countryside between Ringwood (to the west) and Southampton (to the east). Its major town is Lyndhurst on the A35 and A357
Tourist information Main car park, High Street, Lyndhurst **t** (023) 8028 2269 **www**.thenewforest.co.uk

The New Forest represents the largest area of 'wild' vegetation in Britain south of the Scottish highlands: 145 square miles (375 sq km) of light woodland, isolated ponds, deep forest and heath (in fact, despite its name, there's more heath than anything else) inhabited by numerous wild animals including deer (the forest owes its existence to William I's desire to preserve an area of habitat for the royal deer), badgers and the famous New Forest ponies, said to be descended from small Spanish horses captured from the Armada. If all the wild animals evade you, however, you can always check out some captive specimens at the New Forest Otter, Owl and Conservation Park (p.117) and Longdown Dairy Farm in Ashurst (p.119) or the New Forest Owl Sanctuary near Ringwood. At its heart, the forest feels ancient and primordial, the last sprouting remains of a bygone age and, fittingly, the residents of the forest enjoy a range of centuries-old feudal rights including the right to cut peat in the forest (known as 'turbary' in the ancient local dialect), the right to collect firewood in the forest ('estover') and the right to let their pigs forage for acorns ('mast').

To get the best out of your visit, head away from the often heavily congested main roads – an estimated 10 million people visit the forest each year, which works out at over 25,000 a day. Exploring the forest on horseback or by bike is your best bet; the forest boasts over 125 miles of car-free gravel pathways. Whatever your plans, the visitor centre at Lyndhurst, the capital of the forest, can provide you with details of walks, guided tours, horse-riding centres, nature trails and campsites. The centre also has excellent interactive displays (including a 'Feely Log' and a 'Forest Hide' – lift the wooden panels to reveal the secret animal) and an 8m/25ft-long tapestry depicting the history of the region.

You might like to begin your exploration of the forest with a walk to the Rufus Stone, some three miles north of Lyndhurst, which marks the spot where William II (nicknamed 'Rufus' because of his reddish complexion), the son of William the Conqueror, was shot dead by an errant crossbow bolt whilst out hunting with the Royal party. It was, of course, an 'accident' although the man responsible, Sir William Tyrell, quickly fled to France whilst William's brother, Henry, who had accompanied him on the trip, ran equally quickly in the opposite direction to Winchester, where he was crowned king, leaving the body of his brother to be brought home by a passing craftsman.
For bicycle hire and horse-riding see pp.133–4

North Downs

When people are trying to come up with a good countryside day out, the North Downs are often overlooked. People forget that Surrey is the most heavily wooded county in England, with acres and acres of beautiful National Trust-preserved countryside rising west of Guildford and undulating their way into Kent

Box Hill

Getting there Just off the A25, east of Dorking

Surrey's most dramatic viewpoint and the setting for a thousand school trips. The hill covers 324 hectares (800 acres), encompassing wood, heath and downland. The information centre offers guided walks and activities.

Chatley Heath Semaphore Tower

Ockham Common (just off the A3 between Cobham and Effingham) **t** (01932) 458822
Open Mid-Mar–late Sept, Sat–Sun and Bank Hols, school holidays also Wed, 12 noon–5; Oct–Mar 1st Sun of the month 12 noon–5
Adm Adults £2, children £1.50

The country's only surviving semaphore tower, this once formed part of a chain that ran all the way from London to Portsmouth via which the Admiralty could send messages to its warships. There are great views, especially from the telescopes, and you can have a go at manoeuvring the vast semaphore mast. The site is surrounded by 284 hectares (700 acres) of heath and woodland.

Denbies

London Road, Dorking (just off the A24)
t (01306) 876616 **www.denbiesvineyard.co.uk**
Open Jan–Mar Mon–Fri 10–5, Sat 10–5.30, Sun 11.30–5.30; Apr–Dec Mon–Sat 10–5.30, Sun 11.30–5.30 **Adm** Adults £7.25, children £3, under 6s **free**, family £15

The country's biggest vineyard. Take a tour through the winery and watch a 3D film of the wine-making process – suitable for older children.

Devil's Punchbowl

Getting there Just off the A287, 7 miles south of Farnham

A spectacular natural fold in the downs with numerous nature trails through woodland, sandy heaths and scattered ponds.

Hambledon

Getting there Just off the A283, 3 miles south of Godalming

Site of a witch's tree: walk around the tree three times to make the witch appear.

Leith Hill

Near Coldharbour (just off the A25, southwest of Dorking) **t** (01306) 711777

Surrounded by glorious pine, hazel and oak woodland with heather-clad slopes and acres of wild rhododendrons, Leith represents the English countryside at its best. The 18th-century tower at the top of the hill is the highest point in south-east England and the views are magnificent. On a clear day, the view extends all the way to London.

Outwood Post Mill

Getting there Just off M23, J9, 5 miles southeast of Reigate **t** (01342) 843458 **www.outwoodmill.co.uk**
Open Easter–Oct Sun and Bank Hols 2–6
Adm Adult £2, children £1

England's oldest working windmill, built in 1665. Situated 110m (120 yards) up, it must have provided residents with spectacular views of the Great Fire of London in 1666.

South Downs

The North Downs' more famous sibling, this great rolling ridge of chalk hills runs along the southern half of Sussex and Hampshire and contains numerous areas of outstanding natural beauty – as well as a few pylon-blighted eyesores – and is traversed by the South Downs Way, one of the country's great walks, which stretches for 106 miles from Eastbourne all the way to Winchester.

Cissbury Ring

Getting there 3 miles north of Worthing off the A24

Huge Iron Age rampart offering good views out over the coast towards the Isle of Wight.

Devil's Dyke

Getting there 4 miles northeast of Brighton off A23, Estate Office, Saddlescombe Farm, Brighton **t** (01273) 857712

One of the Downs' most famous beauty spots (and a favourite jumping-off point for hang-gliders), it has wonderful views of Brighton and the coast.

For further information on bus tours from Brighton see p.89

Ditchling Beacon

Getting there 6 miles north of Brighton off the B2116

Great views and a sweet country village.

Wilmington

Getting there 4 miles northeast of Eastbourne off the A27

Huge chalk figure the 'Long Man' cut into the hillside. No one knows when or why.

Wilderness Wood

Hadlow Down, near Uckfield **t** (01825) 830509
Getting there Hadlow is 4 miles northeast of Uckfield off the A272
Open Daily 10–5.30
Adm Adults £3.15, children £1.90, under 3s **free**, family £9
Café, picnic area, playground, visitor centre, baby changing facilities, wheelchair access

Spread out over 25 hectares (62 acres) in amongst the hills of the High Weald, there are walking trails (including a discovery trail for children), exhibition sites (where you can watch furniture-making and camp-building), play areas and lots of picnic sites.

SPORT AND ACTIVITIES

Activity centres

Calshot Activity Centre

Calshot Spit, Fawley, Southampton
t (023) 8089 2077 www.calshot.com
Open Daily **Hire** Various, call for details
Baby changing facilities, wheelchair friendly

Run by Hampshire County Council, this is one of the largest activity centres in the UK. Located on a thin peninsula of land jutting out into the Solent, it offers courses in dinghy sailing, power-boating, wind-surfing, canoeing, climbing (on its purpose-built climbing centre), skiing and snow-boarding (on a dry ski slope) and cycling (in its indoor velodrome). Single-day or residential courses available.

Bicycle hire and cycling

AA Bike Hire New Forest

Fern Glen, Gosport Lane, Lyndhurst
t (023) 8028 3349 www.aabikehirenewforest.com
Getting there Near the tourist information centre on the edge of the coach park
Hire Adults £10, children £5 per day (including helmet and accessories)

Quality aluminium-framed mountain bikes, children's bikes, tandems and tag-a-longs.

Deers Leap Park

East Grinstead **t** (01342) 325858
www.deersleappark.co.uk
Open Mar–Sept daily 9–6, Oct–Feb Sat–Sun and school holidays 9–5
Adm Cyclists £4 per day, pedestrians **free**

This is a 93-hectare (230-acre) park with a 10-kilometre (six-mile) all-weather cycle track and a six-kilometre (four-mile) trail through old claypits and woodland and along an old riverbed. Mountain bikes for adults and children can be hired at the Stone Hill entrance.

Forest Leisure Cycling

Village centre, Burley **t** (01425) 403584
www.forestleisurecycling.co.uk
Open Daily **Hire** Adults £11, tandems £20, child £6, child seat (1–4 years) £3

Adult bikes, child trailers, dog trailers and tandems for cycling in the New Forest.

New Forest Cycle Experience

Island Shop, 2–4 Brookley Road, Brockenhurst
t (01590) 624204 www.cycleX.co.uk
Open Daily 9.30–5.30 **Adm** various

Adult bikes, children's bikes, tandems, tag-a-longs and child and dog trailers and can provide details of routes for all abilities through the forest.

Boat and barge hire

Caxton Boat Hire

Tonbridge **t** (01732) 360630
Open Easter–Sept, call for sailing times
Adm Call for details of prices

Barges, cruises and trips on the River Medway.

Dunorlan Park

Tunbridge Wells **t** (01892) 515675

Renovations in progress. Boat hire on lake.

Paddle Steamer Kingswear Castle

Historic Dockyard Chatham, **t** 01634 827648
Open Call for sailing times
Adm Adults £6, children £4, under 3s **free**
(45-minute trip)

Bowling

AMF Bowling Centre

51 Addington Street, Margate **t** 0870 1183024
Open Daily 10am–midnight
Family game (2+2) day £21 (Mon–Fri before 6pm, £26 other times), £3–£4.25 per game, including bowling-shoe hire
Baby changing facilities, wheelchair access

A 24-lane bowling alley.

AMF Whitstable Bowl

Tower Parade, Whitstable **t** 0870 1183037,
www.amfbowling.co.uk
Open Daily 10–midnight
Family game (2+2) day £26 (Mon–Fri before 6pm, £30 other times), £3.35–£4.80 per game, shoes inc.
Baby changing facilities and wheelchair access

A 10-lane bowling alley.

Bowlplex Brighton

Marina Way, Brighton Marina **t** (01273) 818180
Open Daily 9.30am–12 midnight (Sat–Sun later)
Adm Call for prices

Pool tables, 26 bowling lanes and video games.

Bowlplex Portsmouth

Gunwharf Quays **t** (023) 9229 1234
Open Daily 10am–12 midnight (Sat–Sun until 2am)
Adm Call for prices

Pool tables, 26 bowling lanes and video games.

LA Bowl

The Pavilion, The Esplanade, Ryde, Isle of Wight
t 0808 1085353
Open Daily 10am–10.45pm **Adm** Call for prices
Mother and baby room, disabled facilities, fast-food outlets
Arcade machines and a 22-lane bowling alley.

Lloyds Lanes and Laserquest Centre

Broadwater Way, Eastbourne **t** (01323) 50999
Open Daily 10am–late
Adm Bowling: £3.95 per game; Laserquest: £2.75 per game
Fast-food outlets
Laserquest arena, pool tables, video games and 20 bowling lanes.

Climbing

Revolution Climbing

Oakwood Industrial Estate, Broadstairs **t** (01843) 866706 www.revolutionskatepark.co.uk
Open Tues–Wed and Fri–Sat 10–10, Sun 10–8
Adm From £5 per person
Large climbing wall for beginners to experienced climbers. Also a skateboarding park on site.

Go-karting

Teamsport Eastleigh

Barton Estate, Eastleigh (Southhampton) **t** 0870 6000601 www.gokartingforfun.co.uk
Open Call in advance for times and prices
Minimum age eight years.

Horse-riding

Burley Villa School of Riding

B3058, near New Milton **t** (01425) 610278
Open Call in advance for details of times and prices
Pony- and horse-trekking through the New Forest.

Ford Farm Stable

Burley Road, Brockenhurst **t** (01590) 623043
Open Call in advance for details of times and prices
Horse-trekking in the New Forest, lessons and Saturday children's club.

Freewheelin's Trekking

Northcommon Farm, Golf Links Lane, Selsey
t (01243) 602725
Open All year, rides must be booked in advance
Horse-trekking on the South Downs. Half-hour lessons for beginners available.

Willowbrook Riding Centre

Hambrook Hill South, Hambrook, near Chichester
t (01243) 572683
Open All year, rides must be booked in advance
Horse-riding on the South Downs for all ages.

Ice-skating

Planet Ice

The Leisure Park, Basingstoke **t** (01256) 355266
Open/Adm Call for times and prices
Children's lessons and ice hockey games on Saturday nights.

Planet Ice/Ryde Arena

The Esplanade, Key Road, Ryde **t** (01983) 615155
Open Call for times
Adm Call for prices and family disco sessions

Indoor adventure playgrounds

Adventure Warehouse

Terminus Road Industrial Estate, Chichester
t (01243) 839455 www.adventure-warehouse.co.uk
Open Mon–Fri 9.30–6, Sat–Sun 10–6
Adm £3.50 per child (weekends and school holidays £4), adults and non-walking babies **free**
Giant inflatable slide, gorilla mountain, inflatable stranded galleon, ball pools, scramble nets and different slides. Suitable for ages 0–8.

Play Zone

Unit A4, Oak Park Industrial Estate, North Harbour Road, Portsmouth **t** (023) 9237 9999
www.theplayzone.co.uk
Open Daily 10–7
Adm Adults £1, under 12s £4.85 , under 4s £3.20 (weekdays) £3.95 (weekends, school holidays), under 1s **free**
Huge, 600-sq-m (6,500-sq-ft), indoor playground full of giant slides, climbing frames, ball ponds, clamber nets and crawl mazes. For children aged 1–11. Café, baby changing facilities, on-site parking.

Leisure centres

Arun Leisure Centre

Felpham Way, Bognor Regis **t** (01243) 826612
www.inspireleisure.co.uk
Open Daily 9–6
Adm Call for prices
Large pool with a 25m (82ft) waterslide and badminton and squash courts.

Guildford Spectrum Leisure Complex
Parkway, Guildford **t** (01483) 443322
www.guildfordspectrum.co.uk
Open/Adm Call for times and prices
Four swimming pools with flume rides, a bowling alley, an ice rink and a soft play area.

Medina Recreation Centre
Fairlee Road, Newport, Isle of Wight **t** (01983) 523767
Open Limited availability during term time but open all day Sat–Sun and school hols
Adm Call for prices
Two swimming pools including a toddlers' pool, waterslide, badminton, table tennis, trampolining, a climbing wall and theatre/cinema venue.

Westgate Leisure Centre
Cathedral Way, Chichester **t** (01243) 785651
Open Mon–Thurs 1pm–10.30pm, Fri 7am–10.30pm, Sat 7am–8.30pm, Sun 9am–8.30pm
Crèche and cafeteria
Three swimming pools including a toddlers' pool, a 50m (164ft) covered waterslide, squash, badminton, table tennis, short tennis.

Motor sports

Diggerland
Roman Way, Medway Valley Park, Strood, Rochester **t** (08700) 344437 **www.**diggerland.com
Open Sat–Sun, Bank Hols and school hols 10–5
Adm £12.50 per person, under 3s **Free**;
Adventure park themed on JCBs, diggers and dumpers, offering rides for children of all ages and lots of things to drive for ages five and up. There's also a snow park offering skiing, snowboarding and sledging.

Skateboarding

Revolution Skate Park
Oakwood Industrial Estate, Broadstairs **t** (01843) 866707 **www.**revolutionskatepark.co.uk
Open Tues–Wed and Fri–Sat 10–10, Sun 10–8
Adm From £4 per person
Indoor and outdoor areas with ramps for skateboarding, inline skating and BMX riding. Equipment (including skateboards and safety equipment) can be hired.

Summer camps

Camp Beaumont
Old Bembridge School, Bembridge, Isle of Wight **t** (020) 7922 1234 **www.**campbeaumont.com
Open 14 Jul–25 Aug
Adm From £418 for one week (residential centre)
Well-established multiactivity residential centre for kids aged 7–13. Offers a wide range of activities such as fencing, go-karting, swimming, horse-riding, climbing and archery.

Little Canada
Little Canada Centre, New Road, Wootton, Isle of Wight (3D Education) **t** 0870 607 7733
www.3d.co.uk
Open Call for times
Adm From £61–67 (2–5yrs), £92–88 (6–18yrs), £103–124 (adult) for 2 nights.
Well-respected children's activity centre offering a range of expertly organized, supervised activities including abseiling, archery, canoeing, dragon-boating, fencing, quad-biking, 10-pin bowling, trampolining and zip-wiring.

Swimming

Littlehampton Swimming and Sports Centre
Sea Road, Littlehampton **t** (01903) 725451
Open Daily 9–6 **Adm** Call in advance
A 25m (82ft) pool, learner pool and, in summer, an outdoor pool, plus an indoor sports centre.

The Pyramid Centre
Clarence Esplanade, Southsea, Portsmouth **t** (023) 9279 9977 **www.**pyramids.co.uk
Open Please call for times
Adm Adults £4.70, children £3.70
Tropical pools (heated to 29°C/84°F), with superflumes, toddlers' pool, animal slides, and inflatables, video games, gift shop, fast food and licensed café-bar. Family changing rooms and disabled access.

River Park Leisure Centre
Gordon Road, Winchester **t** (01962) 848700
Open Daily 6.30am–11pm
Adm Adults £2.70, children £1.30
Swimming pool, learner pool, 65m (213ft) flume ride, children's adventure playroom.

West Wight Pool
Moa Place, Freshwater, Isle of Wight **t** (01983) 752168
Open Call in advance
Adm Adults £3.15, children £1.90
Two swimming pools and a toddlers' pool, as well as badminton and volleyball courts.

KIDS IN

Watersports

Ardingly Activity Centre

The Lodge, Ardingly Reservoir, Ardingly
t (01444) 892549
www.ardinglyactivitycentre.co.uk
Open Call for details of opening times and prices
   This centre offers courses in dinghy sailing,
canoeing, powerboating and navigation.

Bewl Water Outdoor Centre

Bewl Water Reservoir, Lamberhurst
t (01892) 890716 www.bewlwater.org
Getting there The reservoir is on the A22 south of
Tunbridge Wells
Café, visitor centre, play area, baby changing
facilities, wheelchair access
Open Call for times
Adm Call for prices
   Plenty of watersports on offer. For windsurfing
contact Bewl Windsurfing, t (01892) 891000,
which supplies all the gear. You can also hire
bikes from Bewl Bike Hire, t (01892) 891446, to
cycle the 12-mile route around Bewl Water.

Hove Lagoon Watersports

Kingsway, Hove t (01273) 424842
www.hovelagoon.co.uk
Open Call for details of opening times and prices
   Watersports, wind-surfing, canoeing and
waterskiing for kids and adults.

Neilson Active Holidays Limited

Locksview, Brighton Marina, t (0870) 333 3356
www.neilson.co.uk
Open Call for details of opening times and prices
   Sailing courses at Brighton Marina for all ages
and abilities.

Cinemas

Brighton

Cineworld, Marina Village t 0870 2002000
www.cineworld.co.uk
Brighton Media Centre, 9–12 Middle Street
t 08704 163299 www.mediacentre.org
Duke of York's Cinema, Preston Circus
t (01273) 602503
The Odeon, Kingswest Centre, West Street
t 0871 2244007 www.odeon.co.uk

Broadstairs

Windsor, Harbour Street t (01843) 865726
www.windsorcinemas.co.uk

Canterbury

Odeon, 43–5 St George's Place t 0871 2244007
www.odeon.co.uk

Chichester

Cineworld, Chichester Gate t 0871 2208000
www.cineworld.co.uk
New Park Film Centre, New Park Road t (01243) 786650
www.chichestercinema.org

Dover

Silver Screen Cinema, t (01304) 22800
www.silverscreencinemas.co.uk

Eastbourne

Curzon, Langney Road t (01323) 731441
www.eastbournecurzon.net

Guildford

Odeon Multiplex, Bedford Road t 0871 2244007
www.odeon.co.uk

Hastings

Odeon, Queens Road t 0871 224007
www.odeon.co.uk

Isle of Wight

Cineworld, Coppins Bridge, Newport
t 0871 2208000 www.cineworld.co.uk
Commodore, Star Street, Ryde t (01983) 565064
Medina Theatre, Newport t (01983) 527020
www.medinatheatre.co.uk

Margate

Dreamland Triple Cinema, Marine Terrace
t (01843) 227822

Portsmouth

Carlton, High Street t (023) 92377975
Odeon, London Road t 0871 2244007
www.odeon.co.uk
UCI 6 Cinemas, Port Solent t 0871 2244007
Vue, Gunwharf Quays t 0871 2240240
www.myvue.com

Sevenoaks
Stag Cinemas, London Road **t** (01732) 450175
Southampton
Cineworld, Ocean Village **t** 0871 2002000
www.cineworld.co.uk
Harbour Lights Cinema, Maritime Walk
t 0870 7551237 www.picturehouse-cinemas.co.uk
Odeon Multiplex, Leisureworld, West Quay Road
t 0871 2244007 www.odeon.co.uk
Tunbridge Wells
Odeon Multiplex, Knights Park **t** 0871 224007
www.odeon.co.uk
Winchester
The Screen at Winchester, Southgate Street
t (01962) 877007 www.screencinemas.co.uk

Museums, galleries and science centres

Bentley Wildfowl and Motor Museum
Harveys Lane, Halland, Lewes **t** (01825) 840573
www.bentley.org.uk
Getting there 7 miles north of Lewes and
signposted from the A22, the A26 and the B2192
Open Apr–Oct daily 10.30–5.30 **Adm** Adults £6.50,
children £4.50, under 3s **free**, family (2+3) £21

Motoring museum set in a wildfowl park. There
are more than 1,000 birds living on the park's ponds
and enclosures, with three routes taking you past
assorted ducks, geese and swans. Woodland trails
and miniature steam train.
For further information *see* p.115

Booth Museum of Natural History
194 Dyke Road, Brighton **t** (01273) 292777
www.booth.virtualmuseum.info
Open Mon–Wed and Fri–Sat 10–5, Sun 2–5
Adm Free

The fascinating collection of insects, butter-
flies, fossils and animal skeletons belonging to
Victorian naturalist Edward Thomas Booth.
For further information *see* p.88

Brooklands Museum
Brooklands Road, Weybridge **t** (01932) 857381
www.brooklandsmuseum.com
Getting there Just south of the M3 (J2) and east of
the M25 (J11), 2 miles south of Chertsey
Open Daily 10–5 (winter until 4)
Adm Adults £7, children £5, under 6s **free**, family (2+3)
£18. Concorde Experience: Adults £4, children £2
Tearoom, picnic site

Perhaps the most romantic name in British
racing history, 'Brooklands' conjures up images
of goggles, flying scarves and dashing men
doing daring things in very fast, unsafe cars.
Today, this former racetrack is home to a
motoring museum with plenty of vintage
racing cars on display as well as motorbikes and
even a few planes including a Wellington
bomber rescued from Loch Ness. The most
popular current display is the 'Concorde
Experience' where visitors can tour the interior
of a real, decommissioned Concorde jet and
watch a film on the famous supersonic airliner.

Canterbury Roman Museum
Butchery Lane, Longmarket, Canterbury
t (01227) 785575
Open Mon–Sat 10–5 (last admission 4p), Jun–Oct
also Sun 1.30–5 **Adm** Adults £3, under 18s £1.85,
under 5s **free**, family (2+3) £7.60

Come and see reconstructions of Roman house
interiors, market stalls and floor mosaics.
Interactive computer displays, special 'hands-on'
areas and genuine Roman artefacts.
For further information *see* p.94

D-Day Museum
Clarence Esplanade, Southsea, Portsmouth
t (023) 9282 7261 www.ddaymuseum.co.uk
Open Apr–Sept daily 10–5.30, Oct–Mar 10–5
Adm Adults £6, children £3.60, family £15.60,
under 5s **free**

A series of realistic audiovisual displays vividly
retell the Normandy coast landing of 6 June 1944
and you can even climb aboard one of the actual
landing craft.
For further information *see* p.98

Explosion! – Museum of Naval Firepower
Priddy's Hard, Priory Road **t** (023) 9250 5600
www.explosion.org.uk
Open Apr–Oct daily 10–5.30; Nov–Mar Thurs, Sat
and Sun 10–4.30 **Adm** Adults £5.50, children £3.50,
family (2+4) £15, (1+3) £12.50

The history and development of naval armaments told through touch-screen computers,
gun-deck simulations, torpedos, mines and
audiovisual displays.
For further information *see* p.98

Guildford Discovery Centre

Ward Street, Guilford **t** (01483) 537080
www.scienceworlds.co.uk
Getting there Guildford is situated 35 miles
southwest of London off the A3
Open Tues–Sat 10–5, Sun 2–5
Adm Adults £2.75, children £2.25, under 5s **free**
Gift shop
  Interactive experiments for kids and adults.

★Herstmonceux Science Centre

Herstmonceux, Hailsham **t** (01323) 832731
www.the-observatory.org
Getting there 9 miles north of Eastbourne off
the A271
Open Apr–Oct daily 10–6, Nov–Feb Sat–Sun 10–5
Adm Adults £6.50, children £34.75, under 4s **free**,
family £19.50
Café, shop, picnic areas, on-site parking
  This excellent science centre is set between five
enormous telescope domes with over 70 hands-on
exhibits. You can look at yourself in a 'real' mirror,
which reverses your image so that you can see
yourself as others see you, examine tiny objects
through a TV microscope and find out how lasers
work. There's also an exhibition on astronomy and
a new outdoor Discovery Park with many more
hands-on exhibits and experiments.

Hove Museum and Art Gallery

19 New Church Road, Hove **t** (01273) 290200
www.hove.virtualmuseum.info
Open Tues–Sat 10–5, Sun 2–5 **Adm Free**
  Collection of local history, paintings, toys and
early cinema. Workshop for broken playthings,
working train sets and dolls. Activities include
film-making, puppetry and costume design.
For further information *see* pp.89–90

INTECH

Hampshire Technology Trust Ltd, Romsey Road,
Winchester **t** (01962) 863791
Open Daily 10–4 **Adm** Adults £6.50, children £4,
family £18.90
  Small, interactive science museum, where kids
can build a bridge, operate a crane, turn themselves into a battery and see the effects of a
hurricane on a house.
For further information *see* p.102

Kent Battle of Britain Museum

Aerodrome Road, Hawkinge, Folkestone
t (01303) 893140 www.kbobm.org
Getting there 3 miles north of Folkestone off the
A260 (J13 from the M20)
Open Easter–Sept Tues–Sun 10–4 and Bank Hols
Adm Adults £4.50, children £2.50, under 5s **free**
*Snacks, gift shop, disabled access, guided tours,
on-site parking*
  The country's largest collection of Battle of
Britain memorabilia is housed, appropriately
enough, in this former RAF station. The
remnants of over 600 British and German
planes are displayed alongside full-size replicas
of the Hurricane, Spitfire and ME 109 planes
used during the conflict.

Mechanical Music and Doll Museum

Church Road, Chichester **t** (01243) 372646
Open Jun–Sept Wed 1–4
Adm Adults £2.50, children £1.25
*Gift shop, guided tours, disabled access,
on-site parking*
  Collection of barrel organs, polyphones and
Victorian wax and china dolls.

Milestones Living History Museum

Leisure Park, Churchill Way, Basingstoke
t (01256) 477766 www.milestones-museum.com
Getting there Just north of the M3 (J6)
Open Tues–Fri 10–5, Sat–Sun 11–5 (last admission 4)
Adm £7.25, children £4.25, under 5s **free**,
family £21
Café, shop, on-site parking
  The thoroughly modern Milestones museum,
housed in a stunning glass structure in the
town's famous Leisure Park (where you can also
go ice-skating and bowling), is an attempt to
create an entire replica historic town. Stroll along
historic streets, tour historic factories and browse
historic shops while staff dressed in period
costume guide you through the exhibits. There
are several designated kids' attractions including
an interactive post office, a hands-on history
section and a toy display, where modern toys are
compared with their historic counterparts.

Museum of Army Flying

Middle Wallop, Stockbridge **t** (01264) 784421
www.flying-museum.org.uk
Getting there On the A343 between Andover
and Salisbury
Open Daily 10–4.30
Adm Adults £6, children £4, under 5s **free**,
family (2+2) £18
*Café, gift shop, mother and baby facilities, guided
tours, disabled facilities, on-site parking*

Between Andover and Salisbury in the
delightfully named Middle Wallop, this excellent museum is home to one of the country's
largest collections of military flying machines –
kites, gliders, planes, helicopters, etc. – all
displayed in a series of imaginative dioramas
designed to illustrate the development of
military flying from the First World War to the
present day. For children, however, the highlight
will undoubtedly be the Interactive Science
Centre with its collection of hands-on flying
exhibits (simulators, cockpits and the like) and
the camera obscura which provides wonderful
'secret' views of the surrounding countryside.

Museum of Canterbury and Rupert Bear Museum

Stour Street **t** (01227) 475202
www.canterbury-museums.co.uk
Open Mon–Sat 10.30–5, summer also Sun 1.30–5
Adm Adults £3.30, under 18s £2.20, under 5s **free**,
family (2+3) £8.70

An overview of the major events from the city's
2,000-year history. On the same site enjoy the
adventures of Rupert the Bear, including state-of-
the-art video, computer and hologram displays.
For further information *see* pp.92–3

Royal Marines Museum

Eastney Esplanade, Southsea, Portsmouth
t (023) 9281 9385
www.royalmarinesmuseum.co.uk
Open Jun–Aug 10–5, Sept–May 10–4.30
Adm Adults £4.75, under 16s **free**

Kids get to pretend to be soldiers in this lively
and interactive museum. Jungle Room, multimedia cinema and junior assault course outside.
For further information *see* p.99

Submarine Museum

Haslar Jetty Road, Gosport, Portsmouth
t (023) 9252 9217 **www.**rnsubmus.co.uk
Open Apr–Oct 10–5.30, Nov–Mar 10–4.30
Adm Adults £6.50, children £5, family (2+4) £15

Recreation of the life of the undersea soldier
through exhibits and audiovisuals. Walk down
the decks of HMS *Alliance*, a Second World War
submarine.
For further information *see* p.100

Tangmere Military Aviation Museum

Tangmere, near Chichester **t** (01243) 775223
www.tangmere-museum.org.uk
Open Mar–Oct daily 10–5.30, Feb–Nov 10–4.30
(last admission one hour before closing)
Adm Adults £5, children £1.50, under 5s **free**,
family £11.50
*Gift shop, café, guided tours, disabled access,
on-site parking*

An RAF airfield during the Second World War,
Tangmere is now one of the country's most
important military aviation museums. There's
lots of fearsome-looking (and even more fear-
somely named) hardware on display including a
Meteor, a Hunter, a Hurricane and, of course, a
Spitfire, the most famous fighter plane of them
all. There is even a Battle of Britain flight simulator so visitors can experience what these
machines would have been like in action.

West Gate Museum

St Peter's Street, Canterbury **t** (01227) 789576
www.canterbury-museums.co.uk
Open Mon–Sat 11–12.30 and 1.30–3.30
Adm Adults £1.20, children 70p, under 5s **free**,
family (2+3) £2.80

The West Gate is the last remaining gatehouse from a number that once enclosed the
medieval city of Canterbury. Tour its battlements and look through the murder holes
through which unwelcome visitors were once
bathed in boiling oil.
For further information *see* p.94

★World Naval Base – Chatham Historic Dockyard

Chatham **t** (01634) 823800 **www.chdt.org.uk**
Getting there Chatham is on the north Kent Coast between Rochester and Gillingham on the A229 (J3 from M2)
Open Feb–Oct daily 10–6; Nov Sat–Sun 10–4
Adm Adults £11.50, children £6.50, under 5s **free**, family (2+2) £29.50 (£5 per additional child)
Café, gift shop, disabled access

Founded by Henry VIII and once the Royal Navy headquarters, Chatham's docks have been turned into one of the country's best maritime museums, with lots to see and (more important for kids) do. On arrival, pick up a site plan at the entrance; the museum covers some 32 hectares (80 acres) and it's easy to lose your bearings. Indeed, the sheer size and scale of the place, with its cavernous shipbuilding sheds and ware-houses, is quite awe-inspiring. Check out the Rope-Making Room – officially the largest room in the country – where great, thick quarter-mile long ropes are laid out on the floor and regular demonstrations of rope-making are held.

As well as containing lots of straightforward historical exhibits such as Wooden Walls – a series of waxwork animatronic tableaux designed to illustrate the construction of an 18th-century warship – the museum also provides plenty of opportunity for kids to clamber in and around the exhibits with no less than 15 historic lifeboats to explore – they can run over the decks, pop their heads through the portholes and pretend to steer the ship sitting in the captain's chair. The undoubted highlight of the museum, however, is 'Battle Ships!', a display of three very different fighting vessels: HMS *Cavalier*, Britain's last remaining Second World War destroyer, HMS *Ocelot*, a 1960s spy subma-rine, and the *Gannet*, the last Victorian fighting sloop (a small, extremely manoeuvrable sailing warship mounted with about 20 guns), all of which can be toured and explored in the company of a guide. When the weather is good, trips are offered from the pier aboard a dockyard-produced paddle steamer.

The town of Chatham is also home to Fort Amherst, a well-preserved 18th-century fort surrounded by seven hectares (18 acres) of park-land, with a network of secret tunnels to explore and a battery of guns to pretend to fire.

Theatres

Brighton
Brighton Centre, Kings Road **t** (01273) 290131
Brighton Dome, 29 New Road **t** (01273) 700747
Komedia, Gardner St, Brighton **t** (01273) 647100
New Venture, Bedford Place **t** (01273) 746118
Sallis Benney, Grand Parade **t** (01273) 643010
Theatre Royal, New Road **t** 0870 0606650

Canterbury
The Marlowe, The Friars **t** (01227) 787787

Chichester
Chichester Festival Theatre and **Minerva Theatre**, Oaklands Park **t** (01243) 781312

Edenbridge
Hever Castle Lakeside Theatre t (01732) 866114

Isle of Wight
Anthony Minghella Theatre, Quay Arts Centre, The Quay, Newport **t** (01983) 822490
Apollo, Pyle Street, Newport **t** (01983) 527267
Medina, Fairlee Street, Newport **t** (01983) 527020
Ryde Theatre, Lind Street, Ryde **t** (01983) 568099
Shanklin Theatre, Prospect Road, Shanklin **t** (01983) 868000
Winter Gardens, Pier Street, Ventnor **t** (01983) 855215

Portsmouth
Kings Theatre, Albert Road **t** (023) 9282 8282
New Theatre, Guildhall Walk **t** (023) 9264 9000
Portsmouth Arts Centre, Reginald Road **t** (023) 9273 2236,
Portsmouth Guildhall, Guildhall Square **t** (01705) 824355

Sevenoaks
Stag Theatre, London Road **t** (01732) 450175

Tunbridge Wells
Assembly Hall Theatre, Crescent Road **t** (01892) 530613/532072,
Trinity Arts Centre, Church Road **t** (01892) 678678

Winchester
John Stripe Theatre, King Alfred's Art Centre **t** (01962) 827492
Theatre Royal, Jewry Street **t** (01962) 840440
Tower Arts Centre, Romsey Road **t** (01962) 867986

EATING OUT

Arundel

Black Rabbit
Mill Road **t** (01903) 882828
Open Mon–Sat 11–11 (food 11–9)
Pleasant pub with river views, a children's play area, kids' menu and highchairs. Sunday roasts.

Battle

The Copper Kettle
The Almonry **t** (01424) 772727
Open Apr–Sept Mon–Sat 9.30–4.30, Oct–Mar Mon–Sat 9.30–3.30
Oak-beamed tearoom with a courtyard garden (and open fire) serving baguettes, sandwiches, cakes and hot lunches. Kids' menu and highchairs.

Jempsons Cafe
78 High Street **t** (01424) 772856
Open Daily 9–5
Family-friendly café serving sticky treats and sandwiches. Highchairs available.

Whitehart Inn and Restaurant
Netherfield, near Battle **t** (01424) 838382
Open Mon 12 noon–3, Tues–Sat 12 noon–3 and 6.30–11, Sun 12 noon–3 and 7–10.30
This pub-restaurant offers traditional pub grub (kids' menu) and a garden with a play area.

Beaulieu

Beaulieu Road Inn
Beaulieu Road, near Lyndhurst **t** (023) 8029 2342
www.beaulieuroadinn.co.uk
Open Summer: 11–11; winter: 11–3 and 6–11; food served 12 noon–2.30 and 6–8.30
Country inn serving traditional and modern British cuisine (kids' menu and highchairs) with a large garden, play area and paddock with ponies.

Monty's
Montagu Arms Hotel, Beaulieu **t** (01590) 612324
www.montaguarmshotel.co.uk
Open Daily; food served 12 noon–2.30 and 6–9.30
Upmarket pub-cum-brasserie where you can dine al fresco in summer or lounge by a log fire in winter. Kids' portions and highchairs available.

Bognor Regis

The Beach Restaurant
Esplanade **t** (01243) 840998
Open Daily 10–10; takeaway until 2am Thurs–Sat
Traditional seafront fish and chip shop. Children's menu and smaller portions available.

Brighton

Alfresco
The Milkmaid Pavilion, King's Road Arches
t (01273) 206523 www.alfresco-brighton.co.uk
Open Daily 12 noon–10.30
Pleasant, friendly Italian restaurant overlooking seafront and children's playground, with an outdoor seating area. Very popular with families, especially in summer when it's packed (no room for buggies). Kids' portions and highchairs.

Brown's
3–4 Duke Street **t** (01273) 323501
www.browns-restaurants.com
Open Mon–Sat 11am–11.30pm, Sun 12 noon–11pm
High-quality family restaurant near the Lanes. Separate kids' menu (plus free ice cream) and highchairs.

Café Rouge
24 Prince Albert Street **t** (01273) 774422
www.caferouge.co.uk
Open Mon–Sat 10am–11pm, Sun 10am–10.30pm
Between the seafront and the Lanes, this branch of the family-friendly French café chain offers a kids' menu and highchairs.

Momma Cherri's Soul Food Shack
11 Little East Street **t** (01273) 774545, also 2–3 Little East Street **t** (01273) 325305
www.mommacherri.co.uk
Open Mon 5–10, Tues–Thurs 12–2 and 5–11, Fri 12–2 and 5–12, Sat 11am–12 midnight, Sun 11–9
If you're ravenous after trekking around Brighton's attractions, you could do a lot worse than a heaped plate of momma's 'soul food'. Burgers, buffalo hot wings, jerk chicken, gumbo, jambalaya and breakfasts (complete with grits) are all on offer in this popular joint. Kids' menus.

Harry Ramsden's
1–4 Marine Parade **t** (01275) 690691
www.harryramsdens.co.uk
Open 12 noon–9.30, Fri and Sat till 10pm, Sun till 9pm
For kids who want the usual cod and chips, this branch of the famous northern chain is situated opposite the entrance to the pier and Sea Life Centre and can seat over 100 people. Two kids' menus and highchairs. Eat in or take away.

The Regency Restaurant

131 King's Road **t** (01273) 325014
www.theregencyrestaurant.co.uk
Open Daily 8am–11pm

Traditional seafront fish restaurant with tables on the pavement shaded by coloured umbrellas and a range of locally caught fresh fish and seafood dishes on the menu, plus tempting puddings. Kids' menu and highchairs.

Broadstairs

Broadstairs Pavilion

Harbour Street **t** (01843) 600999
www.pavillion-broadstairs.co.uk
Open Daily 10–10

Large, very child-friendly modern tavern serving baguettes, pastries, ice creams and pub meals. Kids' menu and highchairs. Also a grassy garden.

Canterbury

The Moat Tea Rooms

67 Burgate **t** (01227) 784514
www.moattearooms.co.uk
Open Daily 10–5

Jolly tearoom in a 16th-century building, serving sandwiches, hot savouries, pastries, cream teas.

The Old Weavers House

1 St Peter's Street **t** (01227) 464660
Open Daily 11–11

Traditional cream teas and good solid pub fare are served in this grand 16th-century half-timbered building overlooking the river. There's a riverside patio garden. Kids' portions and highchairs.

Chichester

Ask Pizza

38 East Street **t** (01243) 775040
www.askcentral.co.uk
Open Sun–Thurs 12 noon–11, Fri and Sat 12 noon–11.30

Serves thin-crust Italian-style pizzas and is very welcoming to families. Pasta portions for kids. Highchairs available.

The Bishop Bell Restaurant

The Cloisters, West Street **t** (01243) 783718
Open Summer: Mon–Sat 10–5; winter: Mon–Sat 10–4

Pleasant café-restaurant serving homemade dishes, Cornish pasties, sausage rolls, cottage pies, cakes and assorted snacks. Sunny walled garden. Menu available in Braille; disabled access, baby changing facilities and highchairs available.

King's Head pub

Bognor Road, Drayton **t** (01243) 783576
www.thekingsheadpub.com
Open Daily 11–3 and 6–11

Just outside the town centre. Children under 12 eat free of charge (up to three children) or Sunday roasts for just £1.50 on roast days. One highchair.

Pizza Express

27 South Street **t** (01243) 786648
www.pizzaexpress.co.uk
Open 12 noon–12 midnight daily, Sun until 10.30pm

Family-friendly chain serving thin-crust Italian-style pizzas. Smaller, garlic bread-sized pizzas for kids. Highchairs available.

Chiddingstone

Castle Inn

Chiddingstone **t** (01892) 870247
www.castleinn.co.uk
Open Mon–Sat 11–11, Sun 12 noon–10.30

Friendly medieval inn with a massive garden. Kids are allowed in the restaurant and saloon bar but not the public bar. Menu offers traditional British-European dishes. After your meal take a stroll to the 'Chiddingstone', a large boulder, which children can climb on, or around the pretty village. Kids' menu and highchairs. Food served until half an hour before closing; it has an all-day children's certificate.

Deal

Hare and Hounds

The Street, Northbourne **t** (01304) 365429
Open Mon–Sat 11–3 and 6–11, Sun 12 noon–3 and 7–10.30

Modern pub-restaurant with a family section in the bar, a nice garden and an adventure playground. Food is taken seriously here, with lots of organic choices and a children's menu that features scaled-down versions of adult choices – baby omelettes, mini steak-and-kidney pies, etc. – rather than the traditional nuggets and fish fingers. Highchairs available.

Dover

The Park Inn

1–2 Park Place, Ladywell **t** (01304) 203300
Open Mon–Sat 11–11, Sun 12 noon–10.30

Traditional pub just behind Dover Town Hall with an attractive restaurant. Kids' menu and highchairs, but children must be out by 9pm.

Hastings

Castle Tandoori
43 George Street, Old Town **t** (01424) 429685
Open 12 noon–2 and 5.30–12 midnight
Spicy curries in the heart of the old town.
Children's portions rather than a children's menu.

The Italian Way
25 Castle Street **t** (01424) 435955
Open Daily 10–10
Friendly Italian restaurant with a Mediterranean attitude to children: 'Yes, we take everybody, we are Italian'. There are no children's menus or high-chairs but local families flock here in summer. The kitchen will happily provide children's portions.

Kingfisher
6 Castle Street **t** (01424) 431932
Open Fri–Sat 12 noon–12.30am, Wed 12 noon–11pm
Traditional English dishes. It has a children's menu, highchairs and is very family friendly.

Isle of Wight

Blacksmiths Arms
Calbourne Road, Newport **t** (01983) 529263
Open Daily 11am–11.30pm
Award-winning, child-friendly pub offering a wide selection of international dishes. Kids' menu, indoor play area, garden and highchairs.

Bugle Inn
High Street, Brading, Sandown **t** (01983) 407359
Open All day
Next door to the Isle of Wight Waxworks (p.109), the Bugle is very family friendly and offers a children's menu, an 'all-you-can-eat' Sunday carvery, great outdoor play equipment, highchairs and nappy changing facilities.

Caulkheads
Sandown **t** (01983) 403878
Open All day
Large pub with an indoor play area and a garden with play equipment. Kids' menu and highchairs.

Chequers
Nilton Road, Rookley **t** (01983) 840314
www.chequersinn-iow.co.uk
Open Mon–Sat 11.30–3 and 6–11, Sun 12–3 and 7–10.30
Aimed at families, Chequers was once a customs and excise house and now offers a non-smoking family room, an outdoor play area with a bouncy castle and baby changing facilities. Kids' menu.

The Hare and Hounds
Downende, Arreton **t** (01983) 523446
Open Daily: food: 12 noon–9, Sun 12 noon–4 and 6–9
Pleasant, traditional country pub at the top of Arreton Downs, next to Robin Hill Country Park. It serves a full children's menu and the bar is reputedly made from the gibbet used to hang the notorious local murderer Michal Morey in 1736, who was executed for killing his grandson.

Horse and Groom
Main Road, Ningwood, Newport **t** (01983) 760672
Open Mon–Sat 11.30–3 and 6–11, Sun 12–3 and 7–10.30
This friendly West Wight pub is located three miles east of Yarmouth near Newtown Nature Reserve. Real ales and homemade meals (including vegetarian and children's options) are served and there are two beer gardens, one designed for families, with a children's play area.

Wight Mouse Inn and Clarendon Hotel
Newport Road, Chale **t** (01983) 730431
www.wightmouseinns.co.uk
Open 12 noon–9 Mon–Sat, 12 noon–3 and 7–9 Sun
Very child-friendly pub with an indoor play area ('Pop Zone') for the under 10s and an outdoor play area with swings, climbing frames and, in summer, a bouncy castle. Food is served seven days a week. Kids' menu.

Littlehampton

The Locomotive
74 Lyminster Road, Wick **t** (01903) 716658
Open Food served daily 12 noon–2 and 7–9
Traditional pub with a family room and non-smoking area, a large garden with a play area and a full kids' menu with special kids drinks. Sunday kids' roast.

Portsmouth

Char Bar
25 The Boardwalk, Port Solent **t** (023) 9220 1471; branch: Gunwharf Quays
Open Daily 12 noon–11pm
Every table comes fitted with a gas-fired barbecue on which you cook the meat or seafood of your choice. Strict supervision is obviously necessary but kids absolutely love it. Free fruit juices or milkshakes for kids are served between 12 noon and 6pm. Kids' menu and highchairs.

Sally Port Tea Rooms

35 Broad Street, Old Portsmouth **t** (023) 9282 6265
Open Tues 12 noon–6, Wed–Sun 10–6

Housed in a 17th-century building on a narrow, cobbled street in Portsmouth's old quarter, this tearoom serves traditional fare, including home-made cakes, clotted cream scones and crumpets. **The Dolphin**, **t** (023) 9282 3595), next door, is also good for families.

Shorties

8–9 Bellevue Terrace, Southsea **t** (023) 9283 1941
Open Mon–Thurs 6–11, Fri and Sat 6–12 midnight, Sun 6–10.30

Lively American-style diner serving burgers, spare ribs, fried chicken and steak with mini versions for children. Highchairs provided.

Still and West

2 Bath Square, Old Portsmouth **t** (023) 9282 1567
Open Daily 12 noon–9

A good pub for families who want to sit outside and watch the boats go by.

Rye

Cranberries

105a High Street **t** (01797) 224800
Open Daily 10–5

Small, friendly non-smoking café serving morning coffee, light lunches (jacket potatoes, beans on toast, etc.), sandwiches, main meals (chilli, cottage pie) and homemade desserts.

Old Forge Restaurant

24 Wish Street **t** (01797) 223227
Open Tues–Wed 6.30–11, Thurs–Sat 12 noon–2.30 and 6.30–11

Seafood dishes at competitive prices. There's no children's menu but they're happy to provide half portions and are popular with local families.

The Queen's Head

19 Landgate **t** (01797) 222181
www.queensheadrye.co.uk
Open Daily pub: 11–11; bar meals: 12 noon–3; restaurant: 6.30–9.30pm (till 8 on Sun)

A 17th-century inn with an adjoining olde-worlde restaurant, where a hybrid English-French menu is served. Children's menu and highchairs available. The whole restaurant is non-smoking.

Tunbridge Wells

Frankie and Benny's Restaurant

Knights Park Leisure Development, Longbridge Road **t** (01892) 548285
www.frankieandbennys.co.uk
Open Daily 12 noon–11pm (Sun till 10.30pm)

This restaurant serves up great American diner-style food which kids love (children's menu available), although the service is a bit slow sometimes. It is reasonably priced and customers can learn Italian from the tapes that constantly play in the loos. Kids get a balloon each.

Woods Restaurant

62 The Pantiles **t** (01892) 614411
www.woodsrestaurant.co.uk
Open Daily

A stylish bar and restaurant with an international menu and outdoor eating area. There are high chairs, crayons and colouring sheets and special children's meals as well as half portions of dishes on the regular menu for more adventurous kids.

Whitstable

Pearson's Crab and Oyster House

The Horsebridge **t** (01227) 272005
www.pearsonscrabandoyster.co.uk
Open Mon–Thurs 12 noon–9, Fri–Sat 12 noon–9.30 and Sun 12 noon–2.30

Popular with families, this offers a full children's menu and highchairs.

Winchester

Cathedral Refectory

Inner Close **t** (01962) 857268
Open Mon–Sat 9.30–5, Sun 10–5

Simple, wholesome café food. Children's menu and highchairs are available.

Forte Tea Room

78 Parchment Street **t** (01962) 856840
www.thefortetearooms.co.uk
Open Mon–Sat 9–5.30

This non-smoking tearoom offers Devonshire cream teas, sandwiches, snacks and pasta dishes. They're flexible with portions and also offer highchairs.

The Midwest
Somerset · Dorset · Wiltshire

06

A mystical sort of a place, its landscape dotted with mysterious prehistoric monuments and chalk pictures cut into the hillsides, the Midwest was the first area in England to be settled after the Ice Age and separation from mainland Europe.

It is now famed for its elegant, historic towns – Bath, Glastonbury, Salisbury *et al* – and refined resorts such as Christchurch, Swanage and the fossil-hunting mecca of Lyme Regis. It has livelier areas too: Bristol is a buzzing, cosmopolitan city, as evidenced by its £100-million cultural-cum-science complex, At-Bristol, and the enterprising British Empire and Commonwealth Museum.

Day-trip itinerary

Morning: Tracking down Swindon's industrial past at the fascinating Steam Museum (p.174) and discovering the play area and outlet centre shops. **Lunch:** Grab a sandwich on the train to Bath, saving your appetite for tea at Sally Lunn's (p.183). **Afternoon:** Sipping the Bath water in the Pump Room and learning all about ancient ablutions at the Roman Baths (p.150).

Special events

March
Bath: Shakespeare Festival **t** (01225) 448844
www.bathshakespeare.org.uk
May
Salisbury: The Salisbury Festival **t** (01722) 332977
www.salisburyfestival.org.uk
Bath: International Music Festival
t (01225) 463362 **www.bathmusicfest.org.uk**
Cerne Abbas: Morris men dance on the proud chalk giant on the first day of the month
June
Abbotsbury: Cygnets hatching at the swannery
t (01305) 871858
Dorchester: Carnival **t** (01305) 266861
www.dorchestercarnival.co.uk
July
Bournemouth: Festival of Fun **t** 0845 0511701
www.bournemouth.co.uk
Bristol: Harbour Festival **t** (0117) 9223719
Bristol Children's Festival **t** (01458) 832925
www.childrensworldcharity.org
August
Weymouth: International Fireworks Festival
Glastonbury: Children's Festival **t** (01458) 832925
www.childrensworldcharity.org
Bristol: Bristol Balloon Fiesta **t** (0117) 9535884
www.bristolfiesta.co.uk

Highlights
Ancient monument, Avebury Stone Circle, p.162
Animal fun, Tropiquaria, p.165
Beach holidays, pp.168–73
Fossil-hunting, Lyme Regis, pp.169–70
Hands-on science, At-Bristol, p.152
Hiking, Exmoor, p.176
King Arthur Country, p.158
Spooky caves, Wookey Hole Caves, p.177
Steam trains, West Somerset Steam Railway, p.170
Water fun, Splashdown, Poole, pp.170–1
Zoo mania, Bristol Zoo Gardens, p.153

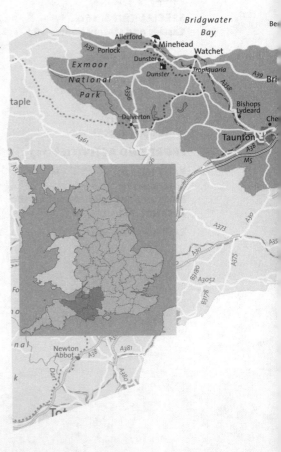

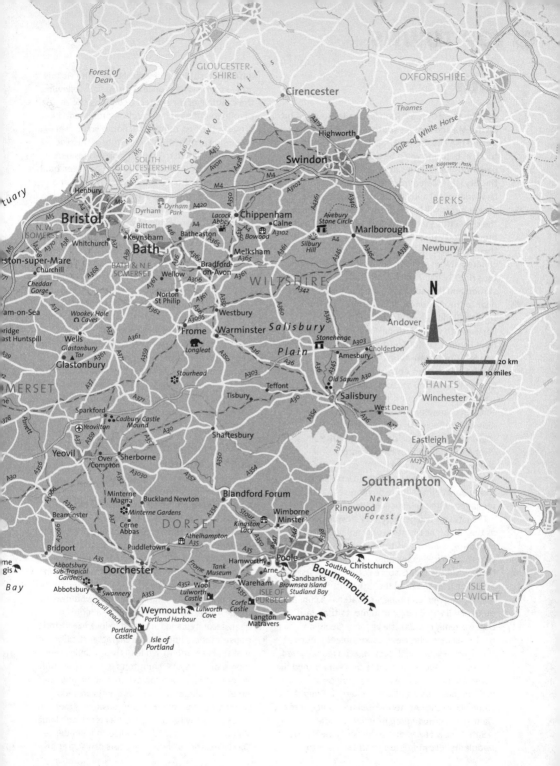

Bath

Getting there By road: Bath is 10 miles south of J18 on the M4 and 12 miles southeast of Bristol on the A4 and the A36. Car parking: Parking is always tricky in Bath and you'd be better off using the park-and-ride facilities at Lansdown, just north of the city (signposted from the A46 and the A420), Newbridge (A4) and Old Down (A367). Double-decker buses will leave you in Queen's Square in the city centre (handy for sights and shops) and provide you with panoramic views of the area as they negotiate the city's steep outlying hills – children always seem to enjoy this rather precipitous ride. By train/coach: Both Bath Spa train station and the bus station are on Manvers Street, near to the city centre. Trains arrive here from London (Paddington), Bristol, Salisbury and Portsmouth while National Express services arrive from London, Bristol, Salisbury, Portsmouth, Oxford and Stratford-upon-Avon

Tourist information Abbey Chambers, Abbey Church Yard **t** 0906 711 2000 **www.**visitbath.co.uk

Bath is beautiful but it has slightly less to offer children than some of the other towns in the area. Kids will certainly like the Roman Baths, the costume museum, the parks and a cruise along the River Avon but many of Bath's charms – the glorious 18th-century architecture, the fine art museums, the narrow lanes lined with antique shops – are perhaps more of interest to adults and teenagers with sophisticated tastes.

The city can also get very, very crowded. Indeed, as the site of the country's only hot spring, it's been attracting hordes of visitors for well over 2,000 years now. The Romans built a bathing complex here, as did the Tudors some 1,000 or so years later, although it wasn't until the 18th century when doctors began prescribing spa water as a cure for a quite bewildering range of ailments, that Bath became really popular. It was these Georgian health seekers, who were responsible for much of the town's elegant architecture, who rediscovered and restored the Roman Baths, and who turned the Pump Room into one of the country's most fashionable meeting places – where you might come across Jane Austen scribbling a quick note or Gainsborough indulging in an idle doodle.

Bath is now poised on the brink of a new wave of popularity following the construction Thermae

Bath Spa, a stunning new facility offering visitors access to the waters once again (p.150). Following the example of the genteel Georgians, the city's air of refinement has been carefully preserved. Upon arriving, the first thing you'll notice is the overwhelming architectural uniformity of the place. There are no modern unsightly blemishes here. Every building, whether old or new, has been built from the same honey-coloured Bath stone and there are strict building regulations in place to make sure nobody bucks the trend. It has proved an inspired decision. Framed by green hills, the city is undeniably beautiful with a certain, timeless (albeit artificially maintained) feel to it. Even the state-of-the-art spa building has had to toe the line, albeit using wraparound glass walls to reflect back the Georgian splendour of its environs.

If, after all this sightseeing, your kids start to get peckish and you'd like to find a healthy bite to eat or organic snacks for your kids to nibble on, try Harvest, 37 Walcot Street, **t** (01225) 465519, and Ben's Cookies, 21 Union Passage, **t** (01225) 460983. Sweet tooths can opt for The Sweet Shop **t** (01225) 428040 on Abbey Green or for something more substantial try The Bath Deli, 7 Margaret's Buildings, **t** (01225) 315666 for sandwiches and high-quality coffees to take away.

Things to see and do

American Museum

Claverton Manor **t** (01225) 460503
www.americanmuseum.org
Getting there 2 miles east of Bath off the A36
Open Mar–Nov Tues–Sun 12 noon–5
Adm Adults £6, children £3.50, family ticket £17.50; grounds only: Adults £4, children £2.50
Café, picnic area, gift shop, mother and baby room, guided tours, limited wheelchair access (phone in advance), on-site parking

The only museum in the country devoted solely to the American way of life, these 18 rooms have been decorated and furnished to look like historic house interiors (including a characteristically minimalist Shaker room), while in the grounds there's a replica of George Washington's garden at Mount Vernon, a teepee, a colonial herb garden and an American arboretum. Various events are held throughout the year, including a Native American Weekend, a Civil War Weekend, a French and Indian War re-enactment and, of course, Independence Day celebrations. Younger visitors can also enjoy

Cinemas and theatres See pp.179, 182

Did you know?

That the water you see in the Roman Baths fell as rain over 10,000 years ago. Over the succeeding centuries it slowly soaked deep into the ground where it became super-heated before being finally forced back to the surface.

some seasonal treats at Christmas and Easter, plus the occasional open-air film show under the trees in summer. Call the Bath Film Festival for details, **t** (01225) 401149, **www.**bathfilmfestival.org.uk.

Bath Abbey

Abbey Churchyard **t** (01225) 422462
www.bathabbey.org
Open Apr–Oct Mon–Sat 9–6, Sun 1–2.30 and 4.30–5.30 ; Nov–Mar Mon–Sat 9–4.30, Sun 1–2.30
Adm Free (recommended donation £2.50)
Shop, disabled access, guided tours

The entrance to Bath Abbey stands 10 metres (11 yards) from the entrance to the Roman Baths and a further five metres (five yards) from the entrance to the Pump Room, making the three visits a perfect afternoon combination. Known as the 'Lantern of the West' since Tudor times, owing to the sheer amount of stained glass adorning its walls, the inside of the Abbey is as grand and dry as most religious buildings. Children will be impressed by its scale but otherwise the abbey holds little of interest to them. Pop around to the south side of the building for a tour of the Heritage Vaults, packed with Saxon and Norman relics and featuring a model of how the abbey would have looked in medieval times.

Bath Boating Station

Forester Road **t** (01225) 321900
Open Apr–Sept daily 10–6; restaurant: lunch, teas in summer and 7am–10.30pm
Café, restaurant and picnic area

You can hire row boats, punts, canoes and traditional wooden skiffs from this restored Victorian structure, which houses a pleasant tea garden and restaurant. Punting tuition available. The Boating Station also runs river trips from Pulteney Bridge.

Bath's Classic City Tour

t (01225) 330444
Fares Adults £9.50, children £5

Open-top bus tours give an excellent introduction to the city. There's a historical overview for older sightseers, you can get on and off as you like and see all the town without tiring little legs. The

tours last 45 minutes, can be joined at 16 stops en route and take in Great Pulteney Street, the King's Circus, the Royal Crescent and the Roman Baths.

Building of Bath Museum

Countess of Huntingdon's Chapel, The Vineyards
t (01225) 333895
www.bath-preservation-trust.org.uk
Open Tues–Sun 10.30–5
Adm Adults £4, children £1.50, under 8s **free**
Shop, free guided tours on Fri at 3pm, disabled facilities

If you're having trouble finding your way around the town, this museum should help you get your bearings. The centrepiece is a huge, scale-model of the city itself with every street and building beautifully rendered in miniature detail. It is fully illuminated so you can press buttons and light up different sections of the town to find out when they were built. Elsewhere, there are exhibits illustrating the different stages of Bath's construction – Celtic, Roman, Saxon, Tudor and Georgian and the techniques and materials these builders used. In the upstairs gallery, there's a children's play corner, where mini architects can design their own edifices using paper and crayons or wooden blocks.

Cinemas and theatres See pp.179, 182

Museum of Costume and Assembly Rooms

Bennet Street **t** (01225) 477785
www.museumofcostume.co.uk
Open Jan–Feb and Nov–Dec daily 11–4, Mar–Oct 11–5
Adm Adults £6.50, children £4.50, family £18 (2+4) under 5s **free**
Shop, parent and baby room, disabled facilities, guided tours, activity trolley with games, quizzes and colouring sheets, holiday activities

A display of changing fashions featuring more than 200 figures dressed in costumes from the 16th century to the present day. Kids can have fun choosing outfits and there'll be much mirth when they find the kind of clothes that were around when you were young. There is a free audio guide. Afterwards take your kids to the Assembly Rooms to gasp at the ornate ceilings and chandeliers.

Postal Museum

27 Northgate Street **t** (01225) 460333
www.bathpostalmuseum.org
Open Tues–Sat 11–4.30 **Adm** Adults £2.90, children £1.50, under 5s **free**, family £6.90
Café, shop

★ *Roman Baths*

Stall Street **t** (01225) 477785
www.romanbaths.co.uk
Open Daily Jan–Feb and Nov–Dec 9.30–5.30,
Mar–Jun and Sept–Oct 9–6, Jul–Aug 9am–10pm
Adm Adults £10, children £6, under 5s **free**
*Café, shop, baby changing facilities, guided tours,
audio guides, activity sheets*

In Roman times, every major town boasted a large public bathhouse. Bathing was one of the Romans' favourite activities, perhaps second only to conquering countries and trying on new togas. To the Romans, bathing was more than just a means of getting clean – it was an important social experience. The bathhouse fulfilled much the same function for the average Roman as the pub, café or gym does for people today. It was an informal meeting place, somewhere for people to come and relax and talk about the day's events. However, when the Roman Empire collapsed in the 5th century AD, so their bathhouses went out of fashion with the locals. The invading Saxon tribes had little need for such fancies and most were either destroyed or left to decay. The bathhouse in Bath was built over and forgotten about until the 18th century when workmen stumbled upon it by accident. Remarkably, it had survived more or less intact and was quickly spruced up and re-opened to the public, whereupon it soon became one of the country's top tourist attractions – something it has remained to this day.

The complex, which looks like a cross between an ancient temple and a modern swimming pool, is beautifully preserved and, wandering through it today, you can really get a feel for what it must have been like in Roman times, full of chattering, gossiping people. On arrival, you are given a self-paced audio guide, which will lead you through the complex and adjoining museum to the hot, bubbling spring itself, which still produces a staggering 250,000 gallons of water a day at a constant temperature of 47°C (116°F) – the bubbles you see are a result of escaping gas rather than the heat. The Romans channelled this water into a whole range of different baths: a large hot bath, a number of small tepid pools and treatment baths as well as a cold, circular plunge pool into which the bathers would jump after their hot dip to freshen themselves up. There would also have been steam rooms and saunas heated by underfloor hypercausts (the

Roman version of central heating). Today, you can see the remnants and remains of all these facilities, and only the main bath and plunge pool still contain water, which flows along lead pipes laid down by Roman engineers. You can explore both, although you should on no account drink the water.

In Roman times, the source of the spring was marked by a shrine to the Goddess Sulis Minerva, where people would come to worship and throw curses written on sheets of lead into the water. You can see examples of these requests for supernatural intervention (most seem to have been the result of quite everyday disputes between neighbours) at the museum along with a bust of the goddess herself. This tradition continues today at the plunge pool, which is littered with coins tossed in by visitors for luck. The museum also contains various models and dioramas showing what the complex would have looked like 1,600 years ago, as well as a number of mosaics and a collection of everyday objects such as coins and hairpins.

The pleasant, pedestrianized square outside the Baths, where you'll also find the Pump Room and Bath Abbey, is frequented by street performers – musicians, jugglers, etc. – and there's a branch of the English Teddy Bear Company guarded by a two-metre (six-foot) bear in a Beefeater uniform.

Tip: The complex can get very crowded, especially in summer, so try to pick your time carefully. Also, do be aware that it takes at least an hour to go round which is tiring for younger children.

Pump Room

Come to the Pump Room, the epitome of 18th-century elegance (it's basically just a very well-to-do tearoom), for a refreshing glass of hot spa water pumped from the same spring that feeds the Roman Baths next door.

Thermae Bath Spa

t (01225) 331234 **www**.thermaebathspa.com
Open 9am–8pm daily
Adm per 90 mins Adults £12, children (12–16) £9

Much delayed and rather over budget, Bath's new spa is finally open allowing visitors to do as the Romans did and enjoy the city's thermal waters first hand. Opened in the summer of 2006, the multi-million-pound complex offers four thermal baths (including two rooftop baths), a spa-water drinking fountain, various treament and massage rooms as well as a a café/restaurant and visitor centre (free entry).

Lively displays on the history of written communication from clay mail to email, housed just down the road from the building at 8 Broad Street where the world's first postage stamp, the Penny Black, was sent on 2 May 1840. Exhibitions chart the history of the British postbox and post-office uniforms. There are interactive computer games, quizzes and worksheets for children, who can sort letters and weigh parcels in an original 1930s' post office. Die-cast miniature historical 'posties' are on sale in the museum shop.

Royal Victoria Park
Adjacent to the Royal Crescent on Royal Avenue

A large, grassy, open space, this is the city's main park and the best place to take kids when they develop cultural overload. Home to the Bath Festival and other family-orientated events in summer, the park has extensive recreational facilities, including skateboard ramps, tennis, bowls, crazy golf and a café. There's a staffed children's playground with roundabout, bouncy castle, slides, swings, sandpit and toilets and a duck pond, an aviary and botanic gardens to wander through.

Shopping

Bath's shops are very much in keeping with its rarefied atmosphere, so don't be surprised to see chocolate-box shopfronts decked out in fine art, haute couture and dazzling jewellery. Broad Street is where you'll find homeware, designer clothes, leather goods and CDs, while Walcot Street houses the more arty end of the retail spectrum. Strictly for kids there's The Dress Up Shop, 118 Walcot Street, **t** (01225) 443393, where kids can play at make-believe while you browse among rows of pirate and princess costumes. A few doors down is Walcot Woollies, **t** (01225) 463966, for knitwear, fleeces and welly boots. Bloomsbury, 15 New Bond Street, **t** (01225) 461049, is fun for all the family. It's the kind of place where you could spend hours gazing at all the amazing and unusual objects, ranging from innovative lighting and furniture designs to jewellery and books. Kids will love the display of Tintin memorabilia and novelty gifts. The Guildhall Market on the High Street is open Mon–Sat for fresh produce, clothing and luggage, jokes and party outfits at discount prices.

Sport and activities *See pp.177–9*

Walking tours
The Huntsman Inn, North Passage t (01225) 335124
Open Apr–Sept; call for details

For an irreverent evening's entertainment, kids and adults can try the 'Bizarre Bath' tour, which leaves the Huntsman Inn at 8pm. To discover more about former Bath resident Jane Austen, there's a tailor-made tour of places she frequented and wrote about in her novels. Tours depart from the Visitor Information Centre in the Abbey Churchyard at weekends and on Bank Holidays throughout the year at 11am. More information is available from the Jane Austen Centre, 40 Gay Street, **t** (01225) 443000, www.janeausten.co.uk.

Around Bath

Bristol, 12 miles northwest (*see* below)
Norwood Farm, 4 miles south (p.167)

Bristol

Getting there By road: Bristol is 122 miles west of London. The two cities are connected by the M4. By train/coach: There are direct train links from London (Paddington or Waterloo), Bath, Birmingham, Exeter and Oxford to Bristol Temple Meads Station and National Express links from London (Victoria, Gatwick and Heathrow), Exeter, Oxford and Stratford-upon-Avon to Bristol Coach Station, which is on Marlborough Street, to the north of the city centre
Tourist information Wildwalk, Anchor Road, Harbourside **t** 0906 711 2191
www.bristol-city.gov.uk or **www.visitbristol.co.uk**

Home of Aardman films, the creators of animated favourites Wallace and Gromit, Bristol, on the River Avon, is the Midwest's largest and arguably most dynamic city. For much of its history, it was a thriving inland port and one of the country's most important trade links with America. Although this trade has long since dried up, the docks are still at the city's heart. As part of an ongoing regeneration programme (costing around £450m), warehouses and cranes have been replaced with arts centres, museums, state-of-the-art attractions (including the outstanding At-Bristol complex), cafés and restaurants, while the harbour is now filled with pleasure craft offering sightseeing trips along the coast and up the rivers Avon and Severn.

Heavily bombed during the Second World War, the city centre is not a particularly beautiful place but it does boast a number of very good museums, an excellent zoo and numerous family-friendly cafés and restaurants. In truth, you'll be far too busy checking out what Bristol has to offer to linger long on the décor. And, in any case, if it's beauty you want, you don't have to go far from the city's borders to find miles of rolling countryside, not to mention the beaches and seaside attractions of the north Somerset coast.

For grumbling stomachs after a busy morning seeing the sights, make a beeline for Royce Rolls Vegetarian Café in Saint Nicholas Market, t (07791) 523014, for an upper-class bite or graze the many food stalls from delis to Caribbean takeaways. There are also lots of café-bars around the Watershed Media Centre (near At-Bristol) including the child-friendly Watershed, t (0117) 9276444.

Things to see and do

★At-Bristol

Anchor Road, Harbourside t (0845) 345 12335
www.at-bristol.org.uk
Open Explore and Wildwalk: daily 10–5; IMAX: Mon–Fri 10–4.45, Sat–Sun 12.30–8.30
Adm Adults £20, children £15, family £62 (access to all attractions over a seven-day period); tickets for single attractions also available

This cavernous cultural complex on Bristol's redeveloped harbourside is fast becoming one of the Southwest's star attractions and deserves at least a day or two of your attention. It comprises a hands-on science centre, 'Explore', where you can take on the power of a tornado, experience rebirth in a giant womb and get inside your own brain; an IMAX 3D cinema showing films about the natural world and animated features; Wildwalk, a mix of live animals and recorded images and displays (including a walk-through botanical house); a planetarium housed in a giant silver sphere; and an open piazza, 'The Millennium Square', lined with cafés and restaurants and decorated with numerous specially commissioned pieces of art including a walk-through fountain, 'The Aquarena'.

Tip: *The water features in the piazza are very tempting to kids on hot days. They are not entirely safe to paddle in, as the far edges can be slippery, but most kids will want to cool off in them. Advise children not to run and bring non-slip aqua shoes, swimwear or a change of clothes. The steps opposite the square are very popular with skateboarders, some of whom are capable of impressive stunts.*

Avon Valley Railway

Bitton Station, Bath Road, Willsbridge
t (0117) 932 5538 Infoline: t (0117) 932 7296
www.avonvalleyrailway.co.uk
Getting there The railway is just off the A431, midway between Bristol and Bath. The nearest station is Keynsham, on the Bristol–Bath line
Open Apr–Oct every Sun, Aug additional midweek service and around Christmas
Fares Adults £5, children £3.50, under 3s **free**, family £13.50
Refreshments and snacks, picnic area, children's play area, converted carriage for wheelchair use, on-site parking at Bitton Station

Steam-train rides operate most Sundays between April and October along this two-mile stretch of the former Midland Railway line just southeast of Bristol. The railway also organizes numerous special event days including Mother's Day, Teddy Bears' Picnics, Santa Specials and, of course, Thomas the Tank Engine Days. The Severn Beach Railway runs from Temple Meads Station from 18 May until 27 September. It's a fine way to take in the sights of the Avon Gorge, visit Clifton and the zoo, or walk the sea wall. Call First Great Western Trains, t 08457 000125, for information.

Boat trips

There are a vast number of sightseeing boat trips on offer at Bristol Harbour. You can choose to go around the harbour itself, up the River Avon and along the coast to Devon, up the River Severn, over to Lundy Island to see the puffins, or across the Bristol Channel to Wales. The Bristol Packet Company, t (0117) 926 8157, offer day trips to Bath, Avon Gorge cruises, plus river trips and dock tours.

If you just want to get from A to B, the most fun option with kids is to board the ferry (turn left out of Temple Meads station and follow the road round until you see the Temple Quay steps), which stops off at various points of the city. It's popular with workers and ideal for family groups, who can buy a round trip family ticket for £12. Trips run daily from April to October (10.10am–6.10pm). Contact the Bristol Ferry Boat Company, t (0117) 927 3416.

Bristol City Museum and Art Gallery

Queen's Road, Clifton **t** (0117) 922 3571
www.bristol-city.gov.uk/museums
Open Daily 10–5, 'Sunday Fundays' on first Sun of
every month **Adm Free**
*Café, shop, mother and baby room, disabled
facilities. Suitable for pushchairs (although the first
floor has a number of small mezzanines which are
not easily navigable)*

Small but surprisingly good city museum with
displays on dinosaurs, Egyptian mummies, wildlife
and natural history and rocks and minerals.
Upstairs are galleries devoted to ceramics, glass-
ware, as well as art ranging from the 16th century
to the present. 'Sunday Fundays' are drop-in family
activity days on the first Sunday of each month
when children may be able to handle a fossil or
meet a real Roman soldier. All children must be
accompanied by an adult. There are also holiday
activities for children and most events are free.
Since entry to the museum is also without charge,
this makes for a very cheap and fun day out.

★Bristol Zoo Gardens

Clifton **t** (0117) 973 8951 **www**.bristolzoo.org.uk
Getting there Take J17/18 from the M5 and follow
the tourist signs, or leave the M4 at J19 and follow
the M32 into the city centre, where the zoo is well
signposted. From Bristol Temple Meads station take
buses no.8 and no.9 (Traveline: **t** 0870 608 2608)
Open Summer: daily 9–5.30; winter: daily 9–5
Adm Adults £10, children £6, under 3s **free**
*Café-restaurant, picnic areas, shop, play area,
mother and baby rooms, disabled facilities,
on-site parking*

Parents may be disappointed to discover that
Bristol Zoo is not, in fact, inhabited by the grumbling camels and chattering lemurs made famous
by Johnny Morris in his delightfully off-the-wall
Animal Magic TV show. Indeed, it may come as a
surprise to learn that (horror of horrors) Johnny
wasn't actually a keeper here at all (or anywhere
else for that matter), he just pretended to be for
the purposes of the show. Nonetheless, once
you've let your disillusionment subside, you'll find
that the zoo is well worth a few hours of your
time. Go early or late to avoid long queues in the
middle of the day. Laid out amongst landscaped
gardens, it is one of the most scenic and modern

Special event
Balloon Fiesta
t (0117) 953 5884 **www**.bristolfiesta.co.uk
Adm Free (car parking £8)
Countless hot air balloons take to the skies at
Ashton Court during the second weekend in
August. Free concerts on the ground too.

zoos in the country. People no longer want to look
at animals living in small, shabby cages, they
want to see them in large enclosures, naturalistic
environments and from unusual viewpoints,
which is exactly what Bristol Zoo provides.

At the Seal and Penguin Coast, you can watch
the animals feeding and cavorting over the fence
or you can view them up close inside the walk-
through underwater tank; in Bug World, you can
put your head into a helmet-shaped enclosure
and watch locusts and spiders scuttling around
just inches from your nose; at Twilight World you
are asked to creep about on a floor covered with
bark chippings, so as not to wake the nocturnal
inhabitants. The zoo's other areas – Gorilla World,
the Reptile House, the Aquarium, the Monkey
House, the Small Mammal House and the Walk
Through Aviary – are equally well thought out,
and there's a hands-on activity centre for kids,
where they can do brass rubbings and have their
face painted to look like a lizard, a tiger or a
butterfly. There are talks every 30 minutes daily in
different zones, so you'll never be lost for something interesting to do. Be sure to check out the
Zoolympics, a series of interactive challenges,
which pit children against animals in the name of
science. Kids can test their speed, height, weight,
and even their ability to stand on one leg, against
members of the animal kingdom. The zoo is set in
splendidly maintained grounds with plenty of
space for kids to run around, plus an excellent
and very popular playground, two restaurants
providing snacks (or more filling meals) and
plenty of picnic spots. A trip to the shop afterwards to buy an adorable cuddly toy animal will
ensure they never forget such an excellent day
out. Surprising as it may seem, the zoo actually
makes a rather good rainy day option with many
of the prime attractions – including Bug World,
the Aquarium, the Gorilla House, the Monkey
House and the seal and penguin enclosures –
designed to incorporate covered viewing areas.

British Empire and Commonwealth Museum

Station Approach, Temple Meads **t** (0117) 925 4980
www.empiremuseum.co.uk
Open Daily 10–5 **Adm** Adults £6.95, children £3.95,
family (2+2) £16, under 5s **free**
*Café, library, research archive, community radio
room, kids play zone outside in summer*

This impressive museum facility charts the rise
and fall of the British Empire from the ruthless-
ness of slavers and imperialists to the creation of
the Commonwealth. The museum documents key
aspects of the period from 1480 to present day
under three headings: 'Trading Fortunes' charts
the voyages of the early traders through an interactive computer display and various cases full of
goods, including a sniff-and-see spice cabinet,
while 'Encircling the Globe' highlights the wealth
and exploitation involved in empire-building.
Exhibits show the effect of mass travel and
increased communication links, as summed up by
the brilliant timeline from penny post to e-mail.
'From colonialism to Commonwealth' deals with
the environmental and social issues surrounding
the spread of empire, as eloquently depicted in the
trade-off of exquisite foreign trinkets for medals
with the heads of monarchs on them. Each room
has a child-height question board that flips over
to reveal the answer. These make for useful
learning tools even if all the kids want to do is
make them spin like a toy windmill. Stop off here
on your way to the station for a very informative
experience that's surprisingly not dry at all.

Bus tours

Take a one-hour tour or buy the all-day hop
on/off ticket. Tours are accompanied by trained
guides. City Sightseeing Bristol, **t** 0870 4440654,
www.bristolvisitor.co.uk, run high-quality guided
bus tours of the city, which take in Bristol Zoo
Gardens, the City Museum and Art Gallery, the
Broadmead Centre and the SS *Great Britain*.
Children travel free (one per accompanying adult)
and there are discounts off the ferry and other
attractions. For details of timetables and other
tours, contact the Bristol tourist information centre
on **t** 0906 711 2191.

Cabot Tower

Brandon Hill, Great George Street **t** 0906 711 2191
Open 8–dusk; call Bristol TIC for details **Adm Free**

Situated in Brandon Hill Park, which is accessible
from Great George Street (off Park Street), Jacob

Wells Road and Berkely Square, this 32m (105ft)
tower commands stunning views of the north
Somerset coast and the Bristol Channel and even
as far as Wales on a clear day. Built in 1897 to
celebrate the 400th anniversary of the navigator
John Cabot's exploratory journey to North America
(he was the first European to set foot on the
American mainland), the tower provides an ideal
diversion for lively kids as they tackle the steep
climb to the top. The surrounding park contains a
network of terraced gardens, pathways, small
waterfalls and steps, and can provide unwilling
climbers with less exalted panoramas of the city.

Castle Park

An open grassy space next to the river, a short
distance from the Broadmead shops, Castle Park
contains a fenced sandy playground built on the
site of a medieval castle (some ruins remain),
where there are a number of wooden, castley-
looking climbing frames.

Cinemas and theatres *See pp.179, 182*

Clifton Suspension Bridge

Visitor Centre, Sion Place **t** (0117) 974 4664
www.clifton-suspension-bridge.org.uk
Open Apr–mid-Oct 10–5; mid-Oct–Mar Mon–Fri
11–4, Sat–Sun 11–5
Adm £2.50 per person for guided tour

The Clifton Suspension Bridge which, like the
SS *Great Britain*, was the work of pioneering local
engineer Isambard Kingdom Brunel, spans the
lovely Avon Gorge in the quiet, scenic part of
Bristol, where there are still several 17th- and
18th-century buildings remaining. It's a wonder of
Victorian technical virtuosity – the 75m/246ft-tall
structure looks as modern and impressive today as
it would have done when first unveiled in 1864. A
short walk from the suspension bridge is the
Clifton Observatory and Caves, **t** (0117) 924 1379,
one of the oldest observatories in Britain. It offers
panoramic views of the local area.

Industrial Museum

Princes Wharf, Wapping Road **t** (0117) 925 1470
www.bristol-city.gov.uk
Open Apr–Oct Sat–Wed 10–5; Nov–Mar Sat–Sun
10–5 **Adm Free**
Shop, mother and baby facilities, disabled facilities

The Industrial Museum celebrates Bristol's
past as a centre of excellence in the development
of transport technology. Exhibits range from

18th-century horse-drawn carriages and steam locomotives to race cars, buses and even a Concorde cockpit (built in Filton, near Bristol).

Shopping

There's so much to see and do that you'll have little time for shopping but, suffice to say, the city contains a huge complex, the Broadmead, which houses the Galleries, with over 100 high street shops under one roof. If you're looking for something more quirky and original, head over to The West End (Park Street, Queen's Road) for some individual fashion ideas and the East Side (Brunswick Square) for fabrics and crafts. Saint Nicholas Market, Corn Street, t (0117) 922 4017, a partly covered selection of stalls alternating between a mouth-watering farmers' market (Wed) and the Nails Street Market clothing emporium (Fri–Sat) are worth a browse.

Sport and activities *See pp.177–9*

SS *Great Britain*, the *Matthew* and the Maritime Heritage Centre

Great Western Dock, Gas Ferry Road
t (0117) 926 0680 **www.ssgreatbritain.org**
Open Apr–Oct daily 10–5.30; Nov–Mar daily 10–4.30
Adm Adults £8.95, children £4.95, under 5s **free**, family (2+2) £24.95
Cafés (there are several good ones outside the heritage centre), picnic area, shop, hard hat guided tours, disabled facilities, pushchair area

The SS *Great Britain*, designed by the great local engineer Isambard Kingdom Brunel, and built in Bristol in 1843, was the first iron-hulled, propeller-driven ship ever built capable of travelling across oceans and spent most of her days of operation transporting emigrants to Australia. Today, she stands in dry dock just south of Bristol's floating harbour and can be visited throughout the year, although renovation work is still being carried out. Visitors can clamber over her decks, visit the sumptuously restored dining room (it's a work in progress but the ornate stencilling and gilding are sufficiently advanced to give you an idea of the ship's grandest quarters), admire the huge bright red propellor and even take the wheel and pretend to steer the ship through the waves. The narrow flights might prove a challenge for very young children, in which case you can steer them on to the deck for a pleasant view of the harbour and

the *Matthew* alongside. She was the 15th-century ship on which John Cabot became the first man to sail to the American mainland in 1497. Perfectly restored, this comparatively small vessel is staffed by volunteers, who help bring to life conditions on board the ship in the late 15th century. The Bristol Ferry Boat Company (p.152) runs a daily service between the ships, the Industrial Museum, Millennium Square, the city centre and Temple Meads train station. The Maritime Heritage Museum, which houses a number of displays detailing Bristol's maritime history, including several life-size recreations of shipboard life, is within walking distance. There is a particularly good section on the *Matthew* covering both the original voyage and the reconstruction carried out in 1997. Some of the exhibits are used for demonstration purposes. Kids are particularly fond of the working steam crane and rides on the steam railway and locally built tug boats. The Bristol Blue Glassworks, which are located next to the SS *Great Britain*, hold demonstrations of glass-blowing at weekends.

Around Bristol

Avon Valley Country Park, 5 miles east (p.174)
Bath, 12 miles southeast (pp.148–151)
Cheddar Gorge, 13 miles southwest (pp.175–6)
Dyrham Park, 12 miles east (pp.254–5)

Dorchester

Getting there By road: Dorchester is 7 miles north of Weymouth, 15 miles west of Bournemouth on the A35 towards Lyme Regis. From the M3 take the M27 to Ringwood and on to Dorchester. By train: There are two train stations – Dorchester South, which has a regular service from London (Waterloo), Bournemouth, Southampton and Weymouth; Dorchester West has a service from Bath and Bristol Temple Meads
Tourist information Unit 11, Antelope Walk
t (01305) 267992 **www.westdorset.com**

Surrounded by rolling countryside (heathland to the east, forest to the west) with lots of pretty Georgian architecture, Dorchester makes a pleasant, albeit rather sleepy, base from which to explore the more headline-grabbing attractions of the Dorset coast. Most of the town's more child-friendly sites are located on or around the High Street, which divides into east and west sections at St Peter's Church. Top of the heap is the **Dinosaur Museum** (Dorchester is only a few miles from Lyme Regis's Jurassic Coast, one of the country's prime fossil-hunting spots), which has a large collection of fossils, some life-size reconstructions of the fearsome beasts, plus various interactive displays including 'feely' boxes and computer quizzes (all crammed into a space no bigger than a large residential house). The **Teddy Bear House**, where you can wander through rooms filled with life-size teddies, will appeal to younger children, although do also be sure to check out the **Tutankhamun Exhibition**, with its full-size tableaux reconstruction of the discovery of the famous Egyptian tomb by Howard Carter in the 1920s. Every detail of the tomb, including the mummy and the famous gold and lapis lazuli headdress, has been painstakingly reconstructed, with spooky sound and lighting effects adding to the overall ambience.

As far as food is concerned, Dorset has a well-established tradition of farmers' markets with 11 taking place across the county on a monthly basis. Dorchester's is at Poundbury, 9am–1pm on the first Saturday of the month. There's another one in Christchurch at Saxon Square (9am–1pm on the first Friday of the month). There's also an annual Dorset Food Week Festival held in October to November. For more details, visit **www**.dorsetforyou.com.

A little bit of history

Don't be fooled by its picturesque appearance. Dorchester is a town with a decidedly murky (not to say gory) past. The area was settled by the Celts some 2,000 years ago. They built a fortified town a few miles southwest of here (known as Maiden Castle; the remains of the town still exist and have become a popular tourist attraction, even though they now only consist of a large, ridged grassy mound from where there are good views of the surrounding countryside). In AD 43, the city was stormed by invading Roman armies, who massacred the inhabitants and founded a new town, *Durnovaria*, on the site of present-day Dorchester, which they furnished with a large amphitheatre where gladiatorial contests were held. After the Romans left, the theatre (known as the Maumbury Rings) continued to be used in the Middle Ages for bear-baiting and public

executions (the last took place in 1706 when a girl accused of being a witch was burned at the stake). In the late 17th century, following the Duke of Monmouth's failed attempt to lead a rebellion against King James II, Dorchester became the site of the infamous Bloody Assizes. The notorious Judge Jeffreys presided over the trials of the rebels, 74 of whom were hung, drawn and quartered, and their heads stuck on spikes and paraded through the county to deter other rebels. Find out about Dorchester's macabre past at the **Dorset County Museum** (there's a children's trail). In summer, you can visit the courtroom where the men stood trial, and sit in one of the cells where they awaited sentence.

These days, Dorchester is best known for its literary connections. This was where the novelist Thomas Hardy wrote many of his famous books (he used it as the basis for Casterbridge in *The Mayor of Casterbridge*) and it has become the unofficial headquarters of the Hardy country tourist industry, attracting thousands of visitors each year.

Things to see and do

Cinemas and theatres *See* pp.179, 182

Dinosaur Museum
Icen Way **t** (01305) 269880
www.thedinosaurmuseum.com
Open Daily Apr–Oct 9.30–5.30, Nov–Mar 10–4.30
Adm Adults £6.50, children £4.75, family £19.95, under 4s **free**
Shop, disabled access, fun sheets for kids

Dorset County Museum
High West Street **t** (01305) 262735
www.dorsetcountymuseum.org
Open Jul–Sept daily 10–5, Oct–Jun Mon–Sat 10–5
Adm Adults £6, children **free** (2 per adult, 3rd £1)
Shop, audio guide

Old Crown Court and Cells
High West Street **t** (01305) 252241
Open Court: all year Mon–Fri 10am–12 noon and 2–4; cells: guided tours mid-Jul–mid-Sept Mon–Fri 2–4.15 (not Bank Hols). Closed for 2 weeks over Christmas and New Year
Adm Free

Sport and activities *See* pp.177–9

Teddy Bear House
Antelope Walk **t** (01305) 266040
www.teddybearhouse.co.uk

Open Mon–Sat 9.30–5, Sun 10–4 **Adm** Adults
£2.95, children £1.95, family (2+2) £8.95
*Shop stocks Steiff, Merrythought and Deans bears
and animals*

★Tutankhamun Exhibition
High West Street **t** (01305) 269571
www.tutankhamun-exhibition.co.uk
Open Apr–Oct daily 9.30–5.30; Nov–Mar
Mon–Fri 9.30–5, Sat–Sun 10–5 (closed 24–6 Dec)
Adm Adults £6.50, children £4.75,
family (2+2) £19.95
Disabled access, audio guides, shop

Around Dorchester
Abbotsbury Swannery, 8 miles southwest (p.164)
Minterne Gardens, 7 miles north (p.173)
Weymouth, 7 miles south (p.164)

Glastonbury

Getting there By road: Glastonbury is 135 miles west
of London via the M3, the A303 and the A361, and 27
miles south of Bristol on the A39. By train/coach: The
nearest train station to Glastonbury is Castle Cary
(on the London Paddington to Plymouth line), a taxi
fare from here costs £25. National Express run daily
coaches from London and there are good bus links
from Bristol, Bath and Wells
Tourist information 9 High Street, The Tribunal
t (01458) 832954 **www.**glastonbury.co.uk

Glastonbury has more myths and legends associated with it than almost anywhere else in the
country. According to the tales, Christ is supposed
to have visited the area early in his life in the
company of his great uncle Joseph of Arimathea –
an episode which is strangely omitted from the
Bible. Following Christ's crucifixion, Joseph is then
meant to have returned to Glastonbury carrying
with him the Holy Grail, a goblet filled with
Christ's blood, and to have founded England's

Can you spot?
*The Glastonbury Thorn, near the main entrance
to Glastonbury Abbey, which, according to
legend, is the descendant of a tree that sprouted
from a staff stuck into the ground by Joseph
of Arimathea.*

Special event
Glastonbury Children's Festival
t (01458) 832925 **Adm** Adults £5,children £7,
3–4-year-olds £5, toddlers £2
Clowns, magicians, fun and games in Abbey Park
(Jul–Aug).

first Christian church, later to become
Glastonbury Abbey. Centuries after, a mortally
wounded King Arthur sailed to Glastonbury to die
(Glastonbury was once an island in a vast inland
lake and thus has been identified by some as the
mythical Isle of Avalon) and the bodies of Arthur
and his queen, Guinevere, supposedly lie under
the ruins of Glastonbury Abbey. Needless to say,
there is absolutely no documentary evidence for
any of these claims – although that doesn't mean
they're not true. There's something strange about
Glastonbury, something which seems to inspire
myth-makers, and which makes people think
important events must have happened here. Lately,
it has become a Mecca for a vague sort of spiritu-
alism, attracting hordes of New Agers and modern
pagans, who come to absorb its famed 'positive
energy'. It's a fascinating and serene place with its
mystical shops and mythical sites all overlooked by
the great bulk of Glastonbury Tor, although considering its fame, it's surprisingly small. Its main
sights, as well as the tourist office and most of the
decent cafés, can all be found on or around the
short High Street including, just to the south, the
ruins of Glastonbury Abbey. Although supposedly
occupying the site of England's first church, most
of what you see dates from the mid 16th century.
Henry VIII had it destroyed as part of his dissolution of the monasteries – the last abbot was hung,
drawn and quartered on top of Glastonbury Tor.
You can see a model of the abbey in the visitor
centre showing how it would have looked in its
prime. The edge of the Abbey grounds is occupied
by the charming Somerset Rural Life Museum,
where you can watch (and occasionally take part
in) a range of traditional rural crafts (cheese-
making, cider-pressing and peat digging). Note the
old-fashioned three-seat toilet, which enabled the
well-bonded family to relieve themselves together.

Just south of the abbey, in the public gardens
on Wellhouse Lane at the foot of the Tor, stands
the Chalice Well, where Joseph of Arimathea
supposedly hid the Holy Grail. This legend

probably arose as a result of the peculiar reddish water produced by the well. Not surprisingly, various healing properties have been attributed to the water. Take a drink as it pours out of the lion's head spout and put these claims to the test.

Things to see and do

Cinemas and theatres *See pp.179, 182*

Glastonbury Abbey

Abbey Gatehouse, Magdalene Street **t** (01458) 832267 www.glastonburyabbey.com
Open Dec–Jan daily 10–4.30; Feb 10–5;
Mar 9.30–5.30; Apr, May and Sept 9.30–6; Jun–Aug 9–6; Oct 9.30–5; Nov 9.30–4.30
Adm Adults £4.50, children £3, under 5s **free**, family £12.50
Shop, snack shop, mother and baby room, disabled facilities, on-site parking

★Glastonbury Tor

The dominant feature of the Glastonbury landscape, the Tor is a great conical grass hill some 160m (520ft) tall, topped by the ruins of a medieval church, which collapsed following a landslide in the 13th century. It is a steep 20-minute climb to the top but well worth it for the views out over the town below and along the vale of Avalon.

Sport and activities *See pp.177–9*

★Somerset Rural Life Museum

Abbey Farm, Chilkwell Street **t** (01458) 831197
Open Apr–Oct Tues–Fri 10–5, Sat and Sun 2–6;
Nov–Mar Tues–Sat 10–5, Bank Hols 10–5 **Adm Free**
Snack shop, gift shop, disabled facilities, on-site parking, not suitable for pushchairs

A little bit of history

King Arthur Country

As England absorbed wave after wave of Angle and Saxon invaders following the collapse of Roman rule in the 5th century AD, the Southwest became a refuge for fleeing Britons. Here, for a few centuries at least, they were safe. Their language and customs could continue to

> **Can you also spot?**
> The graves of Arthur and Guinevere marked in the abbey's graveyard grass.

> **Who was Arthur?**
> There are two King Arthurs. The first was a real historical figure, who lived in the early 5th century AD. He was a fierce Celtic warrior, who fought and won a number of battles against Anglo-Saxon invaders from continental Europe. Little is known about this Arthur; his name survives in just a handful of historical documents, the earliest written at least 200 years after his death. The second Arthur, the famous Arthur, whose exploits have been retold in hundreds of books and films, is a largely fictional character. Though based on the first Arthur, most of the tales about him were made up by English and French writers in the Middle Ages, at least 600 years after the first real Arthur died.

prosper. As time passed, however, and contact between the Southwest and the rest of Anglo-Saxon England grew, so the Britons' way of life began to come under threat. Slowly their customs began to disappear to be replaced by the customs of the dominant Anglo-Saxon society. Cornish, the direct descendant of the ancient British language, began to be spoken less and less until it almost disappeared. There is one aspect of this ancient culture, however, that refused to die out – the legend of Arthur, king of the Britons. Every schoolchild knows how Arthur, with the help of the magical sword Excalibur, Merlin the wizard and his Knights of the Round Table, repelled the invaders and sought the Holy Grail. Not surprisingly, many of the ancient sites and castles in the Southwest claim some sort of link with Arthur although, considering that there are only a tiny number of authentic historical documents bearing his name, these can be regarded at best as tenuous. Still, the stories are great fun and will give your kids something to hold on to and get excited about at what would otherwise be just another ruined building. Sites associated with Arthur include Tintagel Castle (his birthplace, p.205); Stonehenge (supposedly created by Arthur's magician Merlin, p.163); Winchester (where the 'Round Table' hangs on a wall in the town's Great Hall, p.102); Cadbury Castle (the site of Camelot, Arthur's Castle, pp.160–1), Dozmary Pool in Bolventor into which Sir Bedevere threw Excalibur, Arthur's magical sword, as the King lay dying (p.226); and Glastonbury Abbey (where Arthur and his queen, Guinevere, are supposedly buried, *see* left).

Around Glastonbury

Cadbury Castle, 10 miles southeast (pp.160–1)
Cheddar Gorge, 10 miles northwest (pp.175–6)
Fleet Air Arm Museum, Yeovilton, 8 miles south (p.180)
Haynes Motor Museum, 8 miles southeast (p.180)
Wookey Hole Caves, 7 miles northeast (p.177)

Salisbury

Getting there By road: Salisbury is 90 miles west of London on the M3 (J8) A303, A338, 50 miles east of Bristol and 21 miles west of Winchester on the A36, the A354 and the A338. The Beehive park-and-ride service runs to the centre from Amesbury on the A345. By train/coach: Trains run daily from London (Waterloo), Bath, Exeter and Portsmouth. National Express coaches run daily from London, Bath, Bristol and Portsmouth
Tourist information Fish Row t (01722) 334956
www.visitsalisbury.com

On the banks of the River Avon, Wiltshire's capital is an undeniably beautiful place, with picturesque water meadows and a litter of old buildings, some dating back to the 13th century. It is also surprisingly small, with most of its attractions grouped around its central Market Square, and can easily be navigated on foot as part of a walking tour. The town's dominant feature is its magnificent cathedral with its famous spire (at 404ft/123m it is the tallest in England), which can be seen for miles around. The main body of the cathedral was built during the 13th century (c. 1220–66) in a mere 38 years (38 years may not seem that quick but by medieval standards it was practically light speed; most cathedrals took well over 100 years to complete), while the spire was added early in the 14th century. As the original design did not include a spire, its addition caused major architectural problems. It weighs a mighty 6,400 tonnes and, if you look closely at the stone pillars supporting it, you can see that they have become bent under the enormous weight. The interior is dark and spooky with several interesting features to look out for, notably the sculpted tombs of medieval crusader heroes, the clock in the north aisle (built in 1386, this is the oldest, continuously working clock in Europe) and the

model of the cathedral in the north transept surrounded by miniature blacksmiths, carpenters and masons. Guided tours of the cathedral and tower are offered twice daily (at extra cost).

Things to see and do

Cinemas and theatres *See pp.179, 182*

Medieval Hall
West Walk, Cathedral Close t (01722) 412472
www.medieval-hall.co.uk
Open Apr–Sept (performances from 11–5)
Adm Adults £2, children £1.50, under 6s **free**
Refreshments, disabled access
Watch a 40-minute film on the history of Salisbury.

★Old Sarum Castle
Castle Road t (01722) 335398
www.english-heritage.org.uk
Open Apr–Jun daily 10–6, Jul–Aug 9–6, Sept 10–6, Oct 10–5, Nov–Mar 10–4 (closed 24–6 December and 1 January) **Adm** Adults £2.90, children £1.50
Refreshments, gift shop, on-site parking
The original site of the town until it relocated in the 13th century, this large, grassy, corrugated mound two miles north of the city centre is scattered with ruins (a castle, a cathedral and a Bishop's Palace) and offers good views of the city and south Wiltshire countryside. An excellent picnic spot, there are family activities and events laid on at the castle throughout the summer including storytellings, mask-making, Iron Age pottery, a medieval tournament and 'Jurassic Giants', an event at which kids can help archaeologists reconstruct dinosaur skeletons.

★Salisbury Cathedral
The Close, Salisbury t (01722) 555120
www.salisburycathedral.org.uk
Open Jun–Aug daily 7.15am–7.15pm; Sept–May daily 7.15am–6.15pm **Adm Free** (suggested donations: adults £3.25, children £1.50), under 8s **free**
Coffee shop, souvenir shop, wheelchair access to ground floor only
The cathedral's cloisters are the largest in the country and contain some wonderful bas relief friezes depicting early Biblical stories as well as one of the only four surviving copies of the *Magna Carta*. There are free guided tours of the cathedral on most days and a number of self-guiding leaflets. The Cathedral shop stocks a children's Explorer's Guide to the building (available for 99p).

Salisbury and South Wiltshire Museum

The King's House, 65 The Close **t** (01722) 332151
www.salisburymuseum.org.uk
Open Mon–Sat 10–5, Jul–Aug Sun 2–5
Adm Adults £4, children £1.50, family £9.50,
under 5s **free**
*Café, gift shop, mother and baby facilities,
disabled access*

This award-winning museum has interesting
displays on Stonehenge, 16th- and 17th-century
costumes, the Romans and Saxons, and pre-NHS
surgery.

Shopping

To see Salisbury at its best, visit on a Tuesday
or a Saturday when the market is in full swing.
Fruit, vegetables and clothes make up the bulk
of the market's produce, although there are a
few stalls specializing in Italian delicacies.
The Maltings Shopping Centre, **t** (01727) 844226,
adjacent to the central car park and the river,
contains a number of high street shops.
The Wilton Shopping Village on Minster Street,
t (01722) 741211, is the place to go for fashion and
homeware outlet shops.

Sport and activities *See pp.177–9*

Walking tours

Guided tours leave from outside the tourist
information centre twice daily, from May to
September, and on Fridays there is a ghost tour.
Contact Salisbury City Guides on **t** (01722) 320349.
The Wessex Horse Omnibus, **t** (0771) 8046814,
offers quick jaunts through the town, evening
tours and an exciting river ride into the Nadder
and Wylye rivers. Trips leave from the Guildhall in
the Market Square (Apr–Sept Mon–Sat 10.30–5).

Around Salisbury

Cholderton Rare Breeds Farm Park, 10 miles
northeast (p.166)
Farmer Giles Farmstead, 10 miles west (p.166)
Stonehenge, 10 miles north (p.163)

Did you know?
*That a market has been held on the same spot in
Salisbury every week since 1361 (or well over
66,000 times). That's a lot of vegetables!*

SPECIAL TRIPS

Castles and stately homes

Bowood House

Estate Office, Bowood, Calne **t** (01249) 812102
www.bowood.org
Getting there 4 miles southeast of Chippenham and
14 miles northeast of Bath off the A4 and the A342
Open Apr–Oct daily; grounds: 11–6; house: 11–5.30
Adm Adults £7.50, children £5, under 5s £3.80
*Café-restaurant, gift shop, picnic areas, mother and
baby facilities, on-site parking*

The house, which is a typically stately affair
with an exhibition on Dr Joseph Priestly (who
discovered oxygen) and a collection of English
watercolours, sculpture and Napoleonic memorabilia, won't be of much interest to young children,
but the grounds will be. They contain one of the
best adventure playgrounds around, with huge
coloured slides, hanging walkways and a giant
pirate galleon complete with rigging and a crow's
nest for spotting unwanted invaders (like parents
wanting to leave). The site, which is revamped
every year, has been extended to include
spiralling metal flumes, accessed from a wooden
tower and a soft play palace for younger children
to enjoy. Elsewhere, in the Capability Brown landscaped gardens, you'll find a lake, an 8m/25ft-high
cascade, a mock Greek temple, grassy lawns, acres
of shady woodland and, best of all, a spooky cave
(known as the Hermit's Cave), with fossils and
semi-precious stones embedded in the walls.

Cadbury Castle

Contact the council **t** (01935) 841302
Getting there Cadbury is 10 miles southeast of
Glastonbury, off the A303

Do Cadbury's grassy mounds hide a wondrous
secret? Did these 300ft (91m) earth ramparts
once support the mighty weight of Camelot,
castle of the legendary King Arthur? Is it true
that every Christmas Eve, the hillside cracks open
to let the King and his knights gallop down to
the nearby stream to water their horses? That's
what's been claimed. But, then, that's what's
been claimed about a dozen other sites in Wales
and the Southwest. In fact, there seems little
doubt that the mound actually covers the
remains of a 2,500-year-old Iron Age fort, which
is pretty interesting, but not nearly as exciting as
imagining that it contains the sleeping form of
the Once and Future King. That's the thing about
visiting King Arthur country – it's sometimes

more fun thinking about what mysterious thing might be there than it is looking at what actually is there. It's a strenuous climb to the top of the mound from where you can see the 158m (520ft) Glastonbury Tor or, as some say, the mystical kingdom of Avalon. Your kids will probably insist on a piggy back about halfway up.

Corfe Castle

The Square, Corfe, Wareham **t** (01929) 481294
www.corfecastle.org.uk
Getting there On the Isle of Purbeck between Wareham and Swanage, just off the A351
Open Apr–Sept 10–5.30, Oct 10–5, Nov–Feb 10–4
Adm Adults £5 children £2.50, family £12.50 (2+3), £7.50 (1+3)
Café, shop, visitor centre, baby changing facilities, guided tours, disabled access, quiz, trails and family backpacks, children's guide

Corfe Castle, which towers above the tiny stone village of Corfe, was built by the Normans in 1066 and destroyed by Parliamentary troops during the Civil War some half a millennium later. Today, the ruins provide wonderful views of the Purbeck coast and countryside and there are various events and children's activity days organized here during the summer. To see what the castle would have looked like in its heyday, visit the model village in the town (on West Street).

Dunster Castle

Dunster, near Minehead **t** (01643) 821314
www.nationaltrust.org.uk
Getting there Dunster is 3 miles southeast of Minehead on the A396
Open Mar–25 Oct daily 11–5, 26 Oct–2 Nov 11–4; park and gardens: Jan–Mar and end Oct–end Dec 11–4, Apr–Oct 10–5
Adm Adults £7.50, children £3.80, family £18.50; park and garden only: adults £4.10, children £2, family £10
Picnic area, shop, mother and baby facilities, disabled access, on-site parking, buggy park, colouring sheets and activity days

Dunster was restored to fairytale specifications in the 19th century, following a good deal of Civil War damage. Only the 13th-century gateway from the original castle survives. The surrounding 12 hectares (30 acres) of park contain subtropical blooms and offer towering views of Exmoor and the Bristol Channel. It's a steep 10-minute walk from the car park; transport can be arranged.

Kingston Lacy

Wimborne Minster **t** (01202) 883402
www.nationaltrust.org.uk
Getting there The house is on the B3082 Blandford–Wimborne road, 1 mile west of Wimborne. The nearest train station is Poole (8 miles) and buses go from Bournemouth, Poole (passing by the station) and Shaftesbury; alight at Wimborne Square. For more information call **t** (01202) 673555
Open House: Mid-Mar–Oct Wed–Sun 11–5; garden and park: daily 10.30–6 (weekends only Feb–Mar and Fri–Sun Nov–Dec 10.30–4)
Adm Adults £9, children £4.50, family £22
Restaurant with children's meals, shop, mother and baby facilities, restricted disabled access, on-site parking, children's guide, quiz, trails and play area

This grand mansion was built in the 17th century by the fiercely royalist Bankes family when their beloved Corfe Castle was destroyed by the Parliamentarians in 1646. The house was acquired by the National Trust in the 1980s; parts of it are still a little run-down, although there is nonetheless a good deal to see.

Kids get their own guidebook, which will point out the most interesting features of the house and gardens, including the servants' quarters, the Spanish Room and the ancient Egyptian obelisks in the garden. There are also woodland walks through fields grazed by North Devon cattle. Try to come on one of their regular event days when kids can take part in a range of historically themed activities.

Lacock Abbey, Fox Talbot Museum and Village

High Street, Lacock, Chippenham **t** (01249) 730459
www.nationaltrust.org.uk
Getting there 3 miles south of Chippenham off the A350
Open Mar–Nov daily 11–5.30
Adm Adults £7.80, children £3.90, family £20
Restaurant, café, picnic areas, shop, wheelchair access, parking, children's guide, quiz and trail

This well-preserved 13th-century abbey has had a long and abiding association with film. It is where, in 1835, the world's first photographic negative image (of the abbey itself) was taken by local inventor Fox Talbot and more recently it has been used as a location for *Pride and Prejudice*, *Emma*, *Moll Flanders* and the Harry Potter films.

The building now contains a museum of photography and is surrounded by fine gardens. Easter egg hunts, woodland tours and colouring competitions for children are organized throughout the year.

★Longleat

Warminster t (01985) 844400 **www**.longleat.co.uk
Getting there Situated on the A36 Warminster bypass, follow signs between Bath and Salisbury
Open Safari park: Apr–5 Nov daily 10–4; house: all year 10–5.30, guided tours 11–3 (closed 25 Dec)
Adm Passport ticket: adults £19, children £15, valid all season for one visit to each of the attractions
Café, restaurant, picnic areas, mother and baby facilities, guided tours, disabled access, on-site parking

The first private stately home to open its doors to the public, Longleat has firmly established itself as one of the country's very best safari parks, with lions, tigers (including a rare white tiger), monkeys, giraffes, rhinos, elephants and sea lions among its residents. Families without cars can use the Safari Bus service (commentary provided), although there are a few sections of the park which can be tackled on foot. Walking past giraffes, llamas and zebras (although, thankfully, not lions), kids can pretend they are on a real safari out on the African plains. Don't miss the boat trip to see the gorillas on the island – children enjoy feeding the seals and sea lions *en route*. And if the kids become tired of the animals, there is lots more to keep them amused. See if they can find their way out of the 3D hedge maze, take a ride on the narrow-gauge railway or explore the Butterfly Garden. There are exhibitions on Postman Pat and Doctor Who, a King Arthur-themed mirror maze, a Blue Peter maze, and a pets' corner.

Stourhead

Stourton, Warminster t (01747) 841152
www.nationaltrust.org.uk
Getting there Stourhead is 3 miles northwest of Mere (A303), off the B3092, 8 miles south of Frome
Open House: Mar–Oct Fri–Tues 11.30–4.30; tower: daily Mar–Oct 11.30–4.30, Apr–Sept 10–5.30, Oct 10–5, Nov–Feb 10.30–4; gardens: 9–dusk all year
Adm Adults £10.40 children £5.20, family £24.70
Café, picnic area, shop, mother and baby facilities, disabled access, on-site parking, tours

Georgian stately home that does its best to make itself accessible for families, with quiz sheets, events and interesting features in the gardens. These include temples, statues, grottoes and follies – look out for King Alfred's Tower; climb the 221 steps for the great views out over Somerset.

Prehistoric sites

★Avebury Stone Circle

Avebury, near Marlborough, Wiltshire
t (01672) 539250 **www**.nationaltrust.org.uk
Getting there About 10 miles south of Swindon and 22 miles east of Bath, off the A4361 and the A4
Open All year; museum: Apr–Oct 10–6 Nov–Mar 10–4 (closed 24–5 Dec)
Adm Free Museum: adults £4.20, children £2.10, family £10.50 (2+3), £7.50 (1+3)
Restaurant with children's menu, picnic areas, shops, parking, baby changing facilities, children's guide

The trouble with Stonehenge is that as it has become so popular, you're no longer allowed to go right up to the stones. At Avebury, a slightly lesser-known ancient stone monument 19 miles to the north, you can get as close as you like, providing you stick to the designated paths, allowing you to fully appreciate just how big these great monoliths really are and what a feat of engineering it must have been for the ancient people to get them into position without the help of modern tools and technology. There are three circles: two inner ones and one large outer one; the outer one is so large it actually encircles the village and has been cut into quarters (or sectors named northwest, northeast, southwest and southeast) by the two main roads running through it. Built some 3,500 years ago, there are obviously quite a lot of stones missing (many were used by villagers in the Middle Ages to build houses), although the northwest and southwest sectors are more or less complete. Children love following the circle around (careful crossing the roads), counting off the stones, noting the missing ones and, of course, clambering on top of some of the smaller ones. The on-site museum, housed in a 17th-century threshing barn, uses audiovisual technology to describe the building of the site and explore stories pertaining to its use.

If you're particularly interested in ancient sites then the stretch of the A4 just south of Avebury, between Marlborough and Chippenham, will make for some fascinating drives, or walks along

Can you find?
The Barber's Stone, so named because in the 14th century it toppled over and killed a barber who happened to be walking past; and the Swindon Stone, which is the largest of all the stones, weighing a massive 65 tonnes. It is the only stone never to have toppled over (even on to a barber).

the Ridgeway Path, past chalk horses carved into the hillside (p.175) and strange prehistoric burial mounds known as barrows. The most famous of these mounds can be found at West Kennet, just south of Avebury (it's about three-quarters of a mile walk from the road; free entry). The barrow, which was built around 4,000 years ago, is just over 100 metres (328 feet) long and divided into several spooky, explorable chambers (bring a torch), which provided a final resting place for around 50 people. The stones marking the entrance each weigh a mighty seven to 10 tonnes and would have required hundreds of men to haul them into position.

Just north of the barrow is the great turfy flat-tened cone of Silbury Hill, the largest man-made mound in Europe (40m/130ft high). It was built around 2,500 years ago and, as with many ancient sites, its precise purpose remains unknown.

★Stonehenge

Amesbury, Salisbury **t** (01722) 343834
www.english-heritage.org.uk/stonehenge
Getting there 2 miles west of Amesbury on the junction of the A303 and the A344/A360. Salisbury train station is 9.5 miles away. Call Salisbury TIC for buses on **t** (01722) 334956
Open 16 Mar–31 May 9.30–6, 1 Jun–31 Aug 9–7, 1 Sept–15 Oct 9.30–6, 16 Oct–15 Mar 9.30–4
Adm Adults £5.90, children £3, family £14.80 (2+3)
Shop, refreshments, wheelchair access, on-site parking
Please note: *The Stonehenge Project is a combined initiative between English Heritage, the National Trust and the Highways Agency to improve visitor conditions. Stonehenge is currently overshadowed by the A303, which cuts through the heart of the site. Plans are underway to run the A303 through a tunnel, move the car park and restore the surrounding fields to grassland*

One of the world's most famous and mysterious ancient monuments, Stonehenge has been astounding and baffling people in equal measure for centuries. Standing in the centre of Wiltshire's great Salisbury Plain, it consists of a huge outer ring of stones arranged in a series of trilithons (two upright stones with another stone laid as a lintel across the top), inside of which are two concentric horseshoe arrangements of smaller stones and a central altar stone. There's also another ring outside the main ring but only a few of these stones remain. The oldest stones, known as bluestones, which make up the inner horse-shoe, were transported here from the Welsh Coast some 4,000 years ago – presumably by sea, river and then, once on land, on wooden rollers (a round trip of some 240 miles) – a very impressive feat when you consider that each stone weighs around four tonnes. The larger outer stones were added around 1,000 years later and were prob-ably quarried less than 20 miles from the site. Such is their size (each weighs over 40 tonnes) that it has been estimated it would have taken about 600 people to move them into position.

The complex had some sort of religious or mystical significance for whoever built it. The inner stones have been arranged so that they point towards the sun as it rises for the summer solstice on midsummer's day, although no one knows why. In the 18th century, certain scholars believed it had been a site of human sacrifice, although no evidence has been found linking Stonehenge with such practices. Others have claimed that it may have had a more secular use and that its astronomical alignment was simply a means of measuring time. Whatever its purpose, it is still an impressive sight, indeed one of the must-see sights of the entire country.

The demands of conservation mean that you're no longer allowed to wander in among the stones and, in fact, have to stand quite a way back. The entrance fee includes an audio guide, which will fill you in on the background history and the current state of scholarly debate regarding the use of the stones. For the best views, however, you should come just after dawn when, in the swirling early morning mist, you can really get a sense of the stones' mystery and power – features which tend to get rather diluted when you're standing amongst hordes of snapping, chattering tourists.

Animal attractions

★Abbotsbury Swannery

Abbotsbury, Weymouth **t** (01305) 871858
www.abbotsbury-tourism.co.uk
Getting there 10 miles from Weymouth, take the
coast road towards Bridport then follow the signs
from Abbotsbury village
Open Mar–Oct daily 10–6
Adm Adults £7.50, children £4.50. Season ticket
(unlimited entry for 12 months to gardens, swannery and activity barn): adults £28, children £23,
family (2+3) £59
*Café-restaurant, picnic areas, shop, mother and
baby facilities, disabled access, on-site parking*

Over a thousand swans come every year to
the largest swan sanctuary in the country, to
nest in the shelter provided by Chesil Beach. In
early summer, when the nesting is in full swing,
it can seem as if there's nothing but swans as
far as the eye can see – a vast white carpet of
birdlife spread out before you, interspersed
with patches of grey cygnets. As you follow the
paths through the sanctuary, you may see eggs
hatching and lines of cygnets being taken for
walks or swimming lessons by their parents.

Mass feedings of the birds take place every
day at noon and 4pm when visitors are invited
to help. Be warned, however, that this will be a
very different experience from the average
bird-feeding – your local pond with its half-
dozen rather timid specimens hardly compares.
A seething mass of swans descends on the
keepers, which can be a little overwhelming for
very young children, and terribly exciting for
older ones. There are nature trails through the
site including an Ugly Duckling trail for very
young children and you can watch an audiovisual show on the life of swans, which is
shown on the hour throughout the day. When
the swan's feathers moult in August, they are

Did you know?
*That the swannery was first established over 600
years ago as a means of providing swan meat for
the monks in the local abbey. Nowadays, all
swans belong to the Queen and are protected
from being eaten by law.*

collected and used to adorn the helmets of the
Queen's bodyguards. Larger feathers are sent to
Lloyd's of London to be turned into quill pens.
Warning: Parking is a long walk from the site.

★Bristol Zoo Gardens

Clifton **t** (0117) 9747399 **www.bristolzoo.org.uk**
Getting there Take J17/18 from the M5 and follow
the tourist signs, or leave the M4 at J19 and follow
the M32 into the city centre, where the zoo is well
signposted. From Bristol Temple Meads station
take the no.8 and no.9. Traveline **t** 0870 608 2608
Open Summer: daily 9–5.30; winter: daily 9–5
Adm Adults £10, children £6, under 3s **free**,
family £29

The zoo contains a Gorilla World, a Reptile
House, an Aquarium, a Monkey House, a Small
Mammal House, a Walk Through Aviary and more.
For further information *see* p.153

Horse World Centre

Staunton Manor Farm, Staunton Lane, Whitchurch
t (01275) 540173 **www.horseworld.org.uk**
Getting there Off the A37
Open Easter–Sept 10–5; daily 10–4 (closed Monday
from end Sept)
Adm Adults £5.74, children £4.75 under 3s **free**,
family £19.50
*Tea Barn, picnic areas, craft and gift shop, disabled
facilities, on-site parking, nature trail*

From Shetland ponies to Shire horses, all equestrian life is here. The impressive equine complex
also houses a Horse Museum, a Horse World
Theatre, an indoor and outdoor adventure playground with rope bridges, slides and soft play
equipment, plus a small animal centre, 'Noah's
Ark', with goats, lambs and rabbits for children to
play with and cuddle.

★Longleat

Warminster **t** (01985) 844400 **www.longleat.co.uk**
Getting there On the A36, Warminster bypass,
follow signs between Bath and Salisbury
Open Safari park: Apr–5 Nov daily 10–4; house: all
year 10–5.30, guided tours 11–3 (closed 25 Dec)
Adm Passport ticket: adults £19, children £15, valid
all season for one visit to each of the attractions

The stately home's grounds contain a safari
park, the largest hedge maze in the country, a
narrow-gauge railway, a tethered balloon and
much more.
For further information *see* p.162

Monkey World

Longthorns, Wareham **t** (01929) 462537
Infoline: **t** 0800 456600 **www.**monkeyworld.co.uk
Getting there On the Bere Regis–Wool road, off the A31; London Waterloo runs a train service to Wool (Mon–Sat)
Open Daily 10–5; Jul and Aug daily 10–6
Adm Adults £9, children £6.50, family (2+2) £27, family (1+2) £20
Café, gift shop, barbecue areas, baby changing facilities, disabled access, parking, woodland walk

Monkey World is a bit of a misnomer for, while there are indeed plenty of monkeys living here in this 24-hectare (60-acre) park in the heart of the Dorset countryside (including marmosets and macaques), the most prominent and important residents are apes – or, to be precise, chimpanzees. This is one of Europe's leading rescue centres for abused chimps. All the chimps living here have been rescued from dire straits. Some were being used as props by beach photographers, while others were performing in circuses or being experimented upon in laboratories. In each instance, they were snatched from their mothers whilst still young and smuggled out of Africa. At the park, however, they have the chance to return to something like normality. Living in large, naturalistic enclosures, they can learn once again how to bond with other chimps and how to behave in a natural 'wild' way. For this reason, visitors are not allowed to touch them or have close contact with the apes.

Although the centre performs an important role in animal conservation, it is still a fun and welcoming place to visit. Watching the young chimps playing in the nursery, it's difficult to believe that they have been rescued from a life of misery. The centre is also home to orangutans, gibbons and lemurs. If the kids still have some energy, let them loose on the obstacle course (mischievously located by the chimp enclosure), viewing tower and mini motorbikes.

Paignton Zoo Environmental Park

Totnes Road, Paignton **t** (01803) 697500
www.paigntonzoo.org.uk
Getting there A3022 Totnes Road, 1 mile from Paignton; M5/A380
Open Summer: daily 10–6; winter: 10–4.30 (last entry one hour before closing)
Adm Adults £11.35, children £7.60, family £34.10

Restaurant, snack bars, souvenir shop, toilets with baby changing facilities, disabled facilities including electric scooter/wheelchair hire, on-site parking, picnic area and nature trail

Paignton Zoo began life as Torbay Zoological Gardens in 1923, eventually becoming an Environmental Park in 1996 following mixed fortunes and a variety of manifestations. These days, the zoo is an educational and scientific charity dedicated to conserving wildlife across the globe and promoting respect for animals and the environment. The 30-hectare (75-acre) site is divided into zones, which represent forest, savannah, tropical rainforest, wetlands and desert environments. You'll find red pandas, marmots, baboons, monkeys, kangaroos, white rhino, wolves, ostriches, zebras, giraffes, elephants, lemurs, orangutans, gorillas, Asiatic lions and Sumatran tigers, plus numerous rare and endangered species of birds and plants. There are also indoor and outdoor play areas, competitions, face-painting, a miniature railway and a programme of talks and feeding times.

★Tropiquaria

Washford Cross, Watchet **t** (01984) 640688
www.tropiquaria.co.uk
Getting there Just off the A39 between Williton and Minehead
Open Apr–Sept daily 10–6
Adm Adults £6.95 children £5.95
Café-restaurant 'The Parrot's Perch', picnic areas, souvenir shop, mother and baby room, disabled facilities, on-site parking

There are few more imaginative displays of animals in the country than Tropiquaria. This former BBC transmitting station (you can still see the radio masts on the roof and there are examples of early wireless equipment on show) has been transformed in recent years into an amazing ersatz jungle. Its main hall is now a mass of seething, steaming vegetation with palm trees, waterfalls, vines and creepers providing a habitat for various free-roaming animals, insects and birds. As you follow the boardwalk through the jungle, you'll come across iguanas and geckos perched on enormous palm leaves, spiders and giant millipedes scuttling through the undergrowth, snapping turtles and alligators swimming lazily around shallow pools, while flocks of tropical birds fly overhead.

Beneath the hall is an aquarium, full of shoals of colourful fish, while outside there is a landscaped garden and picnic area where turkeys and pot-bellied pigs wander through the tables snaffling any spillages or leftovers. Kids can get much closer to the animals at Tropiquaria than they would at a normal zoo. During one of the regular 'meet the animals' sessions they may even get the chance to hold a tarantula, or have a 4m (12ft) boa constrictor draped around their neck – which is perhaps a little too close for some.

Should you tire of all the animals, there is also a sandpit, trampolines, a children's playground with an adventure fort and pirate ships, and an excellent puppet theatre – shows take place on the hour during the summer and last around 20 minutes; a bell sounds throughout the complex to herald the start of each performance.

Farms

Animal Farm Country Park

Red Road, Berrow, near Burnham-on-Sea
t (01278) 751628 www.animal-farm.co.uk
Getting there Take J22 from the M5 and follow the tourist signs
Open Daily 10–5.30 (until 5pm in winter)
Adm £5.50, under 2s **free**
Café, mother and baby room, on-site parking

Good, solid farm fun with lots of animals for children to stroke, nature trails and play areas (including an indoor play area for toddlers), as well as a small nature reserve in the nearby sand dunes. The farm is just one mile from the beach.

Cholderton Rare Breeds Farm

Amesbury Road, Cholderton, Salisbury t (01980) 629438 www.rabbitworld.co.uk
Getting there The farm can be reached via the A303 from London and the A338 from Salisbury
Open Apr–Nov daily 10–6
Adm Adults £5.50, children £3.95, family £15.50
Café-restaurant, farm shop, mother and baby facilities, disabled access, on-site parking

The centre's function is twofold. Its main role, as home to British Animal Heritage, is to preserve traditional farm breeds for future generations, while its secondary role is to welcome and entertain families – it seems to perform both ably. Small children will love Rabbit World, which is home to more than 50 breeds of rabbit (that's a lot of stroking), and there are goats, sheep and donkeys to meet, as well as a large, shaggy Shire horse. The centre also has a nature trail, picnic areas, a toddlers' play area, adventure playgrounds and it can offer tractor rides and pony rides in summer. Pig racing on summer weekends.

Court Farm Country Park

Wolvershill Road, Banwell t (01934) 822383
www.courtfarmcountrypark.co.uk
Getting there 2 miles from Weston-super-Mare, M5 (J21), follow the brown signs
Open Apr–Oct daily 10–5.30; Nov–Mar 10.30–4.30
Adm Adults £5.75, children £4.25, family £17 (2+2)
Tearoom, gift shop, picnic area, disabled access, toilets, parking

Children of all ages can swing themselves silly in the two large indoor playgrounds, or visit the calves, horses, goats and sheep in the barn. There are bottle-feeding shows twice a day and visitors are invited to walk the goats, groom the ponies and meet the ferrets. There's a pets' corner, play area, tractor playground and sandpit for younger children and tractor rides, pony rides, trampolines and all-terrain Big Cat rides for older ones. In July there's also an Amazing Monster Ocean Maze.

Exmoor Falconry and Animal Farm

West Lynch Farm, Allerford, Porlock t (01643) 862816 www.exmoorfalconry.co.uk
Getting there Allerford is 5 miles west of Minehead, just off the A39
Open Mar–Oct daily 10.30–5; Nov–Feb 10.30–4
Adm Adults £7 children £5.50, under 3s **free** (Nov–Feb all tickets £5)
Shop, snacks, guided tours, disabled facilities, pony rides, hawk walks and experience days, parking

Watch expert bird handlers flying a range of birds of prey over the moors. On one of their special 'Hawking' days, you can even have a go at handling the birds yourself. Exmoor safaris and horse-riding are also offered.

Farmer Giles Farmstead

Teffont, Salisbury t (01722) 716338
www.farmergiles.co.uk
Getting there From Salisbury take the A36 to Wilton and the A30 to Shaftesbury, then at Barford St Martin take the B3089 towards Hindon and follow the brown signs at Teffont

Open Mar–Nov 10–6; winter weekends 10–dusk
Adm Adults £4.50, children £3.50, family £14
'Old Barn' restaurant (traditional farm food), picnic areas, farm shop, guided tours, mother and baby facilities, disabled access, parking, vineyard

Farmer Giles has got pretty much everything you'd want from a day out at the farm – indoor and outdoor play areas, pigs, Shetland ponies, Shire horses, donkeys, sheep (with lambs to bottle-feed in early summer), a pets' corner, tractor rides (you get to sit in a trailer full of hay bales) and over 150 dairy cows. There is even an opportunity to have a go at hand-milking the cows – not as easy as it looks.

Farmer Palmer's Farm Park

Wareham Road, Organford, Poole **t** (01202) 622022
www.farmerpalmer.co.uk
Getting there The farm is off the A35, 4 miles from Poole, heading towards Bere Regis
Open Apr–Oct 10–5.30, Nov–Dec Fri–Sun 10–4
Adm Adults £4.95, children £4.75, family £18.50, under 3s **free**
Café, gift shop, guided tours, disabled access, on-site parking, tractor playground, woodland walks

This busy working dairy farm, just four miles outside Poole, welcomes families throughout the summer, when there are lots of opportunities for kids to get close to the animals. They can feed and cuddle the lambs, goat kids and piglets, and groom the ponies. There is also an undercover play area and tractor rides.

Noah's Ark Zoo Farm

Clevedon Road, Wraxhall **t** (01275) 852606
www.noahsarkzoofarm.co.uk
Open Mid-Feb–Mar Sat, Apr Mon–Sat, May–Aug Mon–Sat, Sept–Oct Tues–Sat 10.30–5
Adm Adults £8, children £6, under 2s **free**, family £25
Café, picnic areas, gift shop, disabled access

This small zoo is home to over eighty types of animal including rhinos, giraffes, marmosets, snakes, rabbits, emus and owls. Once the kids have had their fill of animal watching there are trampolines, a sandpit, a drop slide, an adventure playground, an indoor soft play area and the longest hedge maze in the world to investigate. Don't forget to give the educational maze a go too; the route can be worked out by solving a number of animal clues.

Norwood Farm

Bath Road, Norton St Philip, Bath **t** (01373) 834356
www.norwoodfarm.co.uk
Getting there The farm is 4 miles south of Bath on the B3110 Bath–Frome road
Open Mar–Sept daily 10.30–5.30
Adm Adults £5, children £3.50
Café, picnic area, gift shop, disabled facilities

Organic, environmentally friendly show farm set in acres of beautiful countryside. It has over 30 different types of animals, which means that, depending on the time of year, your kids should be able to see some or all of the following: lambs, goat kids, piglets, calves, foals and chicks. There is also a playground, a picnic area and nature trails.

Putlake Adventure Farm

Langton Matravers, Swanage **t** (01929) 422917
www.putlakefarm.co.uk
Open Apr–Oct daily 10–5, Nov–Dec Wed–Sun 10–4.30
Adm Adults £4.50, children £4.25, under 4s **free**, family (2+2) £16.50
Café, picnic areas, disabled facilities, on-site parking

Lots of hands-on farm fun – lambs and goat kids to bottle-feed, chickens to collect eggs from, cows to hand-milk (every day at 4pm) and ponies to ride. There's ferret-racing daily at 1.30pm (the ferrets run down a plastic tube) and tractor rides.

Roves Farm

Sevenhampton, near Highworth, Swindon
t (01793) 763939 **www**.rovesfarm.co.uk
Getting there Roves Farm is off the B40 Highworth–Shrivenham road and is signposted off the A361 and the A420
Open Mar–Oct Wed–Sun and Bank Hols 10.30–5, summer daily
Adm Adults £5.50, children £4.50, under 3s **free**
Café, picnic site, disabled access, on-site parking, nature walks, all-terrain pushchairs for hire

Sheep farm with lambs to bottle-feed in spring and shearing demonstrations in summer. There's a pets' corner, bouncy castle, ball pit and straw bale maze, an adventure playground and an indoor heated toddler play area. Guided walks and tractor rides also offered. Roves Farm also boasts the world's biggest living willow maze and 'Willennium Dome'.

Sea-life centres

SeaQuarium

Marine Parade, Weston-super-Mare **t** (01934) 613361 **www.**seaquariumweston.co.uk
Open Summer daily 10–5 (last admission 4pm); ring for winter opening times
Adm Adults £5.75, children £4.75, under 4s **free**, family £19.99 (2+2)

Overlooking the beach, there's a walk-through sea bed tunnel.
For further information *see* p.172

Sea Life Centre

Lodmoor Country Park, Greenhill **t** (01305) 761070
www.sealifeeurope.com
Open Summer: daily 10–5; winter: Mon–Fri 11–4, Sat and Sun 10–4
Adm Adults £11.50, children £8, under 3s **free**

The centre has all the usual exhibits, including sharks, rays and sea horses, and offers a range of activities for children.
For further information *see* p.173

Beside the seaside

Bournemouth

Getting there By road: Bournemouth is 100 miles from London via the A31 and the M3.
By train/coach: Trains from London run from Waterloo Station. Bournemouth's train station is about one mile east of the town centre. National Express run a regular coach service from London
Tourist information Westover Road **t** 0906 802 0234; accommodation **t** (01202) 451700 **www.**bournemouth.co.uk

There are three sides to Bournemouth: a sleepy side (it is one of the country's most popular resorts with senior citizens); a lively side (its nightlife is second only to Brighton's on the south coast) and a family-friendly side – its beaches, parks and events attract hordes of family holiday-makers during the summer months. Apart from the beach itself, which is one of the cleanest and best maintained in England, there are parks and gardens covering one-sixth of the town's area. At the Lower Gardens, just back from the seafront, you can take a ride in the **Bournemouth Eye** – a tethered balloon that ascends to a height of a 150m

(500ft) every 15 minutes and, in summer, you can watch storytellers, illusionists and comedians at the Pagoda, as part of the town's annual Festival of Fun. The festival runs from late July until the end of August and includes a colourful candlelit display every Wednesday night and free firework events at the end of the pier every Friday. There's also a free Kids Entertain-tent and Game Zones on the beach. 'Kids Free Family Festival' leaflets are available from the tourist office. The beach, which is patrolled by lifeguards, operates a Kidzone safety scheme, which splits the seafront into eight colour-coded sections (kids are issued with matching wristbands). The town's best rainy day attractions are all clustered around the pier. These include an IMAX 3D cinema and the **Oceanarium**, a well-stocked sea life centre. The pier itself is cheerful and bustling and has a small amusement centre at the end, with tea cup rides and radio-controlled cars.

Bournemouth Eye

Lower Gardens **t** (01202) 314539
www.bournemouthballoon.com
Operating times Apr–Sept 7.30–11pm
Adm Adults £10, children £6, under 2s **free**
Wheelchair accessible, illuminated night flights

Oceanarium

Pier Approach, West Beach **t** (01202) 311990
www.oceanarium.co.uk
Open Daily 10–5 (stays open later in the summer)
Adm Adults £7.50, children £5, family (2+2) £21.50, family (2+3) £25.50
Café, gift shop, mother and baby facilities, disabled access

Sheridon IMAX Theatre,

Pier Approach, Bournemouth **t** 01202 200 000
www.bournemouthimax.com
Adm Single/double film: Adult £6/£9, child £4.50/£6.80, family (1+2) £13/£27 , family (2+2) £18/£27

Christchurch

Getting there By road: From London and the southeast take the M3 and the M27, and Southampton via the A337. By train/coach: Christchurch station has regular services from London Waterloo, Poole, Southampton, Bournemouth and Weymouth and there's a bus service from Bournemouth
Tourist information 23 High Street **t** (01202) 471780

www.christchurchtourism.info

Christchurch is a much more stately, sedate resort than neighbouring Bournemouth. It has six safe, sandy beaches stretching across the sweep of Christchurch Bay of which Avon Beach, with its deckchairs and pleasure rides, is probably the best. Just outside the town is the **Adventure Wonderland** (formerly the Alice In Wonderland Park), which has swing boats, go-karts and an astroslide, and is inhabited by costumed characters from the Alice books.

Look out for the town crier on the walkabout in the summer. Dressed in traditional costume and ringing his bell, he will point out all the local sights. Contact the tourist office for dates and times.

Adventure Wonderland

Merritown Lane **t** (01202) 483444
www.adventurewonderland.co.uk
Open Apr–Sept daily 10–6
Adm £9.25, under 3s **free**
Restaurant, gift shop

Lulworth Castle

Wareham, East Lulworth **t** (01929) 400352
www.lulworth.com
Getting there 3 miles northeast of Lulworth Cove
Open Jan–Mar Sun–Fri 10–4, Apr–Sept 10.30–6, Oct–Dec 10.30–4.

Mary Anning

The tongue-twister 'she sells seashells on the sea shore' is about a girl called Mary Anning, who lived in Lyme Regis in the early 19th century. As a child, she used to hunt for fossils and shells on local beaches with her father, which they would then sell to visitors. Unfortunately, Mary's father died when she was still young leaving the young girl and her family facing destitution – in those days, the father was nearly always the family's sole bread winner. Fate lent a hand, however, for in 1811, when just 12 years old, Mary uncovered a complete *ichthyosaurus* (a sea-living reptile about the size of a dolphin) fossil in a rockfall, which she was able to sell for the then princely sum of £24, thereby saving her family from ruin. Encouraged by her success, Mary subsequently went on to become one of the country's first professional fossil-hunters. The *ichthyosaurus* she found is now on display at the Natural History Museum in London.

Adm Adults £8.50, children £4.50, family £21 (2+3), family (1+3) £14
Play area, woodland walks, farm, activity room

This former 15th-century hunting lodge has survived civil war and a fire, which practically destroyed the building. English Heritage has worked to restore the castle, alongside the Weld family, whose ancestors have owned it since 1641. Visitors can now go below stairs, climb the tower, and enjoy half term and summer events, such as jousting, in the grounds.

Lulworth Cove

Getting there The cove is on the Dorset coast, 9 miles east of Weymouth off the B3070, which links to the A352

An almost perfect loop of sand overlooked by high, craggy cliffs, Lulworth is an understandably popular beauty spot and best appreciated outside high summer. There are good coastal walks to the west taking you past sheltered sandy bays and bizarre rock formations to Durdle Door, where a natural rock arch has been formed by the crashing sea. The Lulworth Cove Heritage Centre tells the story of the area's geological formation and has an exhibition on smuggling.

Lulworth Cove Heritage Centre

Main Road, Lulworth Cove **t** (01929) 400587
Open Mar–Oct 10–5, school summer holidays 10–6, winter 10–4
Adm Free
Café, picnic areas, shop, tours, on-site parking

Lyme Regis

Getting there By road: The M5 provides access from the north to Lyme Regis, exiting at Taunton. It is reached from the east via the M3 and the A303 heading for Ilminster or Crewkerne and is linked to Poole by the A35. By train/coach: The nearest train station is in Axminster, 5 miles to the north. National Express coaches run daily from Exeter
Tourist information Guildhall Cottage, Church Street, Lyme Regis **t** (01297) 442138
www.lymeregis.com

England's fossil headquarters – Lyme Regis's elegant shoreline has been dubbed the 'Jurassic Coast' and recognized as a World Heritage Site owing to the number of fossils found among the rockfalls from its 195 million-year-old clay and limestone undercliff. Small molluscs, like ammonites, belemites and trilobites, are the most common finds, although entire dinosaurs, such as the ocean-going *ichthyosaurus* and flying *ptero-dactyl* have also turned up. Guided fossil walks set out from the excellent dinosaur museum, **Dinosaurland**, which has a wide collection of fossils found in the area and can identify any you may find. The town itself makes a pleasant holiday destination, with a good beach, fossil shops, lots of good restaurants and a lively harbour. There's also a small family-run aquarium on the harbour front.

Dinosaurland

Coombe Street **t** (01297) 443541
www.dinosaurland.co.uk
Open Daily 10–5 (Jul and Aug until 6pm)
Adm Adults £4, children £3, under 5s **free**, family £12.50; fossil-hunting walks (time depends on the tides so telephone in advance): adults £5, children £3, under 5s **free**, family £12.50
Gift shop, refreshments

Minehead

Getting there Minehead is on the north Somerset coast off the A39
Tourist information 17 Friday Street **t** (01643) 702624 www.somerset.gov.uk/tourism

Being the site of Britain's first Butlins Holiday Camp, Minehead is full of fish and chip shops, tearooms and places to buy rock, inflatables and buckets and spades. There's a traditional Hobby Horse fertility dance in May and, from here, you can take a steam train ride along the coast to Watchet. The harbour is bobbing with craft and the wide and sandy beach is cleaned daily.

West Somerset Steam Railway

The Railway Station, Minehead **t** (01643) 704996
www.west-somerset-railway.co.uk
Open Mar–Jan, times vary
Adm Day rover: adults £12.40, children £6.20, family £31.20 (2+4), under 5s **free**
Refreshments, shops, buffet car on most trains, wheelchair access to all stations except Doniford Halt, almost all trains include a special coach for wheelchair use, adapted toilets, on-site parking

This charming recreation of a Great Western Railway country branch line is Britain's longest preserved railway. It runs from Bishops Lydeard to Minehead, stopping at no less than 10 stations and passing the Quantock Hills and Bristol Channel en route. You may recognize the perfectly restored station at Crowcombe

Heathfield from its numerous film and television appearances. There are museums and displays of engines and stock at stations *en route* and Santa Specials in December.

Poole

Getting there By road: Poole is on the South Dorset coast next door to Bournemouth (the border is rather fuzzy and you can easily pass from one to the other without realizing it) and can be reached from London via the M3 and the A31. By train: The train station is situated in the centre of the town and there are daily services from most major cities
Tourist information Poole Quay, **t** (01202) 253253 www.pooletourism.com

Next door to Bournemouth, Poole has a lively, Continental feel to it, with al fresco restaurants and a bustling harbour. Its beaches, all five miles of them, are clean, sandy and safe. The best – Sandbanks – has won no fewer than 13 European Blue Flags. In the centre of town, there's a pleasant park surrounding a 22-hectare (55-acre) lake, where you can hire rowboats, pedaloes and remote-controlled cars. There's also an indoor adventure playground (Gus Gorilla's Jungle Playground), a miniature railway and plenty of grassy lawns to run about on. Farmer Palmer's Farm Park is four miles from town (p.167).

Brownsea Island

Poole Harbour, Poole **t** (01202) 707744
www.nationaltrust.org.uk
Open Mid-Jul–Aug daily 10–6, Sept 10–5, Oct 10–4
Adm Landing **free**, adults £4.40, children £2.20, family £11

A 200-hectare (500-acre) harbour reserve.
For further information *see* p.175

★Poole Pottery

The Quay **t** (01202) 666200
www.poolepottery.com
Open Daily 9.30–4.30, later in summer
Adm Factory tour: adults £3.50, children go free (2 children per adult).
Restaurant, tearoom, factory shop, disabled access

Here you can see skilled potters and glass-blowers at work, watch a film on the history of pot-making (more interesting than you'd think) and, best of all, kids can try throwing a pot themselves in the 'Have a Go' area.

Splashdown Tower Park Leisure Complex

Tower Park Leisure Complex, Poole, Yarrow Road,
Poole t (01202) 716000; **www.splashdownpoole.com**
Open Term time: Mon–Fri 2–9, Sat and Sun 10–7;
school hols: Mon–Fri 10–9, Sat and Sun 10–7;
Aug daily 9–7
Adm 2hr/day ticket £8/10, under 5s £4/5, family
(1+3 or 2+2) £30/37
*Restaurant, café, mother and baby facilities,
disabled access, on-site parking*

Housed in the largest commercial leisure
centre in the UK, Splashdown boasts 11 full-on
waterslides with names like Tennessee Twister
and Louisiana Leap, as well as a paddling pool,
a bubble bench and an interactive play zone (for
very young children), spa pools, saunas and an
outdoor sun terrace (for adults). The centre also
contains a 'Quasar 2000' laser battle-zone for
7–16s, a 'Planet' Kidz for 3–12s, as well as a 10-
screen cinema, video games and a 30-lane
bowling alley.

Waterfront Museum

Waterfront Musem, The High Street
t (01202) 262600
Open summer: 10–5; winter: 10–3 **Adm Free**

Currently being redeveloped with funds from
the Heritage Lottery, Poole's revamped
Waterfront Museum will boast a modern glass
and steel frontage, a viewing terrace overlooking
the harbour and spacious display areas with
collections focusing on the history of Poole. Due
to open early 2007.

Swanage

Getting there Swanage is on the tip of the Isle of
Purbeck at the end of the A351. There is a car park
at Norden station and summer parking available
at Harman's Cross Station. By train: The nearest
train station is Wareham, from where an hourly
Wiltshire and Dorset bus service runs to Swanage
Tourist information Shore Road **t** (01929) 422885
www.swanage.gov.uk

Swanage has the same family-friendly air as
Weymouth or Bournemouth and much the same
sort of attractions, albeit on a rather reduced
scale. Its beach, which is wide and sandy and
gently shelved, is the winner of numerous
European Blue Flags and Tidy Britain Group
Awards (pedalos and canoes can be hired and
there's a Punch and Judy theatre and a beach-

side recreation ground) and you can take boat
tours around the bay and out to Brownsea
Island and the Isle of Wight from the restored
L-shaped pier. If you're lucky, you may even see
bottlenosed dolphins gliding alongside the
boat. On the clifftops behind the beach lies the
106-hectare (263-acre) Durlston Country Park, a
perfect spot for picnicking. Look out for the
Great Globe, a 40-tonne representation of the
earth in Purbeck marble. Corfe Castle (p.161) is
just a five-minute drive along the A351 or, if you
fancy arriving in style, a slightly longer steam
train ride on the Swanage Railway (*see* below).
Studland Bay, two miles north of Swanage, is
owned by the National Trust and boasts a long,
well-maintained sandy beach with a car park
(daily charges), a shop, a café, toilets and baby
changing facilities. The heathland to the rear is a
nature reserve with trails, paths and bird hides.

Swanage Railway

Southern Steam Trust, Station House
t (01929) 425800 **www.swanagerailway.co.uk**
Length of line 6 miles
Open All year weekends and school hols; Apr–Oct
daily; Dec Santa Specials
Fares Adults £7.50, children £5.50, family £21
*Souvenir shop, station buffet, buffet car on most
trains, picnic areas, wheelchair access on to trains,
one coach has an adapted toilet*

The Purbeck line (its local name) takes you
on a picturesque six-mile steam train ride from
Swanage to Norden, stopping off at another four
stations (including Corfe Castle) should your
children tire and wish to stop off along the way.

Weston-super-Mare

Getting there Take J21 from the M5 and follow the
signs along the A370. There are direct train links
from Bristol and London and there is a regular bus
service from Clevedon and Bristol
Tourist information Beach Lawns **t** (01934) 888800
www.somerset.gov.uk

Despite its odd Latin name (coined in the early
19th century in an attempt to gain kudos), this is
actually a very traditional English seaside town
with a pier lined with souvenir shops, cafés and
arcades and a two-mile long stretch of sandy
beach, where you can enjoy donkey and pony
rides, hire pedalos, and jump on bouncy castles.
Overlooking the beach is the SeaQuarium, full of

piranhas, sea horses, angel fish and small sharks, while away from the seafront the town's main attraction is the North Somerset Museum, a small museum specializing in reconstructed historic shop interiors, including a dentist's surgery, a dairy and a chemist's, plus galleries devoted to toys and dolls, rocks and minerals and archaeology. Just outside the town is the Helicopter Museum with more than 50 helicopters and autogyra on display (p.181).

North Somerset Museum

Burlington Street **t** (01934) 621028
Open Mon–Sat 10–4.30
Adm Adults £3.90, children **free**

SeaQuarium

Marine Parade, Weston-Super-mare **t** (01934) 613361 **www.seaquariumweston.co.uk**
Open Summer daily 10–5 (last admission 4pm); call for winter opening times
Adm Adults £5.75, children £4.75, under 4s **free**, family £19.99 (2+2)
Café

Constructed rather like the Tardis, this seemingly small building is cunningly designed to accommodate an amazing array of marine life. The centre is buggy friendly and provides quizzes for older children and a soft play area for younger ones.

Weymouth

Getting there By road: Weymouth is on the Dorset coast, 19 miles west of Bournemouth on the A353 and the A354. By train: The train station, which has direct services from London, Southampton and Bournemouth, deposits you almost directly on the seafront
Tourist information Kings Statue, The Esplanade, Weymouth **t** (01305) 785747; **www.weymouth.gov.uk**

Weymouth offers eveything you'd want for a classic seaside holiday: soft, sandy beaches, deckchairs, bucket-and-spade shops, Punch and Judy shows, a pier, swingboats, a helter-skelter and donkey rides. With Lodmoor Country Park to the north, the harbour to the south (where you can take cruises and sightseeing tours along the coast), this is a perfect spot for a family holiday. Whether staying in a hotel, a B&B, a campsite or a holiday park (and Weymouth has plenty of each), the town is geared towards

family entertainment. Weymouth's three-mile beach features a merry-go-round, trampolines, pedaloes, a volleyball court and a sand modeller. Constantly supervised, there's also a lost children centre and a dog ban in operation from May to September. Just back from the waterfront, you'll find the **Deep Sea Adventure** at the Old Harbour, an interactive museum of underwater exploration with lots of hands-on and animated displays, as well as a dedicated kids' play zone, Sharky's Play Area, which has a death slide, ball pits, toddler zone and a café. Across the harbour is **Brewer's Quay**, an old dockside brewery that's been turned into a multi-attraction centre with a shopping village, a hands-on science centre, 'Discovery', 'The Timewalk', a waxwork history of Weymouth, and Weymouth Museum with its maritime collection. The resort's obligatory Sea Life Centre, which specializes in sharks, is located in Lodmoor Country Park.

Brewer's Quay

Hope Square **t** (01305) 777622
www.brewers-quay.co.uk
Open Daily 10–5.30 (end Jul–Aug until 9.30pm)
Adm Free; Timewalk: adults £4.75, children £3.50, family (2+4) £15, family (1+4) £11.50.
Cafés, restaurants, shops, mother and baby facilities, disabled access

Deep Sea Adventure

9 Custom House Quay, Old Harbour
t (01305) 760690 **www.deepsea-adventure.co.uk**
Open Daily 9.30–8 (last admission 6.30pm); until 7pm in winter
Adm Adults £3.75, children £2.75, family £11.95
Café, restaurant, shop, mother and baby facilities, disabled access

Lodmoor Country Park

Greenhill **t** (01305) 788255

A 142-hectare (350-acre) park just north of the town centre, with waterslides, go-karts, a skate park, miniature golf course, miniature railway and Sea Life Centre. It adjoins an RSPB nature reserve and you can follow footpaths down to observation areas to watch the migratory birds who come here to feed in its shallow ponds.

Nothe Fort

Barrack Road **t** (01305) 766626
Open May–Sept daily 10.30–5.30; autumn half term 11–5.30

Adm Adults £5, children £1, under 5s **free**, family (2+2) £11 , family (1+2) £6.50
Café, disabled access

Jutting out from the mainland, this preserved Victorian fort has exhibits on soldiering life with lots of weapons on display (kids can climb in a tank and clamber on top of the cannons) and a network of tunnels to explore. It is surrounded by gardens that slope gently down to a pebble beach.

Portland Castle

Castle Town, Portland **t** (01305) 820539
www.english-heritage.org.uk
Open Apr–Jun daily 10–5, Jul–Aug 10–6, Sept 10–5, Oct 10–4
Adm Adults £3.70, children £1.90
Shop, on-site parking

One of the many coastal defenses erected during Henry VIII's reign, the shining white Portland Castle (it's made of Portland stone) overlooks Portland Harbour. Special events include displays on Tudor family life, Tudor and medieval music concerts, and Civil War re-enactments are held during the summer months.

Sea Life Centre

Lodmoor Country Park, Greenhill **t** (01305) 761070
www.sealifeeurope.com
Open Summer: daily 10–5; winter: Mon–Fri 11–4, Sat and Sun 10–4
Adm Adults £11.50, children £8, under 3s **free**
Café, picnic area, gift shop, disabled access

The Sea Life Centre, which contains all the old favourites (sharks, rays, sea horses and a feely pool), occupies a large park, where you'll find a paddling pool, a play area, a small funfair, as well as plenty of benches (many with tables) and lots of grass for children to run around on. There's also a marine sanctuary within the centre with seal, otter and penguin colonies.

Parks and gardens

★Abbotsbury Subtropical Gardens

Abbotsbury, Weymouth **t** (01305) 871387
www.abbotsbury-tourism.co.uk
Getting there 10 miles from Weymouth, take the coast road towards Bridport then follow the signs from Abbotsbury village

Open Mar–Oct daily 10–6, Dec–Feb 10–4
Adm Adults £7.50, children £4.50. Season ticket (unlimited entry for 12 months to gardens, swannery and activity barn): adults £28, children £23, family (2+3) £59
Café-restaurant, picnic areas, shop, mother and baby facilities, disabled access, on-site parking

This eight-hectare (20-acre) garden is filled with rare and exotic plants that flourish in the mild coastal conditions created by the nearby Chesil Beach, a 15m/50ft-high, 18-mile-long bank of pebbles that acts as a buffer against the worst of the weather. Surrounded by woodland, the central walled garden becomes a riot of colour every summer when the azaleas, rhododendrons, camelias and magnolias are in bloom. There is an Explorer Trail for children taking them through the gardens and woods, as well as an aviary and a small play area.

Hestercombe Gardens

Cheddon Fitzpaine, Taunton **t** (01823) 413923
www.hestercombegardens.com
Getting there The gardens are signposted from Taunton, off the A361
Open Daily 10–6 (last admission 5pm)
Adm Adults £6.60, 2 children **free** per adult
Picnic areas, on-site parking

Hestercombe's formal, landscaped gardens were laid out at the end of the 18th century but were only opened to the public for the first time in 1997. They're a great place for a day trip with lots of big wide lawns for kids to run about on, as well as fountains, cascades, statues and ponds, plus a gnarly old thatched hut that was once supposedly the home of a witch. Occasionally, a fire engine or two may be spotted up at Hestercombe House, which is now the headquarters of the Somerset Fire Brigade.

Minterne Gardens

Minterne Magna, Dorchester **t** (01300) 341370
Getting there The gardens are located on the A352 Dorchester–Sherbourne Road, 2 miles north of Cerne Abbas
Open Mar–Oct daily 10–6
Adm Adults £3, accompanied children **free**

A landscaped 18th-century garden with lakes, cascades and streams. Dogs on leads please.

Woodland Heritage Museum and Woodland Park

Brokerswood, Westbury **t** (01373) 822238
Getting there From Salisbury take the A36 in the Bath direction then turn right at the roundabout by the Bell pub and follow the brown signs
Open Daily 10–5
Adm Adults £3, children £1.50, under 5s **free**
Café-restaurant, picnic areas, mother and baby facilities, train (75p charge), disabled access, parking

This 32-hectare (80-acre) park includes acres of woodland, museums, a lake, mini train and two adventure playgrounds. Barbecues, fishing permits, camping and guided walks are available.

Steam trains

Avon Valley Railway

Bitton Station, Bath Road, Willsbridge
t (0117) 932 5538 Infoline: **t** (0117) 932 7296
www.avonvalleyrailway.co.uk
Getting there The railway is just off the A431, midway between Bristol and Bath. The nearest station is Keynsham, on the Bristol–Bath line
Open Apr–Oct every Sun, Aug additional midweek service and around Christmas
Fares Adults £5, children £3.50, under 3s **free**, family £13.50

Steam train rides along two miles of the former Midland Railway line southeast of Bristol. Special event days and Thomas the Tank Engine Days.
For further information *see* p.152

Steam – the Museum of the Great Western Railway

Kemble Drive, Swindon **t** (01793) 466646
www.steam-museum.org.uk
Getting there Leave the M4 at J16 and follow the brown tourist signs
Open Mon–Sat 10–5
Adm Adults £5.95, children £3.95, under 5s **free**, family £15.20 (2+2) £18.30 (2+3)
Café, disabled access, audio guide available

These majestic old Swindon railway works (which are located next to an outlet shopping centre), now house a huge museum of railway history with audiovisual displays on the people who used to work on the line, an exhibition on the great engineers (such as Isambard Kingdom Brunel) and a collection of vintage locomotives. Children will like the touch-screen games, the steam train simulator ride and the shunter floor puzzle, not to mention the trains you can clamber aboard. An especially nice touch is the workshed beside the museum – viewed from the upstairs gallery – which is full of machinery and tools, as though the workers have just popped off for a quick tea break.

Swanage Railway

Southern Steam Trust, Station House, Swanage
t (01929) 425800 www.swanagerailway.co.uk
Length of line 6 miles
Open All year weekends and school holidays; Apr–Oct daily; Dec 'Santa Specials'
Fares Adults £7.50, children £5.50, family £21

Picturesque six-mile steam train ride from Swanage to Norden.
For further information *see* p.171

West Somerset Steam Railway

The Railway Station, Minehead **t** (01643) 704996
www.west-somerset-railway.co.uk
Open Mar–Jan, times vary
Adm Day rover: adults £12.40, children £6.20, family £31.20 (2+4), under 5s **free**

Britain's longest-preserved railway, which stops at 10 stations.
For further information *see* p.170

Wide open spaces

Avon Valley Country Park

Pixash Lane, Keynsham, Bristol **t** (0117) 986 4929
www.avonvalleycountrypark.co.uk
Getting there Take the A4 from Bath or Bristol and follow the signs
Open Apr–Oct Tues–Sun 10–6 (summer and Bank Hols also Mon)
Adm Adults £6.50, children £5.50
Café, picnic areas, disabled toilets
No dogs allowed

Upon arriving at the park, the kids will probably insist on heading straight to the adventure playground with its fabulous collection of climbing frames, rope bridges, vertical drop slides and undercover soft play area for the little ones. Once they have burnt off some energy, pick up a leaflet from the visitor centre and head off along the riverside trail, stopping here and there for a little pond-dipping. If you're lucky, you may spot a wild mink or even a wallaby or two. There are lots of picnic sites along the way – if you bring your own coal, you may use the barbecues – and the fields alongside the trail are dotted with children's play equipment which, in total, make up a one-mile long children's assault course. Also, look out for the lake where there are row boats for hire, the miniature railway and the pens of farm animals. Don't worry if the weather takes a turn for the worse as a new attraction is a large Playbarn with slides, tunnels and various things to climb.

Brownsea Island

Poole Harbour, Poole **t** (01202) 707744
www.nationaltrust.org.uk
Getting there Regular daily ferries run to the island from Poole Quay, Sandbanks, Bournemouth Pier and Swanage
Open Mar–Jul, Sept daily 10–5; Aug 10–6; Oct 10–4
Adm Landing **free**; adults £4.40, children £2.20, family £11
Café, mother and baby facilities, disabled access, guided tours of nature reserve, smugglers, explorers and history trails for children

This 200-hectare (500-acre) nature reserve in the middle of Poole's natural harbour was the site of Lord Baden-Powell's first ever Scout camp back in 1907. It is home to a wide variety of wildlife, including butterflies, birds and the rare red squirrel, which was once common throughout the mainland but was driven almost to extinction by the introduction of the larger, grey squirrel. Guided walks are available in summer.

★Cheddar Gorge

t (01934) 742343 **www.cheddarcaves.co.uk**
Getting there Between Wells and Weston-super-Mare. Take J22 from the M5 and follow the A38
Open Jul–Aug daily 10–5.30, Sept–Jun 10.30–5
Adm Adults £11.50, children £8.50, family £31.50 (2+2), under 5s **free** (for caves, gorge and bus tour)
Cafés, tearooms, shop, Cheddar cheese shop, mother and baby rooms; not suitable for pushchairs

It may look like a steep cliff valley, but Cheddar Gorge is perhaps best described as a huge outdoor cave, formed when a cavern roof collapsed thousands of years ago. Although it can easily be viewed by car or from one of the open-top tour buses that operate in summer (the B3135 runs right through the middle of the gorge), it's worth stopping to wander along the well-signposted family walks. The views are truly spectacular, particularly from the top of the 274-step Jacob's ladder – you can see all the way to Glastonbury Tor – although it's a steep climb and not recommended for very young children. As you ascend, you'll see boards pointing out the age of the various rocks (they get younger the nearer to the top you get) and the type of creatures that would have existed on the Earth at that time. Be aware that parts of the gorge are very commercialized and along its floor you'll find your route lined with tearooms and gift shops, where you can pick

Chalk figures

Thousands of years ago, the first people to settle in the little piece of midwest England that would one day be called Wiltshire realized that the local countryside's rolling chalk hills could make a great natural canvas. All you had to do was mark out your design, cut away the top layer of turf to expose the bright white chalk beneath and, before long, you had a picture that could be seen for miles around. It was an idea that caught on in a big way, reaching the zenith of its popularity in the 18th century when, for a while, it seemed that every chalk hillside in the country was in danger of being etched out of existence. Indeed, so many of these great outdoor works of art were created that, if you drive around Wiltshire for long enough (particularly along the A4), you're bound to catch sight of at least one. Most, for some reason that's never been fully explained, are pictures of horses (perhaps horses are easy to do), although people, birds and even lions have also been represented. And, while Wiltshire may have the most number of pictures – you'll find chalk horses at Cherhill, Alton Barnes and Manton – the most famous chalk drawings of all are located at Uffington in Oxfordshire, where a mighty 360ft/110m-long horse bestrides the landscape, and at Cerne Abbas in Dorset, where the hillside is decorated with a giant prehistoric chalk man, portrayed carrying a great chalk club and proudly displaying a great (40ft/12m), er, chalk protrusion on which Morris men dance every May Day as part of an age-old (and deeply odd) fertility rite. The best views are from the main A352 road, just north of Cerne Abbas town.

up the ultimate souvenir of your trip, a piece of Cheddar cheese quarried from the face of the gorge. Of even more appeal to children are the amazing Cheddar Showcaves, which consist of two enormous caverns (called Gough's Cave and Cox's Cave) beneath the gorge. You can explore these incredible cathedral-like structures, full of stalactites and stalagmites, glistening pools and sinister shadows, at leisure, although you will need a guide to go into the very deepest caves on a 'Rock Sport' trip (age restrictions apply). The smaller Cox's Cave tends to be the kids' favourite as part of it has been turned into a dark walk fantasy adventure called 'The Crystal Quest' and is lined with models of goblins, dragons and witches. There's also a small museum housing Cheddar man – a 9,000-year-old skeleton, whose DNA corresponds to that of local residents.

Exmoor Falconry and Animal Farm

West Lynch Farm, Allerford, Porlock, Somerset
t (01643) 862816 **www**.exmoorfalconry.co.uk
Getting there Allerford is 5 miles west of Minehead, just off the A39
Open Mar–Oct daily 10.30–5, Nov–Feb 10.30–4
Adm Adults £7 children £5.50, under 3s **free**; Nov–Feb all tickets £5

Watch expert bird handlers flying a range of birds of prey over the moors.
For further information *see* pp.166

★Exmoor National Park

Getting there Stretching across North Devon and West Somerset, Exmoor covers an area of 265 square miles. The A39 runs along its northern coast while the A396 runs south to north through the middle. Buses run throughout the year from Barnstaple, Bridgwater, Exeter, Taunton and Tiverton
Tourist information:
Lynmouth **t** (01598) 752509
Dunster **t** (01643) 821835
County Gate **t** (01598) 741321
Combe Martin **t** (01271) 883319
Dulverton **t** (01398) 323841
www.exmoor-nationalpark.gov.uk

Dartmoor's tamer, softer sibling (it is underpinned by sandstone rather than granite), Exmoor is an equally rewarding place to visit. Much of its landscape has been altered and reshaped by man (parts have been drained and resown with lush grasses) but there are still some wild, windswept parts left and, unlike Dartmoor, it's inhabited by herds of free-roaming deer. As with Dartmoor, it's probably best explored as a car trip interspersed with walks. Guided walks are arranged by the tourist offices. The most famous walk is the Tarka Trail, the route set out by Henry Williamson in his book *Tarka the Otter*. Only a short part of the trail actually passes through Exmoor but it's as much as you're likely to cover. The full trail, along the banks of the Rivers Taw and Torridge and down into Dartmoor, is over 180 miles long. A branch railway line, known as the 'Tarka Line', runs between Barnstaple and Exeter. You're unlikely to see any otters on your travels, as they are shy, nocturnal creatures but there's other wildlife in the park, including foxes, badgers, buzzards, merlins and ravens. Nature walks (or 'safaris') across Exmoor are organized from the Natural History Centre in Malmstead on the northern tip of the moor, just off the A39, and from the Exmoor Falconry and Animal Farm in Porlock, Somerset (p.166).

Exmoor extends to the North Devon–Somerset coast, where you'll find the highest coastal cliffs in England (some are over 250m/800ft high) and the longest stretch of naturally wooded coastline in the British Isles. The resorts of Minehead, Watchet, Combe Martin, Lynton and Lynmouth, are good bases for exploring the moor.

Moors Valley Country Park

Horton Road, Ashley Heath **t** (01425) 470721
www.moors-valley.co.uk
Getting there 10 miles north of Bournemouth
Open Daily 8am–dusk **Adm Free**
Café, restaurant, shop, wheelchair access, on-site parking (£7 maximum charge)

Large country park aimed at families, with a lake, walks, a 400-hectare (1,000-acre) swathe of forest (with a tree-top walkway, forest-play trail, nature trails and a high-ropes adventure course for ages 10 and up), a miniature steam railway, play castle and sandworks for toddlers. Bikes and tandems for hire from £4 for 90 minutes.

Quantock Hills

Getting there The Quantocks are in west Somerset. Taunton, the main town in the area is on the A358 and the A38
Tourist information Paul Street, Taunton **t** (01823) 336344 (for general enquiries); Quantock Centre: **t** (01278) 733642 (for information on the hills)

This is good, family walking country. The 12-mile-long Quantock range which, as with nearby

Exmoor, sits on a layer of soft red sandstone, offers a variety of landscapes to explore, from the beech woodland of its northern and eastern slopes (home to herds of red deer) to the rolling moorland of its more westerly reaches, all scored with a network of ancient paths and trackways. Though challenging in places, none of the range's peaks are higher than 400 metres (1,300ft), thereby offering good views of the Bristol Channel and Exmoor in return for a reasonable expenditure of energy.

Still, if you don't feel like putting your walking boots to the test, you can always take a more leisurely tour of the region aboard the West Somerset Steam Railway (p.170).

Wookey Hole Caves and Papermill

t (01749) 672243 **www.**wookey.co.uk
Getting there The Wookey Hole Caves are just outside the cathedral city of Wells. Take the J22 from the M5 and follow signs along the A38 and the A371, from Bath A39 to Wells
Open Mar–Oct daily 10–5, Nov–Feb 10–4
Adm Adults £10.90, children £8.50, family £34
Cafés, shop, mother and baby room, disabled facilities, on-site parking; not suitable for pushchairs

These marvellously spooky underground caverns, full of dark tunnels, eerie lakes and mysterious flickering shadows, can be visited only as part of a guided tour. It's quite a trip. The guides are well practised at bringing the myths and legends associated with the caves to life and will take particular pleasure in regaling you with tales of the Witch of Wookey, who is supposed to inhabit the cave's dark inner recesses. In fact, the witch is nothing more than a sinister-shaped stalagmite, made all the more menacing by imaginative lighting. You'll also be shown an underground river, the Axe, which has also been carefully lit so that it seems to glimmer a bright crystal blue. Amazingly, no one has ever discovered the river's source.

Just outside the caves stands a Victorian papermill (it holds a display on the history of paper-making and is still churning out sheets of rag paper) and a vintage fairground, with carousels, a maze of mirrors, slot machines and a fairy garden. New attractions here include Dinosaur Valley, a collection of life-size model dinosaurs and King Kong, a teddy-bear exhibition.

SPORT AND ACTIVITIES

Activity centres
Sunsport
Weymouth Sports Club, Redlands Sports Centre, Dorchester Road, Redlands, Weymouth
Postal address: Sunsport, PO Box 1480, Weymouth
t (01305) 787716
Open Booking office: 8.45am–10pm, morning afternoon and all-day sessions available
Adm Varies, call in advance

School-holiday activities, including tennis, cricket, badminton, fundance, football, judo, horse-riding, gymnastics, snooker, sailing and windsurfing.

Bicycle hire
Hayball Cycle Shop
The Black Horse Chequer, 26–30 Winchester Street, Salisbury **t** (01722) 411378
Open Mon–Sat 9–5.30
Adm Rates vary, call in advance

Hires out bikes for riding in and around Salisbury.

The Lock Inn Café
Lower Canal Walk, Frome Road, Bradford-on-Avon
t (01225) 868068 **www.**thelockinn.co.uk
Open Mon–Sat 9am–5.30pm and 6.30–9.30pm
Adm Rates vary, call in advance

Bikes, children's seats, tandems and canoes.

Bowling
Megabowl
Brunel Way, Ashton Gate, Bristol **t** 0871 5501010
www.megabowl.co.uk
Open Sun–Thurs 10am–11pm, Fri–Sat 10am–1am
Adm Adults £5.50, children £4.50/game; family deal: £15 before 12 noon at weekends, £18 all other times.

Lakeside Superbowl
St Nicholas Street, Weymouth **t** (01305) 781444
www.lakeside-superbowl.co.uk
Open Mon and Thurs from 10am, Tues, Wed and Fri from 11am, Sat and Sun from 9am
Adm Rates vary, call in advance

Football
Bournemouth Football Club
Dean Court **t** (01202) 726303 tickets **t** 0870 0340380 **www.**afcb.co.uk
Tickets £6.50–£30
Adm Match times and prices vary, call in advance
Division: 2nd.

Bristol Rovers

The Memorial Ground, Filton Avenue, Horfield
t (0117) 909 6648 www.bristolrovers.co.uk
Tickets £3.50–£20
Open/Adm Call for times and prices
Division: 3rd.

Torquay United

Plainmoor t (01803) 328666
www.torquayunited.com
Tickets £5–£15
Open/Adm Call for times and prices
Division: 3rd.

Go-karting

Avago Karting and Laser-Shooting

Windrush Cottage, West Dean, Salisbury
t (01794) 884693
Open By arrangement
Adm Call for prices
Karts available and laser-shooting for all ages.

Castle Coombe Skid Pan and Kart Track

Chippenham t (01249) 783010
www.coombe-events.co.uk
Open By arrangement
Adm Call for prices
Kart-racing on a 350m (1,150ft) kart track. Adult
meetings on Saturday, junior meetings on the
first and third Sunday of every month.

Horse-riding

Avon Riding Centre for the Disabled

Kings Weston Road, Henbury t (0117) 959 0266
www.avonridingcentre.co.uk
Open Call in advance for opening times,
closed Sunday
Adm Lessons start from £17 per hour
Flat riding and jumping tuition for the disabled
(must be arranged well in advance).

Grovely Riding Centre

Water Ditchampton, Salisbury t (01722) 742288
www.grovely.info
Open Summer: Tues–Sun 10–6; winter: times vary
Adm Rates vary, call in advance for prices
Rides over Wiltshire's chalk downs. All levels of
experience catered for. Book well in advance.

Wellow Trekking Centre at Franks Farm

Wellow, near Bath t (01225) 834376
www.wellowtrekking.com
Open Daily 10–5 **Adm** Call for prices
Horse-riding and pony-trekking.

Ice-skating and skiing

Bristol Ice Rink

Frogmore Street, Bristol t (0117) 929 2148
Open Mon and Wed–Sun 10.30am–10.30pm,
Tues 10.30–3.30 (session times vary in the after-
noon and evening, call to check)
Adm Call for prices
Café, bar, sports shop
Ice-skating lessons and courses offered.

Christchurch Ski and Leisure Centre

Matchams Lane, Hurn, Christchurch
t (01202) 499155
Open Daily 10am–10pm
Adm £5.75/30 minutes
Ski bobbing and rubber tyre 'ringos' on a dry
ski slope.

Indoor play centres

Boomerang

Bowerhill Trading Estate, Melksham t (01225) 702000
www.boomeranguk.co.uk
Open Mon–Fri 9.30–6, Sat 10–7, Sun 10–6
Adm £2.75–3.95
Indoor play centre for 0–11-year-olds. Very popular.

Planet Kids

Megabowl, Brunel Way, Ashton Gate, Bristol
t 0871 550 1010 www.megabowl.co.uk
Open Daily 10–6
Adm £3.50, under 2s £2
Café, mother and baby facilities
Enormous soft play/adventure playground for
the under 10s.

Llama-trekking

UK Llamas

Beaminster t (01308) 868674 www.ukllamas.co.uk
Open/Adm Call for times and prices
Llama treks through the Dorset countryside.
This unusual (if not unique in the UK) way of
getting around the countryside is very popular, so
pre-booking is essential.

Pitch and putt

Ashton Court Estate

Clifton Lodge entrance, Bristol t (0117) 973 8508
Open 7–4
Adm Call for prices
Two-par three 18-hole golf courses.

Quad-biking

Henley Hillbillies

Old Henley Farm, Buckland Newton
t (01300) 345293 **www.henleyhillbillies.co.uk**
Open/Adm Call for times and prices
  Quad-bikes, mini mavriks to ride, clay pigeon shooting and, in the evening, you can watch badgers from a weatherproof observation set.

Water fun parks and leisure centres

Bath Sports and Leisure Centre

North Parade, Bath **t** (01225) 462563
Open/Adm Call for times and prices
  Excellent children's play pool with two long, twisting slides.

Littledown Centre

Chaseside, Bournemouth **t** (01202) 417600
www.littledowncentre.co.uk
Open Mon–Fri 6.30–11, Sat 7.30–8, Sun 7.30–9
Adm Adults £3.10, children £2.50, under 5s **free**
Café, on-site parking
  Two swimming pools with waterslides. Football, trampolining, basketball, badminton and crêche facilities also offered.

Watersports

Rockley Watersports

Rockley Point, Hamworthy, Poole **t** (0870) 7770541
www.rockleywatersports.com
Open/Adm Call for times and prices
  Courses in dinghy sailing, windsurfing and powerboating for all ages and abilities.

Splashdown Tower Park Leisure Complex

Tower Park Leisure Complex, Poole, Yarrow Road, Poole **t** (01202) 716000
www.splashdownpoole.com
Open Term time: Mon–Fri 2–9, Sat–Sun 10–7; school hols: Mon–Fri 10–9, Sat–Sun 10–7; Aug Mon–Sun 9–7
Adm 2hr/day ticket £8/10, under 5s £4/5, family (1+3 or 2+2) £30/37
  The largest commercial leisure centre in the UK – waterslides, paddling pools, interactive play zones for toddlers, and spa pools, saunas and an outdoor sun terrace for adults.
For further information *see* pp.170–1

Cinemas

Bath

Little Theatre Cinema St Michael's Place
t 0870 7551241
Odeon Kingsmead Leisure Complex, James Street
t 0871 2244007

Bournemouth

ABC Cinema 27 Westover Road **t** 0871 2244007
Odeon Cinemas Westover Road **t** 0871 2244007
IMAX 3D cinema Bournemouth Pier
t (01202) 553050

Bristol

Cineworld Hengrove **t** 0871 2208000
The Cube King Square **t** (0117) 907 4190
IMAX 3D cinema At-Bristol, Anchor Road Harbourside **t** (0117) 9155000
Odeon Union Street **t** 0871 2244007
Orpheus Henleaze Northumbria Drive
t 0845 1662381
Showcase St Philips Causeway **t** 0871 2201000
Victoria Rooms Queens Road, Clifton
t (0117) 9545032
Vue The Venue, Cribbs Causeway
t 0871 2240240
Vue Longwell Green **t** 0871 2240240
Watershed Media Centre Canons Road
t (0117) 9275100

Christchurch

Regent Centre t (01202) 499148

Dorchester

Plaza 1 and 2, Trinity Street **t** (01305) 262488

Lyme Regis

Regent Cinema Broad Street **t** 0871 2303200

Poole

Arts Centre Kingland Road **t** (01202) 685222
UCI Tower Park, Mannings Heath **t** 0871 2244007

Salisbury

Odeon Cinema 15 New Canal **t** 0871 2244007

Swindon

Cineworld Greenbridge Retail Centre
t 0871 2208000
Cineworld Shaw Ridge Leisure Park
t 0871 2202000

Weston-super-Mare

Odeon The Centre **t** 0871 2244007

Weymouth

Cineworld New Bond Street **t** 0871 2208000

Museums and science centres

American Museum

Claverton Manor, Bath **t** (01225) 460503
www.americanmuseum.org
Getting there 2 miles east of Bath off the A36
Open Mar–Nov Tues–Sun 12 noon–5
Adm Adults £6, children £3.50, family ticket £17.50.
Grounds only: Adults £4, children £2.50

UK museum devoted solely to recreating
American colonial life (George Washington's
garden at Mount Vernon).
For further information *see* pp.148–9

★At-Bristol

Anchor Road, Harbourside, Bristol **t** 0845 345 12335
www.at-bristol.org.uk
Open Explore and Wildwalk: daily (except 25 Dec)
10–5; IMAX: Mon–Fri 10–4.45, Sat–Sun 12.30–8.30
Adm Adults £20, children £15, family £62 (access to
all attractions over a seven-day period); tickets also
available for single attractions

Complex containing a hands-on science centre,
an IMAX cinema, a mix of live animals and
recorded images and displays (including a walk-
through botanical house), a planetarium and an
open piazza lined with cafés and restaurants.
For further information *see* p.152

Blaise Castle House Museum

Henbury Road, Henbury **t** (0117) 9039818
Open Apr–Oct Sat–Wed 10–5 **Adm Free**
*Shop, disabled access, summer activities, on-site
parking*

This is a small museum of social history
housed in an 18th-century Gothic Revival
building and surrounded by 162 hectares (400
acres) of park and woodland. Children will enjoy
looking at the model trains, toy soldiers and
dolls, as well as seeing what life was like in a
Victorian schoolroom. There are numerous paths
and trails, plus a well-equipped playground.

Bristol City Museum and Art Gallery

Queens Road, Clifton, Bristol **t** (0117) 922 3571
www.bristol-city.gov.uk/museums
Open Daily 10–5, 'Sunday Fundays' on first Sun of
every month **Adm Free**

Displays on dinosaurs, Egyptian mummies,
wildlife and natural history, as well as rocks
and minerals.
For further information *see* p.153

Building of Bath Museum

Countess of Huntingdon's Chapel, The Vineyards
t (01225) 333895
www.bath-preservation-trust.org.uk
Open Tues–Sun 10.30–5
Adm Adults £4, children £1.50, under 8s **free**
Miniature scale model of the city of Bath with
every street and building beautifully recreated.
For further information *see* p.149

Fleet Air Arm Museum

Royal Naval Air Station, Yeovilton, Yeovil
t (01935) 840565 **www**.fleetairarm.com
Getting there Yeovilton is about 3 miles north of
Yeovil on the B3151, just off the A303/A37; M5 (J25)
Open Apr–Oct daily 10–5.30, Nov–Mar Wed–Sun
10–4.30
Adm Adults £10, children £7, family £30
Shop, baby changing, disabled facilities, restaurant

Telling the story of aviation at sea and, in particular, the history of the Royal Naval Air Service,
this museum, founded in 1964, has lots that kids
will enjoy. The viewing gallery holds 40 historic
aircraft and helicopters, as well as weapons,
models and photographs. Kids will particularly
enjoy the journey aboard a 1970s aircraft carrier,
which features a simulated helicopter ride, not to
mention that now that Concorde has ceased
flying this may be the closest your kids will ever
get to these historic craft. There are several interactive zones, a very good flight simulator and a
children's adventure playground. Family events,
such as Easter egg hunts and pirate treasure
trails, are also on offer.

Haynes Motor Museum

Sparkford, Yeovil **t** (01963) 440804
www.haynesmotormuseum.co.uk
Getting there Sparkford is 5 miles north of Yeovil
off the A359; M5 to Taunton (J25) and A358/A303
Open Apr–Oct daily 9.30–5.30 (until 6pm in school
hols), Nov–Mar 10–4.30
Adm Adults £7.50, children £4, under 5s **free**, family
£9.50 (1+1) £22 (2+3)
*Café, picnic area, shop, mother and baby room,
disabled access, guided tours, on-site parking*

Haynes houses a huge collection of gloriously
glossy vintage cars, classic motorbikes and
motoring memorabilia and regularly organizes
trips for enthusiasts (*see* website for details of
membership) to places such as Goodwood and

Castle Donington, where you can watch these speed machines in action. On site, you'll find a Dawn of Motoring Street Scene, a Hall of Motor Sport, a Motorland play park for children and an outdoor picnic area. The pristine millennium exhibition hall houses modern supercars and classics of the future, including the stunning Jaguar XJ220. Family events such as treasure hunts take place throughout the year.

Helicopter Museum

The Heliport, Locking Moor Road, Weston-super-Mare **t** (01934) 635227
www.helicoptermuseum.co.uk
Getting there From J21 of the M5 take the A371; from Weston-super-Mare buses no. 120, 121 and 126 run from outside the Grand Pier
Open Apr–Oct daily 10–5.30, Nov–Mar 10–4.30, summer 10–6.30 (last admission 45 minutes before closing)
Adm Adults £5.30, children £3.30, family £14.50 (2+2) £16.50 (2+3), under 5s **free**
Coffee shop, mother and baby room, disabled facilities, children's play area, guided tours, parking, on-line shop
More than 50 helicopters and autogyra are on display at this well laid out museum. Special event days during the season including Open Cockpit Days, Weston-Super-Helidays and Air Experience Flights.

Industrial Museum

Princes Wharf, Wapping Road, Bristol **t** (0117) 925 1470
www.bristol-city.gov.uk
Open Apr–Oct Sat–Wed 10–5; Nov–Mar Sat and Sun 10–5 **Adm Free**
Eighteenth-century horse-drawn carriages, steam locomotives, race cars and buses.
For further information *see* pp.154–5

Museum of Costume and Assembly Rooms

Bennet Street, Bath **t** (01225) 477789
www.museumofcostume.co.uk
t (01225) 333895 **www**.bath-preservation-trust.org.uk
Open Tues–Sun 10.30–5
Adm Adults £4, children £1.50, under 8s **free**
Costumes from the 16th century to present day.
For further information *see* p.149

Postal Museum

8 Broad Street **t** (01225) 460333
www.bathpostalmuseum.org

Open Mon–Sat 11–5
Adm Adults £2.90, children £1.50, family £6.90
From 'clay-mail to e-mail' exhibition.
For further information *see* p.149

Purbeck Toy and Musical Box Museum

Arne, near Wareham **t** (01929) 552018
Open Daily 12 noon–5pm, closed Mon; Jul and Aug daily 10.30–5.30 **Adm** Adults £3.50, children £2.50, under 3s **free**, family £9.50
Large collection of vintage toys, including a number of end of the pier amusements, some dating back to the 19th century.

★ Roman Baths

Stall Street, Bath **t** (01225) 477785
www.romanbaths.co.uk
Open Daily Jan–Feb and Nov–Dec 9.30–5.30; Mar–Jun and Sept–Oct 9–6; Jul–Aug 9am–10pm
Adm Adults £10, children £6, under 5s **free**
Complex that lets you explore the remnants and remains of all the facilities (i.e. main baths and plunge pools) as laid down by Roman engineers.
For further information *see* p.150

SS *Great Britain*, the *Matthew* and the Maritime Heritage Centre

Great Western Dock, Gas Ferry Road, Bristol **t** (0117) 926 0680 **www**.ssgreatbritain.org
Open Apr–Oct daily 10–5.30, Nov–Mar 10–4.30
Adm Adults £8.95, children £4.95, under 5s **free**, family (2+2) £24.95
Visit the first iron-hulled, propeller-driven ship and the 15th-century ship on which John Cabot sailed to the American mainland.
For further information *see* p.155

Steam – the Museum of the Great Western Railway

Kemble Drive, Swindon **t** (01793) 466646
www.steam-museum.org.uk
Getting there Leave the M4 at J16 and follow the brown tourist signs
Open Mon–Sat 10–5
Adm Adults £5.95, children £3.95, under 5s **free**, family £15.20 (2+2) £18.30 (2+3)
Huge museum of railway history in old Swindon railway works with audiovisual displays.
For further information *see* p.174

Tank Museum

Bovington Camp, Wareham **t** (01929) 405096
www.tankmuseum.co.uk

Getting there London and southeast M3/M27/A31 Bere Regis/Bovington; A354 Blandford/Bovington **Open** Daily 10–5 **Adm** Adults £10, children £7, family £26 (1+3), £28 (2+2), under 5s **free** *Restaurant (with highchairs), model and bookshop, disabled access, audio guides, on-site parking, play and picnic area, family activity trail*

Bovington's Tank Museum has more than 300 tanks (some of which you can climb inside) plus interactive exhibits (including a walk-through, mock-up First World War trench), a dissected tank, motion simulators and audiovisual displays. Watch the tanks in action from July to September (twice a week, days vary), when a 45-minute display takes place with pyrotechnic explosions. Tank rides are also available. Be warned that younger children might not like the noise, which can be intense.

Theatres

Bath
Theatre Royal St John's Place **t** (01225) 448844

Bournemouth
Bournemouth International Centre Exeter Road **t** (01202) 456400 www.bic.co.uk
Pavilion Theatre Westover Road **t** (01202) 456400
Pier Theatre The Winter Gardens **t** (01202) 456400

Bristol
Arnolfini Narrow Quay **t** (0117) 917 2300
Colston Hall Colston Street **t** (0117) 922 3682
Hippodrome St Augustine's Parade **t** 0870 607 7500
Queen Elizabeth's Hospital Theatre Berkeley Place **t** (0117) 9303082
Redgrave Percival Road, Clifton **t** (0117) 315 7600
St George's Great George Street **t** (0117) 923 0359
Bristol Old Vic King Street **t** (0117) 987 7877

Dorchester
Arts Centre School Lane, The Grove **t** (01305) 266926

Poole
Arts Centre Kingland Road **t** 08700 668701

Salisbury
Arts Centre Bedwin Street **t** (01722) 321744
The City Hall Malthouse Lane **t** (01722) 434434
Salisbury Playhouse Malthouse Lane **t** (01722) 320333
Studio Theatre Ashley Road **t** (01722) 414060

Weston-super-Mare
Playhouse High Street **t** (01934) 645544

Weymouth
The Pavilion Complex The Esplanade **t** (01305) 783225

EATING OUT

Bath
Bathtub Bistro
2 Grove Street **t** (01225) 460593
www.bathtubbistro.co.uk
Open Mon 6–11, Tues–Fri 12 noon–2.30 and 6–11, Sat–Sun 12 noon–11

Intimate candle-lit dining experience with friendly staff and international bistro-style cuisine served with decent and very reasonably priced wines. Kids can enjoy omelettes or fish fingers with salad and chips followed by toffee fudge sundaes and mint ice cream. Families with young children should dine early and parties should book in advance to avoid disappointment. Children's menu, highchairs, disabled access.

The Bear
6 –10 Wellsway **t** (01225) 425795
Open Mon–Wed 11–11, Thurs and Sat 11am–12 midnight, Fri 11pm–1am, Sun 12 noon–11pm; food served 12 noon–8.30

Traditional pub offering a 'steak and ale' menu for the adults and a range of children's meals – such as pasta in tomato sauce, sausage and mash, etc. – which come with a drink and ice cream included in the price. The menu features steak specialities, roast lunches and curries, as well as Chinese and vegetarian options. Highchairs and children's menu available.

Beaujolais
5 Chapel Row, off Queen's Square **t** (01225) 423417
Open Mon–Sat 12–2.30 and 6–10.30

A very welcoming restaurant with a walled garden. The menu is predominantly French but the chef is very accommodating to kids' needs and will happily rustle up a quick chicken and chips. Highchairs, children's menu and non-smoking area.

Blathwayt Arms
Lansdown Road **t** (01225) 421995
www.theblathwayt-bath.co.uk
Open Daily

This friendly real ale pub has a huge garden, non-smoking family areas, disabled access and highchairs. There is a children's menu serving up gammon, sausages, crispy whales and other kiddie favourites.

Brown's
Orange Grove **t** (01225) 461199
www.browns-restaurants.com

Open Mon–Sat 11–11.30, Sun 12–11.30

Large branch of the ever family-friendly chain housed in the city's old police station, a stone's throw from the Roman Bath's Abbey and Pump Room. Children get their own menu, which they can colour in with the crayons provided. Diners wishing to smoke eat in what used to be the cells. Highchairs, baby changing facilities and children's menu available.

Café Cadbury
23 Union Street **t** (01225) 444030
Open Daily 8–6

A hybrid coffeehouse–chocolate shop, Café Cadbury aims to provide the best of both worlds – good café food and drinks, and vast supplies of quality chocolates. It's actually aimed at the adult Starbucks crowd, with clean, minimalist décor and posters adorning the walls with words like 'refresh' and 'indulge' printed on them, but children are never averse to a few chocs. Highchairs, baby changing facilities and kids' portions available.

Caffè Piazza
23 The Podium **t** (01225) 429299
www.caffepiazza.co.uk
Open Mon–Sat 8.30am–10.30pm, Sun 10am–10pm

Offers a wide range of authentic Italian pasta dishes and stone-baked pizzas. Kids will enjoy the desserts and watching the colourful fish swim around in their tank. Highchairs, children's menu and non-smoking area.

Demuths
2 North Parade **t** (01225) 446059
www.demuths.co.uk
Open Daily 10–10 (Sat 9am–10pm)

A non-smoking gourmet vegetarian restaurant with highchairs, crayons and children's lunch menus. Children are welcome until 7.30pm.

Eastern Eye
8a Quiet Street **t** (01225) 422323/466401
www.easterneye.co.uk
Open Daily 12 noon–2.30 and 6–11.30

High-quality Indian food is served in resplendent Georgian surroundings at this multi award-winning establishment. Highchairs and children's portions available.

Pasta Galore
31 Barton Street **t** (01225) 463861
Open Mon–Sat 12 noon–2.30 and 6–10.30
(Thurs–Sat until 11pm), Sun 12 noon–2 and 6–10.30

Fresh pasta made on the premises. Vegetarian dishes, pizza, other Italian specialities. Homemade desserts, luxury ice creams. Lunchtime specials. Highchairs, children's portions and non-smoking areas are available.

Sally Lunn's Refreshment House
4 North Parade Passage **t** (01225) 461634
www.sallylunns.co.uk
Open Mon–Sat 10–10, Sun 6–10

Not to be missed – enjoy a cream tea and a little historical sightseeing at the same time. The oldest house in Bath (it was built some time towards the end of the 15th century), Sally Lunn's not only comprises an excellent tea shop (try the famous Sally Lunn Bun, still baked by hand according to her 1680 recipe), but also a museum where Sally's original kitchen can be seen and which kids can visit free of charge. Highchairs, children's menu and colouring sheets.

Around Bath

Bathampton Mill 'Out & Out'
Mill Lane, Bathampton **t** (01225) 469758
www.eatingoutandout.co.uk
Open Mon–Fri 12 noon–2.30, Sat 12 noon–10, Sun 12 noon–9

This refurbished riverside pub serves bar food and restaurant meals including children's dishes. Highchairs, baby changing facilities, outdoor play area and garden.

Bournemouth

Coriander Mexican Restaurant
22 Richmond Hill **t** (01202) 552202
www.coriander-restaurant.co.uk
Open 12 noon–10pm; children welcome until 7pm

Bright and fun Mexican with friendly staff and freshly prepared food. The children's menu ranges from staples like chicken or fish fingers and sausages to more adventurous dishes like enchiladas filled with cheese, chicken or beef chilli, all served with rice or chips for £1 before 5pm, £3.50 after. First-floor non-smoking area and children's menu.

Café Rouge
67–71 Seamoor Road, Westbourne **t** (01202) 757472
www.caferouge.co.uk
Open Mon–Sat 10am–11pm, Sun 10–10.30

Family-friendly French restaurant chain offering a children's menu, with crayons and stickers.

Chez Fred

10 Seamoor Road, Westbourne **t** (01202) 761023
www.chezfred.co.uk
Open Mon–Sat 11.30–2 (Sat until 2.30) and 5–10,
Sun 5.30–9.30

Award-winning fish and chip restaurant. Kids
get their own menu ('Fred's Sprat Pack Meals')
and are given colouring books, pens and toys to
keep them amused. Eat in or take away.
Highchairs available.

The Grove Seafood Restaurant

77 Southbourne Road, Southbourne
t (01202) 566660
Open Lunch: Tues–Fri 12 noon–1.45, Sat–Sun 12
noon–1.30pm; dinner: Tues–Sat 7–10 (last orders
9pm), booking essential for Sunday lunch

Local seafood (including lobster and crab) is a
speciality here. Children's menu available.

Uncle Sam's

148 Old Christchurch Road **t** (01202) 293355
Open Mon–Sat 12 noon–11.30pm, Sun
12 noon–10.30pm

Lively American-style diner serving up simple
children's favourites including burgers, sausages
and chicken nuggets. Highchairs available.

West Beach Restaurant

Pier Approach **t** (01202) 587785
www.west-beach.co.uk
Open Mon–Sat 9am–12 midnight (last orders for
lunch 4 and dinner 10), Sun 9–11

This spacious and airy restaurant specializes in
locally caught seafood. There's a very reasonable
kids' menu for £4.95 featuring tuna steak salads,
cod, chips and peas and other fish dishes. The
open-plan design allows full view of the chefs at
work, which is fun for children, or you can sit out
on the decking just a hop, skip and a jump away
from the water's edge. There's live jazz music on
Thursday evenings. Highchairs and baby
changing facilities.

Bradford-on-Avon

Woolley Grange

Woolley Green **t** (01225) 864705
Open Lunch 12 noon–2, dinner 7–9.30

This extremely family-friendly luxury hotel is an
excellent spot for Sunday lunch. The restaurant is
pleasant and airy and there's a children's den full
of toys (where kids can have their meals served if
they prefer) supervised by helpful, friendly staff,
enabling parents to relax after eating. The kitchen
serves mostly organic, locally grown (and
inevitably expensive) food and is very popular,
so book well in advance. Highchairs and
babysitter available.

For details of the hotel's facilities see p.511

Bristol

Bella Pasta

8–10 Balwin Street **t** (01179) 293278
www.bellapasta.co.uk
Open Mon–Thurs 10–10, Fri–Sat 10–11.30, Sun
10–10.30

Cheery branch of the Italian pasta chain.
Highchairs, children's menu and a non-smoking
area.

Brown's

38 Queen's Road **t** (0117) 930 4777
www.browns-restaurants.com
Open Mon–Sat 11.30–11, Sun 12 noon–11pm

Taking your children to Brown's is a great way
of introducing them to 'proper' restaurants.
This branch, though elegant and grown-up with
potted plants and tasteful furnishings, is also
extremely family friendly and offers a colour-in
children's menu (crayons provided), booths and
a non-smoking section. It's also conveniently situated next door to the Bristol City Museum and
Art Gallery (p.153). The food is standard brasserie
fare. Highchairs and baby changing facilities.

Firehouse Rotisserie

The Leadworks, Anchor Square, Harbourside
t (0117) 915 7323 www.firehouserotisserie.com
Open 12 noon–2.30pm and 6–11pm

Adjacent to the At-Bristol complex (p.152), this
restaurant is convenient but not exactly cheap.
There are tables outside and the menu consists
of bistro-style fare such as spit-roasted chicken,
grilled fish and gourmet pizzas made with fresh
and healthy ingredients.

Sally Lunn Buns

Sally Lunn was supposedly a well-endowed lady
who sold her buns on the streets of Bath. The
buns are made of a rich dough rather like that of
brioche. Try them at Sally Lunn's Refreshment
House (see above), either for tea or with a savoury
stuffing for dinner.

Harry Ramsden's

Cribbs Causeway **t** (0117) 959 4100
www.harryramsdens.co.uk
Open Mon–Thurs 12 noon–9.30,
Fri–Sat 12 noon–10pm, Sun 12 noon–8

Try this branch of the famous chain of 'chippies' for that authentic northern fish and chip taste. There's a children's menu, a play area with toys and, on the first Sunday of each month, children's entertainment – magicians, face painters, etc. – are laid on. Eat in or take away. Children's menu and highchairs available.

Mud Dock Cycleworks and Café

The Grove **t** (0117) 934 9734 **www.**mud-dock.co.uk
Open Call for details

Quirky bike shop and restaurant combo serving original dishes overlooking the docks. Perfect for watching the sunset, especially on nights when the balloon racers do their practice runs. Teenagers will love the DJs playing house music and younger kids will just enjoy the food, the friendly staff and the laid-back atmosphere.

New World Oriental Karaoke Restaurant

Unite House, Frogmore Street **t** (0117) 9293288
www.newworldgroup.co.uk
Open Mon–Wed 12 noon–2.30 and 6.30–11.30,
Thurs–Sat 12 noon–2.30 and 6.30–12

This will definitely go down well with choosy teenagers and sophisticated school kids but be aware that it gets very busy on weekends and pretty noisy too. There's an extensive buffet menu from Chinese to Thai dishes with some vegetarian options. All the latest pop tunes and rock classics are also on the menu.

Pizza Provençale

29 Regent Street, Clifton **t** (0117) 974 1175
www.pizzaprovencale.co.uk
Open Sun–Thurs 12 noon–11pm, Fri and Sat 12–12,

Tuck into French-style pizzas. Kids' portions and highchairs available.

TGI Fridays

Cribbs Causeway **t** (0117) 9591987
www.tgifridays.co.uk
Open Mon–Thurs 12–10.30, Fri and Sat 12–11.30, Sun 12–10.30

All the waiters and waitresses working at TGI's have been carefully selected for their ability to entertain children, the ideal candidate being as adept at magic tricks, juggling and balloon bending as they are at taking orders. Children are given colouring books and crayons and highchairs are available. The American-style food is a bit bland but perfectly acceptable; baby food is free.

Around Bristol

The Stable Door

Horseworld, Staunton Lane **t** (01275) 540173
Open Apr–Sept daily 10–5, Oct–Mar 10–4

Horsey types will love this converted barn restaurant in the grounds of the Horse World Centre (p.164). The rooms are light and spacious and there's a conservatory that backs on to a pretty walled garden. Food ranges from West Country staples such as pasties to ploughman's lunches and there's a children's menu (sausage roll with beans, picnic boxes and sandwiches), plus highchairs and baby changing facilities.

The White Hart

Littleton on Severn **t** (01454) 412275
Open Daily 12 noon–2.30 and 6–11

Excellent country pub with a family room and a beer garden. Highchairs available.

Christchurch

Avon Beach Café

Mudeford **t** (01425) 272162
Open Daily summer: 8.30–7; winter: 9–4

Friendly café set right on the beach – convenient for pitstops throughout the day. There are children's meals, highchairs and baby changing facilities in both male and female toilets.

Boat House River Café and Restaurant

Christchurch Quay **t** (01202) 480033
www.boathouse.co.uk
Open Daily 9am–10pm

Enjoy a morning pastry as you watch the boats drift by on the River Stour. More hearty choices – steaks, fresh fish, etc. – are available at lunchtime and there's a full children's menu (the kitchen is also happy to adapt choices from the adult menu to suit kids' tastes) and a non-smoking section. Roasts are served on Sunday. The restaurant can seat 100 people and there's space for a further 250 diners in the pleasant outdoor area, where you'll also find a crazy golf course.

New Forest Perfumery Gift Shop and Tea Rooms

The Old Courthouse, 11 Castle Street
t (01202) 482893
Open Mon–Sat 10–5 (Sun 11–5 in season)

Tearoom housed in a 12th-century building serving homemade cakes, sandwiches, light lunches and cream teas. There's an adjoining tea garden (with seating for 20) open in summer.

Riverside Inn

Tuckton Bridge **t** (01202) 429210
Open Mon–Sat 11am–11pm, Sun 12 noon–10.30pm

With fine river views from the restaurant, this makes a relaxing spot for a Sunday lunch. There's a menu for children, which comes with crayons and a booklet for colouring in. The food is largely English staples. Highchairs available.

Dorchester

Judge Jeffreys' Lodging

6 High Street **t** (01305) 264369
Open Daily 10–5, Wed–Sat 7.30–10.30

A proper historical setting, this pleasant restaurant opposite the country museum was once the abode of the most notorious judge in British history. He was the man who sentenced more than 70 men to be hanged, drawn and quartered (and many more to be transported) following the failure of the Monmouth Rebellion (p.156). Children can have smaller portions from the main menu or the chef is happy to rustle up a child's meal using fresh ingredients. Highchairs are available and a parent room is in development.

The Old Tea House

High West Street **t** (01305) 263719
Open Apr–Oct Tues–Sun and Bank Hols 10–5; Nov–Mar Wed–Sun 10–4

Cream teas, snacks, homemade soups and 'hot dish of the day' are available from this archetypal country teahouse.

Around Dorchester

Frampton Arms

Moreton (opposite Moreton Station on the B3390) **t** (01305) 852253 **www.framptonarms.co.uk**
Open Mon–Sat 11–2.30 and 6.30–11, Sun 12 noon–3pm and summer 6.30–10.30 (until 7pm in winter)

This pub has a conservatory and restaurant (both non-smoking) situated next to an orchard and serves up traditional English cuisine. Children's menu and highchairs.

Glastonbury

Abbey Tea Rooms Café

16 Magdalene Street **t** (01458) 832852
Open Summer: 10–5.30; winter: 10–5

Snacks, sandwiches, cakes and hot meals (of the lasagne or steak and kidney pie variety). Children's menu and highchairs available. It's non-smoking throughout.

Café Galatea

5a High Street **t** (01458) 834284
www.cafegalatea.co.uk
Open Mon 11–4, Wed–Thurs 11–9, Fri 11–10, Sat 10.30–9, Sun 10.30–9

Vegetarian-vegan very Glastonbury sort of café serving soups, salads, pasta and rice dishes. They're flexible with the size of the portions and have highchairs. It's non-smoking throughout.

Lyme Regis

By the Bay

Marine Parade **t** (01297) 442668
www.bythebay.co.uk
Open Tues–Sat 10.30–9.30 (winter until 9), Sun 10.30–2

Very friendly and amenable restaurant with good fish and meat dishes, plus a carvery every Sunday. There are great views across Lyme Bay to Golden Cap. Children have their own menu (pasta, burgers, fish, etc.) but the kitchen is happy to do smaller portions of adult meals. There are baby changing facilities and highchairs, as well as crayons and colouring sheets for children.

Millside Restaurant

1 Mill Lane, off Coombe Street **t** (01297) 445999
Open Daily 10.30–2 and 7–9.30 (closed Sun evening and Mon in winter)

Mediterranean cuisine served on a pleasant patio at this small villagey restaurant. It opens in the morning for coffee and snacks. They're flexible with the size of the portions and have highchairs.

Poole

Corkers Restaurant
1 High Street, The Quay **t** (01202) 681393
www.corkers.co.uk
Open Daily. Café bar: 8am–12 midnight,
restaurant: for lunch and dinner
Café bar and restaurant (with children's menu
offered in both) overlooking the Quayside.
Highchairs and baby changing facilities available.

Salterns Restaurant
Salterns Hotel, 38 Salterns Road **t** (01202) 707321
Open Daily 7.30–9.30, 12 noon–2pm (3pm Sun) and
7–9.30
Attractive waterside restaurant offering al
fresco dining, French-style cuisine and a
continental atmosphere. Children's menu and
highchairs are available.

Sands Brasserie
Sandbanks Hotel, Shore Road **t** (01202) 707377
Open Wed–Sat 7.30–10pm
Beachside brasserie with views across to
Studland Bay. Just in front is a kiosk selling
snacks and ice creams.

Purbeck

The Blue Pool
Furzebrook, near Wareham **t** (01929) 551408
Open Apr–Oct daily 10–5
The Blue Pool is famed for the lovely shades of
its waters and makes the perfect spot for a family
walk before sitting down to tea. The on-site
tearoom has pine floors and serves cream teas,
snacks, sandwiches, cakes and soup. There's a
small charge for entry to the area but families can
explore the woods and children's play area, visit
the clay pottery museum and browse the toy and
gift shops.

The Greyhound Inn
The Square, Corfe Castle **t** (01929) 480205
Open Daily 11–3 and 6–11.30
This historic inn at the foot of the castle has
a large beer garden and children's room with
games and colouring books. There's also a
children's menu with lasagne, fish, scampi and
vegetarian dishes.

Salisbury

Cross Keys Restaurant
Cross Keys Chequer, Queen Street **t** (01722) 320933
www.thecrosskeysrestaurant.com
Open Mon–Sat 8.45–5
Set in a 14th-century listed building, this café-
restaurant serves cakes and sandwiches, as well
as a full traditional English menu. Children's
menu and highchairs available. Non-smoking
throughout.

Debenhams
Blue Boar Row, Market Place **t** (01722) 333212
Open Daily 9–5.30
On the third floor of a 15th-century building,
this Tudor-themed English restaurant (waitress
service) is supremely family friendly offering
light snacks and hearty English dishes, a full
children's menu, free baby food, baby warmers
for bottles, highchairs, cradle chairs and a baby
changing room.

George and Dragon
85 Castle Street **t** (01722) 333942
Open Food: Mon–Sat 11.30–2.30 and 6.30–9,
Sun 12 noon–2.30
Typical English village pub with a long lawned
garden leading down to the River Avon. Small
children's menu but management are happy to
adapt dishes from the main menu.

Harbour Fish and Chips
11–13 Salt Lane **t** (01722) 411888
Open Mon–Sat 11.30–2.15 and 5–10
Multi award-winning traditional fish and chip
restaurant housed in a Grade II listed building.
Chips are free for toddlers. Eat in or take away.
Highchairs available.

Pizza Express
50 Blue Boar Row **t** (01722) 415191
www.pizzaexpress.co.uk
Open Daily 11–11.30
Large two-floor branch of the family-friendly
pizza chain. There's no children's menu but
they're flexible regarding how many kids share a
pizza and have a selection of starters and smaller
main meals. Highchairs available.

Weston-super-Mare

The Atlantic Fish Bar

69–71 Meadow Street **t** (01934) 629667
Open Mon–Fri 11.30–2.30 and 5–10.30,
Sat 11.30–10.30

Very popular fish and chip restaurant offering a full children's menu and highchairs.

Papa's

20 Waterloo Street **t** (01934) 626565
Open 11.30–10 (takeaway until 10.30pm)

Fresh fish is bought from local markets and they offer a special 'small fry' menu for under 10s. Highchairs available. Eat in or take away.

Weymouth

Perry's

Trinity Road, the Old Harbourside **t** (01305) 785799
www.perrysrestaurant.co.uk
Open Tues–Fri and Sun 12 noon–2, Mon–Sat 7–9.30

Fish and chips. Children's portions served.

Scoffers Pan Pizza

22 Westham Road **t** (01305) 786048
Open 10–late daily

Simple fast food – pizzas, burgers, fish and chips, etc. Children's portions available.

Seagull

Trinity Road, the Old Harbourside **t** (01305) 784782
Open Summer: 11.45–10.30; winter: Tues–Sat
11.45–2 and 4.45–9

Weymouth's oldest fish and chip restaurant offers a full children's menu. Eat in or take away.

Cheddar cheese

During the last 100 years, the method for making cheddar has been copied widely throughout the world. However, until the end of the 19th century, Cheshire cheese was far more common, cheddar still being made in only small quantities and regarded as a luxury. The strong tang and firm texture result from the old practice of small farmers combining their milk to make one very big co-operative cheese, which is then matured for an unusually long time.

The Southwest
Cornwall · Devon

Special events

February
St Ives: Hurling of the Silver Ball **t** (01736) 796297
May
Helston: Furry Dance **t** (01326) 565431
Padstow: 'Obby Oss' **t** (01841) 533449
June
Exeter Festival **t** (01392) 265200
July
Exeter: Open Air Shakespeare Plays **t** (01392) 265200
Falmouth: Carnival **t** (01326) 312300
August
Dartmouth: Royal Regatta **t** (01803) 834224
Falmouth: Regatta: **t** (01326) 312300
Newquay: British National Surfing Championships
t (020) 7371 7773
Sidmouth: International Festival **t** (01395) 579564
Torbay: Regatta and Paignton Children's Festival
t 0906 680 1268 **www.torbay10k.co.uk**
September
St Ives: September Festival **t** (01736) 366077
www.stivesseptemberfestival.co.uk
November
Ottery St Mary: Bonfire Night and 'Rolling of the
Tar Barrels' **t** (01404) 813964

Highlights

Beach holidays p.210
Pony trekking, Dartmoor National Park pp.227–8
Spooky caves, Torquay p.220
Steam trains, Totnes p.223
Surfing, Newquay p.195
Tropical greenery, Eden Project (near St Austell)
    pp.221–2
Water fun, QuayWest, Paignton p.216

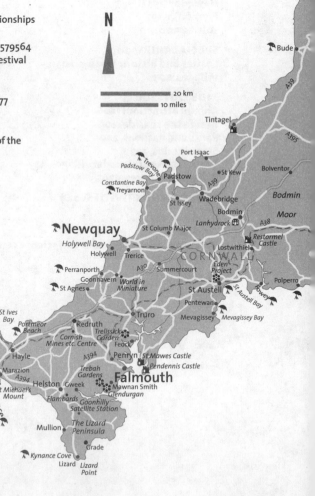

The Southwest is best experienced out of doors. Good for walking (three of the country's great swathes of wilderness can be found here) and beach holidays – the peninsula boasts hundreds of miles of sandy coastline – it enjoys more sunny days per year than any other English region. During the Dark Ages, it provided a refuge for Celtic-British tribes fleeing the invading Angles and Saxons and has a strong Celtic heritage and claims many links with the legendary King Arthur. Today, it is best known as the country's favourite holiday region, a happy collection of country cottages, family hotels, farms, zoos and teashops (serving up Devon's equally legendary cream teas). Whatever your animal fancy, whether it slithers, wriggles, flaps, buzzes or prowls, you'll find it somewhere in the Southwest. From show farms and sanctuaries to sea life centres and aquaria, there are few better places for kids to get up close and personal with members of the animal kingdom.

Day-trip itinerary

Morning: Paignton Zoo Environmental Park (p.216), then a ride on the Paignton and Dartmouth Steam Railway to Kingswear (p.216).
Lunch: Watching ferries at The Royal Dart Bars (p.233).
Afternoon: Cruise up the River Dart to Totnes (pp.201–2). Cream tea at Anne of Cleves tearoom (p.238), then wander around Totnes (p.200). In summer, shopkeepers dress in medieval costume.

Exeter

Getting there By road: Exeter is 170 miles from London, 75 miles from Bristol and 45 miles from Plymouth and can be reached via the M5, the A38 and the A30. By train: Services arrive at its two train stations, Exeter Central and Exeter St David's (which is just outside the city centre), from London Waterloo, London Paddington, Bristol and Salisbury. By bus/coach: The bus station is on Paris Street. There are regular National Express coach services to Exeter from London Victoria, Bristol and Salisbury

Tourist information Civic Centre, Paris Street t (01392) 265700 www.exeter.gov.uk

Exeter, the county town of Devon, is the west country's largest town and main transport hub. Although hardly beautiful – its cathedral and guildhall aside, much of the centre is modern and generic – it is full of character with a thriving university and a lively, youthful ambience. Most of the town's attractions are grouped around the pedestrianized High Street, making it easily navigable by foot (both large and little), and there's a decent selection of department stores, open air markets and shopping malls to explore. In the summer, Exeter Quayside is the place to go for a drink, especially at the weekend when there are often street entertainers, jazz bands and a bouncy castle for the kids. At all times of year, children are well catered for with a variety of activities to choose from – boat trips, cycle rides, special child-friendly guided walks, tours of spooky underground passages, etc. – and the town makes a perfect base for exploring nearby Dartmoor. To find the city at its most vibrant, come in June when the Exeter Festival, a two-week celebration of music, theatre and (best of all) fireworks, is in full swing.

For a deluxe snack or gourmet sandwich, try Michael Caines Boutique, a stylish delicatessen at Cathedral Yard, t (01392) 256200, www.michaelcaines.com. Look out for the locally produced crisps. The deli will even supply an entire picnic hamper. You can eat on the lawns around the cathedral or head out to the wilds of Dartmoor for a perfect outdoor lunch. For basics, there is a Tesco Metro on High Street.

A little bit of history

Two thousand years ago Exeter was a small Celtic settlement made up of just a few simple huts. Despite its lowly status, the Romans, who invaded Britain in the 1st century AD, clearly saw something they liked here, making it one of their main army camps and building it up into one of the most important towns in the whole country. When the Romans left in the early 5th century AD, the town was passed from owner to owner – the Britons were kicked out by the Saxons, who were kicked out by the Vikings, who were kicked out by another lot of Vikings – before being recaptured by Alfred the Great in the 10th century, who ordered a massive rebuilding programme. By the time of the Norman Conquest in 1066, it was once again the Southwest's dominant town – it took William the Conqueror two whole months to break through its walls – and continued to grow throughout the medieval period when it became an important trading port. Although much of it was destroyed in the Second World War, parts of old Exeter do remain, including the medieval Guildhall (still in use), some picturesque Tudor houses, a few parts of the old Roman wall, and, the vast 750-year-old cathedral, which still dominates the city's skyline.

Things to see and do
Boats and bikes

Boat trips on the River Exe and Exeter Ship Canal are offered nearby. Canoes and bikes are available for hire from Saddles and Paddles, 4 Kings Wharf, The Quay, t (01392) 424241, www.saddlepaddle.co.uk. Bike hire for adults costs £14 for a full day, for a child £10 for a full day (child seats are £6). A canoe (carries 2 adults and 2 children) can be rented for £10 (for the first hour, £9 for the second), a single kayak £7 or double kayak £9. The Exeter Canal Trail, which starts on the other side of the river (reached via the Trews Weir Suspension Bridge just south of the quay), offers 14 miles of traffic-free cycling.

Can you spot?
Parliament Street, near the cathedral, one of the narrowest streets in the country: at one end it is just 60 centimetres (25 inches) wide.

Can you spot?

The 'House that Moved': a narrow 15th-century house that once stood near the waterfront. When plans were drawn up for a new city bypass, the house was going to be demolished until the council decided to cut it from its foundations, put it on rollers and move it out of the way. The house now stands 137 metres (150 yards) from where it was originally built.

Cinemas and theatres See pp.231, 232–3

Exeter Quayside

Quay House Visitor Centre, The Quay
t (01392) 271611
Open Easter–Oct daily 10–5 **Adm Free**

Exeter's quays once bustled with activity inspired by a thriving wool trade. Now, as with so many other quayside areas where trade has long since dried up, they have been transformed into a sort of arts-cum-leisure complex. The warehouses and customs buildings have been turned into souvenir shops, cafés, craft centres and pubs, while the Quay House itself is now a heritage centre, where you can find out about the history of the city through a range of exhibits and audiovisual presentations.

Rougemont Gardens

Behind the Royal Albert Memorial Museum, the landscaped Rougemont Gardens provide a nice spot for a picnic and a place for children to let off steam, with good views of the surrounding countryside, particularly the Haldon Hills rising in the west. Open-air performances of Shakespeare plays are put on here every July.

Royal Albert Memorial Museum and Art Gallery

Queen Street t (01392) 665858 www.exeter.gov.uk
Open Mon–Sat 10–5 **Adm Free**
Café, gift shop, mother and baby facilities, disabled facilities

Exeter's main museum has a vast stuffed animal collection, an accessible history section and runs a programme of workshops and children's activities.

Shopping

Exeter has a good selection of shops. The main shopping area is along the High Street, where you'll find an Early Learning Centre for toys, Claire's Accessories for a girly shopping fix, Marks & Spencer and HMV for CDs and computer games. Mothercare and Woolworths are in the Guildhall Shopping Centre. There's a farmers' market in Fore Street on the last Wednesday of the month and a Victorian Christmas market at the end of November.

Sport and activities See pp.229–30

St Peter's Cathedral

Cathedral Close t (01392) 285983
www.exeter-cathedral.org.uk
Open 9.30–5
Adm Free (£3.50 donation)
Refectory restaurant, shop, audiotour and Braille guide, disabled access

Looming down over Exeter's low-rise skyline, this great medieval cathedral, with its two distinctive Norman towers, has been the city's main visitor attraction for well over 700 years now. It is well worth a visit, especially if you can time it so you catch one of the daily guided tours, which take place between March and October at 11am (Mon–Sat), 12.30pm (Jul–Sept Mon–Sat only), 2.30pm (Mon–Fri) and 1.30pm (Sun). A decent children's guidebook is also available. Inside, look out for the flag that Captain Scott took to the North Pole and the 15th-century astronomical clock in the north transept, which was apparently the inspiration for the children's nursery rhyme *Hickory Dickory Dock*. The cathedral houses a fascinating collection of predominantly colonial tombs. Gruesome kids will want to spot the plaque that commemorates 19-year-old Rachel O'Brien, who was burnt alive when her dress caught fire in 1820. Cathedral Close is the place to hang out on a sunny day and have a picnic. It's also home to Mol's Coffee House, where the great Elizabethan sailors, Sir Francis Drake (the first Englishman to sail around the world) and Sir Walter Raleigh (who famously laid his coat over a puddle to prevent Queen Elizabeth I from getting her feet wet), used to meet to discuss their plans for fighting the Spanish Navy.

Tours and guided walks

Enquiries: Exeter City Council, Civic Centre, Paris Street t (01392) 265203

Perhaps the best way to get to know the city is by joining one of the free guided walks provided by Exeter City Council in the company of a 'red coat' guide. As well as tours taking in all the principal sights of the city, the red coats also offer numerous very popular themed tours – 'Ghosts and Legends' (Exeter is supposedly one of England's most haunted cities), 'Murder and Mayhem', 'Exeter through the ages', etc. – as well as a unique torchlight tour of the city's catacombs, which are otherwise closed to visitors. Some tours are up to 90 minutes long, although the council does occasionally organize special children's tours for the 5–10 age range. These are shorter and adopt a more hands-on approach. Most tours leave from Cathedral Yard, outside the Royal Clarence Hotel.

★Underground Passages
Romangate Passage, High Street t (01392) 665887
Open Call for details
Adm Adults £3.75, children £2.75, family (2+3) £11
Gift shop, guided tours

These narrow, winding subterannean passageways were constructed in the 13th century as a means of bringing water into the city. Today, you can explore the spooky network as part of a guided tour which begins with an introductory exhibition and video presentation. The guides are highly entertaining and take great joy in regaling their audience with tales of the ghosts. It is not for the squeamish or claustrophobic. It is advisable to wear a sturdy pair of shoes. Due to development of the surrounding area the underground passages will be closed until autumn 2007. Call **t** (01392) 265206 for up-to-date information.

Around Exeter

Canonteign Falls and Lakeland, 8 miles southwest (p.221)
Castle Drogo, 5 miles west (p.203)
Crealy Adventure Park, 4 miles east (p.224)
Dartmoor, 5 miles southwest (p.227)
Killerton House and Gardens, 6 miles northeast (p.203)

Falmouth

Getting there By road: Falmouth is 12 miles south of Truro off the A394, 10 miles north of the Lizard Peninsula off the B3291 and 58 miles southwest of Plymouth. By train: There are regular branch line

services to and from Truro which is on the main London Paddington–Penzance line. By coach: National Express runs services from London via Truro
Tourist information 11 Market Strand **t** (01326) 312300 **f** (01326) 313457

The focal point of Cornwall's biggest town is its large natural harbour, packed throughout the year with colourful sailing boats, passenger ferries and ocean-going ships. Sightseeing boat trips are offered from the Prince of Wales Pier. Away from the harbour, the town itself is rather non-descript with a typical high street full of the usual souvenir shops and standard seaside cafés. It is home to the brand-new National Maritime Museum, and one mile south of the centre, a castle where medieval-themed entertainments are laid on in summer. Check out the views from the 111-step Jacob's Ladder leading off from the old town square. There's also a good beach and some pleasant hotels.

Things to see and do
★Boat trips
The following companies (which run in season weather permitting) offer sightseeing boat trips to St Mawes and Truro and along the coast to see medieval smugglers' hideouts:
Enterprise Boats t (01326) 374241
www.enterprise-boats.co.uk
St Mawes Ferries t (01872) 862312
www.stmawes-ferry.co.uk

Cinemas and theatres *See pp.231, 232–3*

National Maritime Museum
Discovery Quay **t** (01326) 313 388
www.nmmc.co.uk
Open Daily 10–5 **Adm** Adults £7, children £4.80, under 5s **free**, family (2+2) £18.50
Restaurant, shop, baby changing facilities, parking

Already Falmouth's main tourist attraction, this brand-new interactive museum is seriously hands-on, visually impressive and suitable for all ages. The exhibition kicks off with the help of a series of large screens, where you can feel what it's like to race in a regatta and experience just how frightening a storm at sea can be. Then it charts the rise of the post office's fleet of Packet ships that set sail from here for America and once made Falmouth the second busiest port in the British Empire. You can also watch boat builders repair and restore boats and sail your own on the boating pond. From the lookout across the harbour, you can catch a lift right down to the bottom of the sea. In the base of the tower, which is below the water level, you can watch the tide rise and fall through huge glass windows. If you stay long enough, you can see the tide move five miles. There is a lovely café with an imaginative menu, which also sells baby food and has views across the harbour. You can buy nice souvenirs and gifts at the shop. Look out for the locally made fish-motif jewellery for teenagers and the selection of model boats and pocket-money toys.

★Pendennis Castle

Pendennis Headland **t** (01326) 316594
www.english-heritage.org.uk
Open Apr–Jun and Sept Sun–Mon 10–5, Sat 10–4; Jul–Aug 10–6, Sat 10–4; Oct–Mar daily 10–4
Adm Adults £4.80, children £2.40, under 5s **free**
Souvenir and snack shops, picnic area, mother and baby facilities, disabled facilities, on-site parking

Built as a coastal defence during the reign of Henry VIII, the castle was besieged by the parliamentary forces in the Civil War – it took them over five months to starve the Royalists into submission – and today offers great views along the coast and its sandy beaches. During spring and summer, the castle puts on family entertainments, including an Easter Egg Hunt, a Tudor Kitchen Experience (what Henry VIII used to have for lunch) and a Medieval Jousting Tournament.

Sport and activities *See pp.229–30*

Around Falmouth

Flambards, 1 mile southwest (p.224)
National Seal Sanctuary, 6 miles southwest (p.208)
St Mawes Castle, 3 miles east (p.204)
Trebah Gardens, 3 miles south (p.222)

Newquay

Getting there By road: Newquay is 10 miles northeast of St Agnes off the A3075 and 14 miles southwest of Padstow off the B3276. Traffic congestion can be severe during peak season. By train: It is on the main London–Penzance rail route out of London Paddington. By air: Ryanair fly to Newquay from London Stanstead. By bus/coach: Coaches run daily from London and National

Express services from Plymouth, Bristol and Manchester Contact Western National **t** (01208) 79898
Tourist information Marcus Hill **t** (01637) 854020
www.newquay.org.uk

Thanks to its recent rebranding as the 'surf capital of the UK', Newquay is now a hugely popular resort with thousands coming each summer to ride its big Atlantic breakers. Choppy seas, however, are not its only attraction. It boasts no less than 10 sandy beaches, the most popular of which is probably the 365m (400-yard) rock pool-lined Towan Beach, although this can get very crowded in summer. Lusty Glaze and Porth Beach are usually slightly less congested. All have lifeguards, warning signs, summer dog bans and are cleaned daily during the season.

On rainy days, Newquay has a wide range of indoor attractions. There's a zoo (parts of it are indoors), a good aquarium, a swimming complex, Newquay Waterworld, a waxwork museum, Tunnels Through Time, and a leisure centre, Blue Lagoon, with a tropical fun pool and 10-pin bowling. Should none of these tickle your fancy, you could always head out of town to the Holywell Bay theme park or to the most singular offering of all, Dairy Land Farm World, where cows are milked on a merry-go-round to the sound of classical music!

The town has a young, happening feel to it with lots of bars and nightclubs although occasional

Surf's up!

Newquay's beaches are excellent places to learn how to surf. Children should probably stick to the north-facing beaches around Newquay Bay – Great Western Beach and Tolcarne Beach in particular – where experienced instructors will start them off on bellyboards. Experienced surfers, however, will probably want to try the famed waves of Fistral Beach, which faces directly out into the Atlantic. The waves that break on the sand here have travelled an unbroken 3,000-mile course across the ocean and, when the wind's up, can be pretty fearsome (which, of course, is just how the best surfers like them). Fistral has hosted numerous national and international surfing competitions (*see* pp.229–30 for surf schools).

Tip: For an update on the day's surfing conditions, call **t** 09068 360360.

outbreaks of rowdiness have led to an alcohol ban on the streets. Nonetheless, it's a fun-loving place and despite its recent increase in popularity, it remains an old-fashioned family resort town, albeit a bit tacky. The best family hotels are outside the town centre so you'll need a car. Newquay isn't a great place to shop unless you want to buy some surf gear. You'll need to head for Truro if you're looking for some retail therapy.

Things to see and do

★Blue Reef Aquarium

Towan Promenade **t** (01637) 878134
www.bluereefaquarium.co.uk
Open Daily 9.30–6
Adm Adults £6.99, children £4.99, family (2+2) £19.99, family (2+3) £23.99
Café, snack shop and souvenir shop, mother and baby facilities, disabled facilities

Overlooking Towan Beach, the aquarium is home to all the usual suspects, including sharks, jellyfish, octopuses, seahorse, and there's a walk-through sea-bed tunnel.

Cinemas and theatres See pp.231, 232–3

★Dairy Land Farm World

Summercourt, Newquay **t** (01872) 510246
www.dairylandfarmworld.com
Getting there 4 miles from Newquay on the A3058 Newquay–St Austell road
Open Apr–Oct daily 10–5
Adm Adults £7.75, children £46.75, under 3s **free**, family ticket (2+3) £27
Café, picnic areas, gift shop, mother and baby facilities, disabled facilities, on-site parking

This is where it all started. Dairy Land was the first farm in the country to think of turning itself into a family-orientated tourist attraction. It's still one of the region's top draws, principally because of its spectacular daily milking shows, where you can watch cows being milked on a spinning merry-go-round to the accompaniment of classical music. Rather eccentric. There are also lots of animals to stroke, an assault course, a labyrinth, mini JCBs and trailer rides available as well as an indoor play area with drop slides and ball pools.

Holywell Bay Fun Park

Holywell Bay **t** (01637) 830095
www.holywellbay.co.uk
Getting there Holywell Bay is 2 miles southwest of Newquay on the A3075
Open Apr–Oct 10.30–5.30 (Jul–Aug closes later)
Adm Entry to the park is **free**, individual activities are charged for
Café, snack shops

Go-karts, bumper boats, crazy golf and lots of gentle rides at this small-scale family fun park.

Newquay Waterworld

Trenance Leisure Park **t** (01637) 853828
www.newquaywaterworld.co.uk
Open Daily times vary so call in advance
Adm Adults £4.90, children £3.90, under 5s £1.90, under 2s **Free**
Café, mother and baby facilities, disabled facilities, on-site parking

Next door to Newquay Zoo, Waterworld is one of the best swimming complexes in the Southwest, with an 18m (60ft) water flume, a waterfall, a mushroom fountain, lots of slides and a toddlers' pool.

★Newquay Zoo

Trenance Gardens **t** (01637) 873342
www.newquayzoo.co.uk
Open Apr–Sept 9–6, Oct–Nov 10–5 (last entry 1 hour before closing)
Adm Adults £8.95, children £6, under 4s **free**, family £25
Café, snack and souvenir shops, picnic areas, mother and baby facilities, guided tours, disabled facilities

With lions, penguins, monkeys and zebras among its many residents, Newquay Zoo requires a whole day to do it justice. Start in the morning with a quick trip to the Village Farm, where you can bond with the farm animals and view chipmunks running through tunnels above your head, then it's on to watch the lemurs being fed at 11am. At 12.30, head to the penguin pool and watch the hungry birds gobble their way through buckets of fish. Then, following a spot of lunch yourself, watch a real appetite being satisfied when the big cats are fed at 2.30pm. Finish the day with a quick scoot around the maze and a trip to Waterworld, a large swimming complex with slides and a wave machine, which occupies part of the same site. Small children will enjoy feeding the ducks and meeting Santa at Christmas.

Sport and activities *See pp.229–30*

Tunnels Through Time
St Michael's Road **t** (01637) 873379
www.tunnelsthroughtime.co.uk
Open Easter–Oct Sun–Fri 10–5
Adm Adults £4.40, children £2.20, family £12.80
Gift shop, snacks

Small, low-key waxwork reconstructions of Cornwall's greatest myths and legends with an obligatory gory section 'The Dungeon of Despair'.

Around Newquay

Bodmin Moor, 12 miles northeast (p.226)
Trerice, 3 miles southeast (p.205)

Plymouth

Getting there By road: Plymouth is 46 miles south-west of Exeter and 211 miles from London, off the A38. By train: There are direct train links with London, Exeter, Bristol and Penzance. By coach: National Express coaches run a frequent service from Bristol and London Victoria
Tourist information 9 The Barbican **t** (01752) 306330 www.plymouth.gov.uk

Little of interest may ever have taken place in Plymouth itself, but people are forever leaving it to do exciting things. An important naval base for much of its history, most stories about Plymouth begin with someone setting sail away from it. In 1588, Sir Francis Drake set out from Plymouth to engage the Spanish Armada in battle (he won, having first finished his game of bowls on the Hoe, of course) and, in 1620, this was where 102 pilgrims reboarded a ship called the *Mayflower* with the intention of starting a new life in a vast empty country that would one day be called America (the ship had originally set sail from Southampton but had to stop off at Plymouth for repairs). The ship was anchored just in front of where the aquarium stands today. In the 18th century, Plymouth provided the base for Captain Cook's numerous journeys of discovery (to Australia, the South Seas and Antarctica) and, in the early 19th century, was the main departure point for ships carrying convicts to the penal colonies of Australia.

Can you spot?
Drake's Drum, which supposedly starts beating to summon the great seaman whenever the nation is in danger.

Thanks to the attention of the *Luftwaffe* in the Second World War, little evidence of Plymouth's historic past survives and most of the town is modern and generic. Exceptions include the Barbican, a carefully preserved section of old buildings and narrow streets near the harbour, an Elizabethan captain's cottage and the Royal Citadel, a 17th-century fortress, which looms above the town. Plymouth's most picturesque spot is its famous Hoe, the landscaped area in front of the Sound, the great basin of water formed by the combined estuaries of the Plym, Tavy and Tamar rivers. It is a great place to sit watching sailing boats on sunny afternoons and is dotted with numerous memorials (to Drake, to the defeat of the Armada, to the airmen of the Second World War and to the Navy) and has a reconstructed red and white lighthouse, Smeaton's Tower, which you can climb for the best views of the Sound. Find out more about the town's history at the Plymouth Dome, next to Smeaton's Tower, a modern retelling of the Plymouth story using reconstructions, videos and touch-screen computers, and even follow in the footsteps of one of the town's illustrious fore-bears on one of the numerous sightseeing boat trips offered at the harbour. Other attractions include the National Marine Aquarium, home to sharks, rays and jellyfish, the City of Plymouth Museums and Art Gallery and, outside town, Buckland Abbey, the former home of Sir Francis Drake, where costumed guides will regale you with tales of derring-do on the high seas.

The Barbican is the place to head for a quick snack. Cap'n Jaspers **t** (01752) 2622444 on Fishmarket is a good friendly burger and hot dog takeaway, while there are lots of sandwich takeaways on the waterfront. Monty's, **t** (01752) 252877, just opposite the Aquarium, is a pleasant trendy café with sofas were you can get good, reasonably priced sandwiches all day. The Dolphin Café inside the Plymouth Dome, **t** (01752) 603300, has a great view if you aren't too fussed about the food.

Things to see and do

★Buckland Abbey
Yelverton **t** (01822) 853607
www.nationaltrust.org.uk
Open Apr–Oct Fri–Wed 10.30–5.30, Nov–Mar
Sat–Sun 2–5 (early Dec 11–5)
Adm Adults £7, children £3.50, family £17.50
Café, snacks, gift shop, mother and baby facilities,
disabled facilities, on-site parking
Not suitable for pushchairs; baby carriers for hire

Six miles north of Plymouth stands Buckland
Abbey, a former monastery that was Sir Francis
Drake's home from 1582 (the year he became
Mayor of Plymouth) until his death in 1596, and
remained in the Drake family until 1946. It holds
a good deal of Drake memorabilia. Tours of the
house and its extensive grounds are provided by
guides in Tudor costume. In the summer, there
are craft workshops and activities for children –
you can even relive one of Drake's most famous
moments with a game of bowls on the lawn.

Cawsand Ferry
t (07833) 936863 **www**.cawsandferry.com
Embarkation point Mayflower Steps. Sails to
Cawsand in Cornwall during the summer
months, weather permitting.

Cinemas and theatres *See pp.231, 232–3*

City of Plymouth Museums and Art Gallery
Drake Circus **t** (01752) 304774
Open Tues–Fri 10–5.30, Sat and Bank Hols 10–5
Adm Free
Baby changing facilities, shop, disabled access
The museum has a good natural history section,
a hands-on discovery centre for children and a
good exhibition, 'Tales of the City'. There are kids'
workshops during the school holidays.

Cremyll Ferry
t (01752) 822105 **www**.tamarcruising.com
Embarkation point Admiral's Hard. Sails to
Mount Edgcumbe in Cornwall, all year round.

Crownhill Fort
Crownhill Fort Road **t** (01752) 793754
www.crownhillfort.co.uk
Getting there On the A386 4 miles north of
Plymouth
Open Call for opening times
Adm Adults £5, children £3, family (2+2) £14
Adventure playground, kids' trails

One of the best-preserved forts built along the
South Coast by the Victorians to repel a French
invasion that never happened. Toy soldier
fanatics will enjoy exploring the huge 16-acre
site. The barracks are laid out to give you an idea
of what it would have been like to serve as a
soldier at the fort and kids can dress up in
various Victorian outfits.

Elizabethan House
32 New Street, The Barbican **t** (01752) 304774
Open Apr–Oct 10–5, Tues–Sat
Adm Adults £1.30, children 80p
National Trust shop and information centre
This timber-framed tudor sea captain's house is
the oldest building in Plymouth. Costumed
guides provide nautically-themed tours.

★National Marine Aquarium
Rope Walk, Coxside **t** (01752) 600301
www.national-aquarium.co.uk
Open Apr–Oct daily 10–6; Nov–Mar daily 10–5
Adm Adults £9.50, children £5.75, under 3s **free**,
family (2+2) £27
Café, gift shop, mother and baby facilities, on-site
parking, disabled facilities
There's a Freshwater Pool, a British Coastal Pool,
a Tropical Pool, a Shark Theatre, Europe's largest
collection of seahorses and a Discovery Pool
where children can stroke the rays. Daily talks and
presentations on sharks, rockpool rambles and
creatures of the deep are given and you can
watch divers descend into the Deep Reef to feed
hundreds of fish by hand. The café, which
provides a good, child-friendly menu, overlooks
the Barbican and Plymouth Sound. There's a
special Christmas Grotto in December.

Plymouth Boat Cruises
t (01752) 822797
The main embarkation point is Phoenix Wharf.
Sails past the Naval Dockyard and along the
Tamar and Yealm rivers.

★Plymouth Dome
The Hoe, Hoe Road **t** (01752) 603300
www.plymouthdome.info
Open Apr–Oct 10–5; Nov–Mar 10–4
Adm Dome: adults £4.75, children £3.25, family £13.
Dome and Tower: adults £6.50, children £4,
family £16
Café, gift shop, mother and baby facilities, disabled
facilities, on-site parking

Sir Francis Drake

Who was Sir Francis Drake?

The greatest English sea adventurer of all time, or a low-down stinking, cheating pirate – depending on whether you're English or Spanish, of course.

What difference does that make?

Drake won many sea battles for the English and brought the country much wealth. The trouble is, most of it was stolen from Spain.

So, he was a posh, bullying robber?

Not really. Unusually for the 16th century, Drake was actually a self-made man. Born in 1540, the son of a humble Devon farmer, Drake began his nautical career aged just 13 as an apprentice on a small ship sailing between the North Sea ports. He showed such ability, however, that when his captain died, he left Drake his ship.

How did he become famous?

By being good at what he did. By his late twenties, he was already recognized as one of the best sailors of the age bringing him to the attention of Queen Elizabeth I, who was looking for skilled sailors to take part in her 'secret war' with Spain.

What did she have against Spain?

In the 16th century England and Spain were squabbling over who should control the newly discovered American continents. Elizabeth didn't want to start a proper war with Spain, she just wanted to make sure that Spain kept its paws off America, so she encouraged Drake to attack and plunder those bits of America owned by Spain. Over the next few years, he made many raiding journeys to South America aboard his trusty ship, the *Golden Hinde*, stealing as much Spanish loot as he could. At one point his ship was so laden with gold and treasure that it almost sank.

So he was just a pirate with royal approval?

Well, he was also a great adventurer, becoming the first Englishman to set eyes on the Pacific and the first to sail all the way around the world, returning to Plymouth in 1580 to a hero's welcome, where was knighted aboard his ship by the Queen. He was also Mayor of Plymouth for a while. Nonetheless, despite his success, he carried on with his campaigns against the Spanish. In 1585, he wreaked so much havoc in Spain's West Indian territories that the Bank of Spain went bankrupt.

Spain can't have been too happy.

Correct. By 1587, Philip II, the King of Spain, had had enough. He ordered that a fleet or 'Armada' be built with the intention of invading and capturing England. Drake's reaction was to sail into Cadiz Harbour and set fire to the fleet, an event which became known as the 'singeing of the King of Spain's beard'. The next year, with the Spanish fleet rebuilt and sailing towards England, Drake led the fight in the Channel, deliberately setting fire to English ships and then sailing them into the midst of the Spanish fleet where they caused panic – forcing the Spanish ships to retreat to deeper waters where they were caught in a storm and destroyed.

He saved the country. He must have been popular.

He was, at least with the ordinary people, who bought souvenirs of his likeness by the thousand, turning him into the equivalent of a modern pop or film star. He was not, however, very popular with the aristocracy, who thought he was rather common and unrefined with his West Country accent and manners. The Queen, however, remained his biggest fan and that, after all, was all that mattered.

So did he live to be a ripe old age, forever telling youngsters about his glory days?

No. By the 1590s Drake was a very wealthy man and could have retired into a very easy private life, but he just couldn't let it lie, not where the Spanish were concerned. In the middle of the decade he led yet another expedition against Spain's West Indian territories. This time, however, his luck finally ran out. He contracted a dreadful tropical fever and died within a few days. He was buried at sea in the Caribbean on 28 January 1596.

Overlooking the Sound, in front of Smeaton's Tower (you can buy joint tickets), the Dome has excellent audiovisual displays designed to bring Plymouth's past to life. There are films on the voyages of Sir Francis Drake and Captain Cook and on the city's near destruction by German bombs in the Second World War. You can walk along a reconstructed Elizabethan Street (with obligatory smells), inspect the deck of a 1930s luxury cruise liner, operate a ship's radar, watch live satellite weather transmissions or simply gaze at the boats coming and going on the Sound from two observation platforms.

Can you spot?
The 'Brutus Stone' on Fore Street where the Trojan king supposedly made his famous declaration. It's outside no.51.

Royal Citadel

The Hoe **t** (01752) 773346
Open May–Sept Tues and Thurs guided tours only 2.30pm
Adm Adults £3.50 children £3
No disabled facilities, not suitable for pushchairs

Plymouth was the only town in the Southwest to be held by the Parliamentary forces during the Civil War. The popular story tells that following the restoration of the monarchy, Charles II had this fortress built in 1666 to show the locals just who was boss. However, the more likely (and sensible) motive was to defend the harbour from a possible Dutch invasion. It is still used by the military although guided tours are available. There are wonderful views of the coast from the ramparts.

Shopping

Plymouth has some of the best shops in the Southwest with lots of high street outlets. The main shopping streets all radiate off Armada Way, where there's a Virgin Megastore should you wish to stock up on CDs and games. Boots, Mothercare and Marks & Spencer are on Old Town Street and Woolworths is on New George Street. The Early Learning Centre toyshop is on Cornwall Street, where there's also an Adams for kids clothes. There's also a large indoor market, a monthly farmers' market and a good Christmas Craft fair.

Smeaton's Tower

The Hoe, Hoe Road **t** (01752) 603300
Open Daily 10–5
Adm Adults £2, children £1, under 5s **free**
No disabled facilities, not suitable for pushchairs

The former lighthouse at Eddystone Rock was moved to Plymouth Hoe in 1884 and provides impressive views of the Sound and the town. The lighthouse keeper's bed and miniature cooker add character to the place and climbing up the ladders is a challenge – don't do it if you are heavily pregnant or have toddlers in tow.

Sport and activities *See pp.229–30*

Tamar Cruising

t (01752) 822105 **www.tamarcruising.co.uk**

The main embarkation point is Mayflower Steps. Sails past the Naval Dockyard and along the Tamar and Yealm rivers.

Around Plymouth

Dartmoor National Park, 5 miles northeast (p.227)
Dartmoor Wildlife Park, 8 miles northeast (p.227)

Totnes

Getting there By road: Totnes is 6 miles from Torbay on the A361, and 24 miles southwest of Exeter via the A381 then A380. By train: There are good rail links with Plymouth and Exeter. By coach: National Express coaches from Exeter and London stop here, as do local buses from Exeter
Tourist information The Town Mill, Coronation Road **t** (01803) 863168 **www.totnesinformation.co.uk**

The residents of Totnes, a small riverside market town first founded in the Middle Ages, have been very careful to preserve the town's links with the past. There are many 16th-century buildings remaining in the atmospheric part of town known as the Narrows. Indeed, the town museum is housed in a four-storey Elizabethan house – displays range from an exhibition on life in Elizabethan times with period furniture, costumes, kitchen utensils, and even toys, to a room devoted to the inventor and local resident Charles Babbage, who created the world's first mechanical computer – while local shopkeepers

Ghost story

Once upon a time, two sisters, Margaret and Eleanor de Pomeroy, fell in love with the same man. Lady Eleanor, convinced that her more beautiful sister would win the gentleman's hand, grew so fiercely jealous that she decided to lock Margaret up in the castle's deepest dungeon, where she starved to death. Today, Margaret is said to haunt the castle and can occasionally be seen wandering along the ramparts dressed in long, white flowing robes – hence her nickname, the White Lady. If you walk backwards around the old tree (near St Margaret's Tower) whilst making a wish, it is said that your wish will come true – although this is not quite as easy as it sounds as the tree is situated on a rough, sloping bank.

even go so far as to dress up in Elizabethan dress on Tuesdays and Saturdays during the summer. In the 11th-century guildhall (which is still in use), you can visit the former jail cells and courtroom. Overlooking the town is the magnificent 14th-century Totnes Castle (p.202), which provides wonderful views of the surrounding countryside.

There are lots of interesting places within easy reach of the town. Dartmoor and the English Riviera are just a few miles away, and there are boat trips available along the River Dart to Dartmouth. You can also take a trip aboard the South Devon Railway (p.202), which runs from Totnes through seven miles of delightful Dart Valley countryside, to visit the wildlife at Buckfast Butterflies and Dartmoor Otter Sanctuary (p.206).

Totnes is a great place to find something different to pop into your picnic basket. Effings on Fore Street has lots of homemade snacks, local produce and gourmet ready meals for self-caterers. Ticklemore Cheese and Fish on Ticklemore Street sell local produce and there's a farmer's market on High Street every Saturday. There's a big super-market on the edge of town for basics.

A little bit of history

According to legend, Totnes was Britain's very first town. Following the end of the Trojan War and the destruction of Troy some 3,000 years ago, the defeated Trojans set sail looking for a new home led by their prince Brutus. They eventually discovered a beautiful island inhabited by a race of slow-witted giants, whom they quickly defeated. Following their victory, Brutus leapt on to a stone and proclaimed 'Here I stand and here I rest, and this place shall be called Totnes'. He decided to name the island Britain after himself.

Things to see and do

Berry Pomeroy Castle
Berry Pomeroy, Totnes **t** (01803) 866618
Getting there 2.5 miles east of Totnes off the A385
Open Apr–Oct daily 10–6 (or dusk if earlier)
Adm Adults £3.60, children £1.80
Café, parking close to castle

Said to be the most haunted castle in England (but then, aren't they all), Berry Pomeroy lies in ruins atop a wooded crag close to the River Dart. The building itself is a combination of medieval castle and Tudor mansion. When Edward Seymour (brother of Jane Seymour, third wife of Henry VIII)

bought it from Sir Thomas de Pomeroy (the first Duke of Somerset and the Lord Protector during the reign of Edward VI), the castle had already been home to 19 generations of de Pomeroys – that's a lot of potential ghosts. There's plenty of space for picnics and various events, including storytellings and medieval tournaments, which are organized here in summer.

Cinemas and theatres *See pp.231, 232–3*

Dartington Cider Press Centre
Dartington **t** (01803) 847500
www.dartingtonciderpress.co.uk
Getting there 2 miles northwest of Totnes, on the A385, and just off the A38
Open Mon–Sat 9.30–5.30; Sun 10.30–5.30
Adm Free
Restaurants, picnic area, shops, disabled facilities, on-site parking

A complex of 12 shops and two restaurants housed in a group of 16th- and 17th-century buildings on the Dartington Hall estate, just outside Totnes. The shops sell a diverse range of goods, including aromatherapy oils, kitchenware, stationery, books, toys, plants and local cheeses and children can run around in the grounds of the hall, which has one of the finest gardens in Devon. (Plays are performed in the garden in summer, call in advance.) On Fridays and week-ends there are usually street entertainers, such as jugglers and jazz bands, on hand to entertain the crowds.

★Riverlink
Steamer Quay, Totnes, and 5 Lower Street, Dartmouth **t** (01803) 834488 **www.riverlink.co.uk**
Open Apr–Oct daily; call in advance for times
Fares Totnes–Dartmouth return: adults £8.50, children £5.50, family £23; Coastal Cruise: adults £8, children £5, family £22; Round Robin (combined Totnes–Dartmouth river cruise and/or open-top sightseeing bus tour, ferry to Kingswear and trip on Paignton and Dartmouth Steam Railway): adults £14.50, children £9.50, family £41

Cruises from Totnes Steamer Quay down the River Dart passing picturesque villages, the Agatha Christie Estate and Royal Naval College before arriving in Dartmouth, where you can take a ferry to join the Paignton and Dartmouth Steam Railway at Kingswear (p.216) or a coastal cruise to Mew Shore to view seabirds and seals.

Shopping

If high streets full of the same old stores are getting you down, you'll find Totnes a refreshing change. Along the main high street, you'll find a selection of small shops selling unusual clothes, toys and souvenirs. Gazebo at 74 High Street has a good selection of trendy trinkets and toys. Tribe Trading Co, a few doors down, stocks everything you need for babies. There's also a Woolworths for basics and a farmers' market every Saturday.

★South Devon Railway

South Devon Railway, Buckfastleigh Station, Buckfastleigh **t** 0845 345 1420
www.southdevonrailway.org
Open Most days from Apr–Nov, Dec Santa Specials
Fares Adult return £8.80, children £5.30, family £25.40
Café, bookshop, picnic area, wheelchair access, adapted toilets, a restored carriage has been specially adapted for wheelchairs

Also known as the 'Primrose Line', this offers seven-mile steam train rides alongside the otherwise inaccessible banks of the River Dart between Totnes and Buckfastleigh. It is one of the best railways in the country for observing and encountering animals, with herons, swans and kingfishers all living on or around the river and a nationally renowned otter and butterfly sanctuary at Buckfastleigh. There's a small railway museum and play area at Buckfastleigh Station, as well as an observation area where you can watch rolling stock being restored.

Sport and activities *See pp.229–30*

Totnes Castle

Castle Street **t** (01803) 864406
www.english-heritage.org.uk
Open Apr–Aug daily 10–6, Sept 10–5, Oct 10–4;
Adm Adults £2.40, children £1.20
Picnic areas

The castle runs a programme of medieval-themed family entertainment throughout the year, including Medieval Music, Medieval Dancing, Medieval Cookery, Medieval Fun and Games, Medieval Mask-making, Medieval Storytellings and Medieval Entertainment and Combat (fighting knights, jugglers, fire-eaters, children's games, etc.).

Crabbing at Dittisham

Getting there Approximately 13 miles from Totnes. Take the A381 Totnes to Kingsbridge road and at Halwell take the B3207 towards Dartmouth, then the local road to Dittisham, which is a small picture postcard village on the River Dart.

As equipment bring: bacon, string and a small bucket (filled with water). The best crabbing is from the jetty, which is down the steep hill, when the tide is well in. Tie the bacon to the string and weight it with a stone. Drop it into the water so that the bacon sits on the bottom then wait. When a crab grabs the bacon, pull it out and shake it off into the bucket. See how many you can catch. Make sure the children are well supervised at all times – a life jacket is a sensible precaution if you have one. Once you've finished, the crabs should be tipped back into the river ready for next time. In the summer, crabbing competitions are organized during the Dittisham Regatta.

Totnes Museum

70 Fore Street **t** (01803) 863 821
Open Easter–Oct Mon–Fri 10.30–5
Adm Adults £1.50, children 50p, under 5s **free**
Gift shop, guided tours

Elizabethan house with a special exhibition on local resident Charles Babbage, who in the nineteenth century, invented the first calculating device – the precursor of the modern-day computer. Other exhibits cover local history and include a Roman skeleton and some Saxon coins.

Around Totnes

Buckfast Butterflies and Dartmoor Otter Sanctuary, 5 miles northwest (p.206)
Dartmoor National Park, 5 miles northwest (p.227)
Dartmouth Castle, 7 miles southeast (p.203)
Hedgehog Hospital at Prickly Ball Farm, 10 miles north (p.207)
Pennywell Farm, 5 miles northwest (p.209)
Woodlands Leisure Park, 7 miles south (p.225)

Castles and historic houses

Castle Drogo

Drewsteignton, near Exeter **t** (01647) 433306
www.nationaltrust.org.uk
Getting there 12 miles west of Exeter, south of the
A30 via Crockernwell
Open Mar–Oct Mon and Wed–Sun 11–4 (until 5 in
summer) Nov Mon and Wed–Sun 11–4, early Dec
Sat and Sun 12–4
Adm Adults £7, children £3.50, family £17.50; garden
only: adults £4.50, children £2.50
Restaurant, tearoom, picnic area, shop, play area,
mother and baby facilities, Braille guide, audio
guide, disabled access (some restrictions in castle)

Built for the millionaire tea baron Julius Drewe
between 1910 and 1932 and designed by Edwin
Lutyens, Castle Drogo occupies a stunning
position perched high on a 275m (900ft) hill
with wonderful views out across the Teign Valley
and Dartmoor. Although the castle looks
medieval from the outside (find the portcullis,
the turrets with arrow slits and note the
6ft/2m-thick walls), it is actually a comfortable,
modern family home inside – the house was
even built with a lift and a telephone (state-of-
the-art luxuries back in the 1930s). Look for the
newly opened collection of dolls' houses (some
are more than a hundred years old), the Bunty
House in the cottage garden, where the first
owner's grandchildren used to play, and take a
walk through the beautiful grounds. If you feel
like getting active, you can hire a croquet set at
reception for a quintessentially English game of
croquet on the lawn.

Cotehele House and Quay

St Dominic, Saltash **t** (01579) 351346
www.nationaltrust.org.uk
Getting there On the west bank of the River Tamar,
8 miles south of Tavistock, 14 miles north of
Plymouth, off the A390
Open Mar–Sept Sat–Thurs 11–4.30, Oct–Feb
Sat–Thurs 11–4
Adm Adults £8, children £4, under 5s **free**, family
£12. Garden only : adults £4.80, children £2.40.
Café, children's guide, picnic area, shop, mother and
baby facilities, disabled access

Magical Tudor house full of dark, mysterious
rooms (to preserve its authenticity there is no
electricity) surrounded by landscaped gardens
and woodland walks leading down to Cotehele

Quay. From May to September, you can take a one-
hour round-trip boat ride to Calstock Quay.

Dartmouth Castle

Castle Road, Dartmouth **t** (01803) 833588
www.english-heritage.org.uk
Getting there 1 mile southeast of Dartmouth off
the B3205
Open Apr–Jun and Sept daily 10–5, Jul–Aug daily
10–6, Oct 10–4, Nov–Mar Sat and Sun 10–4
Adm Adults £3.70, children £1.90
Picnic areas, souvenir shop, on-site parking

Jutting out over the Dart Estuary, Dartmouth
Castle is beautifully positioned and preserved.
Come on one of its regular event days when you
might be able to hear a story being told, try your
hand at medieval mask-making, or hear the
castle's mighty cannons being fired.

Killerton House and Gardens

Broadclyst, Exeter **t** (01392) 881345
www.nationaltrust.org.uk
Getting there On the west side of the B3181
Exeter–Cullompton road, 6 miles northeast of Exeter
Open Mar–Jul and Sept Wed–Mon 11–5, Aug daily
11–5, Oct Wed–Sun 2–4
Adm Adults £5, children £3 family £17.50
Café, picnic area, shop, play area, disabled access

Eighteenth-century house set in a park with
woods, where there are a number of pretty walks
to choose from. You can visit the National Trust
costume museum, which has more than 9,000
outfits, dating from the 18th century to the
present day, and the discovery centre, where there
are different activities laid on every day, including
'Animal Storytellings' and the 'Dragon Walks'.

Lanhydrock

Bodmin **t** (01208) 265950
www.nationaltrust.org.uk
Getting there 2.5 miles southeast of Bodmin, look
out for signs on the A30, the A38 or the B3268
Open Mar–Sept Tues–Sun 11–5.30, Oct 11–5
Adm Adults £9, children £4.50, family £13.50;
Gardens only: adults £5, children £2.50
Café, picnic area, shop, adventure playground,
disabled access

Interesting house full of unusual objects and
Victorian toys set in 180 hectares (450 acres) of
woods, parkland and gardens. The house is a
five-minute walk from the car park or (for a price)
a two-minute chauffeur-driven classic car ride.

Launceston Castle

Castle Lodge, Guildhall Square, Launceston
t (01566) 772365 www.english-heritage.org.uk
Getting there Launceston, 2 miles east of Bodmin
Moor, can be reached via the A30 and the A388
Open Apr–Sept daily 10–5 (Jul–Aug until 6), Oct
10–4 **Adm** Adults £2.30, children £1.20
Picnic areas, gift shop, on-site parking
Not suitable for pushchairs

Numerous events and activities are put on
during the summer at this ruined 12th-century
hilltop castle, including medieval games,
performances of medieval music, sculpture workshops and even clown workshops, where you can
come and learn the jester's trade. The pretty town
of Launceston, which was once Cornwall's capital,
also has its own steam railway (*see* Launceston
Steam Railway, p.223), which trips its way through
two miles of scenic countryside.

Powderham Castle

Kenton t (01626) 890243 www.powderham.co.uk
Getting there 5 miles south of Exeter, on the A379
Open Apr–Oct Sun–Fri 10–5.30
Adm Adults £7.95, children £5.95, family £22.45
Café, tearooms, picnic area, shop

The family seat of the Earl of Devon, this much
restored medieval castle is set in an ancient deer
park. Special family tours of the ever-so-grand
state rooms take place throughout the day and
there's a 'children's secret garden' to explore,
some friendly animals to meet and a play fort to
clamber around in. There are also a number of
shops, including a farm shop selling West
Country produce, a 'House of Marbles' gift shop
which has a huge range of marbles and other
toys and games, and a well-stocked plant centre.
During August there are daily bird of prey shows
and displays.

Restormel Castle

Restormel Road, Lostwithiel t (01208) 872687
www.english-heritage.org.uk
Getting there Restormel is about 5 miles south of
Bodmin, just off the A390
Open Apr–Sept 10–5 (Jul–Aug until 6), Oct 10–4
Adm Adults £2.40, children £1.20
Snacks, shop, disabled access, on-site parking

Restormel's storybook-like Norman castle is
surrounded by a deep moat and offers wonderful
views from its battlements out over the Fowey
Valley. Storytellings and plays for children are
staged during the year, along with historical activities (medieval games and battle re-enactments).

St Mawes Castle

St Mawes, Truro t (01326) 270526
www.english-heritage.org.uk
Getting there St Mawes lies across the water from
Falmouth on the A3078. A ferry service runs from
Falmouth
Open Apr–Jun Sun–Fri 10–5, Jul–Aug Sun–Fri 10–6,
Sept daily 10–5, Oct–Mar Fri–Mon 10–4
Adm Adults £3.60, children £1.80
Snacks, shop, mother and baby facilities,
on-site parking

Built at the same time as Pendennis Castle in
Falmouth, St Mawes has enjoyed over 450 years
of largely trouble-free existence and is still
largely intact. Like many other castles across the
country, it has been turned into a sort of Tudor
theme park with events such as Elizabethan
dances and battle re-enactments organized
throughout the summer.

★St Michael's Mount

West End, Marazion t (01736) 710507
www.stmichaelsmount.co.uk
Getting there Marazion is 5 miles east of Penzance
off the A394
Open Apr–Oct Mon–Fri 10.30–5.30
Adm Adults £6, children £3, family £15
Café, shop, mother and baby facilities
Not suitable for pushchairs

The castle on St Michael's Mount looks as a
castle should: dramatic, mysterious and almost
utterly impregnable. The mount, which lies off
the Cornish coast near Marazion, is reached at
low tide along a splendidly romantic narrow
brick causeway and at high tide (providing the
sea is calm) by ferry. Once on the island, it's a
pretty steep climb to the top, where there are
superb views of Land's End and the Lizard,
respectively England's most westerly and
southerly points. In the castle, which is decorated
with paintings, tapestries and suits of armour,
you can watch an audiovisual display on its
history. Before the castle was built in the mid-
16th century, the islet was occupied by a
Benedictine priory.

★Tintagel Castle

Tintagel **t** (01840) 770328
www.english-heritage.org.uk
Getting there On the north coast, off the A39
Open Apr–Sept 10–6, Oct 10–5, Nov–Mar 10–4
Adm Adults £4.30, children £2.20, under 5s **free**
Café, shop; not suitable for pushchairs

It's fitting that Arthur, the nation's most charismatic king, should have been born here on this wild, windswept Cornish clifftop. It's a hugely atmospheric place with the ruins perched high above the crashing sea and it takes just a little imagination to picture the young king riding out to battle against the latest Saxon invaders or to hunt for the Holy Grail. As with all Arthurian sites, the evidence linking the castle with the king is practically non-existent. Parts of the site do date back to the 5th century AD (although most of what you see is 12th century), which was just before Arthur was born, but that's about it. But who needs evidence when you've got faith? And faith in the village of Tintagel, where 'Excali*burgers*' are devoured by hungry, believing tourists is very strong indeed. In the village, check out King Arthur's Great Halls with its 72 stained glass windows depicting scenes from the legend. Afterwards, wander down to Tintagel's pebble beach, where you can explore a spooky cavern called Merlin's Cave. Be warned, however, that, although the castle is very family-friendly (storytellings, puppet shows and battle re-enactments are put on during the summer), visiting Tintagel will involve pretty arduous walking and isn't recommended for the very young, although there's a regular Land Rover service between the village and the castle. The nearby resort of Bocastle, which is equally rugged and wind-ravaged, also offers wonderful clifftop views, as well as a small museum of witchcraft and horse- and pony-trekking along the coast.

Trerice

Near Newquay **t** (01637) 875404
www.nationaltrust.org.uk
Getting there 3 miles southeast of Newquay, off the A3058
Open Apr–Oct Sun–Fri 11–5
Adm Adults £6, children £3, family £9
Café, picnic area, shop, mother and baby facilities, disabled access

Extremely child-friendly historic house with an exhibition on the history of the lawnmower in a barn in its gardens. Quizzes and garden trails for children of all ages in the summer.

Villages

Clovelly

Getting there Clovelly is on the North Devon coast near the border with Cornwall, just off the A39
t (01237) 431 781 **www**.clovelly.co.uk
Open Visitor centre: daily 9.30–5
Adm Visitor centre: adults £4.75, children £3.25, under 7s **free**, family (2+2) £14

Cars are banned from Clovelly's narrow, cobbled streets so you'll have to park up outside the village and walk in. It's a bit of an effort as it's a steep downhill walk, but definitely worth it. Although Clovelly can seem a little bit like a theme park, the views in between the flower-covered cottages to the pretty little harbour have graced a million postcards, posters and biscuit tins. If you don't fancy the return journey, there's a Land Rover service back up the hill every 15 minutes or so in season. At the Visitor Centre, you can find out about the history of the village and buy a few overpriced souvenirs (a postcard, a poster, or a biscuit tin perhaps).

The novelist Charles Kingsley lived here as a child and there's a small museum about his life, as well as a fisherman's cottage preserved as it would have been in the 1930s. There are donkey rides in the summer and two hotels if you want to stay longer than an afternoon. Boats run to Lundy Island in good weather, **t** (01237) 431 042, but be aware that the trip is pricey and only suitable for children over seven years of age.

While kids may not get quite the same enjoyment out of Clovelly's picturesqueness as their parents, they will, however, like the Milky Way Adventure Park, an excellent covered family fun park just outside the village.

Can you spot?
The sledges tethered outside many of Clovelly's cottages. With no cars or public transport, these are the only means many people have of getting their shopping home.

The nearest tourist board for the Polperro Visitor Centre is west Looe, **t** (01503) 262110.

Milky Way Adventure Park
Clovelly, Bideford **t** (01237) 431255
www.themilkyway.co.uk
Open Apr–Oct daily 10.30–6, winter Sat–Sun 11–5
Adm Adults £8, children under 1m (3ft) tall £6, under 3s **free**
Café, picnic areas, ice cream shops, gift shop, mother and baby facilities, disabled facilities, on-site parking

There is a suspended rollercoaster, a large indoor adventure playground (for the use of adults as well as children), a soft play area for youngsters ('Toddler Town'), a crazy golf course, a laser target shooting range, a puppet theatre, lots of arcade games and, in summer, flying displays by birds of prey. All children are assured of the chance to stroke or feed a lamb or kid goat.

Polperro
Getting there Polperro is on Cornwall's south coast 15 miles east of St Austell, 5 miles west of Looe, off the A387

Quaint with a capital 'Q', Polperro is so archetypally pretty, with its dinky little streets and cottages clustered around an equally dinky fishing harbour, that you half suspect it of being the artificial creation of some particularly cunning tourist board. Its tiny cottages are genuine however (ironically, despite their wholesome appearance, many were built from the proceeds of smuggling), unlike the even tinier cottages of the Land of Legend and Model Village, a scaled-down version of the town, with a miniature railway wending its way through the buildings. Its sandy beaches are as clean and well maintained as you'd hope and, in High Season, just as crowded as you'd expect. The village's other attractions are a small museum of smuggling and a house covered entirely in shells.

The nearest visitor centre to Polperro is Looe, **t** (01503) 262072.

Land of Legend and Model Village
The Old Forge, Mill Hill **t** (01503) 272378
Open Easter–Oct 9–6
Adm Adults £2.50, children £1.50

Animal attractions
The Big Sheep
Abbotsham, Bideford **t** (01237) 472366
www.thebigsheep.co.uk
Getting there Bideford is just inland from the North Devon coast, off the A39, about 24 miles northwest of Exeter
Open Daily 10–6 (closed Jan–Feb)
Adm Summer/winter adults £7.95/£4, children £6.95/£4, children under 1m (3ft) tall **free**
Café, fast food area, picnic areas, shop, mother and baby facilities, disabled access, on-site parking

Surely you don't want to watch sheep racing around a steeplechase track? If you do, The Big Sheep in Bideford is the place to be. Bideford's sheep centre has been organizing sheep steeplechases (sheeplechases?) for several years now with large crowds regularly turning out to cheer on the woolly runners, each sheep wearing a knitted jockey on its back. They also organize more traditional sheepdog trials and sheep-shearing demonstrations, plus the slightly less traditional duckdog trials, which are the same as sheepdog trials except with ducks. There's also a Woolcraft Centre, a large indoor playground with ball ponds and slides, an Internet café and mountain boarding.

Buckfast Butterflies and Dartmoor Otter Sanctuary
Buckfastleigh **t** (01364) 642916
www.ottersandbutterflies.co.uk
Getting there Buckfastleigh is 5 miles northwest of Totnes. Follow the signs from the A38
Open Apr–Oct daily 10–5.30
Adm Adults £6.50, children £4.95, family (2+2) £19.50
Picnic areas, shop, disabled access, on-site parking

Do you want to watch otters frolicking underwater? You do? Then the Buckfast Butterfly and Dartmoor Otter Sanctuary may be just the place for you. This is a two-part animal experience: start with a quick walk through the undercover tropical garden, full of exotic butterflies and moths, before watching the frolicking otters. There's an underwater viewing tunnel and six large land enclosures. Feeding times are at 11.30am, 2pm and 4.30pm.

Combe Martin Wildlife and Dinosaur Park

Combe Martin, Ilfracombe **t** (01271) 882486
www.dinosaur-park.com
Getting there Combe Martin is on the North Devon coast, just off the A39
Open Mar–Oct daily 10–4 (last admission 3pm)
Adm Adults £12, children £7, family £34
Café, picnic area, gift shop, mother and baby facilities, on-site parking

Don't let the kids get too excited by the name as it's a little misleading. There are no free-roaming T-Rexes here, although you will find the next best thing – life-size animated dinosaur models that roar, snarl and snort – which is as close to the real thing as you probably want to get. The park also contains numerous real animals including a pair of rare snow leopards (you can see how their thick fur and wide feet are perfectly adapted for life in the snowy foothills of the Himalayas) sea lions and penguins, as well as a petting zoo, 12 hectares (30 acres) of woodland, a museum, an Egyptian 'tomb', and a themed train ride, 'Earthquake'.

Donkey Sanctuary

Slade Hall Farm, Sidmouth **t** (01395) 578222
www.thedonkeysanctuary.org.uk
Getting there Sidmouth is on the South Devon coast between Exmouth and Beer. Take the A375 from the A3052 and follow the signs. Good bus links with Exeter
Open Daily 9–dusk **Adm** Free (donations welcome)
Snacks, on-site parking

This is the largest donkey sanctuary in the world with hundreds of old, sick or retired donkeys living an idyllic existence in acres of beautiful countryside. There are lots of walks and nature trails, including one through a nearby nature reserve down to the South Devon coast.

Exmoor Zoological Park

South Stowford, Bratton Flemming, Barnstaple
t (01598) 763352 **www.**exmoorzoo.co.uk
Getting there Follow the signs on the A39
Open Summer 10–6, winter 10–4
Adm Summer/winter adults £7.50/£6.50, children £5.50/£4.50, under 3s **free**, family (2+2) £23.50/£21
Café, picnic areas, gift shop, disabled facilities, on-site parking

Five miles from the North Devon coast and west of Exmoor, this zoo has lemurs, monkeys, capybara, penguins, swans. Children can help at feeding time and there's an assault course.

★Hedgehog Hospital at Prickly Ball Farm

Denbury Road, East Ogwell, Newton Abbot
t (01626) 362319 **www.**pricklyballfarm.co.uk
Getting there Newton Abbot is 10 miles north of Totnes off the A381
Open Apr–Oct daily 10–5
Adm Adults £5.75, children £4.75, under 4s **free**, family £18.95
Café, snacks, picnic areas, gift shop, mother and baby facilities, disabled facilities, on-site parking

Every year, thousands of hedgehogs are injured through people's carelessness. They get hit by cars, caught in traps and poisoned by pesticides. If they're lucky, they might be found before it's too late and taken to the Hedgehog Hospital, where they can be nursed to health and released back into the wild. The hospital takes its job very seriously: it's an animal rescue centre first, and a tourist attraction second, with a mission to educate as well as entertain; you'll find displays on conservation and countryside protection. Still, it's a lot of fun and its prickly residents are undeniably cute; in mid-season, you should be able to see baby hedgehogs being bottle-fed. Next to the hospital is a hands-on farm, where you can take donkey rides, bottle-feed lambs and watch chicks hatching. There's an undercover picnic area.

Living Coasts

Beacon Quay, Torquay **t** (01803) 202470
www.livingcoasts.org.uk
Open Daily 10–6 **Adm** Adults £6.75, children £4.70, under 3s **Free**, family £20.50; joint tickets for Living Coasts and Paignton Zoo also available.
Café, restaurant, shop, disabled access

This environmentally conscious zoo teaches visitors about the fragile nature of coastlands.
For further information *see* p.220

★Looe Monkey Sanctuary

St Martin, Murrayton, Looe **t** (01503) 262532
www.monkeysanctuary.org
Open Apr–Sept Sun–Thurs 11–4.30 and Oct half term
Adm Adults £6, children £3.50, under 5s **free,** family £16.50

Want to watch monkeys swinging through the trees? No problem, the Monkey Sanctuary in Looe can arrange everything.
For further information *see* p.213

★National Seal Sanctuary

Gweek, Helston **t** (01326) 221361
www.sealsanctuary.co.uk
Getting there Gweek is about 10 miles southwest of Falmouth. Follow the signs from the A39
Open Daily 10–dusk
Adm Call for prices
Café, picnic areas, gift shop, mother and baby facilities, play area, disabled facilities, on-site parking

A few seals have made the sanctuary their permanent home. Most, however, are just temporary residents passing through while their ailments and injuries are seen to. The largest sanctuary of its type in Europe, it releases over 30 seals a year back into British coastal waters. With a good audiovisual display on the work of the sanctuary, regular talks by the sanctuary's keepers and lots of feeding-time fun, the sanctuary is both educational and enjoyable. The seals are best viewed at the underwater observatory, where you can see them gliding and skimming through the water. Guided walks are available through the local woods and there's a small farm to visit

★Newquay Zoo

Trenance Gardens, Newquay **t** (01637) 873342
www.newquayzoo.co.uk
Open Apr–Sept 9–6, Oct–Nov 10–5 (last admission 1 hour before closing)
Adm Adults £8.95, children £6, under 4s **free**, family £25

Lions, penguins, monkeys and zebras as well as farm animals and chipmunks .
For further information *see p.196*

★Paignton Zoo Environmental Park

Totnes Road, Paignton **t** (01803) 697500
www.paigntonzoo.org.uk
Open Summer: daily 10–6; winter: daily 10–dusk
Adm Adults £11.35, children £7.50, under 3s **free**, family £34.10

One of Europe's biggest, best and most ground-breaking zoos with over 1,200 animals.
For further information *see p.216*

Paradise Park

Hayle, near St Ives **t** (01736) 751020
www.paradisepark.org.uk
Getting there Hayle is 2 miles southeast of St Ives, just off the A30
Open Mar–Sept daily 10–5, Oct–Feb 10–4

Adm Adults £8.95, children £7.95 (reduced rates in winter)
Cafés, snack shop, souvenir shop, picnic areas, mother and baby facilities, disabled facilities, on-site parking, play area

One of the country's leading conservation zoos, Paradise Park specializes in breeding rare and endangered species and is home of the World Parrot Trust. Watch these glorious multi-coloured birds flying through the Parrot Jungle, a vast naturalistic aviary full of tropical vegetation, waterfalls and streams. Kids are well catered for at the park with a fun farm, play barn and quiz trails and they can help feed the penguins and otters. Watch out for the flying displays by birds of prey in summer and the narrow-gauge railway that trundles its way round the park.

Quince Honey Farm

North Road, South Molton **t** (01769) 572401
www.quincehoney.co.uk
Getting there 12 miles southeast of Barnstaple off the A361, about 18 miles northwest of Exeter
Open Apr–Sept daily 9–6; Oct daily 9–5; Nov–Mar daily shop only 9–5
Adm Adults £3.95, children £2.75, under 5s **free**
Restaurant, farm shop, on-site parking

This is home to the largest Bee Farm in the world. Its amazing observation hives allow you to look right into the heart of a bee colony to the 'nursery', where worker bees tend the eggs and larvae. It's like looking at a miniature alien kingdom. You might even catch a glimpse of the huge, flightless queen bee herself.

Springfields Fun Park and Pony Centre

St Columb Major, Newquay **t** (01637) 881224
www.springfieldsponycentre.co.uk
Getting there Follow the signs along the A30
Open Easter–Sept daily 9.30–5.30, plus weekends and Oct half-term holiday
Adm Adults £6.95, children £5.95, under 3s **free**, family (2+2) £22
Gift shop, disabled facilities, mother and baby facilities, on-site parking

Lots of rides (pony rides, horse and carriage rides, train rides) and plenty of bouncy fun (trampolines, a large bouncy castle) at this six-hectare (15-acre) fun park, plus an assortment of strokable baby animals, including foals, lambs, calves, kid goats, piglets and kittens.

Farms

Dartmoor Miniature Pony and Animal Farm

Moretonhampstead, Dartmoor **t** (01647) 432400
www.miniatureponycentre.com
Getting there 2 miles west of Moretonhampstead, on the B3212 Princetown Road
Open Easter–Oct daily 10.30–dusk
Adm Adults £6.50, children £5.50, family £22

The perfect opportunity for your kids to meet and touch miniature ponies and donkeys, which foal in spring and early summer.
For further information see p.228

★Pennywell Farm

Buckfastleigh **t** (01364) 642023
www.pennywellfarmcentre.co.uk
Getting there Buckfastleigh is 5 miles northwest of Totnes. Follow the signs from the A38
Open Feb half-term holiday and Apr–Oct daily 10–5, Mar Sat–Tues 10–5
Adm Adults £8.95, children £6.95, under 3s **free**, family £29.95
Café, shop, mother and baby facilities, disabled access, on-site parking

One of the new breed of slick, modern show farms, Pennywell pulls out the stops in an effort to entertain the kids with a different activity or event organized every half hour, including games, animal impressions and puppet shows, cow milking and worm charming. You can learn how to spin wool, make willow sculptures, paint your own tile or go pond-dipping (all without extra charge). There is a toddlers' play farm, a pets' area, a Wildlife Barn (with a hedgehog rehabilitation centre), pony rides and the country's longest gravity-powered go-kart ride. Henry Penny's cafe is good for snacks and light meals.

Trethorne Leisure Farm

Kennards House, Launceston **t** (01566) 863324
www.trethornegolfclub.com
Getting there 3 miles west of Launceston just off the A30
Open Daily 10–6; bowling alley: Fri and Sat 10am–11pm
Adm Call for details
Café, picnic areas, gift shop, mother and baby facilities, disabled facilities, on-site parking

Alongside a 57-hectare (140-acre) working farm where kids can help milk cows, bottle-feed lambs and stroke miniature ponies, there's a large indoor play area full of ball ponds and slides, a 10-pin bowling alley and a covered picnic site.

Sea life centres

★Blue Reef Aquarium

Towan Promenade, Newquay **t** (01637) 878134
www.bluereefaquarium.co.uk
Open Daily 9.30–6
Adm Adults £6.99, children £4.99, family (2+2) £19.99, family (2+3) £23.99
Café, snack shop and souvenir shop, mother and baby facilities, disabled facilities

Sharks, jellyfish, octopi, seahorses and more seen througha walk-through sea bed tunnel.
For further information see p.198

★National Marine Aquarium

Rope Walk, Coxside, Plymouth **t** (01752) 600301
www.national-aquarium.co.uk
Open Apr–Oct daily 10–6; Nov–Mar daily 10–5
Adm Adults £9.50, children £5.75, under 3s **free**, family (2+2) £27

Watch hundreds of fish being fed by hand.
For further information see p.196

Beside the seaside

There are lively, bustling resorts such as Newquay and Torquay, quiet fishing towns like Polperro and St Ives, and everything in between. There are soft, sandy beaches and hard shingle coves, zoos and farms, castles and museums, donkey rides and steam trains. Everything, in fact, for a perfect day at the seaside. The beaches of the Southwest are among the cleanest and best maintained in the country. Most of the main ones employ lifeguards and operate dog bans throughout the summer and several have been awarded either a European Blue Flag or Tidy Britain Group Seaside Award (sometimes both) in recognition of the cleanliness of their sand and water. However, although water quality has improved over recent years, it's still better to avoid swimming at any beaches that are close to busy towns. The Devon resorts around the secluded Tor Bay, known as the English Riviera (see right), enjoy the best of the weather and the calmest seas, while those on Cornwall's northern coast tend to be more exposed and weather-beaten, with volatile seas producing the sort of large, rolling waves so beloved by surfers.

Best beaches
Blackpool Sands
Porthmeor
Daymer Bay
Kynanace Cove
The Lizard
Woolacombe
Breakwater Shoalstone, Torbay
Meadfoot, Torbay

Bantham and Bigbury

Getting there The beaches lie on either side of the River Avon, off the A379, south of the Kingsbridge to Modbury road. Bantham is approximately 7 miles from Kingsbridge and Bigbury 18 miles. The nearest visitor centre to Bantham and Bigbury is Kingsbridge **t** (01548) 853195

An ideal kite-flying-cum-sandcastle-building spot. Bantham is a pleasant family beach with lifeguards in attendance and a stretch of explorable sand dunes behind. It attracts lots of surfers in the summer when it can get rather crowded. Although there isn't a café on the beach itself, the Sloop Inn in Bantham village, just half a mile away, is very welcoming to families. Bigbury has the extra attraction of Burgh Island, which is connected to the land by a strip of sand at low tide but when the tide comes in, you can hop aboard the Sea Tractor (a bus with huge wheels) to get there. Burgh Island has a good family-friendly pub – the Richard Inn.

Beer

Getting there Beer is in east Devon, just west of the Dorset border, off the A3052 and the B3174
Tourist information 18 The Esplanade, Seaton **t** (01297) 21660 **www.eastdevon.net/tourism/seaton**

Parents will appreciate Beer's delightful quaintness: its colourful little cottages, the tinkling stream that runs alongside the town's main road and the fishing boats that line its shingle beach. Kids, however, will probably prefer the town's main tourist attraction – the Pecorama Pleasure Gardens – a gentle, villagey children's theme park with a crazy golf course, a small aviary, an assault course, pony rides and a miniature steam railway, which takes passengers on a ride over bridges,

past gardens and through tunnels to the disused Beer Mine and back (which, despite its name, was actually a source of stone rather than ale).

Pecorama Pleasure Gardens
Beer **t** (01297) 21542 **www.peco-uk.com**
Open Apr–Oct Mon–Fri 10–5.30, Sat 10–1; Jun–Sept also Sun 10–5
Adm Adults £5.75, children £3.80, under 4s **free**
Café, gift shop, snacks, mother and baby facilities, disabled facilities, on-site parking

There is a garden theatre under a marquee, where puppeteers, jesters, clowns and magicians perform (whatever the weather) and circus skills workshops where kids can try plate-spinning, juggling, stilt-walking, unicycling, etc. Various charity events are also put on in the summer, (telephone in advance for details). The highlight of a visit is a ride on the miniature railway and the chance to paint a china model. Some activities have additional charges.

★Blackpool Sands

t (01803) 770606 **www.blackpool-sands.co.uk**
Getting there It's signposted from Dartmouth on the A379 between Stoke Fleming and Strete
The nearest visitor centre to Blackpool Sands is the one at Dartmouth **t** (01803) 834224

A crescent of clean, white, soft sand hemmed in by thick woods, Blackpool Sands has an almost tropical island feel to it (in summer at least). Widely acknowledged as one of Devon's most beautiful beaches, it is also officially one of the cleanest – and has the the certificate to prove it, having been awarded a European Blue Flag Award in 2006. It boasts a paddling pool and boating pond and is cleaned daily during the summer when kids can learn how to windsurf. Unfortunately, although it may once have been secluded and unspoilt, its reputation has grown in recent years and in summer it can get very crowded. Try to go either early or late so as to avoid the worst of the crowds. The most peaceful spot is on the far left-hand side of the beach where there are rockpools to explore. The beach has an excellent café.

Brixham

Getting there Situated 5 miles southwest of Torquay, a 15-minute bus ride from Paignton, Brixham also has good road, rail (change train at

★ *The English Riviera*

This is the name given to the section of Devon coastline around Tor Bay comprising the resorts of Brixham (*see* p.211), Paignton (p.216) and Torquay (pp.219–20). Thanks to a happy combination of sunshine (on average, it enjoys more hours per day than anywhere else in the country), the warming effects of the Gulf Stream and a secluded location away from the worst Atlantic storms, the climate here can, at times, be practically balmy. Still, anyone who has been to the French or Italian equivalents may raise their eyebrows at the 'Riviera' tag. It's not exactly steeped in glamour. This is England, after all, where it can be rainy and cold anywhere, even at the height of summer.

Although there are still some quiet, isolated spots, much of Torbay is highly urbanized and very touristy although, if travelling with the family, this is not necessarily a bad thing, as it means its attractions are well practised at entertaining the kids.

Paignton) and bus links (direct) with Exeter. Follow the signs from the M5

Tourist information The Old Market House, The Quay **t** 0870 7070010 www.englishriviera.co.uk

Brixham is the prettiest and most sedate of the Riviera resorts. The town itself is rather old-fashioned, its economy still largely dependent on the daily catch from the fishing boats in the harbour and you can buy fresh fish to take home all along the seafront. It has three attractive sand and shingle beaches, including Shoalstone Beach, which has a sea water swimming pool and is the only one to employ lifeguards. The *Golden Hinde*, a reconstruction of the 16th-century ship on which Sir Francis Drake became the first Briton to sail around the world, stands by the harbour. The boat was originally kitted out in Brixham and kids can happily spend the best part of an afternoon roaming its decks. Sightseeing and fishing boat trips around Torbay are offered nearby and there is a museum, aquarium, country park and a nautically themed attraction, 'The Deep'.

The *Golden Hinde*

The Quay **t** 08700 118700 www.goldenhinde.org
Open Daily 10–6
Adm Adults £5.50 children £5

Bude

Getting there Bude is on the North Cornwall coast between Tintagel and Clovelly, off the A39
Tourist information The Crescent **t** (01288) 354240 www.bude.co.uk

Bude, a popular family surfing resort (it's a bit like a less intense version of Newquay), has three excellent sandy beaches: Crooklets, the main surfing beach (there's a dog ban in operation from Easter to 1 October); the National Trust-owned Sandy Mouth, which is better for beginners and can offer a network of rockpools for non-surfers to explore; and the main family beach, Summerleaze, which has a seawater swimming pool, a mini golf course and a go-kart track. All three employ lifeguards during the summer months.

Dawlish

Getting there Dawlish is on the A379 on the South Devon coast 3 miles southwest of Exmouth and 5 miles northeast of Torquay. There are good rail links with Exeter
Tourist information The Lawn **t** (01626) 215665 www.dawlish.com

Beneath red sandstone cliffs, Dawlish is a rather old-fashioned town that has had a not wholly successful modern facelift, its picturesque cottages now joined by a range of typical seaside attractions – amusement arcades, children's playgrounds and a pitch 'n' putt golf course.

The main beach, which is made up of sand and shingle with some rockpools, is over one and a half miles long and is cleaned daily (supposedly) in summer. It is also the proud possessor of a European Blue Flag, although don't let that mislead you – the beach itself will be as crowded and littered as any other during high summer and the supposed dog ban is somewhat weakly enforced. Nonetheless, nature lovers will like the nearby Dawlish Warren tidal flats in the Exe estuary, which provide a home for thousands of wading birds. The visitor centre offers guided nature walks in summer.

Exmouth

Getting there Exmouth is on Devon's southern coast about 15 miles north of Torbay. Follow the signs along the A377 or A376. Good rail links with Exeter
Tourist information Alexandra Terrace **t** (01395) 222299 www.exmouthguide.co.uk

Exmouth is a friendly, family-orientated holiday resort at the mouth of the River Exe with a long sandy beach and a lively harbour surrounded by cafés and tourist shops. The **Great Exmouth Model Railway** (one of the world's longest model railways) can be found on the seafront. In summer, **boat trips** are offered from the harbour up the river to Topsham, and mackerel-fishing trips (enormous fun) depart from the beach. On the edge of the town, look out for **A la Ronde**, an intriguing 16-sided 18th-century house: the interior is hand-decorated with seashells, seaweed, feathers and coloured sand. A mile southeast of Exmouth is the **World of Country Life**.

A la Ronde

Summer Lane **t** (01395) 265514
www.nationaltrust.org.uk; **Open** Apr–Oct
Sun–Thurs 11–5.30, **Adm** Adults £5, children £2.50
Snacks, gift shop, on-site parking
Not suitable for pushchairs

Exmouth Model Railway,

Seafront, **t** 01395 278 383
www.exmouthmodelrailway.co.uk.
Open Apr–Oct daily 10.30am–5pm
Adm call for prices.

Stuart Line Cruises

Exmouth Harbour **t** (01395) 222144 or 279693,
www.stuartlinecruises.co.uk
Adm Adults from £5, children from £3

World of Country Life

Sandy Bay, Exmouth **t** (01395) 274533
www.worldofcountrylife.co.uk
Open Apr–Oct 10–dusk **Adm** Adults £8, children £7,
under 2s **free**, family £28
Café, gift shop, mother and baby facilities,
on-site parking

This is a 16-hectare (40-acre) family fun park with a small petting zoo, an outdoor adventure playground, an indoor playground shaped like a pirate ship, a motorcycle collection, mini quad-bikes, several steam engines and a reconstructed Victorian street. In summer, there are flying displays by birds of prey and mini safari rides through llama and deer paddocks.

Fowey

Getting there Fowey is on Cornwall's southern coast between Mevagissey and Looe, off the A3082
Tourist information The Post Office, 4 Custom Hill House **t** (01726) 833616 www.fowey.co.uk

Bustling resort (pronounced 'Foy') with miles of sandy beaches. Avoid the crowds by trying the ones further away from the centre of town.

★Ilfracombe

Getting there Ilfracombe is on the North Devon coast, 5 miles from Barnstaple. Take the A39 and the A361
Tourist information The Landmark, The Seafront **t** (01271) 863001 www.ilfracombe-tourism.co.uk

The most popular resort on the North Devon Coast, Ilfracombe offers typical resort fare: sand and shingle beaches, rocky cliffs, a harbour filled with bobbing boats, a lido filled with bobbing children, a small aquarium, candyfloss, rock and fish 'n' chips. The best (less crowded) beaches are away from the town itself towards Woolacombe (winner of both a European Blue Flag and a Tidy Britain Group Seaside Award and a great place to surf), where you can often find exotic shells washed here by Caribbean currents. In summer, sightseeing cruises are run from the harbour to Lundy, a windswept, rocky island famed for its high cliffs, and birdlife, including a colony of puffins – now, unfortunately, an increasingly rare sight.

The 19th-century **Watermouth Castle** or 'Devon's Happy Castle' (as it has subsequently been branded) is situated three miles east of town. Its interior has been turned into a sort of fairytale grotto for kids and is inhabited by numerous plastic gnomes, trolls and goblins. There are also various fairground rides, slides and swings. There's a similar establishment called Once Upon a Time, a few miles west near Woolacombe (pp.225).

Watermouth Castle

Berrynarbor **t** (01271) 867474
www.warmouthcastle.com
Open Easter–Oct daily 10–4 (later Jul–Aug)
Adm Adults £10, over 3s £8.50

Café, gift shop, mother and baby facilities, disabled facilities, on-site parking

Land's End

Getting there 9 miles from Penzance, 18 miles from St Ives, 290 miles from London, 886 miles from John o' Groats, 3,147 miles from New York, Land's End is on the A30. A regular bus service runs from Penzance

John o' Groats to Land's End, northeast tip to southwest tip, the traditional span of Britain – all year round numerous hardy souls plod their way from one to the other on the ultimate UK charity walk. Land's End provides a fitting climax to this epic journey. It's a dramatic place with sheer cliffs overlooking a vast and volatile expanse of ocean (due west, there's no more land until you reach America), although it clearly wasn't dramatic enough for the government, who in the mid 1980s, sanctioned the building of the 16-hectare (40-acre) 'Land's End Complex' – a sort of 'last hurrah' theme park. A glut of souvenir shops, craft centres, cafés and 'experiences' are now on hand to make sure you get the most out of your time at the nation's extremity. Kids will probably find it highly entertaining and while they pet the farm animals, watch the multimedia shows and clamber over the equipment in the adventure playground, you can take some time to appreciate the area's considerable natural beauty. Although there is a charge to enter the **'Land's End Complex'** attractions, remember, the tip itself is still a public right of way. You can get the best out of the place by visiting it in the early evening when the attractions are closed. It's a good place for an evening stroll in summer. There are some good beaches to the north of Land's End. The nearest tourist office to Land's End is Penzance, **t** (01736) 362207.

Land's End Complex

t 0870 4580099 **www.landsend-landmark.co.uk**
Open Daily 10–7 (later in summer)
Adm Free to the site, attractions vary
Cafés, fast food, shopping arcade, mother and baby facilities, disabled facilities, guided tours, on-site parking

Looe

Getting there Looe is on Cornwall's southern coast between Fowey and Plymouth on the B3253, off the A38. Trains run six times a day from Liskeard, which is on the London–Penzance main line, and one of the prettiest branch lines in the country
Tourist information Guildhall, Fore Street, East Looe **t** (01503) 262072 **www.looe.org**

Sand, sea and sharkfishing are Looe's principal attractions. There are miles of sandy beaches (the most secluded are to the east of town), lots of tourist shops and cafés in the narrow streets and, around the working harbour, you'll find several companies offering 'big game' fishing trips and excursions to nearby Looe Island. At high tide when the fishing boats come in, you can sometimes get a close-hand view of local fishermen landing their catch and selling it at the fishmarket. For something completely different, head out of town to the Looe Monkey Sanctuary.

★Looe Monkey Sanctuary

St Martin, Murrayton, Looe **t** (01503) 262532
www.monkeysanctuary.org
Open Apr–Sept Sun–Thurs and October half-term holiday 11–4.30
Adm Adults £6, children £3.50, under 5s **free,** family £16.50
Café, picnic areas, gift shop, mother and baby facilities, disabled facilities, on-site parking

Established in the early 1960s, this small area of woodland is home to a colony of leaping, climbing, clambering South American Woolly Monkeys. All the animals were born in the sanctuary and have a pragmatic tolerance of people, which means you can get right up close. A special enclosure allows visitors to see the monkeys clamber around in the trees, as they would do in the wild. Bats can be watched here too. Down in the cellar of the sanctuary house is a community of horseshoe bats that can be spied on with the aid of infra-red lights and a special camera. Once children have watched the bats and monkeys they will be keen to try out some acrobatic moves before a spot of lunch at the vegetarian 'Tree Top' café which sells burgers, sandwiches, cakes and Cornish ice cream.

★Lynton and Lynmouth

Getting there Lynton and Lymouth are on the North Devon coast between Ilfracombe and Minehead on the A39. There are regular bus services from Barnstaple and Ilfracombe
Tourist information Town Hall, Lee Road **t** (01598) 752225 www.lynton-lynmouth-tourism.co.uk

Perched on a steep wooded gorge where the West Lyn River meets the sea, Lynton is one of the most photogenic resorts in Devon. It is linked to its handsome harbourside sibling, Lynmouth, some 185m (600ft) below it, by a water-operated Victorian cliff railway, **t** (01598) 753486, and together, they make a perfect base for exploring the wooded coastline and northern extremities of Exmoor (Midwest chapter, p.176). A terrible flood here in 1952 killed 34 people and you can see a memorial on the harbourside. The Tarka Trail passes through both towns, as does the Two Moors Way linking Exmoor and Dartmoor, while just outside Lynton lies the beautiful Gly Lyn Gorge. The towns share three beaches, the best of which is the sand and shingle Lee Bay Beach, offering access to the famous Valley of Rocks, a natural rock bowl surrounded by great rocky outcrops.

Mevagissey

Getting there Mevagissey is on the South Cornwall coast, 15 miles east of Truro on the A391
Tourist information St. George's Square, Megavissey **t** 0870 4432928 www.mevagissey-cornwall.co.uk

Mevagissey is a large, lively commercial resort full of tourist shops, arcades, fish and chip restaurants and (in summer especially) hordes of holidaymakers. The town's main attractions, besides its rather crowded beaches, are the **Lost Gardens of Heligan**, just to the north, a Victorian subtropical garden that fell into disrepair between 1914 and 1991, which has since been restored, and the **World of Model Railways**. This consists of 50 model trains that meander their way through a variety of miniature landscapes, which include a ski resort, a fairground and a quaint thatched village.

Lost Gardens of Heligan

Pentewan (just north of the town off the B2373) **t** (01826) 845100 www.heligan.com
Open Mar–Oct daily 10–6 (last admission 4.30); Nov– Feb 10–5

Adm Adults £7.50, children £4, under 5s **free**
Tea room, nursery, picnic areas, mother and baby facilities, disabled facilities, guided tours, on-site parking

World of Model Railways

Meadow Street, Mevagissey **t** (01726) 842457 www.model-railway.co.uk
Open Mar–Oct daily 10–5; Nov–Feb Sun only 10–5
Adm Adults £3.50, children £2.75, 2–5-year-olds £1.75

Mullion

Getting there South of Helston off the A3083

Mullion makes an excellent base for exploring the Lizard Peninsula, England's most southerly point. It's a good size village with shops, a good hotel and a family-friendly pub, The Old Inn. The Lizard is far less touristy than North Cornwall and is a good place to get a flavour of the real Cornwall. Cornwall isn't an easy place with pushchairs, but the quaint harbour at Mullion Cove and the nearby beaches at Poldhu and Gunwalloe are all easily accessible. Kynance Cove, one of Cornwall's most beautiful and wild beaches, is just a couple miles south of Mullion. There's lots for kids to do. From Mullion Cove, you can take a boat trip round Asparagus Island. Call local fisherman Barry Mundy, **t** (01326) 240413, for details (not suitable for children under seven). Wild asparagus really does grow here and all kids will love the giant Lion Rock just off the harbour, which really does look like a huge lion sleeping in the sea. There's also some good walking to be had with kids. On the cliffs near Poldu Cove, you can see where Marconi sent the first transatlantic wireless message to North America in 1901. Predannack Point is remote, magnificent and easily accessible. Turn left up Ghost Hill just before Mullion Cove and park at Predannack Farms. The coastal path from Kynance Cove is another safe walk with small children. Keep a look out for a craggy outcrop overhanging a brook, where buried under a mass of heather is an Iron Age fort. The walls of the hut circles are clearly visible. Even in high summer this stretch of path is a remote spot. Another easy place to walk with small children is along the shore of Loe Pool, which is a salt water lake that is divided from the beach by only a strip of sand dunes. The story has it that King Arthur was given his mighty sword Excalibur here.

Mullion is also within easy reach of some of south Cornwall's big attractions: Flambards theme park, Goonhilly Satellite Station and the National Seal Sanctuary at Gweek. It's close to the home of Europe's largest helicopter base at RNAS Culdrose. You can watch the helicopters from the viewing area on the south east side of the airfield.

The Old Inn at Mullion is a good family pub. In Lizard town south of Mullion, the Polpeor Café, **t** (01326) 290939, is a marvellous old-fashioned spot with splendid views over England's most southerly point. Don't miss the Lizard Pasty Shop on Beacon Terrace, **t** (01326) 290889, also at the Lizard. It's open Tuesday–Saturday, but closes when the day's batch has been sold, usually around 2pm. The nearest tourist office is in Helston, 79 Meneage Street, **t** (01326) 565431

Padstow

Getting there Padstow is on the west bank of the Camel River estuary 12 miles northeast of Newquay on the A389 and the B3276
Tourist information Old Boatyard, North Quay **t** (01841) 533449 www.padstow-cornwall.co.uk

Best known for its May Day 'Obby Oss' festivities and (especially these days) as the headquarters of Rick Stein's seafood empire, Padstow is a delight-fully quaint, typically Cornish coastal town with a working fishing harbour surrounded by pictur-esque cottages. If you want picnic supplies, don't miss the Seafood Deli on South Quay, where you can buy Rick Stein takeaways (open Mon–Sat 10–7 and Sun 10–5). Kids can learn to rustle up dinner Stein-style at the Seafood School. Children's half-day courses, **t** (01841) 433 566, www.rickstein.com, are held in the Easter and summer holidays and are suitable for 8–14-year-olds. Families can also hire a bike from Padstow Cycle Hire, **t** (01841) 533 533, www.padstowcyclehire.com, and cycle up the Camel Estuary, or head off along the coastal path, which begins on the opposite side of the harbour to the car park. Wide, sandy beaches stretch from here right along the estuary – you can take a ferry across to Rock, where there are more miles of fine beaches running up to Polzeath at the mouth of Padstow Bay. Do be aware of the strong currents running along the estuary.

There are plenty of other family-friendly beaches within easy reach of Padstow. Look out for these:

Obby Oss

Every May one of the local men of Padstow is given the honour of becoming the Obby Oss (Hobby Horse), the centrepiece of the town's age-old fertility rite. Dressed in a large, black and white tent-like costume, he is led on a dance through the streets by an equally strangely dressed character known as a 'teaser' (who carries a – how shall we say – symbolically-shaped club) attempting to capture the local women whom he must then envelop beneath his billowing robes and, er, pinch, in order to ensure their fertility.

Constantine Bay

Getting there On the North Cornwall coast, about 3 miles from Padstow off the B3276

Increasingly popular with surfers in recent years, Constantine Bay is home to a beautiful stretch of beach framed by sand dunes (with lifeguards in attendance in summer) and has become a very popular area for family holidays. The Bedruthan Steps, a collection of great, rounded slate outcrops sticking out from a long, sandy beach, are about four miles south. According to legend, they were the stepping-stones of the giant Bedruthan.

Trevone Bay

Getting there This bay is about 2 miles west of Padstow

Trevone Bay has a good sandy beach, rocks to climb on, pools to fish and paddle in and facilities for surfing, as well as cafés, beach shops and ample parking. When you arrive you should head first to the clifftop where, on the right-hand side, you'll find a long hole where in rough weather the sea is pushed up into a foaming spout. From there, walk the few hundred yards down to the Rocky or Shell Beach to hunt for shells. Large conch shells often turn up and you can paddle or hunt for signs of life in the surrounding rockpools (shrimps tend to hide in the seaweed fringing the pools) and even go for a splash in one of the deeper pools.

Treyarnon Bay

Getting there 4 miles southwest of Padstow

Good, long stretch of sand with lifeguards, parking and facilities for surfing. When the tide is low, a natural swimming pool forms in the rocks on the right-hand side.

Paignton

Getting there 2 miles west of Torquay, Paignton also has good road, rail and bus links with Exeter. Follow the signs from the M5. To arrive in style, board the Paignton and Dartmouth Steam Railway at Kingswear

Tourist information The Esplanade **t** 0870 7070010 **www.torbay.gov.uk.tourism**

A quieter, slightly less touristy version of Torquay, Paignton has much the same look as its neighbour without quite the same gloss. Its harbour is smaller and filled with working fishing boats and besides its four sandy beaches (all cleaned daily), the main attractions are the pier (with cafés, restaurants and a mega-slide), Paignton Zoo, the Paignton and Dartmouth Steam Railway and, just along the coast at Goodrington Sands, the QuayWest Waterpark. In August, Paignton plays host to a week-long Children's Festival with entertainment, activities and workshops.

Paignton and Dartmouth Steam Railway

Dart Valley Light Railway plc, Queen's Park Station t (01803) 555872
www.paignton-steamrailway.co.uk
Operating times Jun–Sept daily; Apr, May, Oct selected dates; Dec 'Santa Specials'
Fares Return: adults £9, children £6
Station cafés at Paignton and Kingswear, shop, mother and baby facilities, disabled access, guided tours

Delightful steam train rides, including Santa and Thomas the Tank Engine events, along the Torbay coast and up the River Dart estuary to Kingswear (a seven-mile journey), where you can catch a ferry to Dartmouth and then, if you've still got the sightseeing bug, a riverboat up the River Dart to Totnes. There's a model railway at Paignton to help you get in the mood for your trip.

★Paignton Zoo Environmental Park

Totnes Road, Paignton t (01803) 697500
www.paigntonzoo.org.uk
Open Summer: daily 10–6; winter: daily 10–dusk
Adm Adults £11.35, children £7.50, under 3s **free**, family £34.10
Café, self-service restaurant, shop, mother and baby facilities, disabled access, on-site parking

Although its profile was significantly raised when it featured in the BBC television series

Zookeepers, Paignton has long been one of Europe's biggest, best and most ground-breaking zoos with over 1,200 animals (including gorillas, orangutans, giraffes, tigers, lions and elephants) living in large, carefully designed 'themed' enclosures – Wetland, Forest, Savannah and Desert – in which they are encouraged to act in as natural a way as possible. For instance, rather than have their meals simply handed to them, the lizards and birds of the desert zone have to root out worms stuffed into an artificial termite mound. Everything is sensitively presented with camouflaged viewing areas and information boards, emphasizing the important conservation work carried out by the zoo. It runs a full programme of keeper talks and feeding displays (check details on arrival) and there is a hands-on animal education centre, where children can meet some of the zoo's resident creepy crawlies (such as snakes and tarantulas), try to match the speeds of various animals on a specially calibrated bike, and test their reflexes when confronted with a lion's roar. There's also a Jungle Fun play area, face-painting and a miniature railway, the 'Jungle Express', which circumnavigates the Gibbon lakes.

★QuayWest Waterpark

Goodrington Sands, Paignton t (01803) 555550
www.quaywest.co.uk
Open May, Jul and Aug 10–6, Jun and Sept 11–5
Adm 2hr/all day ticket: adults £8.50/£9.95, children £7.50/£8.95, children under 4 £3.50/£3.95, family (2+2) £29/£35
Fast food restaurants, ice cream stalls, picnic areas, on-site parking

An outdoor waterpark on the seafront with various slides, chutes and pools where the water is heated to a constant 27°C (80°F).
Please note: *Children under 1m (3ft) tall are only permitted in the play pool, swimming pool and submarine play zone.*

Penzance

Getting there By road: Penzance is 9 miles from Land's End and 281 miles from London on the A30 and the A3071. By train: There is a daily service from London Paddington. By coach: National Express runs services daily from London, Bristol and Exeter
Tourist information Station Road **t** (01736) 362207
www.penzance.co.uk

> ### Tell me a story: The Mousehole Cat
>
> In Mousehole (near Penzance), they eat a special fish pie called star gazey pie. It's only eaten on December 23rd, which is known as Tom Bawcock's Eve. It's a gruesome-looking creation with fish heads and tails sticking up out of the top and it's made from seven different kinds of fish. The locals have been tucking in for over 2,000 years. The pie is made to commemorate a terrible winter when the villagers almost starved as Mousehole was cut off by a terrible storm for weeks and weeks. The fishing boats were trapped in the tiny harbour and soon the villagers had nothing to eat. Tom Bawcock was the only fisherman brave (or perhaps foolhardy enough) to set off through rough seas to bring back fish so the villagers could eat. He and his crew battled out across the waves and miraculously managed to catch enough fish to feed the entire village.

Penzance, Britain's most westerley town, has had a very lively history. A witness to countless shipwrecks off its craggy coast, it was almost destroyed by Spanish raiders in the 16th century (most of the buildings you see today date from the Georgian and Regency periods) and, following expansion during the 17th and 18th centuries, became the base for a celebrated artists' community in the late 1900s. You can see examples of their work in the **Newlyn Museum and Art Gallery**. These days, however, it's an out and out tourist town with a lively harbour, an Art Deco sea water swimming pool, a popular shopping centre, tennis courts, a go-kart track and a subaqua centre. Just outside Penzance, to the north of town on the B331, is **Chysauster Iron Age Village**, where you can see the remains of Iron Age dwellings and fortifications.

Chysauster Iron Age Village
t 07831 757934
Open Apr–Oct daily 10–5 (last entry 4.30)
Adm Adults £2.40, children £1.20

Newlyn Museum and Art Gallery
24 New Road **t** (01736) 363715
Open Mon–Sat 10–5 **Adm Free**

Perranporth
Getting there Perranporth is on the North Cornwall coast off the B3285
Tourist information Cliff Road **t** (01872) 573368
www.perraninfo.co.uk

Six miles southwest of Newquay, this has equally good surfing but is much less congested in summer. There is a long, sandy beach surrounded by harsh, rocky scenery.

St Agnes
Getting there 2 miles west of Perranporth, off the A30
Tourist information 5 Church Town **t** (01872) 554150
www.stagnes.com

St Agnes is set on a steep hill with fantastic views out over Cornwall's Atlantic coast, particularly from the top of the 192m (630ft) St Agnes Beacon. There is also a very good beach at Trevaunance Cove and, just west of town, a craft centre named 'Presingoll Barns', where you can watch demonstrations of candle- and fudge-making.

St Ives
Getting there By road: St Ives is on the North Cornwall coast, on the A3074. By train/coach: Trains and National Express coaches run from Penzance and London Victoria
Tourist information The Guildhall, Street-an-Pol **t** (01736) 796297 www.stives-cornwall.co.uk

The archetypal Cornish resort, full of quaint cottages, narrow cobbled streets and bobbing fishing boats. Once a successful fishing village, it became a haven for artists and sculptors in the early 20th century and still attracts hordes of art lovers, especially since the opening of the Tate Gallery of St Ives in the early 1990s. St Ives is famed for its wide sandy beaches, particularly the mile-long Porthmeor Beach, which has won awards for cleanliness. Boat trips and watersports, such as surfing and parascending, are available and there are deckchairs and beach huts for hire. Lifeguards patrol in summer and the beach is cleaned daily during the holiday season. A dog ban is in operation from Easter to 1 October. St Ives has some lovely small shops and excellent restaurants (p.237). It is a lively place to eat out but you can easily picnic on the headland above the town. Pick up supplies on Fore Street, where there are plenty of small shops serving up pasties, local cheese and other delicacies. Kids will like the old-fashioned sweet shops. The Harbour Kitchen, **t** (01736) 797222, on Wharf Road has a good deli section. Porthmeor Beach has a great café right on the seashore.

Tate St Ives

Porthmeor Beach **t** (01736) 796226 **www.tate.org.uk**
Open Mar–Oct Mon–Sun 10–5.20; Nov–Feb
Tues–Sun 10–4.20
Adm £5.75, entry to the shop and café is **free**
Café-restaurant, gift shop, mother and baby
facilities, disabled access

Displays of paintings from the Tate St Ives' collection are changed quarterly. There are regular family workshops and activity packs for kids. The Tate's rooftop café is one of the best places to eat in town offering great views of the coastline.

Salcombe

Getting there Salcombe is on the South Devon
coast on the A381
Tourist information Council Hall, Market Street
t (01548) 843927 **www.salcombeinformation.co.uk**

At first glance, Salcombe seems to exude a rough, rugged sort of glamour with its exposed, weather-beaten clifftops and steeply sloping streets; an image undermined by the town centre's kitschy collection of souvenir shops and tourist businesses. It is very popular with walkers, who come in their thousands each summer to tackle its winding coastal paths, and there are lots of nearby beaches and coves to explore.

Overbecks

Sharpitor, Salcombe **t** (01548) 842893
www.nationaltrust.org.uk
Getting there Salcombe is about 12 miles
southwest of Dartmouth. The museum is sign-
posted from the A379
Open Garden: daily 10–6; museum: Apr–Jul and
Sept Sun–Fri 11–5.30; Aug daily 11–5.30; Oct
Sun–Thurs 11–4.30
Adm Museum and garden: adult £5.50, children
£2.75, family £8.25 ; garden: £5 (children half price),
Picnic areas, gift shop, mother and baby facilities,
disabled access

Edwardian house full of period pieces, curios and (for want of a better word) junk, including a 'rejuvenating machine' and a number of old toys and dolls displayed in a special 'secret room' for children, plus an organized ghost hunt. Outside in the luscious subtropical gardens, there are glorious views out to sea.

Sidmouth

Getting there Sidmouth is on the South Devon
coast between Exmouth and Beer. Take the A375
from the A3052 and follow the signs. There are
good bus links with Exeter
Tourist information Ham Lane **t** (01395) 516441
www.visitsidmouth.co.uk

Well-to-do seaside resort where colourful fishing boats rest on a pebble beach in front of elegant Regency seafront buildings. All is framed by imposing red sandstone cliffs typical of the region. It is pleasant in a gentle, sleepy sort of a way. For a little excitement, try the Vintage Toy Train Shop and Museum, which has a large display of metal and mechanical toys from the period 1925–40, including a number of Hornby train engines and Dinky cars, or pick up a bag of carrots and head off to The Donkey Sanctuary at Slade Hall Farm (p.207). Every summer the peace and quiet is broken by the Sidmouth International Folk Festival, which consists of eight days of music, dance and processions, with an accompanying children's festival. Sidmouth is popular with the over 65s, so although it's fun to visit, it's not the best place to choose as a base for your holiday.

Vintage Toy Train Shop and Museum

Devonshire House, All Saints Road **t** (01395) 512588
Open Mon–Sat 10–5 **Adm Free**
Snacks, disabled facilities, on-site parking

The best time to visit this shop is in the afternoon when the owner is around.

Teignmouth

Getting there Teignmouth is just 5 miles north of
Torbay on the A379. Good rail links with Exeter
Tourist information The Den, Sea Front **t** (01626)
215666 **www.teignmouth-devon.com**

Popular (although rather tired-looking) family holiday resort with a pier, a small zoo, botanic gardens, a lido, a crazy golf course, a kids' paddling pool and a mile-long sand and shingle beach. Lifeguards patrol during the summer and there's a dog ban from 1 May to 30 September.

Grand Pier

The Promenade **t** (01626) 774367
Open Daily all year **Adm Free**
Refreshments, shop

Amusement arcades, gentle fairground-style rides, 10-pin bowling and an indoor soft play area.

★Torquay

Getting there Torquay, the main Torbay resort, has good road, bus and train links with Exeter, 20 miles north. By road: Follow the signs from the M5 – Torquay is off the A380. By train: Trains from Exeter arrive at Torquay via Newton Abbot and run along the coast to Paignton. By coach: The X46 runs hourly between Exeter and Torquay
Tourist information Vaughan Parade **t** 0870 7070010 **www.torbay.gov.uk/tourism**

Torquay is both an exotic alternative to traditional English resorts and a traditional English resort. For every promenade lined with palm trees (they're actually the rather unromantic-sounding New Zealand Cabbage Trees but they look similar), there's a parade of cheap cafés; for every expensive boutique, there's a tacky souvenir shop, and for every modern luxury hotel, there's a crusty old Basil Fawlty-esque bed and breakfast. The town's focal point is the harbour surrounded by shops and restaurants and framed by huge limestone cliffs. At night, the whole of the waterfront is lit up with coloured lights. The main beaches are the sandy Abbey Sands, where you can hire pedaloes and boats, the rock and shingle Anstey's Cove, and the pebble and sand Medfleet Beach. All have warning flags (but not lifeguards) and are cleaned daily. Owing to the high iron content in the surrounding rocks, many of Torbay's beaches have a reddish hue which can, in wet weather, stain light-coloured clothing. Babbacombe beach is the best in the area. It's about two miles from Torquay harbour on the Babbacombe road. Follow the signs, park up where you can, and then hop aboard the mini railway, which takes you down to the beach (as one carriage goes down the other comes up), which is made up of sand and shingle. It has a café, a beach shop selling buckets and spades, toilets, baby changing facilities and sunbeds and deckchairs for hire. During the summer holidays, leave before the main body of the crowd, otherwise you may find yourself waiting for a long time for a space on the train.

Despite its would-be air of refinement and elegance, Torbay is actually the Riviera's most fun town, with plenty for parents and kids to do. You can take a tour of Kent's Cavern, spooky illuminated caves that are Britain's oldest archaelogical site (in July and August you can take an even spookier evening tour by candle-light); wander past the miniature landmarks at Babbacombe Model Village (which include Stonehenge, the Taj Mahal and the Statue of Liberty); stroll along a reconstructed life-size Victorian Street or a First World War trench at Bygones; throw a pot at Babbacombe Pottery, take a boat trip, visit the new Living Coasts Zoo or check out the views from the clifftop railway. It's important to be aware that Torquay can get very rowdy in the evenings and intoxicated teenagers are a common sight.

Torquay is the place for a takeaway. In the suburb of Babbacombe are two of the Southwest's best fish and chip shops – Drakes on 64 Babbacombe Road and Hanbury's on Princes Street. If you want to eat in, Hanbury's has colouring pens and highchairs to keep your kids entertained while they wait for their food to arrive. For snacks, try the Rocombe Farm Shop on Union Street. They sell organic ice cream, sorbets and smoothies in a variety of flavours and sizes as well as local farm produce, such as cheeses, sausages, pasties and pastries, which are perfect for picnics. The Chatterbox Café on Lower Union Street has a good selection of homemade cakes. The new Torquay Waterfront is a pleasant place to stop for a drink or a snack. The café at Living Coasts has one of the best views in the area and turns into a classy restaurant at night if you want to splash out with teens.

Babbacombe Model Village

Hampton Avenue **t** (01803) 315315
www.babbacombemodelvillage.co.uk
Open Jan–Feb and early Nov 10–3.30, Mar and Oct 10–4, Apr 10–5 (until 9.30 half term), May–Aug 10–9.30, Sept 10–9 (until 5 on Sat), Oct 10–4, late Nov and Dec 11–7
Adm Adults £6.90, children £4.50, family £21
Café, shop, mother and baby facilities, free bus from harbour to model village (Jun–Sept)

There are one-and-a-half hectares (four acres) of 1:12-scale models to explore, featuring thatched villages (based on nearby Cockington), Tudor and Georgian buildings, waterfalls and gardens. There is a 'house on fire' with attendant fire engines, a celebrity banquet, a 366m (1,200ft) model railway and even a nudist beach, all enhanced by sound and lighting effects (best seen in the early evening). There is a kids spotter sheet featuring Dennis the Mennace and the *Beano* gang.

Bygones

Fore Street, Marychurch **t** (01803) 326108
www.bygones.co.uk
Open Jan–Mar and Nov–Dec 10–5, Apr–Jun and
Sept–Oct 10–6, Jul–Aug Wed and Thurs 10–9.30
Fri–Tues 10–6
Adm Adults £5.50, children £4.14, under 4s **free**,
family £16
Café, shop

Replica Victorian street with an ironmonger's,
a grocer's, a forge and a sweetshop, as well as a
reconstructed First World War trench, a 1950s
shopping arcade and a giant model railway.

Kent's Cavern Showcaves

The Caves, Wellswood **t** (01803) 215136
www.kents-cavern.co.uk
Open Apr–Sept daily 10–4.30 (evening tours Jul
and Aug); Oct–Mar daily 10–4 **Adm** Adults £6.75,
children £35.25, under 4s **free**, family £22
*Snacks, shop, mother and baby facilities, disabled
facilities, some wheelchair access, guided tours,
on-site parking*

Stalactites and stalagmites galore in this well
presented, albeit rather eerie, archaeological
site. Guided tours take you deep into the heart
of the complex, where you can see illuminated
dioramas showing how prehistoric cave-
dwellers used to live. Look out for Santa and his
sleigh in December.

Living Coasts

Beacon Quay, Torquay **t** (01803) 202470
www.livingcoasts.org.uk
Open Daily 10–6 **Adm** Adults £6.75, children £4.70,
under 3s **free**, family £20.50; joint tickets for Living
Coasts and Paignton Zoo also available.
Café, shop, restaurant, disabled access

Torquay's coastal zoo has a strong environmental message and wants to get visitors to
think about the fragile nature of the world's
coasts. There's a programme of talks and activities to get the kids involved and leave them
contemplating about the effect their seaside
holiday is having on the environment. You can
watch puffins and seals swimming underwater
and see the birds fly free under a huge aviary that
covers the entire site. The zoo also has a colony of
black rats that came to Britain in the 16th century
from Asia. One of the few places black rats survive
is Lundy Island off the North Devon coast, where
they have almost wiped out the sea bird colonies

there. There is a large penguin pool, interactive
games and displays, as well as a play beach for
children. It's quite exposed so pack something
warm if the wind is blowing. The café, however,
must have the best view in Torquay.

Parks and gardens

Better known for its wildernesses, the
Southwest also boasts its fair share of formal
gardens, country parks and botanic gardens, the
most famous of which is the Eden Project in
St Austell, which consists of two huge football
pitch-sized greenhouses full of tropical and rainforest plants.

Arlington Court Gardens

Barnstaple **t** (01271) 850296
www.nationaltrust.org.uk
Getting there 8 miles northeast of Barnstaple on
the A39
Open House: Apr–Oct Sun–Fri 11–5; garden: Sun–Fri
daylight hours, Jul–Aug also Sat
Adm Adults £7, children £3.30, family (2+2) £17.50
*Café, souvenir shop, mother and baby facilities,
disabled access, on-site parking*

The vast grounds of this grand Regency house
contain a huge woodland park, a neat Victorian
garden, a conservatory, paddocks full of Shetland
ponies and Jacob sheep, lakeside nature trails and
an extensive stable block (home to one of the
country's finest collections of carriages and horse-
drawn vehicles), all of which can be toured in
suitably elegant fashion aboard a horse-drawn
carriage. The house itself contains a fascinating
collection of miscellaneous objects, accumulated
by the eccentric owner Rosalie Chichester on her
travels around the world, including model ships,
stuffed birds and exotic shells. Santa and his grotto
bring a touch of seasonal spice in December. Check
out the bat-cam between May and August to get
a look at the roosting horseshoe bats hanging
upside down in the roof of the house.

Bicton Park Botanical Gardens

East Budleigh, near Exeter **t** (01395) 568465
www.bictongardens.co.uk
Getting there 8 miles southeast of Exeter, off the
B3178, between Budleigh Salterton and Newton
Poppleford

Open Summer: daily 10–6; winter: 10–5
Adm Adults £5.95, children £4.95, family (2+4) £19.95
Restaurant, indoor and outdoor play areas, disabled access

Bicton Park contains one of England's finest 19th-century glass buildings, the Palm House, which houses a 250-year-old collection of tropical plants, as well as a Countryside Museum and a woodland railway which (for a small extra charge) will take children on a 25-minute ride around the 25-hectare (63-acre) grounds. There's also a model village, a mini-golf course, a maze and indoor and outdoor play areas.

Canonteign Falls and Lakeland

Lower Ashton, Exeter **t** (01647) 252434
www.canonteignfalls.com
Getting there Lower Ashton is 10 miles southwest of Exeter on the outskirts of Dartmoor. Follow the signs from the A38
Open Mar–Oct 10–6, Nov–Feb 10–dusk
Adm Adults £5.75, children £3.50, family (2+2) £16.50
Restaurant and tearoom, picnic areas, gift shop, on-site parking

This 32-hectare (80-acre) park boasts England's highest waterfall, as well as a great swathe of ancient woodland, a lake, indoor and outdoor picnic areas and a children's assault course.

The Eden Project

St Glazey Gate, Bodelva, St Austell **t** (01726) 811911
www.edenproject.com
Getting there Follow the signposts from the A30, the A390 and the A391. There is a shuttle transfer bus from St Austell station
Open Apr–Oct 9–6 (last admission 4.30) Nov–Mar 10–4.30 (last admission 3)
Adm Adults £13.80, children £5, family ticket (2+3) £234
Restaurant, café, shop, disabled facilities, on-site parking

The Eden Project is the botanical garden to beat all botanical gardens. An old china clay pit the size of 35 football pitches has been converted into the ultimate plant experience. At the bottom of the pit are two futuristic-looking hemispherical glass and steel conservatories or 'biomes'. The largest, at 200m (656ft) long and 45m (145ft). One biome is devoted to tropical plants and the other to warm temperate vegetation. The huge greenhouses let children experience the sheer scale of the rainforest and the wonderful smells and gentle warmth of the Mediterranean. If you can, visit on a summer evening when you can smell the plants at their best. Since it opened in 2001, Eden has become Cornwall's principal tourist attraction. Its critics complain that there's nothing specifically Cornish about it and all it's done is create a traffic problem blocking country lanes around St Austell. While all that is true, children (even under 5s) can learn so much from a visit here that it would be a pity to miss it out of your sightseeing agenda even if you aren't a fan of botanical gardens. Eden isn't just Kew Gardens on sea. It isn't just about admiring huge tropical trees or looking at pretty flowers. Children are encouraged to smell and touch the plants. The project's main aim is to show that plants matter and that they supply our food, drink and everyday materials. There's a strong environmental message and the project sets out to show that we need plants both for our survival and that of our planet. If your kids think food comes from the supermarket, they'll find Eden an eye-opener. They'll be amazed to discover that the tyres on the car are made out of rubber from trees. They'll see coffee beans growing, watch the olives ripening on the trees and be able to finger the sugar canes. Even botanical names are made accessible. The *cola acuminata*, an African tree rich in caffeine seeds, is surrounded by cans of coke. That's how the drink got its name and it's now the best known Latin word in the world. There's an excellent children's interactive guidebook, which is full of things for children to do on site, but you'll need to buy it before you go down into the main part of the garden. You can easily spend the whole day here as there are lots of activities for kids, storytellers and performers. It's an excellent outing for all ages and there is a good restaurant on site. However, Eden can get very crowded during the summer and to see it at its best you need to avoid the crowds. You need space to appreciate the plants. It's better to visit after 3pm but you will need at least two hours to explore both biomes properly.

Look out for the *Children's Green Detective Guide to Cornwall* (Agenda £4.99), an informative easy-to-read environmentally friendly guide for 7–10-year-olds, which is on sale in the shop. The shop also sells a Cornish edition of Monopoly, reflecting the region's desirability among wealthy second-home owners; Mayfair is the Eden Project and it's a pinch cheaper to buy than the £86m needed to build it in the first place.

Escot Fantasy Gardens and Woodland

Escot, Ottery St Mary **t** (01404) 822188
www.escot-devon.co.uk
Getting there Ottery St Mary is about 8 miles east of Exeter. The park is signposted off the A30
Open Daily 10–dusk
Adm Adults £5.50, children £4, under 4s **free**, family £16.50
Café, snack shop, picnic areas, mother and baby facilities, disabled access, on-site parking, pet and aquatic shop, toy shop.

Large estate and gardens with numerous animals, including barn owls, snowy owls and otters (you can watch them being fed every day at 11am and 3.30pm), birds of prey (which are flown daily in summer) and wild boar, which snuffle and root their way around a woodland enclosure. There's also an aquatic centre with tropical and coldwater fish (including koi carp and piranhas), a waterfowl park, a Victorian rose garden, a new maze, a playground and trampolines for children.

Glendurgan Garden

Mawnan Smith, Falmouth **t** (01326) 250906
www.nationaltrust.org.uk
Getting there 4 miles southwest of Falmouth, on the road to Helford Passage
Open Feb–Oct Tues–Sat 10.30–5.30
Adm Adults £5, children £2.50, family (2+2) £12.50
Café, picnic area, shop, play area

Explore the laurel maze and swing round the 'Giant's Stride' maypole. The hamlet of Durgan and its beach are a 20-minute walk through the subtropical gardens.

Long Cross Victorian Gardens

Trelights, Port Isaac **t** (01208) 880243
www.longcrosshotel.co.uk
Getting there Port Isaac is on Cornwall's northern coast, about 10 miles southwest of Tintagel. The gardens are signposted from the A39
Open Daily 12 noon–dusk
Adm Adults £2, children 50p
Tea garden, souvenir shop, disabled facilities, on-site parking

Just inland from the popular resort of Port Isaac, Long Cross is the only public garden on the North Cornwall coast. Laid out to resemble a maze, it can be fun wandering through the neat flowerbeds and water features, although kids will probably prefer to spend some time in the adventure playground and pets' corner. So why not split up and reconvene afterwards at the pleasant tea gardens?

★Trebah Gardens

Mawnan Smith, Falmouth **t** (01326) 252200
www.trebah-garden.co.uk
Getting there About 3 miles south of Falmouth, signposted from the A39
Open Daily 10.30–6.30 (last entry 5)
Adm Summer/winter adults £5.80/£3, children £2/£1, under 5s **free**
Café, picnic areas, souvenir shop, disabled facilities, on-site parking; not suitable for pushchairs

The gardens start just outside a pretty 18th-century house, from where they descend 200 feet down a steep ravine to the Helford River. In between is an exotic mass of thick, lush vegetation. Huge palms and ferns tower overhead, gnarly 100-year-old rhododendrons block your path, while koi carp regard you lazily from their pools. Make your way to the end and you'll be rewarded by the sight of a private beach, where you can have a picnic or take a quick secluded dip while the kids wreak havoc in the 'Tarzan Camp' play area. A range of activities are put on for children, including Easter egg hunts, spring flower trails and Santa trails in December.

Trelissick Garden

Feock, Truro **t** (01872) 862090
www.nationaltrust.org.uk
Getting there 4 miles south of Truro, off the B3289
Open Mid Feb–Oct daily 10.30–5.30; Oct–Jan daily 11–4, **Adm** Adults £5.50, children £2.75, family £13.75
Café, shop, restaurant, disabled access

Perfect location for a picnic with a large park and woodland offering stunning views out to sea. Activities for children all year round.

Steam trains

Lappa Valley Steam Railway

St Newlyn East, Newquay **t** (01872) 510317
www.lappavalley.co.uk
Getting there South of Newquay off the A3075
Fares Adults £8.80, children £7.20, family (2+2) £28
Open Apr–Sept daily 10.30–4.30
Café, picnic area, coin-operated bikes, shop
   The narrow-gauge steam railway takes a
two-mile trip through the beautiful Cornish
countryside. There are also two miniature trains
to ride, a boating lake, a maze, crazy golf and big
adventure playground.

Launceston Steam Railway

St Thomas Road, Launceston **t** (01566) 775665
www.launcestonsr.co.uk
Operating times Easter–Oct Tues–Sun (call in
advance for details of times)
Fares Adults £6.80, children £4.50, family (2+2) £21
Station buffet, disabled facilities, on-site parking
   Four late 19th-century locomotives pull passen-
gers in open-top wagons through the leafy
Cornish countryside. The open daily ticket allows
plenty of opportunity for riverside picnics and
there's a small railway museum at Launceston
Station for kids to explore.

Paignton and Dartmouth Steam Railway

Dart Valley Light Railway plc, Queen's Park Station
t (01803) 555872
www.paignton-steamrailway.co.uk
Operating times Jun–Sept daily; Apr, May, Oct
selected dates; Dec 'Santa Specials'
Fares Return: adults £9, children £6
   Delightful steam train rides, including Santa
and Thomas the Tank Engine events.
For further information *see p.216*

★South Devon Railway

South Devon Railway, Buckfastleigh Station
t (01364) 642338 www.southdevonrailway.org
Open Apr–Nov most days, Dec 'Santa Specials'
Fares Adult return £8.80, children £5.30, family
£25.40
   Seven-mile steam train rides alongside the
banks of the inaccesible River Dart between
Totnes and Buckfastleigh.
For further information *see p.202*

Theme parks and model villages

If you're looking for the latest heart-stopping,
adrenaline-pumping thrills, then you've come to
the wrong place. There's nothing here to match
the hardware on offer at Alton Towers or the
Blackpool Pleasure Beach. Theme parks in the
Southwest tend to be gentle, homely affairs,
more 'family fun' than 'thrills and spills', with
odd, Victorian-sounding names like Flambards.
So, while somewhere like Surrey's Chessington
World of Adventures might try to entice you with
its state-of-the-art vertical-drop rollercoaster,
Dobwalls in Cornwall will invite you to its weekly
sheepdog trials and diesel-train rides. It's a
different sensibility altogether. Visiting a theme
park in the Southwest is a bit like visiting the
biggest, most exciting village fête in the world.

Babbacombe Model Village

Hampton Avenue **t** (01803) 315315
www.babbacombemodelvillage.co.uk
Open Jan–Feb and early Nov 10–3.30, Mar and Oct
10–4, Apr 10–5 (until 9.30 half term), May–Aug
10–9.30, Sept 10–9 (Sat until 5), Oct 10–4, late Nov
and Dec 11–7
Adm Adults £6.90, children £4.50, family £21
   One-and-a-half hectares (four acres) of
1:12-scale models of villages, buildings, waterfalls
and gardens to explore.
For further information *see p.219*

★Bradworthy Gnome Reserve and Wild Flower Garden

West Putford, Bradworthy **t** (01409) 241435
www.gnomereserve.co.uk
Getting there Signposted from J27 of the M5, the
reserve is 7 miles south of Clovelly
Open Mar–Oct daily 10–6 (last entry 5.30)
Adm Adults £2.75, children £2.25, under 3s **free**
*Picnic areas, souvenir shop, mother and baby
facilities, on-site parking*
   Bradworthy's Gnome Reserve is a must for all
small children. Sporting a colourful pixie hat and
carrying a tiny fishing rod they are let loose to
explore two acres of woodland and meadow,
populated by over 1,000 model gnomes and
pixies. They can even visit a real pixie house or sit
with their newfound friends fishing in the ottery.

Crealy Adventure Park

Sidmouth Road, Clyst St Mary, Exeter
t (01395) 233200 www.crealy.co.uk
Getting there From J30 of the M5, take the A3052 and follow the signs
Open Apr–Jul and Oct daily 10–6, Aug 10–7; Nov–Mar Thurs–Sun 10–5
Adm High summer £9.25, summer £8.95; winter £4.95; children under 1m (3ft) **free**
Cafés and fast food, souvenir shops, mother and baby facilities, disabled facilities, on-site parking

Large family complex just outside Clyst St Mary, with go-karts, bumper boats, pony rides, an adventure playground, a rollercoaster, a 'Splash Zone' water-themed playground, a lake and a farm where you can help milk the cows or feed the baby animals. Activities for children, including treasure hunts, sleepovers and craft workshops, are laid on throughout the year.

★Dairy Land Farm World

Summercourt, Newquay **t** (01872) 510246
www.dairylandfarmworld.com
Getting there 4 miles from Newquay on the A3058 Newquay–St Austell road
Open Apr–Oct daily 10–5
Adm Adults £7.75, children £46.75, under 3s **free**, family ticket (2+3) £27

Cows are milked on a spinning merry-go-round to the sounds of classical music.
For further information *see p.196*

Dobwalls

Liskeard **t** (01579) 320325
www.dobwallsadventurepark.co.uk
Getting there Just off the A38, Liskeard is on the main London–Penzance rail line
Open Apr–Sept daily 10.30–5, Oct Sat–Sun
Adm Adults £7.95, 2–3-year-old children £6.75, under 2s **free**
Café, gift shop, snacks, mother and baby facilities, disabled facilities, on-site parking
Not suitable for pushchairs

Dobwalls is the archetypal Southwest theme park. There are no big dippers or log flumes here, just gentle family-friendly entertainments. Its main attractions are two American-style miniature steam and diesel railways, Rio Grande and

Furry Dance

Also (incorrectly) called the Floral Dance, Helston's colourful celebration of the coming of summer is held on the nearest Saturday to 8 May, when the whole town is festooned with flowers, while elegantly dressed dancers (top hats and tails for the boys, puffy dresses and wide-brimmed hats for the girls) twirl their way through the crowded streets.

Union Pacific (your ticket allows you unlimited rides on each), which chug their way through some pretty countryside. Elsewhere, kids are well provided for with an outdoor woodland adventure play area, an indoor 'Krazee Cavern' play area, a rope lattice climbing frame 'The Skydome' and a Go-Kart Driving School. There's also a small zoo and in summer you can watch weekly sheepdog trials.

★Flambards

Helston **t** 0845 6018684 www.flambards.co.uk
Getting there Helston is 10 miles southwest of Falmouth, off the A39
Open Apr–Jul daily 10–5, Aug 10–5.30, Sept–Oct 10.30–4.30
Adm Adults £12.50, children £9.55, under 5s **free**, family £31.50–58.50; reduced prices after 2.15pm
Cafés and fast food, gift shops, mother and baby facilities, disabled facilities, on-site parking

A theme park without a theme, Flambards has a charmingly eclectic range of attractions. Alongside a couple of very nifty rollercoasters, a log flume and swinging pirate ship, you'll find a reconstructed Victorian village with more than 50 buildings to wander through, each decked out with period furniture, decorations and even period food; a reconstructed Second World War Street (shown ravaged by Blitz bombs); a weather station, where you can watch live satellite transmissions from space and an exhibition showing how wedding fashions have changed through the centuries. There is also a petting zoo, an adventure playground, a soft play area for toddlers, an interactive science centre, some sedate fairground rides, a garden centre and the Cornwall Children's Eye (a rival to that large ferris wheel in London). In summer, there are occasional evening firework displays. It's a bit strange but holds together perfectly, giving kids plenty of opportunity to run around and let off steam. The picturesque Georgian town of Helston famed for its annual 'Furry Dance' is just to the north (*see* above).

Milky Way Adventure Park

Clovelly, Bideford **t** (01237) 431255
www.themilkyway.co.uk
Open Apr–Oct 10.30–6, winter Sat and Sun 11–5
Adm Adults £8, children under 1m (3ft) tall £6, under 3s **free**

Ride the rollercoaster, play in a large indoor adventure playground or stroke a lamb or kid goat. **For further information** *see p.206*

Once Upon a Time

The Old Station, Station Road, Woolacombe
t (01271) 867474/863879
Getting there From J27 of M5, the A361 and the A39
Open Apr–Sept Sat–Thurs
Adm Adults £10, children £8.50, under 2s **free**
Café and snacks, gift shop, mother and baby facilities, disabled facilities, on-site parking

Run by the same management as Watermouth Castle in Ilfracombe (p.212), this is a great place to take very young children as it has lots of gentle rides and activities, including carousels, a children's driving school, old penny slot machines, crazy golf and a 'Young Scientists' Room'.

★Woodlands Leisure Park

Blackawton, Totnes **t** (01803) 712598
www.woodlandspark.com
Getting there 7 miles south of Totnes, 3 miles west of Dartmouth, on the A3122
Open Mar–Oct daily 9.30–dusk
Adm Adults and children £8.75 (£9.25 in high season)
Cafés and fast food, gift shops, mother and baby facilities, disabled facilities, on-site parking

Woodlands is aimed squarely at children but that doesn't mean mums and dads won't have a lot of fun, too. Slides are its speciality – waterslides, dry slides, toboggan runs – you name it, it's got it and while they would no doubt disappoint most rollercoaster aficionados, they have just the right thrill factor for youngsters, meaning they're not too scary.

Most of the attractions are water-themed, which means getting splashed at numerous points during your journey – which kids, of course, love. This particularly applies to the Twister, a spiralling, tipping water chute, which should leave you and the kids thoroughly soaked. All age groups are catered for so, while older pre-teens clamber determinedly over the excellent Green Beret commando-style assault course, toddlers can have fun in one of the numerous indoor soft play areas, full of ball ponds and slides, or at the special play zone for under 6s.

All kids will like the zoo with its cute wallabies and not-quite-so-cute llamas (they really do spit when they're annoyed) and the Bee Farm, where you can watch millions of bees furiously making honey in special glass-sided hives.

Clowns, jugglers and other assorted entertainers are on hand to help keep the queues amused in summer.

World of Country Life

Sandy Bay, Exmouth **t** (01395) 274533
www.worldofcountrylife.co.uk
Open Apr–Oct 10–dusk
Adm Adults £8, children £7, under 2s **free**, family £28

A 16-hectare (40-acre) family fun park with a petting zoo, bird of prey displays and the choice of boarding a safari ride through llama and deer paddocks. **For further information** *see p.212*

World in Miniature

Halt Road, Goonhavern, Truro **t** (01872) 572828
Getting there Lies north of Truro on the B3285
Open Mid-May–Oct 10–5
Adm Adults £5.50, children £4.50
Café, gift shops, mother and baby facilities, disabled facilities, on-site parking

A tiny Taj Mahal, a mini Statue of Liberty, a pint-size Wild West Town – the kids will never get a better opportunity to pretend to be giants.

Wide open spaces

The Southwest is famed for its great stretches of wilderness. Bodmin Moor, Dartmoor and Exmoor have come to symbolize a peculiarly English type of windswept natural beauty. The three areas share many characteristics – they are remote and open

Safety tip
Much of the northern part of Dartmoor is now a designated military area which poses its own set of problems. The presence of red flags means that live firing is in progress and that you are under no circumstances to enter the area. White flags means it is safe to enter. Thankfully, live firing usually only occurs in the winter months.

The Beast of Bodmin Moor

In the early 1980s reports emerged of a large, black panther-like cat seen roaming the Cornish moors. Dismissed at first as a hoax or perhaps the ravings of a particularly drunken tourist, soon more and more people started coming forward claiming to have seen the same thing. Could it be true? Could there really be a big cat on the loose in the West Country and, if so, where did it come from? No zoos had reported any missing animals. The 1976 Dangerous Wild Animals Act prohibited the keeping of big cats as pets. Perhaps it was an illegal pet that had been released once it had grown too big to handle, the owner fearing the legal consequences if they reported it. The national press became determined to solve the mystery, sending teams of reporters to hunt for what soon became known as the 'Beast of Bodmin Moor'. With hundreds of amateur sleuths also on the trail, it rapidly turned into a *cause celèbre*. Farmers expressed concern for the safety of their livestock while tourist boards worried about the potential damage that the presence of a dangerous wild animal running loose in the countryside might do to the tourist industry – although, if anything, the mystery served to increase the area's popularity. Before long, the beast had become as famous as that other great mystery creature, the Loch Ness Monster.

Despite all the interest, the 'beast' itself has remained tantalizingly elusive. Unconfirmed sightings have continued to flood in over the last 20 years, occasionally accompanied by some rather (conveniently) blurred photos showing a fuzzy black shape that could be a cat, or a boulder, or a hole in the ground, or anything really. Absolute proof of the beast's existence has been somewhat hard to come by. To this day, it has managed to escape the combined attention of thousands of tourists and press, not to mention an RAF search team. If there's something out there, it's pretty good at hiding itself.

and empty – but are also each subtly different. Dartmoor is harsh and rugged where Exmoor is soft and rolling, while Bodmin Moor has the greatest number of 'mystical' associations, its bleak features the inspiration for centuries of myths and legends. It is worth bearing in mind that, though the moors offer plenty of scope for fun with their zoos, museums and horse-riding centres, they are not called 'wildernesses' without reason, being made up of hundreds of square miles of barren landscape that should on no account be tackled without proper equipment and preparation.

Bodmin Moor

Getting there Bodmin Moor lies in the heart of Cornwall and is bisected by the A30. The A39 runs just to the north
Tourist information Shire Hall, Mount Folly Square, Bodmin t/f (01208) 76616 www.bodminmoor.co.uk

The smallest of the Southwest's trio of 'wildernesses', Bodmin Moor is like Dartmoor in miniature: boggy and rugged with tinkling streams, murky lakes, thick expanses of grassland and, of course, a smattering of bizarrely shaped granite tors, including the famous 'Cheesewring', an improbably shaped 9m/30ft-high granite monolith. It also has a particularly rich collection of myths and legends. Dozmary Pool, near Bolventor, is supposedly the final resting place of Excalibur, King Arthur's magical sword, thrown into the water by Sir Bedevere as Arthur lay dying, whereupon a mysterious hand reached out of the water, grabbed the sword and dragged it down to the depths where it was reclaimed by the Lady of the Lake (who presumably still has it).

Just south of Bolventor, on the A30, is Colliford Lake Park, where you'll find numerous lakeside walks, an adventure play area and an undercover assault course, as well as lots of animals to see, including sheep, cows and poultry. In summer, there are regular craft demonstrations.

★Dartmoor National Park

Getting there Dartmoor consists of 365 square miles of South Devon countryside and is bisected east to west by the B3357 and the B3212. The A30 runs to the north of the moor, the A38 to the south

Tourist information:

High Moorland Visitor Centre, Old Derby Hotel, Tavistock Road, Princetown (open all year)

t (01822) 890414

Haytor **t** (01364) 661520

Postbridge **t** (01822) 880272

Newbridge **t** (01364) 631303

Ivybridge **t** (01752) 897035

Tavistock **t** (01822) 612938

www.dartmoor-npa.gov.uk

This vast swathe of moorland is the largest remaining area of wilderness in southern England. It is a wondrous, if slightly daunting place. The sheer variety of the landscape is breathtaking, covering great expanses of grass-land interspersed with thick, muddy bogs and heather-clad hills, isolated villages seemingly little changed since the Middle Ages, fast-flowing rivers and tiny streams curling around craggy contours, small copses of oak in sheltered valleys, ancient stone clapper bridges and murky ponds, prehistoric ruins, deep, dark gorges and, of course, tors (granite monoliths that are Dartmoor's most famous feature). You'll see them everywhere punctuating the skyline, their silhouettes weath-ered by thousands of years of wind and rain into weird and wonderful shapes. The most famous tor of all is probably Haytor (just off the B3357, near the visitor centre and a short walk from the car park). It consists of a vast collection of rocks jutting though the ground like a row of worn dragon's teeth. From the top you can see all the way across Devon to the coast.

If travelling with kids, it's best to explore Dartmoor from the safety of a car, following the A382, the B3212 or the B3357, stopping off here and there for a few short strolls or as part of an organized pony- or horse-trekking team. Try the **Shilstone Rocks Riding Centre**, **t** (01364) 621281, near Widecombe-in-the-Moor, which offers treks for around £18 an hour (beginners welcome). The Dartmoor National Park Authority, **t** (01822) 890414, organizes walks and activities (such as treasure hunts) for kids while the visitor centres can provide details of the best family routes.

Letterboxing

Although you may not at first be able to spot them, Dartmoor is littered with thousands of 'letterboxes'. These are not remote outposts of the postal service but rather visitor books hidden in tree stumps and under rocks, which together form a sort of informal treasure hunt. Each box comes attached with an ink pad and stamp with which 'letterboxers' (as the people who hunt for these things are known) stamp their record books before heading off in search of the next box. The aim, of course, is to collect as many stamps as possible – you could explain it to your children as being like a mobile version of Pokémon minus the strange Japanese animation. Collect 100 of these stamps and you qualify to join the exclusive '100 Club'. The practise began in the mid 19th century and now has thousands of (often quite obsessive) devotees.

For more information, contact one of Dartmoor's tourist information centres (*see* left).

Walking on the southern part of the moor is less strenuous and easier for children. The park authorities also publish a useful guide *Easygoing Dartmoor*, which has several good walks suitable for pushchairs. The River Teign near Castle Drogo (p.203) is also a good spot for a family walk.

Beautiful though it may be, much of Dartmoor might well prove a little empty and barren for many kids. For a more manageable piece of wilderness head to the Becky Falls Woodland Park, which has marked walks and nature trails through ancient oak woodland and past cascading falls. It also has an animal centre with goats, rabbits and rescued birds of prey (pony rides are offered during the school holidays). More animals can be found at Dartmoor Wildlife Park and the Dartmoor Miniature Pony and Animal Farm, where your kids can interact with Shetland ponies, donkeys (which foal in spring and early summer), pygmy goats and dwarf rabbits. Pony rides across Dartmoor are offered and there is an excellent indoor adventure play-ground, 'Fort Bovey'.

★Becky Falls Woodland Park

Manaton, near Bovey Tracey **t** (01647) 221259

www.beckyfalls.com

Getting there On the Bovey Tracey–Manaton Road, the A382, an easy 4-mile drive from Bovey Tracey and only 30 minutes from Torbay

Safety tips for walking on the moors

The remoteness of the West Country's moors that are both their biggest attraction and greatest danger. These huge swathes of unspoilt wilderness, where you can often walk for miles without coming across a road, a village or indeed any sign of life, are not to be tackled lightly. Even in the more populated regions, the sameness of the landscape means you can easily lose your bearings.

If travelling with children you should:

► Restrict your visit to the warm summer months. Check the weather forecast and be prepared to change your plans at short notice. Be aware that the weather can change very rapidly in this region and, no matter what the prevailing conditions, you should come prepared with wet and warm weather clothing plus copious supplies of food and drink.

► Decide where you are going and when you plan to return. Tell someone and make sure that person can raise the alarm if you don't arrive back in time.

► Stick to your planned route. If setting out from a car, leave a note displayed in the window showing the direction headed in and the name of the feature intended to see.

► Make sure you have the most up-to-date map available. Dartmoor boasts some particularly treacherous terrain, including several bogs.

► Stick to areas close to the road and within easy reach of civilization.

► Make sure you wear stout, fitted walking boots – not sandals or trainers.

► Bring a whistle.

► Make sure your children are wearing name tags.

► Join an organized walk or a pony-trekking tour.

Open Mar–Oct daily 10–6 (or dusk if earlier); winter Sat–Sun, Feb half-term and Christmas school holidays
Adm Adults £5.75, children £4.75, under 5s **free**
Restaurant, tearooms, ice cream parlour, gift shop, picnic area, pets' corner, on-site parking; not suitable for pushchairs

Some 215m (700ft) above sea level, Becky Falls is a 25-hectare (60-acre) private woodland estate with waterfalls tumbling over huge granite rocks. Pushchair access to the nature trails is restricted, so baby carriers are recommended. Pony rides in the summer holidays.

Dartmoor Miniature Pony and Animal Farm

Moretonhampstead, Dartmoor **t** (01647) 432400
www.miniatureponycentre.com
Getting there 2 miles west of Moretonhampstead, on the B3212 Princetown Road
Open Easter–Oct daily 10.30–dusk
Adm Adults £6.50, children £5.50, family £22
Café, gift shop, disabled facilities, on-site parking

Kids can meet and touch all the animals, including the miniature ponies and donkeys, which foal in spring and early summer. Pony rides are offered and there is an adventure playground, an indoor assault course and nature trails down by the lakes, where you can feed the trout. At Sandy Farm, children can learn farming skills, such as driving and riding tractors, loaders and trailers; sorting out hay; mixing the food then feeding the farmyard animals.

Lydford Gorge

Lydford **t** (01822) 820320
www.nationaltrust.org.uk
Getting there At the west end of the village of Lydford, on the western edge of Dartmoor, off the A386
Open Apr–Sept daily 10–5, Oct 10–4
Adm Adults £5 children £2.50, family £12.50
Cafés, gift shops; not suitable for pushchairs

Beautiful mile-long, oak-clad river gorge with wonderful water features, including the 27m (90ft) White Lady waterfall and the Devil's Cauldron, a foaming whirlpool. Lots of wildlife and plants to admire and, unfortunately, lots of people in summer. Be careful, paths can get very slippery.

Exmoor National Park

Getting there Stretching over North Devon and West Somerset, Exmoor covers 265 square miles. The A39 runs along its northern coast while the A396 runs south to north across the middle
Tourist information:
Lynmouth **t** (01598) 752509
Dunster **t** (01643) 821835
County Gate **t** (01598) 741321
Combe Martin **t** (01271) 883319
Dulverton **t** (01398) 3232841
www.exmoor-nationalpark.gov.uk
For further information *see* Midwest chapter p.176

SPORT AND ACTIVITIES

Bicycle hire

Bridge Cycle Hire
Eddystone Road, Wadebridge **t** (01208) 813050
Open Daily 9–5
Adm Adults £8–12, children £6 per day
   Offers budget deals (around £25 for a family of four to cycle the Camel trail to Padstow).

Tarka Trail Cycle Hire
Railway Station, Barnstaple **t** (01271) 324202
Open Daily 10–5 (Jul–Sept until 6pm)
Prices From £30 a day for bikes for a family of 4
   This is an old railway line that has been turned into a cycle path. Traffic free, it runs for 21 miles along the rivers Taw and Torridge and was named after the story of *Tarka the Otter*, which was inspired by the area. You can picnic on the sandy beach at Instow, six miles from Barnstaple; it's a great place for bird-watching.

Go-karts

Go-karting
St Eval, Newquay **t** (01637) 860160
www.cornwallkarting.co.uk
Getting there Off the B3276 north of Newquay
Open Mon–Sat 9.30–6 **Prices** call for prices
   From age six upwards.

Grand Prix Go-Karts
Warren Road, Dawlish Warren **t** (01626) 862521
www.grand-prix-go-karts.co.uk
Open Easter–Oct 10–6; May–Aug 10–10
Adm Single kart £3.50, 2 seater £5 per session
   Two-seater karts for families.

North Devon Karting Centre
Pottington Business Park, Barnstaple **t** (01271) 328460 www.northdevonkarting.co.uk
Open Call in advance for details of times and prices
   On-site parking available.

Horse-riding

Keypitts Stables and Quads
Keypitts Farm, Ilfracombe **t** (01271) 862247
www.keypitts.com
Open Daily, call in advance to arrange horses
Adm From £5 per hour
   Horse-riding and quad-biking for all abilities.

Woolacombe Riding Stables
Eastacott Farm, Woolacombe **t** (01271) 870260
www.woolacombe-ridingstables.co.uk
Open Summer daily 9–6; call for winter hours
Adm Adults and children £15 per hour
   Horse- and pony-riding along the coast including rides for experienced riders along Woolacombe's three miles of sandy beach.

Ice-skating

Plymouth Pavilions' Swiss Lake Ice Rink
Millbay Road, Plymouth **t** (01752) 222200
www.plymouthpavilions.com
Open Call for times and prices
   The centre also boasts a swimming pool with waterslides and a wave machine.

Indoor adventure playgrounds

Ben's Playworld
Stadium Retail Park, St Austell **t** (01726) 815553
www.bensplayworld.co.uk
Open Daily 10–7 (closed Wed and Thurs in winter)
Adm Children (2–12): Sat and Sun £4.50, Mon–Fri £3; accompanying adults: £1/50p
Café, picnic area, mother and baby facilities, disabled facilities, on-site parking
   The largest indoor play area in the Southwest, full of masses of coloured soft things for kids to clamber in, on and around: ball pools, slides, climbing frames, punch bags, etc. There is a maze, a ghosthouse and, in the outdoor play area, mini cars, bikes and a crazy golf course. While kids go mad, parents can watch TV at the café or relax with a free paper.

Surfing

Extreme Academy
Watergate Bay, Newquay **t** (01637) 860840
www.watergatebay.co.uk
Open Call in advance for details of times and prices
   Surfing, power-kiting, wave skiing and mountain boarding for all ages.

Lusty Glaze Outdoor Adventure Centre
Lusty Glaze Beach, Newquay **t** (01637) 872444
Open Call in advance for details of times and prices
   Surf school with special Junior Baywatch courses for 7–14-year-olds. Also abseiling and kayaking. Children's crèche, café and hire shop.

Offshore Extreme

6 Marcus Hill, Newquay **t** (01637) 877083
www.offshore-extreme.co.uk
Open Call in advance for details of times
Prices Half-day sessions start from £20

Britain's oldest surf school, it runs BSA- and BWSF-approved courses for beginners of all ages.

Reef Surf School

27 Agar Road, Newquay **t** (01637) 879058
www.reefsurfschool.com
Open All year round 9–6
Prices Half day (£25), one day (£35; includes board hire)

Shore 2 Surf

West Road, Woolacombe **t** (01271) 870870
www.shore2surf.com
Open All year round 9–6
Prices Call for prices

Surf coaching for children with surfing champion Nick Thorn.

Swimming

Newquay Waterworld

Trenance Leisure Park, Newquay **t** (01637) 853828
www.newquaywaterworld.co.uk
Open Daily; call for times
Adm Adults £4.90, children £3.90, under 5s £1.90, under 2s **free**

The Southwest's best swimming complex.
For further information *see* p.196

Plymouth Pavilions Atlantis Pool

Millbay Road, Plymouth **t** (01752) 222200
Open/Adm Call for times and prices

Waterslides, a wave machine and an ice rink.

★QuayWest Waterpark

Goodrington Sands, Paignton **t** (01803) 555550
www.quaywest.co.uk
Open May, Jul and Aug 10–6, June and Sept 11–5
Adm 2hr/all day ticket: adults £8.50/£9.95, children £7.50/£8.95, children under 1m (3ft) £3.50/£3.95, family (2+2) £29/£35

Outdoor waterpark on the seafront.
For further information *see* p.216

Waves Leisure Pool

The Riviera Centre, Chestnut Avenue, Torquay
t (01803) 299992 **www.rivieracentre.co.uk**
Open Call for times

Adm Adults £3.50, children £2.75, family £11.25
Restaurant, café

Heated pool (to 29°C/84°F), paddling pool, water spray and wave machine.

Watersports

Canoe Adventures

1 Church Court, Herberton, Totnes **t** (01803) 865301
www.canoeadventures.co.uk
Open Year round; book in advance
Prices £158 for entire canoe or £16–20 per seat

These 12-seater Canadian canoes take 10 passengers (adults and children) and a guide on five-hour trips to explore the River Dart and its creeks. Picnics supplied (£4.50 each). The trips leave from Tuctenhay.

ICC Activity Centres

Island Street, Salcombe **t** (01548) 531176
www.icc-salcombe.co.uk
Open Call in advance for details of times and prices

Range of watersports for all ages and levels.

Killarney Springs

Morwenstow, Bude **t** (01288) 331475
www.killarneysprings.com
Getting there Signposted off the A39 between Bude and Clovelly
Open Daily Apr–Oct 10.30–6; Nov–Easter weekends and school holidays 11–4
Adm Call for prices

There's an indoor playground and a wide selection of outdoor activities: water rides, boating lake, go-karts, assault course and farm animals to feed.

Plymouth Outdoor Education Centre

Mountbatten Centre, 70 Lawrence Road, Plymstock, Plymouth **t** (01752) 404567
www.mount-batten-centre.com
Open Call in advance for details of times and prices

Sailing and watersports centre offering lessons and courses for all ages and abilities.

River Dart Adventures

Holne Park Ashburton, Newton Abbot
t (01364) 655915 **www.riverdart.co.uk**
Getting there Off the A38, west of Newton Abbot
Open Daily Apr–Sept 9.30–6
Adm Call in advance for details of prices

Adventure playgrounds and woodland walks, canoeing, climbing and zip wires.

KIDS IN

Cinemas

Exeter
Exeter Picture House 51 Bartholomew Street West
t (01392) 435522
Odeon Sidwell Street t 0871 2244007
Phoenix Arts Centre Bradninch Place
t (01392) 667080

Exmouth
Savoy Rolle Street t 0871 2303200

Dartmouth
The Flavel Flavel Place t (01803) 839530

Padstow
Cinedrome Lanadwell Street t (01841) 532344

Paignton
Apollo Esplanade t 0871 2233475

Penzance
Savoy Cinema Causeway Head t (01736) 363330

Plymouth
ABC Cinema Derry's Cross t (01752) 663300
Plymouth Arts Centre 38 Looe Street
t (01752) 206114
Vue ShaptersRoad t 0871 2240240

Redruth
Regal Cinema 6 Fore Street t (01209) 216278

St Austell
Filmcentre Chandos Place t (01726) 73750

St Ives
Royal Cinema Royal Square t (01736) 796843

Torquay
Central Cinema Abbey Road t (01803) 380001

Totnes
Dartington Arts Dartington Hall t (01803) 847070

Truro
Plaza Cinema Lemon Street t (01872) 272894

Wadebridge
Regal Cinema The Platt t (01208) 812791

Museums, mines, galleries and science centres

The Southwest has lots of options for when the heavens open which, even in this famously sunny region, happens a good deal more often than is strictly necessary. Obviously, the sort of places that most appeal to kids are those offering the greatest amount of interactivity; places like the Cardew Pottery, where they can have a go on a wonderfully messy potter's wheel, or the Goonhilly Satellite Earth Station, where they can press buttons in a sciencey-looking control room and pretend they are appearing in an episode of *Star Trek*. There are also museums and galleries galore, many of which organize hands-on activities for children on weekends and in the school holidays.

The Cardew Pottery
Newton Road, Bovey Tracey t (01626) 832172
www.cardewdesign.com
Open Daily 10–5.30 **Adm Free**
Restaurant, shop
Tour the factory to see the pots being made and have a go at decorating one in the Activity Centre before browsing for the perfect tea brewer in the shop. They come in all shapes and sizes: Winnie the Pooh-shaped pots, lighthouse-shaped pots, telephone-shaped pots, etc. There are four hectares (10 acres) of woodland, lakes and waterfalls, a playground and a mini train.

City of Plymouth Museums and Art Gallery
Drake Circus t (01752) 304774
Open Tues–Fri 10–5.30, Sat and Bank Hols 10–5
Adm Free
Baby changing facilities, shop, disabled access
Natural history section, workshops and a hands-on discovery centre for children.
For further information *see* p.198

Cornish Mines and Engines and Industrial Heritage Centre
Pool, Redruth t (01209) 315027
www.nationaltrust.org.uk
Open Apr–Oct Sun–Fri 11–5
Adm Adults £5, children £2.50, family (2+3) £12.50
Picnic area, shop, disabled access
Learn about the mining history of Cornwall and see the massive engine working.

Dartington Crystal Ltd
Great Torrington t (01805) 626242
www.dartington.co.uk
Open: Visitor centre and shop : Mon–Fri 9.30–5, Sat 10–5 and Sun 10–4; Factory tour Mon–Fri 9.30–5 (last tour 3.15)
Adm Tour and visitor centre: Adults £5, children **free;** Visitor centre only: Adults £2.50 (£1.50 on weekends)
Restaurant, factory shop, disabled access, on-site parking

Watch craftsmen blowing and shaping crystal, then buy one in the factory shop. There is also a visitor centre and a glass exhibition, with hands-on exhibits for young children.

Geevor Tin Mine Heritage Centre

Pendeen, Penzance **t** (01736) 788662
www.geevor.com
Getting there 7 miles west of Penzance
Open Easter–Oct Sun–Fri 10–4; winter 10–3
Adm Adults £7.50, children £4.30, family (2+3) £21

Explore Cornwall's tin mining past in this former mine, which closed in 1990.

★Goonhilly Satellite Earth Station

The Visitor Centre, Goonhilly Downs, Helston
t 0800 679593 **www.goonhilly.bt.com**
Getting there On Goonhilly Downs, 7 miles from Helston on the B3293
Open Feb–Mar and Nov–Dec Tues–Sun 11–4, Apr–May and Oct daily 10–5, Jun–Sept 10–6
Adm Adults £6.50, children £4.50, under 5s **free**, family £14
Café, picnic areas, gift shop, mother and baby facilities, disabled access, on-site parking

Goonhilly is one of the world's foremost satellite tracking centres. Every moment of every day, it receives millions of pieces of information – TV images, phone calls, faxes, etc. – from the spacecraft that orbit the earth. It's all very X-Files, the vast listening dishes rising out of the earth like God's tea set, each named after a character from Arthurian legend: Arthur, Merlin, etc. On a guided tour, you are taken to the control room where you can see this incredible process of information gathering in action, and even have a go at operating one of the tracking devices yourself. You can also take a bus tour of the site (which is also a nature reserve) to get a close-up look at the enormous dishes. There are lots of hands-on activities (e-mailing an alien and having your photo taken in space in a virtual image booth).

Morwellham Quay

Morwellham, Tavistock **t** (01822) 832766
www.morwellham-quay.co.uk
Morwellham Quay port and copper mine
t (01822) 833808
Open Easter–Oct daily 10–5.30, Nov–Easter 10–4.30
Adm Adults £8.90, children £6, under 5s **free**, family £26 (reduced price in winter as activities close, adult £6, children £4)

Restaurant, shops, guided tours, mother and baby facilities, disabled access, on-site parking

Restored 19th-century village inhabited by staff in period costume (you also have the chance to dress up in Victorian clothes), where you can wander through recreated street scenes, ride on an underground train through a copper mine and take the wheel of the *Garlandstone* sailing ship. Period crafts are demonstrated and there's a wildlife reserve running alongside the River Tamar.

Poldark Mine

Wendron, Helston **t** (01326) 573173
www.poldark-mine.co.uk
Getting there 2 miles north of Helston on the B3297
Open Daily 10–5.30 (May–mid-Jul and Sept–Oct closed Sat)
Adm Adults £7.50, children £4.90, family (2+2) £19
Café, shop, playground

Tour one of Cornwall's old tin mines; not suitable for children under four.

★Plymouth Dome

The Hoe, Hoe Road **t** (01752) 603300
www.plymouthdome.info
Open Apr–Oct 10–5, Nov–Mar 10–4
Adm Dome: adults £4.75, children £3.25, family £13; dome and tower: adults £6.50, children £4, family £16

Excellent audiovisual displays bring Plymouth's past to life.

For further information *see* pp.198–9

Wheal Martyn Discovery Centre

Carthew, St Austell **t** (01726) 850362
www.wheal-martyn.com
Getting there 2 miles north of St Austell on the A3274
Open Easter–Nov 10–6
Adm Adults £7.50, children £3.50, family (2+4) £18
Café, shop

St Austell was once a major clay mining town and the museum traces the history of clay mining. There's a special children's trail around the old pit.

Theatres

Exeter

Barnfield Barnfield Road **t** (01392) 271808
www.barnfieldtheatre.org.uk

★*Minack Theatre*

Porthcurno **t** (01736) 810181 **www.minack.com**
Open Exhibition: Apr–Sept 9.30–5.30, Oct–Mar
10–4. Performances: May–Sept only, call for details
Adm Exhibition: adults £2.50, children £1, under 12s
free; performances: adults £6–7.50, children £3–4

It was built in the 1930s by local woman Rowena
Cade, who single-handedly carved the Greek-style
theatre into Porthcurno's cliff face. The sheer rocks
and blue sea provide a stunning backdrop to
performances – especially the evening shows. The
site also contains an exhibition on Ms Cade's life
with models, photographs and audiovisual
displays. The summer season runs from May to
Sept with a full programme of plays, musicals and
operas staged. There are only 750 seats, so you'll
have to book well in advance.

Exeter Phoenix Bradnich Place, Gandy Street
t (01392) 667080 **www.exeterphoenix.org.uk**
Northcott Stocker Road **t** (01392) 493493
www.northcott-theatre.co.uk

Falmouth

Falmouth Arts Centre 24 Church Street
t (01326) 212300 **www.falmoutharts.org**
Princess Pavilion Melvill Road
t (01326) 211222/311277 **www.falmoutharts.org**

Newquay

Lane Theatre t (01637) 876945
www.lanetheatre.co.uk

Penzance

Acorn Theatre Parade Street **t** (01736) 363545
www.acorn-theatre.co.uk
Minack Theatre Porthcurno **t** (01736) 810181
(*see* above)

Plymouth

Theatre Royal Royal Parade **t** (01752) 267222
www.theatreroyal.com

St Austell

St Austell Arts Centre 87 Truro Road
t (01726) 68532

Torquay

Babbacombe Theatre Babbacombe Downs
t (01803) 328385 **www.babbacombe-theatre.com**
Princess Theatre Torbay Road **t** 0870 241 4120

Truro

Hall for Cornwall Back Quay **t** (01872) 262466
www.hallforcornwall.co.uk
Redannick Theatre Redannick Lane **t** (01872) 222272

Ashburton

Café Green Ginger

26 East Street **t** (01364) 653939
Getting there Turn off the A38 Plymouth–Exeter
Road and take the express way into Ashburton
Open Mon, Thurs and Fri 10–5, Sat 9–5, Sun 11–5

A good place to relax after an afternoon spent
tramping on the moors, it serves excellent
meals, snacks and afternoon teas and has a
garden, where children can play during the
summer months.

Old Inn

Widecombe-in-the-Moor **t** (01364) 621207
Open Daily for lunch and dinner

Traditional pub in a 14th-century stone
building, with ponds and streams in the garden.
On-site parking is available.

Rising Sun Inn

Woodland, near Ashburton **t** (01364) 652544
www.risingsunwoodland.co.uk
Open Mon 11.45–3 and 6–11 Tues–Sun 11–3 and
6–11, food served 12 noon–2.15pm and 6–9.15pm
(until 7pm on Sundays)
On-site parking

Traditional country pub specializing in homecooked meals made from local produce. There
is a family dining area with toys (children's
portions and two highchairs available) and a big
garden with an old tractor that kids can climb on
(very popular).

Dartmouth

The Royal Dart Bars

The Square, Kingswear **t** (01803) 752213
Open Mon–Sat 11–11, Sun 12 noon–10.30pm

On the water's edge, next to the ferry port, the
Royal Dart specializes in local fish dishes (particularly crab and lobster) and can offer children's
portions and highchairs in its downstairs riverside bistro (roasts on Sundays). It also has a
balcony from where in summer you can see steam
trains arriving from Paignton (the trains stop
just outside) and ferries leaving for Dartmouth
(which kids love).

Exeter

Ask

5 Cathedral Close **t** (01392) 427 127
www.askcentral.co.uk
Open Mon–Sat 12 noon–11, Sun 12 noon–10.30
 The pizza chain is opposite the cathedral.
Outside tables in an enclosed courtyard.

Mad Meg's

162–3 Fore Street, St Olave's Close
t (01392) 221225 **www.madmegs.co.uk**
Open Mon and Tues 6pm–late; Wed–Sat
11.30am–2.15pm, 6pm–late; Sun 11.30am–4pm
 This medieval-themed restaurant is extremely
child-friendly. There is a children's menu but
they also like to offer children the chance to try
mini versions of grown-up food and are happy
to cut a 250g (8oz) steak in half, for example.
Highchairs available.

Michael Caines Café Bar

St Martins Lane **t** (01392) 223626
www.michaelcaines.com
Open Daily 10–10 (Fri 10–11)
 A trendy, airy, roomy modern restaurant
opposite the cathedral run by local chef Michael
Caines. Cakes, sandwiches burgers and salads for
lunch (from £3.75–10). The evening menu also
includes tapas, mezze and seafood. Highchairs
and all-day children's menu. The big bonus is
under 5s eat free.

Rosticceria Italia

Bedford Street **t** (01392) 432299
Open Mon–Sat 9am–6.30pm
 The friendly and lively Italian-run Rosticceria
does half portions of pasta and pizza for children. Highchairs available.

Falmouth

Pasty Presto

7 Arwenack Street **www.pastypresto.com**
Open Daily 9–5
 Thai green chicken curry or aubergine and feta
pasties. Chase them down with an excellent
espresso and *pain au chocolat* for a cultural mix
in this small café-cum-takeaway, which is in a
lovely old building with a view across the harbour.
They also sell locally produced jams and crisps.

Seafarer's Restaurant

33 Arwenack Street **t** (01326) 312345
Open Daily 6–10.30pm
 Friendly, colourfully decorated fish restaurant.
Local seafood is their speciality, but they also do
steaks, chicken, lamb and vegetarian dishes. There
is a children's menu, highchairs and a non-
smoking section (except on Saturdays).

Holne

The Church House Inn

Holne **t** (01364) 631208
www.churchhouse-inn.co.uk
Open Mon–Fri 12 noon–2.30 and 7–11, Sat and Sun
12 noon–3 and 7–10.30
 This gnarly old moorland pub dates all the way
back to c.1329 and has a friendly, welcoming attitude towards children and families.

Ilfracombe

Atlantis Café and Restaurant

29 St James Place **t** (01271) 867835
Open Daily in summer 6.30–11pm
 Global cuisine with lots of vegetarian options.

Capstone Restaurant

St James Place **t** (01271) 863540
Open Apr–Oct 10.30am–2.30pm and 6.30–10;
Nov–Dec Thurs–Sat evenings only
 Family-run restaurant with specialities including
fresh local lobster and crab. There is a varied menu
and also one for children. Highchairs available.

Lustleigh

Primrose Cottage

t (01647) 277 365
Open Mon–Sat 9.30–5
 Thatched cottage where you can enjoy a top-
class cream tea and homemade cakes. If it's
sunny, eat in the garden by the stream.
There's an excellent family pub, The Cleave,
t (01647) 277223, nearby.

Lynton

Cliff Top Café

t (01598) 753366
Open Whitsun–early Sept daily 11–5
 This licensed café, right next to the cliff railway,
is an ideal spot to have a cake or a light lunch but
there's no ice cream as the Fat Controller doesn't
want it dripping all over his line.

Lee Cottage
Lee Abbey **t** (01598) 752621
Open Whitsun–early Sept daily 11–5

Cakes, scones and sandwiches are served every day during the summer holidays on a grassy lawn overlooking the coast outside this abbey-owned tea cottage. After your meal, wander through some of the abbey's 105 hectares (260 acres) of land down to the beach. Highchairs available.

Malborough
The Port Light
Bolberry Down **t** (01548) 561384
Open Daily 11–2.30, 6.30–11 (closed 1–8 Dec and whole of Jan)

Inland from the coast in a former RAF radar station set some 137m (450ft) above sea level and surrounded by acres of National Trust countryside, it occupies a particularly idyllic location. There's a big field between the pub and the cliff edge, where kids love to fly kites, as well as a dedicated outdoor play area. The restaurant specializes in fish and is very flexible regarding children's portions.

Mullion
The New Yard at Trelowarren
Trelowarren Estate **t** (01326) 221595
www.trelowarren.co.uk
Getting there Close to the Goonhilly satellite station on the B3293
Open Mar–New Year's Eve daily 10.30am–9.30pm (closed Sun evenings)

Top-class restaurant on a 400-hectare (1,000-acre) private estate, with a large courtyard and outdoor seating in summer. The French chef is happy to accommodate children and adjust the dishes to suit. He uses local organic food and fish. Morning coffee, lunch, afternoon tea and dinner.

Roskilly's
Tregellast Barton, St Keverne **t** (01326) 280479
www.roskillys.com
Getting there Signposted off the B3293 west of Goonhilly
Open Daily 11am–5pm

Organic dairy farm, where they make some of the best ice cream in Cornwall, and sell a good selection of homemade goodies. Visit in the afternoon when you can watch the milking (4.15–5.15pm daily). The restaurant is nothing special and expensive, but there are lovely wood-land walks around the farm and barbecues are offered in the evenings in summer.

Newquay
Beach Hut
Watergate Bay **t** (01637) 860877
Open Daily 9am–10.30pm (in winter Tues and Wed closes at 5pm)

On a two-mile-long beach, the hut is part of the Extreme Academy Sports Club and serves beach food to surfers during the day. Children particularly love their hot chocolate drinks, which come with marshmallows on the top. The menu is largely fish-based in summer, but augmented with a few meaty choices and you can also hire surfboards and wet suits and book surfing lessons here.

Señor Dick's
East Street **t** (01637) 870350
www.senor-dicks.co.uk
Open Summer: daily 12 noon–11; winter: Mon–Fri 5–10.30, Sat–Sun 12 noon–10.30

Mexican bar/restaurant which offers a children's menu including mini tortillas and burritos.

Ye Olde Dolphin
39 Fore Street **t** (01637) 874262
www.dolphinrestaurant.co.uk
Open Daily 6–11pm

Good for fish and traditional English food, the Dolphin welcomes families until 9pm. Highchairs and half portions available.

Newton Abbot
Coombe Cellars
Combeinteignhead **t** (01626) 872423
Open Bar 12 noon–11, food served 12 noon–9 or 10pm

Large, friendly, recently refurbished Brewer's Fare pub overlooking the Teign Estuary, comprising a separate restaurant decorated with

---

Devonshire cream tea
Offered by every West Country tearoom worth its salt, the classic Devonshire cream tea consists of homemade scones, cut in half and spread with copious amounts of strawberry jam and thick clotted cream (it should be the consistency of warm butter), washed down with a pot of freshly brewed tea. Try substituting the jam with black treacle, a local variant known as 'Thunder and Lightning'.

Cornish pasties

Cornwall's most famous delicacy consists of a pastry envelope filled with chopped meat and sliced vegetables (usually onions, potatoes and swedes, which are perversely known as turnips in Cornwall) and then baked in the oven. It is thought to have been developed in the 18th century as a sort of portable lunchbox for miners allowing them to carry their meal easily to work, although it may be a good deal older than that. Jane Seymour, one of Henry VIII's wives mentions pasties in a letter written in the mid 16th century. These days, pasties come with a variety of different savoury and sweet fillings – some miners apparently used to have one side of their pasty filled with meat and the other with apples, thereby combining their main meal and pudding – and are eaten by everyone except sailors. Apparently, it is bad luck to take a pasty on a boat.

For possibly the best pasties in the West Country, go to The Pasty Shop (6 Buller Street) in East Looe, where they are prepared and cooked while you wait in a traditional bakery.

nautical memorabilia (anchors, lifebelts, etc.), an outdoor terrace, a lawned garden and a small soft play area. Children's menu, highchairs and mother and baby facilities are available. There is also an outdoor play area with slides and toys.

Padstow

Rick Stein's Café

Middle Street **t** (01841) 532700
www.rickstein.com
Open Mon–Sun; lunch: 12 noon–2.30pm; dinner: 7–9.30pm

The menu offers more than just fish, with plenty of vegetarian options although the fruits of the sea do unsurprisingly take centre stage. The café does a particularly fine cod and chips. Starters £6.50. Main courses £8.50–16. You can just pop in for a cake and a drink too. Half portions for kids. Relaxed atmosphere with plenty of babies kicking about on the comfy cushioned wooden benches.

Penzance

Harris's

46 New Street **t** (01736) 364408
www.harrissrestaurant.co.uk
Open Tues–Sat 12 noon–10pm

Olde-worlde, rather sophisticated two-floor restaurant on a narrow, cobbled street specializing in locally caught fish and seafood dishes (pasta and sausages also offered). Although they are very child-friendly, they don't offer a children's menu or children's portions.

Plymouth

Cap'n Jaspers

Fishmarket, Barbican **t** (01752) 262444
www.capn-jaspers.co.uk
Open Mon–Sat 7.30am–12am, Sun 10am–12am

Good for burgers and hot dogs, the Cap'n is a simple, friendly takeaway (although there are a few tables and chairs if you want to eat in). The boss gives out free lollipops to children and they are very flexible regarding portions.

Dolphin Café

The Hoe **t** (01752) 600608
Open Daily 10–5

Enjoy a cream tea or an ice cream while you watch boats on Plymouth Sound. The café is situated inside the Plymouth Dome.

Tudor Rose Tea Room

New Street **t** (01752) 255502
Open Tues–Sun 9.30–5.30

Teas, cakes and scones are served here and there is a small, enclosed garden.

Around Plymouth

The George

Tavistock Road, Roborough **t** (01752) 771527
Open Daily 12 noon–11; Deep Sea Den: open daily 12 noon–7pm (8pm on weekends), £2 per hour

A friendly pub offering a kids' menu with ice cream and children's drinks, highchairs, colouring sheets and crayons. Deep Sea Den indoor play area and an outside play and picnic area.

The Unicorn

Plymouth Road, Plympton **t** (01752) 337939
Open Mon–Sat 11am–11pm (food served
11am–10pm); Sun bar open and food served
12 noon–10pm; Deep Sea Den open Mon–Sat
10–7pm; Sun 12 noon–7pm (£2 for 1hour)
  Pub food, with a children's menu, colouring
packs, crayons and an indoor play area.

St Ives

On Shore

The Wharf **t** (01736) 796000
Open Daily 8am–11pm
  Friendly staff and an outside terrace with great
views of the harbour. Pasta dishes and pizzas
cooked in wood-burning oven. Generous kids'
portions; basic kids' pizza £3.95.

Porthminster Beach Café

Porthminster Beach **t** (01736) 795352
www.porthminstercafe.co.uk
Open Daily 10am–12 noon, lunch served 12 noon–4pm,
dinner served 6.30–10pm; open for morning coffee,
afternoon tea and snacks at other times
  Popular seafront café serving seafood and fish
dishes, as well as sandwiches, cakes and cream
teas during the day. They are flexible with children's portions and have highchairs. Try to get a
seat on the large terrace overlooking the beach.

Seafood Café

Fore Street **t** (01736) 794 004
www.seafoodcafe.co.uk
Open Daily 12 noon–3pm and 6–11pm
  Relaxed Conran-style spot with an extensive but
simple menu. In the evening, you can select your
own fish and say how you want it cooked and
what you want it served with. Children's menu.

Stokenham

Church House Inn

Stokenham **t** (01548) 580253
Open Daily 11am–11pm, food served 6–9.15pm
  Only locally caught fish and seafood are served
in this well-respected restaurant just inland from
the coast. There is a large family eating area (children's portions and highchairs available) and an
outside play area with slides and swings.

Torquay and Paignton

Drakes

64 Babbacombe Road, Babbacombe
t (01803) 323302
Open Summer: daily 11.30am–11pm; winter: daily
11.30am–10pm; both summer and winter closes
one hour earlier on Sun
  Traditional fish and chips cooked to order
to eat in or take away. Children's menu with
mini favourites (fish fingers, chicken nuggets,
fish cakes, cod, etc.). Highchairs and a non-
smoking section.

Hanbury's

24 Princes Street, Babbacombe **t** (01803) 314616
Open Mon–Sat 12 noon–1.45pm and 4.30–9.30pm
  Voted the Southwest's fish and chip shop of
the year three times in a row during the 1990s,
Hanbury's can provide a children's menu
(mashed potatoes are offered as an alternative
to chips), baby changing facilities and a highchair. Kids get a colouring kit which they can use
to practise for the colouring competition held by
the shop every four months for a £20 prize.

The Igloo

57 Torbay Road, Paignton **t** (01803) 521449
www.theigloopaignton.co.uk
Open Winter: daily 10–6; summer: 10–10
  The Igloo may possibly be the oldest ice cream
parlour in the country and has been winning
certificates of excellence since the 1960s. They
also serve snacks, such as bacon sandwiches,
sausage sandwiches and chicken nuggets (everything is grilled), as well as pies, jacket potatoes
and salads. They are flexible regarding children's
portions and have seating indoors and outside.

Mulberry House

1 Scarborough Road, Torquay **t** (01803) 213639
www.mulberryhousetorquay.co.uk
Open Wed and Thurs 7.30pm–9.30pm; Fri and Sat
12 noon–2pm and 7.30–9.30pm; Sun 12 noon–2pm;
closed to non-guests Mon and Tues
  Restaurant serving classic and modern British
and continental food. Happy to accommodate
children's choices and portions.

Oldway Tearoom

Oldway Mansions, Torquay Road, Paignton
t (01803) 524263
Open Summer: 9–5; winter: 9.30–4.30 (closed Sat)

For an authentic Devonshire cream tea, light lunch, soup, or coffee and pasties, try this olde worlde-style tearoom. It is very buggy and wheelchair friendly with wide doors and aisles, and there are highchairs available. The tearoom is part of Oldway Mansions, the former home of the Singer family (of sewing machine fame) and the building itself is based on the Palace of Versailles (a suitable choice for the 'Sown King').

Totnes

Anne of Cleves

56 Fore Street t (01803) 863186
Open Summer: daily 9.30–5 (no hot food after 4)

Pleasant olde worlde-looking teashop-cum-restaurant serving homemade food, including lasagne and casseroles, etc., as well as cakes, gateaux and scones. There are highchairs and a non-smoking section. Children's meals available.

Smuggler's Inn

Steamer Quay t (01803) 863877
Open Food served daily 12 noon–2pm and 6.30–9.30pm

One-hundred-year-old inn, where you can eat traditional pub fare in a non-traditional pub atmosphere (it is non-smoking and air-conditioned throughout). There is a separate family room and a children's menu.

Willow Garden Restaurant

87 High Street t (01803) 862605
Open Mon, Tues and Thurs 10–5; Wed 10–5 and 7–9.30; Fri 9–5 and 7–9.30; Sat 7–9.30

Vegetarian restaurant with a family area with books and toys and a small, walled garden. Baby changing facilities and highchairs are available and they are happy to heat up babies' bottles.

Around Totnes

The Mill at Avonwick

South Brent t (01364) 72488
Open Daily for lunch and dinner

A great place for a Sunday roast, the mill is set in two hectares (five acres) of beautiful grounds and has a children's play area with trampolines (best tried before rather than after the meal).

Sea Trout Inn

Staverton t (01803) 762274 www.seatroutinn.com
Open Winter: daily 12 noon–2pm; summer: Mon–Sat 11am–11pm, Sun 12 noon–11pm and 6–11pm

This pub-restaurant specializes in homecooked West Country food and fish dishes. In summer, children can play in the fenced garden. There are highchairs and a non-smoking section but kids are not allowed in the main bar.

The Waterman's Arms

Bow Bridge, Ashprington t (01803) 732214
Open Daily 12 noon–2.30pm and 6.30–9.30pm (last orders)

Sit and have your meal by the water at the head of Bow Creek. The pub is half a mile from the village and accommodates all ages.

Truro

Piero's

Kenwyn Street t (01872) 222279
Open Daily 12 noon–3pm and 6–10pm

Relaxed pizza with outdoor seating in an enclosed courtyard.

Thames Valley

Hertfordshire · Bedfordshire Berkshire · Buckinghamshire Oxfordshire · Gloucestershire

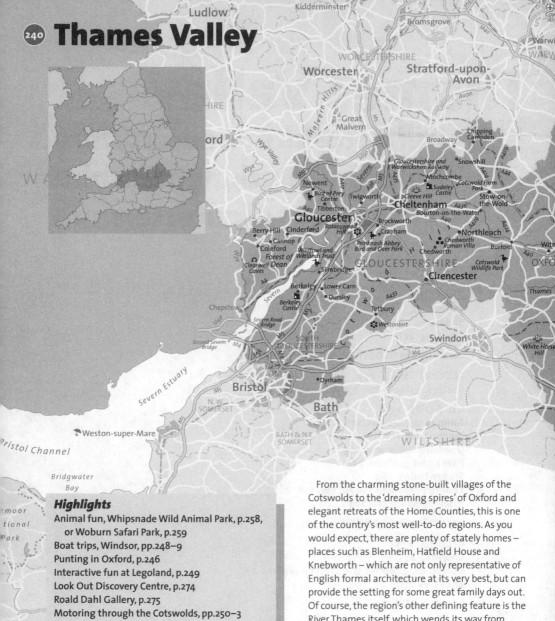

Ludlow
Kidderminster
Bromsgrove
Warwi
WARW
WORCESTERSHIRE
Worcester
Stratford-upon-Avon
ord
HIRE
Wye Valley
Avon
Great Malvern
Chipping Campden
Broadway
Gloucestershire and Warwickshire Railway
Snowshill
Wye
Newent
Cotswold Farm Park
Winchcombe
Cleeve Hill
Sudeley Castle
Bird of Prey Centre
Twigworth
Stow-on-the-Wold
Tibberton
Cheltenham
Gloucester
Bourton-on-the-Water
Robinswood
Brockworth
Berry Hill
Cinderford
Northleach
Cannop
Cranham
Chedworth Roman Villa
Burford
Coleford
Prinknash Abbey Bird and Deer Park
Chedworth
Witn
Forest of Dean
Wildfowl and Wetlands Trust
OXFC
Clearwell Caves
Cotswold Wildlife Park
GLOUCESTERSHIRE
Slimbridge
Cirencester
Chepstow
Berkeley
Lower Carn
Thames
Dursley
Severn
Berkeley Castle
Westonbirt
Tetbury
Severn Road Bridge
Swindon
Second Severn Bridge
SOUTH GLOUCESTERSHIRE
White Horse Hill
Dyrham
Bristol
N.W. SOMERSET
Bath
Weston-super-Mare
BATH & N.E. SOMERSET
WILTSHIRE
Bristol Channel
Bridgwater Bay
moor tional Park
DEVO
Exeter
Lyme Bay
Exmouth

Highlights

Animal fun, Whipsnade Wild Animal Park, p.258, or Woburn Safari Park, p.259

Boat trips, Windsor, pp.248–9

Punting in Oxford, p.246

Interactive fun at Legoland, p.249

Look Out Discovery Centre, p.274

Roald Dahl Gallery, p.275

Motoring through the Cotswolds, pp.250–3

Steam train rides, Gloucestershire and Warwickshire Railway, p.253

Underground adventures at Clearwell Caves, p.269, and Hell Fire Caves, p.268

Walking, the Chilterns pp.267–9

Water fun, Oasis Beach Pool, Bedford, p.272

From the charming stone-built villages of the Cotswolds to the 'dreaming spires' of Oxford and elegant retreats of the Home Counties, this is one of the country's most well-to-do regions. As you would expect, there are plenty of stately homes – places such as Blenheim, Hatfield House and Knebworth – which are not only representative of English formal architecture at its very best, but can provide the setting for some great family days out. Of course, the region's other defining feature is the River Thames itself, which wends its way from Gloucestershire through Oxford and Windsor, and then down through London to the coast. Boat trips are available at numerous points along its length – at Windsor, Reading, Cookham and Henley – and you can also go punting in Oxford and take a cruise along the Gloucester and Sharpness Canal from Gloucester Docks.

Landlubbers, meanwhile, will have to make do with a steam train ride, a day out at Legoland or a trip to one of the region's numerous animal attractions, particularly its three great wildlife parks, Whipsnade Wild Animal Park, Woburn Safari Park and the Cotswolds Safari Park.

Day-trip itinerary

Morning: At Windsor Castle (p.250).
Lunch: At Pizza Express on Thames Street (p.278).
Afternoon: A leisurely cruise from Windsor Promenade up the River Thames (pp.248–9) to Maidenhead (site of the Courage Shire Horse Centre) or a short drive over to Legoland for a very constructive day out (p.249).

Special events

February
Oxford: Chinese New Year **t** (01865) 726871

May
Spring Festival, Newbury **t** (01635) 528766
www.newburyspringfestival.org.uk
Children's Festival, Reading **t** (0118) 939 0771
Windsor: Royal Horse Show **t** (01753) 860633
www.royal-windsor-horse-show.co.uk

June
Chipping Camden: Cotswold Olimpick Games
t (01384) 274041 **www.**olimpickgames.co.uk

July
Cheltenham: Classical Music Festival
t (01242) 227979
Cheltenham Science Festival **t** (01242) 227979
Henley Royal Regatta **t** (01491) 572153
www.hrr.co.uk
River Thames (between Sunbury and Pangbourne):
Swan Upping **t** (01628) 523030

August
Gloucester Festival **t** (01452) 396572

October
Cheltenham Literature Festival **t** (01242) 227979

Gloucester

Getting there By road: Gloucester is about 90 miles from London, 30 miles from Bristol and 40 miles from Birmingham and can be reached via the M5 and the A40. Park-and-ride service 501 from St Oswalds Park (on the old Cattle Market site) and 512 from Quedgeley on the south side of town near the A38. By train: Services arrive from London (Paddington) via Swindon or Bristol. By bus/coach: There are regular National Express coach services to Gloucester from Heathrow, London and Bristol
Tourist information 28 Southgate Street
t (01452) 396572 www.gloucester.gov.uk

One of the most important cities in Roman Britain (when it was called *Glevum*), Gloucester has been playing catch-up ever since, although it did enjoy a brief renaissance in the Middle Ages, when the burial of the murdered King Edward II in the city's cathedral turned it into a pilgrimage centre. Blasted during the Second World War, it was rebuilt with no great care but the city's cathedral managed to escape the attention of the *Luftwaffe* – its elegant tower still dominates the skyline. Not a picture-book town when compared with Cheltenham or the magnificent natural architecture of the Cotswolds, it has an enlivening modernity. There's plenty to occupy little hands and minds at the museums in the renovated docks – particularly the interactive National Waterways Museum. In summer the area comes alive with festival events and music. The city centre still follows the Roman grid layout with four streets (West Gate, East Gate, North Gate and South Gate) radiating out from a central cross, and is pedestrianized and easily navigable, with good high street shopping, particularly along East Gate, the King's Walk shopping centres, and among the covered market stalls, where you can try the famous Gloucester sausage.

Things to see and do

Cinemas and theatres *See pp.273, 276*

Gloucester Cathedral
Chapter Office, 17 College Green **t** (01452) 528095
www.gloucestercathedral.org.uk
Open Daily 7.30am–6pm (5pm in winter)
Adm Free (suggested donation £3)
Café-restaurant, shop, disabled access, guided tours

Kids will find Gloucester Cathedral strangely familiar, although they may not at first be able to put their finger on why. Mention 'Harry Potter', however, and all will become clear. The cathedral has been used for both interior and exterior aspects of Hogwart's School of Wizardry in the films. You'll be pleased to know that, notwith-standing its wizardly associations, it's still well worth a visit with its rows of stained glass windows (including the largest medieval window in Britain), which bathe the interior in multi-coloured light, enormous cylindrical pillars supporting the nave and fan-vaulted cloisters. Look out for the tomb of Edward II, who was murdered in Berkeley Castle in 1327. Guided tours of the cathedral are available (Mon–Sat 10.30am–4pm); additional tower tours operate April to November.

Gloucester City Museum and Art Gallery
Brunswick Road **t** (01452) 396131
Open Tues–Sat 10–5 **Adm Free**
Gift shop, guided tours, disabled access and facilities

Museum with displays of Roman relics, Saxon remains and dinosaurs. There are several dioramas featuring the fearsome kiddies' favourites, plus an art gallery with works by British artists such as Turner and Gainsborough. There are also hands-on exhibits (you can try on a coat of armour) and touch-screen displays. Programme of inventive workshops and events throughout the year.

Gloucester Folk Museum
99–103 Westgate Street **t** (01452) 396868
Open Tues–Sat 10–5 **Adm Free**
Gift shop, picnic areas, disabled facilities

This timber-framed Tudor building has a great collection of artefacts and displays about aspects of local history (farming, Severn fishing and Gloucester parks). Children can sit in a recreated Victorian schoolroom and explore the toy gallery.

Historic Gloucester Walks
Daily two-hour guided tours of city and docks, June–September, leaving from the tourist office, **t** (01452) 396572, www.gloucestercivictrust.org.uk; £2.50 per person.

Can you spot?
The animated clock based on The Tailor of Gloucester story in the East Gate Shopping Centre.

The Docks

As England's most inland port, Gloucester was always going to struggle to keep its foreign trade links viable against fierce competition from its coastal rivals and, from the 16th century onwards, the city was locked in a losing battle with the more handily situated Bristol. Although, by the late 18th century, 600 ships a year were docking at Gloucester, this was nothing compared with the numbers arriving at the Somerset port and, crucially, Bristol's deepwater docks could accommodate much larger ocean-going craft. From the 19th century onwards, Gloucester Docks fell into decline. Happily, today, they have been reborn as a cultural-cum-shopping centre; the grand Victorian warehouses are now home to a shopping mall, a well-respected antiques centre, various bars, cafés and restaurants, as well as several excellent museums, including the Soldiers of Gloucestershire Museum and (best of all for children) the National Waterways Museum.

★National Waterways Museum

Llanthony Warehouse, Gloucester Docks
t (01452) 318200 **www.nwm.org.uk**
Open Museum: daily 10–5; cruises: Apr–Oct 12 noon, 1.30, 2.30 and 3.30pm
Adm Adults £6.60, children £5.25, under 5s **free**
Café-restaurant, gift shop, mother and baby facilities, disabled access and toilets

The name may not sound promising but this is, in fact, an excellent child-friendly museum with three floors full of interactive exhibits and audiovisual displays designed to bring the history of the country's canals and docks to life. You can find out just how hard dock life was when you try the sack-hauling challenge (and how skilful) as you try to steer a narrowboat through a lock without it sinking. You can explore the interior of a narrowboat to see how canal families used to live, try on a diver's helmet, play with model boats in the children's play area and see how your individual share certificate is doing via the touch-screen computers. You can even take a tour of the Gloucester and Sharpness Canal aboard the museum's own sightseeing boat, the *Queen Boadicea II*. There are fun events during the year and seasonal family activities in the school holidays.

Soldiers of Gloucestershire

Custom House, Gloucester Docks **t** (01452) 522682
www.glosters.org.uk
Open Tues–Sun 10–5 (Jun–Sept daily)
Adm Adults £4.25, children £2.25, family £13, under 5s **free**
Gift shop, disabled access

Small regimental museum with a good deal of interactivity for the kids – they can explore a recreated First World War trench and even lead a mock expedition into No-Man's Land.

House of the Tailor of Gloucester

9 College Court **t** (01452) 422856
Open Apr–Oct 10–5, Nov–Mar 10–4
Adm Free
Disabled access
Please note: This attraction is currently closed but is due to reopen early 2007. Call for details

To get you in the mood for your trip to the city, you and your children could read Beatrix Potter's *The Tailor of Gloucester* together, the story of an overworked tailor who, unable to finish a waistcoat for the city mayor, is secretly assisted on the night before it is due to be delivered by a group of friendly sewing mice. It's based on a true story. There was a tailor, John Pritchard, who had been employed to make a waistcoat for the mayor which he couldn't complete in time only to find, as he awoke on the big day, that it had been completed for him. He believed it was the work of

fairies but turned out to be the tailor's assistants, who he had unwittingly locked in his shop overnight, although that doesn't make quite such a good story. You can visit the tailors' house (just north of the cathedral), which has been turned into a Beatrix Potter museum and shop containing dioramas showing scenes from her books, including, of course, the tailor and his helpful mice.

Nature in Art

Museum and Art Gallery, Wallsworth Hall, Twigworth **t** 0845 450 0233
www.natureinart.org.uk
Getting there 2 miles north of the city on the A38
Open Tues–Sun and Bank Hols 10–5
Adm Adults £4.50, children £4, under 8s **free**
Disabled access, shop, coffee shop

This innovative museum, housed in a stately home, holds an unrivalled display of wildlife art from mosaics of exotic birds to abstract landscapes. There's an extensive programme of temporary exhibitions and events, as well as courses (£35 per day) exploring a variety of media and techniques. Visitors also get the opportunity to see artists in action demonstrating their craft, including sculptors, engravers and printmakers. Children's activities are also available in the school holidays (book in advance).

Robinswood Hill Country Park
t (01452) 303206
Getting there Off the A4173, 2 miles south of the city
Open Daily from dawn till dusk **Adm Free**
Café-restaurant, gift shop, toilets, disabled access

These 100 hectares (250 acres) of rolling grassland two miles south of the city centre provide the perfect introduction to the Cotswolds, which start a few miles further east. There are numerous marked trails and the views of the city from the top of the hill are worth the steep climb. Children can also explore the rare breeds farm or enjoy a guided nature walk.

Sport and activities *See pp.270–3*

Around Gloucester

Cheltenham, 7 miles northeast (p.251)
Forest of Dean, 13 miles west (p.269)
National Bird of Prey Centre, 8 miles northwest (p.257)
Prinknash Abbey Bird and Deer Park, 3 miles southeast (p.257)
Shambles Museum, 8 miles northwest (p.264)

Oxford

Getting there By road: Oxford is about 48 miles from London and can be reached via the M40. Oxford's efficient park-and-ride scheme operates daily from five sites: Pear Tree and Water Eaton to the north, A44/A40/M40/M6/M1 and A4260; Thornhill to the east, M40/M25; Seacourt to the west/A420 and Redbridge to the south/A34 (Mon–Sat 5.30am–11.30pm; Sun and from Water Eaton restricted service) . Journey times are between 8–20 minutes. By train: Services arrive frequently from London Paddington. By bus/coach: There are regular National Express coach services to Oxford from London Victoria. The Airline (**t** (01865) 785400

www.theairline.info) operates coach services between Heathrow (every 30 minutes) and Gatwick (hourly) to Oxford both day and night
Tourist information 15 Broad Street **t** (01865) 726871 www.oxfordcity.co.uk

Oxford is more than just a pretty town for tourists (and it is pretty to walk around, with its magnificent college architecture and parks); it's a world-famous centre of culture and learning. Home to one of the country's two most prestigious universities (the other is Cambridge) it has, ever since its foundation in the 13th century, been preparing the great and the good for roles in public life. Tony Blair, Bill Clinton, Margaret Thatcher and even Henry VIII all studied at the university, although the term 'university' is slightly misleading – Oxford actually contains several independently operated colleges, which together form the university and define the shape of the city. Most colleges are open to the public, although to preserve the academic ambience, many operate restricted opening times and charge hefty admission fees. Best for family visits is Christ Church college with its grand dining hall, where Charles I held his parliament, Lewis Carroll ate 8,000 meals and Harry Potter sat under the sorting hat awaiting his fate.

With so much learning and history, you might expect Oxford to be rather dull for children and, approached in the wrong way, it probably would be. But, plan your itinerary carefully and you'll find lots to occupy your days. Oxford actually boasts a good many child-friendly attractions including many lovely parks and gardens, interactive museums, punts and lots of spots providing panoramic views of the 'dreaming spires' and surrounding countryside.

Things to see and do
Botanic Gardens
Rose Lane **t** (01865) 286690
www.botanic-garden.ox.ac.uk
Open Nov–Feb daily 9–4, Mar–Apr and Sept–Oct 9–5, May–Aug 9–6
Adm Adults £2, under 12s **free (free for all in winter)**

Created in 1621, this is the oldest botanic garden in Britain. You can wander through nine small glasshouses filled with tropical and subtropical plants (including palms, orchids and giant ferns), then follow the course of the river, although the turnstiles at either end may prove challenging with a buggy. Halfway along the route and to the left, a wooden bridge leads to the college boathouses. Each house has its own style; if you're lucky you might encounter a training session or even a race.

Bus tours

Red open-top city sightseeing buses run mammoth tours of the key sights and all the colleges every 10–15 minutes (adults £9.50, children £4.50, under 5s free) from Oxford Railway Station, Gloucester Green Bus Station, Pembroke College and the Sheldonian Theatre. Contact The No 1 Shop, Railway Station, Park End Street, t (01865) 790522, **www.citysightseeingoxford.com**

Christ Church

St Aldate's **t** (01865) 276150 **www.chch.ox.ac.uk**
Open Mon–Sat 9–5, Sun 1–5
Adm Adults £4.50, children £3.50
Visitor entrance at Meadow Gate

A great place for Harry Potter-spotting; tell the kids that the steps up into the dining hall were where Maggie Smith greeted the new pupils in *Harry Potter and the Philosopher's Stone*. The dining hall is also Hogwarts Hall, though somewhat modified by the CGI wizards at Warner Bros in order to seat all four of the school's houses.

Christ Church Meadow

Access via St Aldate's, Merton Street, Rose Lane
Open Daily 8am–dusk **Adm Free**

Lovely green space near the city centre with a memorial garden and riverside walks. Look out for practising university crews.

Cinemas and theatres *See pp.273, 276*

Hands-On

The Old Fire Station, 40 George Street
t (01865) 728953
Open Sat and daily during school hols 10–4
Adm Adults £5, children £3.50, family £15

Science museum for children full of interactive games and experiments.

Magdalen College Park

High Street **t** (01865) 276000
Open Daily 1pm–dusk
Adm Adults £3, children £2

Pronounced 'Maudlin'. There's a deer park and river walks through water meadows in the grounds.

Museum of the History of Science

Old Ashmolean Building, Broad Street
t (01865) 277280 **www.mhs.ox.ac.uk**
Open Tues–Sat 12 noon–4, Sun 2–5 **Adm Free**

Displays of scientific instruments (sundials, quadrants, microscopes, telescopes and cameras) dating back to the 16th century (and Einstein's blackboard). There's an education room and library.

Museum of Oxford

St Aldate's **t** (01865) 252761
www.oxford.gov.uk/museum
Open Tues–Fri 10–5, Sat–Sun 12 noon–5
Adm Adults £2, children 50p, family £4
Gift shop, toilets in the town hall, no disabled access, children's trails and school holiday activities

Exhibits range from a mammoth's tooth to Roman and medieval artefacts and a series of evocative room settings, which include an Elizabethan Inn, an 18th-century college room, a Victorian kitchen on washday and a 1930s living room. Kids will enjoy the introductory audiovisual presentation narrated by the *Time Team's* Tony Robinson and they'll be drawn to the Looking for Alice display, which explores the lives of Lewis Carroll and Alice Liddell and the sourcers of inspiration for the books.

The Oxford Story

6 Broad Street **t** (01865) 728822
Open Jan–Jun and Sept–Dec Mon–Sat 10–4.30, Sun 11–4; Jul–Aug daily 9.30–5
Adm Adults £7.25, children £5.25
Gift shop, disabled access

A bizarre and not wholly comfortable experience, as an electric cart winches you up a steep incline past three floors of tableaux depicting scenes from the city's long history – student riots, scientific breakthroughs, etc. – with accompanying sound and lighting effects. It stresses the academic side of things quite strongly, so may not suit very young children, but it's done in an entertaining way. There's a children's commentary and special events are held during the school holidays.

Pitt Rivers Museum

Parks Road **t** (01865) 270927 **www.prm.ox.ac.uk**
Open Daily 12–4.30 **Adm Free**
Shop. Please note: due to building works the upper gallery will be closed until 2007

This elegant Victorian building houses a large ethnographic collection featuring artefacts brought back by Captain Cook from his 18th century journeys of discovery – a witch in a bottle, a puffer-fish lantern, shrunken heads, samurai swords and totem poles are just some of the gruesome horrors bound to attract the children. Kids can take part in informal 'Family Friendly Fun' sessions every Sunday from 2 to 4pm, using backpacks, sorting boxes, quizzes and activity trolleys. Pitt Stops are activity sessions that take place on the first Saturday of every month from 1–4pm. Sessions begin with a short talk and previous topics have included body decoration, puppetry and weapons and armour. Kids can also follow family trails in search of dragons, hats, masks, witches and more.

Port Meadow

Access via Walton Well Road and Thames Towpath
Open Any reasonable time **Adm Free**

The largest green space in Oxford. See horses, cows and geese roaming in this water meadow.

River trips

Punting, the practice of pushing yourself along the river in a flat-bottomed boat using a long wooden pole, is associated with England's two great university towns. The image of young men in flannels and straw hats mucking about in boats on hot summer days has become iconic – as familiar as teashops, beefeaters and cricket on the village green. It's great fun and a little tricky (young children probably won't be able to handle the heavy pole) but, once mastered, provides a wonderful way of seeing the local countryside. Stopping off every 100 metres (100 yards) or so for a picnic and a lie-down is an essential part of the experience. Punts and (for the less adventurous) rowboats for trips on the River Cherwell down past the Botanic Garden and Christchurch Meadow are available for hire from Magdalen Bridge, Folly Bridge and the Cherwell Boathouse (flannels and straw boaters are optional). Sightseeing trips to Iffley, Sandford Lock and Abingdon are also offered from Folly Bridge by Salter's Steamers, **t** (01865) 243421, **www.**saltersteamers.co.uk.

Shopping

Oxford's air of academia has attracted a plethora of bookshops and museum gift shops, as well as more day-to-day stores, such as Boswells of Oxford on Broad Street, **t** (01865) 241244, the city's largest department store, which sells luggage, cookware, gift and toys. There are two main shopping centres in Oxford: Westgate Shopping Centre, Queen Street, **t** (01865) 725455, and Templars Square, Pound Way, Cowley, **t** (01865) 748864. Shops range from traditional family butchers to high street names like Boots the Chemist. The Oxford Covered Market, 39–41 The Covered Market, is the place for fresh meat and fish, cheeses, as well as clothes, records and furniture. Best of all for kids though is Alice's Shop and Tea Rooms, opposite Christ Church college, St Aldate's, **t** (01865) 723793, **www.**sheepshop.com. This is the original Old Sheep Shop in 'Through The Looking Glass' and is where the real-life Alice Liddell used to buy her barley sugar sweets. These days, it's a good place to stock up on Alice trinkets and memorabilia.

Sport and activities *See pp.270–3*

University Museum of Natural History

Parks Road **t** (01865) 272950 **www.**oum.ox.ac.uk
Open Daily 12 noon–5 (not Easter and Christmas)
Adm Free
Picnic area, disabled access, children's page on website

Dinosaur galleries, gemstones, extinct species, and a working beehive (in summer).

University Parks

South Parks Road
Open Daily 8am–dusk **Adm Free**

Twenty-eight hectares (70 acres) of parkland on the west bank of the River Cherwell, with gardens, trees, riverside walks and a duck pond.

Views

With its glorious architecture and history, Oxford is a city of many vistas. Unfortunately, at ground level increased urbanization has obscured many of its best sights but there are more exalted views on offer which allow you to see the 'dreaming spires' in all their glory. Check out the Carfax Tower, **t** (01865) 792653, the 22m/72ft-high remains of a 14th-century church; the University Church of St Mary the Virgin, High Street, **t** (01865) 249111, and Oxford's oldest building, St Michael, at the North Gate, Cornmarket, **t** (01865) 240940, all of which offer panoramic views of the city and surrounding countryside.

Around Oxford

Blenheim Palace, 10 miles northwest (p.254)

St Albans

Getting there By road: St Albans is 18 miles from London, 36 miles from Cambridge and 35 miles from Oxford and can be reached via the M1 and the A6. By train: Services arrive from London Kings Cross (Thameslink) regularly. By bus/coach: There are frequent National Express coaches to St Albans from London Victoria
Tourist information Town Hall, Market Place
t (01727) 864511 www.stalbans.gov.uk

Known as *Verulamium* in Roman times, this pleasant city was renamed St Albans in honour of Britain's first Christian martyr (a Roman citizen who was beheaded here in the 3rd century AD before Constantine converted the Empire) for giving sanctuary to a priest. The remains of the Roman walls, basilica, bathhouse and theatre can be seen in the very pretty *Verulamium* Park on the southwest side of the city and there are numerous Roman relics (mosaics, murals, amphora and jewellery) to be found in the excellent *Verulamium* Museum. St Albans' impressive red-hued cathedral, which sits on top of a mound overlooking the city, was partly built with stone recycled from Roman buildings.

For the full flavour of the city, try the City Trail – a four-mile circular route passing all the historic sites, including Roman *Verulamium*, the conically shaped inn 'Ye Old Fighting Cock', which is reputedly the oldest licensed inn in England, the Kingbury Watermill (its great water wheel still turns) and the medieval Clock Tower. Alternatively, come on a market day (Wednesday or Saturday) when St Peter's Street plays host to one of the largest open air markets (150–200 stalls) in the Southeast. There are several excellent day-trip worthy sites within easy reach of the town, including the Gardens of the Rose (*see* below), Hatfield House (p.255) and Willows Farm Village (pp.261–2).

Things to see and do

Cinemas and theatres *See* pp.273, 276

Gardens of the Rose
Chiswell, Green Lane **t** (01727) 850461 www.rnrs.org
Getting there 18 miles north of London and 2 miles south of St Albans, within easy reach of the M1 (J6), the M25 (J21A) and the A1 (M) (J3/A414)
Open/Adm Call for times and prices

On-site parking, café-restaurant, picnic areas, gift shop, plant sales, guided tours, disabled access. Please note: the Gardens of the Rose are scheduled to reopen after redevelopment in summer 2007

Well worth a detour, this is the world's largest rose collection, with bed upon bed of fabulous blooms (30,000 roses flower here in the summer).

Museum of St Albans
Hatfield Road **t** (01727) 819340
www.stalbansmuseums.org.uk
Open Mon–Sat 10–5, Sun 2–5 **Adm Free**
Picnic area, shop, parking, some disabled access, wildlife garden and pond

Lively displays tell the story of St Albans from Roman times to the present day. The 'Tools of the Trade' exhibition of trade and craft tools will entertain any DIY enthusiasts.

Sport and activities *See* pp.270–3

St Alban's Cathedral
t (01727) 860780 www.stalbanscathedral.org.uk
Open Mon–Fri 8–5.45, Sat 8–5, Sun 8am–7.30pm
Adm Free (donations welcome)
Café, gift shop, guided tours (11.30am and 2.30pm on weekdays; 11.30am and 2pm on Sat and 2.30pm Sun), parking in Westminster lodge on the south side, disabled facilities, toilets

It was erected in the 11th century on the spot where Alban, the country's first Christian martyr, was executed in the 3rd century. As you wander around the building, you get a real sense of how the community would have centred around the cathedral and moved within its corridors and chapels. Within its ruddy coloured walls, look out for the glorious stained-glass rose window, the resplendent High Altar and the multimedia presentation narrated by Nigel Hawthorne, which tells the story of Alban and the construction of the cathedral.

★ *Verulamium* Museum and Park
t (01727) 751810, theatre visits **t** (01727) 835035
www.stalbansmuseums.org.uk
Getting there Follow signs to St Albans from J21a from the M25 or J6, 7 or 9 from the M1, then follow signs to *Verulamium*
Open Mon–Sat 10–5.30, Sun 2–5.30
Adm Adults £3.30, children £2, family £8
Shop, picnic area, disabled access, on-site parking

The museum is set in 40 hectares (100 acres) of attractive parkland, where you can see more

Roman remains including walls, a theatre, a bath-house and a hypocaust system (the Roman version of central heating). Wander through recreated Roman rooms, complete with decorative wall plasters and mosaics (spot the famous half-shell mosaic), look at Roman artefacts (such as coins) through microscopes and find out about everyday life in Roman *Verulamium* in the hands-on discovery areas, touch-screen computers and video presentations. On the second weekend of every month, members of Legion XIIII storm the building to inform willing recruits about Roman equipment and tactics. Children's quiz sheets are available and the extended shop features lots of pocket money souvenirs and toys. The park also contains tennis courts, a crazy golf course, a children's paddling pool and a lake, where you can feed the ducks and stop for an ice cream.

Walking tours

Call the tourist information centre, t (01727) 864511, for details of the scheduled walks offered by local volunteers. These take place from April to October (adults £2, children £1), although there are additional seasonal walks in winter. Topics include Victorian St Albans, Ghostly Sites (not suitable for very young children) and Famous Albanians, as well as the *Verulamium* Walk, which takes in the Roman baths, Mortimer Wheeler's 1930s excavations, the city wall and London Gate.

Around St Albans

Willows Farm Village, just south (pp.261–2)
Hatfield House, 6 miles east (p.255)
Knebworth House, 8 miles northeast (pp.255–6)

Windsor

Getting there By road: Windsor is 20 miles west of London, off the M4 exit 6 and 50 miles northeast of Southampton, off the M3 exit 3. A park-and-ride service runs between Windsor town centre and Legoland operating at least every 30 minutes daily from 10.15am–6.45pm (8.30pm during peak season). Additional park and ride is available from Home Park car park on the Datchet Road (B470) to Windsor town centre Mon–Fri 7–7pm. By bus/coach: Services leave the Greenline coach stop on Buckingham Palace Road at regular intervals throughout day, t 0870 608 7261

Can you spot?

The blue postbox built to commemorate the first ever air mail flight made by Gustav Hemel in 1911 when he took off in a rickety old Bleriot monoplane and flew from Hendon Aerodrome to Shaw Farm Meadow in Windsor to mark the coronation of George V. It's on the corner of High Street and Park Street.

Tourist information Royal Windsor Information Centre, 24 High Street t (01753) 743900 www.windsor.gov.uk
Above the information centre is a small exhibition on the history of the town.

Were its streets not seething with tourists, Windsor would be adorable with its picturesque Georgian houses and demure shops overlooked by the glorious 900-year-old castle. People, however, are an integral part of the Windsor experience. Visit on a fine summer weekend and it can be overwhelming, but on a midweek morning, things are less frenetic. Although its narrow cobbled streets, full of souvenir shops, ice cream parlours and ye-olde tearooms are fun to explore, Windsor is really a three-site town. First and foremost is the castle, which will be upon you as soon as you leave the train station (either one). The official residence of the Queen, it defines the shape of the town, with roads flowing around its fortress walls. North across the river is the adjoining town of Eton, home of the famous public school (and second on our list of must-see attractions), first established in the 15th century, where several prime ministers and members of the Royal Family have been educated (including princes William and Harry). It is open to visitors all year; you can tour the grounds and see the oldest classroom in the world, its ancient desks scored with generations of schoolboy graffiti. If you come in term time, you should be able to see the boys in their distinctively archaic uniform of top hat and tailcoat. School fees cost around £8,000 a term! Nearby there are lots of grassy meadows for picnicking and watching the boats coming and going on the river. You're unlikely to linger long as your kids will want to visit the third site, Legoland (p.249), the exuberant heart beneath the cultured exterior, one of the country's best theme parks, full of rides, games, models, activity centres, rollercoasters and hordes of fun-seeking kids.

Things to see and do

Boat tours – French Brothers Ltd

Clewer Boat House, Clewer Court Road
t (01753) 851900 www.boat-trips.co.uk
Open Easter–Oct for scheduled sailings;
Dec–Easter private hire only (Nov closed)
Fares Adults £4.50, children £2.25 (40-minute trip);
adults £7, children £3.50, family £17.50–£19.25
(2-hour cruise); return trip to Runnymede or
Maidenhead: adults £8.70, children £4.35

Offers 40-minute sightseeing tours around
Windsor's environs, as well as trips downriver to
Runnymede and Hampton Court and upriver to the
picturesque villages of Bray and Maidenhead from
Windsor Promenade. Special trips for children are
also provided along the creeks and backwaters of
Windsor to observe the local wildlife (including the
famous swans). Alternatively, you can hire four-
seater rowboats (£9 for 30 minutes/£15 for 1 hour)
and six-seater motorboats (£35 for 30 minutes) for
a little self-navigation on the Thames from John
Logie Motorboats, Windsor Promenade, Barry
Avenue, t (07774) 983809.

Bus tours

Run by City Sightseeing Open Top Bus Tours in
open-top red buses, they are available from March
to October daily and can be joined at the High
Street, Castle Hill or at either Windsor Central
station or Windsor and Eton Riverside station
(adults £7, children £3.50, family £17.50). Kids Club
passport and colouring pens for children. For a
more elegant, slightly slower, tour climb aboard
one of the horse-drawn carriages (four–eight
seater) lined up at the taxi rank outside the castle
for a 30-minute–1-hour trip round the town. Call
t (01708) 866000 www.city-sightseeing.com.

Cinemas and theatres See pp.273, 276

Legoland

Winkfield Road, Windsor, t 08705 040404
www.legoland.co.uk
Getting there 2 miles from Windsor on the
Windsor to Ascot Road, signposted from J6 of the
M4. The shuttle bus service from Windsor town
centre to Legoland departs from Thames Street
every 15 minutes during opening times
Open 10–6 **Adm** Adults £30, children £23; 2-day
ticket: adults £57, children £45

Can you spot?
As befits this fine royal town, here are two royal
blue things to look out for: can you find the blue
plaque marking the spot where three men were
burnt at the stake in 1543? It's located near the
memorial to George V 'The First Sovereign of the
House of Windsor', on the corner of Datchet Road
and Thames Street.

Seven restaurants/cafés and 11 catering stalls, picnic
areas, mother and baby facilities, wheelchair access,
wheelchair hire available, adapted toilets, on-site
parking, first aid and lost parent facilities

Legoland is among the most imaginative of
Britain's theme parks, and one of the country's
top family attractions. Expect long queues, but if
you time your trip to arrive early or stay late (the
park stays open until at least 7pm in summer),
you'll make the most of it. The theme is Lego, the
Danish multicoloured plastic building bricks that
have become a national institution and have long
been used as prompts for kids to use and develop
their imagination. The park is inspirational too – a
cross between a theme park and an activity
centre, with good rides, including two dragon-
themed rollercoasters (the smaller is the most
exciting) and a log flume, Pirate Falls. More popular
are the interactive zones, such as Lego Traffic, where
children can operate electrically powered Lego cars,
boats and balloons, and the brand new Viking Land.
In the Imagination Centre, kids can make their own
futuristic designs. Older children can create robotic
models or take on the Extreme Team Challenge
waterslide, whilst their younger siblings splash in
Explore Land's Waterworks fountains, dash about in
the indoor and outdoor play zones and enjoy some
gentle boat rides. For a break, head for Miniland and
marvel at the model buildings, complete with mini
tube train and pleasure boats, or stop off for a picnic
and watch the Wave Surfers. There are summer
shows in the Lego Imagination Theatre, where you
can watch a 3D medieval adventure film. Young kids
may prefer a puppet show in the Explore Theatre,
while all the family will enjoy the acrobatic thrills
and spills in the Johnny Thunder Show.

Shopping

With its well-to-do shops and boutiques lining
the pedestrianized triangle of Peascod Street, King
Edward Court and the revamped Windsor Royal
Station, many people come to Windsor to shop.
The interest of younger visitors will be captured by
a few emporia such as Old Boys' Toys, full of model

Can you spot?
Queen Charlotte Street in the cobbled area of Windsor between Market Street and High Street. At 51ft 10in long, it is the shortest street in Britain.

cars, and Miniatures on Parade, which specializes in dolls' houses. If you visit just one shop in Windsor, it should be Hawkin's Bazaar, 134 Peascod Street, **t** 0870 4436011 www.hawkin.com (open Mon–Fri 9–5.30, Sat 9–5.30, Sun 11–4) for a wonderful assembly of old-fashioned curios and oddities (wooden toys and games, automata, wind-up dolls, puppets and kits, kaleidoscopes, theatre sets and musical boxes).

Sport and activities See pp.270–3

Windsor Castle

Windsor, **t** (020) 7766 7304 www.royal.gov.uk
Open Mar–Oct 9.45–5.15 (last entry 4), Nov–Feb 9.45–4.15 (last entry 3)
Adm Adults £13.50, children £7.50, under 5s **free**, family £34.50
Shop, wheelchair access, car parking in town
   The official residence of the Queen and the largest inhabited castle in the world. In 1992, the State Apartments were ravaged by fire but restoration work worth £37 million sorted that out. See the paintings from the Royal collection, including Van Eycks and Rembrandts, plus porcelain, armour and fine furniture. Children should make a beeline for the Queen Mary dolls' house. Visit the tombs of knights and kings in St George's Chapel and try and guess where the Queen and Prince Charles sit during a service (on either side at the back of the choir in curtained booths). From the top of the 12th-century Round Tower you can see 12 counties on a clear day. The Changing of the Guard takes place outside the Palace on alternate days (Mon–Sat 11am; *see* www.royal.gov.uk).

Windsor Great Park

   This vast, 1,950-hectare (4,800-acre) tree-filled green space, **t** (01753) 743900, contains a 15-hectare (35-acre) botanic garden, the Swiss Garden, and a huge lake, Virginia Water, with a 30m (100ft) totem pole on its banks. The paths are well marked, so it is very pushchair friendly. According to legend, the ghost of Herne the Hunter haunts the park on moonlit evenings, dressed in his stag antler headdress riding a black stallion, at the head of a pack of black hounds.

Around Windsor

Thorpe Park, 6 miles southeast (pp.129–30)

THE COTSWOLDS

   The Cotswolds are one of the most beautiful regions in the entire country – a rolling limestone escarpment running for 100 miles between Chipping Campden and Bath. Beautifully unspoilt, it's characterized by a gently undulating stone-walled landscape, clusters of historic villages (many little changed in hundreds of years), honey-coloured cottages, snug pubs, wooded valleys, winding streams, duck-filled ponds and sheep-dotted fields. It has become something of a tourist Mecca and in fine weather its walks and trails (including the Cotswold Way, which runs the entire length of the region) are thick with ramblers. There's so much of it that it's easy to get off the beaten track to admire some of the most dramatic and photogenic scenery in the country. There are good attractions for children (animal parks, model villages, museums) many found in the impossibly picturesque towns of Bourton-on-the-Water, Stow-on-the-Wold and Moreton-in-Marsh (the average Cotswold village is a very hyphenated affair).

★Bourton-on-the-Water

Getting there Bourton is 15 miles east from Cheltenham on the A429, off the A40
Tourist information centre Victoria Street **t** (01451) 820211 www.bourtoninfo.com
   One of the most touristy Cotswolds villages, Bourton is also the most fun for children. Nestling among its cottages is a fine array of attractions to keep kids happy in between countryside rambles. There's **Birdland**, a 28-hectare (70-acre) bird sanctuary home to 130 species of winged beasts including parrots, penguins and flamingos; the **Cotswold Motoring Museum**, with its collection of vintage cars and toys (keep an eye out for Brum; the TV show was filmed here), **Bourton Model Village** and the **Bourton Model Railway**, one of the largest model railways in the country. Bourton also boasts a **Perfume Factory**, where you can see scents being manufactured, and a high street with lots of gift shops including a couple for kitting out your child's dolls' house or model world.
   Bourton may be crowded in the summer but, from a kid's perspective, will probably prove the most popular of all the Cotswold villages. A few miles to the southwest, in the village of Northleach, you'll find **Keith Harding's World of Mechanical Music** with its diverse collection of antique music boxes, automata and musical instruments.

Things to see and do

Birdland Park and Gardens

Rissington Road **t** (01451) 820480
www.birdlands.co.uk
Open Apr–Oct daily 10–6, Nov–Mar 10–4
Adm Adults £5.20, children £3, family (2+2) £15,
under 4s **free**
Café, shop, disabled access, mother and baby room

Bourton Model Railway

Box Bush High Street **t** (01451) 820686
www.bourtonmodelrailway.co.uk
Open Jun–Aug daily 11–5, Sept–May Sat–Sun 11–5
Adm Adults £2.25, children £1.75

Bourton Model Village

The Old New Inn **t** (01451) 820467
Open Summer: daily 9–6; winter: daily 10–4
(last entry 15 minutes before closing)
Adm Adults £2.75, children £2.25, under 4s **free**
Shop, baby changing facilities, children's meals (hotel)

Cotswold Motoring Museum & Toy Collection

The Old Mill **t** (01451) 821255
www.cotswold-motor-museum.com
Open Feb–Nov daily 10–6
Adm Adults £3.50, children £2.45, family £10.85,
under 5s **free**
*Gift shop with official Brum merchandise,
disabled access*

Fundays

Unit 8 Willow Court, Bourton Industrial Park
t (01451) 822999 **www.**fundaysplaybarn.com
Open Daily 10–6
Adm Term-time weekdays: adults £1, 4–11s £4,
under 4s £3, under 1s **free**; school holidays and
weekends: adults £1, 4–11s £4.50, under 4s £4.20,
under 1s £1 (**free** with older siblings)
*Upstairs lounge, café serving adult and children's
meals, baby changing facilities, parking*
Indoor adventure play complex for children up to
11 years of age accompanied by an adult – and the
adults can play along, too! Socks must be worn.

Keith Harding's World of Mechanical Music

High Street, Northleach **t** (01451) 860181
www.mechanicalmusic.co.uk
Open Daily 10–6
Adm 1-hour guided tour: adults £6.50, children £3
under 3s **free**
Shop, disabled access

Perfume Factory

Cotswold Perfumery, Victoria Street
t (01451) 820698 **www.**cotswold-perfumery.co.uk
Open Tours take place Wed and Thurs 10.30am and
2pm. Book in advance
Adm Adults £5, children £3.50
Shop, disabled access, no toilets on site
*Please note: In 2005 the Perfumery Exhibition was
transformed into a factory so visitors could see the
manufacturing process. At present tours take place
on Wed and Thurs but please call in advance of your
visit for up-to-date information*

Cheltenham

Getting there Cheltenham is about 35 miles northeast of Bristol, off the M5 and 35 miles northwest
of Oxford on the A40
Tourist information 77 Promenade
t (01242) 522878 **www.**visitcheltenham.com

Almost as beautiful as Bath, which it closely
resembles, Cheltenham is not quite as interesting. As with Bath, it was founded on the site of
a natural spa and also rose to prominence in the
Regency period when the fashion for 'taking the
waters' was at its height. Constructed in much
the same architectural style as its Somerset rival,
it boasts its own Pump Room, a glorious 18th-
century Greek Revival Building, where you can
sample the salty spa water and test its famed
medicinal properties.

Primarily known as a horse-racing town (the
Gold Cup takes place here every March),
Cheltenham, with its grand architecture and neatly
manicured public parks, provides an elegant base
for exploring the Cotswolds. Its main visitor attractions (besides the race course and Pump Room) are
the Cheltenham Art Gallery, a refined affair with
a tasteful collection of ceramics, porcelain and
William Morris furniture and, outside the town, the
Gloucestershire and Warwickshire Railway.

Things to see and do

Cheltenham Art Gallery and Museum

Clarence Street **t** (01242) 237431
www.cheltenhammuseum.org.uk
Open Mon–Sat 10–5.20 (first Thurs of each month
opens at 11am) **Adm Free**
*Café, gift shop, mother and baby facilities, guided
tours, disabled access*
Galleries on Cheltenham history, the
archaeology and natural history of Gloucester-

shire, and a room dedicated to Edward Wilson, a member of Captain Scott's fateful Antarctic exhibition. A different temporary exhibition is put on each month, suitable for children. Colouring-in sheets, quizzes and display tables are provided and children's events (such as puppet workshops) arranged in summer.

Cleeve Hill

'Area of outstanding natural beauty' offering spectacular views of the surrounding country-side. Good for walks and nature rambles, with rare orchids, wild flowers and butterflies to spot.

Sandford Park

Keynsham Road **t** (01242) 524430
www.sandfordparkslido.org.uk
Open Apr–Aug daily 11–7.30
Adm Adult £3.50, children £1.80, under 5s **free**, family £9

The River Chelt runs through this beautiful park, where you'll find a municipal golf course, a skateboard park, a boating lake and a heated open-air lido comprising a 50m (165ft) pool, a kids' pool, a playground and a poolside café.

Cirencester

Getting there Cirencester is about 10 miles south-east of Cheltenham on the A417 and 15 miles northwest of Swindon on the A419
Tourist information Corn Hall, Market Place
t (01285) 654180 **www.cirencester.co.uk**

This pretty country town was once one of the two most important cities in Roman Britain (the other was *Londinium*). Almost destroyed by the Saxons following the Roman withdrawal, it still has remnants of the old Empire, including the grassed-over ruins of an amphitheatre. The excellent *Corinium* Museum (*Corinium* was Cirencester's Roman name) contains Roman finds and a reconstructed Roman dining room, kitchen and garden. The town was prominent again in the Middle Ages following the expan-sion of the wool trade (most of the Cotswolds villages were built by medieval wool merchants) and remained affluent even when the trade diminished following industrialization.

Quiet and serene most of the time, the town comes to life on Mondays and Fridays when a large market is held in the Market Square. The landscaped park on the western edge of town is worth a visit, especially in warm weather when

you could also visit Cirencester Open Air Baths on Tetbury Road, **t** (01285) 653947, one of the oldest open-air pools in the country, with a main pool and paddling pools for kids. Just south of Cirencester is the Cotswold Water Park, Britain's largest (larger than the Norfolk Broads), 132 lakes, where you can go rowing, sailing and jetskiing. The surrounding parkland offers opportunities for nature walks, fishing, golf and picnicking.

Things to see and do

Corinium Museum

Park Street **t** (01285) 655611
www.coriniummuseum.co.uk
Open Mon–Sat 10–5, Sun 2–5
Adm Adults £3.90, children £2
Café-restaurant, gift shop, mother and baby facilities, disabled access

Plenty of hands-on attractions, audio-visual screens and games to keep families entertained as well as some interesting reconstructions of Roman life (rooms, shops etc.).

Cotswold Water Park and Keynes Country Park

Spratsgate Lane, Cirencester **t** (01285) 861459
www.waterpark.org
Open Daily 9am–9pm; beach: Jun–Sept 1–5
Adm Free

Facilities at the Millennium Visitor Centre include toilets, visitor information, bike and boat hire, a café, fossil display and children's play beach. **For further information** see p.273

Stow-on-the-Wold

Getting there Stow is 16 miles northeast of Cheltenham and can be reached via the A429
Tourist information Hollis House, The Square
t (01451) 831082

Set on a plateau some 240m (787ft) up, this picturesque, occasionally windswept, town is the highest in the Cotswolds. The usual collection of charming stone cottages and houses are here laid out around a large central marketplace that's reminiscent of a medieval piazza (note the narrow alleyways surrounding it). Originally designed to make it easier for farmers to drive their sheep to market, they are now lined with antique shops and souvenir stalls. A good base for exploring the Cotswolds, the town's most child-friendly attraction is probably the Toy and

Collectors Museum on Park Street, which houses a collection of antique toys including a large selection of Victorian bears.

Stow straddles the old Roman Fosse Way, which also takes in Moreton-in-Marsh, a few miles to the north, where a lively market is held every Tuesday when over 200 stalls open for business. Close by in Bourton-on-the-Hill is the Cotswold Falconry Centre, where you can watch eagles, hawks and owls being flown daily and adjacent to this is a newly opened Reptile House.

Between Stow and Moreton lie the tiny villages of Upper and Lower Slaughter which, despite their rather macabre names, are actually among the most picturesque of all the Cotswold villages.

Around the Cotswolds

Cotswold Farm Park
Guiting Power, Stow-on-the-Wold **t** (01451) 850307
www.cotswoldfarmpark.co.uk
Open End Mar–early Sept daily 10.30–5, Oct Sat–Sun 10.30–5
Adm Adults £5.50, children £4.50, family £18
Cuddle animals, meet and greet sheep, cows, pigs, horses and goats. Farm Safari rides available.
For further information *see p.260*

Cotswold Wildlife Park
Bradwell Grove, Burford **t** (01993) 823006
www.cotswoldwildlifepark.co.uk
Open Mar–Sept daily 10–6 (last admission 4.30), Oct–Feb 10–3.30
Adm Adults £9, children £6.50, under 3s **free**
Idyllic acres of woodland and acres with a range of creatures (many endangered species) living in large and natural-looking enclosures.
For further information *see p.257*

Gloucestershire and Warwickshire Railway
The Railway Station, Toddington, Winchcombe
t (01242) 621405 **www.gwsr.com**
Open Mid Mar–Oct Sat, Sun and Bank Hols 10–5; school hols Tues–Thurs, Sat, Sun and Bank Hols 10–5; some Christmas weekends
Fares Adults £9.50, children £6, under 5s **free**, family (2+3) £26
Climb aboard one of the gently puffing steam trains on the Gloucestershire and Warwickshire Railway along a six-mile long stretch of track between Toddington and Winchcombe.
For further information *see p.266*

Castles, palaces and historic houses

Basildon Park
Lower Basildon, Reading **t** (0118) 984 3040
www.nationaltrust.org.uk
Getting there 7 miles northwest of Reading, on the west side of the A329; M4 (J12)
Open Apr–Oct Wed–Sun 11–5; house: 12 noon–5
Adm Adults £5.30, children £2.65, family £13.25
Café with children's menu, picnic area, shop, mother and baby room, disables access, parking, children's guide, quiz and trail

Surrounding an elegant 18th-century Bath stone mansion, this glorious swathe of parkland has numerous marked walks and open spaces. The house contains features that may appeal to children, including the jungle mural that adorns the walls and ceiling of the small tearoom, and a seashell collection. Family events (craft fairs, theatre shows and concerts with fireworks) are held in summer and autumn. Movie fans may recognize the house as Mr Bingley's 'Netherfield' from the screen adaptation of Jane Austen's *Pride and Prejudice* starring Keira Knightley.

Berkeley Castle
Berkeley **t** (01453) 810332
www.berkeley-castle.com
Getting there Just off the A38, midway between Bristol and Gloucester; the M5 (J13/J14)
Open Apr–Sept Tues–Sat 11–4, Sun 2–5; Oct Bank Hols 11–4, Sun 2–5.
Adm Adults £7.50, children £4.50.
Restaurant, guided tours, picnic areas, souvenir shop, on-site parking, plant centre

This imposing-looking castle has been owned by the Berkeley family since 1153, making it the country's oldest inhabited castle. Twenty-four generations of Berkeleys have resided here, resulting in wave after wave of building, so architecturally it's a bit of a jumble. Still, it's a lot of fun to explore, with its craggy Norman central keep, plush stately-home style apartments, exhibition on Edward II (who was murdered here in 1327) and medieval kitchens. It's surrounded by sweeping lawns and manicured gardens. There's a butterfly farm (additional charge), where you can watch the exotic creatures in free flight. Tuesdays are family fun days, when children can encounter aspects of medieval life and participate in seasonal events.

★Blenheim Palace

Woodstock **t** (01993) 811325
www.blenheimpalace.com
Getting there About 6 miles northwest of Oxford, just off the A44
Open Palace: Apr–Oct daily 10.30–5.30; park: 9–6 (last admission 4.45); gardens, maze and butterfly house: mid-Mar–Oct daily 10–6
Adm Adults £14, children £8.50, family £37, under 5s **free**
Shop, restaurants, picnic areas, mother and baby facilities, guided tours, disabled access, parking, miniature railway, children's play area, maze

One of the best-loved stately homes in the country, Blenheim is associated with Britain's great wartime prime minister, Winston Churchill, born here in 1874. The house is vast, covering an area of some six hectares (14 acres) although, despite its bulk, it's still an elegant sight with its delicate sandstone colouring and pinnacles. The interior is opulent, littered with antiques, statues and tapestries, and holds an exhibition on Churchill's life, which includes paintings, manuscripts and letters. However, the house will probably prove less popular with younger visitors than the grounds, which, if anything, are even more magnificent. The gardens surrounding the house are formal and sculpted – landscaped, inevitably, by 'Capability' Brown – and fun to explore with ponds, fountains and water terraces. Beyond this are grand tracts of open parkland, which seem to stretch as far as the eye can see (the estate covers around 800 hectares/2,000 acres), where the kids can run around. Follow the marked walk, which takes you on an hour-long tour of the park passing the large lake on the way (look out for gulping trout) or, if you're feeling tired (some parts are steep and may be hard on little legs), hop aboard the narrow-gauge steam railway, which deposits you at the walled pleasure garden – the highlight for children, with its maze (the largest symbolic hedge maze in the world), giant chess and draughts pieces and model village of Woodstock. There is a butterfly house, with fluttering specimens, and an adventure playground. The restaurants are expensive, so bring a picnic – no great hardship as there are few more elegant spots to enjoy a sandwich and a pork pie.

Chedworth Roman Villa

Yanworth, near Cheltenham **t** (01242) 890256
www.nationaltrust.org.uk
Getting there The villa is situated off the A429, 10 miles southeast of Cheltenham

Open Mar 11–4, Apr–Oct 10–5, Nov 11–4
Adm Adults £5.50, children £3, family £14
Shop, some disabled access, on-site parking

The remains of a 4th-century villa, one of the largest in Britain. The property of a wealthy Roman citizen, the house was equipped with all mod cons (Roman style) including central heating, bath houses and a lavatory. There are well-preserved mosaics, plus an audiovisual presentation, which will help you to picture what the villa would have looked like. Activities for children take place in school holidays and there's a regular programme of living history events and family activity packs.

Claydon House

Middle Claydon, near Buckingham **t** (01296) 730349
www.nationaltrust.org.uk
Getting there 13.5 miles northwest of Aylesbury and signposted from the A413 and the A41; 12 miles from the M40 (J9)
Open Apr–Oct Sat–Wed 1–5
Adm Adults £5.50, children £2.70, family £13
Tearoom, mother and baby room, some disabled access, on-site parking, family and children's guides

Built by the Verney family in the early 17th century, it displays a mixture of styles, its restrained façade concealing a Rococo interior filled with intricate chinoiserie. It's said to be haunted by the ghost of Edmund Verney, Charles I's standard-bearer at the Battle of Edgehill in 1642, searching for his missing hand. Captured by the Roundheads, Edmund had it chopped off before being killed; the body was never recovered. Visit the room where Florence Nightingale stayed when visiting her sister and see her letters detailing events from the Crimean War, where she was employed as a field nurse. Events, including spring walks and children's theatre performances, are held year-round.

Dyrham Park

Near Chippenham **t** (01179) 372501
www.nationaltrust.org.uk
Getting there 8 miles north of Bath, just south of the M4 (J18), off the A46
Open Apr–Oct Fri–Tues 12 noon–4 (gardens until 5)
Adm Adults £9, children £4.50, family £22.50
Restaurant, picnic area, shop, mother and baby facilities, disabled access; suitable for pushchairs, Tracker Packs for families, guided tours

Built in around 1700 for William Blathwayt, the Secretary of War to King William III, the house has a Dutch-looking interior (the king, who had deposed the unpopular James II, was from Holland) with Dutch-style furnishings. Kids will like the restored Victorian kitchen, bakehouse, larders and the pretty Delft-tiled dairy. It's surrounded by lovely rolling grounds, home to deer and peacocks and offering terrific views towards Bristol and Wales.

Greys Court

Rotherfield Greys, Henley-on-Thames
t (01491) 628529 **www.**nationaltrust.org.uk
Getting there 3 miles west of Henley-on-Thames, off the A4130/B481
Open House: Apr–Sept Wed–Fri 2–5; garden: Apr–Jul Tues–Sat 1–5, Aug Wed–Sun 1–5, Sept Tues–Sat 1–5
Adm Adults £5.40, children £2.70, family £13.60; garden only: adults £3.90, children £1.90, family £9.60.
Tearoom, picnic area, shop, baby changing, some disabled access, parking, children's quiz and trail

This beautiful 16th-century house is set in charming grounds that will delight children. There's a brick maze, a wheelhouse (where grey donkeys used to power the wheel that drew water from a well) and, amongst the ruins of a medieval fortified manor, a series of 'secret' gardens linked by 'doorways' in the walls. In the 17th century, the house acted as an informal prison for Robert and Francis Carr, who where banished here by James I after being found guilty of murdering a courtier. The nearby town of Henley-on-Thames is famed for its summer regatta (you can see rowers practising on this stretch of the river all year). Rowboats can be hired for self-guided sightseeing. Seasonal walks and events throughout the year.

Hatfield House

Hatfield **t** (01707) 262823
www.hatfield-house.co.uk
Getting there 21 miles north of London, 7 miles from the M25 (J23), 2 miles from the A1 (J4) and signposted from the A414 and the A100
Open House and gardens: Apr–Sept Wed–Sun 12 noon–5 (Thurs pre-booked guided tours only); park and west gardens: daily 11–5.30
Adm House, park and gardens: adults £8, children £4, family £22; park and gardens: adults £4.50, children £3.50; park: adults £2, children £1
Restaurant, picnic areas, shop, mother and baby room, guided tours, disabled access, on-site parking, children's play area, nature trails

This grand, red-brick Jacobean mansion was built in the early 17th century on the site of the Tudor Palace, where Queen Elizabeth I spent her childhood. A wing of the original palace still survives. The 1,600-hectare (4,000-acre) grounds attract children with their formal gardens of hedges, paths, ponds and fountains, and wilderness areas. See if you can spot the oak tree under which the young Princess Elizabeth learned of her succession following the death of her sister Mary in 1558.

The house is grand inside, with imposing rows of paintings (look for the portrait of Elizabeth) and a vast oak staircase (named the Grand Staircase) decorated with carved figures. Kids will like the National Collection of Model Soldiers, which has more than 3,000 miniature figures arranged in combat position. Craft fairs and theatre productions in the park are among the events that families can enjoy all year.

Knebworth House

Knebworth **t** (01438) 812661
www.knebworthhouse.com
Getting there 2 miles from Stevenage; entrance directly off J7 of the A1
Open End Apr–Sept Sat–Sun and school holidays; park and gardens 11–5; house 12 noon–5
Adm House and grounds: adults £9, children £8.50, family £31 (2+2), under 4s **free**; grounds only: adults and children £7, family £24
On-site parking, café-restaurant, garden terrace tearoom, picnic areas, gift shop, guided tours

Built in the 16th century and originally a simple Tudor mansion, it was covered in over-the-top Gothic adornments (like rearing heraldic dragons and crenellations) in the 1800s at the behest of Victorian author Edward Bulwer-Lytton, a friend of Charles Dickens, who wanted the house to resemble one of the romantic locations from his books. The interior contains paintings and armour (quiz sheets available), but the grounds are the real draw. As you head south from the house, you'll encounter a sunken garden surrounded by trees, a rose garden, a pet cemetery, a wildflower meadow and a small maze. Beyond this is a wilderness area and a 100-hectare (250-acre) park, where red deer roam. The biggest attraction for children is Fort Knebworth adventure playground, with its climbing equipment and slides (including a suspension slide where you travel down clutching on to a rope), four-lane Astroglide,

KIDS OUT

where you travel on a rush mat down a plastic chute, a corkscrew slide and a vertical drop slide. There is a bouncy castle and a miniature railway with looping 15-minute tours of the grounds.

Snowshill Manor

Snowshill, near Broadway **t** (01386) 852410
www.nationaltrust.org.uk
Getting there 2.5 miles southwest of Broadway, signposted from the Broadway bypass off the A44
Open Apr–Oct Wed–Sun 11–5
Adm House and grounds: adults £7.30, children £3.65, family £18.50; garden only: adults £4, children £2, family £10
Café, shop, baby changing and disabled facilities

Within this staid-looking 18th-century manor house is one of the country's greatest collections of clutter: room after room filled with an eclectic array of items amassed by collector *extraordinaire* Charles Paget Wade. Musical instruments, clocks, toys, bicycles, tools, tapestries, mouse traps, animal horns galore. It's as if every attic in the country has been emptied, creating a treasure trove of ephemera. Indeed, space is at such a premium that some of the objects are stuck to the ceiling. Wade himself, who continued collecting until 1951, moved into premises next door when the collection got too big. A quiz sheet is available, and family events, such as Easter bunny trails and Japanese martial arts demos, are organized.

Sudeley Castle

Winchcombe **t** (01242) 602308
www.sudeleycastle.co.uk
Getting there On the A46, just south of Winchcombe; 10 miles from J9 off the M5
Open Mar–Oct Sun–Thurs 10.30–5 (school hols daily)
Adm Adults £7.20, children £4.20, family £20.80
Restaurant, shop, parking, plant centre, picnic area

Henry VIII, Anne Boleyn, Lady Jane Grey and Elizabeth I stayed here, while Catherine Parr lived here and is buried in the chapel. A costume exhibition from TV series *The Six Wives of Henry VIII* is on display in the castle apartments. Remodelled in the 19th century, the apartments are filled with furnishings and paintings by Van Dyck, Rubens and Turner. The lavish grounds (600 hectares/ 1,500 acres) contain the rose-filled Queen's Garden, a Victorian Kitchen Garden, a Tudor Knot Garden (with a water feature modelled on one of Elizabeth I's dresses) and an adventure playground.

Animal attractions

Beale Park

Lower Basildon, Reading **t** 0870 7777160
www.bealepark.co.uk
Getting there About 7 miles northwest of Reading and signposted from J12 of the M4
Open Mar–early Apr and Oct daily 10–5; late Apr–Sept 10–6
Adm Low/high season: adults £6.50/£4.30, children £4.50/£3.30, under 2s **free**, family £18.50–20
Café, picnic areas, mother and baby facilities, disabled access, on-site parking

A beautiful, well-run wildlife park on the banks of the Thames, where rare and endangered species of birds and mammals live in spacious enclosures. There's a deer park, a huge adventure playground, a model boat collection and a narrow-gauge railway offering tours of the park. Boat services run from here to the Thameside promenade in Reading.

Bedford Butterfly Park

Renhold Road, Wilden **t** (01234) 772770
www.bedford-butterflies.co.uk
Getting there Wilden is 4 miles north of Bedford off the A421 (it's signposted), 3 miles from the A1
Open Jan Thurs–Sun 10–4, Feb–Oct daily 10–5, Nov–mid Dec Thurs–Sun 10–4
Adm Adults £4.75, children £3.90, under 3s **free**
Tearoom, gift shop, guided tours, mother and baby room, disabled access, on-site parking

In a small recreated rainforest environment, heated to a constant 28°C (82°F), you can study the life cycle of the butterfly from egg through to caterpillar, chrysalis and fluttering creature. There's a bug room, where you can see giant snails, tarantulas and scorpions. Outside, there's a glasshouse, an adventure playground with a sandpit, tower and play dens, a pygmy goat enclosure and wildflower meadows with nature trails.

Bucks Goat Centre

Langley Farm, Old Risborough Road, Stoke Mandeville **t** (01296) 612983
www.bucksgoatcentre.co.uk
Getting there On the A4010 just south of Stoke Mandeville
Open Daily 10–5 (closes 4 in winter)
Adm Adults £4, children £3, under 2s **free**
Café, picnic areas, farm shop, mother and baby room, tours, disabled access, on-site parking

Dozens of breeds of goats and farm animals to groom, cuddle and feed, plus pigs, a pony, rabbits, donkeys and hens to look at for a spot of variety. For families there's a toddlers' play barn and play area, a fancy dress shop and picnic areas.

Cotswold Wildlife Park

Bradwell Grove, Burford **t** (01993) 823006
www.cotswoldwildlifepark.co.uk
Getting there Burford is about 18 miles west of Oxford, off the A40
Open Mar–Sept daily 10–6 (last entry 4.30), Oct–Feb 10–3.30
Adm Adults £9, children £6.50, under 3s **free**
Café, picnic areas, gift shop, mother and baby room, disabled access, on-site parking

These 65 hectares (160 acres) of woodland and gardens surrounding a Victorian manor house provide an idyllic environment for various creatures, including endangered species such as giant tortoises and red pandas. There are large, natural-looking enclosures for the outdoor animals, which include lions (the rare Asiatic variety), leopards, white rhinos and zebras (with raised viewing areas so little people can have a look), as well as a walk-through aviary, an aquarium, an insect house and a bat house, where you can watch bats flying beneath you from an observation platform. Kids itching to get involved can stroke the animals in the small children's farm, take a rubbing in the brass rubbing centre before hitting the adventure playground with slides and a helter-skelter. There's also a narrow-gauge railway.

★National Bird of Prey Centre

Newent **t** 0870 990 1992 **www.**nbpc.co.uk
Getting there About 12 miles west of Gloucester, signposted from the B4215, off the A40
Open Feb–Nov 10.30–5.30 (or dusk if earlier)
Adm Adults £8.50, children £5.50, under 4s **free**, family £23
Café, gift shop, guided tours, disabled access, mother and baby room, on-site parking

Perhaps the best place in the country to watch birds of prey in flight – you'll see vultures, eagles and falcons taking to the skies and flying from keeper to keeper to pick up titbits of food. Close-up, you can really get a feel for just how large and powerful these magnificent creatures are, particularly when you watch the eagles with their 2m (6ft) wingspans swooping down on to their keeper's outstretched hand, or a falcon diving

from a great height. In between the flying demonstrations, which take place at 12 noon, 2 and 4pm in summer and 12.30 and 3pm in winter, explore the centre's barn-like aviaries, housing over 80 species, and inspect the hawks, falcons and owls at close quarters. The centre organizes falcon, hawk and owl experience days when you can come and learn how to handle and fly the birds yourself (under 16s must be accompanied).

Paradise Wildlife Park

White Stubbs Lane, Broxbourne **t** (01992) 470490
www.pwpark.com
Getting there Broxbourne is about 15 miles east of St Albans, off the A10; M25 (J25) follow signs
Open Mar–Oct daily 9.30–6, Nov–Feb 10–5
Adm Adults £11, children £8, under 2s **free**
Café, picnic areas, baby changing facilities, parking

This park boasts an interesting selection of animals including camels, cheetahs, meerkats, zebras, donkeys, snow leopards, raccoons, coati and tigers. It has a play area with a slide, go-karts, a helter skelter, a 'Pirate's Cove' adventure playground and 'Paradise Lagoon', a toddler jungle, a 'Dinosaur Wood' and a woodland railway. Animal shows, flying displays and talks are also organized.

Prinknash Abbey Bird and Deer Park

Cranham **t** (01452) 812727
www.prinknash-bird-and-deerpark.com
Getting there 2.5 miles northeast of Painswick on the A46; M5 (J11a)
Open Apr–Sept 10–5, Oct–Mar 10–4
Adm Adults £5, children £3.50, under 3s **free**
Café, picnic and play area, gift shop, mother and baby room, on-site parking, disabled access

The largest pets' corner in the country, Prinknash gives children the opportunity to get up close with a variety of animals. You'll see peacocks strutting on the grassy lawns and a lake teeming with waterfowl (swans, ducks, geese) all waiting to be fed bread. You'll find yourself approached by tame fallow deer on the lookout for tasty treats – thrilling children. The park's idyllic grounds are also home to aviaries full of song birds and there's a wonderful two-storey Tudor-style Wendy house for children to play in. At the abbey itself, you can watch pottery demonstrations.

RSPB Nature Reserve

The Lodge, Patton Road, Sandy, Bedfordshire
t (01767) 680551 **www.**rspb.org.uk

Getting there Sandy is about 26 miles north of St Albans on the A1. The reserve is 1 mile east of Sandy, on the B1042 to Potton
Open Park: daily dawn–dusk; visitor centre: 10–5
Adm: Adults £3, children £1, family £6
Refreshments, picnic areas, shop, mother and baby room, disabled access, on-site parking, nature trails

RSPB headquarters with 42 hectares (104 acres) of woodland, heathland and wildlife gardens, where you can see woodpeckers, nuthatches and other woodland birds. Lots of picnic areas.

Shepreth Wildlife Park

Willersmill, Shepreth, near Royston **t** (09066) 800031 **www.**sheprethwildlifepark.co.uk
Getting there Just off the A10 between Cambridge and Royston; **Open** Daily 10–6 (or dusk in spring/winter); **Adm** Adults £7.50, children £5.50, under 2s **free**; Waterworld and Bug City additional charge: adults £1.90, children £1.30
Café, picnic areas, toy and gift shop, children's playroom, kiosk

The emphasis is wholly hands-on at Shepreth, where visitors can hand-feed goats, horses, ducks, geese and even the fish in the lake. There's also a Big Cat House with tigers, lynx and mountain lions on the prowl, a reptile house, a waterworld and bug city teeming with creepy crawlies and lots of grounds to roam around in. Children can also have fun in the toddlers' play area and adventure playground, plus there are pony rides on summer weekends and Bank Holidays.

★Whipsnade Wild Animal Park

Whipsnade, Dunstable **t** (01582) 872171
www.whipsnade.co.uk
Getting there Signposted from the M25 (J21) and the M1 (J9 and J12)
Open Mid-Feb and Oct daily 10–5, Mar–Sept 10–6, Oct–mid-Feb 10–4 (Apr–Oct Sun 10–7)
Adm Adults £13.50, children £10, family £42 (2+2 or 1+3), under-3s **free**
Café, picnic areas, shop, disabled access, mother and baby room, disabled access, on-site parking (£3.50)

It's always more rewarding looking at animals living in large enclosures that closely resemble their natural environments rather than in small, cramped cages. No wildlife park in Britain gives its animals as much space as Whipsnade which, boasts 2,400 hectares (6,000 acres) of paddocks – home to more than 2,500 animals.

There are four ways to tour Whipsnade: on foot, which can be tiring, although you will get to wander among free-roaming wallabies, peacocks and deer; by car, for which you have to pay extra; aboard the Whipsnade narrow-gauge steam railway, for which you also have to pay extra but which takes you on a tour through herds of elephants and rhinos; or, perhaps the best option, aboard the free open-top sightseeing bus, which not only offers elevated views of the animals, but can deposit you at all the best walking spots.

There are lots of animals to see, including Asian elephants, who enjoy Europe's largest elephant paddock; rare white rhinos; hippos, often as not submerged in muddy water; tigers (come at feeding time when you can see them on the prowl – a tiger that's not eating tends to be an indolent tiger); giraffes, iguanas, flamingoes, penguins, wolves and many species of birds including two delightful new hornbills named Horatio and Zazu. If the kids want to get where the action is, the World of Wings flying displays and the Sea Lion Splash Zone guarantee some up close and personal encounters. Just remember to pack a raincoat – those sea lions really do make some waves!

Wildfowl and Wetlands Trust

Slimbridge **t** (01453) 890333 **www.**wwt.org.uk
Getting there Signposted from the M5, J13 or J14, the Trust is about 13 miles south of Gloucester
Open Daily 9.30–5
Adm: Adults £6.75, children £4, family £8.50
Restaurant, café, picnic areas, shop, mother and baby room, guided tours, disabled access, parking

The Wildfowl and Wetlands Trust manages 1,600 hectares (4,000 acres) of protected wetlands across the UK. This centre at Slimbridge was the first to be set up and, thanks to a large investment of lottery cash, is still the best. You follow a zig-zagging path though a vast expanse of soggy wetlands on the hunt for the 8,000 or so waterfowl, who make the park their home at various times of the year (there are more birds here in winter than in summer). Armed with a bag of bird food, your children will no doubt have a whale of a time as flocks of ducks, swans and even flamingoes approach, demanding to be fed. There's also a Tropical House, home to a number of free-flying tropical birds hiding amongst the lush green rainforest-esque vegetation (if you're lucky you may even spot a tiny hummingbird), a new birdwatching tower offering elevated views of the park, the River Severn and a PondZone, where you can go pond-dipping for insect and amphibian life and then examine what you've found, magnified on a TV screen in the Discovery Centre. There are quiz sheets for older children.

★Woburn Safari Park
Woburn Park, Woburn **t** (01525) 290407
www.woburnsafari.co.uk
Getting there Just off the A4012, J13 from the M1
Open Mar–Oct daily 10–5 (last admission 4)
Adm Adults £8.50–£16.50, children £7.50–£13, under 3s **free**
Café, picnic areas, shop, mother and baby room, guided tours, disabled access, on-site parking

The other of Bedfordshire's two great safari parks, Woburn, about 15 miles northwest of Whipsnade, is a more avowedly commercial affair. The animals here have to work slightly harder for their money – be it the elephants being introduced to guests in the showring or sea lions leaping through hoops in the pool – and there are plenty of opportunities for kids to interact with the residents. In the walk-through aviary, they can feed cups of nectar to beautiful, multicoloured lorikeets while, at the Wild World Leisure Area, tame lemurs will take bread from their hands. Best of all, you and the kids can walk through the monkey enclosure inspecting at close quarters the assorted squirrel monkeys (while they, in turn, inspect you).

The car-based parts of your tour (the 'Safari Drive Thru') will be equally exciting, especially when you take a tour through the lion and tiger enclosures. With just the car window to separate you from the fearsome beasts, this provides an adrenaline-pumping experience for both parents and children – even if, as is usually the case, the big cats are doing nothing more aggressive than sleeping in the shade. You'll also see elephants, giraffes, hippos, bears, ostriches, camels, rhinos and penguins on your travels, all living in large enclosures. So large, in fact, that you may not always be able to see a particular enclosure's residents close-up – the bears, in particular, are masters at hiding, which makes the few glimpses you do get all the more rewarding. You can find out a bit more about the animals in the park on the My World Education Centre's computer terminals before burning up a little energy at the park's great collection of play equipment, which includes

an excellent indoor play area shaped like Noah's Ark, full of slides and ball pools; an outdoor adventure playground, the 'Tree-Tops Action Trail'; Swan Lake, where you can take rides in swan-shaped pedalos; the 'Bob-Cat' toboggan run; a 'Tiny Tots Safari' trail and a small steam railway. A full day of fun for two-thirds of what you'd pay at a theme park (even less in winter).

Farms

Bucklebury Farm Park
Bucklebury, Reading **t** (0118) 971 4002
www.buckleburyfarmpark.co.uk
Getting there Bucklebury is 10 miles west of Reading, off the A34 and 3.5 miles from the A4
Open Easter–Sept daily 10–6; Oct weekends only
Adm Adults £5.75, children £4.75, under 3s **free**, family £19
Picnic areas, disabled access, on-site parking

These 24 hectares (60 acres) of beautiful parkland provide an idyllic home to free-roaming red, fallow and Sika deer and to the animals of a small working farm (sheep, pigs, goats, rabbits, geese and poultry). There are nature trails through woodland, an indoor play area and an adventure playground with a play castle.

Cattle Country Adventure Park
Berkeley **t** (01453) 810510 **www.**cattlecountry.co.uk
Getting there 14 miles north of Bristol via the A38 and the B4509; the M5 (J13 and 14)
Open School hols, half term and Bank Hols 10–5; Jul–Aug daily 10–5
Adm Adults and children £6.50, under 2s **free**
Café, restaurant, shop, maze, play areas, farm trail

Dedicated to all things bovine, this lively farm park one mile from Berkeley Castle (p.253) is home to Herefordshire and Gloucester cattle, bison and Gloucester Old Spot pigs. Children are well provided for with indoor and outdoor adventure playgrounds containing slides, trampolines, an assault course, a paddling pool (in summer) and fun, outsized play equipment (big enough for adults to play with, too).

Cogges Manor Farm Museum
Church Lane, Witney **t** (01993) 772602
www.cogges.org
Getting there Witney is about 13 miles west of Oxford, off the A40
Open Apr–Oct Tues–Fri and Bank Hols 10.30–5.30, Sat and Sun 12 noon–5.30 (last admission 4.30pm)

Adm Adults £5.40, children £2.30, family £13.90, under 3s **free**

Café, picnic areas, mother and baby room, disabled access, on-site parking

The aim of Cogges is to provide an all-encompassing Victorian farmyard experience, so visitors can see what farm life was like before the advent of labour-saving devices that turned farming into a mass industry. Not only will you find a working Victorian farm with vintage breeds of horses, donkeys, cows and pigs, but there's also a 13th-century manor house complete with Victorian furniture, fixtures and fittings, a Victorian kitchen, a Victorian dairy and even a Victorian activities room, where children can try on Victorian costumes and play with Victorian toys and games. You can see demonstrations of Victorian cooking, washing and other servants' chores, plus there's a programme of Victorian craft and agricultural events. Even if your interest in Victorian farming isn't great, you will still enjoy the museum's riverside setting. You can picnic on the riverbanks and take walks through the adjoining woodland.

Cotswold Farm Park

Guiting Power, Stow-on-the-Wold **t** (01451) 850307
www.cotswoldfarmpark.co.uk
Getting there About 15 miles east of Cheltenham and 5 miles from the B4682 at Winchcombe
Open End Mar–early Sept daily 10.30–5, Oct Sat–Sun 10.30–5
Adm Adults £5.50, children £4.50, family £18
Café-restaurant, picnic areas, farm shop, mother and baby room, guided tours, disabled access, on-site parking

Home to more than 50 rare (and sometimes rather odd-looking) farm breeds including sheep, cows, pigs, horses and goats – look out for the 'Golden Guernsey' with its huge curved horns and long white beard. There are baby animals to cuddle and feed in the touch barn (including lambs in early summer which can be bottle-fed), a pets' corner, shearing demonstrations in summer and, all year round, you can take an audiotour of the farm entitled 'Animals through the Ages', or hop aboard a tractor for a Farm Safari ride for a game of animal bingo. There's also a well-stocked adventure playground and a tractor driving school, where children get the chance to drive mini tractors and trailers loaded with bales of hay around a mini farm.

Mead Open Farm and Rare Breeds

Stanbridge Road, Billington, Leighton Buzzard
t (01525) 852954 **www.meadopenfarm.co.uk**
Getting there Leighton Buzzard is 10 miles northeast of Aylesbury off the A418; the A5/A505
Open Daily 10–6.30
Adm Adults £5.95, children £4.95, under 2s **free**
Mother and baby room, disabled access, on-site parking

There are over 200 farm animals to meet, including cows, sheep, pigs and goats, plus a pets' corner with rabbits, guinea pigs and chipmunks. There's also a large indoor play barn, wooden outdoor play equipment and mini tractors. Fortnightly falconry displays, monthly reptile roadshows and tractor rides in summer are also fun. Regular activities include pony grooming, bottle-feeding and egg-collecting.

★ Odds Farm Park

Woburn Common, High Wycombe **t** (01628) 520188
www.oddsfarm.co.uk
Getting there About 10 miles north of Windsor and signposted from the A4, the A40 and the A355 (off the M40 J2)
Open Mid-Feb–Jul 10–5.30, Aug–early Sept 10–6, mid-Sept–Oct 10–5.30, Nov–early Feb 10–4.30
Adm Adults £6.50, children £5.50, under 2s **free**
Tearoom, gift shop, picnic area, mother and baby room, disabled access, on-site parking

Famously friendly, Odds Farm is one of the most popular farms in southern England. Although it holds the usual collection of show farm essentials – an animal handling area, a pets' corner, a play barn, an adventure playground, etc. – it's all so imaginatively presented that it's easy to see why it's considered a cut above the competition. Here, you're not expected simply to traipse around the paddocks looking at the animals, but are invited to actively involve yourself in the life of the farm. Activities for children are organized daily, many of which, such as bottle-feeding, egg-collecting and hand-milking, are farm-related – while some, such as face-painting, are not.

The signs on the paddocks are all written in child-friendly language so you can identify the unusual-looking species of cows, sheep and goats (look out for the shaggy highland cattle with their long fringes covering their eyes) and understand the role the farm plays in preserving these breeds for future generations. In summer there are demonstrations of sheep-shearing and sheepdog trials out of doors while in winter most of the animals are safely ensconced within a large, snug barn.

Of course, for the modern show farm, animal displays are no longer enough to attract the public; the play equipment must also come up to scratch and Odds Farm's certainly does. There's a barn full of hay bales, tyres and old tractors for rustic-themed play and an adventure playground with climbing equipment for more modern-style fun and games. There's a special toddlers' area, with a sandpit, mini tractors and a giant blackboard, and, once you've finished learning about farm life and being active, there are plenty of picnic tables and a teashop selling farm produce.

Standalone Farm

Wilbury Road, Letchworth Garden City
t (01462) 686775 **www**.standalonefarm.com
Getting there Letchworth Garden City is about 18 miles north of St Albans, off the A1
Open Daily 11–5
Adm Adults £4.20, children £3.20
Refreshments, picnic area, shop, disabled access, on-site parking

A 69-hectare (170-acre) working farm with pigs, sheep, horses, goats, Jersey cows, geese, ducks and chickens. There are daily milking demonstrations and children can feed the birds. The exhibition barn houses a small natural history collection and a display of small mammals. Outside there are picnic areas, a pets' corner and a children's play area. Also on-site is the Furzedown Rocking Horses workshop, where children can marvel at and play on beautifully crafted wooden toys and horses.

Thurleigh Farm Centre

Cross End, Thurleigh, Bedfordshire **t** (01234) 771597
www.thurleighfarmcentre.co.uk
Getting there 6 miles north of Bedford
Open Daily 9.30–5.30 **Adm** Adults £3.75, children £5.25
Tea shop, play centre, disabled access, on-site parking

Whatever the weather, there's lots to see and do here with sheep, ducks, geese, llamas, rabbits and guinea pigs to meet, plus pony or tractor-trailer rides. There are indoor and outdoor play centres with slides, ball pools, sand pit, swings, trampolines, pedal karts and tractors. Seasonal events include feeding the baby animals in the barn, teddy bears' picnics, Easter egg hunts, pumpkin festivals and Santa in his grotto.

Water Hall Farm

Hitchin Road, Whitwell, Hitchin **t** (01438) 871256
Getting there Off the B651 Hitchin–Whitwell road
Open Weekends and school holidays 10–5
Adm Call for prices
Tearoom, delicatessen, plant and pot shop, on-site parking, indoor and outdoor play areas

Lambs, piglets, rabbits and guinea pigs are all available to be played with at this family-run farm. Kids can also take tractor and trailer rides and have straw fights in the 'Strawbale Battlefield'. There's also a craft and plant centre.

Willows Farm Village

Coursers Road, London Colney **t** 0870 1299718
www.willowsfarmvillage.com
Getting there 3 minutes from J22 of the M25
Open Apr–Nov daily 10–5.30
Adm Jul–Oct weekends and school holidays: adults £9.95, children £8.95; weekdays: Adults £6.95, children £5.95, under 2s **free**
Café-restaurant, picnic areas, farm shop, mother and baby room, guided tours, disabled access, on-site parking

This attraction has lots of animals for children to become acquainted with, including Ben and Bella the Shire horses, pigs and, often as not, piglets, goats and chickens – the smaller ones are often available for a cuddle in the touch barn, where there's a Guinea Pig Village with more than 300 inhabitants. In the afternoon, there are usually flying demonstrations by birds of prey, such as owls and hawks, and the chance to take a 20-minute tractor tour of the farm. Regular events include sheep racing, boat rides and children's theatre productions. Don't forget there's also a tree house, playground bouncy haystacks and trampolines, plus a fairground in summer. Oh yes, and sheepdogs herding ducks...

Woodside Animal Farm and Leisure Park

Mancroft Road, Slip End, Luton **t** (01582) 841044
www.woodsidefarm.co.uk
Getting there Follow the signs from the A5 on to the B450 (J9 from the M1)
Open Apr–Sept Mon–Sat 8–6, Sun 10–6; Oct–Mar Mon–Sat 8am–5pm, Sun 10am–5pm
Adm Adults £6.95, children £5.95
Café-restaurant, mother and baby facilities, disabled access, on-site parking

Large show farm occupying a pleasant woodside setting with over 100 species of farm animal, including goats, sheep and pigs (which can be fed) and rabbits and guinea pigs (which can be cuddled). In early summer, the number of potential cuddles increases with the addition of lambs. There are lots of birds, including storks, cranes and flamingoes and kids can help collect the eggs from the hens in the hen house. Tractor-trailer rides around the complex are offered and are highly recommended; the farm is big and, if tackled on foot, you may struggle to see everything. Special events, including Easter Egg hunts, reptile encounters and magic shows, are organized throughout the year. And, if that's not enough, there are several play areas indoors and out, mini tractors, pony and trap rides, trampolines, crazy golf and bouncy castles for kids to tire themselves silly on.

On the water

Whether you want an elegant guided cruise or to navigate yourself gently downstream, you'll find the Thames and its dependent canals lined with companies offering you the chance to muck about in boats, which, as every reader of *The Wind in the Willows* knows, is the only thing worth doing. Here is a selection of possibilities:

Grand Union Canal

Grebe Canal Cruises

Pitstone Wharf, Pitstone, near Leighton Buzzard
t (01296) 661920 www.grebecanalcruises.co.uk
Open Scheduled services Apr–Oct
Fares Adults £6.20, children £3.20, family £16 (90-minute cruise)

Cruises on narrowboats along the Grand Union Canal through a series of locks into the Chilterns. Choose between a one-and-a-half-hour or a three-hour cruise – cream tea cruises available (Jul–Sept). Self-drive boats for up to 12 people can also be hired.

Leighton Lady Cruises

Brantoms Wharf, Canal Side, Linslade, Leighton Buzzard **t** (01525) 384563
www.leightonlady.freeuk.com
Open Scheduled trips Tues and Thurs 12.30 noon and 2pm throughout Aug
Fares Lunchtime one-hour cruise: adults £2.50, children £1.75; afternoon two-hour cruise: adults £4, children £2

Narrowboat cruises along the Grand Union Canal. Dinner and cream tea cruises available, plus 'Santa Specials' (weekends from mid-Dec until Christmas Eve) and private hire.

Gloucester

National Waterways Museum

Llanthony Warehouse, Gloucester Docks
t (01452) 318200 www.nwm.org.uk
Open Museum: Daily 10–5; cruises: Apr–Oct 12 noon, 1.30, 2.30 and 3.30pm
Adm Adults £6.60, children £5.25, under 5s **free**

Offers 45-minute afternoon cruises (additional charge adults £4.50, children £3.50) along the River Severn and Gloucester and Sharpness Canal aboard the museum's own sightseeing boat, the *Queen Boadicea II*. All-day cruises, noon cruises, tea cruises and disco cruises available.

Oxford

C Howard and Son

Magdalen Bridge, High Street
t (01865) 202643/761586
Open/Fares Call for times and prices

Punts and row boat hire on the River Cherwell. Season runs from Easter to September, weather permitting.

Cherwell Boathouse

Bardwell Road **t** (01865) 515978
www.cherwellboathouse.co.uk
Open/Fares Call for times and prices

Hires out punts, row boats and Canadian canoes.

Oxfordshire Narrowboats

Canal Wharf, Station Road, Lower Heyford, Bicester
t (01869) 340348 www.oxfordshire-narrowboats.co.uk
Open Summer daily 9–5.30 (winter Mon–Sat only)
Fares £110–£140 per boat per day (up to 10 persons)

Three self-drive boats for hire on the South Oxford Canal including a sweet little picnic boat.

Salter's Steamers

Folly Bridge **t** (01865) 243421
www.salterssteamers.co.uk
Open Late May–Sept daily
Fares From £15/1hr for rowboats and punts; £75/£45 day/half day, day boats; trips: various prices

Punts, rowboats and day boats for hire, plus regular steamer passenger services along the Thames. Also branches in Windsor and Reading.

Windsor

Boat tours – French Brothers Ltd

Clewer Boat House, Clewer Court Road
t (01753) 851900 **www.boat-trips.co.uk**
Open Easter–Oct for scheduled sailings;
Dec–Easter private hire only
Fares Adults £4.50, children £2.25 (40-minute trip);
adults £7, children £3.50 family £17.50–19.25 (2hr
cruise); return trip to Runnymede or Maidenhead
adults £8.70, children £4.35
40-minute sightseeing tours around Windsor's
environs, plus trips downriver to Runnymede and
Hampton Court and upriver to the villages of Bray
and Maidenhead from Windsor Promenade.
Special wildlife trips for children along the creeks
and backwaters of Windsor.
For further information *see* pp.248–9

Kris Cruisers

The Waterfront, Southlea Road, Datchet
t (01753) 543930 **www.kriscruisers.co.uk**
Open Apr–Oct 9–5.30
Fares Day boats from £25/1 hr, 12 seaters from £47/1 hr
Self-drive boats for hire just south of Windsor.

Rivertime

Whytegates House, Berries Road, Cookham,
Maidenhead **t** (01628) 780700 **www.rivertime.com**
Fares Call in advance for sailing times and prices
Hires out self-drive electric launches which seat
up to eight people or 12-seater skippered launches.

Thames Rivercruise Ltd

Pipers Island, Bridge Street, Caversham, Reading
t (0118) 948 1088 **www.thamesrivercruise.co.uk**
Open Easter–Sept; call for details of single or round
trips and sailing times
Fares 30-minute round-trip cruise: adults £4, children £3, under 4s **free**
Trips from Reading's Thameside Promenade to
Beale Bird Park at Basildon aboard a 12-seater
launch (see website for other destinations). Also
six- to 10-seater launches for hire.

Open-air museums

★Chiltern Open-Air Museum

Newland Park, Gorelands Lane, Chalfont St Giles
t (01494) 871117 **www.coam.org.uk**
Getting there 13 miles north of Windsor and
signposted from J17 of the M25

Open Apr–Oct daily 10–5 (last admission 4pm)
Adm Adults £7, children £4.50, under 5s **free**, family
£20.50; special prices apply for event days
*Café, picnic areas, gift shop, mother and baby room,
disabled access, on-site parking*
A collection of old and not-so-old farm buildings rescued from all over Buckinghamshire and
reassembled here, where they provide a fascinating insight into the rural life of centuries past.
Children always seem to connect more deeply
with history when it's presented in this sort of
living hands-on way rather than in textbooks or
lectures. There are around 25 buildings to explore,
including a Victorian farm with cows, ducks,
chickens, sheep and horses, an Iron Age house, a
tin chapel, a fully furnished 1940s prefab and
even an Edwardian lavatory. The staff (some of
whom may be in period dress) are always more
than happy to fill you in on the background
history to the exhibits and you can watch demonstrations of traditional arts and crafts such as
blacksmithery. On one of its numerous event
days, including the 'Museum Alive' summer
festival, children can dress up in period costumes
(chain-mail armour for the boys, Victorian
bonnets for the girls), listen to storytellings and
take part in a range of activities, including
puppet-making, kite-making, brick-making,
straw-plaiting and brass rubbing. In addition to
all its historic exhibits, the park has nature trails
through leafy woodland (look out for bluebells in
the spring) and an adventure playground.

Cogges Manor Farm Museum

Church Lane, Witney **t** (01993) 772602
www.cogges.org
Open Apr–Oct Tues–Fri and Bank Hols 10.30–5.30,
Sat and Sun 12 noon–5.30 (last admission 4.30)
Adm Adults £5.40, children £2.30, family £13.90,
under 3s **free**
Working Victorian farm with vintage breeds of
horses, donkeys, cows and pigs. There's also a fine
13th-century manor house to visit.
For further information *see* pp.260

Shambles Museum

Church Street, Newent **t** (01531) 822144
www.shamblesnewent.co.uk
Getting there Newent is 12 miles from Gloucester,
on the B4215
Open Mid-Mar–Oct Tues–Sun and Bank Hols 10–6
or dusk if earlier (last admission 5), Nov–Dec Sat
and Sun only 10–4

Adm Adults £4.35, children £2.75
Refreshments, shop

It seems fitting that such a pretty, unspoilt, historic-looking town should have a museum dedicated to preserving historic buildings. The Shambles is a small recreated Victorian town laid out around a central courtyard, where you can wander along cobbled streets, wend your way through narrow alleys and browse the period shops, which include a pawnbroker, a jeweller and, best of all, a toy shop. There's lots to see, so pick up a guide at the entrance, which will point you towards all the most interesting bits. It's all very charming in a twee sort of way. Once you've had your fill of looking at Victoriana, you could always eat some at the Victorian teashop.

Shuttleworth Collection

Old Warden Aerodrome, Biggleswade
t 01767 627927 **www.**shuttleworth.org
Getting there Old Warden is 6 miles southeast of Bedford off the A600 and 1 mile from the M1 just north of Junction 10
Open Apr–Oct 10–5, Nov–Mar 10–4; call in advance for details of flying days (one or two per month)
Adm Adults £8, accompanied children **free**
Restaurant, shop, disabled access

On its monthly flying days, you can see all sorts of rickety old historic aircraft taking to the skies from the traditional grass airstrip, including a model of the plane in which Louis Bleriot became the first man to fly across the English Channel in 1909 and a Spitfire. There are also numerous vintage motor vehicles and a coach room full of 19th-century horse-drawn carriages. The adjacent Old Warden Park boasts a beautiful 19th-century Swiss Garden laid out around a central lake, a falconry centre, woodland and fairytale gardens and a large children's play area.

Stockwood Craft Museum and Gardens

Farley Hill, Stockwood Country Park, Luton
t (01582) 738714
Getting there Luton is 2 miles east of J11 of the M1
Open Apr–Oct Tues–Sun 10–5, Nov–Mar Sat and Sun 10–4 **Adm Free**
Café, picnic area, shop, disabled access, mother and baby room, on-site parking

Luton's only visitor attraction of any note is this Museum dedicated to Bedfordshire rural life, the highlights of which are the beautiful period gardens (including a 17th-century knot garden), the craft courtyard and the Mossman Collection of horse-drawn vehicles. Pony and cart rides through the park are offered on weekends. Regular events during the year include craft demonstrations, music in the park and children's holiday activities.

Parks and gardens

Stowe Landscape Gardens

Buckingham **t** (01280) 818282/280
Infoline: **t** (01494) 755568
www.nationaltrust.org.uk
Getting there 3 miles west of Buckingham via Stowe Avenue, off the A422
Open Gardens: Mar–Oct Wed–Sun 10–5.30, Nov–Feb Sat–Sun 10.30–4, Dec 10–4; house: guided tours during school holidays and at weekends; call for details
Adm Garden: adults £6, children £3, family £15; house: call for tour prices
Café, picnic area, shop, mother and baby facilities, manual wheelchairs cannot be accommodated, on-site parking, free guided tours of the gardens

These 18th-century landscaped gardens are full of monuments and temples inspired by ancient Greece and Rome. There is the Temple of British Worthies, where kids can try and spot celebrities from British history, a Grotto, an Obelisk and the Congreve Monument with a monkey perched precariously on top. Maps are available to help you plan your route round the fairly extensive gardens.

Wellington Country Park

Odiham Road, Riseley, Reading **t** (0118) 932 6444
www.wellington-country-park.co.uk
Open Mar–Oct and Feb half-term daily 10–5.30 daily (in winter until 4.30) **Adm** Adults £6, children £4, family £18, under 3s **free**
Café, picnic areas, gift shop, disabled access, parking

This 142-hectare (350-acre) country park five miles south of Reading, has marked nature trails through and around meadows, woodland and lakes (row and pedal boats can be hired). For the less active, there's a miniature railway providing good views of the deer park while children are catered for with a small adventure playground, crazy golf, sand pit and animal farm. Themed events take place throughout the year and include craft sessions and seasonal activities, such as firework displays and Easter egg hunts.

★Wyld Court Rainforest

Hampstead Norreys, near Newbury **t** (01635) 202444
Infoline: **t** (01635) 200221 **www.livingrainforest.org**
Getting there 8 miles from Newbury, off the B4009; signposted from the M4 (J13)
Open Daily 10–5.15 **Adm** Adults £6, children (5–14) £4.20 (3–4) £3.30, under 3s **free**, family £17.85
Café-restaurant, picnic areas, gift shop, mother and baby facilities, guided tours, disabled access, parking

A little piece of rainforest in deepest Berkshire – here, under 1,860 sq m (20,000 sq ft) of glass, are three sweaty simulated tropical environments, 'Lowland Tropical', 'Amazonica' and 'Cloudforest', full of dense, lush rainforest vegetation. You take a jungle tour on wooden duckboards past giant ferns and palm trees, brightly coloured almost insect-looking orchids and lily ponds filled with giant 8-feet lilies, all inhabited by free-roaming creatures of the forest: bug-eyed frogs, fluttering brightly coloured butterflies, slow-moving lizards, parrots and toucans, shimmering tropical fish and even leaping, clambering squirrel monkeys. At times, with perspiration running down your neck, it can feel as if you really are lost in the jungle. There are regular talks on conservation and children's events and art workshops are organized in the summer. It has become a popular venue for children's parties. As you explore, remember to feel good about yourself. The project is operated by the Woodland Trust, a conservation charity, and all the profits of this enterprise go towards saving the real rainforests in Central and South America. So, you're not just having a good time, you're also preserving the natural world.

Steam trains

Buckinghamshire Railway Centre

Quainton Road Station, Quainton, Aylesbury
t (01296) 655450 **www.bucksrailcentre.org.uk**
Getting there The railway is 5 miles northwest of Aylesbury and signposted off the A41 and the A413
Open Apr–Oct Wed–Sun 10.30–5.30 and Bank Hols (steam trains every Sun and Wed from 11am); Mar Sat–Sun only
Fares Call in advance for details

Visitor centre, café, gift shop, picnic areas, mother and baby room, on-site parking

Anytime you visit, you'll find a whole host of vintage steam locomotives and engines to explore in the beautifully preserved Victorian station at Quainton Road, although it's probably best to come on one of the centre's special event days. These include a 'Miniature Traction Engine Rally', a 'Steam and Circus Spectacular' and a 'Grand Steam and Vintage Vehicle Show') when you can take a ride along a short length of track. The 'Days Out With Thomas' (Jun–Sept) and the Christmas steam days always prove popular when kids are joined on their journey by a jolly Santa Claus, handing out presents and mince pies as the train happily puffs along. For dads, there's a chance to live out that schoolboy dream by learning to drive a steam engine on one of their special courses.

Chinnor and Princes Risborough Railway

Aylesbury, Buckinghamshire **t** (01296) 433795, timetable **t** (01844) 353535 **www.cprra.co.uk**
Getting there Just off the B4009; 3 miles from the M4 (J6); **Open** Late Mar–Dec Sun and Bank Hols 10–5, Jun–Aug also Sat; **Fares** Adults £7.50, children £3.75, family £19.50, under 3s **free**
Refreshments, shop, disabled access, on-site parking

For families who would rather let the train take the strain, this is a lovely gentle way to enjoy the Chilterns on a seven-mile round trip from Chinnor to just outside Princes Risborough. There are lots of special events to enjoy including Easter egg hunts, teddy bear weekends and Hallowe'en trips.

Didcot Railway Centre

Didcot **t** (01235) 817200
www.didcotrailwaycentre.org.uk
Getting there 10 miles south of Oxford and signposted from J13 of the M4 and the A34 in easy reach of the M40
Open All year Sat–Sun; peak season daily, call for dates; summer: 10–5, winter: 10–4
Fares Steam days: Adults £6.50, children £5.50, family £21. Non Steam days: Adults £4, children £3, family £12
Refreshments, shop, disabled access, on-site parking

A wonderful day out for mini steam enthusiasts. Although the town's industrialized setting is hardly inspiring, you'll barely notice as you examine the 20 or so huge, shiny GWR (Great

Western Railway) locomotives in the engine shed, many of which can be boarded and explored. Kids can stand in the driver's cabin for that all-important pretending-to-drive-the-train experience – still a thrill even in today's virtual reality age. On steam days you can take train rides up and down a short length of track, watch engines being turned around on a turntable and see how mailbags are collected by a moving train or 'Travelling Post Office'. There's also a small collection of railway memorabilia, including several model trains, and the chance to see trains being repaired in the locomotive works. Railway Experience Days, Steam Days and Days Out With Thomas are also available.

★Gloucestershire and Warwickshire Railway

The Railway Station, Toddington, Winchcombe
t (01242) 621405 www.gwsr.com
Getting there Toddington is 13 miles northeast of Cheltenham on the B4632; M5 (J9)
Open Mid-Mar–Oct Sat, Sun and Bank Hols 10–5; school holidays Tues–Thurs, Sat, Sun and Bank Hols 10–5; some Christmas weekends
Fares Adults £9.50, children £6, under 5s **free**, family (2+3) £26
Refreshments, gift shop, on-site parking

Perhaps the most pleasant way to tour the Cotswolds area around Cheltenham is by taking a ride aboard one of the gently puffing steam trains of the Gloucestershire and Warwickshire Railway.

The trains run along a six-mile long stretch of track between Toddington and Winchcombe, passing over bridges, through fields and woodland and past tiny stone villages. You even get to travel through a 693-yard (633m) stretch of the dark Greet Tunnel, something, which never fails to elicit squeals of delight from youngsters. On your journey, look out for the Welsh Mountains rising in the west far away beyond the Vale of Evesham. The whole experience is hugely atmospheric with the smoke billowing from the engine funnel, the smell of engine oil and the guard in his peaked cap blowing his whistle and waving his flag to set the train in motion.

Whilst waiting for your train at Toddington, you can explore the railway's large collection of steam-powered contraptions which, in addition to the trains themselves, also include traction engines and fairground organs. If you're lucky, they may be fired up and playing happily (not to say very

noisily) when you visit. Lots of children's events are laid on throughout the year including Easter egg hunts, 'Santa Specials' and, of course, Days Out With Thomas.

Leighton Buzzard Steam Railway

Pages Park Station, Billington Road, Leighton Buzzard t (01525) 373888 www.buzzrail.co.uk
Getting there Leighton is about 10 miles northeast of Aylesbury, off the A418
Open Mar–Oct Sun; for other times call in advance
Fares Adults £6, children £3, under 2s **free**
Café, gift shop, picnic area, mother and baby room, disabled access, on-site parking

In deepest Bedfordshire the largest collection of narrow gauge locomotives in the country is regularly put through its paces along the tight curves and hard climbs of a country-roadside track. Here you can experience the English light railway as it was 80 years ago, with a wide variety of coaches and wagons in use and on display. The railway regularly organizes special events for children including fancy dress days, the September Steam-Up weekend and other seasonal activities.

Theme parks and model villages

★Bekonscot

Warwick Road, Beaconsfield t (01494) 672919 www.bekonscot.org.uk
Getting there The village is in Beaconsfield which is 2.5 miles from J2 of the M40
Open Mid-Feb–Oct daily 10–5
Adm Adults £5.90, children £3.80, family £17.50
Refreshments, shop, picnic area, on-site parking, playground, toilets, disabled facilities

The country's oldest model village, but still one of the best. First constructed in the 1930s, it's continually being added to and refined and now provides the perfect Lilliputian experience for would-be giants. Follow a set path through the village (actually six different villages), which is quite long, although there are numerous picnic spots and an adventure playground with slides, swings and a climbing castle on hand for when the urge to do finally overcomes the urge to see. A swift jaunt on the light railway might also soothe tired legs and flagging spirits. Children are invariably fascinated by this miniature world – the tiny thatched cottages, churches and schools; the tiny zoo complete with miniscule animals, the tiny harbour with its tiny colourful sailing boats and the model train that wends its intermittent way through the site – while parents will relish the corny names on all the shops. The 'burning' cottage is a particular favourite, as is the fairground with its carousels and helter-skelter. See if you can spot the carp in the brook that trickles over the model water wheel.

Gulliver's Land

Livingstone Drive, Newlands, Milton Keynes
t (01925) 444888 www.gulliversfun.co.uk
Getting there The theme park is signposted from J14 of the M1
Open Apr–mid-Sept 10.30–5; Oct half term 10.30–5. For special Christmas events call in advance
Adm Adults £10.99, children under 1m (3ft) **free**
Café-restaurant, fast food, shop, picnic areas, mother and baby room, on-site parking

Small theme park where the rides, attractions, shows and food are aimed at 3–13-year-olds and which boasts a child-size entrance fee (£10.99), half of what you'd pay at the bigger-name parks. There are several gentle-ish rides, including a log coaster, a log flume plus themed areas – Adventureland, where you can take a Jungle River Ride; Discovery Bay, which has pump carts; Toy Land, which boasts a soft play area for toddlers; and Lilliput Land Castle, the park's centrepiece. The zippy Python is a welcome addition for more adventurous mini types.

★Legoland

Winkfield Road, Windsor t 08705 040404
www.legoland.co.uk
Getting there 2 miles from Windsor on the Windsor to Ascot Road, signposted from J6 of the M4. The shuttle bus service from Windsor town centre to Legoland departs from Thames Street every 15 minutes during opening times
Open 10–6 **Adm** Adults £30, children £23; 2-day ticket: adults £57, children £45

Themed on the famous plastic building bricks, this popular fun park is filled with gentle rides and activity centres. Best for under 10s.
For further information *see p.249*

Can you spot?
The Lego model of St George fighting a dragon. It's located outside the Dragon Knight's Castle.

Wide open spaces

The Chilterns

A sweep of rolling hills stretching across southern Buckinghamshire and beyond, the Chilterns are 30 miles from London and are justly designated an area of outstanding natural beauty (AONB). Throughout the year they attract hordes of walkers, who come to tackle undemanding (indeed, child-friendly) summits, admire the views and explore the various pretty villages – like Thames-side Marlow and Hambleden and the National Trust-owned West Wycombe – that dot the area. The region also boasts several grand landscaped parks, such as the 120-hectare (300-acre) **West Wycombe Park** and **Cliveden**, with its geometric topiary and mazes, not to mention plenty of child-orientated attractions, notably **Whipsnade Wild Animal Park** (p.258); Bekonscot Model Village (the oldest model village in the country); **Odds Farm Park** (pp.260–1), one of the best family farms around; and the **Hell Fire Caves**, a network of natural caves deep beneath West Wycombe Hill. Picnicking families will find sites at Ash Grove, off the A413 west of Old Amersham, Whielden Gate, off the A404 Amersham to Hazlemere Road and at Hodgemoor Woods, between Coleshill and Chalfont St Giles, where there are many picnic areas, forest walks and parking facilities.

Ashridge Estate

Ringhall, Berkhamstead, Herts t (01442) 851227
www.nationaltrust.org.uk
Getting there Just off the B4506, take the M1 (J8/J9) or from the A41 turn off at Tring
Visitor centre Open mid-Mar–Dec Mon–Sun 12–5; monument: open mid-Mar–Oct Sat and Sun 12–5
Adm Monument: £1.30, children 60p
Refreshments, gift shop, on-site parking

This grand area of woodland (18,200ha/4,500 acres) takes in the famous Ivinghoe Beacon, one of the most popular walking spots in the region. The monument is more than 700 ft (230m) tall and on a clear day it is possible to see eight counties from the top. It was once the site of an

Admiralty Beacon – part of a chain between London and the coast lit to warn the capital of potential invaders. Workshops and activity days.

Bluebell Woods

Getting there From J5 of the M40 at Stokenchurch, follow the signs to Christmas Common. It is 5 miles from the turning for the A40, just off the B481 between Stokenchurch and Watlington **Adm Free** *Not suitable for pushchairs, car park*

Bluebell Woods is the site of the Chiltern Sculpture Trail run by the Forestry Commission, a continually changing display of modern, nature-themed art. There is a signposted walk and you can occasionally see the artists at work on their sculptures in the beech wood. Take a pair of wellies.

Cliveden

Taplow, Maidenhead, Buckinghamshire SL6 0JA, **t** 01628 605069
Open Gardens/woodlands Mid Mar–Oct 11–6, Oct–Feb 11–4
Getting there 2ml N of Taplow; leave M4 at exit 7 onto A4, or M40 at exit 4 onto A404 to Marlow and follow brown signs. Entrance by main gates opposite Feathers Inn **Adm** Grounds adults £7.50, children £3.70, family £18.70, woodlands adults £3, children £1.50, family £7.50

Coombe Hill

Getting there Just off the A413 **Adm Free**

At 260m (850ft), this is the highest peak in the Chilterns (by way of comparison, it's only slightly taller than Canary Wharf) and provides good panoramic views and perfect kite-flying conditions. The nearby village of Wendover, with its woodland nature trails and collection of cafés and teashops, provides the perfect base camp for your explorations of the hill.

Country parks

There are numerous country parks nestling on the Chiltern slopes, including the 200-hectare (500-acre) **Black Park Country Park** (off the A412 between Slough and Denham), which boasts untamed woodland, heathland and lakeside walks; the slightly more formal 50-hectare (130-acre) **Langley Park** (off the A412 between Slough and Denham) with its rhododendron garden and arboretum; the watery **Denham Country Park** (off the A40), which surrounds the Misbourne and Colne rivers and Grand Union Canal (it has a children's playground); and, perhaps the most

famous of all, **Burnham Beeches** (off the A355 between Slough and Beaconsfield), a National Nature Reserve made up of dense beechwood forest and inhabited by colonies of free-roaming deer that has provided the location for numerous films including *Robin Hood, Prince of Thieves*.

Dunstable Downs

Dunstable Downs Countryside Centre, Whipsnade Road, Kensworth **t** (01582) 608489
Getting there Between the B4540 and the B4541 Dunstable–Whipsnade road
Open Countryside Centre: Apr–Oct daily 10–5, Nov–Mar Sat and Sun 10–4 **Adm Free**
Picnic areas, mother and baby room, parking, kiosk

Large open area of countryside just east of London and north of Whipsnade that marks the very northern tip of the Chilterns. There are lots of good walks and viewing spots (this is the highest spot in Bedfordshire – you can see right over the Vale of Aylesbury) among the rolling grasslands, plus the remains of a Bronze Age burial site, 'Five Knolls'. On most weekends, you should be able to see groups of kite-flyers clustered on the highest peaks, plus daredevil hang-gliders taking advantage of the perfect thermal soaring conditions.

Hell Fire Caves

West Wycombe Park, High Wycombe
t (01494) 533739 **www**.hellfirecaves.co.uk
Open Mar–Oct daily 11–5.30, Nov–Feb Sat–Sun 11–5.30 **Adm** Adults £4, children £3, family £12
Café, on-site parking

These natural caves were extended in the 18th century at the behest of Sir Francis Dashwood (according to legend, they provided a suitably secret venue for the wildly debauched parties of his notorius Hell Fire Club) and now stretch a third of a mile beneath West Wycombe Hill. With their huge flinty entrance and collection of weird and wonderful tableaux and models, they provide the perfect venue for an afternoon of spooky exploration.

The Ridgeway Path

Claimed to be the oldest path in Britain, the Ridgeway may have been in use for over 5,000 years, although it's difficult to know for sure. It runs from Overton Hill in Wiltshire to Ivinghoe Beacon in Buckinghamshire, taking in the Chilterns and Coombe Hill on the way.

The Thames Path

The section of this 180-mile long route that passes through the Chilterns is mostly flat walking and takes in the scenic villages of Hambleden and Marlow. You can also hire boats for trips along the river (pp.248–9).

West Wycombe Park

West Wycombe, Buckinghamshire HP14 3AJ **t** 01494 513569

getting there 2ml W of High Wycombe. At W end of West Wycombe, S of the Oxford road (A40)
Open Grounds Apr–May 2–6; House/grounds Jun–Aug 2–6 **Adm** adults £6, child £3, family £15. Groups £4.70. Grounds only: £3, child £1.50. Reduced rate when arriving by public transport

Forest of Dean

Tourist Information, Coleford, Royal Forest of Dean **t** (01594) 812388 **www.fweb.org.uk/dean**
Getting there 3 miles southeast of Symonds Yat and signposted from the M5 (Gloucester), and the M4/M48 (Chepstow)

With its lush green landscape of thick oak, pine and beech woodland, wild heathland, tame pasture, hills, gorges, streams and ponds, the forest feels timeless and serene. This is no primeval wilderness, however. The Forest of Dean has spent the last 2,000 years struggling to exist. Exploited for its valuable supplies of iron, charcoal and timber since Roman times, it is scarred with pits, soil heaps, abandoned train tracks and the remains of mines and has required much replenishing over the centuries to bring about its current state of good health. Despite being designated a Royal Forest by William the Conqueror, by the mid-16th century so many trees had been cut down for use in the European shipbuilding industry that the forest was in danger of disappearing altogether. Henry VIII ordered its replanting, while Charles II oversaw the dismantling of the forest's iron mines. By the mid-19th century, however, the forest's oak stocks still hadn't fully recovered prompting the government to order the planting of some 30 million acorns. Miraculously, the forest is still here and the thousands of visitors who explore its leafy depths each year are very thankful that it is.

This is one of the most user-friendly forests in the country with lots of well-marked nature trails traversing its 42 sq mile (110 sq km) area. To get a feel for the place, learn a little of its history and pick up some maps, pop along to the **Dean Heritage Centre** in Soudley, where you'll find a Victorian cottage with a millpond and displays on the people who still make their living from the forest, as well as an adventure playground, farm animals, a blacksmith's miner's cottage, a beam engine, pottery and café.

As you wander along admiring the broad-leafed trees and carpets of wild flowers, look out for evidence of the forest's industrial past – the slag heaps and mine shafts now thankfully almost entirely reclaimed by the forest. One of the most visited sites in the forest is the former iron mine near Coleford known as the **Clearwell Caves**. You can take a tour through nine dark, damp and surprisingly large caverns to look at the bizarre underground rock formations and take part in art workshops using the natural ochres produced here. The oxidized iron ore in the cave wall gives them a reddish hue. Deep-level visits right into the bowels of the caves can also be arranged for groups. You can compare and contrast these caves with the narrower, wood-lined tunnels of the **Hopewell Colliery** in Cannop which is also open for tours. To further acquaint yourself with the forest, take a ride on the Dean Forest Railway through the hilly woodland.

Clearwell Caves

Near Coleford **t** (01594) 832535
www.clearwellcaves.com
Getting there 1.5 miles south of Coleford, off the B4228
Open Mar–Oct 10–5 (special opening Advent (1–24 Dec) and Feb half term 10–5)
Adm Adults £4.50, children £2.80, family £12.90
Café, picnic areas, mother and baby room, guided tours, on-site parking

Dean Forest Railway

Norchard, Forest Road, Lydney, **t** 01594 845 840
www.deanforestrailway.co.uk
Open daily for visiting (call in advance for days when trains are running); **Adm** steam day pass adult £8, children £5, entry free on non steam days

Dean Heritage Centre

Camp Mill, Soudley, Cinderford **t** (01594) 822170
www.deanheritagemuseum.com
Getting there In Cinderford, 6 miles east of Symonds Yat on the A4151
Open Apr–Sept daily 10–6, Oct–Dec 10–4, Jan–Mar 11–4

Adm Adults £4.50, children £2.50, family (2+4) £13
Café-restaurant, picnic areas, shop, mother and baby room, tours, disabled access, parking, craft workshops, seasonal events

Forest of Dean Sculpture Trail

Beechenhurst Lodge, Cinderford **t** (01594) 833057
www.forestofdean-sculpture.org.uk
Getting there The trail starts at Beechenhurst Lodge, just off the B4226
Open All year, dawn–dusk; Beechenhurst Lodge: Apr–Oct 10–6, Nov–Mar 10–5
Adm Free (parking £2)
Café-restaurant, picnic areas, shop, mother and baby room, disabled access, on-site parking

Perhaps the most popular walk in the whole forest is this sculpture trail of Andy Goldsworthy-esque nature-into-art creations, including a huge chair made of tree trunks sitting on a hill, a dome made of charred larch and a grove of silence – wooden signs hanging from the branches proclaim the word 'silence' in many different languages. Stop here for a while to contemplate the gentle sounds of the forest.

Hopewell Colliery Museum

Speech House Road, near Cannop **t** (01594) 810706
Getting there Off the B4226
Open Mar–Oct daily 10–4
Adm Adults £3, children £2
Café, shop, disabled access

Puzzle Wood

t (01594) 833187
Getting there 1 mile south of Coleford on the B4228
Open Easter–Oct Tues–Sun 11–6 (and Bank Hols)
Roman iron mines, shop, tea garden

A maze of woodland walks surrounding some very interesting iron workings; lots of fun and well worth a visit.

Westonbirt Arboretum

Tetbury **t** (01666) 880220
Getting there Leave the M4 at J18 and travel north up the A46, then take the A433 to Tetbury
Open Daily 9–8 (or dusk)
Adm Adults £6.50 (£5 in winter), children £1, under 5s **free**, family £12.50
Café, picnic areas, mother and baby room, disabled access, on-site parking

Miles of beautiful tree-lined paths, perfect for buggies. The arboretum is stunning in autumn.

SPORT AND ACTIVITIES

Activity centres

Forest Adventure Ltd

5 Brummels Drive, Christchurch, Coleford
t (01594) 834661 www.forestadventure.co.uk
Getting there Coleford is 4 miles south of Symonds Yat on the B4228
Open Call in advance for details of times and prices

Rock-climbing, archery, canoeing, kayaking, caving, abseiling, mountain-biking for all ages.

Bicycle hire

Cotswold Country Cycles Bicycle Hire

Longlands Farm Cottage, Chipping Camden
t (01386) 438706 www.cotswoldcountrycycles.com
Getting there Chipping Camden is about 18 miles east of Camden on the B4035
Open 9.30am–dusk
Hire Family (2+2) £35 per day for 4 bikes, cycles £12

Stocks adult bikes, children's bikes, tag-a-longs and panniers; cycle routes through Cotswolds.

Pedalabikeaway

Cannop Valley, Forest of Dean **t** (01594) 860065
Getting there Coleford is 4 miles south of Symonds Yat on the B4228/B4234
Open Apr–Oct Tues–Sun 9–6; Jul–Aug and school hols daily 9–6; Nov–Mar Sat and Sun 9–6
Adm Call in advance for details of prices

Hires out mountain bikes, children's bikes, trikes, tandems, kiddy seats and tag-a-longs.

Boat hire

For information on boat hire *see* pp.248–9

Horse-riding

Backnoe End Equestrian Centre

Keysoe Road, Thurleigh **t** (01234) 772263
Getting there Thurleigh is 2 miles north of Bedford, off the B660
Open Call in advance for opening times and prices

Bourton Vale Equestrian Centre

Fosse Way, Bourton-on-the-Water **t** (01451) 821101
Getting there Off the A429
Open Tues, Thurs and Sat for hacking, lessons; call in advance for details of prices

From age four upwards.

Checkendon Equestrian Centre

Lovegrove's Lane, Checkendon, Reading
t (01491) 680225 www.checkendon.f9.co.uk

Getting there Between Reading and Oxford off the A4074
Open/Adm Call in advance for times and prices
Hacking in the Oxfordshire countryside.

Hill Farm Riding School
Bedford Road, Wilden **t** (01234) 771283
Getting there Wilden is close to Great Barford, 4 miles northeast of Bedford and off the B660
Open/Adm Call in advance for times and prices

Littledean Riding Centre
Wellington Farm, Sutton Road, Littledean, Forest of Dean, near Cinderford **t** (01594) 823955
Getting there Cinderford is about 7 miles east of Symonds Yat, the centre is east of Cinderford on the A4151
Open/Adm Call in advance for times and prices
Trails and hacks through the Forest of Dean; ages from four and upwards.

Old Manor Horse Riding Stable
North Hinksey Lane, North Hinksey, Oxford **t** (01865) 242274
Getting there North Hinksey is on the western edge of Oxford, off the A34
Open/Adm Tues–Sun; call for lessons and prices
Riding for ages six and upwards.

Oxford Riding School
Watlington Road, Garsington, Oxford **t** (01865) 361383 www.ridingschooloxford.com
Getting there Garsington is about 3 miles south-east of Oxford off the B480
Open/Adm Call in advance for times and prices
Riding recommended for ages from six.

Ice-skating and skiing

John Nike Leisuresport Complex
Amen Corner, John Nike Way, Bracknell, Berkshire **t** (01344) 789000 www.bracknellskislope.co.uk
Getting there Bracknell is about 15 miles north of Guildford, off the A322
Open 8am–10pm (session times may vary)
Adm Call in advance for prices
Café, baby changing facilities, disabled facilities and parking.
Olympic-size ice rink, 150m (492ft) dry ski slope and snowbobbing sledges; boarding, blading and skiing lessons are available.

XScape Snozone
602 Marlborough Gate, Milton Keynes, Buckinghamshire **t** 0871 2225670 www.xscape.co.uk

Open Daily 9am–11pm
Adm Adults from £16/hr, children from £13/hr
Indoor ski centre with three slopes, nursery, general and slalom, as well as ski lift. Children must be able to snow-plough and turn to be allowed on the slopes. Lessons and toboggans or bobs for under 3s. Also a 16-screen cinema complex, a bowling alley, a climbing zone, indoor sky-diving, shops, several cafés and restaurants.

Indoor play areas

Fantasy World
Northway House, York Road, Newbury **t** (01635) 580434
Open Mon–Sat 9.30–7, Sun 10–6
Adm Call in advance for prices
Baby changing facilities, disabled facilities, café
Aerial runways, twist slide, rope swings, haunted house and ball pools.

Funtasia
9–15 Warwick Road, Banbury **t** (01295) 250866
Open Term time: Mon–Fri 3–6, Sat and Sun 10–5; school hols: Tues–Sun 10–6
Adm Call for details of prices
Refreshments, baby changing facilities, disabled access, on-site parking
Indoor adventure playground with climbing maze, drop slide, biff-bash bags, rope swings, trapeze bars and inflatable obstacle pirate ship.

Snakes and Ladders
448 Perth Avenue, Slough **t** (01753) 694090 www.snakes-and-ladders.com
Open 10–6 (last admission 5.15)
Adm Before 4.30pm: over 5s £5.50, under 5s £4.50, under 2s 3£.50; after £4.30pm: over 5s £4.50, under 5s £3.50, under 2s £2.50;
Three separate play zones: a toddler area for under 3s, a soft play area (2–5) and an adventure playground (3 up). Ball pools, slides and climbing.

Indoor skydiving

Airkix
Xscape, 602 Marlborough Gate, Milton Keynes **t** 0845 3316549 www.airkix.com
Open Mon–Fri 11–10, Sat, Sun and school hols 8–10
Adm Call in advance for prices
Fancy experiencing the feeling of flying without having to leap from an aircraft? Then this is the place to go. Introductory flights start at £34 and family flight sessions (up to 5 family members) are from £151.99. Not suitable for under 5s.

Leisure centres

Aqua Vale Swimming and Fitness Centre

Vale Park, Park Street, Aylesbury **t** (01296) 488555
www.aquavale.com
Open Mon–Fri 9.30am–10pm, Sat–Sun
8.30am–10pm **Adm** Call for prices
Baby changing, disabled facilities, café
Indoor leisure complex with flumes, 'lazy river',
Jacuzzis, spa pools and a baby pool, plus a 25m
(82ft) sports pool and a 20m (66ft) outdoor pool.

Bourton Mill Waterworld

Engaine Drive, Shenley **t** (01908) 503344
www.bourtonmill.net
Open Daily 7am–10pm (morning lessons); fun
sessions Sat–Sun 11.30am–6pm
Adm Call for prices
Baby changing, disabled facilities, refreshments
A 25m (82ft) main pool with two flumes, a
wave machine and rapids, as well as a baby pool

Coral Reef Water World

Nine Mile Road, Bracknell **t** (01344) 862525
Open/Adm Call for times and prices
Flumes, rapids and a pirate boat as well as a
toddlers' pool.

North Herts Leisure Centre

Baldock Road, Letchworth **t** (01462) 679311
Open/Adm Call for times and prices
*Disabled access and facilities including pool ramp,
baby changing facilities, café*
Leisure pool with wave machine and flumes, as
well as a baby pool for younger visitors.

Oasis Beach Pool

Cardington Road, Bedford **t** (01234) 272100
Open/Adm Call for times and prices
*Disabled access and facilities, baby changing,
café, sauna and gym.*
Large leisure pool with giant waterslides, wave
machine, heated outdoor section, 'lazy-river ride',
'open-air river ride', spa baths and toddlers' pool.

Rivermead Leisure Complex

Richfield Avenue, Reading **t** (0118) 901 5000
Open/Adm Call for times and prices
Café, disabled access, on-site parking
Lagoon pool with wave machine, slides and
beach area, as well as a crèche and a play park.

Willen Lake

Willen Lake, Milton Keynes **t** (01908) 691630
www.whitecap.co.uk
Open/Adm Call for times and prices

Sailing, windsurfing and boating for all ages.

Windsor Leisure Centre

Clewer Mead, Stovell Road, Windsor
t (01753) 850004
Open/Adm Call for times and prices
Leisure pool with wave machine, giant slides,
wild water creek, water cannons, fountains, playzone, parent and toddler sessions and crèche.

Wycombe Sports Centre

Marlow Hill, High Wycombe **t** (01494) 688100
www.wll.co.uk
Open Mon–Fri 6.30am–10.30pm, Sat–Sun 8.30–7.30
Adm Call for prices
Café, disabled access
Heated 50m (164ft) pool (divided into two 25m
(82ft) pools at peak times), teaching pool, outdoor
pool, soft play centre 'Moonbase' (11 and unders).

Outdoor pools

Abbey Meadow Open Air Pool

Abbey Meadow, Abbey Close, Abingdon, Oxon
t (01235) 530678 www.soll-leisure.co.uk
Open/Adm Call in advance for times and prices

Chipping Norton Outdoor Pool

Fox Close, Chipping Norton **t** (01608) 643188
www.chippylido.co.uk
Open Apr–Aug Mon–Fri 4–6.30pm, Sat–Sun 12
noon–7.30 **Adm** Adult £2.80–4, children
£1.80–2.50, family £9–11.50

Letchworth Open Air Pool

Norton Common, Letchworth **t** (01462) 684673
Open May–early Sept Mon–Fri 8–6.30, Sat–Sun
8.30–6.30 **Adm** Call in advance for prices.
Heated 50m (164ft) pool, paddling pool, sun-
bathing areas.

Wolverton Pool

Aylesbury Street West, Wolverton, Milton Keynes
t (01908) 312091
Open Call in advance for opening times
Adm Adults £3.25, children £1.75,
Open-air pool during the summer months.

Quad-biking

Chepstow Quad Trekking Centre

Sedbury, Chepstow **t** 0870 6094439
www.chepstowoutdooractivities.co.uk
Getting there The centre is 1 mile outside
Chepstow, on the Chepstow–Gloucester Road
Open Easter–Oct (weather permitting)
Adm £25 per hour

Countryside trekking on quad-bikes.

Roller-skating

Windsor Roller Rink

Alexandra Gardens, Windsor **t** (01753) 830220

Open Call in advance for opening times and prices
Roller rink with skate and accessory hire. Also bikes for hire by the half day, day and week.

Summer camps

Camp Beaumont

Bishopsgate School, Windsor **t** (01263) 823000
www.campbeaumont.com

Open/Adm Call in advance for times and prices
Multi-activity day camp for 3–15-year-olds, with 50 creative and fun activities such as horse-riding, swimming, football, motorsports and tennis.

Musical holidays

Home Croft, Sun Lane, Harpenden
t (01582) 460978 **www.musicale.co.uk**

Open Call in advance for opening times and prices
Holiday music courses for children of all ages and abilities held at the Dragon School, Oxford.

Watersports

Bray Lake

Maidenhead **t** (01628) 638860 **www.braylake.com**

Open Call in advance for opening times and prices
Wind-surfing, dinghy sailing, canoeing and power-boating.

Cotswold Water Park and Keynes Country Park

Spratsgate Lane, Cirencester **t** (01285) 861459
www.waterpark.org

Open Daily 9am–9pm; beach: Jun–Sept 1–5
Adm Free but hire equipment is individually priced
Café, shop, picnic areas, mother and baby room, guided tours, disabled access, on-site parking
Wind-surfing, jetskiing, sailing, canoeing, camping, birdwatching, fishing, cycling, horse-riding and kayaking at Britain's largest water park. Also play area with fort and diggers, play beach and adventure zone in school holidays.

Stewartby Watersports Club

PO Box 369, Bedford **t** (01234) 767751
www.stewartby.org.uk

Open/Adm Call in advance for times and prices
Wind-surfing, water-skiing and sailing available on the largest expanse of water in Bedfordshire.

Cinemas

Cheltenham

Cineworld Oxford Passage **t** 0871 2008000
www.cineworld.co.uk
Odeon Winchcombe Street **t** 0871 2244007
www.odeon.co.uk

Cirencester

Regal Cinema Lewis Lane **t** (01285) 658755

Gloucester

Cineworld The Peel Centre, St Anns Way, Bristol Road **t** 0871 2002000 **www.cineworld.co.uk**

Hatfield

UCI The Galleria **t** 0871 2244007 **www.uci-cinemas.co.uk**

Luton

Cineworld The Galaxy, Bridge Street **t** 0871 2208000
www.cineworld.co.uk

Milton Keynes

Cineworld Xscape, 602 Marlborough Gate, Avebury Boulevard **t** 0871 220 8000 **www.cineworld.co.uk**
Odeon Midsummer Boulevard
t 0870 2244007 **www.odeon.co.uk**

Oxford

Odeon George Street **t** 0871 2244007
www.odeon.co.uk
Odeon Magdalen Street **t** 0871 2244007
www.odeon.co.uk
Phoenix Picture House Walton Street
t (01865) 554909 **www.picturehouse-cinemas.co.uk**
Vue Ozone Leisure Park **t** 0871 2240240
www.myvue.com

Reading

Film Theatre Whiteknights **t** (0118) 3787151
www.readingfilmtheatre.co.uk
Showcase Cinemas Loddon Road **t** 0871 220100
www.showcasecinemas.co.uk
Vue The Oracle **t** 0871 2240240 **www.myvue.com**

Museums, galleries and science centres

Banbury Museum

Spiceball Park Road, Banbury **t** (01295) 259855
Open Mon–Sat 9.30–5
Adm Free
Shop, café
A hands-on museum focusing on the local area with displays on costumes, Victorian toys

as well as temporary exhibitions, most of which are aimed at schools and families. Children's events are held throughout the year, such as treasure hunt trails, art workshops and design competitions. Adjacent to the museum is Tooley's Boatyard (adults £5.50, children £3.25, under 5s free) where visitors can take part in a tour of a working dock and enjoy a 1-hour boat trip. Tours available (Easter–Sept Sat 3pm).

Gloucester City Museum and Art Gallery
Brunswick Road t (01452) 524131
Open Tues–Sat 10–5 **Adm Free**
   Roman relics, Saxon remains and dinosaurs, hands-on exhibits and touch-screen displays. Programme of inventive workshops and events throughout the year.
For further information *see p.242*

Gloucester Folk Museum
99–103 Westgate Street t (01452) 396868
Open Tues–Sat 10–5 **Adm Free**
   Artefacts and displays about local history (farming, Severn fishing and Gloucester parks). Toy gallery.
For further information *see p.242*

House of the Tailor of Gloucester
9 College Court t (01452) 422856
Open Apr–Oct 10–5, Nov–Mar 10–4 **Adm Free**
Please note: This attraction has been closed, but is due to reopen early in 2007; call for details
   Visit the House of the Tailor of Gloucester (just north of the cathedral) and a Beatrix Potter museum and shop containing dioramas showing scenes from her books.
For further information *see p.243*

★Look Out Discovery Centre
Nine Mile Ride, Bracknell
t (01344) 354400 www.bracknell-forest.gov.uk
Getting there Bracknell is 15 miles northwest of Guildford, off the A322
Open Daily 10–5 **Adm** Adults £5.20, children £3.45, under 4s free, family £13.85, parent and toddler £4.20 (term-time only). Entry half price after 4pm
Café, gift shop, picnic areas, children's play area, tourist information centre, mother and baby room, disabled access, on-site parking
   Superb hands-on science exhibition with over 70 interactive experiments arranged into five themed zones: 'Light and Colour', 'Woodland and Wildlife', 'Forces and Movement', 'Sound and

Music' and 'Body and Perception'. Due to its resounding success, aspects of the centre are currently being enhanced. New developments include a water zone in Woodland and Wildlife, where you can swim under the sea and get up close to an ant colony, and a wormery. Visitors can also make their own Hollywood movies, peer inside an atom or make exciting science discoveries via the centre's regular 30-minute interactive shows. Everything is rendered in brightly coloured plastic and there are helpers on hand to explain the science behind your experiments in easy-to-understand child-friendly terms. Surrounded by 1,050 hectares (2,600 acres) of Crown Estate woodland, you could spend a whole day here. There's also a collection of outdoor play apparatus, including several large plastic mushrooms just outside the centre, and you can hire mountain bikes and safety helmets for rides on a bike trail through the woods – although, be warned, the course is quite tricky with lots of steep hills.

Museum of the History of Science
Old Ashmolean Building, Broad Street
t (01865) 277280 www.mhs.ox.ac.uk
Open Tues–Sat 12 noon–4, Sun 2–5 **Adm Free**
   Sundials, quadrants, microscopes and telescopes.
For further information *see p.245*

Museum of St Albans
Hatfield Road, t (01727) 819340
www.stalbansmuseums.org.uk
Open Mon–Sat 10–5, Sun 2–5 **Adm Free**
   The story of St Albans from Roman times to the present day. Trade and craft tools exhibition.
For further information *see p.247*

★National Waterways Museum
Llanthony Warehouse, Gloucester Docks
t (01452) 318200 www.nwm.org.uk
Open Museum: Daily 10–5; cruises: Apr–Oct 12 noon, 1.30, 2.30 and 3.30pm
Adm Adults £6.60, children £5.25, under 5s free
   Three floors of interactive exhibits and audiovisual displays designed to bring the history of the country's canals and docks to life.
For further information *see p.243*

★The Oxford Story
6 Broad Street t (01865) 728822
Open Jan–Jun and Sept–Dec Mon–Sat 10–4.30, Sun 11–4; Jul–Aug daily 9.30–5

Adm Adults £7.25, children £5.25

Three floors of tableaux depicting scenes from the city's long history with sound and lighting effects for added effect.

For further information *see* p.245

Pitt Rivers Museum

Parks Road **t** (01865) 270927, **www.prm.ox.ac.uk**
Open Daily 12–4.30 **Adm Free**

Large ethnographic collection of artefacts brought back by Captain Cook from his journeys of discovery.

For further information *see* pp.245–6

★Roald Dahl Gallery

Buckinghamshire County Museum, Church Street, Aylesbury **t** (01296) 331441
Open Main museum: Mon–Sat and Bank Hols 10–5, Sun 2–5; Roald Dahl gallery: school holidays and Bank Hols Mon–Fri 10–5, Sat 10–5, Sun 2–5; term-time Mon–Fri 3–5
Adm Adults and children £3.50, under 3s **free**
Café, shop, garden, information point; no pushchairs allowed

There is only one contender for the title of 'all-time children's literature champ' – Roald Dahl, author of such classics as *James and the Giant Peach*, *George's Marvellous Medicine*, *The Witches*, *The BFG*, *Charlie and the Chocolate Factory*, *Danny Champion of the World* and *The Fantastic Mr Fox*. No other author has offered children such a pleasingly subversive view of the world or been as ruthlessly unsympathetic in his portrayal of adults and no other writer has created such a memorable collection of disparate characters loved by generations of children. Dahl spent most of his life (and wrote most of his books) in Buckinghamshire, prompting the county council to create this small hands-on gallery themed on the characters from his books. It's a colourful, lively affair decorated throughout with cut-outs of Quentin Blake's famous illustrations. As you enter, you pass the multicoloured Great Glass Elevator, which will shoot you up into the stars (or, at least, to the next floor) while inside is an imaginative, slightly subversive (hip replacement door handles, labels written in mirror writing) array of games and experiments fully in keeping with the imaginative and quirky nature of the books. You and the kids can tick off the settings and characters from the books together. There's the Giant Peach with the centipede, the ladybird and all the other friendly bugs living inside (which you can examine through microscopes and magnifying glasses); the Fantastic Mr Fox's Tunnel, which you can crawl along, and Miss Catchpole's cupboard. Everywhere you go there are things to press, holes to peer through and games to play. Try the shadow-making machine, create your own jewellery and watch optical trickery demonstrations by Willie Wonka himself. Your visit will be on a timed ticket giving you just one hour to explore the gallery, so it's best to whizz through. If ever there was an attraction designed to get kids away from their Playstations and Gameboys and back to reading, this is it. The gallery is inside the grounds of the Buckinghamshire County Museum, which has improved shop and café facilities. Additions to the museum include a collections showcase featuring a rotating display of the museum's social, historical and archaeological artefacts plus a recreated 18th-century Georgian Room.

Roald Dahl Museum and Story Gallery

81–3 High Street, Great Missenden, Bucks **t** (01494) 892192 **www.roalddahlmuseum.org**
Open Tue–Sun 10–5
Adm Adults £4.95, children £3.50, under 5s **free, family (2+3) £16**
Shop, disabled access, café

Opened in 2005, this attraction is split into two sections. The first is a gallery area with permanent displays on Roald Dahl's life and work, as well some fun temporary exhibitions, and the second is an interactive area on the process of creative writing (suitable for 7–13-year-olds). Enter a reconstruction of the hut in which Dahl wrote his famous stories and learn how to tap into your own creative side. Finish your trip off with a tasty Bogstrotter Chocolate Cake or a Snozzcumber Sandwich at the attached Café Twit.

Soldiers of Gloucestershire

Custom House, Gloucester Docks **t** (01452) 522682 **www.glosters.org.uk**
Open Tues–Sun 10–5 (Jun–Sept daily)
Adm Adults £4.25, children £2.25, under 5s **free, family £13**

Interactive military settings (recreated First World War trenches and expeditions).

For further information *see* p.243

★*Verulamium* Museum and Park

t (01727) 751810 www.stalbansmuseums.org.uk
Getting there Follow signs to St Albans from J21a
from the M25 or J6, 7 or 9 from the M1, then follow
signs to *Verulamium*
Open Mon–Sat 10–5.30, Sun 2–5.30
Adm Adults £3.30, children £2, family £8

Stroll through recreated rooms from the
Roman period, complete with decorative wall
plasters and mosaics, look at Roman artefacts
through microscopes and discover everyday life
in Roman *Verulamium* through touch-screen
computers and video presentations. The park
contains tennis courts, a crazy golf course, a
paddling pool and a lake.
For further information *see* pp.247–8

The Walter Rothschild Zoological Museum

Akeman Street, off the High Street, Tring
t (020) 7942 6171 www.nhm.ac.uk/museum/tring
Getting there Tring is about 13 miles west of
St Albans on the A41
Open Mon–Sat 10–5, Sun 2–5 **Adm** Free
Picnic areas, café, shop, disabled access, parking

You've never seen so many stuffed mammals,
insects, birds and fish together in one place! You
can go right up to the fearsome beasts and
examine them up close – it's quite a thrill to
look a lion straight in the eye. The museum is a
wonderfully atmospheric with its gnarly
wooden cabinets full of stuffed exotica. Look out
for the extinct creatures like the Quagga, the
Moa and the dodo. Activity trails in the school
holidays and regular craft sessions.
Call **t** (020) 7942 6163 to book.

Theatres

Ascot

Novello Children's Theatre 2 High Street,
Sunninghill **t** (01753) 783726
www.novellotheatre.co.uk

Cheltenham

Everyman Regent Street **t** (01242) 572573
www.everymantheatre.org.uk (Everykid Club on
Saturday mornings)
Playhouse Bath Road **t** (01242) 522852

Cirencester

Sundial Theatre Cirencester College, Stroud Road
t (01285) 654228

Gloucester

Guildhall Arts Centre 23 Eastgate Street
t (01452) 505089
The King's Theatre King's Barton Street
t (01452) 300130
New Olympus 162–6 Barton Street
t (01452) 525917

Henley-on-Thames

The Kenton Theatre New Street **t** (01491) 575698
www.kentontheatre.co.uk
The Puppet Theatre Barge Henley Bridge
t (020) 7249 6876 www.puppetbarge.co.uk

Marlow

The Puppet Theatre Barge t (020) 7249 6876
www.puppetbarge.co.uk

Milton Keynes

Milton Keynes Theatre Marlborough Gate
t 0870 0606652 www.miltonkeynestheatre.co.uk
The Stables Stockwell Lane, Wavendon
t (01908) 280800 www.stables.org

Oxford

New Theatre George Street
t (01865) 320770/0870 606 3500
The Burton/Taylor Theatre Gloucester Street
t (01865) 305305
The Old Fire Station Arts and Entertainments
Gloucester Green **t** (01865) 297170
The Pegasus Theatre (Oxford Youth Theatre)
Magdalen Road **t** (01865) 722851
www.pegasustheatre.org.uk
The Playhouse 11–12 Beaumont Street
t (01865) 305305 www.oxfordplayhouse.com

Reading

The Hexagon Queens Walk **t** (0118) 960 6060
Progress Theatre The Mount, Christchurch Road
t 0870 7743490 www.progresstheatre.co.uk

St Albans

Abbey Theatre Holywell Hill **t** (01727) 857861
www.abbeytheatre2.org.uk
Alban Arena Civic Centre, St Peter's Street
t (01727) 844488
Maltings Art Theatre The Maltings
t (01727) 844222

Windsor

Theatre Royal 32 Thames Street **t** (01753) 853888
www.theatreroyalwindsor.co.uk
Windsor Arts Centre The Old Court, St Leonards
Road **t** (01753) 859336 www.windsorartscentre.org

EATING OUT

Cheltenham

Nature in Art
Wallsworth Hall, Twigworth **t** 0845 4500233
www.nature-in-art.org.uk
Open Tues–Sun and Bank Hols 10–5
Excellent café on the A38. The food is homemade and there are board games for children to play.
For further information *see* pp.243–4

TGI Fridays
374 Gloucester Road **t** (01242) 234222
www.tgifridays.com
Open Mon–Fri 12 noon–10.30, Sat–Sun 12 noon–11
Not cheap but great for kids with its bright colours and American-style menu. Children's dishes include macaroni cheese, spaghetti and chicken fingers followed by ice cream or the intriguingly titled 'cup of dirt' chocolate pudding with biscuit chips and gummy worms. Yum.

Gloucester

Cross Hands
t (01452) 863441
This pub is just outside the town in Brockworth, on the A417–A46 roundabout
Open Daily 11.30–10
This pub can offer a family room with high-chairs, nappy changing facilities and a children's menu, as well as a lawned garden and a 'Fun Factory' play area for children.

Orchids
Gloucester Cathedral, 17 College Green
t (01452) 308920
Open Mon–Sat 10–5, Sun 11–5
Gloucester Cathedral's café is very reasonable and, if it's sunny, you could always take your food outdoors to the small eating area. There are highchairs and smaller portions for kids.

Tall Ship Inn
Southgate Street **t** (01452) 522793
Open Mon–Sat 11–11
Family pub offering children's meals situated near the entrance to the docks.

Ye Olde Fishe Shoppe and Restaurant
8 Hare Lane **t** (01452) 522502
Open Mon 11.30–2.30, Tues–Fri 11.30–7, Sat 11.15–6.30
Good-quality fish and chips.

Oxford

Bangkok House
42a Hythe Bridge Street, **t** (01865) 200705
Open Daily 12 noon–3 and 6–11; booking advised
The best prawn soup in town and the most beautiful tables to eat it at. Kids will love gazing at the intricate wooden carvings and trying out milder dishes while their parents feast on delicious Thai food. Close to the station; highchairs.

Browns
5–11 Woodstock Road **t** (01865) 511995
www.browns-restaurant.com
Open Mon–Sat 11–11, Sun 12 noon–11
Pleasant, friendly branch of the extremely family-friendly chain. It can offer a children's menu, highchairs, a non-smoking area, a buggy parking area and nappy changing facilities.

Donnington Doorstep
Townsend Square **t** (01865) 727721
Open Mon–Sat 10–4; cooked meals from 12 noon
Good for a snack or a simple lunch, this drop-in centre has nappy changing facilities, highchairs, toys and activities for children.

Gee's Restaurant
61a Banbury Road, **t** (01865) 553540
www.gees-restaurant.co.uk
Open Daily 12 noon–2.30pm (3.30pm Sun) and 6–10.30pm
This bright Victorian conservatory offers plenty of space for families to spread out over lunch. Kids can choose from simple dishes like spaghetti or chicken and chips. Highchairs available.

Memoirs Café
Carfax Gardens **t** (01865) 790622
Open Daily 7am–6pm
Once you've finished gazing at the views from the top of the Carfax Tower, you can enjoy a pleasant lunch at this small, non-smoking café at its foot. There are baby seats for little ones, too.

Florence Park Family Centre
Rymers Lane **t** (01865) 777286
Open Mon, Thurs and Fri 10–3
Families are welcome to drop in and use the centre's facilities, which include a kitchen for making drinks, parent and baby room, highchairs and toys for children. A snack trolley is available or bring your own sandwiches.

Gourmet Pizza

2 The Gallery, Gloucester Road **t** (01865) 793146
Open Sun–Thurs 12 noon–10.30pm, Fri and Sat
until 11pm

An excellent pizza chain, it offers kids' portions
of pasta, and highchairs.

The Isis Tavern

On the towpath between Donnington Bridge and
Iffley Lock **t** (01865) 247006
Open Daily 11am–11pm (children until 7pm)

Good pub food and a garden with swings.

Old Orleans Restaurant

George Street **t** (01865) 792718
Open Mon–Sat 11–11, Sun 12 noon–10.30

An extremely child-friendly restaurant with
outdoor seating in summer, a children's menu,
highchairs, crayons and a colouring menu to keep
the kids occupied while they wait for their food.

St Albans

Carluccio's

7–8 Christopher Place **t** (01727) 837681
www.carluccios.com
Open Mon–Fri 8am–11pm, Sat 9–11, Sun 10–10

This busy café-food shop is welcoming to families but bring along toys to amuse the kids as
waiting times can get long at weekends. If in
doubt, book a table and browse the Italian deli
counter for wine, oils, pasta and cheeses.
Highchairs, children's menu (chicken with rosemary potatoes, spaghetti with butter or tomato
sauce, and cheese and roast ham focaccia) and
baby changing facilities are available.

Waffle House

Kingsbury Water Mill, St Michael's Village
t (01727) 853502; **Open** Daily 11–6

Waffles are the speciality of this friendly café –
it serves them as starters, main courses and
desserts. Outdoor seating area in summer.

Zizzi

26 High Street, **t** (01727) 850200 **www.zizzi.co.uk**
Open Daily 11am–6pm

Bedfordshire Clanger

This is a pasty with a meat filling at one end and
a sweet one at the other. According to how rich the
person was, the meat would have been bacon,
pork, or steak and kidney; the sweet was probably
apple. A good way of saving on the washing up.

Poor Knights of Windsor

The Poor Knights would probably have enjoyed
tucking into this simple pudding. Slices of stale
bread are soaked in milk and sherry, then rolled in
egg-yolk, fried, and finally topped with cinnamon,
and raspberry or strawberry jam.

Nice pizzas and interesting pasta dishes are
Zizzi's trademarks. There are smaller portions for
kids, highchairs and baby changing facilities.

Windsor

Crooked House Tea Rooms

51 High Street **t** (01753) 857534
Open Daily 9.30am–6pm

Tearoom housed in the oldest free-standing
building in Windsor. The cream teas are a must.

Don Beni

28 Thames Street **t** (01753) 622042
www.donbeni.co.uk
Open Daily 12 noon–11pm

Bright and clean Italian restaurant serving up
pizzas and pasta, plus mouth-watering seafood,
meat and fish dishes. Children are welcome and
highchairs are available. Takeaway service.

Puccino's

31 Windsor Royal Station **t** (01753) 859380
Open Mon–Sat 9–6, Sun 10–6

Part of a relatively new chain with quirky
slogans on the sugar sachets to keep the kids
amused. Pop in for a quick coffee or pizza and
pasta lunch; children's menu and highchairs available. There are other coffee bars in the station but
the friendly service here is a definite bonus.

Pizza Express

7–8 Thames Street **t** (01753) 856424
www.pizzaexpress.co.uk
Open Mon–Sat 11.30am–12 midnight, Sun
11.30am–11pm

Large branch of the family-friendly pizza chain.

Royal Oak

Datchet Road (opposite Windsor and Eton
Riverside Station) **t** (01753) 865179
Open 11am–11pm

This lovely pub is festooned with flowers in the
summer, and has a patio area, children's menu
and highchairs available.

East Anglia
Cambridgeshire · Essex
Norfolk · Suffolk

09

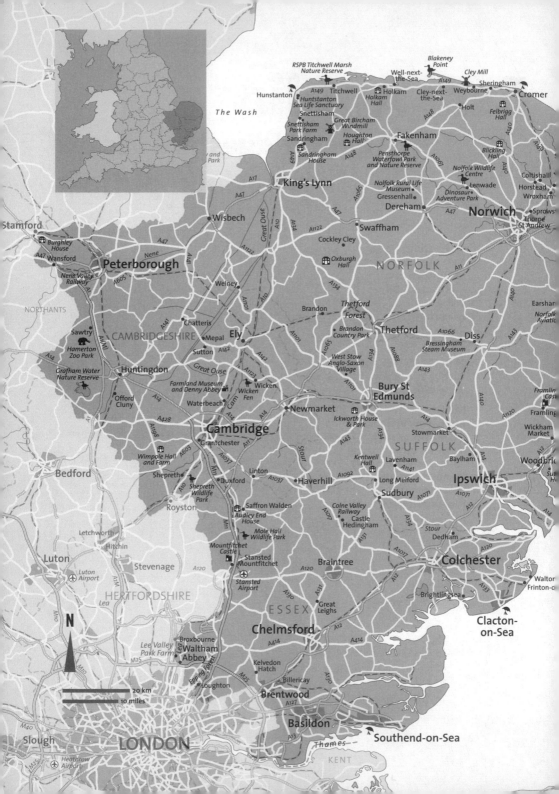

Famously flat, the East Anglian landscape is anything but featureless. Much of Suffolk, particularly around Dedham Vale (the heart of Constable country), is rolling and beautiful and the Suffolk and north Norfolk coasts are among the most picturesque the country has to offer. Then, of course, there are the Broads, the vast network of inland waterways that are the setting for thousands of boating holidays every year, not to mention the historic towns of Cambridge and Colchester (the country's first ever town), as well as the lively resorts of Great Yarmouth, Clacton and Southend-on-Sea. Good for cycling and plane-watching – many of the region's former Second World War RAF bases have been turned into aircraft museums – East Anglia is, above all, a great place for nature lovers, with dozens of nature reserves, including the famous Blakeney Point with its vast colonies of sea birds and seals.

Day-trip itinerary

Morning: Punting along the scenic waterways of Cambridge (p.287).
Lunch: Head for Trumpington Street for family favourites at Browns (p.330).
Afternoon: Drive or take the free bus service from Cambridge train station to Duxford, seven miles south, to see Europe's largest collection of planes and play on its hi-tech simulators (p.328).
Alternatively, you could drive to Linton Zoological Gardens, 10 miles southeast, to meet its assorted tigers, lions, zebras and snakes (p.303).

Special events

May
Bury St Edmunds: Festival **t** (01284) 769505 **www.**buryfestival.co.uk
Stilton: Stilton Rolling **t** (01733) 241206
June
Aldeburgh: Festival of Music and the Arts **t** (01728) 687100
Cambridge: Concerts by Trinity College Choir **t** (01223) 338400
Cambridge: Strawberry Fair **t** (01223) 560160 **www.**strawberry-fair.org.uk
Norwich: Royal Norfolk Show **t** (01603) 748931 **www.**royalnorfolkshow.co.uk
July
Cambridge: Big Day Out **t** (01223) 457555
Hunstanton: Carnival **t** (01485) 532345
King's Lynn: Music and Arts Festival **t** (01553) 767557 **www.**kingslynnfestival.org.uk
Sandringham: Flower Show **t** (01485) 540860
Cambridge: Summer Music Festival **t** (01223) 357851 **www.**cambridgesummermusic.com
August
Cromer: Carnival **t** (01263) 512497 **www.**cromercarnival.co.uk
Southend-on-Sea: Carnival Week **t** (01702) 215120 **www.**southend-on-seacarnival.org.uk
November
Cambridge: Bonfire Night fireworks **t** 0906 5862526

Highlights

Animal fun, Blakeney Point, p.302
Birdwatching, RSPB Nature Reserve Minsmere, p.305
Boating fun, the Norfolk Broads, pp.320–1
Punting on the Cam, p.287
Castle fun, Mountfitchet Castle, p.300
Crabbing, Cromer, p.310
Cycling, the Broads, p.321
Hands-on science, Norwich, p.297
Plane fun, Duxford Airfield Museum, p.328
Rollercoaster fun, Great Yarmouth Pleasure Beach, p.312
Roman fun, Colchester Castle, p.290
Steam train rides, Nene Valley Railway, p.318
Tudor fun, Kentwell Hall, p.300
Water fun, Colchester Leisure World, p.325

East Anglia

Bury St Edmunds

Getting there By road: from Cambridge, which is 30 miles to the west, take the A14 direct; from London's M25 (80 miles southwest) take the M11 north, followed by the A11, and finally the A14. By rail: trains depart regularly from London (King's Cross and Liverpool Street). By bus/coach: National Express runs an hourly service from London to Cambridge, from where (on Emmanuel Street) you can catch bus no. X11 direct to Bury

Tourist information 6 Angel Hill **t** (01284) 764667/757083 **www.stedmundsbury.gov.uk**

A literal kind of a place – it's where St Edmund is buried. He, in case you're wondering, was the last king of East Anglia. He succeeded to the throne in AD 855, when just 14 years old, and died in AD 870 when marauding Vikings had him tied to a tree, shot full of arrows and finally (just to make sure) beheaded. Originally buried in Hoxne, his body was taken to Beadorisworth (as Bury was originally called) in AD 903 for reburial in the newly founded Benedictine monastery and his shrine remained a popular pilgrimage site throughout the Middle Ages. Following the dissolution of the monasteries in the mid 16th century, the abbey was destroyed and its wealth seized by the Crown. It now lies in ruins in the midst of some beautiful landscaped gardens. You can still visit the remains, which are fun to explore in the company of a walkman guide (from the visitor centre), although Edmund's grave and bones have long since disappeared – as has his status as the patron saint of England, bequeathed in the Middle Ages to the dragon-fighting (not to mention un-English) St George. The town's other celebrity tomb, which holds the remains of Mary I, is still standing and can be found in St Mary's church near the 15th-century cathedral, adjoining the abbey grounds.

Bury itself is an attractive market town (cattle, vegetable and fruit markets are held every Wednesday and Saturday) with streets of fine Georgian architecture and a relaxed countryish feel. It is home to a handful of child-friendly attractions, including the Moyse's Hall Museum, with its gruesome collection of exhibits relating to the 'Murder in the Red Barn' (see box opposite) and the Theatre Royal, where you can take back-stage tours. However, it is within reach of several more, notably Ickworth House, West Stow Anglo-Saxon Village and, just outside the town, the 80-hectare (200-acre) Nowton Park.

A little bit of history

In the early 15th century, England had hundreds of monasteries and abbeys, where communities of monks would spend their days praying, farming, making honey and wine, and generally living a rather idyllic existence. The average monastery was a very rich institution filled with precious carvings and sculptures and usually held a good deal of land. England at that time was a Catholic country, which meant that the church and all the monasteries came under the control of the Pope, the head of the Catholic Church in Rome. In 1529, the King, Henry VIII, fell out with the Catholic Church when the Pope refused to grant him a divorce from his first wife Catherine of Aragon. In a fit of anger, Henry decided to remove the English church from the Pope's control and to make himself head of a new 'Church of England'. This meant that, not only could he grant himself a divorce (which he duly did), but that he now owned all the churches' and monasteries' land and wealth. Of course, to Henry, there wasn't much point in owning all that wealth if you couldn't spend it (after all, he had a war with France to finance) and so in the 1540s he ordered that all England's monasteries be dissolved (i.e. abolished), their wealth sold off, and the monks kicked out. The monastery at Bury which, by this time, had become the richest in the country (and a prime target for Henry VIII's greed) was swiftly destroyed and its wealth confiscated by the Crown. It has lain in ruins ever since.

Things to see and do
Cathedral of St James
Angel Hill **t** (01284) 754933
www.stedscathedral.co.uk
Open Daily 8–6
Adm Free (discretionary donation encouraged)
Refectory, shop, mother and baby facilities, guided tours, car park nearby

Though little remains of the adjacent abbey, the city's cathedral, in contrast, is still standing strong and, indeed, is still being added to some 800 years after the first stones were laid. The currently rather stubby-looking tower is as yet unfinished (everything about the structure, it seems, is slightly behind time; it wasn't even

Murder in the Red Barn

One of Bury St Edmunds' most famous events took place in August 1828 when, according to contemporary reports, almost the entire town turned out to see the young squire William Corder stand trial for the murder of local girl Maria Marten.

A few years earlier, the two had been betrothed to be married. Upon the day of the ceremony, William reportedly asked that Maria meet him 'alone' at the red barn on his estate, from where, he said, they would be taken to the registry office. She complied and, for several weeks afterwards, nothing more was seen of the couple until William returned to the area. He told Maria's parents that they had indeed been married and that Maria was now preparing for their imminent move to the Isle of Wight. William then left the area and, for several months afterwards, Maria's parents received letters from him telling them about his and Maria's new life on the island. They received no direct communication from their daughter, however, to whom they had not spoken now since before her wedding day. Maria's mother noticed a curious thing: the letters they received from William, though purportedly sent from the Isle of Wight, all bore a London postmark.

As the months passed, and still no word came from her daughter, Maria's mother became more and more worried, and on three separate occasions had a terrible dream in which she saw William murder Maria and bury her in the red barn. She told her husband about her dreams. Although he was initially sceptical, he agreed to search the barn and, in the very spot that his wife indicated, found the body of his daughter. She had clearly been shot.

A detective was despatched to look for William, who was found living in London with a new wife with whom he had opened a school for girls. William at first denied having even heard of Maria, let alone having promised to marry her. He was arrested, however and, following a search of his premises, was found to be in possession of a pair of pistols.

At the trial William (who by now had admitted his relationship with Maria) claimed that when he met her at the red barn on the supposed day of their wedding, they had had a terrible argument. William had stormed off only to hear a shot ring out behind him. He returned to find that Maria had killed herself with his gun. Fearing the worst, he decided to bury the body and act as if nothing had happened.

The jury chose not to believe him and he was sentenced to death. Whilst awaiting execution, William confessed to the crime and his account of the terrible events now resides in Moyse's Hall Museum, bound in an interesting way (p.284). After the execution, parts of the rope used for the hanging were sold to the crowd as gruesome souvenirs of the event.

designated a cathedral until 1914). It's not a hugely child-friendly place but is still worth a look on a rainy afternoon. Within its impressive hammer-beamed interior, see if you can find the sculpture by Elizabeth Frink; the shields above the Quire (choir), bearing the arms of the barons, who met at the Abbey in the 13th century to enforce the terms of the *Magna Carta*, and the representation of the wolf on the Bishop's throne, put there to guard poor old St Edmund's head. The cathedral holds regular musical events including organ recitals, concerts and choir performances.

Cinemas and theatres See pp.326, 329

Greene King Brewery Museum

Westgate Street **t** (01284) 714297
www.greeneking.co.uk
Open Mon–Sat 10–5, Sun 11–3.30
Adm Adults £3, children **free**

Celebrates 200 years of Greene King beer in Bury St Edmunds. Thirsty families will enjoy the interactive displays on the art of brewing.

Moyse's Hall Museum

Cornhill **t** (01284) 706183
Open Mon–Fri 10.30–4.30, Sat–Sun 11–4
Adm Adults £2.60, children £2.10, residents of Bury St Edmunds **free**
Shop

Dedicated to tracing the history of Suffolk life from prehistory to the present day. The building is a fascinating historical exhibit in its own right. Built in the 12th century, it has been used as a prison, a workhouse and a bridewell (or house of correction) before narrowly avoiding being turned into a fire station in the 19th century. Objections by the local population forced the authorities to alter their plans in 1899 and establish a museum here instead. Kids will be delighted to know that the museum holds a particularly fine collection of gruesome exhibits including numerous torture instruments – a cat o' nine tails, some body irons and a set of stocks – and, in pride of place, various relics relating to the infamous 'Murder in the Red Barn' case from the early 19th century (p.283). In particular, look out for the murderer's own account of the trial bound in his own skin and the preserved section of his scalp; guaranteed to make your skin crawl.

Nowton Park

Nowton Road, Bury St Edmunds **t** (01284) 763666
Getting there The park is a 30-minute walk from Bury, or you can catch a bus from the bus station
Open Daily 8.30–dusk **Adm Free**
Picnic areas, visitor centre, all-weather sports pitch
   Two hundred acres of Victorian-style gardens with three marked walks (from 20–75 minutes) taking in the assorted wildflower meadows, plantations and arboreta. Guided walks every month.

Sport and activities *See pp.322–5*

Theatre Royal

Westgate Street **t** (01284) 755127
www.theatreroyal.org
Open Tours Tues and Thurs 11.30am and 2.30pm, Sat 11.30am
Adm Tours £2.50 per person
   Explore the theatre (owned by the National Theatre in London) on one of the backstage tours given by stewards. More formal tours in summer.

Around Bury St Edmunds

Ickworth House and Park, 2 miles south (p.300)
Kentwell Hall, 11 miles south (p.300)
Rede Hall Farm, 6 miles south (p.308)
West Stow Anglo-Saxon Village, 5 miles northwest (p.316)

Cambridge

Getting there By air: Stansted airport is about 30 miles south of Cambridge and is linked to the city by a regular bus service (and the M11). By road: Cambridge is 55 miles north of London and can be reached by the M11 from the south and A14 from the

Can you spot?
The apple tree by the entrance to Trinity College. According to legend, Sir Isaac Newton was supposed to have 'discovered' gravity whilst sitting under an apple tree in the college grounds. The revelation came when an apple fell on his head. This is supposedly a descendant of that very same tree.

north. Driving into Cambridge city centre, which is largely pedestrianized and ringed by an impenetrable mass of one-way streets, isn't really an option unless you take advantage of the city's excellent park-and-ride scheme. There are five such car parks on the outskirts of Cambridge; Cowley Road/A1309 to the north, Newmarket Road/A1303 to the east, Madingley Road/A1303 to the west and both Babraham Road/A1307 and Trumpington Road/A1134 to the south of the city. Parking is free, buses leave for the city centre every 10 minutes (7am–8pm); an Adult Day Return is £2 with up to 3 children under 16 travelling free per paying adult. For more details, contact Stagecoach Cambus **t** (01223) 423554. By train: There are frequent rail services to London King's Cross (50 minutes) and London Liverpool Street (1 hour 10 minutes). Cambridge station is a mile and a half south of the city centre but served by a regular bus service. By coach: An hourly coach service from London Victoria coach station is provided by National Express
Tourist information The Old Library, Wheeler Street **t** 0870 2254900 www.visitcambridge.org. The centre has a souvenir shop and can provide details of guided walking tours led from here by Blue Badge Guides throughout the year (dramatic tours with costumed characters take place in summer).
   Cambridge, like its great rival Oxford, is principally famous for its university, one of the oldest and most respected in the world. Like Oxford, it's an exceedingly beautiful city with some of the country's most impressive architecture, delightful parks and of course, the River Cam, a great sash of water flowing to the north and west of the city.
   Being smaller and more concentrated than Oxford, it's a great place for pottering, be it on foot, by bike or on the river. The centre of town, where you'll find most of the colleges and university buildings, is largely pedestrianized. The two main thoroughfares, Bridge Street (which turns into Sidney Street, St Andrew's Street and Regent Street) and St John's Street (which becomes Trinity Street, King's Parade and Trumpington

Can you spot?

Magdalene Bridge (pronounced 'Mawdlin'). This is the point where the city began: the Romans built a bridge here when constructing a road between Colchester and Godmanchester, and the town of Cambridge slowly grew up around it. It's now one of the main sites for hiring punts.

Street) are lined with shops, tearooms and book-stores – look out for Galloway and Porter booksellers, 30 Sidney Street, **t** (01223) 367876, which also holds a monthly warehouse book sale, with books for adults from £1 each and a wide range of quality children's titles at bargain prices. Touch Wood Creative Toys, 10 Mill Road, **t** (01223) 507803, sells great gifts for children including wooden toys, kits and games. There's a bustling market held daily on Market Square, selling general produce (fruit 'n' veg, books, clothes, flowers, etc.) from Monday to Saturday, and arts and crafts, antiques and farmers' produce on Sundays. As you might expect of a town so steeped in academia, there are lots of museums, some of which will be of interest to children and, in term time, you can tour the magnificent castle-like college buildings, although this may prove somewhat frustrating as you are usually not allowed to walk on their inviting expanses of neatly manicured grass. Indeed, some of the more popular colleges are becoming increasingly less tolerant of the disruption to study caused by tourists; you may be expected to pay a rather exorbitant entrance fee. For the record, Peterhouse is the oldest college; Trinity, the largest, is famed for its Great Hall and statues of former illustrious students, including Tennyson, Francis Bacon and Isaac Newton; while King's is the most beautiful, with its glorious 15th-century chapel. You may well recognize its stained glass and fan-vaulted interior from the service of lessons and carols broadcast from here every Christmas. In its chapel exhibition, you can read about the history of the college and see a model showing how the chapel ceiling was constructed. Look out for the branch of the English Teddy Company opposite the entrance to King's, guarded by a 2m (6ft) teddy bear dressed in a mortar board and gown.

The city and the surrounding flat countryside are perfect for cycling, which explains the rows and rows of parked bikes you'll see everywhere you go: outside the colleges, alongside the shops, by the railway station, everywhere; it really is the everyday transport of choice here and there are numerous bike hire shops. You can follow the towpath along the banks of the River Cam all the way to the cathedral town of Ely (p.291). The best way to see Cambridge, however, at least in summer, is on a punt, poling yourself along the Cam in a flat-bottomed boat through the 'Backs', the most picturesque part of town (so-called because many of the university buildings 'back' on to it) with its elegant bridges, lush, green riverside vegetation – all overhanging willow trees – and gorgeous views. You can punt yourself all the way to the nearby village of Grantchester if you want, where you can enjoy some refreshment at the Orchard Tea Gardens (a favourite haunt of Rupert Brooke, Maynard Keynes and Virginia Woolf), although do be aware that on summer weekends the river traffic can be pretty fierce with groups of high-spirited youths holding impromptu races.

Despite all the well-preserved history and its studious veneer, Cambridge is no museum city. The large student population helps it to retain its youthful vigour – there are lots of theatres, live music and comedy venues including the famous Corn Exchange opposite the tourist office – and it has a justly deserved reputation as one of the most vibrant cities in southern England.

Things to see and do

Bike hire

City Cycle Hire, 61 Newnham Road
t (01223) 365629 **www.citycyclehire.com**
Open Jun–Sept Mon–Fri 9–5.30, Sat 9–5; Oct–Apr Mon–Fri 9–5
Hire Half day £5, 1 day £8, 1 week £15 (a £25 deposit is also payable)

Bikes, trailer bikes and child trailers for hire by the hour, day or week. Guided cycle tours of the city are also offered between April and September.

Can you spot?

The tower of the church on Benet Street, near the junction with King's Parade, and, in particular, the small, perfectly circular holes cut into the stone near the top of each tower face. Can you guess what these were for? They were put there in the Middle Ages to allow owls to get into the church and catch the church mice.

Can you spot?
The Mathematical Bridge in the grounds of Queen's College; you can see it from the Silver Street Bridge or from aboard a punt on the river itself. So clever was its design – it was originally supposed to have been built without bolts and fastenings – that in the 18th century some engineers took it apart to see how it worked, only to find they couldn't put it back together again. The bridge you see is a copy of the original.

Cambridge Brass Rubbing Centre

Various locations **t** (01223) 871621
Open Call for details/appointment

The centre, which provides access to the largest collection of brass plates in Britain, was until recently housed in the Round Church in Bridge Street. Although currently without a permanent home, the centre's owners do still arrange sessions for families, schools and small groups to do rubbings at Emmanuel Church or at their own home and there are plans to set up at the Fitzwilliam Museum in the near future.

Cambridge and County Folk Museum

2–3 Castle Street **t** (01223) 355159
www.folkmuseum.org.uk
Open Apr–Sept Mon–Sat 10.30–5, Sun 2–5;
Oct–Mar Tues–Sat 10.30–5, Sun 2–5
Adm Adults £3, children £1 (one **free** child with paying adult), under 5s **free**
Gift shop, guided tours, disabled access

Housed in a 16th-century, half-timbered farmhouse, this looks at the non-academic side of life in Cambridge, with displays on the people who have lived and worked in this area for the last 400 years. Activity days for children aged 6–10 are organized on some Saturday afternoons and workshops for 7–11-year-olds are held during the school holidays.

Cambridge Museum of Technology

The Old Pumping Station, Cheddars Lane
t (01223) 368650 www.museumoftechnology.com
Open Easter–Oct Sun 2–5; Nov–Easter first Sun of every month 2–5
Adm £5 (steaming), £3 (non-steaming), under 7s **free**
Shop, disabled access, call for dates of Steaming Days and other special events

Housed in a Victorian pumping station, this is filled with the noisy contraptions of the Industrial Age: boilers, engines and a number of 'hands-on' pumps, a printing room (where you can print your own souvenirs), a collection of early Cambridge wireless instruments and other local artefacts.

Cinemas and theatres *See pp.326, 329*

★Fitzwilliam Museum

Trumpington Street **t** (01223) 332900
www.fitzmuseum.cam.ac.uk/
Open Tues–Sat 10–5, Sun 12–5 **Adm Free**
Café, gift shop, guided tours, mother and baby facilities, wheelchair access

This is the city's most respected museum, parts of which will be of interest to children, although you may want to skip the endless cases full of European porcelain, Chinese vases and Korean ceramics (there's only so much fun to be had by kids from old plates) and head straight to the mummies and painted coffins in the Antiquities Gallery, or the room full of armour and weapons in the Applied Arts section. Free family activity sheets are available at reception.

Great St Mary's Church

Market Hill **t** (01223) 350914 www.gsm.cam.ac.uk
Open Daily 9–4.30 **Adm** £1.75

Climb to the top of the 34m (113ft) tower for great views out over the colleges and nearby marketplace, or clamber up the steep Castle Mound on Castle Hill, just north of the river off Castle Street (it marks the spot where the Norman Cambridge Castle once stood) for views out over the medieval city.

Museum of Archaeology and Anthropology

Downing Street **t** (01223) 333516
Open Tues–Sat 2–4.30; phone to check extended summer hours (Jun–Sept) **Adm Free**

The ground floor 'Rise of Civilization' gallery, full of ancient pots and bits of flint, is only worth a cursory inspection. Instead make a beeline for the ethnographic collection on the first floor, a wonderful array of treasures brought back by 18th- and 19th-century explorers: Native American feathered head-dresses, Eskimo canoes and parkas (made from dried walrus hide), scary African tribal masks and suits of Japanese ceremonial armour, all arranged around a 15m/50ft-high totem pole.

Museum of Classical Archaeology

Sidgwick Avenue **t** (01223) 335153
www.classics.cam.ac.uk/museum
Open University term time: Mon–Fri 10–5, Sat 10–1;
university holidays: Sat 10–1 **Adm Free**

Over 600 casts of some of the major pieces of
sculpture from ancient Greece and Rome.

Punting

The archetypal Cambridge pursuit can be
enjoyed every day between Easter and October.
Punts can be hired from Magdalene Bridge, Mill
Lane, Garret Hostel Lane, the Granta Pub on
Newnham Road and by Jesus Green. A deposit of
around £25 is usually required, while the punts
themselves will cost something in the region of
£6–8 per hour. Chauffeured punt trips are also
available. You'll be shown how to use the pole
before you set off but do be aware that it can be
a pretty wet and soggy experience, especially
during the learning process. However, the Backs
do provide an idyllic space in which to dry off and
have a picnic while you refine your technique –
just remember to stick to the left.

Scott Polar Research Institute Museum

Lensfield Road **t** (01223) 336548
Open Tues–Sat 2.30–4 (except public holidays)
Adm Free
*Shop with children's books on exploration and
polar wildlife*

This museum of polar life and exploration
features original artefacts from Scott's expedition. Sir Ranulph Fiennes' literary defence of
Scott's achievements (published October 2003)
and entitled simply *Captain Scott*, makes a visit
here all the more pertinent.

Sedgwick Museum of Earth Sciences

Downing Street **t** (01223) 333456
www.sedgwickmuseum.org
Open Mon–Fri 10–1 and 2–5, Sat 10–4
Adm Free (discretionary donation encouraged)
Shop, some wheelchair access/assistance available

Houses the oldest geological collection in the
world (although, in geological terms, this is a
pretty slight claim) with various multi-million-
year-old rocks and minerals displayed in antique
walnut cases. It also has a large collection of
fossil dinosaurs. Following redevelopment, the
museum has even more space dedicated to the

weird and wonderful world of nature; new
displays include exhibits on giant dragonflies,
how volcanoes work, and whether there might
be life on other planets.

Sport and activities *See* pp.322–5

University Botanic Garden

Cory Lodge, Bateman Street **t** (01223) 336265
www.botanic.cam.ac.uk
Open Nov–Jan 10–4, Feb and Oct 10–5, Mar–Sept
10–6
Adm (Mar–Oct, weekends and Bank Hols)
Adults £2.50, children £2, under 5s **free**
*Café-restaurant (summer only), picnic areas, gift
shop, mother and baby facilities, guided tours by
arrangement, disabled access*

The 16-hectare (40-acre) University Botanic
Garden, south of Cambridge's centre, was founded
in 1762 and is the city's most beautiful open space
with trees and flowers, several glasshouses, a lake,
a geographical rock garden and rare plants laid
out amid an elegant landscaped setting. It may
prove a little formal for younger tastes, however. If
you're after a spot where kids can enjoy more
uninhibited play, try Jesus Green, to the north of
the city centre near the river, a large, open grassy
space with a play area and an open air swimming
pool in summer. Just to the west, you'll find
Midsummer Common, a huge riverside meadow
that plays host to fairs and circuses in summer
and a large firework display on 5 November.

University Museum of Zoology

Downing Street **t** (01223) 336650
www.zoo.cam.ac.uk/museum
Open Term time: Mon–Fri 10–4.45, Sat 10–1
Adm Free
Wheelchair access

Contains a wide range of natural history
displays including numerous fossils and animal
skeletons, as well as several items collected by
the greatest naturalist of them all, Charles
Darwin, on his famous *Beagle* voyage. Look out
for the 21m (70ft) whale skeleton hanging above
the entrance (it's pretty hard to miss), the moths
from King George III's bedchamber and the
reconstruction of a prehistoric rocky shore with
a killer whale, an extinct, giant ground sloth and
a giant spider crab.

Walking tours

In summer (Jul–Oct Thurs and Sun at 8pm), you can join one of the Ghost Walks, which depart from outside King's College Gatehouse on King's Parade, **t** (01284) 756717, **www**.ghostclub.org.uk/camghost, while in winter Cambridge Junior Explorers, **t** (01223) 246990, **www**.geocities.com/cambridgejuniorexplorers, offer tours of the city for children aged 9–12 in the company of a qualified guide. The tours leave from outside the Guildhall on Market Square at 11am and tickets cost £4 per child (accompanying adult free). Tickets can be purchased from the Tourist information centre, **t** (01223) 457574.

Around Cambridge

Duxford Airfield Museum, 7 miles south (p.328)
Farmland Museum and Denny Abbey, 7 miles northeast (p.327)
Linton Zoological Gardens, 10 miles southeast (p.303)
Shepreth Wildlife Park, 7 miles southwest (pp.305–6)
Wimpole Hall, 8 miles southwest (p.302)

Colchester

Getting there By road: Colchester can easily be reached via the A12 from London, the A137 from Ipswich and the A1037 and A1124 from Cambridge. By rail: There are frequent intercity services between Colchester and London Liverpool Street (50 minutes) and Norwich (1 hour). By bus/coach: Daily National Express coach services link Colchester to all the principal towns and cities in Britain.
Numerous short-stay, long-stay and NCP car parks are located near the centre of town, particularly in the area around Colchester train station. There are 24-hour car parks on Priory Street, Osborne Street and Magdalen Street
Tourist information 1 Queen Street **t** (01206) 282920. The centre can provide details of Blue Guide tours of the city. There are three tours to choose from: a walking tour of the town centre, an open-top bus tour (both available summer only) and a tour of the castle

Colchester's heyday was long ago. Once upon a time it was the most powerful and important city in the whole country. Archaeological evidence has

Can you spot?
Jumbo, the 134ft, 19th-century water tower that dominates the skyline to the west of the city. It was named after the famous elephant of the same name living at that time in London Zoo.

shown that there was a settlement here as far back as the 5th century BC, making it (as the town's tourist signs will constantly remind you) Britain's oldest town. When the Romans invaded in the 1st century AD, they made it the capital of the new province of Britannia (naming it *Camulodunum*) and built the country's first temple and bathhouse here. Sacked by Boudicca and the rampaging Iceni army in AD 60, its influence gradually faded over the succeeding centuries as London (or Londinium as it was then) began her inexorable rise upwards. Although it enjoyed prosperity in the Middle Ages, thanks to a thriving textile industry established by Dutch and Flemish refugees fleeing religious persecution on the European Continent, the only other distinguished episode in Colchester's history came in the Civil War when the town (rather unwisely) declared itself for the Royalist side. This resulted in a three-month siege by the parliamentary forces, during which time the trapped population ate every living thing within the city walls: cats, dogs, rats, mice … everything.

Once the queen of all she surveyed, present-day Colchester is now a rather frumpy old dowager, respected more for what she was than what she has become. Although the self-styled 'cultural capital of Essex' (which is saying something), it no longer enjoys national significance – which is not to say that it is in anyway run-down or decrepit; modern Colchester is, in fact, a very pleasant, middle-ranking university town with lots of old buildings, plenty of good shopping and a youthful atmosphere bolstered by its large student population. It boasts several supremely child-friendly visitor attractions, including a Natural History Museum (p.290), a 1,115 sq m (12,000sq ft) indoor play area 'Go Bananas' (p.324), an excellent park, an award-winning zoo and (I bet you didn't know this) the only international-standard roller-skating rink in Britain (p.325).

There's no escaping the past, however, and remnants and remains of Colchester's illustrious history are everywhere. Around two and a half miles of the Roman wall survives along with the

Boudicca (or Boadicea)

Who was Boudicca?

She was the Queen of the Iceni, a British tribe living in East Anglia during the first few decades of the Roman occupation of Britain.

Why is she famous?

Because she led a bloody revolt against the Romans in AD 60 during which she and her army sacked and destroyed numerous Roman towns and massacred many thousands of Roman citizens.

Why did she do that?

Because of Roman stupidity, basically. The Romans conquered many countries in their time – at its height, the Roman Empire stretched from the north of England to the eastern edges of Europe and Africa – but they didn't always conquer by fighting. Obviously, if the people of a particular country didn't want to be conquered, the Romans would fight them, but the Romans often found it much easier (and a lot cheaper) simply to persuade people to let them rule them.

The Romans' favoured method of persuasion was to do deals with local leaders offering them money and status within the Roman Empire in return for their cooperation. They would even be allowed to continue ruling, except they would now have to do so in the name of Rome. This is exactly what happened in East Anglia in AD 43 when the Romans 'came to an arrangement' with Prasatagus, the Chief of the Iceni (and Boudicca's father). When Prasatagus died, however, the local Roman Governor, Suetonius Paulinus, decided that he'd had enough of deals. He seized Prasatagus'

wealth and land and attempted to turn East Anglia into a slave province. When Boudicca protested, she was publicly flogged. Bad move.

What happened?

Boudicca mobilized the Iceni army and launched a furious assault against the Romans. They destroyed Colchester, the capital of Roman government, and burnt the Temple of Claudius, the ultimate symbol of Roman rule, to the ground (it's now Colchester Castle) before laying waste to London and St Albans. In all, her army killed an estimated 70,000 Romans and tortured many more – pulling a Roman's arms out of their sockets was a favourite Iceni ploy.

So, did she win?

No. When Boudicca started her rebellion, most of the Roman army was busy in Wales putting down an insurrection (they were much less keen on 'deals' in Wales) and so her army actually faced little armed opposition. When the Roman army returned, however, things began to go very wrong for Boudicca. Hers was a rag-bag, disorganized army that had achieved most of its success as a result of the surprising speed of its attacks. Despite outnumbering the Romans by many thousands, in the event it proved no match for the highly disciplined Roman troops.

The two sides met in pitched battle at Epping Forest (p.322): while the Iceni were practically destroyed, the Romans suffered just a few hundred casualties. With the battle lost, Boudicca committed suicide rather than face the wrath of the Romans.

country's largest Roman gateway, and you can visit St Botolph's, the oldest Augustinian priory in the country, where a medieval fair with storytellings and demonstrations of medieval crafts is held in summer. If you visit just one site in Colchester, however, it should be the wonderful Norman castle where you can learn all about Roman Britain at its excellent interactive museum and play in its acres of landscaped parkland.

The heart of the town is the High Street, which still follows the original Roman route, around which are grouped most of the town's attractions. The main shopping area – which is made up of narrow lanes lined with specialist shops, three large covered shopping centres and a

market, held every Friday and Saturday in Vineyard Street – is just to the south while the Dutch Quarter and Castle Park are to the north. The River Colne flows in a loop around the north and east of the town. Remember, Colchester is just a dozen or so miles from the sea and the bustling resort of Clacton is just a short drive or train ride away.

Things to see and do

Cinemas and theatres *See* pp.326, 329

★Colchester Castle and Castle Park

Castle Park **t** (01206) 282939
Open Mon–Sat 10–5, Sun 11–5

Adm Adults £4.90, children £3.10, under 5s **free**, family (2+2 or 1+3) £13
Picnic areas, shop, guided tours, disabled access, on-site parking

At first sight, your kids may think Colchester's great castle looks a bit boxy, with few of the features you usually associate with medieval fortresses. The interior, however, more than makes up for any exterior deficiencies, with a host of bloodthirsty displays on the town's gory past. You can find out all about the warrior queen Boudicca (who burned the original temple to the ground), the devastating Civil War siege and Matthew Hopkins, the notorious Witchfinder General who, in the 17th century, interrogated suspected witches in the castle. The museum houses one of the finest collections of Roman antiquities in the country, with mosaics, tombstones, jewellery, coins and a bronze statue of the messenger God Mercury, although kids will be more excited to try on a toga or Roman helmet.

Stretched out behind the castle are 13 hectares (33 acres) of beautifully landscaped gardens, with a sensory garden, a children's play area, a crazy-golf course, a putting green and a boating lake. It's also home to the Hollytrees Museum (*see* right) and, at the northern end, you can trace part of the city's Roman wall. Punch and Judy shows and children's craft and circus workshops are held here throughout the summer.

Colchester Zoo

Maldon Road, Stanway **t** (01206) 331292
www.colchester-zoo.co.uk
Getting there Follow the brown elephant signs from the A1124 exit from the A12, just south of the town. It's just 10 minutes from Colchester train station by bus or taxi
Open Easter–Sept 9.30–6 (Jul–Aug until 6.30), Oct–Mar 9.30–5
Adm Adults £13.99, children £7.50, under 3s **free**
Café-restaurant, picnic areas, shop, mother and baby facilities, disabled access (please note, the site is hilly and children must be accompanied at all times), on-site parking

Colchester Zoo has been revamped in recent years, which is just as well. Previously the epitome of the depressing cramped city zoo, Colchester's residents, including snow leopards, lion, orangutans, elephants and chimps, now have a good deal more space to roam around in. It's

still not exactly a safari park, but it is a distinct improvement. The zoo is divided into several themed areas: 'Penguin Shores', 'Wilds of Asia', 'White Tiger Valley', 'Lakelands', 'Aquatic Zone' and 'Spirit of Africa', a hi-tech enclosure which is home to giraffes and hippos. There are over 30 animal displays and feeding sessions to choose from every day, including reptile encounters (kids can have a 4m (12ft) boa constrictor draped around their neck), birds of prey flying displays, the penguin parade (you can watch them swimming underwater from a special viewing area) and elephant bath time. There's also a new Jungle Safari Train and 'Calahari Capers' an indoor soft play complex as well as four outdoor adventure play areas for kids to run around in.

Hollytrees Museum

High Street **t** (01206) 282940
www.colchestermuseums.org.uk
Open Mon–Sat 10–5, Sun 11–5 **Adm Free**
Disabled access

If it's history with humour that you're after, you've come to the right place. Hollytrees houses a large, colourful collection of toys and costumes and there's a room dedicated to childhood, which features a giant snakes and ladders game, a crawling tunnel and toddler 'time out' area.

Natural History Museum

All Saints Church, High Street **t** (01206) 282941
www.colchestermuseums.org.uk
Open Mon–Sat 10–5, Sun 11–5 **Adm Free**
Shop, disabled access

Excellent albeit rather small museum of natural history with numerous interactive exhibits, including 'feely boxes' for the kids. Various events, such as 'Animal Magic', at which children can build model animals, and 'Animals Close Up', at which children can examine a range of beasties through microscopes and magnifying glasses, are organized throughout the year.

Sport and activities *See pp.322–5*

Around Colchester

Ely

Getting there By road: Ely is 17 miles from Cambridge and 77 miles from London and lies at the crossroads of the A142 and the A10 King's Lynn–Cambridge Road. By rail: The town is served by trains arriving from both London's King's Cross and Liverpool Street stations (1 hour 15 minutes). By bus/coach: National Express runs a service to Cambridge, from where you can catch a further coach or local bus (approximately 3 hours)
Tourist information Oliver Cromwell's House, 29 St Mary's Street, Ely **t** (01353) 662062 **www**.ely.org.uk

Home to one of England's most glorious cathedrals, Ely (pronounced 'eelee') is a small, pleasant market town and the unofficial capital of the Fens, the vast area of soggy marshland that once stretched between Cambridge and Lincolnshire and which was drained for farming between the 17th and 19th centuries. Before this took place, Ely, which was founded in Saxon times, occupied a small patch of raised dry land; an island in the midst of a vast marsh where people would come to fish for eels (Ely means 'eels') and which could only be crossed by boat or, in muddier parts, using stilts! You can see how things used to be (i.e. very wet) at Wicken Fen, the last remaining area of undrained Fenland and the country's oldest nature reserve, located a few miles south of the town (p.322).

Though a small and relatively unsophisticated town, Ely benefited from its isolated location, which allowed it to hold out against the Norman army following William the Conqueror's invasion until 1071. Once victorious, however, William ordered the building of a cathedral in the town

Oliver Cromwell

The town's most famous former resident was Oliver Cromwell, the man who led the parliamentary forces to victory in the Civil War and who became head of a king-less England between 1649 and 1658. You can visit the timber-framed house, where he lived during the war (which has rooms decorated in period style), and watch videos on his life and the draining of the Fens. The building also houses Ely's tourist information centre.

as a statement of intent. The result was a gloriously grand construction that dwarfed the tiny Anglo-Saxon chapel that had previously stood here and one that was designed both to sing the praises of God and to establish Norman superiority over the Saxons once and for all. Known as the 'Ship of the Fens', the cathedral still towers above the surrounding landscape. Ely was also **Oliver Cromwell's home** town in the 17th century and you can still visit his house.

The town's shopping and market area are well worth a stroll and lead down to a picturesque stretch of riverside overlooked by numerous historic buildings; centuries of seclusion have ensured that much of medieval Ely survives. Its long history and gradual emergence from a world of water is told in the Ely Museum, which is housed in the town's former gaol.

Things to see and do

Cinemas and theatres *See pp.326, 329*

★Ely Cathedral
Chapter House, The College, Ely **t** (01353) 667735 **www**.cathedral.ely.anglican.org
Open Summer: daily 7–7; winter: Mon–Sat 7.30–6, Sun 7.30–5; tours of the Octagon: Apr–Sept several times a day; stained-glass museum: Easter–Oct Mon–Fri 10.30–5, Sat 10.30–5.30, Sun 12 noon–6; Nov–Easter Mon–Sat 10.30–5, Sun 12 noon 4.30
Adm Adults £5.20, children £4.50, under 12s **free**, **free** for all on Sundays; stained-glass museum: adults £3.50, children £2.50, family £7
Refectory, Almonry tearooms, restaurant, café, shops, some disabled access, on-site parking

One of the country's grandest, most distinctive-looking cathedrals, its interior highlights include the painted ceiling, huge imposing Norman arches and, its most beautiful feature, the vast octagonal lantern, a sort of enormous stained glass skylight built in the 14th century and supported by wooden beams cut from the largest oak trees then available. The cathedral also contains a Stained Glass Museum, with many fine medieval and modern examples of this ancient craft on display.

Ely Museum
The Old Gaol, Market Street, Ely **t** (01353) 666655 **www**.elymuseum.org.uk

Did you know?
That when Cromwell died in 1658 he was succeeded by his son who reigned for just two years, before the monarchy was restored in 1660. With the royals back in fashion, Cromwell soon became such a hated figure that his body was removed from Westminster Abbey and hung up at Tyburn (where criminals were executed), while his head was stuck on a pole and placed on top of Westminster Hall, where it remained for the next 20 years.

Open Summer Mon–Sat 10.30–5, Sun 1–5; Winter Mon–Sat 10.30–4 (closed Tues) **Adm** Adults £3, accompanied children **free**
Gift shop, disabled access
    Exhibits detailing the history of Ely and the Fens; 'The Gaol and its Inmates','Trade and Industry', 'The War Years'.

Oliver Cromwell's House

29 St Mary's Street, Ely **t** (01353) 662062
Open Apr–Oct daily 10–5.30; Nov–Mar Mon–Fri 10–4, Sat 10–5, Sun 11.15–4 **Adm** Adults £3.75, children £2.50, family £10
Gift shop, guided tours

Sport and activities *See pp.322–5*

Around Ely

Brandon Country Park and Thetford Forest, 13 miles east (p.317)
Cambridge, 13 miles south (pp.284–8)
Wicken Fen, 7 miles south (p.322)

Ipswich

Getting there By car: Ipswich can be reached easily via the A12 from London and A14 from the Midlands and the North. By train: Intercity trains link Ipswich with London Liverpool Street (just over an hour) and Peterborough from where there are connections to the Midlands and the North. By coach: National Express operates a daily coach service between Ipswich and London Victoria, Manchester, Sheffield and Nottingham. Although largely pedestrianized, there are around 5,800 parking spaces available in the town centre, as well as a park and ride service from the junction of the A12/A14, with connections every 10 minutes to the centre
Tourist information St Stephen's Church, St Stephen's Lane **t** (01473) 258070
www.visit-ipswich.gov.uk

    'Ipswich? you'd be surprised' runs the tourist board's slightly desperate slogan; an overt acknowledgement of the city's problematic image. Glamorous it ain't; it certainly doesn't make it onto most people's list of must-see cities. So, will you be surprised? Well, if you go expecting the worst sort of modern, soulless town with nothing to offer beyond a high street and a shopping centre then, yes, you will be surprised. It's a lot better than that. On the other hand, if you go expecting a moderately interesting, albeit hardly outstanding town, one that makes a decent enough base for exploring the very pleasant local countryside and, in particular, the artist-inspiring Stour Valley, then, no, you won't be surprised at all, as that pretty much sums it up.

    There's a lot more old stuff in Ipswich than you might expect (indeed, you may be surprised). Founded in Saxon times, in around AD 600, the layout of the streets has changed little in the intervening 1,400 years and the Saxon market-place, Cornhill, is still very much the heart of the city. It was also where several Protestants, known as the 'Ipswich martyrs', were burnt to death in the mid 16th century on the orders of the Catholic Mary I. Ravaged by Viking attacks in the 9th and 10th centuries, by around 1150 Ipswich had established itself as a successful inland port, exporting wool and textiles to the Continent, and home to a thriving shipbuilding industry: this was where Edward I's war galleys were constructed. In the 17th century, Ipswich became one of the favoured departure points for emigrants looking to start new lives in the American colonies while, three centuries later, its ships were put to a very different use as part of the evacuation force at Dunkirk. The city's wet dock which, when first built, was the largest in the world, is still (partly) in operation, although many of its warehouses have been turned into pubs and restaurants. The quayside has recently been renovated and should not be missed. Do

Did you know?
That the world's first lawnmower was made in Ipswich.

also look out for the Ancient House, the town's most famous building, which, despite the name, was actually built in the mid 16th century and is decorated with sculpted plasterwork, featuring rooms in period style.

Although much of the city is modern and, to be honest, a bit drab, the town centre itself is fairly pleasant. Largely pedestrianized, it's filled with cafés and restaurants and there are two large, modern shopping malls as well as a more traditional shopping area with specialist shops. The town is particularly good for families with a sporting bent, boasting the Crown Pools (p.325) leisure centre, with beach entry, a wave machine, subtropical greenery and a small indoor activity area, an open-air lido (summer only), a go-kart track and a dry ski slope.

Ipswich is also within easy reach of some idyllic countryside. The Suffolk Heritage Coast, one of the country's most picturesque shorelines, is just a few miles east while, just to the south, running along the border between Suffolk and Essex, is the exquisite Stour Valley (or 'painter's valley' as it's sometimes known), without which the history of British art would have been very different.

Things to see and do

Christchurch Mansion and Wolsey Art Gallery

Christchurch Park **t** (01473) 433554
Open Mar–Oct Tues–Sat 10–5, Sun 10–4.30; Nov–Feb Tues–Sat 10–4, Sun 2.30–4 **Adm Free**

Tudor mansion set in 26 hectares (65 acres) of parkland, where Constables and Gainsboroughs are displayed. Children's activities and workshops in the Wolsey Gallery during the school holidays.

Cinemas and theatres See pp.326, 329

Constable's paintings tours

Bridge Cottage, Flatford **t** (01206) 298260
www.nationaltrust.org.uk
The walks depart May–Sept every afternoon
Adm Adults £2.50, children **free**; advance booking advised, also audio guides £2 per tape (£5 deposit)

In summer, the National Trust arranges guided walks around Dedham Vale, the heart of 'Constable Country', a picturesque valley filled with typically English, leafy scenery, little changed in 200 years. The Constable Trail takes in some of the sites associated with the artist's life – notably the village of Dedham, with its 15th-century flint church and Toy Museum (p.327), where Constable spent much of his childhood – and passing several of the views in his paintings including a lane between East Bergholt and Dedham represented in *The Cornfield*, a section of the River Stour below Flatford Lock as shown in *The White Horse* and the mill in Flatford featured in his most famous picture, *The Haywain*.

Ipswich Museum

High Street **t** (01473) 433550
Open Tues–Sat 10–5 **Adm Free**
Refreshments, shop, disabled access

This excellent museum houses many wonderful objects, including a replica of the Sutton Hoo Viking long ship, one of the greatest archaeological discoveries of the century, which was unearthed near Woodbridge (about seven miles northeast) in 1939 (the original ship and accompanying artefacts are now in the British Museum), as well as the very fork with which a group of cannibals ate the missionary Reverend Baker. The natural history gallery has been arranged to look as it would have done when first unveiled in the 19th century, with stuffed animals placed in beautiful, dark wood glass cabinets. Look out for the gorillas, the first ever seen in Britain and the life-size model of a mammoth (in the Suffolk wildlife gallery), a native of these parts some 12,000 years ago. There is also a collection of world folklore and a 'Romans in Suffolk' exhibition.

Ipswich Transport Museum

Old Trolleybus Depot, Cobham Road **t** (01473) 715666 www.ipswichtransportmuseum.co.uk
Open Apr–Nov Sun and Bank Hols 11–4 (school hols Mon–Fri 1–4)
Adm Adults £3.50, children £2.50, under 4s **free**, family (2+3) £9.50
Shop, disabled access

Housed in a former trolley bus depot, this museum has a large collection of buses, horse-drawn carriages and fire engines, some of which kids can clamber aboard.

Sport and activities *See pp.322–5*

Walking tours

Guided walks are led from the tourist office in the summer (May–Sept Tues and Thurs 2.15pm).

Around Ipswich

Baylham House Rare Breeds Farm, 6 miles north-west (p.307)

Dedham Art and Craft Centre and Toy Museum, 9 miles southwest (p.327)

Orford Castle, 13 miles northeast (p.310)

King's Lynn

Getting there By road: The town is located 45 miles north of Cambridge (via the A14 and the A10) and 105 miles north of London: take the M11/A11/A14. By train: Trains to King's Lynn depart regularly from Cambridge (45 minutes), Norwich via Ely (2 hours) and London King's Cross (1 hour 30 minutes). By bus/coach: There is a frequent bus service from London Victoria via Cambridge (4 hours 20 minutes) and a less frequent one from Norwich (1 hour 25 minutes)

Tourist information Custom House, Purfleet Quay **t** (01553) 763044 www.west-norfolk.gov.uk

The Great Ouse River is both the reason for King's Lynn's existence and the greatest threat to its survival. The town's strategic location three miles inland, where the river flows into the Wash, made it the perfect conduit for Continental trade in the Middle Ages. Goods flowed in and out in such quantities that King's Lynn was once the country's fourth largest city. But its location also made it susceptible to flooding and, throughout its long history, the town has had to cope with periodic submerg-ings, including three particularly devastating floods, in 1953, 1978 and 2000 – you can see just how high the waters reached at St Margaret's Church on Saturday Market Place, where the flood levels are recorded by the west door.

Despite these traumas, much of the old town remains, including several large medieval build-ings and some elegant Georgian town houses, although a significant portion was cleared away in a short-sighted redevelopment scheme in the 1950s. Away from the centre, the town has a

hastily developed, modern feel to it but its small collection of attractions makes it well worth a detour and it provides a good base for exploring the North Norfolk coast.

The town's waterfront was recently redeveloped as part of the millennium scheme for West Norfolk, with the creation of the Green Quay, an interactive exhibition on wildlife in the Wash. Nearby, inside the very grand Trinity Guildhall, parts of which date back to the 15th century, is the Old Gaol House, which offers tours through the history of crime and punishment using an audio guide (with a special children's tour). Around the corner, near St Margaret's Church, is the Town House Museum, where you'll find displays detailing the history of the town. Other sights to look out for in the old part of town include St George's Guildhall (King Street), the largest surviving 15th-century guildhall in England (now the King's Lynn Arts Centre), the Lynn Museum and the restored fishermen's cottages of True's Yard. The town hosts a couple of lively street markets each week, on Tuesdays (at the Tuesday Market Place) and Saturdays (at the Saturday Market Place).

Things to see and do

Cinemas and theatres *See pp.326, 329*

Green Quay

South Quay **t** (01553) 818500
www.thegreenquay.co.uk
Open Daily 9–5 **Adm Free**
Café, shop

Aimed at promoting awareness of the Wash's wildlife and environment: you can watch a film on the local area, see fish and crabs in an aquarium, make rubbings of animal footprints and play interactive computer games. The centre runs half-term art classes, environmental games and photography exhibitions. Call for details.

King's Lynn Arts Centre

27–29 King Street **t** (01553) 764864
Open Mon–Fri 10–2 (not Bank Hols); restricted opening Jul–Aug due to the festival

The largest surviving 15th-century guildhall in England (in Elizabethan times it was a theatre) and the venue for the annual King's Lynn Festival: a week of concerts, exhibitions, dance, films and children's programmes (usually held in July). The arts centre was previously known as St George's Guildhall.

Lynn Museum

Market Street **t** (01553) 775001
Open Tues–Sat 10–5 **Adm** Free

The museum contains a skeleton of a Saxon warrior, a collection of Victorian fairground 'gallopers' and organizes children's activity days – such as a 'What's the Rock?' day (fossil identification), 'Make do and Mend' day (life in the Second World War), and '200 years of dressing up' day – during the school holidays.

Sport and activities *See pp.322–5*

Tales of the Old Gaol House

Saturday Market Place **t** (01553) 774297
Open Apr–Oct Mon–Sat 10–5, Nov–Mar Tues–Sat 10–4 (last admission 1hr before closing)
Adm Adults £2.70, children £1.95, under 5s **free**
Shop, some disabled access

Please note: This attraction may be a little scary for younger children (under 7s)

The personal stereo guided tour begins in a 1930s police station, where you have your fingerprints and mugshot taken before exploring the cells to examine some of the archaic forms of punishment administered in centuries past; kids can put their head and hands in a pillory and even be locked inside one of the dark damp cells for a few moments. You can also read stories about some of the town's most notorious villains, the witches, robbers and highwaymen who fell foul of the law here in times gone by.

Town House Museum

46 Queen Street **t** (01553) 773450
Open May–Sept Mon–Sat 10–5, Oct–Apr Mon–Sat 10–4
Adm Adults £2.60, children £1.50
Herb garden, gift shop, limited disabled access.

Displays recording 1,000 years of King's Lynn life, with rooms furnished in Tudor, Stuart, Georgian and Victorian styles. Children will enjoy the Edwardian school display, where they can practice writing on slate, and the Victorian nursery with dolls' house and replica toys that can be played with.

True's Yard Fishing Museum

North Street **t** (01553) 770479
www.welcome.to/truesyard

Open Mon–Sat 9.30–3.45 (Apr–Oct daily)
Adm Call for details
Tearoom, gift shop

Restored fishermen's cottages and museum illustrating the lives of the fishing folk of King's Lynn (or 'Northenders'), on whose industry much of the town's wealth was founded.

Around King's Lynn

Houghton Hall, 10 miles northeast (p.300)
Hunstanton, 13 miles northeast (pp.312–3)
Long Sutton Butterfly and Wildlife Park, 10 miles west (p.303)
Sandringham House, 7 miles northeast (pp.301–2)

Norwich

Getting there By road: Norwich is 115 miles from London, 63 miles from Cambridge and can be reached via the M11 and the A11 (from London) and the A14, the A11 and the A47 (from Cambridge, the Midlands and the North). By train: Regular train services run to Norwich from London Liverpool Street (1 hour 45 minutes). The station is a 10-minute walk from the centre. By bus/coach: There are regular National Express coaches from London Victoria to Norwich (3 hours) and from Cambridge (2 hours). There are numerous pay and display car parks in and around the city centre, as well as a handful of multi-storeys, including one just off St Giles Street near the City Hall. There are also three NCP car parks just outside the centre; one to the south, two to the north

Tourist information The Forum, Market Place
t (01603) 727927 www.norwich.gov.uk

Norwich is East Anglia's biggest town and the region's unofficial capital. A good-looking old city with plenty of fine architecture, it makes a convenient base for exploring the Norfolk Broads, the vast agglomeration of inland waterways just northeast of the town, and the east Norfolk coast; Great Yarmouth, the area's principal resort, is about 20 miles to the east. Although it may not strike you as overly family friendly at first, Norwich is home to a handful of child-orientated attractions – the best are the Inspire Hands-On Science Centre, Norwich Puppet Theatre and

Bridewell Museum – and is within easy reach of several more.

Founded by the Angles who, with their better-known countrymen, the Saxons, invaded and colonized much of the country in the centuries after the collapse of the Roman Empire, Norwich became the site of a thriving textile industry in the Middle Ages thanks to trade links with the Netherlands and probably enjoyed a closer link with the Low Countries at this time than it did with London. By the early 1700s, it was the country's second most prosperous city but, from this point on, its position began to slip. Slow to adapt to new manufacturing methods pioneered during the Industrial Revolution, it found itself undermined by the large, new textile factories of the northern cities and fell into a slight decline.

These days, however, thanks to a boom in its new hi-tech industries, its star is once again in the ascendant and it is now a busy, lively city, albeit one with with a distinctly olde-worlde village feel to it. The streets still follow the rather jumbled Angle layout (with cobbled alleyways jutting off from the main roads hither and thither) and are lined with medieval buildings; wherever you go, you're seemingly never more than 100 metres (110 yards) from a medieval church. In the middle of the city's pedestrianized centre is the Market Place, the heart of the city, where around 200 stalls are set up for business daily under coloured awnings, selling clothes, jewellery, sweets and fruit and vegetables. While browsing, look out for the starlings darting between your legs looking for scraps.

The town's two principal sites are its main landmarks. The squat Norman castle sits atop a mound just to the south of the city centre, while the magnificent cathedral is to the east. The cathedral spire, the second tallest in the country, hardly dominates the skyline, but you will see it every now and then poking through the rooftops, although the rather random layout of the streets makes it appear rainbow-like – the harder you try to reach it, the further away it seems to get.

Things to see and do

Boat trips

For the clearest and best views of the city's castle and cathedral, take a boat trip along the River Wensum, which flows in a loop around the centre of the town. For information on boat tours through Norwich and the Norfolk Broads, contact Southern River Steamers on t (01603) 624051.

Bridewell Museum

Bridewell Alley t (01603) 629127
Open Feb–Sept Tues–Fri 10–4.30 (Sat 5pm)
Adm Adults £3, children £1.60, family (2+2) £6.90
Shop, not suitable for pushchairs

Good local museum telling the story of Norwich (from small provincial town to economic power-house and back again) with lots of exhibits on the two principal themes of Norwich life: clothes and mustard. Art and craft workshops (where kids can learn block-printing, the techniques of forensic science – such as finger-printing – or how to be a newspaper editor) as well as storytellings, are organized during the school holidays.

Bus tours

During the summer months Guide Friday offers open-top bus tours of the city, t (01789) 294466, www.guidefriday.com. For more general information on public transport contact NORBIC on t 0845 300 6116.

Cinemas and theatres *See pp.326, 329*

City of Norwich Aviation Museum

Old Norwich Road, Horsham St Faith
t (01603) 893080 www.cnam.co.uk
Getting there 2 miles north of the city off the A140
Open Apr–Oct Tues–Sat 10–5, Sun and Bank Hols 12 noon–5; Nov–Mar Wed and Sat 10–4, Sun 12 noon–4
Adm Adults £3.25, children £1.50, family (2+3) £9
Refreshments, shop, disabled access, on-site parking

Military aviation museum with lots of planes on display including a Vulcan Bomber; kids can even sit in the pilot's seat.

Colman's Mustard Shop

15 Royal Arcade t (01603) 627889
www.colmansmustardshop.com
Open Mon–Sat 9.30–5, Sun 11–4 **Adm Free**

No visit to Norwich would be complete without a trip to Colman's Mustard Shop, where you can discover the secret history of mustard and find out how the fiery condiment is made. Kids can follow the cartoon adventures of Jeremiah Colman around the shop, while their parents examine the Art Deco mustard pots and wartime tins.

Inspire Hands-On Science Centre

St Michael's Church, Coslany Steet **t** (01603) 612612
www.inspirediscoverycentre.com
Open Mon–Fri 10–5, Sat and Sun 11–5
Adm Adults £4.50, children £4, family £13,
under 3s **free**
Café, science shop

Small but well-equipped science museum with
a wide range of hands-on exhibits housed in the
medieval St Michael's Church. Kids can step
inside a bubble, build an arch bridge, solve the
sound maze, discover the secrets of lightning
and find out about many other scientific facts.

Norwich Castle

Castle Meadow **t** (01603) 493625
Open Mon–Fri 10–4.30, Sat 10–5, Sun 1–5
Adm Adults £6.50, children £4.60, under 3s **free**
Café, shop

After the Tower of London, this squat, square
little castle (21m/69ft high, 28m/92ft wide) is the
best preserved Norman military fortress in the
country. Built in the mid 11th century, it was
converted into a prison in the late Middle Ages
and was the site of numerous public executions
– the last of which took place in the early 19th
century. You can tour the dungeons to see the
castle's collection of torture instruments and
original plaster casts of the heads of hanged
murderers – cast for phrenological study, the now
discredited science of testing predisposition to
crime by measuring the shape and size of head
and features. The adjacent Regimental Museum,
which is linked to the castle by an underground
tunnel, has galleries full of military paraphernalia
plus a reconstruction of a First World War trench.

Norwich Cathedral

12 The Close **t** (01603) 218231 **www.cathedral.org.uk**
Open Daily 7.30–6 (mid-May–mid-Sept until 7pm)
Adm Free (voluntary donation of £2 requested)
*Restaurant, shop, guided tours, adapted toilets,
some disabled access and parking*

Passing through the great gateway to the city's
medieval cathedral close is like stepping back in
time. In amongst the close's grassy lawns, overhanging trees, narrow alleyways and graceful
architecture – medieval, Georgian, etc. – it's like a
mini town within a town. At its heart is the
honey-coloured, spired cathedral, one of the
country's best. Begun in 1092, it was completed

some 50 years later and built entirely from stone
sailed across from Normandy (the builders clearly
didn't think much of the domestic stone on offer).
You can still see the remains of special channels
dug to float the stones from the river to the site.
The great spire, surrounded by four mini spires,
was added in the 15th century and, at 96m (315ft)
tall, is the second highest in the country (only
Salisbury's is taller). The interior is unusually light
and airy with lots of clear glass filling the nave
with light. There are spectacular stained glass
windows at the west and east ends and a
wonderfully ornate ceiling decorated with round
lattice-like stones: known as bosses, they have
been carved with intricate representations of
biblical stories. You can study them (without the
need to crane your neck) in the mirrors along the
aisle, although it is difficult to pick out that much
detail (the ceiling is a good 18m/60ft up). If you're
particularly interested, check out similar designs
in the cloisters (the largest in the country), only
about 5m (15ft) above your head. Look out for the
huge thick pillars supporting the roof, a speciality
of Norman architecture (in particular the two
either side of the choir which, with their diagonal
line motifs, look as if they're being screwed into
the ground) and the tombs lining the floors of
the side aisles; the thought of walking over dead
bodies always gives kids a spooky thrill. Quiz
sheets for children.

Norwich Puppet Theatre

St James, Whitefriars **t** (01603) 629921
www.puppettheatre.co.uk
Open Mon–Fri 9–5 (box office) and 1hr before the
performance (weekends) **Adm** Performances:
adults £6, children £4; workshops: £6 per child

Award-winning marionette-, glove- and rod-
puppet shows for children aged 3–10 are staged
most Saturdays at 10.30am and 2.30pm. There are
extra weekday shows during the school holidays.
Most are based on fairytales – Cinderella, Jack and
the Beanstalk, Snow White, etc. – although there
are occasional performances of more modern
children's classics such as Roald Dahl's *George's
Marvellous Medicine* and Oscar Wilde's *The Selfish
Giant*. The centre also organizes puppet-making
workshops for children aged 5 and over, where they
can create their own puppets and learn manipula-
tion skills from one of the centre's puppeteers.

SPECIAL TRIPS

Sainsbury Centre for Visual Arts

University of East Anglia, Earlham Road
t (01603) 593199 **www.scva.org.uk**
Getting there Located off the B1108 (Watton Road)
Open Tues–Sun 10–5, Wed 10–8 **Adm Free**

The city's latest pride and joy: a collection of 19th- and 20th-century European art, African tribal sculpture, Egyptian and Asian artefacts housed in a state-of-the-art Norman Foster-designed building on the Norwich University campus. Special events are put on throughout the year.

Sport and activities *See pp.322–5*

St Peter's Hungate Church Museum

Princes Street **t** (01603) 667231
Open Easter–Sept Mon–Sat 10–5 **Adm Free**

Brass rubbings from a number of replica brasses.

Stranger's Hall

Charing Cross **t** (01603) 667229
Open Wed and Sat 10.30am, 12 noon and 4.30pm
Adm Adults £3, children £1.60, under 5s **free**; tickets can be booked on **t** (01603) 493636

A medieval merchant's house turned into a museum of domestic life, with each room decorated and furnished in a different period style (Tudor, Regency, Victorian, etc.).

Walking tours

Sightseeing tours of the city with a Blue Badge Guide. Contact the tourist office, **t** (01603) 666071.

Around Norwich

The Broads, a few miles northeast (pp.320–1)
Dinosaur Adventure Park, 9 miles northwest (p.319)
Wroxham Barns, 7 miles northeast (p.317)

Castles and historic houses

Audley End House

Audley End, Saffron Walden **t** (01799) 522399
www.english-heritage.org.uk
Getting there 1 mile west of Saffron Walden on the B1383. There's a path leading directly to the mansion from Saffron Walden High Street (1 mile)
Open Apr–Sept Wed–Sun and Bank Hols, house: 11–5; grounds: 10–6; Oct, house: Sat 10–3, Sun 10–4; grounds: Sat 10–3, Sun 10–5
Adm House and grounds: adults £8.95, children £4.50, family £22.40; grounds only: adults £4.80, children £2.40, family £12
Café-restaurant, picnic area, gift shop, mother and baby facilities, some disabled access, on-site parking

This exceedingly grand Jacobean mansion, which looks a bit like an enormous square horseshoe, was built by the Earl of Suffolk in the early 17th century. One of the largest houses in the entire country at the time, it was generally considered 'fit for a king'; so fit, in fact, that Charles II actually bought it for £50,000 (an enormous sum of money in those days – the equivalent of many millions today) and used it as a base when attending the horse races at nearby Newmarket. It's a good deal smaller now – the courtyard and east wing (amounting to around two-thirds of the original structure) were demolished in the early 18th century – although still terribly swish with classical concerts held in the gardens landscaped by Capability Brown (who else?) and 30 sumptuously decorated rooms to explore. For kids, the interior highlights will probably be the lavishly furnished Victorian doll's house and the 19th-century collection of stuffed birds and animals (there are over 1,000 on display). A free children's activity sheet is available. However, although interesting, it has to be said that inside the house it's all a bit whispery and quiet and your kids may soon be eager to explore the grounds, where they can run around and make a bit of noise. They'll find sculpted hedges, where they can play hide and seek, walks down by the River Cam and a miniature steam railway, very much aimed at children, with toys and teddies lining the route. Medieval themed attractions and a special 'Children's Day' with puppet and magic shows are put on in summer.

Blickling Hall

Blickling, Norwich **t** (01263) 738030
www.nationaltrust.org.uk
Getting there 15 miles north of Norwich on the
B1354 and signposted off the A140
Open House: Aug–Sept Wed–Sun 1–5 (Aug also
Mon), Oct Wed–Sun 1–4; garden: Aug–Oct
Wed–Sun (Aug also Mon) 10.15–5.15, Nov–Mar
Thurs–Sun 11–4; park and woods: all year daily
dawn–dusk
Adm Adults £8, children £4, family £20; garden
only: adult £5, children £2.50, family £12.50
Restaurant, shop, plant centre, second-hand book-
shop, picnic area, mother and baby room, disabled
access, on-site parking, tours

Grand 17th-century mansion, built on top of the
house where Anne Boleyn, Henry VIII's second
wife, spent much of her childhood. Today, she is
said to haunt the site; her headless ghost has
been seen arriving at the doors of the hall in a
carriage drawn by a team of headless horses.
Pretty spooky. Ghostly goings-on aside, the house
is still well worth a brief detour. Though a touch
stuffy and, as you would expect, richly furnished
with a grand oak staircase, it does have a few
interesting whatnots to look out for including a
statue of Anne (in her pre-headless state), a
tapestry of Peter the Great and a Long Gallery
which has all manner of bizarre creatures
moulded into its plaster ceiling.

Felbrigg Hall

Roughton, Norwich **t** (01263) 837444
www.nationaltrust.org.uk
Getting there 2 miles southwest of Cromer, off the
B1436 and signposted from the A148 and the A140
Open House: Apr–Oct Sat–Wed 1–5; garden:
Apr–Oct Wed–Sun 1–5.30 (Aug daily)
Adm Adults £7, children £3.50, family £17.50
Restaurant, tea room, picnic area, mother and baby
room, disabled access, on-site parking

The last squire of Febrigg bequeathed this
17th-century hall to the National Trust back in the
1960s, since when it has been spruced up and
turned into one of Norfolk's most popular stately
homes. Inside are a number of oddities that
should appeal to the kids. Children's Guide in
hand, see if they can track down the false door,
the extremely elaborate Gothic-style library and
the bath with a difference: designed to preserve
one's modesty whilst servants were in the room,
it enabled bathers to wash without revealing the
more private parts of their body. Do also look out
for the large collection of stuffed rare birds (most
of which you wouldn't be allowed to shoot today)
and the beautiful walled garden and avenue of
beech trees outside.

Framlingham Castle

Castle Street, Framlingham, Woodbridge
t (01728) 724189 **www**.english-heritage.org.uk
Getting there On the B1116 about 20 miles
northeast of Ipswich
Open Apr–Sept daily 10–6; Oct Thurs–Mon 10–5,
Nov–Mar daily 10–4
Adm Adults £4.50, children £2.30, under 5s **free**,
family £11.30
Shop, guided tours, disabled access, picnic area,
on-site parking

Twelfth-century castle that's been a royal residence (this is where, in 1553, Mary I heard of her
succession upon the death of her brother
Edward VI and where she waited while Lady Jane
Grey enjoyed her brief nine-day reign), an
Elizabethan prison, a poorhouse and even a
school. Extremely well preserved, the medieval
curtain wall linking the castle's 13 towers still
survives and you can walk along it. Framlingham
Castle puts on a range of medieval-themed
events over the summer including plays, music
recitals and archery competitions. Activity books
for children are available.

Holkham Hall

Holkham **t** (01328) 710227 **www**.holkham.co.uk
Getting there 3 miles west of Wells-next-the-Sea
on the A149; follow the brown tourist signs
Open House: Jun–Sept Thurs–Mon 1–5; museum:
May–Sept Thurs–Mon 12–5 **Adm** grounds and
farming museum **free**; hall and bygones museum:
adults £10, children £5, family £25

With grand landscaped gardens, farming
museum (delving into Holkham's agricultural
past) and a wonderful collection of paintings by
artists such as Rubens, Van Dyck and
Gainsborough, Holkham is nonetheless principally worth visiting for its Bygones Museum,
which contains over 4,000 domestic and agricultural artefacts – from Victorian matchboxes
to vintage cars, gramophones to fire engines –
housed in a converted stable.

Houghton Hall

Houghton, King's Lynn **t** (01485) 528569
www.houghtonhall.com
Getting there On the A148 King's Lynn–Cromer
Road, 11 miles from King's Lynn
Open Easter–Sept Wed,Thurs, Sun and Bank Hols
11–5.30; house: 1.30–5.
Adm Adults £7, children £3, under 5s **free**,
family £16
*Café-restaurant, gift shop, disabled access,
on-site parking*

A stately home with sweeping landscaped
gardens built by Robert Walpole, Britain's first
prime minister, in the 18th century. It houses the
Cholmondeley (pronounced 'Chumley') Soldier
Museum, which has over 20,000 model soldiers
arranged in a series of spectacular battle scenes.
In the grounds, look out for a small obelisk, which
marks the spot where the village of Houghton
once stood: when Walpole wanted his house built,
he simply had the village moved two miles down
the road.

Ickworth House and Park

The Rotunda, Ickworth, Bury St Edmunds
t (01284) 735270 **www**.nationaltrust.org.uk
Getting there On the A143, 2 miles south of
Bury St Edmunds
Open House: Apr–Oct Fri–Tues and Bank Hols 1–5;
garden: Mar–Sept Fri–Tues 10–5, Oct–Feb Fri–Tues
11–4; park: daily 8–8
Adm House and garden: adults £7, children £3,
family £17; park only: adults £3.40, children 90p
*Café-restaurant, picnic areas, shop, disabled access,
mother and baby facilities, on-site parking*

The people who run Ickworth have done their
best to make the stately home as interesting for
children as possible. You can pick up a 'handy' box
at the entrance full of interesting whatnots and
doodahs – candles, pieces of chandelier, etc. –
which you must match with ones displayed
somewhere in the house. There are also quizzes
and trails and children can take part in a free
'touch' tour of the house. Nonetheless, for all
their efforts, your kids will probably still prefer
the grand Italianate gardens. There is also a deer
park, woodland walks, a family cycle trail and an
adventure playground. There's also a luxury
family hotel in the house's east wing (p.522).

★Kentwell Hall

Long Melford **t** (01787) 310207 **www**.kentwell.co.uk
Getting there 11 miles south of Bury St Edmunds,
off the A134
Open Feb–Dec; call for times
Adm Adults £7.50, children £4.75 (extra charges
apply for special events), under 5s **free**
Café-restaurant, gift shop, on-site parking

Kentwell Hall is a large Tudor Manor house
that, on selected weekends, is turned into a sort
of Tudor theme park when around 250 costumed
volunteers attempt a mass recreation of Tudor
domestic life. All aspects are covered: they cook
Tudor meals in the Tudor kitchen, play Tudor
music in the Tudor minstrels gallery, bake Tudor
bread in the Tudor bakehouse, spin Tudor pots on
the Tudor pottery wheel, make Tudor butter and
cheese in the Tudor dairy and tend to the Tudor-
style animals in the Tudor farmyard, stables,
dovecote and goathouse. The volunteers are even
expected to speak in Tudor style, adopting mid
16th-century speech patterns throughout the
day. It's all tremendous fun and fascinating for
children, who will have lots of opportunities to
join in the fun and games. During the rest of the
year, the house is quieter but, nonetheless, still
well worth a visit. In the house, look out for the
Brueghel-style ceiling in the parlour, which is
decorated with pictures depicting Tudor children's games and, in the grounds, for the Tudor
Rose-shaped maze and (if you fancy getting away
from the overwhelming Tudorishness for a while)
the peaceful woodland walks.

★Mountfitchet Castle and Norman Village

Stansted **t** (01279) 813237
www.mountfitchetcastle.com
Getting there 2 miles from J8 of the M11 and 5
minutes' walk from Stansted Mountfitchet station,
which is on the London–Cambridge line
Open Mar–Nov daily 10–5; toy museum all year
daily 10–4
Adm Adults £6.50, children £5; toy museum: adults
£4, children £3.30. Combined ticket: adults £9.45,
children £7.45
Café, shop, on-site parking

Mountfitchet, a reconstruction of a classic
Norman motte and bailey castle, is a great place
for kids to come and find out what life in a
medieval castle was really like: not all that
pleasant, to be honest. The romanticized image of

dashing knights in armour and princesses in long velvet dresses and strange pointy hats is a long way from the truth. While life for the castle's handful of nobles may indeed have been terribly luxurious, for the majority of people it was just terribly hard. You may be surprised to find an entire replica Norman village inside the castle walls, complete with church, thatched cottages, charcoal burners' hut, pottery kiln and black-smith's forge, but then, in medieval times, castles were more than simple fortresses; in times of siege, they also provided a home for many hundreds of people, most of whom lived in cramped, gloomy, grimy living quarters, here recreated in all their squalor. Inside, animated wax figures dressed in period costume will tell you their rather miserable stories – the blood-spattered victims in the prison have a particularly gruesome tale to tell – while outside, free-roaming farmyard animals, such as goats, hens and tame deer, scrabble about between the houses. Once you've had enough of all the dirt, grime and soot, head to the castle itself to see how the other half lived in the aptly named Great Hall, laid out for a magnificent medieval banquet. Mountfitchet is a fascinating place that will really help to bring history alive for children (it's partic-ularly helpful if they happen to be studying medieval life at school), although it should be noted that, in the interests of authenticity, the site is very hilly and you'll have to put in some serious walking to see everything. On your travels, look out for the replica siege tower (which can be climbed) from where medieval soldiers would have fired arrows and catapulted large stones at potential invaders; your children will no doubt volunteer to help with a reconstruction. For a top day out you could also pay a visit to the House on the Hill Toy Museum, just five minutes up the road, which has more than 80,000 vintage toys displayed on two floors (p.327).

Oxburgh Hall

Oxborough, King's Lynn **t** (01366) 328258
www.nationaltrust.org.uk
Getting there 17 miles south of King's Lynn, off the A134
Open House: Aug–Oct Sat–Wed 1–5 (Oct until 4); garden: Aug daily 11-5.30, Sept–Oct Sat–Wed 11–5.30 (Oct until 4.30), Nov–Feb Sat–Sun 11–4
Adm Adults £6.50, children £3.25, family £17

Restaurant, picnic, shop, mother and baby room, some disabled access, woodland trail, parking

Thanks to a good deal of 19th-century prettifi-cation, this 15th-century manor looks almost castle-esque with its grand battlements and moat. It was owned by the same Catholic family, the Bedingfelds, for over 500 years – hence the priest's hole, which would have been used to hide the family priest when Catholicism was outlawed following the Reformation in the 16th century. The Children's Guide will point out some of the more interesting items on display including the collection of weapons and armour from the Civil War and the display of embroidery sewn by Mary Queen of Scots whilst she was held in captivity by Elizabeth I. Outside, there are attractive woodland walks.

Sandringham House

Sandringham **t** (01553) 772675
www.sandringhamestate.co.uk
Getting there 8 miles northeast of King's Lynn off the A148
Open House: Apr–Oct daily 11–4.45 (Oct until 3); museum: Apr–Oct 11–5 (Oct until 4); gardens: Apr–Oct 10.30–5 (Oct until 4)
Adm Adults £8, children £5, family £21; museum and gardens: adults £5.50, children £3.50, family £14.50
Café-restaurant, gift shop, adventure playground, mother and baby facilities, guided tours, disabled access, on-site parking

This is where the Queen makes her broadcast to the nation at 3pm every Christmas Day and it has a much more relaxed and intimate feel to it than some of the other Royal residences with a good many more family rooms open to the public than at Buckingham Palace or Windsor Castle. It's only a relative distinction, of course. Nobody could describe this grand collection of priceless porcelain, enamelled Russian silver, old master paintings and antique furniture as homely. It's as well-to-do and plush as you'd hope. The house itself is 19th century, although built in the Jacobean style (it was bought by Queen Victoria for her son Edward, the future king, in 1862 – that's some birthday present) and features a display of Oriental arms and family portraits. Over in the converted stable block is a museum which houses a collection of royal cars, a collection of royal photographs, a collection of

KIDS OUT

royal big-game trophies (lions, tigers, etc.) and (of most interest to kids) a collection of miniature cars and dolls made for generations of princes and princesses. Surrounding the house are landscaped gardens and more than 800 hectares (2,000 acres) of rolling country parkland, which provide a home for game birds (who must make themselves scarce every New Year when the Royal Party enjoys its annual hunt).

★Wimpole Hall and Wimpole Home Farm

Arrington, near Royston **t** (01223) 207257
www.wimpole.org
Getting there 8 miles southwest of Cambridge off the A603, J12 from the M11
Open Hall: Mid-Mar–Oct Sat–Wed 1–5 (late Jul–Aug also Thurs), Nov Sat–Sun 1–4; garden: early Mar Sat–Wed 11–4, mid-Mar–Oct Sat–Wed 10.30–5 (late Jul–Aug also Thurs), Nov–Feb Sat–Wed 11–4; park: all year daily dawn–dusk; farm: mid-Mar–Sept Sat–Wed 10.30–5, Nov–Feb Sat–Sun 11–4
Adm Estate: adults £11, children £6, family £28; farm only: adults £6, children £4; garden only: adults £3, children £1.50

The grounds of this grand 17th-century hall contain an adventure playground, woodland walks and a restored Georgian farm.
For further information *see p.308*

Windmills

Great Bircham Windmill

Bircham, King's Lynn **t** (01485) 578393
www.birchamwindmill.co.uk
Getting there The windmill is situated 7 miles southeast of Hunstanton
Open Apr–Sept daily 10–5 **Adm Free**
Tearoom, gift shop, plant stall

Great Bircham is located on one of Norfolk's very few hills (despite what Noel Coward said, they do exist) and can offer great views. Its sails still turn on windy days and it contains a bakery, where you can buy freshly baked bread while the kids entertain themselves with the community of small animals including miniature horses, guinea pigs and pygmy goats, which happily wander around outside. You can also hire bikes here to explore the local countryside (adults £6, children £4).

Animal attractions

Banham Zoo

Kenninghall Road, Banham **t** (01953) 887771
www.banhamzoo.co.uk
Getting there On the B1113: follow the brown tourist signs from the A11 Cambridge–Norwich road and the A140 Ipswich–Norwich road
Open Daily 10–dusk
Adm Adults £11.50, children £7.95, under 3s **free**
Café-restaurant, picnic areas, gift shop, mother and baby facilities, disabled access and parking, guided tours, on-site parking

Run by the same people responsible for the Suffolk Wildlife Park near Lowestoft, these 14 hectares (35 acres) provide a home to some 150 species of animal including red pandas, penguins, seals, lemurs and kangaroos, although it's the zoo's big cats which are very much the feature presentation. You'll see tigers and snow leopards living in large (albeit hardly safari park size) enclosures with glass-fronted windows, which allow you to get within a few inches of the fearsome beasts. You can attend feeding sessions throughout the day (monkeys at 11.30am, seals at 12 noon and tigers at 3.45pm) and there are regular bird of prey flying demonstrations. Tired legs will appreciate the free road train that tours the zoo (with commentary) while at the children's farm, kids can meet and pet the resident miniature donkeys, goats and sheep.

★Blakeney Point

Information Centre, Morston Quay **t** (01263) 740241
www.nationaltrust.org.uk
Getting there Off the A149 Cromer–Hunstanton Road. There's a car park, although access to the beach itself is by foot only from Cley Beach
Open Daily dawn–dusk **Adm Free**
Refreshments (summer), shop, on-site parking (charge)

One of the country's best-known bird sanctuaries, this 3.5-mile-long National Trust sand and shingle spit provides a home for vast colonies of breeding terns, oyster catchers, plovers and redshank, as well as common and grey seals. There are several companies offering seal-watching trips from Morston Quay including:
Bean's Boat Trips **t** (01263) 740505
www.beansboattrips.co.uk

Bishop's Boats **t** (01263) 740753,
www.norfolksealtrips.co.uk
Temple Seal Trips **t** (01263) 740791,
www.sealtrips.co.uk

Colchester Zoo

Maldon Road, Stanway, Colchester
t (01206) 331292 www.colchester-zoo.co.uk
Getting there Follow the brown elephant signs
from the A1124 exit from the A12, just south of the
town. It's 10 minutes from Colchester train station
by bus or taxi
Open Easter–Sept 9.30–6 (Jul–Aug until 6.30),
Oct–Mar 9.30–5
Adm Adults £13.99, children £7.50, under 3s **free**

Snow leopards, lions, orangutans, elephants
and chimps. There are different themes on offer –
'Penguin Shores', 'Wilds of Asia', 'White Tiger
Valley', 'Lakelands', 'Aquatic Zone' and 'Spirit of
Africa', plus a Jungle Safari Train and 'Calahari
Capers', an indoor soft play complex, as well as
four outdoor adventure play areas.
For further information *see* p.290

Grafham Water Nature Reserve

The Wildlife Cabin, Mander Car Park, Huntingdon
t (01480) 812660/811075
Getting there Just west of Perry Village in
Huntingdon, Cambridgeshire. Follow the signs
from the A1
Open Daily dawn–dusk **Adm** Free
*Café, picnic areas, guided tours, disabled access,
on-site parking (Mon–Fri £1, Sat–Sun £2)*

There are nature trails, woodland walks and a
10-mile family cycle trail around this large body
of water, as well as birdwatching hides (you can
see grebes, woodpeckers and sparrowhawks),
bird-feeding stations and a dragonfly pond.

Hamerton Zoo Park

Hamerton Road, near Sawtry **t** (01832) 293362
www.hamertonzoopark.com
Getting there Signposted from the A1 (J15) and the
A14 (junction with the B660)
Open Daily 10.30–6 (winter 4pm)
Adm Adults £7.50, children £5
*Café-restaurant, picnic areas, gift shop, disabled
access, on-site parking*

More than 120 different types of animal have
been given house room at this dedicated
wildlife breeding centre including gibbons, wild-
cats, meerkats, wallabies, cheetahs and

two-toed sloths (the only ones in the entire
country). There's also a children's zoo and indoor
and outdoor play areas.

Linton Zoological Gardens

Hadstock Road, Linton **t** (01223) 891308
www.lintonzoo.com
Getting there 10 miles southeast of Cambridge on
the B1052 just off the A1307. From the M11, take J9
(northbound) or J10 (southbound)
Open Summer: 10–6, winter: 10–dusk (last
admission 1 hour before closing)
Adm Adults £7, children £4.50, under 2s **free**
*Café (summer only), picnic areas, gift shop, disabled
access, on-site parking*

Small, very pretty zoo set in six hectares (16
acres) of beautifully landscaped gardens – look
out for the beds of blooming flowers in summer.
Home to the Cambridgeshire Wildlife Breeding
Centre, the zoo's primary purpose is the conservation of endangered species, but it nonetheless
presents itself in a friendly, entertaining way and
the animal enclosures, though occasionally a bit
on the small side, are well designed; the tiger
enclosure, for instance, has glass windows
allowing you to get right up close. In addition to
visiting the animals, which include zebras, snow
leopards, lions and giant tortoises, kids can
attend animal handling sessions where they can
stroke an owl or have a boa constrictor draped
around their neck; in summer, there's a family
quiz trail and a bouncy castle.

Long Sutton Butterfly and Wildlife Park

Long Sutton, Spalding **t** (01406) 363833
www.butterflyandwildlifepark.co.uk
Getting there Off the A17 between King's Lynn and
Sleeford: follow the brown tourist signs
Open Daily end Mar–Jun 10–5, Jul–mid-Sept
10–5.30, mid-Sept–Oct 10–4
Adm Adults £5.70, children £4.20, under 3s **free**,
family (2+2) £18, family (2+3) £21
*Tearooms, picnic areas, gift shop, guided tours,
on-site parking*

Long Sutton has one of the country's largest
walk-through tropical houses, containing
hundreds of free-flying butterflies, as well as
reptiles and insects. Daily flying demonstrations
by eagles, owls and falcons can be seen at the
on-site Lincolnshire Birds of Prey Centre and kids,
big and small, can exhaust themselves in the
adventure playground and tiny tots' area.

Mistley Place Park Animal Rescue Centre

New Road, Colchester **t** (01206) 396048
www.mistley.org.uk
Getting there 8 miles northeast of Colchester,
8 miles west of Harwich off the A137
Open Daily 10–5.30 **Adm** Adults £3.50, children
£2.50
Coffee shop

Sanctuary for abused, abandoned or injured
domestic and farm animals, with more than
1,500 residents ranging from horses, dogs and
birds to guinea pigs and mice, many of which
roam freely in the centre's 10 hectares (25 acres)
of park. The surrounding area, overlooking the
beautiful Stour Valley, is good for walks.

Mole Hall Wildlife Park

Widdington, Saffron Walden **t** (01799) 540400
www.molehall.co.uk
Getting there 2 miles south of Saffron Walden,
signposted from the B1383
Open Daily 10.30–5.30
Adm Adults £6.30, children £4.30, family £19
Café, gift shop

This wildlife park is set in the grounds of a
moated manor house (private, unfortunately)
which provides a home to a whole range of
animals including otters, chimpanzees and free-
roaming deer. There's also a butterfly house and
water maze.

Norfolk Wildlife Centre

Fakenham Road, Lenwade, Norwich **t** (01603)
872274 www.norfolkwildlife.co.uk
Getting there Just off the A1067, about 10 miles
northwest of Norwich
Open Mid-Feb–Oct daily 10–5
Adm Adults £7.25, children £5.50, under 3s **free**,
Café, gift shop, disabled access, on-site parking

Forty acres filled with the sort of animals found
living (at least once upon a time) in Britain and
Europe, so don't go expecting to see lions, tigers
and elephants. Instead, you'll have to make do
with rather less exotic fare: foxes, wild boar,
badgers and wallabies which, though hardly
mind-bogglingly exciting, are all nonetheless
presented in interesting and imaginative ways.
You can watch badgers (sleeping mainly – they're
nocturnal) through a glass window looking in on
their sett, wander in amongst (and feed) the
wallabies and climb a specially erected tower for
views of the nests built here every spring by

visiting herons. Young children are catered for at
the rabbit and guinea pig village and there are a
couple of large play areas.

North Norfolk Horse Shire Centre

West Runton Stables, West Runton, Cromer
t (01263) 837339 www.norfolk-shirehorse-centre.co.uk
Getting there Follow the brown tourist signs from
the A149 Cromer–Sheringham Road, or the A148
Cromer–Holt Road. West Runton Station is served
by Anglia Railways
Open Apr–Oct Sun–Fri and Bank Hols 10–5
(last admission 3.45)
Adm Adults £6, children £4
Café, picnic areas, gift shop, riding stables, parking

Dedicated to the country's great working
horses, the centre is home to a variety of
different Shire horse breeds and native UK
ponies and has various restored wagons, carts
and pieces of old machinery on display. You can
meet the horses, help feed the foals and farm
animals, watch harnessing and working demonstrations and go for cart rides.

Orford Ness

Quay Street, Orford, Woodbridge
t (01394) 450900 www.nationaltrust.org.uk
Getting there Ferry from Orford Quay. Orford is
14 miles northeast of Ipswich, take the A12, the
B1078, then the B1084
Open Jul–Sept Tues–Sat 10–2, Apr–Jun and Oct
Sat 10–2 **Adm** Adults £6, children £3 under 3s **free**
(ferry crossing included in price)
Guided tours

This isolated shingle spit provides a home to
numerous nesting coastal birds but is accessible
only by ferry (maximum stay three and a half
hours). Children's 'spy-trail'.

The Otter Trust

Earsham, Bungay **t** (01986) 893470
www.ottertrust.org.uk
Getting there Off the A143, 1 mile west of Bungay
Open Apr–Sept daily 10.30–6 **Adm** Adults £6,
children £3
*Shop, tearoom, picnic area, play area, disabled
access, on-site parking*

This is the largest and oldest otter conservation
organization in Britain and the only one dedicated to breeding otters (including both the
British and the Asian short-clawed otter) in order
to return them back into the wild. The trust has,

so far, reintroduced around a hundred captive-bred otters back into the British countryside. Though they're easily the cutest of our native mammals, they're also the shyest, so while you're waiting for them to put in an appearance, get acquainted with some of the centre's other residents: you'll come across geese, grebe and muntjac deer living in and around three large lakes. There is also a children's play area and a number of riverside walks are available.

Pensthorpe Waterfowl Park and Nature Reserve

Fakenham **t** (01328) 851465 **www**.pensthorpe.com
Getting there Signposted from the A1067 Norwich–Fakenham Road
Open Apr–Dec 10–5; Jan–Mar 10–4
Adm Adults £7, children £3.50, family £17.50
Restaurant, countryside shop, binocular hire, disabled access, on-site parking

A wide variety of wildfowl, including spoonbills, oyster-catchers, scarlet ibis and that great British favourite, kingfishers, can be seen here in the idyllic Wensum Valley. The waterfowl on the lakes can be viewed from the swish heated observation gallery and there are wildflower meadows and lakeside nature trails to explore. Children's treasure hunt activity sheets at the entrance.

Pettitts Animal Adventure Park

Church Road, Reedham **t** (01493) 700094
www.pettittsadventurepark.co.uk
Getting there Take the B1140 from Reedham
Open Apr–Oct daily 10–5
Adm Adults £7.95, children £7.95, under 2s **free**, family (2+3) £31
Café, fast-food kiosk, picnic areas, on-site parking

Down at Pettitts Park you can pet pigs, donkeys, goats, tamarins, wallabies, reindeer and many more furry creatures, as well as a few feathered friends (macaws, owls and cockatiel). In addition to the animals there is also a miniature railway, playgrounds and several low-key rides (such as the cup and saucer). Face painting, puppet shows and treasure hunts are organized at weekends.

Redwings Horse Sanctuary

Caldecott Hall, Fritton, Great Yarmouth
t (01508) 481000 **www**.redwings.co.uk
Getting there 1 mile northeast of the village of Fritton on the A143 about 7 miles southwest of Great Yarmouth

Open Daily 10–5 **Adm Free**
Café, shop, disabled facilities, leisure facilities at Caldecott Hall, free on-site parking

Redwings has around 100 horses, ponies and donkeys for children to meet, pet and feed. All the animals living here have been rescued from dire circumstances, be it neglect or potential slaughter. There are marked walks though the paddocks and 'Humane Horse Handling' demonstrations are given every Wednesday at 2pm.

★RSPB Minsmere Nature Reserve

Westleton, Saxmundham **t** (01728) 648281
Getting there Off the A12, about 8 miles north of Aldeburgh
Open Reserve: 9–9 (dusk if earlier); visitor centre: summer 9–5; winter 9–4
Adm Adults £5, children £1.50, family £10 (2+4)
Café, picnic area, shop, mother and baby facilities, guided tours, disabled access, on-site parking

Start off at the visitor centre (which has a tearoom and gift shop), where you can hire binoculars and pick up leaflets before heading off along the trails through heath, woodland and marshes, stopping off every now and then to see what can be seen from the observation hides. Guided walks are available and special events are put on throughout the year.

RSPB Titchwell Marsh Nature Reserve

Main Road, Titchwell, King's Lynn **t** (01485) 210779
Getting there Just off the A419, 6 miles east of Hunstanton
Open Reserve: daily dawn–dusk; visitor centre: 9.30–5 (winter until 4)
Adm Free
Café, picnic areas, guided tours, disabled access, on-site parking (£4, limited space available)

Coastal reserve with hides, a visitor centre, a café and picnic areas. It is particularly good for wading birds such as the avocet (the one with the funny upturned bill).

Shepreth Wildlife Park

Willersmill, Station Road, Shepreth
t (01763) 262234
www.sheprethwildlifepark.co.uk
Getting there On the A10 between Cambridge and Royston, 7 miles south of Cambridge. Shepreth train station is just a 2-minute walk away
Open Daily 10–6 (dusk in winter if earlier)
Adm Adults £7.50, children £5.50, under 2s **free**

Café, burger bar (summer only), picnic areas, souvenir and toy shop, kiosk

Since its foundation in 1979 as a refuge for orphaned and injured British birds and mammals, Shepreth has grown into one of East Anglia's very best animal attractions, with a wide variety of native and exotic wildlife on display, including peacocks, tortoises, wolves, owls, otters, coati, wallabies, squirrel monkeys and capybara (the largest rodent in the world, in case you're wondering, a sort of giant guinea pig). There are lots of interactive opportunities for the kids, too: a special petting field, where kids can meet deer, donkeys and sheep; a fish farm, where huge colourful koi carp will eat from your fingers; a new insect display, 'Bug City', where you can watch leaf-cutter ants building a 'fungus city', before checking out the assorted sting rays, puffer fish and seahorses at the next door Waterworld. You'll also find a children's playroom, a play area with a sandpit, a zip-wire, an adventure fort and a pets' corner. Pony rides are available at weekends in summer.

Suffolk Owl Sanctuary

Stonham Barns, Pettaugh Road, Stonham Aspel
t (01449) 711425 **www.suffolk-owl-sanctuary.org.uk**
Getting there Off the A140 between Ipswich and Norwich
Open Daily 10–5 (winter closes at dusk)
Adm Free (donations appreciated)
Café, picnic areas, crafts shops, on-site parking

Collection of aviaries housing various birds of prey, including owls, vultures, hawks, buzzards, peregrine falcons and eagles. Flying demonstrations held daily at 12.30, 2.15pm and 3.30pm in summer.

Suffolk Wildlife Park

White's Lane, Kessingland, Lowestoft
t (01502) 740291 **www.suffolkwildlifepark.co.uk**
Getting there On the A12, 20 miles south of Great Yarmouth, 5 miles south of Lowestoft
Open Daily 10–5.30 (last admission 1 hour before closing time)
Adm Adults £1.50, children £7.50, under 3s **free**
Café-restaurant, picnic areas, gift shop, mother and baby facilities, disabled access, on-site parking

All African wildlife is here: you'll find lions, cheetahs, giraffes, chimps, hyenas, zebras and ostriches living in this 40-hectare (100-acre) walk-through safari park (you can climb aboard the free road train if you don't fancy tackling the whole thing on foot). Feeding talks and animal handling demonstrations are given throughout the day: at 12.30 you can help feed the giraffes – their great necks swooping down to take the leaves delicately from your hand – before watching the big cats being fed at 3.15pm (thankfully, you are not expected to give the meat directly to the lions or to get the cheetahs to chase after you), while at 4pm you may have the opportunity to handle a snake. Bird of prey flying displays take place on Tuesdays and Wednesdays in summer. There are also explorer trails, play areas, a bouncy castle and a crazy golf course. Various special events aimed at children are laid on over the summer, including their 'Bugs Week', when kids can come and handle a range of creepy crawlies.

Thrigby Hall Wildlife Gardens

Filby, Great Yarmouth **t** (01493) 369477
www.thrigbyhall.co.uk
Getting there 7 miles northwest of Great Yarmouth off the A1064
Open Daily 10–5
Adm Adults £7.90, children £5.90, under 4s **free**
Café, gift shop, picnic area, disabled access, on-site parking

A 250-year-old park providing a dwelling place for various exotic creatures from Asia, including gibbons, red pandas, toucans, otters, monkeys, leopards and crocodiles (living in the Forest House). The monkeys are fed at 3.30pm and the otters at 4pm. There is a children's play area and a tree walk.

Valley Farm White Animal Collection

Wickham Market, Woodbridge **t** (01728) 746916
www.valleyfarmonline.co.uk
Getting there Signposted off the B1078 towards Charlesfield, off the A12
Open Easter–Oct and half-term hols daily 10–4
Adm Free a donation of £2 is suggested

Valley Farm is home to a slightly odd collection of animals, including Camelot the camel, Muffin the mule and Billy and Gruff the goats, as well as the only breeding herd of Carmargue horses (they come from the south of France) in the UK, which are available for rides.

Wildfowl and Wetlands Trust – Welney

Hundred Foot Bank, Welney, Wisbech
t (01353) 860711 www.wwt.org.uk
Getting there 12 miles north of Ely off the A1101
Open Daily 10–5
Adm Adults £3.90, children £2.30, family £10
Tearoom, gift and book shop, binocular hire, disabled access, on-site parking

One of eight Wildfowl and Wetlands Trust centres around the country, Welney is home to thousands of birds. At the visitor centre, find out about the many different species who visit over the course of the year, and watch live video feeds of various parts of the site before setting off along the nature trails to visit the centre's network of hides. Welney is definitely at its most exuberant in winter when great living carpets of ducks and clouds of swans fly in every afternoon to claim their nightly nesting spot, and at its most beautiful in summer, when the wild flower meadows come into bloom. The centre organizes family events throughout the year.

Farms

Barleylands Farm Museum

Barleylands Road, Billericay **t** (01268) 290229
www.barleylands.co.uk
Getting there Just off the A176; take J29 from the M25
Open Daily Mar–Oct 10–5 (last admission 4.30)
Adm Adults £3, children £3
Tearoom, restaurant, shop, mother and baby facilities, disabled access, on-site parking

The museum holds over 2,000 farm-related exhibits, including over 50 tractors (you'll see every size, shape and colour machine imaginable), several steam engines (often set in motion on summer weekends), as well as an animal petting area with goats, pigs and cows. In summer, you have the chance to pick (and of course eat) your own strawberries in the farm's fields and take tractor-trailer rides or a trip on a miniature railway.

Baylham House Rare Breeds Farm

Mill Lane, Baylham **t** (01473) 830264
www.balham-house.co.uk
Getting there 6 miles northwest of Ipswich off the B113
Open Easter–Sept Tues–Sun and Bank Hols 11–5
Adm Adults £4, children £2, under 4s **free**

Picnic areas, gift shop, refreshments, disabled access
Show farm on the site of a former Roman settlement with rare breeds of cattle, pigs, sheep and goats, as well as a children's paddock. Children are given a free bag of animal food, but should bring their own picnics.

Easton Farm Park

Easton, near Wickham Market **t** (01728) 746475
www.eastonfarmpark.co.uk
Getting there About 12 miles northeast of Ipswich, follow the brown tourist signs from the A12
Open Mid-Mar–Sept 10.30–6, Oct half term 10.30–4, Dec Sat and Sun 11–3
Adm Adults £6, children £4.50, family £19
Tearoom, picnic areas, café, gift shop, mother and baby facilities, disabled access, on-site parking

Victorian model farm in the picturesque Deben River Valley. Kids can watch cows being milked in the dairy centre, feed the goats and sheep, take pony and cart rides at weekends and during the school holidays, visit the working blacksmith and play on the toy tractors in the adventure playground.

Hunstanton Sea Life Sanctuary

South Promenade, Hunstanton **t** (01485) 533576
www.sealsanctuary.co.uk
Open Summer daily 10–4; call for winter opening hours
Adm Call in advance for prices
Restaurant, gift shop

Rehabilitation centre for seals. See seal pups being tended to in the seal hospital.

Lee Valley Park Farm

Stubbings Hall Lane, Crooked Mile, Waltham Abbey
t (01992) 892781 www.leevalleypark.org.uk
Getting there 2 miles north of Waltham Abbey off the B194; take J26 from the M25
Open Mar–Oct daily 10–4.30
Adm Adults £4.20, children £3.20, family (2+3) £17
Picnic areas, farm shop, mother and baby facilities, disabled access, on-site parking

Farm animals, a milking exhibition (where you can see over 150 cows being milked each afternoon), an incubation room (where you can see chicks being born), a farm trail, picnic areas, a pets corner and a play area are the main attractions of this twin-farm site.

Marsh Farm Country Park

Marsh Farm Road, Woodham Ferrers, Chelmsford
t (01245) 321552
www.marshfarmcountrypark.co.uk
Getting there Follow the brown tourist signs from
the A130, 9 miles northwest of Southend-on-Sea
Open Mid Feb–Oct Mon–Fri 10–4, Sat–Sun 10–5;
Nov–Dec Sat–Sun only
Adm Adults £5.80, children £3.40, under 3s **free**,
family (2+2) £17
*Café, picnic areas, farm shop, mother and baby
facilities, disabled access*

Various kinds of farm animals, including cattle,
sheep and pigs to feed and an adventure playground with a soft play area for toddlers.

Rede Hall Farm

Rede, Bury St Edmunds **t** (01284) 850695
www.redehallfarmpark.co.uk
Getting there 6 miles south of Bury St Edmunds on
the A143
Open Apr–Sept daily 10–5 (last admission 4)
Adm Call for details
*Café-restaurant, gift shop, mother and baby
facilities, disabled access, on-site parking*

A themed 1940s farm where children can
help bottle-feed lambs and take pony and
wagon rides.

Snettisham Park Farm

Manor Lane, Snettisham, King's Lynn **t** (01485)
542425 **www.**snettishampark.co.uk
Getting there 9 miles north of King's Lynn,
off the A149, close to the church, 4 miles south of
Hunstanton
Open Daily 10–5
Adm Adults £8.75, children, £6.75, family (2+3) £29
Tearoom, shop, indoor and outdoor picnic areas

You can meet and feed a range of farmyard
animals and take a safari through a red deer
park where the deer will happily eat from your
hand. There's also a children's farmyard and a
very good adventure playground.

★Wimpole Hall and Wimpole Home Farm

Arrington, near Royston **t** (01223) 207257
www.wimpole.org
Getting there 8 miles southwest of Cambridge off
the A603. Take J12 from the M11
Open Hall: Mid-Mar–Oct Sat–Wed 1–5 (late
Jul–Aug also Thurs), Nov Sat–Sun 1–4; garden; early
Mar Sat–Wed 11–4, mid-Mar–Oct Sat–Wed 10.30–5
(late Jul–Aug also Thurs during), Nov–Feb Sat–Wed
11–4; park: all year daily dawn–dusk; farm: mid-
Mar–Sept Sat–Wed 10.30–5, Nov–Feb Sat–Sun 11–4
Adm Estate: adults £11, children £6, family £28;
farm: adults £6, children £4; garden: adults £3,
children £1.50
*Café-restaurant, gift shop, disabled access,
on-site parking*

There are three attractions here, each better
than the last. Begin in the grand 17th-century hall,
which, though rather stuffy (few children can get
that excited about a library stuffed with priceless
leather-bound volumes), does contain nooks and
crannies worth seeking out, such as the clever
trompe l'oeil ceiling, the room-size bath and the
servants' quarters. Look out for the row of bells on
the wall, each inscribed with the name of a
servant, which would be rung to summon that
particular domestic 'above stairs'. The children's
guide at the gift shop will point you to all the
most interesting things and can offer a few 'can
you spots?' to help pass the time. The lavish hall
grounds (landscaped by Capability Brown)
contain many marked walks taking you through
woodland and past lakes and follies. You can
picnic anywhere and there's an adventure playground and an enclosed toddlers' area with toy
tractors to ride on. The real highlight of your visit,
however, will be the restored Georgian farm. At
weekends, you can take a wagon ride (pulled by
two enormous shire horses) to the farm from the
stable block near the hall. The farm has been
preserved to look more or less the same as it did
in the 18th century, which translates as weird-
looking traditional breeds (including orange
Tamworth pigs, heavily fleeced Leicester sheep
and White Park cows), thatched-roof barns and
good old fashioned muck. Manure appears to
have been big business in Georgian times and its
thick, pungent smell hangs heavy in the air. Head
to the centre of the farm (doing your best to
avoid the free-roaming geese and chickens as
they peck between your feet), where you'll find all
the headline animals: pigs, sheep, goats and
horses (piglets and lambs, too, in early summer).
Activities such as mucking out the pigs, milking
the goats, collecting eggs and sheep-shearing are
organized and children can try on traditional
farm costumes. There's also a small wagon
museum full of painted carts and barrows.
Special events are regularly organized.

Beside the seaside

Aldeburgh and the Suffolk Heritage Coast

Getting there Take the A12 from London, Colchester or Ipswich and follow the signs east. The nearest train station is Saxmundham, about 10 miles away, from where you can catch the hourly no.81 to Aldeburgh. A taxi from Saxmundham should cost in the region of £10
Tourist information The Cinema, 51 High Street (open Apr–Oct only) **t** (01728) 453637

There could be no greater contrast between the seaside towns of Aldeburgh and Lowestoft and yet both are strangely typical of the region. Suffolk's coast is a peculiar entity. At its north end is Lowestoft, a typically English, typically vibrant, slightly downmarket seaside resort. To the south is the functional freight ferry port of Felixstowe, while in between lie Aldeburgh and the Suffolk Heritage Coast, a 40-mile stretch of some of the most beautifully unspoilt coastline in the whole country, with numerous areas of 'special scientific interest' and clusters of tiny seaside villages, ignored by public transport and only accessible via the minor roads running east of the A12.

Beautifully unspoilt by man that is; the sea is doing its best to do a bit of spoiling, hungrily eating away at the coast. Half of the old town of Dunwich (about six miles north of Aldeburgh) is now underwater (locals say that on stormy nights you can hear the submerged church bells ringing out), although Aldeburgh itself has fared slightly better – the sea still has a few yards to go before it reaches the village – and, for the moment at least, it makes a pleasant, peaceful base from which to explore this grand coastal sweep. You can follow the pebble beach all the way from here to Thorpeness (about three miles north) without seeing a single building (or person) on the way. The town has no specific attractions beyond the Elizabethan Moot Hall (the town's museum) but it still welcomes its fair share of visitors bent on 'getting away from it all' among the painted cottages and historic buildings – watching fishermen winching their boats onto the beach and sampling the excellent cod

and Dover sole served up at the town's trendy collection of restaurants. In June, the town comes to life for its annual music festival, founded by the composer Benjamin Britten, whose grave is in the village churchyard, and again in August for the town carnival, when there's a parade and firework display.

About five miles south of here is **Orford Castle**, a 27m (90ft) 18-sided keep offering fantastic views out over the countryside and North Sea. A range of events, including puppet-making workshops, storytellings, mask-making demonstrations and music recitals, is put on throughout the year and there's a free children's activity sheet available. When the castle was first constructed in the 12th century, it was actually positioned right on the shoreline, but the sea subsequently retreated. You can find out more about the shifting nature of the coastline in these parts at the nearby **Dunwich Underwater Exhibition**, which has finds recovered by divers from the submerged town.

Other local areas of interest include Walberswick, about 10 miles north, which is well known locally for its excellent crabbing (it even holds competitions in summer); Dunwich Heath, five miles north, an area of ancient heathland home to numerous rare breeds of wildlife, including nightjars, antlions, damselflies and red deer (it also has an outdoor playground, and guided walks and nature trails are offered from the information room at the Coastguard Cottages, **t** (01728) 645805, and the nearby Minsmere Beach, which is made up of a mixture of sand and pebbles and makes a pleasant spot for a paddle. Display boards by the beach show where the village of Dunwich originally stood before it fell into the sea. Various events for children, such as beach art and gorse shakes, are organized here during the summer and there is a holiday club for 6–12-year-olds focusing on environmental activities. Minsmere RSPB Nature Reserve is is also nearby (p.305). For the rest of the Suffolk coast, *see* pp.309–10.

Aldeburgh Museum
The Moot Hall t 01728 454 666
Open May–Sept 2.30pm–5pm
Adm £1 (accompanied children free)

Dunwich Underwater Exploration Exhibition

The Craft Shop, Front Street, Orford, Woodbridge
t (01394) 450678
Getting there Orford lies on the B1084, 20 miles northeast of Ipswich
Open Daily 11–5 **Adm** 50p

Orford Castle

Castle Terrace, Orford **t** (01394) 450472
www.english-heritage.org.uk
Getting there On the B1084, 20 miles northeast of Ipswich
Open Apr–Sept daily 10–6; Oct–Mar Thurs–Mon 10–4
Adm Adults £4.50, children £2.30, family £11.30
Shop, on-site parking

Clacton-on-Sea

Getting there The main road into the town is the A133, with Colchester located about 10 miles west and London 55 miles southwest. Regular trains and buses run from Colchester
Tourist information Town Hall, Station Road **t** (01255) 686633 **www.**essex-sunshine-coast.org.uk

Clacton is another in a long line of lively, slightly downmarket seaside resorts offering a range of lively, slightly downmarket English seaside attractions. There's a long sandy beach (although do be warned, according to the European Commission it's one of the dirtiest in the country) with deckchairs and Punch and Judy shows in summer overlooked by rows of amusement arcades, a leisure centre with a swimming pool, dozens of cheap caffs, lots of fast food and a pier with rides, video game parlours, shops, children's play areas, a night-club, a reptile house and an aquarium (with sharks, rays, octopi and a touch pool). The nearby resorts of Brightlingsea, Frinton-on-Sea and (it could only be in England) Walton-on-the-Naze offer somewhat less hectic fare. Walton is particularly renowned for its sea-fishing.

Cromer and the North Norfolk Coast

Getting there Cromer is easily reached via the A148 from King's Lynn (approximately 35 miles) or the A140 from Norwich (approximately 20 miles).

Local bus services run to Cromer from Norwich and there are rail links to both King's Lynn and Norwich
Tourist information Cromer Bus Station, Prince of Wales Road **t** 0871 2003071
www.north-norfolk.gov.uk

There are few better ways to spend a sunny afternoon than crabbing in rockpools and there are few better places to go crabbing than Cromer: all you'll need is a bit of bacon tied on a string and a bucket. The town itself, though once refined, classy and the most fashionable of Victorian resorts is these days rather frayed around the edges. Wind-battered and exposed on low craggy cliffs, Cromer's charms have faded slightly with the years as if the raging sea wind (which comes straight down from the North Pole) has blown all the glamour and elegance from the streets. Its natural attributes, however, still hold strong: its long sandy beach has won several Blue Flag Awards, its rugged coast is good for walks and can offer imposing views out over the sea and, of course, its waters are still home to the crabs that have for so long been the town's biggest draw.

There are also several worthwhile attractions within easy reach of the town including the North Norfolk Horse Shire Centre, a couple of miles west along the coast, which has a large collection of working horses and ponies (p.304). You can see demonstrations of harnessing, pulling and ploughing and kids can take cart rides and meet the animals at the children's farm. A mile or two further west is Sheringham (site of the landscaped Sheringham Park with its rhodo-dendron bushes and viewing towers), where you can clamber aboard the North Norfolk Railway (p.311), while just beyond this is Weybourne, home of the Muckleburgh Collection. Blakeney Point, one of the nation's foremost nature reserves (and home to large colonies of birds and seals), is about five miles west of Weybourne.

In summer, Cromer plays host to a week-long carnival with a Grand Parade, children's activities and firework display and there are variety shows held every day at the end of the pier.

Muckleburgh Collection

Weybourne, Holt **t** (01263) 588210
www.muckleburgh.co.uk
Getting there On the A149 coast road, a few miles west of Cromer

Open Feb–Mar Sun 10–5, Apr–Oct and half-term holidays daily 10–5
Adm Adults £5.50, children £3, under 5s **free**, family £13.50

The largest private collection of military vehicles, uniform, etc. in the country.
For further information *see* p.315

North Norfolk Railway

The Station, Sheringham **t** (01263) 820800
www.nnrailway.co.uk; talking timetable:
t (01263) 820808
Getting there Signposted from the A1082; Sheringham Station is on the opposite side of the road to the Anglia Railways station of the same name
Open May–Sept daily; Apr and Oct closed Mon and Fri, Nov–Dec and Feb–Mar open Sat–Sun only; call for times
Fares Standard steam fares: adults £9, children £5.50, under 4s **free**, family (2+3) £27

Full-size steam and diesel railway known as the Poppy Line.
For further information *see* p.318

Great Yarmouth

Getting there The town can be reached via the A47 from Norwich (17 miles), the A12 to Ipswich (40 miles) and the A143 to Bury St Edmunds (25 miles). There is a rail link with Norwich (30 minutes) and buses connect with Lowestoft and Norwich. National Express, which runs a service from London, has a coach stop at the Market Gates (east side)
Tourist information 25 Marine Parade (Easter–Sept only) **t** (01493) 846345
www.great-yarmouth.gov.uk/tourism

East Anglian resorts tend to be picturesque, unspoilt and rather beautiful. Great Yarmouth then, is not your typical East Anglian resort. With its mass of purpose-built attractions, mess of souvenir shops, fish and chip restaurants and greasy-spoon caffs, it's perhaps best described as grimly functional. Heaving in summer, ghostly in winter, Great Yarmouth is a full-on resort: brash, loud and proudly, defiantly tacky. The acres of caravans and holiday homes that greet you as you enter the town should tell you all you need to know; it's that sort of place. From the slightly faded sign at the train station welcoming you to 'Britain's greatest seaside resort', which obscures the nearby industrial works (all indeterminate tubes and containers, like a giant-size children's science kit) to the '6-for-£1' rock emporiums on the seafront, this is a town determined to make the best of things.

Everything you'd expect to be here is here: the shops selling novelty hats and postcards, the face-painters, the chippies (so many chippies) and the cheap CD and cassette shops that always seem to flourish in these sorts of resorts. The seafront itself provides a grand sweep of simple entertainments: arcade after arcade, bingo halls, crazy golf courses and video game parlours, all lit up with clusters of coloured bulbs that at night give the town the Las Vegas-style appearance it so clearly craves. There are two piers: the Britannia, which has a funfair and a dedicated kids' zone, 'Joyland', with various rides and a hall of mirrors, and the Wellington, which has an entertainment complex, where low-rent TV stars undertake summer seasons. At the western edge of town is the Pleasure Beach, the region's most popular fun park with rollercoasters, log flumes and numerous other rides.

There's nothing particularly seedy or rundown about Great Yarmouth and yet it somehow feels tarnished and out of date, like a 1970s branch of Woolworths. There's an air of desperate nostalgia about everything. The British seaside resort lost its place in the heart of the British holidaymaker to its Spanish equivalent long ago and it shows. The town's two waxwork museums and the tatty, third-hand glamour they offer provide the perfect emblems for the town. It's not that Great Yarmouth is unpopular – come summer and the front will be absolutely heaving with people – just a little unloved; the setting for a make-do rather than a must-have holiday.

That said, kids do love this place. Everywhere they go they'll find games to play, teddies to win, rides to be ridden and 'wobby worlds' to negotiate. On the seafront, or Marine Parade as it is called, there is a Reptile House, 'Amazonia', with lizards, snakes and crocodiles living in a replica jungle; a model village with over 200 miniature buildings, from castles to cottages, set in landscaped gardens; a 36m (120ft) observation tower providing good views of the town from the telescopes at the top; a 'Rock Factory', where you can watch demonstrations of rock-making; and a Sea Life Centre, one of the country's biggest, where you can take a sea-bed stroll past seahorses, sharks and jellyfish. And then, of course, there's the beach, the town's one undoubted highlight: wide, sandy and covered with a smattering of the sort of flat, round stones that are so perfect for skimming. There are lifeguards, warning flags and it's cleaned daily during the summer season. Pony and cart rides along the front are offered from Britannia Pier.

Should you fancy a change of scenery, do be aware that Great Yarmouth lies within easy reach of several day trip-worthy attractions, including the Broads, which start a few miles inland (pp.320–1); Pettitts Animal Adventure Park (seven miles west, p.305); Redwings Horse Sanctuary (seven miles southwest, p.305); and Thrigby Hall Wildlife Gardens (seven miles northwest, p.306).

A little bit of history

In amongst all the modern attractions, elements of Great Yarmouth's past do remain. Despite appearances, this is a town with a history. Founded as long ago as the 11th century, Great Yarmouth boasts one of the most complete medieval walls in the country and, in the 19th century, it was the centre of the European herring industry. It even provided the setting for part of Charles Dickens' *David Copperfield*. On the historic South Quay, you'll find the Elizabethan House and the Tollhouse Museum, where activities for children – such as treasure hunts, storytellings and historically themed craft workshops (mask-making, quill-making, hat design, etc.) – are organized during the school holidays. Nearby are two 17th-century houses, the Old Merchant's House and Row 111. Heritage walks through the town are offered in summer; contact Great Yarmouth Heritage Walks on **t** (01493) 846345.

Amazonia World of Reptiles
Marine Parade, Great Yarmouth **t** (01493) 842202
www.amazonia-worldofreptiles.net
Open Daily 10–5 (7pm in summer)
Adm Adults £4.55, children £3.75, under 4s **free**
Britain's largest collection of reptiles, which includes snakes, lizards and crocodiles, in a lush botanical setting on the seafront at Great Yarmouth.

Elizabethan House Museum
4 South Quay **t** (01493) 855746
www.nationaltrust.og.uk

Open Apr–Oct Mon–Fri 10–5, Sat–Sun 1.15–5
Adm Adults £3, children £1.60,
A 16th-century house with a display on 19th-century domestic life, an exhibition on the execution of Charles I and a toy room for children.

Old Merchant's House and Row 111
Row 111, South Quay **t** (01493) 857900
www.english-heritage.org.uk
Open Apr–Sept daily 12–5
Adm Adults £3.40, children £1.70
A pair of 17th-century houses decorated in period style: late 19th century and Second World War respectively. Visits by guided tour only.

★Pleasure Beach
South Beach Parade **t** (01493) 844585
www.pleasure-beach.co.uk
Open Mar–Sept; call for days and times
Adm Free, charge for individual rides, which can be paid for with tokens (£1 each) or wristbands (£15)
Fast food, tearoom, sweet shops, some disabled access, adapted toilets
The Pleasure Beach was, when it first opened in the early part of the century, a rather gentle, charming little place with a scenic railway, a small joy wheel and little else. In the 90-odd years since, however, it has transformed itself into one of the country's top fun parks and East Anglia's most popular visitor attraction, with 70 or so daredevil rides spread over nine seafront acres. It may no longer be gentle or charming, but it is a lot of fun. Try the new Evolution ride, which spins its passengers a thrilling 20m (66ft) over the ground, upside down. There's also a go-kart track, a log flume, dodgems, an adventure golf course, as well as numerous children's rides (including a carrousel), a boating lake and a traditional, seafront tearoom pavilion. The park's showpiece ride, however, harkens back to its earlier days. It's a traditional wooden roller-coaster that's been operating here since 1932 and can offer that proper, banging-slat, wooden rollercoaster sound.

Tollhouse Museum
Tollhouse Street **t** (01493) 745526
Open Mon–Fri 10–5, Sat and Sun 1.15–5
Adm Adults £3, children £1.60
This was once the town's prison. You can visit the restored dungeons and make brass rubbings.

Hunstanton

Getting there It's on the northwest coast of Norfolk within easy reach of King's Lynn via the A149 (20 miles)

Tourist information Town Hall, The Green **t** (01485) 532610 www.west-norfolk.gov.uk

Norfolk's largest resort after Great Yarmouth, Hunstanton is slightly more genteel. Its Victorian front, which was purpose-built in the mid 19th century by the wonderfully named local landowner Henry Styleman le Strange, still exudes a rather refined air with its elegant gardens and carrstone cottages, despite being lined with the usual collection of arcades and crazy golf courses. In summer, there's a land train to carry visitors between the front's attractions. These include the Oasis Leisure Centre, **t** (01485) 534227, which has a tropically heated outdoor pool with an aquaslide and giant inflatables and the Sea Life Sanctuary, **t** (01485) 533576, one of the best aquariums around, which, in addition to its touch pool, underwater tunnel and array of sharks, seahorses, octopi and jellyfish, has a seal hospital. You can join in the daily feeding sessions and even take a trip out to see the seals living in their natural habitat further along the coast aboard a Second World War amphibian craft. The beach is long, sandy and gently shelved and there are donkey rides and boat trips in summer.

Lowestoft

Getting there Lowestoft lies on the east coast of Suffolk, just south of Great Yarmouth (approximately 10 miles via the A14) and southeast of Norwich (approximately 22 miles via the A146)

Tourist information East Point Pavilion, Royal Plain **t** (01502) 533600 www.visit-lowestoft.co.uk

Britain's most easterly town is a thriving holiday resort. Not quite as touristy as Great Yarmouth, it is still pretty lively. There are six beaches in all, most of which are sandy with some shingle. The most popular, South Beach, has two piers, a children's play area and is patrolled by lifeguards in summer. Youngsters will like 'Mayhem' on the Esplanade (in the same building as the tourist office), a multi-level play area, while older kids will probably prefer a trip to the Pleasurewood Hills theme park, just outside town, with over 50 rides. Look out for the East Anglia Transport Museum, set in a hectare (three

acres) of woodland a few miles southwest of the town (p.315) and Suffolk Wildlife Park (five miles south, p.306).

Mayhem

East Point Pavilion, Royal Plain **t** (01502) 533600 **Open** Summer: daily 9.30–5.30; winter: Mon–Fri 10.30–5, Sat–Sun 10–5 **Adm** Call for prices *Refreshments*

Underwater-themed indoor play area with ropes, scramble nets, tubes, ball pools and a huge slide.

Pleasurewood Hills

Leisure Way, Corton **t** (01502) 586000 www.pleasurewoodhills.co.uk **Open** Times vary so call in advance to check **Adm** Adults £14.50, children £12.50, under 1m (3ft) **free**, family £49 (book online for discount tickets) *Various cafés, fast food restaurants and picnic areas, some disabled access, on-site parking*

This fun park has several adrenaline-inducing rides, such as the 600m/2,000ft-long, 'Enigma' rollercoaster and the spinning 'Wizzy Dizzy', along with a gentler log-flume style affair, the 'Wave Breaker', and a swinging pirate ship. There are also dodgems, a miniature railway, go-karts, mini motorbikes and a special area for under 9s, 'Woody's Little Big Park', which has 10 rides, including a Waltzer and a Sky Diver Slide. If you tire (or run out) of rides then there are three daily shows to watch: a sea lion performance, a parrot show and best of all the 'Castle Theatre Spectacular', which features circus acrobats and clowns.

Southwold

Getting there Situated midway between Lowestoft and Aldeburgh. Take the A12 from London or Colchester and follow the signs for the A1095. By rail: Travel to Ipswich from Liverpool Street, change onto the Lowestoft line and get off at Halesworth, where you can pick up the X99 bus or take a taxi (20–30 minutes)

Tourist information 69 High Street **t** (01502) 724729 www.visit-southwold.co.uk

The heritage resort of Southwold is a haven from the demands of modern society. A sleepy coastal town that's popular with the London country house set, it has a genteel atmosphere and quiet charm that draws visitors back time and time again. Its sand and shingle beach is of Blue Flag standard and lined with colourful beach huts, much sought-after as they can sell for more than £20,000 each. Fortunately, many of them can also be hired by the week, or for the day, t (01502) 724818. There's a full lifeguard service and plenty of traditional fun to be had such as pitch and putt, boating and a model yacht pond all within easy reach of the beach. The privately owned **pier**, re-opened by the Duke of Gloucester in July 2001, has been restored to its original length of 190m (623 feet). It won the 'Pier of the Year' competition in 2002 and, following the construction of a landing stage, it is now possible to travel to and from Southwold on Britain's only sea-going paddle steamer. Contact Waverley Excursions, t (0845) 1304647, for details of these occasional sailings, or visit www.waverleyexcursions.co.uk.

The big name in Southwold is Adnams Brewery, which owns the town's two best hotels (the Crown and the Swan) and still makes its local deliveries of beer and wine by horse-drawn dray.

Everything about the town is understated: the high street has none of the tackiness of larger seaside resorts, the marketplace is little bigger than a handkerchief and the town's diminutive **museum** and **Sailors' Reading Room** hold an eclectic mix of model ships and nautical memorabilia. Southwold harbour, set at the mouth of the River Blythe, is a pretty spot with a decidedly salty tang about it, with fishing smacks bobbing on the water, wooden jetties and the occasional old sea dog repairing his nets. You can buy fresh fish from the rustic fishermen's huts or eat some of the best fish and chips in the area at the Harbour Inn. Cross the river to the neighbouring village of Walberswick via the bailey footbridge or take the tiny passenger ferry.

Alfred Corry Museum

Ferry Road t (01502) 723200
Open Mon–Fri 2–5, Sat–Sun 10–12 noon and 2–5; Nov–Mar Bank Hols and fine weekends only 10.30–12 noon and 2–3.30 **Adm Free**

Lifeboat museum depicting the history of the Southwold lifeboat service.

Electric Picture Palace

Blackmill Road t (07815) 769565
Open Screenings: Fri and Sat 7pm (extra nights in summer and school hols); tours: Sun afternoon

Tickets Stalls £5, circle £6 (seasonal membership fee of £2 required per 4 persons); advance booking necessary; tours (40 minutes): adults £2, children £1; advance booking necessary

Recreated Art Deco cinema with only 66 (authentic cinema) seats. A mini-Wurlitzer organ rises from below the stage during the interval and plays the National Anthem at the end of the show. The cinema screens a number of family films each season, as well as old Ealing Comedies. An usherette will show you to your seats and sell you refreshments in the interval, which only adds to the period feel.

Sailors' Reading Room

East Cliff
Open Daily 9–5 **Adm Free**

Southwold Ferry

Southwold Harbour t (01502) 478615
Open For guided boat trips
Operates Easter–May Sat–Sun 10–12.30 and 2–4.30, Jun–Aug daily **Fares** 40p

Southwold Museum

9–11 Victoria Street t (01502) 726097
www.southwoldmuseum.org
Open Mar–Sept 2–4, Aug also 10.30–12 noon **Adm Free**

Southwold Pier

North Parade t (01502) 722105
www.southwoldpier.co.uk
Open Daily from 10am **Adm Free**

Recently rebuilt traditional pier, with restaurant, café, function rooms and an amusement arcade.

Southend-on-Sea

Getting there Southend lies at the southernmost tip of East Anglia, at the mouth of the Thames estuary, 40 miles east of London (reached by the A127). Trains depart from London Fenchurch Street to Southend Central station regularly (1 hour) and National Express runs a frequent service from London Victoria (2.5 hours)
Tourist information Southend Pier t (01702) 215620 www.southend.gov.uk

Southend, situated on the north bank of the River Thames estuary, is within easy reach of the East End of London; indeed, for decades it seemed as if the two were linked by some sort of vacation umbilical cord. Every Bank Holiday, coachloads of East End families would descend on the Essex town looking to enjoy their annual day in the sun – only to discover that they were once again about to enjoy their annual day in the pub waiting for the rain to clear. The lure of cheap Spanish package holidays may have weakened the bond slightly, but the resort is still going strong and has plenty to offer families looking for that archetypal British seaside experience. There's a seven-mile-long stretch of sandy beach, where you'll find facilities for sailing, water-skiing and wind-surfing; a promenade lined with typically seasidey things: crazy golf courses, arcades, children's playgrounds, etc. (there's a seafront shuttle train in summer), while jutting out from the front is the town's most famous feature, revered since its cockney heyday, Southend Pier, which at over 1.3 miles (2km) is the longest pier in the world – it's quite a walk to the tip although you can hop aboard the pier train if you don't feel quite up to it. Otherwise, the town's most exciting places for children are the Central Museum and Planetarium (*see* below).

Central Museum and Planetarium

Victoria Avenue, Southend-on-Sea **t** (01702) 434449 **www.southendmuseums.co.uk**
Open Museum: Mon–Sat 10–5; planetarium shows: Wed–Sat 11am, 2pm and 4pm
Adm Museum: **free**; planetarium: adults £2.60, children £1.90, family (2+3) £8

Archaeology and natural history displays and the only planetarium in the southeast outside London.

Peter Pan's Adventure Island

Sunken Garden, Western Esplanade **t** (01702) 443400 **www.adventureisland.co.uk**
Open Call for times
Adm Unlimited rides 'Super Saver' wristband £14–19 (over 1.2m/4ft tall), 'Tiny Tots' wristband £8–14 (restricted rides only)

A full-on fun park with several hi-octane thrill rides, including the Thrill River log flume, the Green Scream giant rollercoaster and the Barracuda (which looks like an enormous pair of metal legs; you sit in the feet as they spin over and over), as well as dedicated kiddy-friendly attractions, such as Flying Jumbo rides, junior and senior go-karts and dodgems.

Sea-Life Adventure

Seafront, Southend-on-Sea **t** (01702) 442211 **www.sealifeadventure.co.uk**
Open Daily 10–5 (peak times until 7pm)
Adm Adults £6, children £4.50, family (2+3) £17.50

Large tropical aquarium where talks and regular public feeding sessions are laid on. There's a café too, and there is also a soft play centre (charges apply).

Open-air museums

Cockley Cley Iceni Village and Museum

Cockley Cley, Swaffham **t** (01760) 721339
Getting there 3 miles south of Swaffham off the A1065
Open Apr–Oct 11–5.30 (Aug 10–5.30)
Adm Adults £4, children £2, under 5s **free**
On-site parking, tearoom, gift shop, disabled access

Recreation of an Iceni settlement believed to have existed here 2,000 years ago.

East Anglia Transport Museum

Chapel Road, Carlton Colville **t** (01502) 518459 **www.eatm.org.uk**
Getting there 3 miles southwest of Lowestoft on the B1314, signposted from the A12 and the A146. Nearest train station is at Oulton Broad
Open Easter and May Sun and Bank Hols 11–5.30; Jun–Sept Wed and Sat 2–5, Sun and Bank Hols 11–5.30; Aug daily 2–5
Adm Adults £5, children £3.50, under 5s **free**
Café, picnic areas, bookshop, mother and baby facilities, tours, disabled access, on-site parking

You can clamber aboard trams, steam rollers, lorries, cars, buses and trolley buses, and even go for a ride through a 1930s street scene. Rides are included in the entry price.

Muckleburgh Collection

Weybourne, Holt **t** (01263) 588210 **www.muckleburgh.co.uk**
Getting there On the A149 coast road, a few miles west of Cromer
Open Feb–Mar Sun 10–5, Apr–Oct and half-term holidays daily 10–5
Café-restaurant, shop, disabled access, on-site parking

The largest private collection of military paraphernalia in the country with tanks, missiles, bombs and uniforms on display.

Tank-riding demonstrations every Sunday when kids also have the opportunity to ride in a US personnel carrier.

Museum of East Anglian Life

Iliffe Way, Stowmarket **t** (01449) 612229
www.eastanglianlife.org.uk
Getting there In the centre of Stowmarket opposite the Asda supermarket, signposted from the A14 and the B115. It's a 10-minute walk from Stowmarket train station
Open Apr–Oct Mon–Sat 10–5, Sun 11–5
Adm Adults £6.50, children £3.50, under 4s **free**, family (2+3) £17.50
Restaurant, picnic areas, gift shop, some disabled access, adapted toilets

This 28-hectare (70-acre) site contains just a dozen or so historic buildings and you'll have to put in a lot of walking if you hope to see them all. Nonetheless, the riverside setting is very pretty and all the exhibits are presented in an informative and entertaining way. As you enter, you'll find yourself in Home Close, which is surrounded by various old buildings: Abbots Hall Barn, a stable, a cart lodge and a couple of converted barns where you can see displays and videos on East Anglian farming life. Beyond this is an area of woodland before you reach the charcoal-maker, the adventure playground (look out for Remus, the Suffolk Punch horse whose enclosure is nearby) and, the real highlight of the site, the riverside area, where you'll find a watermill, a Victorian kitchen and a windpump. Demonstrations of traditional crafts, such as basket-making, are given at weekends and family fun days, dressing-up days, treasure hunts, country fairs and craft days are held in the summer.

Norfolk Rural Life Museum and Union Farm

Beech House, Gressenhall, East Dereham
t (01362) 860563 **www**.norfolk.gov.uk
Getting there The museum is 3 miles west of Dereham and is signed from the A47 and B1146
Open Mar–Oct daily 10–5, Nov Sun 11–4
Adm Adults £5.95, children £4.65, under 4s **free**
Café-restaurant, gift shop, picnic areas, guided tours, mother and baby facilities, disabled access, on-site parking

Displays of agricultural and village rural life in a former workhouse adjoining a recreated 1920s farm with working horses (cart rides available)

and traditional East Anglian animal breeds such as large, black pigs, red poll cattle and Norfolk horn sheep. There are regular talks on workhouse life and quizzes and quests for the children taking them all over the museum and farm. In July, kids can help with the annual hay-making.

Sutton Hoo

Woodbridge **t** (01394) 389700
www.suttonhoo.org, **www**.nationaltrust.org.uk
Getting there Off the B1083 Woodbridge to Bawdsey Road, follow signs from the A12. By bus: 83 Ipswich to Bawdsey road (passing Melton railway station). By rail: Melton Station (1.5 miles)
Open Jan–Mar Sat–Sun 11–4, Jul–Aug daily 11–5, Sept–Oct and late Dec Wed–Sun 11–4, Nov–mid-Dec Sat–Sun 11–4
Adm Adults £5.50, children £2.50, family £13.50
Restaurant, shop, baby changing facilities, guided tours, car park

Anglo-Saxon royal burial site where the priceless Sutton Hoo treasure was found in a huge ship grave in 1939. The exhibition hall houses a full-scale reconstruction of the burial chamber and tells the story of the site. The treasure itself is in the British Museum but there are replica displays here. Afterwards visitors can walk the 500 metres (550) yards to the chamber, which is only part of the 100-hectare (245-acre) estate. The shop sells jewellery, ceramics and pocket money gifts based on Sutton Hoo artefacts.

West Stow Anglo-Saxon Village

Visitor Centre, Icklingham Road, West Stow, Bury St Edmunds **t** (01284) 728718
www.stedmundsbury.gov.uk/tourism.htm
Getting there Off the A110, 15 miles northwest of Bury St Edmunds. Follow the brown tourist signs
Open Daily 10–5 (winter 4)
Adm Adults £5, children £4, family (2+3) £15
Refreshments, gift shop, picnic areas, mother and baby facilities, some disabled access, on-site parking

This replica village has been reconstructed on the site of a real Anglo-Saxon village originally built here sometime in the 5th–6th century AD. The seven buildings have been erected using the same techniques, tools and building materials that would have been used by the original builders, so it's pretty authentic. Nothing is roped off, so you're free to examine the buildings from every possible angle (and kids usually do) and meet the pigs and chickens who also live on the site. Original finds from the site are displayed in the visitor centre and the village is surrounded by a 50-hectare (125-acre) country park with acres of woodland, heathland and trails along the banks of the River Lark. Activity days, when kids can try on Saxon costumes and go on guided walks, are organized during the summer.

Wroxham Barns
Turnstead Road, Hoveton **t** (01603) 783762
www.wroxham-barns.co.uk
Getting there 7 miles from Norwich along the A1151
Open Barns: daily 10–5; funfair: mid-Mar–Oct Sat–Sun; Easter school hoidays, May Day, late May–mid-Sept and Oct half term daily; call for times, which vary
Adm Barns: **free**; funfair: individual charges for rides; junior farm: £2.85, under 3s **free**
Tearooms, craft shops, on-site parking

Traditional East Anglian crafts such as decorative glass-making, pottery, woodworking, stitchcraft, furniture-making, printing and cider-pressing, demonstrated in a collection of 18th-century barns. There's also a Junior Farm and, in summer, a traditional fair with swing boats, roundabouts, a ferris wheel and old end-of-the-pier slot machines.

Parks and gardens

Brandon Country Park and Thetford Forest
Visitor Centre, Bury Road, Brandon **t** (01842) 810185
Getting there 1 mile south of Brandon on the B1106 and 12 miles north of Bury St Edmunds
Open Park: daily dawn–dusk; visitor centre: Apr–Sept daily 10–5, Oct–Mar daily 10–4

Brandon Country Park is located within Thetford's thick pinewood forest and boasts a walled garden, four waymarked forest walks (including a 'find the tree' trail and a history trail) and numerous cycle paths. The visitor centre has interactive displays and can provide information and leaflets. The Forestry Commission organizes numerous events in and around Thetford Forest, including Red Deer Safaris, Fungi Walks, Desert Rat Memorial Tours (the 7th Armoured Division hid themselves away in the forest whilst they prepared for the Normandy Landings of 1944) and walks to look at the forest's bat boxes. Contact

the Recreation Department, Forest District Office, Santon Downham, Brandon, **t** (01842) 810271.

Ferry Meadows Country Park
Getting there 3 miles from Peterborough, off the A605 to Oundle. Follow the brown tourist signs to Nene Park
Open All year daily **Adm Free** (car parking charge) Apr–Oct weekends and Bank Hols
Cafés, visitor centre, watersports centre, caravan club, on-site parking

A 200-hectare (500-acre) park within the larger Nene Park ,with two huge boating lakes and several children's play areas. Miniature railway and pony and trap rides are available in summer.

Hinchingbrooke Country Park
Brampton Road, Huntingdon **t** (01480) 451568
Getting there A few miles west of Huntingdon, off the A14
Open All year daily **Adm Free**
Café, picnic areas, on-site parking, fishing, mountain bike course

These 180 acres (72 hectares) of woodland, rivers, lakes and ponds which provide a home to a variety of wildlife, including woodpeckers, herons and foxes. There are numerous marked walks (guided walks are led from the visitor centre most weekends) and the lake has facilities for watersports.

Steam trains

★Bressingham Steam Museum
Bressingham, Diss **t** (01379) 686900
www.bressingham.co.uk
Getting there The museum is just off the A1066, 2 miles west of Diss; follow the brown tourist signs. There's a regular train service to Diss Station, which is on the main line from Norwich to London Liverpool Street
Open Mar, Apr, Sept and Oct daily 10.30–4.30; May, Jun, Jul and Aug 10.30–5.30
Adm Adults £8.50, children £5, under 3s **free**, family £22; steam days: adults £12, children £8, under 3s **free**, family £35
Restaurant, souvenir shop, gardens and plant centre, wheelchair access, adapted toilets, parking

Bressingham offers an array of steam attractions set in two-and-a-half hectares (six acres) of pretty gardens. There are three different narrow-gauge lines: the Nursery Railway, which passes the nearby lake and woodland and gives views of Roydon Church; the Waveney Valley Railway, which runs over watermeadows and through rhododendron banks; and the Garden Railway, home to the 'Alan Bloom', built from scratch by the Bressingham team. You'll also find traction engines, steam wagons, stationary engines and 'The Gallopers', a Victorian steam carousel.

Colne Valley Railway

Yeldham Road, Castle Hedingham t (01787) 461174
www.cvr.org.uk
Getting there 20 miles northwest of Colchester on the A1017, 2 miles north of Sible Hedingham
Open Mar–Dec 11–5; steam days: Mar–Oct most Suns; Jul–Aug extra midweek days
Adm Static viewing: adults £3, children £1.50, family (2+4) £7.50; Steam Days: adults £6, children £4, family (2+4) £20
Pullman restaurant train, buffet, picnic area, wheelchair access to most of the site, on-site parking

This beautifully restored, one-mile-long riverside stretch of the former Colne Valley and Halstead railway offers two very different train-themed experiences. On non-steam days kids and parents can examine the railway's 60 or so vintage engines and carriages, see how the signal box works, try the guard's flag and whistle and (always a thrill) walk along the train tracks – all of which are fun, if a little static. On steam days, you can actually ride one of the puffing steam trains as it trundles along the line. Parents will relish the opportunity to dine in the luxurious Pullman carriage, although kids will probably prefer to picnic on the grass overlooking the Colne River or in the grassy grounds of the adjoining Castle Hedingham, a beautifully preserved Norman keep, where jousting tournaments and re-enactments of medieval sieges are held in the summer. Various special events are laid on throughout the year, including 'Victorian Specials', 'Santa Specials' and Thomas the Tank Engine days.

★Nene Valley Railway

Wansford Station, Stibbington, Peterborough
t (01780) 784444; talking timetable: t (01780) 784404 www.nvr.org.uk
Getting there Wansford station is off the A1 between the A47 and the A605 junctions;

Peterborough NVR station is half a mile from Peterborough BR station and is signposted from the A605 Oundle Road. The nearest mainline railway station is Peterborough
Open End Feb–Oct Sat–Sun, Apr–Oct Wed and Sat–Sun, Jul–Aug Tues–Sun; call for times
Adm Rover fares: adults £10.50, children £5.50, under 3s **free**, family (2+3) £26
Refreshments, souvenir shops, wheelchair access to most locations; most trains have a specially adapted carriage; adapted toilets at Wansford station, parking at Wansford, Ferry Meadow, Orton Mere and Peterborough NVR stations

One of the county's most famous and best loved railways, probably because it's the home of Thomas, everyone's favourite steam engine. It's been the location for dozens of films and TV programmes, including *Octopussy*, *Goldeneye* and *London's Burning*, and recently celebrated its 21st year of operation. It can offer 15-mile round trips from Wansford (where there's a large collection of locomotives and rolling stock from all over Europe), passing through scenic Yarwell and on to Orton Mere, where you can alight for a walk in the 200-hectare (500-acre) Nene Park, with its model railway circling the central lake, before re-embarking for the final leg to the restored Peterborough NVR station. Look out for the haunted tunnel where train drivers have seen the ghosts of 19th-century railway workers...

North Norfolk Railway

The Station, Sheringham t (01263) 820800
www.nnrailway.co.uk; talking timetable: t (01263) 820808
Getting there Sheringham Station is on the opposite side of the road to the Anglia Railways station of the same name and signposted from the A1082
Open May–Sept daily; Apr and Oct not Mon and Fri; Nov–Dec and Feb–Mar open Sat and Sun only; call for times
Fares Standard steam fares: adults £9, children £5.50, under 4s **free**, family (2+3) £27
Buffet at Weybourne, bookshop, souvenir shop, model railway shop at Sheringham, wheelchair access, on-site parking at both stations

Full-size steam and diesel railway, known as the 'Poppy Line', running along a particularly scenic stretch of the North Norfolk coast between Sheringham and Holt with plenty of opportunities for getting off and exploring the wooded countryside. At Holt you can ride the 'Holt Flyer' horse-drawn carriage into the town.

Wells and Walsingham Light Railway

Stiffkey Road, Wells-next-the-Sea **t** (01328) 710630 **www.northnorfolk.co.uk/walsinghamrail**
Getting there Just off the A149, 300 metres (330 yards) east of the A149 Wighton and Walsingham Road junction. Follow the brown signs
Open Apr–Oct daily **Adm** Adults £7, children £5.50, under 4s **free**
Refreshments served from Wells signal box, on-site parking

Steam train rides along the North Norfolk coast, between Wells-next-the-Sea (which, despite its confidently hyphenated name, is actually about a mile inland) and Walsingham; here you can visit the ruins of an Augustinian Priory and the cells or enter a restored Georgian courtroom in the Shirehall Museum (choose between standing in the dock or sitting in the judge's chair).

Theme parks

★Dinosaur Adventure Park

Weston Park, Lenwade, Norwich **t** (01603) 870245/876310 **www.dinosaurpark.co.uk**
Getting there 9 miles northwest of Norwich off the A1067 and signposted from both the A1067 and the A47
Open Mid-Mar–mid-Sept daily 10–5, mid-Sept–mid-Oct Fri–Sun 10–5, end Oct daily 10–5 (last entry 4)
Adm Adults £7.95, children £6.95, under 3s **free**
Restaurant, picnic areas, barbecue area, disabled access, parking, baby changing facilities, shop

At this innovative little adventure park, kids can climb over, around and even inside models of the great beasts. There's a dinosaur trail, with various life-size fibreglass models hidden amongst the foliage, a woodland maze, a 23m (75ft) 'climb-a-saurus' – little ones can climb up into the body, along the neck and take a look out through the fearsome jaws – a crazy-golf course, 'Jurassic Putt', a soft play area for under 5s, 'Tiny Pterosaurs', and an education centre with a fossil workshop. Natural history rambles through the local countryside are arranged and the park has picnic areas with gas-fired barbecues as well as a dinosaur-

themed diner. At the 'Secret Garden', children can meet and stroke a range of smaller, non-extinct animals, including deer, pigs and guinea pigs.

Fritton Lake Countryworld

Fritton, Great Yarmouth **t** (01493) 488288 **www.somerleyton.co.uk**
Getting there On the A143, southwest of Great Yarmouth. The nearest train station is Haddiscoe, just over 2 miles away
Open Apr–Sept 10–5.30; Oct Sat–Sun and half term 10–5.30
Adm Adults £6.70, children £4.60, under 3s **free**
Disabled access, disabled toilets, disabled boats for fishing, on-site parking

Woodland and landscaped gardens surrounding a 60-hectare (150-acre lake), where rowing boats and pedalos can be hired. There's also a Heavy Horse Centre, where Shires and Suffolk Punches give wagon rides, a children's farm, a playground and, in summer, you can take a ride on a miniature railway and watch falconry displays.

Peter Pan's Adventure Island

Sunken Garden, Western Esplanade, Southend-on-Sea **t** (01702) 443400 **www.adventureisland.co.uk**
Open Call for times
Adm Unlimited rides 'Super Saver' wristband £14–£19 (over 1.2m/4ft tall),' Tiny Tots' wristband £8–14 (restricted rides only)

Full-on fun park with hi-octane thrill rides.
For further information *see* p.315

★Pleasure Beach

South Beach Parade **t** (01493) 844585 **www.pleasure-beach.co.uk**
Open Mar–Sept, call for days and times
Adm Free, charge for individual rides, which can be paid for with tokens (£1 each) or wristbands (£15)

East Anglia's most popular visitor attraction.
For further information *see* p.312

Pleasurewood Hills

Leisure Way, Corton, Lowestoft **t** (01502) 586000 **www.pleasurewoodhills.co.uk**
Open Call for times
Adm Adults £14.50, children £12.50, under 1m (3ft) **free**, family £49 (book online for discount tickets)

Hi-tech waterslides and rollercoasters.
For further information *see* p.313

Wide open spaces

The Broads

Broads information centres

The Broads Authority, Thomas Harvey House,
18 Colgate, Norwich t (01603) 610734
www.broads-authority.gov.uk
Beccles
The Quay, Fen Lane, Beccles t (01502) 713196
Great Yarmouth
North West Tower, North Quay, Great Yarmouth
t (01493) 842195 (summer) t (01493) 846345 (winter)
Hoveton
Station Road, Hoveton, Norwich t (01603) 782281
How Hill
Toad Hole Cottage Museum and 'Electric Eel'
Wildlife Water Trail, How Hill, Ludham, Great
Yarmouth t (01692) 678763
Loddon
The Old Town Hall, 1 Bridge Street, Loddon,
Norwich t (01508) 521028
Potter Heigham
The Staithe, Bridge Street, Potter Heigham, Great
Yarmouth t (01692) 670779
Ranworth
The Staithe, Ranworth, Norwich t (01603) 270453

This dense network of inland waterways just
east of Norwich provides the location for
perhaps the ultimate boating holiday: 120 square
miles (310 sq km) of interlinked streams, rivers
and lakes adding up to no less than 125 miles
(200km) of navigable waterways. It's a resolutely
wet landscape. In addition to the waterways
themselves – the region is dissected by six rivers,
including the Bure which is joined by the Ant and
the Waveney before tipping into the sea at Great
Yarmouth – you'll find vast areas of marshland,

Norfolk and Suffolk Broads

The term 'Broads' itself refers to the large
lake-like expanses of water that dot the area.
For centuries they were thought to be purely
natural phenomena until medieval records were
discovered which showed that they were, in fact,
the result of extensive peat excavation in the
Middle Ages. Large holes cut by the peat diggers
filled with water when the sea level rose in the
13th and 14th centuries.

watermeadows, bogs and fens. There's water
everywhere, as far as the eye can see. It's a
fantastic place for nature lovers with its nature
reserves and bird sanctuaries, the whole area
having been given 'national protected status'. The
Broads Information Centres can provide details of
guided tours and a list of bird-watching sites. The
most accessible site is Ranworth, eight miles
northeast of Norwich, where there's a quarter-
mile boardwalk through reed beds and marshes
and a viewing platform from where you can see
herons, crested grebes and terns. At the conservation centre you can see a display on the (natural)
history of the Broads. Check out the Toad Hall
Cottage Museum at How Hill, with its displays of
Victorian country life. Guided wildlife cruises are on
offer at weekends. If you want to explore the area,
take a boat as the waterways are the region's
roads. The Bure Valley Steam Railway covers part
of the Broads on its route from Aylsham to
Wroxham, the 'Capital of the Broads' (combined
train rides and cruises available).

The main centres and booking agents for boat
hire are listed below.

Boating holidays

A boat for two to four people will cost around
£400–600 per week depending on the type of
boat you hire (excluding fuel). Check out:
Norfolk Broads Direct, www.broads.co.uk,
incorporating: Faircraft Loynes, The Bridge,
Wroxham t (01603) 782207; Herbert Woods, Broads
Haven, Potter Higham t (01692) 670711; Brundall
Bay Marina, Brundall, Norwich t (01603) 716606
Blakes Holiday Boating, Hoveton, Norwich (part of
Vacation Rental Group UK) t 0870 2202498
www.holidaycottagesgroup.co.uk
Hoseasons Holidays Ltd, Sunway House, Lowestoft
t (01502) 502588, Bookings t 0870 5434434
www.hoseasons.co.uk
River Ant
Ludham Bridge Services, Ludham Bridge t (01692)
630486 www.ludhambridgeboats.co.uk – Motor
launches, electric boats, dinghies, rowing boats.
Moonfleet Marine, The Staithe, Stalham
t (01692) 580288 www.moonfleetmarine.co.uk
Hire cruisers.
River Bure
Broad Tours Ltd, The Bridge, Wroxham
t (01603) 782207 Motor launches.

Camelot Craft, The Rhond, Hoveton
t (01603) 784620 Sailing school and yacht hire.
Fineway Launch Hire, Riverside Road, Hoveton
t (01603) 782309 Motor launches, electric boats.
River Thurne
Herbert Woods, Broads Haven, Potter Heigham
t (01692) 670711 Motor launches, electric boats.
Whispering Reeds, Hickling **t** (01692) 598314
Dinghies, rowing boats, cruisers and houseboats.
River Waveney
Day Launch Hire, Oulton Broad Yacht Station
t (01502) 513087 Motor launches, rowing boats.
HE Hipperson, Gillingham Dam, Beccles **t** (01502)
712166 Motor launches, electric boats, cruisers
and houseboats.
River Yare
Highcraft, Griffin Lane, Thorpe St Andrew
t (01603) 701701 Motor launches, rowing boats.

Guided boat trips
Electric Eel Wildlife Water Trail
How Hill Nature Reserve, Ludham **t** (01692) 678763
Times Apr, May and Oct weekends, Bank Hols and
school holidays hourly 11–3; Jun–Sept daily 10–5
Fares Call for details
Fifty-minute boats trip taking eight people on an
Edwardian-style electric boat through dykes and
marshes.
Helen of Ranworth
Ranworth Straithe **t** (01603) 270453
Times Mon–Sat from 10.15am
Fares Call for details
Tours of Malthouse Broad and the River Bure.
Liana
Beccles Quay **t** (01502) 713196
Times Apr, May and Oct weekends, Bank Hols and half
term, 11am, 2.15pm and 3.45pm; Jun–Sept daily
Fares Call for details
Explore the Southern Broads and the scenery
and wildlife of the River Waveney on this 12-
seater Edwardian-style electric launch. Trips last
1 hour 15 minutes and must be booked in
advance.
Little Tern
t (01692) 598276
Times/Fares Call for details
Water trail trekking on Hickling Broad National
Nature Reserve for 12 people.

Ra
Barton Broad Nature Reserve **t** (01692) 782281
Times Apr, May and Oct weekends, Bank Hols and
half term, 10am, 11.30am, 2pm and 3.30pm;
Jun–Sept daily
This solar-powered boat takes up to 12 people
(including wheelchair users) on a 1-hour 15-
minute trip around the recently restored Barton
Broad.

Other boat trips
Norfolk Broads Direct – Broad Tours
The Bridge, Wroxham **t** (01603) 782207
Mississippi River Boats, Lower Street, Horning
t (01692) 630262 www.southern-comfort.co.uk
City Boats
Elm Hill and Thorpe Station Quays, Norwich
t (01603) 701701 **www.cityboats.co.uk**
Waveney River Tours
Mutford Lock, Bridge Road, Oulton Broad
t 07817 920592, **www.waveneystardust.co.uk**

Cycle hire points on the Broads
Bungay
Outney Meadows Caravan Park **t** (01986) 892338
Clippesby
Clippesby Hall **t** (01493) 367800
Hoveton
Camelot Craft, The Rhond, Hoveton **t** (07887) 480331
Ludham
Ludham Bridge Boat Service **t** (01692) 630486
Stokesby
Riverside Tea Rooms and Stores **t** (01493) 750470

Train trips
Bure Valley Railway
Norwich Road, Aylsham **t** (01263) 733858
www.bvrw.co.uk
Getting there Aylsham station is midway between
Norwich and Cromer on the A140. Wroxham Station
is adjacent to the Anglia Railways Bittern Line
Wroxham (Hoveton) Station which receives direct
services from Norwich, Cromer and Sheringham
Fares Return: adults £9.50, children £5.50, family
£27 (2 adults, 2 children, £2 extra child); all-day
Rover tickets also available; train and cruise: adults
£15, children £10.50, family £50 (2+2), under 5s **free**
Restaurant, picnic areas, shop, tourist office,
wheelchair access on some carriages, on-site
parking at both stations

Epping Forest

Epping Forest Field Centre, High Beech Road, Loughton **t** (020) 8502 8500 (information centre), **Getting there** Within easy reach of London: take the tube to Loughton (Central Line) or catch one of these buses: 20, 167, 210, 214, 215, 219, 220, 240, 250, 301, 531, 532, 549
Open Mon–Sat 10–5, Sun 11–5 **Adm Free**
On-site parking

Once part of a huge swathe of ancient woodland that stretched from the River Lea to the sea, Epping Forest (on the outskirts of modern London) came into existence 8,000 years ago after the last Ice Age. Six thousand years later, Queen Boudicca (p.289) supposedly fought her last battle here against the Roman Army. Today, this 10-mile crescent is a wonderful mixture of thick dense woodland, grassland, heathland and ponds inhabited by a wide range of wildlife. In autumn, the brambles are thick with blackberries – kids can colour themselves purple from head to toe. The field centre organizes children's activities, including mini safaris, nature trails and pond dippings, and can provide details of walks.

Wicken Fen

Lode Lane, Wicken, Ely **t** (01353) 720274
www.wicken.org.uk
Getting there 8 miles south of Ely (nearest station) and signposted from the A1123 and the A142
Open Fen: daily dawn–dusk; visitor centre: Tues–Sun 10–5; cottage and windpump: from Easter–Oct daily 10–5, Sun and Bank Hols 2–5
Adm Adults £4.50, children £2, family £11
Refreshments, guided walks, on-site parking
Boardwalk suitable for pushchairs

The last remaining patch of unspoilt fenland, this 120-hectare (297-acre) area is the country's oldest nature reserve. Within its confines there's a tiny, original fen cottage, the area's last surviving windpump plus a vast array of wildlife. It's excellent for birdwatching and nature-themed events are organized throughout the year. Trail guides are available and you can hire binoculars to check out the views from Tower Hide.

SPORT AND ACTIVITIES

Activity centres

Horstead Centre

Rectory Road, Horstead, Norwich **t** (01603) 737215
www.horsteadcentre.org.uk
Open For details of times call in advance
Prices Basic weekend: from £44.50; 5-day stay: from £90; autumn activity day: £18.75, children 8+ £13.65

Residential activity centre run by a Christian charitable trust on the edge of the Norfolk Broads National Park, offering a range of programmes, including archery, canoeing, rope-climbing, abseiling, raft-building and sailing.

Lynnsport and Leisure Park

Green Park Avenue, King's Lynn **t** (01553) 818001
Open Mon–Fri 8.30am–10pm, Sat–Sun 8am–9pm
Adm Call for prices

Roller-skating, a BMX ramp, an activity club for 8–16-year-olds, plus facilities for badminton, football, basketball and volleyball.

Maidenhall Sports Centre

Maidenhall Approach, Ipswich **t** (01473) 433622
Open Call in advance for details of times
Adm Vary, call in advance for details of prices

Activities include trampolining, tennis and football. School-holiday day camp for children.

Mepal Outdoor Centre

Chatteris Road, Ely **t** (01354) 692251
www.mepal.co.uk
Getting there Off the A142 between Chatteris and Sutton
Open Daily 10–6 (last admission 4.30); evening activities start at 7pm
Adm Centre and playpark: £2.50, under 2s £1.70; Multi Activity Day (including canoeing, climbing, sailing, trampolining and archery): £20; family activity days: £50 for family of 4
Café, picnic areas, mother and baby facilities, on-site parking

Play park for toddlers, soft play zone for under 5s, adventure play area for 8–14s, holiday clubs for all ages, and day- and week-long archery, sailing, canoeing, wind-surfing and rock-climbing courses. Residential courses too.

Boat hire

For information on punting in Cambridge *see* p.287
For information on boating in the Norfolk Broads *see* pp.320–1

Bowling

Bury Bowl
Eastgate Street, Bury St Edmunds **t** (01284) 750704
Open/Adm Call in advance for times and prices

Kingpin
Family Entertainment Centre, Martlesham Heath,
Ipswich **t** (01473) 611111 **www.**kingpinbowling.co.uk
Open/Adm Call in advance for times and prices
    10-pin bowling, roller-skating and 'Kidz'
Kingdom' adventure play area.

The Kursaal
Eastern Esplanade, Southend-on-Sea
t 0870 5501010
Open/Adm Call in advance for times and prices

Lakeside Bowl
Fen Road, Pidley, Huntingdon **t** (01487) 740968
Open/Adm Call in advance for times and prices

Megabowl
Cowdray Avenue, Colchester **t** 0871 5501010
www.megabowl.co.uk
Open/Adm Call in advance for times and prices

Regent Bowl
92 Regent Road, Great Yarmouth **t** (01493) 856830
www.regentbowl.co.uk
Open Daily 10am–midnight **Adm** Adults £3.40,
children £2.50 per game

Strikes Bowl
Angle Drive, Ely **t** (01353) 668666,
www.strikesbowl.co.uk
Open/Adm Call in advance for times and prices

Cycling

For information on cycling in the Norfolk Broads
see p.321

Alton Cycle Hire
Holbrook Road, Alton Reservoir, Stutton
t (01473) 328873 **www.**altoncyclehire.co.uk
Open Summer: Sat–Sun 10–7 (school holidays
10–6); winter: Sat–Sun 10–4
Adm Hire from £6.50–£10/day.
See also Norfolk Broads pp.320–1

Grafham Water Cycling
Marlow car park, Grafham Water, Huntingdon
t (01480) 812500
Open/Adm Call in advance for times and prices
    Miles of tracks around this reservoir, with nature
reserves and birdwatching sites en route.

Go-karting

Anglia Indoor Karting
12 Farthing Road, Ipswich **t** (01473) 240087
www.angliakarting.com
Open Daily 10–10
Adm 12 laps (+ tuition) £11, 3x12 laps £20
    Youth karting at weekends.

Anglia Karting
The Airfield, Swaffham **t** (01760) 441777
www.anglia-karting.co.uk
Getting there Just outside Pickenham, off the
B1077 in Norfolk
Open Call in advance for details of times and prices
    No age limit as long as children can reach controls.

Indikart Racing
17 Grange Way, Whitehall Industrial Estate,
Colchester **t** (01206) 799511
Open Daily 10–10
Adm Call in advance for prices
    Indoor go-kart track; children aged eight or older.

Wild Tracks Off Road Activity Park
Chippenham Road, Kennet, Newmarket
t (01638) 751918
Open Activity days: first Sun of the month 10–4;
other times by arrangement
Adm Call in advance for details of prices
    Quad bikes, rally karts and motorcross bikes.

Karting 2000
Marine Parade, Great Yarmouth (just south of the
Pleasure Beach) **t** (01493) 854041
Open Call in advance for times and prices
    Cadet kart-racing; children aged eight and over.

Horse-riding

Caister Riding School
Beach House Farm, Yarmouth Road, Caister,
Great Yarmouth **t** (01493) 720444
Open Call in advance for details of times and prices
    Lessons for all ages and abilities.

Caldecott Hall Equestrian Centre
Caldecott Hall, Fritton, Great Yarmouth
t (01493) 488488
Open/Adm Call in advance for times and prices
    Instruction and trekking by arrangement.

Croft Farm Riding Centre
Croft Farm, Thrigby, Great Yarmouth
t (01493) 368275
Open/Adm Call in advance for times and prices
    Hacking and lessons.

Northbrook Equestrian Centre
New Road, Offord Cluny, Huntingdon
t (01480) 812654
Open/Adm Call for times and prices
Lessons for all ages and levels of experience.

Ice-skating
Lee Valley Ice Centre
Lea Bridge Road **t** (020) 8533 3154
www.leevalleypark.org.uk
Open/Adm Call for times and prices

Indoor activity centres
Activity World
Padholme Road, Peterborough **t** (01733) 314446
www.activityworld.co.uk
Open 9.30–5.30 **Adm** weekday £3.50 (adults 50p),
Sat, Sun and school holidays £4.50 (adult £1)
Ball pools, mazes, giant chess and draughts
pieces and crazy golf; 1.5m (5ft) height restriction.

Activity World
Rollerbury, Station Hill, Bury St Edmunds
t (01284) 763799 www.wherekidsplay.co.uk
Open 9.30–6.30 **Adm** Over 1m (3ft) £4.50, under 1m
(3ft) £3.70
Ball pools, mazes, tangle tower, drop slide; 1.5m
(5ft) height restriction.

Big Sky Indoor Children's Play Centre
24 Wainman Road, Shrewsbury Avenue, Woodston,
Peterborough **t** (01733) 390810
Open Daily 10.30–6 **Adm** Call for prices
Slides, inflatables, go-karts and rocket ride.

Funstop
Exchange House, Louden Road, Cromer
t (01263) 514976
Open Daily May–Sept 10–6; Oct–Apr Fri–Sun 10–6
Adm Call for prices
Indoor play centre for under 10s.

Go Bananas
9–10 Mason Road, Cowdray Centre, Colchester
t (01206) 761762 www.go-bananas.co.uk
Open Daily 9.30–6.30
Adm Children £4.20, under 5s £3.50, adult **free**
Café, mother and baby facilities, on-site parking
Three-storey soft play area for 5–12-year-olds;
ball pools, slides, swings, webs and 'spook rooms'.

Jim's Totally Brilliant Play Ltd
Whitehorse Road, Ipswich **t** (01473) 464616
Open Tues–Fri 10–6, Sat–Sun 10–5.30
Adm Call for prices

Huge indoor play area with a 'Nurseryland' for
under 4s and a 'Megazone' for 7s and over.

Kids' Kingdom
Garon Park, Eastern Avenue, Southend-on-Sea
t (01702) 462747
Open Daily 11–7
Adm Call for prices
Large indoor adventure centre with slides,
climbing frames and ball pools.

Kidz' Kingdom
Family Entertainment Centre, Martlesham Heath,
Ipswich **t** (01473) 611333
Open Daily 10–6
Adm Call for prices
Bouncy castles, aerial runway, ball pool, slides,
plus roller-skating rink and 10-pin bowling.

Magic City
13–19 Pier Avenue, Clacton **t** (01255) 421144
Open Fri and Sat 9am–11pm, Sun–Thurs
9am–10.15pm
Adm Call for prices
Ball pools, slides, climbing frames and a special
soft play area for under 5s.

Laser-shooting centres
LaserQuest
2nd floor, 13–15 Bradwells Court, Cambridge
t (01223) 302102 www.laserquestcambridge.tk
Open Daily 10.30–9
Adm Laser Quest: weekdays £3.50 (1 game), £6.25
(2 games); weekends: £4 (1 game) and £7 (2 games)
Café
Laser-shooting games.

Mr B's Quasar Spacechase
5–9 Marine Parade, Southend-on-Sea
t (01702) 603947
Open/Adm Call in advance for times and prices

Rollerworld and Quasar
Eastgates, Colchester **t** (01206) 868868
www.rollerworld.co.uk
Open/Adm Call for times and prices
Café-restaurant, mother and baby facilities, parking
Roller-skating for all ages and abilities plus
laser combat games in the Quasar centre.

Leisure centres
The Brentwood Centre
Doddinghurst Road, Brentwood **t** (01277) 215151
www.brentwood-centre.co.uk
Open/Adm Call for times and prices

Leisure pool and learner pool, plus facilities for tennis, volleyball, badminton and gymnastics.

Bury St Edmunds Leisure Centre

Beetons Way, Bury St Edmunds **t** (01284) 753496
Getting there Follow the signs from the town centre
Open Mon–Fri 7–10.30, Sat 9–7, Sun 9–8
Adm Call for prices
Café, mother and baby facilities, disabled access
Three pools; include teaching pool and flumes.

Clacton Leisure Centre

Vista Road, Clacton-on-Sea **t** (01255) 429647
www.clactonleisurecentre.org
Open/Adm Call for times and prices
A 25m (82ft) pool and indoor adventure play park.

Colchester Leisure World

Cowdray Avenue, Colchester **t** (01206) 282000,
www.colchesterleisureworld.co.uk
Open/Adm Call for times and prices
*Café-restaurant, picnic area, mother and baby
facilities, on-site parking*
Large heated pool with flume rides, spa pools,
'lazy river ride' and water cannons.

Haverhill Leisure Centre

Ehringshausen Way, Haverhill **t** (01440) 702548
Open Mon–Fri 6am–10.30pm, Sat 7.30am–6pm,
Sun 7.30am–9pm
Adm Call in advance for prices
*Café, refreshments, mother and baby facilities,
disabled access, on-site parking*
Two pools, waterslide and adventure play area.

Roller-skating

RollerWorld

Eastgates, Colchester **t** (01206) 868868
www.rollerworld.co.uk
Open Call in advance for times
Adm Rollerblade hire: £1.90; quad skate hire: 90p
Rollercafé, rollershop
England's largest roller-skating rink.

Skiing

Brentwood Park Dry Ski Centre

Warley Gap **t** (01277) 211994
www.brentwoodskicentre.co.uk
Open/Adm Call for times and prices

Suffolk Ski Centre

Bourne Hill, Wherstead, Ipswich **t** (01473) 602347
www.suffolkskicentre.co.uk
Open/Adm Call for times and prices

Swimming

Abbey Indoor Pool

Whitehill Road, off Newmarket Road, Cambridge
t (01223) 213352
Open/Adm Call for times and prices
Small indoor pool and soft play area.

Cambridge Parkside Pools

Gonville Place, Cambridge **t** (01223) 446100
Open Call for times
Adm Adults £3.20, children £1.60
Children's pool and leisure pool with adjustable-
depth floor. Body and float flume rides.

Crown Pools

Crown Street, Ipswich **t** (01473) 433655
Open/Adm Call for times and prices
Competition pool, teaching pool and leisure pool
with wave machine, chutes and inflatables.

Marina Leisure Centre

Marine Parade, Great Yarmouth **t** (01493) 851521
Open/Adm Call for times and prices
Leisure pool with wave machines, water chute
and indoor beach.

Oasis

Seafront, Hunstanton **t** (01485) 534227
Open/Adm Call for times and prices
Tropically heated outdoor pool with an aqua
slide and giant inflatables.

The Splash Leisure Complex

Weybourne Road, Sheringham **t** (01263) 825675
Open/Adm Call for times and prices
Café, shop, saunas, sun terrace
Leisure pool with 45m (150ft) giant waterslide,
wave machine and children's paddling area.

Watersports

Marine Activities Centre

Eastern Esplanade, Southend **t** (01702) 612770,
www.southendmarineactivitiescentre.co.uk
Open/Adm Call for times and prices
Canoeing, jet-skiing, sailing and wind-surfing.

Suffolk Waters Country Park

Bramford, Ipswich **t** (01473) 832327
Open/Adm Call for times and prices
Canoeing, sailing and wind-surfing.

KIDS IN

Cinemas

Aldeburgh
Aldeburgh Cinema 51 High Street **t** (01728) 452996
www.aldeburghcinema.co.uk

Bury St Edmunds
Cineworld Parkway **t** 0871 2208000
www.cineworld.co.uk
Hollywood Cinema Hatter Street **t** (01284) 754477,
(01284) 762586 www.hollywoodcinemas.net

Cambridge
Arts Picture House 38–39 St Andrews Street
t (01223) 504444
Cineworld Clifton Way **t** 0871 2208000
www.cineworld.co.uk
Vue Grafton Centre **t** 0871 2240240
www.myvue.com

Clacton-on-Sea
Flix 129 Pier Avenue **t** (01255) 421188, (01255) 429627

Colchester
Odeon Crouch Street **t** 0870 505 0007, (01206)
710813 www.odeon.co.uk

Ely
Ely Cinema Ship Lane **t** (01353) 666388

Great Yarmouth
Hollywood Cinema Marine Parade **t** (01493)
842043 www.hollywoodcinemas.net

Ipswich
Cineworld 11 Grafton Way **t** 0871 200200
www.cineworld.co.uk
Film Theatre Corn Exchange **t** (01473) 433100
www.ipswichfilmtheatre.co.uk

King's Lynn
King's Lynn Arts Centre King Street **t** (01553)
772864 www.kingslynnarts.co.uk
Majestic Cinema Tower Street **t** (01553) 772603

Lowestoft
Hollywood London Road South **t** (01502) 564567
www.hollywoodcinemas.net

Norwich
Cinema City St Andrew's Street **t** (01603) 622047
www.cinemacity.co.uk
Hollywood Anglia Square **t** (01603) 621903
www.hollywoodcinemas.net
Odeon Wherry Road **t** 0871 2244007
www.odeon.co.uk

Southend-on-Sea
Odeon Victoria Circus **t** 0871 2244007
www.odeon.co.uk

Museums and science centres

Caister Castle Car Collection
Caister-on-Sea, Great Yarmouth **t** (01572) 787251
www.greateryarmouth.co.uk/caister_castle.htm
Getting there 1 mile from Caister-on-Sea just off
the A1064 and about 3 miles north of Great
Yarmouth. Follow the brown tourist signs
Open Late May–Sept Mon–Fri and Sun 10–4.30
Adm Varies, call in advance
*Picnic area, refreshments, disabled facilities,
on-site parking*

The resort of Caister, a few miles north of Great
Yarmouth, boasts a long, sandy beach in addition
to this large collection of vintage motor cars in
the grounds of a 15th-century castle. There are
more than 200 exhibits, including an 1893
Panhard et Levassor, the first 'real' car ever made.

Central Museum and Planetarium
Victoria Avenue, Southend-on-Sea **t** (01702)
434449 www.southendmuseums.co.uk/
planetarium
Open Museum: Mon–Sat 10–5; planetarium
shows: Wed–Sat at 11am, 2pm and 4pm
Adm Museum: **free**; planetarium: adults £2.60,
children £1.90, family £8

Archaeology and natural history displays
and the only planetarium in the southeast
outside London.

Collector's World and Hermitage Hall
Hermitage Hall, Downham Market **t** (01366) 383185
www.collectors-world.org
Getting there Just outside Downham Market,
follow the brown tourist signs on the A1122
Open Daily 11–5
Adm Adults £5, children £4.50, family (2+2) £18
Tearoom, shop, picnic area, free car park

The collection of Eric St John Foti is a fascinating albeit bizarre experience, containing
themed rooms stuffed with memorabilia of such
disparate celebrities as Charles Dickens, Lord
Horatio Nelson, Dame Barbara Cartland and Liza
Goddard. The 'Dickens Experience' features a
Victorian street scene (with sounds and smells)
but don't expect hi-tech animatronics; this is a
charmingly amateur reconstruction, as is the
series of tableaux depicting the ghosts of East
Anglia. For those who wish it were Christmas
every day, there is a 'Nativity Chapel', a 'Mistletoe
Bower', festive teddy bears and Victorian

Christmas decorations. In the grounds, you will find a car museum and a 'Life-of-Jesus' walk.

Dedham Art and Craft Centre and Toy Museum

High Street, Dedham **t** (01206) 322666
www.dedhamartandcraftcentre.co.uk
Getting there 1 mile off the A12 between Colchester and Ipswich
Open Daily 10–5 (summer weekends until 5.30)
Adm Free
Restaurant-tearoom

Watch artists and craftsmen at work and see toys being nursed in the dolls' and toys' hospital.

Ecotech Discovery Centre

Turbine Way, Swaffham **t** (01760) 726100
www.ecotech.org.uk
Getting there Signposted from the A47
King's Lynn–Norwich Road
Open May–Sept Mon–Fri (turbine tours 11am, 1pm and 3pm); winter Mon–Fri (turbine tours at 1pm)
Adm Adults £5, children £3, family £15
Café-restaurant, shop, disabled access, adapted toilets, on-site parking

It calls itself an 'environmental discovery centre' and its aim seems to be to get children interested in the environment by showing them the various potential disasters that have and, indeed, could befall it. You can discover what scientists think happened to the dinosaurs (hit by a meteorite seems to be the most popular explanation), learn about floods, volcanoes and hurricanes and find out how climate change is likely to make all of these increasingly common in years to come. You can also find out what you can do to prevent the world's imminent destruction. Housed in East Anglia's largest timber-framed building, with a computer-controlled heating system to save energy and a rainwater recycling scheme, the centre has certainly put its money where its beliefs are. Although a little worthy and a tad alarmist, it's all presented in a fresh and lively way and is actually a lot of fun. The most fun part of your trip, however, is bound to be your climb to the top of the country's largest wind turbine for fantastic panoramic views out over East Anglia. But, be warned it's more than a whopping 300 steps to get up there.

Farmland Museum and Denny Abbey

Ely Road, Waterbeach, Cambridge **t** (01223) 860988
www.dennyfarmlandmuseum.org.uk
Getting there About 7 miles northeast of Cambridge off the A10
Open Apr–Oct daily 12 noon–5 **Adm** Adults £3.80, children £1.70, under 5s **free**, family £9.60
Café at weekends and during school hols on Thurs, picnic areas, gift shop, some disabled access, adapted toilets, on-site parking

Museum of farming with interactive displays and recreated period interiors (a village shop, a medieval schoolroom and a farmworker's cottage). Family events are put on during the year (falconry displays, art workshops and craft demonstrations (butter-making, printmaking, basket-making, etc.).

House on the Hill Toy Museum

Grove Hill, Stansted **t** (01279) 813237
www.stanstedtoymuseum.com
Getting there 2 miles from J8 of M11 and 5 minutes' walk from Stansted Mountfitchet station, which is on the London Liverpool Street–Cambridge line
Open Daily 10–4 **Adm** Adults £4, children £3.30; combined ticket for Mountfitchet Castle available
Gift shop

The largest private toy collection in the world with more than 80,000 items over two floors (board games, tin toys, teddies, puppets, dolls' houses and action figures including the world's largest collection of Action Man paraphernalia – check out the old-style 'eagle eyes' version) housed in glass cabinets. It's a look-but-don't-touch sort of a place, although there are some push-button interactive toys, a few coin-operated slot machines and the occasional puppet show in summer.

Inspire Hands-On Science Centre

St Michael's Church, Coslany Steet, Norwich
t (01603) 612612 **www.inspirediscoverycentre.com**
Open Mon–Fri 10–5, Sat and Sun 11–5
Adm Adults £4.50, children £4, family £13, under 3s **free**

Small but well-equipped science museum.
For further information *see p.297*

Aircraft museums

During the early years of the Second World War when Britain was under almost constant attack by the German Air Force (who hoped to establish dominance of the skies in preparation for a land invasion), it was the RAF bases of East Anglia and Kent that led the fight back and sent out the planes for the Battle of Britain, which finally thwarted Hitler's plans.

Several of the region's former bases have now been turned into museums, where you can find out more about the conflict and see (and often climb aboard) some of the great flying machines that secured Britain's freedom.

At the Royal Air Force Air Defence Radar Museum, which is housed in an original 1942 building, you can visit a restored Battle of Britain Ground Control Interception room and see films and documentary footage of the war, while at the Norfolk and Suffolk Aviation Museum (which is made up of the 446th Bomber Group Museum, Royal Observer Corps Museum, RAF Bomber Command Museum and the Air Sea Rescue and Coastal Command Museum), there's a vast array of aviation paraphernalia and a World War II hangar with over 25 historic aircraft on display.

Duxford Airfield Museum

Imperial War Museum, Duxford, Cambridge
t (01223) 835000 **www.**iwm.org.uk
Getting there About 7 miles south of Cambridge at J10 of the M11. There's a free bus service from Cambridge train station and the Crowne Plaza
Open Summer: daily 10–6; winter: daily 10–4. For air show dates, call in advance
Adm Adults £13, children **free**; **free** for all after 4.30pm (in summer) and 3pm (in winter)
Café-restaurant, gift shop, disabled access, on-site parking

Run by the Imperial War Museum, Duxford is home to Europe's largest collection of military and civilian aircraft. There are around 140 flying machines in all, ranging from First World War bi-planes to the most modern supersonic jet fighters, all housed in enormous, looming hangars.

Obviously, it's best to visit during one of the museum's numerous airshows when you can see the spectacular craft in action: you'll see jets roaring above your head (seemingly only feet away), recreated bi-plane dog fights and demonstrations of precision formation flying, often as not by the famous Red Arrows. Be warned, though, these shows are incredibly noisy and will probably prove a bit much for very young children. Don't let that put you off altogether, however, as the museum is well worth visiting on non-flying days, too, when kids will actually be able to climb aboard some of the sleek machines – no matter what age you are, it's always quite a thrill to sit at the controls of a jet fighter – and put their dog-fighting skills to the test on the hi-tech Battle of Britain simulator. During the real battle, Duxford was one of the country's main fighter aerodromes and you can find out all about the nation's 'finest hour' at the restored control tower and operations room. There is also a small section dedicated to land warfare, where you can see reconstructions of battle scenes and an adventure playground outside. Trips around the site aboard a narrow-gauge railway are available in summer.

Norfolk and Suffolk Aviation Museum

Buckeroo Way, The Street, Flixton, Bungay
t (01986) 896644 **www.**aviationmuseum.net
Getting there On the B1062, off the A143, 1 mile west of Bungay
Open Apr–Oct Sun–Thurs 10–5; Nov–Mar Tues, Wed and Sun 10–4 **Adm Free**
Picnic areas, shop, mother and baby facilities, guided tours, disabled access, on-site parking

Royal Air Force Air Defence Radar Museum

RAF Neatishead, Norwich **t** (01692) 633309
www.neatishead.raf.mod.uk
Getting there Signed from the A1062 Wroxham–Horning Road
Open 2nd Sat of each month and Bank Hols 10–5, Easter–Sept also Tues
Adm Adults £3, children £2
Refreshments, guided tours, on-site parking

Secret Nuclear Bunker
Kelvedon Hatch **t** (01277) 364883
www.japar.demon.co.uk
Getting there Lies off the A128 Brentwood to
Chipping Ongar Road
Open Mar–Oct Mon–Fri 10–4, Sat–Sun and Bank
Hols 10–5; Nov–Feb Thurs–Sun 10–4
Adm Adults £6, children £4, under 5 **free**, family £15
Refreshments, disabled access

Cunningly concealed beneath an ordinary-
looking bungalow, this now defunct three-storey
bunker is fitted out with a staggering 110 tonnes
of equipment and was designed to support 600
government personnel during a nuclear war. An
audiotour takes you around the site (kids get
their own version) with en-route films, military
uniforms and gas masks to try on plus a
computer quiz at the end.

Theatres
Bury St Edmunds
Theatre Royal Westgate Street **t** (01284) 769505
www.theatreroyal.org
Cambridge
ADC Theatre Park Street **t** (01223) 359547
www.adctheatre.com
Cambridge Arts Theatre St Edwards Passage
t (01223) 503333 **www**.cambridgeartstheatre.com
Concert Hall West Road **t** (01223) 335184
www.westroad.org
Corn Exchange Wheeler Street **t** (01223) 357851
www.cornex.co.uk
The Junction Clifton Road **t** (01223) 511511
www.junction.co.uk
Mumford Theatre A.P.U. East Road **t** 0845 1962320
Clacton-on-Sea
Princes Theatre Town Hall, Station Road
t (01255) 422958
West Cliff Theatre Tower Road
t (01255) 433344
www.west-cliff-theatre-clacton.org.uk
Colchester
Mercury Theatre, Balkerne Gate **t** (01206) 573948
www.mercurytheatre.co.uk

Great Yarmouth
Britannia Pier Theatre Marine Parade
t (01493) 842209 **www**.britannia-pier.co.uk
St George's Theatre King Street **t** (01493) 858387
Ipswich
Corn Exchange King Street **t** (01473) 433100
Regent St Helen's Street **t** (01473) 281580
Wolsey Theatre Civic Drive **t** (01473) 295900
www.wolseytheatre.co.uk
King's Lynn
Corn Exchange Tuesday Market Place
t (01553) 764864
www.kingslynncornexchange.co.uk
King's Lynn Arts Centre 27–9 King Street
t (01553) 764864
For further information *see* p.295
Lowestoft
Marina Theatre The Marina **t** (01502) 533200
www.marinatheatre.co.uk
Seagull Theatre Morton Road **t** (01502) 562863
Norwich
Maddermarket Theatre St John's Alley
t (01603) 620917 **www**.maddermarket.co.uk
Norwich Arts Centre Reeves Yard, St Benedict's
Street **t** (01603) 660352
www.norwichartscentre.co.uk
Norwich Playhouse 42–58 St George's Street
t (01603) 598598 **www**.norwichplayhouse.co.uk
Norwich Puppet Theatre St James, Whitefriars
t (01603) 629921
www.geocities.com/norwichpuppets
For further information *see* pp.297–8
Theatre Royal Theatre Street **t** (01603) 630000
www.theatreroyalnorwich.co.uk
Southwold
Summer Theatre St Edmunds Hall, Cumberland
Road **t** (01502) 722228 **www**.southwoldtheatre.org

Aldeburgh

Regatta

171 High Street **t** (01728) 452011
www.regattaaldeburgh.com
Open Wed–Sat 12 noon–2 and 6–late, Sun lunch only

Smart and trendy bistro with a blackboard showing a daily selection of fresh fish. Modern British and traditional favourites.

Cambridge

Bella Italia

The Mill, Newnham Road, Cambridge **t** (01223) 367507
www.bellapasta.co.uk
Open Mon–Sat 10–11, Sun 11–10.30

Children's menu full of mini Italian favourites, plus colouring books and crayons to keep kids occupied whilst they wait for their food.

Browns

23 Trumpington Street **t** (01223) 461655
www.browns-restaurants.com
Open Mon–Sat 11.30am–11.30pm, Sun 12 noon–11

Housed in Addenbrooke Hospital's former outpatient unit opposite the Fitzwilliam Museum (p.286), this huge branch of the family-friendly chain has a French–American menu and offers a range of children's choices (the hamburgers are particularly good). The dining room is kept cool by overhead fans, there's a mother and baby room and highchairs are provided.

Cambridge Tea Room

1 Wheeler Street **t** (01223) 357503
Open Daily 10–6

Opposite the tourist information centre, this tearoom serves delicious cream teas, baked potatoes and sandwiches.

Copper Kettle

King's Parade **t** (01223) 365068
Open Mon–Sat 8.30–5.30, Sun 9–5.30

A Cambridge institution where generations of undergraduates have come to discuss the meaning of life over coffee and a Chelsea bun. Overlooking the glorious vista of King's College, it is a good place for a 20-minute sandwich pit-stop. No credit cards accepted.

Fitzbillies

52 Trumpington Street **t** (01223) 352500
www.fitzbillies.co.uk
Open Mon–Fri 8.30–5, Sat–Sun 8.30–5.30

Good for cakes and scones.

The Milton Arms

205 Milton Road **t** (01223) 505012
Open Daily 11am–11pm

Outside the centre of town, this is a good family-orientated pub with an outdoor play area.

Rainbow Café

9a Kings Parade **t** (01223) 321551
www.rainbowcafe.co.uk
Open Tues–Sat 10am–9.30

Popular and cheerful vegetarian restaurant with a large menu including several vegan, nut-free and gluten-free dishes. All meals on the menu are available as half portions (£3.95) for children under 12. Jars of organic baby food are provided free for very young diners.

Around Cambridge

The Red Lion

High Street, Grantchester **t** (01223) 840121
Open Daily 11am–11pm

Good pub food (there's a children's menu), a grassy garden and outdoor play area; highchairs are available.

Colchester

Clowns

61 High Street **t** (01206) 578631
Open Daily 11–10

Solid English fare served in impressively large portions. Children's menu and highchairs are provided.

Pizza Express

1 St Runwald Street **t** (01206) 760680
www.pizzaexpress.co.uk
Open Daily 12–11.30

Large, comfy branch of this chain serving thin-crust Italian-style pizzas. Highchairs available.

Red Lion Hotel

High Steet **t** (01206) 577986
Open Daily 12 noon–10

Hearty pub food and cream teas.

Tilly's Tea Rooms

22 Trinity Street **t** (01206) 560600
Open Daily 9–5

Cakes, scones and sandwiches.

Warehouse Brasserie

12 Chapel Street **t** (01206) 765656
Open Tues–Sat 12–2 and 6.30–10

Colchester's swankiest restaurant can provide a very reasonably priced family lunch based around a combination of French and English staples. Kids' portions and highchairs available.

Great Yarmouth

Harry Ramsden's

112 Marine Parade **t** (01493) 330444
www.harryramsdens.co.uk
Open Mon–Wed and Sat 11.30am–9pm, Thurs and Fri 11am–10pm, Sun 12 noon–8pm

Perhaps the best of the town's galaxy of fish 'n' chip shops, this huge 140-seat version of the great northern chain serves large portions of proper, thick-cut, chunky chips, along with a range of choices for children.

The Yankee Traveller

36 King Street **t** (01493) 857065
www.yankeetraveller.co.uk
Open Daily 12 noon–11pm (10.30pm Sunday)

Ribs, fried chicken, steaks and burgers are the specialities of this American-style diner. There's a special children's menu.

Hunstanton

The Lodge Hotel and Restaurant

Old Hunstanton Road, Old Hunstanton
t (01485) 532896
Open Daily 6.30am–8.30pm; Sun carvery 12 noon–2.30pm

Friendly restaurant serving pub food and cream teas with a carvery at weekends. A children's menu is also available.

Ipswich

Ask Pizza

Cardinal Park **t** (01473) 210443
www.yankeetraveller.co.uk
Open Daily 12 noon–11.30pm

Yummy pizzas and pastas are served at this upmarket chain.

Clowns

16 Falcon Street **t** (01473) 230185
Open Daily 11.30–10

Lively, colourful family-friendly restaurant with good children's menu. Highchairs available.

Pizza Express

24–26 Lloyds Avenue **t** (01473) 212651
www.pizzaexpress.co.uk
Open Mon–Thurs 11–11, Fri and Sat 11–12 midnight

Large, cheery branch of the nation's favourite pizza chain.

Around Ipswich

Butley Orford Oysterage

Market Hill, Orford, Woodbridge **t** (01394) 450277
www.butleyorfordoyesterage.co.uk
Open Lunch: daily 12 noon–2.15pm; dinner: Apr–May and mid-Sept–Oct Wed–Sat, Jun–mid-Sept daily, Nov–Mar Fri and Sat only; weekdays 6.20pm–9pm, Sat 6pm–9pm

Seafood restaurant serving fresh fish, landed daily by their own boats at Orford Quay, and oysters grown at the nearby Butley Creek Beds. Expensive, but simple and delicious – especially good as an introduction to shellfish. Children's portions and highchairs are available.

King's Lynn

Rococo

11 Saturday Market Place **t** (01553) 771483
Open Tues–Sat 12 noon–2.30 and 6.30–10.30, Mon 6.30pm–10.30pm only

Well-respected, elegant, modern British restaurant with a surprisingly relaxed, family-friendly atmosphere. Reasonably priced lunches served.

Rose and Crown

Nethergate Street, Harpley **t** (01485) 520577
Open Daily 11–11

Outside King's Lynn, near Houghton Hall, this archetypal village pub serving traditional village pub food has a children's play area and a garden.

Norwich

Adlard's

79 Upper St Giles **t** (01603) 633522
www.adlards.co.uk
Open Mon 7.30pm–10.30pm, Tues–Sat 12.30pm–1.45pm and 7.30pm–10.30pm

Norwich's swankiest restaurant and one of only two in the whole of East Anglia to currently hold a Michelin star. Children will have to be well behaved but are made very welcome. Highchairs are available.

Colchester oysters

For hundreds of years, Colchester and Whitstable were the most important oyster-fishing centres in Britain. It's hard to believe today, but until the 1860s, oysters were so cheap that oyster bars were the contemporary equivalent of fish and chip shops.

> **Treacle tart**
> Norfolk treacle tart should be sticky, flavoured with lemon zest and served with custard for a really tasty treat!

The Assembly House
The Georgian Restaurant, Theatre Street **t** (01603) 626402 www.assemblyhousenorwich.co.uk
Open Mon–Sat 9.30am–late
Home-made scones, pastries and sausage rolls are served in this elegant Georgian dining room. The house holds regular food-themed exhibitions.

Caffè Uno
2–3 Tombland **t** (01603) 615718
www.caffeuno.co.uk
Open Daily 10am–11pm
This excellent Italian restaurant is a stone's throw from Norwich Cathedral (p.297). There's a special children's menu and highchairs.

Courtyard Restaurant
Maids Head Hotel, Tombland **t** (01603) 209955
Open Mon–Fri 7–10am, 12 noon–2 and 7–10pm; Sat 8–10am, 12 noon–2 and 7–10pm; Sun 8–10am, 12 noon–2 and 7–9.30pm
Offers a varied menu including traditional English favourites sausage and mash and shepherd's pie. Children's menu and highchairs available. Call to book on weekends.

Fatso's Speak-easy Restaurant
63–7 Prince of Wales Road **t** (01603) 762763
www.fatsos.net
Open Mon–Thurs 11–11, Fri and Sat 11–11.30, Sun 11.30–10.30
American-style grub (ribs, burgers and fried chicken). Children's menu and highchairs are available.

Jarrolds Department Store
London Street **t** (01603) 660661
Open Mon–Sat 9.15–5.50, Sun 10.30–4.30
This huge department store has three child-friendly eateries. The second-floor self-service restaurant, with views over the market, is the best.

Linzers
67 London Road **t** (01603) 630795
Open Mon–Sat 9–5
Patisserie and pavement café offering a tasty range of cakes and pastries.

Pizza One Pancakes Too!
24 Tombland **t** (01603) 621583
Open Mon–Wed 12 noon–10, Thurs 12 noon–10.30, Fri and Sat 12 noon–11, Sun 12 noon–9
This lively café in the cathedral wall serves pizzas, pastas and French crêpes. Highchairs are available.

Wagamama
408 Chapelfield Plain, Chapelfield **t** (01603) 305985
www.wagamama.com
Open Mon–Sat 12–11pm, Sun 12–10pm
Branch of the popular noodle bar chain. Children's menu available.

Around Norwich

Blue Boar Pub and Restaurant
259 Wroxham Road, Sprowston **t** (01603) 426802
Open Mon–Sat 11–11, Sun 12 noon–10.30
This family-friendly pub just outside the city centre on the Norwich–Wroxham road has an outdoor children's play area and a non-smoking restaurant.

The Green Man
Wroxham Road, Rackheath **t** (01603) 782693
Open Mon–Sat 11–2.30 and 5.30–11, Sun 12–3 and 7–10.30
Pleasant country pub serving excellent hearty meals. Children's menu and highchairs available.

Wroxham

Waterside Terrace Restaurant and Bar
Hotel Wroxham, The Bridge **t** (01603) 782061
Open Summer: 12 noon–9.30; winter: 12 noon–2.30 and 6.30–8.30
Home-cooked meals, snacks and roasts served on a heated outdoor terrace overlooking the river.

East Midlands

Derbyshire · Leicestershire
Lincolnshire · Northamptonshire
Nottinghamshire · Rutland

For centuries a rather featureless and sparsely populated area, the East Midlands only really came into its own following the Industrial Revolution when its county towns of Derby, Nottingham, Northampton and Leicester grew into thriving industrial conurbations. Prior to this expansion, the area had principally been known as the former stamping ground of Robin Hood, the legendary outlaw, who along with his band of merry men, got up to all sorts of adventures in the famous Sherwood Forest. The forest, though much reduced since Robin's time, can still be visited today and, indeed, is just one of several glorious swathes of countryside to be found in the region. From the rolling hills of the Peak District to the woods and dells of the new National Forest, the East Midlands has more than its fair share of beauty spots. There's also plenty for families to do with lively resorts to visit, stately homes to explore, caverns to descend into, steam trains to ride and, at Leicester's brand new National Space Science Centre, even space-ships to fly in.

Highlights

Animal fun, White Post Modern Farm Centre, p.352, or Natureland Seal Sanctuary, Skegness, p.351
Criminal fun, Galleries of Justice, Nottingham, p.341
Cycling, National Forest, p.360, Peak District, p.344 or Rutland Water, p.361
Fisherman Fun, National Fishing Heritage Centre, Grimsby, pp.365–6
Hands-on science, Snibston Discovery Park, p.366
Ice-skating, Nottingham National Ice Centre, p.363
Recreated battle, Bosworth Battlefield, p.355
Robin Hood fun, Tales of Robin Hood, Nottingham, p.342
Space age fun, National Space Science Centre, Leicester, p.337
Stately home fun, Chatsworth, p.348
Underground fun, caves of Nottingham, p.341, Peak District caverns, pp.345–6

Day-trip itinerary

Morning: At the National Space Science Centre in Leicester (p.337).
Lunch: At the Centre or, if you fancy something a bit more adventurous, at the Shireen Indian restaurant back in town (p.368).
Afternoon: Drive to Tropical Birdland, eight miles west of Leicester, to feed the colourful collection of parrots and macaws (pp.351–2).

Special events

February
Leicester: Comedy Festival t (0116) 261 6812 www.comedy-festival.co.uk
March
Ashbourne: traditional 'football' t (01335) 343666
April
Hallaton: Bottle-kicking and Hare-pie Scrambling t (01858) 821270
May
Peak District: Well-dressing t (01629) 813227
June
Leicester: International Music Festival t (0116) 299 8888 www.musicfestival.co.uk
July
Lincoln: Water Carnival t (01552) 873213
August
Leicester: Caribbean Carnival t (0116) 253 3414 www.lccarnival.org.uk
Nottingham: Riverside Festival t (0115) 915 5330
September
Lincoln: International Clowns Festival t (01522) 873213
Chatsworth: Country Fair t (01328) 701133 www.countryfairoffice.co.uk
October
Nottingham: Goose Fair: Traditional funfair t (0115) 915 5330 www.nottinghamgoosefair.co.uk
Nottingham: Robin Hood Pageant t (0115) 915 5330
November
Snibston Discovery Park: traditional Bonfire Night fireworks display t (01530) 510851
Leicester: Diwali t (0116) 299 8888
December
Lincoln: Christmas Market t (01552) 873256

Leicester

Can you spot?
The statue of Richard III in Castle Park overlooking the river.

Getting there By car: Leicester is roughly 80 miles northwest of London, and about 30 miles east of Birmingham. From London take the M1 north; from Birmingham take the M6 westbound, changing at Coventry (J2) for the M69 northeast to Leicester. By train: Trains to Leicester depart regularly from London St Pancras. By bus: National Express operate a service between London and Leicester **Tourist information** 7–9 Every Street, Town Hall Square **t** 0906 2941113 **www.discoverleicester.com**

For Coventry it was cars, for Northampton shoes, while for Leicester it was hosiery (socks and stockings) that turned this small, historic town into a sprawling industrial conurbation. As with the other towns, Leicester suffered wartime damage and in the post-war period saw its bomb-shattered streets replaced by ugly, hastily designed building projects while its core industry underwent a gradual decline. Of the three towns, Leicester has the most to offer families, with a decent collection of attractions including several free museums. During the summer an open-top double decker bus runs between the city's top attractions.

Leicester has made an effort to beautify its more historic areas and the town has a lively ambience bolstered by its large Asian and Afro-Caribbean communities. Truly cosmopolitan, with the reputation for being the country's most racially integrated city, it plays host to many interesting events during the year including elaborate Diwali celebrations when Belgrave Road, the heart of the Asian community, becomes illuminated along its length with coloured lights and fireworks (living up to its nickname, the 'Golden Mile'); the largest city carnival after Notting Hill (first week of August) and Britain's biggest comedy festival outside the Edinburgh Fringe Festival (in February).

The town centre is the Victorian clock tower from where the High Street heads off down towards the Old River Sour passing the remnants of the Roman Baths, known as the Jewry Wall, on the way.

Castle Park overlooking the river is a pleasant place for a stroll and a picnic – kids can climb the mound that once bore the weight of Leicester's medieval castle – although the town's best open space is the Victorian Abbey Park, with flower gardens, Chinese peace garden, miniature railway and boating lake, one mile north of the city centre.

A little bit of history

Founded by the Romans, Leicester was, in the 10th century, one of the major towns of the Danelaw, the part of England controlled by the Vikings. Recently, it has become one of the most multicultural cities in the country, welcoming thousands of refugees fleeing from Idi Amin's Uganda in the 1970s. Despite its topsy-turvy history, however, the town's motto is *semper eadem*, 'always the same'.

Things to see and do
Abbey Pumping Station

Corporation Road, off Abbey Lane **t** (0116) 299 5111 **Getting there** 3 miles north of the city centre, follow the signs from the A568; bus no.54 and 54K run from the centre of town **Open** Apr–Nov Sat–Wed 11–4.30; also open in school holidays, Thurs and Fri **Adm Free** *Guided tours, shop, mother and baby facilities, wheelchair access to museum lower floor and grounds, on-site parking*

Formerly a sewage treatment plant, it has been redeveloped into a museum of public health, where you can find out everything you never wanted to know about waste product disposal.

Mr Big

One of the fattest men who ever lived came from Leicester. Daniel Lambert was born here in 1770 and grew up to be the keeper of Leicester Gaol. Unfortunately, he didn't just grow up, but every other which way as well. Reportedly a normal-sized baby, by his early twenties he weighed over 190kg (420lb) and by the end of his life at age 39, tipped the scales at a mighty 333kg (735lb, or over 52 stone). This despite his claims that he only ate one meal a day! To get his coffin out of his house, his front wall had to be demolished and it took 20 pall bearers to carry it to the graveyard. Find out more about Daniel at the Newarke Houses Museum (*see* opposite).

You can flush an imitation (but disgustingly real-looking) faeces down through a transparent toilet and follow its progress through a series of sealed perspex drains. The plant's narrow gauge railway has also been rebuilt and there are regular demonstration runs of restored locomotives. There is also an interactive exhibition on the science and history of motion pictures during the 1800s.

Cinemas and theatres *See pp.364, 367*

Gorse Hill City Farm

Anstey Lane **t** (0116) 253 7582
Open Summer: 10–4; winter: 10–4.30
Adm Adults £2, children £1
Café-restaurant, picnic areas, souvenir shop, mother and baby facilities, guided tours, disabled access, on-site parking

Working community farm with animals for kids to meet and play with plus an adventure playground.

Great Central Railway

Leicester North Station **t** (01509) 230726
www.gcrailway.co.uk
Open Jun–Sept daily; Oct–May Sat, Sun and some Bank Hols; half term daily
Return fares Adults £12, children £8, under 3s **free**, family (2+3) £30
Refreshments, buffet cars, gift shop, wheelchair access at Quorn and Rothley (at other stations by prior arrangement); specially adapted carriage for wheelchair use, car parks at Quorn and Rothley

Steam train rides are given here every weekend (daily during high season) over eight miles of track between Leicester North and Loughborough Central stopping at two further stations, Rothley and Quorn, on the way. The full journey takes around 30 minutes but you are encouraged to get off and explore at each of the stations, all redecorated to look as they would have done in the 1940s. At Loughborough there are locomotive sheds, where you can see engines being repaired, and at Rothley you can play with a small model railway. Special Thomas the Tank Engine Days are organized during the year. Santa visits in December.

Jain Centre

Oxford Street, Leicester **t** (0116) 254 3091
www.jaincentre.com
Open Mon–Sat 8.30–8.30, Sun 8.30–6.30
Adm Free (donations welcomed)

The Jains are an ancient and obscure Indian sect who believe in the sanctity of all living things, even going so far as to wear masks to prevent themselves from inadvertently swallowing insects. Find out more about the religion, founded around the same time as Buddhism, at this beautifully decorated centre which houses one of the few Jain temples outside the Indian subcontinent.

Jewry Wall Museum

St Nicholas Circle **t** (0116) 2254971
Open Feb–Nov Sat–Sun 11–4.30
Adm Free
Shop, disabled access, on-site parking

On the site of 2nd-century Roman baths, this museum traces Leicester's history from Roman times to the Middle Ages and holds the majority of surviving remnants of Roman Leicester including numerous mosaic pavements (look out for the one depicting a peacock), Fosse Way milestones and painted wall plaster. There is a multimedia exhibition, 'The Making of Leicester', which tells the story of the city's development from the Iron Age to the present day.

★National Space Science Centre

Exploration Drive **t** (0116) 2610261
www.spacecentre.co.uk
Open Tues–Sun 10–5, school holidays also Mon
Adm Adults £11, children £9, family (2+2) £34, (2+3) £42

Dedicated to all things celestial, with hordes of space-related memorabilia on display, including a huge rocket in a stunning 40m/130ft-high see-through tower, a 175-seat multimedia space theatre with state-of-the-art surround sound video, a planetarium (the most technically advanced in Britain) and a Challenger Learning Centre (the first to be built outside the US), where you can train to take part in a simulated space mission. Split into five themed areas, 'Into Space', 'The Planets', 'Orbiting Earth', 'Exploring the Universe' and 'Space Now', the centre has up-to-the-minute technology, interactive displays and several play areas.

Newarke Houses Museum

The Newarke **t** (0116) 225 4980
Open Mon–Sat 10–5, Sun 11–5 (winter until 4)
Adm Free
Closed for refurbishment until early 2007

Housed in two Jacobean houses, it has a wide range of exhibitions focusing on the social history of the city, the centrepiece of which is a Victorian street scene, complete with period shops (and toilets). There are displays on two of Leicester's most famous former citizens: Daniel Lambert and Thomas Cook, the inventor of the package holiday, as well as some pretty period gardens.

New Walk Museum and Art Gallery
New Walk **t** (0116) 2254900
Open Mon–Sat 10–5, Sun 11–5 **Adm Free**
Shop, mother and baby facilities, disabled access

Leicestershire's premier museum and arts venue has a large natural history gallery full of giant dinosaur fossils and a special 'Discovery Room' with plenty of hands-on experiments for kids.

Shopping
Leicester is really one large shopping centre. The best place to park is in the Shires Shopping centre, where there's an Early Learning Centre toyshop, Mothercare and the Disney Store. All the usual big-name shops are along the High Street. There's a huge characterful 700-year-old fruit and vegetable market (Mon–Sat), which also has stalls selling jewellery and sweets. Next to the market is a wonderful four-storey toy and bookshop Dominoes, **t** (0116) 2533363. For something a bit different, pop along to Belgrave Road with its mass of Indian and Pakistani jewellers, clothes shops and music stores.

Sport and activities *See pp.362–4*

Around Leicester
The National Forest: Leicester lies on the doorstep of perhaps the most ambitious environmental project ever attempted in this country (p.360)
Stonehurst Family Farm and Motor Museum, 8 miles north (p.352)
Tropical Birdland, 8 miles west (pp.351–2)
Twycross Zoo, 15 miles west (p.394)

Lincoln

Getting there By road: Lincoln lies 135 miles north of London, about 70 miles east of Manchester and 50 miles northeast of Leicester, and can be reached via the A1, the A46, and the A57. By train: Services depart regularly from London King's Cross via Newark or Peterborough and there are regular services from Sheffield and Nottingham. By bus/coach: You can travel on National Express coaches to Lincoln from London Victoria, Nottingham and Sheffield
Tourist information 9 Castle Hill **t** (01522) 873213
www.lincoln.gov.uk

Lincoln's old town centre is lovely. Perched on a hill – the area is known locally as 'uphill' – and overlooked by a great triple-towered cathedral, it's more picturesque than the approach through the city's rather bland suburbs would suggest and small enough to be easily explored in an afternoon. The only problem is the gradient of the hill itself – the walk from the High Street (located in the part of town known as 'downhill') up the appropriately named Steep Hill to the cathedral will sorely test little legs and buggy pushers.

Uphill Lincoln is where you'll find the city's most important historic sites (linked by a Heritage Trail), including the cathedral, a medieval castle, a 15th-century guildhall, Tudor buildings and the remnants of a Roman wall (Lincoln was one of the four most important towns of Roman Britain), part of which, the 2nd-century Newport Arch, spans one of Lincoln's roads (Bailgate) and is the only Roman arch in Britain still to have traffic going through it.

Back down the hill, you can hire rowboats for pottering along the River Witham (which runs along the southern edge of the city) at Brayford Pool, the old Roman harbour, which is slightly downriver from High Bridge at the bottom of the High Street. Sightseeing river cruises and guided walks of the city (which leave from outside the TIC at 11am and 2pm) are available in summer.

An International Clowns Festival is held in Lincoln every September, with performances and circus skills workshops to attend.

Things to see and do
Cinemas and theatres *See pp.364, 367*

★Lincoln Castle
Castle Hill **t** (01522) 511068
Open Summer: Mon–Sat 9.30–5.30, Sun 11–5.30; winter: Mon–Sat 9.30–4, Sun 11–4
Adm Adults £3.80, children £2.50, under 5s **free**, family (2+3) £9.50
Picnic areas, shop, mother and baby facilities, guided tours, disabled access

The city's second most prominent landmark is set in lovely, adventure-friendly grounds just a short walk west from the cathedral. It's a popular spot with local kids for skateboarding. Lincoln castle, typical of many English castles, is an architectural mishmash. Begun in the late 11th century on the site of a Roman Garrison (parts of which were incorporated into the structure), it was altered and added to until the 19th century. A military fortress until the time of the Civil War, it was then turned into a prison and became the site of numerous public executions attended by thousand-strong crowds in the 1800s. You can visit the dungeons and cells, which are inhabited by gruesome-looking waxwork prisoners and see the prison chapel – a bizarre attempt to combine punishment and redemption – which consists of a series of narrow cells pointing towards a central pulpit, the idea being that the prisoners could see and hear the priest but not each other and the prisoners would, in this way, achieve salvation. (In fact, deprived of any social interaction, most prisoners went mad.) The castle has on display one of only four surviving copies of the *Magna Carta* and offers great views of the town from the Observation Tower perched high on the ramparts. Special events, including medieval battle re-enactments, firework displays and a Christmas market, are held during the year.

The Lawn, a collection of concert halls, exhibition areas, shops and cafés set in lovely landscaped gardens that once bore the weight of the country's first lunatic asylum, can be reached via the castle's west gate. It's principally worth visiting for the Sir Joseph Banks Conservatory, a tropical glasshouse full of birds and butterflies, and the small archaeology museum (it has a hands-on section).

Lincoln Cathedral

Castle Hill **t** (01522) 561600
www.lincolncathedral.com
Open Summer: Mon–Fri 7.15am–8pm, Sat–Sun 7.15–6; winter: daily 7.15am–6pm
Adm Adults £4, children £1, family £30
Café, souvenir shop, guided tours, wheelchair access throughout cathedral, adapted toilets

Lincoln Cathedral was the Canary Wharf of its day. The tallest building in Europe when constructed in the early Middle Ages and a marvel of architectural virtuosity, it has spent the past 700 years watching the surrounding world gradually rise above it. Though no longer the

wonder of Europe (it's not even the tallest cathedral in England any more), in Lincoln itself it's still very much the focus of attention. Sat proudly on a hill overlooking the town's medieval centre, it can be seen from over 30 miles away and is still a magnificent sight.

As with most cathedrals, much of what makes Lincoln glorious – its intricate stonework, stained glass and superb Gothicism – will be lost on children. The guided tours at 11am, 1pm and 3pm from May to October, will help bring some colour to your visit (you're taken up to see the roof), as will the 'Guide for Young People', available at the entrance, which will point children towards all the most interesting features of the interior – much changed since the first stone was laid back in 1072. Look out for the Lincoln Imp, a stone representation of a tiny, cross-legged devil carved in the roof of the Angel Choir which has become the symbol of the city. According to legend, a real imp was caught trying to ingratiate himself with one of the surrounding angels and was turned to stone as a punishment.

The cathedral is at its beautiful best on a sunny day when its stained glass windows bathe the nave in light, or in the evening when the building's exterior detail is picked out by spotlights.

Museum of Lincolnshire Life

Burton Road **t** (01522) 528448
Open Apr–Sept daily 10–5, Oct–Apr Mon–Sat 10–5.30
Adm Adults £2.15, children £1.45, family (2+3) £5.75
Café-restaurant, souvenir shop, mother and baby facilities, disabled access, on-site parking

An antique chemist's shop, a Victorian schoolroom, an Edwardian nursery, a recreated First World War trench, a Second World War tank, a wagon and wheelwright's workshop and a collection of vintage steam engines are the attractions of the region's largest social history museum, a few minutes' walk north of the cathedral. Family fun days in summer.

Did you know?
That Lincoln's factories produced the world's first ever tank, used at the Battle of the Somme in the First World War.

Shopping

Lincoln is really two cities – the upper town around the castle and the lower town, where you'll find all the main shops. Downtown Lincoln is bustling and lively and filled with all the mainstream chain stores. Toys 'R' Us and Mothercare are in the Tritton Retail Park. Uphill has a selection of small tourist shops. Look out for shops selling garments made out of Lincoln Green, the famous local cloth supposedly worn by Robin Hood, and 'Goodies' on Steep Hill, a traditional sweet shop, where you can introduce your children to the joys of Williamesque sticky treats – humbugs, sherbet lemons and bull's eyes. There's a great Christmas market on Uphill if you are in town in December.

Sport and activities *See pp.362–4*

Around Lincoln

Sundown Adventure Land, 13 miles northwest (p.359)
Tattershall Castle, 15 miles southeast (p.350)

Nottingham

Getting there By road: Nottingham lies approximately 100 miles northwest of London, and about 50 miles from Birmingham, and can be reached easily via the M1. By train: Trains to Nottingham depart regularly from London King's Cross–St Pancras, Sheffield and Derby. By bus/coach: There are regular National Express services from London Victoria, Derby and Sheffield
Tourist information 1–4 Smithy Row **t** 08444 775678 www.visitnottingham.com

Erstwhile home of the dastardly sheriff, Robin Hood's sworn enemy, the town of Nottingham (in its fictionalized form) is familiar to all children. Sadly, the real town – a drab agglomeration of modern buildings surrounded and bisected by a serpentine mess of busy roads – may not quite live up to expectations. Dig a little deeper, however, and you'll discover that, though outwardly as grim and gritty as many other Midlands industrial towns, Nottingham is actually a friendly, fun place with lots of history and more. The city becomes a more pleasant place in the evenings and on weekends when the procession of cars that tears around the inner ring road begins to thin out and the streets take on an almost villagey ambience. The city centre is its Old Market Square where you'll find the tourist information office and Council House. According to legend, the Sheriff staged the famous archery competition here, designed to draw Robin Hood into the town to be captured. His plans were thwarted when Robin not only managed to win the competition (by splitting an arrow already lodged in the bull's-eye with one of his own) and claim the prize, but to escape the Sheriff's guards. The Nottingham and Beeston Canal runs along the southern edge of the city before heading off towards Birmingham. Listen out for the huge 10-tonne hour-bell in the dome of the council house, appropriately known as Little John.

A little bit of history

Nottingham was founded 1,400 years ago by the Saxons, who gave it the charming name of Snotingham – perhaps the air didn't agree with them. In the Middle Ages it became an important centre of lace and hosiery production, but remained a relatively small settlement until the early 19th century, when the invention of new industrial practices and machines greatly increased the amount of textiles that could be produced. Soon, huge new factories were being built which, in turn, attracted vast numbers of new workers to the town. Nottingham's population increased five-fold during the early part of the 19th century resulting in a massive building programme that transformed this small medieval town into a sprawling industrial mess full of belching factories and streets full of cheap, slum housing.

Not surprisingly, not everyone was impressed by the changes. The new textile machines didn't require much training to operate and many skilled craftsmen soon found themselves out of a job or had their wages drastically cut. In 1811, the craftsmen decided they'd had enough. They banded together and, wearing masks to conceal their identities, broke into the textile factories and smashed up the new machines. These protests became known as the Luddite riots after the movement's (probably mythical) leader Ned Ludd and were soon hugely popular all over the country.

Thinking that the country was about to sink into anarchy, the government leapt into action and, in 1813, arrested many of the protesters and sent them for trial in York. The ringleaders were hanged while the rest were transported to the penal colonies in Australia. Despite a brief reprisal of machine-smashing in 1816, the rioters ultimately proved unsuccessful – the textile industry continued to modernize and adapt and skilled workers continued to lose their jobs – although they did manage to bequeath a new word to the English language, 'luddite', which has come to mean anyone resistant to change or progress.

The city and its industries continued to expand and modernize until a sudden change in fashions following the First World War virtually killed off the entire lace-making industry. The few lace producers that survive are more of a novelty than a business.

Things to see and do

Brewhouse Yard Museum of Nottingham Life

Castle Boulevard **t** (0115) 915 3600
Open Daily 10–4.30
Adm Weekdays: **free**; weekends and Bank Hols: adults £3, children £1.50, family (2+3) £7
Souvenir shop, disabled access

This group of five 17th-century cottages is filled with period displays designed to show how everyday life for the average Nottinghamshire citizen has changed over the last 300 years with recreated shops (including a 1930s toyshop), a schoolroom and a cottage garden. There are plenty of interactive exhibits including 'feely' boxes and you can visit the nearby caves that were once used as air-raid shelters during the war. A tunnel leads from here all the way to the castle in which Roger Mortimer, the man who murdered Edward II, was supposedly captured by Edward III's troops in 1330.

Cinemas and theatres *See pp.364, 367*

City of Caves

Drury Walk, Broad Marsh Shopping Centre
t (0115) 988 1955 **www**.cityofcaves.com
Open Daily 10.30am–4.30pm
Adm Adults £4.95, children £3.95, family (2+2) £14.95
Shop

The old Saxon town of (S)Not(t)ingham was strategically placed high on a sandstone hill from where it has been spreading outwards (and downwards) ever since. The hill itself is now riddled with a network of man-made caves, tunnels and caverns – some dating back to medieval times – which can be toured and explored in the company of costumed guides. Although they may sound

romantic and mysterious, most of the caves were actually commercial storerooms (albeit old ones) and so it seems entirely fitting that their entrance is now located within the Broad Marsh Shopping Centre on the southern side of the city. Inside the caves which, whatever their origin, look romantic and mysterious, you'll find an underground tannery, a pub cellar, a Second World War air-raid shelter and the remains of a Victorian street, all enhanced with the latest audiovisual trickery.

★Galleries of Justice

Shire Hall, High Pavement, Lace Market
t (0115) 952 0555 **www**.galleriesofjustice.org.uk
Open Apr–Oct Tues–Sun 10–4 (school holidays also Mon); Nov–Mar Tues–Fri 10–3, Sat–Sun 11–4
Adm Adults £7.95, children £5.95, family £22.95
Café, courtyard café in summer, shop, mother and baby facilities, disabled access

If you only have time to visit one Nottingham attraction, let it be this one. In the former Nottingham County Court and Gaol, you are taken on a fascinating tour through the history of crime and punishment that brings to life the child-appealing nastiness of old-style justice. When you enter, you are given a criminal identity number which corresponds to one of the many real criminals to have passed through the court over the years. As you travel through the attraction, look out for the display boards, which will tell you who your particular criminal was, what they stood trial for and what their punishment was (they were always found guilty). Rather than relying on a few hands-on exhibits, the 'galleries' have instead devised ways of involving visitors in the displays right the way through their tour. In the Crime and Punishment Gallery, you can stand in a real 19th-century courtroom dock and hear a reconstruction of the trial of one of Nottingham's 1831 Reform Bill rioters before being taken down to the dark, dingy cells, where you are locked up (for a moment or two) to reflect on the error of your ways. Then, it's out into the exercise yard to try your hand at hard labour. Throughout, costumed guides enthusiastically act out the various judicial roles – warden, judge, policeman, etc. – which help to draw kids into the world of make-believe criminality. At the mock-up of a modern police station, you can see how conditions for prisoners have improved over the last 200 years and, once you've had your fingerprints taken, it's on to a pretend crime scene, where you can try to solve the investigation on a touch-screen computer. Children are invited to put their consciences to the test by voting on the rights and wrongs of capital punishment in the 'A Sense of the Law' exhibition while, at the children's activity centre, they can handle handcuffs and truncheons and dress up as a Victorian bobby, a high court judge or a prisoner. The galleries provide the most comprehensive overview of the criminal process you're likely to get this side of the straight and narrow.

Green Mill and Science Centre

Windmill Lane, Sneinton **t** (0115) 915 6878
www.greensmill.org.uk
Getting there Take bus no.314 from King Street
Open Wed–Sun and Bank Hols 10–4 **Adm Free**
Souvenir shop, disabled and pushchair access to the ground floor of the mill and the science centre, on-site parking

This restored windmill once belonged to George Green, a revered local mathematician, in whose honour a small science centre has opened next door with scores of hands-on experiments for children as well as a special activity area for under 5s. You can also have a go at grinding corn on a millstone.

Nottingham Castle Museum and Art Gallery

Nottingham **t** (0115) 915 3700
Open Daily Mar–Sept 10–5, Oct–Feb 11–4
Adm Adults £3, children £1.50 (includes entry to Brewhouse Yard Museum)
Café, picnic areas, mother and baby facilities, some disabled access

Only the gatehouse from the original 13th-century castle survives today, the rest was destroyed in the Civil War (Charles I rode out from here to set up his standard, making it a prime target for the Parliamentarians) and replaced in 1674 with a large Ducal mansion which was destroyed during the 1831 Reform Bill riots. What remained was turned into a municipal museum and art gallery in 1875, the first outside the

Did you know?
That in olden times, prisoners had to pay for the privilege of being locked up. The more well-off would be kept in tiny, cramped, gloomy cells. Not exactly value for money, until you consider that the poor had to make do with pits in the ground.

Can you spot?
The famous bronze statue of Robin Hood shooting an arrow on Castle Green by the castle gatehouse.

capital. It's worth visiting for the commanding views of the city and its network of man-made underground tunnels (tours in the afternoon). It also contains a good hands-on exhibition on the 'story of Nottingham'. According to legend, Robin Hood was repeatedly imprisoned here (and escaped time and time again).

Shopping

The main shopping area lies between the Broad Marsh and the Victoria shopping centres. For serious shopping head for the latter, where you'll find Gap Kids, Adams for kids' clothes, an Early Learning Centre and Woolworths for toys. Game for computer games is also here, as is the Disney Store and there's a large Boots for baby supplies.

Sport and activities *See pp.362–4*

★Tales of Robin Hood

30–8 Maid Marian Way **t** (0115) 948 3284
www.robinhood.uk.com
Open Daily 10–5.30 (last admission 4.30)
Adm Adults £8.95, children £6.95, family (2+2) £26.95
Restaurant, souvenir shop, mother and baby facilities, disabled access

Cars trundle you past a series of lively dioramas depicting scenes from the life of everyone's favourite fictional outlaw. Watch as he robs the rich, gives to the poor, battles the sheriff and woos Maid Marian. There's a cursory examination of the scant evidence behind the legend while, in the café, you can watch Errol Flynn in green tights on the TVs which also show a stream of clips from other movie versions. Medieval banquets on Friday and Saturday nights.

Wollaton Hall

Wollaton Park **t** (0115) 915 3900
www.wollatonhall.org.uk
Getting there 3 miles west of the centre
Open Apr–Oct 11–5, Nov–Mar 11–4 (closed Fri)
Adm Weekdays: free; weekends and Bank Hols: adults £1.50, children £1
Café-restaurant, picnic areas, souvenir shop, mother and baby facilities, on-site parking

Grand Tudor house perched on a grassy knoll in 200 hectares (500 acres) of landscaped gardens. Home to the city's natural history and industrial museums.

Around Nottingham

American Adventureland, 10 miles west (pp.358–9)
Donington Grand Prix Collection, 10 miles south-west (p.365)
White Post Modern Farm Centre, 12 miles northeast (pp.352–3)

Stamford

Getting there By road: Stamford is 70 miles from London, 50 miles from Birmingham and can be reached from the A1 and the A47. By train: Services to Stamford from London King's Cross. By bus/coach: National Express services connecting Stamford with London Victoria, Leicester and Cambridge
Tourist information Stamford Arts Centre, 27 St Mary's Street **t** (01780) 755611 www.skdc.com

A serious contender for the title of 'most beautiful town in England', Stamford's famously unspoilt appearance led to it becoming, in 1967, the country's first conservation area. Ever since, it has attracted architecture buffs who come to inspect its pristine collection of 17th-century stone buildings and narrow cobbled streets, as well as TV and film crews looking for historical locations. Unfortunately, there's not a great deal for youngsters here, but if the weather is good, you can walk along the riverbank and have fun feeding the ducks. The town museum will help pass an hour or two, as will the landscaped grounds of Burghley House, a grand 16th-century stately home outside the town centre, but Stamford is best as a base for exploring the area. Bourne Wood, eight miles northeast of town, offers pleasant walks; Grimsthorpe Castle, 10 miles north, tame deer to feed; the huge man-made lake of Rutland Water, eight miles west, watersports; while at Clipsham, seven miles northwest, the family can revel in the delights of ornamental topiary. The Fens, stretching from just north of Cambridge to Boston, are also within easy reach. As far as food and shopping are concerned, there's a good farmer's market in Red Lion Square twice a month on Friday mornings. The pedestrianized main street has a decent-sized Woolworths and Adams for kids' clothes.

Things to see and do

Burghley House
Stamford **t** (01780) 752451 **www**.burghley.co.uk
Getting there 3 miles east of town off the B1443
Open Apr–Oct Sat–Thurs 11–4.30
Adm Adults £7.50, children £3.70 (one child **free** per adult), under 5s **free**
Licensed restaurant, shop, guided tours, mother and baby facilities, disabled access, on-site parking

Built for William Cecil, one of Queen Elizabeth I's counsellors, in the mid 16th century, it boasts 240 lavishly appointed rooms. Look out for the Heaven Room with images of dancing angels and nymphs and the ceiling of the Hell Staircase decorated with a cat eating a dinner of sinners.

Cinemas and theatres *See pp.364, 367*

Sport and activities *See pp.362–4*

Stamford Museum
Broad Street, Stamford **t** (01780) 766317
Open Apr–Sept Mon–Sat and Bank Hols 10–5, Sun 1–4 **Adm Free**
Gift shop, disabled access

Slightly dusty displays on the history and archaeology of the town and area – highlights are the life-size models of Daniel Lambert (p.336) and the American midget Tom Thumb (just 3ft 4in (1m) tall).

Around Stamford

Clipsham Yew Tree Avenue, 7 miles northwest (p.356)
Grimsthorpe Castle, 10 miles north (p.349)
Rutland Water, 8 miles west (p.361)

Voting in the 19th century

In the early 19th century only rich men who owned a lot of land could vote. Poor people and women (no matter how rich) had no say in who governed the country. In 1830–31 many people in Nottingham and other areas around the country, who had become rich as a result of businesses started during the Industrial Revolution, rioted for the right to vote. The government relented and passed an Act allowing some members of this new 'middle class' (as these newly rich men became known) to vote. The poor and women were still excluded, however. Women wouldn't be given the right to vote until almost a century later.

Did you also know that until 1870, there was no secret ballot? Rather than write down their choice and slip it inside a sealed box (as happens today), voters had to stand on a platform and say who they were intending to vote for, making it easy for parliamentary candidates to bribe or intimidate them!

In 1951, these 540 square miles (1,400 sq km) of rolling hills and dales became the country's first designated national park. Occupying the southern end of the mighty Pennine range, which stretches from here all the way up the north of England to Scotland, the park is made up of two contrasting landscapes: the harsh, rugged, somewhat bleak moorland of the ominously named Dark Peak (serious, serious walker's country) and the softer, friendlier, more easily navigable limestone hills of the southern White Peak. Made up of great swathes of woodland and grassland interlinked by a vein-like network of walking trails and 18th-century stone walls, White Peak is famed throughout the country for its collection of caves and caverns. Millions of years' worth of rain have eaten great chunks out of the soft limestone filling them with huge, dripping stalactites, mysterious underground streams and sheer walls lined with seams of brightly coloured minerals. These caves are shown to their best effect at the towns of Castleton and Matlock Bath, where you can take tours deep beneath the hills.

Sandwiched between the cities of Manchester, Derby and Sheffield, the park itself boasts no major towns, just lots of nice minor ones and a couple of outstanding stately homes (Chatsworth and Haddon Hall). Buxton, the region's largest town and unofficial capital, lies just outside the park. Local tourist offices can provide details of walks including the Limestone Way which follows a 26-mile-long course through White Peak from Castleton to Matlock. The southern peak district is the easiest walking country and is better suited to family rambles.

Things to see and do

Cycle hire
www.peakdistrict.org
Peak District cycle hire points are located at:
Fairholmes, Derwent **t** (01433) 651261
Information Centre, Station Road, Hayfield,
High Peak **t** (01663) 746222
Mapleton Lane, Ashbourne **t** (01335) 343156
Old Station Car Park, Waterhouses
t (01538) 308609
Parsley Hay, Buxton **t** (01298) 84493
Visitor Centre, Middleton-by-Wirksworth
t (01629) 823204
Open Daily in summer 9.30–6 (dusk if earlier); otherwise call to reserve a bike

Hire Per day: mountain bike, adults £13, children £9, tandem £30, child's buggy or trailer bike £12, child seats £3, helmets **free**; plus a £20 deposit
Guided rides are also offered

Bakewell

Getting there Located on the A6, between Buxton and Matlock
Tourist information The Old Market Hall, Bridge Street **t** (01629) 813227

Bakewell is the largest town within the confines of the Peak District National Park itself and makes a good base for exploring the stately delights of nearby Chatsworth and Haddon Hall.

Things to see and do

The Ranger Centre
Aldern House, Braslow Road **t** (01629) 816200

Guided walks, environmental play schemes, nature fun days, woodland discovery trails and activity days for children.

Buxton

Getting there Situated about 40 miles northeast of Nottingham on the A6
Tourist information The Crescent **t** (01298) 25106
www.highpeak.gov.uk

Attracted to this location once they discovered it was the source of a natural spring producing 1,500 gallons of pure, rock-filtered water every day at a constant 28°C (82°F), the Romans founded a town here, *Aquae Arnemetiae,* in AD 79 – its centrepiece a huge bathing complex. But Buxton didn't reach the zenith of its status, until 1,700 years later when various illustrious members of Georgian society (who, if anything, were even more keen on bathing than the Romans) tried to turn it into the north of England's answer to Bath with its own elegant Georgian terraces, brand-new bathing complex and Pump Room. Unfortunately, it never quite lived up to its Somerset forebear's success (set some 1,000 feet up, this is actually the second highest town in the country and so doesn't possess the sort of mild, gentle, healing climate usually associated with spa towns) and by the 1970s all its bathhouses had been closed down. The old bathhouse is now a small shopping centre with a good Pizza Express restaurant. Buxton is a pleasant town with interesting architecture – notably the 19th-century glass **Buxton Pavilion,** around which are spread some delightful land-

Bakewell Pudding

It's a pudding, not a tart, whatever the rest of the cake-making world might think and its origins go back to the mid 19th century. As with so many other great culinary discoveries, the first Bakewell pudding came about by accident. According to the story, a cook misread a recipe for strawberry tart which resulted in him (or her) spreading the egg mixture on top of the jam instead of on to the pastry. The result was a success with customers and was soon being sold all over the country. Exactly who this fortunately incompetent baker was remains open to debate. Various establishments in Bakewell claim to be the originators of the pudding, although the Old Original Bakewell Tart Shop, The Square, **t** (01629) 812193, the most likely contender, may be trying a little too hard with that name. Try them all (none will set you back more than one pound) and judge whose tastes the most 'genuine'.

scaped gardens, and the old **Pump Room**, which hosts art exhibitions. Sample the warm spring water at **St Ann's Well** (it's still bottled and sold) and see the source. **Pavilion Gardens** is a great place to run around. There's a miniature train, a good modern playground and an artificial lake.

These days, Buxton is principally used as a base for people wanting to explore the wonders of the surrounding countryside and of the Peak District National Park just outside the town's borders. A taster is provided at **Poole's Cavern**, a stalactite-strewn cave (home to Derbyshire's largest stalactite), one mile south of the town centre.

Things to see and do

Pavilion Gardens

St. John's Road **t** 01298 231 114
www.paviliongardens.co.uk
Open Daily Summer 10–5, spring/autumn Mon–Fri 10–4, Sat–sun 10–5, Winter Mon–Fri 10–3, sat and sun 10–5 **Adm** free
café, gift shop, pay and display, car park, play areas, miniature train.

Poole's Cavern

Green Lane **t** (01298) 26978
www.poolescavern.co.uk
Open Mar–Oct daily 10–5, tour lasts about 1 hour
Adm Adults £6.20, children £3.50, family (2+2) £18
Souvenir shop, picnic areas, on-site parking

Castleton

Getting there 10 miles northeast of Buxton, between Chapel-en-le-Frith and Hope

Perhaps the best place to see the spectacular caves that riddle the soft limestone landscape of White Peak, Castleton, which is overlooked by the Norman Peveril Castle, is geared towards the tourist trade with a glut of cafés and souvenir shops on hand to deal with the throngs of walkers and explorers who visit during the summer months. Mam Tor just outside Castleton is a great place to see the Peak District at its best and it's also a wonderful picnic spot. There are four caves within walking distance of the town. Heading west, the first you reach is **Peak's Cavern**, which has the largest natural cave entrance in the country, a vast gaping stony mouth that once provided shelter for an entire village. Tours take you half a mile underground along illuminated passageways until you reach the Great Cave (it measures 45 by 27m or 148 by 89ft) and the Devil's Dining Room where the cave's former owner used to hold subterranean banquets.

Next up is **Speedwell Cavern** which stretches down some 183m (600f)t and is the deepest publicly accessible cave in Britain. A former lead mine, you descend down 105 stone steps to board a boat for a superbly spooky cruise along a quarter-of-a-mile long underground stream, the tunnel ceiling just a few claustrophobic inches from your head.

The final two caves, **Treak Cliff Cavern** and **Blue John Cavern**, are the world's only sources of Blue John, a sparkly semi-precious stone mined here for the past 250 years for use in jewellery. The water-worn caves have thick veins of the mineral running through them – despite the name, it comes in various colours, including red, blue and yellow – and are filled with stalactites and stalagmites and other bizarre rock formations with spotlights creating crazy patterns and shadows.

Things to see and do

Blue John Cavern

Castleton, Hope Valley **t** (01433) 620638,
www.bluejohn-cavern.co.uk
Open Daily 9.30am–5.30pm (dusk in winter)
Adm Adults £7, children £3.50, under 5s **free**, family (2+2) £19

Peak Cavern

Peak Cavern Road, Castleton, Hope Valley
t (01433) 620285 www.peakcavern.co.uk
Open Apr–Oct daily 10–5; Nov–Mar Sat and
Sun 10–5
Adm Adults £6.25, children £4.25, under 5s **free**,
family £18.50
*Souvenir shop, picnic areas, guided tours,
on-site parking*

★Speedwell Cavern

Castleton, Hope Valley **t** (01433) 620512
www.speedwellcavern.co.uk
Open Apr–Oct daily 9.30–5.30; Nov–Mar daily
10–5; boats leave every 15 minutes and the trip
takes about 45 minutes
Adm Adults £6.75, children £4.75, family £23
*Souvenir shop, picnic areas, guided tours,
on-site parking*

Treak Cliff Cavern

Buxton Road, Castleton, Hope Valley
t (01433) 620571 www.bluejohnstone.com
Open Daily 10–5 (last tour 4.15)
Adm Adults £6.50, children £3.50, under 5s **free**,
family (2+2) £18
*Souvenir shop, picnic areas, guided tours,
on-site parking*

Eyam

Getting there Off the A623, about 30 miles
northwest of Nottingham

The small, lead-mining village of Eyam
(pronounced 'eem') has a sad tale to tell. In 1665
the village tailor ordered a consignment of cloth
from London which, upon arrival, was discovered
to be infested with fleas carrying the bubonic
plague, then rife in the capital, which soon began
spreading through the village. Many villagers
wanted to flee but the rector, William
Monpesson, persuaded them to stay, explaining
that it was better the disease be contained
within Eyam where it could burn itself out rather
than be allowed to spread to other areas and
become an epidemic. The villagers agreed. It was
a brave decision; by the time the plague faded
away the following year, well over 300 of the
village's original population of 750 were dead,
including the tailor and the rector's wife. You can
follow the rather depressing Eyam history trail,
which takes in all the sites associated with the
epidemic, including the plague cottages, the
Church of St Lawrence (which contains a
cupboard reputedly made from the box that
carried the original cloth) and the Monpesson
Well, a remote spot outside the village, where
the rector arranged for food deliveries from other
villages to be left. The Eyam Museum has gruesome dioramas showing the bloated, blotchy
plague victims dying in their beds, as well as a
display on the history of the disease.

Things to see and do

Eyam Museum

Hawkhill Road **t** (01433) 631371
www.eyammuseum.demon.co.uk
Open Apr–Oct Tues–Sun 10–4.30
Adm Adults £1.75, children £1.25, family (2+2) £5
Souvenir shop, disabled access

Matlock Bath

Getting there On the A6 between Buxton and
Derby, about 20 miles northwest of Nottingham
Tourist information The Pavilion, South Parade
t (01629) 55082 www.derbyshiredales.gov.uk

On the southeast edge of the Peak District,
Matlock Bath is unashamedly (but not unpleas-
antly) touristy. Though full of cafés, tearooms
and shops, you only have to raise your eyes to
admire its beautiful Derwent Valley setting in
amongst spectacular wooded cliffs and its more
commercial aspects will soon be forgotten. The
town itself boasts a couple of worthwhile attractions, including the **Peak District Mining
Museum**, which tells the story of the region's
lead mines (founded some 200 plus years ago)
and has a number of interactive exhibits on the
hardships and hazards of subterranean employ-
ment – kids can have a go at panning for gold.
One mile south of the town is **Gulliver's
Kingdom**, a child-orientated theme park with
several gentle rides and attractions including an
Alpine Log Flume, a Wild West Street and a Ghost
hotel that will probably be of no interest to
anyone over 10 years old. Most people, however,
come to Matlock Bath to ride its cable car to the
Heights of Abraham Country Park up the valley.

From late August to October, look out for the
Matlock Bath Illuminations, when the river
banks and surrounding cliffs are floodlit and
flotillas of illuminated boats glint their way
down the river.

Things to see and do

Gulliver's Kingdom and Royal Cave

Temple Walk **t** (01629) 57100,
www.gulliversfun.co.uk
Open Easter–Oct Sat–Sun and school hols 10–5
Adm £8.99, children under 90cm (3ft) tall **free**
Some disabled access
Fun-filled theme park.

★Heights of Abraham Country Park

Matlock Bath **t** (01629) 582365
www.heights-of-abraham.co.uk
Open Easter–Oct daily 10–5; Feb half term and
weekends in Mar 10–4.30
Adm Adults £9.50, children £6.50, under 5s **free**
*Café, picnic areas, souvenir shop, mother and baby
facilities, guided tours*

A 28 hectare (70-acre) country park set some
155m (170 yards) above the town of Matlock Bath.
Come to see White Peak's spectacular landscape
and take a tour of the vast natural and man-made
caverns (its most famous feature). There's a five-
minute cable car ride from the town up the side of
the valley to the park; watch the countryside
unfold before you as you rise. At the top, you are
shown an audiovisual display on the formation of
the caves (one, Great Masson Cavern, is natural,
having formed some 350 million years ago; the
other, Nestus Mine, was man-made two hundred
years ago) before being taken down into the
caverns for your creepy tour. Carefully presented to
highlight their spookiness, the caves are illuminated with lights that produce flickering shadows
and dark sinister shapes. In the mine, look out for
waxwork tableaux of miners at work. Afterwards,
head out along the park's walks to check out the
views; the best observation points are Tinker's
Shaft and the Prospect Tower. For kids, there's a
fossil display and model dinosaurs, an explorer
challenge, a play area with a maze and, in summer,
child-orientated entertainments such as Punch
and Judy shows are laid on.

Peak District Mining Museum

The Pavilion **t** (01629) 583834,
www.peakmines.co.uk
Open Apr–Oct daily 10–5, Nov–Mar weekends 11–4
Adm Adults £5, children £4.50, family £11.50
*Picnic areas, mother and baby facilities, guided
tours, disabled access, on-site parking, shop,
refreshments*

Castles and historic houses

★Althorp Park

Althorp, Northampton **t** 0870 167 9000 (24hr
booking line) **www.**althorp.com
Getting there 7 miles west of Northampton off the
A428, follow the signs from the M1
Open Jul–Aug 11–5 (last entry 4)
Adm Adults £12, children £6, under 5s **free**, family
(2+3) £29.50
Café, picnic area, shop, baby changing facilities

Althorp was the home of Princess Diana and is
an extraordinary place to visit. Kids old enough to
remember her funeral in 1997 will find it fascinating. The main attraction is the special (and
riveting) exhibition in the stable block devoted to
Diana's life. Her famous wedding dress and many
outfits are on display and there is a quirky selection of memorabilia from school reports to
Diana's royal passport. The exhibition ends with a
mountain of condolence books signed by thousands of people after her death. Diana is actually
buried on an island in the middle of an ornamental lake in the grounds. There is also a special
avenue planted with one tree for every year of her
life. It's all bound to get the kids asking questions...The house itself is a bit dry and, if you are
trying to economize, it isn't worth the £2.50 to
visit the upstairs. Kids can take a special nature
trail while you visit the house. Diana's brother is
now Earl Spencer, and since he's somewhat of a
celebrity in his own right, it's wonderful fun
gawking at his CD collection and drinks trolley in
the library. He's far from an absentee landlord and
you can usually find him serving in the shop,
which is worth visiting not to buy yet another key
ring but because it's a shop with a difference as it
sells only expensive Di memorabilia. The junior
Spencers are often found selling ice creams and
helping out in the (overpriced) café during the
holidays. The café is bad quality so bring a picnic.

Ashby de la Zouch Castle

South Street, Ashby de la Zouch **t** (01530) 413343
www.english-heritage.org.uk
Getting there On the A50, 20 miles northwest of
Leicester, 12 miles south of Derby. The nearest train
station is Burton-upon-Trent 9 miles away
Open Apr–Jun and Sept–Oct Thurs–Mon 10–5,
Jul–Aug daily 10–6, Nov–Mar Thurs–Mon 10–4
Adm Adults £3.40, children £1.70, family £8.50
Shop, disabled access, on-site parking

Although largely ruined in the Civil War, Ashby de la Zouch castle is still well worth exploring, with grand views (particularly from the 24m (80ft) tower) and spooky tunnels (bring a torch). Various events are staged during the year including many themed on Walter Scott's *Ivanhoe*, which was set in the castle grounds.

Belton House

Grantham **t** (01476) 566116,
www.nationaltrust.org.uk
Getting there On the A607, 3 miles northeast of Grantham. The nearest train station is Grantham, from where you can catch a bus to the house
Open House: Apr–Oct Wed–Sun daily 12.30–5; garden and park: Aug daily 10.30–5, Sept–Oct Wed–Sun 11–5.30, Nov–mid-Dec Fri–Sun 12–4, Feb Sat–Sun 12–4.
Adm Adults £8, children £4.50, family (2+3) £22.50
Restaurant, National Trust shop, mother and baby facilities, very limited disabled access, on-site parking

Eighteenth-century house full of exquisite furniture, tapestries, porcelain, mirrors and royal knick-knacks. There's a children's guide to help bring it all to life and a room with old toys and costumes for kids to dress up in. Outside is a well-equipped adventure playground and miniature train rides in the school holidays. In summer, events include firework concerts, family days and book fairs.

Belvoir Castle

Belvoir, Grantham **t** (01476) 871002
www.belvoircastle.com
Getting there About 7 miles west of Grantham between the A52 and the A607
Open Apr–Sept Tues–Thurs, Sat–Sun and Bank Hols 11–5 (last admission 4)
Adm Adults £10, children £5, family (2+2) £26; Garden only: adults £5, children **free**
Café-restaurant, licensed restaurant, shop, picnic areas, on-site parking

Overlooking the lush vale of Belvoir (pronounced 'beaver'), this haphazard collection of towers, turrets, pinnacles and battlements isn't a 'real' fortress at all but a 19th-century reconstruction of an earlier structure that was severely damaged in the Civil War. Castles expected to withstand attacks tend to be much leaner and less ornamental. It's the ancestral home of the Dukes of Rutland and contains a revered art collection, the highlight of which is Hans Holbein's famous portrait of Henry VIII. There's not a great deal

for children to do in the house, although the gardens offer plenty of scope for running around. To get the most from your visit, try to come on one of the castle's numerous event days when demonstrations of medieval activities such as archery, jousting and dancing are put on. There are free guided tours on weekdays at 12.30 and 2.30pm. The town of Melton Mowbray, famed for its pork pies (p.369) is about 10 miles south.

★Chatsworth

Chatsworth, Bakewell **t** (01246) 565300
www.chatsworth.org
Getting there 8 miles north of Matlock off the B6012 and signposted from J29 of the M1
Open Mar–mid-Dec house: daily 11–5.30; garden: 10.30–6; farmyard and adventure playground: 10.30–5.30; park: all year dawn–dusk
Adm Family pass for all the attractions: £42 or £46.50 (includes a donation, you receive back a £6.30 voucher for use in shops or restaurants). Tickets for individual attractions also available.
Restaurant, snack bar, gift shop, farm shop, mother and baby facilities, disabled access to garden, farmyard shop and restaurant, limited access to the house, on-site parking

'The Palace of the Peaks' has also been described as 'a grand mansion set in 1,000 landscaped acres of Peak District countryside on the banks of the River Derwent'. From a kid's perspective, it sounds pretty dull, but Chatsworth is actually one of the most fun stately homes to visit. The house itself is great fun with 26 sumptuously decorated rooms to explore, nine of which were once used by Mary Queen of Scots. The children's guide, available at the entrance, will point out interesting curios and whatnots – the table hung with stalactites, the *trompe l'oeil* violin 'hanging' on the music room door, the firescreens used to stop 19th-century ladies' make-up from cracking and the fan made from a Rolls Royce jet engine (it can produce quite a breeze). A whistle-stop tour of the interior will serve as the perfect primer for the main attraction – the gardens and the grounds – guaranteed to enchant the most demanding of younger visitors. Your first port of call should be the cascade to the east of the house, one of the estate's most famous features. A sort of artificial low-rise, lake-sized waterfall, it consists of 24 wide steps staggered over 190m (642ft), which together produce a gentle tumble of water. Kids can slip off their shoes and socks and go for a paddle – but owing to the huge amount of water used, it is only switched on for two hours each afternoon. See if you can find the Willow Tree Fountain made from a (very realistic) copper and brass model willow tree with water shooting out of the branches from all angles, then head to the hedge maze and, should you ever get out again, the farmyard, where children can help feed the trout, goat kids and lambs, play on a tractor and watch milking demonstrations before finishing up in the woodland adventure play-ground, which you enter through a 'secret tunnel', to play on its collection of swings, slides, spiral chutes, tree houses, rope walks and commando nets. If you've got energy left, you could tackle some of the estate's five miles of walks and trails. A quick trip back to Bakewell to sample one of the famous puddings and your day is complete. Father Christmas visits Chatsworth in December.

Grimsthorpe Castle

Grimsthorpe, Bourne **t** (01778) 591205
www.grimsthorpe.co.uk
Getting there On the A151, about 10 miles north of Stamford
Open Castle: Apr–Sept Sun, Thurs and Bank Hols 1–6 (last admission 4.30); Aug Sun–Thurs and Bank Hols 1–6 (last admission 4.30); park: daily Apr–May Sun, Thurs and Bank Hols 11–6, Jun–Sept Sun–Thurs 11–6
Adm Castle and park: adults £8, children £3.50, family (2+2) £18.50; park only: adults £3.50, children £2, family £9
Restaurant, picnic areas, shop, guided tours, mother and baby facilities, disabled access, on-site parking

A grand medieval pile filled with fine furniture and elegant state rooms surrounded by rolling grounds, where you can feed herds of tame deer.

Haddon Hall

Bakewell **t** (01629) 812855 www.haddonhall.co.uk
Getting there 2 miles south of Bakewell on the A6. You can catch a bus from Derby
Open Apr and Oct, Sat and Sun, May–Sept daily 12 noon–5; **Adm** Adults £7.75, children £4, under 5s **free**, family (2+3) £20
Restaurant, shop, mother and baby facilities, very limited disabled access, on-site parking (50p per car) Not suitable for pushchairs

Built more than 600 years ago, the medieval manor house of Haddon Hall is well preserved when you consider that it lay abandoned and neglected for around 200 years before being restored in the early twentieth century. The combination of fine architecture and beautiful Peak District setting makes a visit something of a scenic treat and kids will appreciate the house's grand storybook qualities and its rather convoluted, maze-like layout. For instance, to reach the Duke of Rutland's apartments you must pass first through a large gate, up a long drive, over a moated bridge and then climb a steep spiral staircase. Other areas worth seeking out include the 12th-century painted chapel, the banqueting hall with its minstrel's gallery and, best of all, the preserved medieval kitchens – you can still see the grooves worn in the work surfaces by medieval cooks. There are plenty of dark passageways to explore and the upper floors offer great views of the bridge over which Dorothy escaped on the night of her elopement and the surrounding landscaped gardens (full of roses and delphiniums in summer), where special events (i.e. Elizabethan dancing) are held.

Hardwick Hall

Doe Leas, Chesterfield **t** (01246) 850430
www.nationaltrust.org.uk
Getting there 10 miles southeast of Chesterfield off the A6175 and signposted from J29 of the M1
Open New Hall: Apr–Oct Wed, Thurs, Sat, Sun and Bank Hols 12–4.30; Old Hall: Apr–Oct Wed, Thurs, Sat and Sun 10–6; garden: Apr–Oct Wed–Sun 11–5.30; park: daily 8–6
Adm New Hall and gardens: adults £7.80, children £3.90, under 5s **free**, family £19.50; garden only: adults £4, children £2, under 5s **free**, family £10. Old and New Hall: adults £10.60, children £5.30, family £26.50
Restaurant in hall kitchen, National Trust shop, picnic areas, guided tours, mother and baby facilities, disabled access to ground floor of New Hall only, on-site parking (£2 per car)

There are two Hardwick Halls, both built in the 16th century at the instigation of the much married Countess of Shrewsbury (aka 'Bess of Hardwick' and 'Bess the Builder'): the New Hall, a perfectly preserved Tudor mansion, full of antiques, fine furniture and tapestries, and the Old Hall with its largely ruined ghostly *doppel-ganger*, which has big chunks of its roof missing.

They were built within a few years of each other but seem to occupy different centuries like some architectural retelling of *The Picture of Dorian Grey*. The New Hall, with its huge rectangular windows ('Hardwick Hall, more glass than wall', ran the Elizabethan rhyme), is run by the National Trust – and it shows, being rather dry and earnest inside, although there's an I-Spy quiz trail for children (despite the large windows, the interior is deliberately kept dark and gloomy to protect the precious tapestries from sunlight). The English Heritage-controlled Old Hall is more fun with a lively children's audio guide and dark places to explore. From the top floor, there are good views of the surrounding country park with its areas of woodland, orchards, walled courtyards, herb garden and herds of sheep and long-horned cattle. Family events, such as cream tea tours, bat hunts and kite-flying demonstrations, are put on in the summer.

Holdenby House Gardens and Falconry Centre

Holdenby, Northampton **t** (01604) 770074
www.holdenby.com
Getting there 30 miles south of Leicester, 6 miles northwest of Northampton off the A428, J15a/16/18 from the M1
Open Gardens and falconry centre: Apr–Sept Sun 1–5; house: Easter Mon and special event days only 12–5 **Adm** Garden and falconry centre: adults £4.50, children £3, family (2+2) £12
Refreshments, picnic areas, on-site parking

Charles I was briefly held at Holdenby following his defeat in the Civil War. With its grand façade and sweeping lawns it would have made a suitably regal prison. You're not allowed inside the house, (except for special events), but the eight-hectare (20-acre) grounds contain an Elizabethan garden and a falconry centre with regular flying displays by owls, kestrels and hawks. Follow in the footsteps of the unhappy king himself with a stroll along the King's Walk. Visit on one of the house's event days such as their Victorian Easter or the Medieval Weekend (May).

★Sudbury Hall and Museum

Sudbury, Ashbourne **t** (01283) 585337
www.nationaltrust.org.uk
Getting there 30 miles west of Nottingham, 6 miles east of Uttoxeter off the A50
Open Mid-Mar–Oct Wed–Sun and Bank Hols 1–5

Adm Adults £5.50, children £2.50, under 5s **free**, family £13
Tearoom, picnic areas, shop, guided tours, mother and baby facilities, some disabled access

This 17th-century country house contains the National Trust Museum of Childhood with its fascinating range of displays designed to show kids what life was like for Victorian and Edwardian children (of all social backgrounds). Attitudes to youngsters in past times were less tolerant than they are today, especially among the lower classes, as mini adults were made to work for a living. You may find that your kids leave the exhibition showing a new-found appreciation of their ever-so-generous modern parents, especially after the younger ones have tried the chimney sweep climb or sat in a schoolroom presided over by a strict Edwardian schoolmaster. There's a fine collection of 19th-century toys and dolls (some of which can be played with), and mums might be interested to know that the inside of the house doubled as the home of Mr Darcy in the BBC production of *Pride and Prejudice*. The extensive grounds contain lake-side walks and there's a whole host of events each year, including 'Golden Egg Hunts', 'Family Fun Days', 'Peter Pan Quests', 'Activity Days', 'Treasure Hunts', 'Halloween Activities', 'A Victorian Christmas' and a 'Children's Day of Dance'.

Tattershall Castle

Tattershall, Lincoln **t** (01526) 342543
www.nationaltrust.org.uk
Getting there 15 miles southeast of Lincoln on the A153
Open Apr–Sept Sat–Wed 11–5.30; Oct–Nov Sat–Wed 11–4, Nov–Dec Sat and Sun 12–4 **Adm** Adults £4, children £2, family £10
Shop (with refreshments), picnic areas, mother and baby facilities, disabled access

Huge, double-moated, brick tower built in the 15th century for Ralph Cromwell, then Lord Treasurer of England. Look for the dungeons and original lavatories, as well as the spiral stone staircases (designed to force attackers to use their left hands when fighting). You can see all the way to Lincoln Cathedral from the battlements.

KIDS OUT

Animal attractions

Butterfly Farm and Aquatic Centre

Sykes Lane Car Park, North Shore, Rutland Water
t (01780) 460515
Open Apr–Oct 10.30–5 **Adm** Adults £4.50, children
£2.95, under 4s **free**
Disabled access, on-site parking

Butterfly and Wildlife Park

Long Sutton, Spalding **t** (01406) 363833
Getting there Just off the A17, near the
Lincolnshire–Norfolk border
Open Mid-Mar–Jun daily 10–5, Jul–mid-Sept 10–5.30,
mid-Sept–Oct 10–4
Adm Adults £5.70, children £4.20, under 3s **free**,
family (2+2) £18
*Tearoom, tea garden, mother and baby facilities,
disabled access, guided tours, on-site parking*

One of the country's largest tropical houses,
where you can wander amongst free-flying birds
and butterflies, past crocodiles and chameleons
and meet the cute residents of the Furry Friends
House before watching the daily flying demonstrations at the Bird of Prey Centre (home to owls,
falcons and vultures). Afterwards, kids can use up
any remaining energy throwing themselves over
and around the climbing frames, rope ladders,
scramble nets and swing bridges of the adventure playground.

Elsham Hall Country and Wildlife Park

Elsham **t** (01652) 688698 www.elshamhall.co.uk
Getting there It is off the A15, J5 from the M180
Open Easter–mid-Sept Wed–Sun 11–5
Adm Adults £5, children £4, under 3s **free**
*Licensed restaurant, farm shop, disabled access
on-site parking*

Elsham Hall is proof that animal attractions
needn't be large and spectacular to be successful.
Indeed, this small but superbly run wildlife park
offers as much fun as many big city zoos. Set in
lovely grounds with a wild butterfly garden
walkway, an arboretum and a woodland garden,
the park has lots of animals for children to meet
(including sheep, goats, donkeys and llamas) and
there are keeper talks everyday at 1pm, as well as
flying displays by birds of prey in the afternoons
(weather permitting). The highlight of your visit
will probably be the feeding-jetty, from where you
can pop hunks of bread straight into the wet,
gulping mouths of large carp. The park also
doubles as a traditional crafts centre with
demonstrations of pottery, woodturning and
blacksmithery given. Special events for families
are organized in summer, often incorporating
performances at the park's theatre.

Northcote Heavy Horse Centre

Great Steeping, Spilsby **t** (01754) 830286
www.northcote-horses.co.uk
Getting there About 8 miles west of Skegness on
the B1195 (off the A16)
Open Apr–Jun and Sept Sun–Wed 11–3; Jul–Aug
Sun–Fri 11–3 **Adm** Adults £5, children £3.50,
family £15
*Picnic areas, shop, mother and baby facilities,
disabled access*

A veritable temple to large, hairy horses.
Wagon rides are offered in summer.

Otter, Owl and Wildlife Park, Chestnut Centre

Castleton Road, Chapel-en-le-Frith, High Peak
t (01298) 814099 www.otterandowls.co.uk
Getting there 6 miles west of Castleton off
the A625
Open Mar–Dec daily 10.30–5.30, Jan–Feb Sat–Sun
10.30–5.30 **Adm** Adults £6, children £4, under 4s
free, family (2+2) £18
*Café, shop, some disabled access, disabled parking,
on-site parking*

Conservation centre for otters, barn owls, red
squirrels and other endangered forms of native
wildlife set in 20 hectares (50 acres) of parkland.

★Skegness Natureland Seal Sanctuary

North Parade **t** (01754) 764345
www.skegnessnatureland.co.uk
Open Summer: daily 10–5.30; winter: 10–4
Adm Adults £5.50, children £3.60, under 3s **free**,
family (2+2) £16.40

See rescued seals found stranded on the
beaches around the Wash, watch how they are
nursed back to health and returned to the wild.
Other attractions include an aquarium, a
penguin enclosure and a pets' corner.
For further information *see* p.355

Tropical Birdland

Lindridge Lane **t** (01455) 824603
www.tropicalbirdland.co.uk
Getting there 8 miles west of Leicester and
signposted from the A47

Open Mar–Oct 10–4.30, Nov–Feb 10–dusk
Adm Adults £5, children £3.50
Refreshments, picnic areas, shop, on-site parking
  This two-hectare (five-acre) woodland garden is home to more than 85 species of bird, including many tropical varieties living in large walk-through aviaries. Pick up a bag of monkey nuts and watch the colourful parrots and macaws flying out of the foliage to be fed. If you're lucky, one may perch on your arm.

Farms

Ferry Farm Park

Boat Lane, Nottingham **t** (0115) 9664512
www.ferryfarm.co.uk
Getting there Off the A612
Open Apr–Sept Tues–Sun 10-5.30; also Bank Hols and half term
Adm Adults £5.50, children £4.50
Restaurant, gift shop
  Ferry farm features all the usual farm favourites as well as a few more singular animals, including Arnie, the largest Italian Ox in Britain. Venture into the indoor barn during spring to stroke the baby goats and piglets and perhaps even bottle feed a lamb. After checking out all the animals, it's playtime. Head to the adventure playground, scramble over the assault course, hop on the zipline, take a tractor ride and race your family around the go-kart track. Don't worry if it's raining, there is also a large indoor play centre.

Manor Farm Animal Centre and Donkey Sanctuary

Castle Hill, East Leake, Loughborough **t** (01509) 852525 **www**.manorfarm.info
Getting there Signposted from the A60 on the Nottinghamshire–Leicestershire border
Open Sat–Sun and Bank Hols 10–5 (winter until 4) and school holidays Tues–Fri
Adm Adults £4.50, children £3.50, under 2s **free**
Café, picnic area, mother and baby room, disabled facilities
  Everything you could want from a day at the farm – 200 tame animals to meet, 40 hectares (100 acres) of farmland to explore, a straw maze to navigate, a pond to dip in, donkeys and quads to ride and an adventure playground to jump about on. There's an indoor art and craft activity centre for wet days and a café selling farm-made cakes and biscuits.

Sherwood Forest Farm Park

Edwinstowe, Mansfield **t** (01623) 823558
www.sherwoodforestfarmpark.co.uk
Getting there Just off the A6075 between Edwinstowe and Mansfield
Open Apr–Oct 10.30–5.15 **Adm** Adults £6, children £4, under 3s **free**, family (2+2) £18
Tea shop, picnic areas, farm shop, mother and baby facilities, some disabled access, on-site parking
  Horses, sheep, deer, pigs, and goats are just some of the more usual farmyardy-type animals you'll find living on this attractive site alongside a few more exotic companions, such as water buffaloes, wallabies and rare, miniature kune kune pigs. Kids are well catered for with a pets' corner, a guinea piggery, an outdoor adventure playground and an indoor play barn. On certain days, they may be able to see chicks being born in the hatchery and, in summer, take tractor-trailer rides and trips aboard a narrow-gauge railway.

Stonehurst Family Farm and Motor Museum

Bond Lane, Mountsorrel Village, near Loughborough **t** (01509) 413216
Getting there About 8 miles north of Leicester off the A6
Open Daily 9.30–5 **Adm** Adults £3.45, children £2.45, family (2+3) £12.50
Farm teashop and restaurant, disabled access, on-site parking
  All the usual favourites – pens full of friendly animals (sheep, pigs, rabbits, hens, horses and ponies), many of which are happy to be cuddled; a hatchery, where you can watch chicks emerging into the world, a nature trail, a straw-filled play-barn, an activity area, small tractors to ride on and large tractors to ride behind in a trailer.

★White Post Modern Farm Centre

Farnsfield **t** (01623) 882977
www.whitepostfarmcentre.co.uk
Getting there 12 miles northeast of Nottingham and signposted from the A614
Open Daily 10–5
Adm Adults £7.50, children £6.60, under 2s **free**
Farm restaurant, lunch barn, farm shop, pet shop, disabled access, on-site parking
  Working-cum-show farm with lots to look at and plenty for kids to do. You'll find a range of traditional farm breeds – pigs, sheep, chickens,

etc. – living alongside a few more unusual choices such as llamas, snakes and chipmunks. Although it may not be as slick as some of its competitors, it's certainly got lots of character – as exemplified by the handwritten information boards on the paddocks – and younger children will relish the opportunity to feed and pet the animals (they particularly love turning the handle that sends the food up to the top of the Goat Mountain). Watch chicks hatching in the incubation room and walk through the spooky owl barn (it's kept dark so that the nocturnal owls will believe it's night-time) before turning their attention to the farm's indoor soft play area and bouncy castle. Pony rides and talks by the farmer are given in summer.

Beside the seaside

Cleethorpes

Getting there By road: Cleethorpes is about 30 miles from Lincoln off the A46. By train: There are infrequent train services (every couple of hours) from Lincoln. By bus/coach: There is a National Express service from Lincoln and London Victoria
Tourist information 42–3 Alexandra Road **t** (01472) 323111 **www.nelincs.gov.uk**

A bit like Skegness, only less so, Cleethorpes has all the essentials – the bucket and spade shops, the caffs, the crazy golf courses, the leisure centre, the paddling pool, the 10-pin bowling alley, the laser quest, the theme park 'Pleasure Island' and the wide sandy beach. And of late, it's even got pretensions – English Heritage is restoring the front to its Victorian prime and the beach, once listed by the European Commission as one of Britain's dirtiest, now has a Blue Flag Award. In the meantime, you can take a look at its pre-beautified incarnation aboard the miniature steam railway that chugs along the coast. The town's most scenic spot is probably the boating lake, alongside which you'll find the Cleethorpes Humber Estuary Discovery Centre (*see* right), a 'time-travel' exhibition on the history of the town, and 'The Jungle', which houses a collection of tropical animals, including snakes, parrots, monkeys and lizards.

Cleethorpes Coast Light Railway
Lakeside Station, King's Road **t** (01472) 604657, **www.cleethorpescoastlightrailway.co.uk**
Open Mid-Apr–mid-Sept and Oct half term 11–6
Adm Adults £3, children £1.50

Britain's last seafront steam railway potters its way from Kingsway to Lakeside offering good views of the local scenery and the varied wildlife and busy shipping lanes of the Humber Estuary.

Cleethorpes Humber Estuary Discovery Centre
Lakeside, King's Road **t** (01472) 323232, **www.cleethorpesdiscoverycentre.co.uk**
Open Daily 10–5
Adm Adults £1.95, children £1.30, family ticket £5
Café-restaurant, picnic areas, shop, mother and baby facilities, disabled access, guided tours, on-site parking

Holds displays on the marine life of The Wash and John Harrison, the Lincolnshire resident who solved the problem of how to measure longitude at sea. There's also an observation tower offering views out over the Humber Estuary. Family events are organized in summer.

Pleasure Island
Kings Road **t** (01472) 211511
www.pleasure-island.co.uk
Open Apr–Aug daily 10–5; Sept–Oct Sat–Sun 10–5 (Oct half term daily)
Adm £14, under 4s **free**, family £50
Lots of fast food, picnic areas, family bar, sweet shop, souvenirs, disabled access to site, some disabled access to rides, on-site parking

This lively collection of rides, chutes and coasters loosely arranged into six geographically themed areas (Africa, Spain, Morocco, Old England, White Knuckle Valley and Kiddies' Kingdom) is Cleethorpes' most popular attraction. The most intense rides – The Hyper Blaster, Terror Rack, Alakazam and the Boomerang rollercoaster– are all pretty hairy and have strict height requirements (no person under 1.4m/5ft is allowed in), although there are several gentler offerings aimed at pre-teen children, as well as circus shows featuring clowns, jugglers and performing seals.

Skegness

Getting there By road: Skegness is on the east coast of Lincolnshire, about 40 miles from Lincoln, and can be reached via the A52 and the A158. By train: There are infrequent services between Lincoln and Skegness via Sleaford. By bus/coach: You can catch National Express services to Skegness's Richmond coach station from Lincoln and Grimsby

Tourist information Embassy Centre, Grand Parade t (01754) 899887 www.skegness.gov.uk

'Skeggy', as it is affectionately known to locals, is British through and through – a standard bearer for the quintessential working-class, bucket and spade, fish and chip, penny-slot-machine sort of holiday. A wide sandy beach filled with families enjoying donkey rides on sunny (and not so sunny) Bank Holidays; a seafront lined with souvenir shops, greasy spoon caffs and amusement arcades; an entertainment complex where summer seasons headlined by old-style C-list comedians are put on – it's got them all. The presence of a Butlins 'Family Entertainment Resort' just along the coast gives it that final stamp of knees-up authenticity. In summer, the front is lit up by thousands of coloured light-bulbs; in winter, the streets are practically deserted.

The town's principal attractions (besides the front itself) are the Pleasure Beach, which stretches from the Clock Tower (the centrepiece of the annual illuminations) to the pier, and is filled with rides and fairground games (dodgems, a mirror maze, a ghost train, a pirate boat, a 'storm' rollercoaster, mini go-karts and, of course, Romany clairvoyants); the Natureland Seal Sanctuary, on North Parade, where you can watch rescued domestic seals frolicking under-water, and the huge Magic World of Fantasy Island theme park in nearby Ingoldmells which adjoins both the Butlins

Can you spot?
The prime meridian signpost laid into the coastal path. Cleethorpes lies on the 0° longitude line which means you can stand with one foot in the eastern part of the world and one foot in the west.

resort and a large seven-day market (it claims to be Europe's largest).

More serene pleasures are available at the Gibraltar Point Nature Reserve, just south of the town, a three-mile area of salt marshes and sand dunes stretching down to the Wash where guided bird-watching walks are offered.

Butlins Family Entertainment Resort

Roman Bank **t** (01754) 765567
www.butlinsonline.co.uk
Open Jun–Nov 10am–11pm (last admission 4pm)
Adm High/low season adults £7.50/£9.50, children £7.50/£5, under 2s **free**, family £27/£20 (no unaccompanied children)
Fast food, cafés, shops, supermarket, nursery, disabled access, on-site parking

The best thing about this bastion of old-world 1950s-style seaside entertainment is the Splash Subtropical Waterworld, one of the largest indoor leisure pools in the country, full of water rides, flumes, chutes and wave pools. The surrounding collection of attractions nestling in amongst the famously austere rows of wooden chalets include a cinema, a 10-pin bowling alley, a casino and, for the kids, a small funfair with dodgems and a number of fairground shooting games.

★Magic World of Fantasy Island

Sea Lane, Ingoldmells **t** (01754) 872030
www.fantasyisland.co.uk
Open May–Oct 10–dusk
Adm Free, individual charges for rides
Café, fast food, restaurant, snack shops, mother and baby facilities, disabled access, on-site parking

Almost all of the park's rides are housed under a great glass pyramid, which is kept warm enough for palm trees to flourish. There's a lot of hi-adrenalin hardware on display including two huge rollercoasters: the Millennium Coaster (which, wouldn't you just know it, actually careers around the outside of the pyramid) and the Odyssey. There's also the 'Volcanic Eruption', which hurls its passengers 60m (200ft) into the air out of a huge plastic volcano (complete with plastic lava) and the 'Dragon Mountain Descent', Europe's longest water coaster. If the real roller-coasters don't prove thrilling enough, you can always take a virtual coaster ride at the park's IMAX theatre.

★Skegness Natureland Seal Sanctuary

North Parade **t** (01754) 764345
www.skegnessnatureland.co.uk
Open Summer: daily 10–5.30; winter: 10–4
Adm Adults £5.50, children £3.60, under 3s **free**,
family (2+2) £16.40
Snack shop, souvenir shop, mother and baby
facilities, disabled access

Every year Natureland rescues dozens of
stranded seals from the beaches around the
Wash, nurses them back to health and then
returns them to the wild. It's all very heart-
warming and, though ostensibly here as patients,
the seals are happy to perform their full repertoire of aquatic gymnastics for visitors whether
there's a bucket of fish in the offing or not. For
the best views, head to the new underwater
viewing area. Talks are given by keepers at feeding
times (posted by the entrance) and children can
suggest names for new arrivals.

Although the seals are the undoubted stars,
there are plenty of other animal attractions here
including a large aquarium, a penguin enclosure,
a pets' corner for children and a collection of
tropical houses providing a home to crocodiles,
snakes, birds and free-flying butterflies.

Open-air museums

Bosworth Battlefield

Visitor Centre, Sutton Cheney, Market Bosworth
t (01455) 290429
Getting there The centre can be found just off the
A447, about 10 miles west of Leicester
Open Apr–Oct daily 11–5
Adm Adults £3.25, children £2.25, family £8.50
Café, wheelchair access to visitor centre and battle-
field trail, guided tours, on-site parking (£1.50/car)

It was in this large, muddy field that the Yorkist
Richard III, the most notorious of all England's
monarchs, was killed by the troops of Henry
Tudor, thus bringing to an end the 30-year-long
War of the Roses and ushering in a new royal
dynasty that would control the English throne for
over a century. Richard would come to be
regarded, in the literature of the time, as almost
the devil incarnate; a hunchbacked, throne-
stealing, child killer – a view endorsed by
Shakespeare in his play *Richard III*, in which the

king is portrayed as wreaking havoc on the
country as revenge for his physical deformity.

Richard's bad reputation was based on the
events of 1483 following the death of his older
brother, King Edward IV. Instead of becoming the
protector of Edward's son (the newly crowned
12-year-old Edward V) as he had promised his
brother he would, Richard instead imprisoned
the young king, along with his younger brother,
in the Tower of London and declared himself
king. Although there is no evidence linking him
to the crime, it seems highly likely that Richard
then ordered that the two young princes be
murdered to prevent anyone from using them as
figureheads for a revolt.

Obviously, if true, Richard must have been a
pretty ghastly man, but it's also worth remembering that history is always written by the
winners. Had Richard proved victorious on that
fateful day in 1485, then there's every chance that,
over the succeeding centuries, he would have
come to be regarded as a model monarch who
selflessly assumed the reins of government when
the child-king Edward V proved unfit to rule (and,
by the way, whatever happened to him?). Portraits
would have emphasized his beauty, not his
hunched back, for which there is, incidentally,
absolutely no historical evidence.

You can find out more about the life and times
of England's wickedest king at the visitor centre,
which has exhibitions, models and films relating
to the bloody battle (kids can have a go at using
a long bow), and trace the course of the fighting
on the battlefield itself along an illustrated trail
– look out for the memorial stone marking the
spot where Richard fell. A re-enactment of the
battle usually takes place here every summer
along with demonstrations of medieval fighting.

The 4.5-mile-long Battlefield Line, between
Shackerstone and Shenton, passes alongside
the site.

Did you know?
That Richard III, the pantomime villain of
British history, was the last king of England to
die in battle. Knocked from his mount and
wandering the battlefield his last words were,
according to Shakespeare, 'A horse, a horse, my
kingdom for a horse'.

Parks and gardens

Clipsham Yew Tree Avenue

Clipsham, Stamford **t** (01780) 444394 (Forestry Commission)
Getting there Located east of Clipsham, about 7 miles northwest of Stamford off the A1
Open Any reasonable time **Adm Free**
On-site parking

This bizarre but fun attraction is comprised of a lush, green, grassy avenue lined with 150 yew trees that have been carefully clipped into a variety of shapes – animals, people, vehicles, etc. – many of which mark events from national and international history. You'll see topiaried images of deer, elephants and bears as well as a Spitfire cut to commemorate the Battle of Britain, a tribute to the 1969 moon landing, and a royal hedge marking the 40th anniversary of the Queen's accession. There's a treasure trail for kids.

Clumber Park

Worksop **t** (01909) 476592
www.nationaltrust.org.uk
Getting there Situated 4.5 miles southeast of Worksop off the A57 and signposted from the A1
Open Park: all year during daylight hours; kitchen garden: Apr–Oct daily 10–5, Sat–Sun 10–6 **Adm Free** Kitchen garden: adult £2, children **free**
Café, shop, mother and baby facilities, guided tours, disabled access, on-site parking (£3 per car)

The National Trust-owned Clumber Park offers some ,1620 hectares (4,000 acres) of park and woodand to explore. Circumnavigate the vast, 32-hectare (80-acre) lake, wander around the Victorian walled garden or take a stroll along the longest double lime avenue in Europe (more than two miles long). Guided walks leave from outside the conservation centre daily in summer; bicycles can also be hired. Events and activities (Family Fundays, Teddy Bear Picnics, Bug and Bat Hunting days, etc.) are organized regularly.

Ilam Park

Home Farm, South Peak Estate, Ilam, Ashbourne **t** (01335) 350245, **www.nationaltrust.org.uk**
Getting there 4 miles northwest of Ashbourne off the A523
Open Grounds and park daily **Adm Free**
Shop, tearoom, mother and baby facilities, guided tours, limited disabled access, on-site parking (charge)

Laid out on both banks of the River Manifold in the South Peak Estate, this Peak District park with its big swathes of woodland, offers wonderful views of the surrounding valley. Family events (Easter Egg Trails, Children's Nature Days, Landrover Safaris and Pirate Treasure Trails) are held during the year. The park's 19th-century hall is now a youth hostel.

Naturescape Wild Flower Farm

Lapwing Meadows, Coach Gap Lane, Langar **t** (01949) 860592 **www.naturescape.co.uk**
Getting there Northwest of Leicester, off the A46
Open Apr–Sept 11–5.30
Adm Free except mid-Jul–mid-Aug: adults £1.95, children **free**
Tearoom, picnic areas, seed shop, on-site parking

The ideal photo op: 16 hectares (40 acres) of multicoloured wild flower fields and hedgerows, filled with butterflies in summer for your children to look adorable in. There's also a dragonfly pond.

Steam trains and tram rides

Battlefield Line

Shackerstone Station, Shackerstone **t** (01827) 880754
Getting there 3 miles northwest of Market Bosworth. Follow the brown tourist signs from the A444, the A447 and the B585 roads
Open Steam services operate mid-Mar–Nov Sat–Sun and Bank Hols
Fares Adults £7, children £4, family (2+2) £18
Tearoom, buffet on most trains, souvenir shop, some disabled access (call in advance), free on-site parking at Shackerstone Station

This 4.5-mile length of line between Shackerstone and Shenton passes alongside Bosworth Field, site of one of the most famous battles in English history. To find out more about the battle, visit the Bosworth Battlefield Visitor Centre and Country Park (p.355), where you can watch films, look at weapons and tour the battlefield itself or, if trains are more your thing, you can check out the large collection of railway memorabilia and rolling stock at Shackerstone station.

The truth about Robbing Robin

Robin Hood, the guy in the green tights?

That's him. The star of countless books and films and a bulwark of the Nottinghamshire tourist industry, Robin Hood is, along with King Arthur, probably the country's most celebrated legendary figure. The story of the swashbuckling do-gooder who, with his band of merry men, 'robbed from the rich to give to the poor' has long been one of the nation's favourites.

When did he live?

No one is quite sure, some time between the end of the 12th and the end of the 13th century is most people's guess, although, it has to be said that, as with King Arthur, Robin's legend consists mainly of a lot of fantasy wrapped around a very small amount of fact. Most of the stories about Robin are exactly that: stories, devised and embellished by successive generations of writers. Indeed, the earliest known mentions of the character come not in official documents but, rather, in a series of 14th-century ballads which tell of an outlaw who, from his base in the royal hunting forest of Sherwood, fought a number of battles against the authorities of the day and, in particular, the wicked Sheriff of Nottingham. In these early works, no mention is made of his giving anything to the poor or, indeed, of any of the characters – Friar Tuck, Little John or Maid Marian – that are now such an integral part of the legend. These were all later inventions.

So, he was a fictional character?

The lack of hard evidence has led some people to conclude that there wasn't a 'real' Robin at all, that he was simply a literary creation who happened to capture the public imagination. Others maintain that, without a genuine folk memory to draw upon, the character could never have achieved the popularity and longevity that he has.

What is the answer?

Who knows? Did Sherwood Forest's leafy depths really once hide a fugitive who, with popular support, stole from the rich and resisted the government of the day?

If Robin did indeed exist, then there seems little doubt that he would have cut a much less romantic figure that the green-tighted, thigh-slapping character we know from the films. He would have been a serious, professional outlaw and a skilled warrior capable of repelling repeated government attacks.

Any likely candidates?

Interestingly, yes. Though the standard version of the legend casts him as a 12th-century contemporary of Richard I, the most likely hypothesis so far puts forward the claim that Robin may actually have been a supporter of Simon de Montfort.

Who?

Simon de Montfort was a 13th-century noble, who led a rebellion against the unpopular king Henry III, following Henry's decision to raise a tax to pay for his wars with France. Although initially successful, Simon was eventually defeated in battle and his supporters had their land and wealth confiscated. However, they continued to wage their campaign against the king and his laws for years afterwards from hideouts in the country's forests. Was the real Robin, then, not a dandy redistributor of wealth, as portrayed by Hollywood, but rather a desperate protester against unfair taxation and abuse of royal power? If so, it is easy to see how such a character would have captured the public imagination, especially as his outlaw activities would presumably have involved him regularly attacking the country's hated tax collectors.

Where can I find out more?

Whether he was a real historical figure or not, there are many places in Nottinghamshire happy to claim some sort of link with the dandy bowman. These include the Old Market Square in Nottingham, where Robin took part in and won an archery competition (p.340); Nottingham Castle where, at the behest of the dastardly Sheriff, Robin was repeatedly imprisoned (and from where he repeatedly escaped, p.342); the nearby Castle Green, where Robin rescued his comrade, Will Stutely, just before he was about to be hanged (it's also where you'll find Nottingham's famous bronze statue of Robin, p.342); Papplewick Church, seven miles north of Nottingham, where Robin is said to have cut his bow staff from the ancient yews growing in the churchyard; Edwinstowe Church, where Robin and Marian were supposedly married, and the famous Major Oak, where Robin and his men used to hide inside its vast hollow trunk and plan their day's adventuring.

The best place to get acquainted with the legend is probably the 'Tales of Robin Hood' in Nottingham, which uses tableaux, costumed guides and lighting and sound effects to bring the outlaw's story to life (p.342).

Crich Tramway Village

Crich (pronounced 'Cry'), Matlock
t (01773) 854321 **www.tramway.co.uk**
Getting there Off the B5035 about 7 miles
southeast of Matlock Bath signposted from the A6
and the A38
Open Mid–late Feb daily 10.30–4, Mar Sat–Sun
10.30–4, Apr–Oct daily 10–5.30, Nov–mid-Dec
Sat–Sun 10.30–4
Adm Adults £9, children £4.50, family £24
*Café-restaurant, souvenir shop, bookshop, guided
tours, picnic areas, mother and baby facilities,
on-site parking; a special Access tram, originally
built in 1969 for use on the Berlin tramway
network, has been specially fitted out to carry
people with mobility difficulties*

Trips on vintage trams along a one-mile-long
period street and out into the Derwent Valley
countryside. You can take unlimited journeys
which you pay for using vintage pennies. More
trams can be found in the large exhibition hall
plus an interactive display on the history of the
tram. Santa visits on weekends in December.

Great Central Railway

Leicester North Station **t** (01509) 230726
www.gcrailway.co.uk
Open Jun–Sept and half-term holidays daily;
Oct–May Sat, Sun and some Bank Hols only
Return fares Adults £12, children £8, under 3s **free**,
family (2+3) £30

Steam train weekend rides over eight miles
of track between Leicester North and
Loughborough.
For further information *see p.337*

Midland Railway Centre

Butterley Station, Ripley **t** (01773) 747674,
www.midlandrailwaycentre.co.uk
Getting there On the B6179, 1 mile north of Ripley
and signposted from the A38 and M1 J28. Bus no.91
and 92 run from the centre of Derby
Open All year Sat–Sun and Bank Hols; Apr–Oct also
Wed; school holidays daily
Fares Call for prices
*Station refreshments, train buffet and bar, souvenir
shops, wheelchair access to station and coaches,
adapted toilets, on-site parking*

One of the best-equipped railway museums
in the country with an exhibition hall full of
historic locomotives and rolling stock. Steam
and diesel train rides are given along a 3.5-mile-
long length of restored track between Butterley
Station and Swanwick Junction. There's a miniature railway, a narrow-gauge steam line, a
demonstration signal box and a restored
Victorian railwayman's church.

Peak Rail

Matlock Station, Matlock **t** (01629) 580381
www.peakrail.co.uk
Getting there From the M1, take J28, 29 or 30 and
then follow signposts to Matlock. The nearest
mainline train station is Matlock
Open Apr–Oct Sat, Sun and Bank Hols 11–5.30
Fares Adults £6, children £3 (6–16), £1 (3–5), family
(2+5) £17
*Parking at Matlock and Darley Dale Station, shop at
Matlock, shops and buffets at Darley Dale and
Rowsley South, buffets on trains, wheelchair access
onto Brake Van only*

Popular steam railway running through the
rolling Peak District countryside between
Matlock and Rowsley South Station. In summer,
kids can go for donkey rides, play on a bouncy
castle and visit an old-fashioned fair. Thomas The
Tank Engine Days and Santa Specials in season.

Theme parks

American Adventureland

Ilkeston **t** 0845 3302929
www.americanadventure.co.uk
Getting there Between Derby and Nottingham
and signposted from J26 of the M1
Open Apr–Aug and late Oct daily 10–5 (later in
Aug), Sept–early Oct and Nov–Dec Sat–Sun 10.30–5
Adm Adults £12.50, children over 1.5m (4ft 9in) tall
£12.50, children under 1.4m (4ft 6in) tall £4.99 **free**
(book online for discounted prices)
*Fast-food outlets, souvenir shops, mother and baby
facilities, disabled access, on-site parking*

Compared with the other great theme parks of
the Midlands, this is a little bit ordinary with only
a handful of headline-grabbing thrill rides.
Judged on its own terms, however, it's not bad at
all and can provide a very enjoyable day out for
children of all ages (provided you haven't come
straight from Alton Towers that is). There are
over a 100 vaguely Wild West-themed rides

occupying the site of this former colliery (you can see preserved examples of old mining equipment), the best of which are Nightmare Niagara, the world's highest triple log flume, the Missile, a hairy rollercoaster which shoots round six loops and, the biggest draw, the Skycoaster, the park's one truly scary offering – you are fitted into a parachute harness and hoisted 60m (200ft) into the air, given a moment to reflect on the folly of your ways, before being released to enjoy a 50m (170ft) vertical freefall. Bob the Builder fans will love the JCB World and there are also go-karts, dodgems and a huge indoor soft play area for young children, as well as various live shows to watch, including the cowboy-themed extravaganza on the film set like *Silver Street*, which features daredevil horseback stuntriding, Lazy Lil's Saloon Show and Horses of the Wild Frontier.

Magic World of Fantasy Island

Sea Lane, Ingoldmells **t** (01754) 872030
www.fantasyisland.co.uk
Open May–Oct 10–dusk
Adm Free, individual charges for rides

Hi-adrenaline park's rides housed under a great glass pyramid kept warm enough for palm trees to flourish.

For further information *see* p.354

Pleasure Island

Kings Road, Cleethorpes **t** (01472) 211511
www.pleasure-island.co.uk
Open Apr–Aug daily 10–5, Sept–Oct Sat–Sun 10–5 (daily during Oct half-term holiday)
Adm £14, under 4s **free**, family £50

Cleethorpes' most popular attraction – rides, chutes and coasters arranged into geographically themed areas.
For further information *see* p.353

Sundown Adventure Land

Rampton, near Retford **t** (01777) 248274
Getting there 5 miles southeast of Retford off the A57. The nearest train station is Retford from where you can catch a bus to the park
Open Daily 10–5 (6pm during peak times)
Adm £7.50, under 2s **free**
Fast-food outlets, gift shops, disabled access, on-site parking

This gentle, cheerful little leisure park is aimed at the youngest members of the family, with a variety of cutely themed areas to explore – Wild West Street, Pirate Adventureland, Nursery Rhyme Land, Storybook Village, etc., all decorated with colourful tableaux and inhabited by costumed nursery book characters – and several undemanding rides such the Boozey Barrel Boat Ride and the Rocky Mountain Train. There's a small children's farm and occasional Punch and Judy shows. Toddlers and grandparents may find it enchanting; anyone over eight or under 65 may find it a bit dull.

Wicksteed Park

Kettering **t** (01536) 512475
www.wicksteedpark.co.uk
Getting there Just south of Kettering: follow the signs from the A14. From the M1 take J19 from the north, J15 from the south
Open Apr–Oct daily 10–6
Adm Adults £10, children £15 for unlimited ride wristband
Cafés, restaurant, picnic areas, disabled access, on-site parking (£2–6 per car depending on the time of day)

Wicksteed has been around since the early 1920s (an antique roundabout from that time remains) and still retains a very traditional feel to it. There are over 40 fairly sedate rides, which include a rollercoaster and a train ride. Wicksteed offers what used to be known, before the advent of virtual reality and suspension rollercoasters, as family fun, with its dodgems, pirate ship, Lazartag game and boating lake. There's also a pitch 'n' putt course, an aviary, a paddling pool and plenty of space for picnics in among the 60 hectares (148 acres) of parkland and gardens.

Wonderland Pleasure Park

White Post A614, Farnsfield, Mansfield **t** (01623) 882773 **www.**wonderlandpleasurepark.com
Getting there Signposted from the A614 north of Nottingham (about 10 miles)
Open Daily 10–5 (Sat and Sun closes 5.30pm)
Adm £5.50–£7, under 3s **free**, family (2+2) £20–£26 (prices vary according to season)

Near White Post Modern Farm Centre (pp.352–3), this undemanding 12-hectare (30-acre) pleasure park has an adventure playground (the largest in the region), a maze, a pets' corner and can offer rides on miniature trains or (for that extra thrill) on a small caterpillar-themed rollercoaster.

Wide open spaces

The National Forest

t (01283) 551211 **www.nationalforest.org**

The National Forest is one of the most ambitious environmental projects ever attempted in this country. The plan is to try and turn back the clock to a time when most of the country was covered by thick, dense woodland. A huge, 200-square-mile (520 sq km) area of land in Leicestershire, Derbyshire and Staffordshire – which at present contains numerous villages, a few existing areas of forest and many more areas scarred and spoilt by mining and mineral extraction – has been earmarked for replanting. The hope is that eventually some 30 million new trees will be planted, transforming one of the least wooded areas of the entire country. Obviously, it will never be an unbroken canopy stretching from Leicester to Burton-upon-Trent, but it is hoped that one-third of the area (13,500 hectares/33,360 acres) will one day be submerged under leafy forest.

Begun in 1992, the forest exists as isolated pockets of growth and this project will not approach completion for another 30–40 years. If you want some idea of what it may look like in 200 years, visit some of the existing tracts of forest – including remnants of the former Charnwood royal hunting forest – to the northwest of Leicester.

At Newton Linford off the A511, there's Bradgate Country Park, at the heart of whose leafy depths lies the 16th-century home of Lady Jane Grey, who ruled as Queen of England for nine days in 1553, before the rightful heir, Mary I, raised an army and overthrew her. The visitor centre retells her sad story (poor Jane was coerced into becoming Queen by the advisors to Edward VI, who wanted to ensure that, following the Reformation, the country continued with a Protestant ruler. She was beheaded following Catholic Mary's eventual succession) and has displays on the local flora and fauna. The park has miles of waymarked trails on which you may spot some of the fallow deer that still roam these parts. More strenuous walking is offered at the Beacon Hill Country Park, a few miles to the north. The summit of the hill measures some 244m (800ft), rising high and proud above the lovely surrounding 75 hectares (180 acres) of woodland and heathland.

Beacon Hill Country Park

Beacon Road, Woodhouse Eaves, Loughborough
Getting there On the B591, off the A6 between Nottingham (about 10 miles) and Leicester (about 4 miles)
Open Daily dawn–dusk **Adm Free**
Café, picnic area, some disabled access, on-site parking (£1.50 charge)

Bradgate Country Park

Bradgate Park, Newton Linford **t** (0116) 236 2713
Getting there The centre lies 6 miles northwest of Leicester, off the A511
Open Dawn–dusk **Adm Free**
Shop, disabled access

★Conkers

Bowdon Road, Moira, Swadlincote **t** (01283) 216633
www.visitconkers.com
Getting there Situated on the B5003, on the Derbyshire–Leicestershire border, off the A444 and the A5111, J11 or J12 from the M42
Open Summer: 10–6; winter: 10–5
Adm Adults £6.50, children £4.50, family (2+2) £18.95
Restaurant, gift shop, wheelchair access, adapted toilets, picnic areas, guided tours, on-site parking

A veritable wood-fest – the recently revamped centre is set in 50 hectares (120 acres) of parkland and boasts woodland displays, a 'wooden' gift shop 'Once a Tree', a woodland adventure playground 'Hocus Pocus', plus an amphitheatre and forest garden. The centrepiece of the whole site, a structure best described as a kind of wooden Sydney Opera House, houses four interactive zones full of hands-on exhibits based on the seasons and an indoor play centre. There's also a cycle shop and woodland walks and woodcraft workshops are organized.

Cycle hire

Bikes for forest cycling can be hired from:
City Cycles 61 Meadow Lane, Coalville
t (01530) 812727
Conkers Bath Lane, Moira, Swadlincote
t (01283) 216633
Just Bikes 8 The Green, Ashby-de-la-Zouch
t (01530) 415021
Rosliston Forestry Centre Burton Road, Rosliston
t (01530) 515524

Horse-riding

National Forest Hacks are organized by:

Knowlehill Equestrian, Ingleby Lane, Ticknall
t (01332) 862044
Park View Riding School, Anstey Lane, Thurcaston
t (0116) 236 4858

Rutland Water

Tourist information, Sykes Lane, Empingham,
Oakham t (01572) 653026
www.anglianwaterleisure.co.uk
Getting there A few miles south of Oakham, the
county town of Rutland (the country's smallest
county) on the A606

The largest, strangest-shaped man-made lake
in Europe, covering some 1,255 hectares (3,100
acres; it looks a bit like a wonky, spiky horseshoe),
Rutland Water is one of the country's great
outdoor activity centres offering watersports,
sailing, biking, boat trips, fishing, climbing and
miles and miles of nature trails. The tourist office,
your first port of call, can provide all the necessary details. It stands next to the Rutland Water
Butterfly Farm and Aquatic Centre, where you can
walk through clouds of free-flying butterflies
(who will happily land on your hands and arms)
and tickle for carp in the centre's great freshwater
aquariums (trust me, until you've had a carp
nibble your fingers, you really haven't lived).

Cycling

Bikes for cycling around Rutland Water are hired
out by Rutland Cycling www.rutlandcycling.co.uk,
at the following centres:
Normanton Centre, Normanton car park, near
Edith Weston t (01780) 720888
Whitwell Centre, Whitwell car park, near Oakham
t (01780) 460705

Rock-climbing

Rock-climbing for both adults and children
(over 5s) is offered by:
Rockblok, Whitwell Leisure Park t (01780) 460060

Sherwood Forest

Edwinstowe, Mansfield t (01623) 82490
www.sherwoodforest.co.uk
Getting there Located on the B6034, off the A6075,
about 12 miles north of Nottingham
Open Park: daily dawn–dusk; visitor centre:
Apr–Oct daily 10.30–5, Nov–Mar daily 10.30–4.30
Adm Free
*Forest Table restaurant, picnic areas, shop, mother
and baby facilities, disabled access, on-site parking*

The most famous forest in the land, even if
it is now only a fraction of its former size.
Nonetheless, there's a good 182 hectares (450
acres) of woodland and heathland remaining
with many marked trails including one taking you
to the famous Major Oak with its massive 10m
(33ft) girth: According to legend, Robin Hood and
his Merry Men used to hide inside its hollow
trunk and plan their day's adventuring. Robin is
also said to have 'plighted his troth' to Maid
Marian beneath its canopy. The tree, which may
only be around 500–600 years old (and thus too
young to have been used by Robin), is clearly
beginning to feel its age, its sagging branches
supported by a convoluted network of wooden
crutches. The visitor centre, a 20-minute walk
from the tree, has an (inevitable) exhibition on
Robin Hood's Sherwood (or Robin Hode's
Sherwode to be accurate), another of 'Forests of
the World' and holds a special Robin Hood festival
every year in August.

Sherwood Forest Farm Park

Edwinstowe, Mansfield t (01623) 823558
www.sherwoodforestfarmpark.co.uk
Getting there Just off the A6075 between
Edwinstowe and Mansfield
Open Apr–Oct 10.30–5.15
Adm Adults £6, children £4, under 3s **free**,
family (2+2) £18
*Tea shop, picnic areas, farm shop, mother and baby
facilities, some disabled access, on-site parking*

Horses, sheep, deer, pigs, and goats are just
some of the more usual farmyard animals you'll
find living on this attractive site, alongside a few
more exotic companions such as water buffaloes,
wallabies and rare, miniature kune kune pigs. Kids
are well catered for with a pets' corner, a guinea
piggery, an outdoor adventure playground and an
indoor play barn. On certain days, they may be
able to see chicks being born in the hatchery and,
in summer, take tractor-trailer rides and trips
aboard a narrow-gauge railway.

Sherwood Forest Fun Park

Sherwood Forest Country Park, Edwinstowe, near
Mansfield t (01623) 823536
Open Easter–mid-Sept daily 10am–dusk; mid-
Sept–Oct Sat and Sun 10am–dusk **Adm Free**
Small amusement park full of gentle fair-
ground rides and carousels. Good for toddlers.

SPORT AND ACTIVITIES

Bicycle hire

National Forest
For details of National Forest cycle hire *see* p.360

Peak District
For details of Peak District cycle hire *see* p.344

Pitsford Water
Brixworth, Brixworth Country Park
t (01604) 881777 www.pitsfordcycles.co.uk
Bikes to cycle the 7.5-mile cycle path around Pitsford Water and Brampton Valley Cycle Way.

Rutland Water
For details of Rutland Water cycle hire *see* p.361

Bowling

10-Pin Bowling Alley
Kings Road, Cleethorpes **t** (01472) 601006
Open Daily 9am–12 midnight
Adm Adults £3.30, children £2.80 (price per game)

Chesterfield Bowl
Starforth Lane, Haland **t** (01246) 550092
Open Daily 9am–12 midnight, Sat 8am–12 midnight
Adm Adults £3.50, children £3 (price per game), family hour £17

Megabowl
Redfield Way, Nottingham **t** 0871 5501010
www.megabowl.co.uk
Open Mon–Wed 12 noon–12 midnight, Thurs 12 noon–1am, Sat 10am–1.30am, Sun 10am–12.30am
Adm Adults £5.75, children £4.75

Megabowl
Forester's Leisure Park, Sinfin Lane, Derby
t 0871 5501010
Open Daily 12 noon–12 midnight
Adm Adults £5.75, children £4.75
10-pin bowling and laser shooting game.

Nottingham Bowl
Barket Gate, Nottingham **t** 0870 1183026
www.amfbowling.co.uk
Open Daily 10am–12 midnight
Adm Games from £3.15 each

Football

Derby County Football Club
Pride Park Stadium, Pride Park, Derby
t 0870 444 8184 www.dcfc.co.uk
Tours Adults £5, children £4 **Tickets** £22–£32
Guided tours of the 'Rams' stadium offered.

Grimsby Town Football Club
Blundell Park, Grimsby Road, Cleethorpes
t (01472) 605050 www.gtfc.co.uk
Tours Adults £5, children £4 **Tickets** £15–£17
Home of the 'Mariners'.

Leicester City Football Club
Walkers Stadium, Leicester
t 08700 40600 www.lcfc.co.uk
Tours By arrangement **Tickets** £23–£30
The 'Foxes', currently in the English premiership.

Northampton Town Football Club
Sixfields Community Stadium, Upton Way, Northampton **t** (01604) 757773 www.ntfc.co.uk
Tours Adults £5, children £4 **Tickets** £16–£19

Nottingham Forest
The City Ground, Nottingham **t** (0115) 982 4444
www.nottinghamforest.co.uk
Tours Adults £5, children £4 **Tickets** £17–£24

Go-karts

Swain's Centre
Buxton, **t** (01298) 71037 www.swains-centre.co.uk
Open Sat–Thurs 10–4 **Adm** Call for prices
Children aged five and up.

Formula One Indoor Karting
Wymeswold Industrial Estate, Burton on the Wolds, Loughborough **t** (08712) 205050
Open Daily 10–10 **Adm** Call for prices

Horse-riding

A. B. R. S. Lophams Equestrian Centre
Thorn Lane, Goxhill **t** (01469) 530 3814
Open Tues–Sun, depending on light and weather conditions **Adm** Children £10 per hour (age 6 and up)

Caistor Riding School
North Kelsey Road, Caistor **t** (01472) 851613
Open/Adm Call for times and prices

Chestnut Farm Riding School
Brigsley Road, Ashby Cum Fenby, Grimsby
t (01472) 825777
Open/Adm Call for times and prices

Knowlehill Equestrian
Ingleby Lane, Ticknall **t** (01332) 862044
Open/Adm Call for times and prices

Manor Park Equestrian Centre
Wychnor, near Burton-upon-Trent **t** (01283) 791791
Open/Adm Call for times and prices

Park View Riding School
Anstey Lane, Thurcaston **t** (0116) 236 4858
Open/Adm Call for times and prices

RG Equestrian Enterprise
Cottagers Plot, Laceby **t** (01472) 276427
Open/Adm Call for times and prices

Silver Shoe Riding Stables
73 Sea View Street, Cleethorpes **t** (01472) 200477
Open/Adm Call for times and prices

Ice-skating

Grimsby Leisure Centre
Cromwell Road, Grimsby **t** (01472) 323100
Open Daily 8–10 **Adm** Call for prices
Ice-skating, swimming, badminton, netball, etc.

★National Ice Centre
Lower Parliament Street, Nottingham
t (0115) 853 3000
Open Call for times **Adm** Adults £3.80–£4.50, under 5s £2.20 (inc skate hire), family £20 (inc. skate hire); skate hire £1.50
England's premier ice-skating venue, with two Olympic-sized rinks. Leisure skating and ice dance.

Laser-shooting

Quasar
Megabowl, Forester's Leisure Park, Sinfin Lane, Derby **t** 0871 5501010 **www.megabowl.co.uk**
Open Mon–Fri 2pm–late, Sat–Sun 10am–late
Adm Adults £4.50, children £3.50 per game

Quaser Elite
22 Cranbrook Street, Nottingham **t** (0115) 958 9178
www.laserfun.co.uk
Open Mon–Fri 11–9, Sat 9–9, Sun 10–8 **Adm** £4/game

Motorsports

Buggyland
National Autosports Centre, Adbolton Lane, Nottingham **t** (01949) 861155 **www.buggyland2.com**
Open Weekends; school hols daily **Adm** Call for prices
Special children's track for ages 6–12.

Silverstone Circuit
Silverstone, Towester **t** (01327) 850206
www.silverstone-circuit.co.uk
Open/Adm Call for events and prices
Home of the British Formula 1 Grand Prix.

Rock-climbing

Rockblok
Whitwell Leisure Park, Rutland Water
t (01780) 460060
Open Daily 9–5 **Adm** Adults/children £15 per hour

Roller-skating

Roller World
Mansfield Road, Derby **t** (01332) 345828
Open/Adm Call for times and prices

Skateboarding

Derby Storm Skate Park
Storm Sports Centre, Shaftesbury Street, Derby
t (01332) 201768
Open Daily 12 noon–10pm **Adm** £2 per hour
BMX and skateboard park.

Skiing

John Nike Leisuresort Swadlincote Ski Centre
Hill Street, Swadlincote **t** (01283) 217200
www.swadlincoteskislope.co.uk
Open Mon–Fri 10–10 **Adm** Call for prices
A 160m (525ft) dry ski slope and a 650m (2,133ft) toboggan run. Alpine restaurant and ski shop.

Swimming

Cleethorpes Leisure Centre
Kingsway, Cleethorpes **t** (01472) 323200
Open/Adm Call for times and prices
Large leisure pool with aqua-glide and waves.

Danes Camp Leisure Centre
Channel Road, Hunsbury **t** (01604) 705469
Open Call for times **Adm** Adults £2.80, children £2
Fun pool with giant flume ride, beach boat slide and rain cloud; crèche and school holiday fun.

Grimsby Leisure Centre
Cromwell Road, Grimsby **t** (01472) 323100
Open Call for times **Adm** Adults £2.50, children £1.95
Swimming, ice-skating, badminton, netball, etc.

Leicester Leys Leisure Centre
Beaumont Way, Leicester **t** (0116) 233 3070
Open Call for times **Adm** Adults £2, children £1
Leisure pool with flumes and a wave machine.

Victoria Park Leisure Centre
Manners Road, Ilkeston **t** (0115) 944 0400
Open Call for times **Adm** Adults £2.50, children £1.95
Leisure pool with flume and artificial rain storms.

Water Meadows
Tichfield Park, Bath Street, Mansfield
t (01623) 463880
Open/Adm Call for times and prices
Leisure pool with waves, flume, geysers and beach.

Watersports

Bosworth Water Trust

Far Coton Lane, Market Bosworth **t** (01455) 291876
www.bosworthwatertrust.co.uk
Open Dawn–dusk **Adm** £2 per car

A 20-hectare (50-acre) leisure park with eight
hectares (20 acres) of lakes. Dinghying, boardsailing and fishing. Saturday morning kids' club.

Carsington Water

Visitor centre, Ashbourne **t** (01629) 540696
www.carsingtonwater.co.uk
Open Visitor Centre: daily 9.30–dusk
Adm Call for prices

Sailing, dinghying, canoeing, wind-surfing,
mountain biking and fishing. Children's playground, bird hides and a wildlife centre.

National Watersports Centre

Adbolton Lane, Holme Pierrepont, Nottingham
t (0115) 982 1212
Open/Adm Call for times and prices

A 2,000m (6,562ft) regatta course set in 110
hectares (270 acres) of park with a man-made
water slalom course and water ski lagoon.

Nene Whitewater Centre

Bedford Road, Northampton **t** (01604) 634040
www.nenewhitewatercentre.co.uk
Open/Adm Call for times and prices

White-water rafting sessions for groups of four
and more (children aged 14 up only) and a 'taster
session' for children aged 9–16 (who must be able
to swim a minimum of 50m/164ft).

Rutland Water

Tourist Office, Sykes Lane, Empingham, Oakham
t (01572) 653026 www.rutnet.co.uk
Open/Adm Call for times and prices

The largest man-made lake in Europe. Sailing,
biking, boating, fishing, climbing and walking.
For further information *see* p.361

Tallington Lakes

Barholm Road, Tallington, Stamford
t (01778) 347000 www.tallington.com
Open/Adm Call for times and prices

Jet-skiing, ski-boating and sailing. Also a café,
picnic area, refreshments and parking.

Watermead Country Park

Wanlip Road, near Syston **t** (0116) 267 1944
Open/Adm Call for times and prices

A 93 hectare (230-acre) water park with woodland walks, sailboarding, sailing and fishing.

Cinemas

Chesterfield

Cine World Alma Leisure Park, Derby Road
t 0871 2208000 www.cineworld.co.uk

Derby

Metro Green Lane **t** (01332) 347765
www.metrocinema.org.uk
Showcase Foresters Leisure Park, Osmaston Park
Road **t** 0871 2201000
www.showcasecinemas.co.uk
Odeon Meteor Centre, Mansfield Road
t 0871 2244007 www.odeon.co.uk

Kettering

Odeon Pegasus Court **t** 0871 2244007
www.odeon.co.uk

Leicester

Bollywood (Indian films), Melton Road
t (0116) 268 2555
City Cinema Abbey Street **t** (0116) 251 9699
www.citycinemaleics.com
Odeon Aylestone Road **t** 0871 2244007
www.odeon.co.uk.
Phoenix Arts 21 Upper Brown St **t** (0116) 255 4854
www.phoenix.org.uk
Piccadilly Cinema Green Lane Road **t** (0116)
2518880 www.piccadillycinema.co.uk
Vue Meridian Leisure Park, Braunstone **t** 0871
2240240 www.myvue.com

Lincoln

Odeon Valentine Road **t** 0871 2244007
www.odeon.co.uk

Loughborough

Curzon Cattle Market, Loughborough
t (01509) 212261 www.curzoncinema.com

Mansfield

Odeon Park Lane **t** 0871 2244007
www.odeon.co.uk

Melton Mowbray

Regal King Street **t** (01664) 562251
www.regal-melton.co.uk

Northampton

Cineworld Weedon Road, Broad Street **t** 0871
2002000 www.cineworld.co.uk
Forum Western Favell Centre, Wellinborough Rd
t (01604) 401006
Vue Dodderidge Street **t** 0871 2240240
www.myvue.com

Nottingham

Cineworld Forman Street **t** 0871 200 2000
www.cineworld.co.uk
Broadway Nottingham Media Centre, Broad Street
t (0115) 952 6611 **www.broadway.org.uk**
Savoy Derby Road **t** (0115) 986 6766
www.savoycinemas.co.uk
Screen Room Hockley, Lenton **t** (0115) 924113
www.screenroom.co.uk
Showcase Redfield Way, Lenton **t** 0871 2201000
www.showcasecinemas.co.uk

Skegness

Embassy Centre Grand Parade, Skegness
t (01754) 768333
Tower Lumley Road **t** (01754) 763938

Museums, galleries and science centres

Abbey Pumping Station

Corporation Road, off Abbey Lane, Leicester
t (0116) 299 5111
Open Apr–Nov Sat–Wed 11–4.30, school holidays
also Thurs and Fri **Adm Free**
   Museum about public health, with waste
product disposal demonstrations.
For further information *see* p.336

Cleethorpes Humber Estuary Discovery Centre

Lakeside, King's Road, Cleethorpes **t** (01472) 323232,
www.cleethorpesdiscoverycentre.co.uk
 Open Daily 10–5
Adm Adults £1.95, children £1.30, family £5
   Marine life displays and an observation tower
offering views out over the Humber Estuary.
For further information *see* p.353

Denby Pottery Visitor Centre

Derby Road, Denby, Ripley **t** (01773) 740799
Getting there On the B6179, off the A38, just south
of Ripley
Open Craftroom tour: daily 11, 2 and 3; factory
tours: Mon–Thurs 10.30 and 1; shop: Mon–Sat
9.30–5, Sun 11–5
Adm Craftroom: adults £3.95, children £2.75 (no
under 6s); factory tour: adults £5.25, children £4.25
*Café, factory shop, guided tours, mother and baby
facilities, disabled access, on-site parking*
   Watch skilled craftsmen at work in the factory,
browse the shop and (best of all) try throwing a

pot or painting a plate for yourself; there's an
extra charge for firing. Small children's play area.

Donington Grand Prix Collection

Donington Park, Castle Donington **t** (01332) 811027
www.doningtoncollection.com
Getting there Off the A42, J23A/24 from the M1
Open Daily 9–5 **Adm** Adults £7, children £2.50,
under 6s **free**, family (2+3) £14
Restaurant, souvenir shop, free on-site parking
   The world's largest collection of Grand Prix
racing cars, housed in five large halls. All the big
names of F1 are represented – McLaren, Williams,
Ferrari *et al.*

★Galleries of Justice

Shire Hall, High Pavement, Lace Market,
Nottingham **t** (0115) 952 0555
www.galleriesofjustice.org.uk
Open Apr–Oct Tues–Sun 10–4, school holidays also
Mon; Nov–Mar Tues–Fri 10–3, Sat–Sun 11–4
Adm Adults £7.95, children £5.95, family £22.95
   Fascinating tour through history of crime and
punishment that brings to life the child-
appealing nastiness of old-style justice.
For further information *see* pp.341–2

Green Mill and Science Centre

Windmill Lane, Sneinton **t** (0115) 915 6878
www.greensmill.org.uk
Open Wed–Sun and Bank Hols 10–4 **Adm Free**
   Restored windmill with a science centre and
scores of hands-on experiments and activities.
   For further information *see* p.342

Museum of Lincolnshire Life

Burton Road **t** (01522) 528448
Open Apr–Sept daily 10–5; Oct–Apr Mon–Sat
10–5.30
Adm Adults £2.15, children £1.45, family (2+3) £5.75
   The region's largest social history museum.
For further information *see* p.339

★National Fishing Heritage Centre

Alexandra Dock, Grimsby **t** (01472) 323345
www.nelincs.gov.uk
Getting there Grimsby is on the A180 on the
Lincolnshire coast. Once in the town, follow the
brown tourist signs to the dock. The nearest train
station is Grimsby and there's a regular bus service
Open Apr–Oct Mon–Fri 10–5 (Mon until 4), Sat–Sun
11–3; Nov–Mar Mon–Fri 10–4, Sat–Sun 11–3 (last
entry 1hr before closing time)

Adm Adults £6, children £4, family (2+2) £12
*Café, shop, guided tours, disabled access,
free on-site parking*

Replica boats, house and shop interiors,
waxwork dioramas and hands-on displays on the
hard life of the North Sea fisherman. Kids can
stand on a replica deck as it pitches from side to
side and feel cold icy winds blowing on their
faces, as well as try their hand at net-making
and knot-tying. A special children's section,
'Codswallop', has fishing-related games to play
and stories. Craft exhibitions and Pirate Days
throughout the year. Outside the centre, join a
tour of a genuine trawler, the *Ross Tiger*, on
which 12-man crews would undertake three-
week trips up beyond the Arctic Circle. Go below
decks to see the cramped sleeping quarters and
hear the deafening noise of the engine room.

★National Space Science Centre

Exploration Drive **t** (0116) 2610261
www.spacecentre.co.uk
Open Tues–Sun 10–5, school holidays also Mon
Adm Adults £11, children £9, family (2+2) £34,
(2+3) £42

Space-related memorabilia and interactive fun
displays for kids.
For further information *see* p.337

Nottingham Castle Museum and Art Gallery

Nottingham **t** (0115) 915 9700
Open Mar–Sept daily 10–5, Oct–Feb 11–4
Adm Adults £3, children £1.50 (includes entry to
Brewhouse Yard Museum)

Hands-on exhibition on the city of Nottingham.
For further information *see* p.342

★Snibston Discovery Park

Ashby Road, Coalville **t** (01530) 278444
Getting there Coalville is on the A5111. Take J22
from the M1. In the town follow the brown tourist
signs. Buses run to the site from both
Loughborough and Leicester
Open Apr–Sept daily 10–5, Oct–Mar Mon–Fri 10–3,
Sat–Sun 10–5 **Adm** Adults £6, children £4, family £18
*Self-service restaurant, shop, guided tours, disabled
access, on-site parking*

Excellent interactive science centre on the site of
a former colliery. Inside the exhibition hall there
are a wide range of experiments and displays
designed to entertain and educate children about
scientific principles. Children are invited to participate in a variety of seemingly impossible tasks –
to stand inside a tornado, make their own
rainbow, light a bulb with their bare hands, play
with lightning, create an earthquake or cycle
alongside a skeleton. The hall is arranged into a
number of themed areas – Science Alive, Science
of Light, Wild Water, Transport, Extractions,
Engineering and Textiles & Fashion – and there are
explainers on hand to talk kids through the
science behind the fun and games. There's also a
Virtual Reality gallery (£1 extra) and an outdoor
science play area decorated with statues, where
kids can muck about with building blocks and
follow nature trails through areas of landscaped
parkland. Guided tours of the colliery available.

★Tales of Robin Hood

30–8 Maid Marian Way, Nottingham
t (0115) 948 3284 **www.**robinhood.uk.com
Open Daily 10–5.30 (last admission 4.30)
Adm Adults £8.95, children £6.95, family (2+2)
£26.95

Scenes from the life of the fictional outlaw.
For further information *see* p.342

Toys of Yesteryear

Peak Village Outlet, Chatsworth Road, Rowsley
t (01629) 732111 **www.**toysofyesteryear.co.uk
Getting there Located between Bakewell and
Matlock off the A6
Open All year Sun 10–5; Apr–Oct Mon–Sat
10–5.30; Nov–Mar Mon–Sat 10–4.30
Adm Adults £3, Children £2, under 4s **free**, family
£8.50
Toyshop

The museum contains a collection of vintage
toys from 1900–'70s (Steiff, Hornby, etc.) and, best
of all, a full-size model of Chitty Chitty Bang Bang.
Pedal cars, traditional wooden games and antique
toys can be bought in the attached shop.

Wind in the Willows

Peak Village, Rowsley **t** (01629) 733433
Getting there About 6 miles north of Matlock Bath,
heading towards Bakewell off the A6. You can catch
bus no.R61 from Matlock Bath train station
Open Apr–Sept daily 10–5.30; Oct–Mar 10–4.30
Adm Adults £3.50, children £2, under 4s **free**
Shop, disabled access, on-site parking

Dioramas and displays on Kenneth Grahame's
famous animal tale, plus an exhibition on the
lives of badgers, moles, toads and weasels.

Woolsthorpe Manor

23 Newton Way, Woolsthorpe-by-Colsterworth,
Grantham **t** (01476) 860338
www.nationaltrust.org.uk
Getting there 7 miles south of Grantham off
the A1 via the B676
Open Apr–Sept Wed–Sun and Bank Hols 1–5, Oct
Sat–Sun 1–5
Adm Adults £4.50, children £2.20, under 5s **free**,
family £11.20
Guided tours, some disabled access, on-site parking
  Small interactive science museum in the
17th-century farmhouse where Sir Isaac Newton
was born.

Theatres

Cleethorpes

Memorial Hall Grimsby Road **t** (01472) 691838

Derby

Assembly Rooms Market Place **t** (01332) 255788
www.assemblyrooms-derby.co.uk
Derby Playhouse Theatre Walk, Eagle Centre
t (01332) 363275 www.derbyplayhouse.co.uk

Grimsby

Grimsby Auditorium Cromwell Road **t** 0870
0602331 www.grimsbyauditorium.com

Leicester

De Montford Hall Granville Road **t** (0116) 233 3111
www.demontforthall.co.uk

Northampton

Derngate Guildhall Road **t** (01604) 628411
www.royalandderngate.com
Royal Theatre Guildhall Road **t** (01604) 628411
www.royalandderngate.com

Nottingham

Nottingham Playhouse Wellington Square
t (0115) 941 9419 www.nottinghamplayhouse.co.uk
Theatre Royal Theatre Square **t** (0115) 989 5555
www.royalcentre-nottingham.co.uk

Skegness

Embassy Centre Grand Parade **t** (01754) 768333
www.embassytheatre.co.uk

Stamford

The Arts Centre t (01780) 763203
www.stamfordartscentre.com

Bakewell

Australian Bar/Diner

Granby Road **t** (01629) 814 909
Open Daily 11am–11pm (last orders 9pm)
  This lively place is, despite its singular menu
(kangaroo and ostrich meat anyone?), very
family-orientated, with an excellent-value
children's menu full of vegetarian options,
Boomerang burgers and Shark Sticks. Highchairs.

Bakewell Pudding Parlour

Wye House, Water Street **t** (01629) 815107
Open Summer: Mon–Fri 9–5.30 Sat–Sun 9–8;
winter: Mon–Fri 9–5.30 Sat–Sun 9–6.30
  Serves hot sandwiches and cakes (including
the famous puddings) baked on the premises.
There's a children's menu and highchairs.

Byways Tea Rooms

Water Lane **t** (01629) 812807
Open Mon–Fri 9–4, Sat 9–4.30, Sun 9.30–4.30
  Serves snacks, toasties, cakes and biscuits
throughout the day and is very popular with
families. A box of toys and highchairs.

The Old Original Bakewell Pudding Shop

The Square **t** (01629) 812193
www.bakewellpuddingshop.co.uk
Open Summer: daily 9–9; winter: daily 9–6
  The source of the famous pudding (so they
say), offering a choice of three children's menus,
baby changing facilities and highchairs.

Castleton

Cheshire Cheese Inn

Edale Road, Hope **t** (01433) 620381
Open Mon–Fri 12 noon–3 and 6.30–11,
Sat 12 noon–11, Sun 12 noon–4 and 6.30–10.30
  Small, English inn happy to cater for all
children. Highchairs available.

The Castle

Castle Street **t** (01433) 620578
Open Pub: daily 11.30–11; restaurant: Mon–Sat
12 noon–10, Sun 12 noon–9.30
  Children are welcome in this family-friendly
restaurant (especially on Sundays when there's a
roast) but not the tap room (bar). Kids' portions
and highchairs available.

> ### Pikelets
> These thick raised pancakes can be eaten as a
> snack with butter straight from the pan or toasted.

Ye Olde Nag's Head Hotel

1 Cross Street **t** (01433) 620248
Open Breakfast: 8am–9.30am; snacks and coffee
all day from 8am; pub: Mon–Fri 11–11, Sun 11–10.30;
restaurant: 12 noon–2.30 and 7–8.30

English food and a friendly, tolerant attitude to
youngsters in the bar and restaurant. Flexible
menu and portions. Highchairs available.

Cleethorpes

Wellow Hotel

Kings Road **t** (01472) 695589
Open Mon–Sat 11–11, Sun 12 noon–10.30; bar meals:
Mon–Fri 12 noon–3 and 5–9, Sat and Sun 12 noon–9

A traditional English pub with a family dining
room, children's menu and an outdoor play area.

Derby

Bartlewood Lodge

Dale Road, Ockbrook **t** (01332) 677198
www.bartlewoodlodge.co.uk
Open Mon–Sat 11.30am–10pm, Sun 12 noon–10pm

Well-situated pub outside the city on a hill overlooking the surrounding countryside. The food is
good, solid pub fare and there's a Charlie Chalk Fun
Factory (with ball pool and slide) and crazy golf.

Sarah's Restaurant

Eagle Centre, 8 Cope Castle Square **t** (01332) 371429
Open 7.30am–5pm

Pies and jacket potatoes are the speciality.
Children's menu (with free drink) and highchairs.

Grimsby

Granary Restaurant

1st Floor, Haven Mill, Garth Lane **t** (01472) 346338
www.granarygrimsby.co.uk
Open Mon–Fri 11–2, Wed–Sat 7–12 midnight (last
orders 9pm)

Introduce children to the joys of winkle-picking
at this long-established seafood restaurant.

Leicester

City Stadium

Filbert Street (entrance through the main reception at City Stadium) **t** 0800 542 6282
Open Daily, lunch from 12 noon, dinner from 7pm

Great for 'Foxes' fans; you can have a family
meal overlooking the pitch and do a tour of
the stadium.

Mem-Saab

98 Vaughan Way **t** (0116) 253 0243
www.mem-saab.co.uk
Open Mon–Sat 5.30–11pm

Well-to-do Indian restaurant with children's
portions, highchairs and a non-smoking area.

Peking Restaurant

16 Charles Street **t** (0116) 262 3376
www.thepeking.co.uk
Open Mon–Sat 12 noon–3, 5pm–12am; Sun
12 noon–12 midnight

Cantonese, Szechuan and Peking cuisine
for all ages. Children are always rather partial
to *dim sum*, which is a speciality here.
Highchairs provided.

Shireen

161 London Road **t** (0116) 233 3640
Open Sun–Thurs 12 noon–2 and 6–11.30;
Fri 6–12.30; Sat 12 noon–2 and 6–12.30

Children are welcome in this Leicester curry
house (which specializes in Indian and Bangladeshi
cuisine). There isn't a children's menu, but they'll
suggest choices and provide smaller portions.

Stones

29 Millstone Lane **t** 0845 6500777
www.stonesrestaurant.co.uk
Open Mon–Sat 12 noon–3 and 6.30–late (last
orders 12 midnight)

Very good Mediterranean restaurant. There's
no children's menu but you can order child-size
tapas. Highchairs available.

Vermont Restaurant

Holiday Inn, 129 St Nicholas Circle **t** (0116) 242 8723
Open Daily 7–10.30pm

In the city centre, popular with families at
weekends. They do a special Sunday 'Splosh and
Nosh' deal: if you book a family Sunday lunch, you
can use the hotel's swimming pool, Jacuzzi, sauna
and steam room free of charge. The cuisine is
modern British and there is a children's menu.

Lincoln

Dennetts on Ballgate Street is *the* place in town
for ice cream.

Browns Pie Shop

33 Steep Hill **t** (01522) 527330
Open Coffee from 11, lunch 12 noon–3, dinner 5.30–10

Near the cathedral, Browns serves big chunky
pies cooked according to time-honoured
regional recipes and provides highchairs.

Jews House

15 The Strait **t** (01522) 524851

Open Tues–Sat 11.30am–2pm and 7pm–late

This 12th-century building (the oldest occupied house in Europe) is full of antique trimmings – exposed wooden beams, a cast-iron open fireplace, etc. It welcomes more families for lunch than for dinner and is all non-smoking (apart from the upstairs coffee lounge). No kids' menu, but the chef rustles up simple dishes on request.

Mediterranean

14 Bailgate **t** (01522) 546464

Open Mon–Fri 12 noon–2.30 and 6–10pm, Sat 12 noon–2.30 and 6–10.30pm, Sun 12 noon–4pm and 6–9.30pm

Family restaurant serving up a wide selection of Mediterranean dishes. It's good for lunch and occasionally runs 'kids free' deals. Highchairs.

Mansfield

Forest Table Restaurant

Sherwood Forest Country Park and Visitor Centre Edwinstowe **t** (01623) 823202

Getting there On the B6034, off the A6075

Open Park: daily dawn–dusk; visitor centre: Apr–Oct daily 10.30–5; Nov–Mar 10.30–4.30

Child-friendly café at the epicentre of the Robin Hood industry. After your meal, you can join the merry men at the visitor centre's Robin exhibition.

Market Bosworth

Henry's Restaurant

9a Main Street **t** (01455) 292865

Open Tues–Sat 7–10pm; Sun 12 noon–12.30am

Specializing in exotic fish and vegetarian dishes, and very child-friendly (0–4-year-olds eat for free and it's half price for 5–11-year-olds). Children's portions and highchairs available.

Matlock Bath

The Fishpond

204 South Parade **t** (01629) 581000

Open Pub: Mon–Sat 11–11, Sun 12 noon–10.30; restaurant: Mon–Fri 12 noon–2.30 and 5.30–9, Sat and Sun 12 noon–9

Traditional pub with indoor/outdoor eating areas, beer garden, children's menu and highchairs.

The Princess Victoria

South Parade **t** (01629) 57462

Open Pub: daily 12 noon–11; restaurant: daily 12 noon–4 and 7–9

Tasty homecooked meals – steaks, scampi, Sunday roasts, etc. – a children's menu and lots of vegetarian options. Highchairs available.

Melton Mowbray

Ye Olde Pork Pie Shoppe and The Sausage Shop

8–10 Nottingham Street **t** (01664) 482068

www.porkpie.co.uk

Open Mon–Sat 8–5

Melton Mowbray's oldest bakery and *the* place to pick up a traditional English pork pie or watch the pies being made. There's an equally famous sausage shop next door.

Moira

Heart of the National Forest Visitor Centre Restaurant

Enterprise Glade **t** (01283) 216633

Open Daily 10–6

Family-friendly restaurant in this excellent organic-looking visitor centre (children's menu, highchairs with woodcraft workshops, brass rubbings, organized woodland walks and a woodland adventure playground outside).

Nottingham

Branaghan's Restaurant and Bar

Bostock Lane, Long Eaton **t** (0115) 946 2000

Open Mon–Sat 12 noon–3 and 5–11; Sun 12 noon–10.30

American-themed restaurant and bar with a children's menu (burgers, hot dogs, etc.) Family Day on Sundays when kids eat for free (one per paying adult) and are entertained by 'Zozo' the clown. Highchairs are provided.

Café Rouge

31 Bridlesmith Gate **t** (0115) 958 2230

www.caferouge.co.uk

Open Mon–Sat 10am–11pm, Sun 10am–10.30pm

Cheerful branch of the French café-restaurant chain. Kids' menu is £3.95 (main course, ice cream and a free drink) and comes with a page to colour in. Crayons and stickers provided. Highchairs available.

Melton Mowbray pork pies

The chief reason for the fame of Melton Mowbray pies was that traditionally the pigs were fed on the whey left over from making Stilton, and also from the mild, deeply annatoed Leicestershire cheese (today only made in the big creameries).

Fellows Morton and Clayton

54 Canal Street **t** (0115) 950 6795
www.fellowsmortonandclayton.co.uk
Open Mon 11.30–2.30, Tues–Fri 11.30–2.30 and
5.30–9.30, Sat 11.30–10.30, Sun 12 noon–6

Nottingham's oldest brewery pub. Children are
welcome in the restaurant (the bar doesn't have
the appropriate licence), which offers a kids'
menu, highchairs and a garden.

Frankie and Benny's

29 Upper Parliament Street **t** (0115) 979 9736
Open Mon–Sat 12 noon–11, Sun 12 noon–10.30

'New York'-themed Italian diner serving up big,
tasty pizzas, pastas and salads. Separate children's
menu. Kids get balloons, crayons and activity
packs to help them pass the time. Highchairs.

The Hard Rock Café

11 King Street **t** (0115) 947 4201 www.hardrock.com
Open Sun–Thurs 12 noon–11pm, Fri 12 noon–1am,
Sat 11–1am

A central venue popular with teenagers. Noisy
on Saturday nights. Children's meals and balloons.

The Loch Fyne Restaurant

17 King Street **t** (0115) 9886840 www.lochfyne.com
Open Mon–Thurs 9am–9.30pm, Fri 9am–10pm,
Sat 10am–10pm, Sun 10am–9.30pm

Small seafood restaurant (oysters a speciality)
that's well thought of by local families.
Highchairs and children's portions available.

Ye Olde Trip to Jerusalem

1 Brewhouse Yard **t** (0115) 9473171
www.triptojerusalem.com
Open Restaurant: Mon–Sat 11–6, Sun 12 noon–6;
pub: Mon–Sat 11–11, Sun 12 noon–10.30

Hewn from the rock below Nottingham Castle,
this watering-hole first opened in the 12th century.
Children are welcome in the restaurant (but not
the bar). Children's menu.

Sonny's

3 Carlton Street, Hockley **t** (0115) 947 3041
Open Restaurant: Mon–Fri 12.30–2.30 and
6.30–10.30; bar: food Mon–Sat 11–11 and Sun
10.30–10.30

Hip and groovy with modern British menu and
minimalist décor. Will happily serve up simpler
meals for children and provide highchairs.

La Vecchia Romagna

112–14 Derby Road **t** (0115) 941 9443
Open Daily 12 noon–3 and 6–11

Warm and friendly Italian family restaurant.
Reasonable lunchtime set menu for £5.95;
children's portions and highchairs.

Wagamama

The Cornerhouse, Burton Street **t** (0115) 9241797
www.wagamama.com
Open Mon–Sat 12 noon–11pm, Sun 12 noon–10pm

Branch of the popular noodle bar. Children's
menu available.

The Wollaton Arms Innkeeper's Fare

Trowel Road, Wollaton **t** (0115) 985 5494
Open Sun–Thurs 12 noon–9, Fri–Sat 12 noon–10

Traditional English pub that's happy to welcome
familes until 9.30pm each evening. There is a
children's menu, an indoor Deep Sea Den play area
and an outdoor playground in the garden.

Skegness

La Bella Napoli

123 Roman Bank **t** (01754) 765825
Open Daily 12 noon–2 and 6–11

Family-friendly Italian restaurant. Highchairs
and smaller menu portions available.

The Winning Post Diner

Burgh Road **t** (01754) 898111
Open Daily 8am–7.30pm

All-day breakfasts, traditional English lunches
(including a three-course Sunday roast), afternoon teas, evening meals and children's meals.

Stamford

The pizza chains Ask and Pizza Express have
two venues in town: **Ask**, 10 St John's Street,
t (01780)765455; **Pizza Express**, St Martins,
t (01780) 767902.

The George

71 St Martins **t** (01780) 755171
Open Restaurant: 12 noon–2 and 7–10; bistro: 11–10.30

This old coaching inn houses two restaurants –
the Garden Lounge bistro is easily the most child-
friendly. Flexible about portions and can provide
highchairs. The more formal A La Carte restaurant
is suitable for children aged 12 and over.

Heart of England
Herefordshire · Shropshire
Staffordshire · Warwickshire
West Midlands · Worcestershire

Riding rollercoasters at Alton Towers, exploring the medieval fair at Warwick Castle, skiing at the Tamworth Snow Dome, there's plenty here for children. This is the country's industrial heartland where, in the late 18th century, a technical revolution began that would change the world forever. At its centre is Birmingham, the world's first industrial city and the country's second largest metropolis, a thriving cultural centre filled with family attractions – Thinktank Museum of Science and Discovery, Cadbury World, the National Sea Life Centre and more.

This region is full of surprises, with numerous expanses of wonderful rolling countryside to explore, particularly in the counties of Shropshire, Herefordshire and Worcestershire and beautiful historic towns to visit, such as Hereford, Ludlow, Shrewsbury and Worcester. Not forgetting, of course, Stratford-upon-Avon, birthplace of the country's most famous man of letters, William Shakespeare.

Day-trip itinerary

Morning: A quick whizz around Warwick Castle (pp.392–3). Hop on a train to Stratford-upon-Avon (10 miles away).
Lunch: Sandwiches and cakes at Bensons of Stratford (p.412).
Afternoon: Explore the Teddy Bear Museum (p.387). If the weather is fine, go for a cruise on the River Avon (p.385), otherwise take a bus tour (p.385).

Special events

April
Shrewsbury: Children's Book Festival
t (01743) 281200
Stratford-upon-Avon: Shakespeare's birthday
t (01789) 293127
May
Hereford: May Fair t (01432) 268430
Hay-on-Wye: Children's Festival t (0113) 230 4661
Ludlow Castle: Festival of Crafts t (01584) 873355
Shrewsbury: West Midlands Show t (01743) 281200
Warwick: Medieval Festival t 0870 442 2000
June
Ludlow: Shakespeare Festival t (01584) 875053
Royal Air Force Museum, Cosford: Royal Air Force Open Day t (01902) 376200
Shrewsbury: Carnival t (01743) 281200
Warwick: Carnival t (01926) 492212

Highlights
Animal fun, Twycross Zoo, p.394
Chocolatey fun, Cadbury World, pp.375–6
Civil War fun, Boscobel House, pp.390–1
Exploring, Hawkstone Park, p.400
Getting lost, Amazing Hedge Puzzle, Symonds Yat, p.387
Hands-on science, Thinktank Museum of Science and Discovery, Birmingham, p.377
Industrial Age fun, Ironbridge Gorge Museum, pp.398–9
Medieval fun, Warwick Castle, pp.392–3
Rollercoaster riding, Alton Towers, pp.401–2
Steam train fun, Shakespeare Express, p.377
Storytelling, Mythstories, Shrewsbury, pp.383–4
Water fun, Waterworld, Stoke-on-Trent, p.406

August
Eastnor Castle: Children's Fun Week
t (01531) 633160
Kenilworth: Town and Country Festival
t (024) 7669 6969
September
Ludlow: Ludlow Marches Food and Drink Festival
t (01584) 875053 www.foodfestival.co.uk
November
Ironbridge Gorge Museum: Traditional Bonfire Night celebrations t (01952) 432166

Birmingham

Getting there The city lies directly in the centre of the UK, making it accessible from virtually anywhere. By air: Birmingham International Airport is situated 8 miles southeast of the city centre and welcomes both transatlantic and European flights. By road: Birmingham is 60 miles from Manchester and about 100 miles from London, and can be reached via the M6, M1, M5, M40 and M42. By train: Birmingham New Street station is in the city centre. Trains depart regularly from London Euston, Bristol Temple Meads and Manchester. There is also a connection to the city's airport. By bus/coach: There are frequent connections from London Victoria, Bristol and Manchester **Tourist information** The Rotunda, 150 New Street **t** 0870 2250127 **www.beinbirmingham.com**

Birmingham has been undergoing a major face lift, which has done a lot to improve its image, although it's still not surprising that it's regularly voted the most unattractive city in the land. It is not really one of the country's greatest tourist assets. It is staggeringly ugly in parts and you'll find most people in England look down on the city. It was seemingly always thus. During the Industrial Revolution, when Birmingham was the brightest furnace burning in Britain's 'workshop of the world'; the city of a thousand trades, where everything from train tracks and guns to gold rings and chocolate bars was produced, it was still unable to command the capital's respect. Birmingham may have been making all the money but London still had the nation's parliament, the Royal family and all the fine buildings. London regarded Birmingham in much the same way that an aristocratic landowner of the time would have regarded a newly rich cotton-mill owner: as a vulgar, uncouth (but essentially useful) upstart. The twin evils of mass industrialization and extensive wartime damage, followed by some particularly hasty and unsympathetic redevelopment, have resulted in an architectural infrastructure that can most charitably be described as grimly functional. Combine this with some of the most crazy road planning to be found anywhere in the country (as exemplified by the infamous Spaghetti Junction, a knotted mess of tarmac made by the haphazard conjunction of the M5, M6 and M42 motorways) and you can

begin to understand why, for many, Birmingham will always be the last word in poor taste.

Birmingham is fighting back. It now has one of the most stylish department stores in the country. The futuristic Selfridges in the new Bull Ring would look at home in Milan or New York. It's covered in 15,000 aluminium discs and was inspired by a Paco Rabanne chain-mail dress. It's a good place to get kids thinking about architecture. You'll find every store you'll ever need in the centre or on the pedestrian streets that radiate off it. Large tracts of the city centre are car free, so it's easier to see and admire some of the huge 19th-century buildings in Victoria Square, which were built with the profits of the Industrial Revolution.

In terms of dining, there are plenty of cafés and restaurants in the centre of town but the food hall in Selfridges is the place to eat. Once you've seen the sushi, champagne and caviar bars that sit alongside the most mouth-watering cakes and pies, you won't be sniffy about Birmingham again.

Birmingham is Britain's second most populated city, which means that, unless there's some weird demographic anomaly at work, there are more children here than anywhere else outside London. This would certainly explain the city's impressive number of child-friendly attractions. In how many other cities can you take a steam train ride, stroll along a see-through tunnel past sharks and rays, wander through a tropical glasshouse, take a trip on a narrowboat and visit a chocolate factory all on the same day? The presence of so many families, whose future is clearly invested in the city, also goes some way to explaining the massive regeneration programme currently taking place here, seen to its best effect at the redeveloped canalside area at Brindleyplace, where the new National Sea Life Aquarium is located, and the soon-to-be-opened Millennium Point on the east side of the city.

It may not be beautiful (yet), it may not be inspiring, but Birmingham is actually a fun place. Despite, or perhaps because of, its endless winding stream of roads, Birmingham is not very car friendly and, if at all possible, you should try to come by train or coach. The main train station, New Street, where all the Intercity services arrive, is just one minute's walk from the pedestrianized Victoria Square which marks the city centre. The National Sea Life Centre, National Indoor Arena and Ikon Gallery, as well as the new Brindleyplace waterfront development (lots of pleasant bars and cafés), can be found to the west of the square alongside the Birmingham and Fazeley Canal while the Jewellery Quarter (Birmingham is still the country's leading producer of gold jewellery) is to the northwest.

Things to see and do

Birmingham Botanical Gardens and Glasshouses

Westbourne Road, Edgbaston **t** (0121) 454 1860
www.birminghambotanicalgardens.org.uk
Open Apr–Sept Mon–Sat 9–7, Sun 10–7; Oct–Mar Mon–Sat 9–5, Sun 10–5
Adm Mon–Sat: adults £6.10, children £3.60, under 5s **free**, family £18; summer, Sun and Bank Hols adults £6.40, children £3.60, under 5s **free**, family £19
Café, licensed pavilion restaurant overlooking main lawn, picnic area, shop, mother and baby facilities, guided tours, disabled access, on-site parking

In terms of the diversity of plant life on display, these gardens aren't as good as those at Kew or Edinburgh, but they're not far behind and are perhaps more child friendly than either of their more illustrious rivals. There are six hectares (15 acres) of lawns, flowerbeds (including banks of azaleas and rhododendrons) and trees to explore. You're free to wander where you want – there are no 'keep off the grass' signs – although you could also choose to follow the orienteering course, for which you'll need to pick up a map and a stamp card at the entrance. Use the map to find your way around a collection of marker points, where you can use the ink stamps provided to mark your card. Complete your card and you'll be awarded a prize. As with most botanic gardens, the highlights at Birmingham are definitely the swelteringly hot glasshouses, which are filled with a mass of lush, tropical plants – lilies, palms, banana, cocoa, dates, etc. It's like being in a real rainforest, especially when the sprinklers come on, filling the air with a light, drizzly mist. Try not to stand too near the nozzles unless you want to end up with some very soggy children. The gardens also contain numerous aviaries filled with exotic birds, a waterfall, a collection of tiny bonsai trees (always a big hit with children) and a pretty good adventure playground. Brass band concerts are given on the bandstand overlooking the main lawn on most Sundays during the summer. One of

the best times to visit is at Christmas when Santa himself is there and there are carol singers.

Birmingham Museum and Art Gallery

Chamberlain Square **t** (0121) 303 2834
www.bmag.org.uk
Open Mon–Thurs and Sat 10–5, Fri 10.30–5, Sun 12.30–5 **Adm Free**
Edwardian tearoom, shop, mother and baby facilities, guided tours, disabled access, loop system for the hard of hearing, wheelchair hire

Best known for its outstanding collection of pre-Raphaelite art (reputedly the world's largest), the museum also contains displays of silverware, jewellery and ceramics, as well as galleries devoted to natural history, archaeology and (best of all for kids) science with a number of hands-on experiments for them to try. Various activities for children, such as 'designing money' or 'learning to write hieroglyphics', are organized during the summer holidays. Family trail sheets are available and there are good themed guided tours on offer. There are family activities (art workshops, etc.) held every weekend (1–4pm) and daily (11–4) during school holidays.

Birmingham Nature Centre

Pershore Road, Edgbaston **t** (0121) 472 7775
Open Apr–Oct 10–5 (last admission 4pm); Nov–Mar Sat–Sun 10–4 **Adm** Adults £1.80, children **free**, 24 per cent discount to adults accompanying children under 5
Café, shop, mother and baby facilities, wheelchair access, on-site parking

This 2.5-hectare (6.5-acre) site is home to otters, beavers, foxes, lynxes, deer, snowy owls and other creatures living in a mixture of indoor and outdoor enclosures. There's a special Lilliput Village for under 5s with rabbits, guinea pigs, pygmy goats, ducks and a play area.

★Cadbury World

Linden Road, Bournville **t** 0845 4503599
www.cadburyworld.co.uk
Getting there Off the A38 on A4040 ring road; follow the brown and white tourist signs. Trains run to Bournville Station from Birmingham New Street or you can catch one of buses no.83, 84 or 85 from Birmingham city centre
Open Daily 9–5
Adm Adults £12.50, children £9.50, under 4s **free**, family (2+2) £39, (2+3) £47 (booking recommended)

Self-service restaurant, chocolate shop, wheelchair access to most of the factory apart from the packaging plant, on-site parking, audio guides

Surely this must be every child's dream come true: the chance to tour a real chocolate factory just like Charlie. Before you let the youngsters get too excited, however, it's worth bearing in mind that, though very enjoyable in its own way, Cadbury World doesn't quite live up to the Willie Wonka-esque heights of Roald Dahl's classic tale. Not only is there a distinct lack of strange, magical creatures stirring big vats of bubbling liquid, but you're not even allowed to watch the chocolate-making machines in action. You can take a tour of the packaging plant to see chocolate bars being wrapped (this, in itself, can be a bit hit-and-miss as the plant is by no means constantly operational) but you can't help feeling that, by being denied entry to the inner sanctum in this manner, you're somehow missing out on the best bit. These caveats aside, Cadbury World does provide a very enjoyable and surprisingly informative day out. You can learn all about how, in the 16th century, the Spanish Conquistadors discovered the Aztecs and Mayans of South America eating a strange, bitter substance made from cocoa plants – kids may be surprised to find out that chocolate in its raw state doesn't taste sweet or even particularly nice – which they brought back to Europe where, mixed with sugar to suit the more delicate European palates, it was soon all the rage in the royal courts. It remained a luxury treat until the 19th century when a Birmingham Quaker family, the Cadburys, decided to build a chocolate factory with the intention of providing cheap mass-produced chocolate for the working classes. As avid advocates of temperance reform, they hoped their confectionery would become an alternative treat to alcohol in the diet of the poor (better fat than drunk seems to have been their logic in those days before obesity). Such was the success of the family's chocolate bars (with both drinkers and non-drinkers) that they were soon able to open up other factories and, by the 20th century, had established a chocolate empire. After the history, it'll be time to move on to the more interactive and child-friendly areas to meet the giant creme-egg characters, play on the chocolate-themed climbing equipment and ride through the chocolate world of 'Cadabra' in a cocoa bean-shaped car – all the while munching on free chocolate bars. You can watch luxury chocolates being carefully hand-made and, while kids stuff themselves silly, parents can wallow in the nostalgia of old sweet wrappers and TVs showing a constant stream of vintage adverts.

Cinemas and theatres *See pp.406, 408*

Museum of the Jewellery Quarter
75–79 Vyse Street **t** (0121) 554 3598
www.bmag.org.uk
Open Tues–Sun and Bank Hols 11.30–4
Adm Free
Café, shop, mother and baby facilities, guided tours, wheelchair access

In the mid 19th century, Birmingham was the world's largest jewellery producer and, even if this trade has declined somewhat in recent decades, its famous and historic Jewellery Quarter is still thriving. At this excellent museum you can visit a preserved jewellery factory (not as glamorous as you might think, with workers crowded into tiny spaces producing an endless stream of earrings, brooches and rings) and see displays on the growth and decline of the trade.

★National Sea Life Centre
The Water's Edge, Brindleyplace **t** (0121) 643 6777
www.sealife.co.uk
Open Daily 10–6 (last admission 5)
Adm Adults £9.95, children £6.95, under 4s **free**,
Café, shop, mother and baby facilities, guided tours, disabled access

If it's not the best sea life centre in the country, then it's a strong contender. It's the first of the generally excellent chain to be located inland and the first to feature a completely transparent underwater tunnel offering 360° views of its vast ocean tanks, where sharks, rays and other exotic creatures surround you on all sides. Though very hi-tech, with lots of interactive computer screens and a replica of the *Titanic*, which you visit in a 'mini-sub', it's the spectacular sea creatures – and there are more than 3,000 here on display – that are still very much the main attraction. Many of these are perhaps best categorized under the heading 'beautiful but deadly': tiny green poison arrow frogs, intricately camouflaged stone fish, puffy-faced porcupine fish and, most deadly (and beautiful) of all, lion fish, which have so many fins and spines that they look like rather spiky, crumpled silk scarves. There's also a touch-pool, where kids can get interactive with the weird-looking rays and a soft play area for under 5s.

Parties Afloat

Gas Street **t** (0121) 236 7057
Open Easter–Oct Sat–Sun and Bank Hols; school holidays daily **Fares** Various prices
Sightseeing trips with commentary.

Second City Boats

Gas Street Basin **t** (0121) 2399811
Open Daily **Fares** Various prices
Take a canal trip from Gas Street Basin or Holiday Wharf. Birmingham is said to have more canals than Venice although they're not quite so charming – warbling gondoliers tend to be a bit thin on the ground in the Midlands. The city's waterways do provide a great way of seeing the city. The newly redeveloped waterfront areas at Brindleyplace, the Water's Edge and Mailbox are the most visible evidence of Birmingham's recent revitalization and have, together, brought a real fizz and excitement to the area. Trips last 1 hour 90 minutes, 2 hours or a day and can include a waterside city tour combined with a visit to the Sea Life Centre, Black Country Museum or Cadbury World.

The Shakespeare Express

Snow Hill Station **t** (0121) 708 4960
www.vintagetrains.co.uk
Open Jul–Sept every Sun, rest of year some Suns
Fares Single: adults £10, children £5, under 5s **free**
Some disabled access
The fastest steam trains (50-minute journeys) between Birmingham Snow Hill Station and Stratford-upon-Avon (pp.384–5) every Sunday in the summer.

Sherbourne Wharf Heritage Narrowboats

Sherbourne Street **t** (0121) 455 6163
www.sherbournewarf.co.uk
Open Easter–Oct daily 11.30–4; rest of the year: weekends only **Adm** Call for prices
Sightseeing cruises with commentary on board a historic narrowboat. 'Search for Santa' trips (weekends) from late November until Christmas.

Shopping

The main shopping area is largely pedestrianized and has every shop you'll ever need. The new Bull Ring shopping centre is the thing to see, especially the swanky new Selfridges department store. The Bull Ring is also home to Boots the Chemist, a large Borders bookshop, Claire's Accessories for yet another pair of earrings, Gap and H&M for kids' clothes, the Early Learning Centre and Lego store for toys and the list goes on.

Sport and activities *See pp.403–6*

Thinktank Museum of Science and Discovery

Millennium Point, Curzon Street **t** (0121) 202 2222
www.thinktank.ac
Open Daily 10–5 (last admission 4)
Adm Museum only: adults £6.95, children £4.95, under 3 **free**, family (2+2) £20; IMAX only: adults £6.50, children £4.50; Planetarium: £1 extra per person. Museum and IMAX: adults £11, children £8
Café, gift shop, disabled access
A modern museum where science and history come to life. There are special exhibits on the machines that made Birmingham an industrial powerhouse, which show how getting about was made easier by the development of the steam engine and later planes. Medicine and Biology are also covered in an easily accessible hands-on way. A special kids' club organizes activities, including sleepovers. There are family events every weekend and during school holidays. The museum also charts the history of Birmingham, while in the 'Kids in the City' gallery, under 7s can find out what it's like to do a job like Mum and Dad. Then look into the future and see how we'll be living when the kids are grown up. It's also the home of Birmingham's IMAX cinema and a brand-new planetarium with regular family shows and events.

Tyseley Locomotive Works

Warwick Road, Tyseley **t** (0121) 707 4960
www.vintagetrains.co.uk
Getting there 3 miles south of the city centre off the A41 Warwick Road
Open Sat–Sun 10–4, some Bank Hols
Adm Call for details
On-site parking, shop
Steam train rides along a short stretch of line are given (call for details). There are also numerous static locomotives to admire as well as a restored workshop.

Walking tours

Graveyard and ghost tours of the city take place all year (adults £5, children £3). Contact the tourist office.

Around Birmingham

Black Country Living Museum, 10 miles west (pp.397–8)
Dudley Zoo and Castle, 10 miles west (p.394)
National Motorcycle Museum, 8 miles southeast (p.407)

Bridgnorth

Getting there By road: Bridgnorth is on the A458 between Shrewsbury and Birmingham. By train: The nearest station is in Wolverhampton, 16 miles away; trains run direct from Birmingham every 15–20 minutes. By bus/coach: There are good bus connections with Wolverhampton (no.890), Shrewsbury and Kidderminster
Tourist office Listley Street, Bridgnorth **t** (01746) 763257 www.virtual-shropshire.co.uk

Bridgnorth, a picturesque, rather striking town near the Shropshire–Staffordshire border, has a small but very decent collection of attractions (most notably, the Severn Valley Railway which runs between here and Kidderminster) that make it well worth a visit. The town itself is split into two levels: the Low Town, which sits on the banks of the River Severn, and the older High Town, which can be reached either by climbing 185 stone steps or (much more fun) aboard Britain's steepest and oldest funicular cliff railway (first opened in 1892), which runs between Castle Walk and Bank Street. High Town has lovely gardens (offering great views of the Severn Valley countryside) surrounding the tilting remains of the town's medieval castle, which was largely destroyed during the Civil War. The High Street, which is also located, appropriately enough, in High Town, is where you'll find the tourist office, the Town Hall (which sits on a wooden arch in the middle of the street) and the Costume and Childhood Museum, **t** (01746) 764636, which has a wide range of antique toys and dolls, as well as a complete Victorian nursery.

Things to see and do

Bridgnorth Cliff Railway

Castle Terrace **t** (01746) 762052
www.bridgnorthcliffrailway.co.uk
Open Summer: Mon–Sat 8–8, Sun 12–8; winter: Mon–Sat 8–6.30, Sun 12–6.30

Can you spot?
Lavington's Hole, a small tunnel cut into Castle Hill. It was dug by the parliamentary forces during the Civil War when Bridgnorth was held by royalist troops, the intention being to fill it with explosives and then blow the hill (and the Royalists perched on top of it) up. Luckily for the town, the Royalists surrendered before the hole was complete.

Fares 80p return, under 6s **free**
This jaunty funicular, which links the Low Town to the High Town, is the country's oldest.

Cinemas and theatres *See* pp.406, 408

Dudmaston

Dudmaston, Quatt, Bridgnorth, Shropshire **t** (01746) 780866 www.nationaltrust.org.uk
Getting there 4 miles southeast of Bridgnorth on the A442
Open House: Apr–Sept Tues, Wed, Sun and Bank Hols; 2–5.30; garden: Apr–Sept Mon–Wed and Sun 12 noon–6 **Adm** House and garden: adults £5, children £2,50, under 5s **free**, family £5; garden: adults £2, children **free**
Café, shop, disabled access, on-site parking, baby changing facilities

There are no specific attractions here, no adventure playgrounds, mazes or show farms, nothing to match the array of entertainments on offer at somewhere like Chatsworth. Rather, the joy of Dudmaston comes from sampling the simpler pleasures of life – walking through meadows and woods, playing on neatly manicured lawns, climbing trees, collecting acorns and watching swans swimming on the lake. The gardens surrounding the 17th-century mansion house are a real walker's paradise with trails leading off hither and thither – through the Dingle (an area of damp woodland), around the lake and out into the far reaches of the estate; the longest is a good five miles. The house itself contains a collection of 17th-century flower portraits that once belonged to Francis Darby of Coalbrookdale.

Ray's Farm Country Matters

Billingsley, Bridgnorth **t** (01299) 841255
www.raysfarm.com
Getting there 5 miles south of Bridgnorth, off the B4363
Open Feb Sat–Sun and half term 10–5.30, Mar–Oct daily 10–5.30, Nov Sat–Sun (no farm walks) 10–4

Adm Adults £5.50, children £4, under 2s **free**;
Nov **free** for all
Refreshments, gift shop, picnic area, guided tours, on-site parking , some disabled access

A country farm that actually feels properly countryish. There are no play areas or toy tractors here. Instead, kids will have to make do with living, natural attractions and, in particular, the assorted sheep, horses, deer and llama, who have made the farm their home. Santa visits in December. Adjoining the site is a delightful woodland walk decorated with various carved creatures designed to represent the 'Spirit of the Woods'.

Severn Valley Country Park

Avaley **t** (01746) 781192
Getting there About 6 miles south of Bridgnorth. Follow the signs from the A442
Open Park: daily dawn–dusk; visitor centre: Apr–Oct Wed–Sun 12 noon–5; Nov–Mar Wed–Sun 11–4 **Adm Free** (including car park)
On-site parking, tea shop (at weekends)

A scenic country park spread out over both banks of the River Severn with numerous pushchair-friendly marked trails including a woodland trail, a riverside trail, a history trail and a poetry trail on which you are encouraged to write a poem that will then be laminated by the visitor centre and posted on a display board along the trail. The park also offers good views of the puffing steam trains of the Severn Valley Railway.

★Severn Valley Railway

The Railway Station, Bewdley **t** (01299) 403816
www.svr.co.uk
Open May–Sept daily, rest of year weekends
Adm Day return ticket with unlimited travel Bridgnorth–Kidderminster: adults £11.80, children £5.90, under 5s **free**
Parking available at Bridgnorth and Kidderminster stations, train buffet and bar facilities, gift shops; specially converted carriages are available for groups of up to 15 visitors in wheelchairs

Steam train trips through the forested country-side between Bridgnorth in Shropshire and Kidderminster in Worcestershire passing over the 61m/200ft-high Victoria Bridge on the way. The journey takes just over an hour and involves stopping at seven stations, each restored to look as it would have done during the heyday of steam

with period advertisements and posters adorning the walls. Kidderminster Station has a collection of railway memorabilia and a miniature railway (rides are given on weekends) while at Country Park Hall you can get off for a walk and a picnic in the beautiful Severn Valley Country Park.

Sport and activities *See pp.403–6*

Walking tours

Depart from tourist office
Open Apr–Oct Fri and Sat 2.15pm
Adm Adults £2, children £1

The tourist office can provide details of various guided tours of the town.

Around Bridgnorth

Long Mynd, 18 miles west (pp.402–3)
Shrewsbury, 20 miles northwest (pp.382–4)

Hereford

Getting there By road: Hereford is 140 miles from London, 58 miles from Birmingham, 52 miles from Stratford-upon-Avon and 26 miles from Worcester and is reachable via the A38, the A49 and the A4103. By train: Hereford Station is served by Birmingham New Street Station and London Paddington. By bus/coach: National Express operate services to Hereford from London and Birmingham
Tourist office 1 King Street **t** (01432) 268430
www.visitorlinks.com

A deeply traditional market town at the heart of a deeply traditional farming region, Hereford's main industry is the same today as it was 200 years ago – cider production – and there's still a lively livestock and general produce market held here every Wednesday, which is the only time this otherwise rather sleepy town really comes to life (at the markets, look out for the white-faced Hereford Cattle, the town's most famous export). The town lies on the banks of the River Wye – Bishop's Meadow, across the town's Victorian suspension bridge, is particularly good for walks and picnics – and its architecture is principally Georgian, albeit with a few medieval interludes, most notably the magnificent cathedral.

Things to see and do

Cider Museum and King Offa's Distillery

Pomona Place, Whitecross Road **t** (01432) 354207
www.cidermuseum.co.uk
Open Tues–Sat and Bank Hols Jan–Mar 11–3,
Apr–Oct 10–5, Nov–Mar 12 noon–4
Adm Adults £3, children £2, under 5s **free**
Café, souvenir shop, disabled access, on-site parking

Ask anyone to name the drink they most associate with Herefordshire and the chances are they
will say cider. The image of the country worker
chomping on a corn stork in between gulps of
industrial-strength cider has become an icon of
Englishness, as familiar as cricket on the village
green and bicycling bobbies. At Hereford's Cider
Museum you are taken on a whistle-stop tour
through the history of cider-making on which
you'll see the cider cells with their huge oak vats,
the press house and beam presses, a recreated
cooper's (barrelmaker's) workshop and a working
cider-brandy (also known as 'applejack') distillery.
You can also visit the enormous, modern
Poulner's Cider Mill to watch bottles of cider
happily trundling off the production line.

Cinemas and theatres *See* pp.406, 408

Guided walks

The tourist office can provide details of the
daily guided walks of the city given by members
of the Hereford Guild of Guides in summer.
Scenic coach tours of the local countryside are
also available.

Hereford Cathedral

Cathedral Close **t** (01432) 374200
www.herefordcathedral.org
Open Cathedral: daily 7.30–5.30 (Sun until 3.30);
Mappa Mundi and Chained Library Exhibition:
Mon–Sat 10–4.30, Apr–Oct also Sun 11–3.30
Adm Cathedral free; *Mappa Mundi* and Chained
Library Exhibition: adults £4.50, children £3.50,
under 5s **free**, family (1+3) £6 (2+3) £10
Café, souvenir shop, guided tours
*Please note: Tower closed for refurbishment until
further notice.*

Hereford's red sandstone cathedral, which sits
in grounds overlooking the River Wye, is something of an architectural hotchpotch with arches
that date back to Norman times, a 14th-century
tower (there are good views from the top) and
numerous 19th-century adornments. Its most
treasured possession is the extraordinary *Mappa
Mundi*, a 13th-century map of the world showing
Jerusalem lying at the heart of a flat earth with
England hovering at its outer extremities. In the
1980s, when the cathedral was in urgent need of
repair, it was thought that the map might have to
be sold. However, thanks to a massive fundraising
effort (which resulted in a multi-million-pound
donation by the American philanthropist John
Paul Getty Junior), the money was found to keep
the map at the cathedral and it now resides in a
purpose-built exhibition centre. The map is an
encyclopedia of history, geography and the
animal kingdom. Kids usually like the way the
map is wildly inaccurate, but to get the best out
of it, they'll need to know their Old Testament.
There's a family funday every August. The centre
also houses the world's largest medieval Chained
Library (so named because the books are literally
chained to the shelves) holding some 1,500 works
dating from the 8th to the 14th century.

The Old House

High Town **t** (01432) 260694
Open Apr–Sept Tues–Sat 10–5, Sun and Bank Hols
10–4; Oct–Mar Tues–Sat 10–5 **Adm Free**
Souvenir shop

Archetypal Jacobean black-and-white house
furnished throughout in authentic 17th-century
style. There's a wonderful children's corner with
books, games and dressing-up clothes.

Shopping

The pedestrianized High Town is the city's focal
point and main shopping area, although it now
faces stiff competition from the new Left Bank
Village shopping complex overlooking the river.
Mothercare is in the Orchard Shopping Centre
while Adams for kids' clothes is in the Maylord
Centre; otherwise shopping is a bit dull.

Sport and activities *See* pp.403–6

Waterworks Museum

Broomy Hill **t** (01432) 344062
www.waterworksmuseum.org.uk
Open In steam: Easter–Aug last Sunday of
month and Bank Hols 2–5; no steam: Easter–Sept
Tues 11–4
Adm Adults £3, children £1
*On-site parking, disabled access, adapted toilets,
refreshments*

See the huge pump engines of this former Victorian pumping station 'in steam'. Children's quiz sheets and colouring cards availalble.

Around Hereford

Eastnor Castle, 10 miles east (p.391)
Shortwood Family Farm, 8 miles north (p.396)
Symonds Yat, 15 miles south (p.387)

Ludlow

Getting there By road: The town lies near the border of England and Wales, 30 miles west of Birmingham, about 160 miles from London and 20 miles from Hereford, just off the A49. By train: There are regular connections between Ludlow and Shrewsbury or Hereford. By bus: Service no.435 runs to Ludlow from both Shrewsbury and Hereford about every two hours
Tourist office Located in the 19th-century Assembly Rooms on Castle Street **t** (01584) 875053 **www.ludlow.org.uk**

The presence of more than 500 listed buildings – including numerous half-timbered Jacobean structures – makes Ludlow, on the banks of the River Teme, one of the prettiest towns in the Midlands; prettier even than pretty Shrewsbury 30 miles to the north. Its dominant feature is its castle, built in the 11th century by the Normans to control the Welsh, which adjoins the Market Square lying at the heart of a grid of medieval streets. Broad Street boasts the greatest number of historic buildings with plenty of well-preserved Tudor and Georgian examples on display and it's also where you'll find the Broadgate, the remnants of the town's medieval wall. The Linney Riverside park, beneath the castle, is a good spot for a picnic and a stroll, while the Ludlow Assembly Rooms organizes children's activities in the school holidays and contains an arts centre and cinema. The famous Ludlow Festival, when Shakespeare plays are performed in the open air at the castle, takes place in late June–early July every year while the slightly less well-known Ludlow Marches Food and Drink Festival (look out for the sausage-making competition) kicks off during the second week of September.

Can you spot?
The Feathers Hotel on the Bull Ring between Corve Street and Old Street, a very handsome 16th-century inn adorned with grotesque wooden gargoyles. Also look out for the jolly misericords (carving under the seats in the choir) in St Lawrence's Church representing mermaids and barmaids.

Things to see and do

Cinemas and theatres See pp.406, 408

★Ludlow Castle

Castle Square **t** (01584) 873355
www.ludlowcastle.com
Getting there In the centre of Ludlow town; the train station is 2 minutes' walk away
Open Jan Sat–Sun 10–4, Feb–Mar and Oct–Dec daily 10–4, Apr–Jul and Sept daily 10–5, Aug daily 10–7 **Adm** Adults £4, children £2, under 6s **free**, family (2+4) £11
Picnic areas, disabled access, gift shop

Although largely ruined, there's still enough of Ludlow Castle left to provide a good afternoon's worth of entertainment. Constructed in the 12th century along classic motte and bailey lines – the town's people would have sought shelter within the castle walls in the event of an attack – the castle became a royal palace in the 14th century, a seat of government under Edward IV (it was also where his son, the unfortunate Edward V, lived prior to his imprisonment in the Tower of London) and, in the 16th century, was the home of Prince Arthur, the brother of Henry VIII, and his wife Catherine of Aragon (who would later marry, and of course, be divorced by, Henry following Arthur's death), before being abandoned in the early 18th century. It has remained uninhabited ever since with the result that much of it is, as you would expect, in a pretty poor state of repair – the moat, for instance, has long since disappeared. Nonetheless, all its major walls are standing and, even after nearly 300 years of neglect, it's still an impressive and monumental structure with lots of interesting places for kids to examine and explore – low doors, tiny rooms, fireplaces, arrowslit windows, spiral staircases, etc. You can climb the gatehouse to the battlements for impressive views out over the River Teme and picnic on the rolling lawns that surround the site.

Henry VIII and the Reformation

Did you know that in the 16th century it was against church law for a man to marry his brother's widow? In order to marry Catherine of Aragon (his brother Arthur's widow), Henry VIII had to get special permission from the Pope in Rome who, at that time, was the head of the English church (England being a Catholic country). When Henry decided (after several years of marriage) that he no longer wanted to be married to Catherine but wanted to marry Anne Boleyn instead, he argued that the Pope had been wrong to grant his permission for the union and that his marriage to Catherine should therefore be annulled. When the Pope refused, Henry declared that the Pope was no longer the head of the English church and that he, Henry, had now taken over and had furthermore (surprise, surprise) decided to award himself a divorce so that he could marry Anne (and another four wives after her). Allowing Henry to skip from wife to wife wasn't the only consequence of his break from papal authority. It kickstarted an entire religious revolution known as the 'Reformation' that led to England becoming a Protestant country and to its parliament conjuring up lots of anti-Catholic laws, most of which weren't repealed until the 19th century – some are, amazingly, still in place; even today, the Monarch cannot be a practising Catholic (or, for that matter, marry one). Henry also used the Reformation as an excuse to break up many of the country's Catholic religious orders and to seize the wealth and land of the abbeys and monasteries where they lived.

If you want to learn a little about the history of the place, you should pick up an audio guide and children's leaflet, as there's a distinct lack of information boards. Lots of events are organized at the castle throughout the summer including typically historical fare like battle re-enactments and Shakespeare plays, as well as a few more specifically child-orientated activities – facepainting and conker championships, for instance.

Ludlow Museum

Castle Street **t** (01584) 875384
Open Easter–Oct Mon–Sat 10.30–1 and 2–5, Jun–Aug also Sun **Adm Free**
Café, souvenir shop, disabled access

The town's history from the Middle Ages until the present day.

Shopping

Ludlow Market has been held every week on Castle Square for the past 800 years and is a great source of homemade cakes and cheeses, as well as antiques and crafts (open Mon, Fri and Sat 9–5, Easter–Sept and Dec and Wed). Also look out for the Red Balloon Family Bookshop, 4 Old Street, **t** (01584) 872149. Otherwise, for a big shop you'll need to drive to Shrewsbury or Birmingham.

Sport and activities *See* pp.403–6

Walking tours

Depart from the cannon by the castle entrance **t** (01584) 874205
Open Easter–Sept Sat–Sun 2.30pm, daily during Ludlow Festival

Guided tours of the city led by members of the Ludlow Historical Research Group. The tourist office can also provide details of walks on the nearby Long Mynd (pp.402–3). There's some excellent biking country around Ludlow (p.403 for cycle hire details).

Around Ludlow

Berrington Hall, 7 miles south (p.390)
Secret Hills, Shropshire Discovery Centre, 7 miles northwest (p.407)
Stokesay Castle, 6 miles northwest (p.392)

Shrewsbury

Getting there By road: The town lies 35 miles from Birmingham, 40 miles from Hereford and can be reached via the A49 and the A5. By train: Regular direct trains from Birmingham and Hereford. By bus/coach: National Express runs services from London, Birmingham and Hereford to Shrewsbury
Tourist information The Music Hall, The Square **t** (01743) 281200 www.shrewsburyguide.info

There can be few other towns whose shape is so clearly defined by water as Shrewsbury. It's almost entirely encircled by a looping meander of the River Severn. In fact, the river would only have to change course by a few hundred yards to turn the town into an island – and, in late 2000, with the rain beating down and much of the town under several feet of water, it seemed as if it was threatening to do exactly that. Historically, the town's geographic isolation has at least made it easy to defend against attack; something which

Can you spot?

The statue of Shrewsbury's most famous son, Charles Darwin, which stands outside the library across the road from the castle. Darwin was the man who first came up with the theory of evolution, which postulated that every living species was the result of natural selection over millions of years rather than divine creation. When the idea of erecting a memorial to the great Victorian scientist was first mooted in the late 19th century, the spire of St Mary's Church fell down prompting the vicar to proclaim that it was a message from God warning the towns-people not to celebrate such heresy. The townspeople decided that it was probably the result of dry rot and built one anyway.

both the Normans (who built a castle here) and King Charles I (who hid here during the Civil War) were quick to pick up on (although, strangely, not the Romans, who had their base at nearby Wroxeter (p.393). Inhabited since the 5th century, Shrewsbury really came into its own in the late Middle Ages when it grew rich on the back of a thriving wool trade with nearby Wales and, by the 18th century, had become very well-to-do indeed, its famous public school educating a steady stream of high society offspring. Although its status has diminished slightly in recent centuries, it remains affluent, prosperous and rather posh, an exclusive enclave whose isolation protects it now, not against attack, but against encroach-ments by the modern world. A huge proportion of Shrewsbury's architecture was built in previous centuries with many Tudor, Jacobean and Georgian buildings lining the picturesque cobbled streets that still follow the rather higgledy-piggledy medieval layout. There are some 600 historic buildings here which means that many of Shrewsbury's modern shops, cafés and pubs occupy listed premises (when was the last time you saw a McDonald's occupying a medieval building?). As with many old towns, Shrewsbury's heart is still its market square (a daily fruit 'n' veg and general produce market is now held in the Elizabethan Market Hall over-looking the square), radiating out from which are various roads bearing the name of the trade practised there in medieval times – Fish Street, Butcher Row, Milk Street, etc. – although where Gullet Passage and Grope Lane got their names from is anyone's guess.

Shrewsbury's strange, olde-worlde appearance, with its dark, explorable alleys, known as 'shuts', shooting off from the main streets hither and thither, should greatly appeal to children. There's a signposted trail leading you past many of the town's more interesting buildings including St Mary's Church, one of the three tallest churches in England (the cast-iron holding its stained glass in position was produced at nearby Ironbridge, p.398); Rowley's House Museum, which contains displays on the Romans, medieval and modern Shrewsbury; Clive House (on College Hill), the former home of derring-do British statesmen and former Shrewsbury mayor, Clive of India and, guarding the only land approach to the town, the town's sandstone castle, which now houses the Shropshire Regimental Museum.

The town's considerable archaic beauty is enhanced each year by the famous Shrewsbury flower show, which is centred on the lovely river-side Quay Park occupying the town's southwest corner. Many of the town's homes and businesses join in with their own ornate flower box displays.

Things to see and do

Boat trips

Porthill Bridge, The Quarry t (01743) 365849
Open May–Oct 11.30–5.30
Adm Call for prices

Sightseeing boat trips and row boats and canoes for hire are on offer from Riverking.

Cinemas and theatres *See pp.406, 408*

Guided tours

t (01743) 281200
Open May–Sept daily, Oct Mon–Sat 2.30pm
Adm Adults £2, children £1

These historical tours of the town leave from outside the tourist office in the Square.

★Mythstories

Morgan Library, Aston Street, Wem, north of Shrewsbury t (01939) 235500 www.mythstories.com
Open Apr–Aug Mon–Fri 2.30–6.30, Sept–Nov Sat–Sun 11–4 **Adm Free**
Café

A strange but rather charming place dedicated to myths, fables and legends – Egyptian folk tales, Indian epics, Canadian hunting stories, ancient Greek myths and even local legends. Although there are lots of pictures and the odd bit of interactivity – children can crawl through the reeds of a pretend pond to retrieve some animal stories – this is essentially a series of reading rooms with the majority of stories displayed on boards on the wall or in the volumes of the medieval-style chained library. It's quite heartening to see groups of children sitting in silent contemplation of the latest opus – many of which have been suggested by local schoolchildren – and to realize that, even today, not every form of kids' entertainment needs to make an electronic beeping sound.

There are occasional live storytellings and children can browse the centre's website and even contribute their own story or provide an illustration for an existing one.

Shrewsbury Museum and Art Gallery
Barker Street, Shrewsbury t (01743) 361196
Open Jan–Sept Mon–Sat 10–5, Sun 10–4; Sept–Dec Tues–Sat 10–4
Adm Free
Souvenir shop

Contains displays on the local history of the region including numerous items recovered from the nearby Roman settlement of Wroxeter (p.393), as well as a costume gallery and a medieval gallery.

Shopping
Full of old-world charm, Shrewsbury is a pleasant place to shop. Start at the Charles Darwin Centre, where you'll find Woolworths, Mothercare, Boots, Gamezone and Marks and Spencer.

Shrewsbury Castle and Shropshire Regiment Museum
Castle Gates, Shrewsbury t (01743) 358516
Open Jan–mid-Sept Tues–Sat 10–5 and Sun 10–4, mid-Sept–Dec Tues–Sat 10–4 **Adm** Adults £2.50, children **free**
Souvenir shop, disabled access

Small military museum set in the town's 12th-century castle (which was largely rebuilt in the 18th century). It's surrounded by very pleasant gardens.

Sport and activities See pp.403–6

Around Shrewsbury
Long Mynd, 10 miles south (pp.402–3)
Wroxeter Roman City, 5 miles southeast (p.393)

Stratford-upon-Avon

Getting there By road: Stratford is 20 miles from Birmingham, 80 miles from London and 10 miles from Warwick. By train: The best service direct to Stratford from London is from Paddington with Thames Trains; services also run from Birmingham via Warwick – you can catch the Shakespeare Express steam train from Birmingham Snow Hill Station every day in summer (*see* opposite). By bus/coach: National Express run services from Warwick and London Victoria
Tourist office Bridgefoot **t** 0870 1607930
www.shakespeare-country.co.uk. Ask for a copy of the leaflet 'Children's Stratford'

Stratford to most people, of course, means just one thing, William Shakespeare. This is where the country's most famous and celebrated dramatist was born, where he lived for twenty-odd years before moving to London and married, and where he returned later in life having made his fortune. The association has turned this small, pretty but otherwise unremarkable market town into one of the country's top tourist attractions, its streets welcoming in summer an almost ceaseless procession of coaches come to disgorge their Will-obsessed human cargo. Join the throng and take a tour through five of the buildings where Shakespeare spent much of his early and later life. Once you've seen how he lived, you can catch a performance of his work at one of the three theatres in Stratford operated by the Royal Shakespeare Company: the Royal Shakespeare Theatre, The Swan Theatre and The Other Place, all of which overlook an idyllic stretch of the River Avon (backstage tours).

Children, of course, can quickly overdose on Shakespeareana; one house should probably do it – Mary Arden's with its animals and hawk displays will probably prove the most popular. Thankfully, the town does boast alternative distractions when framed sonnets become too much to bear. There's a very good teddy bear museum (owned by the author and former MP Gyles Brandreth), full of furry favourites; a brass rubbing centre; and a Butterfly Farm with more than 1,500 free-flying butterflies. The Shire Horse Centre, where you can watch parades by the great shaggy beasts and meet friendly farmyard animals, is south of Stratford.

Things to see and do

Avon Cruises

Swan's Nest Lane **t** (01789) 267073
www.avon-boating.co.uk
Open Easter–Oct daily
Fares Guided cruises: adults £3, children £2; boat hire per hour: adults £2.50, children £1.50

Offers 30-minute guided river trips on motorized river launches plus punts and rowing boats for hire. You can jump on board a cruise at any point along its route. If you're lucky, you may even see boats being built back at the workshops.

Bus tours

t (01789) 294466 **www**.guidefriday.com
Open Tours daily 9–4
Fares Adults £9, children £4, family £22

1-hour-long open-top double-decker bus sightseeing tours of Stratford are run by Guide Friday.

Cinemas and theatres See pp.406, 408

Guided walks

Stratford Town Walks **t** (01798) 292478/293127
www.stratfordtownwalk.co.uk
Adm Adult £5, children £3

A variety of walks, including ghost walks every Monday, Thursday and Friday evening. Evening ghost cruises are also on offer.

Mary Arden's House

Station Road, Wilmcote **t** (01789) 204016
www.shakespeare.org.uk
Open Jun–Aug Mon–Sat 9.30–5, Apr–May and Sept–Oct Mon–Sat 10–5, Nov–Mar 10–4
Adm Adults £6, children £2.50, family £15
On-site parking, café, picnic area, shop, guided tours

The former home of the playwright's mother, this is perhaps the most child friendly of the five Shakespeare houses. There's a Victorian farm and you can see displays of falconry daily in summer.

Royal Shakespeare Company

Waterside **t** (01789) 403492 **www**.rsc.org.uk
Tour times Mon–Fri 1.30 and 5.30 (matinée days 11.30); Sat 11.30 and 5.30; Sun 12 noon and 1pm
Adm Adults £5, children and concs £4

These 45-minute tours of the Royal Shakespeare Company and Swan Theatre are available all year round – you can stand on the stage, watch the scenery being changed and see how the costume department gets the fake blood to look so realistic. The RSC puts on special children's productions every winter, but tickets need to be booked well in advance. RSC productions are usually excellent and, with a little bit of pre-performance explanation, kids as young as 10 can enjoy a good Shakespeare play.

The Shakespeare Express

Snow Hill Station **t** (0121) 708 4960
www.vintagetrains.co.uk
Open Jul–Sept every Sun, rest of year selected Sun
Fares Single: adults £10, children £5, under 5s **free**

The fastest steam trains in the land (50-minute journeys).
For more information see p.377

The Shakespeare Houses

The Shakespeare Birthplace Trust, the Shakespeare Centre, Henley Street **t** (01789) 204016
www.shakespeare.org.uk
Tours All five houses: adults £14, children £6.50, family ticket (2+3) £29

The Shakespeare Houses tour takes you around the five buildings in Stratford-upon-Avon where the bard spent much of his early and later life. These are the small house on Henley Street, where he was born in 1564 (decked out with period furniture, it contains an interactive display on his life and a garden planted with trees and flowers mentioned in the plays); the home of his mother, Mary Arden (there's a Victorian farm and falconry displays are given daily in the gardens); the thatched Tudor farmhouse where Will's bride Anne Hathaway lived; New Place, which in the early 17th century was one of the largest houses in Stratford and was bought by Will with wealth accrued in London (the building was destroyed in the 18th century although the foundations and Elizabethan knot garden survive) and Hall's Croft, the home of Dr John Hall, who married Shakespeare's daughter.

Shopping

Stratford is a good town to shop in. The main chain stores all have branches in town. Marks and Spencer and Mothercare are on Bridge Street. Daisy Chain on Red Lion Court has unusual toys and children's clothes.

Sport and activities See pp.403–6

Was Shakespeare really Shakespeare?

He's the most famous playwright in the world. His works have been staged and filmed more times than any other author and yet the man himself remains something of a mystery. Little documentary evidence of Shakespeare's life survives. It is known that he was born in Stratford-upon-Avon in 1564, the son of a local glovemaker; that at age 18 he married a local girl, Anne Hathaway and, in his mid twenties, moved to London. He became an actor and later a playwright before returning to live in Stratford at the end of his life, where he gave up writing to concentrate on business.

Beyond that, details are sketchy and many questions remain unanswered. Who, exactly, was Shakespeare? What prompted this working-class lad from the Midlands to seek his fortune in the theatres of Elizabethan London and, perhaps more intriguingly, where did he find the inspiration to write his collection of plays that are still being performed around the world 400 years later?

Very few personal documents relating to Shakespeare's private life have survived. There is not one single existing copy of a Shakespeare play or poem in his own handwriting. Indeed, he seems to have been strangely unconcerned with preserving his own work. His will contains no mention of any manuscripts or books (although it does mention his 'second best bed', which he left to his wife) and his works weren't even compiled into an anthology until 1623, some six years after his death. This has led some people to question whether the low-born man from the Midlands was indeed the same man responsible for some of the finest works in the English language. How, they ask, could a man with little education (Shakespeare's own father could neither read nor write) have transformed himself into a writer of such stature? Some have even argued that 'Shakespeare' was in fact a pseudonym used by one of the other (higher-born and better educated) men of letters of the time – Sir Francis Bacon and Christopher Marlowe have been put forward as possible alternatives.

The Marlowe theory would seem to be undermined by the small fact that Marlowe was actually murdered in a bar brawl early in Shakespeare's career. Conspiracy theories abound, however, and it has been claimed that Marlowe faked his own death in order to avoid being jailed for a criminal charge he was on at the time.

It is known that Marlowe was a close friend of Sir Thomas Walsingham, one of the most powerful men in the country and one of the few capable of arranging Marlowe's 'disappearance'. It should also be noted that Christopher Marlowe had worked as a spy for the government and so may have had other reasons for wanting to duck out of public view at the time.

Once officially declared dead, the conspiracy theorists believe that Marlowe, still wanting to continue working as a playwright, hired a young, jobbing actor on the London theatre scene called William Shakespeare to act as a front for his work, in the same way that blacklisted writers did in America in the 1950s.

Shakespeare and the English language

Shakespeare wasn't just a playwright, he was perhaps the single greatest linguistic innovator in the history of the English language who fundamentally changed the way English was written and spoken. He coined well over 2,000 words, many of which are still in use today. Everytime you're 'critical', tell a 'barefaced' lie or find something to be 'excellent', you have Shakespeare to thank. Mountaineers would never reach the 'summit', money-savers could never be 'frugal' and the wind would never 'gust' without Shakespeare's help. He was the first to 'castigate', 'hint' and 'hurry' and the first to describe things as 'monumental', 'majestic' or 'obscene'.

As a phrase-maker, he was even more influential: 'one fell swoop', 'my mind's eye', 'play fast and loose', 'to be in a pickle', 'more in sorrow than in anger', 'flesh and blood', 'cruel to be kind' – these are all phrases regularly uttered in everyday discourse that were first introduced to the language by the Bard of Avon.

Stratford Brass Rubbing Centre

The Royal Shakespeare Theatre Summer House, Avon Bank Gardens **t** (01789) 297671
www.stratfordbrassrubbing.co.uk

Open Summer: 10–6; winter: 11–4
Adm Free, each rubbing costs £1.95–£19.95 depending on size
Shop, garden, disabled access, on-site parking

Stratford-upon-Avon Butterfly Farm

Tramway Walk, Swan's Nest Lane **t** (01789) 299288
www.butterflyfarm.co.uk
Open Summer: 10–6; winter: 10–dusk
Adm Adults £4.95, children £3.95, family (2+2)
£14.95
Restaurant, shop, disabled access, on-site parking
   Europe's largest butterfly farm is also home to
an Insect City, full of stick insects, beetles and
leafcutter ants, as well as a spider-infested
Arachnoland (look out for tarantulas and giant
scorpions) in addition to the many tropical butterflies fluttering around the centre's rainforest and
waterfalls. There is also an adventure playground.

Teddy Bear Museum

19 Greenhill Street **t** (01289) 293160
www.theteddybearmuseum.com
Open Daily 9.30–5.30
Adm Adults £2.95, children £1.95, family (2+3) £9.50
Shop
   Thousands of bears (including Paddington and
Sooty) in a house that once belonged to Henry VIII.
Children's quiz sheets are available.

Around Stratford-upon-Avon

Ragley Hall, 7 miles west (p.392)
Stratford Shire Horse Centre, 2 miles southeast
(p.384)
Warwick Castle, 10 miles northeast (pp.392–3)

Symonds Yat

Getting there By road: Symonds Yat lies a few
miles from the Welsh border, 16 miles from
Hereford, 55 miles from Birmingham and 60 miles
from Oxford, and is reachable via the A40
between Monmouth and Ross-on-Wye. By train:
The nearest stations are either Hereford or
Gloucester; trains depart regularly from London
Paddington and Birmingham New Street to
Gloucester. By bus/coach: The no.38 bus runs
between Hereford and Gloucester, stopping at
Ross-on-Wye midway, from where you can catch
bus no.34 to Symonds Yat. Both buses run regularly
Tourist information Ross-on-Wye: Swan House,
Edde Cross Street **t** (01989) 562768
www.visitorlinks.com

   This famous beauty spot set on a bend of the
River Wye is divided into two parts: Symonds
Yat East and Symonds Yat West, which are
linked by an unusual hand-pulled rope ferry.
Though it's a touch touristy in places, and can
get very crowded in summer, it's an undeniably
beautiful place. So idyllic, in fact, that it even
attracts pairs of rare peregrine falcons, who
nest in holes in the rockface high up the side of
the river gorge. Bring a pair of binoculars and
you should be able to see them coming and
going between April and August. The RSPB has
even set up an observation area.
   There are views galore here – those from the
top of Yat Rock (Symonds Yat East) are particularly
impressive – and you can easily lose yourself for a
few hours on one of the many walks and nature
trails that traverse the area, wending your way
alongside the river and then deep into the heart
of the wooded gorge. If you really want to lose
yourself, you should head to Jubilee Park which, in
addition to its Chinese watergarden and fairytale-
themed adventure playground ('Fairytaleland'),
boasts a fiendishly difficult hedge maze planted
to commemorate the Queen's Silver Jubilee in
1977 and a museum of hedge-making history.
The great red ruins of the Norman Goodrich
Castle are a few miles north of the town.

Things to see and do

★Amazing Hedge Puzzle

Jubilee Park, Symonds Yat West, Ross-on-Wye
t (01600) 890360 **www.**mazes.co.uk
Open Jan–Feb and Nov–Dec 11–3.30, Mar and Oct
11–4.30, Apr–Sept 11–5.30 (peak times until 6.30)
Adm Adults £3.75, children £2.50, under 5s **free**
*Cafés, mother and baby facilities, disabled access,
on-site parking, puzzle and game shop*
   For some reason, England has, over time,
become the unofficial headquarters of the
hedge maze. While other countries are content
to have the odd maze here and there as a
novelty, the average Englander (especially the
average Englander with a bit of spare land)
seems to regard it as his or her patriotic duty to
cryptically arrange hedges. Every respectable
stately home has at least one small maze. To
find out a little bit more about this strange
obsession, and to try one of the country's best
mazes, you should visit the Amazing Hedge
Puzzle in the leafy surrounds of Symonds Yat.

At the Museum of the Maze, you can trace the history of the man-sized puzzle from the Minotaur's labyrinth in Ancient Greece passing through pagan-planting rituals to the medieval Crusader period (when mazes became symbols of Christian pilgrimage) and on to the 17th and 18th centuries when designing an intricate maze was considered the height of landscape gardening.

Afterwards, you can put the centre's skill to the test at its own maze, planted in 1977 to celebrate the Queen's Silver Jubilee. Laid out in a circular pattern, with tall hedges preventing any surreptitious peeking, it shouldn't take you more than 20 minutes to reach the centre, where there is a viewing platform allowing you to see how lost your companions are. Jubilee Park also contains an oriental water garden and a fairytale-themed adventure playground, **Fairytaleland**,t (01600) 890471 (**open** April–Oct 10–6, Nov–Mar 10–4).

Cinemas and theatres *See pp.406, 408*

Goodrich Castle

Goodrich, Ross-on-Wye **t** (01600) 890538
www.english-heritage.org.uk
Getting there 2 miles north of Symonds Yat off the A40
Open Mar–May and Sept–Oct daily 10–5, Jun–Aug daily 10–6, Nov–Feb Mon and Thurs–Sun 10–4
Adm Adults £4.50, children £2.30, under 5s **free**, family £11.30
Shop, free audio guide, on-site parking, café

On an August Bank Holiday, with the sun shining behind it, Goodrich Castle looks like nothing so much as Dracula's summer retreat: a jagged, sinister silhouette perched high on a rocky outcrop overlooking the River Wye. Built of great blocks of ruddy red sandstone in Norman times, it was laid siege to for four-and-a-half months in the Civil War, during which time great holes were knocked in its battlements by the locally made cannon 'Riotous Meg'. It's still one of the most complete medieval castles in Britain. Indeed, it has aged rather well, avoiding all the ghastly prettifying that was inflicted on the country's castles in the 18th and 19th centuries. There's a maze of small rooms, passageways and dungeons to explore, murder holes to peer through, towers to climb and grand views to be viewed. The free audio guide will help you get your bearings, while the free children's activity sheet will help to bring the place alive.

Did you know?
That the Peregrine Falcon is the fastest of all the birds of prey. It hunts by 'stooping', that is, dropping from a great height on to its prey, usually a small bird, which it kills by driving its claws in at speed. During the stoop, the falcon can reach speeds of up to 275mph. Peregrines are particularly fond of pigeons, which led, in the Second World War, to the government ordering a cull of the falcon, fearing the loss of carrier pigeons carrying vital messages.

Kingfisher Cruises

c/o The Saracens Head, Symonds Yat East
t (01600) 891063
Open Mar–Oct daily 11–6
Offers 45-minute sightseeing cruises with commentary along River Wye. Closes for winter.

Sport and activities *See pp.403–6*

Symonds Yat Canoe Hire

Symonds Yat West **t** (01600) 890883
Open Call for times
Hire From £7/hour (£18/day) for 1-person kayak, £8/hour (£25/day) for 2-person canoe
Hires out two-, three- or four-man Canadian canoes and one- or two-man kayaks for river trips.

Around Symonds Yat

Gloucester, 13 miles east (p.242–4)
Hereford, 15 miles north (p.379–85)

Worcester

Getting there By road: Worcester is 113 miles from London, 27 miles from Birmingham, 26 miles from Stratford-upon-Avon and 57 miles from Oxford, just off the M5 (J7) and can be reached via the A422, the A449, the A44, the A4103 and the A38. By train: Worcester's Shrub Hill station has links with London Paddington, while Foregate Street Station receives trains from Birmingham. By bus/coach: National Express coaches stop on the edge of the city where they connect with a city bus service taking passengers into the city centre; call County Bus Line **t** (0345) 125436. By boat: Worcester stands on the banks of the River Severn and Worcester–Birmingham Canal, some moorings available
Tourist information The Guildhall, High Street **t** (01905) 726311 **www.visitworcester.com**

Worcester lies on the east bank of the River Severn. Prone to floods – including some particularly comprehensive submergings in the autumn and winter of 2000 – the city has managed more or less successfully to restrict the amount of building alongside the river, which is flanked by meadows and fields and overlooked by the city's defining feature, its great medieval cathedral.

The river (when it's not flooded) affords plenty of opportunities for walking and boating. You can take sightseeing boat trips, hire rowing and motor boats and walk part of the Severn Way – the longest riverside walk in Britain – from Hallow to Topascope.

Despite the presence of a few half-timbered buildings, much of the town is modern and generic, although there are several nice parks – including Cripplegate Park, Gheluvelt Park and, on the edge of the city, the 60-hectare (140-acre) Worcester Woods Country Park.

A little bit of history

During the Civil War, Worcester was on the side of Charles I and the Royalists (also known as 'Cavaliers', the ones with long hair and colourful clothes) and witnessed two bloody battles, the second of which, 'the Battle of Worcester', finally won the war for the parliamentary forces (also known as 'Roundheads', the ones with short hair and simple, black and white clothes). After this defeat, the future King Charles II was forced into hiding in France by way of Boscobel House in Shropshire (pp.390–1). In recognition of its loyalty, Worcester was given the name 'The Faithful City' after the monarchy was restored in 1660 and has remained avowedly monarchical ever since. Its 18th-century Guildhall is a veritable monument to royalty with a façade adorned with carved likenesses of Charles I, Charles II and Queen Anne, as well as one of Oliver Cromwell, the leader of the Roundheads, shown hung up by his ears.

Things to see and do

Bickerline River Trips
South Quay **t** (01905) 831639
Depart Mar–Oct daily every hour 11–5
Adm Adults £4.50, under 12s £2.25, under 3s **free**
Offers 45-minute sightseeing trips along the River Severn.

Cinemas and theatres *See pp.406, 408*

City Museum and Art Gallery
Foregate Street **t** (01905) 25371
Open Mon–Fri 9.30–5.30, Sat 9.30–5
Adm Free
Café, disabled access
Organizes art workshops; 'Big Art for Little People' for 3–6 and 6–9-year-olds, and 'First Marks' for 0–3-year-olds.

Commandery Civil War Centre
Sidbury **t** (01905) 361821
Getting there Five minutes' walk from the city centre
Open Mon–Fri 10–5, Sat 10–1 and 1.30–5
Adm Call for details
Café, shop, guided tours
Please Note: The Commandery is currently closed for refurbishment but is due to re-open early 2007 with new interactive displays. The shop and visitor centre will remain open during this refurbishment period.

The country's only dedicated Civil War museum is housed in this 15th-century building, which was the Royalist headquarters during the Battle of Worcester in 1651. You can see various artefacts dating from the time of conflict, as well as waxworks dressed in Royalist and parliamentary military regalia, and watch a video reconstruction of the battle. Activities for children are often organized during the school holidays.

Guided walks
Depart from the Guildhall, **t** (01905) 726311/222117
www.worcesterwalks.co.uk
Open Apr–Sept Mon–Fri 11am **Adm** £3
Guided walking tours by Green Badge Guides.

Shopping
The main high street runs through the centre of town, changing its name every few hundred yards. There are plenty of good shops and several shopping centres. In the Crowngate Centre, you'll find Mothercare, and the Early Learning Centre is on Friary Walk if you need toys. For something a bit different, try Formative Fun on Charles Street, which sells educational games, toys, books and software. For souvenirs, head for the famous factory shops of the Royal Worcester Pottery. Every Christmas there's a special Victorian Street market in the city centre.

Sport and activities *See pp.403–6*

SPECIAL TRIPS

Worcester Cathedral

College Green **t** (01905) 28854
www.cofe-worcester.org.uk
Open Daily 7.30–6 **Adm Free** (recommended donation £3); guided tours: adults £4, children £1.50 (book in advance)
Tearoom, shop, cloister, disabled access

The construction of Worcester's grand sandstone cathedral was as painfully slow as with most medieval churches. Begun in the 11th century (the spooky crypt dates from this time) on the site of a Saxon monastery, it was finally completed some 300 years later. Its most notable features are its tower – at 52m (170ft), it's one of the tallest in the country – and, inside the cathedral itself, the tomb of King John, perhaps the most unpopular king ever to rule the country (with the exception of Richard III). John so antagonized his nobles during his reign with his constant demands for money that they forced him to sign a document, the *Magna Carta*, limiting his power (which John ignored). On his death bed, John apparently became worried about his chances of making it into heaven, such was his catalogue of sins, and so asked to be buried between the tombs of Saint Wulfstan, founder of the cathedral, and Saint Oswald, thinking that lying in amongst such exalted company might improve his chances. As a further insurance, he asked to be buried disguised as a monk. As you wander along the nave, look out for the carvings of fruit adorning the pillars. Started by expert masons from Lincoln in 1348, they had to be completed by inferior craftsmen when the Lincoln men died of the Black Death.

Worcester Woods Country Park

A422 Spetchley Road **t** (01905) 766493
Open Daily 10–5 **Adm Free**
Information centre, on-site parking, café, BBQ hire

These 60 hectares (140 acres) of dense forest, primordial woodland and wild flower meadows are found on the outskirts of the city with waymarked trails, play and picnic areas.

Around Worcester

Great Malvern, 5 miles southwest (p.403)
Severn Valley Railway (p.379)
West Midlands Safari Park, 8 miles north (pp.394–5)

Castles and historic houses

Berrington Hall

Berrington, Ashton **t** (01568) 615721
www.nationaltrust.org.uk
Getting there 7 miles south of Ludlow off the A49 in Herefordshire
Open House: end Mar–Sept Sat–Wed 1–4.30; garden: end Mar–Sept Sat–Wed 12–5, Nov–mid-Dec Sat–Sun 12–4.30
Adm Adults £5.30, children £2.65, family £13.25; garden only: adults £3.70, children £1.85
'Servants Hall' restaurant, Edwardian tearoom, picnic areas, shop, mother and baby facilities, guided tours, disabled access, on-site parking

The National Trust has done its best to present this elegant neoclassical, 18th-century stately home in an entertaining way for families with quiz sheets and trails taking you through the house (look out for the Victorian nursery and laundry) and I-Spy sheets leading you through the Capability Brown-landscaped gardens, where you'll find a well-equipped adventure playground and a large lake.

Boscobel House

Boscobel Lane, Bishop's Wood **t** (01902) 850244
www.english-heritage.org.uk
Getting there It's on an unclassified road between the A41 and the A5, J3 from the M54
Open Apr–May and Sept–Oct Mon and Thurs–Sun 10–5, Jun–Aug daily 10–6 (last admission 1hr before closing)
Adm Adults £4.80, children £2.40, family (2+3) £12
Tearoom, picnic area, shop, some disabled access, on-site parking

Come to this pretty timber-framed hunting lodge to see perhaps the most famous hiding place in English history. In 1651, Charles Stuart, the future Charles II, was running for his life. Around 10 years earlier, the country had descended into a civil war between the Royalist forces of his father, Charles I, and the parliamentary forces led by Oliver Cromwell. After bloody battles, the latter proved victorious and in 1649 Charles I was beheaded in London and the monarchy abolished. Cromwell became the new ruler of the country as Lord Protector. Two years later, with the remnants of the Royalist army defeated at the Battle of Worcester, the hunt was on for the young prince Charles. Cromwell was worried that, as long as an heir to the throne survived, so the Royalists would always have a focus around which to unite and launch further attacks. Charles fled to Boscobel House pursued by the parliamentary army, where he hid in an oak tree for a whole day while soldiers hunted for him below. With the coast clear, he then sought refuge within the house itself, which was owned by a Royalist-supporting family, who hid him in a priest's hole. Many country houses had priest's holes – tiny hidden chambers where Catholic priests could perform mass in secret – Catholicism having been outlawed in England for over a century at this time. The prince managed to escape to France, where he hid out for the next 10 years until, with Cromwell dead, the country decided it wanted a king again and asked him to come back. He agreed and, in 1660, was crowned King Charles II in London. Boscobel can be visited only as part of a guided tour on which you are taken to see the very priest's hole where Charles was hidden. Kids are even invited to climb inside the cramped space. The hole itself is located inside a closet which, when the troops came searching, would have been filled with cheese to put the dogs off the royal scent. You can also see a 300-year-old descendant of the famous Royal Oak in the house grounds and collect an acorn or two from around its (fenced) base – they're supposed to be lucky. A number of special events are organized at the house during the year, most, unsurprisingly, themed on the Civil War. You can listen to Civil War music, meet Charles II and his courtiers dressed in their restoration finery, find out about taking the King's shilling to enlist in the navy and learn about the gruesome horrors of Civil War field surgery.

Eastnor Castle

Eastmor, Ledbury **t** (01531) 633160
www.eastnorcastle.com
Getting there 2 miles east of Ledbury on the A438
Open Easter–Jun and Sept–mid-Oct Sun and Bank Hols 11–5; Jul–Aug Mon–Fri and Sun 11–5
Adm Castle and grounds: adults £7, children £4, family (2+3) £18; grounds: adults £3, children £1
Tearoom, picnic areas, shop, mother and baby facilities, guided tours, on-site parking, some disabled access

In the 19th century, when medieval glamour was all the rage, it became the fashion for aristocrats to have their stately homes built to look like castles, adorned with a whole range of unnecessary features such as battlements and arrow-slit windows. Eastnor, a grand chocolate-box,

Did you know?
That 'The Royal Oak' is one of the most popular pub names in England. If you see a pub of that name, take a look at the painted sign outside. Look closely at the tree and you should after a while be able to pick out the image of the young prince hiding in its branches.

multiturreted creation in the Malvern Hills is one such home; its fairytale-like, slightly unreal appearance wholly in keeping with its Regency provenance. Notwithstanding its feudal pretensions, Eastnor has a beauty and a grandeur all of its own. Set in grounds containing a 120-hectare (300-acre) deer park, an arboretum, a lake, an adventure playground, a children's maze and nature trails, the castle's walls are covered in Virginia creeper (vivid scarlet in autumn) while its lavish Italianate-cum-Gothic interior is filled with antique furniture, tapestries and suits of armour.

★Kenilworth Castle

Castle Green, Kenilworth **t** (01926) 852078
www.english-heritage.org.uk
Getting there In Warwickshire on the western edge of Kenilworth town off the A46
Open Jan–Mar daily 10–4, Apr–Aug 10–6, Sept–Oct 10–5, Nov–Feb 10–4
Adm Adults £4.95, children £2.50, family (2+3) £12.40
Tearoom (open in summer), picnic area, shop, disabled access, on-site parking, free audio guide

This gloriously grizzled ruddy monster with its 6m/20ft-thick walls is the largest ruined castle in the country. It was built sometime in the 12th century and you can still see the remains of the Norman keep, as well as the Strong Tower and Great Hall added in later centuries. In the 16th century, it was often frequented by Elizabeth I, who came here to meet with her favourite Robert Dudley, the Earl of Leicester. At that time, the castle would have stood in the middle of a great lake, now replaced by lawns although a Tudor Barn and Tudor Garden still survive (the barn houses the castle shop, café and a small interactive museum with a model showing how Kenilworth used to look). Following the Civil War, the castle was left to fall into disrepair.

This is no wet weather option. Every part of the site is open to the elements and a great deal of the soft red sandstone has been eaten away by centuries of wind and rain. The lack of preserved formality means that you can tour the castle and grounds more or less at will. Free audio guides are available and there's a free children's activity leaflet and lots of events and activities (medieval combat demonstrations, plays, medieval music performances, sheepdog demonstrations and Halloween tours) to attend during the year.

Ragley Hall

Alcester **t** 0800 0893 0290, **t** (01789) 762090
www.ragleyhall.com
Getting there 1.5 miles southwest of Alcester off the A435, J3 from the M42
Open Apr–Oct Thurs–Sun and Bank Hols; house: 12.30–5; park: 10–6 (park daily Jul–Aug)
Adm House and garden: adults £7, children £4.50, family (2+4) £23; gardens: adults £4.50, children £3
Café-restaurant, picnic areas, souvenir shop, mother and baby facilities, disabled access, on-site parking

There's a lot more for kids to do outside Ragley's grand Palladian mansion than in it. Unless your children are fans of baroque plasterwork, it makes sense to leave the hall till last (children's pamphlets points out a few of the house's more arresting eccentricities) and head straight to the Adventure Wood, a two-level maze made up of a complicated network of interconnecting rope bridges, tunnels and pathways. Find your way to the centre and your kids will be rewarded with climbing equipment to play on. Nearby is a large adventure playground divided into two sections – a section for under 12s, with swings, slides and rope walks, and a more daunting one for over 12s. From here, it's on to the lake for a stroll (look out for free-roaming peacocks), a picnic and a quick game on the grass (there's a handy kiosk selling bats, balls and frisbees). Afterwards, take a trip to the stables to see the resident horses and admire the collection of ornate carriages and the display of Edwardian toys and dolls.

Stokesay Castle

Stokesay, Craven Arms **t** (01588) 672544
www.english-heritage.org.uk
Getting there 6 miles northwest of Ludlow off the A49 **Open** Mar–Apr and Sept–Oct Thurs–Mon 10–5; May–Jun daily 10–5; Jul–Aug daily 10–6; Nov–Feb Fri–Mon 10–4
Adm Adults £4.80, children £2.40, family (2+3) £12
Refreshments, gift shop, disabled access, on-site parking

Not actually a castle but one of the best-preserved medieval manor houses in the country.

> **Did you know?**
> That, according to local tradition, Stokesay's elegant appearance is the very reason why it has managed to stay so well preserved. Legend has it that, after robbing the house, a band of medieval burglers were unable to bring themselves to set fire to it, so overwhelmed were they by its beauty.

Supremely picturesque, with its exposed wooden beams, shutters and cruck-framed roof, it's made up of three distinct buildings – the main house, a church and a gatehouse (which contains a gift shop). The house itself has been built in a court-yard pattern with a central well and contains various rooms worth exploring, including kitchens and a vaulted hall – it also offers grand views from the top floor of the idyllic local countryside. Pick up a free audio guide when you enter (there's a special one for children) or attend one of the range of events (medieval music demonstrations and living history reconstructions of events from Civil War) put on in summer.

★Warwick Castle

Warwick **t** 0870 442 2000
www.warwick-castle.co.uk
Getting there 2 miles from the M40 (J1), off the A429 in Warwick town centre. The nearest train station is Warwick, five minutes' walk away, which operates a direct service from London Marylebone
Open Jan–Mar and Oct–Dec 10–5, Apr–Sept 10–6
Adm Adults £17.95, children £10.95, under 4s **free**, family (2+2) £48 (discounted tickets during off-peak periods)
Two restaurants, gift shops, limited wheelchair access, disabled parking, on-site parking; house unsuitable for pushchairs

Set glorious on the banks of the River Avon, this has got to be the country's most well-presented castle – a cross between a medieval fortress, an interactive museum and a historical pageant. It's run by the Tussaud's Group, who have brought the place to life with their patented brand of waxwork kitsch. There has been a castle on this spot as far back as the 10th century, when it was home to Ethelfleda, daughter of Alfred the Great, although most of what you see is 14th century with a few 19th-century adornments. It's made up of a main house linked to a series of asymmetrical towers – the largest, Caesar's tower, is 45m (147ft tall) – by a crenellated curtain wall and is surrounded by 24 hectares (60 acres) of picnic-perfect landscaped gardens, where free-roaming peacocks strut their haughty stuff. The castle's interior has been divided into a series of lively exhibits in which costumed guides lead you through some of the more notable episodes from the castle's medieval heyday. You can visit the Ghost Tower said to be haunted by the spirit of Sir Fulke Greville, murdered here by his servant in 1628, descend into the dungeon to see the terrifying collection of torture instruments used to extract confessions from French prisoners during the Hundred Years' War and tour the ramparts to see the Murder Holes through which boiling tar was poured on potential invaders. The castle reached the height of its status and importance in the 15th century when it was the home of Richard Neville, the Earl of Warwick, one of the major players in the Wars of the Roses. During his illustrious career, he helped depose both the Lancastrian Henry VI and the Yorkist Edward IV (earning himself the nickname 'The Kingmaker') before being killed in battle by Edward's troops in 1471. The Kingmaker exhibition in the castle's undercroft makes full use of the Tussaud's Group's visual and sound trickery to create an atmospheric tableaux showing the preparations for the Earl's final battle. The castle is highly interactive throughout; the owners clearly having realized that in today's virtual reality world, dusty displays guarded by hordes of 'do not touch' signs don't really cut it. At the new Death or Glory Exhibition, which showcases the castle's magnificent collection of medieval armour and weapons (one of the largest in Europe), you can attempt a few thrusts and parries with a mighty broadsword, try on a knight's helmet and see how longbows were used. By the 19th century, the country's civil wars had all been fought and fortresses were no longer in demand so Warwick's mighty walls became the setting for lavish society parties rather than fearsome battles. The Royal Weekend Party – 1898 is a waxwork recreation of one of these swanky soirees showing Daisy, the Countess of Warwick, playing the elegant hostess to a group of society notables, including the Prince of Wales and a young Winston Churchill. You can also see the opulent great hall and state rooms adorned with priceless furniture and paintings by Rubens and Van Dyck.

Visit the castle between May and September, when its river island plays host to a medieval festival. You can watch knights jousting or engaging in hand-to-hand combat, see demonstrations of archery and bird of prey handling and participate in a range of games. The Doll Museum, which occupies a half-timbered Tudor house near the castle entrance, is also well worth a visit; it holds a large collection of antique toys and dolls.

★Witley Court

Great Witley t (01299) 896636
www.english-heritage.org.uk
Getting there 10 miles northwest of Worcester on the A443
Open Mar–Oct daily 10–5 (Jun–Aug until 6pm), Nov–Feb Thurs–Mon 10–4 **Adm** Adults £5.20, children £2.60, under 5s **free**, family £13
Souvenir shop, visitor centre, picnic spots, on-site parking, children's activity sheets

One of England's greatest country homes less than a century ago, Witley is now its most spectacular ruin following a devastating fire in 1937. A vast amount of the structure still stands and you can take a ghostly tour of the interior in the company of the free audio guide, which will fill you in on the background history and tell you what each of the ruined rooms was used for. The house's deteriorated condition allows you to marvel at its sumptuousness without fear of bumping into the antique furniture and kids are free to prod and poke things to their heart's content. The gardens are in slightly better nick – partly landscaped with woodland trails and some huge old fountains, two of which have been restored to working condition and can be seen shooting mighty jets of water into the sky between April and September.

Wroxeter Roman City

Wroxeter, Shrewsbury t (01743) 761330
www.english-heritage.org.uk
Getting there 5 miles southeast of Shrewsbury on the B4380
Open Mar–Oct daily 10–5 (Jun–Aug until 6pm), Nov–Feb Wed–Sun 10–4
Adm Adults £4 children £2, under 5s **free**, family £10
Refreshments, shop, on-site parking

Most of the remains of Roman Britain's fourth largest city are still buried beneath Wroxeter's fields, although you can see the remnants of the bathing complex. Tour it in the company of a guide who will help to bring the collection of walls alive. There's a free children's activity sheet and often there are special Roman activity days when you can come face to face with a Roman soldier.

Animal attractions

Dudley Zoo and Castle

The Broadway, Dudley **t** (01384) 215300
www.dudleyzoo.org.uk
Getting there In Dudley, off the A4123 about
10 miles from central Birmingham, near the M5 (J2)
Open Easter–Sept daily 10–4, Sept–Easter 10–3
Adm Adults £9.95, children £6.75, under 4s **free**,
*Licensed restaurant, shop, wheelchair access
(although it's steeply sloped in places), not suitable
for pushchairs, on-site parking (£2.50)*

In the Middle Ages, kings and noblemen often
used to keep small zoos at their castles. Dudley
has managed to put a modern spin on this practice of being a zoo with a small pet castle.

It's by no means the best zoo in the Midlands –
laid out on a hillside, it can be pretty hard on little
legs with a helter skelter-like maze of pathways
to follow (although there is a chairlift in summer
and a land train making a circuitous journey to
the top) and some of the presentation is a bit
uninspired. Nonetheless, it has its moments. The
chimpanzees, orangutans, tigers and giraffes are
all fun and the Tropical Bird House, where birds fly
freely in a replica rainforest, is excellent. There's
also an adventure playground, a funfair and face-
painting for the kids in summer and, at the ruined
castle at the hill's summit, you can visit an imaginative interactive exhibition on medieval life and
check out the great views of the surrounding
wooded countryside.

★Twycross Zoo

Twycross, near Atherstone **t** (01827) 880250
www.twycrosszoo.com
Getting there In Warwickshire on the A444 near
Market Bosworth
Open Mar–Oct daily 10–5.30; Nov–Feb daily 10–4
Adm Adults £8.50, children £5, under 3s **free**, family
£22; rides in the Pirates' Cove £1.50, miniature
railway £1
*Café-restaurant (children's meals served), picnic
areas, gift shop, disabled access, on-site parking*

Twycross is home to a whole range of different
animals including giraffes, sea lions, elephants,
penguins, camels, lions and tigers, although it's
principally known for its primate collection which
holds representatives of all four ape species
(gorillas, chimps, orangutans and gibbons in case
you were wondering), plus numerous monkeys.

Come in the early morning when the gibbons and
howler monkeys are in full cry – their eerie calls
echoing around the park – and you could almost
be in the midst of the steamy Sumatran jungle
(as long as you closed your eyes). Twycross is an
important breeding centre and at its ape nurseries, you can see the cute babies playing with
boxes and sacks while their parents tackle the
more serious climbing equipment – ropes, tyres,
etc. – in the outdoor enclosures. A full programme
of feeding demonstrations is put on every day
and you should look out for the elephant sessions
in particular, when you can watch the great
beasts stuffing loads of vegetables into their
mouths using their long prehensile trunks. If
you're lucky, you may also see them having their
nails clipped. The complex also contains a pirate
themed adventure playground (very much aimed
at young children) with some gentle rides, bouncy
castle, mini golf and a miniature railway. Kids can
also take donkey rides in summer.

West Midlands Safari Park

Spring Grove, Bewdley **t** (01299) 402114
www.wmsp.co.uk
Getting there On the A456 between Kidderminster
and Bewdley. From the M5 take J3 from the north,
J6 from the south
Open Mid-Feb–Oct daily 10–4 (Bank Hols and peak
times until 5)
Adm Zoo: adults and children £8.99 (free return
visit with ticket), under 4s **free**; leisure park:
unlimited ride wristband £8.75
*Spring Grove House restaurant, fast food, picnic
areas, mother and baby facilities, disabled access,
on-site parking*

While the prospect of seeing a real lion may
once have been enough to send kids dizzy with
excitement, the modern media-savvy child tends
to expect a little bit more for its money. The
plethora of safari documentaries on TV means
that the average youngster has seen more than
their fair share of gruesome animal kills. Indeed,
they have probably gorged themselves on spectacular wildlife footage to such an extent that the
image of a lion bringing down a wildebeest and
then tearing it apart in a furious frenzy of blood
and bone is now regarded as pretty routine stuff.

Not only does the modern audience expect its
animals to perform – hence the prevalence of sea
lion shows and animal handling sessions at the
nation's menageries – it also expects to be

offered a range of alternative distractions for when it tires of the assembled creatures and their determination to act as little like their all-action TV counterparts as possible. Today's zoos, therefore, tend to be hybrid creations – a combination of menagerie, hands-on-science centre and leisure park. The West Midland Safari Park fits this template perfectly.

One half of the site is given over to the safari animals – still (just) the headline attraction – which include lions, tigers, elephant, rhinos, camels, giraffes, zebras and emus all roaming freely in large naturalistic enclosures, which are split into three sections: African, American and Eurasian. Obviously, despite the park's best intentions, the animals can't be expected to perform on demand and, as you drive through, you may find that some are a touch on the shy side. Don't despair, you can repeat your journey through the park as many times as you want in order to catch up with its more recalcitrant inhabitants. Of course, having food handy is always a good way of making sure the animals put in an appearance and in the deer park you are actually allowed to feed the animals through the car window with food available from the ticket office by the entrance (remember, you can do this in the deer park, *not* in the lion enclosure) and the monkeys are always more than willing to get acquainted, food or no food – do make sure that you keep your windows tightly shut in their enclosure, however, as they seem to have some sort of unofficial competition going on to see who can steal the most car parts.

Families looking for those all-important modern zoo ingredients – interactivity and entertainment – should head first to the pets' corner, where children can pet and stroke a range of animals before attending a sea lion show at the Seal Aquarium. Hippo feeding displays take place every afternoon, when you can watch these great behemoths chomping down on whole cabbages with their tusk-like teeth while, at the Reptile House, you can watch crocodiles and alligators swimming from an underwater viewing area.

Once you've had your fill of living attractions, you can head to the leisure park which, though on the small side, does have three rollercoasters (the most intense of which is the Twister Coaster), a vertical drop ride, a log flume a pirate ship and dodgems. Cartoons are shown in the Undercover Dome.

Farms

Acton Scott Historic Working Farm

Wenlock Lodge, Acton Scott, Church Stretton
t (01694) 781306 www.actonscottmuseum.co.uk
Getting there About 17 miles south of Shrewsbury and signposted from the A49
Open Apr–Oct Tues–Sun and Bank Hols 10–5
Adm Adults £4.85, children £2.50, under 5s **free**
Farm café, shop, picnic areas, mother and baby facilities, disabled access, on-site parking

Come here to see what rural life in Shropshire was like 100 or so years ago. The picturesque cobbled farm has been carefully preserved to look as historically accurate as possible – there are horses working the land and powering the mill, and a costumed farmer's wife demonstrating bread-making in the kitchen while the resident blacksmith, farrier and wheelwright get on with what they do best. There are lots of animals (traditional breeds only of course), including sheep, Tamworth pigs, ducks and chickens, many of which roam freely and will tamely approach you looking for food. Look out for the beehive, where regular talks are given by the farm beekeeper. Demonstrations of rural crafts such as brick-making, basket-weaving and spinning are given at weekends and there's a small play area for younger children, as well as a marked walk through fields and meadows.

Ash End Home Farm

Middleton Lane, Middleton, Tamworth
t (0121) 329 3240 www.ashendhouse.fsnet.co.uk
Getting there Follow the signs from the A4091 to J9 from the M42
Open Daily 10–5 (or dusk); Jan Sat–Sun only
Adm Adults £4.50, children £4.90 (free animal food and activity pack included)
Café-restaurant, picnic area, mother and baby facilities, disabled access, on-site parking

At Ash End, the buzz word is 'interaction'. Children are encouraged to get in the pens and bond with many of the smaller animals and are even given a bucket of feed to help smooth the introductions. Potential new pals include goats, lambs, rabbits and chicks – which children can watch emerging into the world at the hatchery – although the farm's larger residents (its cows, pigs and horses) are spared the indignity of such intrusion (but can still be fed). Every child that visits is guaranteed a pony ride and, at the end of the day, can help the farmer collect the eggs from the hen house. They can even take one home as a souvenir (don't panic, it won't hatch – you can eat it for tea). Undercover activities such as badge-making and pot-throwing are organized during the school holidays and there's a picnic barn plus the obligatory collection of play equipment.

★Hoo Farm Animal Kingdom and Christmas Tree Farm

Preston-on-the-Weald Moors, Telford
t (01952) 677917 www.hoofarm.com
Getting there Just off the B5060 in Shropshire. Follow the signs from the A442 or A518; J6 from the M54
Open Late Mar–early Sept daily 10–6; early Sept–Nov Tues–Sun 10–5 **Adm** Adults £5.25, children £4.75, under 2s **free**, family £22
Picnic area, farm shop, mother and baby facilities, disabled access

Hoo Farm is the perfect example of the modern show farm – carefully designed, well-presented and with a strong emphasis on entertainment. In other words, it's as much about the 'show' as the 'farm'. Every effort has been made to make sure kids have fun. Idly wandering around looking at the animals is simply not allowed. Here, you don't merely feed the hens, you attend an exhibition showing how the birds have developed from eggs, 'The Egg Experience'; you watch bees making honey through glass-sided hives and sheep racing round a steeplechase track. Even the choice of animals is deliberately eye-catching. In addition to the usual farm breeds (like goats and pigs), you'll see more exotic specimens such as camels, llamas, ostriches and racoons. Nonetheless, for all the effort put into presenting the animals, the sad fact is that the most popular attractions here will probably be the coin-operated cars, the Junior Quad-bikes (for 6–9-year-olds only), the bouncy farm and the Junior Rifle Range. There is also an indoor play area for the little ones and a games room with pool, table-football and air hockey for old children and adults. For something more idyllic, try one of the marked walks through local pine woods or, in summer, a horse and cart ride.

Ray's Farm Country Matters

Billingsley, Bridgnorth **t** (01299) 841255
www.raysfarm.com
Getting there 5 miles south of Bridgnorth, off the B4363

Open Feb Sat–Sun and school holidays 10–5.30, Mar–Oct daily 10–5.30, Nov Sat–Sun (no farm walks) 10–4
Adm Adults £5.50, children £4, under 2s **free** (Nov free for all)
Refreshments, gift shop, picnic area, guided tours, on-site parking , some disabled access.

Sheep, horses, deer and llama.
For further information *see* p.378

Shortwood Family Farm

Shortwood, Pencombe, Bromyard **t** (01885) 400205
www.shortwoodfarm.co.uk
Getting there About 12 miles northeast of Hereford, between Burley Gate and Bodenham, 1.5 miles from the A417
Open Easter–Oct daily 10am–dusk (Sept–Oct Sat–Sun only)
Adm Adults £5.50, children £3.50
Shop, light meals and snacks available weekends and holidays

Kids can take part in farmyard activities (collecting eggs, milking the cows, feeding the pigs, cuddling the calves and lambs, etc.), meet the farm's donkeys and Shire horses, watch demonstrations of sheep-shearing and, on special occasions, join a badger-watching trip. Trailer rides are available.

★Shugborough Estate and Farm

Shugborough, Milford, near Stafford
t (01889) 881388 www.nationaltrust.org.uk
Getting there On the A513 between Stafford and Lichfield in Staffordshire. From the M6 take J13
Open Mid-Mar–Oct Mon–Sun 11–5
Adm Adults £10, children £6, under 5s **free**, family £25
Café-restaurant, picnic areas, mother and baby facilities, disabled access, on-site parking (£3 per vehicle)

The main attraction at this grand 18th-century stately pile will undoubtedly be the restored Georgian farm – it's best described as a cross between a working farm, a museum and a theme park. Everyone, from the farmers to the milk-maids, dresses in period costume and there are lots of animals to meet and feed as well as plenty of opportunities for kids to get involved in farm-related activities, such as bread-making and milking (unfortunately, kids are only allowed to tackle a wooden cow as the real things are left to the experts). They can also watch flour being ground in the restored corn mill and play interactive games designed to teach them about farm life. The mansion house, home to Lord Lichfield, is terribly posh, with fine furniture and antiques but if you want your kids to get the most out of the place, join a guided tour. The Staffordshire County Museum has plenty to offer children with its working laundry, kitchens, coach house (complete with carriages) and schoolroom. The enormous grounds and parkland (the drive itself is over two miles long) provide scope for uninhibited play. Special events, including concerts, firework displays, car shows, craft fairs and Victorian circuses, are put on in summer.

Small Breeds Farm Park and Owl Centre

Kingswood, Kington **t** (01544) 231109
www.owlcentre.com
Getting there Just south of Kington, near the Welsh border off the A44 and A411
Open Easter–Oct 10–5.30
Adm Adults £5.50, children £3.50
Refreshments, farm shop, disabled access, on-site parking, picnic areas

A farm with paddocks and pens filled with cute miniature animals like Dexter cows (which can grow to be a mighty 80cm/32in tall), kune kune pigs, rabbits, guinea pigs, chipmunks and squirrels, plus breeds of small waterfowl. There's a separate owl centre. It's great for kids who like stroking and petting animals as they can really get involved in a way that wouldn't be possible with larger breeds.

Stratford-upon-Avon Butterfly Farm

Tramway Walk, Swan's Nest Lane **t** (01789) 299288
www.butterflyfarm.co.uk
Open Summer: 10–6; winter: 10–dusk
Adm Adults £4.95, children £3.95, family (2+2) £14.95

Europe's largest butterfly farm plus all manner of weird and wonderful insects.
For further information *see p.387*

Sea Life Centres

★National Sea Life Centre

The Water's Edge, Brindleyplace **t** (0121) 643 6777
www.sealife.co.uk
Open Daily 10–6 (last admission 5)
Adm Adults £9.95, children £6.95, under 4s **free**

The first sea life centre in the country to feature a completely transparent underwater tunnel offering 360° views of its vast ocean tanks.
For further information *see p.376*

Open-air museums

Avoncroft Museum of Historic Buildings

Reddith Road, Stoke Heath, Bromsgrove
t (01527) 831363 **www.**avoncroft.org.uk
Getting there 2 miles south of Bromsgrove off the A38, J1 from the M42
Open Mar Tues–Thurs, Sat and Sun 10.30–4; Apr–Jun Tues–Fri 10.30–4.30, Sat and Sun 10.30–5; Jul–Aug daily 10.30–4; Sept–Oct Tues–Sun 10.30–4
Adm Adults £6, children £3, family (2+3) £15
On-site parking, café, picnic areas, gift shop, guided tours, disabled access

This pleasant, grassy open air site has 25 historic buildings to explore, all of which have been rescued from potential destruction and reassembled here. Some are very old – the modern reconstruction of Worcester Cathedral's Guest Hall is topped by the original 700-year-old roof – while some, including the 1940s prefab, are representative of a more recent past. The children's favourite is the windmill – you can go right inside to see where the corn is ground – followed close behind by the blue Dr Who-esque police box and the collection of vintage telephone kiosks. Demonstrations of traditional crafts, such as blacksmithery, pottery, woodturning and brick-making, are given in summer from time to time. There's also an active learning centre, where you can find out how building techniques have changed through the ages, a play area and (again in summer only) a miniature train giving tours of the site on weekends.

★Black Country Living Museum

Tipton Road, Dudley **t** (0121) 557 9643
www.bclm.co.uk
Getting there 10 miles west of Birmingham off the M5. Take J2 west onto the A4123 and follow the brown and white signs. The nearest station is Tipton, where you can catch the Dudley–Stourbridge bus which stops outside the museum
Open Mar–Oct daily 10–5, Nov–Feb Wed–Sun 10–4
Adm Adults £11, children £6, under 5s **free**, family (2+3) £30
Restaurant, shop, guided tours, mother and baby facilities, wheelchair access and hire, on-site parking (£1 per car)

Dedicated to showing what life was like at the height of the Industrial Revolution, this 10-hectare (26-acre) site is one of the best open-air museums in the country with dozens of historic buildings recovered from sites all over the Black Country and then painstakingly reassembled here. Upon arrival, you are scooped up by a tram and taken to the reconstructed Canal Street Village, which is populated by an assortment of (very enthusiastic) costumed guides and craftsmen demonstrating the skills (for both work and life) needed to survive in 19th- and early 20th-century industrial England. You can watch metal being banged into shape at the ironworks, see a trapmaker and horse-brass caster at work, visit a recreation of a damp and dirty drift mine and tour the villages's pubs, shops and houses – look out for the tiny, cold, outside toilets. Children can sit in a dark and chilly Victorian schoolroom while a schoolmaster in mortarboard and gown takes a lesson (woe betide any bad behaviour), buy sweets from the sweet shop, cakes from the baker and fish 'n' chips from the pub before taking a trip to the special playground, which contains an assortment of vintage fairground rides, including the 'Slip' or helter-skelter and the 'Ark', which in the 1920s was the very latest in high-speed excitement. There's also a cinema showing flickery, black-and-white Laurel and Hardy films and an old-fashioned fairground with painted carousels. Afterwards, take a 45-minute trip along the Dudley Canal through its spooky tunnels. To heighten the atmosphere, the tunnel lights are turned out at several points during your journey which may scare (or delight) very young children.

Hatton Country World

Dark Lane, Hatton, Warwick **t** (01926) 843411
www.hattonworld.com
Getting there Off the A4177 Warwick–Solihull road, J15 from the M40
Open Daily 10–5 **Adm** Adults and children £5.75 (Sat–Sun £8.25), under 2s **free**
Café, restaurant, picnic areas, mother and baby facilities, disabled access, on-site parking

A rustic shopping centre with more than 30 shops selling traditional craft and antiques in a series of Victorian farm buildings, with a family farm, pets' corner, falconry displays, pony riding, guinea pig village, adventure playground, maze, mini tractors, Punch and Judy shows, a soft play area and a fairground (with carousel) attached. Nature trails lead from here to the Canal Locks.

★Ironbridge Gorge Museum

Ironbridge **t** (01952) 884391
www.ironbridge.org.uk
Getting there In the Severn gorge, just south of Telford. Follow the brown and white tourist signs from J4 off the M54. The nearest railway station is Telford, 5 miles away
Open Daily Apr–Oct 10–5, Nov–Mar 10–4
Adm Passport ticket: adults £14, children £9.50, under 5s **free**, family (2+5) £46
Cafés at Blists Hill, Museum of Iron and Jackfield Tile Museum; picnic areas, souvenir shops, guided tours, mother and baby facilities; good disabled access to Blists Hill and the Museum of the Gorge, limited access elsewhere; on-site parking

This atmospheric industrial museum encompasses an area of six square miles made up of 10 separate attractions, including Abraham Darby's original ironworks, a museum of iron, a museum of tobacco pipe-making and a decorative tile museum, as well as other factories and workshops. Your first port of call should be the Museum of the Gorge, which can provide you with a rough overview of the history of the area, as well as a few suggested itineraries (ranging in length from an hour to a whole day). You can also see a 12m (40ft) model showing what the gorge would have looked like 200 years ago. From here, its just a short walk to the famous jet black Iron Bridge itself, the first such bridge ever built, still standing strong after 200 years of wear-and-tear and still giving wonderful views up and down the gorge. For kids, the museum highlights will definitely be the new hands-on engineering museum, which is great for all ages and the spooky Tar Tunnel, a 275m (300-yard) passageway cut into the hillside in the late 18th century to exploit a natural spring of bitumen, and Blists Hill, the main attraction, a complete reconstructed Victorian village spread out over a square mile (2.5 sq km) site. You'll find everything from offices, banks and pubs to doctors' surgeries, bakers' shops and pigsties, all inhabited by staff in period costume demonstrating how life was lived here during the Industrial Age and regaling you with stories. At the bank, you can change your money for Victorian currency (sixpences, pennies and farthings) to spend in the shops on freshly baked bread, boiled sweets and cast-iron goods. You can also visit a number of workshops – a blacksmith, a locksmith, a carpenter, a candlemaker, etc. – to watch traditional crafts being performed, while at the foundry you can see a spectacular reminder of the town's origins as you watch red-hot molten iron being poured into casts. Be sure to check out the Victorian fairground with its swingboats and occasional Punch and Judy shows.

Notwithstanding the rest of the museum, Blists Hill provides a wonderful day out in its own right and is surprisingly accessible for pushchairs. It also boasts several good picnic spots overlooking the river, as well as numerous food shops.

A little bit of history

It could be argued that it was at the small, Shropshire town of Coalbrookdale in the Severn Gorge that the modern world began. For it was here, in 1709, that Abraham Darby perfected his technique for using coke in the smelting of iron ore, making possible the mass production of reliable cast iron. It may not sound like a thrilling development – it hardly ranks up there with Columbus's discovery of America or the Wright brothers' first flight in terms of excitement – but, in its own way, it was just as important. Without Darby's invention, Britain would never have industrialized and neither would have America, France, Germany or Japan. Without industrialization, many of the things that we now take for granted living in the modern world – cars, TVs, trains, tubes, tractors, electrical appliances – would not have been invented. Without industrialization, most people would still be living the same life as their early 18th-century forebears – in the countryside, working the fields. The growth of cities and the corresponding movement of the population from rural to urban areas was a direct result of industrialization and the invention of the factory.

Darby had no idea of what the long-term consequences of his invention would be; he was simply trying to make a better kind of cast iron. Although people had been using it for centuries, inefficiencies in the smelting process had meant that the iron produced was brittle and liable to break when put under strain. Darby's method weaned out these imperfections, resulting in a much stronger metal that could, for the first time, be used as a proper building material. It was put to the ultimate test by his grandson, Abraham Darby III, who built a bridge, the first

iron bridge in the world, over the Severn Gorge in 1781. It was considered such an achievement by the people of Coalbrookdale that they changed the name of their village to Ironbridge to celebrate it. The fact that the bridge is still standing some 200 years later is testament to the quality of old Abe's invention.

Ironbridge was, by the early 19th century, thanks to the Severn Gorge's abundant supplies of coal, iron ore, limestone and timber, the largest producer of iron in the world, its workshops busy churning out the first-ever iron rails, boats, trains, wheels and building frames. Soon, other industries began to exploit the gorge's natural resources and factories began to spring up producing goods such as china, glass bottles, tiles and clay pipes, turning the whole area into a hive of frenzied activity. By the early 20th century, it was all over. Once the epicentre of a changing world, the industrial storm had, as the new century dawned, passed Ironbridge by. The town and its surrounding industries fell into decline until in the 1960s someone came up with the idea of turning the area into a museum.

Originally conceived on a modest scale, Ironbridge Gorge Museum is now the largest open air museum in the country and one of Britain's few World Heritage sites – a fitting tribute to Abraham Darby's revolutionary idea.

Lunt Roman Fort
Baginton, Coventry **t** (024) 76785173
Getting there In Baginton, near Coventry Airport
Open Easter–Oct Sun and Bank Hols; school holidays (not Christmas) daily 10.30–4.30
Adm Adults £2, children £1, family £5
Picnic area, gift shop, guided tours, disabled access

Reconstruction of a wooden 1st-century Roman Fort (on the site of an original fort) where you can watch realistic demonstrations of Roman military training and fighting (the legions even shout and swear at each other in Latin).

Royal Air Force Museum, Cosford
Cosford, Shifnal **t** (01902) 376200
www.rafmuseum.org.uk
Getting there On the A41, 1 mile south of J3 of the M54 in Shropshire
Open Daily 10–6 (last admission 4) **Adm Free**
Restaurant, picnic areas, shop, mother and baby facilities, gift shop, disabled access, on-site parking

Perhaps the country's best aviation museum after Duxford (p.328), it has a huge collection of aircraft housed in three enormous hangars. Amazement will kick in as you arrive and wander under and around the civilian aircraft in Hangar 1, their vast bulk looming down above you. You can experience what it's like to fly with the Red Arrows in a flight simulator (extra charge and height restrictions apply). Hangar 2 holds a collection of prototype and experimental aircraft, while in Hangar 3 you'll find all the excitingly named military aircraft; all the Spitfires, a Lincoln bomber, Hurricanes, Victors, Vulcans and Lightnings, as well as over 50 rockets and missiles, including a large Polaris missile cut into sections.

Parks and gardens

Birmingham Botanical Gardens and Glasshouses

Westbourne Road, Edgbaston **t** (0121) 454 1860 **www**.birminghambotanicalgardens.org.uk
Open Apr–Sept Mon–Sat 9–7, Sun 10–7; Oct–Mar Mon–Sat 9–5, Sun 10–5
Adm winter Mon–Sat: adults £6.10, children £3.60, under 5s **free**, family £18; summer, Sun and Bank Hols: adults £6.40, children £3.60, under 5s **free**, family £19

Hot glasshouses filled with masses of lush, tropical plants and much more.
For further information *see* p.375

Coombe Country Park

Visitor centre, Brinklow Road, Binley, Coventry **t** (0247) 645 3720
Getting there On the B4027 between Coventry and Rugby
Open Park: daily dawn–dusk; visitor centre: summer 9.30–5, winter 9.30–4 **Adm Free**
Café, restaurant, picnic areas, shop, mother and baby facilities, guided tours, most of the park is wheelchair accessible with all weather pathways in place and easyrider vehicles available free of charge (these must be booked at least a day in advance), on-site parking (charge)

These 160 hectares (400 acres) of woodland, historic parkland and beautiful formal gardens have lots to offer children. The Discovery Centre for younger visitors has interactive games (tell different woodland scents, types of tree bark and

fish apart), pond-dipping and insect-collecting kits. Special activities are organized for kids throughout the year as well as an adventure playground (near the visitor centre), a lake (unfenced) full of friendly ducks and an arboretum full of enormous, imported American redwoods.

Dudmaston

Dudmaston, Quatt, Bridgnorth, Shropshire **t** (01746) 780866 **www**.nationaltrust.org.uk
Getting there 4 miles southeast of Bridgnorth on the A442
Open House: Apr–Sept Tues, Wed, Sun and Bank Hols 2–5.30; garden: Apr–Sept Mon–Wed and Sun 12 noon–6 **Adm** House and garden: adults £5, children £2.50, under 5s **free**, family £5; garden: adults £2, children **free**

A real walker's paradise.
For further information *see* p.378

★Hawkstone Park

Weston-under-Redcastle, Shrewsbury **t** (01939) 200611 **www**.hawkstone.co.uk
Getting there Off the A49, between Shrewsbury and Whitchurch
Open Apr–Oct 10–3.30 daily; Nov–Mar Sat–Sun 10–2.30
Adm Adults £5.95, children £3.95, family (2+3) £17
On-site parking, café, picnic areas, shop, mother and baby facilities, guided tours

Hawkstone's collection of bizarre follies laid out amongst 40 hectares (100 acres) of gardens and dense woodland provided an appropriately magical setting for a recent BBC production of *The Chronicles of Narnia*. It was created in the 18th century by Sir Rowland Hill, fell into neglect in the 19th century and was recently rediscovered and restored to its original splendour. Today, this Grade 1 listed site provides the perfect setting for an afternoon of adventure and exploration (allow three or four hours for the full circuit) as you wind your way along twisty, turny paths; past dramatic cliffs, towers and castles; down tunnels, passageways and underground stone grottos; through isolated arches and secret valleys; and over twisted tree roots and gnarly wooden bridges. It's hilly, so bring your stoutest pair of shoes, as well as a torch to explore the underground features – which will, of course, add to the sense of adventure. Look out for the Gingerbread House, 'rustic' sofas and the 112-feet-tall obelisk and its 152 steps to the top, from where you can see 13 counties.

Severn Valley Country Park

Aveley, Bridgnorth **t** (01746) 781192
Getting there About 6 miles south of Bridgnorth.
Follow the signs from the A442
Open Park: daily dawn–dusk; visitor centre:
Apr–Oct Wed–Sun 12 noon–5; Nov–Mar Wed–Sun
11–4 **Adm Free** (including car park)
On-site parking, teashop (weekends only)
Scenic country park with visitor centre.
For further information *see* p.379

Steam trains

Cadeby Steam and Brass Rubbing Centre

The Old Rectory, Cadeby, Nuneaton **t** (01455) 290462
Getting there Cadeby is on the A447, 6 miles north
of Hinckley
Open Call for times **Adm Free** (donation requested)
Refreshments, on-site parking
The Cadeby Light Railway was founded by the
late Reverend Teddy Boston, the original 'Fat
Clergyman' of the Thomas the Tank Engine books,
and is one of the smallest fully operational
passenger railways in the world. It is also home to
a number of other attractions, including a large
model railway and a popular brass rubbing centre
housed in the nearby 13th-century Church of All
Saints. The railway hosts various special events
throughout the year including a Morris Dance
Day in May and a Teddy Bears Picnic in June.

★Severn Valley Railway

The Railway Station, Bewdley **t** (01299) 403816
www.svr.co.uk
Open May–Sept daily, rest of year Sat–Sun
Adm Day return ticket with unlimited travel
Bridgnorth–Kidderminster: adults £11.80,
children £5.90, under 5s **free**,
Steam train trips through forested countryside.
For further information *see* p.379

Tyseley Locomotive Works

Warwick Road, Tyseley **t** (0121) 707 4960
www.vintagetrains.co.uk
Getting there 3 miles south of the city centre off
the A41 Warwick Road
Open Sat–Sun and some Bank Hols 10–4
Adm Call for prices
Steam train rides along a short stretch of line.
For further information *see* p.377

Theme parks

★Alton Towers

Alton **t** 08705 20 4060 **www**.altontowers.com
Getting there Signposted from the M1; J28 from
the north, J23A from the south; and from the M6:
J16 from the north, J15 from the south. The nearest
train stations are Alton, Luton and Stafford. Virgin
Trains, Midland Mainline, Central Trains and
National Express Coaches organize packages
Open Late Mar–Oct daily 9.30–5.30 (peak days
9.30–7); Nov–early Mar, special weekend hotel
packages, including Christmas and New Year
Adm Peak time: Adults £20.50, children (4–11)
£19, under 1m (3ft) tall **free**
*Fast-food restaurants, shops, two on-site hotels,
one with an indoor water park complex (p.405),
mother and baby facilities, wheelchair access to
park, all rides and facilities, adapted toilets, on-
site parking (£4 per car), lost parent services*
Alton Towers is the undisputed champion of
British theme parks, offering an unparalleled
array of hi-octane, adrenaline-fuelled, heart-in-
the-mouth thrill rides. Only the brave will take on
the big five – Air (the flying roller coaster), Rita
(the incredibly fast roller coaster), Nemesis (the
inverted roller coaster), Oblivion (the vertical
drop roller coaster) and the Ripsaw (the one that
spins you upside down and squirts you in the
face with water). Alton is not all about teenage
kicks, however; there are plenty of things for the
little ones as well. Brand new for 2006 were two
very popular attractions, both of which are suitable for 4–10-year-olds: the Driving School where
children can guide their mini cars around traffic
lights and roundabouts; and Charlie and the
Chocolate Factory, a boat ride through Willy
Wonka's enchanted world. After checking out
these new arrivals, prepare to do battle at the
Ribena Berry Bish Bash, where kids armed with
missile launchers play shoot 'em-up games.
Daredevil school kids will also like Duel – The
Haunted House Strikes Back, a spooky adventure
ride where you take on the ghouls for a spot of
target practice. Toddlers, meanwhile, can ride on
the tractors and join in with a singsong in the
barn at Old McDonald's Farm before heading
over to the Cred Street Theatre to watch Bob the
Builder 'fix it' in a live show. There's masses of fast
food and, at the end of each season, the park

hosts a series of firework spectaculars. Alton Towers does have more sedate attractions. There are delightful gardens with a conservatory and pagoda, where you can wander whilst waiting for your heartbeat to come back down under 200.

A few words of caution: the park does what it does well and is deservedly popular but it is not the cheapest day out imaginable, so it's worth scanning the papers for vouchers offering reduced entry. Furthermore, the queues in summer will inevitably be long, although fastpass tickets that allow you to return at a specified time are now available for the top attractions. In the meantime, you can enjoy some of the park's less glamorous offerings; its log flumes, white-water raft rides and live shows, which at any other park, would be the feature attractions. Look out for 'Hex', located in The Towers, a combination of haunted house, live show and virtual reality ride. It has to be said that not all the park's attractions are of a uniformly high standard. With so much attention and energy spent on its showpiece rides, a few of the lesser areas and smaller rides have become frayed around the edges and could do with a lick of paint.

★Drayton Manor Park

Tamworth **t** (01827) 287979
www.draytonmanor.co.uk
Getting there On the A4091, just off J9 and 10 (M42)
Open Late Mar–Oct 10.30–6 (later in summer, earlier in autumn) **Adm** Adults £20.95, children (under 12) £16.95, under 4s **free**, family (2+2) £66, (2+3) £83. Discounted tickets available on weekdays (excluding school holidays)
Lots of fast food, self-service café, mother and baby facilities, on-site parking

The 'manor' at Drayton was once the home of the Victorian Prime Minister Robert Peel (he who invented the Metropolitan Police; the force acquired the nicknames 'bobbies' and 'peelers' as a result) and has long since been demolished.

One of the country's top theme parks, its vast collection of attractions is spread over 100 hectares (250 acres), including more than 100 rides, the best of which rival Alton Towers or Chessington. The park's most thrilling ride is probably 'Apocalypse', sending its passengers on a near-vertical drop down a 55m (180ft) tower during which they experience over 4gs of down force. Almost as intense is 'Shockwave', Europe's only stand-up roller-coaster. Height restrictions apply to both. Smaller

children are catered for at Robinson's Children's Corner with a giant slide and a small rollercoaster, and the Golden Nugget Wild West, where would-be cowboys can practise their quick-draw skills against each other.

Even the most demanding water ride fan will enjoy 'Stormforce 10', a simulation of a lifeboat launch involving lots of flying spume and spray, and the white-water rafting themed 'Splash Canyon', while young children and nervous adults are catered for at the pirate raft ride, which glides gently past various kitschy pirate tableaux.

The park's only real disappointment is its zoo, which feels rather tacked on and has only a handful of lions, monkeys and parrots living in cramped enclosures. It seems like a good deal more care has gone into presenting the model monsters of the nearby 'Dinosaurworld' than the real creatures in the zoo. The farm is better. It's home to spotted pigs, barn owls and fallow deer and there are free falconry displays on weekends.

Wonderland

Telford Town Park, Telford **t** (01952) 591633
www.wonderlandtelford.co.uk
Getting there Exit J4 or 5 from M54 and follow signs from Telford
Open Mid-Jan–Mar and Oct–Dec Sat–Sun 10.30–4, Apr–Sept daily 10.30–6
Adm Adults £5.50, children £5.50, under 2s **free**, family (2+3) £24.75
Tearoom, picnic areas, gift shop

Wonderland is a nursery rhyme themed park aimed exclusively at the smaller members of the family. Under tens will enjoy the maze, the soft play centre, the gentle rides and wandering among the fairytale scenes, and will be entertained by the clowns and puppet shows. Visit in December to meet Santa and take a ride on his sleigh.

Wide open spaces

Long Mynd

Getting there Church Stretton is 10 miles south of Shrewsbury on the A49
Tourist office Church Street, Church Stretton **t** (01694) 723133

The Long Mynd is a range of hills running north–south about 10 miles south of Shrewsbury.

Though dauntingly high in places, they are hardly the fearsome peaks suggested by their Victorian nickname 'Little Switzerland' or by the word 'mynd', which means 'mountain' in Welsh.

At 520m (1,695ft), the highest peak will be beyond the reach of youngsters but there's lots of scope for family walks along the lower slopes, which offer breathtaking views of the Shropshire countryside and are dotted with tiny, picturesque villages, where you can stop for refreshments in the local tearooms.

The village of Church Stretton is the main base for exploring the area from where the Carding Mill Valley Trail heads up to the summit. The tourist office can provide advice on routes and there are lots of cafés, tearooms and shops hiring out mountain bikes (see opposite).

Malvern Hills
Getting there Great Malvern is 8 miles from Worcester on the A449
Tourist information 21 Church Street, Great Malvern **t** (01684) 892289

Great Malvern, once one of Victorian England's most elegant and popular spa resorts, is now the largest of a cluster of towns on the lower slopes of the Malvern Hills, the mountainous-looking collection of pointed peaks that rise out of the surrounding flat plains. The town has a few attractions including a museum detailing the history of the town and the (supposedly) curative powers of its spring water, which still pours out of St Anne's Well; the home of Edward Elgar (who wrote 'Land of Hope and Glory') and a medieval priory. These days, it's visited by thousands of walkers who come here yearly to tackle the nearby hills. Although not recommended for young children, there's nothing here that the 10 and over age range should find too daunting.

Great Malvern provides good access to the range's highest peaks: Worcestershire Beacon (419m/1,374ft) and Herefordshire Beacon (334 m/1,095ft), which is also the site of an Iron Age camp. The views from both are spectacular. You can see from the plains of the Midlands in the east to the sharp, jagged Welsh mountains in the west.

Visit the tourist office for details of maps and route details. Only hire bikes from here if you are experienced mountain bikers, as the terrain is tough going.

SPORT AND ACTIVITIES

Activity centres
Ackers Trust
Golden Hillock Road, Small Heath, Birmingham **t** (0121) 772 5111 www.ackers-adventure.co.uk
Open Apr–Oct Mon–Fri 10–9, Sat, Sun and Bank Hol Mon 10–5; Nov–Mar Mon–Fri 10–10, Sat, Sun and Bank Hols 10–6. **Adm** Call for prices
Skiing, climbing, canoeing, abseiling and archery.

Stoke-on-Trent Festival Park
Etruria, Stoke-on-Trent, Staffordshire **t** (01782) 206696 www.festival-park.co.uk
Open Call for details of opening times and prices
Bowling, indoor skiing, pool and laser games.

Bicycle hire
Pearce Cycles
Fishmore, Ludlow, Shropshire **t** (01584) 876016 www.pearcecycles.co.uk
Open Mon–Sat 9–5.30
Prices Bike: half day £8, whole day £15; child seat £5; tag-a-long £10 (day), £5 (half day)
For town and country cycles.

Pedal Away
Trereece Barn, Llangarron, Ross-on-Wye **t** (01989) 770357 www.pedalaway.co.uk
Open Daily 10–5
Prices Bike: adults £10 (half day), £15 (full day), children £5 (2 hours), £7 (full day); baby seat £3; helmets **free**
Mountain bikes, recumbents, hybrids, tandems, trikes and kiddy trailer/seats for hire. Cycle holidays.

Terry's Cycle Hire
6 Castle Hill, All Stretton, Church Stretton **t** (01694) 723302
Open Call for opening times and prices
Mountain bike hire for cycling the Long Mynd.

Wheely Wonderful Cycling
Petchfield Farm, Elton, near Ludlow **t** (01568) 770755 www.wheelywonderfulcycling.co.uk
Open Easter–Oct 9–6
Hire Adult £3.50 (per hour), £15–£18 (per day), children £3.50 (per hour), £8–£10
Hires bikes for cycling on the nearby Long Mynd and can also provide special 'hill-free' route maps. Cycling holidays also offered.

Bowling

AMF Bowling and Megazone

Brixton Way, Harlescott, Shrewsbury
t 0870 1183032 www.amfbowling.co.uk
Open 10–12 midnight **Adm** Adults £3.25, children £3.45
10-pin bowling and children's adventure play area.

AMF Bowling

Birmingham Road, Wolverhampton
t 0870 1183032 www.amfbowling.co.uk
Open 10–12 midnight **Adm** Adults £4, children £2.85

Megabowl

17 Star City, Watson Road, Birmingham
t 0871 5501010 www.megabowl.co.uk
Open 12 noon–12 midnight (Sat–Sun opens 10am)
Adm From £6 (adults) and £5 (children)

Megabowl

Festival Park, Etruria, Stoke-on-Trent
t 0871 5501010 www.megabowl.co.uk
Open 12 noon–12 midnight
Adm Adults £5.75, children £4.75

Megabowl

Crosspoint Business Park, Olivier Way, Coventry
t 0871 5501010 www.megabowl.co.uk
Open Mon–Fri 12noon –12 midnight, Sat–Sun 10–12
Adm From £9.75 (adults) and £7.25 (children)

Megabowl

Tenpin, Greyfriars Place, Stafford t 0871 5501010
www.megabowl.co.uk
Open Mon–Fri 12 noon–12 midnight, Sat–Sun
10am–1am
Adm From £5.75 (adults) and £4.25 (children)

TGS Bowling

Station Approach, Hereford t (01432) 352500
www.tgsbowling.co.uk
Open 10am–12 midnight
Adm Adults from £4.95, children £3.85
10-pin bowling, pool and bouncy castle.

Bowlxtreme

Droitwich Road, Worcester
t (01905) 757475 www.bowlxtreme.co.uk
Open 10am–12 midnight
Adm Adults £3.50, children £2.75

Football

Aston Villa Football Club

Villa Park, Trinity Road, Birmingham
t (0121) 327 2299 www.avfc.co.uk
Tickets £18–£30
Once best, now struggling Midlands club.

Birmingham City Football Club

St Andrews, Birmingham t (0121) 772 0101
www.bcfc.com
Tickets £13–£22

Coventry City Football Club

Highfield Road Stadium, King Richard Street,
Coventry t (024) 7623 4000 www.ccfc.co.uk
Tickets £19–£25
Perennial relegation-battlers who show few
signs of returning to the top flight.

West Bromwich Albion Football Club

The Hawthorns, Halfords Lane, West Bromwich
t (0121) 525 8888 www.wba.co.uk
Tickets £15–£25
The division-hopping 'Baggies' count Frank
Skinner among their celebrity fans.

Wolverhampton Wanderers Football Club

Molineux, Waterloo Road, Wolverhampton
t (0121) 446 4422 www.wolves.co.uk
Tickets £15–£20

Go-karting

Fast Kart

King Street, Fenton, Stoke-on-Trent
t (01782) 250450 www.fastlanekarting.co.uk
Open Daily 10am–10.30pm
Adm Adult/child £10 for 15 laps (over 12s only)

Grand Prix Karting

Birmingham Wheels Park, Adderley Road South,
Birmingham t (0121) 327 7617
www.grandprixkarting.co.uk
Open Sat–Sun 2–4 **Adm** Call for prices
Indoor and outdoor (floodlit) racetracks. Karts
range in power from 20–75cc. Over 14s only.

Heritage Motor Centre

Banbury Road, Gaydon t (01926) 641188
www.heritage-motor-centre.co.uk
Open Daily 10–5
Adm Museum: adults £8, children £6, under 5s **free**,
family (2+3) £25; Go-Karts: museum visitors: adults
£4.80, children £3; non-museum visitors: adults £8,
children £5; Miniature Roadway: museum visitors:
£1.80; non-museum visitors: £3
Next door to the world's largest collection of
historic British cars, this centre offers go-karts for
ages 8 up. There is also a miniature roadway for
3–7-year-olds and an adventure playground.

JDR Karting

Sheriff Street, Shrub Hill t (01905) 616996
Open Daily 12–12 **Adm** £4.50 per person per game

Horse-riding

International Warwick School of Riding

Guys Cliffe, Coventry Road, Warwick
t (01926) 494313 **www.**warwickriding.co.uk
Open/Adm Call for times and prices
  Lessons, hacks and daily riding in the countryside.

Ice-skating

Planet Ice

Croft Road, Coventry **t** (02476) 630693
www.planet-ice.co.uk **Open** 11–5
Adm £3.50–6, skate hire £1.50

Solihull Ice Rink

Hobs Moat Road, Solihull **t** (0121) 742 5561
www.solihullicerink.co.uk
Open School holidays 11–6, or family skating times
Adm Adults and children £4–£6

Indoor adventure playgrounds

Tumble Jungle

Wharfside Leisure Complex, Lifford Lane,
Birmingham **t** (0121) 2480600
Open/Adm Call for times and prices
  Indoor play area with café.

Jungle Mania

4 Station Approach, Hereford **t** (01432) 263300
Open Fri–Wed from 10am; call for closing times
Adm Call for prices
  Indoor adventure playground for 0–12-year-olds.

Laser games

Laser Quest

High Street, Amblecote, Stourbridge **t** (01384) 443939
www.lasergames.co.uk
Open Mon–Fri 12 noon–10pm, Sat–Sun 10–10
Adm £4 per person per game (£4.50 weekends)

Mega Zone

Westley Road, Acocks Green, Birmingham
t (0121) 764 4764
Open Daily 12–12 **Adm** £5 per person per game

Leisure centres

Coventry Sports Leisure Centre

Fairfax Street, Coventry, Warwickshire
t (024) 7625 2525 **www.**coventrysports.co.uk
Open/Adm Call for times and prices
  Gymnastics, football, drama and dance classes for
children aged two and up. Pool and soft play area.

Dimensions Fantasy Pool

Scotia Road, Burslem, Stoke-on-Trent, Staffordshire
t (01782) 233500
Open/Adm Call for times and prices
  Volleyball, hockey, cricket, football, badminton,
short tennis and a tropically-heated leisure pool.

Rock-climbing

Creation Climbing Centre

The EPIC Centre, 582 Moseley Road, Birmingham
t (0121) 4498000 **www.**creationwall.co.uk
Open Mon–Fri 10–10, Sat–Sun 10–7
Adm Adults £5.25–£6.30, children £3.80–£4.80
  Next to Millennium Point, indoor climbing.

Skiing

Ackers Trust

Golden Hillock Road, Small Heath, Birmingham
t (0121) 772 5111 **www.**ackers-adventure.co.uk
Open/Adm Call for times and prices
  Dry-slope skiing, snowboarding, tobogganing,
climbing, canoeing, abseiling and archery.

Ski Centre

Festival Park, Etruria, Stoke-on-Trent
t (01782) 204159
Open/Adm Call for times and prices

Tamworth Snow Dome

Leisure Island, Castle Grounds, River Drive,
Tamworth **t** 08705 000011 **www.**snowdome.co.uk
Open Daily 9am–11pm **Adm** Call for prices
  Europe's only indoor snow centre. Skiing, snowboarding and tobogganing on real snow for all
ages. Non-skiers must take an hour's tuition
before going on the slopes. Free equipment.

Swimming

Cariba Creek Waterpark

Splash Landings Hotel, Alton Towers
t 0870 460 6545 **www.**alton-towers.co.uk
Open Mon–Sun 11.30–8
Adm Adults, children £12, under 4s **free**, family £37.50
  At an Alton Towers hotel, this waterpark offers a
whirlpool, an outdoor steam pool, a toddler pool,
a watercoaster and slides.

Coventry Sports and Leisure Centre

Fairfax Street, Coventry **t** (024) 7625 2525
www.coventrysports.co.uk
Open Mon–Fri 10–8, Sat–Sun 9–6
Adm Call for prices

A 50m (164ft) pool, paddling pool and splash pool with a 64m (210ft) flume, rapids and fountains.

Dimensions Fantasy Pool

Scotia Road, Burslem, Stoke-on-Trent
t (01782) 233500
Open Daily; times vary, so call in advance
Adm Adults £4.75, children £3.50

Tropically heated pool with Dragon slide. Sunday is 'Family Fun' day. Children aged under eight must be accompanied by an adult. Volleyball, hockey, cricket, football, badminton and short tennis facilities.

Stratford-upon-Avon Leisure Centre

Stratford-upon-Avon **t** (01789) 268826
Open/Adm Call for times and prices

Swimming pool, activity centre (with crawl-through tubes and a ball pool) and skate park.

Waterworld

Festival Park, Stoke-on-Trent **t** (01782) 205747
www.waterworld.co.uk
Getting there On the Festival Park site at Etruria
Open Daily 9–6
Adm School holidays: £8.50, under 5s £5; Sat–Sun £7.95, under 5s £5; school term: £6.50, under 5s £4
Café, mother and baby facilities, snacks, disabled access, on-site parking

Tropically heated waterpark with rides, flumes and 'Nucleus', a 115m (375ft) water coaster.

Watersports

Ackers Trust

Golden Hillock Road, Small Heath, Birmingham
t (0121) 772 5111 www.ackers-adventure.co.uk
Open/Adm Call for times and prices

Canoeing and kayaking.

Bosworth Water Trust Leisure and Water Park

Far Caten Lane, Wellsborough, Nuneaton
t (01455) 291876 www.bosworthwatertrust.co.uk
Open Daily 9am–dusk
Adm Call for prices

A 200-hectare (50-acre) leisure park offering boardsailing, dinghying, rowing, sailboarding, canoeing and fishing. Wetsuits can be hired.

Symonds Yat Canoe Hire Ltd

Symonds Yat West **t** (01600) 891069
Open Summer daily 10–6
Adm Call for hire prices

Two-, three- and four-seat Canadian canoes and kayaks for hire.

KIDS IN

Cinemas

Birmingham

AMC Ladywood Middleway,
t 0870 7555657 www.amccinemas.co.uk
Cineworld Broad Street **t** 0871 2002000
www.cineworld.co.uk
Cineworld Great Park **t** 0871 2002000
www.cineworld.co.uk
Electric Cinemas Station Street
t (0121) 6437879 www.theelectric.co.uk
IMAX Think Tank, Curzon Street
t (0121) 202 2222 www.imax.ac
Odeon New Street **t** 0870 50 50 007
www.odeon.co.uk
Showcase Kingsbury Road, **t** 0871 2201000
www.showcasecinemas.co.uk
UGC Arcadian Centre, Hurst Street **t** (0121) 622 3323
Vue Star City, 100 Watson Road, Nechells
t 0871 2240240 www.myvue.com

Bridgnorth

The Majestic Whitburn Street **t** (01746) 761815

Coleford

Studio Cinema High Street **t** (01594) 833331
www.circlecinemas.co.uk

Coventry

Showcase Gielgud Way, Walsgrave **t** 0871 2201000
www.showcasecinemas.co.uk
Odeon Croft Road **t** 0871 2244007
www.odeon.co.uk
Warwick Arts Centre Gibbet Hill Road
t (024) 76524524 www.warwickartscentre.co.uk

Hereford

Courtyard Theatre Edgar Street **t** (01432) 359252
www.courtyard.org.uk
Odeon Commercial Road **t** 0870 505007
www.odeon.co.uk

Ludlow

Ludlow Assembly Rooms Arts and Entertainment
Centre, 1 Mill Street **t** (01584) 878141
www.ludlowassemblyrooms.co.uk

Shrewsbury

Cineworld Multiplex Cinema Old Potts Way
t 0871 2208000 www.cineworld.co.uk
Old Market Hall The Square **t** (01743) 281281
www.oldmarkethall.co.uk

Stoke-on-Trent

Forum Theatre Bethesda Street, Hanley
t (01782) 232799
Odeon Festival Park, Etruria **t** 0871 2244007
www.odeon.co.uk

Stratford-upon-Avon
The Picture House Windsor Street **t** (01789) 415500
www.picturehouse-cinemas.co.uk

Tamworth
Odeon Bolebridge Street **t** 0871 2244007
www.odeon.co.uk

Worcester
Odeon Foregate Street **t** 0871 2244007
www.odeon.co.uk
Vue Friar Street **t** 0871 2240240 **www**.myvue.com

Museums, galleries and science centres

Birmingham Museum and Art Gallery
Chamberlain Square, Birmingham **t** (0121) 303 2834
www.bmag.org.uk
Open Mon–Thurs and Sat 10–5, Fri 10.30–5, Sun
12.30–5 **Adm Free**
   Outstanding collection of pre-Raphaelite art,
history, archaeology and science.
For further information *see* p.375

★Cadbury World
Linden Road, Bournville **t** 0845 4503599
www.cadburyworld.co.uk
Getting there Off the A38 on A4040 ring road;
follow the brown and white tourist signs. Trains
run to Bournville Station from Birmingham New
Street or you can catch one of buses no.83, 84 or 85
from Birmingham city centre
Open Daily 9–5
Adm Adults £12.50, children £9.50, under 4s **free**,
family (2+2) £39, (2+3) £47 (booking recommended)
   Learn how the Spanish Conquistadors discovered
the bitter substance made from cocoa plants.
For further information *see* pp.375–6

Ceramica
Market Place, Burlem **t** 01782 832001
www.ceramicauk.com
Open Tues–Sat 9.30–5 Sun 10.30–4.30
Adm Adults £4.10, children £2.90, family (2+2) £11.90
Shop
   Find out how clay is transformed into ceramics, dig
for evidence of the past and 'fly' over the Potteries.

Cider Museum and King Offa's Distillery
Pomona Place, Whitecross Road, Hereford
t (01432) 354207 **www**.cidermuseum.co.uk
Open Tues–Sat and Bank Hols Jan–Mar 11–3,
Apr–Oct 10–5, Nov–Mar 12 noon–4
Adm Adults £3, children £2, under 5s **free**

Discover more about the drink most associated
with Herefordshire – cider.
For further information *see* p.380

Heritage Motor Centre
Banbury Road, Gaydon **t** (01926) 641188
www.heritage-motor-centre.co.uk
Getting there 2 minutes from J12 of the M40
Open Daily 10–5; school hol workshops **Adm** Adults
£8, children £6 under 5s **free**, family (2+3) £25
Café, shop, disabled access, picnic area
   Largest collection of British classic cars in the
world. Mini roadway, quad-bike circuit, and a chance
to get behind the wheel of a 4x4 Land Rover.

National Motorcycle Museum
Coventry Road, Bickenhill, Solihull **t** (01675) 443311
www.nationalmotorcyclemuseum.co.uk
Getting there Located off the A45 near the
National Exhibition Centre, J6 from the M42
Open Daily 10–6 **Adm** Adults £6.95, children £4.95
under 5s **free**, family (2+2) £20
Restaurant, gift shop, disabled access, on-site parking
   More than 650 gleaming speed machines.

Secret Hills, Shropshire Hills Discovery Centre
Ludlow Road, Craven Arms **t** (01588) 676000
Getting there 7 miles northwest of Ludlow off
the A4119
Open Summer: daily 10–5.30; winter: 10–4.30
Adm Adults £4.50, children £3, under 5s **free**, family
(2+3) £13.50
Café, shop, disabled access, on-site parking
   Eco-friendly, grass-roofed building which
displays, celebrates and explains natural world.
Life-size mammoth and simulated balloon rides.

Thinktank Museum of Science and Discovery
Millennium Point, Curzon Street, Birmingham
t (0121) 202 2222 **www**.thinktank.ac
Open Daily 10–5 (last admission 4) **Adm** Museum
only: adults £6.95, children £4.95, under 3s **free**,
family (2+2) £20; IMAX only: adults £6.50, children
£4.50; museum and IMAX: adults £11, children £8;
planetarium: £1 extra per person
   Science and history come to life in this hands-
on museum, which also has an IMAX cinema.
For further information *see* p.377

Walsall Art Gallery
Lichfield Street, Walsall **t** (01922) 654400
www.artsatwalsall.org.uk

Getting there In Walsall, signposted from the M6 and A34

Open Tues–Sat 10–5; Sun, Bank Hols 12–5 **Adm Free** *Shop, café, baby facilities, guided tours, disabled access* Award-winning modernist-style gallery building. Interactive area for children, plus European art including works by Van Gogh, Matisse and Epstein.

Theatres and concert halls

Birmingham

Alexandra Theatre Station Street t 0870 607 7533
Birmingham Repertory Theatre Broad Street t (0121) 236 4455 www.birmingham-rep.co.uk
Birmingham Symphony Hall Broad Street (within the ICC building) t (0121) 780 3333
Crescent Theatre Brindley Place t (0121) 643 5858 www.crescent-theatre.co.uk
Midlands Arts Centre Cannon Hill Part t (0121) 440 3838 www.macarts.co.uk

Coventry

Belgrade Theatre Belgrade Square t (01247) 655 3055 www.belgrade.co.uk
Criterion Berkeley Road South t (0124) 7667 5175 www.criteriontheatre.co.uk

Hereford

Courtyard Theatre Edgar Street t 0870 1122330 www.courtyard.org.uk

Kenilworth

Priory Theatre Rosemary Hill t (01926) 855301 www.priorytheatre.co.uk

Ludlow

Ludlow Assembly Rooms, 1 Mill Street t (01584) 878141 www.ludlowassemblyrooms.co.uk

Shrewsbury

The Music Hall Theatre, The Square t (01743) 281281 www.musichall.co.uk

Stoke-on-Trent

Regent Theatre Piccadilly, Hanley t 0870 0606649 www.regenttheatre.co.uk

Stratford-upon-Avon

Royal Shakespeare Theatre Waterside t (01789) 403404 www.rsc.org.uk

Warwick

The Dream Factory Shelley Avenue t (01926) 419555

Worcester

Huntingdon Hall Crowngate t (01905) 611427 www.huntingdonhall.com
Swan Theatre The Moors t (01905) 27322 www.huntingdonhall.com/swan

EATING OUT

Birmingham

Birmingham is one of *the* places in England to enjoy a curry – the country's unofficial national dish – its contribution to the cuisine being the Balti (based on Kashmiri cuisine with a Midlands twist). These dishes are usually served in a bowl ('balti' means bowl) without rice, with nan bread provided to soak up the juices. There are more than 50 Balti restaurants in Birmingham, most of which can be found on Sparkbrook, Sparkhill and Balsall Heath (together they make up the city's famous Balti Mile). Although they don't tend to go in much for children's menus and activity packs, most curry houses are family friendly; however your children will have to be prepared to be a little adventurous – even the mildest kormas are full of spicy flavour.

During the day head for the Bull Ring, where there are lots of sandwich shops and cafés with outdoor seating. Selfridges food hall has a wide selection of snacks and is worth a visit just to look. It's divided into small café stands and sells everything from sandwiches to champagne and caviar. If you're feeling daring, there's also a Yo! Sushi bar, where the kids will love watching the dishes go round on the conveyor belt.

The Bucklemaker!

30 Mary Ann Street, St Paul's Square t (0121) 2002515 www.thebucklemaker.co.uk
Open Mon–Fri 12 noon–2.30 and 5.20–10.20, Sat 7–10.30; winter also Sun 12 noon–2.30
Located in a collection of 17th-century cellars, this child-friendly restaurant offers a tapas menu and an à la carte menu (with vegetarian options). Don't miss the happy hour between 5.30 and 7.30, when you can get four tapas dishes for the price of three, as well as cheap wine.

Caffé Uno

126 Colmore Row t (0121) 212 0599 www.caffeuno.co.uk
Open Mon–Sat 10am–11pm, Sun 11–10.30
Pizza, pasta, pastries and ciabatta sandwiches. Children's menu and activity funpacks to help pass the time. Baby changing facilities available.

Celebrity Balti House

44 Broad Street t (0121) 6438969 www.celebritybalti.co.uk
Open Daily 6pm–12.30am
Renowned Balti house that welcomes curry lovers of all ages. There's no children's menu but

the chefs are happy to adapt dishes to younger tastes (smaller portions, reduced spiciness, etc.).

La Galleria Restaurant and Wine Bar Bistro

Paradise Place, Paradise Circus **t** (0121) 236 1006
Open Restaurant: Mon–Sat 12–2.30 and 6.30–11;
wine bar-bistro: 12–2.30 and 5.30–11

Family-run Italian restaurant and bistro specializing in fresh fish dishes. Child-size portions of spaghetti and pizza. Highchairs provided.

Maharaja Restaurant

23–5 Hurst Street **t** (0121) 622 2641
www.maharajarestaurant.co.uk
Open Mon–Sat 12 noon–2pm and 6–11pm

This highly respected, multi-award-winning restaurant in the heart of Birmingham's theatre district has been serving up curries for nearly 30 years now and is very popular with families.

Le Petit Blanc Brasserie

9 Brindley Place **t** (0121) 633 7333
www.lepetitblanc.co.uk
Open Daily 11am–11.30pm

A Raymond Blanc restaurant with Kids' French-International menu. Highchairs and colouring packs also available.

Rajnagar International Indian Restaurant

256 Lyndon Road, Olton, Solihull
t (0121) 742 8140 www.rajnagar.com
Open Sun–Thurs 5pm–12.30am, Fri–Sat 5pm–1am

There are two family-friendly Rajnagar restaurants side by side – one is non-smoking. Both specialize in Bangladeshi and Indian cuisine and offer children's portions and highchairs.

The Reservoir

Solihull **t** (01564) 702220
Open Daily 11–11; food: Sun–Thurs 12 noon–9.30pm, Fri and Sat until 10pm; children welcome until 7pm

Traditional pub fare with lots of family-friendly amenities – a bright and airy family dining room with computers, a children's menu, highchairs, mother and baby facilities and an outdoor play area overlooked by a shady terrace.

Sports Café

240 Broad Street **t** (0121) 633 4000
Open Daily 12 noon–2am

Munch your burgers, ribs, hot dogs and similar American fare in the presence of sporting memorabilia. There are pool tables, a mini basketball court and an interactive games area to help you while away the time, although it can get crowded and noisy during major sporting events

shown live on three giant screens and 150 TVs. Children's menu available.

Wagamama

The Bullring, Edgbaston Street **t** (0121) 6333033
www.wagamama.com
Open Mon–Sat 12–11pm, Sun 12–10pm

Branch of the popular noodle bar chain. Children's menu available.

Bridgnorth

Bassa Villa Bar and Grill

48 Cartway **t** (01746) 763977
Open Easter–end Sept Mon–Fri 12 noon–2.30pm and 6–10pm; Sat 11am–10pm; Sun 10am–9.30pm; winter: Mon–Fri 6–10pm only, Sat–Sun 12 noon–10pm

Housed in a 16th-century building on the banks of the River Severn, the Bassa Villa has a menu that includes Indian, French and Chinese dishes. Children are welcomed with half portions and highchairs can be provided.

The Quays Tea Rooms

45 Cartway **t** (01746) 767231
Open Mon, Thurs and Fri 10.30–5; Sat 10–5.30; Sun and Bank Hols 11–5.30; Mar–Sept Tues–Sun (long school hols daily); winter closed Mon–Tues

These 350-year-old tearooms occupy an idyllic riverside setting. The food is classic homemade fare – jacket potatoes, cakes, soups, etc. – all available in child-size portions. The gardens are beautiful. Highchairs available.

Six Ashes Tea Rooms and Restaurant

Bridgnorth Road, Broad Oak, Six Ashes
t (01384) 221216
Open Tues–Sun 10–5, Fri–Sat 7–10 (Fri and Sat bookings essential)

It's breakfast until 1pm followed by traditional afternoon favourites – scones, cakes, homemade soups, etc. – every day except Sunday, when a full roast lunch is laid on. Children are welcomed in this non-smoking establishment, with half portions and highchairs available.

The Tudor Room Restaurant

Northgate **t** (01746) 761973
Open Mon–Fri 9am–10pm, Sat and Sun 8.30am–10pm

An upstairs restaurant serving swanky evening fare and a downstairs café churning out tasty homecooked breakfasts and snacks housed in a Tudor building next to the historic Northgate. Children's meals and highchairs are provided.

Cosford

Royal Air Force Museum
Cosford, Shifnal **t** (01902) 376200
www.rafmuseum.org.uk
Open Drinks and snacks 10–5, hot food 12 noon–2pm
Watch planes landing and taking off from the airfield while you eat (you don't have to visit the museum). Children's meals and highchairs.

Hereford

The restaurant scene in Hereford is set to improve now that the big chains are moving in (a sad statement about British provincial cuisine – and a contrast to Ludlow, see right). Caffe Uno is on Bridge Street and is soon to be joined by a Pizza Express on the other side of the road.

The Bay Horse Inn
236 Kings Acre Road **t** (01432) 273351
Open Mon–Fri 12 noon–3pm and 5.30–11pm; Sat 12 noon–3pm and 6–11pm; Sun 12 noon–3pm and 7–10.30pm
Local homemade fare (including a cracking good traditional Sunday roast) with dedicated children's menu. Kids can romp in the indoor play area and there's a conservatory and attractive gardens.

The Bell Inn
Tillington Road, Tillington **t** (01432) 760395
Open Mon–Fri 11am–3pm, 6–11pm; Sat 11am–11pm; Sun 12 noon–5pm, 7–10.30pm (no children after 9.30pm, no food served on Sun evening)
Excellent, varied menu with vegetarian dishes and children's meals available, a play area, highchairs. Special children's drinks.

England's Gate Inn
Bodenham **t** (01568) 797286
Open Mon–Sat 10am–11.00pm, Sun 12 noon–10.30
A 15th-century pub set in idyllic countryside with outdoor seating and play area. Traditional British menu and separate kids' version.

Nutters
Capuchin Yard, off Church Street **t** (01432) 277447
Open Mon–Sat 9–6
Vegetarian café and coffee shop notable for its supremely healthy fare and its location in the heart of the oldest (Saxon) and prettiest part of the city, right by the cathedral. There's a pleasant outdoor seating area and highchairs are available.

TGS Hereford Limited
Station Approach **t** (01432) 352500
Open Daily 10am–12am (no children after 7)
American restaurant in a 10-pin bowling centre with a children's play area, garden patio, video games and free bouncy castle in the summer. The menu offers English, US and Mexican choices and there's a special children's menu available. It's a bit tacky but your kids will like it. Highchairs provided.

Ludlow

Ludlow is something of a foodies' Mecca, boasting no less than four Michelin-starred restaurants, more than any other UK town outside London. Not bad for a town with a population of barely 8,500. Although these are not really suitable for children, there are plenty of others that are.

Aragons and The Kitchen Door
5 Church Street **t** (01584) 873282
Open Daily 8–7 (open slightly later in the summer)
A good attitude complemented by good food. The regular menu features pizzas, pasta and vegetarian options (smaller portions available) and there's a children's menu. Often caters for children's parties. Highchairs available.

The Cookhouse Restaurant
Bromfield **t** (01584) 856565
www.go2.co.uk/cookhouse
Open Restaurant: 10am–11pm; cookhouse, café (breakfasts and light lunches): opens 9am (winter 10am) – café turns into a bistro in the evening. No food 3–6pm
Upmarket restaurant-cum-café two miles outside town offering smaller portions of selected dishes such as salmon, pasta and chicken breast. Highchairs are available. Very generous portions.

De Greys
5–6 Broad Street **t** (01584) 872764
www.degreys.co.uk
Open Mon–Thurs 9–5, Fri–Sat 9–5.30; restaurant: Tues–Sun 7pm–9pm
Another surprisingly child-friendly choice, this elegant 1920s Art Deco café welcomes families during the day – when it's Ludlow's most refined tearoom – and in the evening, when it transforms into a restaurant specializing in fresh fish dishes. Children's menu and highchairs available.

Hibiscus Restaurant
17 Corve Street **t** (01584) 872325
www.hibiscusrestaurant.co.uk
Open Lunch: Wed–Sat 12.30–2pm; dinner: Mon–Sat 7.30–10pm

The poshest choice available to families in Ludlow is run by Claude Bosi, the chef responsible for Overton Grange's Michelin star. Surprisingly child friendly, the kitchen will happily adapt the classical and modern French menu for children's simpler tastes and offer children's portions.

Ludlow Fish and Chip Bar and Restaurant
14 Upper Galdeford **t** (01584) 879300
Open Mon–Thurs 12 noon–2pm and 5–11pm; Fri 12 noon–2pm and 5–12 midnight; Sat 12noon–2.30pm and 5–12 midnight; Sun 5–11.30pm

A better class of fish and chips. Kids can get a 'Children's Box' (kid's meal, drink, lollipop or other lolly and some little toys). Eat in or take away.

The Old Bakehouse
6 Tower Street **t** (01584) 872645
Open Mon–Fri 9.15–3, Sat 9–5m

Cakes, soups and snacks during the day; hot meals on Saturday evenings. Everything is home-cooked except the bread. Children are welcome.

The Sun Inn
Corfton, Craven Arms (6 miles from Ludlow on the Ludlow to Bridgnorth Road)
t (01584) 861239
Open Mon–Sat 11am–2.30pm and 6–11; Sun 12 noon–3pm and 7–10.30pm

This award-winning pub is one of the few pubs around to have taken the trouble to get a Children's Certificate from the local magistrate legally allowing children to be in the pub until 9pm. Hearty pub food with a full children's menu and a large garden with climbing frames and swings. Highchairs available and staff will warm up baby food.

Ross-on-Wye
Barn Owl Restaurant
Orles Barn Hotel, off Wilton Roundabout
t (01989) 562155
Open Mon–Sat 7am–9pm, Sun 12 noon–2.30pm

'Trio of African Game' (fillets of impala, kudu and springbok in a gin and juniper sauce), 'Gourmet of Ostrich fillet' (flame-grilled with redcurrant and orange sauce) and 'Backstrap of African crocodile' (served in a light, fresh watercress sauce) are just some of the tempting

delights on offer at this South African restaurant. Barbeques are held in summer months, when you can cool off in the heated outdoor pool.

Shrewsbury
Ask
22 High Street **t** (01743) 242172
www.askcentral.co.uk
Open Mon–Sat 12 noon–11pm, Sun 11am–10.30pm

This reliable chain has a stylish new restaurant in the centre of town.

The Beaten Track
Old Potts Way **t** (01743) 233941
Open Mon–Sat 11am–11.30pm, Sun 12 noon–10.30pm

Offering quality pub fare, it has a Playbarn (£1.25, open 9am–9pm) and runs a Kids' Disco on Friday nights. Children's menu and highchairs.

The Goodlife Wholefood Restaurant
Barracks Passage, 73 Wyle Cop **t** (01743) 350455
Open Mon–Sat 9.30am–4.30pm

Inexpensive, child-friendly healthy eating with children's portions and highchairs available.

Radbrook Hall Hotel Family Restaurant
Radbrook Road **t** (01743) 236676
www.radbrookhallhotel.co.uk
Open Restaurant: Mon–Fri 12 noon–2pm and 6–9.30pm; Sat 12 noon–3pm and 6–9.30pm; Sun 12 noon–9.15pm; bar: Mon–Sat 11.30am–11pm; Sun 12 noon–10.30pm (over 14s only)

'Global cuisine' menu specializing in 'sizzling dishes' (children's portions). Carvery on Sundays.

Sol Brasserie
82 Wyle Cop **t** (01743) 340560
Open Tues–Fri lunch and dinner; Sat all day

Trendy spot serving good-quality and good-value simple food that's likely to appeal to kids – mushroom risotto, lamb kofta and cheese on toast, as well as small and large portions of all the dishes.

Stratford-upon-Avon

In warm weather, pack a picnic and eat it on the lawns by the river in front of the theatre. Marks and Spencer on Bridge Street is the easy place to buy supplies but if you want to buy something

Staffordshire Oatcakes
Staffordshire Oatcakes are not like biscuits but a kind of pancake. They are delicious served hot and rolled around a piece of Cheshire cheese, so that all but the middle of the cheese melts.

different, there's a farmers' market with a medieval feel selling local goats' cheese and dead rabbits. As Stratford has a large community of foreign language and drama students, there are plenty of inexpensive places to eat and all the main family-friendly chains are represented – **Caffé Uno** on Wood Street, **Café Rouge** on Sheep Street and **Pizza Express** on Ely Street.

Ask Pizza and Pasta

Unit 10, Old Red Lion Court, Bridge Street t (01789) 262440 **www**.askcentral.co.uk
Open Daily 10am–11pm

This branch of the national chain has a friendly, contemporary feel and can offer an extensive range of Euro-style pizza, pasta and salad dishes including many vegetarian options. Children are made welcome with half portions and highchairs are available. Outdoor tables in a small courtyard in season.

Bella Italia

32 Wood Street t (01789) 297261
www.bellapasta.co.uk
Open Daily 12 noon–11pm

Large pasta chain offering a kids' menu, highchairs and a non-smoking section. Kids are provided with colouring sets and balloons.

Bensons of Stratford

4 Bards Walk t (01789) 261116
www.bensonsrestaurant.co.uk
Open Mon–Fri 10–5.15, Sat 8.30–5.30, Sun 10.30–5

Elegant but still very child-friendly establishment offering sandwiches from its café and cakes from its patisserie. Children's portions available.

Hamiltons

8 Waterside t (01789) 209109
Open Daily 10.30am–11pm

This roomy, stylish restaurant just opposite the theatre is a good place for a pre-theatre dinner. The inexpensive children's menu kicks off with garlic ciabatta and has roast chicken or pasta options. Big choice of light snacks. Main meals from £11.75.

Othello's

19 Chapel Street t 0870 400 8182
Open Daily lunch and dinner

Imaginative kid's menu and a wide selection of light sandwiches, pasta and salads (in both small and large portions); a good pre-theatre option. Small, enclosed courtyard and friendly staff.

Sorrento... A Taste of Italy

8 Ely Street t (01789) 297999
www.sorrentorestaurant.co.uk
Open Lunch: Tues and Wed 11.30–1.45pm; dinner: Mon–Sat 6–10pm

The restaurant displays a warm, welcoming Mediterranean attitude towards families. The chef is very flexible and will happily provide child-friendly meals and portions. Children are welcome in the lounge and bar.

Worcester

The Fox Inn

Bransford Court Lane, Bransford t (01886) 832247
Open Pub: Mon–Sat 11.30am–11pm, Sun 12 noon–10.30pm; play area: 10.30am–9pm

This pub has indoor play areas (£2 for 45–55 minutes), a children's menu with fun packs (masks, colouring books, etc.) and highchairs.

Hodson's Coffee House and Restaurant

100 High Street t (01905) 21036
Open Daily 9am–5pm

Traditional cuisine, light meals, snacks and a wide selection of vegetarian choices. It provides pram parks, child seats and baby changing facilities.

The Ketch Inn

Bath Road, Broomhall t (01905) 820269
Open Pub: 11–8.15; indoor play area: Mon–Thurs 9.30–8, Fri and Sat 9–8

This pub has an outdoor play area and an indoor 'Deepsea Den' play area with a ball pool (£1.50 per hour). Children's portions available.

The Swan

Whittington, J7 M5 off the A44 t (01905) 351361
Open 11.30am–11pm, food 12 noon–9.30pm

Country pub with beer garden and play area.

Swan With Two Nicks

28 New Street t (01905) 28190
www.theswanwithtwonicks.co.uk
Open Daily 11–5

Sixteenth-century pub offering delicious homemade food.

> ### Worcester Sauce cheese
>
> Just along the road from Lea and Perrins' factory (manufacturers of Worcester Sauce) is Broomhill Farm, where Colin and Alyson Anstey make Worcester Sauce-flavoured cheese. They originally started it as a joke and were quite surprised when it turned out to be a bestseller.

The Northwest
Cumbria · Lancashire · Merseyside
Cheshire · Greater Manchester

by Terry Marsh

12

The Northwest

From the glorious poet-inspiring countryside of the Lake District to the wonderfully preserved historic architecture of Chester, by way of the rollercoasters and arcades of Blackpool, the charms of the Northwest are nothing if not eclectic. Its most well-known cities are Liverpool and Manchester, both of which have undergone a good deal of redevelopment in recent years and offer a wealth of cultural heritage: Liverpool FC and Manchester United, the country's two most successful football teams; the 'Mersey Sound' and 'Madchester', two of the most influential musical styles of the last 40 years, not to mention an abundance of museums, restaurants and shops.

With shimmering lakes, rolling hills, state-of-the-art science centres, zoos, piers, beaches, steam railways, museums and wildlife parks, it's little wonder that the Northwest is one of the country's most popular holiday destinations.

Day-trip itinerary

Morning: At the World of Beatrix Potter in Windermere (p.434) or, for older children, at Windermere Outdoor Adventure Watersports Centre (p.434).

Afternoon: Board one of Windermere Lake Cruises vintage steamers (pp.433–4) where you can take lunch whilst you enjoy a cruise down to the southern tip of the great lake. Disembark at Lakeside for a ride on the Lakeside and Haverthwaite Steam Railway (p.433) before, if there's time, finishing the day at the Aquarium of the Lakes in nearby Newby Bridge (p.433).

Special events

February
Manchester: Chinese New Year Celebrations
t (0161) 832 7271
April
Liverpool: Grand National horse race
t (0151) 523 2600 www.aintree.co.uk
May
Chester: May Festival Race Meeting
t (01244) 304600
Liverpool: Liverpool Show t (0151) 233 1102
June
Appleby-in-Westmoreland: Horse Fair
t (017683) 51177
Carlisle: Festival of Nations t (01228) 625600
Chester: Midsummer Watch Parade
t (01244) 402330

Highlights
Accessible art, Manchester Art Gallery, p.426
Animal fun, Knowsley Safari Park, p.438, or
   Chester Zoo, p.419
Hands-on science fun, Jodrell Bank Science Centre,
   Planetarium and Arboretum, p.449–50
Museum of Science and Industry, Manchester,
   pp.427–8
Museums, Albert Dock, pp.421–2
Rollercoaster riding, Blackpool Pleasure Beach, p.417
Boat trips and walking, the Lake District,
   pp.429–34

July
Blackpool: Kids Megafest and Blackpool Carnival
t (01253) 395976
Liverpool: Merseyside International Street Festival
t (0151) 709 3334 www.brouhaha.uk.com
Liverpool: Summer Pops t 08707 460000
August
Grasmere: Lakeland Sports and Show
t (01539) 432127
Liverpool: International Beatle Week Festival
t (0151) 236 9091 www.cavern-liverpool.co.uk
Liverpool: Matthew Street Festival t (0151) 236 9091
www.mathew.st
September
Blackpool: Illuminations t (01253) 478222
Southport: Air Show and Military Display
t (01704) 395511 www.southportairshow.com
October
Manchester: Food and Drink Festival
t (0161) 228 0006 www.foodanddrinkfestival.com
November
Lancaster: Bonfire Night fireworks display and
beacon lighting t (01524) 32878
December
Keswick: Victorian Fair t (017687) 72645

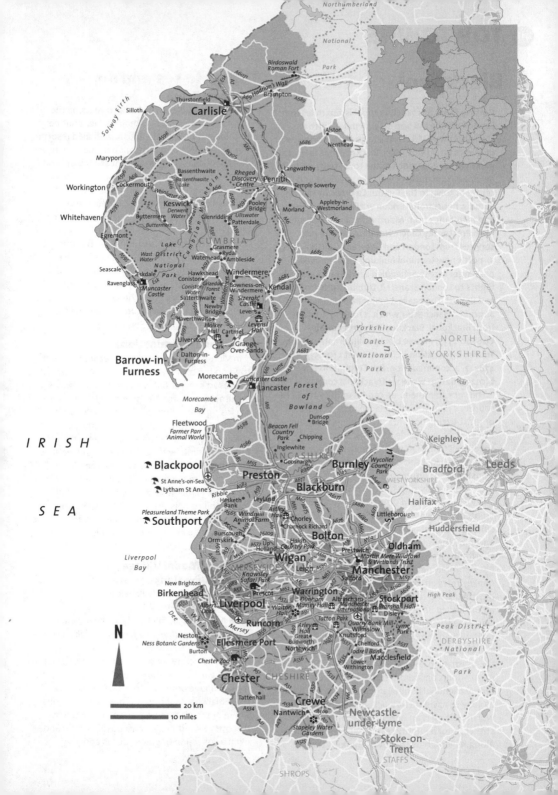

Blackpool

Getting there By road: Blackpool is 240 miles from London via the M6 and M55, 56 miles north of Liverpool (M58, M6, M55) and 50 miles northwest of Manchester (M61, M55). Blackpool has many car parks within easy reach of the town centre. A new link road from the M55 will take you right into the centre of town to the Central Car Park. By rail: It's about 4 hours from London via Preston, one hour and 15 minutes from Manchester and 30 minutes from Preston. By coach: National Express run services from London and Chester. By air: Blackpool airport's new terminal building has improved passenger access. Scheduled services include daily flights to London Stansted, Dublin, the Isle of Man, and Belfast. The nearest major international airport is Manchester which is roughly 30 miles from Blackpool. Blackpool Airport enquiries **t** 08700 273777 **www.**blackpoolinternational.com **Tourist information** 1 Clifton Street **t** (01253) 478222; accommodation: 87a Coronation Street **t** (01253) 621891 **www.**visitblackpool.com

The veritable knees-up capital of Britain and the country's largest resort, Blackpool is a brash, bright, buzzing bonanza of all things tacky but fun. Like many seaside resorts, it enjoys a two-speed existence. Quiet and almost ghostly in winter, with just 100,000 permanent residents, it transforms in summer into a glittering, gaudy metropolis attracting some eight million visitors all looking for a good time. They're rarely disappointed. It may not be one of the country's great cultural hot spots and its climate, largely influenced by the volatile Irish Sea, is perhaps most charitably described as changeable, but Blackpool has definitely got a certain something. From donkey rides on the beach to a coiffure-destroying trip to the top of its famous tower, it is an unrivalled British seaside resort. With its piers, trams, beaches, rollercoasters, arcades, bingo halls, fish and chips shops, candyfloss sellers and stacks of bargain guesthouses, it offers perhaps the ultimate in cheap, unpretentious entertainment – loud, boisterous but always determinedly family friendly. Though large, there are few towns as easy to navigate as Blackpool. Everything worth visiting is on or near the seafront, which stretches for a mighty seven miles and is served along its length by the town's famous trams.

Things to see and do

Blackpool Beach

Over the course of the last 250 years, as the town has grown from a small hamlet built next to a 'black pool' into the most developed resort in the country, the one constant has been the beach. Blackpool boasts a magnificent stretch of sand which, on hot summer days, despite competing attractions, still acts as a powerful magnet to visitors hoping to snooze away the afternoon, indulge in a few impromptu games or go for a paddle. The sands stretch from the tranquil, wide-open spaces of Bispham in the north through the bustling Central Beach, with its donkeys, ice cream, deckchairs and seafood stalls, to Squire Gate in the south, and is patrolled by life guards and cleaned daily during the season. A dog ban is in operation between the North Pier and the South Pier from May to September.

★Blackpool Illuminations

In Victorian times, Blackpool became the first town in the country to 'go electric'. A century later, the resort's love affair with light endures. Every autumn, when other seaside resorts are thinking of closing down, Blackpool chooses instead to decorate its entire seafront with a mass of coloured lights; an event which the tourist office bills (rather modestly) as 'the greatest free show on earth'. The show, which can be seen from September to November, certainly gets bigger and more elaborate every year with over half a million bulbs now used and fibre optics and computer-controlled displays helping to enhance the overall spectacle. For the full effect, take the tram along the front.

Blackpool Model Village

East Park Drive t (01253) 763827
www.blackpoolmodelvillage.com
Open Apr–Dec 10–dusk
Adm Adults £4.50, children £3.75, family £14
Café, shop, baby changing facilities, disabled access, parking

Set in a hectare (two-and-a-half acres) of land-scaped gardens on the edge of Stanley Park, the model village offers visitors a welcome break from Blackpool's more commercial attractions. There are miniature houses and cottages to discover, a windmill, a lighthouse, a castle and even a collection of greenhouses and a

Did you know?

Every year, Blackpool Pleasure Beach's seven million visitors consume one million ice cream cones, 550,000 burgers and 2.5 million plates of chips and, perhaps as a result, use 20,000 packets of toilet roll.

suspension bridge. Children can enjoy seasonal treasure hunts and follow a quiz around the village or just take it easy in the park.

Blackpool Piers

Open Daily **Adm** Individual charges for attractions

An English seaside resort is nothing without a pier and Blackpool, as befits the nation's premier resort, boasts no less than three, each supporting an array of lively attractions. The North Pier, its façade now restored to its former Victorian splendour, is famed for its theatre (where the resort's requisite 'summer season' is held), restaurants and bars and is one of the resort's favourite sunbathing spots, while the newly refurbished Central Pier, **t** (01253) 623422, boasts a showbar and a new big wheel. The South Pier, with its famous marquee-style frontage, also has its own theatre, as well as numerous shops and amusement arcades.

★Blackpool Pleasure Beach

Ocean Boulevard **t** 0870 444 5566
www.blackpoolpleasurebeach.com
Open Mar and Nov–Dec Sat and Sun, Apr–Oct daily (times vary, call in advance)
Adm Free, but individual charges for attractions or discount sheets of ride tickets or wristbands:
£15–£29 for unlimited rides
Restaurants, cafés, bars, good baby changing facilities in the Beaver Creek area, large car and coach parks, railway station

The rollercoaster capital of Britain and home of the Pepsi Max Big One – Europe's tallest, fastest, all-round nastiest rollercoaster – the Pleasure Beach is the current Big Daddy of British tourist attractions. Welcoming more than seven million visitors a year, it has over 150 rides (including no fewer than 10 rollercoasters) which are graded A, B and C according to their perceived 'thrillability'. There are also lots of shows to watch – ice shows, magic shows, circus shows, comedy shows, etc. – as well as dozens of arcades and lots of (mainly fast-food) restaurants. With so many visitors, queues are an inevitable part of the experience. Those for the four top rides – Big One, Grand National, Valhalla and Bling – are liable to be very

long although, as it's free entry, you shouldn't have to queue to get into the park itself. So, while you wait for the crowds to thin out, you can try some of the park's lesser offerings such as the rock-climbing walls, ghost trains, bungee trampolines, dodgems and the gentle rides of Beaver Creek, a special theme park aimed at young children. Highlights for kids include the Eddie Stobart Convoy, with five miniature heavy goods vehicles and the Alice Ride, which explores the dark fantasy of Lewis Carroll's storybook world. Be aware that most of the main 'A' rides have rigid height requirements, usually 130cm (52 in). Rather unusually, one of the more popular attractions at the Pleasure Beach is not a ride but a museum of oddities. Ripley's, **t** (01253) 341033, **www.**ripleysblackpool.com, contains a quirky collection of illusions, artworks and freaks of nature, such as the stuffed two-headed calf. It's the fertility statue that gains the most attention though, from women anyhow, with Ripley's claiming to have had over 1,000 letters and emails from females who fell pregnant shortly after touching the statue's belly. Admission is £7 for adults, £4 for children and £16 for a family of four, which is a bit stiff but half-price vouchers are often available from the website.

Blackpool Sea Life Centre

Central Promenade **t** (01253) 621258
www.sealife.co.uk
Open Daily (closed 25 Dec) 10–9 (10–6 out of season)
Adm Prices vary, call for details
Café, shop, disabled access

Offers a pioneering, state-of-the-art look at the world's marine life. Highlights include the 'Lost City of Atlantis' where you can watch the largest captive sharks in Europe (they can grow up to 2.4m/8ft) from the safety of a sea-bed tunnel; the octopi and starfish of the 'Superheroes of the Sea' exhibition; the ever-popular touch pool and 'Claws', a crustacean display featuring the massive Japanese Giant Spider Crab (with its fearsome nine-foot claw span).

Did you know?

In 1998, the American coaster-aficionado Richard Rodriguez set a new world record by spending a staggering 1,013 hours (or just over 42 days) riding continuously on a Blackpool Pleasure Beach rollercoaster.

★Blackpool Tower and Circus

The Promenade **t** (01253) 622242
www.theblackpooltower.co.uk
Open Daily 10–11 (closed 25 Dec and 1 Jan)
Adm Adult £14.95, children £11.95 (£9.95 during
weekdays in winter), family Saver tickets: £36–60.
Ringside circus: Adult £16.95, children £13.95
Cafés, restaurants, shop

Comedian Peter Kay opted for Blackpool Tower
as the venue for his hilarious live show and it's no
wonder when you consider the building's rich
history for popular entertainment.

Built in 1895 and modelled on the Eiffel Tower,
Blackpool's most famous landmark stands a
considerable 158m (518ft) high and, even after all
these years, is still an impressive sight, especially
when seen against the low-rise Blackpool skyline.

Following a £3 million face-lift, the tower now
offers seven floors of attractions including a
circus, an aquarium, a 'Jungle Jim's' playground, a
dinosaur ride and, of course, the beautiful
Edwardian Tower Ballroom as featured on TV in
countless editions of *Come Dancing*. The tower's
prime attraction, however, is still the grand
panoramic views it offers of the coast and Irish
Sea. A high-powered lift will shoot you to the
top in a few seconds, where you can try the aptly
named 'Walk of Faith' – a 5cm/2in-thick glass floor
117m (385ft) above ground.

Blackpool Trams

Officially opened on 29 September 1885,
Blackpool's world-famous trams still provide
both the best way of seeing the sights (especially
during the illuminations) and the most convenient way of getting around the town. The route
runs for 12 miles, taking in the entire promenade,
and is served by a variety of stock ranging from
finely restored vintage cars to customized
feature trams.

Blackpool Zoo Park

East Park Drive **t** (01253) 830830
www.blackpoolzoo.org.uk
Getting there 2 miles east from Blackpool
Promenade and signposted from J4 of the M55
Open Daily 10–5.45 (last admission 5), Jul–Aug Wed
until 9
Adm Zoo: adults £11, children £7, under 3s **free**,
family (2+2) £32 (2+3) £38; zoo and dinosaur safari:
adults £13.50, children £10.50, under 3s **free**, family
(2+2) £42 (2+3) £50

*Café, refreshment kiosks, picnic areas, mother and
baby room, disabled access, on-site parking, shop,
first-aid centre*

One of the most modern zoos in Europe with
a carefully planned environment of spacious
moated pens, lakes and islands providing a
home to more than 400 animals, including lions,
tigers, sea lions, zebras, elephants, yak, giraffes
and apes. Every half hour there is a talk and
feeding session at one of the enclosures – seals
at 11.15am and 2.30pm, big cats at 3.30pm – and
there's also a children's zoo, a farmyard, adventure playground and a new dinosaur safari with
life-size models.

Cinemas and theatres *See pp.447, 453*

Louis Tussaud's Waxworks

Central Promenade **t** (01253) 625953
www.blackpool.vispa.com
Open Easter–Oct 10–6 (summer until 8)
Adm Adults £8.95, children £5.95, family £11
Refreshments, disabled access

This museum offers 3D wax portraits of
famous – and infamous – personalities from
the worlds of royalty, film, pop music and football including those generational icons Posh 'n'
Becks. Kids will particularly like Arnie as the
Terminator and pop idols Britney, Kylie and
Madonna. You can have a photo taken with your
favourite star at the end.

Sandcastle Waterworld

South Promenade **t** (01253) 340709
www.sandcastle-waterworld.co.uk
Open Call for times
Adm Standard (use of slides and pools): adults
£10.50, children (6–13) £8.50, (2–5) £6.50, family £25;
hyperzone wristband: adults £3, children £2.50
Café, disabled access, shops

Of all Blackpool's many attractions, reliable
warm weather is most certainly not one of them.
So, if you feel the need for a burst of tropical heat,
make your way here where you can swim in the
heated pools, slide down the various water rides
and chutes and relax in the poolside 'sun spots'
while you wait for the weather outside to clear.
The two most intense rides can be found in the
hyperzone (extra fee applicable). Here you'll find
the world's longest rollercoaster waterslide, the
'Masterblaster' and the 'Sidewinder' a vertical-
drop waterslide There's also a Sleepy Lagoon fun
pool for kids.

Sport and activities *See pp.445–6*

Around Blackpool

Farmer Parr's Animal World and Fylde Country Life Museum, 10 miles north (p.439)
Lytham St Anne's, 8 miles south (p.440)
Martin Mere Wildfowl and Wetlands Trust, 12 miles north (p.438)
Windmill Animal Farm, 8 miles north (p.439)

Chester

Getting there By road: Chester lies close to the border with North Wales, 190 miles from London, 85 miles from Birmingham and 18 miles from Liverpool, just south of the M57 and M62. By train: There are direct services from London (Euston), Birmingham, Manchester and Liverpool. By coach: National Express services run regularly from London and other major cities
Tourist information Town Hall **t** (01244) 402111; Chester Visitor and Craft Centre, Vicar's Lane **t** (01244) 351609 (*see* below) **www.**visitchester.com
Genuinely beautiful, with its grand, encircling wall (parts of which date back to Roman times) and streets of 'black and white' medieval architecture, Chester attracts more than its fair share of tourists. The inevitable bustle of the summer months, however, barely detracts from its charms. Filled with interesting sights, shops and restaurants, Chester is a gem of a city with a lively, vibrant atmosphere – as exemplified by the street performers who entertain the crowds in its pedestrianized centre. Small and compact, it's easily explored on foot and, for the best introduction to the city, you should start with a walk around the magnificent medieval walls (the most complete in England), which offer wonderful views of the surrounding area. The town centre, which still follows the Roman grid layout, is marked by the medieval High Cross, where the town's four main thoroughfares (Watergate Street, Foregate Street, Northgate Street and Bridge Street) meet and where the Town Crier proclaims the daily news to the populace by shouting at the top of his voice for around 15 minutes at 12 noon (every Tuesday–Saturday from May–August). The streets here are lined

Did you know?
That Chester's Eastgate Clock, which was built in 1897–99 for Queen Victoria's Diamond Jubilee, is, after Big Ben, the most photographed timepiece in the world. An estimated 50 million photos have been taken of it since its construction.

with shops occupying rows of two-storey, almost ridiculously picturesque timber-framed buildings, known as The Rows, which give the town a decidedly medieval appearance.

Things to see and do
Boat trips
Sightseeing boat trips along the River Dee are offered from The Groves, a leafy riverside promenade just south of the wall, which leads to the pleasant Grosvenor Park to the east of the city.

Bithells Boats
Boating Station, Souters Lane **t** (01244) 325394 **www.**showboatsofchester.co.uk
Open Apr–Oct 10–5.30, Nov–Mar Sat–Sun 11–4 (weather permitting); cruises: summer daily at 12 noon, Jul–Aug also Wed and Sat at 8pm
Daily 30-minute river cruises plus two-hour evening trips and cruises to Ironbridge and Eaton Hall, home of the Duke of Westminster.

Chester Visitor and Craft Centre
Vicar's Lane **t** (01244) 351609 **www.**chestercc.gov.uk
Open May–Oct Mon–Sat 10–5.30, Sun 10–4; Nov–Apr Mon–Sat 10–5, Sun 10–4
Adm Free
Café, disabled access, baby changing facilities
This is probably the biggest visitor information centre in Britain and has displays on the history of Chester (including a life-size Victorian street scene and video show) and offers brass rubbing and guided walks of the town in the company of a Roman soldier. You can also pick up maps, guides and souvenirs and book concert and show tickets.

★Chester Zoo
Upton-by-Chester **t** (01244) 380280 **www.**chesterzoo.org
Getting there Just over 3 miles northeast of Chester, off the A5480; there are signs from the M56 and A41; from the M53 take J12 or 14
Open Summer 10–6, winter 10–4 (last entry 1hr before closing)

Adm Adults £14.50, children £10.50, under 3s **free**, family ticket (2+2) £47.50
Restaurants, cafés, picnic areas, shops, disabled access

Britain's largest zoo is home to over 5,000 animals spread out over 44 hectares (110 acres) of large, natural-looking enclosures. With more than 40 per cent of its species classified as endangered, Chester is at pains to point out the importance of its captive breeding programme, the success of which is shown by the hordes of baby animals running around its enclosures.

Chester takes its role as an educator seriously and, as with all good teachers, understands that the best way to get people interested in something is by entertaining them. At its regular keeper talks, members of the public are invited to examine some of the zoo's smaller residents and there are feeding displays throughout the day (a timetable is posted by the entrance). Otherwise, the zoo's showpiece attractions are the Penguin Pool (you can watch the birds cavorting underwater from a special viewing area); the Twilight World, which contains the largest artificial bat enclosure in the world with more than 200 free-flying bats (it's a little eerie but kids do love this); the Monkey Islands (home to mandrills, lion-tailed macaques and the largest colony of chimps in Europe) and the Islands in Danger exhibition, which showcases island-bound endangered species, such as komodo dragons and birds of paradise. Recent additions include miniature monkeys, a newlook aviary, the Tsavo Black Rhino Experience, which allows the resident rhinos more room for manoevre and Bears of the Cloud Forest, a South American Spectacled bear enclosure. Beside the Ark Restaurant is the Children's Fun Ark made from natural materials with rope swings, slides and two themed play areas – one for toddlers and ones for ages up to 14.

Do remember, when planning your itinerary, that the zoo is very large – its 11 miles of pathways will test even the keenest of animal lovers – although you can cut down on your journey time by using the zoo's zippy monorail or the waterbus, which provides close-up views of the lemurs and Tamarin Islands in summer. There's also plenty of space for picnics for when you feel the need to refuel and lots of open space to wander round.

Cinemas and theatres See pp.447, 453

See pp.447, 453

Question
Q: Other than the fact that it is the oldest horse race in the country, do you know what else makes Chester's famous Rodee race unique?
A: It's the only race to be run in an anti-clockwise direction.

Dewa Roman Experience
Pierpoint Lane, Bridge Street **t** (01244) 343407
www.dewaromanexperience.co.uk
Open Mon–Sat 9–5, Sun 10–7
Adm Adults £4.25, children £2.50, under 5s **free**, family (2+3) £12
Gift shop, disabled access

Chester is the descendant of a Roman fortress, known as *Dewa Castra*, built here some 2,000 years ago and which now lies largely buried beneath the modern city. This long-forgotten past is revealed and explained at the town's excellent interactive Roman museum, where you can discover what life was like aboard a Roman galley, wander along a replica Roman street, examine Roman artefacts recovered locally, operate a miniature siege engine, try your hand at mosaic-making and don a Roman suit of armour – it's a lot flimsier than the medieval knight's version but is still heavy enough to fell a child. The scent and feely boxes dotted throughout the museum are bound to be a big hit with the kids as well.

Grosvenor Museum
27 Grosvenor Street **t** (01244) 402008
Open Mon–Sat 10.30–5, Sun 1–4 **Adm Free**
Refreshments, shop, disabled access

The Grosvenor Museum tells the story of the city and surrounding area from prehistory to modern times with particular emphasis on Roman Chester. You can learn about the building of the Dewa fortress and hear stories told by Roman soldiers. Beyond the Roman exhibition rooms and the shop, the museum embarks on a whistlestop tour of domestic Britain from the Georgian drawing room to the 1920s children's nursery. There's a kitchen from 1900, an Edwardian bathroom and a Victorian parlour and schoolroom. It's a bit of a mishmash but one that works delightfully well thanks the 'talking tableaux' of household servants and gentry. Kids can colour in activity sheets and make use of the discovery room upstairs at weekends, where there are objects to handle, computer displays and cases of finds.

Roman Soldier Wall Patrol

Open Tours depart Chester Visitor Centre Jun–Aug Thurs–Sat 1.45pm; Tourist Information Centre, Town Hall Jun–Aug daily 2pm
Adm Adults £4.50, children £3.50, family £13

Visitors are invited to patrol Fortress Deva in the company of Caius Julius Quartus. Dressed in full battle gear, your guide brings to life tales of Roman skirmishes and military endeavours – just be careful you don't end up joining the legion. Ghost walks and Pastfinder tours also available.

★ Walking the wall

It should take around one and a half hours to circumnavigate the city atop its great encircling wall. Originally erected by the Romans in the 2nd century, but much rebuilt in the Middle Ages and again following the Civil War, it is wonderfully preserved and remains the most complete city wall in the country with only a small section missing by the River Dee. On your travels, see if you can spot the Rodee (to the west), the country's oldest horse-racing circuit, where, appropriately enough, the country's oldest horse race is held in May (*see* above); the Eastgate, which stands over Foregate Street guarding the eastern approaches to the city; the remains of the Roman amphi-theatre (to the east), which would have once staged gladiatorial contests and could hold up to 10,000 people; and the Roman Gardens (also to the east), where you'll find the famous 'Wishing Steps' – run all the way up and down (whilst holding your breath) to make your wish come true.

Shopping

All of the main thoroughfares in Chester are lined with shops and you should really take a morning out just to explore them, but be aware that the Rows are on a raised level that is not pushchair friendly. The Mall – Grosvenor Shopping Centre, 2 Newgate Street, **t** (01244) 342942 (open Mon–Sat 9–5.30pm, Sun 11–5pm) – has a baby and maternity wear shop Blooming Marvellous, Claire's Accessories, a Bear Factory for younger kids and Footlocker for their older siblings. Chester Market, 6 Princess Street, **t** (01244) 402340 (open Mon–Sat 8–5.30) has 100 stalls laden with local produce. There's also an outdoor market in Town Hall Square (open Sundays 9.30am–4pm).

Sport and activities *See* pp.445–6

Around Chester

Jodrell Bank Science Centre, Planetarium and Arboretum, 25 miles east (pp.449–50)
Ness Botanic Gardens, 9 miles northwest (pp.441–2)
Stapeley Water Gardens, 21 miles southeast (p.442)

Liverpool

Getting there By road: Liverpool is 210 miles from London and 100 miles from Birmingham via the M6 and 35 miles from Manchester via the M62. By train: Intercity trains arrive at Liverpool Lime Street station from Manchester and London (Euston). By coach: The National Express station is in Norton Street and there are regular services from Manchester, London and Birmingham
Tourist information Queen Square Centre **t** (information) 0906 680 6886 **t** (accommodation) 0845 601 1125 www.visitliverpool.com

Just a few years ago, you would have found few guidebooks willing to recommend a trip to the Beatles' home city. Once the country's second most important port and a bulwark of Imperial Britain, Liverpool's fall from grace over the latter half of the 20th century was nothing if not spectacular. Thriving and prosperous until the Second World War, the docks fell into decline soon after taking the city with them and turning the area into a byword for urban deprivation. Following riots and record unemployment in the 1980s, the city's fortunes were eventually turned around, in part by tourism. The waterfront, which had once financed Liverpool's growth, would begin to do so again as the buildings and warehouses of the 19th-century Albert Dock were transformed into one of the North of England's premier attractions, with shops, TV studios, bars, restaurants and a collection of award-winning museums. Liverpool's resurrection is, however, as yet incomplete. Still with more than its fair share of problems – poverty, poor housing, unemployment – it is once again alive and looking to the future with an eye to its status as European City of Culture in 2008.

Things to see and do

★Albert Dock

Suite 7, The Colonnades, Albert Dock
t (0151) 708 7334 www.albertdock.com
Open Daily 10–5.30 (museums close at 5) **Adm Free**

If you spend any time in Liverpool, you're sure to visit the Albert Dock. First opened in 1846 by Prince Albert to store tea, silk, tobacco and spirits from the Far East, these restored brick warehouses now make up one of the finest groupings of Grade I Listed Buildings in the country. Derelict and run-down following the decline of the docks, they were transformed in the 1980s into a thriving cultural complex comprising shops, cafés and restaurants, alongside museums and exhibitions designed to highlight and celebrate the culture and history of the area. These include the five-storey Merseyside Maritime Museum, the Anything to Declare? HM Customs and Excise National Museum, The Beatles Story and Tate Liverpool. Buskers and jugglers are on hand to entertain the crowds and you should look out for historic ships that visit the dock from time to time and, of course, Fred the Weatherman's floating map. Make sure children don't breach the barriers though – the dock water is deep and ice cold.

Anything to Declare? HM Customs and Excise National Museum

Merseyside Maritime Museum, Albert Dock
t (0151) 478 4499
Open Daily 10–5 (last admission 4) **Adm Free**
Café, shop, disabled access to some areas

Housed on the ground floor of the National Maritime Museum, this provides a somewhat lighthearted look at the art and practice of smuggling (hollowed-out shoes, animals stuffed down underpants, etc.), tracing its development from the small-scale efforts of the Middle Ages – when it enjoyed a rather romantic image – to the hi-tech multi-million-pound operations of today. Kids will be entertained by the museum's interactive offerings: they can try and detect counterfeit goods, 'spot a smuggler' from a computer line-up of suspicious characters and watch sniffer dog demonstrations on designated days. On a more serious note, there's an exhibition showing the damage that smuggling does to the animal world and the number of goods linked to endangered species seized every year by customs officials.

The Beatles Story

Britannia Vaults, Albert Dock t (0151) 709 1963
www.beatlesstory.com
Open Daily 10–6
Adm Adults £8.99, children £4.99, under 5s **free**, family £25; combined ticket available for The Beatles Story and Liverpool Football Club
Shop, disabled access, parking

Lively and moving tribute to the city's most famous musical sons, telling the story of how the loveable mop tops rose from the Merseyside back-streets to achieve global domination within the space of a decade. There are videos, dioramas and heaps of memorabilia to look at (including costumes from the film *A Hard Day's Night*); you can even visit a reconstruction of the legendary Cavern Club and hear a recording of one of the group's early performances. For kids too young to remember Beatlemania, there's a mocked-up Yellow Submarine. Each year Liverpool plays host to a seven-day International Beatles Festival when tribute bands from all over the world descend on the city to belt out their evergreen hits.

The Beatles tours

Various companies offer tours of the Beatles' homes, schools, places of birth and landmarks; call for details of times and prices. Check out:
Beatles Magical Mystery Tour t (0151) 2399091
www.cavern-liverpool.co.uk
Beatles Car Tours t (0151) 9313075
Cavern City Tours t (0151) 236 9091, t 0871 222 1963
Liverpool Beatles Tours t (0151) 2817738

National Trust tours of Paul McCartney and John Lennon's former homes (adults £10, accompanying children **free**) depart from the National Conservation Centre at 10.30am and 11.20am, and from Speke Hall at 1.50pm and 3.55pm. Infoline for Speke Hall, Mendips and 20 Forthlin Road: t 08457 585702; call t (0151) 708 8574 for morning tours and t (0151) 427 7231 for tours in the afternoon. Pre-booking is advised.

Cinemas and theatres *See* pp.447, 453

City Sightseeing Tours

t (0151) 933 2324 www.city-sightseeing.com
Operating hours Every 30 minutes from Albert Dock **Adm** Adults £6, children £3, under 5s **free**, family (2+2) £15

A 50-minute bus ride around the city centre on an open-top double decker with live commentary and hop-on, hop-off service.

Croxteth Hall and Country Park

Croxteth **t** (0151) 228 6910 www.croxteth.co.uk
Open Easter–Sept daily 10.30–5; farm, shop and
café: Oct–Easter Sat–Sun only **Adm** Hall: Adults
£2.30, children £1.50; farm: adult £2.30, children
£1.50; garden: adult £1.50, children 90p; family
ticket to hall, farm and garden £11
*Café, gift shop, disabled access, baby changing
facilities, on-site parking*

Run by Liverpool City Council, the Edwardian
home of Lord Sefton is now filled with period
displays and inhabited by jolly-looking
mannequins of its former residents. Outside in the
park, you'll find a Victorian walled garden with
rows of fruit trees, a wooden adventure playground
with a separate toddler area, lots of picnic spots
and a special area for ball games. There's also a
farm with pigs, cows, hens, horses and sheep.

Duck Tours

Anchor Courtyard, Britannia Pavilion, Albert Dock
t (0151) 708 7799,
www.theyellowduckmarine.co.uk
Operating hours Daily 11–dusk (tours depart hourly)
Adm Adults £11.95, children £9.95, under 2s **free** but
not allocated a seat, family (2+2) £34 (discounted
tickets during off peak times)

These land/river tours aboard amphibious
vehicles are not the cheapest way of seeing the
city but they're the most unusual. Passengers are
likely to get wet so come prepared!

Grand National Experience

Aintree Race Course **t** (0151) 5232600
www.aintree.co.uk
Open Mid-Apr–mid-Oct Tues–Sun (excluding race
days) 10–5 **Adm** Adults £7, children £4
Café, gift shop, disabled access

The long history of the country's most famous
horse race (p.424), which has been run every year
since 1839, is explored at this new visitor centre
where you can visit the Weighing Room, try on a
jockey's uniform, take a guided tour of the race
course (extra charge) and put your riding skills to
the test on the Grand National Simulator (extra
charge) – you can feel what it's like to go over the
infamous Beechers Brook.

Joseph Williamson Tunnels

t (0151) 709 6868 www.williamsontunnels.co.uk
Open summer: Tues–Sun 10–6; winter: Thurs–Sun
10–5 **Adm** Adults £3.50, children £2, family £10

Can you spot?
The Liver Birds. A pair of huge, 18 feet high (but
still rather elegant-looking) copper cormorants
which sit atop the twin clocks of the Royal Liver
Building (the first building in the world to be
made from reinforced concrete) and which have
become emblems of the city.

Guided tours, café, toilets, partial disabled access

Take a 45-minute guided tour through this
intriguing maze of tunnels (30 have so far been
discovered) designed by philanthropist Joseph
Williamson between 1815 and 40. The tunnels
were originally built as a kind of 19th-century
work experience project aimed at giving employ-
ment to the city's poor. Local enthusiasts have
been tracing their whereabouts for around 10
years and there is an exhibition area detailing
their search. Special events take place underground throughout the year.

Liverpool Football Club Museum and Stadium Tour

Anfield Road, Liverpool **t** (0151) 260 6677
www.liverpoolfc.tv
Open Daily 10–5 **Adm** Museum and tour: adults £9,
children £5.50, family £23; museum only: adults £5,
children £3, family £13

Mini football fans will enjoy an energetic day
out at the museum of the four times European
Cup winners: scoring goals in the penalty-
shooting gallery, composing their own match
commentary and stepping out onto a recreation
of the Kop (which, before seating was introduced,
was the world's largest stand). They are then
taken behind the scenes on a tour of the stadium
itself on which they can inspect the players' baths,
walk down the tunnel to the simulated roar of
45,000 fans, touch the legendary 'This is Anfield'
sign and settle down in the Liverpool dugout.

Liverpool Museum

William Brown Street **t** (0151) 478 4399
www.liverpoolmuseum.org.uk
Open Daily 10–5 **Adm** Free
*Café, shop, baby changing facilities, limited parking,
disabled access and facilities, lift*

This is a grand hotch-potch of a museum with
five floors of displays covering subjects as diverse
as land transport, natural history, antiquities,
ethnology, space and time worldwide. The
Natural History Centre is well worth a visit with
its thousands of creepy crawlies and fossils, some

of which can be handled plus a brand new aquarium with tropical fish and microscopes to give a close up view of tiny sea creatures. There's also a planetarium, which presents hi-tech shows exploring stars, comets and the Solar System. In the Weston Discovery Centre children can handle objects that are up to 5,000 years old and take part in activities such as weaving or making stone axes. Regular family events take place on weekends and in the school holidays.

★Mersey Ferries

Pier Head **t** (0151) 2272660
www.merseyferries.co.uk
Operating times Mon–Fri 10–3, Sat–Sun 10–6
Prices Return: adults £4.95, children £2.75, under 5s **free**, family £13.20

Taking a trip aboard this particular attraction is almost like a rite of passage for travellers of a certain age and, before long, you'll no doubt be belting out 'So Ferry 'cross the Mersey' in your best Gerry and the Pacemakers voice to your children's utter bemusement. Fittingly, for so famous a ferry service, it's also the oldest in Europe, having been started some time in the early 13th century. There are actually two services, both of which leave from Pier Head (about a five minutes' walk from the Albert Dock): a no-frills shuttle service during peak hours for workers and a leisurely tourist service offering audiotours of the city as you make your way to Seacombe, where there's an aquarium (joint tickets available) and Woodside, where you can at times take a ride on a vintage tram.

★Merseyside Maritime Museum

Albert Dock **t** (0151) 478 4499
www.merseysidemaritimemuseum.org.uk
Open Daily 10–5 **Adm Free**
Café, shop, limited disabled access, baby facilities

A lovely mix of maritime nostalgia: at the five-storey Merseyside Maritime Museum, you can find out all about Liverpool's docks, which were for so long the lifeblood of the city. The rigours and hardships of dockyard life are vividly brought to life and there are displays on the Merchant Navy, emigration (you can explore the reconstructed hull of an emigrant ship to see the awful conditions emigrants had to put up with on the long journey to the New World), luxury cruisers, as well as a whole gallery filled with model boats. Although there's more than a hint of rose-tint about many of the displays, the museum doesn't

Grand National

Every April, Liverpool's Aintree course plays host to the country's most famous horse race, the Grand National. For reasons no one really understands, this particular steeplechase has captured the public imagination like no other. Even people who have no interest in either horse-racing or gambling decide, come the big day, to wager a pound or so on some no-hoper picked out of the newspaper with a pin and then settle down to watch the horses hurtling over the course's fiendishly difficult collection of fences. The only guarantee is that there will be numerous fallers – horses finishing the race without their jockeys is a common sight. Indeed, it is presumably the rather random nature of the event, with favourites seemingly as liable to take a tumble as long-shots, which is part of its appeal.

shrink from confronting the darker aspects of Liverpool's past as shown by its hard-hitting display on Liverpool's once thriving slave trade. The ground floor is given over to the Anything to Declare? HM Customs and Excise National Museum (p.422). There are quiz sheets and regular family activities, as well as a children's play space in the upper gallery with toys so that the little ones can take some time out.

Sport and activities *See pp.445–6*

Tate Liverpool

Albert Dock **t** (0151) 702 7400 **www.tate.org.uk**
Open Tues–Sun 10–5.50, Jun–Aug also Mon
Adm Free (charge for special exhibitions)
Café, gift shop, disabled access

Housed in an appropriately modernist-style converted warehouse with lots of natural light, this is the North of England's premier collection of modern art, with works by Damien Hirst, Andy Warhol, Francis Bacon, Lucian Freud and Henry Moore. Activities are put on for families to help children get the most out of what might otherwise seem like just another gallery. Every Sunday afternoon (except the last of each month), there are Art Quests with free games, craft activities and trails for children. On the last Sunday of the month, Great Art Adventures are organized. Led by artists these take a hands-on approach to art, involving games and practical activities in the galleries themselves.

Walking tours

There are several tours of the city available that will appeal to kids, from Sunday City Walks, t (0151) 237 3925, to sightseeing buses. No doubt teenagers will want to opt for a Beatles tour while younger children might prefer to make a big splash on the 'Yellow Duckmarine'.

Around Liverpool

Knowsley Safari Park, 12 miles east (p.438)
Pleasureland Theme Park, 18 miles north (p.441)

Manchester

Getting there By road: Manchester is 200 miles from London and 85 miles from Birmingham via the M6 and 40 miles from Leeds via the M62.
By train: It's easily accessible from all the country's major cities and towns and has two mainline rail stations, Piccadilly, east of the city centre, and Victoria station to the north. London Euston to Manchester takes just over 2.5 hours. By coach: The city's coach station is in Chorlton Street, near to the Piccadilly bus station. National Express run services from most major towns and cities. Manchester Airport is the busiest outside London. Just 10 miles south of the city centre, it is a 20–25-minute journey by direct rail link or motorway
Tourist information Town Hall Extension, Lloyd Street t 0871 2228223 t 0906 871 5533 (infoline) **www.**manchester.gov.uk. For 'Family Friendly' information on facilities in Manchester t (0161) 234 4525 **www.**manchestercitycentremanagement.co.uk

It's all go in Manchester. No other city in the country is regenerating faster. As new attractions open by the month, and old historic areas are spruced up, there's now a real buzz about what is fast becoming England's second largest city.

It wasn't always thus. Once one of the country's great industrial towns and one of the world's major centres of textile production, Manchester was at one time seen as emblematic of all the worst excesses of industrial capitalism, with a skyline dominated by belching factories and streets of slum housing. Today, although it still has its more deprived areas and its fair share of social problems, it is definitely a city on the up. Having finally said goodbye to large-scale industry, Manchester

Did you know?
That Britain's (and probably the world's) first ever bus service was started in Manchester by John Greenwood in 1824. The route ran from Pendleton to Manchester.

began reinventing itself with a vengeance in the 1980s and '90s, a process helped, rather than hindered, by an IRA bomb, which destroyed parts of the main shopping district in 1996. Most of the recent redevelopment has been centred around two main areas: the Castlefield canalside area to the south of the city centre (*see* below) and the Millennium Quarter, where you'll find the Printworks entertainment complex and Urbis: Museum of Urban Life (p.428). Manchester's image has been further enhanced by a vibrant music scene and the success of Manchester United, who in the 1990s claimed six league championships and two European trophies, thus confirming their status as the biggest, richest, most widely supported football team in the world. More recently, Manchester City have once again become a major player, having settled into their brand-new stadium, inherited from the 2002 Commonwealth Games. The stereotypical image of a run-down, post-industrial city is long gone. Manchester is now a multicultural metropolis with the country's second largest Chinatown district (*see* Chinese Arts Centre p.426), its own Imperial War Museum (p.449), The Lowry Centre arts complex (p.450) and lots of spruced up galleries and museums to explore.

Things to see and do
Boat trips

Sightseeing boat trips along the River Irwell and Manchester Ship Canal are offered by The Irwell and Mersey Packet Boat Company, t (0161) 736 2108. City Centre Cruises, t (0161) 902 0222, do a Sunday lunch cruise departing Castlefield at 1pm, taking in the Bridgewater Canal and Manchester Ship Canal (adults £19.95, children £9.95). Call for details and for weekend hourly boat trips elsewhere.

★Castlefield Urban Heritage Park
Castlefield Visitor Centre, 101 Liverpool Road, Castlefield t (0161) 834 4026 **www.**castlefield.org.uk
Open Daily; visitor centre open Mon–Fri 10–4; Sat, Sun and Bank Hols 12 noon–4 **Adm Free**

Designated an urban heritage park in the 1980s, the city's industrial canal basin has seen its

Did you know?
That Manchester-based soap opera Coronation
Street has been broadcast for more than 40 years
– the longest-running TV soap in the world.

previously derelict wharves and warehouses
transformed into smart new visitor attractions –
including Bridgwater Hall (the home of the Hallé
Orchestra), the excellent Museum of Science and
Industry (*see* right) and even a reconstructed
Roman fort – waterside cafés, bars, restaurants
and swanky apartment complexes. Boat trips
down the canal are available and the Castlefield
Visitor Centre can provide self-guided heritage
walks along the area's historic towpaths. There is
also a seasonal outdoor events programme, which
encompasses the Castlefield-on-sea weekend in
July (www.manchesterlive.co.uk) when aquatic
performers and beach lovers descend on the area
to ensure the surf is most definitely up.

Chinese Arts Centre

Market Buildings, Thomas Street **t** (0161) 832 7271
www.chinese-arts-centre.org
Open Mon–Sat 10–6, Sun and Bank Hols 11–5
Adm Free
*Disabled access, baby changing facilities,
teahouse, shop*

Located in Manchester's thriving Northern
Quarter, the centre displays contemporary visual
arts from a broad variety of media. Changing
exhibitions cover architecture, design, fashion,
installation, painting, photography, printmaking,
sculpture, and video. The centre also has an 'Art
Cart' stocked with materials and activities for
kids to use, costumes, masks and kites for hire
and family workshops every other Sunday.

Cinemas and theatres *See* pp.447, 453

Greater Manchester Police Museum

Newton Street **t** (0161) 856 3287
Open Tues 10.30–3.30 **Adm Free**

The city's rather jolly police museum is set in a
Victorian police station and traces the development of the force from the advent of the 'peelers'
(the country's first police force, introduced in the
1820s by the then Home Secretary, Robert Peel) to
the present day. There are old uniforms, weapons
and equipment to look at, costumes and hats to
try on and you can explore the macabre-looking
cells designed to hold up to 12 criminals at a time.
Kids can investigate whether their ancestors

were part of the Manchester underworld by
using the museum's criminal tracking resources.

★Manchester Art Gallery

Mosley Street **t** (0161) 235 8888
www.manchestergalleries.org
Open Tues–Sun and Bank Hols 10–5 **Adm Free**
*Café and restaurant, baby changing facilities in
both male and female toilets, disabled access and
facilities, lifts, shop, family audio guide, free guided
tours at weekends from 2–3pm*

After extensive refurbishment, it has simply
become a great place to take the kids. Children
will particularly like the sign that says 'please
do touch' above the bronze statue of a panther
and the Clore Interactive Gallery, where they
can create their own artworks out of junk,
arrange coloured plastic shapes on a lightbox,
design postcards, play on computer screens or
try on costumes to explore mirror images or
recreate famous paintings. Older children will
also enjoy viewing the Pre-Raphaelite collections and the displays of 20th-century British
art. Children's events and activities in the
school holidays and family workshops once a
month on Sundays.

Manchester Museum

The University of Manchester, Oxford Road
t (0161) 275 2634 **www.museum.man.ac.uk**
Getting there On the B5117 main route into
Manchester, 2 miles from Oxford Road railway station
Open Tues–Sat 10–5, Sun, Mon and Bank Hols 11–4
Adm Free (some activities £1)
Shop, mother and baby room, café

Following refurbishment, the museum has
gained three new galleries, which are accessed
through a new courtyard and entrance hall. A
steel and glass walkway now links the two
museum buildings (dating from 1885 and 1912),
the first of which was designed by local architect
Alfred Waterhouse, who also built the Natural
History Museum in London. First of the new
galleries is Living Cultures, which features artefacts from around the world that are of cultural
significance, including early hunting implements
and examples from the museum's extensive
archery collection. The Story of Money traces the
development of coinage from bartering through
to electronic banking, while Rocks and Minerals
displays fossils and crystal formations to
dramatic effect. Other sections of interest to

children are the Vivarium and Aquarium, with living reptiles in recreated savannah and rainforest settings; the Egyptology Gallery – the largest in the country outside the British Museum – which contains a large collection of mummies; the Science For Life Gallery, which uses interactive exhibits to explore the mysteries of the human body and medical science; and the Zoology Gallery, overlooked by a huge skeleton of a sperm whale, where you can see displays of those perennial children's favourites, dinosaurs. Children's events are put on in school holidays, there are storytelling sessions for under 5s on Fridays (11am–12 noon) and weekend craft events.

Manchester United Football Club Museum and Tour Centre

Manchester United Football Club, Old Trafford **t** (0161) 868 8000, **t** (0161) 868 8631 (Tour Centre) **www**.manutd.com
Open Daily Mon–Sat 9.30–5, Sun 9.40–4.30
Adm Tour and museum: adults £9.50, children £6.50, family (2+3) £27. Museum only: adults £6.50, children £4.25, family (2+3) £17.50
Café, shops

The museum traces the club's meteoric rise from its humble beginnings in 1878 as the Newton Heath Lancashire and Yorkshire Railway Cricket and Football Club to its current position as the most famous football club in the world. The museum was opened in 1998 by Pele, the man who is widely regarded as the greatest player of all time. Your tour begins with a look at the trophy collection (which is bursting at the seams following all the club's recent successes) and a wander past exhibitions looking at the club's two greatest managers – Sir Matt Busby and Sir Alex Ferguson; its greatest players – Best, Charlton, Law, Cantona *et al*, as well as the club's darkest hour – the 1958 Munich air tragedy in which half the team perished. From here, it's on to the heart of the club itself – the part guaranteed to get fans really salivating – to look at the players' lounge and dressing room (spot the peg of your favourite player) before being taken on a tour of the cavernous stadium itself (unfortunately, you're not allowed to step on to the pitch).

Metrolink

t (0161) 205 2000 **www**.metrolink.co.uk
The Manchester tram system is a great way for families to get about the city, connecting Bury in

the north with Altrincham to the south (via Old Trafford) and Piccadilly Station with Salford Quays and Eccles. There are one-day MetroMax family tickets (2+3) available (Mon–Fri £6.20, Sat–Sun £10) and special seats for parents with pushchairs. Bury Metrolink is just a short walk away from the East Lancashire Railway (p.442) and there's a shuttle bus service to the Trafford Centre shopping complex, **t** (0161) 749 1717, from the Stretford Metrolink car park.

★Museum of Science and Industry

Liverpool Road, Castlefield **t** (0161) 832 1830 (24-hr information line) **www**.msim.org.uk
Open Daily 10–5 **Adm Free**; train rides: adults £1, children 50p; some charges for special exhibitions
Restaurant (with hot water to heat baby food and milk), café, gift shop, disabled access, baby changing facilities, parking, pushchair friendly

Once upon a time, Manchester was one of the shining lights of industrial Britain. The spiritual home of the factory, it now provides the perfect setting for a museum dedicated to tracing the history of industrial invention. From spinning jennies to supersonic jets, this is nothing less than a complete overview of the inexorable progress of physical science. Located in the redeveloped industrial area of Castlefield, its centrepiece is an 1830 railway station – the oldest such building in the world – around which is grouped a collection of 19th-century brick warehouses filled with the great metallic behemoths of the industrial age: steam engines, railway locomotives (including the Beyer Garratt locomotive, one of the largest ever built), vintage cars and, appropriately enough for a city founded largely on the back of the textile industry, looms.

Train trips are available along a short stretch of line on weekends and Bank Holidays between 12 noon and 4pm. You'll find displays on electricity, the history of photography and TV, and a four-storey transport gallery with an Air and Space section that runs the gamut from biplanes to space stations.

Although largely concerned with the technologies of the past, the museum's highly interactive displays make use of modern technology with buttons to press and levers to pull. There's a hands-on gallery (Xperiment!) full of science-related activities a soft play zone for toddlers and the Morphis Simulator ride (adults £2, children £1.50).

On the first Friday of the month, there are 'Xperitots' sessions (10–11am) where under 5s can enjoy creative activities, music and storytelling. Mechanically minded activity workshops for older kids during the school holidays.

People's History Museum

The Pump House, Bridge Street **t** (0161) 839 6061
www.peopleshistorymuseum.org.uk
Getting there Near Salford Central railway station, just off Deansgate
Open Tues–Sun 11–4.30 **Adm Free**
Café with highchairs and bottle warming facilities, mother and baby room, disabled access, shop

Dedicated to championing the cause of the man on the street, this museum looks at popular political causes throughout history – trade union rights, the closure of the Yorkshire coal mines, votes for women, etc. It's a diverse selection that has resulted in the museum acquiring the largest collection of political banners in the world. Free guided tours are offered on the second and last Friday of every month. Family-friendly workshops take place in the school holidays.

Shopping

Manchester has long been attracting high street names – Selfridges (in the Trafford Centre, *see* under Metrolink), Habitat and Heals have all seen fit to stake their claim. The 1996 IRA bomb played its part in reshaping Manchester's retail districts, most notably in The Corn Exchange, once an eclectic mix of stalls and shops, which has been reborn in glass, steel and chic boutiques as the Triangle. The Arndale Centre, however, where you'll find a lively market and the Early Learning Centre for toys, merely needed a facelift. For designer clothes, head for King Street and Kendalls department store on Deansgate, where you'll also find a huge Daisy and Tom children's emporium complete with carousel. Affleck's Palace and the thriving selection of outlets in Manchester's Northern Quarter is where the hip kids will be happiest though – especially if they're looking for cutting-edge fashion or state-of-the-art fishtanks. Try Aquatech, 59 Church Street, **t** (0161) 834 8787, or for that rare piece of vinyl, visit Factory Records, 53 Church Street, **t** (0161) 834 8341.

Question

Q: How many lakes are there in the Lake District?

A: Surprisingly, just one. Bassenthwaite Lake is the only 'official' lake; all the rest are categorized as meres, tarns or waters.

Sport and activities *See* pp.445–6

Urbis: Museum of Urban Life

Cathedral Gardens **t** (0161) 605 8200
www.urbis.org.uk
Open Sun-Wed 10–6, Thurs–Sat 10–8 **Adm Free** (charges for some exhibitions)

Urbis resembles either a giant glass boot or an artist's impression of the iceberg that sank the Titanic. Neither aspect is very flattering, especially since the building stands bluntly in the middle of one of the largest open spaces in the city. Inside there are lots of ideas connected to urban living from video boxes about people's experiences in cities to making your own identity cards. Kids will like the glass elevator and the chance to record their own opinions of city life, while parents will enjoy the chance to sit down and take an audiovisual trip around some of the world's greatest cities.

Whitworth Art Gallery

Oxford Road **t** (0161) 275 7450
www.whitworth.man.ac.uk
Getting there Take any bus from Oxford Road Station
Open Mon–Sat 10–5, Sun 2–5 **Adm Free**
Café, picnic area, shop, mother and baby room, disabled access

This collection of British watercolours, prints, sculptures, textiles and wallpaper caters well for children. Regular family activities are planned thoughout the school holidays.

Around Manchester

Haigh Country Park, 20 miles west (p.444)
Jodrell Bank Science Centre Planetarium and Arboretum, 20 miles south (pp.449–50)
Quarry Bank Mill and Styal Country Park, 10 miles south (pp.451–2)
Tatton Park, 12 miles south (p.437)
Wigan Pier, 20 miles west (p.452–3)

THE LAKE DISTRICT

This poet-inspiring landscape is recognized as one of the country's most beautiful. The lush, green hills, dales, tinkling waterfalls, grey limestone villages, peaks and vast shimmering lakes (Coniston Water, Derwent Water, Ullswater and Windermere) of the region have become an icon of England, as emblematic as Big Ben or the White Cliffs. The Lake District National Park (the country's largest) is set within 855 square miles (2,200 sq km) and has six national nature reserves, 16 lakes, more than 50 dales, 100 sites of 'special scientific interest', 150 mountains and nearly 400 towns and villages. It makes for some wonderful walking – its hills are, away from the central mountains, more rolling than challenging – and, although it enjoys a typically English (wet) climate, it attracts tourists all year round. An estimated 14 million people visit the park each year, mostly during the summer months when queue-like processions can form on the major walking routes. The tourist offices stock literally hundreds of walking and cycling guides, many listing routes suitable for families. Parts of the park, particularly in the east towards the Pennines and around the volcanic dome of Scafell and the Cumbrian mountains, are pretty steep and the weather in these parts can close in quickly, even in summer. The region's popularity means that its major towns – Keswick, Ambleside and Windermere – are geared up for the family market and can offer lots of kids' attractions; little ones can quickly tire of sublime scenery.

Lake District Visitor Centre

Brockhole, Windermere **t** (01539) 446601
www.lake-district.gov.uk
Getting there On the A591 between Windermere and Ambleside
Open Apr–Oct 10–5, Nov Sat–Sun 10–5; grounds and gardens: all year **Adm Free**
Café, gift shop, on-site parking
With information on walks, events, attractions and activities throughout the Lake District, this should definitely be your first port of call. It's also an ideal place to take the kids when it's raining. There are two floors of interactive displays and audiovisual programmes and an adventure playground for when the sun comes out. The centre organizes lake cruises, special events, guided walks and children's activity trails.

Ambleside

Getting there Located just north of Windermere, 2 miles south of Grasmere on the A592
Tourist information Central Buildings, Market Cross **t** (01539) 432582
Two miles north of Windermere, Ambleside makes a good base for exploring the southern lakes. Pretty and almost stereotypically quaint with picturesque limestone cottages, you'll find it filled during the summer and autumn months with hardy-looking types who come here to do some serious hiking in the nearby peaks – hence the many outdoor equipment shops lining its narrow stone streets. The park information centre at Brockhole, **t** (01539) 446601, just south of the town, has attractive gardens, an adventure playground and an audiovisual display on the national park.

Things to see and do

Lakeland Safari Tours

23 Fisherbeck Park, Butterworth **t** (01539) 433904
www.lakesafari.co.uk
Open In summer
Adm Half day £22, full day £33
Half- or full-day tours around the Lake District aboard a six-seater vehicle in the company of a Blue Badge Guide.

Hawkshead and Coniston

Getting there Hawkshead lies between Lake Windermere and Coniston Water, 20 miles west of Kendal on the B5285. Coniston is about 4 miles west on the A593
Tourist information Hawkshead: Main car park, Main Street **t** (01539) 436545; Coniston: Ruskin Avenue **t** (01539) 441533
Hawkshead is a superbly preserved 16th-century village that lies roughly equidistant between Lake Windermere and Coniston Water (it's four miles east of the sailing centres at the northern tip of Coniston). Festooned with flowers in summer, and largely free of cars, it's one of the park's main holiday centres and is very popular with Beatrix Potter enthusiasts (her former home lies just to the south of the town). The nearby village of Coniston, which lies in the shadow of the 812m (2,633ft) 'Old Man' mountain can offer pony rides, **t** (01539) 441391, and is surrounded by a network of eminently explorable walking trails. Its eponymous lake is

the park's third largest and has been in the news following the discovery of the wreck of the *Bluebird*, the late Sir Donald Campbell's super-powered speedboat which tragically crashed and sank in 1966 as the inventor attempted to break the water speed record. Filled with pleasure craft for much of the year, the lake provides a refuge for an array of wildlife and many water birds.

Things to see and do

The Beatrix Potter Gallery

Main Street, Hawkshead **t** (01539) 436355
www.nationaltrust.org.uk
Open Apr–Oct Sat–Thurs 10.30–4.30 (last entry 4); timed ticket system in operation
Adm Adults £3.60, children £1.80, family £9
Not suitable for pushchairs or wheelchairs

A changing exhibition of original watercolours by children's favourite Beatrix Potter, including numerous unpublished pictures of her famous animal characters (Peter Rabbit, Jemima Puddleduck, Squirrel Nutkin *et al*), as well as original manuscripts of her stories. A children's quiz sheet and guide to the author are available. You might like to combine a visit here with a trip to Hill Top in Sawrey, just south of Hawkshead, where you'll find the 17th-century house in which Beatrix Potter wrote most of her stories and which has been preserved much as she left it with her original furniture and china.

Coniston Boating Centre

Lake Road **t** (01539) 441366
Open In summer, call for price details
Picnic area, café, parking, toilets

Sailing dinghies, row boats, kayaks and canoes.

★Coniston Launch

Coniston **t** (01539) 436216
www.conistonlaunch.co.uk
Open In summer
Sailings Daily mid-Mar–mid-Nov and 26 Dec–2 Jan
Adm Varies according to whether you are taking a full tour or stopping off; family return £14

Small, family-run firm running a ferry service to various jetties up and down the lake, from where you can disembark to explore the lakeside on foot. Look out for Brantwood, the idyllically situated home of the 19th-century social reformer John Ruskin, which is surrounded by 100 hectares (250 acres) of woodland. The company also offers themed sightseeing tours including one taking in

Did you know?
That the Lake District is not only an extremely beautiful area, it's also a record-breaking one. It's home to the country's highest peak (Scafell Pike – 978m/3,120ft high), its deepest lake (Wastwater – 79m/258ft deep), its longest lake (Windermere – 17km/10 miles long), its steepest road (Hardknott Pass, which ascends at a thigh-burning 33 per cent gradient or 1:3) and even the country's ugliest face puller or 'gurner' who is crowned following the annual championships at Egremont.

the sights associated with Sir Malcolm and Sir Donald Campbell's attempts to break the world water speed record on the lake and one based on Arthur Ransome's children's classic *Swallows and Amazons* (which was set here). Ransome was originally a war reporter but, after covering the Russian Revolution, he decided that he'd had enough. He married Trotsky's secretary and retired to the Lake District. Coniston Water inspired him to write for children and, after a trip around the lake with the enthusiastic guide, you'll really believe that the mountain really is Kanchenjunga and that you've just found Wild Cat Island (tours Mar–Oct Wed 3.40pm; school holidays also Sun). They are popular for birthday parties so it's advisable to book well in advance. Expect to pay around £27 for a family of four. The tour is only suitable for kids over six years of age.

Grizedale Forest Park

Hawkshead **t** (01229) 860291 **www.grizedale.org**
Getting there The visitor centre is 2 miles southwest of Hawkshead on the road between Hawkshead and Satterthwaite
Open Daily (closed 25 Dec and 1 Jan) **Adm Free** (parking £3 per day)
Tearoom, shop, exhibition

Hunt for over 80 wood and rock sculptures hidden throughout the forest. You can hire bikes, visit the craft centre and the adventure playground.

Steam Yacht Gondola

Coniston **t** (01539) 441288,
www.nationaltrust.org.uk
Open In summer
Sailings Apr–Oct daily once an hour 11–4
Adm Return tickets adults £5.90, children £2.90, family £14.50, under 2s **free**

First launched way back in 1859, this remarkably well-preserved steam-powered yacht still offers sightseeing tours of the lake.

Kendal

Getting there Kendal is about 10 miles southeast of Windermere on the A6
Tourist information Town Hall, Highgate **t** (01539) 725758

Famed for its legendary mint cake, a sticky concoction of boiled sugar and peppermint oil, which possesses such astounding energy-giving properties that it was enthusiastically consumed by Sir Edmund Hillary during his pioneering ascent of Everest and, even today, can be found packed inside the luggage of all hikers worth their salt. The town behind the cake is rather less celebrated. Compared with some of the other major towns of the region, it is a little staid and lies on the outskirts of the national park, failing to attract the crowds that swarm around its competitors – although its surrounding limestone fells are popular with the hiking fraternity. Nonetheless, it's worth a detour for its ruined castle, where Catherine Parr (Henry VIII's luckiest wife, who survived him) was born, its museums and bustling, untouristy ambience. The grand stately homes of Holker Hall (p.435) and Levens Hall (pp.435–6) are within easy reach of the town.

Things to see and do

Kendal Leisure Centre

Burton Road, Kendal **t** (01539) 729777
theatre: **t** (01539) 729702
Open Daily 7.40am–10pm
Adm Prices vary depending on the facility required
Café, bar, free parking, theatre

The premier sports and entertainment centre in South Lakeland with facilities for swimming, squash, badminton and a fitness room.

Kendal Museum of Natural History and Archaeology

Station Road, Kendal **t** (01539) 721374
www.kendalmuseum.org.uk
Getting there 10 minutes from the M6 (J36)
Open Mid-Feb–Dec Mon–Sat 10.30–5 (winter until 4)
Adm Adults £2.70, children **free**
Shop, some wheelchair access, on-site parking

One of the country's oldest museums with a varied collection of displays on wildlife, natural history and social history. There are prehistoric tools, fossils (look out for the dinosaur footprints) and lots of stuffed animals including a fully grown

> **Did you know?**
> That the Lake District is where you'll come across the country's biggest (amateur) liar. The title is bestowed on whoever can tell the most convincing tall story at the 'lying championships' held at the village inn of the small town of Santon Bridge. Politicians, lawyers, journalists and other 'professional' liars are banned from competing.

polar bear. It's pretty hands-on, with touch-screen computers showing you what life was like in Kendal 500 years ago, and a variety of activities are laid on for children: Roman pottery, Roman sandal-making and medieval tiling. Quizzes and trails (such as a Creepy Crawly Trail) are also laid on. Along with the Museum of Lakeland Life (*see* below), Kendal Museum runs a Saturday club with activities for children based on the collections.

Museum of Lakeland Life

Abbot Hall, Kendal **t** (01539) 722464
www.lakelandmuseum.org.uk
Open Nov–Mar Mon–Sat 10.30–4, Apr–Oct Mon–Sat 10.30–5
Adm Adults £3.75, children £2.75, family £11
Café, picnic area, some disabled access, on-site parking

Dedicated to tracing the history and development of the Cumbrian people, this contains several replica period rooms including a Victorian parlour and a recreation of the study of Arthur Ransome (author of *Swallows and Amazons*), a host of old toys and games, as well as displays looking at traditional local crafts and skills such as patchwork and embroidery. Work sheets are available for children and activity clubs are organized every Saturday (*see* Kendal Museum).

Keswick

Getting there Keswick is just north of Derwent Water on the A591
Tourist information Moot Hall, Market Square **t** (01768) 772645 www.keswick.org

Pleasant and picturesque in a cobbledy sort of way, Keswick, a stone's throw from Derwent Water, is the most popular of the northern lake towns. Though slightly overdeveloped, it has all the ingredients for a top family holiday – a jolly collection of museums, two landscaped parks, good walking in the local area (look out for the Castlerigg ancient stone circle just outside the town), a lovely tea garden and the watersports and sailing of Derwent Water itself (*see* Keswick Launch, below).

Things to see and do

Cars of the Stars Motor Museum

Standish Street, Keswick **t** (01768) 773757
www.carsofthestars.com
Open Easter–Nov and Feb half term daily 10–5
(weekends only to 25 Dec)
Adm Adults £4, children £3
Gift shop, guided tours, disabled access
   Famous vehicles from TV and films on display
include Chitty Chitty Bang Bang, several
Batmobiles, the Flintstone's prehistoric car, the
Trotters' van from *Only Fools and Horses*, Herbie
and James Bond's Aston Martin.

Cumberland Pencil Museum

Southey Works, Keswick **t** (01768) 773626
www.pencils.co.uk
Open Daily 9.30–4 (longer hours in peak season)
Adm Adults £3, children £1.50, family (2+3) £7.50
Gift shop, disabled access, parking
   The history of pencil-making from the discovery
of graphite in Borrowdale in the 1500s through
the early cottage industry that produced the
famous Cumberland pencils to the modern high-
speed processes. There's a children's drawing
corner, brass rubbings and changing exhibitions.
Look out for the largest pencil in the world – it's
more than 8m (25ft) tall.

Keswick Launch

Keswick **t** (01768) 772263
www.keswick-launch.co.uk
Sailings Every 30 minutes **Adm** Adults £6.50,
children £3.25, under 5s **free**, family (2+3) £15
Offers 50-minute trips around the lake. Row boats
can also be hired for around £8.50 per hour for up to
2 people or £9.50 an hour for a family (2+3)

Trotters World of Animals

Coalbeck Farm, Bassenthwaite, Keswick
t (01768) 776239 **www.trottersworld.com**
Getting there 5 miles north of Keswick off the A591
and A66
Open 10–5.30 (or dusk if earlier) **Adm** Adults £5.95,
children (3–14) £4.50, under 3s **free**
Tearoom, gift shop, free car park, picnic areas
   Home to llamas, lar gibbons, lemurs, rabbits,
ponies, snakes and lizards, deer and birds such as
peacocks, owls and assorted pheasants, this has
been designed with families in mind. There are
daily demonstrations of milking and bird of prey
flying and your kids can delight in hugging a

bunny, bottle-feeding a baby goat or milking a
Jersey cow. When they tire of all that, there's the
soft play and climbing area (ages 4–12) with a
separate ball pool for under 4s, plus tractor or
pony rides around the 10-hectare (25-acre) site.

Whinlatter Forest Park

Whinlatter **t** (017687) 78469
Getting there Whinlatter visitor centre is on the
B5292, just off the A66 to Cockermouth, a little
over 3 miles northwest of Keswick
Open Daily (closed 25 Dec and 1 Jan) **Adm Free**
Tearoom, forest shop, visitor centre
   England's only mountain forest park with an
adventure playground and waymarked trails.

Penrith

Getting there Penrith is a few miles north of
Ullswater, just off the M6 (J40), A66 and A686
Tourist information Robinson's School, Middlegate
t (01768) 867466
   The largest of the lake towns (outside the
confines of the park proper), Penrith is busy and
bustling and less overtly touristy than many of its
neighbours. Close to the Pennines and just a few
miles north of Ullswater, it offers its fair share of
outdoor pursuits, but is also good for shopping, its
distinctive red sandstone buildings housing a
range of specialist shops, where you can pick up
traditionally made cheeses, pottery, woollen goods
and curly Cumberland sausages (though the best
place to go for these is Waberthwaite). The main
shopping areas are the covered Devonshire Arcade
and the pedestrianized Angel Lane. If it's sunny,
visit the ruins of the town's medieval castle, which
is surrounded by a pleasant park. The gentle
attraction of the Lowther Leisure and Wildlife Park
is about six miles south, while Eden Ostrich World
(pp.437–8) and Acorn Bank Garden and Watermill
(p.441) are about six miles east.

Things to see and do

Penrith Museum

Middlegate **t** (01768) 212228
Open Mon–Sat 10–4, Apr–Oct also Sun 1–4.45
Adm Free
Disabled access
   Overview of the history, archaeology and
geology of Penrith and the Eden Valley. Kids will
like the handling sessions, medieval cauldron,
Roman pottery and the old wooden rocking horse.

Rheged Discovery Centre

Redhills **t** (01768) 868000 **www.rheged.com**
Open Daily 10–5.30
Adm Movie: Adults £5.95, children £4, family (2+3) £17; extra movie: £4, children £2.75; mountaineering exhibition: adults £5.95, children **free**; movie and exhibition: adults £9.95
Two cafés, food bar, food hall, shops, disabled access, mother and baby facilities, on-site parking

A hi-tech look at a traditional world, this discovery centre (named after an ancient Celtic kingdom) aims to provide a complete overview of Cumbrian life. Set into the hills, in Britain's largest grass-covered building, the centre's showpiece is a film retelling 2,000 years of Lake District history on a six storey-high cinema screen. Over in the mountaineering exhibition, you can dress up as a mountaineer, learn how Ordnance Survey maps are compiled and see films, photos and interactive displays on the challenging sport. There are several shops within the centre including a bookshop, a toyshop, a paper mill (you can have a go at making paper), chocolate workshop and Create store (open weekends and school holidays), where children can paint pottery to take home. There is also an indoor play area (charges apply).

Ullswater Cruises

The Pier House, Glenridding, Patterdale **t** (01768) 482229 **www.ullswater-steamers.co.uk**
Sailings Mar–Oct daily, Easter–Sept full service
Fares Adult return: £7–10.30, children £3.50–5.15

Offers cruises from Pooley Bridge at the northern tip of Ullswater (about five miles south of Penrith) to Glenridding at its southern tip (about nine miles) aboard *My Raven* or *My Lady of the Lake*, two 19th-century steamers that have been converted to oil. The lake is surrounded by beautiful countryside with a network of well-worn walking paths taking you past its most scenic parts, including the famous 20m (65ft) Aira Force waterfall on its western banks.

Windermere

Getting there On the eastern shore of Lake Windermere on the A592
Tourist information Victoria Street, Windermere **t** (01539) 446499

The most resort-like of the lake towns came into being in the mid 19th century when the railways reached the shore of the country's largest lake.

Now spread out for a mile or so along the lake's eastern side, the town of Windermere has become the region's principal urban centre, with a range of attractions on offer and, though a little touristy and overpriced, makes a good base for a family holiday. You can use the services of Windermere Lake Cruises to visit some of the other attractions grouped around the lake including the Aquarium of the Lakes in Newby Bridge and the Lakeside and Haverthwaite Steam Railway in Lakeside.

Things to see and do

Aquarium of the Lakes

Lakeside, Newby Bridge **t** (01539) 530153
www.aquariumofthelakes.co.uk
Getting there Newby Bridge is on the southern shores of Lake Windermere, 10 miles south of the town of Windermere on the A590, J36 from the M6
Open Apr–Oct daily 9–6, Nov–Mar 9–5
Adm Adults £7, children £4.50, family £22–30.50; combined ticket for Windermere Lake Cruises available (*see below*)
Café, gift shop, disabled access

Just a short walk from the steamer stop, this boasts the UK's largest collection of freshwater fish, a recreated bay, seashore and lake bed (complete with otters), which you observe through a see-through tunnel.

★Lakeside and Haverthwaite Steam Railway

Haverthwaite, near Ulverston **t** (015395) 31594
www.lakesiderailway.co.uk
Getting there Lakeside is at the southern tip of Windermere. From J36 of the M6 follow the A590 west to Haverthwaite near Newby Bridge
Open Easter–end Oct daily 10.30–5 **Fares** Return: adults £4.90, children £2.45; combined ticket for Windermere Lake Cruises available (*see below*)
Restaurant, souvenir shop, car parking

A serious contender for the title of the country's most scenic railway. From Haverthwaite Station, steam locomotives haul vintage coaches through the beautiful Cumbrian countryside to Lakeside, where you can continue your journey aboard one of the Windermere Lake Cruises.

★Windermere Lake Cruises

Bowness-on-Windermere **t** (01539) 531188
www.windermere-lakecruises.co.uk
Sailings Daily (except 25 Dec) from Lakeside, Bowness and Ambleside during daylight hours

Adm Return trips: adults £7.30–£13.25, children £3.75–£6.65, family £10–£34

There are a variety of cruises to choose from including a 45-minute island cruise taking in wooded islets, mountains and secluded bays, a buffet cruise or a shorter trip to the Lake District National Park Visitor Centre in Brockhole. Rowing boats and motor boats available for hire.

Windermere Outdoor Adventure Watersports Centre

Rayrigg Road **t** (015394) 729777
www.southlakelandleisure.org.uk
Open Mid-Mar–end Nov daily 9–5. Evenings and weekends by pre-booked arrangement
Adm Call in advance for details

Courses in dinghy sailing, kayaking, open canoeing, wind-surfing and keelboat sailing.

Windermere Steam Boat Museum

Rayrigg Road **t** (01539) 445565
www.steamboat.co.uk
Open Apr–Jun and mid-Sept–early Nov 10–4.30, July–mid-Sept 10–5
Adm Museum: adults £4.75, children £2.50, family £9.50; boat trips: adults £5.50, children £2.50
Gift shop, disabled access, on-site parking

Pristine collection of ancient steam and motor boats. Pride of place is *Dolly*, the world's oldest mechanically powered boat, which was recovered from the murky depths of Ullswater in 1962, some 65 years after she sank. Lake trips aboard a small steam launch are offered and various events such as boat rallies and model boat regattas organized.

World of Beatrix Potter

Crag Brow, Bowness-on-Windermere
t (01539) 488444 www.hop-skip-jump.com
Getting there Located in the town centre, which is 10 miles west of Kendal, off the A591
Open Apr–Sept daily 10–5.30, Oct–Mar 10–4.30 (closed 25 Dec, 1 Jan and 10–30 Jan)
Adm Adults £6, children £3 (under 4s **free**)
Tearoom, shop

Hi-tech recreations of scenes from Beatrix Potter's colourful children's books. You'll see Peter Rabbit wreaking havoc in Mr McGregor's garden, Mrs Tiggywinkle pottering around her kitchen and Jemima Puddleduck hiding from Mr Fox. It's particularly good for young children, who will take delight in the Tailor of Gloucester tearoom, where you can have a snack amongst an array of Beatrix Potter's characters.

Castles and historic houses

Arley Hall and Gardens

Great Budworth, near Northwich **t** (01565) 777353
www.arleyhallandgardens.com
Getting there Arley Hall is about 7 miles north of Northwich, 10 minutes from the M6 (J9) and M56
Open Hall: Easter–Sept Sun and Tues 12 noon–5; gardens: Apr–Sept Tues–Sun and Bank Hols 11–5, Oct Sat–Sun only
Adm Grounds, gardens and chapel: adults £5, children £2, under 5s **free**, family £12; hall (extra): adults £2.50, children £1, under 5s **free**, family £7; farm, hall and garden: adults £8.50, children £5, under 5s **free**, family £23
Restaurant, shop, nursery, on-site parking

Beautiful Jacobean estate with fine architecture and elegant gardens. See daily milking demonstrations and birds of prey flying displays at nearby Stockley Farm (reached aboard a tractor and trailer that leaves every hour from the hall car park). Special events, such as the famous Arley Garden Festival, are held at the estate throughout the year.

Astley Hall

Astley Park, Chorley **t** (01257) 515927
www.chorley.gov.uk
Getting there Astley Park is just on the edge of Chorley town centre off the A581, J8 from M61
Open Park: daily; hall: Apr–Oct Tues–Sun 12–5; call for details of winter opening
Adm Park: **free**; hall: call for details
Gift shop, picnic areas, mother and baby room, guided tours, on-site parking

A quiz trail takes you around this grand Elizabethan hall, which has exhibits for children including a dressing-up box and a hands-on zone where they can examine historical objects and write with a quill pen. Outside is a lake, where you can feed the ducks, a pets' corner with goats, pigs and rabbits, plus picnic and kick-about areas.

★Carlisle Castle

t (01228) 591922 www.english-heritage.org.uk
Getting there Carlisle is in the extreme northwest corner of England on the A595, A69 and A7, just south of the M6 (J43 and 44)
Open Daily Apr–Sept 9.30–6, Oct–Mar 10–4
Adm Adults £4.10, children £2.10, under 5s **free**
Refreshments, gift shop

Lying near the border with Scotland in what has historically been one of the most fiercely contested patches of land in the entire country, Carlisle's grand, sinister-looking castle has enjoyed a turbulent past, bearing witness to numerous attacks. Built on the orders of William II in the late 11th century after the Norman army's capture of the town from the Scots, it would come to be seen north of the border as a hated symbol of English colonial aggression. It was laid siege to in the Middle Ages by William Wallace and Robert the Bruce, was a prison for Mary Queen of Scots in the 16th century and, in 1745, was briefly captured by the Jacobite army of Bonnie Prince Charlie during its abortive invasion of England, before being brought back under English control by the Duke of Cumberland (also known as 'Butcher' Cumberland on account of the ruthless way he treated his enemies). Much altered over the last 900 years, the castle is well preserved, with lots of passageways and winding staircases to explore, as well as period-style rooms. Kids will be drawn to the dungeons, where they can see the terrible graffiti scratched into the walls of the condemned cells and the 'licking stones', a gruesome relic of the castle's murky past: after the Jacobite army's defeat, many Scottish soldiers were thrown into the castle's dungeons, where they were kept without food or water while they awaited punishment. They kept themselves alive by licking the moisture on the cell's stones – all in vain as every prisoner was executed.

Dunham Massey Hall, Park and Garden

Altrincham **t** (0161) 941 1025 **www.**nationaltrust.org.uk
Getting there 3 miles southwest of Altrincham, off the A56, M6 (J19) and M56 (J7)
Open House: Apr–Oct Sat–Wed 12–5; garden: Apr–Oct daily 11–5.30
Adm Adults £6.50, children £3.25, family £16.25; house or garden only: adults £4.50, children £2.25; park only: cars £3
Restaurant with children's menu, shop, on-site parking, picnic area, baby changing facilities

Early Georgian mansion with a grand Edwardian interior and a fascinating Victorian kitchen set in a 100-hectare (250-acre) wooded park with children's trails taking you past ancient trees (some with trunks over eight feet across), a restored water-powered Elizabethan sawmill and millpond, and herds of free-roaming deer. Excellent family events throughout the year. The park is beautiful in autumn and winter, when there are carol-singing events and bird walks.

Holker Hall and Gardens

Cark-in-Cartmel, Grange-over-Sands
t (01539) 558328 **www.**holker-hall.co.uk
Getting there 14 miles southwest of Kendal on the B5278; signposted from the M6 (J36) and the A590
Open Apr–Oct Sun–Fri 10–5.30; hall and motor museum close at 4.45pm
Adm All-inclusive tickets: adults £10.50, children £6, under 6s **free,** family £29; individual tickets available
Café with children's menu and bottle warming, shop, food hall, picnic area, baby changing facilities, disabled access, on-site parking

Owned by Lord and Lady Cavendish, this grand Victorian stately pile provides children's guides and activity sheets for exploring the hall and grounds. The 10 hectares (25 acres) of award-winning gardens have lovely water features (look out for the world's largest slate sundial) and there's a 50-hectare (125-acre) deer park and an adventure playground. The prime attraction is the Lakeland Motor Museum, with its collection of vintage vehicles (from classic cars to tractors) and a Bluebird exhibition with replica vehicles, which details the life and times of Sir Malcolm and Donald Campbell who broke 21 world speed records for Britain.

Lancaster Castle

Castle Parade, Lancaster **t** (01524) 64998
www.lancastercastle.com
Getting there Lancaster is 45 miles north of Manchester, off J34 of the M6
Open Daily 10–5; admission by guided tour only at 30-minute intervals, duration 45 minutes (court sittings permitting)
Adm Adults £5, children £4, children £14
Shop, limited disabled access

One of the best-preserved, most energetically presented medieval castles in the country, parts of which are still used as a prison, Lancaster's fortress makes great play of its gruesome past. See the spot where, in 1612, several women accused of being witches were tried, convicted and condemned to die; a display of torture instruments in the dungeon; the 'Hanging Corner', where prisoners were executed before a baying mob; and the Crown Court, where poor petty criminals were sentenced to transportation to the penal colonies in Australia. The Shire Hall, with its colourful display of heraldic shields, will come as a relief.

Levens Hall and Topiary Gardens

Levens **t** (015395) 60321 **www.levenshall.co.uk**
Getting there About 5 miles south of Kendal on the A6 and signposted from the A590 and A591
Open Apr–mid Oct Sun–Thurs; garden and tearoom: 10–5; house: 12–5 (last admission 4.30); steam collection: Sun and Bank Hols in season 2–5
Adm Adults £9, childen £4, family (2+3) £23; gardens only: adults £6, childen £3, family £17.50
Café, shop, disabled access to gardens, shop and restaurant only, on-site parking

The grounds of this fine Elizabethan estate will strike a chord with children. The world-famous topiary gardens, first laid out in 1694, contain a fascinating collection of bizarrely shaped leafy sculptures that should interest all age groups. There's also a lovely fountain garden and, on Sundays and Bank Holidays, rides on a miniature steam engine.

Lyme Park

Disley, Stockport **t** (01663) 762023
www.nationaltrust.org.uk
Getting there On the A6, 6.5 miles southeast of Stockport and 9 miles northwest of Buxton
Open House: Apr–Oct Fri–Tues 1–5, Bank Hols 11–5; gardens: Apr–Oct daily 11–5, Nov–early Dec Sat–Sun 12–3; park: Apr–Oct daily 8–8.30; Nov–Mar 8–6
Adm House and garden: £6.50, children £3.30, family £17
Restaurant and tearoom with children's menus, coffee and toyshop, baby changing facilities, some disabled access and facilities, on-site parking (£4.50)

Grand country estate with 600 hectares (1,400 acres) of moorland, woodland and park on the edge of Stockport. At its centre is an Italianate mansion, where the Legh family have lived for 600 years. It's sprawling and cluttered inside; look out for the collection of clocks. Surrounding the house are seven hectares (17 acres) of gardens, with an orangery and a wilderness garden; beyond this is a deer park (home to red deer), a curious dovecote, a hunting lodge (redecorated in early 19th-century style; open second and fourth weekends of the month), an adventure playground and the lake from which Mr Darcy emerged in the BBC production of *Pride and Prejudice*.

★Muncaster Castle, Garden and Owl Centre

Ravenglass **t** (01229) 717614 **www.muncaster.co.uk**
Getting there On the coast, 1 mile south of Ravenglass on the A595, and 19 miles south of Whitehaven; *see* Ravenglass and Eskdale Railway (p.443)

Open Gardens and owl centre: daily 10.30–6 (dusk in winter); castle: mid-Mar–Oct Sun–Fri 12 noon–5
Adm Gardens, maze, owl centre and castle: adults £9, children £6, family £25; gardens, maze and owl centre: adults £6.50, children £4.50, family £20
Restaurant, refreshments, shops, mother and baby room, disabled access, on-site parking

The castle has been owned by the same family since the 13th century and, according to legend, will remain in their possession just so long as they can keep a 'magical' drinking bowl intact (the bowl is kept safely under lock and key). Though majestic and refined and filled with 800 years' worth of artefacts and treasures (the audiotour will explain the colourful history behind many of the items on display), kids will be much more interested in what is going on outside at the World Owl Trust and the Owl Centre Works, which is home to over 150 birds and which holds 'Meet the Birds' sessions with daily talks and flying displays (Mar–Oct). You can also watch closed-circuit TV pictures of nesting owls. The centre is surrounded by gardens full of rare plants and colourful flowers, and there are trails and walks through natural woodlands, as well as a large wooden play area, a wildlife pond and a maze aimed at children who, to enter, will have to assume the role of a vole making its way across the countryside – to find the exit, they must scratch off the correct answers on the card provided as they go.

Sizergh Castle and Garden

Sizergh **t** (015395) 60951 **www.nationaltrust.org.uk**
Getting there 3.5 miles south of Kendal, off A590
Open Apr–Oct Sun–Thurs; garden and shop: 12–5; castle and tearoom: 1–5
Adm Adults £6.20, children £3.10, family £15.50; garden only: adults £4, children £2
Tearoom, picnic tables, refreshment kiosk in car park, shop, baby changing facilities, disabled access, on-site parking. The castle is not suitable for baby backpacks or pushchairs; hip carrying seats are on loan

Built around a 14th-century defensive tower and home to the Strickland family for over 750 years, Sizergh Castle houses a fine collection of Elizabethan carvings, panelling, furniture and portraits (children's discovery sheet available). The garden is largely 18th century and contains a treasure hunt that will keep the kids occupied while mums and dads enjoy the scenic views. A children's guide to the castle is also available.

★Tatton Park

Knutsford **t** (01625) 534400 Infoline: (01625) 534435
www.tattonpark.org.uk
Getting there 12 miles south of Manchester; sign-posted from the M56 (J7), M6 (J19), A56 and A50
Open Garden: Tues–Sun 10–5; mansion:
Tues–Sun 1–4
Adm Mansion and gardens: adults £3.50, children £2, family £9; discovery saver card: adults £5, children £3, family £13.50; car park £4
Café, gift shop, disabled access, on-site parking

Although Tatton Hall is rather stuffy, the grounds are anything but. Spread out over 24 hectares (60 acres), they boast a fiendishly difficult maze, a recreated 1930s rare breeds farm, where traditional farming practices are observed, and which is home to four Shire horses (including a Blue Roan Clydesdale), donkeys, pigs and an abandoned fallow deer; colourful flowerbeds, a collection of huge, towering American redwood trees; a sailing and watersports centre, where you can hire boats for pottering about on the estate's two lakes and an adventure playground filled with swinging tyres, rope bridges and plank walks. The grounds are also home to free-roaming deer and, on summer weekends, you can take horse and carriage rides and tractor rides through the woods. Activities most weekends and special events (historic costumed tours, classical concerts with firework finales, craft fairs, teddy bear fairs and family fun days) throughout the year.

Walton Hall Gardens

Walton Lea Road, Higher Walton, Warrington
t (01925) 261957 (hall), **t** (01925) 601617 (rangers), **t** (01925) 602336 (heritage centre)
www.warrington.gov.uk
Getting there Just outside Warrington off the A56, J11 from the M56
Open Park: daily 8–dusk; other facilities:
Easter–end Sept daily 10.30–6; end Sept–Easter 10.30–4.15; call for details **Adm Free**
Café-restaurant, gift shop, disabled access, guided tours, on-site parking (pay and display)

The 19th-century (albeit Elizabethan style) Walton Hall provides an ideal setting for a family day out with extensive lawns, picnic areas, orna-mental gardens, a heritage centre, children's zoo and woodland trails – see if you can spot any of the squirrels, weasels, nuthatches, tree creepers and woodpeckers that live in these parts.

Animal attractions

Blackpool Zoo Park

East Park Drive **t** (01253) 830830
www.blackpoolzoo.org.uk
Getting there 2 miles east from Blackpool Promenade and signposted from J4 of the M55
Open Daily 10–5.45 (last entry 5pm); Jul–Aug Wed until 9pm
Adm Zoo: adults £11, children £7, under 3s **free**, family (2+2) £32 (2+3) £38; Zoo and dinosaur safari: adults £13.50, children £10.50, under 3s **free**, family (2+2) £42 (2+3) £50

Modern zoo with more than 400 animals, spacious moated pens, lakes and islands. Children's zoo, farmyard and adventure playground.
For further information *see p.418*

Bowland Wild Boar Park

Chipping, Preston **t** (01995) 61554
www.wildboarpark.co.uk
Getting there About 2 miles from Chipping in the Forest of Bowland, 10 miles from Preston and 8 miles from Clitheroe
Open Easter–Oct 10.30–5.30
Adm Adults £4, children £3, under 2s **free**, family (2+2) £12
Café, picnic area, river walks, play area

A chance to see wild boar, Longhorn cows, owls, llamas, goats and deer. Kids can feed baby animals.

★Chester Zoo

Upton-by-Chester **t** (01244) 380280
www.chesterzoo.org
Open Summer 10–6 (last entry 5); winter 10–4 (last entry 3) **Adm** Adults £14.50, children £10.50 (under 3s **free**), family ticket (2+2) £47.50

Britain's largest zoo (more than 5,000 animals) spread out over 45 hectares (110 acres) of natura-listic enclosures.
For further information *see pp.419–20*

Eden Ostrich World

Langwathby Hall Farm, Langwathby, Penrith
t (01768) 881771 **www.ostrich-world.com**
Getting there Located in the village of Langwathby, on the A686, 6 miles east of Penrith, J40 from the M6
Open Mar–end Oct 10–5
Adm Adults £4.95, children £3.95, under 3s **free**, family tickets £16
Tearoom, indoor and outdoor picnic areas, gift shop

Home to a large collection of ostriches, as well as llamas, suckler cows, deer, walllabies, pigs, Shire horses, Shetland ponies and various breeds of sheep. There's also an adventure play area with a giant maze for kids, a pets' corner and tractor rides.

★Knowsley Safari Park

Prescot **t** (0151) 430 9009 **www.**knowsley.com
Getting there Leave the M62 at J6, then the M57 at J2; the park is signposted
Open Mar–Oct daily 10–7 (last admission 4pm); Nov–Feb daily 10.30–4 (last entry 3; closed 25 Dec)
Adm Adults £10, children £7, family (2+2) £30
Restaurant, café, gift shop, baby changing facilities, disabled access, on-site parking, picnic area, first aid

Opened in 1971 by the 18th Earl of Derby, this was the first safari park in Britain to be built near a major city – just eight miles from the centre of Liverpool. Moats and electric fences prevent the wild animals from putting in any unexpected appearances in the high street, however.

In the mid 19th century, the 13th Earl of Derby kept one of the largest private collections of animals in the world on this site. Members of the public could visit, in groups of no more than six, with the written permission of the Earl. Today, the park's authorities are more accommodating. The full 'Safari' experience takes you on a five-mile ride through the park's enclosures, which are home to elephants (the largest herd in Europe), lions, tigers, wildebeest, buffalo, zebra and rhinos (known collectively, appropriately, as a 'crash'; the park is one of only a handful in the world to have successfully reintroduced captive bred rhinos back into the wild), as well as ostriches, camels and a troop of baboons. Elsewhere in the park is a children's funpark with traditional rides such as a carousel, dodgems, the Pirate Ship, Viper rollercoaster and Zebra Jeeps; there's also a small steam railway and a show area for daily sea lion performances.

Martin Mere Wildfowl and Wetlands Trust

Burscough, Lancashire **t** (01704) 895181
www.wwt.org.uk
Getting there 10 miles from Southport, 6 miles from Ormskirk. Signposted from the M61, M58 and M6
Open Mar–Oct daily 9.30–5.30; Nov–Feb 9.30–4 (closed 25 Dec)
Adm Adults £6, children £3.80, under 4s **free**, family £15.55
Café, shop, binocular hire, lectures, disabled access and facilities, baby changing facilities

With over 1,600 ducks, geese and swans in residence, Martin Mere is perfectly suited to studying wildfowl in close proximity. As well as penned enclosures, where rare species may be observed at close range, Martin Mere has a number of strategically positioned hides dotted about the surrounding fields and meres. The Trust run inventive, animal-inspired events throughout the year.

★Muncaster Castle, Garden and Owl Centre

Ravenglass **t** (01229) 717614 **www.**muncaster.co.uk
Open Gardens and owl centre: daily 10.30–6 or dusk in winter; castle: mid-Mar–Oct Sun–Fri 12 noon–5
Adm Gardens, maze, owl centre and castle: adults £9, children £6, family £25; gardens, maze and owl centre: adults £6.50, children £4.50, family £20

The World Owl Trust and the Owl Centre Works are home to more than 150 birds, which kids can observe on closed-circuit TV. Daily flying displays between March and October.
For further information *see* p.436

South Lakes Wild Animal Park

Crossgates, Dalton-in-Furness **t** (01229) 466086
www.wildanimalpark.co.uk
Open Summer daily 10–5, winter 10–4.30
Adm Adults £10.50, children £7, under 3s **free**,
Getting there About 2 of miles north of Barrow-in-Furness, just south of the A590; M6 (J36)
Café, indoor and outdoor picnic areas, gift shop, adventure play area, safari railway, on-site parking

One of Europe's top conservation centres, the South Lakes Wild Animal Park is home to zebras, rhinos, cheetahs, apes and monkeys, tigers and lions, who you should be able to see at feeding times clambering up six-metre (20ft) wooden poles to claim their hunks of meat. There are tiger-feeding sessions daily at 2.30pm, lion-feeding at 4.25pm and lemur-feeding at 2pm (Easter–Oct).

Farms

Cheshire Ice Cream Farm

Drumlan Hall, Newton Lane, Tattenhall
t (01829) 770446,
www.cheshirefarmicecream.co.uk
Getting there Tattenhall is 38 miles southwest of Manchester via the A51
Open Daily 10–5.30 (winter 5pm) **Adm Free**
Tearoom, ice cream parlour, gift shop

Working dairy farm selling its own brand of tasty, traditionally made ice cream in 30 flavours.

You can meet the resident pigs, sheep, rabbits and watch the dairy herd being milked. There's also an adventure playground and an indoor play barn for under 6s.

Farmer Parr's Animal World and Fylde Country Life Museum

Wyrefield Farm, Rossall Lane, Fleetwood
t (01253) 874389
Getting there Fleetwood is about 10 miles north of Blackpool off the A584, 100 yards from the A585
Open Daily 10–5
Adm Adults £3.25, children £2.50, family £10 (ticket includes Animal World, pottery and museum)
Tearoom, shop, baby changing facilities, playground, picnic area, on-site parking

More than eight hectares (20 acres) of farmland, with a large collection of farm animals, cattle, horses, sheep, poultry and pets, as well as a few more unusual residents such as llama, emu and even wild boar. There's a rare breeds indoor barn, a good play area and children can help bottle-feed the lambs in summer. The museum displays historic agricultural equipment, as well as a wartime army jeep and a jail.

Trotters World of Animals

Coalbeck Farm, Bassenthwaite, Keswick
t (01768) 776239 **www.**trottersworld.com
Getting there 5 miles north of Keswick off the A591 and A66
Open 10–5.30 (or dusk if earlier) **Adm** Adults £5.95, children (3–14) £4.50, under 3s **free**

Llama, lemurs, rabbits, ponies, snakes and lizards, deer and peacocks, owls and pheasants live on this 10-hectare (25-acre) site.
For further information *see* p.432

Windmill Animal Farm

Red Cat Lane, Burscough **t** (01704) 892282
www.windmillanimalfarm.co.uk
Getting there About 8 miles north of Blackpool off the A59; M6 (J27) A5209
Open Easter–Sept daily 10–5, Oct–Easter Sat and Sun 10–4
Adm Adults £4.50, children £3.50, under 2s **free**, family £13
Café, shop, baby changing facilities, adventure playground, ball pool, wheelchair access, car park

The farm offers kids a chance to experience the everyday running of an actual working farm as they watch, feed, touch and interact with the animals in the company of the farmer. There are

Scottish Highland cattle, Jacob sheep and pigs, rabbits, horses, goats and Shetlands ponies to meet and the farm also has a marvellous children's play area suitable for all ages, an indoor play barn, as well as pedal tractors for younger visitors.

Sea-life centres

Aquarium of the Lakes

Lakeside, Newby Bridge **t** (01539) 530153
www.aquariumofthelakes.co.uk
Open Apr–Oct daily 9–6, Nov–Mar 9–5
Adm Adults £7, children £4.50, family £22–£30.50;

The UK's largest collection of freshwater fish observed through a see-through tunnel.
For further information *see* p.433

Blackpool Sea Life Centre

Central Promenade **t** (01253) 621258
www.sealife.co.uk
Open Daily (closed 25 Dec) 10–9 (10–6 out of season)
Adm Prices vary, call for details

Takes a sophisticated look at marine life. Highlights include the 'Lost City of Atlantis' and the octopi and starfish in the 'Superheroes of the Sea' exhibition.
For further information *see* p.417

★Blue Planet Aquarium

Longlooms Road, Little Stanney, Ellesmere Port
t (0151) 3578804, **t** 0906 941 0088 (24-hr helpline)
www.blueplanetaquarium.com
Getting there Ellesmere lies on the south bank of the Mersey Estuary, just north of the M53, J10
Open Apr–Oct daily 10–6; Nov–Mar Sat, Sun and Bank Hols 11–5 (closed 25 Dec)
Adm Adults £10.95, children £7.75, under 3s **free**, family (2+2) £35
Café, gift shop, free car park

This huge aquarium is one of the best places in the country for children to get acquainted with creatures from the deep. The centrepiece is the huge see-through tunnel set in a vast, three-million-gallon tank, where you can see sharks and stingrays swimming on all sides and perhaps even a diver or two at feeding time. The displays are arranged according to habitat – mangroves, freshwater rivers, tropical oceans, etc. – and hold more than 3,000 species of fish in total, as well as numerous amphibians and reptiles, including fierce-looking caymans, a sort of miniature crocodile and even a family of otters. New additions inlcude a reef tank with bright tropical fish and coral reef. There are plenty of opportunities for kids to interact with displays. They can touch fish and rays and (if they're feeling really brave) even handle a toad or (for the super-brave) a cockroach. Quiz sheets are available and, in summer, free face-painting is offered.

Beside the seaside

The Northwest has seaside resorts for all tastes, from the boisterous, fun-loving atmosphere and excitement of Blackpool (pp.416–9) to the more relaxed charms of neighbouring Southport and Lytham St Anne's with miles of sandy beaches and plenty of typical seaside amusements on offer – donkey rides, tram rides, arcades, boating pools, illluminations, fish and chip shops, zoos, etc. Up until a couple of years ago, the waters of the Northwest were among the most polluted in the entire country but now 36 of the areas beaches have reached EU standards, compared with only three in 2002. In addition, Blackpool Sands, Southport and Formby – a National Trust site with miles of rolling sand dunes, a lively guided walks programme and a red squirrel sanctuary, t (01704) 878591 – have all achieved Blue Flag beach status.

Lytham St Anne's

Getting there The Lancashire coast is easy to get to from the M55. There are buses every few minutes between St Anne's-on-Sea and Blackpool, with 'promenade service' bus no.1 running direct to Pleasure Island and the pier in summer
Tourist information 290 Clifton Drive South, Lytham St Anne's t (01253) 725610

Lytham is a good deal quieter than Blackpool (after all, so are most resorts) and seems to operate according to an entirely different set of priorities. At Lytham, they stress the quality of life, not merely the intensity of experience. Its attractive shopping square, pretty three-mile stretch of sandy beach and elegantly maintained parks and gardens evoke a more traditional, calmer approach to leisure, much welcomed by holidaymakers looking for a break from the hustle and bustle of louder resorts. Fun-seekers shouldn't despair entirely, however. Despite the town's best efforts, there are a few lively amusements to be found – including the pier and The Island entertainment complex – which actually complement the town's gentler pleasures rather well. The beach is cleaned daily in summer,

when there's also a dog ban in operation.

The Island
South Promenade t (01253) 781381
Open Mon–Thurs 10–8, Fri 12 noon–10, Sat–Sun 10–10
Adm Free; charges for individual attractions
Cafés, fast-food outlets, large Italian restaurant, mother and baby room, disabled access
Entertainment complex with cinema, swimming pool, putting, miniature train, 10-pin bowling, arcades and rides.

St Anne's-on-Sea Pier
t (01253) 711649
Open Daily; call for times
Adm Free; charges for individual attractions
A traditional seaside pier with entertainment in abundance – children's rides, shops, amusement arcades, cafés and restaurants – everything you'd expect really.

Southport

Getting there By road: Southport is situated on the coast between Liverpool (20 miles) and Blackpool (30 miles). From the south, take the M6, the M58 then the A570; from the north, take the A59 at Preston. By rail: There are regular direct rail services from Liverpool and Manchester. By coach: National Express runs services from London and most surrounding major towns
Tourist information 112 Lord Street t (01704) 533333
www.visitsouthport.com

Compared with some of Lancashire's other seaside resorts, Southport has a prosperous, almost elegant air to it. Relaxed, informal and agreeable, rather than brash and breezy, it nonetheless boasts its fair share of boisterous seaside attractions. Other than Pleasureland, its excellent theme park, the main entertainment for kids lies along the seafront, where there's a boating lake, and beyond, where the resort's famously 'endless' stretch of beach runs out into Liverpool Bay. Don't go expecting shimmering white sands, however. The coastline in these parts is more muddy than golden with natural sand dunes and coastal woodlands providing a haven for an array of wildlife including natterjack toads, red squirrels and sand lizards; think nature walks rather than sun-bathing.

Model Railway Village

Kings Garden, Lower Promenade **t** (01704) 538001
www.southportmodelrailway.co.uk
Open Apr–Sept daily 10–5 (summer 11–6)
Adm Adults £2.95, children £2.50, under 1s **free**,
family £10
*Café, all-weather tea gardens, shop, mother and
baby room, disabled access*

A chance to play at being giants: set in six hectares
(one-and-a-half acres) of sheltered gardens, this
model village has more than 200 buildings served by
a 500m/1,640ft-long Garden Gauge Railway which
wends its way over, round and through the site.
There's also a children's play area.

★Pleasureland Theme Park

Marine Drive, Festival Coast **t** 0870 220 0204
www.pleasureland.uk.com
Open Easter–mid-Sept and Oct half term daily 11–5
(10–5 in summer); March Sat–Sun only
Adm Adult wristband: £18, children £12
*Restaurant, cafés, gift shop, baby changing facilities,
disabled access, first aid and lost parent centre*

Previously the epitome of the old-fashioned
leisure park, full of gentle rides and rickety old
rollercoasters, Pleasureland, which is situated right
on the beach itself, has in recent years been
running fast to catch up with its better known
rivals. Its current pride and joy is the Traumatizer, a
suspension rollercoaster, which takes its passengers on a hair-raising journey through loops,
corkscrews, rolls, inversions and flipovers. There's
also the almost equally scary Space Shot, the Wild
Cat, the Tidal Wave swing boat and the Mistral for
big thrills, as well as the Cyclone, a wooden rollercoaster, which first saw action way back in 1937 (but
which was still thrilling enough in 1996 to be voted
the third best rollercoaster in Europe by a group of
American coaster aficionados). Despite its revamp,
Pleasureland remains at heart a deeply traditional
establishment that manages to keep its visitors in
touch with the spirit of fairgrounds past. You can
take a trip down memory lane aboard the 1954
Gulliver Carousel, the 1923 River Boat Journey and
(one of the real grand old men of British funparks) a
1914 rollercoaster – don't panic, it was fully renovated in 1996. The park also contains several water
rides, three go-kart tracks and the 'Sultan Towers' –
a children's play area with a bouncy castle, mini
rollercoaster, a junior Ferris wheel, Viking boats and
Flying Camels.

West Lancashire Light Railway

Station Road, Hesketh Bank **t** (01772) 815881
www.westlancs.org
Getting there The main station can be found opposite the Becconsall Hotel at Hesketh Bank, midway
between Preston and Southport; catch the 102 bus
Open Apr–Oct and Bank Hols daily at 20-minute
intervals 12–5; plus seasonal specials
Fares Call for details
Refreshments, shop

One of Britain's best-preserved narrow-gauge
railways plus railway equipment.
For further information *see* p.443

Parks and gardens

Acorn Bank Garden and Watermill

Temple Sowerby, nearr Penrith **t** (017683)
61893/61467 **www**.nationaltrust.org
Getting there Acorn Bank is just north of Temple
Sowerby, 6 miles east of Penrith on the A66,
reached from the M6 (J40)
Open Apr–end Oct Wed–Sun 10–5
Adm Adults £3.20, children £1.60, family £8
*Restaurant with children's menu, baby changing
facilities, shop, wheelchair access*

A delightful garden with sheltered orchards,
pond and beck, a famous herb garden and fine
displays of shrubs, flowers and herbaceous
borders. Look out for newts in June, enjoy woodland walks in springtime and pop over for an
apple in October. You could combine a trip here
with a visit to the nearby Eden Ostrich World in
Langwathby (pp.437–8) and the fine lakeland
town of Penrith (p.432).

Ness Botanic Gardens

University of Liverpool, Ness, Neston
t (0151) 353 0123 **www**.nessgardens.org.uk
Getting there Midway between Neston and
Burton on the Wirral, 5 miles from the end of the
M56 and 6 miles from the M53 (J4)
Open Mar–Oct daily 9.30–5, Nov–Feb daily 9.30–4
(closed 25 Dec)
Adm Adults £5, children **free** (reductions in winter)
Restaurant, café, gift and plant shop, picnic area

Set in 25 hectares (62 acres) of ground overlooking the Dee Estuary, the Ness Botanic
Gardens contain a vast range of plants from

around the world. There are two nature trails around the assorted water gardens, herbaceous borders and flower beds, as well as a wooden fort adventure playground and picnic site.

Stapeley Water Gardens

London Road, Stapeley **t** (01270) 623868
www.stapeleywatergardens.com
Getting there 1 mile south of Nantwich on the A51 to Stone (signposted from J16 on the M6)
Open Gardens: mid-Mar–mid-Sept Mon–Sat 9–6 (Wed until 8pm), Sun 10–4; mid-Sept–mid-Mar Mon–Sat 9–5, Sun 10–4; Palms Tropical Oasis: mid-Mar–mid-Sept Mon–Sat 10–6, Sun 10–5, mid-Sept–mid-Mar Mon–Sat 10–5, Sun 10–5
Adm Gardens: **free**; Palms Tropical Oasis: adults £4.45, children £2.60 under 3s **free**
Disabled access (wheelchairs available), car park, angling centre and garden centre

Twenty-six hectares (64 acres) of gardens, lakes, pools and fountains. In the Palms Tropical Oasis, housed in a 9m/30ft-high glasshouse, kids can pretend to be lost in the jungle as they fight their way through a dense array of rainforest vegetation to meet the glasshouse's collection of piranhas, pythons, tarantulas, macaws, koi carp and tropical marine fish.

Williamson Park and the Ashton Memorial

Lancaster **t** (01524) 33318
www.williamsonpark.com
Getting there Lancaster is easily reached by road along the A6 or the M6 and is on the main west coast railway line
Open Apr–Sept daily 10–5; Oct–Mar 10–4
Adm Adults £3.25, children £1.50
Café, shop, some disabled access, car park, picnic areas

Williamson Park occupies a commanding position overlooking the historic city of Lancaster and offers spectacular views across Morecambe Bay to the Lakeland Fells. The 22 hectares (54 acres) of magnificent parkland can be explored using woodland walkways and broad avenues lined with neat arrangements of trees, shrubs and flowers. The terraced paths and undulating landscape echo the shape of the disused quarry beneath, which provided stone for many of Lancaster's historic buildings. Entertainment for children is provided by a new play area and there are plenty of lawns for games and picnics. The Edwardian Palm House now serves as a Tropical

Butterfly House, where exotic species flutter amongst lush foliage in the warm, humid atmosphere of a tropical forest. There's also the Mini Beasts Centre, a 'cave' full of lizards, spiders, snakes and a variety of creepy-crawlies and, right next door, a free-flying foreign birds enclosure.

Steam trains

East Lancashire Railway

Bolton Street, Bury **t** (0161) 764 7790
www.east-lancs-rly.co.uk
Getting there Metrolink from Manchester to Bury
Open Jan–Nov Sat–Sun trains run hourly from 9–5; May–Sept additional services Wed–Fri, call for details of times and special/steam events
Fare Day Rover: adults £15, children £11, family £40
Refreshments, shop, museum

The museum at Bury station houses a collection of road and rail vehicles including a fire engine, traction engine and an ice cream tricycle. Then it's all aboard for a trip steam train ride to peaceful Summerseat (as pretty as it sounds) and lunch at the Waterside Inn, **t** (01706) 822065, where children's meals and highchairs are available, plus there are swings outside and great river views. Alternately, head on to Ramsbottom and Rawtenstall for a real taste of rural Lancashire.

Lakeside and Haverthwaite Steam Railway

Haverthwaite, near Ulverston **t** (015395) 31594
www.lakesiderailway.co.uk
Getting there Lakeside is at the southern tip of Windermere. From J36 of the M6 follow the A590 west to Haverthwaite near Newby Bridge
Open Easter–end Oct daily 10.30–5 **Fares** Return: adults £4.90, children £2.45; combined ticket for Windermere Lake Cruises available

The country's most scenic railway through the beautiful Cumbrian countryside to Lakeside. For further information *see* p.433

Model Railway Village

Kings Garden, Lower Promenade, Southport **t** (01704) 538001
www.southportmodelrailway.co.uk
Open Apr–Sept daily 10–5 (summer 11–6)
Adm Adults £2.95, children £2.50, under 1s **free**, family £10

Model village with more than 200 scale model buildings arranged in the shape of a town and served by a 500m (1,640ft) Garden Gauge Railway. **For further information** see p.441

Ravenglass and Eskdale Railway

Ravenglass **t** (01229) 717171
www.ravenglass-railway.co.uk
Getting there On the A595 coast road between Barrow-in-Furness and Whitehaven
Open Easter–Oct daily, Nov–Dec and Feb half term Sat–Sun only
Fares Round trip: adults £9, children (5–15) £4.50
Restaurant, picnic areas, gift shop, mother and baby room, disabled access, on-site parking

Affectionately known as 'La'al Ratty', England's oldest narrow-gauge steam railway runs from the old Roman port of Ravenglass for seven miles along the Eskdale Valley to Eskdale, often up gradients as steep as 1:35. Three miles from the railway and the splendid Muncaster Castle is Waberthwaite, a small village beside the A595. Here you'll find the finest Cumberland sausages, hams and bacon, in Richard Woodall's shop, **t** (01229) 717237, which is by appointment to Her Majesty the Queen.

South Tynedale Railway

Alston **t** (01434) 381696, **t** (01434) 382828 (talking timetable) **www**.strps.org.uk
Getting there Take the A686 or the A689 to Alston (leave the M6 at J40). The station is on the Hexham road, a short distance from Alston town centre
Open Easter–Oct Sat–Sun (Jul–Aug daily)
Fares Return: adults £5, children (3–15) £2.50; single: adults £3, children £1.50; all day: adults £8, children £4
Picnic area, souvenir and book shop, wheelchair access, free parking

The journey on England's highest narrow-gauge railway begins in Alston, 20 miles south of Hadrian's Wall (pp.473–5), and continues through the bracing North Pennines countryside to Kirkhaugh. The trains are pulled by steam and diesel locomotives from Britain and overseas.

West Lancashire Light Railway

Station Road, Hesketh Bank **t** (01772) 815881
www.westlancs.org
Getting there The main station is opposite the Becconsall Hotel at Hesketh Bank, midway between Preston and Southport; catch the 102 bus
Open Apr–Oct and Bank Hols daily 12–5, at 20-minute intervals; seasonal specials
Fares Call for prices
Refreshments, shop

In the 1950s and '60s, Britain's narrow-gauge railways, which had formerly been popular forms of transport for the agricultural, mining and building industries, began disappearing as the country's road network was expanded. The West Lancashire Railway was founded to gather and preserve as many as possible of these delightful little railways before they vanished completely. It has a huge collection of railway equipment on display, although the highlight here is definitely the line itself, which runs from Hesketh Bank near Preston to Southport. The carriages are often pulled by the railway's pride and joy, an 1898 Hunslet steam engine called *Jonathan*.

Theme parks and model villages

★Blackpool Pleasure Beach

Ocean Boulevard **t** 0870 444 5566, **t** (01253) 341033
www.blackpoolpleasurebeach.com
Open Mar and Nov–Dec Sat–Sun, Apr–Oct daily (times vary, call in advance)
Adm Free, but individual charges for attractions or discount sheets of ride tickets or wristbands: £15–£29 for unlimited rides

More than 150 rides (including no fewer than 10 rollercoasters) plus shows to watch – ice shows, magic shows, circus shows, comedy shows etc.
For further information see p.417

Camelot Theme Park

Park Hall Road, Charnock Richard, Chorley
t (01257) 453044 **www**.camelotthemepark.co.uk
Getting there Between Wigan and Preston, just a short drive from the M6 (J27 northbound and J28 southbound) or the M61 (J8)
Open Apr–Oct daily 10–5
Adm Adults and children £16.50 (unlimited rides), children under 1m (3ft) **free**, family (2+2 or 1+3) £56
Free parking

Jolly 50-hectare (130-acre) theme park where the majority of the attractions are themed on Arthurian legends – Excalibur swing boats, Pendragon's Plunge log flume, Camelot Castle family entertainment centre and, of course,

Merlin's Playland. No doubt the epic success of JK Rowling's Harry Potter books has had a positive effect on visitor numbers and the latest additions, Merlin's School of Wizardry with its masterclass in magic show, the Playland Express train and the Cup and Sorcerer should prove to be even more of a draw. Older children will love the the spinning rollercoaster, The Whirlwind, the terrifying Rack and the Gauntlet coaster for big thrills between quiet spells. Excellent, hell-for-leather jousting exhibitions are put on in the Knights Arena and there's a rare breeds farm for non-magical types.

Gulliver's World

Shackleton Close, Warrington **t** (01925) 444888
www.gulliversfun.co.uk
Getting there 5 minutes from the M62 (J8/9); M6 (J21a)
Open Easter–end Aug daily 10.30–5 (4.30 in term time); Sept–Oct weekends only; Dec Thurs–Sun to 24 Dec 10.30–6
Adm Adults and children £9.99, children under 90cm (3ft) **free**
Café-restaurant, fast food, shop, picnic areas, disabled and baby changing facilities, on-site parking, pushchair hire

Small theme park where all the rides, attractions, shows and food are aimed at 3–13-year-olds and which boasts a suitably child-size entrance fee (just £9.99), much less than what you'd pay at one of the bigger name parks. There are several low-key rollercoasters, a log flume, plus various gentle rides for younger children. The most recent addition to the park is the Lost World, a dinosaur-themed adventure zone with a children's play area, discovery centre, observation tower with walkways and several prehistoric rides and T-Rex snack shop.

★Pleasureland Theme Park

Marine Drive, Festival Coast, Southport
t 0870 220 0204 **www**.pleasureland.uk.com
Open Easter–mid Sept and Oct half term daily 11–5 (10–5 in summer); Mar weekends only
Adm Adult wristband: £18, children £12

Previously the epitome of the old-fashioned leisure park, it has caught up with its better known rivals and now offers plenty of scary rides and high-octane attractions for adults and kids alike.
For further information *see* p.441

Wide open spaces

Croxteth Hall and Country Park

Croxteth, Liverpool **t** (0151) 228 6910
www.croxteth.co.uk
Open Easter–Sept daily 10.30–5; farm, shop and café: Oct–Easter Sat–Sun only
Adm Hall: Adults £2.30, children £1.50; farm: adult £2.30, children £1.50; garden: adult £1.50, children 90p; family ticket to hall, farm and garden £11

Edwardian home of Lord Sefton, filled with period displays and inhabited by jolly mannequins of its former residents.
For further information *see* pp.422–3

Grizedale Forest Park

Hawkshead **t** (01229) 860291 **www**.grizedale.org
Open Daily (closed 25 Dec and 1 Jan)
Adm Free (parking £3 per day)

Hunt for more than 80 wood and rock sculptures hidden throughout the forest. You can hire bikes (which should at least speed up the process), visit the craft centre and the adventure playground.
For further information *see* p.430

Haigh Country Park

Haigh **t** (01942) 832895 (country park),
t (01942) 831107 (golf)
Getting there On the outskirts of Wigan, 20 miles west of Manchester, via the M6 (J27 or J5) and A6
Open Grounds open daily (hall not open to public)
Adm Free
Café, picnic area, gift shop, disabled facilities, on-site parking

There are 100 hectares (250 acres) of woodland and parkland surrounding Haigh Hall, the former home of the earls of Balcarres. Grounds contain a children's play area, a crazy-golf course, a model village, a miniature railway and a craft gallery, where children can take part in artistic pursuits such as stencilling and finger-puppet-making.

Lake District National Park

The country's largest national park (855 square miles/2,215 sq km of land) contains six nature reserves, 16 lakes, more than 50 dales, 100 sites of 'special scientific interest', 150 mountains and nearly 400 towns and villages. It attracts an estimated 14 million tourists every year and makes for some wonderful walking through both rolling and steep hills.
For further information *see* p.429

SPORT AND ACTIVITIES

Activity Centres

Noah's Ark Soft Play Centre
1st Floor, 36–40 Burrowgate, Penrith
t (01768) 890640
Open Mon–Fri 10–3.45 (Wed closes 1pm),
Sat 10–4.45, Sun 10.30–3.45
Adm Call for prices
An indoor soft play centre with a giant Noah's Ark
and animals, a rope walk and ball pool to drop into.

Fun For Kids
Parkside Road, Kendal **t** (01539) 735556
Open Mon–Fri 9.30–6, Sat 9.30–6, Sun 10–6
(sometimes closes at 4pm for parties)
Adm £2.50 per hour
Soft play centre with rocking horses, ball pools,
foam furniture, climbing frames and a slide.
Suitable for very young children (up to three years).

Bowling

Barrow Superbowl
Hollywood Park, Barrow-in-Furness
t (01229) 820444 **www.super-bowl.co.uk**
Open Daily 10am–late
Adm Adults £4.20, children £3.20 (including
shoe hire)
This bowling alley has 24 air-conditioned lanes
with 12 lanes adapted to suit the needs of children.

Megabowl
Parrs Wood, Wilmslow Road, Manchester
t 0871 5501010 **www.super-bowl.co.uk**
Open Mon–Fri 12 noon–12 midnight, Sat–Sun
10am–1am
Adm Adults £6, children £5 (including shoe hire)
A 26-lane alley suitable for children.

AMS Bowling
Miry Lane, Wallgate, Wigan **t** (01942) 820225
www.amfbowling.co.uk
Open Mon–Fri 12 noon–12 midnight, Sat–Sun
10am–12 midnight
Adm Adults from £3.70, children from £3.15
This 10-pin bowling alley has 26 lanes all fitted
with bumpers, and there's an on-site diner.

Cycling

Manchester Velodrome: The National Cycling Centre
Stuart Street, Clayton, Manchester
t (0161) 223 2244 **www.manchestervelodrome.com**
Open Call for times
Adm £12 for 2 hours
Britain's premier cycling venue, where even
Olympic champions come to train and where the
2002 Commonwealth Games cycling events were
held. Offers a range of cycling courses for all ages
and abilities, plus badminton, basketball and
netball courts for hire.

Football

Bolton FC
Reebok Stadium, Burnden Way, Lostock, Bolton
t (01204) 673673 **www.bwfc.co.uk**
Open All day, call for details
Tickets £10–£39

Everton FC
Goodison Park, Goodison Road, Liverpool
t (0151) 330 2200 **www.evertonfc.co.uk**
Open All day, call for details
Tickets £14–£32

Liverpool FC
Anfield, Anfield Road, Liverpool **t** (0151) 263 2361
www.liverpoolfc.tv
Open All day, call for details
Tickets £17–£33

Manchester City
City of Manchester Stadium, Rowsley
Street, Manchester **t** (0161) 231 3200
www.mcfc.co.uk
Open All day, call for details
Tickets £12–£37

Manchester United
Old Trafford, Sir Matt Busby Way, Old Trafford,
Manchester **t** (0161) 868 8000 **www.manutd.com**
Open All day, call for details
Tickets £27–£37

Go-karting

Wigan Indoor Karting Centre
Unit 3, Eckersley Mill Complex, Swan Meadow Road
t (01942) 829696
Open Daily 12 noon–9pm
Adm £5 for 7 minutes, £10 for 15 minutes

Leisure centres

Kendal Leisure Centre
Burton Road, Kendal **t** (01539) 729777/729702
Getting there On the A65, just south of Kendal
Open Daily 7.45am–11pm, swimming 7.45am–9pm
Adm Call for prices
The premier sports and entertainment centre in South Lakeland, with facilities for swimming, squash and badminton, and a fitness room. Café, bar, free parking.

Manchester Aquatics Centre
Booth Street East **t** (0161) 275 9450
www.manchesteraquatics.com
Open Mon–Fri 6.30am–10pm, Sat 7am–6pm, Sun 7am–10pm; family fun sessions: Wed 7pm–10pm, Fri 4pm–9pm, Sat–Sun 9am–6pm
Adm Call for prices
This modern facility was built for the Commonwealth Games in 2002 and houses a 23m (75ft) pool and a 25m (82ft) pool, as well as a leisure pool with children's slides and lagoon. Café, disabled access and baby changing facilities.

Sunset Leisure Centre
Stanwix Park Holiday Centre, Silloth
t (016973) 32666
Open Daily 9am–9pm
Adm Call for prices
Superb leisure facility boasting an indoor pool with an array of water features, sauna, spa, steam room, gym and bowling alley.

Outdoor pursuits

Chorlton Water Park
Maitland Avenue, Chorlton, Manchester
t (0161) 881 5639
Getting there M60 (J5) then A5103 Princess Road and A5145, follow signs
Open Daily, call for details of watersports
Adm Free; canoeing: adults £2.60, children £1.25; sailing: adults £3.40, children £2
A lovely place to get away from it all, with woodland walks, footpaths and watersports on the lake. There's a children's play area, picnic spots and the surrounding parkland has Green Flag status.

Water Park Lakeland Adventure Centre
Coniston, High Nibthwaite **t** (01229) 885456
Getting there On the southeastern side of Coniston Water
Open/Adm Call for times and prices
This outdoor adventure centre offers full- and half-day courses in canoeing, sailing, climbing, orienteering, kayaking and ghyll (waterfall) scrambling. Book in advance.

Watersports

Windermere Outdoor Adventure Watersports Centre
Rayrigg Road, Windermere **t** (015394) 729777
www.southlakelandleisure.org.uk
Getting there On the A592, 1 mile south of the Cooks Corner roundabout, signposted Bowness
Open Mid-Mar–end Nov daily 9–5; evenings and weekends by pre-booked arrangement
Adm Call for prices
The centre is located on the east shore of Windermere. Courses in dinghy sailing, kayaking, open canoeing, wind-surfing and keelboat sailing.

Cinemas

Carlisle
City Mary Street **t** (01228) 594409
www.lonsdalecitycinemas.co.uk
Vue Botchergate **t** 0871 2240240 www.myvue.com

Chester
Odeon Northgate Street **t** 0870 505 0007
UGC Chester Court Greyhound Park, Sealand Road
t 0870 155 5158

Ellesmere Port
Vue Cheshire Oaks **t** (0151) 356 2261
t 08702 40 60 20

Liverpool
Fact Wood Street **t** (0151) 7074450 www.fact.co.uk
Odeon Allerton Road **t** (0151) 7245095
www.odeon.co.uk
Odeon London Road **t** 0871 2244007
www.odeon.co.uk
Showcase East Lancs Road **t** 0871 2201000
www.showcasecinemas.co.uk
Cineworld Montrose Way, Edge Lane Retail Park
t 0871 2002000 www.cineworld.co.uk

Manchester
AMC Cinemas Great Northern Warehouse 16,
Deansgate **t** 0870 7555657
www.amccinemas.co.uk
Cineworld Parrs Wood, Wilmslow Road, Didsbury
t 0871 2002000 www.cineworld.co.uk
Corner House 70 Oxford Street **t** (0161) 200 1500
www.cornerhouse.org
Odeon Dantzic Street **t** 0871 2244007
www.odeon.co.uk
Odeon The Dome **t** 0871 2244007
www.odeon.co.uk
Red Cinema Lowry Centre, Salford Quays, Salford
t 0871 2240240
Showcase Hyde Road, Belle Vue **t** 0871 2201000
www.showcasecinemas.co.uk

Southport
Vue, Ocean Plaza **t** 0871 2240240 www.myvue.com

Wigan
Cineworld Anjou Boulevard, Robin Park
t 0871 555150 www.cineworld.co.uk

Museums, galleries and science centres

Anything to Declare? HM Customs and Excise National Museum
Merseyside Maritime Museum, Albert Dock, Liverpool
t (0151) 478 4499
Open Daily 10–5 (last entry 4) **Adm Free**
Looks at the art and practice of smuggling from the Middle Ages to the hi-tech multi-million-pound operations of today.
For further information see p.422

The Beatles Story
Britannia Vaults, Albert Dock, Liverpool
t (0151) 709 1963 www.beatlesstory.com
Open Daily 10–6
Adm Adults £8.99, children £4.99, under 5s **free**, family £25; combined ticket available for Beatles Story and Liverpool Football Club
Moving tribute to the Fab Four.
For further information see p.422

The Beatrix Potter Gallery
Main Street, Hawkshead **t** (01539) 436355
www.nationaltrust.org.uk
Open Apr–Oct Sat–Thurs 10.30–4.30 (last admission 4); timed ticket system in operation
Adm Adults £3.60, children £1.80, family £9
Exhibition of the original watercolours by children's author Beatrix Potter, including many previously unseen pictures of her animal characters.
For further information see p.430

The Boat Museum
Ellesmere Port **t** (0151) 355 5017
www.boatmuseum.org.uk
Getting there Ellesmere is just north of the M53 (J9)
Open Apr–Oct daily 10–5, Nov–Mar Sat–Wed 11–4
Adm Adults £7.10, children £5.25, under 5s **free**, family (2+3) £20.65; boat trips: adults £2.50, children £2.25
Free car park, disabled access, café, toilets, parent and baby room
The world's largest collection of traditional canal boats (all displayed on the water), as well as Georgian and Victorian warehouses filled with exhibits on the waterways, their industry and people. See displays on domestic life from the 1840s to the 1950s in a collection of restored dock-workers' cottages, chat to a blacksmith working in his forge and take a boat trip round the dock. There

are family workshops and events throughout the year and 'Santa Cruises' at weekends in December.

British Commercial Vehicle Museum
King Street, Leyland, Preston t (01772) 451011
www.commercialvehiclemuseum.co.uk
Getting there About 7 miles south of Preston, J28 from the M6
Open Apr–Sept Sun, Tues–Thurs and Bank Hols 10–5; Oct Sun 10–5 **Adm** Adults £4, children £2, family £10
Gift shop, café, disabled access, on-site parking
Lively museum with around 100 historic and commercial vehicles from all over Europe on display (vans, horse-drawn carriages, buses) including the world-famous Popemobiles.

Cars of the Stars Motor Museum
Standish Street, Keswick t (01768) 773757
www.carsofthestars.com
Open Easter–Nov and Feb half term daily 10–5, weekends only until 25 Dec
Adm Adults £4, children £3
Famous vehicles from TV and films on display.
For further information *see* p.432

★Catalyst: The Museum of the Chemical Industry
Gossage Building, Mersey Road, Widnes
t (0151) 420 1121 www.catalyst.org.uk
Getting there Catalyst is located in Widnes, just minutes from the Runcorn/Widnes Bridge; M62 (J7), M56 (J12) and follow the brown tourist signs
Open Tues–Fri, Bank Hols and school holidays also Mon 10–5; Sat and Sun 11–5
Adm Adults £4.95, children £3.95, under 5s **free**, family £15.95
Shop, restaurant, wheelchair access, free car park
Excellent science museum packed with hands-on experiments, touch-screen computers, quizzes and puzzles, all designed to explore and explain the often-overlooked chemical industry. You can melt a crystal, split a molecule and watch sparks fly, design a medicine, travel in a glass lift, send a sticky liquid glooping its way through a collection of pipes and valves, discover how synthetic scents are made and lie on a special heat-sensitive sheet and watch a thermal image of yourself gradually appearing. There are free Science Clubs for 11–14-year-olds on the second Saturday of every month. Book in advance.

Cumberland Pencil Museum
Southey Works, Keswick t (01768) 773626
www.pencils.co.uk
Open Daily 9.30–4 (peak season extended hours)
Adm Adults £3, children £1.50, family (2+3) £7.50
The history of pencil-making from the discovery of graphite to the modern high-speed processes.
For further information *see* p.432

Dewa Roman Experience
Pierpoint Lane, Bridge Street, Chester t (01244) 343407 www.dewaromanexperience.co.uk
Open Mon–Sat 9–5, Sun 10–7 **Adm** Adults £4.25, children £2.50, under 5s **free**, family (2+3) £12
Gift shop, disabled access
Discover what life was like on board a Roman galley, wander along a replica Roman street and examine Roman artefacts found locally.
For further information *see* p.420

The Dock Museum
North Road, Barrow-in-Furness t (01229) 894444
www.dockmuseum.org.uk
Getting there Take the A590 or the A595 to Barrow and then follow the brown and white signs
Open Easter–Oct Tues–Fri 10–5, Sat and Sun 11–5; Nov–Easter Wed–Fri 10.30–4, Sat and Sun 11–4.30
Adm Free
Coffee shop, museum shop, lift to all floors, wheelchair access, free car parking, tours, picnic area
Built over an original Victorian graving dock, this sleek, super-modern-looking museum explores the history of Barrow, showing how it grew from a small village into one of the world's major centres of iron, steel and ship production. There are lots of ships on display (including a Trident submarine), as well as interactive displays and an adventure playground. Craft workshops, storytelling sessions and special events throughout the year.

Gallery of Costume
Platt Hall, Wilmslow Road, Platt Fields, Rusholme, Manchester t (0161) 224 5217
Open Last Sat of every month 10–5 **Adm Free**
Georgian mansion filled with displays representing 400 years of changing fashions – from ruffs and bodices to flapper dresses and platform heels. It is widely acknowledged as one of the finest collections of its kind in the country.

Grand National Experience

Aintree Race Course, Liverpool **t** (0151) 5232600
www.aintree.co.uk
Open Mid-Apr–mid-Oct Tues–Sun (excluding race days) 10–5 **Adm** Adults £7, children £4

Explore the long history of the country's most famous horse race.
For further information *see* p.423

Greater Manchester Police Museum

Newton Street, Manchester **t** (0161) 856 3287
Open Tues 10.30–3.30 **Adm Free**

Trace the development of the force from the advent of the 'peelers' in the 1820s by the then Home Secretary, Robert Peel, to the present day.
For further information *see* p.426

Grosvenor Museum

27 Grosvenor Street, Chester **t** (01244) 402008
Open Mon–Sat 10.30–5, Sun 1–4 **Adm Free**

The story of the city and surrounding area from prehistory to modern times (particular emphasis on Roman Chester).
For further information *see* p.420

Hack Green Secret Nuclear Bunker

Nantwich, Cheshire **t** (01270) 629219
www.hackgreen.co.uk
Getting there 12 miles from Crewe, signposted from the A530 Whitchurch Road
Open Mid-Mar–Oct daily 10.30–5.30, Nov and Jan–mid-Mar Sat–Sun 11–4.30 (Feb half term daily)
Adm Adults £6.50, children £4.50, under 5s free, family £19
Café, shop

For over 60 years the existence of this bunker in Cheshire was known only to a select few. It started its military life as a radar station (one of just 21 in Britain) during World War II before being bought in the 1970s by the Home Office and expanded at a cost of 32 million to make it safe for government VIPs to sit out a nuclear strike. Nowadays, visitors can not only experience what it would have been like inside the bunker during a nuclear war (pretty grim, in truth, but not as grim as on the outside), but can also view an impressive collection of military memorabilia and audiovisual displays

Imperial War Museum North

The Quays, Trafford Wharf Road, Trafford Park, Manchester **t** (0161) 836 4000 www.iwm.org.uk
Getting there M60 (J9) and then Parkway (A5081) towards Trafford Park; M602 (J2) and follow signs

Open Mar–Oct daily 10–6, Nov–Feb 10–5 **Adm Free**
Restaurant-café, parking, disabled access and facilities, baby changing facilities, picnic space (open at weekends and in school hols)

Opened in July 2002, the museum was created to give northern audiences access to the national collections including items from the wartime photographic, film, video and sound archives. Designed by world-renowned architect Daniel Libeskind, the IWM North focuses on the impact of war on people's lives. There are three film shows daily, one entitled 'Children and War' (at 10.30am, 1.30pm and 4.30pm) and a multiscreen audio-visual experience, 'The Big Picture', which is shown at hourly intervals during the day. In addition there are museum guides or 'Interactors' on hand to discuss and perform aspects of the material, hold workshops and conduct tours. There's a children's trail and free drop-in events are held at weekends and in school holidays, plus special events to tie in with the temporary exhibitions.

★Jodrell Bank Science Centre, Planetarium and Arboretum

Lower Withington **t** (01477) 571339
www.jb.man.ac.uk
Getting there Jodrell Bank lies 20 miles south of Manchester on the A535, J18 from the M6
Open Mid-Mar–end Aug daily 10.30–5.30; Nov–mid-Mar Mon–Fri 10.30–3, Sat–Sun 11–4.30
Adm Adults £1.50, children £1, under 4s **free**; shows £1 extra
Café, restaurant (can be hired for birthday parties), bookshop, disabled access, picnic area

The enormous Lovell Radio Telescope (the second largest in the world) is one of the country's great scientific landmarks, a 76m/249ft-high, 3,200-tonne (3,150-ton) metallic saucer staring at the sky, searching for signs of life on other planets. The adjoining science centre is one of the best in the country with eight galleries filled with displays and models designed to reveal the secrets of the universe. Though there's plenty of interactivity, you'll need to have your brain in gear if you're to get the most out of the museum as the science is by no means dumbed down and it will probably go right over the heads of very young children – who will have to make do with the centre's small play area. Older ones will have a whale of a time as they get to grips with the physical universe. They can see telescopic images of galaxies, listen to Albert Einstein explaining his theory of relativity, investigate the forces of gravity and magnetism through a series of hands-on experiments and watch a space show in the 150-seat planetarium. There's also a 3D theatre for visitors to experience the universe from an even more intimate perspective. The 35-acre arboretum provides a peaceful space in which to wander whilst you contemplate your newfound astronomical knowledge.

Kendal Museum of Natural History and Archaeology

Station Road, Kendal **t** (01539) 721374
www.kendalmuseum.org.uk
Getting there 10 minutes from the M6 (J36)
Open Mid-Feb–Dec Mon–Sat 10.30–5 (winter until 4)
Adm Adults £2.70, children **free**
Fossils, tools, dinosaur footprints and stuffed animals.
For further information *see* p.431

Lakeland Motor Museum, Holker Hall

Cark-in-Cartmel, Grange-over-Sands
t (01539) 558328 www.holker-hall.co.uk
Getting there 14 miles southwest of Kendal on the B5278; signposted from the M6 J36 and the A590
Open Apr–Oct Sun–Fri 10–5.30; hall and motor museum close at 4.45
Adm All-inclusive tickets: adults £10.50, children £6, under 6s **free**, family £29; Individual tickets available.
Collection of vintage vehicles on display.
For further information *see* p.435

Liverpool Football Club Museum and Stadium Tour

Anfield Road, Liverpool **t** (0151) 260 6677
www.liverpoolfc.tv
Open Daily 10–5 **Adm** Museum and tour: adults £9, children £5.50, family £23; museum only: adults £5, children £3, family £13
Score goals, compose your own match commentary and step out onto a recreation of the Kop.
For further information *see* p.423

Liverpool Museum

William Brown Street, Liverpool **t** (0151) 478 4399
www.liverpoolmuseum.org.uk
Open Daily 10–5 **Adm Free**
Natural history, antiquities, ethnology and space.
For further information *see* pp.423–4

Louis Tussaud's Waxworks

Central Promenade, Blackpool **t** (01253) 625953
www.blackpool.vispa.com
Open Easter–Oct 10–6 (summer until 8)
Adm Adults £8.95, children £5.95, family £11
3-D waxworks of famous personalities.
For further information *see* p.418

The Lowry Centre

Pier 8, Salford Quays (box office) **t** 0870 7875780
www.thelowry.com
Getting there M60 (J12) then M602 (J3) and follow the brown Lowry logo signs
Open Sun–Fri 11–5, Sat 10–5
Adm Free (donations appreciated); theatre tickets individually priced (family tickets for some shows)
Restaurant-cafés, shop, disabled access and facilities, baby changing facilities, parking
This entertainment complex caters for a variety of performing arts from dance and ballet to comedy, music and drama, with two theatres, a suite of galleries, various cafés and a restaurant. Family trails are available for the galleries, and there's a children's activity corner with art materials based around the current exhibitions.
Children aged 5–11 can take part in Playhouse activities on Saturdays and during half term. Summer theatre productions in the plaza include kids' shows and outdoor performances. Visit the outlet centre next door.

★Manchester Art Gallery

Mosley Street, Manchester **t** (0161) 235 8888
www.manchestergalleries.org
Open Tues–Sun and Bank Hols 10–5 **Adm Free**
Create your own artwork out of junk and other materials or recreate famous paintings.
For further information *see* p.426

Manchester Museum

University of Manchester, Oxford Road, Manchester
t (0161) 275 2634 www.museum.man.ac.uk
Getting there On the B5117 main route into Manchester, 2 miles from Oxford Road railway station
Open Tues–Sat 10–5, Mon, Sun and Bank Hols 11–4
Adm Free (some activities £1)
Culturally significant artefacts from around the world, living reptiles and mummies.
For further information *see* p.426

Manchester United Football Club Museum and Tour Centre

Manchester United Football Club, Old Trafford
t (0161) 868 8000 **www**.manutd.com
Open Mon–Sat 9.30–5, Sun 9.40–4.30
Adm Tour and museum: adults £9.50, children
£6.50, family (2+3) £27; museum only: adults £6.50,
children £4.25, family (2+3) £17.50
    Tracing the club's history and meteoric rise.
For further information *see* p.427

★Merseyside Maritime Museum

Albert Dock, Liverpool **t** (0151) 478 4499
www.merseysidemaritimemuseum.org.uk
Open Daily 10–5 **Adm Free**
    Lovely mix of maritime nostalgia.
For further information *see* p.424

Mendips – John Lennon's Childhood Home

Woolton, Liverpool
t 0870 900 0256 **www**.nationaltrust.org.uk
Getting there Minibus from Speke Hall and Albert
Dock (pp.421–2); no access by car
Open Apr–Oct Wed–Sat, Nov–mid-Dec Sat only
Adm Combined ticket with Paul McCartney's
Childhood Home (*see* right): adults £12, children £1
    The house where John Lennon lived from the
ages of five to 23, has been bequethed to the
National Trust by Yoko Ono, who oversaw the
restoration process. The décor has been restored
using replicas, period furnishings and original
items from the house. Tours depart from Albert
Dock at 10.30am and 11.20am and from Speke Hall
at 2.15 and 3.55pm.

Museum of Lakeland Life

Abbot Hall, Kendal **t** (01539) 722464
www.lakelandmuseum.org.uk
Open Nov–Mar Mon–Sat 10.30–4, Apr–Oct
Mon–Sat 10.30–5
Adm Adults £3.75, children £2.75, family £11
    The history and development of Cumbrian people.
For further information *see* p.431

★Museum of Science and Industry

Liverpool Road, Castlefield, Manchester **t** (0161) 832
1830 (24-hour information line) **www**.msim.org.uk
Open Daily 10–5
Adm Free; train rides: adults £1, children 50p; some
charges for special exhibitions
    Tracing the history of industrial invention.
For further information *see* p.427

Museum of Transport

Boyle Street, Cheetham **t** (0161) 205 2122
www.gmts.co.uk
Getting there About 1 mile north of the city centre;
Metrolink: Piccadilly or Victoria to Woodlands
Road; bus no.135 from Piccadilly or Victoria to
Queens Road
Open Wed, Sat, Sun and Bank Hols 10–5 (Nov–Feb
10–4) **Adm** Adults £4, children £2, under 5s **free**,
family £10
Tearoom, shop, disabled facilities
    One of the largest collections of transport and
associated memorabilia in the country with over
80 beautifully restored vintage buses and coaches,
one of which is said to be haunted.

Paul McCartney's Childhood Home

20 Forthlin Road, Allerton, Liverpool
t 0870 900 0256 **www**.nationaltrust.org.uk
Open Apr–Oct Wed–Sat, Nov–mid-Dec Sat only
Tours Minibus from Speke Hall and Albert Dock
(p.421–2); no access by car
Adm Combined ticket with Mendips (*see* left):
adults £12, children £1
    The 1950s terraced house where Paul McCartney
used to live and where, with John Lennon, he wrote
many of the early Beatles' songs, including 'Love
Me Do' and 'I Saw Her Standing There'. Many of
these songwriting sessions were conducted while
the boys were playing truant from school – look
out for the drainpipe which Paul used to climb up
and sneak back into the house without his dad
noticing. Displays within the house include
photographs by Sir Paul's brother (Michael) and
early Beatles memorabilia.

People's History Museum

The Pump House, Bridge Street, Manchester **t** (0161)
839 6061 **www**.peopleshistorymuseum.org.uk
Open Tues–Sun 11–4.30 **Adm** Adults £1 (Friday **free**),
children **free**
    Celebrates the cause of the man on the street.
For further information *see* p.428

★Quarry Bank Mill and Styal Country Park

Estate Office, 7 Oak Cottages, Styal **t** (01625) 527468
www.quarrybankmill.org.uk
Getting there 10 miles south of Manchester, just
over 1 mile north of Wilmslow, off the B5166;
2 miles from the M56 (J5)
Open Mill: Mid-Mar–Sept daily 11–5, Oct–mid-Mar
Wed–Sun 11–4; Apprentice House and garden: mid-
Mar–Sept Tues–Sun, Oct–mid-Mar Wed–Sun;

admission by timed ticket **Adm** Adults £8.50, children £4.70, family £19; mill only: adults £5.75, children £3.70, family £15
Restaurant, picnic areas, gift shop, mother and baby facilities, disabled access, on-site parking
A good hands-on introduction to the Industrial Revolution: visit an 18th-century working mill; watch steam engines and a 50-tonne water wheel in action, visit the preserved cottages of a 19th-century workers' village, where guides in period dress will explain the exhibits and demonstrate how life in the industrial north was lived some 150 years ago – kids can try curling up on one of the tiny, hard beds of the pauper children who were expected to work back-breaking 12-hour shifts six days a week. Afterwards, head out into the country park itself which has acres of woodland and lovely riverside walks. Seasonal events, such as Easter Trails and Halloween activities, as well as craft workshops and environmental displays.

Rheged Discovery Centre

Redhills, Penrith **t** (01768) 868000 **www.rheged.com**
Open Daily 10–5.30
Adm Movie: Adults £5.95, children £4, family (2+3) £17; extra movie: £4, children £2.75; mountaineering exhibition: adults £5.95, children **free**; movie and exhibition: adults £9.95
A hi-tech overview of Cumbrian life.
For further information *see* p.433

Sellafield Visitors' Centre

Sellafield, Seascale **t** (019467) 27027
www.sellafield.com
Getting there On the Cumbrian coast off the A595, approximately 60 miles from the M6
Open Apr–Oct daily 10–5, Nov–Mar 10–4 (closed 25 Dec) **Adm Free**
Restaurant, shop, disabled facilities, car park
Find out all about nuclear power in 10 galleries of interactive experiments, quizzes, shows and displays that trace the history of nuclear physics and provide an uncritical look at the nuclear energy and reprocessing industry. The 'Sparking Reaction' exhibition, designed by the Science Museum in London, explores all aspects of electricity generation, including non-nuclear options, such as coal, gas and renewable technologies. Family events and activity tables for children on weekends and in the school holidays.

Tate Liverpool

Albert Dock, Liverpool **t** (0151) 702 7400
www.tate.org.uk
Open Tues–Sun 10–5.50 (Jun–Aug also Mon)
Adm Free (charge for special exhibitions)
Café, gift shop, disabled access
North of England's premier modern art collection.
For further information *see* p.424

Tullie House Museum and Art Gallery

Castle Street, Carlisle **t** (01228) 534781
www.tulliehouse.co.uk
Getting there Carlisle is in the extreme northwest corner of England on the A595, A69 and A7, just south of the M6 (J43 and 44)
Open Apr–Jun and Sept–Oct Mon–Sat 10–5, Sun 12–5; Jul–Aug Mon–Sat 10–5, Sun 11–5; Nov–Mar Mon–Sat 10–4, Sun 12–4 **Adm** Adults £5.20, children £2.60, under 5s **free**, family £14.50
Garden restaurant, baby changing facilities, wheelchair access and facilities, play area, picnic area
Founded by the Celts, conquered by the Romans, settled by the Saxons, taken over by the Vikings, seized by the Scots, stolen by the Normans, held by the English against repeated Scottish attacks, the city of Carlisle has enjoyed a volatile history. Find out all about it (and that of the surrounding Border Lands) at this excellent, inventively presented museum. Housed in a Jacobean mansion, its lively displays make full use of modern technologies. Good sections on the Romans (kids can try a Roman crossbow) and nearby Hadrian's Wall, as well as a fascinating study of the Reivers, a band of brigands who robbed and pillaged in the border area during the Middle Ages and who supposedly invented the practice of blackmail. Programme of natural history talks and walks. ArtyFacts activity bags and toy boxes are available for children.

Whitworth Art Gallery

Oxford Road, Manchester **t** (0161) 275 7450
www.whitworth.man.ac.uk
Open Mon–Sat 10–5, Sun 2–5 **Adm Free**
British watercolours, prints, sculptures and textiles.
For further information *see* p.428

★Wigan Pier
Wallgate **t** (01942) 323666 **www.wlct.org**
Getting there Wigan is 205 miles from London,
90 miles from Birmingham and 20 miles from
Manchester and can be reached via the M6 and
A6. Its train station has direct services from
London (Euston), Birmingham and Manchester
Open Mon–Thurs 10–5, Sun 11–5
Adm Day pass: Adults £5.25, children £4.25, under
5s **free**, family (2+2) £14.75
Café, picnic areas, disabled access, on-site parking
  Don't expect amusement arcades and
candyfloss sellers: the pier (as made famous in
the contrasting compositions of George Formby
and George Orwell) is not an over-sea walkway
but a heritage centre, named 'The Way We Were',
on the wharfs next to the Wigan stretch of the
Leeds–Liverpool Canal. It shows what life was like
in the industrial north at the turn of the 20th
century – you'll see a mill filled with machinery, a
seaside pier lined with 'what the butler saw'
machines, a replica mine, a Victorian marketplace
and period buildings – pubs, schools, shops –
populated by costumed characters. Also located
here is the 'Trencherfield Mill Engine', the largest
original working mill steam engine. The separate
Opie Museum of Memories is filled with sweets,
comics, jukeboxes, bikes, clothes) designed to
illustrate how domestic life has changed over the
last 70 years. Check out the interactive memory
area and test your memory skills. Finally, take a
stroll along the canalside towpaths to the
Waterways Gardens.

Windermere Steam Boat Museum
Rayrigg Road, Windermere **t** (015394) 45563
www.steamboat.co.uk
Open Apr–Jun and mid-Sept–early Nov 10–4.30,
July–mid-Sept 10–5
Adm Museum: adults £4.75, children £2.50, family
£9.50; boat trips: adults £5.50, children £2.50
  Collection of ancient steam and motor boats.
For further information *see* p.434

World of Beatrix Potter
Crag Brow, Bowness-on-Windermere
t (01539) 488444 **www.hop-skip-jump.com**
Open Apr–Sept daily 10–5.30, Oct–Mar 10–4.30
(closed 25 Dec, 1 Jan and 10–30 Jan)
Adm Adults £6, children £3 (under 4s **free**)
  Recreations of scenes from her books.
For further information *see* p.434

Theatres
Bolton
Octagon Theatre Howell Croft South **t** (01204) 520661
www.octagonbolton.co.uk
Chester
Gateway Theatre Hamilton Place **t** (01244) 340392
www.chestergateway.co.uk
Kendal
Brewery Arts Centre 122A Highgate **t** (01539) 725133
www.breweryarts.co.uk
Keswick
Theatre by the Lake Lakeside **t** (01768) 74411
www.theatrebythelake.com
Liverpool
Empire Theatre Lime Street **t** 0870 606 3536
Everyman Theatre and **The Playhouse** Hope Street
t (0151) 709 4776 **www.everymanplayhouse.com**
Neptune Theatre Hanover Street **t** (0151) 709 7844
Royal Court Theatre 1 Roe Street **t** 0870 7871866
www.royalcourtliverpool.co.uk
The Unity Theatre 1 Hope Place **t** (0151) 709 4988
www.unitytheatreliverpool.co.uk
Manchester
Coliseum Theatre Fairbottom Street, Oldham
t (0161) 624 2829 **www.coliseum.org.uk**
Contact Theatre Oxford Road **t** (0161) 274 0600
www.contact-theatre.org
Green Room 54–6 Whitworth Street West
t (0161) 615 0500 **www.greenroomarts.org**
Library Theatre St Peter's Square **t** (0161) 234 1919
www.librarytheatre.com
Opera House Quay Street **t** 0870 401 9000
Palace Theatre Oxford Street **t** 0870 401 3000
Royal Exchange Theatre St Ann's Square
t (0161) 833 9833 **www.royalexchange.co.uk**
Southport
Arts Centre Lord Street **t** (01704) 540011
www.seftonarts.co.uk
Little Theatre Hoghton Street **t** (01704) 530521
www.southport-littletheatre.co.uk
Southport Theatre Promenade **t** 0870 6077560
www.southporttheatre.com
Wigan
Mill at the Pier Theatre Wigan Pier, Wallgate
t (01942) 5243974
Wigan Little Theatre Crompton Street **t** (01942) 242561
www.wiganlittletheatre.co.uk

Blackpool

The Cottage
31 Newhouse Road **t** (01253) 694010
Open Daily 11.45–2 and 5–9.45pm (Mon–Tues closes 9pm, winter Sun 8pm)
  Good-quality seaside fish and chips; highchairs.

Harry Ramsden's
Promenade **t** (01253) 294386
www.harryramsdens.co.uk
Branches Liverpool: Brunswick Way, off Sefton Street **t** (0151) 709 4545; Manchester: 1 Water Street **t** (0161) 832 9144
Open Sun–Thurs 11.30–8, Fri–Sat 11.30–9
  Huge branch of the famous fish 'n' chips chain. Two special children's menus (Postman Pat: £2.99; Cool Kids: £3.99). Eat in or take away. Highchairs.

La Fontana
17 Cliffton Street **t** (01253) 622231
www.lafontanarestaurant.co.uk
Open Sun–Thurs 5.30–11.30, Fri–Sat 5.30–12
  Popular Italian restaurant with a children's menu (all dishes £3.95 including free ice cream).

Outside Inn
Whithills Business Park, Hallam Way **t** (01253) 798477 www.outsideinnblackpool.co.uk
Open Daily 10–10
  Unusual pub restaurant that looks like a small village. Children's menu and soft play area.

West Coast Rock Café
5–6 Abingdon Street **t** (01253) 751283
Open Mon–Sat 12 noon–2am, Sun 12–12
  Mexican restaurant with highchairs and a special kids' menu consisting of mini burritos and fajitas.

Chester

  Chester is not well endowed with child-friendly restaurants. Its cafés are geared up for workers not tourists, and some pubs declare themselves 'family hostile'. The visitor centre is good for lunch. Vito's Italian and the 3 Kings Studios and Tearooms on Lower Bridge Street are worth a try. For savoury snacks, biscuits and decorated cakes, head for PA Davies on Bridge Street (opposite the *Dewa* Roman Experience), **t** (01244) 320247. If you're out and about in Cheshire, call in at the Cheshire Smokehouse, Vost Farm, Morley Green, Wilmslow, **t** (01625) 548499, for smoked nuts, cheeses and meats, fresh bread and salads for picnics.

Lobscouse
  Traditionally associated with Liverpool, this nourishing dish is hard to come by in its original form because it was a sailor's dish of meat stewed with vegetables and ship's biscuit. These days, the ship's biscuit is omitted, but lobscouse was for many years a staple diet in some of the poorer parts of Merseyside and may well have given rise to the nickname for Liverpudlians as 'scousers'.

The Blue Bell Restaurant
65 Northgate Street **t** (01244) 317758
Open Mon–Fri 12 noon–2.30 and 6–9.30, Sat 10–2.30 and 5.30–10, Sun 12 noon–2.30 and 6.30–9
  Friendly restaurant; open for lunch and dinner.

The Boathouse Inn
The Groves **t** (01244) 328709
Open Food served: Mon–Sat 11–9, Sun 12 noon–9
  Large, friendly pub by the river, with healthy portions, family room, highchairs and kids' menu.

Franc's
Cuppin Street **t** (01244) 317952
Open Daily 12 noon–11pm
  Cosy restaurant serving great food, with kids' portions, highchairs and baby changing facilities.

Keswick

Maysons
33 Lake Road **t** (017687) 74104 www.maysons.bz
Open Easter–Oct daily 10–9, rest of year Sun–Mon 10–4.30; takeaway 10–5
  A good choice of vegetarian and meat dishes, delicious coffee and cakes. The takeaway over the road sells toasted panini, drinks, sweets and ice creams. Highchairs available.

Liverpool

  Liverpool's museums all have decent cafés attached, the best of which is Café Maritime in the Merseyside Maritime Museum, **t** (0151) 478 4437.

De Coubertins Sports Bar and Grill
43 North John Street **t** (0151) 284 1996
Open Daily 11am–9pm (later at weekends)
  A real find, with more than 500 sporting exhibits on the walls including Pele's shirt, Mohamed Ali's boxing shorts and Michael Owen's England shirt. Friendly staff and a large restaurant area for families, with booth seating. The kids' menu (£2.95 for drink, meal and ice cream) includes such staples as pizzas, fish fingers, burgers and hot dogs. Adults

can choose from a selection of meat dishes with names like 'They Think it's All Over', 'Golden Boot' and 'Fowl Tackle', not to mention the '1966' burger.

Mister Ms
Atlantic Pavilion, Albert Dock t (0151) 707 2202
Open Tues–Sat 12 noon–3, Mon–Sat 6–10.30

Upmarket seafood restaurant on the docks, suitable for older kids in the early evening (reserve), while younger kids are welcome for lunch (fine chunky fish and chips); they'll enjoy looking at the fish in the tank, but not as much as you will savour eating their (the fishes') relations.

Sapporo Teppayaki
134 Duke Street **t** (0151) 7053005
www.sapporo.co.uk
Open Mon–Sat 12–11, Sun 12–10.30

A fun, trendy Japanese restaurant where diners get to watch their food being prepared by skillful chefs who perform various theatrical fire and knife stunts. Smaller portions can be ordered .

Simply Heathcotes
Beetham Plaza, The Strand **t** (0151) 236 3536
www.heathcotes.co.uk
Branches: Manchester Jacksons Row **t** (0161) 835 3536, Preston: Longridge **t** (01772) 784969 (the 14-year-old flagship restaurant), Winckley Square **t** (01772) 252732
Open Lunch: Mon–Sun 12 noon–2.30; dinner: Mon–Fri 6–10, Sat 6–11, Sun 6–9.30

Paul Heathcote's restaurants are a a homegrown institution in these parts. This branch does not deviate from the winning formula of modern British cuisine served in relaxed surroundings. There's a children's menu for £6.99 (choose from pasta with five sauces, fish, sausage or chicken with chips or mash, or roast chicken followed by any dessert from the *à la carte* menu), highchairs and baby-changing facilities. Children will be happily occupied with pens, crayons and paper.

Manchester

There are more restaurants in Manchester than you've probably had hot dinners and many of them are extremely family friendly. Of the many café-bars that welcome kids during the day, Atlas (corner of Deansgate, near the station), **t** (0161) 834 2124, and Dukes 92 in Castlefield, **t** (0161) 839 8646, really stand out. Both have space outdoors, although Dukes is close to the canal and therefore kids must be supervised at all times.

For sandwiches the place to go is Philpotts, **t** (0161) 832 1419, on Brazennose Street, a pedestrianized area between Albert Square and Deansgate.

Caffé Uno
Albert Square **t** (0161) 834 7633
www.caffeuno.co.uk
Open Mon–Thurs 12 noon–10.30pm, Fri–Sat 12 noon–11pm, Sun 12 noon–10pm

Long, open-plan Italian restaurant with a separate menu for the kids (£3.95 for pasta/pizza main course, drink and ice cream) and decent dishes for adults such as salmon, tiger prawns and steaks. There are balloons, crayons and paper for the kids and lots of tables outdoors in summer.

Croma
1 Clarence Street, just off Albert Square
t (0161) 237 9799 **www.**cromamanchester.co.uk
Open Mon–Sat 12 noon–11, Sun 12 noon–10.30

Set on three levels, Croma is the ideal place for a relaxed family lunch. Staff are helpful and friendly and the menu features a range of upmarket pizza and pasta dishes. Best of all, kids the are encouraged to crayon on disposable tablecloths.

Est Est Est
Ridgefield Road **t** (0161) 833 9400
Open Mon–Thurs 12 noon–10.30pm, Fri–Sat 12 noon–11pm, Sun 12 noon–10pm

Family-friendly Italian with a kids' menu for £5.95 (choose from lasagne, spaghetti bolognese or chicken, or opt for the DIY pizza). Children can have fun decorating their own chef's hat with crayons before customizing their own pizzas with their choice of toppings. Great fun atmosphere for the kids with highchairs, baby changing facilities and colouring sheets.

Le Petit Blanc
55 West King Street **t** (0161) 832 1000
www.lepetitblanc.co.uk
Open Mon–Sat 11am–11pm, Sun 11am–10.30pm

A chip off the Blanc block, this offers fine family dining, as well as a children's menu and complicated models of a 2CV for kids to colour in and for baffled parents to construct.

Market Restaurant
104 High Street, Northern Quarter **t** (0161) 834 3743
www.market-restaurant.com
Open Wed–Fri 12 noon–9.30pm, Sat 7–9.30pm

Recent winner of the Manchester Food and Drink Festival Chef of the Year, this small, friendly restaurant in Manchester's Northern Quarter is a real find. There's a frequently changing menu of seasonal dishes sourced from the local farmers' market and the chef is happy to do children's portions from the main menu. Open for lunch as well as dinner.

The Pacific

58–60 George Street **t** (0161) 228 6668
Open China: 12 noon–12 midnight; Thailand: daily 12 noon–3pm (Thai buffet, booking essential); 6–12 midnight (stairs only to upper level)

Younger sibling of the Manchester veteran Pearl City, this boasts a Chinese restaurant downstairs and a Thai one above. The downstairs is a credit to Chinatown but the stylish upper floor goes one better. There are big tables and lots of room for families. The lunchtime 'all you can eat' Thai buffet is utterly irresistible with lots of salad and fruit, as well as tasty noodle dishes and curries for more adventurous appetites. Just save some room for the mouthwatering desserts!

Yang Sing Restaurant

34 Princess Street **t** (0161) 236 2200
www.yang-sing.com
Open Mon–Thurs 12 noon–11.45pm,
Fri–Sat 12 noon–12.15am, Sun 12 noon–10.45pm

Arguably the finest Chinese restaurant in Britain, offering a stunningly good menu. Kids' portions available Hugely popular, so reserve.

Around Manchester

Smith's Restaurant

1–3 Church Road **t** (0161) 7887343
Open Tues–Wed and Sat 5.30–10pm, Thurs–Fri 12 noon–2 and 5.30–10pm, Sun 5–9

Child friendy non-smoking restaurant serving international cuisine. Children's menu and activity packs available.

> ### Kendal mint cake
>
> This famed northern sweet is a high-energy glucose confection (it was taken to the summit of Everest in 1953, and on many other Himalayan expeditions) but was the result of an accident when Joseph Wiper was boiling sugar in his sweet shop in 1868. It now comes in all shapes and sizes, and different flavours too, including chocolate-covered...

> ### Lancashire hot pot
>
> This traditional recipe has many variants, but the authentic hot pot is made from lamb neck chops, lamb's kidneys, onions, potatoes, stock and lard. In its original form, the recipe included oysters, too. It is a warming dish to serve up on a winter's evening.

Southport

Café Arden

75 Eastbank Street **t** (01704) 546094
Open Tues–Sat 9.30–4

Basic seaside chippy offering a separate kids' menu. It also serves a number of vegetarian dishes.

Gallery Grill

5–7 Eastbank Street **t** (01704) 536734
Open Mon–Sat 9.30–6, Sun 11–5

Kids' menu, consisting mainly of burgers, fish fingers and sausages, all served with chips.

Swan Restaurant

52 Stanley Street **t** (01704) 530720
Open Mon–Fri 11.30–2 and 4–8pm (Fri 9pm), Sat 11.30–9, Sun 12 noon–8

Fish 'n' chippy with a range of kids' meals. Highchairs and baby changing facilities available.

Wigan

Papa Luigi's

Wigan Lane **t** (01942) 231558
www.hilton-leisureltd.com
Open Tues–Fri 12–2 and 6–10.30, Sun 5–9pm

All things Italian (pasta, pizzas) and a few that aren't (steaks, fried chicken); half portions for kids.

Wiggin Tree

Parbold Hill, Parbold **t** (01257) 462318
Open Mon–Sat 11am–10pm, Sun 12 noon–10pm

Perched on a hill north of Wigan, this restaurant is a local landmark. Range of child-friendly dishes. Highchairs and baby changing facilities available.

Windermere

Queen's Head

Troutbeck **t** (01539) 432174
www.queensheadhotel.com
Open Mon–Sat 11–11, Sun 12 noon–10.30pm

A cosy pub with flagstones and a log fire, on the A592 just north of Windermere. Children's menu offering salmon fishcakes and spag bol. Highchairs and baby changing facilities available.

The Northeast
Northumberland · Durham
Tyne and Wear · Yorkshire
East Riding of Yorkshire
by Dennis Kelsall

The Northeast

Though less well known as a holiday destination than many other parts of England, the Northeast has all the ingredients necessary for a great family holiday. There are the beaches and funfairs of resorts like Scarborough and Whitby, the heritage museums and big-city bustle of the great industrial towns of Newcastle and Leeds, the fabulous Jorvik Viking Centre and strange medieval architecture of York and, of course, the imposing bulk of Hadrian's Wall, Roman Britain's greatest monument.

It is the countryside, however, that is perhaps the region's greatest glory, with a landscape as varied and attractive as any in England. Two great stretches of Heritage Coast combine beaches, rock pools and dunes with miles of exhilarating cliff paths whilst inland, three National Parks encompass some of the country's finest unspoilt moorland, hill, forest and river scenery, providing a landscape that is ideal for cycling and walking.

Highlights

Castle Museum, York, p.468

Viking fun, Jorvik Viking Centre, York, pp.468–9

Digging for bones, DIG archaeological resource centre, York, p.468

Hands-on science fun, Eureka! The Museum for Children, Halifax, p.494, or National Museum of Photography, Film and Television, Bradford, p.496

Roman fun, Hadrian's Wall, pp.473–5

Industrial fun, North of England Open Air Museum, Beamish, p.484

Puffin-spotting, Farne Islands, pp.479–80

Spooky tours, Dracula tour of Whitby, pp.482–3

Train fun, National Railway Museum, p.469, or North Yorkshire Moors Railway, pp.485–6

Tropical gardens, Roundhay, p.465

Underground fun, White Scar Caves, Ingleton, p.490

Walking, Yorkshire Dales National Park p.488

Day-trip itinerary

Morning: At the Jorvik Viking Centre in York (p.468).

Lunch: Take a stroll down Parliament Street and watch the street performers en route to Betty's Café Tearooms (p.500), or have a picnic in the Museum Gardens, which are a five-minute walk from York Minster.

Afternoon: If you're feeling energetic, climb to the top of York Minster (pp.469–70), or catch the mini road train to the National Railway Museum (p.469).

Special events

February
York: Jorvik Viking Festival t (01904) 543403
www.vikingjorvik.com

April
Whitby: Gothic Weekend t (01947) 602674
www.topmum.co.uk

June
Durham Regatta t (0191) 384 3720
www.durham-regatta.org.uk
Scarborough: Scarborough Fayre t (01723) 373 333

July
Durham: Summer Festival t (0191) 384 3720
Harrogate: Great Yorkshire Show t (01423) 541000
www.yas.co.uk
Harrogate: International Festival t (01423) 562303
www.harrogate-festival.org.uk
Leeds: Rhythms of the City t (0113) 242 5242

August
Leeds: Carnival t (0113) 242 5242
www.leedscarnival.co.uk
Kingston-upon-Hull: Sea Shanty Festival
t (01482) 223559

September
Newcastle: Great North Run t (0191) 277 8000
www.greatrun.org
York: Festival of Food and Drink t (01904) 554488
www.yorkfestivaloffoodanddrink.com

October
Whitby: Captain Cook Festival t (01947) 602674

November
York: St Nicholas Fayre t (01904) 621756
www.yuletideyork.com

Durham

Getting there By road: Durham is about 230 miles north of London, 15 miles south of Newcastle and can be reached via the A1 (M) and the A19. There is a £2 congestion charge to drive into the city centre. People carriers with roof boxes will need to park in the open air car park by the riverside. By train: The city lies on the main London Kings Cross–Scotland rail network and services pass through frequently. By bus/coach: National Express coaches run regularly from Newcastle and London Victoria
Tourist information 2 Millennium Place **t** (0191) 384 3720 **www.durhamtourism.co.uk**

The first thing the kids will notice about Durham is its size. The city centre is clustered on the hill around the castle and cathedral. It may be small but there are lots of things to see and do here, with excellent museums and good restaurants. The town is home to one of the country's main universities and has a student atmosphere reminiscent of Oxford and Cambridge. Since a congestion charge was introduced to get into the old town, it's virtually car free. To make sure you see everything, join one of the many guided tours run by the tourist office. The botanical gardens, Oriental museum and heritage centre are worth a visit, and most children will enjoy a boat trip on the river – either take a cruise or hire a rowing boat. The surrounding countryside is inviting, with highlights including High Force in Upper Teesdale, one of England's largest waterfalls, and Hamsterley Forest, for walks, a forest drive or pony-trekking. There are special events throughout the summer, the most spectacular being the June Durham Regatta.

A little bit of history

Durham was founded more than 1,000 years ago, when Lindisfarne's monks fled Viking raids, bringing with them the remains of St Cuthbert (known locally as 'Cuddy'). The city rapidly assumed an importance that it has retained ever since. Prosperity grew from the gifts and trade of pilgrims, and power came with William the Conqueror's creation of the Prince Bishops, who ruled the north. Two great symbols of that age remain in Durham's castle and cathedral and around the Palace Green. Many old buildings that were formerly almshouses or official residences are now part of the city's university.

Q: Can you see what kind of birds are at the feet of St Cuthbert on one of the murals?
A: They're eider ducks, locally called Cuddy Ducks.

Things to see and do

Cinemas and theatres *See pp.492, 497*

Crook Hall and Gardens

Frankland Lane, Sidegate **t** (0191) 384 8028
www.crookhallgardens.co.uk
Open Easter weekend, May Sun and Bank Hols, Jun–early Sept Wed–Sun 11–5
Adm Adults £4.50, children £4, family £14
Tearoom, plant shop, limited disabled access to hall

A tranquil spot on the banks of the River Wear, this listed medieval hall (check out the haunted Jacobean Room) overlooks one-and-a-half hectares (four acres) of gardens, where kids can run about. The grass maze is fun.

Durham Castle

Palace Green **t** (0191) 334 4099
www.durhamcastle.com
Open Easter–Sept daily; Oct–Easter Mon, Wed, Sat and Sun; call for tour times
Adm Adults £5, children £3.50, family £12
Guided tours, not suitable for pushchairs

This magnificent building was begun in 1072 under William the Conqueror and, for almost 800 years, was the seat of the powerful Prince Bishops. The castle is one of the country's finest surviving Norman fortifications, thanks to repair and restoration in the 18th century and in the 1930s after the whole building nearly collapsed. The castle, a student hall of residence, is only accessible by a 45-minute guided tour (suitable for older children) that takes you through the history and present life of the castle, including the 15th-century kitchen, which is still in use.

★Durham Cathedral

Palace Green **t** (0191) 386 4266
www.durhamcathedral.co.uk
Open Jun–Aug Mon–Fri 9.30–8, Sun 12.30–8; Sept–July Mon–Fri 9.30–6, Sun 12.30–5.30
Adm Free (suggested donation £4 per adult); call for opening times and admission prices for the Tower, Treasures of St Cuthbert, Monks' Domitories and audiovisual display
Please note: the Monks' Dormitory is currently closed; due to re-open April 2007
Restaurant, bookshop, disabled facilities

Can you spot...?
Look out for the sanctuary ring on the cathedral door, clasped in the mouth of a ferocious beast. Many years ago you could claim the protection of the church by simply clasping it.

Founded in 1093 as a shrine to St Cuthbert, this great Norman cathedral took only 40 years to build and stands in a commanding position encircled by the River Wear. The lawns around the cathedral are the place to hang out and relax. Inside, the beauty of the carved arches and pillars is quite breathtaking, along with the colourful stained-glass windows and effigy tombs. The saint's remains lie buried behind the high altar – originally he was buried on Lindisfarne, but in AD 793 the monks carried his relics over to the mainland after Viking raids made the island unsafe. You'll see objects that were buried with Cuddy in a Treasures of St Cuthbert display. Look out for the tomb of the Venerable Bede, the first English historian. In good weather, you can climb 325 steps to the top of the tower for views of the city. There's an excellent kids' trail, too.

Ghost Walks
Tourist Information Centre, Millennium Place
t (0191) 384 3720
Open Jun–Sept daily 6.30pm; Jul–Aug also Mon at 8.30pm
Adm Call for prices
These not-too-scary 90-minute historic tours are very popular, so buy your tickets in advance.

Light Infantry Museum and Art Gallery
Aykley Heads **t** (0191) 384 2214
www.durham.gov.uk/dli
Getting there Off the A691, northwest of the city centre
Open Apr–Oct daily 10–5, Nov–Mar 10–4
Adm Adults £3, children £1.25, family (2+2) £7
Refreshments, internet café, picnics, shop, mother and baby facilities, disabled facilities, on-site parking
This museum traces the proud 200-year history of the county's regiment, its soldiers and families at home and abroad. Find out about the wartime experiences of children on the homefront and, in the 'Horrible Histories' zone (created after local author Terry Deary's series of books), get spooked in the creepy crawling tunnel, dress up in uniform and clamber onto a bren gun carrier – but watch out for the dead rats in the soldiers' uniforms and eerie noises coming from

the 'Dreadful Dugout'. The art gallery has regular shows of work by traditional and modern artists and craftspeople. The museum often runs craft sessions for families.

The Old Fulling Mill (Museum of Archaeology)
The Banks **t** (0191) 334 1823
www.dur.ac.uk/fulling.mill
Open Apr–Oct daily 11–4, Nov–Mar Fri–Mon 11.30–3.30
Adm Adults £1, children 50p, family (2+2) £2.50
Shop
The museum houses archaeological material, mostly from the northeast of England. There are well preserved medieval finds from Durham City and a hands-on gallery for children. Special school-holiday events are organized for kids.

The Oriental Museum
Elvet Hill **t** (0191) 334 5694
www.dur.ac.uk/oriental.museum
Open Mon–Fri 10–5 Sat–Sun 12 noon–5pm
Adm Adults £1.50, children 75p, family (2+2) £3.50
Shop, café
The only museum in the UK devoted to art and archaeology from the Orient. It's part of the university and organizes lots of events for kids.

Prince Bishop River Trips
Prince Bishop, Brown's Boathouse, Elvet Bridge
t (0191) 386 9525
Getting there Near Prince Bishop shopping centre
Open Summer daily; call for times
Fares Adults £4.50, children £2
Refreshments, rowing boats for hire
This cruise along the Wear has a lively and informative commentary, looping around Durham for brilliant views of the castle and cathedral.

Shopping
Durham is a tiny city so don't expect too much. Mothercare is in the Prince Bishop Shopping Centre and there's a lively covered market by the gates. Marks and Spencer is on Silver Street and the Early Learning Centre toyshop is in the Millburngate Shopping Centre.

Sport and activities *See pp.490–2*

Around Durham
Hall Hill Farm, 8 miles west (p.478)
North of England Open Air Museum, 10 miles north (p.484)

Kingston-upon-Hull

Getting there By road: Kingston-upon-Hull lies 50 miles east of Leeds on the A63 and about 145 miles north of London. By train: Local trains provide connections to the national rail network in York and Leeds. By bus/coach: There is a regular National Express service from Leeds, York and London Victoria

Tourist information 1 Paragon Street **t** (01482) 223559 **www.**hullcc.gov.uk

Approach the city by way of the spectacular Humber Bridge (if possible), which has one of the longest spans in the world. The city itself has a long history, an ancient harbour and a wealth of museums and parks. Parents will be delighted to know that Hull's museums, apart from The Deep, are all free of charge. The Fish Trail discovery walk around the old town (leaflet available from the tourist office) is marked by a series of pavement brasses and sculptures. Children can take rubbings of the fishes. There are two visitors' boats in the marina and a wealth of maritime attractions. For letting off steam and encountering animals, there are Pearson and East Parks. In summer, there is a wonderful Sea Shanty Festival, with a host of international performers against a backdrop of sails.

Things to see and do

The *Arctic Corsair*

River Hull between Drypool Bridge and Myton Bridge **t** (01482) 324223
Open Apr–Oct Wed and Sat 10.30–4.30, Sun 1.30–4.30 (last tour at 3)
Adm Free
Not suitable for children under 6

From Hull boats set sail into the treacherous waters on the Arctic Circle. The boat is moored alongside the museums and on board you can find out what it was like to live and work on a boat like this in the freezing waters of the Arctic.

Cinemas and theatres *See pp.492, 497*

The Deep

Size Point **t** (01482) 381000 **www.**thedeep.co.uk
Open Daily 10–6 (last admission 5) **Adm** Adults £8, children £6, under 4s **free,** family £25
Café, shop, disabled access

On the waterfront near the old town in a spectacular modern building, The Deep's main feature is a discovery centre looking at the evolution of the world's oceans from the beginning of time through interactive displays. In the aquarium, divers swimming with the fish explain how they live and feed in their natural environment. There's a brand new 'Hullaballoo' play area with lots of hands-on learning activities.

Hands-on History Museum

South Church Side **t** (01482) 613902
www.hullcc.gov.uk/museums
Open Mon–Sat 10-5 Sun 1.30–4.30 **Adm Free**
Baby changing facilities, shop

The museum, housed in an old Tudor schoolroom, is aimed at children aged 5–11 and sets out to support the National Curriculum history course – there are lots of reference books lying around if you want to read up! However even the smallest child will have fun dressing up in real Victorian costume or working the water pump. The ground floor looks at everyday life in Victorian Britain. Upstairs there's a collection of life-size replicas from Tutankhamun's tomb made for the British Empire Exhibition in 1924 and a real Egyptian mummy, which once belonged to a friend of Bram Stoker, who kept it in his house in Whitby, where Stoker was inspired to write the novel *Dracula*. The mummy inspired him to write another thriller about a mummified princess but the museum has recently found out that the 'mummy princess' is actually a man!

Hull and East Riding Museum

36 High Street **t** (01482) 613902
Open Mon–Sat 10–5 Sun 1.30–4.30 (last admission 30 minutes before closing) **Adm Free**

Brings history alive for the smallest child. There's a life-size model of a woolly mammoth, a recreation of an Iron Age village, a real Viking longboat, and a reconstruction of a Roman town and villa. There are reference books for kids to find out more about each of the rooms.

Maritime Museum

Queen Victoria Square **t** (01482) 613902
www.hullcc.gov.uk/museums
Open Mon–Sat 10–5, Sun 1.30–4.30 (last admission 15 minutes before closing) **Adm Free**
Shop, baby changing facilities

In this impressive Victorian building, displays tell stories of the ships and crews that ventured into the North Sea in search of trade and fish. Don't miss the huge skeleton of a white whale.

Museums Quarter

36 High Street **t** (01482) 613902
www.hullcc.gov.uk/museums
Open Mon–Sat 10–5 Sun 1.30–4.30 **Adm Free**
Shops, baby changing facilities, picnic areas in the museum gardens

Home to Wilberforce House, the Hull and East Riding Museum and Streetlife Hull Museum of Transport (*see* opposite and below).

Shopping

The city has a swanky new shopping centre at Princes Quay. You'll find the Disney Store, Gap Kids and the Virgin Megastore for a CD fix. There is a giant Toys 'R' Us at the nearby Kingston Retail Park next to Mothercare World and branches of all the main department stores and high street chains on Whitefriargate and Prospect Street, which radiate off Queen Victoria Square next to Princes Quay. Trinity Market is the place to buy food.

Sport and activities *See* pp.490–2

The *Spurn Lightship*

Hull Marina **t** (01482) 613902
Open Mar–Oct Mon–Sat 10–5, Sun 1.30–4.30
Adm Free

Built in 1927, this floating lighthouse guided shipping through the treacherous waters of the Humber Estuary. On board, the 'crew' tells how its predecessors spent their tours of duty.

Streetlife Hull Museum of Transport

36 High Street **t** (01482) 613902
Open Mon–Sat 10–5 Sun 1.30–4.30 **Adm Free**

A collection of buses, trams and cars, interactive displays and sounds and smells to bring the past to life. You can actually climb on board the buses.

Wilberforce House Museum

36 High Street **t** (01482) 613902
Open Mon–Sat 10–5 Sun 1.30–4.30 **Adm Free**

William Wilberforce, the man who led the campaign to abolish slavery, was born in this house 250 years ago. The exhibits are more likely to interest older children, but expect more child-friendly displays following a major revamp of the museum for the 2007 bicentenary of abolition.

Around Kingston-upon-Hull

Bridlington, 24 miles north (p.480)
Cleethorpes, 18 miles southeast (p.353)
Sewerby Hall, 26 miles north (p.473)

Leeds

Getting there By road: Leeds is on the eastern fringe of the Pennines, 30 miles northwest of Manchester, about 45 miles east of Hull, and 160 miles north of London and it can be approached via the M1 and M62. By train: Transpennine and regional rail services connect with the national rail network in Manchester and York. There are direct trains from London King's Cross. By bus/coach: National Express coaches run a regular service from Manchester and London and a new super-tram service makes local travel easy
Tourist information The Arcade, Leeds City Station **t** (0113) 242 5242 **www.**leedsliveitloveit.com

Arguably Europe's fastest growing city, Leeds continues to enjoy a prosperity founded on the medieval wool trade. Many famous companies began trading here (including Marks and Spencer from a stall in Kirkgate Market and Waddingtons). The city is cosmopolitan, with a wealth of arts and entertainment (the West Yorkshire Playhouse is the largest provincial theatre in the country), shops, chic hotels, bars and cafés. Galleries, museums and heritage centres abound , as well as several stately homes and parks on the outskirts. Leeds is also home to the nation's collection of armour and the National Museum of Photography, Film and Television (p.496) is nearby in Bradford. It's well located for test cricket, premier league football and super-league rugby. The starkly beautiful Pennine moors are a short drive away, with miles of footpaths and cycle tracks and fresh air for weary heads.

Things to see and do

Armley Mills Industrial Museum

Canal Road, Armley **t** (0113) 263 7861
Getting there On the A65, 2 miles west of Leeds
Open Tues–Sat and Bank Hols 10–5, Sun 1–5
Adm Adults £3, children £1
Picnic areas, shop, disabled facilities, on-site parking

This used to be one of the world's largest woollen mills and, on 'working weekends', exhibits are set in motion – water wheels turning, steam engines hissing, 'mules' spinning. There are demonstrations of mechanical printing methods, and an exhibition tracing the history of cinema projections. Silent films play in the 1920s cinema.

Cinemas and theatres *See pp.492, 497*

Kirkstall Abbey and Abbey House Museum

Abbey Road, Kirkstall **t** (0113) 230 5492
Getting there On the A65, 3 miles from Leeds
Open Abbey: daily 8am–dusk; museum: Tues–Fri
10–5, Sat 12 noon–5pm, Sun 10–5
Adm Abbey **free**; museum: adults £3.50, children
£1.50, family (2+3) £5
*Café, picnic areas, shop, mother and baby facilities,
disabled facilities*

The site of this medieval monastery is one
of the best-preserved in Britain. After the
Dissolution, much of the roof, windows and
stonework was taken for local buildings, and it
gracefully fell into a ruin much admired by artists
and poets of the Romantic period. The museum
traces the lives of the monks in one of its
galleries, but its main feature is a recreation of
three streets showing how life was for Victorian
residents of Leeds or 'loiners'. In the chemist's, it is
revealed how former so-called remedies would
today be classed as illegal substances.
Nineteenth-century toys, games and nursery
rhymes play in the interactive children's gallery.

★Royal Armouries Museum

Armouries Drive, The Waterfront **t** (0113) 220 1916
www.royalarmouries.org
Getting there Follow the brown tourist signs to
Leeds centre, then 'finger' signpost (15 minutes' walk)
Open Daily 10–5 **Adm** Free
Restaurant, café, shop, disabled facilities, parking

The royal collection of arms and armour is
found in five themed galleries: War, Tournament,
Self-Defence, Hunting and Arms and Armour of
the Orient. There are multimedia and interactive
exhibits, live demonstrations of martial arts and
cowboy shoot-outs and, especially for children,
storytellers, actors and hands-on experiences like
handling swords, wielding battle axes and
shooting crossbows. Outside, spectacular
jousting tournaments and hunting displays are
held from April to September. In the Menagerie
Court, you'll find falcons, hunting dogs and
horses. In the Craft Court, swordsmiths, leather-
workers and gunmakers demonstrate their skills.
The museum also organizes sleepovers for kids.

Shopping

Leeds has some of the best shops in the
country. The city centre is one huge shopping
complex but remains a characterful place with
its Victorian arcades and market. Parking is best
in the marketplace car park. The main shopping
drag is Briggate, where you'll find the classy new
Harvey Nichols department store, TopShop, GAP
and Marks and Spencer, plus Borders bookshop,
t (0113) 2424400, which has kids' activities in the
school holidays. The Early Learning Centre
toyshop is in Bond Street Mall and H&M is on
Albion Street. For designer boutiques, go to the
new Corn Exchange centre.

Sport and activities *See pp.490–2*

Temple Newsam House and Park

Temple Newsam Road **t** (0113) 264 5535
www.leeds.gov.uk/templenewsam
Getting there 4 miles east of the city off the A63
Open House: Apr–Oct Tues–Sun 10.30–5, Nov–Mar
Tues–Sun 10.30–4; farm: Apr–Oct Tues–Sun 10–5,
Nov–Mar Tues–Sun 10–4 **Adm** House: adults £3.50,
children £2.50, under 5s **free**, family £9; farm:
adults £3, children £2, under 5s **free**, family £8
*Tearoom, shop, disabled facilities, on-site parking
(£3.50), picnic area*

Europe's largest rare breeds centre (486
hectares/1,200 acres) has over 400 animals to
watch, touch and smell. There are engaging
exhibitions depicting life on the farm; on work
days, the kids can help the laundry maids, see
the blacksmith at work or watch trees being
sliced into planks in the saw-mill. Inside the
opulent house, there's the country's largest
collection of Chippendale furniture. Outside,
there's a putting green and playground, not
forgetting the spacious grounds of the house. It
can be muddy outdoors so pack your wellies.

Thackray Medical Museum

Beckett Street **t** (0113) 244 4343
www.thackraymuseum.org
Getting there Next to St James' University
Hospital, 1 mile east of the city centre
Open Daily 10–5 **Adm** Adults £5.50, children £4,
under 5s **free**, family £18
Café, shop, disabled facilities, parking (£4)

From the workings of the human body to
medical developments of the last 150 years, this
mesmerizing museum explores what makes us
tick. Gory and disgusting, it is almost guaranteed
to delight the kids. One exhibition promises to
'literally have you in stitches'. 'Pain, Pus and Blood'

The Geordie dialect

The name 'Geordie' generally applies to people who are from the northeast (and Northumbrians will tell you that their dialect is slightly different). The hard-to-understand accent has similarities with Scandinavian languages, perhaps dating back to the times of Viking occupation. Geordies are fiercely proud of their land and language.

Some words and phrases

How there, marra!/What cheor! Hello!
Why aye! Of course *and* Hello
What're ye dein in there? What are you doing?
It's varra caad oot by It's very cold outside
Aa've prog'd me thoom wiv a needle
I've pricked my thumb
He's a greet sackless cuddy He's a big stupid donkey
Blather skite One who talks senselessly
Linins Underpants
Parnicketty Fussy
Not reet iv his head He's mad
My eye! That's nonsense

Around Leeds

Colour Museum, 10 miles west (p.494)
Harewood House, 7 miles north (p.472)
National Coal Mining Museum for England, 10 miles south (p.495)
National Museum of Photography, Film and Television, 10 miles west (p.496)

Newcastle-upon-Tyne

Getting there: Newcastle-upon-Tyne is approximately 100 miles northeast of Manchester, 245 miles north of London and 48 miles east of Carlisle, and can be reached via the A1(M), the A19 and the A69. By train: There are frequent services on the main London–Scotland rail network. By bus/coach: There are regular National Express coach services from London Victoria, Manchester and York
Tourist information 132 Grainger Street **t** (0191) 277 8000 www.newcastle.gov.uk

The ancient capital of the kingdom of Northumbria, England's northernmost city, is known for the warmth and hospitality of its inhabitants; the River Tyne's impressive bridges, especially the new Millennium Bridge; the remains of a Norman keep (the 'new castle', after which the city is named); and an elegant medieval cathedral.

Founded by the Romans, who recognized its potential as a military position, in later times the city became a thriving industrial port – coal, loco-motives and shipbuilding were big business – and gained its many grand 19th-century buildings. In the early 20th century, Newcastle suffered a decline along with many other English industrial towns. Now however, the traditional industries are being replaced, most noticeably by shops, and the city centre has a fresh face after much cleaning and restoration, and bold new develop-ments such as the revamped Quayside area. There are many guided walks around the city, and a trail created especially for children, which explores the city's Victorian heart, Grainger Town. Older kids should enjoy the river cruise beneath the city's great bridges; the Tyne Bridge, which opened in 1928, was the world's largest single-span bridge in its day. At Jesmond Dene, a lovely woodland park close to the city's heart, escape the hustle

tells how surgery took place without anaes-thetics. 'Hannah's Ordeal' is a leg amputation and, in 'Having a Baby', visitors strap on an 'empathy belly' to find out how it feels to be pregnant.

★Tropical World and Roundhay Park

Princes Avenue, Roundhay **t** (0113) 266 1850
www.roundhaypark.org.uk
Getting there Off the A58, 3 miles north of Leeds; take bus nos.2, 10 or 12 from the city
Open Summer 10–6; winter 10–4
Adm Adults £3, children £2, under 8s **free**
Café, picnic areas, shop, disabled facilities, parking

Keep your eyes open for scaly iguanas, frogs, snakes, hairy tarantulas and piranhas! At Tropical World an alien landscape of plants, animals and birds are housed in a variety of environments, including a South American House with rain-forest pools and brightly coloured tropical birds; a Nocturnal House with spooky fruit bats, monkeys and bush babies; a Butterfly House with over 60 species of butterfly and moth; and an Australasia House with underwater displays and a tropical insect collection. The adjacent 285-hectare (700-acre) Roundhay Park has nature walks, picnic and games areas, an adventure playground, lakes, land train, wooded parkland and gardens.

and bustle and follow the pathways of nature and history trails. If visiting in June, don't miss the annual 'Hoppings' Fair (named after the 'hopping' or dancing that took place), which is held on the Town Moor during the last full week of the month and is said to be the largest non-permanent fair in the world.

Things to see and do

Baltic Centre for Contemporary Art

South Shore Road, Gateshead **t** (0191) 478 1810
www.balticmill.com
Open Daily 10–6 (Wed until 8)
Adm Free
Restaurants and café, shop, disabled access, unisex baby changing facilities

A relatively new venue for exhibitions and artists' workshops. The riverside restaurant and café are great places to eat and there are family activities, kids' workshops and courses on offer.

Castle Keep

Castle Garth, St Nicholas St **t** (0191) 2327938,
Open Apr–Oct daily 9.30–5.30, Nov–Apr 9.30–4.30
Adm Adults £1.50, children 50p, under 4s **free**

The 'new castle' was built in 1080 on the site of a Roman fort by the illegitimate son of William the Conqueror. Originally made of wood, it was rebuilt in stone by Henry II, who added the fine Norman keep; the roof and battlements are from the 19th century. Climb up the spiral stairs for views of the city.

★Centre For Life

Times Square, Scotswood Road **t** (0191) 243 8210
www.life.org.uk
Open Mon–Sat 10–6, Sun 11–6 (last admission 4)
Adm Adults £7.50, children £4.95, family (2+2) £22.50, under 4s **free**
Café, shop, disabled facilities, nearby parking (70p)

Housed in an unusually shaped building designed to look like a leaf, this place is billed as the city's most exciting attraction. Part of the International Centre for Life, it focuses on the big questions of life – human, plant and animal – in a basic but fun way. Find out about courtship and mating in 'The Tunnel of Love', our monkey ancestors in 'The River of Life', see live theatre in 'The Secret of Life' and explore your brain in the 'Sensory Zoo'. There's also the world's longest motion simulator ride and interactive computer games, such as 'virtual volleyball', to be tested out.

Cinemas and theatres *See pp.492, 497*

Discovery Museum

Blandford House, Blandford Square
t (0191) 232 6789 **www.**twmusuems.org.uk
Open Mon–Sat 10–5, Sun 2–5 **Adm Free**
Café, shop, mother and baby facilities, disabled facilities

Explore science, technology and Tyneside's history in this hands-on museum, which has a complete ship as its centrepiece. The fully restored 44-tonne *Turbinia* was, in 1894, the first to be powered by a steam turbine invented and built by a local man, Charles Parsons. Described as one of Britain's greatest engineers, he also invented the means to power electric street lighting in 1895.

Laing Art Gallery

New Bridge Street **t** (0191) 232 7734
www.twmusuems.org.uk
Open Mon–Sat 10–5, Sun 2–5 **Adm Free**
Café, shop, mother and baby facilities, disabled facilities

Alongside the permanent collection, there's the Procter and Gamble Children's Gallery, a paradise for the under 5s with puzzles and a soft play area.

Shopping

The Metro Centre, one of Europe's largest shopping centres, is the best place to shop; you'll find all the big high street names here. It's on the A1 west of Gateshead. It also has a huge indoor play area. In the city centre, shops are concentrated on Northumberland Street and for toys you'll find the Early Learning Centre in Eldon Square shopping centre, alongside Miss Selfridge and shops selling computer games and CDs. Boots the Chemist is on Grey Street. There's an Internet Exchange cyber café on Market Street.

Sport and activities *See pp.490–2*

Walks and tours

If you fancy a stroll, catch the no.21 bus from Pilgrim Street to come face-to-face with the Angel of the North. Unwind at the quayside: kids will love watching the Millennium Bridge opening up. City Sightseeing's open-air bus tours depart from the railway station, **t** (0871) 6660000, **www.**citysightseeing.co.uk. There are more than 30 guided city walks organized by the tourist office, **t** (0191) 2778000, that take in attractions such as the old walls and the Tyne bridges.

TOP TOWNS | SPECIAL TRIPS | KIDS OUT | SPORT AND ACTIVITIES | KIDS IN | EATING OUT

Can you spot?

The 'Angel of the North' overlooking the A1 at Gateshead. The giant steel sculpture by artist Antony Gormley symbolizes the regeneration of the northeast. At 20m (65ft) tall and weighing 200 tonnes (197 tons), it is nearly as big as a Boeing 747 airliner.

Tyne Leisure Line Ltd

Quayside **t** (0191) 296 6740/6741
www.tyneleisureline.co.uk
Open Summer Sat 10–3, 1hr cruise **Adm** Adult £6, children £4, family £16

Sightseeing along the River Tyne with themes like 'Tyne Fascination' and 'Geordie Heritage'. Call in advance for additional information.

Around Newcastle

Bede's World and St Paul's Church, 9 miles east (p.493)
Gibside, 7 miles southwest (pp.484–5)
New Metroland, 3 miles south (p.487)
***Segedunum* Roman Fort and Museum**, 1 mile east (p.474)
Souter Lighthouse, 10 miles southeast (p.475)
Washington Wildfowl and Wetlands Centre, 9 miles south (p.477)

York

Getting there By road: York is 70 miles south of Newcastle, 58 miles northeast of Manchester and 23 miles northeast of Leeds, and is accessible via the A64 and the M1. Park-and-ride facilities are signposted from the main approaches to the city. By rail: It lies on the east coast mainline and is served by direct trains from London Kings Cross. By bus/coach: There are regular National Express coaches from all major cities
Tourist information De Grey Rooms, Exhibition Square **t** (01904) 550099 **www.**visityork.org

York is one of the country's most attractive and historic towns; the site has had a resident community for almost 2,000 years and has been occupied many times. The Romans (who called the city 'Eboracum'), the Saxons (who called it 'Eoforwic') and the Normans all left their mark – to say nothing of the Vikings, who ruled what they called 'Jorvik' for almost a century. Today, the wonderful Jorvik Centre and ARC bring Viking

Britain vividly to life. It's a great city for kids and there's enough to do to make it an ideal place for a short break. It has lots of family-friendly hotels and restaurants, which is no surprise as York is the city where many famous name chocolate bars were invented. For much of the medieval period, York was England's second city. Its many, sagging, half-timbered houses and narrow, twisting streets and alleyways, including the famous Shambles, date from then. Also built at this time, 800-year-old Minster Cathedral is the city's most famous landmark, and the largest Gothic cathedral in northern Europe. The Georgians also made their mark in the 18th century and at elegant Fairfax House you can catch a glimpse of their splendidly refined style.

A grisly attraction for the more bloodthirsty, York Dungeon shows the gruesome history and fate of York's infamous villains, such as Dick Turpin and Guy Fawkes. If you want to be spooked, join the Ghost Hunt of York for a supernatural stroll around the spiritually infested nooks and crannies of the city. A day city tour is also fun or sit back and cruise the Ouse taking in the riverside sights. If you plan to fit in a lot of sightseeing, buy a York Pass (from **www.**yorkpass.com or tourist offices) which entitles you to free entry to 29 of York's popular attractions as well as offering restaurant, entertainment and shopping discounts. Family passes start at £54 for 1 day rising to £92 for 3 days for 2 adults and 2 children.

Things to see and do

Association of Voluntary Guides

t (01904) 640780
www.york.touristguides.btinternet.co.uk
Tour times Daily 10.25, Apr–Sept also 2.15, Jul–Aug also 6.45 **Adm** Free

Two-hour tours of the city, leaving from outside the Art Gallery on Exhibition Square.

Barley Hall

2 Coffee Yard **t** (01904) 610275)
www.barleyhall.org.uk
Open Tues–Sun 10–4
Adm Adults £4.50 under 10s **free**
Shop

Step back in time at York's finest medieval townhouse. Kids can dress up in medieval costume, handle glass and pottery and sit on the furniture.

Can you spot?
Whip-Ma-Whop-Ma-Gate – York's shortest street – measuring 32m (35 yards). It means 'neither one thing nor the other' and dates from Saxon times.

★Castle Museum

The Eye of York **t** (01904) 687687
www.yorkcastlemuseum.org.uk
Open Daily 9.30–5 **Adm** Adults £6.50, children £3.50, under 5s **free**, family £18. All tickets are valid for a return trip within 12 months.
Shop, café, picnic areas, disabled facilities, no pushchairs (buggy park and loan of free backpacks and carrycots available)

Once a prison where executions took place (you can see the cell where the highwayman Dick Turpin was held), these buildings now house furnished rooms recreating life from Jacobean times to the 1950s, along with a collection of military armour and arms. The most popular attraction here is Kirkgate, a reconstruction of a cobbled Victorian Street lined with shops. Recently renovated and extended, it now boasts a number of interactive displays. Costumed characters inhabit the street during the summer, when you can head to the sweetshop to meet the sweetmaker and sample some of his tasty treats, stop for a chat with the policeman and try not to get a telling-off by teacher in the new school room.

Cinemas and theatres *See* pp.492, 497

Clifford's Tower

The Eye of York **t** (01904) 646940
www.english-heritage.org.uk
Open Apr–Sept daily 10–6, Oct 10–5, Nov–Mar 10–4
Adm Adults £3, children £1.30, family (2+3) £7.50

Clifford's Tower is a reminder that history wasn't all about jolly Vikings and steam trains. The Normans arrived in York in 1068 and built an imposing castle to impress the locals. It was a great example of a classic motte and bailey castle, although all that's left of it today is the mound underneath Clifford's Tower. The tower has a sad history and was the scene of the worst pogrom in English history. Anti-Semitism was rife during the Crusades and in March 1190 the city's Jews took refuge in the tower from a marauding mob. When they were offered a choice between baptism and death, they committed mass suicide rather than face being murdered by the crowd below: the tower was burned to the ground and the rioters killed whoever tried to escape. The

tower you see today was actually built 50 years later but visitors often claim to have seen blood pouring down the walls. The red stains are, in fact, due to iron oxide in the stone. Surprisingly though, no other stone from the mine in Tadcaster bears the same stains.

DIG

St, Saviour's Church, St Saviourgate **t** (01904) 543403 **www.digyork.co.uk**
Open Daily 10–5 **Adm** Adults £5.50, children £5, family (2+2) £16; joint ticket with Jorvik: adults £11, children £8.30, family £32

DIG is a hands-on educational attraction run by the York Archaeological Trust (which also runs the Jorvik Viking Centre, *see* below). Here, kids don't just get to learn about archaeological techniques, they get to play at being archaeologists – digging for artefacts, examining finds, recording evidence, analysing human remains, making reconstructions and more, all in the company of professional archaeologists. It's a popular attraction and spaces are limited; book in advance.

The Dungeon

12 Clifford Street **t** (01904) 632599
www.thedungeons.com
Open Apr–Sept daily 10.30–6.30 (last admission 5.30); Oct–Mar 10.30–5.30 (last admission 4.30)
Adm Adults £11.95, children £6.95
Not suitable for young children

Learn the dark and gory truth about York's past. Follow a creepy tour guide, to see the effects of the Black Death as it ravages the city's 14th-century streets. Accompany the highwayman Dick Turpin on his final journey to the gallows and witness the terrible punishments and tortures doled out to the evil villains of the past.

The Ghost Hunt of York

t (01904) 608700 **www.ghosthunt.co.uk**
Tour times Daily at 7.30pm from the Shambles; booking not necessary **Adm** Adults £5, children £3
Route suitable for wheelchairs and pushchairs

York is England's most haunted city, so come walk the streets of ghostly York with a Victorian gentleman guide, who will entertain, mystify and thrill you with his repertoire of stories and illusions. Audience participation is encouraged.

★Jorvik Viking Centre

Coppergate **t** (01904) 543402 **www**.jorvik.co.uk
Open Daily 10–5 **Adm** Adults £7.75, children £5.50,
under 5s **free**, family (2+2) £21.95, (2+3) £26.50; joint
ticket with DIG: adults £12, children £8.30, family £32
Café, shop, audio guide, disabled facilities

Step into a simulated time machine and go back
over 1,000 years to a reconstruction of the Viking
city of Jorvik with a nine-year-old Viking boy as
your guide. The ride rises above the banks of the
River Foss to give a panoramic view over the
rooftops towards the Viking equivalent of York
Minster before descending into the streets, where
animals scratch about backyards and traders go
about their business. A blast of heat hits you as
you pass the blacksmith's furnace and the smells
of a cesspit greet you as you pass. Back in the
present, visitors can witness how excavation finds
are preserved for future generations. If visiting
during school holidays, pre-book to avoid queues.

★National Railway Museum

Leeman Road **t** (01904) 621261 **www**.nrm.org.uk
Open Daily 10–6 **Adm Free**; Yorkshire Wheel:
adults £6, children £4, under 4s **free**
*Restaurant, café, picnic area, shop, disabled facilities,
on-site parking, gift shop*

The world's largest museum of its kind, which
tells the complete story of rail from Stephenson's
Rocket to the Eurostar. Thousands of exhibits and
demonstrations explain every aspect of railway
operation. Rides on miniature and full-size steam
trains (subject to the weather and availability)
are included in the admission, there's a railway-
themed play area, or you can have a go at the
real thing by building an engine or operating a
signal box. Arts and drama-related activities are
usually held in the school holidays and sometimes Thomas the Tank Engine pays a visit. In
summer, you can catch the mini road train from
outside the Minster to get to the museum. For
great views of the city and surrounding landscape take a ride on York's answer to the London
Eye, the Norwich Union Yorkshire Wheel which
lifts its passengers 54m (177ft) into the sky.

Shopping

York has some excellent shops and a good daily
outdoor market. The Shambles is one of the best-
preserved medieval shopping streets in Europe.
Borders Bookshop, **t** (01904) 653300, on Davygate
organize kids' activities at the weekend and
during summer holidays, while the Discovery Store
next door has some unusual toys and games. Gap
is also on Daveygate. Christmas Angels on Low
Petergate sells wooden toys and Christmas decorations all year round. The Virgin Megastore is on
Coney Street. Boots and Marks and Spencer are in
the Coppergate shopping complex. Mothercare
and Toys 'R' Us are in Clifton Moor shopping centre
on the outer ring road, north of York city centre.

Sport and activities *See pp.490–2*

Treasurer's House

Minster Yard **t** (01904) 624247
www.nationaltrust.org.uk
Open Mid-Mar–Oct Sat–Thurs 11–4.30 **Adm** Adults
£5, children £2.50, family (2+2) £12.50
*Tearoom, mother and baby facilities, disabled
facilities, special events*

Once the residence of the Minster's Treasurers,
this charming Georgian townhouse and secluded
garden were restored and furnished by its last
occupant, Frank Green, who lived here until 1930.
An activity sheet helps children explore the history
of the house and the site, which goes back to
Roman times. Ghost cellar tours are available daily.

Yorkboat

The Boat Yard, Lendal Bridge **t** (01904) 628324
www.yorkboat.co.uk
Open Mid-Feb–Nov daily 10.30–3.30
Adm Adults £6.50, children £3.30, under 5s **free**
Refreshments, running commentary

Yorkboat have two landings, one at King's Staith
and the other at Lendal Bridge, and run a series of
trips along the Ouse including a ghost cruise with
a costumed storyteller.

★York Minster Cathedral

Deangate **t** (01904) 557200 **www**.yorkminster.org
Open Mon–Sat 9–5, Sun 12 noon–3.45; Undercroft,
Treasury and Crypt: Mon–Sat 9.30–5, Sun
12 noon–5; Tower: Mon–Sat 10–5, Sun 12 noon–5
Adm Cathedral: adults £5, children **free**; Cathedral,
Undercroft, Treasury and Crypt: adults £7, children
£2; Tower: adults £3.50, children £2
Café, shop

The building stands on the site of a chapel
founded by the Northumbrian King Edwin on his
conversion to Christianity in AD 627. Begun in 1220,
it took 250 years to complete. The intricacy of its
carved stonework and stained glass is renowned,
and that it survives today is a miracle for the

Can you spot?
On the ceiling in the Minster, some ceiling 'bosses' (ornamental knobs) that don't look very medieval. Can you see the one with an astronaut on it? Some of the original bosses were destroyed in the 1984 fire, and the new ones to replace them were designed by children who won a competition organized by Blue Peter.

central tower partly collapsed during the 15th century and fires (in 1840 and 1984) caused serious damage. Careful restoration has ensured that most of the building still stands. There's a kids' guide to the cathedral on sale in the shop. Climb the central tower for fantastic views over the city, or visit the Foundations Museum to discover its history. Free tours offered (Mon–Sat).

York Model Railway

Tea Room Square, York Station **t** (01904) 630169
Open Mar–Oct 9–6 (last entry 5.30); Nov–Feb 10.30–5 (last entry 4.30) **Adm** Adults £4, children £2.50, under 4s **free**

It covers one-third of a mile of track and can have up to 14 model trains whizzing through it at any one time.

Walks and tours

The best time to walk along the city walls is in the early evening when there are fewer tourists around. The safest section runs behind the Minster from Bootham Bar to Monkgate, where it is fully fenced on the inside. Admission is free.

Yorwalk

3 Fairway, Clifton **t** (01904) 622303
www.yorkwalk.co.uk
Tour times Daily; call for times
Adm Adults £5, children £2, under 6s **free**; Minster and St Nicholas tours: adults £8, children £2 (includes entry to Minster and Chapter House)

A range of walking tours ('Essential York', 'Secret York', 'Roman' or 'Medieval York') begin at the Museum garden gates on Museum Street and last about two hours each.

Around York

Beningbrough Hall, 8 miles northwest (right, opposite)
Castle Howard, 16 miles northeast (p.471)
Murton Park and Yorkshire Museum of Farming, 5 miles east (p.478)
Yorkshire Air Museum, 9 miles east (p.497)

SPECIAL TRIPS

Abbeys, castles, historic houses and sites

★Alnwick Castle

The Estate Office, Alnwick **t** (01665) 510777
www.alnwickcastle.com
Getting there In Alnwick town centre, off the A1 and 35 miles north of Newcastle
Open Apr–Oct daily 10–6; state rooms: 11–5
Adm Adults £8.50, children £3.50, under 5s **free**, family £3
Restaurant, shop, some disabled access, parking

The Duke of Northumberland's family home since the 1300s, this dramatic castle was known as 'the Windsor of the north' by the Victorians – the second-largest inhabited castle in the country. Wander through lavish rooms and visit archaeology displays in the ancient towers on the Percys' volunteer army. There's a wonderful garden, but kids will be more impressed that scenes from *Harry Potter and the Philosopher's Stone* were filmed here. Look out for the walking sticks with handles crafted into animals' heads.

Bamburgh Castle

Bamburgh **t** (01668) 214515
www.bamburghcastle.com
Getting there Off the B1340 and 45 miles north of Newcastle on the A1
Open Mid-Mar–Oct daily 11–5
Adm Adults £6, children £2.50, under 5s **free**
Tearoom, shop, mother and baby facilities, parking (£1)

Strikingly positioned on a rocky outcrop overlooking a wide stretch of beach, Bamburgh looks every bit the royal castle that it once was. The Victorian restoration was undertaken by Tyneside industrialist Lord Armstrong, and an exhibition shows his inventive genius. A collection of armour from the Tower of London is also on display and there are some unusual things to see: how would you like to ride on a wooden bicycle? The grim and dingy dungeons are said to house a horrible toad, once an ancient, wicked queen, who was transformed as a punishment for her evil spell. See if you can find the Bamburgh Beast.

Beningbrough Hall

Beningbrough, York **t** (01904) 472027
www.nationaltrust.org.uk
Getting there 8 miles northwest of York, off the A19 in Beningbrough

Do you know?
*How The Strid at Bolton Abbey got its name.
Confined within a narrow gorge less than 2m (6ft)
wide, it was a feat of daring to stride ('strid')
across. Don't be tempted as its treacherous waters
are 10m (33ft) deep and a slip would be fatal!*

Open House: Jul–Aug Fri–Wed 12–5, Sept–Oct
Sat–Wed 12–5; garden: Jul–Aug Fri–Wed 11–5.30,
Sept–Oct Sat–Wed, Nov–Mar Sat–Sun 11–3.30
Adm Adults £7, children £3.50, family £16
*Restaurant, shop, mother and baby facilities,
disabled facilities, on-site parking*

Children have their own guides to help them
get the most from visiting this early 18th-century
mansion. Highlights include more than 100
portraits from the National Portrait Gallery and a
magnificent staircase. Younger children will
probaby be more interested in finding out about
the Victorian life that went on 'below stairs', as
revealed in the laundry, and how they got by
without bathrooms, as well as exploring the
walled gardens and wooden playground outside.
Family events, like treasure hunts and garden
games, are held regularly throughout the year.

Bolton Abbey

Estate Office, Bolton Abbey, Skipton **t** (01756)
718009 **www.boltonabbey.com**
Getting there Off A59, 5 miles east of Skipton,
20 miles northwest of Leeds
Open Daily 9–dusk **Adm** £5 per car (disabled £3.50)
Café, picnics, shop, disabled facilities, on-site parking

Bolton Abbey is centred on the wonderfully
atmospheric ruins of a 12th-century Augustinian
priory and the extensive estate offers riverside,
woodland and moorland walks through some of
England's loveliest countryside. Chug your way to
nearby Embsay (p.485) on the steam train, which
leaves from Bolton Abbey station.

Brodsworth Hall

Brodsworth, Doncaster **t** (01302) 724969
www.english-heritage.org.uk
Getting there On the B6422 in Brodsworth, about
30 miles south of York (A64–A1)
Open House: Apr–Sept Tues–Sun and Bank Hols
1–5, Oct Sat–Sun 12–4; gardens: Apr–Oct daily
10–5.30, Oct–Mar Sat–Sun 10–4
Adm Adults £6.60, children £3.30, under 5s **free**;
garden only: adults £4.60, children £2.30
*Tearoom, picnic area, shop, guided tours, mother and
baby facilities, disabled facilities, on-site parking*

An amazing house that has survived almost
intact from the Victorian era, where children can
gain a fascinating insight into the lives of the
people who lived here. The lavish furnishings
and decoration of the rooms that were inhabited by the family and their guests are in sharp
contrast to the almost spartan living conditions
of their servants. There are activity sheets for
younger visitors.

★Castle Howard

Coneysthorpe, near Malton, York **t** (01653) 648444
www.castlehoward.co.uk
Getting there Off the A64, 15 miles north of York
Open House: Mar–Oct daily 11–4; grounds and
gardens: daily 10–4.30
Adm Adults £9.50, children £6.50, family £25.50;
gardens only summer/winter: adults £7/3.50,
children £5/1.50, family £18.50
*Tearoom, café, picnic area, shops, disabled facilities,
on-site parking, no pushchairs in the house*

Horace Walpole described it as 'sublime'. Set in
more than 405 hectares (1,000 acres) of magnificent parkland, this splendid Baroque house
contains lavish period furnishings and decorations; paintings by famous artists adorn the
walls. Outside, huge gardens spread about fountains and lakes (upon which you can take a boat
ride on a Victorian-style motor launch) and
there's an adventure playground and a lakeside
café. In the summer special events are held. Call
for more information.

Chillingham Castle and Gardens

Chillingham, Alnwick **t** (01668) 215359
www.chillingham-castle.com
Getting there Off the B6346, 12 miles northwest of
Alnwick, 42 miles north of Newcastle
Open May–Sept 1–4.30 (Sun–Fri) **Adm** Adults £5,
children £2
Tearoom, shop, on-site parking

This ancient medieval border fortress is reputedly haunted by two ghosts, one of whom is a
little boy. The rooms are furnished with a fascinating assortment of artefacts from all over the
world. Dungeons and a scary torture chamber
will thrill the kids, but you'll enjoy the delightful
Italianate walled garden, landscaped avenues and
woodland walks. Ongoing restoration is revealing
the castle's true character. Combine your visit
with a trip to see the Wild Cattle of Chillingham
(p.476).

Cragside House, Garden and Estate

Rothbury, Morpeth **t** (01669) 620333 or 620150,
www.nationaltrust.org.uk
Getting there The house lies 1 mile east of
Rothbury, 24 miles north of Newcastle
Open Estate and garden: Apr–Oct Tues–Sun
10.30–7, Nov–mid-Dec Wed–Sun 11–4
Adm Estate and gardens: adults £6.50, children £3,
family £16; discounted tickets Nov–Dec
*Restaurant, picnic and play area, shop, mother and
baby facilities, disabled facilities, on-site parking*

This marvellous house was built for Tyneside
industrialist Lord Armstrong, whose inventive
genius is quite in evidence here: it was the first
house ever to be lit by hydroelectricity and you
can discover how he used water to provide
power for a lift or to work a roasting spit in front
of the kitchen fire. There are wonderful gardens
(popular with red squirrels) terraced down to the
river, where there's a museum of Armstrong's
achievements, and woodland walks lead to the
lakes, which provided the house with its power.
The gardens also feature a maze and an
adventure garden.

Dunstanburgh Castle

Craster, Alnwick **t** (01665) 576231
www.nationaltrust.org.uk
Getting there 9 miles northeast of Alnwick
(30 miles north of Newcastle): park in Craster then
follow the coastal footpath 1 mile north
Open Apr–Sept daily 10–6, Oct daily 10–4,
Nov–Mar Thurs–Mon 10–4
Adm Adults £2.70, children £1.40
Shop, on-site parking

The gaunt ruins of Dunstanburgh, dramatically
overlooking the sea, make an ideal destination for
a great family day out so pack a picnic and follow
the mile-long path from Craster above the rocky
shore to the castle, where the kids can explore its
ancient nooks and crannies. It is possible to
manoevre a pushchair along the cliff path. Walk
back the way you came, or take an alternative
path that follows the coastline about half a mile
inland from the sea, returning to the car park
through a delightful wooded glen.

Fountains Abbey and Studley Royal

Studley Park, Fountains, Ripon **t** (01765) 601005
www.fountainsabbey.org.uk
Getting there Off the B6265, 4 miles west of Ripon

Open Abbey: Nov–Feb daily 10–4, Mar–Oct 10–5;
mill: Jan–Feb 10.30–3.30, Mar–Oct 10–5, Nov–Dec
10.30–3.30; park: daily dawn–dusk
Adm Adults £6.50, children £3.50, family £17.50;
park only: £2 per car
*Restaurant, shop, guided tours, mother and baby
facilities, disabled facilities, on-site parking*

Once the largest monastic houses in Britain, the
ruins of Fountains Abbey form the centrepiece of
a magnificent 18th-century landscaped park with
water features, ornate temples and follies. Look
out for the deer, which roam free in this former
medieval hunting park. There is a quiz guide to
help kids find their way around, an indoor play
area and organized activities (pond-dipping,
mini-beast searches) in summer. The abbey is
floodlit in the evening from August until October
and at Christmas there are carol singers.

★Harewood House

Harewood, Leeds **t** (0113) 218 1010
www.harewood.org
Getting there 7 miles north of Leeds on the A61
Open Apr–Oct daily; house: 11–4.30; grounds and
gardens: 10–6; bird gardens: 10–5.30
Adm Adults £11.30 (£13.15 on weekends), children
£6.50 (£8.15 weekends), family £37 (£44.50 weekends); grounds only (including the bird garden):
adults £8.80 (£10.90 on weekends), children £5.90
(£7.25 weekends), family £32.25 (£37.25 weekends)
*Café, refreshments, picnic areas, shop, disabled
facilities, on-site parking*

One of the finest 18th-century mansions in the
country. In the landscaped grounds you'll hear
strange noises from the bird gardens – hoopoes,
flamingos and a bird called a 'laughing thrush' –
and see penguins being fed in the afternoon.
There is a huge adventure playground, known
locally as the estate's 'animated ant heap', and
special events are frequently organized.

Newby Hall

Ripon **t** 0845 4504068 www.newbyhall.co.uk
Getting there 16 miles northwest of York, off the A1
and the B6265
Open Apr–Sept Tues–Sun (Jul–Aug daily); gardens:
11am–5.30pm; house: 12 noon–5pm **Adm** House
and gardens: adults £9.20, children £6.40; garden:
adults £6.90, children £5.20
*Restaurant, picnic area, mother and baby facilities,
disabled facilities, on-site parking, shop*

Did you know?
In 1930 Hull-born Amy Johnson became the first woman to fly solo from England to Australia. Her achievement is celebrated in an exhibition at Sewerby Hall.

This fine 17th-century house was designed by Robert Adam and has some splendid furniture as well as containing important collections of sculpture and tapestries. Outside there are extensive grounds including water and rock gardens. There is an adventure play area and a miniature railway, as well as special woodland discovery walks to explore.

Sewerby Hall

Church Lane, Sewerby, Bridlington **t** (01262) 673769
www.eastriding.gov.uk/sewerby
Getting there 24 miles north of Hull and 2 miles northeast of Bridlington, off the B1255 towards Flamborough
Open Hall: Apr–Oct 10–5; gardens and zoo: daily dawn–dusk
Adm Adults £3.50, children £1.50, family (2+2) £9
Tearoom, picnic area, shop, disabled facilities, on-site parking, hall not suitable for pushchairs

Perched high on cliffs overlooking the North Sea, this grand Georgian hall stands surrounded by 20 hectares (50 acres) of parkland. Exhibitions include one celebrating the achievements of Amy Johnson. Look for squirrels in the gardens outside, with their splendid Monkey Puzzle trees; dangle in the adventure playground; bowl or pitch-and-putt your way across the green and 12- or 18-hole courses; or make a beeline for the zoo, with its monkeys, llamas, goats, penguin- and fantail pigeon-feeding. Special events include bands.

Skipton Castle

Skipton **t** (01756) 792442 **www.skiptoncastle.co.uk**
Getting there 35 miles west of York off the A59; the castle is in the town centre
Open Daily Mar–Sept 10–6, Oct–Feb 10–4
Adm Adults £5.40, children £2.90, under 5s **free**, family £15.90
Café, picnic area, shop, nearby parking

One of the best-preserved medieval castles in the country, Skipton was restored after suffering considerable destruction during the Civil War. Climb to the top of the watchtower and explore the depths of the dungeons, taking in bedchambers, state rooms and kitchens on the way.

Wallington House

Cambo, Morpeth **t** (01670) 773600
www.nationaltrust.org.uk
Getting there 12 miles west of Morpeth on the B6342
Open House: Apr–Aug Wed–Mon 1–5.30, Sept–Oct Wed–Mon 1–4.30; garden: Apr–Sept daily 10–7, Oct daily 10–6, Nov–Mar daily 10–4 (or dusk); grounds: daily during daylight hours **Adm** Adults £8, children £4, family (2+4) £20; garden and grounds only: adults £5.50, children £2.75, family £14
Tearoom, picnic area, shop, mother and baby facilities, disabled facilities, on-site parking

Armed with quizzes and their own guidebooks, children can show parents around this wonderful house. Amongst its delights are some strikingly detailed and colourful murals, which depict different periods or events in Northumbrian history. No doubt you'll be led to the toy collections and the amazing dolls' houses which are furnished in remarkable detail. The extensive grounds provide refreshing walks and places for picnics and there is an adventure playground in the woods.

Warkworth Castle

Warkworth **t** (01665) 711423
www.english-heritage.org.uk
Getting there Off the A1068, 7 miles south of Alnwick, 25 miles north of Newcastle
Open Castle: Apr–Sept daily 10–5, Oct 10–4; Nov–Mar Sat–Mon 10–4
Adm Adults £3.40, children £1.70, family (2+2) £8.50; hermitage: adults £2.30, children £1.80
Parking, picnics, audio guide, disabled facilities

These impressive ruins overlooking the River Coquet star in Shakespeare's *Henry V*, for Warkworth was the home of the Earls of Northumberland and brave Harry Hotspur. There's lots to see and children get an information sheet to help them in their exploration. Afterwards, you can follow the riverbank upstream to investigate the hermitage. The story goes that the chambers were cut out of the rock in the cliff face by hermits during the Middle Ages and served as a chapel and cells in which they lived.

★Hadrian's Wall

From Wallsend-on-Tyne in the east to Bowness-on-Solway in the west, Infoline and public enquiries: **t** (01434) 322002 **www.hadrians-wall.org**

These ruins extend across the width of the country and represent the most spectacular Roman remains in Britain (*see* box, right). There are several museums along its length exhibiting some of the items that the Romans armies left behind.
Forts and visitor centres (east to west):

Arbeia Roman Fort and Museum

Baring Street, South Shields **t** (0191) 456 1369
www.twmuseums.org.uk
Getting there On the south side of the Tyne estuary, 13 miles from Newcastle
Open Apr–Sept Mon–Sat 10–5.30, Sun 1–5;
Oct–Mar Mon–Sat 10–4
Adm Free Time Quest: adults £1.50, children 80p
Refreshments, picnic area, shop

Built in AD 16 and occupied for nearly 300 years, *Arbeia* guarded the approaches to the Tyne Estuary. Excavated remains and reconstructions show what life was like in Roman Britain and in the summer archaeologists can be seen at work uncovering more of the site. In the Time Quest, you can have a go at weaving Roman-style.

Segedunum Roman Fort and Museum

Buddle Street, Walls End **t** (0191) 2369347
www.twmuseums.org.uk
Getting there On A187, 3 miles east of Newcastle
Open Apr–Oct daily 10–5, Nov–Mar 10–3
Adm Adults £3.95, children **free,**
Parking, café, shop, mother and baby facilities, disabled facilities

This marked the eastern end of the wall and reconstructions, which include a bath house and frescoed latrines, give children a vivid picture of ancient Roman life. Climb the observation tower for an aerial view of the fort.

Corbridge Roman Site and Museum (*Corstopitum*)

Corbridge **t** (01434) 632349
www.english-heritage.org.uk
Getting there Off the A69, 1 mile northwest of Corbridge and 15 miles west of Newcastle
Open Apr–Oct daily 10–5.30 (Oct until 4pm),
Nov–Mar Sat and Sun 10–4
Adm Adults £3.80, children £1.90
Shop, audio guide, disabled facilities, on-site parking

This fort served as a major depot; the granaries are the best-preserved in the country. Corbridge grew into a sizeable town, with the camp surrounded by shops and civilian houses. The museum has been built in the style of a Roman

---

The Romans and Hadrian's Wall

Begun in AD 122 on the orders of Hadrian, the wall marked the northern limit of Roman occupation and was the only one ever built throughout the whole Empire. A remarkable achievement, its 73 miles spanned the country from the Solway to the Tyne and took 15 years to complete. Along its length were turrets, milecastles and forts, which served as guardposts, gateways and supply depots for the patrolling troops. Many of the forts have been excavated and the finds have revealed an amazing amount of detail about the lives of the people who lived and worked here. You can trace the Wall west from Newcastle: take the A69 and then the B6528 out of the city to join the B6318 beyond Heddon, which then follows its course to the Cumbrian border. In many places, the structure remains impressive and some of the turrets and milecastles are visible from the road. Look out, too, for the Vallum, a great ditch and earthwork, which ran parallel beside it and formed a secondary line of defence. The Hadrian's Wall Bus runs daily between Newcastle and Carlisle from May until September, stopping at all the major sites along its length. Call **t** (01434) 344777 or **t** (01228) 606003 for timetable information and prices.

---

house and, with an activity book, children can find out about the domestic life of the period.

Chesters Roman Fort and Museum (*Cilurnum*)

Chollerford, near Hexham **t** (01434) 681379
www.english-heritage.org.uk
Getting there 3 miles north of Hexham on the B6318
Open Apr–Sept daily 9.30–6, Oct–Mar 10–4
Adm Adults £3.80, children £1.90
Parking, café, shop, disabled facilities

You will find stables here for this barracks housed the cavalry. Kids will find the bath house down by the river interesting, where the soldiers relaxed and enjoyed alternating hot rooms and cold plunges, the equivalent of our saunas today.

Housesteads Roman Fort and Museum (*Vercovicium*)

Bardon Mill, Hexham **t** (01434) 344363
www.nationaltrust.org.uk
Getting there 14 miles west of Hexham on the B6318
Open Apr–Sept daily 10–6, Oct–Mar 10–4
Adm Adults £3.80, children £1.90, family £9.50
Parking (charge), refreshments, picnics, shop, disabled facilities

This is the best-preserved of all the forts and, armed with activity books, youngsters will get a good impression of what it was like to live here by wandering along the ancient streets past the military headquarters, barracks, storehouses and even a hospital. The building that seems to hold the most fascination is the 24-seater loo, which even in those days was flushed by running water.

Chesterholm Fort and Museum (*Vindolanda*)
t (01434) 344277 **www.**vindolanda.com
Getting there 9 miles west of Chollerford off the B6318
Open Mid-Nov–Jan daily 10–4, Feb–Mar and Oct–Nov 10–5, Apr–Sept 10–6 **Adm** Adults £4.95, children £3, family £14; combined *Vindolanda* and Roman Army Museum tickets available.
Parking, café, picnics, shop, video display, disabled facilities

Here, not only the fort, but also civilian houses, shops and a Roman temple have been excavated. See the archaeologists at work in summer and visit the adjoining museum to see the exciting finds. Reconstructions bring some of the buildings back to life and one of them shows what Hadrian's Wall would have looked like. *Vindolanda* was the name of a Roman commanding officer who was killed during a rebellion of the British tribes just before Hadrian's Wall was built. His tombstone was found here.

The Once Brewed National Park Centre
Military Road, Bardon Mill **t** (01434) 344396
Getting there 14 miles west of Hexham on the B6318
Open Mar–Oct daily 9-30-5; Nov–Feb Sat–Sun 10–3
Adm Free
Refreshments, picnics, shop, video display, disabled facilities, on-site parking

The interpretation centre gives a good description of Hadrian's Wall, as well as providing useful information about the surrounding countryside. This is an ideal place to begin a walk, where the children can learn about some of the things to look out for during the day.

The Roman Army Museum (*Carvoran*)
Greenhead **t** (01697) 747485 **www.**vindolanda.com
Getting there On the B6318, west of Chollerford and 30 miles west of Newcastle
Open Feb–Mar, Oct–Nov daily 10–5, Apr–Sept 10–6
Adm Adults £3.95, children £2.50, family £11
Café, picnics, shop, disabled facilities, on-site parking

If your kids want to leave home, bring them here, for they can 'sign on' as a soldier in the Roman army. Audiovisual and imaginative displays show them what life was like in the army and some of the jobs they would have had to do whilst on patrol along Hadrian's Wall.

Birdoswald Roman Fort (*Banna*)
Gilsland, near Haltwhistle **t** (01697) 747602
www.english-heritage.org.uk
Getting there Off the B6318, 35 miles west from Newcastle on the A69
Open Mid-Mar–Nov daily 10–5.30 (Nov shorter hours); exterior only in winter
Adm Adults £3.80, children £1.90, family (2+2) £9.50
Café, shop, guided tours, disabled facilities, on-site parking

Even after the Romans left, people continued to live here and archaeologists have learned quite a lot about life in Britain after the occupation. Kids will enjoy looking around the visitor centre before walking along a really impressive section of the wall to the nearby milecastle at Harrow's Scar.

Lighthouses
Souter Lighthouse
Coast Road, Whitburn **t** (0191) 529 3161
www.nationaltrust.org.uk
Getting there 6 miles southwest of Newcastle on the A183
Open Apr–Oct Sat–Thurs and Bank Hols 11–5
Adm Adults £4, children £2.50, family (2+4) £10.50
Tearoom, picnic area, shop, disabled facilities, limited access for pushchairs

Built in 1871 this was the first lighthouse in the country to have an electric lantern. See the engine room (where the keeper lived), send a message in Morse code and climb up on to the lamp platform for a fantastic view on a fine day.

St Mary's Lighthouse
St Mary's Island, Whitley Bay **t** (0191) 200 8652
Getting there On the A193, 2 miles north of Whitley Bay and 5 miles northeast of Newcastle
Open Apr–Oct daily; Nov–Mar Sat–Sun and school holidays (times depend upon the tides)
Adm Adults £2, children £1, family £4.50
Refreshments, picnic area, shop, disabled access, on-site parking

You can only get to this lighthouse when the tide is out and originally the lighthouse keeper would have been cut off from the land for part of the day. Explore the nearby nature reserve on a guided walk and discover some of the plants and wildlife that inhabit the beach and cliffs.

Animal attractions

The Big Sheep and the Little Cow

The Old Watermill, Aiskew, Bedale **t** (01677) 422125
www.farmattraction.co.uk
Getting there Situated near Bedale, signposted
from Bedale Bridge
Open Mar–Sept 10.30–5, Oct Sat–Sun and half
term 10.30–5; tours on the hour 11–4; play barn
open all year 10.30–5.30
Adm Adults £5, children £6.50, family £21; play barn
only adults £2.50, children £4

Set amongst traditional water meadows, this
working farm will delight children of all ages,
with the biggest sheep and littlest cows they
have ever seen. Guided tours give lots of opportunities for close contact with the many animals.
After all that, there are pony rides, quad bikes
(over 6s), a play area and homemade ice cream to
sample, as well as a large indoor play area with
separate toddler area.

Blue Reef Aquarium

Grand Parade, Beaconsfield, Tynemouth
t (0191) 258 1031 **www.**bluereefaquarium.co.uk
Getting there Lies beyond the end of the A1058,
on the seafront
Open Daily 10–5
Adm Adults £5.99, children £3.99 family (2+2)
£17.50, family (2+3) £21.50
*Refreshments, shop, mother and baby facilities,
disabled facilities, on-site parking*

A tunnel beneath the water gives children a
diver's eye view of the sharks and other fish,
which are normally hidden deep beneath the
waves. There are some weird and wonderful
things, from starfish and anemones to rays and
conger eels, and the touch tank is a great
favourite with children. Kids have their own
interactive trail to follow, where they encounter
many different types of fish.

Chillingham Wild Cattle

Chillingham Castle **t** (01668) 215250
www.chillingham-wildcattle.org.uk
Open Apr–Oct Mon and Wed–Sat 10–12 noon
and 2–5, Sun 2–5 **Adm** Adults £4.50, children £1.50

Believe it or not, these cows are actually wild.
They're the descendants of herds that once
roamed all over the country. When the park was
enclosed in the 13th century, the cows were
walled in, and since then, they've had no contact
with any other cows or had any close contact
with people. Vets are never called to look after
them; they won't touch cattle cake or oats and, if
any of the herd does come into immediate
contact with a human, the rest of the cows will
kill it. They're the only cattle in the world to have
remained completely pure. You can visit the park
with a warden and admire the cows from a
distance. Much of the park looks like it did in
medieval times and a visit is a bit like stepping
into a time machine.

Falconry UK Bird of Prey and Conservation Centre

Sion Hill, Kirby Wiske, Thirsk **t** (01845) 587522
www.falconrycentre.co.uk
Getting there Off the A167, 6 miles south of
Northallerton
Open Mar–Oct daily 10.30–5.30
Adm Adults £5, children £3, under 3s **free**, family
(2+2) £14
Gift shop, refreshments

Children can learn at first hand about the
lives of these magnificent birds and the importance of preserving their natural environments.
Many of them can be seen at close quarters and
the trained handlers give exciting demonstrations of the birds' flying and hunting skills.

Honey Farm

East Ayton, Scarborough **t** (01723) 865198
Getting there Off the A170, 5 miles west of
Scarborough
Open Daily 9–5 **Adm** Adults £2.95, children **free**,
concessions £1.50
*Tearoom, shop, mother and baby facilities, disabled
facilities, on-site parking*

Beekeepers escort you through this fascinating
exhibition revealing the secret world of bees and
how we exploit them. Lively explanations and
displays show exactly how bees make honey and
why they are so important to the countryside. You
will see exactly what goes on inside a hive and
how the honey and beeswax is collected. There is
a chance to taste different types of honey, visit
some of the farm's animals, play on toy tractors or
let off a bit of steam in the play area.

Staintondale Shire Horse Farm

Staintondale, near Scarborough **t** (01723) 870458
www.shirehorsefarm.yorks.net
Getting there Off the A171, 8 miles northwest of
Scarborough

Open Mid-May–mid-Sept Sun, Tues, Wed, Fri and Bank Hols 10.30–4.30 **Adm** Adults £5, children £3
Café, picnic area, shop, mother and baby facilities, disabled facilities, on-site parking

For horse lovers of all ages. Shire horses were once a common site on farms and in towns and cities, carrying out the jobs done by tractors and lorries today. Children can meet these magnificent animals and learn all about how they are trained for heavy work by their handlers. Smaller, but no less endearing, are the ponies that give kids rides around the farm. There are lots of videos and displays showing aspects of life on the farm and a wonderful clifftop walk.

Tropical Butterfly House, Wildlife and Falconry Centre

Hungerhill Farm, Woodsetts Road, North Anston, Sheffield **t** (01909) 569416
www.butterflyhouse.co.uk
Open Apr–Sept Mon–Fri 10–4.30, Sat–Sun 10–5.30; Oct–Mar Mon–Fri 11–4.30 or dusk, Sat–Sun 10–5
Adm Adults £5.99, children £4.99, family £20.99
Café, picnic area, shop, disabled facilities, on-site parking

If children keep their eyes open, they will see a lot more than butterflies in this lush tropical paradise. Stick insects, ladybirds and midwife toads all help keep unwanted pests under control and flying between the trees are many brightly coloured birds that live off the seeds produced by the great variety of plants. Watch where you tread, for there are also three 1.5m/5ft-long iguanas wandering through the undergrowth. Other exotic reptiles and amphibians live in display tanks; don't miss the amazing birds of prey at the Falconry Centre. New additions to the centre include a play area and an activity centre where children can paint pots and do brass rubbing.

Washington Wildfowl and Wetlands Centre

District 15, Washington **t** (0191) 416 5454
www.wwt.org.uk
Getting there On A1231 between Washington and Sunderland
Open Summer: daily 9.30–5; winter: 9.30–4
Adm Adults £5.95, children £3.95, family £15.50
Café, picnic area, shop, guided tours, mother and baby facilities, disabled facilities, on-site parking

Interactive exhibits introduce kids to the fantastic variety of birdlife that visits the centre.

However, the real thrills are gained by actually watching them. As well as observing from hides, children can get really close to some of the birds, particularly when it is time for the ducks', geese and herons' eggs to hatch. Nature trails lead through woods and grasslands and past ponds, where you never know what you will see.

Farms
Bill Quay Farm

Hainingwood Terrace, Bill Quay, Gateshead
t (0191) 433 5780
Getting there Off the A185 in Felling, east of the junction with the A184
Open Daily 12–5 **Adm Free** (donations welcome)
Refreshments, picnic area, farm produce shop, mother and baby facilities, on-site parking

This friendly, suburban farm is an adventure for younger children, where many of the smaller animals are quite inquisitive and seem to expect to be stroked. See if you can match the animal sculptures dotted around the place to their real-life counterparts. There is also a nature trail to follow through the woods leading down to the river, so bring a picnic and enjoy the day here.

Cherryburn

Station Bank, Mickley, near Stocksfield
t (01661) 843276 www.nationaltrust.org.uk
Getting there 10 miles west of Newcastle, off the A695 north of Mickley Square
Open Mid-Mar–Oct Thurs–Tues 11–5
Adm Adults £3.50, children £1.75, under 5s **free**
Refreshments, picnic area, shop, disabled facilities, on-site parking

Born here in 1753, Thomas Bewick later won recognition as an artist, wood engraver and naturalist. Restored and furnished to reflect mid-18th-century country life, Cherryburn and its farm includes an exhibition illustrating his life and a working printing press. Younger children will also enjoy the many animals to be seen in the farmyard.

★Flamingo Land Theme Park and Zoo

Kirby Misperton, Pickering **t** 0870 752800
www.flamingoland.co.uk
Getting there 15 miles west of Scarborough, 19 miles northeast of York and 4 miles south of Pickering, off the A169
Open Park: Apr–Oct daily from 10; zoo: daily; closing times depend on the season

Adm Adults/children £19, under 3s **free**, family £70
Shows, animals and rides for all the family.
For further information *see* p.486

Hall Hill Farm

Lanchester, Durham **t** (01388) 731333
www.hallhillfarm.co.uk
Getting there 4 miles southwest of Lanchester on
the B6296, 11 miles west of Durham
Open Apr–Sept daily 10.30–5; Sept–Oct Sat–Sun
10.30–5; Dec 'Santa Weekends'
Adm Adults £4.40 children £3.30, family (2+2)
£13.50
Refreshments, picnic area, shop, mother and baby
facilities, disabled facilities, on-site parking

Bring the children at Easter time to see the
new-born lambs – perhaps even get the chance
to help bottle-feed them. There is lots to see at
any time of the year, with day-old chicks, piglets,
goats, ponies, deer and cattle, as well as more
exotic beasts like llamas. Special events include
Santa days, teddy bears' picnics and sheep dog
demonstrations. There are tractor-trailer and
donkey rides, mini tractors and a play area.

Hazel Brow Farm

Low Row, Richmond **t** (01748) 886224
www.hazelbrow.co.uk
Getting there On the B6270, 15 miles west of
Richmond
Open Apr–Sept Tues–Thurs, Sat–Sun 11–4.30
Adm Adults £4, children £3.75
Café, shop, picnic area, on-site parking

Deep in the heart of the beautiful North
Yorkshire Dales, kids can experience life on a
traditional dairy farm. Enthusiastic helpers are
always appreciated for feeding the animals and
filling milk bottles for the next day's delivery. The
cows come in for milking at 5pm every day, and in
April the year's new lambs make their appearance. There is plenty to do, with sheep dogs, pigs,
pony rides and a riverside nature trail to explore,
as well as displays, videos and old equipment.

Murton Park and Yorkshire Museum
of Farming

Murton Lane, Murton **t** (01904) 489966
www.murtonpark.co.uk
Getting there 3 miles east of York, off the A166
Open Mar–Oct daily 10–5, Nov–Feb 10–4 with
reduced facilities and admission charges
Adm Adults £4, children £2, under 3s **free**, family
(2+4) £10

Café, picnic area, shop, disabled and baby changing
facilities, on-site parking

Set within four hectares (10 acres) of park, old
buildings, tools and machinery take you through
the seasons – younger children will enjoy seeing
the animals. There's a village from Dark Age
Britain and a Roman fort to see and, at weekends
and Bank Holidays, the Derwent Valley Light
Railway (once known as 'The Blackberry Line').

Nature's World

Ladgate Lane, Acklam, Middlesbrough
t (01642) 594895 www.naturesworld.org.uk
Getting there On the B1380, 4 miles south of
Middlesbrough
Open Apr–Sept 10–5, Oct–Mar 10.30–3.30
Adm Summer: Adults £4, children £2, family (2+2)
£10; winter: adults £3, children £1.50, family (2+2)
£7, under 4s **free**
Tearoom, picnic area, shop, mother and baby
facilities, disabled facilities, on-site parking

There are more than 100 exciting projects and
exhibition areas to help your children discover
how to work with nature to achieve a sustainable
future. Explore the inner workings of a compost
heap, or learn what organic cultivation means,
and finally visit the 'wee only' toilet, built out of
straw, where 'donations' are collected and piped
into the reedbeds. There are scale models
depicting aspects of the local area including the
River Tees and its famous transporter bridge.
Continuing the enviromental theme, there are
nature trails, lots of things to 'have a go' at and
animals' and children's play areas.

Temple Newsam House and Park

Temple Newsam Road **t** (0113) 264 5535
www.leeds.gov.uk/templenewsam
Getting there 4 miles east of the city off the A63
Open House: Apr–Oct Tues–Sun 10.30–5, Nov–Mar
Tues–Sun 10.30–4; farm: Apr–Oct Tues–Sun 10–5,
Nov–Mar Tues–Sun 10–4
Adm House: adults £3.50, children £2.50, under 5s
free, family £9; farm: adults £3, children £2, under
5s **free**, family £8

Europe's largest rare breeds centre (486
hectares/1,200 acres).
For further information *see* p.464

★Tropical World and Roundhay Park

Princes Avenue, Roundhay **t** (0113) 266 1850,
www.roundhaypark.org.uk

Getting there Off the A58, 3 miles north of Leeds; take bus nos.2, 10 or 12 from the city
Open Summer 10–6, winter 10–4
Adm Adults £3, children £2, under 8s **free**

Scaly iguanas, frogs, snakes, hairy tarantulas and piranhas plus a variety of plants and birds.
For further information *see* p.465

Whitehouse Farm

North Whitehouse Farm, Morpeth **t** (01670) 789998 or 789571 **www.whitehousefarm.ndo.co.uk**
Getting there By the junction of the A1 and the A197, southwest of Morpeth
Open Tues–Sun 10–5
Adm Adults £6.75, children £5.75, family (2+2) £22.50
Café, picnic area, shop, mother and baby facilities, disabled facilities, on-site parking

This place will delight children, with lots of small animals and chicks to cuddle and help feed. There are tractor rides, play areas, go-karts, children's entertainment, face painting and even candle-making and a toboggan slide.

Sea-life centres

The Deep

Size Point, Kingston-upon-Hull **t** (01482) 615789
www.thedeep.co.uk
Open Daily 10–6 (last entry 5) **Adm** Adults £8, children £6, under 4s **free**, family £25
Café, shop, disabled access

Explore the evolution of the world's oceans from the beginning of time and see lots of fish.
For further information *see* p.462

Sea Life and Marine Sanctuary

Scalby Mills Road, Scarborough **t** (01723) 373414
www.sealife.co.uk
Open Summer: daily 10–6; winter: daily 10–4
Adm Adults £6.50, children £4.75

Displays, tanks and touch pools bring you face to face with the fascinating creatures of the deep.
For further information *see* p.482

Beside the seaside

Bamburgh

Getting there North of Newcastle off the A1
Bamburgh's wide sandy beach runs for miles and, if it's warm enough to paddle, it's great for

toddlers as the sea is shallow and there's a stream to spend the afternoon damming. There's no front and no chip shops, just mountains of sand dunes. It's totally unspoilt and a wonderful place for a picnic on the beach while Bamburgh Castle (p.470) is the perfect inspiration for sandcastle building. There are a lot of good self-catering properties in the area but few hotels. Just south of Bamburgh at Seahouses, you can catch a boat to the Farne Islands, where Grace Darling lived. She set out to save the victims of a shipwreck and shot to stardom in the 19th century. Seahouses is a good place to try fish and chips and there's a Sea Shanty Festival, **t** (01665) 720884, with live music, storytelling and face painting in late summer. The nearest tourist office is Berwick, **t** (01289) 330733, which is open all year.

Grace Darling Museum

Radcliff Road Bamburgh **t** (01668) 214465
Open Easter–Sept 10–5
Adm Free (donations accepted)
Please note: the museum is currently closed for refurbishment and is due to open May 2007

One of the Victorians' favourite heroines, Grace Darling is buried in Bamburgh churchyard. She lived in the Longstone Lighthouse on the Farne Islands, which lie just off the coast. It's always been a dangerous place for shipping and, as long ago as the 9th century, monks kept a warning beacon alight on the islands. On the night of 7 September 1838 there was a fierce storm and a terrible wreck and 23-year-old Grace and her father rowed through the storm to save the passengers and crew. It made Grace an overnight sensation – Wordsworth wrote a poem about her and she was invited to recreate the rescue on the London stage! Opposite the church, there's a small museum, where you can see the boat she used in the rescue and the hats that endless admirers sent her. Unfortunately, she was plagued by unwanted fans until her untimely death from tuberculosis, which only added to her fame.

★Farne Islands

Farne Islands, Northumberland
Island Manager **t** (01665) 720651
Information Centre: **t** (01665) 721099
www.farne-islands.com
Getting there Several boat trips leave Seahouses, some of which allow landing on either Inner Farne

or Staple Islands; enquire at the ticket offices on the harbour for details

Boatmen J Hanvey, **t** (01665) 720388, and Billy Shiel, **t** (01665) 720308. Both offer landing trips lasting two to three hours and cruises for one to two hours

Landings (weather permitting): Apr–Sept (May–Jul is breeding season) daily 10–6; Staple Island: 10.30–1.30; Inner Farne: 1.30–5

Fee Boat fare: adults £12, children £9; landing fee: adults £5.20, children £2.60

Café, disabled facilities on Inner Farne, parking at Seahouses

These offshore islands are protected as one of Britain's finest wildlife sanctuaries, a haven for seals and birds. The islands are found in two groups: the Inner (closer to Seahouses) and the Outer. The seals breed in autumn, but you're likely to see them through the year basking on the rocks at low tide. Late spring or early summer is the best for the birds, when you'll see puffins, cormorants, eider (the 'Cuddy Duck') and kittiwakes, plus many more, noisily chattering and feeding their young. If you land on the islands, remember to wear a hat – the Arctic terns do not always take kindly to visitors during the breeding season.

Bridlington

Getting there Located 41 miles east of York and 30 miles north of Hull, Bridlington is on the A166/A164 or the A165

Tourist information Prince Street **t** (01262) 673474

Bridlington is a medium-sized traditional holiday town, lively and bustling with things to do. It's a good place for a camping or caravan holiday. Fishing boats bring in their daily catch to the 900-year-old harbour, which sits between the town's beautiful beaches: stretching away to the north and south, they have both won cleanliness awards. There are funfairs, pools, seaside games, boats, a model village and you can take the seafront road train into the town to explore the ruined Priory, shops and the market, held three days a week. Exhilarating cliff walks can be sought at nearby Flamborough Head and Bempton

Can you spot?
On the Farne Islands, the statue next to the priory church of St Aiden, founder of the priory, and the first person to live on Inner Farne.

RSPB Reserves, **t** (01262) 851533 – remember your binoculars to see the puffins, gannets, kittiwakes and cormorants that nest on and in the eroded chalk cliffs during the breeding season that runs from April until August.

Beside the Seaside Museum

34–5 Queen Street **t** (01262) 608890
www.bridlington.net/besidetheseaside
Open Mar–Oct daily 10–5
Adm Adults £2, children £1, under 5s **free**
Disabled facilities

If you're still wondering what a quintessential English family seaside holiday is about, this is the place to find out. From saucy postcards to slot machines, they have it all. Have a go at steering a virtual reality boat around the bay, puppeteering in a Punch and Judy show, and try out the 'Tubes of Mystery' to feel something – ugh – strange.

Bridlington Leisure World

Promenade **t** (01262) 606715
www.bridlington.net/leisureworld
Open Daily; call for times
Adm Individual charges for each activity

Let the children burn off their energy here. A fabulous water-based entertainment centre with wave pool, tropical rainstorm and a black-hole waterslide, where sound and lighting effects add to the excitement. There's a teaching pool if you want to get the children used to the water. While they have fun, you can tone up or relax in the health and fitness zone. Then it's on to the soft play area for a nice sit down.

John Bull's World of Rock

Lancaster Road, Carnaby **t** (01262) 678525
www.john-bull-confectioners.co.uk
Getting there 2 miles southwest of Bridlington, off the A165
Open Mid-Apr–Oct Mon–Fri 11–12 and 1–3.30
Adm Adults £1.50, children £1 (**free** in winter)
Café, shop, on-site parking

At this long-established firm, they will share their secrets for getting the letters into the rock and kids can make their own chocolate lollies.

Filey

Getting there Filey is situated 35 miles northeast of York on the A64 and 7 miles south of Scarborough, off the A165
Tourist information John Street **t** (01723) 518000

Did you know?
Another name for the puffin is the 'Sea Parrot'.

Described as 'an English seaside resort at its best', Filey is a peaceful and elegant Edwardian town, which retains a charm that has made it a favourite for many years. Head down from the town through 'the Ravine' (a wooded slope) to the sheltered sandy beach, which stretches for five miles. Along at the Coble Landing, you can watch the colourful Yorkshire 'cobles' (small, flat-bottomed boats) being dragged across the beach after a day's fishing. The marvellous views from Filey sweep south to Flamborough Head and north to Filey Brigg – the area is extremely popular with birdwatchers and for sea-fishing. For children, things to do are in plenty: they can lose themselves in play areas, paddling pools, at pitch and putt, and have donkey rides along the beach.

Holy Island

Getting there Holy Island lies off the Northumberland coast, 14 miles southeast of Berwick-upon-Tweed. The causeway to the island is only passable at low tide from Beale and you should check safe crossing times with local tourist information offices before beginning your journey. A car park lies on the Beale side of the causeway and has tide and crossing information
Tourist information Berwick **t** (01289) 389004
www.lindisfarne.org.uk

Also known as Lindisfarne, Holy Island is visited by over 500,000 visitors every year, who come to visit the castle and priory, walk, paint, take photos, fish and watch birds. The extensive dunes and sands, which surround the island, are an important nature reserve and attract a wealth of species of bird, insect and plantlife. Discover some of its secrets by following a nature trail – information boards placed along the route tell a little of the island's history but bring a baby carrier as this isn't pushchair country. With the castle and priory to visit yourselves, a tranquil village to explore, and of course miles of beach, the island holds everything necessary for a whole day out of doors.

Lindisfarne Castle

t (01289) 389244 **www.**nationaltrust.org.uk
Getting there 15–20 minutes' walk from the village
Open Apr–Oct (times depend on the tides)
Adm Adults £5.20, children £2.60 family (2+2) £13; garden only: adults £1, children **free**

Romantically placed on a craggy headland, which looks out at the Northumberland coast, Lindisfarne Castle was transformed at the beginning of the 20th century into a delightful residence by the Arts and Crafts architect, Edwin Lutyens. Gertrude Jekyll designed the pretty walled garden outside. With the help of activity sheets, children will love exploring its intimate rooms, narrow passages and staircases.

Lindisfarne Priory

t (01289) 389200 **www.**english-heritage.org.uk
Open Apr–Sept daily 9.30–5, Oct 9.30–4; Nov–Jan Mon, Sat and Sun 10–2; Feb–Mar daily 10–4
Adm Adults £3.70, children £1.90

Children's activity sheets and a well laid out exhibition introduce the history of this ancient priory and the story of how Christianity came to Northumbria. Founded in the 7th century by St Aiden, it was also associated with St Cuthbert and was an important pilgrimage destination for many centuries. The ruins date from its refoundation as a Benedictine house by monks from Durham in the 12th century. Look out for the white-cowled ghost of a monk!

Scarborough

Getting there Located 40 miles northeast of York and 50 miles southeast of Middlesbrough, Scarborough is on the edge of the North York Moors National Park. Trains run from York but if you come by car, you will find the park and ride scheme convenient
Tourist information Scarborough Harbour
t (01723) 373333

With its fine medieval castle overlooking the busy harbour, Scarborough is a lively and well-loved seaside resort with a friendly atmosphere. The local fishing fleet and pleasure boats wend their way to and from the harbour, Victorian lifts run up and down the cliffs giving fine views, and there are safe, sandy beaches to nestle in between. Punch and Judy shows, crazy golf and putting, a miniature railway and donkey rides are on offer. Should the sun fail to shine, there is plenty to occupy you inside.

Atlantis

Peasholm Gap, North Bay **t** (01723) 372744
Open Spring Bank Hols–early Sept daily 10–6
Adm Adults and children £6.90
Café, mother and baby facilities

Can you find?
In Scarborough Castle, Henrietta *hanging from* the ceiling in the Ship Room. She's a model of a three-masted Dutch merchant ship.

This giant aqua-fun centre has just about everything to keep kids happy in the water (outdoor heated pools, giant waterslides and river rapids), plus video arcades and a children's play area (on dry land).

Kinderland

Burniston Road **t** (01723) 354555
www.kinderland.co.uk
Open Mid-Apr–Aug 10–6, Sept 10–5
Adm All day/half-day adults £3.50/£2.50, children £5.50/£3.30; family (2+2) £14, (2+3) £17
Café, picnic area, shop, mother and baby facilities, disabled facilities

Being out of doors, this activity park is best saved for a fine, sunny day. There are swings, trampolines, boats, carts, a sandpit, climbing frames and much more to keep children up to the age of 12 amused all day.

Scarborough Castle

Castle Road **t** (01723) 372451
www.english-heritage.org.uk
Open Apr–Sept daily 10–6, Oct–Mar Thurs–Mon 10–4
Adm Adults £3.50, children £2.60, family £8.80
Refreshments, picnic area, shop, audio guide, disabled facilities

This impressive castle was founded by two Viking brothers, who named their new fort Skardaborg. Standing on a rocky headland 90m (300ft) above the town, its outer walls enclose eight hectares (19 acres) and the keep still stands three storeys high. Children's activity sheets are available.

Scarborough Pleasure Steamers

Lighthouse Pier, Harbour **t** (01723) 363605
Sailings Summer daily 11.30–3.30 (once an hour)
Fares Adults £2.95, children £1.60
Refreshments, shop, disabled facilities

Enjoy a leisurely cruise along the coast.

Sea Life and Marine Sanctuary

Scalby Mills Road **t** (01723) 373414
www.sealife.co.uk
Open Summer: daily 10–6; winter: daily 10–4
Adm Adults £9.95, children £7.95, family £32.80

Refreshments, shop, mother and baby facilities, disabled facilities, on-site parking

A close encounter of a watery kind. Displays, tanks and touch pools bring you face to face with strange and fascinating creatures of the deep. There are otters and a seal sanctuary, which looks after pups that have been injured or abandoned.

Terror Tower

21 Foreshore Road **t** (01723) 501016
www.terrortower.com
Open Summer: daily 12 noon–6; winter: Sat–Sun 10–10 **Adm** Adults £2.50, children £1.50 (over 10s only)
Shop

Not for the faint-hearted. Film sets, hi-tech light and sound, animatronics and live actors take you through those scary moments from the movies.

Whitby

Getting there Whitby is 45 miles northeast of York and can be reached by rail from Middlesbrough along the Esk Valley
Tourist information Langborne Road **t** (01723) 383637

A charming and attractive port, which sits in a valley at the mouth of the River Esk, Whitby is a melting-pot for traditional seaside fun, history and the supernatural. Below the North Cliff's bustling promenade is a fine beach with attractions around the harbour. Wander through the narrow alleys and quaint streets of the old town (on the east cliff), where you will still find Whitby jet being worked, a black gem that Queen Victoria made fashionable. You can learn about the town's (and indeed England's) famous navigator Captain James Cook at the Memorial Museum – but watch out if you're at the ruined abbey when the sun sets for this was the place that inspired Bram Stoker, while on a family holiday, to write his novel *Dracula*. Pack a copy for teenagers as it's a surprisingly easy, if spooky, read. The main action in the book happens in St Mary's Church next to the abbey. Just south of Whitby is the tiny fishing village of Robin Hood's Bay, which was once a haunt for smugglers. It's only a moment's drive from Whitby up on to the North Yorkshire Moors, so this is a great place to combine a beach holiday with a spell in a remote cottage hideaway.

Captain Cook Memorial Museum

Grape Lane **t** (01947) 601900
www.cookmuseumwhitby.co.uk

The Jurassic Coast

The Yorkshire coast is one of the best places to find fossils in England. The coast is so porous that it is easily eroded and in 1993 a hotel in Scarborough fell right off the cliff into the sea. Around 200 million years ago, England was covered by a huge sea that teemed with great marine reptiles – *ichthyosaurs*, *plesiosaurs* and crocodiles; then around 170 million years ago, the sea receded and land dinosaurs arrived. As the cliffs fall away, they reveal their bones and fossils and you can see dinosaur footprints at Burniston and Scalby Bays or indoors at the Wood End Museum in Scarborough. There are lots of fossil hunts and events for budding palaeon-tologists during the summer. It's not difficult to find an ammonite – a coiled shell imprinted in the rock. Call **t** (01723) 373333 for details. Dinosaur hunts are also organized by Wood End Museum, **t** (01723) 367326. You can see more fossils in Whitby Museum, Pannet Park, **t** (01947) 602908), **www**.whitby-museum.org.uk. If you do go fossil hunting, check tide times and stay away from the bottom of the cliffs. Keep hammering to a minimum and keep a record of where you found what – you never know but you could be on to something really big!

Open Feb Sat–Sun 11–3; Mar daily 11–3, Apr–Oct 9.45–5 **Adm** Adults £3.50, children £2.50, family £9.50 *Shop*

Apprenticed to the Whitby ship owner Captain John Walker, this is where the young James Cook lived when not at sea learning his trade. Amidst Georgian furnishings, children can find out about his life and some of the discoveries he made in the distant Pacific Ocean and southern seas. The tourist office sells an excellent children's guide to Captain Cook country.

★Dracula Experience

9 Marine Parade **t** (01947) 601923
Open Summer: daily 10–10; winter: Sat–Sun 12 noon–5
Adm Adults £1.95, children £1.50, family (2+2) £6

Most youngsters won't realize that it was to Whitby that Dracula's coffin was brought from distant Transylvania. Eerie scenes and weird light and sound effects portray the story.

Whitby Abbey

t (01947) 603568 **www**.english-heritage.org.uk

Open Mid-Mar–Sept daily 10–6, Oct daily 10–5, Nov–Mar daily 10–4
Adm Adults £4, children £2, family (2+2) £10
Picnic area, shop, on-site parking

Still impressive in ruins, this magnificent 13th-century abbey was built on the site of the one originally founded by St Hilda in AD 657. Activity books and an intriguing, hands-on visitor centre help children to discover its history and explore where the monks used to live and work.

Open-air museums

★Hartlepool Historic Quay

Jackson Dock, Hartlepool **t** (01429) 860077
www.thisishartlepool.com
Getting there Situated in the town centre and signposted from the A179
Open Daily 10–5
Adm Adults £7, children £4.25, family (2+2) £18.50
Coffee shop, shop, mother and baby facilities, disabled facilities, on-site parking

If you don't want to take the king's shilling, keep an eye open for the press gang as you wander around the quayside shops, market, gaol and the admiral's house. The harbour area takes you back to the time of Cook and Nelson, with live action sequences, floating ghosts and its centrepiece, the HMS *Trincomalee* (**open** summer daily 10–5, winter 10.30–4), a restored 1817 battleship, where you can see what life in the 19th-century British navy was like. There's also an Adventure Playship and Virtual Reality Pod; nearby is the Hartlepool Museum, where kids will find sea monsters and mermen,

Captain Cook

Born in Marston in 1728 and brought up on a farm, Cook worked briefly in a shop before going to sea. He learned his seamanship as an apprentice on trading boats sailing from Whitby before joining the Navy, where he rose to the rank of Commander. At 40, he embarked on the first of three epic voyages to the South Seas and the Pacific on board the *Endeavour*. His achievements were extraordinary, charting New Zealand, much of Australia and the northwest coast of America, as well as discovering many new islands. Sadly, he was killed in 1779 during a fracas with some natives on the island of Hawaii.

and can clamber aboard a fishing coble, the traditional boat of the area.

This is a real adventure for young and old alike. Put on miners' hats and lamps and walk through the old tunnels to discover what life was like underground for Victorian lead miners. On the surface, see the crushing mill and washing floor, where the ore was prepared for smelting and a giant waterwheel that powered the machinery. Have fun being amateur prospectors for the day, searching for lumps of lead, 'fool's gold' or fluorspar.

Murton Park and Yorkshire Museum of Farming

Murton Lane, Murton **t** (01904) 489966
www.murtonpark.co.uk
Getting there 3 miles east of York, off the A166
Open Mar–Oct daily 10–5, Nov–Feb 10–4 with reduced facilities and admission charges **Adm**
Adults £4, children £2, under 3s **free**, family (2+4) £10

Inside the grounds are a village from Dark Age Britain and a Roman fort to see.
For further information *see* p.478

★North of England Open-Air Museum

Beamish, Durham **t** (0191) 370 4000
www.beamish.org.uk
Getting there Off the A693 at Stanley, 8 miles south of Newcastle
Open Apr–Oct daily 10–5, Oct–Mar (town and tramway only) Tues–Thurs and Sat–Sun 10–4 (last admission 3pm) **Adm** Summer: adults £16, children £10, under 5s **free**; winter: all £6
Tearooms, refreshments, picnic area, shop, mother and baby facilities, disabled facilities, on-site parking

Beamish takes you literally back to the northeast of the early 1800s and 1900s. At Pockerley Manor, experience rural life in 1825; visit houses, shops and public buildings in the village, where characters in period dress will tell you about their lives. Children's favourites include watching sweets being made, a ride on an electric tram car or an 1825 steam train (a replica of Stephenson's Locomotion 1, the first public passenger-carrying steam train in the world) and traditional breeds of animal at Home Farm. Special summertime events (ploughing contests, traditional festivities) are regularly held.

Parks and gardens

Alnwick Garden

Denwick Lane, Alnwick **t** (01665) 511350
www.alnwickgarden.com
Getting there 30 miles north of Newcastle. Follow signs from centre of Alnwick town
Open Daily summer 10–7, winter 10–4
Adm Adults £8, children **free** (up to 4 children free per adult)
Café, on-site parking, shop

Opened in 2002 and still being expanded, Alnwick boasts grand landscaped grounds with huge water cascades (perfect for splashing around in – you may want to bring a change of clothes), a maze, a poison garden (guided tours only, pointing out the lethal plants), a woodland walk and miniature tractors to ride.

Bolam Lake Country Park

Belsay **t** (01661) 881234
Getting there Signposted off A696, 15 miles northwest of Newcastle
Open Visitor centre: Sat–Sun and school holidays 1–5; park: daily dawn–dusk **Adm Free** (charge for car park)
Picnic area, shop, disabled facilities, on-site parking

A beautiful spot with a 10-hectare (25-acre) lake and guided trails (available from the Visitor Centre) for you to follow. The birdlife which inhabits the park has become quite tame (although you should probably stay at arm's length from the mute swans); with patience, you'll find thrushes, sparrows, various species of tit and even nuthatches literally eating from your hands.

Druridge Bay Country Park

Red Row, Morpeth **t** (01670) 760968
Getting there Off the A1068 at Hauxley, 3 miles south of Amble and 19 miles north of Newcastle
Open Daily 8.30–dusk; visitor centre: weekends and school hols **Adm Free** (charge for parking)
Café, picnic area, shop, on-site parking

This three-mile stretch of beach and dunes along the Northumbrian coastline attracts a wide range of birdlife; the freshwater Ladyburn Lake is popular with wind-surfers and sailors, too. Visit the Visitor Centre for pointers on the reserve's flora and fauna.

Can you spot?
The Column of Liberty at Gibside. It was built after the 1745 Jacobite Rebellion and is taller than Nelson's Column.

Gibside

Near Rowlands Gill, Burnopfield, Newcastle
t (01207) 541820 www.nationaltrust.org.uk
Getting there 7 miles southwest of Newcastle, on the B6314 at Rowlands Gill
Open Grounds: Mar–Oct daily 10–6, Nov–Apr 10–4; chapel: Mar–Oct 11–4.30
Adm Adults £5, children £3, family (2+4) £15
Tearoom, picnic area, shop, on-site parking

A 'forest garden' landscaped in the 18th century, this estate was once the home of the Queen Mother's family and is presently being restored. Acres of spacious woodland, streams (remember your wellies) and riverside walks spread for 16 miles. It's also home to red squirrels, deer, kingfishers and herons, and is extremely child friendly. Special children's days are frequently held.

Tyne Riverside Country Park

Front Street, Prudhoe, Newcastle **t** (01661) 834135
Getting there 10 miles west of Newcastle
Open Visitor centre: weekends and school holidays 11–4 **Adm Free**
Picnic area, shop, disabled facilities, on-site parking

A pleasant base for countryside activities, with walks and a cycleway. It's also an important place for birds and butterflies.

Steam trains and boat trips

Amble by the Sea

Puffin Cruises, Amble **t** (01665) 711975
Getting there In the harbour at Amble, 9 miles southeast of Alnwick
Open/Adm Summer daily; call for details

Puffin cruises leave Amble harbour on the Coquet Estuary to sail around the RSPB reserve on Coquet Island. If you go during the nesting season, take your binoculars and you will be able to see more than 20,000 pairs of birds that go there to breed.

★Embsay and Bolton Abbey Steam Railway

Embsay Station, Skipton, and Bolton Abbey Station, Skipton **t** (01756) 710614, timetable information **t** (01756) 795189
www.embsayboltonabbeyrailway.org.uk
Getting there Embsay is 1 mile north of Skipton; Bolton Abbey is 7 miles east of Skipton
Open Easter–Oct Sat–Sun 10.30–5 (summer school holidays up to 7 days a week), Nov Sun 10.30–4
Fares Return tickets: adults £6, children £3, family £16
Café, disabled facilities, on-site parking

Only reopened in 1996, steam trains now once again ply the five miles between Embsay and Bolton Abbey – it makes a fine start to a day out at the latter (p.471). A collection of steam and diesel trains and historic carriages are also on display.

★Farne Islands

Island Manager **t** (01665) 720651, Information Centre **t** (01665) 721099 www.farne-islands.com
Getting there Several boat trips leave Seahouses, some of which allow landing on either Inner Farne or Staple Islands; enquire at the ticket offices on the harbour
Boatmen J Hanvey, **t** (01665) 720388, and Billy Shiel, **t** (01665) 720308. Both offer landing trips lasting two to three hours and cruises for one to two hours
Landings (weather permitting): Apr–Sept (May–Jul is breeding season) daily 10–6; Staple Island: 10.30–1.30; Inner Farne: 1.30–5
Fee Boat fare: adults £12, children £9; landing fee: adults £5.20, children £2.60
For further information *see* pp.479–80

Keighley and Worth Valley Railway

Station Road, Haworth, Keighley
t (01535) 645214/647777 www.kwvr.co.uk
Getting there In Haworth village
Open Sat–Sun and Bank Hols 9–5.30; last week Jun and first week Sept also Mon–Fri 11.30–5.30 (until later in summer)
Fares Call for prices
Café, disabled facilities, on-site parking

The track was laid in 1867 to serve the valley's mills and runs for five miles between Keighley and Oxenhope. The trains stop at four stations along the way including Oakworth, which was used as a location for the film *The Railway Children*, and Haworth, where the Brontës lived (p.493). Visit the museums at Ingrow and Oxenhope or the Vintage Carriages Trust, where children can learn more about the great age of the train.

★North Yorkshire Moors Railway

Pickering Station, Park Street, Pickering
t (01751) 472508 www.nymr.demon.co.uk
Getting there In the centre of Pickering
Open Easter–Oct daily, Nov Sat–Sun; some days in
Dec and Feb half term **Fares** Day Rover tickets:
adults £14, children £7, family £30
Café, shop, mother and baby facilities, disabled
facilities, on-site parking

Passing through some of the North Yorkshire
Moors' finest countryside, the track runs for 18
miles between Pickering and Grosmont. Scenes
from the film *Harry Potter and the Philosopher's*
Stone were shot on the line. If you buy Day Rover
tickets, you can stop at the stations along the
way, from which there are some beautiful woodland and moorland walks, or you may prefer to
explore the villages (at Grosmont you'll see the
engine sheds). There are many special events like
visits from Thomas the Tank Engine and Santa
specials in December.

Heatherslaw Light Railway

Ford **t** (01890) 820244
Getting there 12 miles south of Berwick
Open Mar–Jun and Sept 11–3, Jul and Aug 11–4
Fares Adults £5.50, children £3.50 under 5s **free**
Shop

It winds along the riverbank past the reeds and
the herons and you can spot bunnies in the fields.

Skipton Canal Cruises

Pennine Boat trips, Wharf Office, Coach Street,
Skipton **t** (01756) 790829
www.yorkshirenet.co.uk/pennine boats
Getting there On the canal wharf, by the town centre
Open Apr and Oct daily 1.30pm and 2.30pm; May,
Jun and Sept 11.30am, 1pm, 2.30pm and 3.45pm
Fares Adults £5, children £2.50
Refreshments

A delightful sail from Skipton through Yorkshire's
countryside, along the Leeds and Liverpool Canal.
Built in the latter part of the 18th century, it was
the trans-Pennine motorway of its day, carrying
goods and people cheaply and quite quickly across
the breadth of England and creating a continuous
water route between the Irish and North Seas.

Tanfield Railway

Old Marchley Hill, Tanfield **t** (0191) 388 7545
www.tanfield-railway.co.uk
Getting there Beside the A6076, 7 miles south of
Newcastle
Open Sun, summer also Wed–Thurs
Fares Adults £6, children £3 family (2+2) £15
On-site parking

Tanfield first opened in 1725 as a horse-drawn
colliery tramway. Passenger trains now give
exciting rides through some beautiful wooded
countryside – don't miss the Causey Arch, the first
large railway bridge ever to be built.

Theme parks

★Flamingo Land Theme Park and Zoo

Kirby Misperton, Pickering **t** (01653) 668287
www.flamingoland.co.uk
Getting there 15 miles west of Scarborough,
19 miles northeast of York and 4 miles south of
Pickering, off the A169
Open Park: Apr–Oct daily from 10; zoo: daily **Adm**
Adults and children £14.50, under 3s **free**, family £54
Café, shop, mother and baby facilities,
disabled facilities

Shows, animals and white-knuckle rides for all
the family. There are play areas and roundabouts
for younger children, plus the stomach-churner
rides, which sort out the kids from the grown-
ups. Keep your feet on the ground at seven
spectacular family shows including the scary
Tomb of Terror and performing sea lions and
parrots (Rodney, Maureen and Fraser). Don't
forget the zoo and children's animal farm with
over 1,000 animals, including tigers, meerkats,
rhinos, giraffe, hippos, penguins and pink
flamingos – the largest flock in the country.
Leisure facilities (swimming pool with slide,
tennis courts and gym) are available at extra cost.

Kinderland

Burniston Road, Scarborough **t** (01723) 354555
www.kinderland.co.uk
Open Mid-Apr–Aug 10–6, Sept 10–5
Adm All day/half-day adults £3.50/£2.50, children
£5.50/£3.30; family (2+2) £14, (2+3) £17

Active outdoor activity park.
For further information *see p.482*

Lightwater Valley Theme Park

North Stainley, Ripon **t** 0870 458 0070
www.lightwatervalley.co.uk
Getting there 3 miles north of Ripon on the A6108
Open Easter–Oct; call for days and times
Adm £15.95 (over 1.2m/4ft), £14.50 (under 1.2m/4ft),
free (under 1m/3ft), family £58
Café, shop, disabled facilities, on-site parking

Highlights include the 'Ultimate', Europe's
longest rollercoaster, the new Skyrider, plus tidal
waves and twister. Tots have their own ferris
wheel, ladybird coaster, swan rides, a train, and
there's even a zoo.

New Metroland

Yellow Quadrant, 39 Garden Walk, MetroCentre,
Gateshead **t** (0191) 493 2048
www.metroland.uk.com
Getting there Found in Gateshead MetroCentre,
2 miles from Newcastle, signposted from the A1
Open Mon–Fri 12–8 (shool holidays 10–8), Sat 10–8,
Sun 11–7 **Adm** Day pass £9.90 or individual rides
are priced 1.95–2.40 each
Café, disabled facilities, on-site parking

Europe's largest indoor family funfair with a
huge range of attractions, from the latest block-
buster rides to old favourites like dodgems.
Younger children have fun on rides like the 'Terrific
Train' or 'Happy Helicopters'. Good for all ages.

Wet 'n' Wild

Rotary Way, Royal Quays, North Shields
t (0191) 296 1444 **www.wetnwild.co.uk**
Getting there 3 miles from Newcastle on A187,
2 miles north of Tyne Tunnel. Follow signs for the
ferry terminal
Open Wed–Thurs 12–7.30, Sat 10–8, Sun 10–7;
school hols, Jul–early Sept Mon–Sat 10–8, Sun 10–7
Adm weekend and school hols: over 1.2m (4ft) tall
£8.95, under 1.2m (4ft) £5.20, under 2s **free**,
spectators £3.10; term-time reductions Mon–Fri
and after 6pm; call for details
Café, shop, on-site parking

Terrific water fun at its best for all ages, from
shallow toddler pools and mini slides to mind-
boggling monster-size flumes and raft rides. Kids
even get to be the ball in a giant pinball game.
Adults may prefer to relax while the kids get on
with it – try the hot Jacuzzi tubs, or drift along
the Sleepy Creek on an inflatable ring.

Wide open spaces

This beautiful area is protected within three
national parks, two heritage coasts and many forest
areas. Each has its own distinct characteristics; all
provide exciting opportunities for day trips and are
made accessible by a network of footpaths and
cycle tracks. If an area is new to you, seek out one of
the many visitor centres, which provide information
on the local flora and fauna. For short, easy walks
and bike rides (which often include suitable spots
for a picnic), there are waymarked trails and ranger-
led walks. If you are inexperienced, be careful not to
underestimate the terrain or be over-confident in
your own or your children's ability. Make sure that
you are carrying or wearing appropriate equipment
or clothing and footwear and, if you are not sure
where you are going, talk over your plans with the
rangers. *See p.228 for moor-walking safety tips.*

Allen Banks

Bardon Mill, Hexham **t** (01434) 344218
www.nationaltrust.org.uk
Getting there 25 miles west of Newcastle, 3 miles
west of Haydon Bridge, south of the A69
Open Daily dawn–dusk **Adm free**
Picnic area, on-site parking

This wonderful wilderness garden, created in
the early 19th century, offers lovely walks and
great picnic sites on the banks of the River Allen.

Brimham Rocks

Summerbridge, near Harrogate **t** (01423) 780688
www.nationaltrust.co.uk
Getting there 22 miles west of York, between the
B6265 and the B6165
Open Daily 8am–dusk **Adm** Cars £3
Refreshments, shop, on-site parking

These mysterious rocks of millstone grit have
been sculpted by ice and wind erosion over the
millennia to create the weird 200-tonne Idol Rock,
which balances precariously on a narrow pedestal.
Look out for moorland flora (bilberries, heather,
lichen) and fauna (jackdaws, grouse, rabbits and
perhaps red deer). Special events in the summer.

★ Yorkshire Dales National Park

www.yorkshiredales.org.uk

The 700-square-mile (1,800 sq km) park has some of England's finest and most visited countryside. Its craggy cliffs, dry gorges, limestone pavements, bubbling waterfalls, seemingly endless potholes and lush pastures giving way to wild moorland are a haven for outdoor enthusiasts.

If you aren't the hardy type, don't despair. One of the best ways to explore is by car and the 70-mile-long Settle to Carlisle Railway is one of the country's most scenic train journeys. Skipton and Ilkley make good bases for exploring the southern Dales and are with easy reach of both Leeds and York if the weather is poor. There's a good selection of family-friendly hotels and restaurants (pp.498–500).

If you are short of time but want to get a taste of what's on offer, Ilkley is just a 45-minute drive from Leeds. Its main attraction is the moor, made famous by the song *'On Ilkla Moor B'aht'at'*. You can pick wild raspberries and blueberries on the moor in summer. Watch out though, this is one of the country's top spots for UFO sightings!

Some of the most stunning scenery in the Dales lies just to the north of Ilkley. From Bolton Abbey take the B6160 to Burnsall. This is real Postman Pat country, crisscrossed by dry stone walls. The drive from Grassington to Malham Cove is one of the best in the Dales. Two hundred years ago this extraordinary 90m/300ft-high limestone amphitheatre had a giant waterfall cascading over it, which inspired Charles Kingsley to write the *Water Babies*. From the visitor centre, you can walk to Janet Foss waterfall and Gordale Scar, a natural limestone cavern.

Aysgarth Falls National Park Centre

Aysgarth, Leyburn **t** (01969) 662910
Getting there 40 miles northwest of York, 7 miles west of Leyburn, off the A684
Café, on-site parking

From the Aysgarth Falls National Park Centre, an easy walk takes you past one of the most dramatic sequences of waterfalls in the area, seen at their best during the winter months when rainfall is at its heaviest. There's a great interactive display which explains how the cascades were formed.

Grassington National Park Centre

Hebden Road, Grassington, Skipton
t (01756) 751690
Getting there Found on B6265, 35 miles northwest of York and 9 miles north of Skipton
On-site parking

The centre lies beyond a pleasant, cobbled village, just a short walk from a tumultuous waterfall.

Hawes National Park Centre

Station Yard, Hawes **t** (01969) 666210
Getting there 46 miles northwest of York and 16 miles west of Leyburn, on the A684
On-site parking

Hawes, the country's highest market town, makes a good base for exploring the northern Dales. Its excellent Dales Countryside Museum (in the old station) shows how life in the region has changed over the centuries. You can see demonstrations of traditional crafts such as rope-making and peat-cutting, look at a collection of steam engines and at Gayle (just at the other end of the village) and watch Wallace and Gromit's favourite cheese being made at the **Wensleydale Cheese Visitor Centre**, Wensleydale Creamery, Gayle Lane **t** (01969) 667664 www.wensleydale.co.uk.

Malham National Park Centre

Malham, Skipton **t** (01729) 830363
Getting there Just off the A65, 12 miles northwest of Skipton, 30 miles northwest of Leeds
On-site parking

Reeth National Park Centre

The Literary Institute, The Green, Reeth
t (01748) 884059
Getting there On the B6270, 42 miles southwest of Newcastle
On-site parking

Set in a particularly attractive village, the Reeth National Park Centre has exhibitions on mining – once a major industry in the Dales – and local wildlife. In spring and early summer, the hay meadows surrounding the village become filled with carpets of wildflowers.

Danby Moor National Park Centre

The Moors Centre, Lodge Lane **t** (01439) 772737
Getting there Off the A171 outside Danby, 15 miles west of Whitby
Open Apr–Oct daily 10–5 (Aug 10–5.30); Nov–Dec and Mar 11–4; Jan–Feb Sat–Sun 11–4
Café, shop, disabled facilities, on-site parking

In the beautiful Esk Valley, this is ideal for walks, bike rides and picnics. The centre has an interesting landscape exhibition and runs many special events days for families throughout the year, like learning skills for kite-making and survival.

Ingleton Waterfalls

Ingleton **t** (01524) 241930
www.ingletonwaterfalls.co.uk
Getting there 57 miles northwest of York and 25 miles northwest of Skipton, off the A65
Open Daily 9am–dusk **Adm** adults £3.50, children £1.50 family (2+3)£7
Refreshments, picnic area, on-site parking

This well laid-out circular walk provides easy access to two of the most spectacular valleys in the area. Follow the courses of the Twiss and Doe, the two rivers that meet at the village through beautiful wooded valleys and past a series of waterfalls.

Kielder Castle Visitor Centre

Kielder Water **t** (01434) 250209
Getting there At the northwestern end of the lake
Open Mar–Oct daily 10–5 (Aug and Bank Hols 10–6); Nov–Dec weekends 11–4
Café, picnic area, shop, disabled facilities, parking

Exhibitions explain forest management and describe its birds. Bike hire, waymarked trails, guided walks, a forest drive and a play area.

Kielder Forest Park

Tourist information (north of Bellingham) **t** (01434) 220643
Getting there About 40 miles northwest of Newcastle and the A68. The lake is signposted off the B6320 from Bellingham

Britain's largest forest and one of the biggest man-made lakes in Europe create a large range of opportunities for both land- and water-based recreation. Forest and lakeside offer walks and bike rides, which range from easy to strenuous backpacking expeditions. Choose from water activities ranging from leisurely cruises aboard the *Osprey* to windsurfing and sailing (*see* Calvert Trust, p.490).

Leaplish Waterside Park

Kielder Water **t** (01434) 250312
Getting there Lies on lake's southeastern shore
Adm Charges for some activities
Restaurant, picnic area, shop, wheelchair facilities, on-site parking

The main centre for water-based activity, with boat cruises, boat hire and a swimming pool. Watch flying displays at the Bird of Prey Centre, where you can handle the birds. You can hire bikes, play crazy golf, and even stay the night on the campsite.

Northumberland National Park

t (01665) 578248 **www**.nnpa.org.uk

The park's emblem, a curlew, symbolizes the lonely moorland, rolling hills, woods, forests and Kielder Water, Britain's largest artificial lake, that constitute much of its area. Rich in prehistory and tales of border warfare, its most famous monument is Hadrian's Wall (pp.473–4). Contact the park authorities about their special walks and activities programme, 'Great Days Out', **t** (01665) 578248, **www**.nnpa.org.uk.

North York Moors National Park

www.moors.uk.net

Wild and windswept, these moors are covered with purple heather between July and September. The national park's 550 square miles (1,400 sq km) encompass everything from the high cliffs and sheltered coves of its heritage coastline to the rolling hills and deep wooded valleys of its western fringes. Grand views are offered aboard the North York Moors Railway between Pickering and Grosmont (18 miles).

Stump Cross Caverns

Greenhow, Pateley Bridge **t** (01756) 752780
www.stumpcrosscaverns.co.uk
Getting there 30 miles northwest of York and 5 miles west of Pateley Bridge on the B6265
Open Apr–Oct daily 10–6; winter Sat–Sun, midweek by appointment only
Adm Adults £5, children £3.95, under 4s **free**
Tearoom, shop, on-site parking

Discovered by 19th-century lead miners, they have been sealed off by debris since the last Ice Age. Archaeologists have found the remains of prehistoric animals, but even older are the fantastic stalactites and stalagmites. Levelled paths and floodlights enable you to see the spectacular (and slippery) limestone trails oozing and dripping from the cave sides and ceilings.

The Once Brewed National Park Centre

Military Road, Bardon Mill **t** (01434) 344396
Getting there 14 miles west of Hexham on the B6318
Open Mar–Oct daily 9.30–5, Nov–Feb Sat–Sun 10–3

An ideal base for exploring the southern part of Northumberland National Park while Rothbury is a good starting-point for exploring the Cheviot Hills. For further information *see* p.475

Rothbury Visitor Centre

Church House, Church Street, Rothbury
t (01669) 620887
Getting there 22 miles north of Newcastle, 12 miles southwest of Alnwick on the B6341
Open Mid-Mar–Oct daily, Nov–mid-Mar weekends
Shop, disabled facilities, on-site parking

An ideal base for exploring the Coquetdale Valley, Simonside Hills and Lordenshaws.

Sutton Bank National Park Centre

Sutton Bank, Thirsk **t** (01845) 597426
Getting there 6 miles east of Thirsk on the A170, 20 miles north of York
Open Apr–Oct daily 10–5 (Aug 10–5.30); Nov–Dec and Mar daily 11–4; Jan–Feb weekends 11–4
Café, shop, disabled facilities, on-site parking

Exciting exhibition that teaches children to read the landscape, and gadgets and hands-on exhibits introduce them to 'Jurassic' National Park. Short walks and bike hire (try out the 'Ride and Seek' bike trail). Nearby is England's most northerly White Horse (*see* p.175).

★White Scar Caves

Ingleton **t** (01524) 241244
www.whitescarcave.co.uk
Getting there 55 miles northwest of York and 2 miles northeast of Ingleton beside the B6255
Open Feb–Oct daily 10–dusk; Nov–Jan Sat–Sun (weather permitting)
Adm Adults £6.95, children £3.95, family (2+2) £20
Café, picnic area, shop, on-site parking

Described as Britain's longest show cave, the underground tour takes you into a magical world past streams, waterfalls and thousands of beautiful stalactites and strange rock formations.

SPORT AND ACTIVITIES

Adventure sports

Calvert Trust

Kielder Water, Hexham **t** (01434) 250232
www.calvert-trust.org.uk
Getting there Between Kielder and Falstone, 32 miles from Hexham
Open All year, daily
Adm From £5 per activity (+VAT unless disabled)

Supervised by qualified instructors, the centre offers a range of adventurous activities including climbing, abseiling, canoeing, sailing, archery, horse-riding and orienteering.

Leaplish Waterside Park

Getting there On the lake's southeastern shore
Adm Charges for some activities
Restaurant, picnic area, shop, wheelchair facilities, on-site parking

Boat cruises, boat hire and swimming. For further information *see* p.489

Outdoor Trust

30 West Street, Windy Gyle, Belford
t (01668) 213289 **www**.outdoortrust.co.uk
Open All year **Adm** £30 for a day's watersports
Getting there In Belford, 49 miles north of Newcastle

Qualified instructors lead residential and non-residential activity sessions and courses from one day to a full week in a range of sports that include canoeing, wind-surfing, climbing, hill-walking, and orienteering (booking essential).

Teeside White Water Course Centre

Four Seasons, Tees Barrage, Stockton-on-Tees
t (01642) 678000 **www**.4seasons.co.uk
Open Mar–Oct; call for times
Adm £8.50 a day

White-water canoeing at all levels. Unaccompanied children must be at least eight years of age.

Bowling

A.M.F. Bowling Ltd

Merrion Centre, Merrion Way, Leeds
t 0870 1183020 **www**.amfbowling.co.uk
Open Mon–Fri and Sun 10am–12 midnight, Sat 9.30–12 midnight **Adm** Adults £3.70–£4.50, children £3.15–£3.60

A.M.F. Bowling Ltd

Newcastle Bowl, Westgate Road, Newcastle-upon-Tyne **t** 0870 1183025 **www**.amfbowling.co.uk

Open Tues, Fri and Sat 10am–12 midnight; Mon, Wed, Thurs and Sun 12 noon–12 midnight
Adm Adults £3.40–£4.10, children £2.50–£2.75

Hollywood Bowl
Valley Centretainment, Broughton Lane, Sheffield
t (0114) 244 4333 **www.hollywoodbowl.co.uk**
Open daily 10–12 midnight
Adm Adults £2.60–£4, children £1.80–£3

Motor sports

Diggerland
Langley Park, County Durham
t 08700 344437 **www.diggerland.com**
Open Sat–Sun and school holidays 10–5
Adm Call for prices
　Drive a JCB digger.

F1 Racing
Pepsi Max Race Way, Kathryn Avenue Monks Cross, York **t** (01904) 673555 **www.karting.uk.com**
Open Mon–Fri 11–7, Sat–Sun 10–7
Adm Call for prices

Cycling

Kielder Cycle Hire
Kielder Water **t** (01434) 220643
Getting there At the northwestern end of the lake
Open Mar–Oct daily 10–5 (Aug and Bank Hols 10–6); Nov–Dec Sat–Sun 11–4
　Bike hire, waymarked trails, guided walks.
For further information *see* p.489

Trailways Cycle Hire
The Old Railway Station, Hawsker, Whitby
t (01947) 820207 **www.trailways.fsnet.co.uk**
Open Easter–Nov 10–6 or dusk
Adm Call for prices
　Situated beside the quiet Whitby–Scarborough Coastal Trail (once the railway line), Trailways offers trailer bikes, buggy trailers and bikes of all sizes for hire, with periods from two hours upwards. You can visit beauty spots like the fishing village of Robin Hood's Bay or Ravenscar, stopping at a tearoom or a pub on the way.

Go-karting

Madtrax Tynetees
Plantation House, East Cowton, Northallerton
t 0800 0521888 **www.madtrax.co.uk**
Open/Adm Call for times and prices

Scarborough Kart 2000
1 Orchard Court, Dunslow Road, Scarborough
t (01723) 583210,
Getting there Outside Scarborough, off the A64
Open Daily 10am–11pm **Adm** Call for prices

Teesside Karting
Middlesbrough Road, Middlesbrough **t** (01642) 231117
www.teesidekarting.co.uk
Open Wed–Sun 10–7
Adm Adult/child £15/£10 for 15 minutes

Horse-riding

North Humberside Riding Centre
Humberside Lane, Easington **t** (01964) 650250
Open Daily from 8.30am
Adm Adult/child £17 per hour

Ice-skating

Whitley Bay Ice Rink
Hillheads Road, Whitley Bay **t** (0191) 291 1000,
www.whitleybayicerink.co.uk
Open 10–12 noon, 2–4 and 7–9
Adm Adults £4.50, children £4, skate hire £1.50

Jet ski

Fosse Hill Jet Ski Centre
Catwick Lane, Brandesburton, near Driffield
t (01964) 542608 **www.fossehill.co.uk**
Getting there Off the A165, east of Brandesburton
Open Daily 10–dusk **Adm** Call for prices
　Jet ski hire, a quad-bike track, an adventure playground and a relaxing lakeside walk.

Leisure centres

Bridlington Leisure World
Promenade **t** (01262) 606715
www.bridlington.net/leisureworld
Open Daily; call for times
Adm Call for prices, by activity
　Fabulous water-based entertainment centre.
For further information *see* p.480

Richard Dunn Sports Centre
Rooley Avenue, Odsal, Bradford **t** (01274) 307822
Open/Adm Call for times and prices
　The fastest interactive water slide in the country, a gentle tyre ride along the Zambezee and a hippo pool for tots.

KIDS IN

Swimming

Atlantis
Peasholm Gap, North Bay **t** (01723) 372744
Open Spring Bank Hol—early Sept daily 10–6
Adm Adults and children £6.90
Giant aqua-fun centre.
For further information *see* p.482

Leeds International Pool
Westgate, Leeds **t** (0113) 214 5000
Open/Adm Call for times and prices
Equipped with a 50m (164ft) pool, diving boards to 10m (33ft) and a learner pool, as well as fitness and physiotherapy suites and sunbeds, the centre offers a wide range of recreational, swimming and fitness facilities at all levels.

Whitby Indoor Swimming Pool
West Cliff, Whitby **t** (01947) 604640
Open Call for details of times
Adm Adults £2.70, children £1.70, under 5s **free**
Refreshments, mother and baby facilities
A 25m (82ft) heated pool and a learner pool.

Skateboarding

Exhibition Park
Claremont Road, Newcastle **t** (07947) 254624
www.exhibitionpark.co.uk
Open Dawn–Dusk **Adm** Free
Exhibition Park in the centre of Newcastle with a skateboarding/BMX'ing area.

Tennis

South Leeds Tennis Centre
Middleton Grove, Leeds **t** (0113) 395 0010
www.tennisleeds.co.uk
Open 8.30am–9.30pm
Adm Call for latest prices.
The centre offers playing and coaching facilities at all levels and for all ages and there is a fully equipped crèche.

Cinemas

Bradford
Cineworld Vicar Lane **t** 0871 2208000
www.cineworld.co.uk
NMPFT Pictureville **t** (01274) 202030
www.nmpft.org.uk

Bridlington
The Forum The Promenade
t (01262) 676767 www.forumcinema.co.uk

Kingston-upon-Hull
Odeon Kingswood Leisure Park, Ennerdale Link Road **t** 0871 2244007 www.odeon.co.uk

Leeds
Northern Morris Cinema Cottage Road
t (0113) 2751606 www.nm-cinemas.co.uk
Hyde Park Picture House Brudenell Road, Headingley **t** (0113) 2443801
Vue The Headrow **t** 0871 2240240
www.myvue.com

Newcastle-upon-Tyne
The Gate Newgate Street **t** 0871 4714714
www.empirecinemas.co.uk
Odeon Russell Way, MetroCentre, Gateshead
t 0871 2244007 www.odeon.co.uk
Tyneside Cinema 10 Pilgrim Street **t** (0191) 2328289
www.tynecine.org

Scarborough
Hollywood Plaza North Marchine Road
t (01723) 507567 www.hollywoodplaza.co.uk

Sheffield
Odeon Arundel Gate **t** 0871 2244007
www.odeon.co.uk
Vue The Oasis, Meadowhall Centre
t 0871 2240240 www.myvue.com

York
City Screen Coney Street **t** (01904) 541144
www.picturehouse-cinemas.co.uk
Helmsley Arts Centre Meeting House Court
t (01439) 771700 www.helmsleyarts.co.uk
Vue Stirling Road, Clifton Moor
t 0871 2240240 www.myvue.com

Museums, galleries and science centres

Armley Mills Industrial Museum
Canal Road, Armley, Leeds **t** (0113) 263 7861
Getting there On the A65, 2 miles west of Leeds
Open Tues–Sat and Bank Hols 10–5, Sun 1–5
Adm Adults £3, children £1

Watch exhibitions of mechanical motion in action – water wheels turning, steam engines hissing and 'mules' spinning.
For further information *see* p.463

Bede's World and St Paul's Church

Church Bank, Jarrow **t** (0191) 489 2106
www.bedesworld.co.uk
Getting there Off the A185, near the south end of the Tyne Tunnel
Open Mon–Sat 10–5.30, Sun 12 noon–5.30 (winter until 4.30)
Adm Adults £4.50, children £3, family (2+2) £10
Café, shop, mother and baby facilities, disabled facilities, on-site parking

A monk at the monastery of Jarrow during the eighth century, Bede became one of the greatest scholars of his day. He wrote the first ever book about the history of the English people, which remains our most important source of information about Anglo-Saxon England. Amongst the ruins of the monastery where he lived, go back to the period for a glimpse of what life was like for both monks and the ordinary people. You can even try on Saxon clothes and listen to Latin, the language of the Church. There are regular events and living history displays and a farm with many rare breeds.

Beside the Seaside Museum

34–5 Queen Street, Bridlington **t** (01262) 608890
www.bridlington.net/bethseaside
Open Mar–Oct daily 10–5
Adm Adults £2, children £1, under 5s **free**

Saucy postcards, slot machines, virtual boats and Punch and Judy shows.
For further information *see* p.480

Josephine and John Bowes Museum

Barnard Castle, Durham **t** (01833) 637163
www.bowesmuseum.org.uk/
Getting there In the town of Barnard Castle, 19 miles southwest of Durham
Open Daily 11–5 **Adm** Adults £7, children **free**
Café, shop, disabled facilities, on-site parking

This magnificent 'French château' was conceived by John Bowes, a Durham industrialist and his wife, Josephine, to display their amazing collection of art, furniture and local antiquities. Paintings by El Greco, Tiepolo, Canaletto and Turner accompany other treasures: toys, dolls, dolls' houses, teddy bears, games and puzzles;

rooms exhibiting women's 19th-century dress; ceramics, English period interiors and a hands-on display of local archaeological finds, especially geared towards children. Don't miss the extraordinary silver swan!

Did you know?
The names of the Brontë sisters – Charlotte, Emily and Anne.

Brontë Parsonage Museum

Church Street, Haworth, Keighley **t** (01535) 642323
www.bronte.org.uk
Getting there On the A6033, about 16 miles west of Leeds
Open Apr–Sept daily 10–5.30, Oct–Mar 11–5 (closed early Jan–early Feb)
Adm Adults £5, children under 16 £2, under 5s **free**, family £12
Shop, disabled facilities, on-site parking

To find so many talented writers in one family is unique and even if the kids have never heard of the Brontës before, they'll find their story fascinating. The museum is very accessible to children (there's a children's guide) and most kids find the small books that the Brontë children wrote when they were young and the collection of items from their childhood intriguing and easy to identify with. Their tragic early deaths adds a gruesome tinge to the visit – you can see the sofa Emily died on. In fact, almost half the children in Haworth died before the age of six. There was terrible sanitation in the town and a dangerous seepage from the overflowing graveyard. The shop sells kids' versions of the novels, as well as the original classics. The best way to get to the parsonage is to catch the Keighley and Worth Valley steam railway from Keighley Station (p.485). There's a small park not far from the station in Haworth, where you can stop for a picnic and an old-fashioned sweet shop at the top of the hill.

Captain Cook Memorial Museum

Grape Lane, Whitby **t** (01947) 601900
www.cookmuseumwhitby.co.uk **Open** Feb Sat–Sun 11–3, Mar daily 11–3, Apr–Oct 9.45–5 **Adm** Adults £3.50, children £2.50, family £9.50

Discover the life and some of the discoveries made by this famous English explorer.
For further information *see* p.483

Q: How many creatures can you spot in the camouflage tank?
A: It is home to five anole lizards, four reed frogs, an osculated skink and two veiled chameleons.

★Castle Museum

The Eye of York **t** (01904) 687687
www.yorkcastlemuseum.org.uk
Open Daily 9.30–5 (term time Fri opens 10am)
Adm Adults £6.50, children £3.50, under 5s **free**, family £18; all tickets are valid for a return trip within 12 months

Once a prison where executions took place, these buildings now house furnished rooms recreating life from Jacobean times. See the cell where Dick Turpin was held and wander through intriguing collections of all sorts.
For further information *see* p.468

★Centre For Life

Times Square, Scotswood Road, Newcastle-upon-Tyne
t (0191) 243 8210 **www.life.org.uk**
Open Mon–Sat 10–6; Sun 11–6 (last admission 4)
Adm Adults £7.50, children £4.95, family (2+2) £22.50, under 4s **free**

Discover the quirks of human, plant and animal life.
For further information *see* p.466

Colour Museum

Perkin House, 1 Providence Street, Bradford
t (01274) 390955 **www.sdc.org.uk**
Getting there Bradford city centre, near the Metro interchange
Open Tues–Sat (except Bank Hols) 10–4
Adm Adults £2, children £1.50, family (2+3) £4
Shop, disabled facilities

Fun-packed galleries containing hundreds of demonstrations, displays and brain-tingling tricks and illusions showing you how light and colour work: it's an eye sensation, with many things for you to try out yourself. Workshops are held often in dyeing, printing and mask-making (call for more information).

Discovery Museum

Blandford House, Blandford Square, Newcastle-upon-Tyne **t** (0191) 232 6789
www.twmusuems.org.uk
Open Mon–Sat 10–5, Sun 2–5 **Adm Free**
Science, technology and Tyneside's history.

For further information *see* p.466

Eden Camp Modern History Museum

Malton **t** (01653) 697777 **www.edencamp.co.uk**
Getting there Midway between York (18 miles) and Scarborough (22 miles), off the A64
Open Daily 10–5
Adm Adults £4.50, children £3.50
Prisoners' canteen, officers' mess tearoom, shop, mother and baby facilities, on-site parking

Once a prisoner-of-war camp, this museum shows the social side of the war through themed displays. There are more than 30 huts to select from covering the Blitz and various aspects of the Second World War. Among the items on display are military weapons and vehicles and a sing-along puppet show in the music hall. Ask what 'Soup of D-Day' is in the Prisoners' Canteen.

★ Eureka! The Museum for Children

Discovery Road, Halifax **t** (01422) 330069
www.eureka.org.uk
Getting there Near Halifax station
Open Daily 10–5
Adm Adults £6.95, children £6.95, under 2s £1.95, family (2+3) £29.50
Café, shop, disabled facilities, on-site parking

This interactive museum is designed for children aged three to 12. Four separate galleries explore health and the body, communications, working life, and how things operate. There's also a special discovery gallery for under 5s. Children get the chance to broadcast the news, be a cashier in the shop, fill a car at the petrol station and use a computer to design and race a bike. Leave the kids to learn about themselves and the world about them while you research some 'How does it work?' questions. The museum also operates a nursery for 0–5-year-olds and a holiday club for 5–11-year-olds on weekdays.

Hands-on History Museum

South Church Side, Kingston-upon-Hull
t (01482) 613902 **www.hullcc.gov.uk/museums**
Open Mon–Sat 10-5, Sun 1.30–4.30 **Adm Free**
'Victorian Britain', 'Story of Hull and Its People' and 'Ancient Egypt exhibitions'.
For further information *see* p.462

Killhope, The North of England Lead Mining Museum

Cowshill, Weardale, St John's Chapel, Bishop Auckland **t** (01388) 537505
www.durham.gov.uk/killhope/
Getting there On the A689 at the top of Weardale, 34 miles west of Durham
Open Apr–Oct daily 10.30–5
Adm Site and mine: adults £6, children £3 (over 4s only in mine), family £17; site only: adults £4.50, children £1.70, family £11, under 4s **free** (not allowed down the mine)
Café, shop, mother and baby facilities, disabled facilities, on-site parking

Experience life as a lead miner. Above ground there's a waterwheel, mining machinery and an example of the meagre accommodation miners had to endure, while down in the mine, visitors don hard hats, wellies and lamps to find out what working conditions were really like (not very nice).

Kirkstall Abbey and Abbey House Museum

Abbey Road, Kirkstall, Leeds **t** (0113) 230 5492
Getting there On the A65, 3 miles from Leeds
Open Abbey: daily 8am–dusk; museum: Tues–Fri 10–5, Sat 12 noon–5pm, Sun 10–5
Adm Abbey **free**; museum: adults £3.50, children £1.50, family (2+3) £5

Recreation of three Victorian streets in Leeds.
For further information *see* p.464

Laing Art Gallery

New Bridge Street, Newcastle-upon-Tyne
t (0191) 232 7734 **www.twmuseums.org.uk/laing**
Open Mon–Sat 10–5, Sun 2–5 **Adm Free**

Procter and Gamble Children's Gallery for under 5s and much much more.
For further information *see* p.466

Light Infantry Museum and Art Gallery

Aykley Heads, Durham **t** (0191) 384 2214
www.durham.gov.uk/dli
Getting there Off the A691, northwest of the city centre
Open Apr–Oct daily 10–5, Nov–Mar 10–4
Adm Adults £3, children £1.25, family (2+2) £7

The 200-year history of the county's regiment.
For further information *see* p.461

Magna

Sheffield Road, Templeborough, Rotherham
t (01709) 720002 **www.visitmagnatrust.co.uk**

Open Daily 10–5 **Adm** Adults £9.95, children £7.95, under 5s **free**, family (2+2) £25
Café shop adventure playground

The museum aims to make science an adventure and encourages kids to discover scientific principles by way of hands-on activities. In this part of the world much of the museum concentrates on steel production and huge blast furnaces. Wear warm clothes as it can be very cold in the museum in winter. There are family workshops during the school holidays and the museum is a popular spot for kids' birthdays.

Maritime Museum

Queen Victoria Square, Kinston-upon-Hull
t (01482) 613902 **www.hullcc.gov.uk/museums**
Open Mon–Sat 10–5, Sun 1.30–4.30 (last entry 15 minutes before closing) **Adm Free**

Displays of the ships and crews that ventured into the North Sea plus a white whale skeleton.
For further information *see* p.462

Museums Quarter

36 High Street, Kingston-upon-Hull **t** (01482) 613902
www.hullcc.gov.uk/museums
Open Mon–Sat 10–5, Sun 1.30–4.30 **Adm Free**

Contains the Hull and East Riding Museum, Streetlife Hull Museum of Transport and Wilberforce House.
For further information *see* p.463

National Coal Mining Museum for England

Caphouse Colliery, New Road, Overton, Wakefield
t (01924) 848806 **www.ncm.org.uk**
Getting there On the A642 at Overton, 6 miles southwest of Wakefield
Open Daily 10–5
Adm Free
Café, picnic area, shop, disabled facilities, on-site parking

Go down the mine to see what it was like during the 19th century, when children worked underground. A cage takes you 137m (450ft) down one of Britain's oldest working shafts, accompanied by tour-guide miners. On the surface see a working steam winder, colliery train, pithead baths and exhibitions – kids will love the pit ponies and Shire horses. Follow a nature trail, or let loose in the children's play areas.

National Glass Centre

Liberty Way, Sunderland **t** (0191) 515 5555
www.nationalglasscentre.com
Getting there About 8 miles from Newcastle, off
the A183 in Sunderland, on the banks of the Wear
Open Daily 10–5 **Adm Free**
*Café, shop, mother and baby facilities, disabled
facilities, on-site parking*

Sunderland was once one of Britain's most
important glass-manufacturing towns.
Here you can watch glass-makers, blowers and
artists demonstrate their crafts. An exhibition
gallery traces the history of this intriguing
substance with science-oriented activities for kids
from exploring the world of optic fibres and
kaleidoscopes to looking through telescopes,
microscopes and the like.

★National Museum of Photography, Film and Television

The Art Mill, Upper Parkgate, Little Germany,
Bradford **t** 0870 7010200 **www.nmpft.org.uk**
Getting there Bradford is 6 miles west of Leeds;
the museum lies close to the city centre, off
Westgate (B6144)
Open Tues–Sun and school hols 10–6
Adm Museum **free** (charges for IMAX, ride
simulator and cinemas)
*Café, picnic area, shop, disabled facilities,
on-site parking*

From the shadowy images of the first photographs to the brilliant resolution of today's
hi-tech multimedia images, the story of photography, film and television is told through
countless exhibits and interactive demonstrations. Children can have a go at animation or
making a TV programme; fiddle with periscopes
and a camera obscura in the Magic Factory, and
see films in the thrilling IMAX cinema, with its
giant five-storey-high screen. Free workshops for
5–12-year-olds in the holidays.

★National Railway Museum

Leeman Road, York **t** (01904) 621261 **www.nrm.org.uk**
Open Daily 10–6 **Adm Free**; Yorkshire Wheel: adults
£6, children £4, under 4s **free**

Thousands of exhibits and demonstrations to
explain every aspect of railway operation.
For further information *see* p.469

The Old Fulling Mill (Museum of Archaeology)

The Banks, Durham **t** (0191) 334 1823
www.dur.ac.uk/fulling.mill
Open Apr–Oct daily 11–4, Nov–Mar Fri–Mon 11.30–3.30
Adm Adults £1, children 50p, family (2+2) £2.50

Archaeological material from northeast England.
For further information *see* p.461

The Oriental Museum

Elvet Hill **t** (0191) 334 5694
www.dur.ac.uk/oriental.museum
Open Mon–Fri 10–5, Sat–Sun 12 noon–5pm
Adm Adults £1.50, children 75p, family (2+2) £3.50

The only museum in the UK devoted to art and
archaeology from the Orient. It's part of the
university, which organizes lots of events for kids.
For further information *see* p.461

★Royal Armouries Museum

Armouries Drive, The Waterfront, Leeds
t (0113) 220 1916 **www.royalarmouries.org**
Getting there Follow the brown tourist signs to
Leeds centre, then 'finger' signpost (15 minutes' walk)
Open Daily 10–5 **Adm Free**
Royal collection of arms and armour.
For further information *see* p.464

Saltburn Smugglers' Heritage Centre

Old Saltburn, near Ship Inn, Saltburn-by-the-Sea
t (01287) 625252
Getting there 40 miles north of York and about
16 miles northwest of Whitby, off the A174
Open Apr–Sept daily 10–6
Adm Adults £1.95, children £1.45, family £5.80
Shop, disabled facilities, on-site parking

Tales of smuggling are brought alive in this
recreation of the smugglers' world. Sounds and
smells add to the atmosphere and you'll see
some of the tricks they used in avoiding the
government men. Go for a ride on Britain's oldest
water-powered cliff railway, which still ferries
passengers up and down the nearby 36m
(120ft) cliffs.

Streetlife Hull Museum of Transport

36 High Street, Kingston-upon-Hull **t** (01482)
613902 **www.motorsnippets.com Adm Free**

Two hundred years of transport history.
For further information *see* p.463

Thackray Medical Museum

Beckett Street, Leeds **t** 0113 244 4343
www.thackraymuseum.org
Getting there Next to St James' University
Hospital, 1 mile east of the city centre
Open Daily 10–5 **Adm** Adults £5.50, children £4,
under 5s **free**, family £18.00

Explores the human body and the medical
developments of the last 150 years.
For further information *see* pp.464–5

Wilberforce House Museum

36 High Street, Kingston-upon-Hull **t** (01482) 613902
Open Mon–Sat 10–5, Sun 1.30–4.30 **Adm Free**

The birthplace of the slavery abolitionist
William Wilberforce; 2007 marks the bicentenary
of abolition in Britain.
For further information *see* p.463

The World of James Herriot

Skeldale House, 23 Kirkgate, Thirsk **t** (01845) 524234
www.hambleton.gov.uk
Getting there Thirsk town centre, 19 miles north
of York
Open Mar–Oct daily 10–5, Nov–Feb daily 10–4
Adm Adults £4.99, children £3.50, family £13.60

Home-cum-surgery where 'James Herriot' (Alf
Wight in reality) worked as a country vet 50 years
ago. Learn about the work of a vet and how
things have changed since Herriot travelled
between the neighbouring farms in his Austin 7.
Interactive displays show you what the insides of
a horse look like, or go on to sets used for the TV
series and try operating the cameras.

Yorkshire Air Museum

Elvington Airfield Industrial Estate, Halifax Way,
Elvington, York **t** (01904) 608595
Getting there At Elvington on the B1228, 6 miles
southeast of York
Open End Mar–Oct daily 10–5, Nov–Mar 10–3.30
Adm Adults £5, children £3, family (2+2) £14
Refreshments, disabled facilities, on-site parking

Based around a former bomber station, the
museum has a fine collection of Second World War
planes including the world's only complete Halifax
and a Mosquito undergoing reconstruction.
Displays explore aspects of the air war and there is
a gallery looking at airships. The tower has been
restored and you can see the crew's quarters and
the mess used by the French airmen stationed here.

Theatres and concert halls

Bradford

Alhambra Theatre Morley Street **t** (01274) 752375
www.bradford-theatres.co.uk
St George's Hall Bridge Street **t** (01274) 752000
www.bradford-theatres.co.uk

Bridlington

Spa Theatre and Royal Hall South Marchine Drive
t (01262) 678258 www.bridlington-spa.co.uk

Durham

Gala Theatre Claypath **t** (0191) 332 4041
www.galadurham.co.uk

Leeds

Leeds Grand Theatre and Opera House
46 New Briggate **t** 0870 1214901
www.leedsgrandtheatre.co.uk
West Yorkshire Playhouse Playhouse Square,
Quarry Hill **t** (0113) 213 7700
www.wyplayhouse.co.uk

Newcastle-upon-Tyne

Northern Stage Barras Bridge
t (0191) 230 5151 www.northernstage.co.uk
Theatre Royal Grey Street **t** 0870 905 5060
www.theatreroyal.co.uk

Scarborough

Futurist (Theatre and Cinema) Foreshore Road
t (01723) 365789 www.futuristtheatre.co.uk
Spa Complex (including Grand Hall and Theatre)
South Bay **t** (01723) 376774
www.scarboroughspa.com

Sheffield

Merlin Theatre 2 Meadow Bank Road
t (0114) 255 1638
Montgomery Theatre Montgomery Hall, Surrey
Street **t** (0114) 272 0142

York

Barbican Centre Barbican Road **t** (01904) 656688
Grand Opera House Cumberland Street
t (01904) 671818
Joseph Rowntree Theatre Haxby Road
t (01904) 602440 www.jrtheatre.co.uk
Theatre Royal St Leonard's Place **t** (01904) 623568
www.theatre-royal-york.co.uk
Youth Theatre Yorkshire 54a Nunthorpe Road
t (01904) 639707

Bolton Abbey

Bolton Abbey Tea Cottage
Next to the Abbey t (01756) 710495
www.boltonabbey.com
Open Summer daily 11–5; winter Sat–Sun only
Eat on the terrace with great views of the abbey.

The Devonshire Arms Hotel
Bolton Abbey t (01756) 710441
www.thedevonshirearms.co.uk
Open Daily for lunch and dinner
This Michelin star-rated restaurant has a children's menu but family dining is more fun in the modern relaxed bistro, where the kids can try the delicious homemade chicken nuggets. The adult and child portions are generous in typical Yorkshire fashion and main courses are between £10–15. Activities for children (at weekends and on Bank Holidays), books and colouring pens are available.

Bridlington

Busy Bees
35 Chapel Street, Bridlington t (01262) 673630 (also branches on West Street and the Promenade)
www.busybeesfishandchips.co.uk
Open Daily
Child-friendly fish 'n' chips restaurant with lots of character. The children's menu features fatty favourites such as sausage or chicken nuggets with chips (both £3.15 including drink).

Burnsall

The Devonshire Fell
Burnsall t (01756) 792000
www.devonshirefell.co.uk
Open Call for times
The top-class menu offers small or large portions so older kids who feel the children's menu is below them needn't blow your budget (chargrilled chicken salad is £5). The children's menu is basic but homemade. Special *tapas* takeaway service.

Wharfeview Tearooms
The Green t (01756) 720237
Open Sat–Wed 9.30–530
Yorkshire at its best – large portions of well-cooked food at a reasonable price in a relaxed family café; the owners' kids wait on the tables. An ideal place to refuel after a walk on the moors.

Durham

Durham is an excellent place to eat out with kids, with plenty of inexpensive, studenty places to pick up snacks like Pizza Express on Saddler Street and plenty of takeaways. Eat your picnic by the cathedral or by the river. Next to the swimming baths there is a good playground and picnic tables. Vennel's Café on Saddler Street is a good place for a quick sandwich or pasta dish and has outdoor tables in an enclosed 16th-century courtyard. It's very popular with students.

Bella Italia
20–21 Silver Street, Durham t (0191) 386 1060
www.bellapasta.com
Open Sun–Thurs 11–10, Fri–Sat 11–10.30
Italian restaurant with views of the River Wear. There is a children's menu and highchairs.

Hollathan's
16 Elvet Bridge t (0191) 386 4618
www.hollathans.com
Open Daily
Easygoing café-restaurant (a popular spot for brunch) with highchairs for tots and sofas for you. Big selection of reasonably priced burgers, salads, sandwiches, wraps and pizza. Kids' portions of pasta and risottos.

Harrogate

Red Lion
South Stainley, near Harrogate t (01423) 770132
Open Food served Sun–Thurs 12 noon–9.30 (Fri–Sat until 10)
An old coaching inn, north of Ripley Castle. There are kids' menus and highchairs, with an outside playground and indoor 'Adventure Island'.

Hexham

Riverdale Hall Hotel
Bellingham, near Hexham t (01434) 220254
www.riverdalehallhotel.co.uk
Open Bar snacks 12 noon–2pm, dinner 6.45–9.30
Victorian country house not far from Kielder Water. Kids' menu, half portions and highchairs.

Ilkley

If you are self-catering, don't miss Lishman's Butchers on the Leeds Road, who make their own sausages. If the weather is good, you'll want to take your lunch in a backpack. The Ilkley Sandwich Co. on Brook Street in the central car park sell excellent snacks and sandwiches – eat them on the moor or by the River Wharfe. Betty's Café on The Grove, t (01943) 608029, is a good place to eat in and a great place to buy snacks, bread and cakes, as well as something special to take home as a present.

Balti Chef

19 Church Street t (01943) 603050
Open Daily 6–11pm

Branch of the famous Bradford curry house. There's no kids' menu but it's a relaxed, family-friendly place and good value for money.

La Sila

The Grove Promenade t (01943) 601908
Open Mon–Sat 12 noon–2pm and 6–11.30pm

Lively Italian pizza joint with great ice cream.

Kingston-upon-Hull

The Princess Quay shopping centre has a food court for snacks and there are plenty of outdoor tables along the waterfront if the sun shines.

Ask

6 Princes Dock Street t (01482) 210565
www.askcentral.co.uk
Open Daily

The prime spot in town on the water's edge serves good-quality pizzas.

Leeds

Get in the mood by stopping for a coffee at the Harvey Nichols Espresso Bar in Victoria Arcade. It's an indoor courtyard so is safe for the kids to run around and watch the fountain while you relax. Pizza Express has a great venue on Crown Street behind the Corn Exchange and there are plenty of coffee bars along Briggate.

Bella Italia

145 Briggate t (0113) 245 4630 www.bellapasta.com
Open 11am–11pm

Opposite Marks and Spencer on the main pedestrianized shopping street, it's the best place to take a break from shopping. Kids' menu and friendly staff.

Flying Pizza

60 Street Lane, Roundhay, Leeds t (0113) 266 6501
www.theflyingpizza.co.uk
Open Daily 12.30–2.30pm and 6–11pm

High-quality traditional Italian food.

The Original Harry Ramsden's

White Cross, Guiseley, Leeds t (01943) 874641
www.harryramsdens.co.uk
Open 11.30am–10pm (closes earlier in winter)

Famous for being the only fish 'n' chip shop in the country where you can dine beneath chandeliers. Others have since opened around the country, but this is the original – and the best!

Newcastle

The best place to eat is along the Quayside or along Stowell Street in Chinatown, where there are lots of buffet restaurants. Most of the big chains are along Quayside and there is a wide variety of pizza joints – Pizza Express is on Dean Street, t (0191) 221 0120. There are also a number of traditional cafés serving teas and fry-ups. A lot of Newcastle's restaurants offer early-bird deals and good-value set lunch menus. The Baltic Centre is a good place for a snack lunch; there is outdoor seating by the river in summer.

Est Est Est

The Quayside t (0191) 2602291
www.estestest.co.uk
Open Daily 12 noon–10.30pm

Modern pizza restaurant with a kids' menu and a good selection of dishes besides pizza and pasta.

La Tasca

106 Keelman Square t (0191) 230 4006
www.latasca.co.uk
Open Daily 12 noon–11pm

Inexpensive tapas restaurant with dishes to suit kids. It's next to the Millennium Bridge so it's a fun evening venue when the bridge is lit up. Outdoor seating in summer and highchairs.

L Robson and Sons Ltd

Craster, Alnwick, near Newcastle t (01665) 576223
Open Tues–Sun 12 noon–1.30pm (last orders) and 6.30–8.30pm (last orders); closed Mon

Traditionally cured in smokehouses that are 130 years old, Craster kippers are amongst the finest you will taste anywhere. Eat in or take away.

Scalini's

Great North Road, Gosforth nr Newcastle
t (0191) 2268855 www.scalinisgosforth.co.uk
Open daily for lunch and dinner

Italian restaurant with a children's menu and free ice cream. Children's entertainment is staged at lunch time on Sunday.

Northallerton

Betty's Café Tearooms

188 High Street **t** (01609) 775154

Open Mon–Sat 9–5.30, Sun 10–5.30

Beautiful old-fashioned tea room in a Grade II listed building. The large children's menu includes hot dishes such as fish fingers, sausage and pasta as well as sandwiches, ice creams and cakes.

Ripon

Brymor Ice Cream Parlour

High Jervaulx Farm, Masham **t** (01677) 460377

www.brymoredairy.co.uk

Open Daily 10am–6pm

Thirty flavours of ice cream, drinks and snacks.

Scarborough

Florio's

37 Aberdeen Walk **t** (01723) 351 124

Open Evenings only

Cheerful pasta and pizza joint. In the summer, try the cooler Pizza Hut on Huntriss Row.

Whitby

Beacon Farm Ice Cream

Beacon Farm, Sneaton **t** (01947) 605212

Open Summer daily 11–5, winter Sat–Sun only

Homemade ice cream, snacks and kids' play area.

Trenchers

New Quay Road **t** (01947) 603212

www.trenchersrestaurant.co.uk

Open Mar–Oct 11am–8.30pm

Fish restaurant with kids' menu. There are also several vegetarian options on offer.

Elizabeth Botham & Sons

35 Skinner Street **t** (01947) 602823

www.botham.co.uk

Open Mon–Sat 8.30am–5.15pm

This bakery-cum-teashop is good for a light lunch or tea. Excellent value kids' menu. Takeaway service.

York

York's students mean there are lots of inexpensive but fun places to eat out. All the big family-friendly chains have places in town: Café Rouge is on Low Petergate, **t** (01904) 673293, and Pizza Express on 17 Museum St, **t** (01904) 672904, is on the riverbank. There's a large Marks and Spencer in the Coppergate shopping centre if you want basic sandwiches and supplies. You can picnic in Museum Gardens on Museum Street but it's also fun to eat your sandwiches and watch the street performers. There's an internet café, York Internet Exchange, on Stonegate, **t** (01904) 638 808. Borders Bookshop, **t** (01904) 653300, on Davygate has a good coffee shop. Piglets Swinegate Court East, **t** (01904) 65448, is ideal for a cake or a sandwich (open Monday–Saturday).

Betty's Café Tearooms

6–8 St Helens Square **t** (01904) 659142

Open Daily 9am–9pm

'Little Rascals' menu, highchairs, bibs, beakers and great mother and baby facilities. Branches in Northallerton and Ilkey.

Russell's Restaurants

34 Stonegate **t** (01904) 641432

26 Coppergate **t** (01904) 644330

Open Daily 10am–11pm

Traditional English fayre. Yorkshire pudding, roasts and bread and butter puddings are the specialities. Kids' menus and highchairs available.

Villa Italia

69 Micklegate **t** (01904) 670501,

www.villaitalia.co.uk

Open Daily 12 noon–2pm and 6–10.30pm

Warm and friendly ambience in this family-run Italian restaurant. Good deals at lunchtime.

Yorkshire pudding

The famous accompaniment to traditional roast beef. Whereas the modern idea of Yorkshire pudding is that it should be light and puffy, in the days when meat was roasted on spits, the pudding was placed directly underneath the meat to catch the juices and was thus tastier but soggier.

Where to stay

After the destination itself, choosing where to stay is probably the most important decision you can make regarding your holiday. The good thing about England is that there's plenty of family-friendly accommodation to choose from with everything from luxury hotels to cheap and cheerful campsites on offer, although this can, of course, provide its own set of difficulties. The sheer range of alternatives can be a little bewildering and it pays to take a little time and make sure you get things right.

When deciding what sort of accommodation you want, it's worth weighing up the following: cost, facilities, local amenities, privacy and space.

HOTELS

The important thing is to find a hotel that's not just child friendly or parent friendly, but family friendly. It can be a difficult trick to pull off. Many hotels don't even bother trying but have instead simply imposed a blanket ban on under 12s, while others go to the opposite extreme and create a world of soft play equipment that is difficult to escape from.

The perfect family-friendly hotel should have all the facilities parents expect (large, well-equipped bedrooms, comfortable public rooms where they can relax, a babysitting service or crèche and a decent restaurant serving cuisine as well as chips), all the stuff kids need (highchairs, cots, suitable mealtimes, a supervised activity area filled with toys and games, a swimming pool and garden) but should, above all, display a welcoming attitude with staff prepared to go out of their way rather than merely tolerate younger visitors. Thankfully a few such hotels do exist.

Family-friendly hotel checklist

Does it offer:
▶ special family packages or discounts?
Do remember that many British hotels charge per person rather than a room rate, so cramming everyone into the same room doesn't always make sound economic sense. When booking, always check whether prices are per room or per person. Many hotels allow children sharing their parents' room to stay free of charge.

▶ a choice of family rooms with three or more beds?
▶ rooms with interconnecting doors?
▶ a constantly monitored baby-listening service?
▶ access to whatever leisure facilities there might be? Nothing is guaranteed to put a damper on a child's spirits more than being told they can't use the swimming pool.
▶ cots and highchairs?
▶ children's meals? Are they healthy, served at a conveniently early time, in a family-friendly location, and if not, are children welcome in the restaurant?
▶ designated play areas for children? If there's an outdoor play area, is it safe and supervised?
▶ supplies of toys, books and computer games?
▶ a babysitting service?
▶ a crèche?
▶ organized activities for children?
▶ qualified child-care staff?

Hotel chains

Most hotel chains are keen to supplement their weekly business income with family trade at weekends and in the school holidays. Several companies offer a range of competitive packages and deals for families, as well as activity programmes and children's menus in their restaurants. Babysitting, baby-listening, cots and highchairs often come as standard. Novotel, the French-owned chain, offer Themed Breaks, which include family entry to nearby attractions (the chain operates hotels close to the National Railway Museum in York, Cadbury World in Birmingham and the National Marine Aquarium in Plymouth), while the Forte Group (who own the Travelodge chain among others) have, in the past, offered discounts of up to 50 per cent on some of their London hotels, a deal which includes reduced entry for kids to a West End show. Hilton hotels also offer a Family Breaks package, which comes with a welcome pack of money-off vouchers for attractions and shows, as well as goodie bags for the kids and a family playroom (p.502).

The hotel chains below have a policy of welcoming families (given prices are a rough guide only and are per person per night unless otherwise stated).

Best Western

t 0845 67050 www.bestwestern.co.uk
Price From £90 (prices vary enormously, depending on the size and facilities of the hotel, this is by no means the minimum in all Best Western hotels)

The country's largest hotel group operates over 400 three- and four-star properties in the UK. Children's menus are available at most hotels. Kids normally stay free when sharing a family room with their parents. Call your desired location for details.

Campanile

t (020) 8569 6969 www.campanile.fr
Price From £29.95–£46.95

The French-owned chain offer budget accommodation in 16 locations (among them Birmingham, Coventry, Hull, Liverpool, Manchester, Newcastle-upon-Tyne and Milton Keynes). Most hotels have an outdoor play area and one child under 12 can stay free in the parents' room; interconnecting rooms are available. There's a full children's menu in the on-site café.

Corus

t 0845 6026787 www.corushotels.com
Price From £60

Operates more than 70 three-star hotels in Bedford, Birmingham, Canterbury, Coventry, Derby, Exeter, Leicester, London, Manchester Airport, Oxford and Sheffield. Family offers at certain times of year, when under 15s stay free in their parents' room (one adult per child). Call for details.

Hilton

t 0870 590 9090 www.hilton.co.uk
Price £98 per room; under 5s stay **free** at most hotels

Hilton have always been extremely good hotels to stay in with kids but have recently set out to attract families with family and kids' welcome packs, a goodie bag for each child and family splash-hours in the indoor pool (selected hotels). Most hotels have family rooms, a children's menu (under 5s eat free and under 16s eat half price from the main menu) and room service. A lot of hotels have play areas, Playstations in the rooms and offer special family break rates.

Holiday Inn

t 0870 400 9670 www.holiday-inn.co.uk
Price Double s from £60

Under 12s stay and eat free and under 19s stay free when sharing with their parents. Some hotels are specifically family friendly with entertainment areas, family rooms and free adjoining rooms at weekends. Children's menus and in-room children's movies. There are over 100 hotels in the UK and Ireland. Holiday Inn Express hotels are convenient for short stays, they don't have as many amenities as the larger hotels, but the self-serve breakfast is handy with kids and the rooms are nice and clean.

Luxury Family Hotels

t (01225) 860150 www.luxuryfamilyhotels.co.uk
Price From £150

Operates hotels in Bradford-upon-Avon and Malmesbury (Wiltshire), Weymouth (Dorset), Fowey (Cornwall) and Ickworth (Suffolk).

Moat House Hotels

t (01708) 730522 www.moathousehotels.com
Price From £22 (per person per night)

Operates three- and four-star hotels (many with leisure facilities) in Cheltenham/Gloucester, Cambridge, Chester, Liverpool, London, London Gatwick, Manchester, Newcastle, Nottingham, St Albans, Stoke-on-Trent, Stratford-upon-Avon, Winchester, Windsor and York. Operates seasonal family offers. Call for details.

Novotel

t 0870 609 0962 www.novotel.com
Price From £55 (rates are b&b, for a minimum 2-night stay, Fri–Sun only, subject to availability)

Owned by the French Accor group, Novotel is one of the most child-friendly chains around, offering a range of family deals (kids stay for free in their parents' room), special kids' menus and indoor play areas (some have outdoor play facilities as well). They operate three- to four-star hotels in Birmingham (Airport and Centre), Bradford, Coventry, Edinburgh, Glasgow, Ipswich, Leeds, London (Heathrow, Euston, City South, Tower Bridge, Waterloo, West and Excel), Manchester (Centre and West), Milton Keynes, Newcastle, Nottingham/Derby, Plymouth, Preston, Sheffield, Southampton, Stevenage, Wolverhampton and York.

Premier Lodge

t 0870 2428000 www.premiertravelinn.com
Price From £47 per room per night

One of the newer budget hotel groups, Premier Lodge offers 140 hotels nationwide, each with a fully licensed restaurant or pub next door. Some have family rooms (others are undergoing refur-

England hotel websites
www.theaa.com/getaway (AA Hotel Guide)
www.expedia.co.uk
www.HotelsGreatBritain.com
www.hotels.uk.com
www.s-h-systems.co.uk (UK Hotel and Guest
House Directory)
www.thisistravel.com
www.visitbritain.com
www.ukhotelsearch.com

bishment to include these soon), where up to two children can stay free in their parents' room.

Swallow Hotels

t 0845 600 4666 **www.**swallowhotels.com
Price From £54.99 per person for 2 night stay during summer

Operate 78 hotels scattered throughout England, many with play areas and crèches. Children under 14 stay free when sharing their parents' room or half price in their own room (selected hotels only). There are also children's menus on offer and kids eat for half price.

Thistle

t 0870 4141516 **www.**thistlehotels.com
Price From £45 per person per night b&b

Operates four-star hotels in Birmingham, Brighton, Bristol, Cheltenham, Exeter, Liverpool, London (24 in total), Manchester, Middlesborough, Newcastle and Stratford-upon-Avon. Up to two children (under 16) stay free when sharing their parent's room and children (under six) eat free in the restaurant. Children 6–16 are charged £5 each for breakfast or £10 for breakfast and dinner.

Travel Inn

t 0870 242 8000 **www.**premiertravelinn.com
Price From £47 per room per night

Operates budget hotels (usually with an adjoining family restaurant) right across the country including Birmingham, Blackpool, Bristol, Cheltenham, Chessington, Chester, Colchester, Coventry, Derby, Dover, Durham, Exeter, Gloucester, Grimsby, Hastings, Hereford, Ipswich, King's Lynn, Leeds, Leicester, Lincoln, Liverpool, London, Lowestoft, Manchester, Newcastle, Norwich, Nottingham, Oxford, Plymouth, Poole, Portsmouth, Ross-on-Wye, Salisbury, Sheffield, Southampton, Southend-on-Sea, Sunderland, Weston-super-Mare, Weymouth, Whitstable, Worcester and York.

Travelodge

t 08700 850950 **www.**travelodge.co.uk
Price From £42.95 per room per night

Operates budget hotels (usually with adjoining family restaurant) in Birmingham, Bristol, Cambridge, Exeter, Ipswich, Lincoln, Liverpool, London, Ludlow, Manchester, Norwich, Nottingham, Oxford, Salisbury, Sheffield, Southampton and Weston-super-Mare.

Luxury hotels

The terms 'luxury' and 'children' needn't be mutually exclusive. Until about 12 years ago, the idea of taking the kids to a top-notch hotel was a complete non-starter. That was until Nigel Chapman opened the Woolley Grange in Bradford-on-Avon, a hotel dedicated to providing the best of both worlds – old-fashioned country house opulence for parents and fun and games for the kids, with neither age group allowed to curtail the enjoyment of the other. Woolley Grange proved such a success that Chapman was soon able to open a further four 'Luxury Family Hotels' – Fowey Hall in Cornwall, the Old Bell in Malmesbury, Moonfleet Manor in Weymouth and Ickworth House in Suffolk. All have enjoyed a similar success and the template proved so popular that it is being copied by other (formerly exclusively 'adult') luxury hotels including selected properties in the Pride of Britain Hotels group, **t** 0800 0892929, **www.**prideofbritainhotels.com.

Stylish hotels

Price is an important factor when choosing a family holiday but it doesn't have to cramp your sense of style. There are increasingly more small hotel groups offering value for money accommodation with desirable fixtures and fittings that are fully appreciative of family needs. Here are some of the best:

Alias Hotels

www.aliashotels.com
Price Doubles from £100 per night

There are currently three hotels in the group: Barcelona in Exeter, Kandinsky in Cheltenham and Seattle in Brighton. The rooms are spacious, with power showers, huge tubs and bathrobes, plus funky lights, brilliant décor and a comfortably laid-back attitude. They are happy to advise on leisure activities in the area and have children's options in the restaurant and a baby-listening service. Weekend break offers are available.

Hotel du Vin

www.hotelduvin.com

Price Doubles from £100, large doubles from £125 and suites from £150 per night (£10 per extra bed)

The storybook 'princess and the pea' would have no trouble sleeping in one of these hotels: you literally melt into beds of Egyptian cotton. There are seven hotels so far, in Birmingham, Brighton, Bristol, Harrogate, Henley-on-Thames, Tunbridge Wells and Winchester. All have large double rooms with power showers and some have accommo-dating loft suites and leisure facilities. The hotels don't have specific family facilities but they are in the most fashionable buildings in the most fash-ionable parts of town. They do children's meals on request.

Malmaison

www.malmaison.com

Price From £125 (weekdays) £79 (weekends); prices for extra beds vary according to the hotel

These hip hotels in the choicest spots of Birmingham, Manchester, Leeds, Oxford, Liverpool, London, Newcastle and Scotland are buzzing with life, are happy to adapt meals for children and can arrange for a local babysitting service on request.

Bed and breakfasts

A great British institution, the term 'bed and breakfast' (abbreviated to b&b) is used to describe a great variety of usually quite cheap accommoda-tion, ranging from rooms in private houses and farms to large guesthouses that provide all the facilities of a hotel (minus a restaurant).

It's worth bearing in mind, however, that whilst at their best offering a cheap, homely place to stay, b&b's do have their drawbacks. Lower prices neces-sarily mean fewer facilities. It is less usual to find a b&b offering a babysitting service or, indeed, any of the other services regularly provided by hotels that help to take the strain off parents on holiday. Also with rooms located in people's private houses, you face the extra hazard of having to adapt to the daily rituals of the residents. On the other hand, sharing a private residence can work to your advantage as the owners will necessarily have a good knowledge of the local area and can give you insider tips on all the attractions.

It could take quite a while to find a b&b that is genuinely family friendly, but it might help your search to ask some of the following questions:

▶ Are there cots and highchairs available?

▶ Is it possible to make separate children's meals at a time that suits them?

▶ Are the children expected to eat with the adults or at separate tables?

▶ Is there space for children to run around?

▶ Is there a comfortable lounge for adults to relax in once the children have gone to bed?

Agencies that can help you in your search for a family-friendly b&b:

London

www.visitlondon.com

Official London Tourist Board website.

Host and Guest Service **t** (020) 7385 9922

www.host-guest.co.uk

Extensive list of London b&bs, plus UK-wide and farm accommodation, some specifically for families.

London Bed and Breakfast Agency

t (020) 7586 2768 www.londonbb.com

Very reasonable rates for desirable properties.

Countrywide

www.visitbritain.com

Official British Tourist Board website.

Bed and Breakfast (GB) London **t** 0871 7810834

www.bedbreak.com

Bed and Breakfast Nationwide **t** (01255) 831235

www.bedandbreakfastnationwide.com

Discover Britain Holidays **t** (01905) 613 7464

Britain's Finest **t** (01488) 684321

www.britainsfinest.co.uk

Not all properties are suitable for families and some have age restrictions but many are welcoming family-run establishments.

Books and Guides

AA Family Friendly Places to Stay, Eat and Visit £12.99

AA Bed & Breakfast Guide £11.99

Bed & Breakfast Guest Accommodation in England (Where to Stay) (ETC) £11.99

The Best Bed & Breakfast: England, Scotland, Wales (UKHM) £10.50

The Good Bed and Breakfast Guide (Which? Guides) £15.99

RECOMMENDED HOTELS

The following hotels go out of their way to welcome and provide facilities for families. Though arranged according to the same geographical template as the rest of the guide, with the country split into 10 regions – London, the Southeast, the Midwest, the Southwest, Thames Valley, East Anglia, the Heart of England, East Midlands, the Northeast and the Northwest – it's been impossible to give equal weight to each region. The Southwest has almost double the number of child-friendly hotels of any other area, once again confirming its reputation as *the* place for family holidays in England.

Prices are based on two adults and two children sharing a family room but are only meant as a rough guide. Hotels prices rise and fall with the season and many offer special deals.

London

A good place to begin your search is the official visitor organization, Visit London, **t** (08456) 44 30 10, **www.**visitlondon.com, which lists hundreds of family-friendly hotels, bed and breakfasts and flat-hunting agents in the capital. The British Visitor Centre, 1 Lower Regent Street, SW1 (Mon–Fri 9–6.30, Sat–Sun 10–4) can supply a free list of budget hotels and has a hotel booking service run by First Option Leisure Breaks, **t** (020) 7808 3861.

If money is no object, you could go the five-star route – The Ritz, the Savoy, Claridges, the Dorchester, etc. They're all centrally located with family suites and excellent facilities and all offer a guaranteed supply of petting and pampering – but will charge £400 plus a night for a family of four. Even then there's no guarantee that your kids will be welcome in the restaurants and public rooms. At the other end of the scale are budget hotels. A good one in the centre of town should cost around £100 a night, for which you should get a TV, shower or bath, phone and breakfast (even cheaper if you're sharing a bathroom with other guests).

The well-known international hotel chains are virtually guaranteed to be a safe bet. True, this type of hotel can be rather impersonal – their principal clients are businessmen, not families – but you can be sure that the rooms will be clean and well-equipped and the service reliable. Many

hotels also offer a range of competitive packages and deals for families, as well as activity programmes and children's menus in their restaurants, and some provide babysitting, baby listening, cots and highchairs as standard. **Novotel**, the French-owned chain, offer Summer Fun Breaks, which include family entry to a nearby attraction, while the Forte Group (who own the **Travelodge** chain among others) have, in the past, offered discounts of up to 50 per cent on some of their London hotels, a deal which includes reduced entry for kids to a West End show.

Last but not least are smaller independent hotels that go out of their way to welcome and provide facilities for families on holiday.

Best Western
t 0845 67050
www.bestwesternhotels.com
Price Doubles from £90 (prices vary depending on the size and facilities of the hotel; prices are much steeper in some of the Best Western hotels)

Choice Hotels
t 0800 444444
www.choicehotelseurope.com
Price Doubles from around £100

This hotel group, which includes Comfort Inns, Quality Inns and Sleep Inns, offers a range of family deals (at the time of going to press, a four-night family break for two adults, two children could be had for as little as £255). All rooms have Playstations and DVD players; the restaurants offer an 'Adventure Kids' menu. Some hotels have a pool.

Holiday Inn
t 0870 400 9670 **www.holiday-inn.co.uk**
Price Doubles from £60

Family-friendly chain where children under 17 stay for free and under-12s eat for free. A range of family deals are available.

Novotel
t (020) 8283 4500
www.novotel.com
Price Doubles from £115

One of the most child-friendly chains around. Kids stay for free in their parents' room, get breakfast for free, are given games when they arrive and also have a special indoor play area. Most hotels also have an outdoor play area and some have a pool. All Novotel restaurants offer a children's menu and a 'children's corner', where kids can go play, leaving their parents to enjoy coffee and a few moments' peace after they've finished eating.

Queens Moat Houses
t (01708) 730522
www.moathousehotels.com
Price Doubles from £120. *See* p.502

Thistle
t 0870 4141516
www.thistlehotels.com
Price Doubles from £120. *See* p.503

Travel Inn
t 0870 238 3383
www.travelinn.co.uk
Price £44.95 (all rooms)
Travel Inn also operate 'London Family Leisure Deals' offering a room and breakfast for up to two adults and two children, plus free entry to selected attractions (including the Tower of London, Madam Tussaud's and the London Dungeon) for £95.

Travelodge
t 0800 850 950
www.travelodge.co.uk
Price From £47 (all rooms). *See* p.503

22 Jermyn Street
22 Jermyn Street, SW1
t (020) 7734 2353
www.22jermyn.com
⊖ Piccadilly Circus
Price Doubles from £220, suites from £350
Small luxury hotel behind Piccadilly Circus, which welcomes children with their own newsletter, 'Kids' Talk', and a supply of games, children's videos, a list of local child-friendly restaurants and even teddy bear dressing-gowns; 24-hour room service; extra beds and cots available.

Ashley Hotel
15–17 Norfolk Square, W2
t (020) 7723 3375
www.ashleyhotels.com
⊖/⇌ Paddington
Price Doubles £65, family rooms from £80
Cheap and cheerful family-run hotel (50 rooms) in three warren-like houses on a quiet square near Paddington Station. The family rooms are quite cramped (with tiny en-suite shower rooms), but from £80 per night, they are still good value. Special rates for children sharing with parents and no charge for babies.

The Athenaeum
116 Piccadilly, W1
t (020) 7499 3464
www.athenaeumhotel.com
⊖ Green Park
Price Doubles from £180, apartments from £380
An upmarket hotel-apartment complex set in a row of elegant Piccadilly townhouses that prides itself on its family friendliness. All the rooms are sumptuously appointed – if a bit chintzy – and each apartment comes complete with sofas, TV, video, hi-fi, washing machine and kitchen, allowing you to live a totally self-contained existence (but with the hotel's facilities on call 24 hours a day). Guests are entitled to free use of the Athenaeum spa, gym and CD and video library.

Concorde Hotel
50 Great Cumberland Place, W1
t (020) 7402 6169
⊖ Marble Arch
Price Doubles from £90, triples from £99
With the same owners as the equally family-friendly Bryanston Court next door, this small, friendly hotel has a large, comfortable lounge and well-appointed bedrooms. There are cots, high-chairs and a babysitting service available. They have furnished apartments with kitchens in an adjacent building that are popular with families.

County Hall Travel Inn Capital
Belvedere Road, SE1
t 0870 2383 300
www.travelinn.co.uk
⊖/⇌ Waterloo
Price Mon–Fri £92 per room, Fri–Sun £85
Centrally located, excellent value hotel above the London Aquarium, next to the new London Eye and just across the Thames from the Houses of Parliament. Part of the Travel Inn chain, it provides reliable, no-frills accommodation with extra cots. Children's menu available.

Crescent
49–50 Cartwright Gardens, WC1
t (020) 7387 1515
www.crescenthoteloflondon.com
⊖/⇌ Euston
Price Doubles from £95, family room £118
One of several hotels on this Bloomsbury Crescent just north of the British Museum and the pick of the bunch. The rooms are basic, but cheap

for the location. Ground-floor rooms available (but no lift to upper floors). No charge for children under two; cots and highchairs available and babysitting by arrangement.

Durrants Hotel

George Street, W1
t (020) 7935 8131
www.durrantshotel.co.uk
⊖ Bond Street
Price Doubles from £185, family from £199

Smart, very traditional family-run hotel (90 rooms) housed in an 18th-century building behind the Wallace Collection and close to Bond Street. It has a comfortable lounge, a good restaurant (dinner from 6pm) and can arrange a babysitting service. Extra cots and highchairs available.

Dolphin Square Hotel

Dolphin Square, Chichester Street, SW1
t (020) 7834 3800
www.dolphinsquarehotel.co.uk
⊖ Westminster
Price Suites from £100 (prices rise in high season)

One of the few all-suite hotels in London, the Dolphin Square combines the benefits of an apartment complex with the facilities of a top-notch hotel. In the heart of London on the north side of Parliament Square, next to the river and set in its own gardens, it boasts a grand selection of one-, two- and three-bedroom suites, an 18m (59ft) pool, tennis courts, shopping mall and spa.

Edward Lear

28–30 Seymour Street, W1
t (020) 7402 5401
www.edlear.com
⊖ Marble Arch
Price Doubles from £50, family from £74 (prices go down the longer you stay)

Friendly hotel 50 yards from Oxford Street, housed in two 18th-century townhouses that were once the home of the nonsense verse writer (and composer of *The Owl and the Pussycat*) Edward Lear. His illustrated limericks adorn the public rooms. The bedrooms are quite spacious but not en-suite and there's no charge for under 2s or for children under 13 sharing their parents' room at weekends. Extra cots available.

Goring

Beeston Place, Grosvenor Gardens, SW1
t (020) 7396 9000
www.goringhotel.co.uk
⊖/≋ Victoria
Price Doubles from £200, family from £470

In the heart of Royal London, near Buckingham Palace and the great parks, this grand, traditionally British establishment does its best to accommodate the needs of families. The public rooms are furnished in country house style with open fires in winter, the bedrooms are sumptuous with all mod cons, there's a large private garden and guests can use the local health club. Babysitting service available.

Grange Blooms Hotel

7 Montague Street, WC1
t (020) 7323 1717
www.grangehotels.com
⊖ Russell Square
Price Doubles from £155

Lovely small hotel set in an 18th-century townhouse near the British Museum. There are no specific children's facilities, but it welcomes families and the staff are friendly and helpful. There's a pretty, paved, walled garden, 24-hour room service, babysitting (on request) and extra cots are available. Under-10s stay for free in their parent's room.

Hart House Hotel

51 Gloucester Place, W1
t (020) 7935 2288
www.harthouse.co.uk
⊖ Baker Street ⊖/≋ Marylebone
Price Doubles from £110, family rooms from £135

Smart b&b in a West End Georgian mansion. The rooms vary in size – those near the top tend to be the larger and brighter – and are decorated in a variety of styles (antique to modern). Toys are provided, there are extra cots and a babysitting service.

Hilton Metropole

225 Edgware Road, W2
t (020) 7402 4141
www.hilton.com
⊖ Marble Arch
Price Doubles from £150 (prices rise in high season)

Recently refurbished and extended, a superb family choice. Kids stay for free in their parents' room and there's a swimming pool, a children's menu in the restaurant and a babysitting service (plus great views out over London from the 23rd floor). Highchairs and video games available.

Parkwood
4 Stanhope Place, W2
t (020) 7402 2241
www.parkwoodhotel.com
⊖ Marble Arch
Price Doubles from £66.50, family from £79 (prices go down the longer you stay)

Owned by the same people as the Edward Lear, this small hotel just a few yards from Hyde Park boasts large, bright family rooms, as well as a gallery of pictures by children who have visited the hotel. Extra beds, cots and highchairs available plus babysitting by arrangement.

Pippa Pop-Ins
430 Fulham Road, SW6
t (020) 7385 5706
⊖ Fulham Broadway
Price Call in advance

This friendly establishment is just for children. Up to 12 kids can stay here for between a night and a week. Activities are organized on weekends and during the school holidays. Children (aged 2–5) can attend the day nursery and there's an after-school service, where they can be picked up and given tea and homework supervision until collected by their parents. There's a second hotel 'Pippa Pop-Ins on the Green' at 165 New King's Road, SW6.

Hotel La Place
17 Nottingham Place, W1
t (020) 7486 2323
www.hotellaplace.com
⊖ Baker Street
Price Doubles from £125, family from £160

Small, family-owned hotel near Madame Tussaud's with a good restaurant (supper served 6–8.30 pm, highchairs available), pleasant rooms and a welcoming atmosphere. Babysitting available.

The Southeast

Ashford
Eastwell Manor
Eastwell Park, Boughton Lees **t** (01233) 213000
www.eastwellmanor.co.uk
Price Doubles from £190

The hotel is grand, stately and set in 25 hectares (62 acres) of grounds. The real draw for families will be the Victorian stable block, a minute's walk from the main house, which has been turned into 19, one- to three-bedroom cottage apartments, each with its own garden and garden furniture (hired on a self-catering basis). Facilities include an indoor pool (which children over three can use for two one-hour sessions a day), heated outdoor swimming pool, croquet lawn, tennis courts and petanque. There are two restaurants; one offers fine dining (largely adult orientated) and the other is a more informal brasserie, which opens on to a terrace in summer. Babysitting service available.

Brighton
Alias Seattle
Brighton Marina Village **t** (01273) 679799
www.aliashotels.com
Price Doubles from £100 (midweek)

Ship-shaped haven right on the marina with portholes, model yachts and sailor mannequins for decoration. The rooms are spacious and light and have great balconies with funky plastic chairs that the kids can fashion into slides and seesaw. The rooms have huge shower heads, cavernous baths, fluffy towels, bathrobes, big windows, quality bedding and a DVD-in-surround-sound on the plasma screen. Baby listening service available.

Brighton Marina House Hotel
8 Charlotte Street **t** (01273) 605349
www.brighton-mh-hotel.co.uk
Price Doubles from £65, family rooms £79

Victorian bed and breakfast by the sea that is undergoing an upgrade. It's very comfortable and perfectly adequate for a short stay. Located in a quiet side street, parts of the hotel have good sea views and there's a bright breakfast room where you can enjoy a 'full English' (vegan and vegetarian alternatives also available). Several bedrooms have been decorated according to particular themes (there's a Tudor Room, a Scandinavian Room and an Eastern 'Pavilion' Room). Some have four-poster beds, as do several of the family rooms, which can incorporate one or two extra beds.

Hilton Brighton Metropole
Kings Road **t** (01273) 775432 www.hilton.co.uk
Price £70–£140 (per person per night)

Superbly placed for the beach, shops and main attractions, this spacious hotel has a vast dining/breakfast room, 324 en-suite bedrooms and a leisure centre. Family rooms are huge and there's an indoor children's play area, a swimming pool and an Odeon cinema just around the corner.

Dove

18 Regency Square **t** (01273) 779222
Price From £65

There are nine comfortable rooms in this Regency house b&b, located in a historic seafront square. Toys, games and a babysitting service.

De Vere Grand Hotel

King's Road **t** (01273) 244300
www.grandbrighton.co.uk
Price From £210 per room per night, £20 extra per child, £10 for a cot

Perhaps the most famous hotel in Brighton, the mighty Grand was built in 1864 and contains over 200 luxuriously appointed en-suite rooms (70 family), a sauna, solarium, gym, Jacuzzi/spa and heated indoor pool. It's located right on the seafront facing the Palace Pier (many of its rooms have sea views) and boasts an excellent restaurant.

Brockenhurst

Watersplash

t (01590) 622344
www.watersplash.co.uk
Price Doubles from £54–£69

In the heart of the New Forest, within easy reach of Beaulieu and Paultons Park theme park, it makes a good, solid base for a family holiday. The house is Victorian (but much altered over the past 100 years) and has been in the same family for over 50 years. There are six large family rooms at the top of the house with sloping ceilings and views out over the leafy garden, where you'll find a heated pool with a terrace and picnic area. An outdoor children's play area, indoor games room (with toys and board games) and a baby listening service are available. Early high teas for children can be served in the restaurant on request. Highchairs available.

Canterbury

Thanington Hotel

140 Wincheap **t** (01227) 453227
www.thanington-hotel.co.uk
Price Doubles £80–£120

The most child-friendly of Canterbury's hotels with two good-sized family rooms, a swimming pool, games room (with half-size snooker table, darts and board games) and a smallish garden. Opposite the hotel is a park with a playground and plenty of grassy lawns to run about on.

Deal

Sutherland House Hotel

186 London Road **t** (01304) 362853
www.sutherlandhousehotel.co.uk
Price Doubles £55–£65 per room, children £10 each

This Edwardian hotel has only five rooms (two can accommodate an extra bed at no extra cost) but it is in a lovely quiet location and set within beautiful gardens. They are happy to adapt meals for children in the restaurant. Ideal for visiting East Kent attractions such as the castles at Deal (p.112), Walmer (p.113) and Dover (p.96), as well as the Dover Museum and Bronze Age Boat (p.96).

Eastbourne

The Grand Hotel

King Edward's Parade **t** (01323) 412345
www.grandeastbourne.co.uk
Price From £170 (discount for longer stays)

A dignified hotel in keeping with the upmarket feel of the resort. At the western end of the seafront, it can offer 20 large family rooms (out of 152), many with sea views, large public rooms adorned with flowers, indoor and outdoor swimming pools (both heated) and a well-respected restaurant, the Mirabelle (children's portions available). It's a short walk down to the beach. Children's high teas are available and kids get welcome packs at their own dedicated check-in desk.

Gosport

The Anglesey Hotel

24 Crescent Hotel, Alverstoke **t** (023) 9258 2157
www.angleseyhotel.co.uk
Price From £69.50

Located on the end of a Georgian crescent only a degree or two less grand than the Royal Crescent in Bath, it has stunning views of the Solent from its upper floors, six family rooms and five doubles. The hotel is walking distance of Stokes Bay and the Alver Valley for watersports and nature walks and is convenient for the Explosion! – Museum of Naval Firepower (p.98) and Portsmouth Historic Dockyard.

Hastings

Beauport Park Hotel

Battle Road **t** (01424) 851222
www.beauportparkhotel.co.uk
Price From £130 per room, forest lodge: £150;
discounts for 2-night stays in season, child bed in
parents' room **free**

A Georgian hotel occupying an idyllic setting in
33 acres of parkland outside Hastings. Choose to
stay either in one of the two large family rooms in
the hotel or in the Scandinavian-style lodges in the
grounds (perfect for families of up to five people).
Sporting facilities include outdoor heated swimming pool, tennis courts, grass badminton court,
boule and croquet pitches, giant outdoor chess set,
and large, grassy lawns. The riding school next door
will happily arrange family treks. A children's menu
is served in the award-winning garden restaurant.

Isle of Wight

Clarendon Hotel and Wight Mouse Inn

Chale, Ventnor **t** (01983) 730431
www.wightmouseinns.co.uk
Price From £50 per person per night b&b

Pleasant, family bed and breakfast in a 17th-
century former coaching inn on the southwest
slopes of St Catherine's Down overlooking Chale
Bay and the Needles. There are nine large family
rooms, a good restaurant (early teas and highchairs available), a sun lounge and a friendly,
welcoming atmosphere – particularly in the
adjacent Wight Mouse pub which is very child
friendly with three games rooms, an indoor play
area 'Mouse World', the 'Chilled Mouse' for cold
drinks and ice creams, and an outdoor play area
with swings, climbing frames and, in summer, a
bouncy castle. There are half price reductions for
children sharing the parental room. Hotel-orga-
nized activities include horse-riding, paragliding
and fossil-hunting. Baby listening service available.

Old Park Hotel

St Lawrence, Ventnor **t** (01983) 852583
www.childrenwelcomehotel.co.uk
Price Call for details

The island's most southerly hotel is a large
Victorian house (with a modern wing) and pleasant
gardens with subtropical greenery. There are several
family suites (with master bedroom and separate
children's room), an indoor swimming pool, supervised soft play area, plus a self-catering cottage and

apartment in the grounds. It's a 10-minute walk to
the nearest rockpool-lined beach. In summer,
there's a programme of entertainment (juggling
workshops, supervised play sessions, magic shows,
discos and a nightly badger watching from the bar).

Seaview Hotel and Restaurant

High Street, Seaview **t** (01983) 612711
www.seaviewhotel.co.uk
Price From £105 per room

Its public rooms adorned with nautical pictures, it
is the quintessential seaside hotel – clean, cosy,
comfortable and a short walk from the rock pools
and sand of Priory Bay. The 16 bedrooms vary in size
and there's one family room, but even the smaller
ones are comfortable and some have sea views.
Children under 12 sharing with their parents can
stay at a reduced price. A children's menu is available in both hotel restaurants (one is non-smoking),
which specialize in local seafood – early high teas
are served for younger children. The hotel also offers
self-catering accommodation in an 18th-century
fisherman's cottage and arranges sailing lessons.

Portsmouth

Best Western Innlodge Hotel

Burrfields Road **t** 0870 125 3535
www.bw-innlodge.co.uk
Price From £49

Comfortable but rather faceless, it is located on
the outskirts of the city and offers 73 en-suite
rooms (10 family), a decent restaurant (children's
menu and highchairs available), a large garden and
a supervised children's activity room.

Sally Port Inn

57–8 High Street, Old Portsmouth **t** (023) 92821860
Price Family room (2+2) £89 b&b

Nice olde-worlde pub in Portsmouth old town
with great views of the harbour.

Southampton

Busketts Lawn Hotel

174 Woodlands Road, Woodlands **t** (023) 8029 2272
www.buskettslawnhotel.co.uk
Price From £80

Simple, informal hotel on the edge of the New
Forest within easy reach of Southampton. Its 14
en-suite rooms (three family) are well-furnished
and there's a heated outdoor pool, garden, croquet
lawn and a non-smoking restaurant.

The Midwest

Bath

Bath Spa Hotel

Sydney Road **t** 0870 400 8222
www.macdonaldhotels.co.uk/bathspa
Price From £254 per room

   Sheer elegance reigns supreme in this high-quality establishment. Children are free to roam the beautiful and peaceful grounds, complete with secret cave, fountains and ponds. There's a spacious terrace for al fresco dinners, lunches and breakfasts with a children's menu and highchairs. Rooms are spaciously sumptuous with space for extra beds and children's CDs and videos are available for guests. There's a big indoor pool with an outdoor sun terrace and Bath's chocolate box attractions are a short distance away down the hill.

Royal Crescent

16 Royal Crescent **t** (01225) 823333
www.royalcrescent.co.uk
Price From £210

   It is bang in the middle of the famous Royal Crescent, one of Bath's main tourist attractions and one of the country's finest examples of Georgian architecture. Considering its location, it's surprisingly child friendly with eight large family rooms (all with CD and video players), toys, a spacious garden, indoor swimming pool, outdoor plunge pool and a river launch. The hotel even has its own hot air balloon and will happily arrange flights.

Bournemouth

Chine

Boscombe Spa Road **t** (01202) 391737
www.bw-chinehotel.co.uk
Price From £140

   Run by the same people as the Sandbanks in Poole, the Chine is equally family friendly with easy access to the beach and pier. Set in its own gardens with good sea views, it can offer 13 large family rooms (out of 69), a good restaurant serving a French–English menu (a children's menu is also available), indoor and outdoor heated pools, croquet lawn, putting green, sauna, solarium and indoor and outdoor children's play area.

Laguna Hotel

Suffolk Road South, Westcliff **t** (01202) 767022
www.lagunaholiday.com
Price From £26 per person per night

   Cheap, cheerful but very serviceable seaside b&b just back from the seafront. Families are well catered for with two large family rooms, a heated indoor swimming pool, a games room with pool and table tennis, indoor and outdoor play areas. Highchairs are available in the dining room. Self catering appartments also available.

Bradford-on-Avon

Woolley Grange

t (01225) 864705 **www.woolleygrangehotel.co.uk**
Price From £145 for a small double, £210 for a standard double

   The Woolley Grange is the flagship establishment of the 'Luxury Family Hotels' group, who have spent the past 10 years proving that it's possible to combine the facilities of top-notch hotel accommodation with a real family-centric attitude. The Woolley Grange offers the best of both worlds – lots of entertainment for the children and an elegant, restful space for adults. The bedrooms are cosy and snug with all the family facilities yet elegant and refined. The public rooms are charming with fresh flowers, antiques and log fires in winter. Children are supremely well catered for with a variety of facilities aimed at different age groups. The huge 'Woolley Bears' den in the old stable block for 7s and under is filled with toys and games (open 10–6) while 8s and over are steered towards the 'Hen House', where there's television, videos, Nintendo and board games. Outside, there are facilities for badminton and croquet, as well as a heated swimming pool , trampolines and six hectares (14 acres) of grounds for children to play in. There are also separate eating arrangements to suit the different generations. Children can eat in the crèche without their parents in tow at a time that suits them (i.e. early), while parents can relax, alone, in the evening in the award-winning restaurant. If you prefer, the whole family can join up for a meal in the Victorian conservatory. The only downside to your stay will be the price. Expect to pay something in the region of £400–£500 for a weekend for a family of four.

Bristol

The Avon Gorge

Sion Hill, Clifton **t** (0117) 973 8955
www.avongorge-hotel-bristol.com
Price From £126

Overlooking the Clifton Suspension Bridge in the most picturesque part of Bristol, it has 76 en-suite rooms (six are designated family rooms), many with views of the Avon Gorge. There's a children's activity area and a very good restaurant with high-chairs available.

Premier Apartments

30–38 St Thomas Street **t** (0117) 954 4800
www.premierapartments.co.uk
Price From £65 per night (discounts for longer stays)

If you fancy a home away from home, these tidy self-catering units come with all the amenities a family could want. The apartments are very spacious and feature a living room with CD player and TV, bedrooms (one and two beds available), bathroom and kitchen with washing machine, fridge, sink, cooker and crockery. There's a range of takeaway menus to alternate with nights out in the city and the (occasional) homecooked meal. There are secure gates to the entire complex and small railed balconies on the upper floors.

Frome

Babington House

Babington, Kilmersdon **t** (01373) 812266
www.babingtonhouse.co.uk
Price From £190

Sister of the hip, members-only Soho House in London (whose members can enjoy reduced rates), this is a very trendy, terribly luxurious, but surprisingly child-friendly hotel. There's a nursery supervised by trained staff, a flexitime restaurant and home-baked pizzas on call during the day. The service and atmosphere are friendly and relaxed, despite its ultra-fashionable status, and there are indoor and outdoor swimming pools, tennis courts, a private arthouse cinema and beauty treatments available. The public rooms are terribly modern – all brushed steel and suede pillows – while the bedrooms are tastefully furnished and contain thoughtful touches such as toasters and DVD players. Delightful, but at a price.

Malmesbury

The Old Bell

Abbey Row **t** (01666) 822344
www.oldbellhotel.com
Price from £125

This ivy-covered coaching inn in the centre of Malmesbury (next to the Abbey) has a paddling pool, an outdoor play area, a games room with computers and a supervised 'den' full of games and toys. The house is a Grade I listed building and retains many original features (it claims to be England's oldest hotel, along with around 20 other establishments around the country). The bedrooms are decorated in styles ranging from antique Edwardian (in the main house) to modernist Japanese (in the old Coach house). Children sharing with their parents stay free of charge. Baby listening service available.

Poole

Sandbanks

15 Banks Road **t** (01202) 707377
www.sandbankshotel.co.uk
Price From £65 per person per night (child discounts available)

It may be a functional, purpose-built seaside hotel, but what it lacks in beauty, it makes up for in family friendliness with lovely views over Poole Bay and the yacht harbour. Thirty of its 100 plus rooms have been set aside for family use and there's a soft play room, an outdoor playground and children's entertainers are laid on during the school holidays. Kids even get their own 'Wipe Clean' food bar serving up dishes of gloopy favourites (and are welcome in the main restaurant). The hotel has access to a Blue Flag Award accredited beach, where you'll find a pirate ship play area.

Swanage

Knoll House

Studland **t** (01929) 450450 **www.knollhouse.co.uk**
Price From £97 (various rates for children depending on age; call for details)

Set in 40 hectares (100 acres) of grounds with wonderful views out over Studland Bay and easy access to a beautiful National Trust-maintained sandy beach (400 yards/366m from the house), it is very family friendly with 30 comfortable family suites, each with a separate children's bedroom and baby listening device. There's also a play room with table tennis, pool, table football and board games; a heated outdoor pool; tennis courts and an adventure playground with a climb-aboard pirate ship, tube slides, climbing nets and towers. Children are served their meals early in the colourfully decorated children's dining room, after which parents can enjoy a relaxed dinner in the (child-free) restaurant while their kids are supervised in the playroom. Facilities are available round-the-clock for parents with their own food and bottles.

Swindon
The Pear Tree
Church End, Purton (01793) 772100
www.peartreepurton.co.uk
Price From £110

When you imagine a country retreat far away from the stresses of daily life, you're probably thinking of somewhere just like the Pear Tree. Flowery borders on immaculate lawns, rabbits gambolling in the fields, church bells tolling – it's all here. This very friendly family-run hotel offers spacious accommodation with heaps of individual character and plastic ducks in the bathrooms that visiting children may adopt for a small fee (a donation goes to the local wildlife trust). Meals are locally sourced at very reasonable prices and they're happy to accommodate junior tastes. Breakfast is a suitably protracted affair with porridge, eggs and Wiltshire sausages among the many items available. After that it would be rude not to take a stroll in the gardens before heading off to discover the delights of the West Country.

Wellington
Bindon Country House Hotel
Langford Budville, Wellington, Somerset
t (01823) 400070 **www.bindon.com**
Price From £145 (children £10 per night each)

If you have ever wondered what it is like to be to the manor born, Bindon is the place to play out your aristocratic dreams. The present house was built around the time of the English Civil War and its current owners have restored it to an immaculate, though thankfully not exclusive, state. There are three hectares (seven acres) of grounds to explore with a heated outdoor swimming pool, tennis court and Langford Heath Nature Reserve just a short walk away for family outings.

West Lulworth
Cromwell House Hotel
Lulworth Cove **t** (01929) 400253
www.lulworthcove.co.uk
Price From £40.50 per person per night (children **free** or half price depending on age)

The century-old Cromwell occupies an idyllic location overlooking Lulworth Cove. The best views are from the heated outdoor swimming pool, set high above the building to catch the maximum sunshine. Furnished in classic country-house style with bright, cheerful décor, it has 14 rooms, of which three are suitable for families (one has a four-poster bed). Cream teas are served in the dining room where, in the evening, you can tuck into crabs and lobsters caught by local fishermen.

Weymouth
Moonfleet Manor
Fleet **t** (01305) 786948
www.moonfleetmanorhotel.co.uk
Price From £160

Another of the super child-friendly 'Luxury Family Hotels', the Moonfleet Manor is perhaps the least visually arresting of the four. It does, nonetheless, have plenty to offer families, with facilities for bowling, squash, tennis, indoor skittles and swimming (toddlers' and learners' pool too). There's also a special indoor supervised 'Four Bears' den with computer games, table tennis, pool and videos. One-year-olds get their own 'Tiny Tots Corner'. The 48 bedrooms are sumptuous and elegant; the public rooms are classic Edwardian style.

Wookey Hole
Glencot House
Glencot Lane **t** (01749) 677160
www.glencothouse.co.uk
Price From £115 (cots **free**; children aged 3–10 £20 for extra bed)

Victorian mansion (albeit built in Jacobean style), set in seven hectares (18 acres) of leafy gardens next to the trout-filled River Axe (where guests can fish). Though the public rooms may be grand and antique-looking with carved ceilings, dark wood panelling and lots of European *objets d'art* lying around, the hotel is well-practised at welcoming families, with an indoor swimming pool and facilities for tennis, table tennis and croquet. There are 13 rooms of which two are very large family rooms.

The Southwest

Brixham
Berryhead
Berryhead Road **t** (01803) 853225
www.berryheadhotel.com
Price From £120

The Berryhead doesn't go hugely out of its way to entertain children but it's very friendly and located just outside Brixham in perhaps the most picturesque part of the 'English Riviera'. The house was built in 1809 as a military hospital and was later the home of the Reverend Henry Francis Lyte, who wrote *Abide with Me* (perhaps best known these days as the FA Cup Hymn). Its seven well-equipped family rooms have lovely views of the Torbay coast and there are two-and-a-half hectares (six acres) of gardens and lawns to run about on, as well as plenty of walks in the adjacent National Trust-owned Berryhead Country Park. Its indoor swimming pool, croquet lawn and petanque court (a French game similar to bowls) are available to all guests and you might also like to check out the nearby seawater swimming pool. It's just a short walk to Brixham Marina, where deep-sea fishing trips can be arranged. Half portions for children in the restaurant.

Cawsand
Wringford Down
t (01752) 822287 **www.cornwallholidays.co.uk**
Price From around £75–£90 (2 adults and 2 children aged 3–7); one week self catering £350–£700

Wringford Down specializes in families with young children. The main body of the hotel is 18th century (with various modern adornments including a very nice conservatory) and there are just 12 bedrooms (all designed for families), as well as a games room with toys and table tennis, a play-barn with ball pool, padded playpen, sandpit, trampoline, climbing ropes and a heated indoor swimming pool. The garden has lovely views and a tennis court, and there are animals to meet including goats, rabbits and Shetland ponies. Donkey rides are offered in summer.

Constantine
Trengilly Wartha Inn
Nancenoy **t** (01326) 340332 **www.trengilly.co.uk**
Price Double from £84, £10 for extra bed (cot £5)

This beautiful old pub tucked away in a wooded valley is perfect for getting away from it all. There's good food and a friendly welcome. It's open all year round and has two ground floor family rooms. The restaurant has a children's menu and highchairs. You can eat in the garden in summer and in winter there is a cosy family room. It's an ideal base for exploring the Lizard peninsula.

Dawlish
The Langstone Cliff Hotel
Mount Pleasant Road, Dawlish Warren
t (01626) 868000 **www.langstone-hotel.co.uk**
Price From £126

A popular three-star hotel set in seven hectares (19 acres) of grounds just back from the sea. It may not be the most relaxing of choices, with entertainments and dances organized almost daily in summer, but there are plenty of facilities for families. Forty-six of its 68 rooms have been designed for family use (many have balconies and sea views) and there's a toddler room filled with toys for younger children, while older children can play in either of two games rooms (with snooker and table tennis), or on the lawns and wooded areas of the grounds. The hotel also has a heated indoor pool, a baby-listening intercom connected to reception and hires children's entertainers during the school holidays – there's a children's party held every week in summer. Under 10s stay free and there is a special single family supplement. Early children's suppers are available or parents can choose to bring their children into the restaurant for a later sitting. Warren beach is just 500m (1,640ft) from the hotel via a public footpath.

Exeter
The Royal Clarence Hotel
Cathedral Yard **t** (01392) 221111
www.corushotels.com/royalclarence
Price From £80

The hotel has a great location right opposite the cathedral, where the kids can run around. There's a top-class restaurant run by local chef Micheal Caines, where they are happy to welcome children but you'll probably be happier in the hotel's café-bar, which has a relaxed student atmosphere, high-chairs and children's menu. Kids under 15 stay free and there is a reduced price for children in their own room.

Falmouth
The Falmouth Hotel

Castle Beach **t** (01326) 312671
www.falmouthhotel.co.uk
Price From £80, children (4–8) £15, children (9–14) £25 when sharing a room with parents

The hotel is seconds away from the beach with great views across the bay and within walking distance of the National Maritime Museum. There are family rooms and the hotel is welcoming to its junior guests and has a relaxed attitude. The restaurant has a kids' menu and there's an indoor swimming pool. The hotel has a large garden and there are self-catering cottages attached to the hotel. Baby listening service available.

Royal Duchy Hotel

Cliff Road **t** (01326) 313042 **www.**royalduchy.com
Price From £160

Overlooking Falmouth Bay, the hotel is just a short walk from the centre of town and the beach. It can offer six large family bedrooms (several with sweeping coastal views), a sun terrace, a heated indoor pool, a children's paddling pool, a games rooms with table tennis and other assorted amusements and a pleasant restaurant, serving half portions for children (highchairs available).

Fowey
Fowey Hall

Hanson Drive **t** (01726) 833866
www.foweyhallhotel.co.uk
Price From £150

Fowey Hall offers the usual 'Luxury Family Hotel' comforts. There's a 'Four Bears' den for children full of toys, games and computer games, and a cellar playroom with table tennis, table football and pool. The house itself, which sits above a river estuary overlooking the English Channel (there are lots of good coastal walks nearby), is a listed mansion and a typically Cornish affair. Built in 1899, it is said to have provided the inspiration for Toad Hall in Kenneth Graham's *Wind in the Willows*. Its bedrooms (named after characters from the book) are as swish and as elegant as you'd expect – there are 24 in all including 11 suites for families – and

the two restaurants are perfectly willing to accommodate children. The two hectares (five acres) of grounds boast a covered, heated pool with sunbathing area, as well as tennis and badminton courts. Children sharing their parents' room stay free of charge.

Hope Cove
The Cottage

t (01548) 561555 **www.**hopecove.com
Price From £75, children (0–6) £8.50, (7–12) £18

Run by the same family for over 20 years, The Cottage has a safe, homey feel to it. Many of its 35 en-suite rooms have balconies and coastal views and there are five family rooms, an attractive garden with swings, a playroom with table tennis and computer games and access to a sandy beach. The hotel restaurant specializes in seafood and can provide highchairs.

Lynmouth
Tors Hotel

t (01598) 753236 **www.**torslynmouth.co.uk
Price From £106

A stone's throw from the wilds of Exmoor, the Tors stands in two hectares (five acres) of woodland overlooking the pretty coastal town of Lynmouth. Inside it's small and comfortable with 33 en-suite rooms (most with views and five family rooms), two games rooms, a heated outdoor swimming pool and a good, non-smoking restaurant (children's menu and highchairs available).

Mawgan Porth
Bedruthan Steps Hotel

t (01637) 860555 **www.**bedruthan.com
Price From £146, suites from £174

A bright, shiny modern hotel overlooking a celebrated beach. Nearly all of its 75 rooms are suitable for families (many have second bedrooms), although the Seaview Villa Suites, which have their own terraces, are perhaps the best (and certainly the most expensive). The hotel has several play areas, where children can let off a little steam, including an adventure play area with a ball pool, tube slide, rope ladder and biff-bash bags; a games room with table tennis, pool and skittles; a football site; an indoor swimming pool and, in summer, a bouncy castle. Children also have the chance to join one of four clubs – Tadpoles, Minnows, Dolphins or Sharks – and take part in a range of activities such as nature walks, treasure hunts and painting. There's even a special room for teenagers (a rarity in hotels) with a jukebox, table tennis, table football and computer games. The heated outdoor swimming pool enjoys a leafy garden setting and is adjoined by a learners' paddling pool.

Mullion

Polurrian Hotel

Lizard Peninsula t (01326) 240421
www.polurrianhotel.com
Price From £118

Perched high on the clifftops and painted in traditional seaside white, the Polurrian occupies an idyllic stretch of coastline close to the country's southernmost point. It's just above a lovely beach, which isn't private despite the hotel's claims in its publicity but never gets too busy as there is no road. It's very family orientated with 22 family rooms (including several very large two-bedroom suites), many with sea views; an activity room with Playstation, table football and pool table; an indoor swimming pool (where supervised fun hours for youngsters are organized), lovely gardens with tennis courts, cricket nets and lots of space for playing football and rounders. Special events for children, such as discos, Easter Egg hunts and football tournaments, are organized in summer and the hotel can hire out mountain bikes and wet suits. The restaurant, which specializes in seafood (and offers sea views), is very accommodating to families and can provide early high teas.

Newquay

Crantock Bay

West Pentire, Crantock t (01637) 830229
www.crantockbayhotel.co.uk
Price From £118

With access to a popular surfing beach, the Crantock Bay is a friendly, professionally run hotel well-practised at entertaining families with lots of child-friendly facilities. It has 33 en-suite rooms (three family), some with sea views (extra cots available), an indoor swimming pool with a separate paddling pool for kids, tennis courts and a children's activity area with a wooden fort, swings and climbing trees. Kids can also meet the animals (which include donkeys and pigs) in the field next to the hotel and can be provided with early evening dinners (as early as 5pm if you want). A baby listening service is also available.

Headland Hotel

Fistral Beach, t (01637) 872211
www.headlandhotel.co.uk
Price From £200

Overlooking the British surfing mecca of Fistral beach, this grand Victorian establishment can offer no fewer than 56 family rooms (out of 107), indoor and outdoor swimming pools (both heated), tennis courts, pool tables, a croquet lawn and surfing play areas. There's also a good restaurant offering high teas for children and, throughout, the hotel has a jolly, family-friendly atmosphere. Kids might like to know that the hotel was where the TV version of Roald Dahl's *The Witches* was filmed. There are also self-catering cottages for families.

Sands Family Resort

Watergate road, Porth t (01637) 872864
www.sandsresort.co.uk
Price From £1,450 per week, full board

The Sands Resort on the north Cornwall coast is more of a giant holiday complex than a hotel. In high season, rooms are rented on a weekly basis only. There are lots of special deals throughout the year but this isn't the kind of place you just drive up to and ask for a room. Decorated in bright, shiny colours, the hotel is aimed squarely at families offering a huge range of activities – squash, tennis, junior tennis, football, pool, racketball, basketball, skateboarding, swimming in a heated outdoor pool, table tennis, table football, as well as a variety of typically seaside entertainments (quizzes, football tournaments, discos). It has four age-branded children's clubs, which run all day and in the evening, and entertainments including a visit from the animals of Newquay zoo. Parents, however, aren't allowed to leave the hotel while the children are in the clubs and kids who won't settle will be asked to leave. You can hire buggies and there is a launderette. Most of the huge bedrooms are open-plan suites that have been specifically designed for family use, with a separate children's area, microwave, fridge and a baby monitor. Sadly the restaurant can feel a bit like a canteen and the food isn't great. Early dinners for children (or families) are served in the back part of the restaurant. It's five minutes' walk from the lovely sandy Porth beach and families can also use the Watergate Bay Beach Hut Café during the day. Newquay, the country's most popular surfing resort, is just a few miles away.

Watergate Bay

Watergate Bay **t** (01637) 860543
www.watergate.co.uk
Price From £90

With its own private stretch of sandy beach and a shed-load of facilities, this is almost a resort in its own right. Near Newquay, it offers 27 large family rooms (baby listening service in every room) and simple, knees-up seaside entertainment for all generations – concerts and dancing for adults, Punch and Judy shows, fancy dress competitions and swimming galas for kids. There's a large play-room for children with toys and games, tennis and badminton courts (short tennis for young kids), an outdoor swimming pool (with paddling pool), a small indoor pool and a very child-friendly coffee shop serving chips and chicken nuggets.

North Bovey

The Ring of Bells Inn

North Bovey, Dartmoor, Devon **t** (01647) 440375
www.ringofbellsinn.com
Prices From £80

Old-fashioned thatched inn in the heart of Dartmoor. North Bovey is a lovely village with a large green. The rooms are large enough for extra beds and cots. There's an interesting kids' menu but the kitchen will rustle up whatever the kids want. Some of the family rooms have four-poster beds. The restaurant uses local produce and in good weather you can eat outside in the courtyard.

Padstow

Treglos Hotel

Constantine Bay
t (01841) 520727 www.treglos-hotel.co.uk
Price From £152

On the north Cornwall coast, close to the lovely sandy beaches of Constantine Bay, stands a rather higgledy-piggledy building that contains a very comfortable family hotel. The décor is cosy, the food hearty and there's plenty to entertain the kids including a children's playroom with toys and computer games, a landscaped garden with play equipment, an indoor swimming pool, as well as facilities for table tennis, croquet, table football and pool. There are 12 family rooms as well as four self-catering apartments. Early children's meals are served in the restaurant at 5.30pm (no kids after 7pm) and parents with babies and young children have a special breakfast service from 8 to 8.30am.

Penzance

Rose Farm

Chyanhal, Buryas Bridge **t** (01736) 761808
www.rosefarmcornwall.co.uk
Price Doubles £35 per person, family room £30 per person over 11 years, under 11s £15

In the peaceful hamlet of *Chyanhal* (which means 'place by the moor' in Cornish) in the middle of a working farm, stands this picturesque old farmhouse with three very cosy rooms for hire. Each is completely private with its own entrance and pleasantly furnished – one even has a 17th-century four-poster bed. The house itself is set in beautiful gardens and there are lots of animals to meet including cattle, horses, Shetland ponies, sheep, ducks, geese, hens and pot-bellied pigs. Do also be sure to check out the farm's own collection of ancient, mystical standing stones – the farm is supposedly criss-crossed by ley lines. It's very friendly; the owners are happy to help devise itineraries, and there are hearty homecooked breakfasts to enjoy. The Cornish coastal path is within easy reach.

Plymouth

Holiday Inn

Cliff Road, The Hoe **t** (0870) 400 9064
www.holidayinn.co.uk
Price From £100

The hotel may not look much from outside – it's a 1960s tower block but it has amazing views over the harbour and is right next to the Hoe, where kids can run around and visit the lovely Seaton's Tower. Kids eat free in the restaurant, which serves good-quality food.

Polperro

Talland Bay Hotel

Porthallow **t** (01503) 272667
www.tallandbayhotel.co.uk
Price From £205

With its lush gardens leading down to the sea, this 16th-century stone manor house has an almost tropical feel to it, from the outside at least. Inside it's deeply traditional – oak panelling, open fires, antiques, etc. – but still very family friendly with 19 large, comfortable rooms (two family), a heated outdoor pool, a games room for kids and a croquet lawn. It's over 5s only in the restaurant – early high teas are served for younger children.

Roseland

Driftwood

Rosevine nr Porthscatho **t** (01872) 580644
www.driftwoodhotel.co.uk
Price From £210

Light airy hotel with great clifftop views. The hotel has a California meets Cornwall feel. There's a small private beach and fresh modern food. Kids are welcome in the relaxed laid-back atmosphere and stay for £10 (if under 12) or £15 (if over 12) including breakfast, in their parents' room. High teas are available.

Nare Hotel

Carne Beach, Veryan **t** (01872) 501111
www.narehotel.co.uk
Price From £330

Very well-to-do seaside hotel perched high on a clifftop overlooking a sheltered cove and within easy reach of a sandy beach (where you can go sailboarding). There are 38 large, airy rooms, some with balconies and sea views, comfortable public rooms adorned with fresh flowers and pleasant, sheltered gardens, where you'll find a swimming pool and facilities for tennis. Children are served their own early suppers in the dining room. Horses can be hired for canters along the beach from the nearby Manor Stables and the hotel also has its own 7m (22ft) crabbing boat for hire.

The Rosevine Hotel

Rosevine, Portscatho **t** (01872) 580206,
www.rosevine.co.uk
Price From £215

Run by the Makepeace family, who also own the Soar Mill Cove in Devon, the Rosevine is one of the latest additions to Cornwall's burgeoning luxury hotel industry. The Makepeaces have young children themselves and have therefore ensured that the hotel is endowed with lots of family-friendly facilities including a children's indoor paddling pool, a swimming pool, a well-stocked playroom and an outdoor playground. Cots, highchairs, changing mats and baby listeners are provided free of charge. The Makepeaces are particularly proud of the hotel's subtropical gardens, which overlook Porthcurnick beach and lead down to the Cornish coastal path. Some rooms have private terraces and there are several family suites available. Children (under 18 months) sharing their parents' room stay free of charge.

St Austell

Carlyon Bay

Sea Road, Carlyon Bay **t** (01726) 812304
www.carlyonbay.co.uk
Price From £185

A perfect base for exploring the nearby Eden Project (pp.221–2), perhaps the most ambitious botanical garden yet created in this country, which features three of the largest conservatories in the world. Set in 100 hectares (250 acres) of gardens, this lovely ivy-covered house has 14 large family rooms (some with views of the bay), a supervised nursery where children's activities are arranged, an outdoor children's play area, tennis courts, and indoor and outdoor swimming pool (both heated) and an excellent golf course. The hotel even has its own collection of subtropical blooms, which flourish in the Southwest's warmer climate.

Salcombe

Gara Rock

East Portlemouth **t** (01548) 842342
www.gara.co.uk
Price From £114

A clifftop hotel housed in a former coastguard station, the Gara Rock has 17 family-sized bedrooms and 20 self-catering apartments. The owners take great pains to make sure that kids are entertained, organizing daily activities in summer with a qualified supervisor employed to lead children (aged 3–12) in a range of games, craft workshops and nature walks (£5 per child). Occasional events, such as clown shows, discos and barbeques, are also laid on. Otherwise, kids can devise their own fun in the hotel games room (which has table football and table tennis), the heated open air swimming pool (with adjoining paddling pool) or at the small adventure playground. Early suppers for kids are served in the restaurant and there's a babysitting (and listening) service available.

Soar Mill Cove Hotel

Soar Mill Cove, Malborough **t** (01548) 561566
www.makepeacehotels.co.uk
Price From £240

Occupying a particularly picturesque spot of National Trust-owned coast in south Devon, the Soar Mill is a lovely, traditional seaside hotel – the sort of place where you can still see lobster pots being hauled onto the beach and deer roaming the local hillsides. With numerous sandy bays dotting the local area, it makes a great base for coastal walks. All of its 21 spacious rooms can offer either sea or garden views (many have balconies or patios) and kids are well catered for with a games room (pool and table tennis), an outdoor swimming pool, an outdoor play area, grass tennis courts and a tame Shetland pony and donkey for them to meet (and feed carrots to). A children's menu is served from 5–5.30pm in the restaurant and parents can use the hotel washing room, cots, highchairs, changing mats and baby listeners at no extra cost. Children under 18 months old stay in their parents' room free of charge.

Saunton
Saunton Sands Hotel
Near Barnstaple **t** (01271) 890212
www.sauntonsands.co.uk
Price From £215

With Woolacombe and Croyde Bay within easy reach, this makes an ideal base for exploring the north Devon coast. It's a very elegant hotel, stark white in colour with parasolled recliners lining its heated outdoor pool, crisply decorated public rooms and an air-conditioned restaurant (children's menu and highchairs available). There are 39 rooms, many with good views of the coast (the hotel can provide access to five miles of sandy beaches), as well as 15 self-catering apartments, a nursery full of toys (with a nanny in attendance from 10 to 5 daily), an outdoor play area and hard tennis courts. The hotel will happily arrange activities such as horse-riding or surfing.

Thurlestone
Thurlestone Hotel
Near Kingsbridge **t** (01548) 560382
www.thurlestone.co.uk
Price From £224

This is a great family-run hotel occupying an idyllic south Devon location, a five-minute walk from the beach. Indeed, it's been in the same family for over 100 years, during which time they have clearly perfected the art of entertaining children. The hotel organizes a full programme of activities for kids under the auspices of its Dolphin Club (a registered play scheme) involving mini golf, volleyball, magic shows and videos. There's also a playroom, an indoor swimming pool (heated with adjoining paddling pool), an outdoor adventure playground with swings, climbing frames and a slide, not to mention tennis and badminton courts.

A communal children's supper is served from 5.15 to 6pm leaving parents free to enjoy their evening meal in the non-smoking restaurant. The bedrooms are well appointed and all offer either country or, if preferred, sea views and the baby-listening service extends to the 16th-century pub next door. The pub was reputedly built with timbers recovered from a Spanish Armada galleon sunk by Sir Francis Drake and the English navy in the 1580s.

Torquay
Toorak Hotel
Chestnut Avenue **t** (01803) 291666
www.tlh.co.uk
Price From £128

With its 29 large family rooms (out of 92), indoor pool complex, gardens, tennis courts, croquet lawn, games room, kids' clubs and children's play area, this grand seaside-white hotel is a good, solid choice. Children's menu available in the restaurant where they call toddlers 'sir'. There are two cheaper hotels in the complex and self-catering apartments as well.

Totnes
Sea Trout Inn
Staverton **t** (01803) 762274
www.seatroutinn.com
Price From £88

A cosy, unpretentious choice in the heart of the Dart Valley, the Sea Trout has 10 large, rather rustic bedrooms (two with sofa beds, cots available), in addition to its family-friendly restaurant. There's also a fenced garden and a self-catering cottage.

Wadebridge
Hustyns
St Breock Downs **t** (01208) 893700
www.hustyns.co.uk
Price From £90; cottages from £880 per week

Luxury modern family-friendly hotel set in 75 hectares (180 acres) of countryside and woodlands, where kids can ride the ponies and feed the ducks and fish. Leisure club, swimming pool, outdoor playground and indoor games room with plenty of toys and videos. The large rooms can easily accommodate extra beds and cots, or you can choose a luxury cottage. The hotel is 15 minutes from Padstow and has bikes for all ages so you can cycle to the seaside. Activities for children aged four to 10 are organized on site and older kids can go on excursions to Lusty Glaze, where they can learn to abseil and surf. The family-friendly bistro serves up local organic produce. Unfortunately, under 5s are not allowed in the fine dining restaurant but the hotel has a babysitting service and offers high teas.

Woolacombe Bay

Woolacombe Bay Hotel
t (01271) 870388
www.woolacombe-bay-hotel.co.uk
Price From £150

A good family-friendly choice, the Woolacombe Bay is a large Victorian hotel located next to a sandy beach and surrounded by green hills with a long stretch of grass running from the house down to the beach. It boasts 65 well-furnished rooms, many with fine sea views; large indoor and outdoor pools (with flumes, both heated); a crèche for 0–5-year-olds and a children's club for 5s and over, which organizes various activities (bouncy castle fun, horse-riding, archery, kids aerobics, walks, football, plus the odd disco). There's also a large play area with table tennis, computer games, pool and videos; a laundry room; tennis courts and two-and-a-half hectares (six acres) of grounds to play in. Children's meals are served in the non-smoking bistro; high teas also available. Unfortunately, the child-friendly atmosphere is let down by the restaurant – family dining is at 7pm prompt and after that any child will be charged £25 even if they don't eat. Fortunately, the hotel also has a large number of self-catering apartments.

Thames Valley

Calcot

Calcot Manor
Near Tetbury **t** (01666) 890391
www.calcotmanor.com
Price Family suite £270, family room £235

A great base for exploring the Cotswolds, the very grand Calcot Manor – log fires in the lounge, a smattering of antiques – was originally a Cistercian abbey and still has a few remaining 14th-century features. There are nine family rooms, including a

few two-bedroom suites in the Granary Barn (baby listening service available); a children's 'Playzone' staffed by nannies with a dedicated area for babies and younger children (play kitchen, dolls, puppets) and a separate floor for over 8s with comfortable sofas, a mini cinema, games consoles and a Beyblade arena. Outside, there's a small swimming pool, two tennis courts and an outdoor play area with climbing equipment. Parents can meanwhile book into the spa, which houses a pool, sauna, steam room, garden spa pool, fitness room, exercise studio, treatment and relaxation rooms. Older children are welcome in the evening in the hotel restaurant, which is very smart and opens on to a conservatory decked out with flowers from the estate garden. Otherwise, families can choose to dine together in the Gumstool Inn or opt to book the kids in for high tea and then make use of the listening service. The owners have recently bought another 90 hectares (220 acres) of land which, once it has been developed, will allow families the chance to picnic in the lovely countryside.

Cheltenham

Old Farmhouse Hotel
Lower Swell **t** (01451) 830232 **www.oldfarm.co.uk**
Price From £70

Very welcoming to families with 12 comfy rooms located in an assortment of farm buildings. It's quiet, friendly and simple and the owners are happy to help devise itineraries for touring the Cotswolds. Highchairs, cots, z-beds, baby listeners and supplies of games and toys are all available. Children under 14 staying in their parents' room are charged a flat rate of £10 per night.

Great Milton

Le Manoir aux Quat' Saisons
Church Street **t** (01844) 278881 **www.manoir.co.uk**
Price From £575

For a truly stylish (expensive), family holiday, you could try this terribly well-to-do 15th-century Oxfordshire manor house. Owned by renowned chef Raymond Blanc and set in 11 hectares (27 acres) of parkland with lovely sculpture-adorned gardens, you could be forgiven for thinking that the hotel is strictly for adults only. However, they make a supreme effort to make little ones feel as comfortable as possible with games, toys and a special kids' menu in the excellent (as you'd expect, considering the provenance) restaurant. The public rooms are typical country house affairs – antiques, deep-cushioned sofas, fresh flowers, open fires, etc.

Maidenhead

Cliveden

Taplow **t** (01628) 668561 **www.clivedenhouse.co.uk**
Price From £295

A posh treat – this sister hotel of the Royal Crescent in Bath is as luxurious as they come. Surrounded by a 150-hectare (375-acre) National Trust-maintained estate, you approach along a grand, gravelled boulevard before entering one of the most aristocratic-looking hotels around, the sort of place you feel should still be hosting house parties and high society soirées. Indeed, considering just how swish its 39 bedrooms actually are (with maid-unpacking service and a butler's tray, for people who like that sort of thing) and just how lavish its public rooms (with their paintings, antiques and tapestries), it's surprising how family friendly Cliveden actually is. Children are welcomed in the terrace restaurant during the day and in the conservatory restaurant at any time and there are wonderful gardens to explore, indoor and outdoor swimming pools (both heated) and facilities for tennis, riding, and boating on the River Thames.

Painswick

Painswick Hotel

Kemps Lane **t** (01452) 812160
www.painswickhotel.com
Price From £196

This 18th-century whitewashed mansion in the heart of a beautiful Cotswold village (home to over 100 listed buildings) has 19 rather grand rooms (including two large family rooms), several with good views of the valley; public rooms decorated with antiques and fine furniture, plus the odd individual touch (look out for the model battleship in the library) and a lovely garden for youngsters to romp about in. It's more child friendly than it looks from outside with friendly staff and a welcoming lack of pomposity considering its rather exclusive surroundings.

In the village, pay a visit to the church of St Mary, the grounds of which have been planted with 99 yew trees (according to local legend, the Devil will steal away the 100th yew should it ever be planted) and the Rococo Gardens, laid out in

the 1740s with a maze and a nature trail, which should keep kids happy for an afternoon.

Watford

The Grove

The Grove, Chandler's Cross **t** (01923) 807807
www.thegrove.co.uk
Price From £240 (superior), £320 (superb)

Self-styled as 'London's Country Estate', this former stately home once welcomed Queen Victoria and King Edward VII among its illustrious guests. Due to years of neglect, the house itself has few period features, though externally and in the reception rooms, it retains its former grace. Thankfully its quirky, modern refurbishment has thoroughly saved the day. There are 211 hotel rooms (mostly in an adjoining modern block) and 16 suites combining traditional trappings (chandeliers and chaise longues) with modern materials (perspex and hallogens). Bedrooms have balconies and enormous free-standing baths with fat feet but kids will mostly appreciate the box of toys and books, as well as the range of videos (available from reception) to play on the huge plasma TV screen. Within the grounds, there's a championship standard golf course, a jogging track, croquet lawn, tennis courts, spa and indoor pool. Families can hire mountain bikes or wander along the banks of the Grand Union Canal before taking a dip in the black-tiled pool. An outdoor pool and Ofsted-inspected nursery and crèche for babies from three months up are further elements of this hotel's charms.

Westonbirt

Hare and Hounds

Near Tetbury **t** (01666) 880233
www.bestwestern.co.uk
Price From £120 (kids stay in parents room free)

A pleasant, welcoming choice housed in a former farmhouse near the Westonbirt Arboretum (with adjoining coach house), the Hare and Hounds, with its 31 large bedrooms (three family), makes a good base for touring the Cotswolds. There are four hectares (10 acres) of gardens with wide grassy lawns to run about on, a family-friendly, non-smoking restaurant and facilities for pool, table tennis, tennis and croquet.

East Anglia

Aldeburgh

Wentworth Hotel

Wentworth Road **t** (01728) 452312
www.wentworth-aldeburgh.com
Price From £130

Not a dedicated family hotel *per se*, it is very accommodating and can easily adapt any of its 31 bedrooms (some of which are located in Darfield House across the road) to the needs of a small family – the ones with en-suite annexes are perhaps most suitable. The hotel occupies an idyllic location overlooking a famously unspoilt stretch of shingle coastline – the sort of place where fishing boats are still hauled on to the beach. High teas and kids' half portions are served in the non-smoking restaurant. The Minsmere Nature Reserve is a short drive away.

Blakeney

Blakeney Hotel

Holt **t** (01263) 740797
www.blakeney-hotel.co.uk
Price From £154

With the North Norfolk Railway, the North Norfolk Shire Horse Centre, the Muckleburgh Collection, as well as the bird life and seals of Blakeney Point all within easy reach, this award-winning 59-room (11-family) hotel overlooking a National Trust-owned harbour makes a perfect base for exploring Norfolk's picturesque northern coast. The bedrooms are comfortable (with views out across the marshes to Blakeney Point), with bunk beds and cots available in the family rooms; there's an indoor pool, a games room with table tennis and pool and a garden with a play area. Children's high teas are served before dinner.

Cambridge

Arundel House

Chesterton Road **t** (01223) 367701
www.arundelhousehotels.co.uk
Price From £120

Set on the banks of the River Cam, this terraced hotel overlooks Jesus Green and is five minutes' walk from the town centre. It has its own garden and there is plenty of green nearby for kids to run around in. The restaurant has a separate children's menu and there is a comfortable bar and lounge.

Royal Cambridge

Trumpington Street **t** (01223) 351631
www.theroyalcambridgehotel.co.uk
Price From £145; under 14s **free** (sharing with parents) or half price (own room)

Just half a mile from the station, this Georgian hotel is in the heart of the city (the famous 'Backs' are only yards away). The hotel has its own bar/lounge, free parking and a restaurant with highchairs and a children's menu.

Hunstanton

Le Strange Arms Hotel

Golf Course Road, Old Hunstanton **t** (01485) 534411
www.bw-lestrangearmshotel.co.uk
Price From £110

Several of the rooms in this three-star hotel have impressive sea views and the grounds lead down to a pleasant, sandy beach. There are family rooms and suites, two children's rooms and a play area. The Ancient Mariner Inn next door has its own rival restaurant and offers light snacks.

Ickworth

Ickworth House

Bury St Edmunds, Suffolk, **t** (01284) 735350
www.ickworthhotel.com
Price From £180, family suite £400

Not many hotels can boast they are part of a visitor attraction, but the east wing of the 18th-century Ickworth House has been transformed into a family-friendly haven. As the youngest sibling of the Luxury Hotels Group, the Ickworth combines lovely surroundings and fine food with family features. There's a staffed crèche for little ones and an activity club for older kids. Families can also enjoy the swimming pool and tennis courts and the acres of parkland for nature walks and bike rides. The house, which is one of the most family friendly around, has grand gardens, a deer park, woodland walks, a family cycle trail, an adventure playground and quizzes and trails to occupy young minds and bodies (p.300).

King's Lynn

Red Cat Hotel

Station Road, North Wootton **t** (01553) 631244
www.redcat.co.uk
Price Double £55, family rom £65

Inexpensive, country-style b&b, it is full of character and has been welcoming visitors since the

19th century. The interior is filled with antique touches, including the eponymous mummified red cat itself, which is displayed in the hotel bar alongside other local historical curiosities. The family rooms have double and bunk beds (extra cots available) and there's a children's playground.

Norwich

Maid's Head Hotel

Tombland **t** 0870 6096110
Price From £110

In the centre of Norwich, within sight of the cathedral, the Maid's Head Hotel is a characterful place with seven family rooms. With no baby listening facilities and only a small garden, the hotel is not ideal for travelling with younger children, but given its location and good value for money (children under 15 stay for free), it may be suitable for an overnight stay.

Norwich Sports Village

Drayton High Road, Hellesdon **t** (01603) 788898
www.norwichsportsvillage.com
Price From £65

About 10 minutes' drive from the centre of Norwich, this complex has its own aqua park (complete with white water rapids and a 168m/550ft-long flume as well as a toddler pool), two restaurants and a three-storey play area for the under 10s (with ball pool, slides and its own restaurant). Two additional restaurants and an assortment of reasonably priced family sized rooms (equipped with SKY TV), tennis, badminton and squash courts, make this a good base from which to explore Norwich and the surrounding countryside.

Southwold

The Crown

90 High Street **t** (01502) 722275
Price From £120

Pleasant hotel with two family rooms and a big restaurant, which offers a children's menu. The staff go home early, so no baby listening, but the rooms are comfortable and the service friendly.

Swaffham

Strattons

Ash Close **t** (01760) 723845
www.strattonshotel.com
Price From £160

Strattons is small but perfectly formed with just six individually decorated rooms, each with their own distinct theme (Venetian, Victorian, Tuscan, Sea, Palladian and Red) housed in a Queen Anne-style villa. There are lots of toys and games and a pleasant garden, where children can play with the hotel's numerous resident cats.

East Midlands

Ashbourne

Izaak Walton Hotel

Doveridge **t** (01335) 350555
www.isaakwaltonhotel.co.uk
Price From £205

This ivy-covered 17th-century three-star hotel has 34 rooms (some with Jacuzzi). There is a very good restaurant with children's menus and large gardens to explore. Children under 10 sharing their parents' room pay half price. Fishing (the hotel is close to the River Dove) packages are available.

Buxton

Roseleigh Hotel

19 Broad Walk **t** (01298) 24904
www.roseleighhotel.co.uk
Price From £64

The owners have their own young family and are very accommodating. They have four family rooms, a highchair and a cot. Under 5s stay for free and 6–16-year-olds are half price. The hotel is on the pedestrianized Broadwalk and overlooks the pavilion garden's duck pond and is moments away from the playground. There's no evening meal available but it's a short walk to the centre of town or you can picnic in the park.

Corby

Holiday Inn

Geddington Rd **t** (01536) 401020
www.holiday-inn.co.uk
Price From £70

Located in lovely countryside and handy for Stamford and Leicester, this four-star luxury hotel has 105 bedrooms, a children's fun house, an indoor swimming pool, and two restaurants (formal and informal). It can get a bit overrun with business people at times, but the atmosphere is relaxed and friendly. Special weekend offers available.

Leicester

Holiday Inn

129 St Nicolas Circle **t** 0870 4009094
www.holiday-inn.co.uk
Price From £78

In the centre of Leicester, this functional chain hotel is happy to welcome children and is in easy reach of all the main attractions. There's an indoor swimming pool and a good restaurant.

Nottingham

Langar Hall

Church Lane, Langar **t** (01949) 860559
www.langarhall.com
Price From £150

A great English tradition, Langar Hall has been in the same family since the early 19th century and there's a great sense of continuity and refinement about what goes on here. The public rooms are terribly elegant and filled with antiques, the service is polished and there are 10 spacious and comfortable bedrooms, some overlooking the gardens and croquet lawn. They'll happily knock up children's meals in the non-smoking restaurant. Indoor and outdoor play areas and babysitting service.

Stamford

The George

71 St Martin's **t** (01780) 750750
www.georgehotelofstamford.com
Price From £210

This stylish old coaching inn has an excellent restaurant and there are tables in the courtyard in summer. It's a really atmospheric hotel close to the river, where you can have fun feeding the ducks.

Heart of England

Alton

Alton Towers Hotel

Alton, Staffordshire **t** 0870 4585195
www.altontowershotels.com
Price From £247 (off-peak), £381 (peak), (2+2) family (including access to the Splash Landings Water Park and Alton Towers Theme Park)

The Alton Towers hotel has 167 Discovery Rooms, all offering a welcome pack for the kids on arrival, en-suite bathrooms, tea and coffee-making facilities, hairdryers, satellite TV, baby listening and a giant teddy bear to cuddle. Themed rooms sleeping two adults and up to four children include The Coca-Cola Fizzy Factory Bedroom, which is decked out in red and white and features giant ice cubes and a fridge stocked with Coca-Cola. The Oblivion Bedroom is a bit like the ride it's named after – sleek, steely, hi-tech and exhilarating and the Gothic-style Nemesis Bedroom will definitely appeal to kids with a liking for Buffy and Batman. For an ultimate indulgent break, book The Chocolate Bedroom and enjoy your very own chocolate dispenser. Guests also have unlimited entry to the theme park for the duration of their stay, early ride times for key rides and entry to the luxury Spa and the Cariba Creek Water Park (p.405) in the sister hotel Splash Landings next door. Here things are more relaxed and a Caribbean theme runs throughout from the buffet-style restaurant (overlooking the pool complex) to the bright bedrooms with their parrot design bedding.

One-night packages including accommodation at either Splash Landings or the Alton Towers Hotel, Continental breakfast, entry to the theme park and Cariba Creek and exclusive resident benefits (including Early Ride Time, show seat reservations and discount voucher booklet) start at around £247 for a family of four.

Birmingham

Crowne Plaza Birmingham

Central Square, Holliday Street **t** 0870 400150
Price From £90

A good, central, comfortable base for exploring the local sites. There are a mighty 188 family rooms on offer (out of 284), as well as an indoor swimming pool (with children's pool), sauna, solarium and gym. Rooms have two double beds and space for a cot. Large families will need interconnecting rooms. Children's menu and highchairs in the restaurant.

Novotel Birmingham Centre

70 Broad St **t** (0121) 643 2000
Price From £79

The family-friendly chain have a brand-new hotel in the city centre with secure underground parking. All rooms are family rooms and two childern stay free per room. There is a children's menu in the restaurant and small play area. It's cheaper to book online than by telephone.

Jury's Inn
245 Broad Street **t** (0121) 606 9000
www.jurysinns.com
Price From £119

In the city centre, this hotel is a good bet with children, families and is part of the family-friendly Irish chain. Children's menu available.

Bridgnorth
Old Vicarage Hotel
Worfield **t** (01746) 716497
www.oldvicarageworfield.com
Price From £175

In the leafy Shropshire countryside, this comfy, multi award-winning Edwardian hotel has 14 large rooms, all of which are suitable for a small family, although there's only one designated family room (the ground floor rooms have their own gardens). The public rooms have that archetypal English country house look with plush sofas and dark wood furniture. There are large lawns for kids to run around. The restaurant is non-smoking throughout and can provide half portions for children. Baby listening service available.

Broadway
Lygon Arms Hotel
High Street **t** (01386) 852255
www.paramount-hotels.co.uk
Price From £224

Built in 1532, the Lygon Arms Hotel can count Charles I and the man who sentenced him to death, Oliver Cromwell, among its former guests. With its great hall (and minstrel's gallery), oak panelling, wooden beams and 65 antique bedrooms (many with four-poster beds), it looks like a castle. Its network of dark, explorable passageways particularly appeals to children. Every child is given a fun pack, a bottle of lemonade and bag of bath goodies. The restaurant has a children's menu (over 8s only in the evening) and can provide colouring books and crayons. A room service children's menu and babysitting service are also available. The hotel has lovely gardens with floodlit tennis courts and a heated outdoor swimming pool.

Evesham
Evesham Hotel
Coopers Lane, off Waterside **t** (01386) 765566
www.eveshamhotel.com
Price From £168 (children £2 per year of their life)

Run by husband and wife team John and Sue Jenkinson, the Evesham is a 40-bedroom family hotel housed in a 16th-century building. It prides itself on its idiosyncratic approach with teddy bear key fobs and *pterodactyl* eggs offered on the menu. As the hotel blurb puts it, 'well-behaved children are as welcome as well-behaved grown-ups'. All the bedrooms are individually named and have supplies of games for kids and teddy bears on tap. The Alice in Wonderland suite is perhaps the best, decorated as it is with images from Lewis Carroll's classic book – caterpillars, Cheshire cats, etc. – with space for a Mad Hatter's Tea Party under the eaves, where only children can go. There's a large garden with a play area, as well as an indoor fun pool, table football, pinball machines and table tennis.

Ludlow
The Feathers Hotel
Bull Ring **t** (01584) 875261
www.feathersatludlow.co.uk
Price From £100

Not just a decent hotel, it's one of Ludlow's best known landmarks; an elegant half-timbered, 17th-century building with wonderful carved, wooden gargoyles. It boasts 40 en-suite rooms of varying sizes (three family) and a very good restaurant.

Stratford-upon-Avon
The Falcon Hotel
Chapel Street **t** 0870 8329905
www.corushotels/thefalcon
Price From £102

Lovely old timbered hotel in the city centre with 9 family rooms. Under 12s stay free of charge in their parents' room but the main attraction is the lovely walled garden where the kids can play safely. The hotel is five minutes' walk to the Royal Shakespeare Company theatre.

Faviere Guest House
127 Shipston Road **t** (01789) 293764
www.faviere.com
Price From £22 per person

This lovely relaxed guesthouse is run by a couple with their own children. They have a Continental approach (the husband is Spanish) and are happy to help and give advice about what to see and do in town. They have three family rooms. Under 3s stay free and 3–12-year-olds stay half price. It's next to the butterfly farm, close to the riverside and just 10 minutes' walk to the theatre.

Welcombe Hotel and Country Club

Warwick Road **t** (01789) 295 252
www.welcombe.co.uk
Price From £225

Set in a Jacobean manor house overlooking 325 hectares (800 acres) of landscaped parkland (some of which was once owned by Shakespeare himself), there are 64 en-suite rooms and its high-quality restaurant serves up a combined English–French menu. It adjoins a golf course and has a swimming pool and floodlit tennis courts, babysitting and listening services. No children in the dining room after 7pm.

Warwick

The Aylesford Town House Hotel

1 High Street **t** (01926) 492817
www.aylesfordhotel.co.uk
Price From £90–£100

Small Georgian hotel that's full of character. The kids will love the sloping floors. If you need a cot call in advance as they need to order it in. There are three family rooms and a room with a four-poster that can take two extra beds. Warwick is a nice place to stay as it's decidedly less touristy than Stratford but has plenty of charm.

The Northwest

Ambleside

Rothay Manor

Rothay Bridge **t** (01539) 433605
www.rothaymanor.co.uk
Price From £135

Rothay is a Regency style hotel near Lake Windermere. Family run, it has several ground floor suites, each with its little terrace and garden. Guests can use the nearby leisure club free of charge and the hotel has a swimming pool and an excellent restaurant where high teas and half portions are provided. Baby listening service available.

Appleby-in-Westmoreland

Appleby Manor

Roman Road **t** (01768) 351571
www.applebymanor.co.uk
Price From £134

A handy base for exploring both the Lake District and Yorkshire Dales, Appleby Manor can offer nine large family rooms (out of a total of 30) with double and bunk beds (extra cots available), a smart restaurant (children's portions and high-chairs available) and a welcoming, family-friendly atmosphere. The house itself is Victorian with good views of Appleby Castle and Eden Valley, and there's a heated, indoor swimming pool and a games room with pool and table tennis. Pony-trekking is offered nearby.

Blackpool

Imperial Hotel

North Promenade **t** (01253) 623971
www.paramount-hotels.co.uk
Price From £57 per person per night

It looks like a typical Victorian seaside resort hotel but inside it's thoroughly modern with a gym, indoor swimming pool and 181 rooms, many with sea views. It's also right on the front, thereby providing easy access to the town's principal attractions, and has a children's club.

Sparkles Hotel

37 Station Road, South Shore **t** (01253) 343200
www.sparkles.co.uk
Price From £130 (single parents half price and seasonal offers available)

This award-winning bed and breakfast is owned by the eponymous Mrs Sparkle. During the break-fast hour, between 8.30 and 10am, children are fed, taken to play in the Cinderella lounge and then regaled with stories and nursery rhymes. Between 8.30 and 9.30pm has been designated 'Panto Time' with games and dressing up. Every bedroom has been designed with children's needs in mind, such as the teddy-bears' picnic rooms and the Barbie room, with collections of toys, games and books. Activities such as 'Fun with Puppets', 'Disco Hour' and 'Games Galore' are laid on during the holidays.

Keswick

Armathwaite Hall

Bassenthwaite Lake **t** (017687) 76551
www.armathwaite-hall.com
Price From £160

Armathwaite Hall is a supremely well-equipped, 17th-century mansion in the heart of the Lake District. It is overlooked by Skidday Mountain and surrounded by 160 hectares (400 acres) of land, containing a deer park and woodland with numerous marked walks and bike trails. There are four family rooms (out of 43) as well as three self-catering properties. The hall has its own equestrian centre with more than 20 horses. You can also hire quad-bikes. Its also has a farm, Trotters World of Animals (p.439), and organized activities. There are facilities for croquet, tennis, fishing, riding, archery, clay pigeon-shooting and a heated indoor pool.

Hilton Keswick Lodore

Borrowdale **t** (017687) 77285
www.hilton.co.uk
Price From £98

Beautiful lakeside hotel overlooking Derwent Water with 16 hectares (40 acres) of gardens, 71 large, well-equipped rooms, pleasant public rooms, where open fires roar in winter, a leisure club with facilities for tennis and squash, an indoor pool, a games room for kids and a good, family-friendly restaurant. Nanny service available.

Liverpool

International Inn

4 South Hunter Street **t** (0151) 709 8135
www.internationalinn.co.uk
Price From £15 per person per night

Not much to look at from the outside, Liverpool's recently built independent hostel is a real gem of a place. There are self-catering facilities, a TV lounge, games room, kitchen, laundry, bike and bag stores and internet access. The rooms are clean, bright and spacious with both dormitory and double rooms available.

Manchester

Rossetti

107 Piccadilly, Manchester **t** (0161) 247 7744
www.hotelrossetti.co.uk
Price From £110

Just a few minutes' walk from the station, the Rossetti is conveniently placed but do be prepared to see the world and his wife pass by from the foyer bar. Upstairs it's a different matter with spacious rooms, big bathrooms and windows overlooking the city (an especially beautiful sight at night). There are kitchenettes on each floor, stocked with breakfast items and endless quantities of ice. Best of all with the kids tucked into their designer beds, parents can head down to the basement bar with the baby listening device in hand for some low-key lounging and top tunes.

Penrith

Beckfoot House

Helton **t** (01931) 713241
Price From £79

A few miles from Ullswater, Beckfoot is a grand 19th-century stone house surrounded by spruce, rolled lawns and manicured trees. There are three large family rooms (each with a double bed, two single beds and, if need be, extra cots), an adventure playground and games and toys for the kids.

Center Parcs Holiday Village

Whinfell Forest **t** 08700 673030
www.centerparcs.co.uk
Price From £130 low season, £715 high season

Swish holiday resort six miles from Penrith, with cycling, tennis courts, football, swimming pool, bowling alley and watersports lake. Kids' clubs and activities for all ages (from sports tournaments to face painting), as well as a variety of restaurants.

The Northeast

Bellingham

Riverdale Hall

Near Hexham **t** (01434) 220254
www.riverdalehall.co.uk
Price From £190

This hotel will prove particularly popular with cricket fans – the Cocker Family have had their own cricket pitch installed. There's also a putting green, a croquet lawn and, for that continental flavour, a petanque court. Children are well catered for with a heated indoor swimming pool, a games room and gardens to roam about in. The hotel's 11 family rooms are large and spacious (some have four-poster beds) and some have their own balcony. The restaurant specializes in seafood.

Bolton Abbey

The Devonshire Arms Country House Hotel

Bolton Abbey **t** (01756) 710441
www.devonshirehotels.co.uk
Price From £350

This lovely old coaching inn on the Bolton Abbey estate is surrounded by wonderful countryside. The hotel does nothing specific for children but welcomes them in a relaxed continental style. The Michelin star restaurant even has a children's menu. Some of the family rooms are split-level adding an element of fun but all rooms are large and can take extra beds and cots. There's an excellent bistro with an imaginative children's menu and a swimming pool. There are chickens in the grounds and a helicopter landing pad for a quick getaway!

Burnsall

The Devonshire Fell Hotel

Burnsall **t** (01756) 729000
www.devonshirehotels.co.uk
Price From £155

This small, old Victorian hotel has been so stylishly refurbished that it will be a big hit with fashion-conscious teenagers. It's the sister hotel of the Devonshire Arms and again welcomes kids in a relaxed fashion without treating them differently to any other guest. Burnsall is a pretty village in the heart of the Dales and this is the ideal place to stay if you want to get away from it all.

Durham

Royal County Hotel

Old Elvet **t** (0191) 3866821
www.marriot.com
Price From £100

By the riverside this hotel has an olde-wordly charm but a modern attitude to families and no pretensions like banning kids from the restaurant after 7pm. There's a babysitting service and all the amenities you'd expect from a major hotel chain.

Hexham

De Vere Slaley Hall

Slayley near Hexham **t** (01434) 673350
www.devereonline.co.uk
Price From £150

Luxury country house hotel set in huge grounds with a swimming pool. There's a good choice of room sizes, interconnecting rooms for families and a babysitting service. This is a good choice if you like hotels that welcome families but find kids' clubs a bit of a turn off. Here the kids can spend hours exploring the 400 hectares (1,000 acres) of woodlands and moors on the estate.

Hull

Holiday Inn Hull Marina

Castle Street **t** 0870 400 9043
www.holidayinn.co.uk
Price From £90

Overlooking the marina and within easy walking distance of the shops and museums, this is the best choice in Hull. The bedrooms are large and kids under 19 stay free in their parents' room. There are 19 family rooms and an indoor pool. The restaurant has a kids' menu (kids eat free), highchairs and outdoor tables beside the marina in summer. There are special weekend rates for families.

Ibis

Forensway **t** (01482) 387 500
www.ibishotel.com
Price From £47

The best budget option in the city centre (close to Princes Quay) but the rooms are small and there's only space for one extra bed alongside the double bed. Under 12s stay free in parents' room.

Leeds

Novotel Leeds Centre

4 Whitehall Quay **t** (0113) 242 6446
www.novotel.com
Price From £79

The French family-friendly chain offers the best option in Leeds right in the city centre. Children's menu in the restaurant and a small play area.

Newcastle

Hilton Gateshead

Tyne Bridge **t** (0191) 4900700
www.hilton.co.uk
Price From £140

This hotel is in the city centre on the quayside, within easy walk of all the main restaurants and attractions. The company is keen to attract families and has all the facilities you'd expect from a major chain. There's also a swimming pool.

Scarborough

Hotel St Nicolas

St Nicholas Cliff **t** (01723) 364101
Price From £60

Scarborough has lots of hotels but most are full of pensioners. While there are plenty of over 65s, here the bet is they are visiting with their grandchildren. The hotel has a friendly, relaxed atmosphere and St Nicholas Cliff is in the centre of town overlooking the beach. There's a swimming pool, kids' entertainment, children's menu and baby listening service.

York

Dean Court

Duncombe Place **t** (01904) 625082
www.deancourt-york.co.uk
Price From £170

Next to the Minster, it used to be a clergy house and now has 37 comfortable bedrooms (two family). A good base for exploring the medieval heart of the city. The restaurant has a children's menu and there is a toybox with a variety of games and distractions

Hilton

1 Tower Street **t** (01904) 648111
www.york.hilton.com
Price From £150

Opposite Clifford's Tower (p.468). Playroom at weekends, children's menu, interconnecting rooms.

Novotel York

Fishergate **t** (01904) 611660 **www.novotel.com**
Price From £75 (all rooms sleep four)

Modern hotel on the riverbank, one minute's walk from Clifford's Tower (p.468). Interconnecting rooms for families, small indoor pool, playground, car park and indoor play area. The restaurant has a children's menu and highchairs. Special weekend rates are available.

Lastingham Grange

Lastingham **t** (01751) 417345
www.lastinghamgrange.com
Price From £195

This 17th-century farmhouse has been run by the same family for over 40 years. Each of its 12 rooms is different and the public rooms offer wonderful views of the National Park with open fires in winter. There's an adventure playground for children in the garden with a sunken rose garden.

The Youth Hostel Association (YHA) has reported a year-on-year growth for family bookings over the past decade. Annual family membership (including children up to 18) of the YHA costs £22.95 (£15.95 for a single-parent family), which entitles you to stay in youth hostels not just in Britain, but all over the world. They can also provide a list of family-friendly hostels in England and publish guidebooks for hostelling in Europe and America. Many hostels now actively seek out family groups and have installed the amenities to attract them, offering family rooms with four to six bunks (with duvets and bedside lamps), central heating, carpets and even en-suite facilities. The rule of 'one night and you're out' no longer applies; lights can now stay on until the heady hour of 11.30pm (sometimes later) and families are even exempt from participating in the chores and tasks which used to be such a fundamental (and unenjoyable) part of the hostelling experience. Unlike individual travellers, families can stay inside the hostel during the day if they want. At mealtimes, you can go self-catering or eat from the hostel menu – some are very impressive with children's menus on offer. With very competitive prices – a night for a family of four (self-catering) can cost as little as £40 – families are now the fastest-growing sector of the hostel market.

YHA t 0870 770 8868 **www.yha.org.uk**

Self-catering

For a stay of weeks, or even months, consider the self-catering option as it can provide a cheaper and more flexible alternative to hotel accommodation.

Cottages

Blakes **t** 08700 781300
www.blakes.co.uk

Over 2,000 bargain properties throughout the UK.
Classic Cottages **t** (01326) 555555
www.classic.co.uk

Cottages throughout the Southwest from £150 per week.
Country Holidays **t** 08700 781200
www.country-holidays.co.uk

Over 3,000 properties (cottages, farmhouses, oast houses, fisherman's cottages) throughout the UK.
English Country Cottages **t** 08700 781 100
www.english-country-cottages.co.uk

Good bookings service and well-trained staff.

Helpful Holidays **t** (01647) 433593
www.helpfulholidays.com
 Cottage properties in the Southwest, including
several with heated indoor swimming pools.
Hoseasons **t** (01502) 502588 **www.hoseasons.co.uk**
 Over 1,000 bargain properties throughout the UK.
Norfolk Country Cottages **t** (01603) 871872
www.norfolkcottages.co.uk
 Good range of cottages in the Norfolk area.
Rural Retreats **t** (01386) 701177
 Luxury cottages throughout the country.
Toad Hall Cottages **t** (01548) 853089
www.toadhallcottages.com
 Cottages in the Southwest from £225 per week.

Cottage websites
Premier Cottages Direct
www.premiercottages.co.uk
Recommended Cottage Holidays
www.recommended-cottages.co.uk
UK Holiday Cottages Online **www.oas.co.uk**
Cottages 4 You **www.cottages4you.co.uk**

Historic houses
Landmark Trust **t** (01628) 825925
www.landmarktrust.co.uk
National Trust Enterprises **t** (01373) 828602
(enquiries) 0870 4584422 (bookings)
www.nationaltrust.org.uk

Farms
 Farms provide a very competitive form of accommodation. Prices for a family of four start at £160
per week in low season rising to £500 in summer.
Cartwheel
t (01392) 877842 **www.cartwheel.org.uk**
 A consortium of more than 200 farm-based
holidays including self-catering cottages, b&bs and
campsites.
The Farm Bureau
t (024) 7669 6909 **www.farmstayuk.co.uk**
 This co-operative of accommodation-offering
farms has also produced a glossy brochure 'Stay on
a Farm', with plenty of options across the country.
Farm and Cottage Holidays
t (01237) 479146 **www.farmcott.co.uk**
West country properties.
Norfolk and Suffolk Farm Holiday Group
t (01359) 231013 **www.farmstayanglia.co.uk**
 Represents more than 60 properties on working
farms.

Home exchange

Home Base Holidays **t** (020) 8886 8752
Homelink International **t** (01344) 842642
www.homelink.org.uk
Latitudes House-Swap Register **t** (01273) 581793
Find a Property **www.findaproperty.co.uk**

Caravanning and camping

Caravanning
 Caravanning has obvious benefits. It comes in at
a relatively low cost (from around £45 for three
nights). Free from rigid schedules, you can take your
pick of stop-off points along the way allowing your
family to play and to eat whatever and whenever
they choose. Many caravan sites do not require you
to make a reservation and many also have their own
permanent collection of caravan homes (usually
perched on cement blocks), which you can hire.

Camping
 These days, camping does not have to mean
roughing it. Organized campsites are equipped with
toilet and shower blocks, shops and entertainment,
making them ideal for families. Most have all mod
cons and some even have their own separate toilet
tent. Sites such as these give a great deal of thought
to families, often providing organized children's
activities, babysitting and baby equipment rental.

Contacts
Visit Britain t (020) 8846 9000
 Provides a list of camping and caravan parks.
Camping and Caravan Club t (024) 7669 4995
www.campingandcaravanningclub.co.uk

Websites
Cades **www.cades.co.uk**
Canvas Holidays **www.canvas.co.uk**
Eurocamp **www.eurocamp.co.uk**
Keycamp **www.keycamp.co.uk**

Camping and caravanning checklist:

► Is it possible to book a pitch away from the road and (if camping) in the shade?
► Does the site have shower and toilet facilities?
► Does the site have a children's play area?
► Can the site provide a babysitting service?

Boating

Blakes and Hoseasons are the country's principal agents for boat hire, both offering trips on such famous stretches of water as the Rochdale Canal, Wey Navigation and, of course, the Norfolk Broads.
Blakes Holiday Boating, Hoveton, Norwich (part of Vacation Rental Group uk) t 0870 1971000 www.holidaycottagesgroup.co.uk
Hoseasons Holidays Ltd, Sunway House, Lowestoft t (01502) 500505; bookings t 0870 5434434
See East Anglia p.320 for more boating options.

Family resorts

Family resorts aim to offer an all-encompassing holiday experience. Rather than choosing your accommodation as a base from which to explore the local attractions, here the resort *is* the attraction. Everything you want from your holiday – somewhere to stay, places to eat, activities to enjoy, entertainments to watch – is provided on-site. The family resort market in England is dominated by three names, Butlins, Pontin's and Center Parcs.
Butlins t 0870 242 1999 www.butlinsonline.co.uk
Center Parcs t 08705 200 300 www.centerparcs.com
Pontin's t 0870 604 5602 www.pontins.com

Children's camps

Of course, there's no need for the whole family to go on holiday together. There are now dozens of activity camps offering residential courses for children (usually aged 6–16) in a range of sporty, outdoorsy and educational pursuits – horse-riding, archery, tennis, mini motorbikes, go-karting, football, netball, drama, arts and crafts, music, even

computer skills. The camps, most of which are rural-based, provide a safe and secure environment in which youngsters can run around and let off steam while parents take things easy at home. When booking, check that the camp is a member of the Adventure Activities Licensing Authority (AALA), www.aala.org, and/or the British Activity Holiday Association (BAHA), www.baha.org.uk, whose job it is to ensure the camps meet current safety standards and that instructors hold the relevant licences to teach climbing, watersports, trekking and caving. Admission prices vary greatly, depending on the length of the stay, whether it's a residential stay or not, the time of year, the activities selected and the number of days involved.

Activity camps
Adventure and Computer Holidays Ltd
t (01306) 881299 www.holiday-adventure.com
Price Varies depending on age, activity and duration of course; call for details
Outdoor activity, sports and computer skills day courses in Dorking, Surrey for 4–14-year-olds.
ATE Superweeks
t 08454 561205 www.ate.org.uk
Price Call for details
Outings, day trips and sport. There are six UK locations to choose from, including a castle.
Camp Beaumont
t (01603) 284280 www.campbeaumont.com
Price Call for details
One of the most famous names in the world of children's activity holidays, it operates purpose-built centres (for ages 6–17 in separate age groups) in Norfolk, the Isle of Wight (p.135), Staffordshire and Wales. Each centre runs trips to a number of local attractions (Blakeney Point, Dinosaur Isle Museum, Alton Towers and Snowdonia). The venues offer a range of activities (archery, climbing, motorsports and watersports), plus some have themed weeks ('starmaker', 'movie maker', 'wizards and witches school' and 'secret agent'), where the emphasis is on building skills and confidence.
PGL
t 0870 551551 www.pgl.com
Price Call for details
One of the leading summer camp companies in the UK, PGL organizes adventure days, residential activity weeks (ages 7–17) and Active Family weeks.

EAC Activity Camps

t 0845 1130 022
www.eac-summer-activity-camps.co.uk/
Price Call for details

Selection of summer activity holidays at rural residential locations and day camps (ages 5–15).

Field Studies Council

t 0845 3454071 **www.**field-studies-council.org
Price Call for details

Weekly conservation courses for 8–16-year-olds with plenty of outdoor activities; 17 centres in the UK in beautiful countryside and coastal locations.

The Horstead Centre

t (01603) 737215 01603 **www.**horsteadcentre.org.uk
Price Call for details

Residential activity centre on the edge of the Norfolk Broads National Park offering a range of programmes including archery, canoeing, rope-climbing, abseiling, raft-building and sailing.

Junior Choice Adventure (JCA)

t 08705 133773 **www.**travelclass.co.uk
Price Call for details

JCA's online brochure service is available for a range of activity camps and environmental programmes in Somerset. They also run skiing and snowboarding holidays for schools and groups.

Kids Klub

t (01449) 742700 **www.**kidsklub.couk
Price From £299 per week

Residential summer camps based in Hertfordshire, Nottinghamshire and Suffolk. Extras include trips to West End shows (from Herts), horse-riding (Suffolk) and theme park visits (Notts). Ages 6–17.

Mepal Outdoor Centre

t (01354) 692251 **www.**mepal.co.uk
Price Call for details

Weekly courses in archery, sailing, canoeing, wind-surfing and rock-climbing. Day visits or residential courses available. Nature trail, trampolines and a play area on site.

Mill on the Brue

t (01749) 812307 **www.**millonthebrue.co.uk
Price Call for details

Residential, day and half-day courses in canoeing, camping and outdoor activities in an idyllic location near the River Brue in Somerset. Ages 7–15.

XUK

t (020) 8371 9686 (day camps) **t** (020) 8922 9739 (residential) **www.**campsforkids.co.uk
Price Call for details

Cross Keys (formerly Experience UK) organize Easter, summer holiday and half-term activity camps for 3–17-year-olds in and around North London and East Anglia. The biggest draw are the driving lessons for kids aged 12 and over and the outward bound expeditions.

Index

Main page references are in **bold**.
Map page references are in *italics*.

INDEX: STE–WAL

Steam Boat Museum **434**, 453
steam trains
  day trips from London 63
  East Anglia **317–19**, 321
  East Midlands 337, 353, **356–8**
  Heart of England 378, 379, **401**
  Midwest 152, 170, 171, **174**
  Northeast **485–6**
  Northwest 433, **442–3**
  Southeast 63, 106, **126–7**
  Southwest 202, 216, **223**
  Thames Valley 253, **265–6**
Stockwood Craft Museum 264
Stokesay Castle 392
Stonehenge 163
Stonehurst Family Farm 352
Stourhead 162
Stow-on-the-Wold 252–3
Stowe Landscape Gardens 264–5
Stranger's Hall 298
Stratford-upon-Avon 384–7
  Butterfly Farm **387**, 397
Streetlife Hull Museum **463**, 496
Studley Park 472
Stump Cross Caverns 489
Styal Country Park 451–2
Submarine Museum 100, 138
Sudbury Hall 350
Sudeley Castle 256
Suffolk
  Heritage Coast 309–10
  Owl Sanctuary 306
  Wildlife Park 306
  see also East Anglia
summer camps
  Southeast 135
  Thames Valley 273
Sundown Adventure Land 359
supermarkets 22
surfing 195, 229–30
Surrey see Southeast
Sussex see Southeast
Sutton Bank National Park Centre 490
Sutton Hoo 316
Swaffham, hotels 523
Swanage 171
Swanage Railway **171**, 174
swimming
  East Anglia 325
  East Midlands 363
  Heart of England 405–6
  London 71–2
  Northeast 492
  Southeast 135
  Southwest 230
  Thames Valley 272
  see also watersports
Swindon
Symonds Yat 387–8

Tales of the Old Gaol House 295
Tanfield Railway 486
Tangmere Military Aviation Museum **95–6**,
  139

Tank Museum 181–2
Tate Liverpool **424**, 452
Tate St Ives 218
Tattershall Castle 350
Tatton Park 437
Technology Museum (Cambridge) 286
Teddy Bear House 156–7
Teddy Bear Museum 387
teenagers 7
Teignmouth 218
telephones 25–6
Temple Newsam House 464, 478
tennis 72, 492
Terror Tower 482
Thackray Medical Museum **464–5**, 496
Thames Festival 36
Thames Path 17, 69, 269
Thames Valley **239–78**, 240–1
  animal attractions 256–62
  boat trips 262–3
  cinemas 273
  Cotswolds 250–3
  eating out 277–8
  festivals and events 241
  hotels 520–1
  itineraries 241
  museums and galleries 263–4, 273–6
  parks and gardens 264–5
  sports and activities 270–3
  steam trains 253, **265–6**
  theatres 276
theatres
  East Anglia 329
  East Midlands 367
  Heart of England 408
  London 40, 41, 50, 56, 65, **79–80**
  Midwest 182
  Northwest 453
  Southeast 140
  Southwest 232–3
  Thames Valley 276
Thetford Forest 317
Thinktank Museum of Science and Discovery
  377, 407
Thomas à Becket 92
Thorpe Park 129–30
Thrigby Hall Wildlife Gardens 306
Thurleigh Farm Centre 261
Thurlestone, hotels 519
time 26
Tintagel Castle 205
tipping 26
Titchwell Marsh Nature Reserve 305
toddlers 7
toilets 26, 34
Tollhouse Museum 312
Tor Bay 210
Torquay 219–20
Totnes 200–2
tour operators see travel agents
tourist information 26, 34
Town House Museum 295
Toys of Yesteryear 366
trains see railways; steam trains

trams 418
Transport Museum (Cheetham) 451
Transport Museum of East Anglia 315
travel **6–18**
  choosing your holiday 6–7, 8
  entry formalities 12
  getting around 13–18
  getting there 10–12
  with infants 6–7, 33
  insurance 22–3
  around London 30–2
  with primary school children 7
  with teenagers 7
  with toddlers 7
  when to go 20
travel agents 6, 8–9
  disabled travellers 25
travelling times 14
treacle tart 332
Treak Cliff Cavern 346
Treasure Island 121
Treasurer's House 469
Trebah Gardens 222
Trelissick Gardens 222
Trerice 205
Trethorne Leisure Farm 209
Trevone Bay 215
Treyarnon Bay 215
Trooping the Colour 35
Tropical Birdland 351–2
Tropical Butterfly House 477
Tropical World **465**, 478–9
Tropiquaria 165–6
Trotters World of Animals **432**, 439
True's Yard Fishing Museum 295
Tulley's Farm 119
Tullie House Museum 452
Tunnels Through Time 197
Tussaud, Madame Marie 38
Tutankhamun Exhibition 157
Twycross Zoo 394
Tyne Riverside Country Park 485
Tyne and Wear see Northeast
Tyseley Locomotive Works **377**, 401

Ullswater 433
Underground Passages (Exeter) 194
Underwater World 122
Union Farm 316
University Museum of Zoology 287
Urbis: Museum of Urban Life 428

Valley Farm White Animal Collection 306
Ventnor 107
  Botanic Gardens 108
Vercovicium 474–5
Verulamium Museum and Park **247–8**, 276
Victory, HMS 99
Vindolanda 475
visas 12
voting rights 343

Walberswick 309
walking 16–17